CALENDAR
OF THE
PATENT ROLLS

Preserved in the Public Record Office

Elizabeth I
Volume VII
1575–1578

LONDON
HER MAJESTY'S STATIONERY OFFICE
1982

ISBN 0 11 440115 2*

CONTENTS

PREFACE

This volume continues the Calendar of Patent Rolls on the plan described in the preface to the first volume of the calendar for this reign (1558–1560). The text was prepared in draft by a number of Assistant Keepers and the whole was edited by the late Mr J. H. Collingridge, C.B.E., of this Office, who also compiled the subject entries for the index. The persons and places entries are mostly the work of Mrs J. M. Trier.

PUBLIC RECORD OFFICE

CALENDAR OF PATENT ROLLS
18 ELIZABETH I

17 November 1575–16 November 1576
PART I
C. 66/1137

(Except where otherwise noted, all these grants are dated at Westminster.)

1.) 3 *Feb.* 1576. Pardon for Peter Hudson late of Hanley Castle and [*m.* 1] Francis Glover *alias* Browne of Great Malverne, co. Worcester, 'yomen', indicted for manslaughter in that they assaulted William Braunche at Estnor, co. Hereford, on 16 May, 17 Eliz., so that he died there on 4 June (*details given*). By Q.

2.) 10 *Feb.* 1576. Pardon for Robert Leighe late of Naworthe, co. Cumberland, indicted, with Leonard Dacre of Naworthe, for rebellion at Geltemore in Hayton, co. Cumberland, on 20 Feb., 12 Eliz., after which he fled into Scotland (*details given*). On report of his penitence. [*m.* 2] By p.s.

3.) 3 *Feb.* 1576. Pardon for Catherine Harris late of Fromeselwoode, co. Somerset, 'spinster', indicted at the gaol delivery of Yvelchester held at Charde before Roger Manwood, a justice of the Common Pleas, and John Jefferay, one of the Queen's serjeants at law, and their fellows, justices of gaol delivery, on Monday in the fourth week of Lent, 17 Eliz., for the theft of goods (*described*) from the house of William Leversage at Valleis in Fromeselwoode on 18 Jan., 17 Eliz. She pleaded not guilty, was convicted and was sentenced, but for divers causes was committed back to gaol. At the suit of Roger Harris, her brother. By p.s.

4.) 28 *Jan.* 1576. Grant to Charles Wyndham of the wardship and marriage of John Wyndham, kinsman of John Wyndham, knight, to wit, the son of John Wyndham, deceased, his son; with an annuity of £13 6s. 8d. from 13 March, 16 Eliz., when John the grandfather died. [*m.* 3] By Q.

5.) 9 *Feb.* 1576. Grant to William Roche of the wardship and marriage of Richard Dowson, son and heir of Henry Dowson, 'yoman'; with an annuity of £3 6s. 8d. from 30 April, 2 Eliz., when Henry died. Yearly value of the inheritance £11 16s. By Q.

6A.) 9 *Feb.* 1576. Grant to Thomas Sowthe of the wardship and marriage of Robert Ormesbye, son and heir of John Ormesbye; with an annuity of 10s. from 2 Jan., 5 Eliz., when John died. Yearly value of the inheritance £11 6s. 8d. [*m.* 4] By Q.

6B.) 3 *Feb.* 1576. Grant to Nicholas Upton and John Upton of the wardship and marriage of Edward Fagge, son and heir of Robert Fagge; with an annuity of 26s. 8d. from 18 June, 16 Eliz., when Robert died.   By Q.

7.) 25 Nov. 1575. Creation of the office and several offices of 'broker' or 'brokers' in London and elsewhere in England. And grant for 23 years, for his service, to William Cecill, K.G., master of the court of Wards, baron of Burghley, treasurer of England, of the sole power to appoint brokers in London and elsewhere in England; and the survey and government of the same brokers for the greatest good of the Queen's subjects in respect of all changes, exchanges and re-changes both into and out of the realm and all other trading whatsoever; without rent or account; no other person to intermeddle in the premises without his licence under penalty of £1,000 to the Queen's use.   [m. 5]
      By patent, 9 March, 17 Eliz., the office of keeper of the same change, exchange and re-change was granted inter alia to the same lord Burghley for 23 years at a yearly rent of £30, with power to appoint all brokers. It is reported that the grant will promote little or nothing for the public good unless lord Burghley is granted the sole power of appointing brokers, because the business of the said change, exchange and re-change may be hindered in many ways as regards the common weal by the multitude and abuse of such brokers.   By Q.

8.) 7 Dec. 1575. Grant for life to Baldwin Wake of the office of a gunner in the Tower of London; with wages of 12d. a day, payable at the Exchequer. On surrender in Chancery by John Flemynge of a patent, 3 April, 5 Edw. VI, granting him the office for life. By p.s.

9.) 6 Dec. 1575. Grant for life to William Knolls, a gentleman pensioner, of the office of marshal of the marshalsea of the Queen's Bench; as formerly held by John Wykes, Thomas Brandon, knight, Charles Brandon or William Nawnton. For his service.   By p.s.
      Vacated, because surrendered 24 June, 1 James I, by Knolles by the name of lord Knolles; signed: E.Bruce; W.Knollys.

10.) 12 Dec. 1575. Grant for life to Robert Bonnyard of the office of fletcher or archer (flechiarii sive archiarii nostri) of Rye, Sangate, Deale and Sandowne and in the town below 'le Peere' and in the town below Dover castle; wages of 6d. a day, payable by the paymaster of the Queen's castles; as formerly held by George Hunt by grant of Edward VI.   By p.s.

11.) 11 Feb. 1576. Grant for life to George Whitton, the Queen's servant, of an annuity of £18; from the death of Alonso de Salablanca, Spaniard, who by patent obtained a like annuity for life from the Queen; payable at the Exchequer. For his service to Henry VIII, Edward VI, Queen Mary and the present Queen.   [m. 6]
                                                                                                By p.s.

12.) 9 Dec. 1575. Grant for life in survivorship to Thomas Lichefild, the Queen's servant, and Margaret his wife of an annuity of £100, payable at the Exchequer, from Christmas last. In consideration of the surrender of a fee and wages of 40 marks a year, payable by the cofferer, and a fee or livery of £40 6d. a year, payable in the great wardrobe, both appointed by the Queen to be paid to Lichefild for life; and for his services. By p.s.

13.) 5 Dec. 1575. Grant for life to Christopher Hatton, captain (prefectus) of 'the yeomen of our garde', a gentleman of the privy chamber, of an annuity of £400 from Michaelmas last, payable at the Exchequer. For his service.   By p.s.

14.) 25 Nov. 1575. Protection for one year for Thomas Steynton and Ferdinand Steynton, his son, of London, merchants.   By p.s.

15.)   29 *Dec.* 1575.   Licence for four years for William Wilson of Markate Rayson, co. Lincoln, to buy, keep and sell again 4,000 todds of English wool; the licence to have the amounts bought endorsed on it within a twelvemonth.   *English.*   [*m.* 7]

By p.s.

16.)   1 *Dec.* 1575.   Grant for life to Francis du Bignon of an annuity of 8*d.* a day from Michaelmas last, payable at the Exchequer. In consideration of his long service to Henry VIII in his wars beyond the seas and since in other martial services, for which the Queen means to yield him some relief, being a stranger born.   *English.*   By p.s.

17.)   1 *Dec.* 1575.   Licence of 10 years to the mayor of Cork in Ireland, and sufficient persons appointed by warrant under his hand and seal, to buy in England 300 quarters of wheat a year when a quarter may be at any such time bought at the price of 16*s.* or less and ship the same to Cork for the behoof of the mayor, bailiffs and citizens of the said city; provided that the custom and subsidy be duly paid. The mayor reports that there is not enough corn growing in the parts of Ireland adjoining Cork for the sustentation of the inhabitants, who have always heretofore been furnished from England of so much corn as did supply the want thereof in Cork.   *English.*   By p.s.

18.)   10 *Feb.* 1576.   Licence for Thomas, earl of Sussex, councillor, lord chamberlain, to send hoys, plates and other vessels and mariners from England to Cane or elsewhere in Normandy, to bring over 500 tons of stone 'of the growth and cutt of that place' to be employed on certain buildings which he has in hand; notwithstanding stat. 13 Eliz. prohibiting hoys or plates to   [*m.*8]
cross the seas. The river leading up to Cane is very shallow and only hoys and plates drawing but little depth of water can go thither.   *English.*   By p.s.

19.)   28 *Nov.* 1575.   Grant for life in survivorship to Matthew Salwey and Edmund Englishe of an annuity of £50, payable at the Exchequer, from Lady Day last.

On surrender in Chancery by the undermentioned persons of annuities, amounting in all to £53 15*s.* a year, granted to them for life as follows:-

(1) By patent of the court of Augmentations, 9 Dec., 30 Hen. VIII, to Ralph Bent, formerly a monk in the monastery of Vale Royal, co. Chester,—100*s*, payable by the receiver of the court of Augmentations in the county.

(2) By patent of the court of Augmentations, 10 March, 31 Hen. VIII, to John Wiseman, formerly a monk in the priory of St. Neots, co. Huntingdon,—106*s.* 8*d.*, payable by the receiver of the court of Augmentations in the county.

(3) By patent of the court of Augmentations, to William Wisbiche *alias* Boucker, formerly a monk in the monastery of Peterborough, co. Northampton,—£6, payable by the receiver of the court of augmentations in the county.

(4) By patent of the court of Augmentations, 2 Feb., 31 Hen. VIII, to Robert Bayte, formerly a monk of the monastery of Thorney, co. Cambridge,—40*s.* payable by the receiver of the court of Augmentations in the county.

(5) By patent of the court of Augmentations, 1 Sept., 2 Edw. VI, to John Porter, formerly a minister in All Saints college, Maydeston, co. Kent,—100*s.*, payable by the receiver of the court of Augmentations in the county.

(6) By patent, 27 June, 2 & 3 Ph. & Mary, to Henry Grave, a yeoman in ordinary of the chamber,—£12 3*s.* 4*d.*, payable by the receiver for the court of Augmentations in the county of Oxford.   [*m.* 9]

(7) By patent, 18 Feb., 2 Eliz., to Henry Fraunces—£18 15*s.*, payable at the Exchequer.

In consideration that the crown will be discharged of £3 15s. a year of the said sum of £53 15s.　　　　　　　　　　　　　　　　　　　　By p.s.

20.) 28 *Nov.* 1575. Grant for life to William Pratte of the office of usher of the court of Wards; yearly fee of £5, with 20s. a year for his vesture, payable by the receiver general of the court, from Lady Day last; as formerly held by Quintin Sueinton, Thomas Bates or George Lawrence.　　　　　　　　　　　　　　　　　　　　　　　　　By Q.

21.) 30 *Nov.* 1575. Protection for one year for Nicholas Seyntler *alias* Sellinger of Eastwell, co. Kent.　　　　　　　　　　　　　　　　　　　　　[*m.* 10]
　　　　　　　　　　　　　　　　　　　　　　　　　　　　By p.s.

22.) 21 *Nov.* 1575. Pardon for Tristram Tirwhit late of Lincoln, indicted together with Peter Evers late of Lincoln and Thomas Gower, 'goldesmyth', Miles Roase, 'goldesmyth', Anthony Ellis, 'yoman', and Ralph Harrington, 'yoman', all of Lincoln, for misprision of treason in that they counterfeited Portugese gold coins, called 'Portagues', at Lincoln on and about 5 March, 16 Eliz., and uttered the same at Lincoln and other places, co. Lincoln, on and about 20 March, 16 Eliz. (*details given*) contrary to stat. 14 Eliz.　　　By p.s.

23.) 5 *Dec.* 1575. Grant for life to Reginald Morraunt, the Queen's servant, of the office of chief gunner at Windsoure castle; with wages of 8d. a day, payable at the Exchequer, from Michaelmas 13 Eliz.　　　　　　　　　　　　　　　　　　　　By Q.

24.) 5 *Dec.* 1575. Grant for life in reversion to Francis Southwell, an equerry of the stable, of the office of registrar and keeper of the register or registers of decrees and orders in Chancery, granted by patent, 13 June,　　　　　　　　　　　　[*m.* 11]
11 Eliz., to Martin James for life; as held by Ralph Standishe, John Adams, William Naylor or James. For his service.　　　　　　　　　　　　　　　　　By p.s.
　　Vacated, because surrendered 15 *May* 18 *Eliz.*; *signed* Wyllm Cordell; Francis Sowthwell.

25.) 25 *Jan.* 1576. Release to lady Elizabeth Mervyn, widow, late the wife of John Mervyn, knight, executrix of Richard Perkyns, one of the executors of William Moore, of the forfeiture of the marriage and arrears of an annuity　　　　　[*m.* 12]
of £28 16s. 8d. due to Moore under a grant of the wardship of Thomas Lisle, son and heir of Lancelot Lisle, as witnessed by an indenture in the court of Wards, 14 March, 1 Edw. VI, for which Moore had no patent.　　　　　　　　　　　　　　　　By Q.

26.) 20 *Jan.* 1576. Presentation of Thurston Shawe, clerk, to the vicarage of Stonehouse, Gloucester dioc.　　　　　　　　　　　　　　　　　　　　By p.s.

27.) 19 *Nov.* 1575. Presentation of Nicholas Crumpe, M.A., to the portion of Tydcombe in Tyverton church, Exeter dioc., void by death.　　　　　　　　By p.s.

28.) 15 *Dec.* 1575. Presentation of Robert Awfilde, B.A., to the church of Burton on the Water with the chapel of Slaughter inferior, Gloucester dioc.; void by the full loss (*plenam amissionem*) of the last incumbent.　　　　　　　　　　　　　　By p.s.

29.) 14 *Feb.* 1576. Presentation of John Whetcombe, clerk, M.A., to the rectory of Swanewiche, Bristol dioc.　　　　　　　　　　　　　　　　　　By p.s.

30.) 1 *Dec.* 1575. Presentation of Thomas Cooke, clerk, to the rectory of Swanwiche *alias* Sanwiche with the chapel of Northe [*sic*] Sanwiche annexed in the isle of Purbeck, co. Dorset, Bristol dioc.   By p.s.

31.)   13 *Feb.* 1576.   Presentation of James Fernyside, preacher, to the rectory of Whikham, Durham dioc.   By Q.

32.)   6 *Feb.* 1576.   Grant for life to John Calverley, LL.B., of the canonry or prebend in Rochester cathedral void by the death of John Richedale.   By p.s.

33.)   6 *Dec.* 1575.   Grant for life to William Chaderton, S.T.P., of the canonry or prebend in the collegiate church of St. Peter, Westminster, void by the resignation of Robert Ramsden.   By p.s.

34.)   3 *Feb.* 1576.   Pardon for Edmund Savage late of the city of Gloucester. It was found by an inquisition taken before Luke Garnance, coroner of the city on 17 Dec., 15 Eliz., at Gloucester on the body of John Allwood   [*m.* 13]
that Savage wounded Allwood in self defence at Over, co. Gloucester, in the house of Richard, bishop of Gloucester, so that he died there on 17 Dec. (*details given*).

35.)   11 *Feb.* 1576. Pardon for Richard Warynge late of Marlowe Magna, co. Buckingham, 'haberdassher', indicted at the general gaol delivery of Aylesbury held at Little Brickhill, co. Buckingham, on Monday in the first week of Lent, 17 Eliz., before Christopher Wraye, knight, chief justice of the Queen's Bench, and Gilbert Gerrard, attorney general, justices of gaol delivery, for the felonious killing of Thomas Myller at Marlowe Magna on 18 Oct., 16 Eliz. He pleaded not guilty and the jury found that he killed Myller in self defence (*details given*).

36.)   17 *Feb.* 1576.   Pardon for Nicholas Singlehurst, late of Westminster, 'yoman'. It was found by an inquisition (*jury named*) taken at New Windesor, co. Berks, before John Wheteley, mayor and coroner of the town, on 20 Dec., 18 Eliz., on the body of Robert Rutter that Singlehurst killed Rutter in self defence at New Windesor on 19 Dec. last (*details given*).   [*m.* 14]

37.)   11 *Feb.* 1576.   Pardon for Thomas Bawldwyn late of Sheffeilde Parke, co. York. It was found by an inquisition taken at Sheiffield, co. York, before William Calverd, a coroner in the county, on 24 Dec., 18 Eliz., on the body of John Wigeley late of Sheffeild, 'yoman', that Bawldwyn killed Wigeley in self defence at Sheiffield on 23 Dec. (*details given*), after which he was arrested at Sheiffield Lodge in Sheiffielde.

38.)   21 *Nov.* 1575.   Pardon for Richard Frauncys late of Studley, co. Warwick, 'laborer', indicted at the gaol delivery of the county of Warwick held before James Dyer, knight, chief justice of the Common Pleas, and Nicholas Barham, one of the Queen's serjeants at law, justices of assize and gaol delivery, on 15 July, 17 Eliz., at Warwick for manslaughter. It was found by an inquisition taken before Henry Rogers, a coroner in the county, on 16 July, 17 Eliz., on the body of John Lucas at Studley that Fraunceys feloniously wounded him on 28 June, 17 Eliz., so that he died there on 2 July; he pleaded not guilty and the jury found that he killed Lucas in self defence (*details given*).

39.)   13 *April* 1576.   *Gorhambury.*   Pardon for Henry Ridley late of Rabye, co. Durham, George Horseley late of Aclington Parke, co. Northumberland, and James Swynnowe late

of Thornehill in the liberties of Norham, co. Durham, for the undermentioned treasons and
all other offences committed before   [*m*. 15]
1 July, 12 Eliz. Thomas, earl of Northumberland, late of Topcliff, co. York, Charles, earl of
Westmoreland, late of Branspeth, co. Durham, Leonard Dacre late of Harlesey, co. York,
Edward Dacre late of Morton, co. York, Richard Norton late of Norton Conyers, co. York,
John Swynborne, late of Chopwell, co. Durham, Thomas Markenfeild late of Markenfeild,
co. York, Christopher Nevell late of Kyrkbymoreside, co. York, Francis Norton late of
Baldersbye, co. York, Robert Tempest late of Holmesyde, co. Durham, William Smythe
late of Eshe, co. Durham, Thomas Hussey late of Topcliff aforesaid and Brian Palmes late of
Murton, co. Durham, were indicted with others for that they conspired and rebelled against
the Queen at Branspeth on 18 Sept., 11 Eliz.; afterwards on 14 Nov, 11 Eliz., they together
with William Norton late of Hartford, co. York, the said Ridely, John Welberye late of
Branspeth, Thomas Haill late of Durham, 'draper', the said Horseley, Ralph Swynnowe late
of Durham and the said James Swynnowe, levied war against the Queen from 14 Nov. to 16
Nov. at Durham, and at Branspithe and Darneton, co. Durham, with 300 men and more; the
earls of Northumberland and Westmorland, Richard Norton, Swynborn, Nevell and
Marmaduke Blackston on 14 Nov. at Durham issued a traitorous proclamation (*recited in
English*); and Leonard and Edward Dacre received and abetted the said earls at Branspeth on
16 Sept., 11 Eliz. Further by an inquisition taken before John Walshe, a justice of the
Common Pleas, Christopher Wraye, one of the Queen's serjeants at law, Henry Gaites,
knight, George Bowes, knight, William Tankard, Lawrence Meres, Thomas Layton and
others, justices appointed by patent to inquire concerning treasons and other offences
therein specified, on 17 July, 12 Eliz., at York castle it was found that the said earls, Richard
Norton, Swynborn, Markenfeild, Egremont Rattcliff late of York, Thomas Jenney late of
York, Robert Calton late of Thriske, co. York, 'yeoman', Michael Thirkeld late of Topcliff,
Michael Tempest late of Holmesyde, Ridley, Robert Browne late of Nisham, co. Durham,
George Pringley late of Farne Acres, co. Durham, Welbery, Horseley, William Welden late
of Welden, co. Northumberland, George Carre late of Wytton, co. Northumberland,
Robert Collingwood late of Alberweke, co. Northumberland, Thomas Erington late of
Walweke Grange, co. Northumberland, the said Ralph and James Swynnowe, Thomas
Taylor late of Tadcaster, co. York, 'yeoman', Richard Cowper late of Huton, co. Durham,
                                                                              [*m*. 16]
'yeoman', Robert Heighington late of Richemond, co. York, Christopher Shawe late of
Claydon *alias* Clayton, co. Durham, 'yeoman', Peter Kirke late of Eglescliff, co. Durham,
'yeoman', Cuthbert Armorer late of Belford, co. Northumberland, Cuthbert Fenwyke late
of Southshells, co. Durham, John Ridley late of Branspeth, 'yoman', John Cowper late of
Kesweke, co. York, 'taylour', and William Mallam late of Elslake, co. York, were indicted
for rebellion against the Queen at Wetherby, co. York, on 18 Nov., 12 Eliz., with 4,000 men
and more.   By p.s.

40.)   30 *June* 1576.   Order to all justices and others to suffer Edward and Francis Bacon,
sons of Nicholas Bacon, knight, councillor, keeper of the great seal, to pass with their
servants, six horses or geldings, £60 and other baggage and necessaries. The Queen has
licensed them to depart overseas for three years for their increase in knowledge and
experience. *English*.   By Q.
        The warrant thereof remains with the keeper of the great seal by his order.

41.)   30 *April* 1576.   *Gorhambury*   Licence for John Mabbe the younger, a goldsmith of
London, to sell certain jewels and 'goldsmythes wares of gold' specified in a schedule hereto
annexed (*recited*) notwithstanding stat. 18 Eliz. forbidding the working or selling of gold of

less fineness than 22 carats and the charging for workmanship of more than 12 pence for the ounce of gold.   [m. 17]
At his suit: long before the act he had the said jewels and goldsmith's ware made for the service of the Queen and her nobility, the workmanship of which is so costly that, if they might not be sold, it would be to his utter undoing.   *English.*   By p.s.
     [*Printed together with the schedule of jewels and their descriptions,*   [m. 18]
in Rymer, Foedera (*The Hague,* 1741), *vol.* VI, *part* IV, pp. 167–169.]

42.)   16 *Feb.* 1576.   Pardon for the undermentioned persons indicted for felonies (*details given*) as follows:— Christopher Heighington late of Heighington, co. Durham, 'yoman', indicted with Thomas Vavasor late of Denton, co. Durham, 'yoman', and Christopher Walton late of Stillington, co. York, 'yoman', for the several robberies of Robert Robinson, John Burrell and Richard Thompson in the highway at Cokkerton, co. Durham, on 11 Dec., 7 Eliz.; John Hewson *alias* Hewitson late of Bradsawe, co. Derby, 'yoman', for the
                                                                                      [m. 19]
theft of a horse belonging to John Towneson of Horseley, co. Derby, 'yoman', at Tanfeld in the West Riding, co. York, on 24 May, 14 Eliz.; Elizabeth Wilson late of Kirkby Moreside, co. York, 'spynster', for breaking and entering the house of Francis Strickland at Kyrkby Moresyde and stealing money belonging to him on 20 June, 14 Eliz.; John Stowte late of 'le Olde Towne' in the regality of Hexham, 'yeoman', for that he on 2 May, 12 Eliz., (1) burgled the house of Henry Dawson at Readburne Sheilde in East Allendell, co. Northumberland, put him, George Tod and Alice Dawson his wife, in fear and stole horses belonging to him and (2) burgled the house of Rowland Littell at Rysegrene in East Allendell, put him and Janet his wife in fear and stole a sword belonging to him; Robert Browne of Great Kelke in the East Riding, 'laborer', for the theft of goods belonging to Martin Walker of Kelke, 'laborer', at Kelke on 28 Nov., 15 Eliz.; John Blenkerne late of Murton, co. Westmorland, 'yoman', for inciting and abetting Oswald Hourde late of Barton, co. Westmorland, 'yoman', on 20 March, 15 Eliz., when he burgled the house of William Richeson, 'yoman', at Ellerhorne, St. Michael, co. Westmorland, put him and his servants in fear and stole horses and goods belonging to him; John Spayne late of Akam in the regality of Hexham, co. Northumberland, 'yoman', indicted with Gavin Rede of Kaylyff Close in the liberties of Redisdale, co. Northumberland, 'yoman', for breaking and entering the close of William Smyth of Akam, 'yoman', on 3 Sept., 14 Eliz. and stealing cattle belonging to him; Archibald Armestrange late of Eske, co. Cumberland, 'yoman', for stealing 4s. 5d. and a ring belonging to Thomas Tooke from the person of Bridget Tooke, his wife, at Carlyll on 10 Jan., 15 Eliz.; and Peter Blackett late of Wykham in the county of the bishopric of Durham, 'laborer', for burgling the house of John Wightman of York, 'inholder',   [m. 20]
at York in Colyergate on 22 Nov., 16 Eliz., and stealing 10s. belonging to Henry Killingale. By consideration of Richard Harper, a justice of the Common Pleas, and Christopher Wraye, a justice of the Queen's Bench, justices of assize in the county of York.   By Q.

43.)   27 *Feb.* 1576.   Pardon for John Vliedson late of Cottingham, co. York, 'yoman', indicted at a special gaol delivery held before Thomas Gargrave, knight, Henry Gate, knight, William Farefax, knight, Lawrence Meres and Thomas Eynns, justices of oyer and terminer in the county, at York castle on 25 Nov., 18 Eliz., for that he broke and entered the closes of Henry Browne of Rowley at Rowley, co. York, and Thomas Jackson of Wawdbey the younger at Wawdbey in the East Riding, co. York, and stole horses severally belonging to them on 23 Aug., 17 Eliz. (*details given*). At the suit of Walter Jobson the elder of Kingeston on Hull, alderman.   By Q.

44.)   16 *May* 1576.   Grant for life in reversion to Edmund Cotton, one of the sons of John

Cotton, knight, of the office of registrar and keeper of the register or registers of decrees and orders in Chancery,   [*m.* 21]
granted by patent, 13 June, 11 Eliz., to Martin James for life. On surrender in Chancery by Francis Southwell of a patent, 5 Dec., 18 Eliz., granting him the same office for life in reversion.   By p.s.

Vacated, because surrendered 1 March, 35 Eliz., by the said Edmund at Dublin before Charles Calthrop, Roger Wilbram, Henry More and Richard Massingberd, commissioners by virtue of the Queen's writ; signed: Jo. Puckering C.S.

45.)   13 *April* 1576.   *Gorhambury.*   Pardon for James Bell late of Bradshawe, co. York, 'yoman', and Isabel his wife. The said James, James Rayner late of Kingewell, co. York, 'lynnen weaver', Francis Elleson late of Bradshawe, 'yoman', Walter Cromocke late of Ilkeley, co. York, 'tanner', Isabel, John Cromocke   [*m.* 22]
late of Ilkeley, 'tanner', and Robert Mayson late of Halton, co. York, 'yoman', were indicted for making counterfeit sixpences about 20 Sept., 13 Eliz., at Bradshawe and uttering the same about 1 Oct., 13 Eliz., at Scipton and elsewhere, co. York, (*details given*).   By p.s.

46.)   10 *May* 1576.   Pardon for William Spencer late of Westminster, co. Middlesex, for manslaughter. It was found by an inquisition (*jury named*) taken before Robert Hogeson, coroner of the city, on 17 April, 18 Eliz., on the body of Roger Wilkinson late of London at London in the parish of   [*m.* 23]
St. Thomas the Apostle in Vyntry ward that Spencer (accompanied by Richard Marche, his servant) wounded Wilkinson on 11 April, 13 Eliz., in the parish of St. Michael Paternoster in Vintry ward so that he died in the said parish of St. Thomas on 15 April (*details given*).
                                                                                                    By p.s.

47.)   16 *May* 1576.   Pardon for Richard Whetehill (*alias* Wheteley *alias* Whestthall) late of London, indicted, with Thomas Wilcox late of London 'yoman', for that on 30 Oct., 17 Eliz., in the highway at Hanwell, co. Middlesex, they stole horses and goods (1) belonging to John Harewood and (2) belonging to George Whitton from the keeping of Robert Tossell, Whitton's servant, (*details given*). At the suit of Thomas, earl of Sussex, councillor, lord chamberlain.   By p.s.

48.)   16 *April* 1576.   *Gorhambury.*   Pardon for John Overs late of London, 'yoman', indicted for that in the highway at Stanwell, co. Middlesex, on 16 Dec., 18 Eliz. he robbed Thomas Yate of £40 belonging to William Pettey. At the suit of James Woodforde, a clerk of the spicery.   [*m.* 24]
                                                                                                    By p.s.

49.)   27 *April* 1576.   *Gorhambury.*   Denization for Agnes Harvy, wife of James Harvy, alderman of London, and Agnes Harvy, their daughter, both born at Antwerp in the obedience of the King of Spain; to pay customs as aliens, and not to live in Berwick or Portesmouth without the Queen's special licence; without fine or payment for the third part of their goods.   By p.s.

50.)   16 *April* 1576.   *Gorhambury.*   Protection for one year for Thomas Parker, 'haberdassher', and William Parker, draper, citizens of London, *alias* merchants, brothers and co-parceners. They are indebted to the Crown; and several of their creditors intend to sue them for payment.   By p.s.

51.)   23 *Jan.* 1576.   Grant to John Baylye and Robert Blunt, cappers,   [*m.* 25]

and their deputies authorised in writing of authority to search for offenders against stat. 13 Eliz. for the continuance of the making of caps, and to compound with such persons for offences against the statute; so that they do not compound for any offence before it be committed. Also grant of monies arising from such compositions; and power to give compounders a discharge of penalties incurred. Also grant, for the relief of decayed towns, of all forfeitures by reason of offences against the statute; and order to all mayors and other rulers of cities, boroughs and towns corporate to assist the grantees to levy the moiety of forfeitures which is appointed by the statute to be distributed among the poor inhabitants. Provided that   [m. 26]
the grantees bestow yearly among the poor cappers of London, Exetur, Bristoll, Monmouth, Hereforde, Rosse, Bridgenorth, Bewdeley, Gloucester, Worcester, Chester, Nantwiche, Newe Castle, Utcester, Stafforde, Lichfeild, Coventrie, Yorke, Beverley, Richemond, Darby, Leicester, Northampton, Shrewsbury, Wellington, Southampton and Cantorburye such monies as they receive for such forfeitures over and above all necessary charges; and to account yearly for the same at Bewdley, co. Worcester, before five auditors to be appointed yearly, one by the mayor of Coventrye, one by the mayor of Hereforde, one by the bailiffs of Lychfield, one by the bailiffs of Shrewsbury and one by the bailiffs of Stafford; money found remaining in the grantees' hands to be employed upon such cappers in the cities and towns named as the auditors shall appoint; certificate of the account to be made every Michaelmas term into the Exchequer to the Queen's remembrancer. The patent to be void, if monies received shall not be employed for the relief of the poor cappers as is before expressed, or if hereafter the grant shall seem to the Queen or the Privy Council to be incommodious.

It is reported that the statute has not of late been duly put in execution, whereby the trade of making caps is greatly decayed. *English.*   By p.s.

52.)   12 *May* 1576.   Grant to John Maynerd, Matthew Spencer and Walter Hedley, the Queen's servants, their executors and assigns of a moiety of the arrears of rents and issues of the manors of Tuxwell, Bower, Fyshed, Weston and Drayton, Mochelney and the rectory of Mochelney, co. Somerset, and out of all lands in the said places, which were due to Edward VI from the beginning of his reign and withheld   [m.27]
from him, Queen Mary and the present Queen; and power to sue for the same in the Queen's name or their own as the Crown might have done. For their service. *English.*   By p.s.

53.)   2 *March* 1576.   Pardon for John Gyles and Richard Manningham, both of London, free of the fellowship of merchants adventurers of England, for their respective marriages to Anne Hawkes, daughter of John Hawkes of Andwarpe, merchant, and Jane Hendrick, daughter of Lucas Hendrick of Andwarpe, merchant, aliens born, by which marriages Gyles and Mannyngham have acquired lands beyond the seas; provided they sell the said lands within such time as the governor, assistants and fellowship of the said merchants appoint and shall henceforth keep their wives and families resident within the realm unless some necessary occasion to be allowed by the said governor, his deputy and assistants shall force them to the contrary. By patent, 18 July, 6 Eliz., it was *inter alia* ordained that if any person free of the fellowship should marry a woman born out of the Queen's dominions or should obtain lands in Holland, Zealand, Braband, Flaunders or other places adjoining, he should *ipso facto* be disfranchised of the fellowship. *English.*   By p.s.

54.)   24 *April* 1576.   *Gorhambury.*   Protection for three years for Robert Christmas and all sureties standing bound with or for him. *English.*   [m. 28]
                                                                                              By p.s.

55.)   9 *May* 1576.   Licence for three years for the bailiffs, burgesses and commonalty of the town of Great Yarmouth, co. Norfolk, by their deputies and factors specially named by writing sealed with consent of the bailiffs, burgesses and commonalty to buy in the county of Norfolk 6,000 quarters of malt and barley and 4,000 quarters of wheat, and export them in ships of the Queen's realm or of outward parts being with her in amity from the harbours of Lynne, Great Yarmouth or their members, co. Norfolk, after paying the customs payable in the year 10 Eliz.; from the present date; provided the market price of malt and barley in the ports at the time or seven days before does not exceed 10*s.* a quarter and that of wheat 15*s.* a quarter; and, if the grains aforesaid shall exceed the said several prices at any time within the three years, the effect of the licence shall cease for that time, and the licensees may transport the residue at any time within five years from the present date when the prices shall not exceed the rates above rehearsed; the licence to have the amounts shipped endorsed upon it and to be left, when expired, with the officers of the port where the last amount was shipped; a yearly particular account of the grain carried, of the profits arising and of the employment thereof about the haven to be made before auditors appointed by William, lord Burghley, treasurer, and Robert, earl of Leicester, master of the horse, or either of them and presented to the said lord or earl to be sent to the Privy Council. For the relief of their charges about the repair of the haven there, which is greatly decayed.   *English.*   By p.s.

56.)   29 *March* 1576.   *Gorhambury.*   Licence for Matthew Lullis and Peter Seris, merchants of London, their deputies and assigns to export in ships of the Queen's realm or of outward parts being with her in amity 2,000 cloths and 'carsies', accounting three 'carsies' to the cloth, as well of such cloths as are commonly called 'Kentyshe clothes or Suff' cloths, Worcester, Glocester, Somersett or Wilshier clothes commonlye called sortynge clothes' of whatever price   [*m.* 29]
dressed or undressed, as of any other kind of cloths of any other country, from the port of London, duty free; the licence to have the amounts shipped endorsed upon it, that it may be left, when expired, with the officers of the port.   *English.*   By Q.

57.)   28 *Feb.* 1576.   Appointment of Edward Fitton, knight, the Queen's servant, to be vice-treasurer and general receiver of the Queen's revenues in Ireland with a yearly fee of £66 13*s.* 4*d.* Irish, payable from 30 Sept. last; and also to be treasurer of the wars in Ireland, with a fee of 6*s.* 8*d.* sterling a day from 30 Sept. last, payable from the revenues of his office; with 20 horsemen at 9*d.* sterling a day wages each and 20 footmen at 8*d.* sterling a day wages each and 20 footmen for the ward of the Alone at 6*d.* a day wages each, payable from 30 Sept. last out of the said revenues; power to make payments out of the revenues received ordinary and extraordinary as the cause shall require, that is to say, by warrant from the Queen or for all ordinary payments by warrant from the deputy of Ireland only and for all extraordinary payments by warrant from the deputy with the advice of the Council there; he may make his account every year during his time of office before the deputy or chancellor of Ireland, the barons of the Exchequer and auditor there or before such other to whom the Queen's commission shall be given to take it, so as the deputy or the chancellor or the deputy and the chief baron of the Exchequer there be always two of the commissioners; and all acquittances made by the said commissioners (or three of them, the deputy and auditor being two) shall be as good a discharge as if made by the Queen under the great seal of England.   *English.*   By p.s.

58.)   3 *July* 1576.   Licence for five years and two months for Thomas   [*m.* 30]
Allyn of London, the Queen's servant, to export from London, Southampton, Bristall, Chester, Chichester, Sandwiche or Ippiswiche 1,600 dickers and 8 raw hides and 850 dickers 6 hides of tanned leather, parcel and residue of 2,000 dickers of salt hides and 1,000 dickers

of tanned leather which Edward, lord Clinton, high admiral, had licence for seven years by patent, 22 Nov., 13 Eliz., to export from the ports aforesaid; reserving to the Crown only the customs and subsidies payable if the same hides and leather had been transported in the year 13 Eliz., viz., for every dicker of leather or raw hides 5*s.* 5*d.*; he may under this licence export such number of calfskins as seems good to him, so that every ten dozen of calfskins be reckoned as one dicker of the said quantity of hides and leather; any true transcript or duplicate of this grant passed in due form to be given the same credit as the original patent; the licence to have the amounts shipped endorsed on it that it may be delivered to the customer of the port where the last part shall be shipped; from the present date; the chancellor or keeper of the great seal may, at the licensee's request, seal and deliver to him seven transcripts or duplicates of this licence. At his suit; on surrender of a patent, 22 July, 16 Eliz., by which it appears that the admiral assigned to Allen his interest in the patent, 22 Nov., 13 Eliz., since which date it appeared by endorsement on the patent that there had been shipped 294 dickers 2 hides of salt hides and 58 dickers of tanned leather, and on surrender thereof Allen had licence by the said patent, 22 July, 16 Eliz., to export 1,705 dickers 8 hides of raw hides and 942 dickers of tanned leather, residue of the 2,000 dickers of salt hides and 1,000 dickers of tanned leather; it appears by endorsement on Allen's patent that there have been shipped thereunder 105 dickers of raw hides and 92 dickers 2 hides of tanned leather, so that there remain unshipped 1,600 dickers 58 [*sic*] raw hides and 850 dickers 6 hides of tanned leather. *English*.   By p.s.

59.)   9 *July* 1576.   Grant for 20 years to Thomas Cornewalleys, 'gromeporter' of the household, of power to licence in London and Westminster and the suburbs of the same persons to keep 'houses of playe' and to use 'all kinde of games and playes' therein excepted or not excepted in the statutes against unlawful games; from the present date; provided that every such licenced person shall enter into recognisance not to use any 'cosonages, fraude or deceyte in playe' in his said house nor suffer apprentices or suspected persons to frequent his house and play or to use any kind of betting there; provided also that the licences be made by writing tripartite indented, one part to be delivered by the grantee into Chancery; the grantee to have all   [*m.* 32]
penalties due to the Crown as from Lady Day last for offences against the said statutes within the said cities and suburbs, which penalties may nevertheless be 'moderated, mytigated and qualifyed' by him; provided that such compositions between the grantee and offenders shall be put in writing indented bipartite, which shall be sufficient to acquit compounders against the Crown in the Exchequer and other courts; order to all officers and others to assist the grantee in summoning juries and witnesses for the better finding out of such as shall obstinately stand in defence and denial of their offences. For his service; and because he complains that his office of groom porter is utterly decayed by reason of the negligent execution of the statutes against unlawful games, which without any oversight are most commonly used in all cities, towns and villages and specially in London and Westminster to the utter extinguishment of artillery and other exercises. *English*.   By p.s.
    Vacated because surrendered 22 July, 38 Eliz.; *signed*: Tho. Egerton, C.S.; Thomas Cornwaleys.

60.)   28 *July* 1576.   *Gorhambury*.   Licence for seven years for Ralph Bowes and Thomas Bedingfelde, the Queen's servants, to import playing cards; from Michaelmas next; no other persons to import playing cards or to distribute   [*m.* 33]
any other than such as the licensees shall bring in or allow to be sold or cause any to be made; offenders to forfeit all cards brought in, sold or made, one half to the Crown and the other to the licensees, and suffer punishment for contempt; duties to be paid. In consideration of 100 marks payable at the Exchequer yearly at Lady Day or within one month after, the first

payment to be made at Lady Day 1577 or within one month after, for which they are bound in the Exchequer. *English.*   By p.s.

61.) 9 *July* 1576. Licence for four years for Robert, earl of Leicester, councillor, to alienate all lands comprised in grants to him and his heirs *inter alia*, to hold by service of the fortieth part of a knight's fee, (1) by patent, 19 April, 14 Eliz., of the manors of Arusteley and Caveliock, with the townships of Maghenlleth, Llanydlos and Caersons, and other lands in Arustely and Caveliock, co. Montgomery, and (2) by patent, 9 June, 5 Eliz., of the lordship or lordships of Denbigh and Denbighlande, the castle of Denbigh, the borough of Denbigh, the forest of Denbigh, the manor of Chirke and Chirkland and other lands, co. Denbigh; from the present date; he may on every such alienation reserve and create such tenures as he pleases whether by rent and fealty, by fealty only or by other services of him and his heirs as of any manor of his or otherwise, notwithstanding the statute of Westminster III of *Quia emptores* or any other law.   By Q.

62.) 10 *July* 1576. Grant for life, for his service, to William Littleston of Barnestable, co. Devon, the Queen's servant, of an annuity of £30, payable out of the customs and subsidies in the ports of Exeter and Dartmouth, co. Devon; from Michaelmas 1574; the grant to be void, if he should hereafter receive any greater preferment from the Crown.   By p.s.

63.) 25 *June* 1576. Pardon for Peter Girlyngton and Anthony Girlyngton, both of Burton, co. Lincoln. It was found by an inquisition taken before   [*m.* 34] Christopher Barde, a coroner in the county, on the body of Henry Crosbye on 10 Feb., 18 Eliz., at Tupholme, co. Lincoln, that they and Archibald James late of Glantworth, co. Lincoln, 'yoman', at Tupholme on 8 Feb., 18 Eliz., attacked Crosbye and James feloniously killed him (*details given*).   By Q.

64.) 25 *June* 1576. Lease for 21 years to Thomas Hellerd of lands (*named*) in Cottingham, co. York, parcel of the manor of Cottingham and of lands late of Charles, earl of Westmorland, exchanged; with reservations; from Lady Day last; yearly rent £10 15s. 5d. (*detailed*)   [*m.* 35] In consideration of the surrender by him of a patent, 14 June, 12 Eliz., leasing the premises to him for 21 years from Lady Day then last at the same rent; and for a sum within a sum of £20 paid at the Exchequer by Thomas Elwald and him.

                                                   By warrant of the commissioners.

65.) 20 *June* 1576. Lease for 21 years to Thomas Browne of lands (*named with tenants' names*) in Southwarke, co. Surrey, late of Battle abbey, co. Sussex; with reservations; from the termination of a lease therof by patent of the court of Augmentations, 13 May, 36 Hen. VIII, to his father, William Browne the King's servant, for 50 years from Michaelmas then next at a yearly rent of a peppercorn; yearly rent £17 10s. 8d. (*detailed*).   [*m.* 36]
                                                                             By p.s.

66.) 25 *June* 1576. Grant to William Meringe, knight, of the wardship and marriage of William Rigges, son and heir of Edmund Rigges; with an annuity of £6 13s. 4d. from 8 April, 11 Eliz., when Edmund died, until the death of Anne late the wife of William Rigges, the ward's grandfather, and of Anne Rigges, late the wife of Edmund, his mother, and thereafter an annuity of £10.   By Q.

67.) 25 *June* 1576. Lease for life in succession to Richard Younge,   [*m.* 37] Catherine his wife and Catherine their daughter of lands (*named with tenants' names*) in St.

Neots, co. Huntingdon, parcel of the manor of St. Neots and of lands assigned to the Queen before her accession, late of the monastery of St. Neots; with reservations; from Lady Day last; yearly rent 58*s.* 6*d.*   [*m.* 38]

On the surrender by Richard and Catherine his wife of a patent of the Exchequer, 8 July, 12 Eliz., leasing the premises to him, his said wife and Paul Younge, their son, for life in succession from Michaelmas next at the same rent. For a fine of 58*s.* 6*d.* paid at the Exchequer by Richard.   By warrant of the commissioners.

68.)   10 *July* 1576.   Lease for 21 years to William Addyson, a soldier of the town of Berwick, of (1) the rectory of Newarke, co. Nottingham, a barn called 'the tyeth lathe' there and the tithes of corn, hay, wool and lambs there, (2) the small tithes in Newerke, once in the tenure of John Markham and George Garlande, and (3) lands in Ferlington, co. York, once of the late chapel of Farlington in Sherif Hutton, co. York; with reservations; (1) and (2) (the said rectory and tithes in Newarke) from St. Mark's Day 1584, being the termination of a lease of (1) by the priory of St. Catherine without the walls of Lincoln by conventual indenture, 21 April 1530, to Thomas   [*m.* 39]

Hobman of Saxelby, co. Lincoln, husbandman (*agricole*), Cecily his wife and Roger their son for 30 years from St. Mark's Day 1554 at a yearly rent of £17, and (3) from Michaelmas 1583, being the termination of a lease thereof by patent of the exchequer, 5 Dec., 5 Eliz., to Elizabeth Watson, widow, for 21 years from Michaelmas then last at a yearly rent of 18*s.*; yearly rents (1) and (2) £7 and (3) 18*s.*; the lessee to pay to the vicar of Newarke a yearly stipend of £10. For his service.   By p.s.

69.)   5 *Nov.* 1576.   Presentation of Richard Hancock, clerk, to the perpetual vicarage of Hartburne, co. Northumberland, Durham dioc., void by the resignation of Richard Stancliff; in the Queen's gift *sede vacante*.   By p.s.

70.)   30 *Oct.* 1576.   Presentation of John Mason, clerk, to the rectory of West Illesley, co. Berks, Salisbury dioc.; in the Queen's gift by lapse.   By p.s.

71.)   6 *Nov.* 1576.   Grant for life to Bartholomew White of an annuity of 12*d.* a day from Michaelmas last, payable at the Exchequer. For his service in war.   By p.s.

72.)   10 *Nov.* 1576.   Presentation of Robert Cansfeld, M.A., to the rectory of Bifford, co. York, York dioc., void by death.   By p.s.

73.)   6 *Nov.* 1576. Presentation of Cuthbert Bradford, clerk, to the rectory of Howghton, co. Southampton, Winchester dioc.; in the Queen's gift by lapse.   By p.s.

74.)   5 *Nov.* 1576. Appointment for life of Henry Fane to assist   [*m.* 40]
the warden of the Cinque Ports with the said warden's lieutenant in Dover castle, co. Kent, as William Oxenden, deceased, lately did in the said castle; with wages of 2*s.* a day from Lady Day last, payable by the receiver general in the said county. For his service.

75.)   30 *Oct.* 1576.   Order to all archbishops, bishops, deans and archdeacons in England and especially Henry Tutchener, archdeacon of Dorset, Bristol dioc., to institute Thomas Cooke to the rectory of Sanwiche *alias* Worthswanwich in the archdeaconry of Dorset, to which Cooke was presented by patent, 1 Dec., 18 Eliz., and to induct him or his proctor thereto.   By p.s.

76.)   2 *Nov.* 1576.   Grant for life to John Rolfe, the Queen's servant, of an annuity of £20

from Easter last, payable at the Exchequer; the grant to be void if he shall be promoted by the Crown to any office or living of the yearly value of £20 or more. For his service.

By p.s.

77.)   3 *Nov.* 1576.   Presentation of Stephen Townesend, clerk, S.T.B., the Queen's chaplain, to the rectory of Testocke *alias* Taystocke *alias* Tavestocke, Exeter dioc.; in the Queen's gift by the minority of William, earl of Bath, kinsman and heir of John the late earl.

By p.s.

78.)   30 *Aug.* 1576.   *Gorhambury.*   Grant for life to John Morgan of the office of bailiff of the hundred of Dyvenock, co. Brecon; no sheriff or other minister of the Crown to intermeddle in the office so long as Morgan and his deputy shall behave well in the execution thereof; with the accustomed wages and the like, payable out of the profits of the hundred by himself or by the sheriff of the county.   By p.s.

79.)   5 *Nov.* 1576.   Grant to Francis Walsingham, the Queen's secretary,   [*m.* 41] of the gift of the canonry or prebend in Canterbury cathedral which shall next be void; so that he may present thereto Robert Havenden, M.A., and no other; if this grant cannot take effect by reason of a former grant or otherwise, it shall extend to the second, third or fourth vacancy; so that the patronage thereof shall not revert to the Crown until Hovenden has been presented by the grantee.   By p.s.

80.)   5 *July* 1576.   Lease for 21 years to Edmund Standen, a clerk of the petty bag of Chancery, of lands (*tenants named*) in Est Moulsey and West Moulsey, parcel of the manor of Moulsey Matham and Est Moulsey *alias* Moulsey Prior, co. Surrey, parcel of the honour of Hampton Courte; with reservations; from Lady Day last; yearly rent 44s. 8d. For a fine of £4 5s. 4d. paid at the Exchequer.   By warrant of the commissioners.

(Membranes 1d. to 10d. are blank.)

81.)   16 *Dec.* 1575.   Commission to Henry Sidney, K.G., president of the   [*m.* 11d] council in the principality and marches of Wales, deputy of Ireland, Adam, archbishop of Dublyn, Nicholas Bagnall, knight, marshal of the army there, John Plunkett, knight, chief justice of the Queen's Bench in Ireland, Lucas Dyllon, chief baron of the Exchequer, Nicholas White, master of the rolls there, Francis Agarde, Thomas Jenison, auditor of Ireland, and Lancelot Alforde, surveyor of the Queen's lands in Ireland, (or five of them, of whom the deputy, the archbishop, Dyllon, White, Jenison and Alforde are to be four) to take the accounts of Edward Fiton, knight, treasurer at the wars and undertreasurer and receiver general of the revenues in Ireland, from his   [*m.* 12d.] first entry into the offices until Michaelmas last; upon determination of his said accounts, a just declaration of account shall be made thereof, engrossed on parchment to remain to the Queen's use of record under the commissioners' hands and seals, and one part or parts or the just declaration thereof delivered to Fiton for his discharge, which shall be as good a discharge as if signed by the Queen and sealed with the great seal of England; a third part of the said treasurer's account of the wars to be engrossed and sent into England to remain in the Exchequer there of record. At his suit. *English.*   By Q.

82.)   9 *Feb.* 1576.   Commission to Nicholas Brockett, Edmund Bardolfe, Giles Crowe, Walter Tooke, deputy feodary in the county, and Michael Berisforde (or two of them, Tooke being one) to inquire *post mortem* Francis Rogers in the county of Hertford.

The like to the following, viz.—

83.)   28 *Jan.* 1576.   John Ashecome the elder, Richard Hyde, Richard Radishe and Thomas Nooke, feodary of the county, (or two of them); *p.m.* Thomas Gifford; co. Berks.

84.)   28 *Jan.* 1576.   Jerome Corbett, John Broke and Thomas Staunton, feodary of the county, (or two of them); *p.m.* John Wanerter; co. Salop.

85.)   30 *Jan.* 1576.   William Gerard, Peter Warberton, Robert Turbridge, William Ashton and John Billott, feodary of the county, (or two of them); *p.m.* Anthony Gravenor; co. Denbigh.

86.)   4 *Feb.* 1576.   George Ratclif, knight, Thomas Gray, knight, Robert Middleton and John Lawson, feodary of the county, (or two of them); *p.m.* John Shaftoo; co. Northumberland.

87.)   4 *Feb.* 1576.   Edmund Dockwra, Griffin Curteys, Richard Pickeringe and Thomas Noke, feodary of the county, (or two of them); *p.m.* Thomas Dolman; co. Berks.

88.)   4 *Feb.* 1576.   John Scudamore, James Warrecombe, James Boyle, James Garnans and John Parry, deputy feodary of the county, (or two of them); *p.m.* Richard Harford; co. Hereford.

89.)   6 *Feb.* 1576.   John Langley, Richard Malthouse, Henry Townsend, Thomas Smyth and Michael Berisford, feodary of the county, (or two of them); *p.m.* Roger Colte; co. Kent.

90.)   9 *Feb.* 1576.   Roger Yonge, John Elston and Thomas Noke, feodary of the county; *p.m.* Thomas Essex; co. Berks.

91.)   9 *Feb.* 1576.   John Hiegham, Robert Gurden, Francis Clopton, Thomas Poley and Thomas Andrewes, feodary of the county, (or three of them); *p.m.* Lionel Talmage; co. Suffolk.

92.)   9 *Feb.* 1576.   Arthur Gregory, feodary of the county of the city, George Willughby, Richard Over and Ralph Joyner (or two of them); *p.m.* Thomas Essex; co. city of Coventry.

93.)   9 *Feb.* 1576. Richard Dudley, Francis Sandes, Robert Sandes and Henry Tolson, feodary of the county, (or two of them); *p.m.* Thomas Barwoys; co. Cumberland.

94.)   10 *Feb.* 1576.   Ralph Barton, feodary of the county, Thomas Bullocke, feodary of the honour of Tickhill, parcel of the duchy of Lancaster, and Charles FitzWillyam; *p.m.* Robert Moreton; co. Nottingham.

95.)   14 *Feb.* 1576.   Thomas Dabridgecourte, William Purefey, Humphrey Davenporte and Arthur Gregorye, feodary of the county, (or two of them); *p.m.* Anthony Stoughton; co. Warwick.

96.)   24 *Jan.* 1576.   Francis Hastinges, Francis Browne, Thomas Roos and Robert Braham, feodary of the county, (or two of them); *p.m.* William Brodgate; co. Leicester.

97.)   26 *Jan.* 1576.   John Ayre, William Jurdane and William Grove, feodary of the county, (or two of them); *p.m.* Edward Baynarde; co. Wilts.

98.)   16 *Jan.* 1576.   *Hampton Court.*   William Necton, Eustace Webbe, deputy feodary of the county, and Edward Welshe (or two of them); *p.m.* Richard Blunt; co. Surrey.

99.)   3 *Feb.* 1576.   Richard Lygon, William Childe, feodary of the county, Thomas Hanford and John Alderford; *p.m.* William Pynnocke; co. Worcester.

100.)   15 *Feb.* 1576.   Thomas Tey, Edward Waldegrave, George Knightley, John Glascoke, feodary of the county, and William Ram (or two of them); *p.m.* Francis Cockeyn *alias* Cockyn; co. Essex.

101.)   2 *Jan.* 1576.   John Lawson, feodary of the county, Henry Welton, Ralph Booteflower, Robert Newton and Cuthbert Rydley (or two of them); *p.m.* Richard Newton of Eltringham; co. Northumberland.

102.)   18 *Nov.* 1575.   William Catesby, knight, Thomas Tressam, knight, and William Rudd, feodary of the county, (or two of them); *p.m.* Ralph Leycester, knight; co. Northampton.

103.)   3 *Dec.* 1575.   Godfrey Bossevile, Francis Roodes and Anthony Kyme, feodary of the county, (or two of them); *p.m.* Richard Slater, 'yoman'; co. Lincoln.

104.)   3 *Dec.* 1575.   William Aucher, Arnold Haddes, Giles Crowe, James   [*m.* 13*d.*] Austyn and Michael Berisford, feodary of the county, (or two of them); *p.m.* Henry Crippes, knight; co. Kent.

105.)   3 *Dec.* 1575.   The same (or two of them); *p.m.* Christopher Harflette *alias* Sepvaunce; co. Kent.

106.)   3 *Dec.* 1575.   Thomas Scotte, knight, Arnold Haddes, William Ager and Michael Berisford, feodary of the county, (or two of them); *p.m.* Gervase Carkaredge; co. Kent.

107.)   3 *Dec.* 1575.   William Aucher, Arnold Haddes, Giles Crowe, James Astyn and Michael Berisforde, feodary of the county, (or two of them); *p.m.* Thomas Pepper; co. Kent.

108.)   16 *Dec.* 1575.   Anthony Morton, Edward Trovell, William Uvett, James Garnans and John Parrye, feodary of the county, (or two of them); *p.m.* Richard Harford; co. Hereford.

109.)   16 *Dec.* 1575.   William Mohun, Richard Chamond, Richard Tryvanyan and Thomas Browne, feodary of the county, (or two of them); *p.m.* Edward Trevanyon; co. Cornwall.

110.)   10 *Dec.* 1575.   Robert, lord Ogle, Cuthbert Collingwood, knight, Thomas Graye, knight, John Hedworth, John Lawson, feodary of the county, and Henry Wiclif (or three of them); *p.m.* Anthony Mitford of Pounteland; co. Northumberland.

111.)   14 *Dec.* 1575.   Robert Powell, Simon Kemsey, Richard Prynce and Thomas Staunton, feodary of the county, (or two of them); *p.m.* Arthur Chambers; co. Salop.

112.)   6 *Feb.* 1576.   Commission to Richard Malthouse, Henry Townsend, Thomas Smyth and Michael Berisford, feodary of the county, (or two of them, the feodary being one) to inquire *post mortem* Richard Wilson, son and heir of Nicholas Wilson, a minor in the Queen's ward, in the county of Kent.

The like to the following,—

113.)   11 *Feb.* 1576.   George Danvers, Robert Doyley the elder, John Cupper, George Whitton and Thomas Bickardes, feodary of the county, (or two of them); *p.m.* Bartholomew Belson, son and heir of Richard Belson; co. Oxford.

114.)   28 *Nov.* 1575.   Oliver St. John the elder, William Langhorne, Giles Blofield and Richard Faldo, feodary of the county, (or two of them); *p.m.* John Cobbe, son and heir of Thomas Cobbe; co. Bedford.

115.)   *Undated.*   Commission to Christopher Heydon, knight, William Buttes, knight, and Christopher Daubney, feodary of the county, to inquire better *post mortem* Christopher Calthorpe in the county of Norfolk; sitting at days and places to be appointed by Jerome Bowes, knight, and Edward Devereux (so that Bowes shall make known the day and place to Devereux 12 days before the sitting). By an inquisition taken before the same commissioners by virtue of a commission of *melius inquirendum* on 21 Sept. last at Holte Markett it was found that he held lands (*tenants named*) in Cokthrope, parcel of the manor of Netherhall in Styfkey; but by what service certain of them are held is not specified, and the jury did not know whether he held further lands of the Crown in Cokthorpe, Bynham, Langham and Styfkey.

116.)   6 *Feb.* 1576.   Commission to Thomas Andrewes, feodary of the county, John Thurston and Reginald Rowse (or two of them, the feodary being one) to inquire better *post mortem* George Veasey in the county of Suffolk.   [*m.* 14*d.*] By an inquisition taken before Thomas Colbye, John Copledicke, William Robertes and

Francis Boldero by virtue of a commission to them and Richard Wingfeld it was found that he held lands in Westleton, Thorington, Brampfeld, Blybrough and Wenhaston and that Marion Veysey is his daughter and heir; but of whom or by what services the lands are held is not specified.

117.)   14 *Feb.* 1576.   Commission to Anthony Smethley, feodary of the East Riding, co. York, William Ingleby, Marmaduke Constable and William Danyell (or two of them, the feodary being one) to inquire *post mortem* Walter Griffith what further lands he held in the county of York than those specified in an inquisition heretofore taken.

118.)   8 *Feb.* 1576.   Commission to William Hunston, William Yaxley, William Savell, Anthony Pickeringe and Arthur Kyme, feodary of the county, (or two of them, the feodary being one) to inquire *post mortem* Richard Westland what further lands he held in the county of Lincoln than those specified in an inquisition heretofore taken.

119.)   16 *Jan.* 1576.   *Hampton Court.*   Commission to John Forster, knight, Francis Russell, knight, Thomas Graye, knight, Cuthbert Carnabie and John Lawson, feodary of the county, (or two of them, the feodary being one) to inquire touching the idiocy of John Fenwick in the county of Northumberland.

120.)   9 *Feb.* 1576.   Commission to Robert Graye, George Wyatt, John Eveleighe, feodary of the county, and Hugh Wyatt (or two of them, the feodary being one) to inquire touching the lunacy of Alexander Beaple in the county of Devon.

121.)   16 *Jan.* 1576.   (*No place.*)   Commission to John Southcote, a justice   [*m.* 15*d.*] of the Queen's Bench, and Richard Harpur, a justice of the Common Pleas, to determine in the guildhall of London an appeal of error in the record, process and judgment of a suit concerning a plea of account on the receipt of divers goods brought by Richard Whytinge against Bartholome Talyofer before the mayor and aldermen of London in the chamber of the guildhall; at the suit of Talyofer.

122.)   26 *Jan.* 1576.   Commission to John Southcote and Thomas Gawdy, both justices of the Queen's Bench, to determine in the guildhall of London an appeal of error in the record, process and judgment of a suit concerning a plea of trespass on the case brought by Lewis Tyrrye against James Hawes, knight, before the mayor and aldermen of London in the chamber of the guildhall; at the suit of Tyrrye.

123.)   16 *April* 1576.   *Gorhambury.*   Commission to the bishop of London, the dean of St. Peter's collegiate church, Westminster, the dean of St. Paul's cathedral and the archdeacons of Middlesex and Essex for the time being, Christopher Wraye, knight, chief justice of England, James Dyer, knight, chief justice of the Common Pleas, William Cordell, knight, master of the rolls, John Southcotte and Thomas Gawdye, judges of the Queen's Bench, Thomas Sackeforde and Thomas Wilson, masters of the requests, Gilbert Gerrard, attorney-general, Thomas Damsell, Rowland Heyward, William Allen, John Ryvers and James Hawes, knights, William Fleetewood, recorder of London, David Lewes, Thomas Yale, John Gybon, William Drurye, Thomas Marten, Robert Forde and Bartholomew Clerke, doctors of civil law, William Knolles, marshal of the Queen's Bench prison, and his successors and his and their deputies there, Francis Sandbache, John Eve, Richard Best and Michael Moselley, attorneys of the Queen's Bench, John Langley, William Bonde, Francis Barnam, Richard Pype, James Harvye, Thomas Blancke, William Kympton, Wolfstan Dyxe, George Barnes and Edward Osborne, aldermen of London, Master Crowley and

Master Wager, preachers of God's Word, Thomas Highgate, William Gerrarde, William Wightman, John Page and [—] Lyon in the county of Middlesex, John Catesbye, William Scotte and John Scotte in the county of Surrey, Thomas Mylles and William Spencer, serjeants at arms, Thomas Cure, Thomas Wey, William Evance, Oly [—] [sic] Burr, William Lyger and William Gardyner of Southwark, co. Surrey, Richard Barnes, Matthew Felde, Anthony Calthropp, John Wever and Thomas Shippam, mercers, Nicholas Backehowse, Richard Yonge, Ralph Wodcocke, Ferdinand Poyntes, William Smyth and Hugh Morgan, grocers, Nicholas Wheler, William Barnarde, Martin Caltropp and William Raignoldes, drapers, Thomas Ware and John Allott, fishmongers, John Mabbe, Andrew Palmer and Thomas Gardyner, goldsmiths, Thomas Starkye, Thomas Awdley and Ralph Carkett, skinners, Thomas Browne, Richard Hyll and Thomas Spencer, merchant taylors, Robert Offley, Thomas Sares, William Stone and George Bond, haberdashers, Anthony Cage and William Gybons, salters, William Roo and Richard Morryce, ironmongers, William Abraham, vintner, John Clerke, Thomas Bayarde, Robert Howse and Nicholas Parkynson, clothworkers, Richard Peacocke and Ralph Pratte, leathersellers, John Draper and [—] Treue, alebrewers, (or three of them) to call before them at least four times a year in the city or suburbs of London or in the marshal's lodging in the Queen's Bench prison all prisoners in the prisons of the Queen's Bench and their creditors, to examine their several petitions and made a final determination therein [m. 16d.]
on the prisoners' own bonds, if it seems good, for default of sureties, and to punish creditors disobedient to the commissioners' orders; if any creditors be bankrupt, fled overseas, dead or of purpose absent and have not authorised by letter of attorney or otherwise someone whereby the Queen's pleasure in the premises may be the better be accomplished, the commissioners may take order for the enlargement of the prisoner as in other like causes of debt they have to do between prisoners and creditors present before them; the marshal and his deputies shall permit all persons within the prison to go at all times with their lawful keepers to all places in the Queen's dominions to treat with their creditors or otherwise provide for their deliverance, as accustomed; provided that the marshal or his substitutes have always their prisoners so licensed in such sure custody that they may be produced at their creditors' lawful demand; provided that this patent shall not give authority to make a composition between any persons or to discharge any prisoner without the consent of the parties at whose suit prisoners are detained, except the commissioners find the creditor unreasonable. By advice of the Privy Council; at the prisoners' suit. *English*. By Q.

124.) 27 *March* 1576. *Gorhambury*. Commission to lord Burghley, treasurer, K.G., Francis, earl of Bedford, Ambrose, earl of Warwick, master of the ordnance, Robert, earl of Leicester, master of the horse, Henry, lord Hunsdon, governor of Barwike and warden of the East Marches towards Scotland, K.G., James Croft, knight, controller of the household, Thomas Smyth, knight, and Francis Walsingham, the two principal secretaries, and Walter Mildmay, knight, chancellor of the Exchequer, all councillors, (or four of them, the treasurer, lord Hunsdon, one of the secretaries or Mildmay being one) to take the account of Valentine Browne, knight, from the date of his last account to the [m. 17d.]
date of the presents; they shall on determination of the account cause all monies found due to be paid into the Exchequer, advertise the Queen of the state of the account, and give Browne for his discharge a copy of his account or declaration signed and sealed by them and signed by the auditors of the prests. He has had of the treasurer great sums of money to be employed in the Queen's affairs and has received to her use corn, victuals and other things for which he stands accountable. *English*. By Q.

125.) 13 *July* 1576. Appointment during pleasure of William, lord Burghley, treasurer, chancellor of the university of Cambridge, Richard, bishop of Ely, John Whitgifte, Andrew

Perne and Edward Hawford, doctors of theology, and Henry Harvye, Thomas Ithell and
[—] Binge, doctors of civil law in the said university, (or four of them, Burghley, the bishop
or Ithell being one) to be delegates or commissioners to visit St. John's College, Cambridge,
to remove delinquents (but only with the express consent of Burghley and the bishop), to
reform the statutes and to do all other things which are requisite.   By Q.

(The rest of the dorse is blank.)

PART II

C. 66/1138

126.)   28 *Nov.* 1575.   Denization for Nicholas Ragemy, born a Spanish   [*m.* 1]
subject; to pay customs as an alien, and not to live in Berwik or Portesmouth without the
Queen's special licence.

> By the keeper of the great seal by virtue of the Queen's
> warrant; for 6*s.* 8*d.* in the hanaper.

The like, for the following, for the fines specified, viz.—

127.)	2 *Jan.* 1576.	Alexander Moco, Spanish subject, born in Valencia.	6*s.* 8*d.*
128.)	5 *Dec.* 1575.	Henry Wynckan, subject of the duke of Cleves.	6*s.* 8*d.*
129.)	19 *Nov.* 1575.	John Lyon *alias* Lyen, Scottish subject.	10*s.*
130.)	5 *Dec.* 1575.	Anthony Monard, Spanish subject, born in Warrey.	13*s.* 4*d.*
131.)	18 *Nov.* 1575.	Arnold Elsam, subject of the duke of Cleves.	10*s.*
132.)	24 *Nov.* 1575.	John Cowte, Scottish subject.	10*s.*
133.)	21 *May* 1576.	James Seres, Spanish subject, born in Holland.	6*s.* 8*d.*
134.)	22 *Nov.* 1575.	Roger van Peene, Spanish subject.	10*s.*
135.)	30 *Jan.* 1576.	Anthony Gheven, Spanish subject, born in Turnolte.	10*s.*
136.)	9 *Feb.* 1576.	Peter Seres, Spanish subject, born in Antwerp.	10*s.*
137.)	9 *Feb.* 1576.	Edward Arnold, Spanish subject, born in Harlinge.	6*s.* 8*d.*

138.)   6 *March* 1576.   Order to all justices and others to permit the bailiffs, good men and
burgesses of the town of Dunwich to enjoy the liberties granted them by charter, 7 May, 14
Hen. III, whereby it was granted that they should be quit of toll and other dues (*named*) and
all other customs and exactions throughout the King's power.

139.)   24 *May* 1576.   Order to all sheriffs and others to permit the men and tenants of the
manor and town of Elesford, co. Kent, to be quit according to custom, as tenants in ancient
demesne, of contributions to expenses of knights of Parliament, of juries etc. except in the
court of the manor and town (unless they hold lands of another tenure whereby according to
statute they ought to be put thereon) and of toll and other dues (*named*). They are found to be
tenants in ancient demesne by a certificate of the treasurer and chamberlains sent into
Chancery and remaining in the Chancery files.

140.)   11 *Feb.* 1575.   Presentation of William Lyre, clerk, to the   [*m.* 2]
vicarage of Wendeover, Lincoln dioc.

The like for the following clerks, viz.—

141.)   9 *Feb.* 1576.   Thomas Butler to the vicarage of Overton under Ardern, Lincoln
dioc.

142.)   8 *Feb.* 1576.   Robert Vause to the rectory of Southfambridge, London dioc.

143.)   11 *Feb.* 1576.   John Masson to the rectory of Rolston, Salisbury dioc.

144.)   11 *Feb.* 1576.   Robert Sherington to the rectory of St. Margaret in Fryday Streate,
London, London dioc.

145.)   14 *Feb.* 1576.   Richard Clerk to the rectory of Kyrkby Malary, Lincoln dioc.

146.)   13 *Feb.* 1576.   Thomas Hyde, M.A., to the rectory of Sadington, Lincoln dioc.

147.)   9 *Feb.* 1576.   Thomas Hyde, M.A., to the vicarage of Marston Lawrence, Peterborough dioc.

148.)   11 *Feb.* 1576.   John Masson to the rectory of Rolston, Salisbury dioc.

149.)   5 *Dec.* 1575.   Owen Johns to the rectory of Marston Sicca, Gloucester dioc.

150.)   8 *Feb.* 1576.   Joshua Hutton to the vicarage of Reculver, Canterbury dioc.

151.)   30 *Jan.* 1576.   James Lawrence to the vicarage of Canfford, Bristol dioc.

152.)   28 *Jan.* 1576.   William Bentley to the rectory of Wirlingham, Norwich dioc.

153.)   26 *Jan.* 1576.   John Coxe to the rectory of Fely, Exeter dioc.

154.)   30 *Jan.* 1576.   William Stannynoyght to the rectory of St. Martin, Oxford, Oxford dioc.

155.)   3 *Feb.* 1576.   Edmund Welles to the vicarage of Estewinche, Norwich dioc.

156.)   30 *Dec.* 1575.   Richard Rawelyn to the vicarage of Stranton, Durham dioc.

157.)   7 *Jan.* 1576.   *Hampton Court.* Gilbert Dutton to the rectory of Dogmersfeld, Winchester dioc.

158.)   2 *Jan.* 1576.   Richard Turnebull to the rectory of Wadingworth, Lincoln dioc.

159.)   20 *Jan.* 1576.   John Farbrace to the vicarage of Elmisted, Canterbury dioc.

160.)   9 *Dec.* 1575.   John More to the vicarage of Chalke, Canterbury dioc.

161.)   16 *Dec.* 1575.   James Smyth to the rectory of Weston, Norwich dioc.

162.)   23 *Nov.* 1575.   Anthony Wright to the rectory of Huntyngdon, peculiar of Canterbury.

163.)   4 *Jan.* 1576.   *Hampton Court.* James Chapman to the vicarage of Chesterton, Oxford dioc.

164.)   23 *Nov.* 1575.   Christopher Walker to the rectory of Duston, Carlisle dioc.

165.)   23 *Nov.* 1575.   Thomas Bonde to the rectory of Acryse, Canterbury dioc.

166.)   17 *Nov.* 1575.   John Motley, M.A., to the vicarage of Ringmere, peculiar of Canterbury.

167.)   23 *Nov.* 1575.   William Malkyn to the rectory of Syresham,   [*m.* 3]
Peterborough dioc.

168.)   23 *Nov.* 1575.   James Powell to the vicarage of Monmouth, Hereford dioc.

169.)   23 *Nov.* 1575.   Christopher Dixe to the rectory of Eaton Hastinges, Salisbury dioc.

170.)   23 *Nov.* 1575.   John Taverner to the rectory of Wodeyton, Oxford dioc.

171.)   23 *Nov.* 1575.   William Lawson to the vicarage of Baburham, Ely dioc.

172.)   28 *Nov.* 1575.   John Darlaye to the rectory of Stokeashe, Norwich dioc.

173.)   5 *Dec.* 1575.   Thomas Esterbe to the vicarage of Seham, Durham dioc.

174.)   5 *Dec.* 1575.   John Wynne to the vicarage of Wardon, Durham dioc.

175.)   5 *Dec.* 1575.   Richard Stinte to the rectory of Mongham Magna, Canterbury dioc.

176.)   5 *Dec.* 1575.   Mardoch Bownell to the rectory of Cranesford, Canterbury dioc.

177.)   8 *Feb.* 1576.   William Duxfeld to the vicarage of Warkewooth, York dioc.

178.)   27 *July* 1576.   *Gorhambury.*   Order to all sheriffs and others to permit the tenants of the manor of Newport, co. Essex, to be quit according to custom, as tenants in ancient demesne, of toll and other dues (*named*) and of contributions to expenses of knights of Parliament. They are found to be tenants in ancient demesne by a certificate of the treasurer and barons sent into Chancery *temp.* Henry IV and remaining in the Chancery files.

179.)   8 *Aug.* 1576.   *Gorhambury.* Licence for four years for Henry, earl of Huntington, K.G., president of the council of the North, to buy in England 8,000 broad woollen cloths, long or short, dressed or undressed, wrought or unwrought, white or coloured, or as many kersies or other kind of cloth as are 'answerable' to the said long or short cloths; and to export to friendly countries the same 8,000 cloths or kersies answerable to the same

unwrought and undressed, that is to say, 'not rowed, first coursed and shorne or otherwise wrought'; from the present date; duties to be paid after three years as by merchants Englishmen born and citizens of London; various   [m. 4]
statutes touching the export of wool (named) notwithstanding; the licence to have the amounts shipped endorsed upon it and to be left, when expired, with the customers of the port where the last amount shall be shipped; the licensee to be bound in the Exchequer or the custom house for payment of sums due hereby; the Queen undertakes that no licence to export woollen cloths or kersies contrary to the statutes before mentioned will be granted
                                                                                    [m. 5]
during the four years of the present licence; power for the licensee to cause searches to be made for breaches of the statutes aforesaid and any others concerning the export of woollen cloths or kersies unwrought or undressed, and grant of one half the sums due to the Crown for breaches so discovered; the keeper of the great seal or chancellor to issue such commissions and process in respect of the present grant as the licensee shall require. *English*.   By Q.

180.)   27 *July* 1576.   *Gorhambury*. Grant to the master, wardens and commonalty of the mistery of clothworkers of London of power to search   [m. 6]
all packs, trusses and other things wherein any cloth is bestowed, suspected to be packed contrary to stat. 8 Eliz. touching clothworkers and cloths ready wrought to be shipped oversea and other statutes to like effect, when the same shall be waterborne either in lighters or other vessels that take into them such packs or trusses at any quay or wharf or on board any ship before the same ship shall be fully laden; also—that the handicraftsmen clothworkers of London for whose relief the statutes were chiefly made may have no cause to complain, and for the better understanding what cloths shall henceforth be shipped by the merchants adventurers or others by force of any licence—order that the merchants adventurers shall forthwith show to the master and wardens of the clothworkers such licences as they have remaining in force, and that customers and other officers shall, upon request of the said master and wardens, show them all such licences in force as have been or shall be granted for exporting cloths undressed, so that they may be satisfied that such cloths as by the statute are appointed to be dressed are dressed; the governor or his deputy, assistants and generalty of the merchants adventurers in London may appoint for the port of London two freemen of their company by writing under seal, and the said master and wardens of the clothworkers may appoint for the said port two, three or four freemen of their company, which persons so appointed shall be sworn before the governor or his deputy and assistants of the merchants adventurers resident in London and the master and wardens and two or four of the assistants of the clothworkers (and, if there be any default of the merchants adventurers in appointing, the four persons appointed by the clothworkers shall be sworn before the said master, wardens and assistants of the clothworkers only), the tenor of which oath shall be that they shall without malice or favour search such packs of woollen cloths as shall be waterborne for transport over the sea by force of any licence granted since the stat. 8 Eliz. suspected not to have the tenth cloth dressed according to the same statute; it is lawful for two of the said persons, to wit, one of the merchants adventurers and one of the clothworkers (or, if the merchants adventurers do not appoint, two or more of the persons appointed by the clothworkers), to search at the port of London; for the search elsewhere in the realm the master and wardens of the clothworkers may appoint as many more persons of the said handicraft as they think needful, to be sworn in form aforesaid before the master, wardens and assistants of the clothworkers only; provided that at the port of London the persons appointed to make search do at their coming on board specify the name of the owner or mark of the packs which they shall mind to search, and finding anything done contrary to statute shall have power to seize the cloths until the

statutory penalties be answered, and that all forfeitures shall be employed according to the statute; officers having the custody of any cocket touching cloths to be searched shall show them on request by the persons appointed to search; no cloth dressed with the 'gigge mill' shall be allowed for any tenth cloth ordered by the said statute to be   [m. 7] dressed; whenever the said persons shall search any pack and not find anything contrary to statute, they shall forthwith re-pack the same at their charges. *English.*   By p.s.

181.)   20 *Sept.* 1576.   *Gorhambury.*   Grant to Richard Grinfelde of Chelswell, co. Berks, of all the goods and chattels of Geoffrey Shakerley late of Biston, co. Chester, son and heir of Peter Shakerley of Shakerley, co. Lancaster, and Richard Anderton late of Vale Royall, co. Chester, forfeited by outlawry of the said Geoffrey and Richard Anderton.   By p.s.

182.)   10 *Aug.* 1576.   *Gorhambury.*   Grant for life to Edmund Knyvett late of Buckenham Castell, co. Norfolk, of the offices of (1) bailiff of the manor of Barkynge, co. Essex, once of the monastery of Barkinge, and (2) collector and receiver of the said manor both of the South part and of the North part; from the death, forfeiture or surrender of William Nutbrowne, to whom by patent, 16 October, 13 Eliz., were granted *inter alia* for life the office of bailiff and collector of the quit rents of the manor of Barkinge both of the South part and of the North part, with a yearly fee of £7 13s. 4d., and the office of bailiff and collector of the rents of the marsh lands within 'le sex levelles' between Bowebridge and Mockinge Milles, co. Essex, with a yearly fee of £10 for the same office and for the office of surveyor of repairs and works of the said marshes; yearly fee of £14, payable out of the issues of the manor and the rest of the premises by himself or   [m. 8] the receiver general of the county.   By p.s.

   Vacated, because surrendered 3 Sept., 26 Eliz., by John Wylford of London, holder of the interest in the said patent of William Hunnys by grant of Margaret Rookes of London, widow, executrix of Edward Rookes, late citizen and fishmonger of London, to which Edward the said Knyvett granted his interest, as appears by several indentures in the Chancery files; signed: G. Gerrard; Joh. Wilford; Ri: Garth.

183)   30 *July* 1576.   *Gorhambury.*   Grant to George Scott, the Queen's servant, of the gift of the canonry or prebend in Canterbury cathedral which shall next be void, for one vacancy only; so that he may present thereto John Langworth, M.A., preacher of God's Word.

                By p.s.

184.)   30 *Aug.* 1576.   *Gorhambury.*   Protection for one year for Edmund Bury of Worcester, 'clothier'.   By p.s.

185.)   26 *Sept.* 1576.   *Gorhambury.*   Licence for Arthur Wake, M.A., prebendary of Christ Church cathedral, Oxford, to be absent from his prebend and all his other ecclesiastical preferments and to receive the fruits thereof as if in continual residence; from the present date so long as he shall reside in France with the Queen's ambassador, with whom he   [m. 9] is now with the Queen's licence setting out thither.   By p.s.

186.)   20 *Aug.* 1576.   *Gorhambury.*   Grant for life, to Charles Lister, the Queen's servant, of the office of keeper of 'the Litle Parke of Windesore', co. Berks; from the death, forfeiture or surrender of John Truchild, the office having been granted by patent, 25 Feb., 1 Eliz., to John Westcote, now deceased, and him for life in survivorship; wages of 4d. a day, payable out of the issues of the honour and castle of Windesore by the clerk or receiver there; with herbage and pannage of the park. For his service.   By p.s.

187.)   8 *Aug.* 1576.   *Gorhambury.*   Pardon for John Colliforde late of Waishefeild, co. Devon, 'laborer'. At the general goal delivery of Exeter castle, co. Devon, made before Roger Manwood, a justice of the Common Pleas, and John Jefferey, one of the Queen's serjeants at law, and their fellows, justices of gaol delivery, at the said castle on 5 Aug., 17 Eliz., he was indicted for that on 21 March, 17 Eliz., he with others burgled the house of John Beryman at Shebbeare, co. Devon,   [*m.* 10] assaulted him, Elizabeth his wife, Anthony Whitlocke and Alice Pernacott, Beryman's servant, and stole money and goods (*described*) belonging to Beryman; he pleaded not guilty and was convicted and sentenced, and afterwards for divers causes was committed back to gaol. At the suit of John Babbage.   By p.s.

188.)   10 *Oct.* 1576.   *Gorhambury.*   Pardon for Richard Baker *alias* Tanner late of Taunton, co. Somerset, 'husbandman'. It was found by an inquisition taken at Charde, co. Somerset, at the assizes held there on 14 March, 17 Eliz., before Roger Manwood, a justice of the Common Pleas, and John Jeffrey, then the Queen's serjeant at law, and their fellows, justices of the peace and of oyer and terminer in the county and of gaol delivery of Yevelchester prison, (*jury named*) that Baker burgled the house of Robert Henley, 'marchaunte', at Taunton on 18 Dec., 17 Eliz., and stole cloth (*described*) belonging to him.   By p.s.

189.)   10 *Aug.* 1576.   *Gorhambury.*   Pardon for Philip Morgan and John Stone, both late of London, 'yeomen', indicted for the theft of sheep (*described*) belonging to (1) William Pye on 8 June, 18 Eliz., and   [*m.* 11] (2) William Redmer on 11 May, 18 Eliz., at Ratcliff, co. Middlesex. At the suit of Ralph Hope, yeoman of the robes.   By Q.

190.)   27 *Aug.* 1576.   *Gorhambury.*   Pardon for Walter *alias* Watkin ap Rosser late of Llanvyhangell Cum Dee, co. Brecon, 'yoman' for stealing nine lambs between 10 and 26 June, 18 Eliz.   By Q.

191.)   23 *Aug.* 1576.   *Gorhambury.*   Licence for life for John Molt of Baintree, co. Essex, 'yoman', to keep a tennis court and a bowling alley   [*m.* 12] in or adjoining his house for himself and his friends, and to play therein with round bowls, half bowls and other bowls and any other pastime devised to be used in the said alley or tennis court; provided that he shall expel and seek to punish offenders offering any 'cosonage' or fraud, that no apprentices, unseemly or 'unlikelye' persons shall be suffered to play for gain, and that no rogues or the like be suffered to loiter thereabouts or to play or to use any betting there; power to apprehend such persons and deliver them to the next justice, constable or other head officer.   *English.*   By p.s.

192.)   13 *Aug.* 1576.   *Gorhambury.*   Appointment during good behaviour of Thomas Hankye to be yeoman of the wardrobe within the principality of Wales and officer and clerk for drawing and framing all bills of complaint for debt exhibited before the council there; with fees as heretofore; no other person to intermeddle with the drawing or framing of the said bills without his consent. The drawing of such bills has of late time customarily been bestowed on a person or persons attending on the said council, and by the said council's order no one shall intermeddle therewith except such as should be by the Queen or said council thereto specially appointed; by means of which order the multitude of feigned suits is better avoided and the Queen's subjects in their lawful suits better served.   *English.*

                                                                        By p.s.

193.)   12 *Oct.* 1576.   *Gorhambury.*   Grant for life to Nicholas Alexander of the room of an almsknight in the college of St. George in Windesore castle which shall next be void. In consideration of many years' service to the Queen and her progenitors in the wars and of great losses sustained by him to his utter undoing. *English.*   By p.s.

194.)   20 *July* 1576.   *Gorhambury.*   Grant for life to Robert Tildesley of the room of an almsknight in the college of Windesore castle which   [*m.* 13] next be void. For his long service. *English.*   By p.s.

195.)   12 *Oct.* 1576.   *Gorhambury.*   Grant for life to Thomas Wilkes, the Queen's servant, of the office of a clerk of the Privy Council; with an annuity of £50, payable at the Exchequer, from Midsummer last.   By p.s.

196.)   25 *Sept.* 1576.   *Gorhambury.*   Grant during pleasure to Richard Cawndishe, the Queen's servant, of an annuity of £40, payable at the Exchequer, from Midsummer last. For his service.   By p.s.

197.)   14 *Sept.* 1576.   *Gorhambury.*   Grant for life to Edward Grant, M.A., master of the Queen's grammar school of Westminster, of the canonry or prebend in the collegiate church of St. Peter, Westminster, which shall next be void.   By p.s.

198.)   27 *July* 1576.   *Gorhambury.*   Presentation of Nicholas Baldwyn, M.A., to the rectory of Riton, Durham dioc., void by death and in the Queen's gift by the vacancy of the bishopric of Durham.   By p.s.

199.)   7 *Sept.* 1576.   *Gorhambury.*   Presentation of Walter Harte, priest, to the rectory of Okeforde, Exeter dioc., void by the resignation of Simon Harte and in the Queen's gift by the minority of Hugh Pollarde, son and heir of Lewis Pollarde.   By p.s.

200.)   23 *July* 1576.   *Gorhambury.*   Presentation of Edward James, M.A., clerk, to the perpetual vicarage of Bovytracye, Exeter dioc., void by   [*m.* 14] the death of William Merig.   By p.s.

201.)   31 *Aug.* 1576.   *Gorhambury.*   Presentation of Robert Grene, a chaplain of the chapel royal, to the rectory of Walkington, York dioc., void by the death of John Newcome.   By p.s.

202.)   27 *July* 1576.   *Gorhambury.*   Grant for life to John Wolwarde, M.A., of a canonry or prebend in Rochester cathedral, void by the death of John Ellis.   By p.s.

203.)   27 *July* 1576.   *Gorhambury.*   Presentation of John Thorneborowe, M.A., to the rectory of Marnehull, Bristol dioc., void by lapse.   By p.s.

204.)   8 *Aug.* 1576.   *Gorhambury.*   Presentation of John Hottofte, clerk, a chaplain in the chapel royal, to the rectory of Pawlerspury, Peterborough dioc., void by lapse.   By p.s.

205.)   27 *July* 1576.   *Gorhambury.*   Protection for one year for George Southacke of London, merchant. Because he has suffered very great losses overseas.   By p.s.

206.)   30 *Jan.* 1576.   Grant in fee simple to John Mershe of London   [*m.* 15] and William Mershe of London of the following, all concealed from the Crown,—the house and site of the hospital of St. Leonard of Stoke by Newark, all lands reputed parcel thereof before the foundation of the same by King Philip and Queen Mary, and lands in Stoke, Elston and Cotham, late of the said hospital, (reserving to the Crown two cottages in Stoke called 'le Bedehouses' where live two poor men called lay brothers, to the intent that they may remain there for life and thereafter two other poor men appointed by the Crown or the treasurer of England for ever) and lands (*named with tenants' names*) in Sawnby, given for a light there, in or by Nottingham, late of St. George's guild there, and in Blyth, late of the monastery there, all in the county of Nottingham; lands (*named*) in Haseop *alias* Hassesopp, late of the monastery of Beauchief (? *Bello Campo*), all lands given for chantries and the like in the church of Assheborne and in the chapel of the Glorious Virgin Mary in the manor of Hoghe, and lands (*named with tenant's name*) in Asheleyhey in the parish of Wirkesworth, late of (1) St. Helen's chantry there and (2) the chantry of Muggenton, co. Derby, all in the county of Derby; lands (*tenant named*) by Gateshed in the county of the bishopric of Durham, late of Robert Tempest, attainted of treason; a yearly rent of 22s. out of lands called 'le Glene' in the parish of St. Olave in Southwark, co. Surrey, once given by William Chester, merchant of the staple, to wit, 20s. for an obit in the church of St. Botolph without Algate and 2s. for the priest of the said church to pray for the souls of Chester, his wife and others; 'le churchehouse' in Framefeild *alias* Frankfeild, co. Sussex, given for superstitious uses in the church there; lands (*tenant named*) in Hawridge, co. Buckingham, given for superstitious uses in the church there; lands (*named with tenant's name*) in Careforde and Petworth, co. Sussex, late of the guild of Petworth; lands (*named with tenants' names*) in Benyfeild, late granted *inter alia* by patent, 19 Feb., 16 Eliz., to Christopher Fenton and Bernard Gylpyn, their heirs and assigns and formerly of the hospital of St. John of Jerusalem, in Peterborough, given for guilds and the like in the church there, in the parish of St. Giles in Northampton, given by Mr. Permynter, clerk, for an obit in St. John's hospital there, in Blysworth, late of St. John's hospital in Northampton, in Northampton, once of St. Mary's

[*m.* 16]

guild in All Saints church there, in Piddington (including 'le churchehouse' and a cottage once a chapel), in the lordship of Hartwell, given for a lamp in the church there, in Eston next Stamford (*tenants including* Richard Johnson, curate there), late of (1) St. Mary's guild and (2) Holy Trinity guild in the said town, in Milton *alias* Midleton, given for a lamp in the church there, in Passenham and Cosgrave, late of Snelshall priory, and in Okeley Parva, all in the county of Northampton; lands (*named*) in Swepston, co. Leicester, (1) late of St. Paul's chapel and (2) given for a light in the church there; lands (*tenant named*) in Neitherseale, co. Leicester, given for a light in Mersham church, co. Derby; lands (*described*) in the parish of St. Margaret in Leicester (in the tenure of John Lum, clerk, vicar of St. Margaret's church), given for superstitious uses in the said church; lands etc. (*tenants named*) in Hackleton in the parish of Piddington, late of the monastery of St. Andrew in Northampton and leased by conventual indenture, 10 Feb., 18 Hen. VIII, to Thomas Chipsey for 70 years from Michaelmas then next at a yearly rent of 3s. 4d., in Hartwell in the parish of Roode, late of the monastery of St. James, Northampton, or of Hartwell chapel, and in Wellingborough *alias* Wendlingborough, late of the guild of Corpus Christi, St. George, St. Mary and St. Catherine there or other superstitious uses, all in the county of Northampton; lands (*named*) in Nymsfeilde, co. Gloucester, late of 'the chauntrye or free chapell' of Kynley in Nymsfeild; lands (*tenant named*) in Dewchurche Magna within the lordship of Kilpeck, co. Hereford, late of 'the nunry of Aconbury *alias* Acornbury', co. Hereford; lands (*named with tenants' names*) in Great Bedwynne, given for prayers for departed souls in the church there, in Highworth, given for 'le   [*m.* 17]

roode' there, in Bradford, given for lamps and the like in the church there, and in Busshoppes Cannynges, given for masses and the like, all in the county of Wilts; the free chapel or rectory of Brimpton Coorte *alias* the chapel of St. Leonard, co. Berks, and all tithes and lands belonging thereto given for a priest celebrating in the said chapel on the feast of

St. Lawrence; lands (*named*) in Whitechurche, cos. Berks and Oxford, given for masses, obsequies and dirges there; lands (*tenant named*) in Henlye upon Theames, co. Oxford; lands and tithes (*named with tenants' names*) in Coldswell *alias* Coldeshill, cos. Berks and Wilts, late of the monastery of Edyngton; 'the churche house' in Hampsted Mershall, co. Berks, given for superstitious uses; tithes (*tenant named*) within the bounds of the parish, chapelry or rectory of Little Brothton *alias* Broughton, co. Wilts, late of Farleigh priory, co. Wilts; lands (*named with tenant's name*) in Boyton, co. Wilts, given for a lamp in the church there; lands (*named with tenants' names*) in Barkley and Beckington, cos. Wilts and Somerset, late of Westbury chantry; lands (*named with tenants' names*) in Blubery, co. Berks, late of the monastery of Redinge, and in Hungerford, co. Berks, given by [———] Jennyns for an obit and light in Hungerford church; lands (*named with tenants' names*) in Pottorne (including a chapel), given for oblations, in Bulkington and Worton, and in Baydon, given for a light in the chapel there, all in the county of Wilts; a chapel and garden without 'the Utter Northgate' in Gloucester in the parish of St. John the Baptist, given for a priest celebrating in the chapel; lands (*named with tenant's name*) in Farnham Royall, cos. Berks or Buckingham; lands (*named with tenant's name*) in Beckingfeild, co. Hertford [*sic*], given by John Clack for obits and the like in Saynt Giles Chafont church in the said county; lands (*tenants named*) in Alesheath, Burton and Thornehill, co. Wilts, and in Malmsbury, co. Wilts, (*described*), late of St. Mary's chapel there and parcel of the monastery of Malmsbury; lands etc. (*named with tenants' names*) in Kethermoster, given for 'the Trynyty service'   [*m.* 18] in Kethermoster church and other superstitious uses, in Pipleton, given by Thomas Mounslowe and John Pykham for lights in Pipleton church, by Walcot within the lordship of Alisborowe, late of the monastery of Pershore, co. Worcester, in Pershore, late of the same monastery, in Badsey, given for lights in Badsey church in Ufnam, given for lights in the church there, in Midlelitleton, given for lights in the said church, in Seynt Marye Witton, late of the monastery of Kensam, co. Gloucester [*sic*], in Martyn Huscentrye, given for lights in Martyn Huscentry church, in Crowle, given for lamps and lights in Crowle church, in Pershore and Pipleton, late of the monastery of Pershore, and in Orleton, given for obits there, all in the county of Worcester; lands etc. (*named with tenants' names*) in Northampton in St. Giles's parish, late of St. Clement's guild, in Maydeforde, late of Cannonsashbye priory, in the river Willand (a fishery from Holtbridge to Rockinhame Dike), late of the monastery of Peterborough, and in Moulton, given for obits and lights, all in the county of Northampton; lands etc. (*named with tenants' names*) in Whitwicke, given for lamps and   [*m.* 19] lights in Whitwick church, in Shepsteade, late of the monastery of Pré, Leicester, and in Tilton, given for superstitious uses, all in the county of Leicester; lands (*named with tenants' names*) in Longnore in the parish of Austenfeilde, co. Stafford, late of (1) the monastery of Delacrise and (2) Longnore chapel; lands (*tenants named*) in Whittelton in the parish of Stokesey, late of the monastery of Hamond, co. Salop, in Langunford, given for lamps or lights in Langunford church, in Hutton in the parish of Eton, late of the hospital of St. John of Jerusalem, in Shabrye (including 'the hall of Shabrye'), given for St. Mary's service in Shabry church, in Cleve, given for a priest in Cleve church, and in Tilford and Witmore in the parish of Burford, late of the hospital of St. John of Jerusalem, all in the county of Salop; lands (*named with tenants' names*) in Whitton, given for an obit in Whitton church, in Tyde Saynt Mary, parcel of the chantry of Tyde Saynt Gyles, co. Cambridge, and in Grauntham, parcel of St. George's guild there, all in the county of Lincoln; a cottage in the parish of St. Swithin, Lincoln, given by George Skynner for a mass priest in the parish of Ryfam, co. Lincoln; lands (*tenant named*) in Birchewood in the parish of Alfreton, co. Derby, given for lights and the like; lands (*described with tenants' names*) in Stanes, late of the royal free chapel of SS. Mary and Stephen in the palace of Westminster, in Istelworth, late of Shene priory, co. Surrey, or the monastery of Syon, co. Middlesex, and in Stanwell (including a messuage now called 'the vicaredge'), given for a candle burning on the altar of Stanwell church at the time of mass and the time of St. Mary's antiphon, all in the county of Middlesex; a graveyard or void place by the church late of the Austin friars of London to the South, late of the said house of friars; lands (*named with tenants' names*) in Springefeild and Bromefeilde, given for an anniversary in Waltham Parva church, in Waltham Parva, given for an anniversary and obit in the said church, in Great Wendon and Little Wendon or elsewhere, late of the chantry or chapel of Kneysworth, co. Cambridge, all in the county of Essex; a rent of lands (*tenant named*) once of John Warde, given for three 'lez tapers' or 'prickettes' in Elmestede church, co. Kent; lands (*named with tenants' names*) in Fryerninge, co. Essex, given (1) for superstitious uses there, (2) by [——] Dowe, widow, for an obit in the church there and (3) for superstitious uses   [*m.* 20]

in the said church, and in Shenfeild, given for 'a torche' burning at the elevation of the sacrament in Shenfeilde church, co. Essex; lands (*named with tenants' names*) in Crundell, given by [——] Hobert for obsequies and masses in Crundell church, in Saltwood, given by William White and [——] Fittell for lights, wax and the like in the church there, and in Reculver and the borough of Hothe, given for 'le torche' at Easter in Hothe chapel, all in the county of Kent; lands (*named with tenants' names*) in Belchanger, co. Essex, given for superstitious uses in the church there, and in Stanstede Munfitchet, co. Essex, (1) 'the guildhall house', (2) given for lights in the church there, (3) given for an obit there and (4) once of a chapel; lands (*named with tenants' names*) in Buckton, given for lights in Buckton chapel, in Eston, late of 'le nunerye of Nunamadyke'; in Flamborough ('le guilde house'), in Moreley in the parish of Batley, given by Thomas Lymonelde to pray for his soul, in Packlington ('Saynt Helens Garthe'), in Edstone, late of Keldham priory, co. York, in Ardeslowe in the parish of Wakefeild, given for an obit there, in Righton, late of the late chapel of Righton, in Wyton, given for a priest in Wyton chapel, in Hutterfeilde, late of Kirklees priory, co. York, in Carleton in Coverdale (once called 'Saynt Thomas chapell'), in Leedes, given for 'Our Ladyes service' in Leedes, and in Warthill, given for a light in Warthill church, all in the county of York; lands (*tenants named*) in Eglestone, co. Durham, late of the monastery of Mountgrace in Egleston, co. York; lands (*named with tenants' names*) in Kirkby Grindlife, given for an obit in Kirkham Abbey, in Kirkeby Averblous, Kirkeby Grindelif and Midleton on le Wolde, late of St. John of Jerusalem, in Haxby, given for a priest in Haxby chapel, in Santon, in North Cave, in Westlutton, given for a priest in the chapel of Lutton aforesaid, in Conyston, late of the monastery of Thorneton, in Skirlaugh, late of the monastery of Swyne, in   [*m.* 21]

Easte Rounton in the parish of Rudby, given for a light in Rudby church, in Oughton, once of Bramley chapel, in Elslake in the parish of Broughton, once of Denton chapel, in York (a house called 'le guilde' or brotherhood of Corpus Christi without Micklegate Barr with all possessions of the guild in the city and its suburbs) and in Naburne, Stamforth Brigges and Buttercrame, late of the said guild of Corpus Christi, in York, late of a chantry in the church of St. Martin in Micklegate there, in the graveyard of St. Martin Micklegate in York, by Busshophill Kirk in York, given for an obit, in York, given for a priest in the church of St. Martin aforesaid, in York, given for a priest in the church late of St. George in Micklegate, in Clementhorpe by York ('Scropp chappell garth'), in Fishergate by York, given for a guild, in Huby and Easingwolde in the forest of Galters, late arrented to Richard Petyven and his heirs for ever and to William Petyven and escheated because the said Richard died without an heir, in Belingley in the parish of Darfeilde, given for 'le Ladye service', in Neither Cudworth and Royston, given for 'le Ladye preist' in Royston church, in Thormomby (some within the lordship of Rascall), in Catfosse in the parish of Siglestron *alias* Silstorne, late of 'le Lady guilde' in Silstron church, in Askarigge, given for St. Mary's light in the church there, in Farnlay next Horrockstones, late of the monastery of Bolton, co. York, in Spradbrough next Donkaster, and in Thorpe in the parish of Baddisworth, all in

the county of York; lands (*named with tenants' names*) in Honyden *alias* Hunden and Barneston *alias* Barnerdistone and elsewhere ('Rogerons Landes'), given for superstitious uses, in Bury St. Edmunds, in Barnestone *alias* Barnardiston and Hunden, given for salt to make holy water for the church there, in Wethersfeilde, given for obits and the like, in Barnerdiston, given to find straw in Barnardiston church, in Wythersfield ('Hanchett chappell'), given for a place of 'le pylgrymage of Our Ladye' or one 'le annett', in Haverell and Keddington, given for guilds and the like, and in Longmelforde, given for a term of years by William Clopton, knight, deceased, or others for a priest celebrating the 'Jesus service' and for obits and the like in the church of Melforde aforesaid,   [*m. 22*]
all in the county of Suffolk; lands (*named*) in Sturmere, co. Essex, given for guilds and the like; lands (*named with tenants' names*) in Great Bradle (including 'the Ildehall'), in Little Bradley or elsewhere belonging to the late college of Denston or college of Bury St. Edmunds, co. Suffolk, and in Rusham in the hamlet of Winckfeilde ('the chapell yarde'), all in the county of Suffolk; lands (*tenants named*) in Posenall *alias* Possenhall and Calerton *alias* Calloughton, co. Salop, given for a chaplain in Much Wenlock church, co. Salop; lands (*named with tenants' names*) including an old chapel called 'Mapperley chappell') in Mapperley, co. Derby, late of Mapperley chantry; lands (*named*) in Dulwiche in the parish of Camerwell, co. Surrey, late of Barmondsey priory, co. Surrey; the chapel of St. Mary of Broughton in the parish of Claverley *alias* Clareley Holme and lands (*tenants named*) in Broughton or elsewhere, co. Salop, given by [——] Chicknell for a priest in the said chapel; lands (*named with tenants' names*) in Shirborne and in Alveston *alias* Alston in the parish of Folke or elsewhere, co. Dorset, once of the monastery of Shirborne; lands (*named with tenants' names*) in Kethermoster and a field called Elernefeilde, given for superstitious uses in Churchill church, co. Worcester, in Elmesbridge, given for a light in Elmesbridge church, in Priors Stooke ('Seynt Godwoldes chapell') and in Fecknam, given (1) for a priest in Fecknam church and (2) for obits and the like in the same church, all in the county of Worcester; lands (*named with tenant's name*) in Much Wenlock, co. Salop; lands (*tenants named*) in Normanton, co. Rutland, ('Sepulcher Close') and in Ketton, co. Rutland, given by one Porter of Collyweston for drink in 'le Rogacion Weeke' in Ketton; lands (*tenants named*) in Desborough, co. Northampton, late of the chantry or chapel of Rothwell, and in Wickden *alias* Wicken *alias* Wickhamond, co. Northampton, late of the monastery of Snelshall; lands (*tenants named*) in Anstye, co. Leicester, (*named*), given for an obit in Anstye chapel, and in Frisbye and Galbye,   [*m. 23*]
co. Leicester, late of Huncotte chantry; lands (*tenant named*) in Tenberye, co. Worcester, given for lamps and the like in Tenberye church; lands (*named with tenants' names*) in Harlaxston *alias* Hurleston, given for priests and the like, in Gedney, late of the monastery of Crowland, co. Lincoln, in Kirton (*named*), bequeathed by Humphrey Heyland to Humphrey Heylande under a condition that he should yearly keep an obit in Kirton church, in Fishetoft (a close called 'Chapelgrene'), in Quapplade *alias* Whaplood, given for a chaplain in Whapelode chapel, and in Silkwillowbye, late of Sympryngham priory, all in the county of Lincoln; a chapel on Newton Heathe *alias* Foxwistheathe, co. Chester, founded by Humphrey Newton and William Newton in honour of the Blessed Trinity and St. Mary, and all its possessions; lands called 'the Spitle Croftes' (*tenants named*) in Frodesham, co. Chester; lands (*tenants named*) in Lentwarden, co. Hereford, late of St. Mary's service there, and in Leompster, co. Hereford, (*named*), given for a light in Leompster church; lands (*tenants named*) in Bucknyll and in Lingen, co. Salop; all lands in Keythorpe and Blaston, co. Leicester, late of the chantry of Stoke Faston, co. Leicester, whereof John Robertson and William Warton were late chaplains, or given for chaplains or priests there praying for the souls of John Boyville and others departed; lands (*tenant named*) in Waton in the parish of Stoke-gabriell, co. Devon; lands (*named with tenants' names*) in Roode, cos. Wilts and Somerset, given for obits and the like in Roode church; 'the chauntrye house' (*tenant named*)

in Endforde, co. Wilts; lands (*named*) between Northtudworth and Southtudworth, cos.
Southampton and Wilts; lands (*tenants named*) in Beckington, cos. Wilts and Somerset, given
for obits and the like in Beckington church; lands (*named*) in Hawkley in the parish of
Newton Vallans, co. Southampton, and the advowson of the vicarage of Newton Vallans
and Hawkeley *alias* Hackley; lands (*described with tenants' names*) in Cirencestre, co.
Gloucester; lands (*named with tenant's name*) in Wickleis, Longnore and Bolholmes in the
parishes of Bawkyn and Kingston Lisley or elsewhere, cos. Wilts and Berks, given by lord
Lisley for priests and the like in Bawkyn and Uffington churches, cos. Wilts and Berks; lands
(*tenant named*) in Orcheston, co. Wilts, late of the monastery of Edington, co. Wilts; lands
(*named with tenants' names*) in Blidworthe, given to priests in Blidworthe church for lights
before St. Lawrence's image and the like, in Edingley, given to Edingley church by John
Woodhouse for lamps and the like, in Caunton (a barn called 'Kirke Lath', which was once
'le Guildehouse' and belonged to 'Seynt Johns Guilde' and 'Trynytie guilde'), in Westhorpe
next Southwell (where stood a free chapel now destroyed called 'Seynt Katheryns chappell'
used for oblations, pilgrimages and the like), in Gibsmore in the parish of Blesbye, given to
the vicar of Blesbye for masses and the   [*m*. 24]
like in Blesbye church, in Calverton in the forest of Sherwood, given for lamps and the like
in Calverton church, in Aslacton (including a cottage which until the year 1 Edw. VI was the
free chapel of Holy Trinity), given for masses and the like in the said chapel, in Colson
Bassett, given for bells and the like in Colson Bassett church, in Skarryngton, given for
lamps and the like in Skarryngton church, and in Welley, given for lamps and the like in
Welley church, all in the county of Nottingham; a chantry at St. Nicholas's altar in Knesall
church founded by John Chapman late of York, notary public, deceased, the chantry-
priest's dwelling and all lands of the said Chapman in Knesall, Ampton and Allerton in
Sherwood, co. Nottingham, and in Fokerthorpe, Eskrike and Northdalton, co. York, given
for the founding of the chantry; lands (*named with tenants' names*) in Knesall, given for obits
and the like in the church there, in Cotgrave, given before the year 1 Edw. VI and in Queen
Mary's time for lamps, lights called 'sergeis, rowelles, sepulchre lightes and torches' for
images called 'Alhallowes', 'bawdrickes' and the like in Cotgrave church, in Upton next
Hayton, belonging until the year 1 Edw. VI to a free chapel in Upton afterwards destroyed,
in Blithe, late of the monastery of Blithe, in Blythe and Alcottes, late of the chantry or the
stipendiary of Blithe, in Gotam, given by one Seynt Andrewes to the church fabric and for
lamps and the like in Gotam church, in Halam, given for lamps and the like in the free chapel
of Normanton, co. Nottingham, and in Snenton and Bridgforde, given by the ancestors of
Henry Perpoynte for lights before the images of St. [——] and St. Edmund in Snenton and
Holme churches and the like there, all in the county of Nottingham; lands (*described with
tenants' named*), (1) late of Thomas Knyfton, attainted of treason, (2) late of the chantry of St.
James on Nottingham bridge and (3) bequeathed by Robert Fisher to St. George's guild or
brotherhood in Nottingham for an obit there; and all lands in Barrowe and Atterley, co.
Salop, late of the monastery of Wenlock.   [*m*. 25]
Yearly value, according to the several particulars thereof, £24 4s. 10½d. To hold as of the
manor of Eastgrenewich, co. Kent, in socage, and by yearly rents of (1) 50s. out of the late
hospital of Stoke and the premises in Stoke, Elston and Cotham, co. Nottingham, that the
two poor men called lay brothers may have the said rent, to wit, each of them 20s. a year for
his sustenance and 5s. for his livery for life, (2) 20s. out of the premises in Carford and
Petworth, co. Sussex, (3) out of the premises in Passenham, co. Northampton, 4s., (4) 17d.
out of the premises called 'Rogerons Landes' in Hunden and Barneston, co. Suffolk, (5) 17s.
out of the premises in Posenall, co. Salop, (6) 7s. 4d. out of the premises in Callerton, co.
Salop, and (7) 4s. to the Crown as in right of the chantry of Normanton next Southwell) out
of the premises in Halam, co. Nottingham. Issues from the time when the premises should
have come to the Crown. The patent to be sufficient warrant for officers of the courts of the

Exchequer and the duchy of Lancaster to issue process in the Queen's name for the recovery of rents, profits and arrears, and pay moneys recovered to the grantees, and for the grantees to have the same to their use and to dispense, compound and discharge in respect of such process. If any of the premises shall be withheld from the grantees' possession, they may have by gift of the Crown other concealed lands to the same value. The grant to be void in respect of any of the premises which were not concealed on and before 1 Nov., 16 Eliz., when the said John Mershe and Francis Greneham of London at their own charges procured the discovery thereof.   [m. 26]

In consideration of promises in letters under the Queen's signature dated at Grenewiche, 1 Nov., 13 Eliz., touching lands to be granted to the said John Mershe and Greneham and the heirs and assigns of John; and for £290 18s. 6d. paid at the Exchequer by the said John and William Mershe.   By Q.

207.)   1 Oct. 1576.   Licence for Thomas Gresham, knight, and Anne his wife to alienate lands in Wedmore, Marke, Wokey, Meare, Stoke Gifforde, Chelton, Panborowe, Blackeforde, Allerton and Sonde and common of pasture in moors (named) there, co. Somerset, to John Durban. For 8s. 1d. paid to the Queen's farmer.

208.)   20 Sept. 1576.   The like for Lewis Mordaunte, knight, lord Mordaunte, Elizabeth his wife, Henry Darcye, knight, and Catherine his wife to alienate lands in Brymbem alias Brymham, Warsall and Lareton, parcel of the manor of Brymbem, co. York, to Edmund Norton.   For 26s.

209.)   20 Sept. 1576.   The like for John Smythe and Dorothy his wife to alienate lands in Wynesley, Hartwith, Felbeck and Lareton, parcel of the manor of Brymbem alias Brymham, co. York, to John Ellys. For 10s. 8d.

210.)   27 July 1576.   Gorhambury.   Grant in fee simple to Andrew   [m. 27] Palmer, citizen and goldsmith of London, and Alexander Kinge of London of the following, all concealed from the Crown,—lands (tenants named) in Eyton in the parish of Salley, co. Derby, (named), given for lamps in Eyton chapel, and in Balbrough, co. Derby, given by Geoffrey Hydes to pray for his soul; lands etc. (tenants named) in Darrington, given for lights and repairs of the altar in Darrington church, in Busby in the parish of Stokesley (a cottage once a chapel), in Wynterborne (tithes of corn or rents of the same), late of the monastery of Furnes, co. Lancaster, in Pomfrett, given for an obit, in Coniston and Swindon, late of St. Leonard [sic] in York, in Southe Skerlaie (a cottage called 'Chauntrye Howse'), in Heslington, late of the monastery of Fountaunce, co. York, in Rowton in Northe Skarley (named), late of the monastery of Swyne, co. York, in Thormondby alias Thornabie in the parish of Staynton, given for lamps in Thormondby chapel, in the lordship of Malhumm, in the lordship of Thresfeilde (named), in the parish of Burnsall (named), late of Richard Norton, attainted of treason, in Brompton, given for lamps and lights in Brompton church, in Bongate next Rippon, given for 'le guylde' in Ryppon church, in Osmotherley, late of the monastery of Mountgrace, co. York, in Estroungton, Westeroungton, Gysburgh, Ingleby Grene Howe, Armecliff, Arsam in the parish of Acklam, Brompton next Northalverton, Hutton, Rydby, Martyn, Carleton, Wherlton, Yaram, Thornabie in the parish of Staynton, Ilton, Estcottam, Virbye, Rydcar, Marche, Westgate in the parish of Gysborughe, Kukby cum Broughton, Faceby, Hevatt and Whorleton in the parish of Swainbie [sic], Dighton and Uxsall, late of the priory of St. John of Jerusalem or Mount St. John, in Kirkbie Malzerde, late of the guild in Kyrkby aforesaid, in York (described), in the Queen's hands by escheat or given by Isabel Fawcett, widow, for an obit in St. John the Evangelist's church there, in York (described), Wakefielde, Sandall and Crygleston, given for

'le Ladye service' in Wakefielde church, in York (*described*), late of the monastery of Holy
Trinity there, and in the parishes of Stowsler and Kirkby (*named*), given   [*m. 28*]
for masses and lights in Stowsler church, all in the county of York; two tenements in the
parish of St. Botolph without Bushoppes Gate, London, in the several tenures late of
Richard Glascock and [——] Richardson and now of Enoch Williamz and Nicholas
Bottrell, late of the priory or new hospital of St. Mary without Busshoppes Gate; a garden
and a lodge built therein in the parish of St. Stephen Colmanstrete, London, in Goughes
Alley (between a garden once in the tenure of Robert Riche on the South and land belonging
to the monastery of Rowley, co. Oxford, on the North), now in the tenure of John Ritche,
late of the said monastery; a ruinous tenement late built on the churchyard of St. Stephen
Colmanstrete, London, (between the tenement of Robert Wolman on the North and St.
Stephen's church on the South), late in the tenure of Robert Smyth; a tenement and garden,
in the tenure once of [——] Stacey and now of George Chapman, a piece of land belonging
to the same tenement on which are now built four tenements, now or late in the several
tenures of John Reynoldes and others, and a garden there on which is built a lodge, now or
late in the tenure of William Blounte, in Estsmythfilde in the parish of St. Botolph without
Algate, London, (between a tenement and lands late in the tenure of Thomas Browne on the
East and South, lands once of the monastery of St. Mary Graces by the Tower of London on
the North and the highway on the West), late of the said monastery; a tenement and garden
and a rod of land adjoining in Hollywell Lane in the parish of St. Leonard in Shorditch, co.
Middlesex, now in the tenure of Maurice Longe, late of the monastery of Hollywell; a
garden (1 rd. enclosed with hedges, ditches and walls) in Saynt Johns Streete, co. Middlesex,
(between a tenement in the tenure of John Preston on the East and a tenement occupied by
Thomas Norton on the West), now in the tenure of Edward Randall, late of the priory of St.
John of Jerusalem; a close (10 ac.) in Haggerston in the parish of St. Leonard in Shorditche,
in the tenure late of Richard Haddon and now of Thomas Haddon, his son, bequeathed by
Roger Barker to Joan Barker, his wife, an alien born, and her heirs, beyond a yearly rent
payable to the prebendary of Hoxton in St. Paul's, London; a tenement and garden, a close
(2 ac.) and a piece of void land on which are now built four tenements in Mile Ende in the
parish of Stebunheathe, co. Middlesex, now in the several tenures of William Hickes and
others, late of John Nevill, knight, attainted of treason, beyond a yearly rent payable to lord
Wentworth at his manor of Stebunheathe; a toft and piece of void land late a tenement and
garden, in the tenure once of Robert Ivey and now of no one, and a piece of void land on
which are now built nine tenements, now in the several tenures of Charles Hobson, Thomas
Harryson, James Johnson, John Stevenson, William Reste, Thomas Perte and others,
without the site of the priory or new hospital of St. Mary without Byshoppesgate, London,
in the parish of St. Leonard in Shorditche (between a tenement now in the tenure of Joan
Jackson, widow, on the North, a cross in the stone wall of the priory on the South, the
highway from London to Shorditche on the West and the said site on the East), late of the
said priory; a piece of void land on which are now built three tenements, now in the several
tenures of Robert Jones, Richard Knevitt and John Davis, and a piece of land, now
occupied by Roger Somers, next the site of the said priory of St. Mary without Busshops
Gate in the parish of St. Botolph there, co. Middlesex, (between a cross in the stone wall of
the priory on the North and 'le barres' there on the South), late of the said priory; two
tenements and two gardens within the site of the said priory, now or late in the several
tenures of Roger Wilkinson and Paul Wilkinson, late of William Wilde, an alien born; a
tenement and garden in Estsmythfilde in the parish of St. Botolph without Algate, London,
co. Middlesex, late in the tenure of Cornelius Lambertson, an alien born, and now occupied
by James Reynoldes; a ruinous chapel in Slapton, co. Devon, given by Guy Brian, knight, to
the rector and the chief fellowship of Slapton; lands (*named*, in the tenure of the prebendary
of Uscum) in Uscum, given for two 'lez tapers' before the altar cross and two 'lez tapers' on

'le highe alter' in the church there; lands (*named with tenants' names*) in Frome Selwood (including 'le churche house'), given for superstitious uses (1) in the church there and (2) in the church of

[*m.* 29]

Marston, co. Somerset, in Bagurndy in the parish of Willowe, late of the monastery of St. Augustine next Bristol, and in Rode and Wilberton, given for superstitious uses in Roode church, all in the county of Somerset; lands (*named with tenants' names*) in Sechey and Westwiche, co. Norfolk, late of Blackborough priory, co. Norfolk; lands (*named with tenant's name*) in Besthorpe in the said county, given for holy bread in the church there; lands (*named*) in Besthorpe, in Girton and in Normanton on Sore, all in the county of Nottingham, given for obits and the like in the church of Normanton aforesaid; lands (*named with tenants' names*) in Derby, co. Derby, late of the monastery of Darley, co. Derby; lands (*named with tenants' names*) in Birmingham and Bordisley, given by William Lynche and Agnes his wife for superstitious uses in the church of St. Martin in Birmingham or in some chapel there, in Birmingham, given to the guild of the Holy Cross there, in Lapworth (including a cottage once 'Oure Lady chappell') and in Brincklowe *alias* Brinckley, given for superstitious uses in the church there, all in the county of Warwick; lands (*tenants named*) in Luddington (*named*), in Nether Toynton (*named*), given for a light before St. Mary's image in the church there, in Maringe on the Hill, given for a light and lamp before St. Benet's image in the church there, in Hornecastell, given to St. Catherine's chantry in the church there, in Southhicam, late of Fosse priory, and in Spaldinge, late of the monastery of Spaldinge, all in the county of Lincoln;

[*m.* 30]

the tithes of the demesne lands of the manor of Welbery *alias* Welbury *alias* Westbery, co. Hertford, and lands (*named with tenants' names*) in the parish of Offley, co. Hertford, all late of the chantry of Chalgrave, co. Bedford; lands in Middlewich (*Medio Wico*), co. Chester, late leased to William Hillton for a term of years and late of the nunnery in Chester; lands (*tenants named*) in Langleybury *alias* Langleyburiell (*named*), given for lamps and the like in Langleyburie church, in Bulkington (including a small decayed chapel once called 'Sainte Audries chappell'), in Stoke *alias* Hanginstoke, given for lamps in Hangingstoke church, and in Windesley, given for lamps there, all in the county of Wilts; a water called Istunblin and an island called Ynyssedwifell (*described*) in Trifflis, Llan Saint Yatrin, Llanginsfrin Ygirthe or elsewhere, co. Carnarvon; lands (*named with tenants' names*) in Hydon, co. Montgomery, (a former chapel called 'le Palmant' of Hydon), in Hydon in the parish of Castell in Kyrrynyon, co. Montgomery, and in Nantford *alias* Nantforth in the said parish, late of the nunnery of Llandigan, co. Montgomery; lands (*named*) in the parish of St. Thomas or St. Ishmael, co. Pembroke, (in the tenure of John Parrott, knight below-mentioned), late of the monastery of St. Thomas the Martyr of Haverforde Weste, and in Nerberth, co. Pembroke, (*tenants named*), some given for a priest and other superstitious uses in Templeton chapel; lands (*named with tenants' names*) in Chertsey *alias* Chersey, co. Surrey, late of the monastery of Chertsey; lands

[*m.* 31]

(including the site of a chapel) in Caldwell *alias* Cawdwell and Wickham, co. Leicester, given for obits and the like in Cawdwell church; lands (*tenants named*) in Kingesclere, Woodlandes or elsewhere, co. Southampton, given for a 'Jesus masse' and the like in the parish of St. Lawrence in Readinge, co. Berks, and in Ringwood, co. Southampton, given for 'Our Ladie lighte'; lands (*named with tenants' names*) in Iwood next Shepey, co. Kent, granted *inter alia* by patent of Henry VIII to Thomas Wyat, knight, and his heirs, to hold by service of the tenth part of a knight's fee and by a yearly rent of 4s; the tithes of lands called 'le Friez *alias* Frise', co. Oxford, (*tenant named*), late of the monastery of Osney; Caldicot chapel and lands (*named*) in Caldicot and Nether Heyforde or elsewhere, co. Oxford, belonging thereto; lands (*tenants named*) in Neither Heyford aforesaid; lands (*tenants named*) in Brydsett *alias* Brisiert *alias* Sainte Clementes, co. Oxford, given for superstitious uses in St. Clement's church; lands

(*named*) in Wydeforde *alias* Wydforde, late of the monastery of Barmondsey, co. Surrey, in Wynge (in the tenure of [——] Grevis, vicar of Winge), given for lamps in the church there, and in Sherington, given for a mass and the like in the church there, all in the county of Buckingham; lands (*named with tenant's name*) in Shilton, co. Warwick, given by Richard Jeffcockes for an obit; lands (*named with tenants' names*) in Westgrenested, in Seale, in Bramber, in Cowfolde, in Ashehurste, in Bramber, Stayninge, Sompertinge and Amningdon (demesne lands of the manor of Bidlington) and in Cowfolde, all in the county of Sussex; lands (*tenants named*) in Hollywell in the parish of Shutlington, co. Bedford, late of the monastery of Coldwell, and in Edworth, co.   [*m.* 32]
Bedford, ('the Towne Howse'), in the Queen's hands by the dissolution of chantries and the like; lands etc. (*tenants named*) in Esthannye (*named*), belonging to the Queen by escheat, in Dreyton (tithes), late of the monastery of Abington, in Botley, given for superstitious uses in the church of St. Aldate (*Sancti Abbatis*) in Oxford, and in the parish of St. Aldate (*Sancti Aldoti*) (*named*), late of the monastery of Abington, all in the county of Berks; lands (*described with tenant's name*) in Melcombe Regis, co. Dorset, late of St. Mary's brotherhood there; the rectory or prebend of Ichyn *alias* Abbassam Ichyn, co. Southampton, and appurtenances thereof (*tenant named*), late of the monastery of St. Mary, Wynton; Barlee chapel and lands (*tenants named*) in Stauley or elsewhere, co. Derby, belonging to the Queen by the dissolution of chantries and the like; and lands (*tenant named*) in Eaton, co. Leicester, given for superstitious uses in Eaton church. Yearly value, according to the several particulars thereof, £10 8d. To hold as of the manor of Estgrenewich, co. Kent, in socage. Issues from the time when the premises   [*m.* 33]
should have come to the Crown. The patent to be sufficient warrant for officers of the courts of the Exchequer and the duchy of Lancaster to issue process in the Queen's name for the recovery of rents, profits and arrears, and pay moneys recovered to the grantees, and for the grantees to have the same to their use and to dispense, compound and discharge in respect of such process. If the title to any part of the premises shall hereafter be lawfully taken from the grantees' possession, they may have by gift of the Crown other concealed lands to the same value. The grant to be void in respect of any of the premises which were not concealed on and before 30 Dec., 13 Eliz., when John Parrott, knight, at his own charges procured the discovery thereof.

At the suit of Parrott: for £100 6s. 8d. paid at the Exchequer by him; and for his service.

By Q.

211.)   8 *June* 1576.   *Gorhambury*.   Lease for 21 years to George Middleton of rents of assize of the manor of Warton, co. Lancaster, of the yearly value of 57s. 5d., and lands there (*named with tenants'*   [*m.* 34]
names) parcels of the said manor, parcel of Richemondes Landes and late of William, marquess of Northampton, deceased; with reservations, including certain parcels of land (*specified*); from Lady Day last;   [*m.* 35]
yearly rent £38 4s. 10d. (*detailed*); the lessee to pay on the decease or alienation of a tenant double the yearly rent of the premises in such tenant's tenure by way of fine or ingress, beyond the rent hereby reserved; also to do suit at the Queen's court in the manor and bear and do all other charges and services according to the custom of the manor; also with all other tenants to take his corn to the Queen's mill there to be ground, as accustomed; the lease to be void (i) if in   [*m.* 36]
any dispute between the lessee and the other tenants or occupiers he shall not obey the order of the treasurer and the chancellor of the Exchequer in this behalf, (ii) if he shall change any custom of the manor or take a greater fine or ingress on the death or alienation of a tenant than is hereby reserved or (iii) if he shall not permit the tenants or occupiers and their wives

and children to enjoy their several tenements as they have done at any time within the past 30 years.   For a fine of £70 14s. 10d. paid at the Exchequer.   By p.s.

212.)   11 *July* 1576.   Grant to Robert, earl of Leicester, councillor, his heirs and assigns of lands (*named with tenants' names*) in (1) Dynlley, Bodeloge, Llanlysney, Clynocke, Llanilhayan, Elerneon,   [*m.* 37]
Glasverin, Gorse Elerneon, Penterghe, Duyforth and Duyarth, Cader Elway, Nantekele, Penaunt and Penevet, Penmaghno, Bettws,   [*m.* 38]
Dolothellon, Gwedyr, Cwmllanerche, Llanrichwyn and Treveriew, Bodvaio and Treworth, co. Carnarvon, and (2) Festiniock, Aberllilrwlande,   [*m.* 39]
Llanvrotha, Nanmore, Llanyhangell y Trayther, Lladanog, Llanbeder, Llanvayer, Llanendwyn, Llanthowye and Llanenthem, Llandogwey,   [*m.* 40]
Llanabre, Llanelltied, Llanaber, Llandeckwin, Trawsweneth, Werne,   [*m.* 41]
Maientorge, Penanllewe, Gwernevell, Kiltalgarth, Penmayn, Penauron, Rewdocke, Selour, Keswyn, Maistrefaunt, Pennall, Trevrio, Kevenros, Morva Minoge, Nanmey *alias* Nanvy, Kewen Rawen[1] and Garth Gwynvaure, co. Merioneth, all unlawfully enclosed or encroached; to hold as of the manor of Estgrenwich, co. Kent, in socage; yearly rents
                                                                                                      [*m.* 42]

(1) £6 8s. 5¾d. and (2) 32s. 6d.; if the grantee shall because of the lawful interest of any person be prevented from enjoying the issues of any part of the premises, the rent shall upon complaint by the grantee be apportioned by the barons of the Exchequer and the grantee shall be discharged of the rent thereof. For his service.   By Q.

(Membrane 1d. *is blank.)*

213.)   3 *Sept.* 1575.   *Gorhambury.*   Commission during pleasure   [*m.* 2d]
to Nicholas Bacon, knight, keeper of the great seal, William, lord Burghley, treasurer of England, and Thomas, earl of Sussex, lord chamberlain, all councillors, Edmund, bishop of Norwiche, Thomas, lord Wentworth, Henry, lord Crumwell, Roger, lord Northe, William Cordell, knight, master of the rolls, Christopher Heydon, knight, Thomas Seckforde, a master of the requests, the dean of Norwiche for the time being, Robert Wyngfeild, knight, Ambrose Germyn, knight, William Buttes, knight, William Walgrave, knight, Robert Bell, John Still, D.D., William Foulke, D.D., William Blaverhasset, Nicholas Bacon, Drew Drury, Robert Ashefeild, Ralph Shelton, John Heigham, the chancellor of Norwiche for the time being, Matthew Carewe, doctor of law, John Birde, Edward Flowerdewe, William Heydon, Francis Wyndham, Robert Germyn, Thomas Andrewes, Thomas Pooley, Nathaniel Bacon, John Reynoldes and Charles Calthroppe (or four of them, the bishop or the chancellor being one) to inquire in the diocese of Norwich concerning offences and misdemeanours against the acts 1 Eliz. for the supremacy of the Crown over the state ecclesiastical and for the uniformity of common prayer, the act 5 Eliz. for the assurance of the Queen's power over all states and subjects within her dominions and the act 13 Eliz. to reform certain disorders touching ministers of the Church, also of all heretical opinions, seditious books, contempts and slanderous words set forth against the Queen or any her officers contrary to the said acts within the diocese of Norwich, and of all abettors of such offences; also to search out and punish persons wilfully absenting themselves from church and the divine service by law appointed by censures of the Church or any other ways appointed by the said acts or any laws ecclesiastical of the realm; power—because there is great diversity in the persons to be called before the commissioners, some dwelling afar and

---

[1] Illegible in the roll; reading from the warrant (in Chancery Warrants II (C. 82), 1303).

some being fugitive,—to command all justices and others within the diocese by letters to apprehend persons to be 'convented' before the commissioners, and to take such bonds for appearance as the commissioners by letters shall prescribe; also power, in case any such person be not able or shall refuse to give bond, to give commandment to the justices or others to commit him to ward until the commissioners take further order for his enlargement; also power to take of offenders and suspects recognisances for appearance as aforesaid and for performance of the commissioners' orders; Anthony Alcocke to be the commissioners' registrar, or in his absence or default any other notary or notaries public whom the bishop shall judge meet; the bishop to limit to the registrar such allowance as shall be thought meet, also to appoint a messenger or messengers to attend upon him (the bishop) in this behalf, and to limit to them allowances; the bishop also from time to time to appoint a receiver of fines assessed by the commissioners; for the receiver's account, there shall be two paper books indented, the one to remain with the receiver and the other with the registrar, in which shall be entered all fines assessed, every entry being signed by the commissioners; the commissioners by bills signed to assign to the receiver and their registrar, messengers and officers for their charges such sums as shall   [*m. 3d.*]
be thought convenient; also every Michaelmas term to certify into the Exchequer the receiver's name and a note of the fines by him received, that he may be charged thereby on his account; for 'the better credyte and more manyfest notyce' of the Commissioners' doings, a seal engraved with the rose and crown over the rose and the letter E before and the letter R after the same with a ring about the seal containing as follows—*Sigill: commissar: Reg: ma: ad: cas: ecclesiast:* shall be affixed to their letters missive, processes and judgments. *English.*   By p.s.

214.) 13 *Aug.* 1576. *Gorhambury.* Commission to William Strickland, John Carlill, William Lutton, Stephen Lekenby and Anthony Smethley, feodary of the East Riding, co. York, (or two of them, the feodary being one) to inquire *post mortem* Francis Lutton in the said county.

The like to the following, viz.—
215.) 12 *Sept.* 1576. (*No place*). William Fairefax, knight, John Vavasor, William Wickliff, Christopher Wandesford, Anthony Caterick and [——] Willyamson, feodary of the North Riding, co. York, (or three of them, the feodary being one); *p.m.* Thomas Pudsey; co. York.
216.) 13 *July* 1576. Henry Curwen, knight, Lancelot Pickeringe, George Salkeld and John Brisco (or two of them); *p.m.* Elizabeth Bradley, late the wife of Thomas Bradley; co. Cumberland.
217.) 9 *July* 1576. Rowland Lacon, Jerome Corbett, Andrew Charleton, Richard Cressett, Robert Eyton, Richard Prince, Thomas Staunton, feodary of the county, Adam Mytton and Francis Hoorde (or two of them, the feodary being one); *p.m.* Edward Wonwoode; co. Salop.
218.) 9 *July* 1576. The same; *p.m.* William Norton; co. Salop.
219.) 9 *July* 1576. The same; *p.m.* Robert Cole; co. Salop.
220.) 9 *July* 1576. The same; *p.m.* Peter Banyster; co. Salop.
221.) 9 *July* 1576. The same; *p.m.* Thomas Twyford; co. Salop.
222.) 30 *June* 1576. Thomas Mallett, Richard Pollard, John Lancaster and John Coles, feodary of the county, (or two of them, the feodary being one); *p.m.* John Howe; co. Somerset.
223.) 28 *June* 1576. James Warnecombe, Richard Wigmore, Thomas Harley, and John Parrye, deputy feodary of the county, (or two of them, Parry being one); *p.m.* John Strete; co. Hereford.

224.) 28 *June* 1576.   John Salisbury, John Edwardes, Robert Pauleston, William Almer and John Belott, feodary of the county, (or two of them, the feodary being one); *p.m.* John Yardeley; co. Denbigh.

225.) 8 *Nov.* 1576.   Richard Pates, Christopher George, feodary   [*m.* 4*d.*] of the county, Richard Broke and John Baker (or two of them, the feodary being one);   *p.m.* Richard Lawrence; co. Gloucester.

226.) 28 *Nov.* 1576.[1] Brian Hamond, feodary of the West Riding, co. York, Edmund Eyer, Robert Bellamy and William Mason (or two of them, the feodary being one); *p.m.* Roger Fretwell; co. York.

227.) 28 *Nov.* 1576.[1] John Eveleigh, feodary of the county, John Courteney and Richard Chanon (or two of them, the feodary being one);   *p.m.* William Cooke; co. Devon.

228.) 29 *Nov.* 1576.[1]   Richard Cressett, Thomas Staunton, feodary of the county, Francis Lawley and Robert Acton (or two of them, the feodary being one); *p.m.* Richard Lenthall; co. Salop.

229.) 20 *July* 1576. *Gorhambury.* Rowland Lacon, Jerome Corbett, Richard Cressett, Andrew Chorlton, Thomas Staunton, feodary of the county, and Adam Mytton (or two of them, the feodary being one); *p.m.* John Rollesley; co. Salop.

230.) 23 *July* 1576. *Gorhambury.* Christopher Brome, knight, Alexander Denton, Robert Doyley the elder and Thomas Ricardes, feodary of the county, (or two of them, the feodary being one); *p.m.* John Denton; co. Oxford.

231.) 16 *July* 1576.   Lawrence Smythe, knight, Peter Warberton, Thomas Tutchett, John Cotton and John Warde (or three of them, Ward being one); *p.m.* James Paver; co. palatine of Chester.

232.) 12 *July* 1576.   Thomas Cave, Thomas Skevington and William Braham, feodary of the county, (or two of them, the feodary being one); *p.m.* William Poole; co. Leicester.

233.) 12 *July* 1576.   Clement Sisley, Christopher Chibborne, Francis Stonard and John Glascocke, feodary of the county, (or two of them, the feodary being one); *p.m.* Anthony Cooke, knight; co. Essex.

234.) 13 *July* 1576.   Robert Bradford, escheator of the county, William [*sic*] Hamond, feodary of the West Riding, co. York, Richard Tempest and Thomas Waterton (or two of them, the feodary being one); *p.m.* James Pilkynton, bishop of Durham; co. York.

235.) 8 *Oct.* 1576. *Gorhambury.* John Zouche, knight, William Grove, feodary of the county, and Lawrence Huyde (or two of them, the feodary being one); *p.m.* John Samborne; co. Wilts.

236.) 8 *Oct.* 1576. *Gorhambury.* Robert Wroth, John Stonard, Thomas Powle and John Glascoke, feodary of the county, (or two of them, the feodary being one); *p.m.* William Franckland, citizen and 'clothworker' of London; co. Essex.

237.) 15 *Oct.* 1576. *Gorhambury.* Edmund Dockwray, Griffin Curtys and Thomas Noke, feodary of the county, (or two of them, the feodary being one); *p.m.* Gilbert Stocker, 'mercer'; co. Berks.

238.) *Undated.*   John Huband, knight, James Parry, Anthony Washborne, John Lyggen and John Parry, deputy feodary of the county, (or two of them, Huband or John Parrye being one); *p.m.* Richard Browne; co. Hereford.

239.) 1 *Oct.* 1576. *Gorhambury.* James Warncombe, John Abrall, John Delabere and Thomas Kerry, feodary of the county, or his deputy (or two of them, the feodary or deputy feodary being one); *p.m.* James Bedill; co. Hereford.

240.) 1 *Oct.* 1576. *Gorhambury.* Charles Somersett, knight, David Lewes, LL.D., William Harbarte of Saynt Julyans, William Morgan of Lanternam, Rice Morgan and John Gybon, LL.D., (or three of them, Somersett, Lewes or Gybon being one); *p.m.* Thomas

---

[1] Entry stated to be of the year 19 Eliz.

Morgan of Pencoye, knight, Charles Herbertt, knight, David Phillip Powell and Thomas Huntley of Hadnocke; co. Monmouth.

241.) 1 *Oct.* 1576. *Gorhambury.* Nicholas Arnolde, Giles Poole, Nicholas Poynes, William Wintre and John Tracye, knights, George Fetiplace, Richard Pates, John Trye, Thomas Smythe of Camden, Gabriel Bleeke, Thomas Atkins, Richard Barnam, Humphrey Ashefelde and Christopher George, feodary of the county, (or three of them, Arnolde, Poole, Pates, Fetiplace or George being one); *p.m.* George Bunne of Bixwere, William Warren of Stowe Graunge, William Hickes and Richard Tyndale; co. Gloucester.

242.) 1 *Oct.* 1576. *Gorhambury.* John Lyttelton, knight, Ralph Sheldon, Gilbert Littleton, Walter Blonte, Edmund Coles, John Talbott of Grafton, John Talbott of Sallopp, Arthur Sallowey, [——], escheator of the county and William Childe, feodary of the county, (or three of them, John Lyttelton, Sheldon or Childe being one); *p.m.* James Webbe, John Hunckes the younger, Thomas Haye and William Sparye; co. Worcester.

243.) 15 *Nov.* 1576. John Manners (esquire), Thomas Stanhope, knight, Peter Rosse, William Auger and Richard Repington, feodary of the county, (or two of them, the feodary being one); *p.m.* Mary Mynors, late the wife of Edward Mynors; co. Stafford.

244.) 24 *Oct.* 1576. *Gorhambury.* John Sowthcote, a justice of the Queen's Bench, Thomas Mildmay, Thomas Lucas, Thomas Barrington and William Walgrave, knights, Thomas Meade, serjeant at law, Thomas Powle, George Nicholes, Henry Goldinge, William Cardnall, Francis Stoner, escheator of the county, and John Glascoke, feodary of the county, (or two of them, Southcote, Meade, Powle, Nichols or Glascoke being one); *p.m.* Francis Jobson, knight, Thomas Stevins and Edward Blackwell; co. Essex.

245.) 30 *Oct.* 1576. George Norton, knight, John Yonge, knight, Hugh Smythe and John Coles, feodary of the county, (or two of them, the feodary being one); *p.m.* William Lotsham; co. Somerset.

246.) 30 *Oct.* 1576. The same; *p.m.* the same; co. Somerset.   [*m. 5d*]
Vacated, with a note: Vacat quia antea.

247.) 15 *Nov.* 1576. John Manners (esquire), Thomas Stanhope, knight, Peter Rosse, William Auger and Richard Repington, feodary of the county, (or two of them, the feodary being one); *p.m.* Edward Minors; co. Stafford.

248.) 15 *Nov.* 1576. Thomas Parry, Thomas Fortescue, John Chayny and Thomas Noke, feodary of the county (or two of them, the feodary being one); *p.m.* John Smythe; co. Berks.

249.) 15 *Nov.* 1576. Nicholas Poynes, knight, John Yonge, knight, Maurice Sheppard, Christopher George, feodary of the county of the city, and John Seymer (or two of them, the foedary being one); *p.m.* Hugh Partridge; co. city of Bristol.

250.) 28 *July* 1576. *Gorhambury.* William Cordell, knight, master of the rolls, William More, knight, Thomas Browne, knight, John Vaughan and Eustace Webbe, deputy feodary of the county, (or two of them, Webbe being one); *p.m.* Richard Polsted; co. Surrey.

251.) 15 *Aug.* 1576. *Gorhambury.* Thomas Fanshawe, William Aylyffe and John Glascoke, feodary of the county (or two of them, the feodary being one); *p.m.* Henry Mewtas; co. Essex.

252.) 20 *Sept.* 1576. *Gorhambury.* Nicholas Arnolde, Giles Poole, Nicholas Poynes, William Wynter and John Tracye, knights, George Fetyplace, Richard Pates, John Trye, Thomas Smythe of Camden, Gabriel Bleke, [——] Atkyns, Richard Barnam, Humphrey Ashefeld and Christopher George, feodary of the county, (or three of them, Arnold, Poole, Pates, Fetyplace or George being one); *p.m.* Richard Wigett of Shennyngton, William Jones of Newland, Philip Erwithe of Engleshbucknor and Henry Brayne of Stanton; co. Gloucester.

253.) 20 *Sept.* 1576. *Gorhambury.* The same; *p.m.* Walter Payne, Thomas Dawnt, John Tyson and John Haylye; co. Gloucester.

254.)   20 *Sept.* 1576.   *Gorhambury.*   Charles Somersett, knight, William Morgan, knight, David Lewes, LL.D., William Harbert of Saynt Julyan, William Morgan of Lanternam, Rice Morgan and John Gibon, LL.D., (or three of them, Somersett, William Morgan, Lewes or Gibon being one); *p.m.* William Johns ap Evan, William Morgan of Tredegre, Morgan David ap Gwillym of Llanhangell and Reginald ap Powell of Perthhier; co. Monmouth.

255.)   20 *Sept.* 1576.   *Gorhambury.*   The same; *p.m.* Thomas ap Powell of Wytchurche, Walter ap Probart of Penclace, James Gunter of Aburgavenny and John Morgan of Maughan; co. Monmouth.

256.)   20 *Sept.* 1576.   *Gorhambury.*   James Whytney, knight, John Huband, knight, John Skydmore, John Harley, James Warnecomb, Edward Croftes, John Garnannes, Thomas Kerle, Fabian Phillippes, John Apparrey and John Parry, deputy feodary of the county, (or three of them, Huband, Skydmore, Warnecombe, Kerle, Phillippes or Parry being one); *p.m.* James Barrowe, John Warnecombe, Rowland Bradshawe and Lewis Parye; co. Hereford.

257.)   20 *Sept.* 1576.   *Gorhambury.*   Fulk Grevill, John Huband, Thomas Lucye and William Catesbye, knights, George Digby, [——] Anderson, Edward Eglonby, Thomas Dabscott, Clement Fisher and Arthur Gregorye, feodary of the county, (or three of them, Grevill, Huband, Lucye, Anderson, Dabscott or Gregorye being one); *p.m.* John Hunckes the younger, [——] Stanford, Thomas Wolfe and Hugh Marrowe; co. Warwick.

258.)   20 *Sept.* 1576.   *Gorhambury.*   John Manners (esquire), Francis Willoughbye, knight, Francis Leake, knight, Nicholas Powtrell, serjeant at law, John Berryn, Richard Cooke, escheator of the county, and Ralph Barton, feodary of the county, (or three of them, Manners, Willoughby, Powtrell or Barton being one); *p.m.* John Hersey, knight; co. Nottingham.

259.)   14 *Dec.* 1575.   *Gorhambury.*   William Wightman, Christopher Riche, Thomas Hughes and William Necton, feodary of the county, (or two of them, the feodary being one); *p.m.* Thomas Heigate; co. Middlesex.

260.)   17 *Nov.* 1576.[1]   James Whitney, knight, John Huband, knight, John Skydamore, John Harley, Edward Crofts, John Garnnans, Thomas Kerle, Fabian Phillippes, James Apparry and John Parrye, deputy feodary of the county, (or three of them, Huband, Skydmore, Kerle, Phillipps or Parry being one); *p.m.* Richard Barrowe, Jane Carrell, late the wife of Edmund Carrell, Rowland Bradshawe and Lewis Parry; co. Hereford.

261.)   31 *Oct.* 1576.   James Warnecombe, James Doyle, John   [*m.* 6*d.*] Baskervile, Walter Baskervile and John Parrye, deputy feodary of the county, (or three of them, Parrye being one); *p.m.* Walter, earl of Essex; co. Hereford.

262.)   4 *Aug.* 1576.   *Gorhambury.*   Thomas Cecill, knight, Adrian Stokes, Francis Cave, Francis Harrington and Robert Braham, feodary of the county, (or two of them, the feodary being one); *p.m.* Thomas Neale, a minor; co. Leicester.

263.)   12 *Oct.* 1576.   *Gorhambury.*   Robert Drewry, knight, George Peckham, knight, William Fleetewood, William Hawtry, Roger Alforde, Thomas Farmer and Peter Palmer, feodary of the county, (or three of them, Drewry, Fleetwood, Hawtry, Farmer or Palmer being one); *p.m.* Thomas Abbott, Thomas White, Henry Ferrers and [——] Browne; co. Buckingham.

264.)   12 *Oct.* 1576.   *Gorhambury.*   Thomas Gawdy, a justice of the Queen's Bench, Christopher Haydon, knight, William Bottes, knight, Nicholas Straunge, knight, Robert Bell, William Paston, Drew Drewry, Henry Woodhowse, Francis Wyndham, Clement Paston, Edward Flowerdewe, Philip Appleyard, John Carewe and Christopher Dawbeney, feodary of the county, (or three of them, Gawdy, Heydon, Bell, Drewry, Wyndham,

---

[1] Entry stated to be of the year 19 Eliz.

Flowerdewe or Dawbeney being one); *p.m.* Edward Waters, Henry Valenger, [——] Carter of Walton the elder and [——] Bexwell *alias* Shordiche; co. Norfolk.

265.)   7 *Nov.* 1576.   Thomas Moore, knight, Thomas Lyfelde and Ralph Bossevile, feodary of the county, or his deputy (or two of them, the feodary or deputy feodary being one); *p.m.* Henry Mellys; co. Surrey.

266.)   30 *Nov.* 1576.[1]   John Brockett, William Tooke, auditor general of the court of Wards, George Ferrys and Walter Tooke, feodary of the county, (or two of them, William Tooke being one); *p.m.* Richard Rede, knight; co. Hertford.

267.)   1 *Dec.* 1576.[1]   Edmund Dunche, Thomas Richardes, feodary of the county, and John Holowell (or two of them, the feodary being one); *p.m.* Ralph Haley; co. Oxford.

268.)   1 *Dec.* 1576.[1]   Edward Flowerdewe, Richard Cooke, Christopher Daubney, feodary of the county, and John Dobbes (or two of them, the feodary being one); *p.m.* Thomas Brampton; co. Norfolk.

269.)   8 *June* 1576.   *Gorhambury.*   Richard Barkeley, knight, John Tracye, knight, Thomas Throgmerton, Edward Veell and Christopher George, feodary of the county, (or two of them); *p.m.* Edward, lord Windesor; co. Gloucester.

270.)   4 *June* 1576.   Christopher Yelverton, Robert Spencer, Richard Fawkenor and William Rudde, deputy feodary of the county, (or two of them, Rudde being one); *p.m.* John Randall; co. Northampton.

271.)   16 *April* 1576.   *Gorhambury.*   John Birche, a baron of the Exchequer, Rowland Hayward, knight, John Marshe, William Wightman, Francis Newdigate, Christopher Riche and William Necton, feodary of the county, (or three of them, Birche or the feodary being one); *p.m.* Thomas Foxe; co. Middlesex.

272.)   2 *May* 1576.   *Gorhambury.*   John Trye, Henry Poole, John Highford, Paul Tracye, Humphrey Ashefeld, William Bassett and Christopher George, feodary of the county, (or two of them, the feodary being one); *p.m.* Anthony Marton; co. Gloucester.

273.)   2 *May* 1576.   *Gorhambury.*   James Whitney, knight, John Dalabar, Richard Mynors, Thomas Kirle and John Parry, deputy feodary of the county, (or two of them, Parry being one); *p.m.* Thomas Marbill; co. Hereford.

274.)   1 *May* 1576.   *Gorhambury.*   John Radclyffe, James Anderton, Christopher Anderton and Gilbert Moreton, feodary of the county palatine, (or two of them, the feodary being one); *p.m.* John Radyshe; co. palatine of Lancaster.

275.)   12 *May* 1576.   Cuthbert Collingwood, knight, Thomas Graye, knight, James Ogle and John Lawson, feodary of the county (or two of them, the feodary being one); *p.m.* John Fenwicke; co. Northumberland.

276.)   12 *May* 1576.   Oliver, lord St. John, Henry, lord Cheynie, Lewis Dyves, Ralph Austrie and Richard Faldo, feodary of the county, (or two of them, the feodary being one); *p.m.* lady Agnes Calveley, late the wife of Richard Chetewood; co. Bedford.

277.)   10 *May* 1576.   William Button, Giles Escourte, John Eyre, Thomas Escourte and William Grove, feodary of the county, (or two of them, the feodary being one); *p.m.* John St. John; co. Wilts.

278.)   12 *May* 1576.   Edward Onley, Thomas Morgan, feodary of the county, William Chauncey, John Dryden, Thomas Onley and William Rudde (or two of them, the feodary being one); *p.m.* Richard Colles; co. Northampton.

279.)   14 *April* 1576.   *Gorhambury.*   William Tooke, auditor general of the court of Wards, George Horsey, Thomas Dockwra and Walter Tooke, deputy feodary of the county, (or two of them, William Tooke being one); *p.m.* John Pygotte of Tewinge; co. Hertford.

280.)   2 *May* 1576.   *Gorhambury.*   Edmund Coles, John Alderford, William Childe,

---

[1] Entry stated to be of the year 19 Eliz.

feodary of the county, John Badger and John Bridges (or two of them, the feodary being one); *p.m.* John Callowe; co. Worcester.

281.)   2 *May* 1576.   *Gorhambury.*   Thomas Tresham, knight, Roger Chernocke, Edward Dalyson, William Rudd, deputy feodary of the county, Richard Langtree and Giles Cheyney (or three of them, Rudde being one); *p.m.* Ralph Curson; co. Northampton.

282.)   2 *May* 1576.   *Gorhambury.*   Thomas Palmer, knight, Edward Fennar, George Goringe, Henry Goringe, Richard Lewknor and Edward Middleton, feodary of the county, (or three of them, the feodary being one); *p.m.* Thomas Culpepper; co. Sussex.

283.)   26 *May* 1576.   Thomas Scotte, knight, Thomas Wootton, William Cromer, Thomas Potter, John Rudston, Stephen Slanye, William Onslowe and Michael Berisford, feodary of the county, (or two of them, the feodary being one); *p.m.* Francis Barnham, alderman of London; co. Kent.

284.)   1 *June* 1576.   William Metham, Anthony Thorold, Robert Saunderson, Edward Sapcotes and Anthony Kyme, feodary of the county, (or two of them, the feodary being one); *p.m.* John Dyon; co. Lincoln.

285.)   29 *May* 1576.   Richard Bolles, Thomas Kyme, Thomas Quadringe   [*m.7d.*] and Anthony Kyme, feodary of the county, (or two of them, the feodary being one); *p.m.* Thomas Elward, a minor; co. Lincoln.

286.)   29 *May* 1576.   Edmund Hall, John Harington, Francis Harington and Anthony Kyme, feodary of the county, (or two of them, the feodary being one); *p.m.* John Haselwood; co. Lincoln.

287.)   1 *June* 1576.   Richard Pates, Christopher George, feodary of the county of the city, John Smyth and Peter Romney (or two of them, the feodary being one); *p.m.* Robert Moreton, a minor; co. city of Gloucester.

288.)   2 *May* 1576.   Robert Staunforde, Richard Brooke, Richard Repington, feodary of the county, Thomas Waryng and William Fynny (or three of them, Repington or Warynge being one); *p.m.* John Laweson; co. Stafford.

289.)   2 *April* 1576.   *Gorhambury.*   John Birche, a baron of the Exchequer, William Fleetewood, recorder of London, William Wightman, George Asheby, William Gerrard and William Necton, feodary of the county, (or three of them, Birche or the feodary being one); *p.m.* Richard Holford; co. Middlesex.

290.)   2 *April* 1576.   *Gorhambury.*   The same; *p.m.* William Cornyshe; co. Middlesex.

291.)   2 *April* 1576.   *Gorhambury.*   The same; *p.m.* John Leake; co. Middlesex.

292.)   2 *April* 1576.   *Gorhambury.*   The same (Necton being described as feodary of the city); *p.m.* Joan Taylor, widow; city of London.

293.)   2 *April* 1576.   *Gorhambury.*   Richard Bolles, Anthony Kyme, feodary of the county, Robert Townley and Alexander Skynner (or two of them, the feodary being one); *p.m.* Anthony Stringer; co. Lincoln.

294.)   7 *April* 1576.   *Gorhambury.*   Henry, lord Norrys, Christopher Saunders, Anthony Pallard and Thomas Ricardes, feodary of the county, (or two of them, the feodary being one); *p.m.* Anthony Carleton; co. Oxford.

295.)   17 *May* 1576.   John Kytchen, Christopher Rithe, William Necton, feodary of the city, and Jasper Cholmeley (or two of them, the feodary being one); *p.m.* John Draper, citizen and innkeeper of London; city of London.

296.)   17 *May* 1576.   Francis Stonerd, escheator of the county, John Glascoke, feodary of the county, Edward Bell and Thomas Wiseman (or two of them, the feodary being one); *p.m.* Thomas Leveson; co. Essex.

297.)   24 *April* 1576.   *Gorhambury.*   Alexander Hampden, Michael Hawtre, John Kynge and Edward Betham, deputy feodary of the county, (or two of them, the feodary being one); *p.m.* William Howell; co. Buckingham.

298.)   2 *May* 1576.   *Gorhambury.*   Humphrey Ashfeld, John Trye, Nicholas Thorpe,

George Huntley, Henry Poole, John Highford and Christopher George, feodary of the county (or two of them, the feodary being one); *p.m.* George Twysell; co. Gloucester.

299.)   2 *May* 1576.   *Gorhambury.*   The same; *p.m.* Thomas Twisell; co. Gloucester.

300.)   2 *May* 1576.   *Gorhambury.*   The same; *p.m.* Edward Twisell; co. Gloucester.

301.)   2 *May* 1576.   *Gorhambury.*   The same; *p.m.* Thomas Birte; co. Gloucester.

302.)   2 *May* 1576.   *Gorhambury.*   The same; *p.m.* Thomas Sandford; co. Gloucester.

303.)   2 *May* 1576.   *Gorhambury.*   The same; *p.m.* Richard Watkyns; co. Gloucester.

304.)   2 *May* 1576.   *Gorhambury.*   The same; *p.m.* William Elland; co. Gloucester.

305.)   2 *May* 1576.   *Gorhambury.*   The same; *p.m.* Edward Tybbottes; co. Gloucester.

306.)   31 *March* 1576.   *Gorhambury.*   Arthur Manwaringe, knight, William Gerrard, Peter Warberton of Arley, Jerome Corbett, Peter Warberton of Lincolnes Ynne, William Ashton and Richard Hurleston, feodary of the county palatine, (or two of them, the feodary being one); *p.m.* Anthony Gravenor; co. palatine of Chester.

307.)   31 *March* 1576.   *Gorhambury.*   Arthur Manwaringe, knight, William Gerrard, Peter Warberton of Arley, Jerome Corbett, Peter Warberton of Lincolnes Ynne, William Asheton and John Billott, feodary of the county, (or two of them, the feodary being one); *p.m.* Anthony Gravenor; co. Denbigh.

308.)   28 *Feb.* 1576.   Edmund Hall, George Jon, Alexander Skynner and Anthony Kyme, feodary of the county, (or two of them, the feodary being one); *p.m.* Lawrence Baker *alias* Robinson; co. Lincoln.

309.)   3 *March* 1576.   John Ayre, Thomas Escourte and Robert Grove, feodary of the country (or two of them, the feodary being one); *p.m.* Michael Quinton; co. Wilts.

310.)   5 *March* 1576.   Edward Gage, Ralph Hare, Edward Middleton, feodary of the county, and Thomas Churchar (or two of them, the feodary being one); *p.m.* Richard Nye; co. Sussex.

311.)   19 *April* 1576.   *Gorhambury.*   Thomas Stanhope, knight, John   [*m.8d.*] Biron, Robert Merkham, William Dabridgcourt and Ralph Barton (or two of them); *p.m.* John Haselwood; co. Nottingham.

312.)   24 *April* 1576.   *Gorhambury.*   Henry Wallopp, knight, Henry Gifford and Richard Hore, feodary of the county, (or two of them, the feodary being one); *p.m.* John Gifford; co. Southampton.

313.)   19 *May* 1576.   William Tooke, auditor general of the court of Wards, Rowland Lytton, Nicholas Bristowe, Henry Cooke and Walter Tooke, deputy feodary of the county, (or two of them, William Tooke being one); *p.m.* John Butler, knight; co. Hertford.

314.)   20 *Feb.* 1576.   Richard Bolles, Thomas Kyme, Alexander Skynner and Anthony Kyme, feodary of the county, (or two of them, the feodary being one); *p.m.* Richard Denton; co. Lincoln.

315.)   20 *Feb.* 1576.   The same; *p.m.* Robert Cracrofte; co. Lincoln.

316.)   19 *March* 1576.   Thomas Gargrave, knight, Robert Bradford, Walter Jobson the younger, William Ingleby and William Hamand, feodary of the West Riding, co. York, (or two of them, the feodary being one); *p.m.* John Wayneright; co. York.

317.)   30 *June* 1576.   Edward Boughton, Arthur Gregory, feodary of the county, Richard Rowley and Thomas Wilmer (or two of them, the feodary being one); *p.m.* William Radborne; co. Warwick.

318.)   28 *June* 1576.   James Altham, Richard Swyfte, John Vavasor and John Glascoke, feodary of the county, (or two of them, the feodary being one); *p.m.* Simon Adams; co. Essex.

319.)   3 *July* 1576.   Hugh Wyate, John Eveleighe, feodary of the county, Richard Channon and Vincent Calmadye (or two of them, the feodary being one); *p.m.* Thomas Velley; co. Devon.

320.)   4 *July* 1576.   Roger Prydeaux, Edward Emeredithe, Edward Whiddon and John

Eveleigh, feodary of the county, (or two of them, the feodary being one); *p.m.* Leonard Loveyse; co. Devon.

321.)   4 *July* 1576.   William Tooke, auditor general of the court of Wards, Richard Gadbury, William Necton, feodary of the city, and Nicholas Spencer (or two of them, the feodary being one); *p.m.* John Luke; city of London.

322.)   3 *July* 1576.   William Deverox, knight, Humphrey Bradburne, knight, Edward Holte, Clement Fisher and Richard Repington, feodary of the county, (or two of them, the feodary being one); *p.m.* John Ferrers; co. Stafford.

323.)   9 *July* 1576.   Thomas Henley, Levin Buskyn, Thomas Fludd and Michael Berisford, feodary of the county, (or two of them, the feodary being one); *p.m.* Richard Tomyowe; co. Kent.

324.)   9 *July* 1576.   Nicholas Powtrell, serjeant at law, Thomas Markham, James Washington, Ralph Barton, feodary of the county, William Poole and John Thornehagh (or two of them, the feodary being one); *p.m.* Francis More; co. Nottingham.

325.)   9 *July* 1576.   Rowland Lacon, Jerome Corbett, Andrew Charlton, Richard Cressett, Robert Eyton, Richard Prynce, Thomas Staunton, feodary of the county, Adam Mitton and Francis Hoord (or two of them, the feodary being one); *p.m.* Robert Detton; co. Salop.

326.)   4 *June* 1576.   William Garnons, John Parry, deputy feodary of the county, Anthony Washeborne and George Vaughan (or two of them, Parry being one); *p.m.* Hugh ap Parry; co. Hereford.

327.)   23 *May* 1576.   John Arundell of Treryse, John Trevanyon of Cary Heys, William Courteney of Devyoke, Hugh Roscarrocke and Thomas Browne, feodary of the county, (or two of them, the feodary being one); *p.m.* Richard Roscarrocke; co. Cornwall.

328.)   9 *March* 1576.   Walter Tooke, deputy feodary of the county, William Tooke the younger and Thomas Pagett (or two of them, Walter Tooke being one); *p.m.* Humphrey Stafford, knight; co. Hertford.

329.)   27 *Feb.* 1576.   Thomas Waterton, Richard Tempest, Robert Bradforde, escheator of the county, and William Hamond, feodary of the West Riding thereof, (or two of them, the feodary being one); *p.m.* James Pylkington, bishop of Durham; co. York.

330.)   25 *June* 1576.   James Padgett, Thomas Weste, Thomas Clerke, deputy of Edmund Clerke, escheator of the county, and Richard Hore, feodary thereof, (or two of them, the feodary being one); *p.m.* John Foster; co. Southampton.

331)   7 *July* 1576.   Thomas Cecill, knight, Edmund Hall, George Quarles and William Rudd, deputy feodary of the county, (or two of them, Rudd being one); *p.m.* Robert Wingfeld the elder; co. Northampton.

332.)   10 *July* 1576.   John Eveleighe, feodary of the county, Richard Reynoldes, Thomas Wyse and Christopher Harryse (or two of them, the feodary being one); *p.m.* Margaret Buller, widow; co. Devon.

333.)   10 *July* 1576.   Richard Pates, Christopher George, feodary of the county of the city, and Richard Bingham (or two of them, the feodary being one); *p.m.* Thomas Robertes, clerk; co. city of Gloucester.

334.)   10 *July* 1576.   Owen Hopton, knight, John Southcote, a justice of the Queen's Bench, William Fletewood, recorder of the city of London, Bernard Randolphe and William Necton, feodary of the county, (or two of them, the feodary being one); *p.m.* Edward, lord Windesor; co. Middlesex.

335.)   5 *Nov.* 1576.   Commission to William Tooke, auditor general of the court of Wards, Francis Stoner, Thomas Wyseman and John Glascocke, feodary of the county, (or two of them, Tooke or Glascocke being one) to inquire *post mortem* Robert Denny, a minor in the Queen's ward, son and heir of Henry Denny, in the county of Essex.   [*m.* 9*d.*]

336.)   12 *Oct.* 1576.   *Gorhambury.*   Commission to Henry, lord Clynton, Christopher Wraye, knight, chief justice of the Queen's Bench, Robert Mounson, a justice of the

Common Pleas, Robert Tyrwytt, knight, Anthony Tharrolde, Thomas Saintpole, Robert Care the elder, Stephen Thymblebly, Robert Savile, Edmund Hall, William Marbury, Richard Topclyf, Thomas Grantham and Anthony Keyme, feodary of the county, (or three of them, Clynton, Wraye, Mounson, Tharrolde, Carre, Sainthole, Thymbleby or Keyme being one) to inquire better *post mortem* William Manby in the county of Lincoln. By inquisition taken at Hornecastle on 14 May, 15 Eliz., before the said Tharolde, then escheator of the county, it was found that he held divers lands in the county; but it is reported that they are held otherwise and by other or more services and are of a greater yearly value than is specified in the inquisition.

The like, of *melius inquirendum*, to the following, viz.—

337.)   12 *Oct.* 1576.   *Gorhambury*.   The same; *p.m.* William Wesman; co. Lincoln.

338.)   20 *Feb.* 1576.   Richard Bolles, Thomas Kyme, Alexander Skynner and Anthony Kyme, feodary of the county, (or two of them, the feodary being one); *p.m.* Richard Larkes; co. Lincoln.

339.)   29 *May* 1576   Richard Bolles, Thomas Kyme, Thomas Quadrynge and Anthony Kyme, feodary of the county, (or two of them, the feodary being one); *p.m.* Richard Kedby; co. Lincoln.

340.)   7 *July* 1576.   William Gerrard, William Necton, feodary of the city, Leonard Scutedamore and Thomas Holcrofte (or two of them, the feodary being one); *p.m.* Thomas Walker, citizen and 'letherseller' of London; city of London.

341.)   16 *July* 1576.   *Gorhambury*.   Thomas Henley, George Moulton, William Lambert, Thomas Fludd and Michael Berisford, feodary of the county, (or three of them, the feodary being one); *p.m.* Richard Tybald; co. Kent.

342.)   18 *May* 1576.   Commission to Humphrey Ferrys, Edward Holte and Arthur Gregory, feodary of the county, (or two of them, the feodary being one), to inquire better *post mortem* Thomas Bracebridge in the county of Warwick. By inquisition taken before William Deverox, knight, Edward Holte and [—] Langworth, commissioners, it was found that he died seised of the manor of Kingesbury and that Thomas Bracebridge was his son and heir, but of whom the manor was held the jury did not know.

343.)   7 *Nov.* 1576.   Commission to Thomas Gawdey, a justice of the Queen's Bench, Christopher Haydon, knight, William Buttes, knight, Nicholas Straunge, knight, William Paston, Robert Bell, Drew Drewry, Henry Woodhouse, Francis Wyndham, Clement Paston, Edward Flowerdew, Philip Appleyard, John Carewe and Christopher Dawbney, feodary of the county, (or three of them, Gawdey, Haydon, Bell, Drewrey, Wyndham, Flowerdewe or Daubney being one) to inquire better *post mortem* Edward Waters of Lenn Regis in the county of Norfolk. By   [*m.* 10*d.*] inquisition taken before Henry Cornewallys, Christopher Yelverton and Christopher Dawbeney, commissioners, it was found that he held lands in Lynne Regis and Dowsilgate; but it is reported that they are held otherwise and by other or more services than are specified in the inquisition.

344.)   12 *Oct.* 1576.   *Gorhambury*.   Commission to Henry, lord Clynton, Christopher Wray, knight, chief justice of the Queen's Bench, Robert Mounson, a justice of the Common Pleas, Robert Tirwytt, knight, Anthony Tharrolde, Thomas Saintpole, Robert Carre the elder, Stephen Thymbleby, Robert Savile, Edmund Hall, William Marbury, Richard Topclyf, Thomas Grantham and Anthony Keyme, feodary of the county, (or three of them, Clynton, Wraye, Mounson, Tharrolde, Carre, Saintpole, Thymbleby or Keyme being one) to inquire better *post mortem* Anthony Mawer in the county of Lincoln. By inquisition taken before George Mounson, late escheator of the county, it was found that he was seised of the manor of Garnethorpe and other lands in Garnethorpe, Ludnaye and Wharfholme and that they are held of the heirs of the late duke of Suffolk as of his soke of Gayton by fealty only; but it is reported that they are held otherwise and by other or more services than is specified in the inquisition.

345.)   12 *Oct.* 1576.   *Gorhambury.*   Commission to Fulk Grevill, knight, John Huband, knight, Thomas Lucy, knight, William Catesby, knight, George Didby, Edward Eglionby, Edmund Anderson, Thomas Dabscott, Clement Fyssher and Arthur Gregory, feodary of the county, (or three of them, Grevill, Huband, Lucye, Anderson, Dabscott or Gregory being one) to inquire better *post mortem* lady Jane Braye, late the wife of Edward Bray, knight, lord Braye, in the county of Warwick. By inquisition taken before the said Eglionby and Gregorye, commissioners, it was found that she held the manors of Mountforde Wellesborne, Griffe and Colton and other lands, but it is reported that they are held by other or more services than are specified in the inquisition.

346.)   1 *Dec.* 1576.[1]   Commission to John Gifford, John Coffyn, John Eveleighe, feodary of the county, and Balthazar Butler (or two of them, the feodary being one) to inquire better *post mortem* Thomas Pomerey, knight, in the county of Devon. By inquisition taken before John Marwood, late escheator of the county, it was found that he was seised *inter alia* of the manor of Lancrasse *alias* Lankarsse, held of the heirs of Edward, late earl of Devon, as of his honour of Okehampton, and   [*m.* 11*d.*] of lands in Higheaunton; but by what services the lands are held is not specified in the inquisition.

347.)   30 *Nov.* 1576.[1]   Commission to James Ryvett, Richard Kempe, William Tymperley and Henry Reynoldes (or two of them) to inquire better *post mortem* William Duncon in the county of Suffolk. By inquisition taken before John Dobbes, late escheator of the county, it was found that Duncon died seised *inter alia* of lands in Mendlesham, whereof Thomas Andrewes and John Pretyman long before Duncon's death were seised in their demesne as of fee and by charter, 30 Dec., 10 Eliz., enfeoffed thereof Edward Keme, William Spurdance and Swithin Elinger and their heirs to the use of Duncon and Catherine then his wife for life in survivorship and thereafter to the use of his heirs male by her with remainder to the use of his right heirs, and that Andrewes and Pretyman long before Duncon's death were seised in their demesne as of fee of other lands in Mendlesham and by another charter of the date aforesaid enfeoffed thereof Duncon and Richard Duncon, his son, and their heirs.

348.)   16 *May* 1576.   Commission to Anthony Smethley, feodary of the East Riding, co. York, William Ingleby, Walter Jobson the younger and Thomas Elwood (or two of them, the feodary being one) to inquire better *post mortem* Gerard Eylwyn in the county of York. By inquisition taken before Christopher Tomlynson, late escheator of the county, *temp.* Henry VIII it was found that he held *inter alia* divers lands in Thornegunbold, Hedon and Ryhill; but by what services is not specified in the inquisition.

349.)   21 *May* 1576.   Commission to Henry Gates, knight, Richard Cholmeley, knight, and Thomas Willyamson, feodary of the North Riding, co. York, (or two of them, the feodary being one) to inquire better *post mortem* Robert Percy in the county of York. By inquisition taken before William Hamond, late escheator of the county, it was found that he was seised in his demesne as of fee of the reversion of the manor of Ryton and of lands in

---

[1] Entry stated to be of the year 19 Eliz.

Newmalton, Kyrkby Mysperton and Japton Magna; but of whom or by what services they are held is not specified in the inquisition.

350.) 19 *March* 1576. Commission to Thomas Grenewood, Anthony Busterd, George Whitton, John Chamberleyne and Thomas Ricardes, feodary of the county, (or two of them, the feodary being one) to inquire better *post mortem* Thomas More in the county of Oxford. By inquisition taken   [*m.* 12*d.*]
before Anthony Throkmorton and the said Ricardes, commissioners, it was found that Moore held of the Crown lands in Wretchwike and Burcester *alias* Byssyter and that he died on 10 March, 16 Eliz.; but who is his heir is not specified in the inquisition.

351.) 11 *July* 1576. Commission to Francis Leeke, knight, Francis Curson, Henry Foljambe, Ralph Barton, feodary of the county, Geoffrey Pole and Edmund Stephenson (or two of them, the feodary being one) to inquire better *post mortem* John Poge in the county of Nottingham. By inquisition taken before Nicholas Powtrell, serjeant at law, William Dabridgecourte and the said Barton, commissioners, it was found that he held lands in Hayton, Clarebrough, Mysterton, Walkringham, Stockwith and Westretford and that John Poge is his son and heir; but it is reported that they are held by other or more services than is specified in the inquisition.

352.) 20 *July* 1576. *Gorhambury.* Commission to John Zouche, knight, Francis Wortley, Anthony Gell, feodary of the county, Ralph Sacheverell, Richard Perkyns and Alan Berysford (or two of them) to inquire better *post mortem* John Rollesley in the county of Derby. By inquisition taken before Nicholas Strelley, late escheator of the county, it was found that he held lands in Little Rollysley, Yolgreve, Anparke, Carsington, Hopton, Workesworthe, Knyveton *alias* Kneton and Ryley and that Maud Rollesley is his daughter and heir; but it is reported that they are held otherwise or by other or more services than are specified in the inquisition.

353.) 5 Nov. 1576. Commission to Ralph Sheldon, John Folyett, Robert Wyche and William Chylde, feodary of the county, (or two of them, the feodary being one) to inquire on the idiocy of John Fellowe in the county of Worcester.

    The like to the following, viz.—

354.) 26 *Nov.* 1576.[1] Thomas Lovelace, George Moulton, William Lambert and Michael Berysford, feodary of the county, (or two of them, the feodary being one); idiocy of Edward Weldyshe; co. Kent.

355.) 14 *May* 1576. William Barbott of Swansey, Miles Button and Griffith Williams (or two of them); idiocy of Thomas Sevyer; co. Glamorgan.

356.) 30 *June* 1576. Thomas Cecill, knight, Robert Winckfeld,   [*m.* 13*d.*]
John Winckfeld and William Rudd, deputy feodary of the county, (or two of them, Rudd being one); idiocy of John Uxex; co. Northampton.

357.) 12 *July* 1576. Lawrence Levett, John Asheborneham, Francis Bolton and Edward Middleton, feodary of the county, (or two of them, the feodary being one); idiocy of John Abyrge *alias* Byrge; co. Sussex.

358.) 5 Oct. 1576. *Gorhambury.* Commission to Richard Barkeley, knight, John Younge, knight, William Rede and Christopher George, feodary of the city, (or three of them, the feodary being one) to inquire on the lunacy of Alice Robertes, widow, late the wife of Thomas Robertes of Bristoll, in the city of Bristoll.

---

[1] Entry stated to be of the year 19 Eliz.

The like to the following, viz.—

359.) 28 *July* 1576. *Gorhambury*. Richard Goodrick, George Woodrowe, Charles Jackson, Thomas Waterton and William Hamonde, feodary of the county, (or two of them, the feodary being one); lunacy of William Copley, son and heir of Philip Copley; co. York.

360.) 28 *July* 1576. *Gorhambury*. The same; lunacy of Philip Copley of Spradborrowe; co. York.

361.) 28 *July* 1576. *Gorhambury*. Gervase Clyfton, knight, Thomas Stanhope, knight, Robert Markham, Edward Stanhope and Ralph Barton, feodary of the county, (or two of them, the feodary being one); lunacy of William Copley, son and heir of Philip Copley; co. Nottingham.

362.) 7 *Nov.* 1576. John Waade, mayor of the city, George Norton, knight, Hugh Smythe, Christopher George, feodary of the city, and Thomas Kelke, (or three of them, the mayor and the feodary being two); lunacy of Alice Robertes, widow, late the wife of Thomas Robertes of Bristoll; city of Bristoll.

363.) 28 *June* 1576. William More, knight, Henry Barkley, D.C.L., John Cowper and Eustace Webbe, deputy feodary of the county, (or two of them, Webbe being one); lunacy of John Ashburnham; co. Surrey.

364.) 30 *July* 1576. *Gorhambury*. Robert Corbett, Richard Steynton, William Wyllyston and Thomas Staunton, feodary of the county, (or three of them, the feodary being one); lunacy of William Alkyngton; co. Salop.

365.) 8 *Nov.* 1576. Commission to Roger Manwood and Robert Mounson, justices of the Common Pleas, to determine in the guildhall of London an appeal of error in the record and process of a plea of trespass on the case brought by Henry Lane, skinner, against Richard Procter, grocer, before James Harveye, alderman, late a sheriff of London, in the court of the city and afterwards, at Procter's suit, by order of John Ryvers, knight, then mayor, in the court of the city transferred before the said Ryvers, then mayor, and the aldermen of the city in the chamber of the guildhall; at the suit of Procter.

366.) 8 *Oct.* 1576. *Gorhambury*. Commission to John Dalston the elder, Richard Dudley, Henry Tolson, feodary of the county, John Sowthake the elder and Francis Sandes (or two of them, the feodary being one) to inquire *post mortem* Thomas Barwys in the county of Cumberland what further lands he held. It is reported that he held of the Crown in chief more lands in the county than are specified   [*m.* 14*d.*] in an inquisition late taken.

367.) 28 *Nov.* 1576.[1] Commission to William Hylton, knight, Henry Bramlynge, mayor of Newcastle on Tyne, David Carnabye and Henry Anderson (or two of them, Hylton or Carnabye being one) to inquire *post mortem* Anthony Mytford in the county of Northumberland; Gilbert Errington to inform Christopher Morpethe or Robert Hallyman of the day and place of meeting 10 days beforehand.

The like to the following, viz.—

368.) 12 *Oct.* 1576. *Gorhambury*. William More, knight, Thomas Rychefeld and Robert Bossevyle, feodary of the county, or his deputy (or two of them); *p.m.* John Pordam; co. Surrey.

369.) 24 *Nov.* 1576.[1] Arthur Bassett, knight, John Chichester of Raleigh, John Eveleigh, feodary of the county, and George Wyat (or two of them, the feodary being one); *p.m.* John Darte; co. Devon.

370.) 24 *Nov.* 1576.[1] Cuthbert, lord Ogle, Thomas Graye, knight, James Ogle and John

[1] Entry stated to be of the year 19 Eliz.

Lawson, feodary of the county, (or two of them, the feodary being one); *p.m.* Guy Annsley; co. Northumberland.

371.)   24 *Nov.* 1576.[1]   James Whytney, knight, James Apparrye, John Delabere and John Apparrye, deputy feodary of the county, (or two of them, the deputy feodary being one); *p.m.* John Apparrye of Wormebridge; co. Hereford.

372.)   22 *Nov.* 1576.[1] William Gerrarde, Philip Scudamore, William Necton, feodary of the city, and Thomas Holcroft (or two of them, the feodary being one); *p.m.* William Spencer; city of London.

373.)   26 *Nov.* 1576.[1]   Thomas Andrewes, feodary of the county, John Ryvett, Charles Sekeford and Francis Saunders (or two of them, the feodary being one); *p.m.* George Derehaugh; co. Suffolk.

374.)   26 *Nov.* 1576.[1]   Peter Dormer, Peter Palmer, feodary of the county, and Edward Betham (or two of them, the feodary being one); *p.m.* Simon Egerton; co. Buckingham.

375.)   24 *Nov.* 1576.[1]   Thomas Offeley, knight, Thomas Fanshawe, William Tooke, Ralph Bossevyle, Edward Heron and William Necton, feodary of the city, (or two of them, Tooke, Bossevyle or Necton being one); *p.m.* Robert Trappes, mercer; city of London.

376.)   26 *Nov.* 1576.[1]   Richard Barkeley, knight, Edward Barkeley, Christopher George, feodary of the county, and Richard Byrde (or two of them, the feodary being one); *p.m.* Thomas Hodge; co. Gloucester.

377.)   12 *May* 1576.   Edward Onley, Thomas Morgan, feodary of the county, William Chauncey, John Dryden, Thomas Onley and William Rudde (or two of them, the feodary being one); *p.m.* Wibert Wattes; co. Northampton.

378.)   9 *July* 1576.   Rowland Lacon, Jerome Corbett, Andrew Charlton, Richard Cressett, Robert Eyton, Richard Prynce, Thomas Staunton, feodary of the county, Adam Mytton and Francis Hoorde (or two of them, the feodary being one); *p.m.* Thomas Powes; co. Salop.

379.)   2 *May* 1576.   *Gorhambury.*   Thomas Tresham, knight, Roger Chernock, Edward Dalyson, William Rudde, deputy feodary of the county, Richard Langtree and Giles Cheyney (or three of them, Rudde being one); *p.m.* John Baro; co. Northampton.

380.)   2 *May* 1576.   *Gorhambury.*   The same; *p.m.* John Ball; co. Northampton.

381.)   5 *Nov.* 1576.   Commission to lord Wentworthe, Francis Knolles, knight, councillor, treasurer of the household, James Croftes, knight, controller of the household, Ralph Sadler, knight, chancellor of the duchy of Lancaster, Walter Myldmaye, knight, chancellor and undertreasurer of the Exchequer, William Cordell, knight, master of the rolls, John Southcott, a justice of the Queen's Bench, Roger Manwood, a justice of the Common Pleas, Gilbert Gerrard, attorney general, Thomas Bromley, solicitor general, Thomas Seckford and Thomas Wyllson, masters of Requests, Owen Hopton, knight, lieutenant of the Tower of London, William Damsell, knight, receiver general of the court of Wards, Rowland Haywarde and Lionel Duckett, knights, aldermen of London, Thomas Gresham and William Moore, knights, William Fleetewood, recorder of London, David Lewes, judge of the Admiralty, Richard Kyngsmyll, attorney of the court of Wards, Robert Hopton, knight marshal of the household,   [*m.* 15*d.*]
Henry Knolles, Thomas Randolphe, master of the posts, Henry Killigrewe, Peter Osborne and Thomas Powle, clerk of the crown, (or four of them) to search out offenders in respect of counterfeitings and falsifying of money and all murders, felonies, burglaries and other grievous offences throughout the realm; power to summon before them and order the apprehension of all offenders and suspects, to order their imprisonment for trial according to law, to take recognisances for further appearance and to certify examinations to the justices of assize and gaol delivery or justices of oyer and terminer before whom offenders

---

[1] Entry stated to be of the year 19 Eliz.

are to be tried, or to the chief justice of the Queen's Bench if he shall by letters signed send for the same; also power to allow costs to persons by their order bringing up prisoners or persons to be examined, a bill signed by the commissioners being sufficient warrant for payment of the same at the Exchequer up to the sum of £6 13s. 4d. for one prisoner, and, if the charges shall seem to require a further sum, to require allowance thereof by means of the Privy Council. It is reported that such offences are being committed more accustomably than heretofore.   *English.*   By Q.

(*The rest of the dorse is blank.*)

PART III

C. 66/1139

382.)   28 *May* 1576.   Lease for 21 years to James Butler, clerk, of the rectory, church and chapel of Aldringham and Thorpe, co. Suffolk, late of Charles,   [*m.* 1] duke of Suffolk, formerly of the monastery of Laiston, co. Suffolk; with reservations; from Lady Day last; yearly rent £7 11*s.* 6*d.*; the lessee within seven years to build a sufficient mansion house for the curate of Alsingham and Thorpe at the discretion of the surveyor of the county; the lessee shall not alienate the lease to any other person except to the next incumbent or an ecclesiastical person fit to celebrate divine service there and for such consideration for the lessee's charges as the treasurer and chancellor of the Exchequer shall adjudge or as shall have been agreed between the lessee and the alienee. By warrant of the commissioners.

383.)   15 *June* 1576.   *Gorhambury*.   Lease for 21 years to George Brydiman, the Queen's servant, of all lands in Shrewsbury (*Salop'*) or elsewhere, co. Salop, late of the fellowship of drapers there and in the Crown's hands by stat. 1 Edw. VI for the dissolution of chantries and the like; with reservations; from Lady Day last; yearly rent, from the time when he shall obtain possession, £15 15*s.* 2*d.*   By p.s.
        Vacated, because surrendered 12 *Dec.*, 19 *Eliz.*; *signed*: Wyll'm Cordell; George Bredyman.

384.)   12 *June* 1576.   *Gorhambury*.   Presentation of William Stearne, clerk, to the vicarage of Gillinge, Chester dioc., void by death.   By p.s.

385.)   15 *June* 1576.   *Gorhambury*.   Presentation of Thomas Freman, clerk, M.A., preacher of the Divine Word, to the church of Mynchinhampton *alias* Michelhampton, Gloucester dioc., void by the deprivation of Thomas Taylor or otherwise; in the Queen's gift by the minority of Frederick Windsor,   [*m.* 2] son and heir of Edward, late lord Windsor.   By p.s.

(386.)   16 *June* 1576. Pardon for (1) John Slade late of London, indicted for that he broke and entered the house of Ralph Fitche, 'vyntener', in the parish of Christ Church in Farringdon Within ward, London, on 21 Oct., 17 Eliz. and stole a silver cup belonging to Fitche, (2) William Storrye late of London, 'yoman', indicted for that he robbed John Keyne (*alias* Keyme) in a highway called Hodge Lane at Whitechappell, co. Middlesex, of a kerchief and 5*s.* belonging to him on 10 Feb., 18 Eliz., and (3) Richard Nicolson *alias* Nicolles late of London, 'carpenter', indicted for that he with others burgled the house of Joyce Pomase, widow, in the parish of St. Leonard in Shorditche, co. Middlesex, on 10 Feb., 18 Eliz., and stole goods and money (*described*) belonging to her and to James Haynes.   By Q.

387.)   14 *June* 1576.   *Gorhambury*.   Grant for life to Richard Browne of the office of clerk of the peace in the county of Essex.   By Q.

388.)   4 *June* 1576.   Presentation of Arthur Boorne, clerk, to the portion of Tydcombe, Exeter dioc., void by resignation; in the Queen's gift by the minority of Jonathan Trelanye.
                                                                              By Q.

389.)   18 *June* 1576.   *Greenwich.*   Grant to Henry, earl of Arundell, K.G., councillor, of
the wardship and marriage of John Jackman, son and heir   [*m.* 3]
of Edward Jackman, late alderman of London.   By p.s.

390.)   24 *April* 1576.   *Gorhambury.*   Grant for life to William Herle, the Queen's servant,
of an annuity of 100 marks, payable at the Exchequer. For his service.   By p.s.

391.)   21 *May* 1576.   Pardon for James Danby of Brayworth, co. York, and Thomas
Danby, his son for the forgery of a deed under James's seal dated 5 March, 2 Eliz.,
containing a conveyance of lands belonging to James in the parish of Leake to Thomas
Gargrave, knight, and others, at any time before the present date since the death of William
Danby, elder son of James. On information of Henry, earl of Huntingdon, president of the
council in the North, that they did the offence not of malice, but by the instigation and craft
of others.   By p.s.

392.)   19 *May* 1576.   *Inspeximus* and confirmation of a patent of confirmation, 12 Dec., 1
Edw. VI, inspecting and confirming a patent of confirmation, 22 Nov., 21 Hen. VIII,
inspecting and confirming a patent, 26 May, 3 Hen. VI   [*m.* 4]
[*Calendar of Patent Rolls*, 1422–1429, p. 285] inspecting and confirming divers charters and
patents granting liberties to the mayor and burgesses of Marleberg,   [*m.* 5]
co. Wilts.
   Also grant to them of liberties as follows—The borough and town to be a free borough
by the name of the mayor and burgesses of the borough and town of Marleberg. Incorporation of the mayor and burgesses. Power, for the better support of the borough and town,
to acquire lands to the yearly value of 100 marks not held of the Crown in chief or of others
by knight service. To have a gaol in the borough. Power to commit to the common gaol of
the county of Wilts persons arrested for treason, murder, felony and suspicion of felony
within the borough. Power to make ordinances for the government of the inhabitants and
the victualling of the borough, so that such ordinances be not repugnant to the laws of the
realm or the Crown's prerogative. To have all such courts, jurisdictions and profits as they
have heretofore lawfully enjoyed. John Lovell, now mayor, and his successors and two
other burgesses to be nominated by the mayor (or two of them, the mayor being one) to be
justices of the peace there, so that they do not proceed to the determination of any felony
without the Queen's special command. The mayor to be escheator, coroner and clerk of the
market there, being   [*m.* 6]
sworn before the old mayor and the burgesses; no other justice, escheator, coroner or clerk
of the clerk of the market to intermeddle there for the performance of his office.   By p.s.

393.)   7 *June* 1576. Lease for 21 years to Nicholas Adams of (1) the tithes of corn in
Wylome, now or late in the tenure of John Swinborne, parcel of the rectory of Haltwysell,
co. Northumberland, and (2) a fishery in the Tyne in Wylome, now or late in the tenure of
John Swinborne, once belonging to the monastery of Tynmouthe; from Michaelmas next;
yearly rents (1) 66*s.* 8*d.* and (2) 53*s.* 4*d.* For a fine of £24 paid at the Exchequer.
                                          By warrant of the commissioners.

394.)   19 *May* 1576.   Grant for life to Toby Houghton of the office of receiver of the
revenues of lands in the counties of Suffolk and Cambridge late in the survey of the court of
Augmentations and now in that of the Exchequer; with a yearly fee of £50 and 20*s.* for
portage on every £100 paid by him into the Exchequer, payable out of the issues of his
office; from the death of Thomas Badby, the present holder, to whom   [*m.* 7]
the office was granted by patent, 17 July, 3 Eliz., for life.

Vacated, because surrendered 11 *Nov.,* 22 *Eliz.; signed*: Wyll'm Cordell; Thoby Houghton.

395.)   28 *May* 1576. Lease for 21 years to Robert Garthome of (1) a tenement in Hombleton, parcel of the manor of Hombleton, co. York, and once of the monastery of Kirkestall,
co. York, (2) the tithes of corn, hay, wool and lambs of lands in Brustwick called Braymer
Demeasnes, co. York, and (3) the tithes of hay of Bramer in Elsternewicke, co. York, parcels
of the rectory of Brustwick and once of the monastery of Kirkestall, and (4) lands (*named*) in
Hombleton, once of the monastery of Thorneton, co. Lincoln; with reservations; from
Lady Day last; yearly rents (1) £6 13*s.* 4*d.*,   [*m.* 8]
(2) and (3) 18*s.* 4*d.* and (4) 9*s.* 8*d.* (*detailed*). In consideration of the surrender by him of leases
thereof for 21 years as follows—(*a*) by patent, 6 Nov., 8 Eliz., to the said Garthome of the
premises in (1) from Michaelmas then last at the same rent, (*b*) by patent of the Exchequer,
18 Sept., 8 Eliz., to John Harrison of the premises in (2) and (3), then or late in the tenure of
Robert Garthome, from Lady Day then last at yearly rents of (2) 13*s.* 4*d.* and (3) 5*s.* and (*c*) by
patent of the Exchequer, 7 Nov., 8 Eliz., to Christopher Canaby *inter alia* of the premises in
(4), then or late in the tenure of Robert Garthome, from Michaelmas then last at a yearly rent
for them and other lands of £4 13*s.* 8*d.*; and for a fine of £8 8*d.* paid at the Exchequer.
                                                        By warrant of the commissioners.

396.)   2 *June* 1576. Grant to Bernard Dewhurst of the wardship and marriage of Margaret
Mitford the younger, daughter and heir of Jasper Mitford; with an annuity of 33*s.* 4*d.* from 5
Oct., 9 Eliz., when Jasper died. Yearly value of the inheritance of £6 15*s.* 6*d.*   By Q.

397.)   28 *May* 1576. Lease for 21 years to Thomas Kitson of lands (*named with tenants' names*)
in Warton, co. Lancaster, parcel of the manor of Warton, once parcel of Richemondes
Landes and late of William, late marquess of Northampton, deceased; with reservations;
from Lady Day last;   [*m.* 9]
yearly rent 109*s.* 4½*d.* (*detailed*); the lessee to pay on the death or alienation of a tenant double
the yearly rent of the premises in such tenant's tenure; also to do suit and service at the
Queen's court in the manor and suit at the Queen's mill in the manor and to bear and do all
other charges and services according to the custom of the manor; also, if there shall be any
dispute between the tenants and him by reason of this patent, to obey the order of the
treasurer and the chancellor of the Exchequer in this behalf; the lease to be void if he shall
cause any tenants of certain of the premises to be expelled. For a fine of £10 18*s.* 9*d.* paid at
the Exchequer.   By warrant of the commissioners.

398.)   2 *June* 1576.   Grant for two years to Christopher Bland of Rippon, co. York, of a
yearly rent of 5*s.* out of the Queen's lands in the county of York. For the termination of the
uses in the undermentioned indenture and that the assurances by the said indenture or
otherwise may be annulled in the presence of Bartholomew Kemp, John Osborne, Francis
Whitney and Richard Goodrick, servant[s?] of Nicholas Bacon, knight, keeper of the great
seal: by indenture, 26 Aug., 11 Eliz., Thomas Merkinfeilde of Merkinfielde, co. York,
covenanted with Robert Aske of Aughton, co. York, and Christopher Wyvell of Burton
Parva, co. York, that all his lands in England should henceforth be held only to the uses
specified in the indenture, to wit, to the use of the same Thomas until he should convey by
deed to Aske and Wyvell or either of them an annuity of 3*s.* 4*d.* for two years and thereafter
or in default of the same and after his death to the successive uses of his first-born son, of his
second, third, fourth, fifth and sixth sons in tail male successively, of William and John
Merkinfielde, his younger brothers, in tail male successively, and of the right heirs of his
first-born son; it was further covenanted in the indenture that the same Thomas should have
power in his lifetime to dispose of any of the premises to any person for life or a term of

years; also it was covenanted that if the same Thomas during his life should by deed in the presence of four trustworthy persons convey to 'Aske and Wyvell or either of them or any person who should at that time be a parishioner dwelling in the parish of Rippon, co. York, a yearly rent of 5s., the uses specified in the indenture should be of   [m. 10] no effect; afterwards the said Thomas was indicted of the treason and outlawed and his attainder confirmed by act of Parliament, 2 April, 13 Eliz., and all the conditions to which he was then entitled passed to the Queen.   By Q.

399.)   19 *May* 1576. Lease for 10 years to Robert, earl of Leicester, baron of Denbigh, councillor, knight of the orders of the garter and of St. Michael, master of the horse, of (1) 'the Quenes fynes' or 'the Kinges fynes' and all other moneys payable to the Crown in the 'hamper' of Chancery for licences of alienation of lands in England and Wales and all 'fynes upon pardons' and all moneys and forfeitures due to the Crown in the 'hamper' of Chancery or the Exchequer in respect of alienation of lands without licence and (2) 'the Quenes fynes' or 'the Kinges fynes' in Chancery for the suing forth of writs of covenant whereon fines are to be levied; (1) from the present date and (2) from Lady Day last; yearly rents (1) £1,086 10s. 7¼d. and (2) £1,346 12s., payable in the said 'hamper'; the lessee may compound with every person for the assessing or releasing   [m. 11] of the sums hereby granted, and neither the Crown nor any other shall during the term make such composition without the lessee's consent; he may also by indenture release persons from fines and the like hereby granted; warrants or bills made by the lessee or his deputies authorised by indenture to be sufficient warrant to the chancellor or keeper of the great seal for passing under the great seal patents of licences for alienation and of pardons concerning the premises, paying for the same the ordinary fees accustomed; warrants or bills made by the lessee or his deputies sufficiently authorised by deed enrolled in Chancery to be sufficient warrant to the chancellor and other ministers of the Crown for the issuing of commissions,
                                                              [m. 12]
writs and processes necessary, made according to the course of the Exchequer, concerning the trial of the Crown's title to the premises; the lessee may have free access to all records of the Crown for the proving of any tenure held of the Crown and may have copies of records without payment; if any of the rents are in arrear for six months, the patent shall be void for as much only of the premises for which the rent is in arrear; the lessee may by deed enrolled in Chancery surrender his interest in the premises or any   [m. 13] part thereof.   *English*.   By Q.

400.)   4 *June* 1576. Lease for 21 years to John Jakes of lands (*named with tenants' names*) in Balderby, co. York, parcels of the manor of Balderby and once of the monastery of Fountaunce, co. York; with reservations; from Lady Day last; yearly rent 175s. 7d. (*detailed*); the lease to be void in respect of any part of the premises from which the lessee shall expel any of the present tenants, or whereof he shall not by deed make them leases for his whole term and at the rents hereby reserved before Christmas next so long as they pay among themselves his costs about obtaining this patent.   [m. 14]
In consideration of the surrender by the said John of his interest in the premises, Henry Blackborne, John Thekeston, Lancelot Jakes and Lancelot Browne having by deed, 11 May last, bargained and sold to him their several interests in the same by virtue of indentures whereby the said Blackborne, Thekeston, Lancelot Jakes and John Jakes aforesaid, Lancelot's son, and Browne had leases of the same from Francis Norton, assign of Richard Norton of Hertford, co. York, his father, to whom by indenture of the court of Augmentations, 1 Feb., 35 Hen. VIII, the manor of Balderbye was leased *inter alia*, woods reserved, for 40 years from the feast of St. Wilfrid in the winter then last at a yearly rent (for all the hereditaments in Balderby leased except the tithes of corn and hay) of £44 16d.; and in

consideration of £18 paid back by John Jakes aforesaid to John Warde on behalf of the Queen, which sum Warde had paid at the Exchequer for the fine of a lease of lands in Oldacre and Hurworth in the bishopric of Durham, which lease was adjudged void, as appears by a bill signed by Christopher Smyth, clerk of the pipe, and annexed to the particular on which this patent issued. By warrant of the commissioners.

401.) 11 *June* 1576. *Gorhambury*. Pardon for Thomas Wollsey late of Stopporte, co. Chester, indicted for that he (1) broke and entered the house of Peter Leighe, knight, at Lyme in Handeley, co. Chester, on 6 Jan., 17 Eliz., and stole a cup (*described*) belonging to him and (2) burgled the house of Alexander Holme at Stapport on 19 March, 17 Eliz., put Henry Heywood, Holme's servant, in fear and stole cloth (*described*) belonging to Holme. At the suit of Eleanor Savage, wife of John Savage, knight. By p.s.

402.) 22 *May* 1576. Grant to Robert Freake of the wardship and marriage of Elizabeth Blunt, daughter and heir of Richard Blunt; with an annuity of £6 13s. 4d. from 17 Nov., 18 Eliz., when Richard died. By Q.

403.) 26 *May* 1576. Grant to William Waldgrave of the wardship and [*m.* 15] marriage of Waldegrave Abell, son and heir of John Abell; with an annuity of £10 from 26 June, 17 Eliz., when John died. By Q.

404.) 21 *May* 1576. Lease for 21 years to Thomas Randolphe of two tenements in the parish of All Hallows in Honye Lane, London, late of Elsingspittle priory in London, now or late in the several tenures of (1) Edward Tailor and (2) Thomas Foteman, citizen and 'letherseller' of London; from Lady Day last; yearly rents, from the time when he shall have possession, (1) £5 16s. 8d. and (2) £5 6s. 8d. In consideration that Randolphe has reported that a lease thereof by conventual indenture, 12 Feb., 26 Hen. VIII, to the said Edward Tailor late of London for 80 years (1) from Lady Day then next and (2) from Lady Day 1550 at the same rents is void in law. By warrant of the commissioners.

405.) 15 *June* 1576. *Gorhambury*. Lease for 21 years to Richard Smyth [*m.* 16] of mills and lands (*named*) in Redborne, co. Hertford, parcel of the manor of Redborne, parcel of the lands assigned to the Queen before her accession and formerly of the monastery of St. Albans, co. Hertford; with reservations; from Michaelmas next; yearly rent £8. In consideration of the surrender by Smyth of the interest in the premises of William Horne of Redborne, 'yoman', to whom they were leased by Robert, abbot, and the convent of the monastery by indenture, 9 Oct., 29 Hen. VIII, for 50 years from Michaelmas then last at the same rent; and for a fine of £16 paid at the Exchequer. By warrant of the commissioners.

406.) 24 *May* 1576. Lease for life in succession to William Samwell, Mary his wife and John Samwell, their son, of the park of Restormell, co. Cornwall; parcel of the duchy of Cornwall; with reservations, including Rostormell castle; from Lady Day last; yearly rent £28 and heriot the best beast. In consideration of the surrender by the said John of a patent, 27 May, 4 Eliz., leasing the premises to Francis, earl of Bedford, for 21 years from [*m.* 17] Lady Day then last at the same rent; and for a fine of £84, to wit, £50 paid to John Benson in recompense of a fine paid by him for a lease of lands in Catton, co. York, which is void by law as appears by a bill signed by Christopher Smyth, clerk of the pipe, and annexed to the particular upon which the present patent issued, and £34 paid at the Exchequer. By p.s.

407.) 21 *May* 1576. Lease for 21 years to Walter Stricklond of (1) the tithes of wool and lambs in Wyntringham, Newton, Lynton and Knapton, parcel of the rectory of Wyntringham on the Wold, co. York, once of the monastery of Malton, co. York, (2) lands (*tenants named*) in Eston, co. York, once of the monastery of Bridlington, co. York, and (3) (*named with tenants' names*) in Eston aforesaid, once of Marricke priory; with reservations; from

[*m.* 18]

Lady Day last; yearly rents (1) £6, (2) £8 2*s.* 8*d.* and (3) 10*s.* In consideration of the surrender by Stricklond of leases of the premises (1) and (2) above for 21 years from Michaelmas then last at the same rents by patents, (1) 29 March, 5 Eliz., *inter alia* to John Hothome and (2) 9 Nov., 8 Eliz., to Stephen Lekynbye; and for a fine of £20 2*s.* 8*d.* paid at the Exchequer.

By p.s.

408.)   4 *June* 1576. Grant to George Strateforde of the wardship and marriage of Henry Strateford, son and heir of Richard Strateford; with an annuity of £6 13*s.* 4*d.* from 26 Dec., 17 Eliz., when Richard died. Yearly value of the inheritance £18 13*s.* 10*d.*   By Q.

409.)   4 *June* 1576. Lease for 21 years to Robert Markeham of (1) a portion of tithes and a house (*tenant named*) in Bottisford, co. Leicester, and (2)   [*m.* 19]
the tithes of corn and hay in Plouger *alias* Plougarth, co. Leicester, all late of the monastery of Beyver *alias* Belver, co. Lincoln; with reservations; from Lady Day last; yearly rents (1) 26*s.* 8*d.* and (2) 106*s.* 8*d.* In consideration of the surrender by Markeham of an indenture, 8 Feb. 1530 [/31], whereby Thomas Kingesburye, prior, and the convent of Bever leased the premises to Christopher Ploughe of St. Albons, co. Hertford, 'yoman', for 51 years from Lady Day then next at the same rents; and for a fine of £20 paid at the Exchequer.

By warrant of the commissioners.

410.)   2 *June* 1576. Lease for 21 years to William Wilkinson of the site of the manor of Midleton, Co. York, and all lands belonging thereto, once of the provostry of St. John, Beverley, co. York; with reservations; from Lady Day last; yearly rent £9; the lessee to leave at the end of the term at the Crown's election certain lands in the fields of Middleton sown by view of four trustworthy men to be appointed by the Crown or its officers or the value thereof as appraised at rates (*specified*) by the said men. In consideration of the surrender by Wilkinson of an indenture, 4 Jan., 13 Hen. VIII, whereby Thomas Dalbie, clerk, late provost, and the chapter of the collegiate church of St. John, Beverley, leased to Vincent Appulbie of Middleton the manor and lands belonging thereto for   [*m.* 20]
60 years from the feast of St. Mark then last at the same rent; and for a fine of £27 paid at the Exchequer.   By warrant of the commissioners.

411.)   22 *May* 1576. Grant to John Serle, 'yoman', of the wardship and marriage of Thomas Somner, son and heir of Christopher Somner; with an annuity of 20*s.* from 1 Dec., 13 Eliz., when Christopher died.   Yearly value of the inheritance £4.   By Q.

412.)   22 *May* 1576. Grant to David Lewes, justice of the Admiralty, of the wardship and marriage of John Thomas, son and heir of John Thomas; with an annuity of £6 13*s.* 4*d.* from 30 July, 17 Eliz., when John the father died.   Yearly value of the inheritance £23 17*s.* 9*d.*

By Q.

413.)   28 *May* 1576. Pardon for William Fynche late of Redburne,   [*m.* 21]
co. Hertford, 'yoman' and Isabel his wife indicted for (1) the murder of Dorothy Fourde, 'spinster', a guest in Fynche's house at Redborne, on 27 Aug., 15 Eliz., (*details given*) and (2) the theft of goods (*described*) belonging to the said Dorothy on the same date there. At the suit of Richard Rede, knight, Edward Verney, Robert Stepnethe, Robert Spencer, John

Puckeringe, John Bristowe and Richard Alexander, justices of the peace in the county, who consider them to be not guilty; also at the suit of Nicholas Fynche, William's father.

By p.s.

414.) 4 *June* 1576. Lease for 21 years to John Knight of the site and capital messuage of the manor of Northbarsted and all lands heretofore occupied therewith in Northbarsted, co. Sussex, late of the archbishopric of Canterbury and in the Queen's hands by exchange between Henry VIII and   [*m.* 22]
Thomas, late archbishop; with reservations; from Lady Day last; yearly rent £22; the lessee to provide entertainment four days a year for the Queen's steward and surveyor if they shall so often come to survey the premises or hold courts. In consideration of the surrender in Chancery by Knight of a patent, 26 March, 13 Eliz. leasing the premises to him for 21 years from Michaelmas then last at the same rent; and for a fine of £22 paid at the Exchequer.

By p.s.

415.) 19 *May* 1576. Grant to Everard Digbie of the wardship and marriage of Anthony. Collie, son and heir of Anthony Collie; with an annuity of £13 6s. 8d. from 27 Nov., 17 Eliz., when Anthony the father died.   By Q.

416.) 26 *May* 1576. Grant to John Waters of the wardship and marriage of John Gardener, son and heir of John Gardener; with an annuity of £10 from Lady Day 1578, when the lands came into the Queen's hands.   [*m.* 23]

By Q.

417.) 4 *June* 1576. Grant to Edward Mountagu, knight, Roger Mountague and William Mountague of the wardship and marriage of John Woode, son and heir of Robert Woode; with an annuity of £5 from 7 Aug., 17 Eliz., when Robert died.   By Q.

418.) 19 *May* 1576. Grant to Eleanor Sturges, widow, and Leonard Spencer of the wardship and marriage of Francis Sturges, son and heir of Francis Sturges; with an annuity of £8 from 1 Feb., 17 Eliz., when Francis the   [*m.* 24]
father died.   By Q.

419.) 21 *May* 1576. Lease for 21 years to William Robinson of York, merchant, of (1) lands (*tenants named*) in Catton Northby, Dalton and Crakehall, co. York, late of St. Mary's chantry in Topcliffe church, (2) lands (*tenants named*) in Raynton, co. York, (3) lands (*named with tenants' names*) in Raynton and (4) lands (*named with tenants' names*) in the manor of Balderby, co. York, which premises in Raynton and   [*m.* 25]
Balderby were once of the monastery of Fountaunce, co. York, and (5) lands (*tenants named*) in Raynton, once of St. Leonard's hospital or priory in York; with reservations; from Lady Day last; yearly rents (1) £4 16s. 4d., (2) 40s. 1d., (3) £4 7s. 6d., (4) £13 8s. 8d. and (5) 5s. In consideration of the surrender by Robinson of patents of the Exchequer, (*a*) 14 May, 6 Eliz., leasing the premises in (1), by the name of St. Mary's chantry in Topcliffe church, to Henry Bordman from Lady Day then last, (*b*) 9 Dec., 15 Eliz., leasing the premises in (2) to Andrew Sayer from Michaelmas then last and (*c*) 7 May, 9 Eliz., leasing the premises in (3) and (5) to Edmund Norton from Lady Day then last, in each case for 21 years at the same rent, and also of his surrender by deed, 16 May, 18 Eliz., enrolled in Chancery, of the interest in the premises in (4) of John Dudley and Thomas Swifte, to whom they were leased *inter alia* by patent, 18 April, 12 Eliz., at the same rent for 21 years from the termination of the interest of Richard Norton in the manor of Balderby and of the termination of any other leases or grants of the same   [*m.* 26]

premises; and for a fine of £18 17s. 8d. paid at the Exchequer.   By p.s.

420.) 26 *May* 1576. Grant to Henry Gate, knight, of the wardship and marriage of Richard Josseline, son and heir of Richard Josseline; with an annuity of £13 6s. 8d. from the death of lady Dorothy Josseline, widow, late the wife of Thomas Josseline, knight, grandfather of Richard the son, or from the death of Anne Josselin, widow, mother of Richard the son, whichever occurs first.   By Q.

421.) 8 *June* 1576. *Gorhambury.* Pardon for John Stradling of Lantwit, co. Glamorgan. Jenkin Jevan and Jenkin Mors, both of Lantwit, 'laborers', and he were indicted by inquisitions taken before David Kemes, a coroner in the county, (1) at Lantwit on 29 May, 4 & 5 Ph. & Mary, on the body of Richard Fleminge for the murder or felonious killing of Fleminge on 23 May, 4 & 5 Ph. & Mary, and (2) at Cardif on 16 June, 4&5 Ph. & Mary, on the body of Thomas ap John Thomas David ap Hoell   [*m.* 27] for the murder or felonious killing of the same Thomas on 23 May aforesaid.   By p.s.

422.) 22 *May* 1576. Protection for one year for Thurstan Tyldesley.   By p.s.

423.) 2 *June* 1576. Lease for 21 years to Thomas Wigmore of the grange of Mardief *alias* Mardif, co. Cardigan, and lands etc. there (*named with tenants' names*) with a custom called 'the comortha' amounted to £6 16s. 6d. every three years, all late of the monastery of Talley, co. Carmarthen; with reservations; from Lady Day last; yearly rent £9 2s.   [*m.* 28]
          By warrant of the commissioners.

424.) 7 *June* 1576. Lease for 21 years to William Pattenson of lands (*tenants named*) in (1) Bywell, parcels of the barony of Bywell, (2) Ovington, parcels of the manor of Ovington and of the barony of Bywell, and (3) Rydinge in le Lye, parcels of the barony of Bulbeck, all in the county of Northumberland and late of Charles, late earl of Westmorland, attainted of treason; with reservations; from Lady Day last; yearly rents (1) £7 14s. 7¼d.,   [*m.* 29] (2) 32s. 8d. and (3) 26s. 9d. (*all detailed*); the lessee to serve the Queen by himself or sufficient men with horses and arms in the North when summoned by her warden or lieutenant according to the custom of the country, to occupy the premises by himself or sufficient men, and to fence the premises as ordered by the steward of the Queen's court or other her commissioners there; the lease to be void in respect of any parcels of the premises from which the lessee shall expel the present tenants, or whereof he shall not before Christmas next make them leases by deed for his whole term and at the same rents, so long as they pay him among themselves his charges about obtaining this patent. For a fine of £10 14s. ¼d. paid at the Exchequer.   By warrant of the commissioners.

425.) 29 *May* 1576. Commission for three years for Gaven Carewe, Robert Denys, Arthur Chambernon and Humphrey Gilbert, knights, and Bernard Drake (or three of them, Carewe or Denys being one) and their deputies to take up within 20 miles of Culliton Havon at Seaton, co. Devon,—towards the making and repair of which haven a patent was granted in the year 17 Eliz. for the collection of money throughout the realm—stone, timber and other necessaries for the making of the haven, also to press workmen for the same, to dig pits on common grounds to burn lime in, to make trenches and foundations for the works, to build 'woorke howses' for the workmen and to take up carriage by sea and land, for such prices agreed with the parties as shall be thought reasonable by any three justices of the peace nearest to the place where the provisions shall be made; no person to be used as a deputy unless he shall be authorised under the hands and seals of the commissioners and shall bring with him the commission or a true copy thereof testified under their hands; no person to be impressed that shall be in any other man's service by the year or has taken any work in hand to be accomplished within a time limited until the covenant and work shall be finished; none of the provisions aforesaid to be taken from any persons that have provided the [*m.* 30] same for their necessary uses to be occupied in their own buildings, either in houses, ships or otherwise; no carriage to be taken up from any man in times when he is to carry his own corn or hay. *English.*   By p.s.

426.) 28 *May* 1576. Grant to William Breerton, brother of Jane Leighe, wife of Edward Leighe of Baguley, co. Chester, of the recognisance and the obligation below mentioned and all claims of the Crown in respect thereof. Out of compassion for Jane: she has lived apart from her said husband for about 20 years, being for most of that time chiefly relieved by Urian Brierton, her father; at last being driven by necessity to complain to the archbishop of York and other the Queen's commissioners in causes ecclesiastical she was before them divorced from her husband and had assigned to her an annuity of £20; for payment of which the said Edward was bound to the Crown by recognisance, 10 March, 14 Eliz., in £200 to pay to her or her attorney during his and her lives £10 every Midsummer and £10 every Martinmas in 'Ryles chappell' in the parish church of Willmeslowe, Chester dioc.; afterwards by an obligation, 24 Aug., 16 Eliz., the said Edward, John Torkinton of Torkinton, co. Chester, and Richard Tarvin of Baguley, yeoman, were bound to the Crown in £200 for the appearance of Edward before the commissioners for causes ecclesiastical in the province of York at York on 15 Oct. then next; both which recognisance and obligation Edward has forfeited by not making any payment to Jane and not appearing before the commissioners. *English.*   By p.s.

427.) 23 *May* 1576. Protection for John Bradbury the younger of Eastsmythfield, co. Middlesex, 'beerebruer', and John Bradbury the elder, citizen and butcher [*m.* 31] (*lanii*) of London; to be void if they or either of them shall not within one year compound for the payment of their debts.   By p.s.

428.) 2 *June* 1576. Lease for 21 years to John Warde of the rectory of Middleham Episcopi in the bishopric of Durham, late of the monastery of Durham, the glebe lands belonging thereto, the tithes of corn in Middleham *alias* Busshopps Middleham, Corneforthe, Thirslington and Mauntforthe *alias* Maunceforthe in the said bishopric and all appurtenances of the rectory; with reservations; from Michaelmas next; yearly rent £23 15s. 4d.; the lessee to occupy the [*m.* 32] premises by himself or a sufficient man, to find an able man or men to serve with horse and arms in the North when required by the warden of the East marches according to the custom of the country, and to fence the premises as ordered by the commissioners for the severing of the Queen's lands there or the steward of her manor of Middleham Episcopi. In consideration of the surrender by Warde of a patent, 25 Jan., 7 Eliz., leasing the premises to Robert Cotton for 21 years from Lady Day then next at the same rent; and for a fine of £26 13s. 4d. paid at the Exchequer.   By p.s.

429.) 30 *May* 1576. Grant to William Smythe of Ashe in the county palatine of Durham and Margaret his wife and the assigns of them or the survivor of them for ever of lands (*tenants named*) in Barneton *alias* Barmeton, Ashe, Ushawe, Hewghe, Rowley, Estharrington, Westharrington, Middle Harrington and [*m.* 33] Offerton *alias* Ufferton in the said county palatine (of the yearly value of £28 19s. 10d. or thereabouts and now or late charged with an annuity of 26s. 8d. to Robert Stocdale for life, a yearly rent of 5 marks to the bishop of Durham for lands in Ashe, an annuity of 5 marks to Elizabeth Norton in fee simple and an annuity of 40s. to Oliver Ashe for life, and so of the clear yearly value of £19 or £20 6s. 8d. or thereabouts). At Margaret's suit, for the relief of her and George Smythe, infant son of William and her: the said William on the day of his attainder for his offence committed in the rebellion in the North was seised of the premises for life as in right of Margaret; which premises and all his other possessions were forfeited to the Crown by his attainder, so that he and Margaret have none of the said lands left to live on, albeit he is by the Queen's late pardon granted to him restored to the benefit of her laws. *English*.   By p.s.

430.)   15 *June* 1576. *Gorhambury*. Grant for seven years to Ralph Lane, the Queen's servant, of all forfeitures arising from breaches of the statutes against the transportation out of the realm of gold, silver, coin, bullion, jewels or other treasure; from the present date; power to search out   [*m.* 34] offences committed heretofore or during the term and to compound with offenders; also in the Queen's name or his own to sue for forfeitures and grant discharges of the same by writing signed and sealed; persons to whom such a discharge shall be made, the same being enrolled in Chancery, may sue from the Crown a patent of pardon, and it shall be a sufficient warrant to the chancellor or keeper of the great seal to pass the patent without any payment other than the ordinary fees due to the officers of Chancery for a single   [*m.* 35] pardon; at the grantee's request commissions shall be issued under the great seal or the Exchequer seal to him, his assigns and deputies or any of them with two or three justices of the peace in any country to inquire into such offences; power for the grantee, his assigns and deputies to have in the Queen's name access to all custom houses, ships and places to search for offences and seize treasure and the like forfeited; the patent to be void if it be found by inquisition or the examination of two sufficient witnesses in the Exchequer that the grantee has compounded with any person for the transporting of gold, silver or bullion out of the realm before the offence is committed or has consented to the same. *English*.   By p.s.

(*The dorse of this roll is blank.*)

PART IV

C. 66/1140

431.)   24 *Nov.* 1575.   Grant to John Greves of the wardship and marriage   [*m.* 1]
of John Merkhame, kinsman and heir of Geoffrey Merkham, to wit, the son and heir of John
Markham, son and heir of Geoffrey; with an annuity of £3 from 12 May, 10 Eliz., when
Geoffrey died. Yearly value of the inheritance £11.   By Q.

432.)   29 *Nov.* 1575.   Grant to Walter Osborne of the wardship and marriage of Robert
Brookes, son and heir of John Brookes; with an annuity of £8 from 1 June, 13 Eliz., when
John died. Yearly value of the inheritance £17 10*s.*   By Q.

433.)   1 *Dec.* 1575.   Grant to Andrew Kynge of the wardship and marriage of John
Brograve, son and heir of Henry Brograve; with an annuity of   [*m.* 2]
£10 from 12 Aug., 16 Eliz., when Henry died.   By Q.

434.)   3 *Dec.* 1575.   Grant to Arthur Harryes of the wardship and marriage of Sarah
Stephen, daughter and heir of John Stephen; with an annuity of £4 from 13 Dec., 17 Eliz.,
when John died. Yearly value of the inheritance £14 16*s.* 8*d.*   By Q.

435.)   5 *Dec.* 1575.   Grant to Thomas Staunton, feodary of the county of Salop, and
Lancelot Ridley of the wardship and marriage of Francis Byllingsley, son and heir of John
Byllingsley; with an annuity of £3 from 7 July,   [*m.* 3]
16 Eliz., when John died.   By Q.

436.)   29 *Nov.* 1575.   Grant to Joan Calton, widow, of the wardship and marriage of
Francis Calton, son and heir of Nicholas Calton; with an annuity of £6 13*s.* 4*d.* from 24 Feb.,
17 Eliz., when Nicholas died.   By Q.

437.)   1 *Dec.* 1575.   Grant to Walter Tooke of the wardship and marriage of Edmund
Alleyne, son and heir of John Allyn the younger; with an annuity of £3 6*s.* 8*d.* from 1 Dec.,
15 Eliz., when John Alleyn the elder, father   [*m.* 4]
of John the younger, died.   By Q.

438.)   29 *Nov.* 1575.   Grant to Nicholas Maynarde of the wardship and marriage of John
Hele, son and heir of Hugh Hele of Newton Ferrars; with an annuity of 26*s.* 8*d.* from 26
June, 15 Eliz., when Hugh died. Yearly value of the inheritance £13 17*s.* 8*d.*   By Q.

439.)   1 *Dec.* 1575.   Grant to Elizabeth Cheke, widow, of the wardship and marriage of
Thomas Cheke the younger, kinsman and heir of Thomas Cheke the elder, to wit, the son
and heir of James Cheke, son of Thomas the   [*m.* 5]
elder; with an annuity of £3 from 22 Oct., 16 Eliz., when Thomas the elder died. Yearly
value of the inheritance £20 6*s.* 8*d.*   By Q.

440.)   24 *Nov.* 1575.   Grant to Richard Cooke of the wardship and marriage of William

Waldbie, son and heir of William Waldbie; with an annuity of 26s. 8d. from 26 June, 9 Eliz., when William the father died. Yearly value of the inheritance £11 11s. 8d.   By Q.

441.) 5 *Dec.* 1575.   Grant to Thomas Staunton of the wardship and marriage   [*m.* 6] of Thomas Mynton, son and heir of Thomas Mynton, 'yoman'. Yearly value of the inheritance 40s.   By Q.

442.) 30 *Nov.* 1575.   Grant for life to Jasper Cholmeley of the offices of (1) steward and keeper of the courts of the manors of Westham and Brettes, co. Essex, and (2) steward of the manor of Clerkenwell, co. Middlesex, once of the monastery of Clerkenwell; (1) from the death of Robert Hodgeson, to whom it was granted for life by patent, 22 Jan., 7 Eliz., and (2) from the present date, having been granted during pleasure by patent of the Exchequer, 31 May, 8 Eliz., to John Devicke which pleasure is hereby terminated; with yearly fees of (1) £4, payable out of the issues of the manors of Westham and Brettes, and (2) 40s., payable out of the issues of the manor of Clerkenwell.   By Q.

443.) 30 *Nov.* 1575.   Grant for life to John Sonkeye of (1) the office of   [*m.* 7] woodward and keeper of the woods in the county of Salop in the survey of the Exchequer, granted by patent of the Exchequer, 16 Jan., 10 Eliz., to Robert Hodgeson during pleasure, which pleasure is hereby terminated, and (2) the office and offices of bailiff of the hundreds of Eynsforde and Forhowe, co. Norfolk; no sheriff or minister of the Crown to intermeddle in the offices of bailiff so long as Sonkye or his deputies behave well in the execution thereof; with (1) a yearly fee of 100s., payable out of the issues of the county of Salop, and (2) the fees and allowances accustomed, payable out of the issues of the hundreds or by the sheriff of Norfolk.   By Q.
      Signed (in margin): John Sonkye.

444.) 24 *Nov.* 1575.   Grant for life to Margery Burden, wife of John Burden, of an annuity of £24, payable at the Exchequer, from Christmas last.   [*m.* 8]
In consideration of the surrender by Francis Colby of a patent, 31 Oct., 1 Mary, granting him an annuity of 40 marks, payable at the Exchequer, for life.   By p.s.

445.) 30 *Dec.* 1575.   Pardon for Robert Hichecock late of London *alias* late of Caversfeld, co. Buckingham, Jane Biddele late of Caversfeld, 'spynster', wife of Robert Biddell, John Hichecock late of Compton, co. Warwick, 'gent' *alias* late of Caversfeld, 'yeoman', Robert Wynter late of Caversfeld, 'laborer', Robert Pillesworth late of Caversfeld, 'yeoman', John Baillye late of Caversfeld, 'laborer', and George Stretley late of Bampton, co. Oxford, for all offences concerning the death of Rumbold Bennett and all offences touching the detention of messuages or lands at Caversfeld. They are indicted, with others, for murder in that John Hichecock shot Bennett with a gun at Caversfeld on 13 Oct., 16 Eliz., so that he died on 18 Oct., 16 Eliz., at Edgecote, co. Buckingham, and the others were present abetting him (*details given*).   By p.s.

446.) 24 *Nov.* 1575.   Grant for life to Simon Mason of the room of a yeoman waiter in the Tower of London which shall next be void, with wages of 8d. a day, a livery coat and a watch livery; the grant not to prejudice any person to whom a former grant of the like room has been made. *English.*   By p.s.

447.) 20 *Dec.* 1575.   *Hampton Court.* Grant for life to Adam Dynmore of the room of an almsknight in the collegiate church within the castle of   [*m.* 9]

Wyndesore, void by the resignation, hereby accepted, of John Dudeley. For his service. *English*. By p.s.

448.) 18 *Jan.* 1576. *Hampton Court*. Licence for four years for Henry Wallop, knight, to export from the port of Southampton, co. Southampton, to friendly countries 300 quarters of wheat and 200 quarters of barley yearly of his own growing within the said county only; from the present date; duties to be paid; provided that the licence may by the Queen's special letters to him be restrained in time of dearth; the officers at the port to endorse upon the licence the amounts shipped and to deliver it to the Exchequer when expired. To encourage others to follow the example of Wallop, who has lately broken up for tillage 700 acres of warren ground. By p.s.

449.) 27 *Nov.* 1575. Licence during pleasure for John Alderyche, Robert Sucklyng, Thomas Layer and Simon Bowde, aldermen of Norwyche, to buy [*m.* 10] wool grown within the Queen's dominions and to sell it to inhabitants of the said city to be made into any kind of cloth or other merchandise within the city and not elsewhere, notwithstanding stat. 5 Edw. VI touching the buying of wool; provided that, if any of the licensees shall sell any wool (other than such sorts as they might before the making of this patent lawfully buy and sell) to persons not dwelling in Norwich and shall not for every such offence pay a penalty of double the value of the wool to the receiver general of the county of Norfolk within one month, the patent shall as regards him be void. For the relief of the said city and that the Queen's subjects there may be trained in the trade of making divers goods now made by strangers there. *English*. By p.s.

450.) 21 *Jan.* 1576. Grant to Edward Dyer, the Queen's servant, and his deputies and assigns authorised by writing under his hand and seal of power in the Queen's name and in the name of Dyer to pardon and release persons resident in the Queen's dominions exercising the trade of tanner or tanning of leather from all offences and penalties, from the present date until other provision is made by the Queen or Parliament, under the following clauses of stat. 5 Eliz. touching the tanning and dressing of leather:—(1) no tanner after Michaelmas then next to put on sale any hide gashed, slaughtered or cut as in the statute is mentioned; (2) none to suffer any hide to lie longer in the lime than when the hair falls off or put into the lime after the hair may be taken off; (3) none to use any liquor, stuff or workmanship in the tanning but only lime, culver dung or hen dung and that in cold water and oozes made of cold water and oak bark only; (4) none to suffer his leather to hang or lay wet in frost until it be frozen; (5) none to tan any hide putrified, rotten or tainted by long lying; (6) none [not] to renew and make strong their oozes as often as should be [*m.* 11] requisite; (7) none to tan any ox hide, steer hide or cow hide but whole without cutting of any bellies called wombs; (8) none after Michaelmas then next to put on sale any tanned hide which is raised by the tanning or otherwise or by using anything otherwise than by the statute is appointed; (9) no person using the mistery of tanning to tan after Midsummer then next any bull hide, horse hide or sheep skin or dispose of any such tanned. Persons to whom any such release or discharge shall be made by the grantee by indenture or otherwise under his hand and seal, shown to the chancellor or keeper of the great seal, may sue for a further discharge in that behalf by patent (every patent containing 10 or 12 men and not more), paying the ordinary fees; in which patents a proviso shall be contained that, if the Queen or Privy Council shall by proclamation or otherwise declare the dispensations contained in the patent to be harmful to the realm, the same being notified by any of the Privy Council in writing to the grantee, the same shall be void for anything afterwards to be done and for all things done before the notification shall remain in full strength. Until other order shall be taken by Parliament the grantee may, for such consideration as to him shall be thought convenient, grant in the Queen's name or Dyer's by indenture liberty to any person resident in the Queen's dominions using the trade of tanning to tan and use hides as before the said statute notwithstanding any of the clauses before mentioned, working leather as they ought to do by any other clause of the statute in these premises not specially rehearsed and dispensed; every person so licensed may dry their leather in the temperate heat of the summer sun, the said statute or anything in these presents to the contrary notwithstanding; every such grant and licence to contain a proviso as in the patents before mentioned to be made. No courts or officers of the Crown to admit without the grantee's consent any action upon any article in which the grantee has power to dispense. No person to seize any hide or leather by reason of any article under this grant dispensed, on pain of imprisonment for one month upon the grantee's request. Bonds   [*m.* 12] and obligations heretofore made by tanners for tanning according to the statute may be taken into the grantee's hands and at his pleasure may be redelivered to the obligors to be cancelled. The patent to be construed to the benefit of the grantee and persons to whom dispensations shall be made by him. The patent to be void, if the grant shall at any time hereafter by the queen or Privy Council be declared hurtful to the realm, the same being first notified to the grantee by any of the Privy Council in form abovesaid, but anything before the same notification licensed under the patent shall remain lawfully dispensed. The grantee shall not constrain any persons to any composition or agreement against their will.

Upon complaint by tanners to the Queen and Privy Council that the clauses of the statute which are specified above are impossible to be performed or inaptly worded, Dyer being their suitor in that behalf. *English.*   By Q.

451.)   3 *Feb.* 1576.   Grant for life to Richard Wyndebank, the Queen's servant, of an annuity of £27 7s. 6d., payable at the Exchequer, formerly granted by patent, 3 Feb., 1 & 2 Ph. & Mary, to Nicholas de Mesnyl for life from   [*m.* 13] Michaelmas then last and hereby declared void from Christmas 1573 because of de Mesnyl's absence abroad without licence; from Christmas 1573. For his service. *English.* By p.s.

452.)   30 *Dec.* 1575.   Licence for three months for Christopher Whytbye of Kinges Towne upon Hull, co York, and his deputies bearers hereof to ask alms within the city and suburbs of London and the city of Westminster, whereby he may return to his trade of a seafaring man. In consideration of losses sustained by him upon the seas. *English.*
                                                                                      By p.s.

453.)   24 *Dec.* 1575.   Grant for life to Thomas Tompson of the office of a gunner in the Tower of London, void by the death of his father Edward Tompson; wages of 12d. a day, payable at the Exchequer, from Midsummer last.   By Q.

454.)   9 *Jan.* 1576.   *Hampton Court.*   Presentation of Geoffrey Downes, clerk, M.A., to the rectory of Busshoppes Bourne and Barham, Canterbury dioc., void by the resignation of Thomas Wylloughbye, clerk, the Queen's chaplain, and in the Queen's gift *sede vacante.*
                                                                                      By p.s.

455.)   2 *Jan.* 1576.   Presentation of Edmund Lylly, M.A., to the rectory of Northe Hewys in the deanery of Plimton, co. Devon, Exeter dioc., by lapse   [*m.* 14] void and in the Queen's gift.   By p.s.

456.)   20 *Jan.* 1576.   Grant during good behaviour to Thomas Greeke of the office of a baron of the Exchequer; from the death of James Lorde, late a baron of the Exchequer.
                                                                                      By p.s.

457.)   30 *Nov.* 1575.   Grant to William Frye of Stockland, co. Dorset, of the advowson of the vicarage of Yartcombe, Exeter dioc., when it shall next be void, for one vacancy only; that he may present thereto Thomas Major, clerk M.A.   By p.s.

458.)   18 *May* 1576.   Pardon for Thomas Hewes late of London, 'yoman', indicted for that he with others at Hartley, co. Kent, on 9 June, 17 Eliz., (1) broke and entered the house of Thomas Crips and stole goods (*described*) and £13 6s. 8d. belonging to him and (2) broke and entered the house of James Crips and stole £11 6s. belonging to him. At the suit of Anne Busshopp, wife of John Busshopp and sister of Hewes.   By Q.

459.)   17 *May* 1576.   Grant to Maud Launde, widow, of the wardship and marriage of John Lande the younger, son and heir of John Lande;   [*m.* 15] with an annuity of 46s. 8d. from 4 Dec., 17 Eliz., when John the father died. Yearly value of the inheritance £14 7s. 7½d.   By Q.

460.)   27 *Feb.* 1576.   Grant to Thomas Cecill of the wardship and marriage of Edward, lord Zouche, Seyntmaure and Cantilupe, son and heir of George, lord Zouche, Seyntmaure and Cantilupe; with an annuity of £60 from 19 June, 11 Eliz., when George died, until the death of Margaret, lady Zouche, late the wife of George, or Susan, lady Zouche, late the wife of John, lord Zouche,   [*m.* 16] Seyntmaure and Cantilupe, great grandfather of Edward, and thereafter a further annuity of £26 13s. 4d.   By Q.

461.)   2 March 1576.   Pardon for Richard Sparckes late of Gloucester, 'bocher', indicted for the theft of heifers (*details given*) (1) on 7 Oct., 16 Eliz., at Sandhurste in the county of the said city belonging to Walter Kente, (2) on the same date at Sandhurste belonging to Edward Hayward and (3) at Gloucester on 4 Oct., 16 Eliz., belonging to John Woodwarde the younger. By consideration of Edward Saunders, knight, chief baron of the Exchequer, and William Lovelace, serjeant at law, justices of assize in the county of the said city.   By p.s.

462.)   12 March 1576.   Grant for life to Nicholas Annesley, a yeoman for   [*m.* 17] the mouth of the office of the cellar, of the office of bailiff and collector of the manors of Timberwood, Raynehurst, Blackmanston [and] Windhill in the hundred of Hoo, of the manor in the isle of Grayne and of lands in Highame, Chalke and Stocke and the parishes of All Hallows and St. Mary in the hundred of Hoo, co. Kent, late of Thomas Wiatt, deceased, and in the Queen's hands by exchange; with a yearly fee of £10 16s. 8d., to wit, for the manors of Timberwood and Rainehurst £8, the manor of Blackmanston 13s. 4d., the manor of Windhill 20s. and the manor in the isle of Grayne 23s. 4d., payable out of the issues of the premises; as formerly held by John Wilkyns, deceased. For his service.   By p.s.

463.)   2 March 1576.   Grant for life in survivorship to Henry Mackwilliam, a gentleman pensioner, and lady Mary his wife, late the wife of John Cheke, knight, a gentlewoman of the privy chamber, of the offices of (1) keeper of the house and mansion called Seynte James next Westminster, co. Middlesex, (2) keeper of the wardrobe there, (3) keeper of the gardens and orchards there and of a close of land newly enclosed with a ditch (42 ac.) next the mansion, between it and the common way from London to Kensington, and (4) bailiff of the fairs called Seynte James Fayer and of the Queen's lands in the parishes of St. Margaret, Westminster, St. Martin by Charinge Crosse and St. Giles in the Fields, co. Middlesex, to the North of the way from Charinge Crosse to Knightsbridge; as held by William Morrant or Richard Cooke, deceased, or John Astley and Catherine his wife; with a yearly fee of 8d. a day, payable out of the issues of the premises. On surrender in Chancery by the said Astley of a patent, 27 May, 2 Eliz., granting the offices to him and Catherine, now deceased.

By p.s.

464.)   29 *March* 1576.   *Gorhambury.*   Grant for life to Walter Trymmell, a groom of the chamber, of the offices of (1) chief steward of the lordship, liberty and franchise of Hexham and Hexhamshire, co. Northumberland, late of the   [*m.* 18]
archbishopric of York, and (2) bailiff of the same; as held by John Erington, deceased; with yearly fees of (1) £6 13s. 4d. and (2) £13 6s. 8d., payable out of the issues of the premises by himself or the receiver general of the county, from Michaelmas last; provided that the warden of the Middle marches towards Scotland shall have the execution of the said offices and such direction as is fitting or accustomed for the better government of the people there and 'lez borders'. For his service.   By p.s.
    Vacated because surrendered 10 *Feb.,* 40 *Eliz.; signed:* Tho. Egerton C.S.; 'sign' WT Walteri Trymmell'.

465.)   19 *March* 1576.   Pardon for Richard Hawdenbye *alias* Awdenbye *alias* Hornebie and Robert Hawdenbie *alias* Awdenbye *alias* Hornebye *alias* Haldenbye, both late of Stamforde, co. Lincoln. Richard is indicted for that he with a man unknown robbed John Bucke of Thetforde in the isle of Elie and Francis Newton of Chatteres in the same isle, co. Cambridge, 'drovers', in the highway at Northwickam in the parts of Kesteven, co. Lincoln; of £72 13s. 8d. in silver and £40 in gold belonging to them (*details given*) and John Babthorpe late of Stanforde afterwards received and abetted Richard. At the suit of Bucke and Newton.

By p.s.

466.)   4 *April* 1576. *Gorhambury.* Grant for life to John Duddeley of the office of particular surveyor of lands in the county of Suffolk in the survey of the Exchequer; with a yearly fee of £13 6s. 8d. and expenses,   [*m.* 19]
payable by the receiver of the said court in the county; from the death of William Humberston, late holder of the office.   By p.s.

467.)   2 *March* 1576.   Pardon for Rice Lloid *alias* Rice Lloyd ap David ap Meredith and Mereddith Lloid *alias* Mereddith Lloid ap David ap Mereddith, both late of Llanbaderne Vaur, co. Cardigan, for thefts of horses belonging to William Williams at Hereford, co. Hereford, on 11 Oct., 16 Eliz. (*details given*).   By p.s.

468.)   11 *May* 1576.   Grant for life to John Welles, the Queen's servant, of the office of a courier or post; with wages of 2s. a day, payable at the Exchequer, from Christmas last. For his service.   By p.s.

469.)   26 *March* 1576.   *Gorhambury.* Grant for life to Walter Hayte, clerk, preacher of God's Word, of a canonry or prebend in Rochester cathedral, void by the death of John
                                                                              [*m.* 20]
Ellys.   By p.s.

470.)   27 *March* 1576.   *Gorhambury.*   Grant for life to Richard Harreys, M.A., of a canonry or prebend in Worcester cathedral, void by the death of John Ellys.   By p.s.

471.)   27 *April* 1576.   *Gorhambury.* Grant for life to Edward Bassano of wages of 20d. a day, as his father Anthony Bassano, deceased, had, payable at the Exchequer, from Michaelmas last. For his service in the art of music.   By p.s.

472.)   23 *March* 1576.   *Gorhambury*.   Grant to Thomas Asheton, S.T.P., of the advowson of the parish church of Hanburye, co. Worcester, for the next vacancy only.   By p.s.

473.)   27 *April* 1576.   *Gorhambury*.   Grant for life to Henry Nevelle, knight, the queen's servant, of the offices of (1) keeper of the houses of the upper bailiwick within the castle of Windesor, (2) keeper of the leads within the castle and (3) keeper of the great butts within the castle; with (1) the wages and profits accustomed, (2) wages of 2d. a day and (3) wages of 2d. a day, from Michaelmas last, payable out of the issues of the castle by the constable or clerk thereof or their lieutenants; as held by Walter Ruding, deceased, and formerly by John Tamworth, Thomas Welden, Thomas Ward or Robert Little. For his service.   By p.s.

474.)   28 *Feb*. 1576.   Grant for life in survivorship to John Bynckes and Richard Stanton of the office of a messenger in ordinary at the receipt of the Exchequer; with wages of 4½d. a day, payable at the Exchequer,   [*m*. 21]
and with their several liveries yearly and 'lez rydinge jorneys' both in the receipt of the Exchequer and in Chancery as they now have or heretofore had. On surrender by Bynkes of a patent, 3 Oct., 1 Eliz., granting him the office for life. For their service.   By p.s.

475.)   30 *April* 1576.   *Gorhambury*.   Grant for life to Michael Cobbe of the office of serjeant at arms, held by Thomas Hale, deceased; with wages of 12d. a day, payable at the Exchequer; from the death of Hale.   By p.s.

476.)   27 *April* 1576.   *Gorhambury*.   Grant for life to Francis Ingolesbe of the office of keeper of the arms or armour at Estgrenewiche, co. Kent, held by Henry Parker, deceased; with wages of 20d. a day, payable at the Exchequer, and his dwelling in a house in 'le Tyltyarde' of Estgrenewiche and herbage or pasture there; from Christmas last.   By p.s.

477.)   13 *April* 1576.   *Gorhambury*.   Grant in fee simple to Thomas Kery, a clerk of the privy seal, that he may hold two fairs on his manor of Launsdowne, co. Somerset, one on the feast of St. John 'Port Latyne' until vespers of the morrow of the same feast and the other from midday on the eve of St Lawrence for the three days following. At his suit.   By p.s.

478.)   1 *March* 1576.   Pardon for Richard Posterne late of Mynton, co. Salop, 'yeoman', indicted for the manslaughter of Edward Wright at Mynton on 17 Aug., 17 Eliz. (*details given*). At the suit of Thomas Scryven of Frodisley, co.   [*m*. 22]
Salop.   By p.s.

479.)   26 *March* 1576.   *Gorhambury*.   Order that henceforth there shall not be more than four persons admitted as attorneys in the court of Marshalsea; and appointment of William Danby, Thomas Holforde, Hugh Brooker and John Byll to be sole attorneys in the said court; when any of them shall die, discontinue from the exercise of their office or by reason of any just matter of offence be disallowed by the steward and marshal of the court, some other sufficient person may be admitted by order of the steward and marshal in his place. For the reformation of disorders by reason that a greater number of persons than heretofore 'unorderlye' come to the court as attorneys.   *English*.   By p.s.

480.)   23 *April* 1576.   *Gorhambury*.   Grant for life to John Dighton of the office of escheator of the country of York.   By p.s.

481.)   4 *April* 1576.   *Gorhambury*.   Licence for five years for Richard   [*m*. 23]
Chapman, keeper of the park at Hampton Court, to buy 500 tods of English wool yearly and

drape and sell the same again in England only; from the present date; the licence to have the amounts bought endorsed upon it. *English.*   By p.s.

482.)   26 *Feb.* 1576.   Grant for life to John Preston, a page of the 'squillery', of a fee of 6*d.* a day, payable at the Exchequer, from Lady Day, 16 Eliz. For his relief, upon recommendation of the chief officers of the household; in consideration of his long service, and for that by reason of divers impediments and sicknesses he is not able to serve the Queen as to that place belongs. *English.*   By p.s.

483.)   16 *April* 1576.   *Gorhambury.*   Grant for life to William Devonshere of the custody and keeping of the stables and stable yard at Redynge and 'the pondhest' on the South side of the old stable and the stable yard adjoining the new stable, with the gate between the town and the said stable yard, and the lodgings called 'the Almery'; with a yearly fee of £12 3*s.* 4*d.* (£6 20*d.* for the keeping of the stables and the rest of the premises and £6 20*d.* for his charges in cleaning and carrying away the soil of the stables), payable at the Exchequer, from Michaelmas last. *English.*   By Q.

484.)   15 *May* 1576.   Protection for one year for Ralph Boswell, citizen and 'haberdasher' of London.   [*m.* 24]
                                                                             By p.s.

485.)   20 *April* 1576.   *Gorhambury.*   Protection for one year for William Herle of London.   By p.s.

486.)   16 *March* 1576.   Pardon for Robert Jackson late of Annesley, co. Nottingham, clerk, for the manslaughter of Simon Write late of Annesley. At the suit of Jane Jackson, wife of Robert.   By p.s.

487.)   9 *May* 1576.   Grant for life to lord Henry Seymor of the annuity of 100 marks, payable at the Exchequer, held by his brother, Edward, lord   [*m.* 25] Seymor, deceased, to whom it was granted by patent, 7 Nov., 14 Eliz. for life; from the death of Edward. For his service.   By p.s.

488.)   27 *Feb.* 1576.   Grant for life to Henry Cary, the Queen's servant, of the offices of (1) escheator and feodary of all lands belonging to the duchy of Cornwall in the counties of Cornwall and Devon and (2) constable of the castle of Launceston *alias* Dunhed, co. Cornwall; with the usual fees; payable by the receiver general of the duchy; as held by Edward Trevanyon, deceased.   By p.s.

489.)   20 *April* 1576.   *Gorhambury.*   Grant to Gawin Carewe, knight, the Queen's servant, of the advowson of the rectory of Pit and the portion of Clare in the parish church of Tyverton, co. Devon, Exeter dioc., in the Queen's patronage by the minority of Jonathan Trelawnie, for the next turn only during Trelawnie's minority (and so also from heir to heir if Trelawnie shall die).   By p.s.

490.)   20 *April* 1576.   *Gorhambury.*   Grant for life to John Maplesden, M.A., of a canonry or prebend in Rochester cathedral, void by the death of John Symkyns.   By p.s.

491.)   20 *April* 1576.   *Gorhambury.*   Presentation of Thomas Crosse, clerk, M.A., to the vicarage of Sutherton, Lincoln dioc., void by the resignation of David Wood.   By p.s.

492.)   5 *March* 1576.   Protection for one year for Peter du Perry of London, merchant,
                                                                              [*m.* 26]
alien born. Because of great damages which he has suffered by Frenchmen of the town of St.
Malo (*Sancti Mallos*); at the suit of sieur de la Mothe Fenelon, French ambassador. By p.s.

493.)   27 *Feb.* 1576.   Presentation of John Watkyns, M.A., to the deanery in Hereford
cathedral, void by the death of John Ellize.   By p.s.

494.)   13 *April* 1576.   *Gorhambury.*   Presentation of John Collyns, M.A., to the rectory
of Northhuishe in Plimpton deanery, Exeter dioc., void and in the Queen's gift by lapse.
                                                                                By p.s.

495.)   16 *Feb.* 1576.   Grant for life to John Rugg, M.A., of a prebend or canonry in St.
Peter's collegiate church, Westminster, held by Thomas Aldrich, deceased.   By p.s.

496.)   16 *March* 1576.   Presentation of John Woolton, clerk, to the rectory of Spaxton,
Bath and Wells dioc., void and in the Queen's gift by lapse.   By p.s.

497.)   10 *May* 1576.   Grant for life to Thomas Lamben of an annuity of £36, payable at the
Exchequer, from Christmas last. For his service in the wars in Ireland and elsewhere to
Henry VIII, Edward VI, Queen Mary and the present Queen.   By p.s.

498.)   9 *May* 1576.   Grant for life to Gawin Smyth, 'le dromme player', of a fee of 12*d.* a
day, late held by William Garson, deceased, the Queen's 'le dromme', payable at the
Exchequer, from Michaelmas last.   By p.s.

499.)   17 *May* 1576.   Grant for life to John Stallens of the office of a   [*m.* 27]
gunner in the Tower of London; with wages of 6*d.* a day, payable at the Exchequer; as soon
as any of the offices of gunners in the Tower of the wages of 6*d.* a day shall be void; the patent
not to be to the prejudice of any person to whom the Queen has heretofore granted the like
office.   By Q.

500.)   23 *April* 1576.   *Gorhambury.*   Grant during pleasure to Edmund Tremayn, a clerk
of the Privy Council, of the office of receiver general of lands in the counties of Devon,
Cornwall and the city of Exeter late in the survey of the court of Augmentations and now in
that of the Exchequer; from Lady Day last; with fees at the discretion of the treasurer,
chancellor and under-treasurer of the Exchequer, payable out of the issues of the office.
                                                                                By p.s.

501.)   4 *April* 1576.   *Gorhambury.*   Pardon for Francis Birchley late of Ware, co. Hertford, 'mercer', indicted for that he with others stole horses severally belonging to Christopher Browne, John Penred and Richard Dane,   [*m.* 28]
all of Hartford, at Hertford on 31 July, 6 Eliz. (*details given*). At the suit of Dorothy Birchley,
Francis's wife.   By p.s.

502.)   2 *April* 1576.   *Gorhambury.*   Grant for life to Henry Gifford, the Queen's servant,
of the office of ranger or 'rydingfoster' in the New Forest, co. Southampton; with wages of
6*d.* a day, payable out of the issues of the county; as held by Edward Creswell, deceased;
from Cresswell's death. For his service.   By p.s.

503.)   23 *April* 1576.   *Gorhambury.*   Appointment during pleasure of William Gerrard, a justice in South Wales and one of the council in the marches of Wales, to be chancellor of Ireland; from the present date; with fees and the like as held by Robert Weston, deceased, late chancellor of Ireland, payable out of the customs in the ports of Dublin, Drogheda and Dundalke or, if the said customs do not suffice, by the treasurer, undertreasurer or receiver general of Ireland.   By p.s.

504.)   23 *April* 1576.   *Gorhambury.*   Grant for life to George Howard, knight, usher of the privy chamber and master of arms, of an annuity of 200 marks, payable at the Exchequer, from Christmas last. For his service to Henry VIII, Edward VI, Queen Mary and the present Queen.   By p.s.

505.)   17 *Feb.* 1576.   Presentation of Simon Hart, clerk, to the portion of Clare in Tiverton church, co. Devon, Exeter dioc., void by the resignation of Edward Cornewall or by lapse or otherwise; in the Queen's gift by the   [*m.* 29] minority of Jonathan Trelawney, son and heir of John Trelawney.   By p.s.

506.)   20 *April* 1576.   *Gorhambury.*   Grant to John Pearce, bishop of Rochester, great almoner, in augmentation of the Queen's alms, of all goods of felons *de se* and deodands in England and Wales belonging to the Queen; from 15 April last, so long as he shall be almoner.   By p.s.

507.)   9 *May* 1576.   Grant for life to Thomas Milles, the Queen's servant, of the office of a serjeant at arms, held by Fulk Mostyn, deceased; with wages of 12*d.* a day, payable at the Exchequer; from Mostyn's death. For his service.   By p.s.

508.)   9 *April* 1576.   *Gorhambury.*   Grant during good behaviour to John Hamonde of the office of usher or porter of the mint in the Tower of London, when it shall be void by the death of Richard Farr or otherwise; with an annuity of £10, payable by the undertreasurer or warden of the change, coinage and mint in the Tower.   By p.s.
     Vacated, because surrendered, 13 *Jan,* 20 *Eliz., that the office might be granted to Robert Knolles; signed*: Wyll'm Cordell; *and* be me John Hamond.

509.)   11 *April* 1576.   *Gorhambury.*   Grant for life to Hieremias Nenner, 'Almayne', of an annuity of £40, payable at the Exchequer, from Lady Day 1576, with an allowance of 2*s.* a day for him and his servant for so many days as they shall be directed by the master of the ordnance or the lieutenant of the same to work for the Queen. In consideration of the service he is to do about the office of the ordnance in the Tower of London and at the house called the Mynorites and elsewhere.   *English.*   By p.s.

510.)   15 *May* 1576.   Appointment during pleasure of John Jeffreys, the Queen's [*m.* 30] serjeant at law, to be a justice of the Queen's Bench.   By p.s.

511.)   10 *May* 1576.   Presentation of William Redman, S.T.B., to the archdeaconry of Canterbury in Canterbury cathedral; in the Queen's gift *hac vice*, the temporalities of the archbishopric of Canterbury being in her hands at the time of the archdeaconry being void.
                                                                    By p.s.

512.)   16 *April* 1576.   *Gorhambury.* Presentation of Thomas Cott, M.A., preacher of God's Word, to the perpetual vicarage of Catterick, Chester dioc.   By p.s.

513.)   12 *July* 1576.   Grant to Edward Dyer, the Queen's servant, and his deputies and assigns authorised by writing under his hand and seal of power in the Queen's name and in the name of Dyer to pardon and release persons resident in the Queen's dominions exercising the trade of tanner or tanning of leather from all offences and penalties, both before and after the present date, under the following clauses of stat. 5 Eliz. touching the tanning and dressing of leather:— [*nine clauses recited, as in the grant to Dyer of* 21 *Jan.* 1576 (*no.* 450 *above*)]. Persons to whom any such   [*m.* 31] release or discharge shall be made by the grantee by indenture or otherwise under his hand and seal, shown to the chancellor or keeper of the great seal, may sue for a further discharge in that behalf by patent (every patent containing 10 or 12 men and not more), paying the ordinary fees. The grantee may, for such consideration as to him shall be thought convenient, grant in the Queen's name or Dyer's by indenture liberty to any person resident in the Queen's dominions using the trade of tanning to tan and sell hides and leather as before the said statute notwithstanding any of the clauses before mentioned, working leather as they ought to do by any other clause of the statute in these premises not specially rehearsed and dispensed; every person so licensed may dry their leather in the temperate heat of the summer sun, the said statute or anything in these presents to the contrary notwithstanding. Also—whereas by stat. 5 Eliz. mayors and others having authority to appoint searchers and sealers of leather and leather wares are charged with penalties for the offences and negligences of such searchers and sealers, whereby without their own default they are in peril of great loss, especially in London (where the quantities of leather brought to be sold are so great that no searcher or sealer is able to give sufficient bonds for the indemnity of the mayor and aldermen), and whereas, if the indemnity of the said mayors and others in the premises is not provided for, the present grant for the relief of tanners cannot take effect—grant to the mayor and aldermen of London and all mayors and others to whom the appointing of searchers and sealers by the said statute is appointed that they may be discharged of all penalties for offences or defaults committed during such time as this patent shall remain effectual by any searcher or sealer contrary to stat. 5 Eliz.; and licence to all searchers and sealers of leather and made wares to seal and allow all leather and made wares wrought contrary to any points by these presents dispensed, so that they be otherwise wrought according to statute; all mayors and others having power to appoint sealers or searchers shall yearly see the same take their oaths to do their offices in all points according to the statute except in such points as be dispensed with or licensed to be dispensed with by these presents, and shall yearly take bonds of them to the Queen's use in such sums as in their discretions shall be thought convenient to execute their offices according to the statute other than in such things as by these presents are or may be dispensed with, and that only in such persons as shall be dispensed with by the grantee or by the Queen. The patent to be sufficient discharge to all curriers,   [*m.* 32] cordwainers, saddlers and other artificers using the currying, cutting or dressing of leather dispensed by the grantee during the time that the patent shall remain of force to procure, use and sell leather tanned, dispensed, searched and sealed as aforesaid (except only for bull hides and horse hides, which shall not be converted into boots, shoes or slippers). No courts or officers of the Crown to admit without the grantee's consent any action upon any article in which the grantee has power to dispense, nor against the mayor and aldermen of London or others aforesaid concerning any act or default of any searcher or sealer or other matter exonerated by this patent. No person to seize any hides, leather, boots, shoes or other wares as is aforesaid or pursue any action by reason of any article by these presents dispensed, on pain of imprisonment for one month upon the grantee's request. Bonds and obligations heretofore made by tanners for tanning according to the statute may be taken into the grantee's hands and at his pleasure may be redelivered to the obligors to be cancelled. The patent to be construed to the benefit of the grantee, the mayor and aldermen of London and persons to whom dispensations shall be made by the grantee. The grantee shall not constrain

any persons to any composition or agreement against their   [m. 33]
will.

     Upon complaint by tanners to the Queen and her Council that the clauses of the statute
which are specified above are impossible to be performed or inaptly worded, Dyer being
their suitor in that behalf.   *English.*   By Q.

514.)   13 *July* 1576.   Grant to Thomas Awdley of the wardship and marriage of Thomas
Awdley, son and heir of Christopher Awdley; with an annuity of 26s. 8d. from 5 June, 17
Eliz., when Christopher died. Yearly value of the inheritance £4 17s. 10d.   By Q.

515.)   16 *July* 1576.   Grant to Catherine Carus, widow, of the wardship and marriage of
Elizabeth Carus, daughter and heir of Thomas Carus; with an annuity of £6 13s. 4d. from 9
Sept., 17 Eliz. when Thomas died.   [m. 34]
                                                                              By Q.

516.)   16 *July* 1576.   Grant to Francis Cox of the wardship and marriage of Thomas Hale,
son and heir of Humphrey Hale; with an annuity of 26s. 8d. from 20 Nov., 3 & 4 Ph. &
Mary, when Humphrey died. Yearly value of the inheritance £4 7s.   By Q.

517.)   12 *July* 1576.   Grant to Robert Carter of the wardship and marriage of Mary and
Joan Burcome, daughters and co-heirs of Thomas Burcombe; with an annuity of 20s. from
28 Oct., 11 Eliz., when Thomas died. Yearly value of the inheritance £3 6s. 8d.   By Q.

518.)   16 *July* 1576.   Grant to William Walter of Wymbleton of the wardship and marriage
of Robert Baynard, son and heir of Edward Baynard; with an   [m. 35]
annuity of £20 from 12 Dec., 18 Eliz. when Edward died.   By Q.

519.)   16 *July* 1576.   Pardon for John Babthorpe late of Radwell, co. Hertford, indicted
for that at Radwell in the highway on 1 Sept., 17 Eliz., he (1) with others robbed George
Parryshe of £59 belonging to him, (2) robbed Richard Parkyns of 35s. 8d. belonging to him
and (3) robbed Thomas Clarke of 12s. belonging to him.   By p.s.

520.)   13 *July* 1576.   Presentation of Francis Bunney, M.A., to the rectory of Eglescliffe,
Durham dioc., void by death.   [m. 36]

521.)   13 *July* 1576.   Presentation of Thomas Sickyllmore, M.A., to the rectory of Slade-
borne, co. York, York dioc., void by death.   By p.s.

522.)   24 *July* 1576.   *Gorhambury.*   Erection of the office of hostager or host for hosting
and lodging merchants strangers now within the realm or hereafter coming into London or
any other place within the realm; and grant for 21 years to William Tipper of London,
merchant, of the said office. From Midsummer next. No persons after Michaelmas next to
host, lodge or sojourn any merchants strangers, but only such as shall be appointed
thereunto by the grantee; on pain of the Queen's displeasure and forfeiture of £20 for every
offence. Appointment of Tipper and such persons as he, his assigns or any of them shall
appoint in London and other places to be free hosts for the hosting and lodging of all
merchants strangers. Power for Tipper and his assigns during the term by writing sealed and
signed to appoint such persons as they think convenient in every place to be hosts for the
hosting of merchants strangers, and likewise to appoint persons to be their deputies in the
office; which persons shall be free hosts for such merchants strangers and during such time

as they shall be appointed may do everything appertaining to the office as Tipper might if present himself. Power for Tipper, his executors, assigns and deputies to take to their own use all fees and the like which by any free host of merchants   [m. 37] strangers may be taken by force of any custom or law. Paying a yearly rent of 40s. at the Exchequer. The mayor and sheriffs of London and the head officers of other places shall admit to be free hosts and to use the trade of hostage of merchants strangers all persons, and no others, which hereafter during the term by Tipper, his executors and assigns or their deputies under Tipper's hand and seal shall be appointed. Provided that the merchants of Italy being Italians born now dwelling in the realm may host and dwell together as heretofore, using no colour or deceit by hosting any other merchants strangers. Provided also that this grant be not prejudicial to the house in London called 'the Styllyarde or Guylde Hall Tewtonicorum' and the merchants there inhabiting together, but that they may in like manner host together as in times past. Power for Tipper and his assigns or their deputies appointed as is aforesaid to search out offences henceforth committed against any laws touching the hosting, lodging and sojourning of merchants strangers and both for the Crown and for themselves to prosecute offenders, causing all penalties due to be levied to the use of the Crown; and grant to Tipper and his assigns of a moiety of all sums so levied. Also power during the Queen's pleasure for Tipper, his executors and assigns to put in execution stat. 32 Hen. VIII concerning strangers born that be artificers and others and to prosecute offenders; and grant to them, towards their costs, of a moiety of all forfeitures recovered by them in every such suit. The chancellor, keeper of the great seal and the treasurer, chancellor and barons of the Exchequer shall from time to time, as occasion shall serve, at the request of Tipper, his executors or assigns issue commissions to such persons as he or they shall think convenient to inquire into the truth of such articles and things as Tipper, his executors or assigns shall deliver in writing touching the better execution of the present grant. Without fine or fee.

For the enforcement of the laws forbidding merchants strangers to be lodged or hosted with any other stranger, but only with Englishmen, to the intent that their doings and confederacies in trade might be better understood and looked to; which laws have not for a long time been duly put in execution, by reason whereof 'many secrett and undyrecte practyses' have been used among merchants strangers, and the prices of foreign wares advanced and those of wares of the realm diminished.   *English*.   [m. 38]
                                                                                                                By p.s.

Vacated, because surrendered 30 *March*, 24 *Eliz.; signed*: G. Gerrard *and* per me Will'm Tipper.

523.)   21 *July* 1576.   *Gorhambury*.   Grant for life to Edward Horsey, the Queen's servant, his deputies and assigns of licence and power, for such considerations paid to the grantee's use as to him shall be thought convenient, by indenture tripartite in such form as in a former patent, 23 April, 12 Eliz., granted to Horsey is expressed, to grant licences to keep such number of taverns over and above the number limited by stat. 7 Edw. VI in the cities and towns permitted by the statute as follows:—in the city of London three; in the city of Westminster three; in the cities of Chester and Oxforde two each at the most; in every other city, borough, port and market town permitted by the statute to have a tavern one above the number permitted; in Seynte Katheryns, Ratclyffe and Lymehowse, co. Middlesex, one each; in every thoroughfare, clothing town, haven town and fisher town not permitted by the statute to have a tavern one each. Power for persons so licensed to sell wines by retail by the gallon or less or greater measure during their lives at their own prices. This patent or the enrolment of the same together with one part of the indenture tripartite made as aforesaid and certified into Chancery shall be sufficient warrant to the chancellor or keeper of the great seal to deliver to the said persons jointly or severally such patents as they desire according to the tenor of these presents and of the said indentures tripartite.

Because of the proof had of Horsey, his deputies and assigns in the execution of the patent, 23 April, 12 Eliz., and for his service. That the wealth, traffic and trade of cities and towns which have become more populous and rich since the passing of the statute may be continued, and the ease of travellers and residents there maintained, which otherwise would not stay or use their assemblies and traffic there unless order be provided that the same may be done without breach of the law. *English.*   By p.s.

524.)   23 *July* 1576.   *Gorhambury.*   Licence for six years for William Nutshawe of South-ampton, merchant, to buy 300 quarters of wheat at not more than 2*s.* 4*d.* a bushel and 200 quarters of barley at not more than 15*d.* a bushel in the counties of Sussex and Dorset and export the same to friendly countries; from the   [*m.* 39] present date; customs only to be paid; if the prices of wheat and barley shall at any time during the term exceed those above limited, the licensee may at any time after the six years' end buy and transport them, so as the same exceed not at the first buying the prices aforesaid. *English.*   By p.s.

525.)   25 *July* 1576.   *Gorhambury.*   Grant to Lawrence Hollyngshed and Agnes his wife of the undermentioned bond, forfeited to Queen Mary by the attainder of Thomas, late archbishop of Canterbury. For their relief: Richard Reade, John Coxe and Lawrence Wether, salters, John Juxson, merchant taylor, and Edward Morton, grocer, citizens of London, by a bond, 24 Oct., 29 Hen. VIII [*English*], bound themselves to the said archbishop in £2,000 for the just administration of the will of John Smythe, late citizen of London, by Juxson and Reade,   [*m.* 40] his administrators during the nonage of Thomas, John, Richard, Francis, Joan and the said Agnes, Smythe's children; the £2,000 belongs to the Crown because Juxson and Reade did not faithfully administer or deliver to Smythe's children the residue of his goods; Agnes is sole survivor of Smythe's children and now his administratrix.   By p.s.

526.)   20 *July* 1576.   *Gorhambury.*   Grant to Thomas Betsworth of the wardship and marriage of John Cobden, son and heir of William Cobden the younger; with an annuity of 13*s.* 4*d.* from 14 Feb., 4 Eliz., when William died. Yearly value of the inheritance £3 6*s.* 8*d.*   By Q.

527.)   14 *Aug.* 1576.   *Gorhambury.*   Pardon for Thomas Laverock late of Bysshop Mylne in Medomsley, co. Durham, 'yoman', for manslaughter. It was found by an inquisition (*jury named*) taken before Anthony Dixon, coroner of James, bishop of Durham, of Chester ward, co. Durham, on the body of John Meybourne at Ponthopp in Medomsley on 2 Oct., 14 Eliz., that he feloniously wounded Meybourne at Ponthoppe on 24 Aug., 14 Eliz., so that he died on 1 Oct at Ponthoppe   [*m.* 41] (*details given*); he was also indicted for that he feloniously wounded the said Meabourne on Aug. 24 at Hamesterley, co. Durham, so that he died on 1 Oct. in his house at Ponthoppe.   By p.s.

528.)   20 *Aug.* 1576.   *Gorhambury.*   Pardon for John le Pastourell the younger of Ner-mount, 'yoman'. At the suit of Thomas Leighton, captain of the isle of Guernzey: it is reported by Leighton and other trustworthy persons dwelling in the isle that it was found by examinations of divers persons taken there that le Pastourell caused the death of the wife of John la Pere, one of la Pere's sons and a girl called Simone Mangeur by accidentally upsetting his cart in which they were into the sea (*details given*); by the customs and laws of the isle he should suffer the penalty of death, though by the laws of England such an act ought to be adjudged misadventure only.   By p.s.

529.)   10 *Aug.* 1576.   *Gorhambury.*   Order that William Absolon, M.A., a chaplain in ordinary and keeper of the privy oratory (*oratorii secreti*), be admitted and sworn a fellow or chaplain of the hospital of Le Savoye, co. Middlesex, and then forthwith admitted master of the same; and grant to him for life of the office of master. The said office of master is void by the death of Thomas Thurland and the places of three of the fellows or chaplains are void by death or secession, one chaplain only remaining; so that by the statutes of the said house no election of another master or other fellows can be made and the nomination of both master and fellows or chaplains belongs to the Queen.   By p.s.

(*The dorse of this roll is blank.*)

PART V

C. 66/1141

530.)   13 *Nov.* 1576.   Pardon for Thomas Kynge of Steplelangford, co.   [*m.* 1]
Wilts, 'tayler', for murder. It was presented by an inquisition (*jury named*) taken at Chippen-
ham, co. Wilts, at the general session of the peace held on 30 June, 9 Eliz., before John
Thynne, knight, Richard Kingesmyll and Edward Baynard, justices of the peace and of oyer
and terminer in the county, that John Rowdon, 'smyth', Kynge, Robert Lorde, 'husbond-
man', and John Gastling, 'laborer', all of Steplelangford, co. Wilts, feloniously wounded
Bartholomew Illsley at Hanginge Langford on 29 May, 9 Eliz., so that he died there on 30
May (*details given*).   By Q.

531.)   13 *Nov.* 1576.   Lease for 21 years to Christopher Smyth, the Queen's servant, of (1)
the rectory of Flampsted, co. Hertford, once in the tenure of Robert Tyrwytt, knight, and
now or late in the several tenures of William Skipwith, knight, and Smyth, late of Thorneton college, co. Lincoln, and (2) the tithes of corn (*tenants named*) in Southelkington, co.
Lincoln, late of the monastery of Nunormesby, co. Lincoln; with reservations; from (1)
                                                                                          [*m.* 2]
Lady Day 1607 and (2) Lady Day 1591; yearly rents (1) £32 and (2) £6 13s. 4d. For his
service; and for a fine of 100 marks paid at the Exchequer.   By p.s.

532.)   28 *June* 1576.   Lease for 21 years to Henry Anderson of Newcastle on Tyne, merchant, of the tithes of corn and hay in Elstwick, co. Northumberland, and a tithe barn and
castle [*sic*] there, late of the monastery of Tynemouth; from Lady Day last; yearly rent £6. In
consideration of the surrender by Anderson of an indenture, 18 May, 17 Hen. VIII, whereby
John, once bishop of the church of Poleten, commendatory of Tynemouth, and the convent
of the same place leased the premises (by the name of the tithe of grain of Elstwicke and a
tithe barn with 'le garth' adjoining) to John Blaxton of Newcastle on Tyne, merchant, and
Barbary his wife (which Barbary still survives) for life in survivorship from Lammas then
next at the same rent; and for a fine of £13 6s. 8d. paid at the Exchequer.
                                              By warrant of the commissioners.

533.)   9 *July* 1576.   Lease for life in succession to Alexander Ley and Robert Ley and
Stephen Ley, his sons, of the rectory of Waldishe, co. Dorset,   [*m.* 3]
late of Vaux college by New Salisbury, co. Wilts; with reservations; yearly rent 106s. 8d. In
consideration of the surrender by Robert Mone of a patent, 24 May, 7 Eliz., leasing the
rectory of Waldishe and a tenement there for 21 years from Lady Day then last at the same
rent; and for a fine of £10 13s. 4d. paid at the Exchequer by Alexander.
                                              By warrant of the commissioners.

534.)   7 *July* 1576.   Lease for 21 years to Thomas Beverley of the rectory of Eaton, co.
Bedford, late of the priory of St. John of Jerusalem in England,   [*m.* 4]
with reservations; and implements etc. (*detailed*); from Michaelmas next; yearly rent £56 13s.
4d.; the lessee to deliver back the implements etc. to the surveyor or other officers of the
county at the end of the term; also to pay all charges out of the rectory. In consideration of
the surrender in Chancery by Beverley of a patent, 30 May, 7 Eliz., leasing the premises to

Humphrey Aderley for 21 years from Michaelmas then next at the same rent; and for a fine of £113 6s. 8d. paid at the Exchequer.   By p.s.

535.)   4 *July* 1576.   Grant to John Meyre of the wardship and marriage of William New-ton, kinsman and heir of William Newton of Pownall, co. Chester, to wit, the son and heir of William Newton the younger, son and heir of the said William Newton the elder; with an annuity of £6 13s. 4d. from 4 May,   [*m.* 5]
16 Eliz., when William the elder died.   By Q.

536.)   9 *July* 1576.   Grant for life to Ralph Bowyer, one of the serjeants at arms, of the office of a serjeant at arms, and that he shall be a serjeant at arms, as he now is, and be in attendance on the Queen's person outside the time of any Parliament and during every Parliament in attendance on the speaker elected by the Commons; with 12d. a day, payable at the Exchequer, from Lady Day last; also with livery of the suit of the other serjeants at arms, to be received yearly at the great wardrobe at Christmas; as formerly held by Thomas Hale, deceased, late holder of the office, or John St. John. For his service.   By p.s.

537.)   10 *July* 1576.   Lease for 41 years to Robert Byndlose of two water corn mills called 'Castle Mylne' and 'Barnehill Mylne' and a 'le kylne' in Kyrkebye in Kendall, co. Westmor-land, parcel of the lordship or barony of Kendall, late of Helen, marchioness of Northamp-ton, and in the Queen's hands by exchange, and all waters, wastes etc. and multure of the Queen's tenants in Skaylthwaitrigge, Hutton, Hey, Helsyngton and elsewhere, co. West-morland, now or late in the tenure of William Lucas; with reservations; from Lady Day last; yearly rent £6 13s. 4d. In consideration that Byndlose offers to undertake the rebuilding of one of the mills, which is now almost laid waste.   By warrant of the commissioners.

538.)   5 *July* 1576.   Lease for 21 years to Henry Carye, K.G., baron of Hunsdon, of all granges and lands in Anderby and all lands in Warlabye in the said parish of Anderbye, co. York, late of Leonard Dacre, attainted of treason; with reservations; from Lady Day last; yearly rent £23 3s. 2d.; the lessee   [*m.* 6]
discharged of all other charges except 13s. 4d. for the fee of the bailiff of the premises. For a fine of £69 9s. 6d. paid at the Exchequer.   By p.s.

539.)   10 *Nov.* 1576.   Pardon for John Welbery (*alias* Wellerbye) late of Branspeth, co. Durham, for all treasons and the like committed before 1 April, 12 Eliz. He is indicted by inquisitions taken (1) before William, lord Ewre, Gilbert Gerrard, attorney general, Thomas Bromley, solicitor general, George Bowes, knight, Thomas Calverley, Thomas Layton and others, justices of oyer and terminer, at Durham castle, co. Durham, on 31 March, 12 Eliz., and (2) before John Walshe, a justice of the Common Pleas, Christopher Wraye, one of the Queen's serjeants at law, Henry Gaite, knight, George Bowes, knight, William Tankard, Lawrence Meres, Thomas Layton and others, justices of oyer and ter-miner, at York castle, co. York, on 17 July, 12 Eliz., for complicity in the   [*m.* 7]
rebellion in the North (*details given*). At the suit of Henry, lord of Hunsdon, governor of Berwick and warden of the East marches towards Scotland.   By p.s.

540.)   3 *July* 1576.   Lease for 21 years to William Thomlinson the elder and William Thomlinson the younger, his son, of lands (*named with tenants' names*) in Wheldrake, co. York, late of the monastery of Fountaunce in   [*m.* 8]
the archdeaconry of Richemond; with reservations; from Lady Day last; yearly rent 105s. 10½d. (*detailed*). In consideration of the surrender by them of a patent, 10 Nov., 3 Eliz.,

leasing the premises to William Thomlynson for 21 years from Lady Day then last at the same rent; and for a fine of £15 17s. 7½d. paid at the Exchequer.

By warrant of the commissioners.

541.)   8 *Nov.* 1576.   Grant to lady Elizabeth Guildford, widow, of the wardship and marriage of Henry Guldeforde, son and heir of Thomas Guldeforde, knight; with an annuity of £33 6s. 8d. from 15 June, 17 Eliz., when Thomas died, until the death of lady Mary, late the wife of John Guildeforde, knight, grandfather of Henry, or until the death of the said lady Elizabeth, mother   [*m.* 9] of Henry, whichever first shall happen, and thereafter a further annuity of £6 13s. 4d.

By Q.

542.)   7 *July* 1576.   Pardon for Nicholas Osencrofte late of Bungey, co. Suffolk, 'carpenter'. He was indicted at the gaol delivery of Burye St. Edmunds held on Wednesday in the second week of Lent, 17 Eliz., before Christopher Wraye, chief justice of the Queen's Bench, and Gilbert Gerrard, attorney general, justices of assize and gaol delivery, for that (1) he with Henry Keble late of Bungey, 'cowper', at Bungey on 31 Oct., 16 Eliz., broke and entered the close of Robert Gooche and stole a boar belonging to him and (2) he with Keble and John Pygeon late of Twayghte, co. Norfolk, 'labourer', burgled the house of William Linsted in the parish of St. Peter in Southelmham, co. Suffolk, on the feast of SS. Simon and Jude,   [*m.* 10]

16 Eliz., assaulted Joan wife of Linsted and stole £10 belonging to him; Osencrofte pleaded not guilty and was convicted. At the suit of certain trustworthy lieges asserting that he always lived honestly and barely earned a living by his labours for himself, his wife and children before the said crimes, which it is likely that he was driven to commit by the other malefactors, who have lately been hanged for their crimes.   By Q.

543.)   9 *July* 1576.   Lease of 21 years for William Lacye of (1) the rectory of Westharptre and a dovecote there, co. Somerset, late of the monastery of Keynesham, and (2) a water mill (*named with tenant's name*) in Pennesforde, co Somerset, late of Farleighe priory; with reservations; from Lady Day last; yearly rents, from the time when he shall enjoy possession, (1) £6 6s. 8d. and (2) 20s.   By warrant of the commissioners.

544.)   7 *July* 1576.   Grant to Michael Locke of the wardship and marriage of Julius Adelmare, son and heir of Cesar Adelmare; with an annuity of 20s. from 20 Sept., 11 Eliz., when Cesar died. Yearly value of the inheritance 53s. 4d.   [*m.* 11]

By Q.

545.)   25 *June* 1576.   Lease for 21 years to Richard Statham of (1) lands in Skirpenbecke, co. York, late of the monastery of Whitbye, and (2) lands (*tenant named*) in Little Staynton in the bishopric of Durham, late of the monastery of Blauncheland; with reservations; from Lady Day last; yearly rents (1) 60s. and (2) 53s. 4d. For a fine of £11 6s. 8d. paid at the Exchequer. On surrender by William Horseley of an indenture, 8 Jan., 30 Hen. VIII, whereby Henry, abbot, and the convent of the monastery of Whitbye leased to George Lawson of York, knight, the premises (1) above, then or late in his tenure, for 21 years from Martinmas then last at the same rent.   By warrant of the commissioners.

546.)   3 *Nov.* 1576.   Presentation of Thomas Carter, clerk, M.A., to the rectory of Stone, Rochester dioc.   By p.s.

547.)   15 *Nov.* 1576.   Lease for 21 years to Thomas Cotton, the Queen's   [*m.* 12]
servant, of (1) the barns and buildings of the rectory of Marske, co. York, and the tithes of
corn of the said rectory, (2) the tithes of fish at Redcarr, co. York, (3) the barns and buildings
of the rectory of Stranton and the chapel of Seton in the bishopric of Durham and the tithes
of corn of the said rectory and chapel, (4) the barns and buildings of the rectory of Harte and
the chapel of Hartipole in the said bishopric and the tithes of corn, wool and lambs of the
said rectory and chapel and (5) the tithes of fish at Hartilpole in the said bishopric; with
reservations, including the tithes of hay, formerly in the tenure of William Rokesbye, parcel
of the rectory of Marske, and the tithes of corn of Breereton, formerly in the tenure of the
vicar there, parcel of the rectory of Stranton and chapel of Seton; from Lady Day last; yearly
rents (1) and (2) £26 13s. 4d., (3) £17 6s. 8d. and (4) and (5) £22. In consideration of the
surrender in the Exchequer by the said Thomas of a patent, 16 Dec., 1 Edw. VI, leasing to
John Cotton, the King's servant, the premises (by the name of the tithes of corn of the
rectory of Marske, the tithes of fish at Redcarre, the tithes of corn of the rectory of Stranton
and chapel of Seton, the tithes of corn, wool and lambs of the rectory of Harte and chapel of
Hartilpole and the tithes of fish at Hartilpoole), with like reservations, at the same rents for
21 years from the termination of a lease thereof for 21 years by patent, 21 Nov., 32 Hen.
VIII, to Thomas Leigh; and for a fine of £66 paid at the Exchequer.   By p.s.

548.)   15 *Nov.* 1576.   Lease for 21 years to Robert Potter of the site and capital messuage
of the manor of Rewsales in Estmersey, co. Essex, late of Giles Capell, knight; with reservations; from Michaelmas last; yearly   [*m.* 13]
rent £13 6s. 8d. In consideration of the surrender in Chancery by Potter of a patent, 20 April,
3 Eliz., leasing the premises to John Walden for 21 years from Michaelmas then last at the
same rent; and for a fine of £26 13s. 4d. paid at the Exchequer.
                                                   By warrant of the commissioners.

549.)   15 *Nov.* 1576.   Lease for life in succession to Alice Lawrence and Edward Lawrence
the younger, son of Edward Lawrence the elder and the said Alice, of (1) a portion of the
tithes of wool, lambs and corn in the parish of Winfred, co. Dorset, (2) a barn in Knighton,
co. Dorset, and a close adjoining the same and (3) a yearly rent of 40s. payable by the rector
of Wynfred, all parcels of the parsonage of Wynfred and late of the monastery of Byndon,
co. Dorset; with reservations, including the tithes in Westburton in the said parish and the
tithes on the demesne lands there late in the occupation of the abbot and convent of Byndon;
from Michaelmas last; yearly rent £30 13s. 4d. In consideration of the surrender in the
Exchequer by the said Edward Lawrence   [*m.* 14]
the elder of an indenture, 28 Jan., 27 Hen. VIII, whereby John, abbot, and the convent of
the monastery leased the premises to Thomas Trenchard and Henry Trenchard (the said
tithes in Westburton and on the demesne lands reserved) for 80 years from Lady Day then
last at the same rent; and for a fine of £30 13s. 4d. paid at the Exchequer by Alice.   By p.s.

550.)   27 *Oct.* 1576.   Pardon for Richard Horton late of Rochester, co. Kent, 'miller',
indicted and convicted for treason in that on 1 Jan., 18 Eliz., at Rochester he made and
uttered four counterfeit 'twelve pennye peeces'.   By p.s.

551.)   7 *July* 1576.   Foundation of the free grammar school of Queen   [*m.* 15]
Elizabeth in Carmarthen, co. Carmarthen, of the foundation of Walter, earl of Essex, viscount Hereford, lord Ferrers of Charteley, K.G., Richard, bishop of St. Davids, James
Crofte, knight, councillor, controller of the household, Griffith Rece and Walter Vaughan,
aldermen of the town of Carmarthen, and Robert Toye, a burgess of the said town; with a

master and an usher. Appointment of the mayor of the town, at present Griffith ap Jevan, Griffith Rece and Walter Vaughan, aldermen, Robert Toye, burgess, William Davyes, alderman, Hugh Owen, recorder of the town, Jenkin David ap Jevan Phillipp, Robert Birte, Richard Phillippes, Richard Lewys and Griffith ap Jevan, aldermen, and John ap Harrye, David ap Jevan Taylor, Richard Lewes Hopkyn, Lewis David ap David, Edward Middleton, Henry Owen, David Edwardes, Martin Davys and Nicholas Roche, burgesses of the town, to be the first and present wardens and governors of the school; the mayor to be warden and governor during his mayoralty, the others to be wardens and governors for life. Incorporation of the governors. Whenever a warden and governor dies, the survivors may elect another in his place; in default of such an election within six weeks, the bishop of St. Davids may appoint; so that the person chosen be resident in the town. Power for the wardens and governors to appoint the master, usher and scholars and, (after the death of the present wardens and governors) with the advice and consent of the bishop of St. Davids; to make statutes in writing for the gover-   [*m.* 16] nance of the school; if they do not appoint a suitable person to vacancies in the places of master, usher and scholars within three months the bishop of St. Davids may appoint. Licence for the wardens and governors to acquire lands to the yearly value of £60 not held of the Crown in chief or otherwise by knight service.

At the suit of the earl and other founders above-mentioned.   By p.s.

552.)   7 *July* 1576.   Grant in fee simple to Edward, earl of Lincoln,   [*m.* 17] K.G., councillor, and William Raven of Horsepoole Graunge, co. Leicester, of the following (*tenants of the lands named*)—lands (*named*) in Wymonswolde, Burton, Prestwolde, Cotes and Hoton, co. Leicester, given for an obit in Wymondswolde church and late of John Nevell, knight; the chantry or chapel of Busbye in Stokesley and lands (*named*) once belonging thereto in Stokesley, Carleton and Facebye, co. York, all leased by patent of the Exchequer, 21 Jan., 10 Eliz., to George Bedlington for 21 years at a yearly rent of 72*s.* 7*d.*; lands (*named*) in Normanton on Sore, co. Nottingham, leased by patent, 7 Nov., 8 Eliz., to Edward Southworth at a yearly rent of 3*s.*; lands in Fenton, co. Lincoln, once of the hospital of St. John of Jerusalem; lands in Ludwell, co. Oxford, once of the monastery of Godstowe, co. Oxford; lands in Plymouth, co. Devon, once of Dabernons and Paynters chantry in Plymouth; lands in Southmolton and Northmolton (*named*), co. Devon, given to a chantry founded by John Knyghte and John Morles for the maintenance of a chaplain   [*m.* 18] in Southemolton church; all lands in Milton, co. Oxford, late of Thomas Pope, knight, exchanged, and late leased to Richard Gill at a yearly rent of 48*s.* 2*d.*; lands in Birmyngham, co. Warwick, once of Studley priory; lands (*described*) in Birmyngham, once of the guild or first chantry of Birmyngham; lands (*named*) in Shete or elsewhere in Petersfelde or elsewhere, co. Southampton, once of the monastery of Keynsham; lands (*named*) in Havant, co. Southampton, once of a brotherhood founded in Havante; lands (*described*) in Bridgewater, co. Somerset, late leased to Richard Randall at a yearly rent of 3*s.* 4*d.*; lands (*described*) in Orcheston St. George, co. Wilts, once of the monastery of Mayden Bradley and leased at several yearly rents of 13*s.* 4*d.* and 3*s.* 6*d.*; lands (*named*) in Katherington, co. Southampton, once of the monastery of Nuneaton, co. Warwick; a portion of tithes in Bachley, co. Southampton, once of the monastery of Christchurche Twyneham, co. Southampton, and leased at a yearly rent of 6*s.* 8*d.*; lands (*described*) in Alborne, co. Wilts, late leased *inter alia* by the Crown to James Yaet *alias* Yeate at several yearly rents of 10*s.* 4*d.* and 9*s.* being

[*m.* 19] in the Crown's hands by stat. 1 Edw. VI for the dissolution of chantries and the like; lands in Ulcebye, co. Lincoln, once of Thorneton college, co. Lincoln; lands in Farunton *alias* Farnedon and Thorpe, co. Nottingham, leased at a yearly rent of 7*s.* and once of the monastery of Haverholme; lands in Fennycompton, co. Warwick, parcel of lands of William Petifer,

attainted of felony, (brother of Robert Petifer) and leased at a yearly rent of 40s.; lands in the parish of St. George in Norwich, co. Norfolk; leased at a yearly rent of 13s. 4d., once of Horsehame St. Faith priory, co. Norfolk; lands (*described*) in Nottingham, once of (1) St. Mary's guild in the parish of St. Nicholas there and (2) Holy Trinity guild in the parish of St. Mary there; lands in Carcolston, co. Nottingham, once of the monastery of Thurgarton, co. Nottingham; lands in Kynlett, co. Salop, once of Dynmore preceptory, co. Hereford; lands (*named*) in Cleoburye Mortymer, co. Salop, once of the monastery of Wigmore; lands and services etc. in the grange of Custoda, co. Carmarthen, leased at a yearly rent of 7s., once of the monastery of Talley, co. Carmarthen; a mill etc. (*named*) in the grange of Kevenblaith, co. Carmarthen, once of the monastery of Talley, of a yearly rent of 12d.; lands in Huccles-cote in Ibstocke, co. Leicester, once of Ulvescrofte priory, co. Leicester, leased at several rents of 5s. 4d. and 6s.; the rectory of Tutburye, co. Stafford, once of the monastery of Tutburie; and the   [*m.* 20]
manor of Garford, co. Berks, once of the monastery of Abendon, co. Berks. Advowsons and lead, except lead in gutters and windows, reserved. To hold the manor of Garford by service of the fortieth part of a knight's fee   [*m.* 21]
and the rest as of the manor of Estgrenewich, co. Kent, in socage. Issues from Lady Day last. The grantees charged with the yearly payment of 20s. 1d. out of the premises in Southmol-ton and Northmolton to divers chief lords, £5 10s. out of the rectory of Tutburie for the stipend of the priest or curate there and 7s. 6d. out of the same rectory to the archdeacon of Stafford for synodals.

At the suit of the said earl: in consideration of the capital messuage of Newhall and other lands in Pinchebecke, co. Lincoln, bargained and   [*m.* 22]
conveyed to the Crown by him; and for his service.   By Q.

553.)   2 *July* 1576.   Licence for three years for Charles, lord Howard of Effingham, K.G., or his deputies or assigns whether Englishmen or strangers born, to buy and export to friendly countries 4,000 broad woollen cloths or kerseys (counting three kerseys for one broad cloth), both the sorts called Kentish cloth or Suffolk cloth or any other sort, both white and coloured, every part thereof unwrought and undressed; from the present date; paying at the full end of one year after the transportation of any of the cloths for customs and the like such sums as merchants Englishmen born and citizens of London pay for like merchandise; notwithstanding stats. 17 Edw. IV, 3 Hen. VII, 3 Hen. VIII, 5 Hen. VIII, 27 Hen. VIII, 33 Hen. VIII and 8 Eliz. touching   [*m.* 23]
the export of cloth, stat. 5 Hen. VIII concerning the entering of merchandise in customers' books and stats. 1 and 11 Hen. VIII touching the payment of customs by denizens; the number of cloths transported to be endorsed on the patent that it may be left, when expired, with the customers of the port where the last part shall be shipped; no similar licence to be granted to anyone else during the term; licence also during the term to search for breaches of the statutes concerning the export of unwrought woollen cloths or kersies, with grant
[*m.* 24]
of half the penalties for such breaches; the licensee may have such commissions and process for the Queen's service in that behalf, and also as many patents in form aforesaid for the transportation of the said 4,000 cloths, as by him are required.   *English.*   By p.s.

554.)   11 *July* 1576.   Grant for life to Edmund Rokrey, S.T.B., of a canonry or prebend in Rochester cathedral, late held by John Calverley, deceased.   By p.s.

555.)   11 *July* 1576.   Presentation of John Jennynges, B.A., preacher of God's Word, to the vicarage of Campden, Gloucester dioc., void by the   [*m.* 25]
resignation of Nathaniel Harford.   By p.s.

556.)   10 *July* 1576.   Presentation of Nicholas Bonde, M.A., to the rectory of Fulbecke, Lincoln dioc., void and in the Queen's gift by lapse.   By p.s.

557.)   25 *June* 1576.   Presentation of Richard Phillippes, clerk, B.A., to the rectory of Norlewe *alias* Northlewe, Exeter dioc., void by the death of John Curteys, clerk.   By p.s.

558.)   19 *June* 1576.   *Greenwich.*   Appointment for so long as the bishopric of Durham, void by the death of James the last bishop, shall remain in the Crown's hands of Thomas Calverley, chancellor of the county of Durham, to be keeper of the great seal of the bishopric of Durham; order to the treasurer to cause a great seal for the bishopric to be made for Calverley's use during the time aforesaid.   By Q.

559.)   10 *July* 1576.   Grant for life to Robert Davis, the Queen's servant, of the office of a serjeant at arms in ordinary, held by Richard Tegyn, deceased; with wages of 12*d.* a day from Lady Day last, payable at the Exchequer; as formerly held by Tegyn or Henry Burrell. For his service to Henry VIII, Edward VI, Queen Mary and the present Queen.   By p.s.

560.)   10 *July* 1576.   Presentation of Christopher Shutte, M.A., to the perpetual vicarage of Gigleswike, York dioc., void by death.   By p.s.

561.)   22 *June* 1576.   Lease for 47 years to Thomas Smalebroke, son of   [*m.* 26]
Richard Smalebroke, deceased, of lands (*described with tenants' names*) in Birmyngham, co.
Warwick, late of the guild or first chantry at Birmyngham;   [*m.* 27]
with reservations; from Michaelmas last; yearly rent £10 12*s.* 6*d.* (*detailed*). In consideration of the surrender in the Exchequer by Thomas of three several patents of the Exchequer, 28 Nov., 5 Eliz., whereby the premises were leased to his said father, *inter alia* for 60 years from Michaelmas then last at yearly rents   [*m.* 28]
(*detailed*) of £3 18*s.*, 76*s.* 6*d.* and 58*s.*   By warrant of the commissioners.

562.)   25 *June* 1576.   Lease for 21 years to John Bennett of (1) two water mills in Ewelme, co. Oxford, parcel of the manor of Ewelme and of the lands assigned to the Queen before her accession, and (2) lands (*tenant named*) in Fordyngton, co. Dorset, parcel of the manor of Fordyngton and of lands of the duchy of Cornwall;   [*m.* 29]
with reservations; from Lady Day last; yearly rents (1) £7 6*s.* 8*d.* and (2) 12*s.* 5½*d.* In consideration of the surrender by Bennett of a patent, 9 Nov., 8 Eliz., leasing the premises (1) above to Anthony Carleton for 21 years from Michaelmas then last at the same rent; and for a fine of £9 16*s.* 6*d.* paid at the Exchequer.   By warrant of the commissioners.

563.)   23 *June* 1576.   Lease for 21 years to Philip Hall of the manor or grange of Wyndgate *alias* Wyndgate Grange, co. Durham, and all its appurtenances in Kellowe in the said bishopric, once of the priory of Durham cathedral; with reservations; from Martinmas 1598 or the termination of a lease thereof   [*m.* 30]
by patent, 11 July, 3 & 4 [*recte* 4 & 5][1] Ph. and Mary; to Christopher Hall at a yearly rent of £12 10*s.* for 21 years from Martinmas 1577 or the termination of a lease thereof by conventual indenture, 21 Nov. 1537, to the said Christopher and Beatrice his wife for 40 years from Martinmas then last at the same rent; same rent; the lessee to find an able man to serve with horse and arms in the North, when needed, according to the custom of the country, and to

---

[1] *Cf. Calendar,* 1557–1558, p. 83.

fence the premises as ordered by the steward of the Queen's courts there. For a fine of £25 paid at the Exchequer.   By p.s.

564.)   30 *June* 1576.   Grant for life to Ralph More of the keeping of the stables at St. Albans late of the monastery there, with the lodgings and ground there enclosed belonging to the same and the use of the lodgings belonging to the same late called 'the Prior of Tynmouthes lodginge'; with a yearly fee of £12 3s. 4d. (£6 20d. for the keeping of the stables and £6 20d. for his charges in cleaning and carrying away the soil therof), payable at the Exchequer, from the death of James Thomasyn, deceased, who had the keeping of the stables.   *English.*   By Q.

565.)   28 *June* 1576.   Lease for 21 years to William Graye, John More and William Smyth *alias* Carter of lands (*tenants named*) in (1) Thorkleby and (2)   [*m.* 31] Ganstede, co. York, all late of Swyne priory, co. York; with reservations; from Lady Day last; yearly rents (1) 42s. and (2) 40s. and 22s. In consideration of the surrender by them of a patent, 15 March, 5 Eliz., leasing the premises to Robert Naylom and Leonard Edmundes for 21 years from Michaelmas then last at the same rents; and for a fine of £5 4s. paid at the Exchequer.   By warrant of the commissioners.

566.)   30 *June* 1576.   Grant for life to John Watson of the office of a gunner in the Tower of London, now held by Thomas Serjaunte; with wages of 8d. a day, payable at the Exchequer; from the death, forfeiture or surrender of Sarjaunt, to whom it was granted by patent, 28 Nov., 13 Eliz., for life. For his   [*m.* 32] service overseas.   By p.s.

567.)   25 *June* 1576.   Pardon for John Quasshe late of Iselington, co. Middlesex, indicted for that in the highway at Brandon, co. Suffolk, on 9 Feb., 17 Eliz., he robbed William Howes, Robert Skarlett and Thomas Boddam of goods belonging to Skarlett (*details given*).
                                                                                    By p.s.

568.)   3 *July* 1576.   Grant to Thomas Knevett, a groom of the privy chamber, of all the plate, money, jewels and other chattels forfeited to the Crown   [*m.* 33] by the attainder of Thomas Grene late of London, 'goldesmyth', for treason in clipping coin; power to sue for the same in the Crown's name or his own; if there shall be difficulty in gaining possession, he may convey the premises or any parcel thereof back to the Crown in the Exchequer, and the barons of the Exchequer shall cause them to be recovered in the Crown's name and after recovery deliver them to him.   By p.s.

569.)   2 *July* 1576.   Lease for 21 years to William Strachie and William   [*m.* 34] Spencer of the rectory of Normanton, co. Nottingham, once of the monastery of Worksoppe, co. Nottingham; with reservations; from Lady Day last; yearly rent £10, from the time when they shall obtain possession. In consideration that they will endeavour at their own costs to make void a pretended lease thereof for 90 years by indenture, 24 Aug., 30 Hen. VIII, to Richard Whalley.   By warrant of the commissioners.

570.)   26 *June* 1576.   Pardon for William Spence *alias* Spencer and Nicholas Bedle late of London, 'yomen', indicted for that they with others broke and entered the houses of (1) Thomas Crips and (2) James Crips at Hartley, co. Kent, on 9 June, 17 Eliz., and stole goods and money (*described*) severally belonging to them.   By p.s.

571.)   5 *Nov.* 1576.   Lease for 21 years to Matthew Poyntz of (1) lands   [*m.* 35] (*named with tenants' names*) in Kyngeswood, co. Wilts, parcel of the manor of Kyngeswood, (2) lands (*named with tenants' names*) in Kyngeswood, parcel of the said manor, (3) the rectory of Kynlett and (4) the rectory of Chelmarshe, co. Salop, both once of the monastery of Wigmore, (5) a decayed chapel in the parish of Llatwide, co. Glamorgan, and lands (*named*) in the parish of Llanmayell, co. Glamorgan, (6) a messuage in the parish of St. Mary in Bedford, co. Bedford, once of the monastery of Wardon, co. Bedford, (7)   [*m.* 36] a garden in the said parish of St. Mary, once of the monastery of Caldwell, co. Bedford, (8) lands (*named*) in Estdereham, co. Norfolk, and (9) the toll of a market and two fairs yearly in Southmolton, co. Devon, parcel of 'Richmondes Landes', and all profits leased with the same toll for a yearly rent of 32*s.*; with reservations; (1) from the termination of a lease thereof by Thomas Weare, abbot, and the convent of the monastery of Kyngeswood by indenture, 26 July, 11 Hen. VIII, to Thomas Poyntz late of Aldersley, co. Gloucester, at a yearly rent of £10 4*d.* (*detailed*) for 60 years from Lady Day then last as regards one parcel thereof and as regards the rest from Lady Day next after the several deaths, surrenders or forfeitures of tenants for life; (2) from the termination of a lease thereof by William Bewdley, abbot, and the convent of the monastery of Kyngeswood by indenture, Midsummer 29 Hen. VIII, to John Seaverne *alias* Plommer of Aldersley, 'clothmaker', for 60 years from that date at a yearly rent of 28*s.*; (3) and (4) from the termination of a lease thereof by conventual indenture, 8 May, 29 Hen. VIII, to Catherine Blunte, widow, for 60 years; (5) and (7) from Michaelmas 1594, having been leased (5) by patent, 5 Dec., 15 Eliz., to John Turbervile for 21 years from Michaelmas then last at a yearly rent of 8*s.* 11*d.* and (7) by patent, 10 Oct., 13 Eliz., to Geoffrey Laurence for 21 years at a yearly rent of 2*s.*; (6) and (8) from Lady Day 1589, having been leased (6) by patent, 9 Jan., 11 Eliz., to Richard Hodgeson for 21 years from Michaelmas then last at a yearly rent of 13*s.* 4*d.* and (8) by patent, 2 June, 10 Eliz., to John Browne, Henry Skarlett, Richard Atley, Thomas Butham and John Marshall for 21 years from Lady Day then last at a yearly rent of 8*s.*; and (9) from Lady Day 1582, having been leased by patent, 19 May, 3 Eliz., to Thomas Hunt, Richard Stephens *alias* Bagbere, Richard Paynter and others for 21 years; yearly rents (1) £10 6*d.* (*detailed*), (2) 28*s.*, (3) £4, (4) £4, (5) 8*s.* 11*d.*, (6) 13*s.* 4*d.* , (7) 2*s.*, (8) 8*s.* and (9) 22*s.*; the lessee to pay yearly out of (4)   [*m.* 37] 28*s.* 8*d.* for the stipend of a curate in Chelmarshe. At the suit of Hugh Parler: in consideration that Parler has surrendered an annuity of £14 granted to him by patent for life; and in consideration of the surrender of his interest in a lease of a manor in Barrowe called Downehall, co. Lincoln, of the yearly value of £8 made by the Crown to Brian Cotes.

By p.s.

572.)   12 *Nov.* 1576.   Lease for 21 years to Francis Russell, knight, of lands etc. (*tenants named*) in (1) Bywell, parcel of the barony of Bywell, (2) Ovington (including the site of the manor and common of pasture for the tenants of Welton), parcels of the manor of Ovington, parcel of the barony of Bywell, (3) Bromley (*named*, and including commons in the respective tenures of   [*m.* 38] the inhabitants of Ferne, Fawderby and Hely), parcels of the manor of Bromley, parcel of the barony of Bywell, and (4) Rydynge and Le Lye, parcels of the barony of Bulbecke, all in the county of Northumberland and late of Charles, late earl of Westmorland, attainted of treason; with reservations; from Lady Day last; yearly rents (*detailed*) (1) £1 5*s.* 8*d.* , (2) £7 6*s.* 2*d.*, (3) £9 12*s.* and (4) £7 19*s.* 6*d.*; the lessee to pay also yearly 26*s.* 8*d.* out of the site of the manor of Ovington to the Crown as in right of the chantry of Brauncepeth;   [*m.* 39] the lessee by himself or sufficient men with horse and arms to serve in the North when summoned by the Queen's warden or lieutenant according to the custom of the country, to inhabit and cultivate the tenements by himself or sufficient men, and to fence the premises as ordered by the steward of the Queen's courts or other her commissioners there; the lease to be void in respect of any parcels of the premises from which the lessee shall expel the present tenants, or whereof he shall not before Christmas next make to the present tenants leases by deed of the parcels in their several tenures for the whole term and at the same rent, so long as they pay him among themselves his costs about obtaining this patent. For a fine of £52 6s. 8d. paid at the Exchequer.   By warrant of the commissioners.

573.)   15 *Nov.* 1576.   Lease for 21 years to William Babthorpe, knight, of the rectory of Draxe and appurtenances thereof (*described with tenants' names*) in Draxe, Newland, Langredd, Camyforde, Newhey and Rusholme, co. York, and a close at Stanthill and a barn built thereon called 'le tythe lathe', co. York, all once of Draxe priory; with reservations; from Michaelmas last; yearly   [*m.* 40] rent £22 12s.; the Crown to discharge the lessee from £6 13s. 4d. payable yearly to the vicar of Draxe. In consideration of the surrender by Babthorpe of a patent, 3 March, 3 Eliz., leasing the premises to him for 21 years from Michaelmas then last at the same rent; and for a fine of £45 4s. paid at the Exchequer.   By p.s.

574.)   27 *Oct.* 1576.   *Hampton Court.*   Lease for 21 years to Francis Skelton and John Carlell of (1) the site and capital messuage of the manor of Speton, co. York, and lands (*named*) and the tithes of corn and hay in Speton belonging to the said site and (2) the chapel of Bucton, co. York, all once of the monastery of Bridlington, co. York; with reservations; from Michaelmas last; yearly   [*m.* 41] rents (1) £10 9s. 6d. and (2) £14; the lessees to provide entertainment at the manor for the Queen's steward and surveyor coming to hold courts and make a survey. In consideration of the surrender in the Exchequer by Skelton and Carlell of a patent, 13 June, 3 Eliz., leasing the premises to Thomas Warcoppe for 21 years from Lady Day then last at the same rents; and for a fine of £24 9s. 6d. paid at the Exchequer.   By p.s.

575.)   11 *July* 1576.   Grant in fee simple to Anthony Lewkenor, a footman in ordinary, of lands in Slyngesby, co. York, late in the tenure of William Jennyson, attainted of treason; lead, except in gutters and windows, reserved; to hold in socage as of the manor of Estgrenewich and by a yearly rent,   [*m.* 42] after the death of Lewkenor, of 53s. 4d.; issues from Michaelmas last.

     Grant also to Lewkenor of all the goods and chattels late of Jennyson, remaining at Slyngesby and of the value of £30 14s.

     For his service.   By p.s.

576.)   12 *Nov.* 1576.   Lease for 21 years to Ralph Harbottell of three salt pits in the manor of Cawpon, co. Northumberland, and all coal in the fields and common of Cawpon, now or late in the tenure of Thomas Harbottell, with liberty to take the same coal as of old time accustomed, late of Thomas, late earl of Northumberland, attainted of treason, with 'wayleve' and 'stayleve' for the said mine and pits and wood for 'le tymbrynge' of the pits to be taken in adjoining woods by assignment of the Queen's officers there; from Michaelmas last; yearly rent £6 13s. 4d. For a fine of £20 paid at the Exchequer.
     By warrant of the commissioners.

577.)   4 *July* 1576.   Grant in fee simple to Ambrose, earl of Warwick, of (1) the manor of Thirkelbye Magna and lands (*named*) in Thirkelbye Magna and Thirkelbye Knolle, co. York, late in the tenure of Francis Fulthroppe, all late of John Fulthroppe, attainted of treason, (2) the manor of Rosedale, co. York, and the site and demesne lands of Rosedale priory (*named*), now or late in the tenure of Thomas Williamson, all late of Charles, late earl
     [*m.* 43]

of Westmorland, outlawed for treason, and (3) the advowson of the rectory of Melsambye, co. York; to hold as of the manor of Estgrenewiche, co. Kent, in socage; the Crown to discharge the grantee from the payment out of the manor of Thirkelbye Magna of annuities of 53s. 4d. to Thomas Fulthroppe, one of the said John's brothers, 53s. 4d. to Robert Fulthroppe, another of his brothers, and £6 to Lucy Fulthroppe, one of the said John's daughters, for their several lives; issues from 1 Nov. last. The premises were conveyed *inter alia* by patent, 23 Feb., 13 Eliz., to the said earl of Warwick in fee simple, to hold by service of the fortieth part of a knight's fee; by indenture, 25 Nov., 15 Eliz., enrolled in Chancery, he conveyed them to the Crown.   By p.s.

578.)   15 *Nov.* 1576.   Grant for life to John Saunders, M.A., of a canonry and prebend in Bristol cathedral, void by the resignation of Thomas Wethered, clerk.   By p.s.

579.)   26 *Oct* 1576.   *Gorhambury.*   Lease for 21 years to William   [*m.* 44] Whethill, citizen and merchant taylor of London, of the rectory of Edwardston, co. Suffolk, late of Colne priory, co. Essex; with reservations, including profits of court and the advowsons of the vicarages of Edwardston and Little Waldingfelde; from Lady Day 1583, being the termination of a lease thereof by patent, 31 Aug., 4 Eliz., to Francis Jobson, knight, for 21 years from Lady Day then last at a yearly rent of £20; same rent; the lessee to provide entertainment for the Queen's steward there coming to hold courts. For his service.
                                                    By p.s.

580.)   30 *Oct.* 1576.   Lease for 21 years to William Ridley of lands (*named*) in Hexhamshire, co. Northumberland, late of the archbishopric of York;   [*m.* 45] with reservations; from Michaelmas last; yearly rent £7 6s. 8d. In consideration of his surrender of a patent, 23 Oct., 8 Eliz., leasing the premises to him for 21 years from Michaelmas then last at the same rent; and for a fine of £13 6s. 8d. paid at the Exchequer.
                                          By warrant of the commissioners.

581.)   15 *Nov.* 1576.   Lease for 40 years to William Emery and Thomas Mercer of an inn called 'le Swanne with Two Neckes' in the parish of St. Lawrence in Old Jewry, London, in the tenure once of [—] Okes, widow, and now or late of Robert Medley, given by Simon Benyngton for a stipendiary priest in the church of St Lawrence aforesaid; from Michaelmas next; yearly rent £11. In consideration that the lessees will repair the inn, now ruinous.
                                          By warrant of the commissioners.

582.)   26 *Oct.* 1576.   *Gorhambury.*   Licence for 16 years for Henry Middlemore, a groom of the privy chamber, to export 200 tons of beer yearly, counting six score to the hundred for filling beer, in the ports of London, Sandwiche   [*m.* 46] or Ipswiche; the usual custom and subsidy to be paid and no impost or other sum; from the present date; notwithstanding stat. 1 & 2 Ph. & Mary to restrain carrying corn, victuals and wood oversea; the licence to have the amounts shipped endorsed on it that it may be left with the customer of the port where the last shipment shall be made and may be returned by him into the Exchequer to be cancelled.   *English.*   By p.s.

583.)   15 *Oct.* 1576.   *Gorhambury.*   Licence for 10 years for Simon Bowyer, a gentleman usher daily attendant of the chamber, to buy and sell again 500 sarplers of English wool; from the present date; the licence to have the amounts bought endorsed upon it within a twelvemonth. For his service.   *English.*   By p.s.

584.)   3 *July* 1576.   Lease for 21 years to John Dodington of the site   [*m.* 47]

or capital messuage and demesne lands of the manor of Salforde Priors, once of the monastery of Kenelworth, co. Warwick, all appurtenances of the said site in Salforde Priors, Donyngton and Cubbington, co. Warwick, or elsewhere and the tithes of corn, mills, woods, underwoods, lambs, wool and hay of the premises; with reservations, including a rent of £13 13s. 4d. out of certain lands in Woodbenyngton; from Lady Day last; yearly rent, from the time when the lessee shall obtain possession, £49 18s. 5d.; if it shall be proved that the premises are now or have been leased at a greater yearly rent than that hereby reserved, the lessee shall pay such greater rent or this lease shall be void; if it shall be proved that the rent hereby reserved is greater than has heretofore been answered, the lessee shall yearly have allowance at the Exchequer of the amount by which it is in excess; the lessee to provide entertainment for the Queen's steward and surveyor coming to hold courts of the manor or survey the same. By conventual indenture, 24 Feb., 29 Hen. VIII, the manor aforesaid, all lands of the monastery in Salforde Priors, Donyngton and Cubbington, the advowson of the vicarage of Salforde aforesaid and all other appurtenances of the manor (except profits of courts and the like and the said　　　　　　　　　　　　　　　　　　　　　　　[m. 48]
rent of £13 13s. 4d.), with the tithes aforesaid of the premises, were leased to William Grey for 99 years from Lady Day then next at the same rent; which indenture is void as is supposed.　　　　　　　　　　　　　　　　　　　　　　　　　　　　　By p.s.

585.)　10 *July* 1576.　Licence for 12 years for Henry Lee, knight, the Queen's servant, by himself, his servants, factors, assigns, deputies and attorneys the Queen's subjects born, to buy in England and export to friendly countries 200,000 calf skins wrought, tanned or dressed; from the present date; not more than 20,000 skins to be transported in any one year; duties payable before the last session of Parliament only to be paid; amounts shipped to be endorsed on the patent by the customer of the port or his deputy within two months, that it may be returned, when expired, by the officer of the place where the last shipping shall be made into the Exchequer to be cancelled. For his service.　　　　　　　　By p.s.

586.)　12 *Nov.* 1576.　Grant to Thomas Roche of the wardship and marriage of Thomas Rogers, son and heir of Thomas Rogers; with an annuity of 26s. 8d. from 6 Jan., 15 Eliz., when Thomas the father died. Yearly value of the inheritance £5 10s. 8d.　　　　　By Q.

(*Ms. 1d. to 40d. are blank.*)

587.)　10 *July* 1576.　Commission for Andrew Perne, S.T.D., dean of Ely　　[m. 41d.] cathedral, John Whitgifte, S.T.D., Thomas Seckford, a master of the Requests, Henry Harvie, LL.D., Thomas Ithell, LL.D., Edward Leades, LL.D., Robert Bell, William Humberston, Edmund Hall, Thomas Andrewes, John Bell, S.T.B., John Parker, M.A., Robert Shute, Richard Anger, Edward Styward, William Styward, John Styward and William Adams (or four of them, Perne or Harvy being one) to survey the lands and hereditaments of Ely cathedral; inquisitions to be returned into Chancery; the keeper of the great seal or chancellor shall at their discretion, at the suit of the dean and chapter of the cathedral, issue without further warrant commissions according to the tenor of the present commission, 20s. only being payable for every such commission for all fees. The dean and chapter have complained that the possessions of the cathedral have not been surveyed for many years, by reason whereof divers rents and services have been withheld and lands concealed.　　　　　　　　　　　　　　　　　　　　　　　　　　　　　By p.s.

(*The rest of the dorse is blank.*)

PART VI

C. 66/1142

588.) 24 *Nov.* 1575. Lease for 80 years to Robert Woorseley of Both,   [*m.* 1]
co. Lancaster, of (1) the rectory of Michelchurche *alias* Mikelkirke, co. Lancaster, now or
late in the tenure of William Kirkby, (2) lands (*named*), now or late in the tenure of the vicar
of Michelchurche, and (3) a barn there, now or late in the tenure of the said William,
belonging to the rectory; with reservations; from the termination of a lease thereof by
patent, 4 Nov., 14 Eliz., to Henry Kirkby at yearly rents of (1) £27 4*s.* 4*d.*, (2) 8*s.* and (3)
3*s.* 4*d.* for 21 years from the termination of a lease thereof *inter alia* by patent, 28 Dec., 5 Eliz.,
to William Doddington for 21 years from Michaelmas then last at the same rents; same rents.
At the suit of Anne, wife of Henry, lord of Hunsdon.   By p.s.

589.) 22 *Nov.* 1575. Lease for 21 years to Anthony Tailboys of a messuage called
Barmeston *alias* Barmeton and lands in Barmeston in the bishopric of Durham, now or late
in the tenure of Margaret Hall or her assigns,   [*m.* 2]
late of John Swinborne, attainted of treason; with reservations; from Michaelmas last;
yearly rent 44*s.* 4*d.*; the lessee to pay yearly 22*s.* 4*d.* to the dean and chapter of Durham
cathedral for free rent; the lessee to occupy the premises by himself or a sufficient man, to
find a sufficient man to serve with horse and arms when required by the warden or lieutenant
of the marches there as accustomed, and to fence the premises as ordered by the steward of
the Queen's court there. In consideration of the surrender by Tailboys of a patent of the
Exchequer, 20 Nov., 16 Eliz., leasing to John Lane the premises, then or late in the tenure of
Thomas Morey and Margaret Hall or her assigns by assignment of Richard Hall and the said
Margaret, his wife, with reservations, for 21 years from Michaelmas then last at the same
rent.   By the commissioners by virtue of the Queen's warrant.

590.) 30 *Nov.* 1575. Lease for 21 years to Tristram Swadell of the rectory of Sledmer, co.
York, once of the monastery of Kirkehame, co. York; with   [*m.* 3]
reservations; from Michaelmas last; yearly rent £21; the lessee to pay the stipend of a curate
in Sledmer church. In consideration of the surrender by Swadell of a patent, 12 June, 3 Eliz.,
leasing the rectory to Richard Holte for 21 years from Michaelmas then last at the same rent;
and for a fine of £42 paid at the Exchequer.   By p.s.

591.) 30 *Nov.* 1575. Lease for 21 years to John Guylpyn of lands (*named with tenants'*
names) in Newsome in the parish of Kyrkby Wyske, co. York, once of the monastery of
Fountaunce, co. York, and since the dissolution of the monastery withheld from the Crown
and claimed by certain persons as their own lands rendering to the Crown a bare yearly rent
of £6 3*s.* 8*d.* by the name of free rent; with reservations; from Michaelmas last; yearly rent
£6 3*s.* 8*d.* In consideration that Guylpyn sued out at his own costs a commission and an
       [*m.* 4]
inquisition by virtue thereof before John Genkins and Hugh Bethell taken at York castle on
23 Sept. last returned in the Exchequer whereby it found that the buildings of the premises
are decayed, and that he undertakes to maintain them and to take a lease of the premises at
the rent aforesaid.   By the commissioners by virtue of the Queen's warrant.

592.)   28 *Nov.* 1575.   Grant to the inhabitants of Kirkbie in Kendall, co. Westmorland, of liberties as follows—The town shall be a free borough and the inhabitants shall be a corporation by the name of the alderman and burgesses of the borough of Kirkbie in Kendall; with an alderman and 12 chief burgesses. Appointment of Henry Wilson, inhabitant of the borough, to be the first and present alderman until Michaelmas next and thereafter until another burgess be appointed and sworn in his place; and of Henry Fysher, Robert Wylkinson, Miles Foxe, Christopher Bindlos, Henry Dyxson, Miles Braken, Adam Eskrigge, Edward Potter, Edward Swainson, Richard Spedye, Thomas Willson and Robert Jopson, inhabitants of the borough, to be the first and present chief burgesses during good behaviour. There shall be two serjeants at mace to be attendant on the alderman for the execution of process and other business; who shall be appointed yearly by the alderman and burgesses on Monday before Michaelmas and sworn before them, and shall bear maces gilt or silver and adorned with the arms of England everywhere within the borough before the alderman. The alderman and burgesses shall have there a man learned in the common law called the recorder or steward of the said town, elected by them at their pleasure; Robert Brigges being hereby appointed steward or recorder during their pleasure. Also to have a court of record to be held before the alderman, the recorder or steward and three of the burgesses (or two of them), for actions not exceeding £20, on Thursday every third week in a chamber there called 'le Courte Lofte' or another house there as seems fit to the alderman and burgesses; process to be as in the Common Pleas or in   [*m.* 5] any other court of record in a city, borough or town incorporate; the alderman and burgesses to have the profits of the court. Also to have, besides the fairs accustomed there, two fairs yearly, one on the eve of the feast of St. Mark for two days and the other on the eve of the feast of SS. Simon and Jude for two days. Also to have view of frankpledge of the inhabitants yearly in the guildhall of the borough. The boundaries of the borough to be as of old accustomed; and the alderman and burgesses may make perambulations to survey and limit the same. The alderman and burgesses to have the assize and assay of bread, wine, ale and other victuals, fuel and wood there. Also to have power by the alderman and chief burgesses to make and enforce ordinances for the borough; so that they be not repugnant to the laws of the realm. The burgesses to have power yearly on Monday before Michaelmas to elect two of the chief burgesses, of whom all the inhabitants assembled   [*m.* 6] may elect one to be alderman for one year; the alderman elect to be sworn before admission to the office before the last alderman or in his absence before the recorder or steward; if an alderman shall die or be removed, the chief burgesses may elect two of their number, of whom the inhabitants may elect one as alderman for the rest of the year, to be sworn as aforesaid. Whenever one of the said 12 burgesses shall die, be removed or dwell outside the borough, the remainder may elect another of the inhabitants in his place, to be sworn before the alderman. Whenever the recorder or steward shall die or be removed, the alderman and burgesses may within 20 days elect another man learned in the law in his place, to be sworn before the alderman and burgesses. The alderman, the recorder or steward and one of the principal burgesses to be during their time of office justices of the peace; and the alderman, the recorder or steward and the senior man of the 12 chief burgesses to have power to inquire touching all offences which ought to be inquired about before the keepers and justices of the peace in any county of England; so that they do not proceed to the determination of any capital offence without the Queen's special order; the justices of the peace of the county of Westmorland not to intermeddle save in default of the alderman, recorder and senior burgess. If anyone elected to the office of alderman, burgess or other lower officers of the borough (except the offices of recorder and common clerk) shall refuse, having notice of election, to serve, he shall forfeit £10 to the burgesses, and the alderman and burgesses may commit him to the borough gaol until he pay. No one having served as alderman shall within four years following be elected alderman again. Licence for the

alderman and burgesses to acquire lands to the yearly value of £20 not held of the Crown in chief or of the Crown or any other by knight service. Provided that nothing in this patent shall deprive George,   [*m.* 7]
earl of Cumberland, sheriff of the county of Westmorland by hereditary right, or his heirs or assigns of any liberties or profits.

At the suit of the inhabitants.   By p.s.

593.)   9 *Dec.* 1575.   Lease for 21 years to Philip Constable of the rectory of Garton, co. York, once of Kirkeham priory, co. York, the tithes of wool and lambs in Garton, parcel of the rectory, and all other appurtenances thereof; with reservations; from Michaelmas last; yearly rent £35 7s. 8d. In consideration of the surrender by Constable of a patent, 25 April, 3 Eliz., leasing the premises to Thomas Woode for 21 years from Michaelmas then last at the same rent; and for a fine of £60 paid at the Exchequer.   By p.s.

594.)   15 *May* 1576.   Lease for 21 years to John Lane of Kettering, co. Northampton, of five mills   [*m.* 8]
(*described*) in Ketteringe; with reservations; from Michaelmas next; yearly rent £10. In consideration of his surrender of a patent, 5 July, 5 Eliz., leasing to him the premises, by the name of four mills (*described*), parcel of the manor of Kettering, for 21 years from Lady Day then last at the same rent; and for a fine of £10 paid at the Exchequer.
                               By the commissioners by virtue of the Queen's warrant.

595.)   9 *March* 1576.   Lease for 21 years to Henry Leonerde of Dovor,   [*m.* 9]
'brewer', of lands (*described with tenants' names*) in Dovor, (1) once of the late house or hospital called 'le Masondewe' there and (2) once of the late house called 'le Archepreistes' there; from Michaelmas last; yearly rent, (1) 132s. (*detailed*) and (2) 16s. In consideration of the surrender by Leonerde of the interest of John Wheler, Henry Harwoode and John Portewaye in certain of the premises in (1) and in the premises in (2) by virtue of a patent, 20 Aug., 4 & 5 Ph. & Mary, whereby the same were leased *inter alia* to them for 21 years from Michaelmas then next at yearly rents of (1) 62s. 4d. and 8s. 4d. and (2) 16s.; and for a fine of £14 16s. paid at the Exchequer.
                               By the commissioners by virtue of the Queen's warrant.

596.)   16 *April* 1576.   *Gorhambury.*   Lease for 21 years to Leonard   [*m.* 10]
Edmondes of lands (*tenants named*) in (1) Thorkelebye and (2) Ganstede (*named*), co. York, once of Swyne priory, co. York; with reservations; from Lady Day last; yearly rents (1) £4 2s. and (2) 22s. In consideration of the surrender by Edmondes by deed, 14 April, 18 Eliz., enrolled in Chancery, of the interest in the premises of Robert Naylor and him (which Naylor is dead, by reason whereof his interest has come to Edmondes) by patent, 15 March, 5 Eliz., leasing the premises to them for 21 years from Michaelmas then last at the same rents; and for a fine of £10 8s. paid at the Exchequer.
                               By the commissioners by virtue of the Queen's warrant.

597.)   16 *April* 1576.   *Gorhambury.*   Lease for 21 years to John Carlell of the chapel of Besingby, co. York, once of the monastery of Bridlington, co. York; from Lady Day last; yearly rent £10 14s. 4d.; the Crown to discharge the lessee from all other payments. In consideration of the surrender by Carlell   [*m.* 11]
of the interest of James Cookeson by virtue of a patent of the court of Augmentations, 6 April, 7 Edw. VI, whereby the chapel was leased to him, then the King's servant, at the same rent for 21 years from the termination of a lease thereof under the great seal, 25 Oct., 30 Hen. VIII, to Brian Leighton for 21 years from Michaelmas then last; and for a fine of £21 8s. 8d.

paid to the Queen's use to Richard Hebborne by way of reward for his labour and charges about her works at Sherifhutton castle, co. York, over the past three summers having no allowance therefor, as appears by the particular books of her works with the auditor of the county, and by testimony of Henry, earl of Huntingdon, president of the council in the North.   By the commissioners by virtue of the Queen's warrant.

598.) 12 *March* 1576. Lease for 60½ years to Robert Honywoode of the rectory of Goodneston, the messuage and barns called 'le personage of Goodneston', the tithes of corn in Goodneston next Wingham, co. Kent, and all lands in Wingham of the provost and canons of the late college of Wingham belonging to the said rectory; with reservations, including the house there called 'le vicaridge' and all lands annexed thereto and all courts and the like; from Michaelmas last; yearly rent £24; the lessee to pay all charges. Edmund Cranmer, clerk, provost, and the canons of the said   [*m.* 12] college by indenture, 1 Aug., 36 Hen. VIII, leased to Christopher Nevinson, LL.D., the said parsonage, tithes and lands (the vicarage reserved) for 91 years from Lady Day then next at the same rent; after Nevinson's death Anne his wife and executrix, having the said term, married Thomas Wyseman; Wyseman by writing, 26 Jan., 15 Eliz., conveyed it to Roger Manwoode, a justice of the Common Pleas; Manwoode by writing, 29 Jan., 16 Eliz., conveyed it to Honywood; and, because the indenture made by the college has by misadventure been lost, Honywood by writing, 25 Nov. last, enrolled in the Common Pleas, has surrendered his interest that he may have a new lease for the rest of the term.

By p.s.

599.) 24 *Feb.* 1576. Lease for 21 years to Robert Ledome of a tenement in Barmeton *alias* Barmeston in the parish of Hawghton in the bishopric of Durham, late of John Swinborne, attainted of treason; with reservations; from Michaelmas last; yearly rent 66s. 8d.; the lessee to pay all charges; also to find a sufficient man with horse and arms to serve in the North when required by the warden of the East marches as accustomed, and to fence the premises as ordered by the steward of the Queen's court there. In consideration of the surrender by Ledome of an indenture, 5 April, 3 Edw. VI, whereby the said John Swynborne of Chopwell, co. Durham, leased the tenement to Richard Hall and Margaret his wife for 21 years from the death of William Cragges, the late tenant, at the same rent; and for a fine of £10 paid at the Exchequer.   By the commissioners by virtue of the Queen's warrant.

600.) 27 *July* 1576. *Gorhambury.* Lease for 21 years to Robert Cotton,   [*m.* 13] yeoman of the wardrobe of beds, of (1) lands (*tenants named*) in Otteryngham, co. York, parcel of the manor of Otteryngham, once of the monastery of Melsa *alias* Meux, co. York, (2) lands (*named*) in Warhorne, Orleston and elsewhere,   [*m.* 14] in Warhorne and Orleston, in Bilsington, in Snave and in Strongwer Warhorne, parcels of the manor of Warhorne, co. Kent, late of Thomas Wyatt, knight, exchanged, (3) lands (*named with tenants' names*) in Leedes and Hollingborne, co. Kent, late of the monastery of Leedes, (4) lands (*tenants named*) called Frithe of Drossecoydes and Frithe of Buladulyn in the commote of Iscor', co. Caernarvon, parcels of the principality of North Wales, (5) lands (*named with tenant's name*) in Wingham, co. Kent, late of the late archbishop of Canterbury, (6) lands (*named*) in Newbiggyng in Teisdale and in Middleton in Teisdale, parcels of the lordship of Barnardcastell, in the bishopric of Durham, and (7) lands (*tenants named*) in Alderton *alias* Aldrington, co. Northampton, parcels of the manor of Alderton, now annexed to the honour of Grafton, co. Northampton; with reservations; (1) from Michaelmas 1579 or the termination of a lease thereof by patent, 10 Dec., 4 & 5 Ph. & Mary, to Roger Strete for 21 years from Michaelmas then next at a yearly rent of £4 2s.; (2) from the death of Anne, duchess of Somerset, to whom the manor of Warhorne was granted by

patent, 20 [*recte* 27] Feb., 2 & 3 Ph. & Mary, *inter alia* for life; (3) from Lady Day 1585, having been leased by patent of the Exchequer, 28 June, 6 Eliz., to Richard Lambe *inter alia* for 21 years from Lady Day then last at yearly rents of 9*s*. (Leedes) and 37*s*. 7*d*. (Hollingborne); (4) from Michaelmas 1592, having been leased by patent, 12 April, 8 Eliz., to William Warde, Lewis Lloyde and William Edwards *inter alia* for 21 years from Michaelmas 1571 at yearly rents of 68*s*. 8*d*. (Drossecoyde) and 47*s*. 4*d*. (Baladulyn); (5), (6) and (7) from Michaelmas 1589, having been leased severally by patents of the Exchequer (5) 27 May, 10 Eliz., to Thomas Palmer for 21 years from Michaelmas then last at a yearly rent of 53*s*. 4*d*., (6) 5 Feb., 11 Eliz., to Cuthbert Baynbrigge for 21 years from Michaelmas then last at yearly   [*m*. 15]
rents of 7*s*. 6*d*. (Midleton in Teisdall) and 28*s*. and 4*s*. (Newbyggynge in Teisdall) and (7) 28 Feb., 11 Eliz., to Richard Bradley for 21 years from Michaelmas then last at yearly rents of 21*s*. 4*d*. and 32*s*. 2*d*.; yearly rents (1) £4 2*s*., (2) £9 5*s*. 4*d*., (3) 46*s*. 4*d*., (4) £5 8*s*., (5) 53*s*. 4*d*., (6) 39*s*. 6*d*. and (7) 53*s*. 6*d*.; the lessee to cause the premises in Newbigging to be occupied, to find a sufficient man or sufficient men with horse and arms to serve in the North when commanded by the warden or lieutenant of the marches and to bear all other services and charges for the said premises according to the custom of the country, also to fence them as ordered by the steward or other the Queen's commissioners there. For his service.

By p.s.

601.)   25 *July* 1576.   *Gorhambury*.   Lease for 31 years to Richard Warde,   [*m*. 16] cofferer of the household, of (1) a water mill called Sandford Myllne with the tolls and customs belonging thereto, lands etc. (*named*) in the lordship of Sonnyng and Wymershe in the parish of Hurste, co. Berks, and all lands in Sonnynge, Wymershe and Hurste which Richard Restwolde late held of the bishop of Salisbury by copy of court roll of the manor of Sonnynge, (2) 'the Easte Parke' in Sonnyng (*described*) and (3) the herbage of 'le Holme Parke' in Sonnyng with 'lez lawndes' and meadows (*named*) belonging thereto, all parcels of the manor of Sonnynge and Eye and late of the bishop of Salisbury;   [*m*. 17] with reservations; (1) from Lady Day 1602, having been leased by Edmund, late bishop of Salisbury, by indenture, 1 May 1522, to Ralph Thompson for 80 years from Lady Day then last at a yearly rent of £3 6*s*. and 17*s*. 6*d*. for eel silver; (2) from Michaelmas 1606, having been leased by John, late bishop of Salisbury, by indenture, 22 Nov., 36 Hen. VIII, to John Sandes of Sonnynge (woods with all regalities except fishings reserved) for 61 years from Michaelmas then next at a yearly rent of 53*s*. 4*d*.; (3) from Michaelmas 1583, having been leased by John, late bishop of Salisbury, by indenture, 30 Sept., 32 Hen. VIII, to John Barnabye for 43 years from Michaelmas then last at a yearly rent of £6 and 10 cartloads of hay, to be delivered into the bishop's barn in Sonnyng, or 40*s*. at the bishop's choice; yearly rents (1) £4 3*s*. 6*d*., (2) 53*s*. 4*d*. and (3) £8. For his service.   By p.s.

602.)   20 *Sept*. 1576.   *Gorhambury*.   Assignment to William Killigrewe, a groom of the privy chamber, of a lease to the Queen (at her special instance and in consideration of a certain sum paid by her) by Thomas Hearle, master   [*m*. 18] or warden, and the fellows chaplains of the college of St. Mary, Manchester, co. Lancaster, of the foundation of King Philip and Queen Mary by indenture, 12 Dec., 18 Eliz., of the tithes of corn in (1) Hulme by Stopforde, (2) Blakeley, (3) Cleyton *alias* Clayton, Fayleswourth and Drylesden, (4) Ancotes, (5) Gorton, (6) Bexwicke, (7) Denton and Haughton, (8) Harperhey, (9) Kerdsall, (10) Kerdmanshull, (11) Rusheholme, (12) Heyfeilde, (13) Brownage, (14) Ordshall, (15) Manchester, (16) Broughton, (17) Chetham, (18) Lenshulme *alias* Leyshulme with Hulmesmore, (19) Chorleton, (20) Tetlowe, (21) Diddesburye and Wythington and (22) Salforde, co. Lancaster, at a yearly rent of £86 14*s*., to wit, for (1) 15*s*., (2) £6, (3) £10, (4) 18*s*., (5) £8, (6) 15*s*., (7) £10, (8) 28*s*., (9) 13*s*. 4*d*., (10)

30s., (11) £5 6s. 8d., (12) 10s., (13) 26s., (14) £3 6s. 8d., (15) 53s. 4d., (16) £5, (17) 50s., (18) £3, (19) 53s. 4d., (20) 22s., (21) £16 and (22) £3 6s. 8d., for 40 years from the termination of a lease thereof by patent of the duchy of Lancaster, 16 March, 3 Edw. VI, to Robert Bull for 31 years from Easter then last; without payment to the Crown so long as he holds the premises by virtue of the lease to the Crown and pays the rent to the college, and thereafter rendering to the Crown £86 14s. yearly; also grant to him of a bond whereby the warden and fellows are bound to the Crown in £700 to perform covenants mentioned in the indenture (which indenture and bond are held in the Exchequer) and all rights of the Crown therein against the college; if the indenture and lease shall be void in law, then, notwithstanding that the premises should have come to the Crown by stat. 1 Eliz. for the dissolution of colleges and the like, the assignee may after the expiry of Bull's lease have the premises for the whole term of 40 years.   For his service.   By Q.

603.)   20 *July* 1576.   *Gorhambury*.   Lease for 21 years to Henry Knolles, the Queen's servant, of the manor and the rectory of Lewesham, co. Kent, once of Shene priory, co. Surrey, and afterwards parcel of lands exchanged with John, late earl of Warwick; with reservations, including wards, marriages and the like and three meadows of the yearly value of 26s. 8d., parcel of the manor; from Lady Day last; yearly rent £33 3s. 3d.; the lessee to provide entertainment for the   [*m.* 19]
Queen's surveyor and steward coming to the manor to hold courts or make a survey; he shall within three years deliver to the auditor of the county new rentals of the premises altering the names of the tenants who have departed from their tenures or died, and shall renew the bounds of the demesne lands; he shall also renew the rentals every seven years and shall deliver the rentals, writings of lands and court rolls to the same auditor at the end of the term; he shall also at the end of the term leave sown with good corn as many acres of land as Robert Cheseman and Bernard Cavell of Cheseherste received at their entry into the premises under a lease made to them by the priory; the Crown to discharge him of a yearly pension payable to the bishop of Rochester. On surrender by Knolles by deed, 4 July last, enrolled in Chancery, of his interest in the premises, except the three meadows above reserved, by virtue of a patent, 8 May, 5 Eliz., leasing the manor and rectory *inter alia* to him for 21 years from Michaelmas 1566 or the termination of the interest of Edmund Fourde at the same rent. For a fine of £30 paid at the Exchequer.   By p.s.

604.)   3 *Aug.* 1576.   *Gorhambury*.   Confirmation of the estate of John Worseley of Appledercombe in the isle of Wight, co. Southampton, and Thomas Worseley and Richard Worseley, his sons, in the manor or priory of Appledercombe, by virtue of a grant thereof by Dorothy Comberford, abbess, and the convent   [*m.* 20]
of the monastery of minoresses without Algate, London (whose right the Crown now holds) by indenture, 17 Dec., 19 Hen. VIII, to John Worseley, knight, and Anne his wife, their heirs and assigns in fee farm (all lands in Wolvelegh, co. Berks, reserved) at a yearly rent of £56 13s. 4d., £6 13s 4d. to be paid as relief or heriot on the death of each successive holder of the lands, with covenants for cesser in case of non-payment of the rent or the relief; and pardon for them of any breaches of the said covenants; reserving to the Crown the said rent and relief; the grantees covenant that for every default in payment within one month of the rent or relief they shall forfeit £5; the Crown covenants not to take advantage of any condition in the said indenture, and also that the grantees can pay the rent and relief to the receiver of Crown revenues in the isle of Wight or his deputy. For the service of the said John Worseley of Appledercombe.   By p.s.

605.)   30 *July* 1576.   *Gorhambury*.   Lease for 21 years to James Walley of (1) lands called 'Bodehowse' in Selsey, co. Sussex, given for lights in the church there, (2) lands (*tenant named*) in Femersham, co. Bedford, late of the monastery of Caldwell, (3) lands (*tenant named*) in Aspley Gyes, co. Bedford, late of chantries and the like in the Crown's hands by act of Parliament, and (4) a coney warren in Milbroke, co. Bedford, parcel of the honour of Ampthill, co. Bedford; with reservations; from Lady Day last; yearly rents (1) 8*d*., (2) 6*d*., (3) 2*s*. and (4) £7; the lessee to discharge the Crown   [*m.* 21] of the wages of the keeper of the warren and all other charges out of the warren; he shall have in the Queen's woods near the warren sufficient 'trappewood' for the warren, as accustomed. In consideration of his surrender in Chancery of a patent, 30 Oct., 8 Eliz., leasing the warren to him for 21 years from Michaelmas then last at the same rent; and for a fine of £14 12*s*. 8*d*. paid at the Exchequer.

> By the commissioners by virtue of the Queen's warrant.

606.) 23 *July* 1576. *Gorhambury*. Lease for 21 years to Arthur Dyneley of the site and capital messuage of the manor of Houghton and all lands and pastures in Pountefracte park belonging to the said messuage as accustomed, co. York, once of the monastery of St. Oswald, co. York; with reservations; from Michaelmas next; yearly rent £10; the lessee to provide entertainment for the Queen's steward and surveyor coming to the manor to hold courts or make a survey. In consideration of his surrender of a patent, 26 June, 6 Eliz., leasing the premises to him for 21 years from Lady Day then last at the same rent; and for a fine of £20 paid at the Exchequer.

> By the commissioners by virtue of the Queen's warrant.

607.) 17 *July* 1576. Lease for 21 years to John Hawforde of (1) a   [*m.* 22] messuage (*tenant named*) in Kegworth, cos. Leicester and Nottingham, and (2) two water corn mills there (*tenant named*), parcels of the jointure of Helen, marchioness of Northampton; with reservations; from Lady Day last; yearly rent £11. In consideration of the surrender by Hawforde of an indenture, 20 Nov., 15 Eliz., whereby the marchioness leased the premises to Richard Jones for her life at yearly rents of (1) £3 and (2) £8; and for a fine of £11 paid at the Exchequer.

> By the commissioners by virtue of the Queen's warrant.

608.) 20 *Aug.* 1576. *Gorhambury*. Grant in fee simple to Robert, earl of Leicester, baron of Denbigh, knight of the garter and of St. Michael, master of the horse, councillor, of a market every Wednesday in his town or borough of Kenelworthe, co. Warwick, and a yearly fair there on the eve, day and morrow of the feast of the Nativity of St. John the Baptist.   By p.s.

609.) 30 *July* 1576. *Gorhambury*. Lease for 21 years to Roger Dalton of lands (*tenants named*) in Osgarbye, co. York, parcels of the manor of Osgarbye and late of John Wyvell, attainted; with reservations; from Lady Day   [*m.* 23] last; yearly rent £8 5*s*. 10*d*. In consideration of the surrender by Dalton of a patent, 23 May, 4 Eliz., leasing to Richard Woode the premises by the name of lands (*tenants named*) in Osgarbye, parcels of the manor of Osgarbye, and lands (*tenants named*) [in Kayton, co. York, parcels of the same manor,][1] for 21 years from Lady Day then last at the same rent (*detailed*); and for a fine of £16 11*s*. 8*d*. paid at the Exchequer.

> By the commissioners by virtue of the Queen's warrant.

610.) 30 *July* 1576. *Gorhambury*. Lease for 40 years to Edward Bigges of two water

---

[1] The locality is not specified in this patent; but *cf*. the enrolment of the patent of 23 May, 4 Eliz. [*Calendar*, 1560–1563, p. 361].

mills called Rookholte Mylles and Temple Mylles under one roof in Hackney and Leighton, cos. Middlesex and Essex, on 'the Sherestreame', and all lands now or late in the tenure of John Mustyan, parcel of the manor   [m. 24] of Hackney, late of the hospital of St. John of Jerusalem in England; from Lady Day last; yearly rent £11 6s. 8d.; the lessee to pay all quit rents and other charges ordinary and extraordinary. In consideration of the surrender by Bigges of an indenture, 1 June 1531, whereby William Weston, knight, prior, and the knights of the hospital leased to the said John Mustian of Westham, co. Essex, 'myller', the premises, by the name of Rokeholte Mylles *alias* Temple Mylles, 7 ac. of meadow called Hartlake in the meadow of Hackney and all other lands theretofore leased with the mills to Henry Knyght late of Stratford at Bowe, co. Middlesex, 'myller', for 60 years from Lady Day then last at the same rent.

By the commissioners by virtue of the Queen's warrant.

611.)   20 *July* 1576.   *Gorhambury*.   Lease for 21 years to George, earl of Shrewsbury, K.G., of rents of 70 quarters of barley and 6 quarters of wheat yearly reserved on a lease *inter alia* of the rectory of Sutton on Trent, co. Nottingham, to John Knyfton for 40 years; from Lady Day last; yearly rent £16. In consideration of the surrender by the said earl in Chancery of a patent, 20 July, 11 Eliz., leasing to Thomas Knyfton the premises, by the name of 70 quarters of barley and 6 quarters of wheat reserved on a lease of the said rectory for 40 years to William Matteley, for the years remaining of the said 40 years at the same rent; and for a fine of £16 paid at the Exchequer.   By p.s.

612.)   23 *July* 1576.   *Gorhambury*.   Commitment for 30 years (by mainprise in the Exchequer) to Thomas Cleburne of the farm or keeping of a close called Hayeclose in Englewood forest, co. Cumberland; from Lady Day last; yearly rent £6 13s. 4d. and 5s. beyond of increase; provided that, if anyone will give more of increase for the farm, Cleburne shall be bound to pay so much if he wishes to have it.   By treasurer's bill.

613.)   20 *July* 1576.   *Gorhambury*.   Commitment for 30 years (by mainprise in [—]) to Richard Kyrkebryde of the farm or keeping of a tenement called Ellerton in Englewood forest, co. Cumberland, once in the tenure of   [m. 25] John Belson and now in that of Kyrkebryde; from Lady Day last; yearly rent 101s. and 6s. 8d. beyond of increase; provided as above (*no.* 612).   By treasurer's bill.

614.)   30 *July* 1576.   *Gorhambury*.   Lease for 21 years to Richard Williams of a yearly rent of 24 quarters and 2 'lez bolles' of barley payable by the tenants in the township of Ambell, co. Northumberland, once of Tynmouth priory; from Lady Day last; yearly rent £6 2s. 6d. For a fine of £6 2s. 6d. paid at the Exchequer.

By the commissioners by virtue of the Queen's warrant.

615.)   8 *Nov.* 1576.   Pardon of alienation for Rowland Baugh, Nicholas Tykerynge, 'yoman', and Thomas Tykerynge, his son, Thomas Sambage, 'husbondman', Ralph Savage, John Hadock, 'husbondman', James Davys, 'husbondman', John Cotterell, 'husbondman', John Wyatt, clerk, and Thomas Brevell the younger, 'husbondman', to whom by indenture, 21 June, 17 Eliz., Miles Sandes, John Popham, George Fetyplace and Matthew Smythe conveyed lands (*named with tenants' names*) in Snowshill, co. Gloucester. For £5 paid to the Queen's farmer.

616.)   1 *Oct.* 1576.   The like: Thomas Myldmaye, knight, and Frances his wife in Michaelmas term, 17 Eliz., conveyed by fine in the Common Pleas to Francis Wyndam the manors of Asshewood in Pentney and West Bylney, lands in Pentney, West Bilney, Watton,

Estwalton and Gayton Thorpe *alias* Ayleswithorpe and the rectories of Pentney and West Bylney, co. Norfolk.   For £40.

617.)   7 *Nov.* 1576.   The like: Henry Knyvett and Elizabeth his wife in Michaelmas term, 15 Eliz., conveyed by fine in the Common Pleas to John Stumpe and William Knyvett and the heirs of Stumpe lands in Brinkworth, Braydon and the forest of Braydon, co. Wilts.   For 14*s.* 5*d.*

618.)   7 *Nov.* 1576.   The like: Henry Knevett and Elizabeth his wife in Hilary term, 14 Eliz., conveyed by fine in the Common Pleas to Hugh   [*m.* 26] Bampfeilde a capital messuage and lands in Charleton, co. Wilts.   For £6 13*s.* 4*d.*

619.)   1 *Oct.* 1576.   Licence for Stephen Hadnoll and Margaret his wife to alienate lands (including an iron mill) in Cleburye Mortymer, co. Salop, to William Norton.   For 14*s.* 5*d.* paid to the Queen's farmer.

620.)   1 *Oct.* 1576.   The like for the same to alienate lands in Cleburye Mortymer to Richard Bysshopp.   For 9*s.* 1*d.*

621.)   8 *Nov.* 1576.   Pardon of alienation: by indenture, 7 June, 18 Eliz., John Jackson and Asculph Clesbie conveyed *inter alia* to William Waller a third part of (1) the manors of Skelton, Brotton, Langbarghe, Marske, Eston and Yarme and lands in Skelton, Brotton, Langbarghe, Marske, Redker, Upletham, Eston, Yarme, Tunstall, Tampton, Broughton, Whorleton, Hornebie, Apleton, Allethorne, Hackforthe, Ormstable Burton, West Brompton, East Brompton, Newton, Morker, Thorneton Stewerde, Crakall Parva, Aldwerke, Skipton Bridge, Northottrington and Northalverton, co. York, (2) the manor of Kirkbye Neshefill *alias* Kirkbye in Ashefelde, co. Nottingham, and (3) the manor of Belford
                                                                                        [*m.* 27]
and Wuller *alias* Wolmer, co. Northumberland.   For £33 10*s.* paid to the Queen's farmer.

622.)   1 *Oct.* 1576.   Licence for John Marston to alienate a tenement in 'le Olde Chaunge' in the parish of St. Vedast *alias* Saynt Faister, London, in the tenure of Thomas Tounley, 'vyntner', to Henry Goodere.   For 20*s.* paid to the Queen's farmer.

623.)   1 *Oct.* 1576.   The like for Henry, earl of Arundell, John Lumley, knight, lord Lumley, and Jane his wife and Thomas Sackvile, knight, lord Buckhurst, and Cecily his wife to alienate lands in Gorynge, co. Sussex, and the rectory and the advowson of the vicarage of Gorynge (all liberties and franchises of the earl reserved) to Thomas Mychell.   For £3 6*s.* 8*d.*

624.)   1 *Oct.* 1576.   The like for Fitz Ralph Chamberleyne and Dorothy his wife, Richard Skipwith, William Mallowes, George Agar and Paul Pope and Catherine his wife to alienate the manor of Bechewood *alias* St. Gyles in le Wood and lands in Flamstede, Stodham and Gaddesden, cos. Hertford and Bedford, to Richard Smythe and Thomas Smythe and the heirs and assigns of Richard.   For £3 6*s.* 8*d.*

625.)   1 *Oct.* 1576.   The like for Thomas Pygott and Valentine Pygott to alienate the manor of Bradwell and lands in Bradwell and Wolverton *alias* Wolvrington, co. Buckingham, to Francis Haydon and Arthur Longeville and the heirs of Arthur to the use of Arthur and Judith his wife, as Judith's jointure, during her lifetime and thereafter of Arthur and his heirs.   For £6 13*s.* 4*d.*

626.) 1 *Oct.* 1576. The like for William Cardynall and Joan his wife [*m.* 28] to alienate lands (*named*) in Colchester, co. Essex, to John Pye and Thomas Barker to the use of Alice Maynerd for life and thereafter of Elizabeth Maynerd and her heirs and assigns. For 28*s.* 2*d.*

627.) 1 *Oct.* 1576. The like for Clement Fynche to alienate the rectory of Seynt Jeames in the isle of Grayne, co. Kent, with the advowson of the vicarage of the same to William Cobham, knight, lord Cobham. For £4 9*s.*

628.) 1 *Oct.* 1576. The like for Reginald Knathchebull to alienate the manor of Saltwood and lands in Saltwood, Heth, West Heth, Lymme, Aldyngton, Newington, Postling, Stamford, Mersham, Ruckinges, Bilsington, Woodchurche and Kyngesnothe, co. Kent, to John Cryspe and Richard Vyncent and the heirs and assigns of Cryspe. For £6 13*s.* 4*d.*

629.) 13 *Nov.* 1576. The like for William Anstie and Anne his wife to alienate the manors of Bromehame *alias* Bromehame Baynton, Chippenham and Chippeham Stanley and lands in Bromeham *alias* Bromeham Baynton, Bromeham Clenche, Wotton Rivers, Milton Chirrell, Calne, Chippenham and Stanley, co. Wilts, to Edward Baynton, knight. For £10.

630.) 1 *Nov.* 1576. The like for Edward, earl of Oxford, to alienate lands (*named with tenants' names*) [*m.* 29] in the parish of Thornecombe, co. Devon, to Thomas Walker. For 31*s.* 8*d.*

631.) 20 *Sept.* 1576. The like for William Inglebye, knight, and Anne his wife and William Inglebye and Catherine his wife to alienate lands in Hartwith and Lareton, parcel of the manor of Brymbem *alias* Brymham, co. York, to James Bucke. For 11*s.* 6*d.*

632.) 20 *Sept.* 1576. The like for the same to alienate lands in Hartwith and Lareton, parcel of the manor of Brymbem *alias* Brymham, to Thomas Haxebye and Jenet his wife and the heirs and assigns of Thomas. For 10*s.*

633.) 20 *Sept.* 1576. The like for the same to alienate lands in Hartwith and Lareton, parcel of the manor of Brymbem *alias* Brymham, to Stephen Snawe. [*m.* 30] For 6*s.* 9*d.*

634.) 20 *Sept.* 1576. The like for the same to alienate lands in Wynesley and Lareton, parcel of the manor of Brymbem *alias* Brymham, to John Raynerd and Helen his wife and the heirs and assigns of John. For 6*s.* 3*d.*

635.) 20 *Sept.* 1576. The like for Lewis Mordaunte, knight, lord Mordaunte, and Elizabeth his wife and Henry Darcye, knight, and Catherine his wife to alienate lands in Bewerley *alias* Beverley and a moiety of the manor of Bewerley *alias* Beverley, co. York, to Thomas Benson. For £9 2*d.*

636.) 6 *Nov.* 1576. The like for Nicholas Clyfton and Anne his wife to alienate the manor of Clyfton and lands in Clyfton, Chaseley *alias* Chatisley, Horgell, Chappell, Crombe Symondes *alias* Erles Crome and Defforde, co. Worcester, to Francis Clyfton. For 33*s.* 4*d.*

637.) 28 *May* 1576. The like for Wistan Browne to alienate a third part of the manors of Warmyster and Westbury *alias* Mawdittes in Westburye, co. Wilts, and of the hundred of Warmyster to George Tuchett, lord Awdley, and James Mervyn, knight. For £11 13*s.* 9*d.*

638.)   1 *Oct.* 1576. The like for Amyas Powlett, knight, and Margaret   [*m.* 31]
his wife to alienate (1) the manors of Monken Seale *alias* Seale Monachorum, Loosebeare
and Stockley Pryerton, lands in Monkenseale *alias* Zeale Monachorum, Loosebeare,
Marydowe, Bowe, Lapford, Cheryton Episcopi, Nymprowlande, Bawdeley, Colridge,
Wynkeleigh, Brassheford, Stokeley Pryerton, Kyrton *alias* Credyton, Sandford, Stockeley
and Stockelinche, free warren and view of frankpledge in Monkenseale, Lapford and
Cheryton Episcopi, free warren and view of frankpledge in Stockeley Pryerton and
Credyton and the advowson of Zeale Monachorum church, co. Devon, (2) the manor of
Marshwood *alias* Marshoode *alias* Marshton, lands in Marshood, Whitchurche, Catherston
Lewson, Stock Atram, Wotton Fitzpayne, Wotton Abbatis, Colwaye, Pillesden, Wyle,
Staunton Gabriell, Chidiocke and Symondesboroughe, Marshwood park, and free warren
and view of frankpledge in Marshood, co. Dorset, and (3) the manor of Wynsford Ryvears,
lands in Wynsford Ryvers, Wynsford Bozome, Hawkeridge, Exton, Exford and Dulverton
and free warren and view of frankpledge in Wynsford Ryvers, co. Somerset, to Thomas
Forteskue and Thomas Rawe and the heirs and assigns of Forteskewe.   For £24.

639.)   20 *Sept.* 1576.   The like for William Inglebye, knight, and Anne his wife and
William Inglebye and Catherine his wife to alienate lands in Hartworthe, Wynnesley and
Lareton, parcel of the manor of Brambem *alias* Bramham, co. York, to Robert Harcastell
and Christopher Hardcastell, his son, and the heirs and assigns of Christopher.   For 5*s.* 6*d.*

640.)   28 *May* 1576.   The like for Thomas Wilford and Mary his wife, Catherine Browne
and John Tufton and Christian his wife to alienate a third part of the manors of Warmyster
and Westburye *alias* Mawdittes in Westburye, co. Wilts, and of the hundred of Warmyster,
to George Tuchett, lord Audley.   For £11 13*s.* 9*d.*

641.)   20 *Sept.* 1576.   The like for John Singleton and James Singleton to alienate lands in
Wynnesley and Lareton, parcel of the manor of Brymbem   [*m.* 32]
alias Brymham, co. York, to Robert Longe.   For 8*s.* 1*d.*

642.)   20 *Sept.* 1576.   The like for William Inglebye, knight, and Anne his wife and
William Inglebye and Catherine his wife to alienate lands in Hartwith and Lareton, parcel of
the manor of Brymbem *alias* Brymham, co. York, to William Hardcastell and Margaret his
wife and the heirs and assigns of Hardcastell.   For 2*s.* 9*d.*

643.)   20 *Sept.* 1576.   The like for the same to alienate lands in Wynnesley and Lareton,
parcel of the manor of Brymbem *alias* Brymham, to Thomas Burnett.   For 12*s.* 6*d.*

644.)   20 *Sept.* 1576.   The like for John Smythe and Dorothy his wife to alienate lands in
Wynnesley, Hartwith, Felbeck and Lareton, parcel of the manor of Brymbem *alias*
Brymham, co York, to James Brathwaite.   For 18*s.*

645.)   1 *Oct.* 1576.   The like for Robert Whyte to alienate a house, manor or capital
messuage called Bordley Hall in Nether Bordley in Craven, lands (*named with tenants' names*)
in Nether Bordley and Over Bordley, lands   [*m.* 33]
(*tenant named*) in Bumsall, Over Bordley, Nether Bordley, Hetton, Kirkbye and Malholme,
10 parts of a great close called Mascells Close divided into 26 parts in Hetton, Malhame or
the parish of Burnesall, 10 parts of unenclosed waste lands in Hetton, Over Bordley, Nether
Bordley and Malhame or in Burnesall divided into 26 parts, a sheep pasture for 'le flock
rayke' called Highe Marke and all his other lands in Craven, co. York, to John
Proctor.   For £3 13*s.* 4*d.*

646.)   1 *Oct.* 1576.   The like for Edward, earl of Oxford, to alienate lands (*tenant named*) at Syndersforde in the parish of Thornecombe, co. Devon, parcel of the manor of Thornecombe, to John Coffer.   For 7*s.* 2*d.*

647.)   23 *Oct.* 1576.   The like for Henry, earl of Arundell, John Lumley, knight, lord Lumley, and Jane his wife and Rowland Haywarde, knight, to alienate the manor of Stretton *alias* Churchestretton and lands in Stretton *alias* Churchestretton, Allstretton, Lytelstretton, Botfelde and Mynton, co. Salop, to Richard Warren and Francis Bowyer to the use successively of Haywarde and Joan his wife for life, of John Thyne and Joan his wife in tail and of the right heirs of Haywarde.   For £6.

648.)   14 *Sept.* 1576.   *Gorhambury.*   Grant to Adam Blande, skinner, the Queen's servant, and Humphrey Blande and the heirs and assigns of Adam of—(1) 'the Brotherhedd Hall' in Layton, co. Bedford, (*tenant named*); (2) the rectory of Bodewred *alias* Bodwred, co. Anglesey, once of Penman priory; (3) the rectory of Wrotton and the rectory of Wereham, co. Norfolk, once of the monastery [*sic*] of Westdereham and Sholdeham or one of them, co.
[*m.* 34]
Norfolk; (4) lands (*named with tenant's name*) in Woodham Mortimor, co. Essex, once of Bileigh priory, co. Essex; (5) lands (*named with tenants' names*) in the manor of Mouncton, co. Brecon, once of Brecknock priory; (6) lands (*tenants named*) in Hemmyngfad Greye, co. Huntingdon, once of the monastery of Chatteras; (7) lands (*named with tenants' names*) in Burye, co. Suffolk, once of the monastery of Burye St. Edmunds; (8) lands (*tenants named*) in Esterkele and Westerkele, co. Lincoln, once of the hospital of St. John of Jerusalem; (9) lands (*tenant named*) in Wolley, co. Huntingdon, once of Stonley priory, co. Huntingdon; and (10) lands (*tenant named*) in Barnebye in the parish of Blythe, co. Nottingham, once of the monastery of Blithe. To hold as of the manor of Estgrenewiche, co. Kent, in socage. Issues from Michaelmas 1574. The grantees charged with the yearly payment out of (2) for proxies and synodals of 20*d.* to the bishop of Bangor and 15*d.*   [*m.* 35]
to the archdeacon of Anglesey. The grantees at their own charges to cause the cures of Wrotton and Wereham churches to be served as is fitting.

In compensation for the rectory of Brokeworthe, co. Gloucester, which being of the yearly value of £4 19*s.* 4*d.* was by patent, 5 April, 16 Eliz., and in consideration of divers lands conveyed by Robert, earl of Leicester, councillor, to the Crown in exchange, granted to the said earl *inter alia* in fee simple, but, because it was granted by another patent of Henry VIII to John Guynes and his heirs, the earl cannot have it; at the suit of the said Adam; and for Adam's service.   By p.s.

649.)   8 *Oct.* 1576.   Pardon of alienation: Nicholas Webbe by fine in the Common Pleas in Easter term, 18 Eliz., acquired from Thomas Essex lands in Badburye, co. Wilts.   For 26*s.* paid to the Queen's farmer.

(The dorse of this roll is blank.)

PART VII

C. 66/1143

650.)   16 *Dec.* 1575.   Lease for 21 years to Robert Bocher of the   [*m.* 1]
site and capital messuage of the manor of Dengmershe, co. Kent, the dead stock belonging
to the same site and all appurtenances heretofore leased therewith to Thomas Stughill and
William Bucher, deceased, the said Robert's father, late of the monastery of Batle, co.
Sussex; with reservations, including lands (*named*), the rent and customs of the manor with
perquisities of courts and hundreds there and all liberties once granted by charters of the
Kings of England to the said monastery, the place accustomed for courts and hundreds
there, with salage, fish called 'craspeis', 'sturgeons', 'purpris' and whales, cabins by the sea,
profits of the cabins and fishings, with wreck of the sea, savings and findings on the
demesnes of the manor, and fisheries (*named*); from Michaelmas last; yearly rent £22; the
lessee to repair and maintain sea walls and drains (*described*), to pay all tenths and subsidies
granted to the Crown and all water scots assessed on lands of the manor, and to provide
entertainment   [*m.* 2]
for the Queen's steward and surveyor coming to the manor to hold courts and make a
survey. In consideration of the surrender in Chancery by the said Robert of a patent, 16
Dec., 12 Eliz., leasing the premises to his father for 21 years from Michaelmas then last at the
same rent; and for a fine of £22 paid at the Exchequer.   By p.s.

651.)   16 *Dec.* 1575.   Lease for 21 years to Richard Vaughan, Thomas Gwynne, Jevan ap
Robert and Margaret Thomas of (1) the town of Penmen in the commote of Gaffogion, (2)
the town of Towen and (3) the hamlet of Pengogo, (4) the town of Tyndowith and the
hamlet of Cruckgarren and (5) the town of Penmer Vyneth (*alias* Pennervineth) in the
commote of Kemytmayne, all in the county of Carnarvon and parcels of the principality of
North Wales; with reservations; from Michaelmas last; yearly rents (1) 31s., (2) 117s. 6d., (3)
19s. 5d., (4) 70s. 8d. and (5) 58s. 10d. In consideration of the surrender by the said Richard,
Thomas, Jevan and Margaret of a patent, 12 July,   [*m.* 3]
9 Eliz., leasing the premises to Robert Vaughan and Thomas Gwynne for 30 years from
Lady Day then last at the same rents; and for a certain sum paid at the Exchequer.   By p.s.

652.)   30 *Dec.* 1575.   Lease for 21 years to John Carlile of lands (*tenants named*) in Newham
and Staxbye in the parish of Whitbye, co. York, parcels of the manor of Staxbye, late of the
monastery of Whitbye; with reservations; from Michaelmas last; yearly rent £6 17s. 1½d.
                                                                                   [*m.* 4]
(*detailed*), also rendering yearly rents and payments for 'lez multure sylver' for lands (*named*)
which the tenants ought and have been wont to pay; the lease to be void in respect of any
parcel of the premises from which the present tenant shall be expelled by the lessee or of
which the tenant shall not be given a lease by him before Midsummer next for the whole
term at the rent specified, so long as the tenants will pay the lessee among themselves his
costs about obtaining this patent. In consideration of the surrender by Carlile of a patent, 8
July, 3 & 5 Ph. & Mary, leasing the premises to him for 30 years from Lady Day then last at
the same rent; and for a fine of £13 14s. 3d. paid at the Exchequer.
                    By the commissioners by virtue of the Queen's warrant.

653.)   16 *Dec.* 1575.   Lease for 21 years to Ralph Conyers of the capital tenement and site of the mansion of Leyton in the bishopric of Durham and lands (*named*); with reservations; from Michaelmas last; yearly rent during the lives of George and Mary Conyers £14 13*s.* 4*d.*; the lessee   [*m.* 5]
to discharge the Crown from the yearly payment of £10 for the annuity of George Conyers for his life, 100*s.* out of a close (*named*) for the annuity of Mary Conyers, widow, Ralph's mother, for her life, £26 13*s.* 4*d.* for the third part of the lands aforesaid in Leyton granted to the said Mary Conyers, wife of Cuthbert Conyers, Ralph's father, for life and 53*s.* 4*d.* due to the Crown in right of the late monastery of Blaunchlande, co. Northumberland, and also from the payment of £21 payable, as it is said, from time to time to John Eden; after the respective deaths of George and Mary Conyers the lessee shall pay to the Crown the annuities now severally payable to them. In consideration of the surrender by the said Ralph in Chancery of a patent, 18 Feb., 17 Eliz., leasing the premises to Thomas Cotton for 21 years from Michaelmas then last at a yearly rent of £59; and because he has undertaken to pay the said annuities to George and Mary Conyers.   By p.s.

654.)   20 *Jan.* 1576.   Lease to Henry Sacheverell of Grais Inne, co.   [*m.* 6]
Middlesex, of the manors of Morley, Hopwell, Snitterton, Calowe and Bolton, co. Derby, the manor of Saddington, co. Leicester, and lands in Morley, Hopwell, Snytterton, Calowe, Bolton, Smalley, Kiddesley, Kilborne, Horseley, Woodhowse, Chadsden, Sandie Acre, Thurlaston, Aston on Trent, Chelaston, Willington, Darbye, Querndon, Duffeilde, Belper, Wyndeley, Thurnediche, Risley, Workesworthe, Bonsall, Mattock, Windslee, Alsopp in le Dale, Hartington, Alporte, Staunton, Staunton Lez, Holbroke and Spendon, co. Derby, late of John Sacheverell and forfeited because he had departed into foreign parts and abides there contrary to statute; wards, marriages, goods of felons and outlaws and advowsons reserved; from Michaelmas last, during the life of the said John, so long as the premises remain in the Crown's hands by his forfeitures; yearly rent £200; the lessee to cut the underweeds of the premises at fitting seasons, to enclose them after cutting, and to leave sufficient 'lez staddles' in every acre of woodland according to statute; also to bear all charges. On surrender after grave consideration of a patent, 27 June, 15 Eliz., (hereby pronounced void) leasing the premises to   [*m.* 7]
George Rolleston during the forfeiture of the said John at the same rent. By advice of the treasurer, the chancellor of the Exchequer and the barons there.   By p.s.

655.)   30 *Dec.* 1575.   Lease for 21 years to Walter Serle of lands (*named with tenants' names*) (1) in the lordship of Haveringe in the parishes of Hornechurche and Navestock, co. Essex, (2) in the said lordship in the parish of Hornechurche and (3) in the liberties of Havering and Navestock in the parish of Navestock, all late of Brian Tuke, knight; with reservations; from Michaelmas last; yearly rents (1) £7 6*s.* and (2) and (3) 60*s.* In consideration of the surrender by Serle of the interest of Richard Hale, to whom by patent, 10 March, 4 & 5 Ph. & Mary, the premises were leased for 30 years from Michaelmas then next at the same rents; and for a fine of £20 12*s.* paid at the Exchequer.   [*m.* 8]
                     By the commissioners by virtue of the Queen's warrant.

656.)   9 *Feb.* 1576.   Foundation of the free grammar school of William Lambe in Sutton Vallens, co. Kent; with one master. The said William Lambe of London, 'clothworker', to be governor of the school during his life, and after his death the master and four wardens of the guild of the Assumption of the mistery of 'clothworkers' in London to be governors. Incorporation of the governors. Power for Lambe as governor during his life, and after his death for the master and wardens of the guild in 'their courte of assistantes', to appoint the master and make ordinances for the school. Licence for the governors to acquire for the

maintenance of the school and the relief of the poor in Sutton Vallens lands to   [*m.* 9]
the yearly value of £50.

At the suit of Lambe.   By p.s.

657.)   16 *Dec.* 1575.   Lease for life in succession to George Rodney, Lucretia Rodney, his daughter, and Honor Rodney, his daughter, of the rectory of Boltonsboroughe, co. Somerset, once of the monastery of Glaston, co. Somerset; with reservations; from the present date; yearly rent £8 10*s.* In consideration of the surrender by George of a patent, 4 Feb., 5 Eliz., leasing the rectory to John Dodington for 21 years from Michaelmas then last at the same rent; and for a fine of £17 paid at the Exchequer by him.

By the commissioners by virtue of the Queen's warrant.

658.)   7 *Dec.* 1575.   Lease for 21 years to Edmund Norton of lands   [*m.* 10]
(*tenants named*) in (1) Balderbye, co. York, (*named*), parcels of the manor of Balderbye and once of the monastery of Fountaunce, co. York, and (2) Kirkeby, co. York, late of Michael Tempest, attainted of treason; with reservations; from Michaelmas last; yearly rents (1) 175*s.* 7*d.* (*detailed*) and (2) 20*s.* For a fine of £39 2*s.* 4*d.* paid at the Exchequer by Norton and Thomas Yeoman.

By the commissioners by virtue of the Queen's warrant.

659.)   7 *Dec.* 1575.   Lease for 30 years to John Thynne, knight, of the manor of Kingeston Deverall, co. Wilts, the reversion and fee whereof belongs to the Crown by exchange between Edward VI and Edward, late   [*m.* 11]
duke of Somerset; from the termination of a lease thereof by the said duke by indenture, 24 July, 1 Edw. VI, *inter alia* to Thynne, by the name of John Thynne, steward of the duke's household, for 50 years from Michaelmas then last at a yearly rent of £22 13*s.* 4*d.*; same rent; without fine or fee.   By p.s.

660.)   20 *Jan.* 1576.   Lease for life in survivorship to Mary Corbett, wife of Richard Corbett, Francis Palmes and Vincent Corbett of lands etc. (*tenants named*) in Wardington, co. Oxford, parcels of the manor of Wardington and purchased from John, late earl of Warwick; with reservations; from late Michaelmas last; yearly rent £24. 9*s.* 7½*d.*   [*m.* 12]
For a fine of £33. 6*s.* 8*d* paid at the Exchequer by the said Richard Corbett.   By p.s.

661.)   13 *Feb.* 1576.   Lease for 40 years to Esay Yarner of two water mills called 'Stapull Mills' in Wendlingborough *alias* Wenlingborough, co. Northampton, parcel of lands assigned to the Queen before her accession, once of the monastery of Crowlande, co. Lincoln, and now annexed to   [*m.* 13]
the honour of Grafton; with reservations; from Michaelmas last; yearly rent £6. In consideration of the surrender by the said Esay of a patent, 29 May, 12 Eliz., leasing the mills to John Yarner for 21 years from Lady Day then last at the same rent; and because he offers to undertake the repair of the mills which are in great decay.

By the commissioners by virtue of the Queen's warrant.

662.)   7 *Dec.* 1575.   Lease for 21 years to William Hobbye and Anthony Hodgkyns of portions of tithes (*tenants named*) in (1) Wynchelcombe, co. Gloucester, once of the monastery of Winchelcombe, and (2) Gretton, co. Gloucester, once of the monastery of Tewkesbury, co. Gloucester; from Michaelmas last; yearly rents (1) £6 11*s.* 4*d.* and (2) 7*s.*; the lessees to pay yearly stipends of £10 for a curate in Winchelcombe church and 6*s.* 8*d.* for a priest hired to assist there. In consideration of the surrender in Chancery by the said Anthony, as possessor under the will of Henry Hodgkyn, his grandfather, of a patent, 3

July, 3 Eliz., leasing *inter alia* to the said Henry the premises in (1) for 21 years from Lady Day then last at the same rent; and for a fine of £21 2s. paid at the Exchequer.

By the commissioners by virtue of the Queen's warrant.

663.)   9 *Feb.* 1576.   Lease for 21 years to Robert Boston of the rectory of Hunstanstowe *alias* Hunstanton, co. Norfolk, and the site and other appurtenances thereof, now or late in his tenure and formerly in that of Henry Whitereson, once of the monastery of Haugh-monde, co. Salop; with reservations; from Michaelmas last; yearly rent £8. For a fine of

[*m.* 14]

£8 paid at the Exchequer.

By the commissioners by virtue of the Queen's warrant.

664.)   30 *Jan.* 1576.   Lease for 21 years to Edward Batley of lands (*named with tenants' names*) in (1) Barrowe and Thorneton, co. Lincoln, parcels of the manors there and once of Thorneton college, and (2) Ripham, co. Lincoln, once of the monastery of Barlinges; with reservations; from Michaelmas last; yearly rents from the time when he shall obtain possession (1) 157s. 4d. (*detailed*) and (2) 6s. 8½d. Because he offers at his own costs to prove void an indenture, 2 Oct., 30 Hen. VIII, whereby John, abbot, and the convent of the monastery of Thorneton leased certain of the premises to James Hudson and Anne his wife for 60 years.

By the commissioners by virtue of the Queen's warrant.

665.)   20 *Jan.* 1576.   Lease for 21 years to Thomas Harrys of a   [*m.* 15]
capital messuage in Fencote in the halimote of Stoke, co. Hereford, a tenement (*tenant named*) in Fencote and the herbage of a hereditament called Westwoode *alias* Westwoode Park (*tenant named*), once of the cell or priory of Leomynster, co. Hereford, belonging to the monastery of Readinge, co. Berks; with reservations; from Michaelmas last; yearly rent 50s. 4d. For a fine of £10 16d. paid at the Exchequer.

By the commissioners by virtue of the Queen's warrant.

666.)   9 *Dec.* 1575.   Lease for 21 years to John Williams of tithes in Powlett *alias* Pawlett and Gauntesham, co. Somerset, late of the monastery of St. Augustine; from Michaelmas last; yearly rent £14 from the time when he shall obtain possession. In consideration that he will at his own costs make void in law a conventual indenture fraudulently, it is reported, leasing the premises to Robert Williams.   By p.s.

667.)   9 *Feb.* 1576.   Lease for 21 years to Nicholas Conyers of lands (*named with tenants' names*) in Staxbye, co. York, once of the monastery   [*m.* 16]
of Whitbye, co. York; with reservations; from Michaelmas last; yearly rents 40s. and 61s. In consideration of the surrender by the said Nicholas of a patent, 16 May, 3 Eliz., leasing the premises to George Conyers for 21 years from Lady Day then next at the same rents; and for a fine of £15 3s. paid at the Exchequer.

By the commissioners by virtue of the Queen's warrant.

668.)   30 *Jan.* 1576.   Lease for 21 years to Henry Wilson, alderman, and the burgesses of the borough of Kirkebye in Kendall, co. Westmorland, of two parts of the toll in the said borough, late of William, marquess of Northampton, deceased; from Michaelmas last; yearly rent £10. In consideration of the surrender by them of the interest in the premises of Christopher Philipson of Staveley, co. Westmorland, to whom the said marquess and Elizabeth his wife (for them and the heirs of the marquess) by indenture, 8 Feb., 4 Edw. VI, leased *inter alia* the toll of the town of Kirkbye Kendall, then in the occupation of Philipson and late in that of William Collyns, deceased, for 31 years from Whitsunday then next at the same rent; and for a fine of £30 paid at the Exchequer.

By the commissioners by virtue of the Queen's warrant.

669.)   30 *Dec.* 1575.   Lease for 21 years to Henry Cheyney, knight, lord Cheyney, of the manor of Gaddesden with Fruthesden, cos. Hertford   [*m.* 17]
and Buckingham; with reservations, including wards, marriages, goods of felons and outlaws and advowsons; from Lady Day next; yearly rent £15. 10*s.* 4¼*d.* For a fine of £31 8½*d.* paid at the Exchequer.   By p.s.

670.)   20 *Jan.* 1576.   Lease for 21 years to Edward Turnor of the tithes in Braken, co. York, late of Watton priory, co. York; from Michaelmas last; yearly rent £7. In consideration of the surrender by Turner by deed, 10 Nov. last, enrolled in Chancery of the interest of William Foster, to whom by patent, 11 Jan., 5 Eliz., the said tithes were leased *inter alia* for 21 years from Michaelmas then last at the same rent; and for a fine of £14 paid at the Exchequer.

By the commissioners by virtue of the Queen's warrant.

671.)   9 *Dec.* 1575.   Lease for 21 years to Thomas Bowleys of the chapel of Cloughton, co. York, the tithes of wool and lambs in Cloughton and elsewhere belonging to the chapel and all other tithes of wool and lambs in Cloughton or elsewhere, co. York, late of the monastery of Bridlington, co. York, and leased to Ralph Bawde with the chapel for a yearly rent of £7 10*s.*; from Lady Day last; yearly rent £7 10*s.* For a fine   [*m.* 18]
of £30, to wit, £21. 6*s.* 8*d.* paid at the Exchequer by a tally levied on 2 Dec. last and £8 13*s.* 4*d.* paid to Robert Bradley in repayment of a fine paid by Bradley to the Queen for a lease of lands in Potterspurie, co. Northampton, which never issued because a previous lease thereof was in being, as appears by a bill signed by Christopher Smythe, clerk of the pipe, annexed to the particular on which this patent issued.

By the commissioners by virtue of the Queen's warrant.

672.)   26 *Jan.* 1576.   Commitment for 21 years (by mainprise of Peter Charde and Tildesley Monke in the Exchequer) to Peter Charde of the farm or keeping of lands in Barghe, co. Rutland, given without licence by William Megetson of Barghe to the chaplain there for the finding of a priest to celebrate in the said chapel; from Lady Day last; yearly rent 3*s.* 8*d.* and 12*d.* of increase; provided that, if anyone will give more of increase for the farm, Charde shall be found to pay so much if he wishes to have it.

By treasurer's bill.

673.)   30 *Dec.* 1575.   Lease for 21 years to Stephen Harvye of the tithes of corn in Westcotes and in Westfeilde by Leicester, co. Leicester, now or late in the tenure of John Ruddinges, once of the monastery of Pré, Leicester; from Michaelmas last; yearly rent from the time when he shall obtain possession of £8.

By the commissioners by virtue of the Queen's warrant.

674.)   27 *Feb.* 1576.   Grant in fee farm to Anthony Rotsey and William Fissher, their heirs and assigns of the reversions and rents of the lands comprised in leases for 21 years as follows:—

(i) By patent, 5 Dec., 14 Eliz., to James Boreman of all lands in the county of Devon once of the chantry of Washeborne, co. Devon,   [*m.* 19]
founded by predecessors of the bishop of Exeter, from Michaelmas then last at a year rent of £5 14*s.* 9*d.*

(ii) By patent, 9 Jan., 10 Eliz., to Dunstan Braye and Walter Jennynges *inter alia* of the capital messuage of Henton Marchaunte,   [*m.* 20]
co. Southampton, and lands (*named with tenants' names*) in Henton Dawbney and Hormere at a yearly rent of £7 3*s.* 10*d.*

(iii) By patent, 9 July, 16 Eliz., to Thomas Haywarde and Alice his wife of lands called 'the Amners Grounde' in Wenlocke and other lands (*named*), parcels of the manor of Much Wenlocke, co. Salop, once of the monastery of Wenlock and leased to one Thomas Heywarde by conventual indenture at a yearly rent of 22*s.*, at the same rent. (Also reciting a lease by patent, 8 May, 5 Eliz., to Richard Fermour and Richard Southerne *inter alia* of copyhold lands in Wenlocke and lands called Amners Grounde, then or late in the tenure of one Thomas Harwarde, once of the monastery of Wenlocke, for 21 years at a yearly rent for all the lands specified in the lease of £26 11*s.* 10*d.*)

(iv) By patent, 28 May, 17 Eliz., to Thomas Edmondes *inter alia* of lands (*tenant named*) called Paynters and Dabernons in Plymouthe, late of Dabernons and Paynters chantry in Plymouth, co. Devon, from Michaelmas then next at a yearly rent of 40*s.*, parcel of a rent of £8 10*s.* 3*d.* for them and all other lands specified in the lease.[1]

(v) By patent of the Exchequer, 9 Nov., 7 Eliz., to William Iveson *inter alia* of a portion of the tithes in Beckton, co. Southampton, from Michaelmas then last at a yearly rent of 6*s.* 8*d.*

(vi) By patent of the Exchequer, 2 June, 9 Eliz., to Lawrence Bradebent *inter alia* of lands (*tenants named*) in Keyworthe, co. Nottingham, late of the monastery of Lenton, co. Nottingham, from Lady Day then last at a yearly rent of 29*s.* 10*d.* (*detailed*).

(vii) By patent, 3 Feb., 5 Eliz., to Christopher Warcopp of (*a*) the capital messuage in Great Busbye, (*b*) lands (*named with tenants' names*) in Busbye in 'le Northriddinge', (*c*) lands (*named*) in Carleton in 'le Northriddinge' and (*d*) the site of the manor of Facebye and lands (*named with tenants' names*) in Facebye, all in the county of York and parcels of the duchy of York, from Michaelmas then last at yearly rents of (*a*) £6, (*b*) £6 14*s.* 4*d.* (*detailed*), (*c*) £4 15*s.* 9*d.* and (*d*) £11 6*s.* 11*d.* (*detailed*).

(viii) By patent of the Exchequer, 4 May, 6 Eliz., to Richard Hebborne *inter alia* of lands (*named*) in Great Busbye, co. York, parcel of the duchy of York, at a yearly rent of 10*s.*

Also grant of—(1) the chantry of Wasshebourne, co. Devon;   [*m.* 21]
(2) the manor, capital messuage, grange, farm or hereditament of Henton Merchaunte in Katherington and elsewhere, co. Southampton, late of the monastery of St. Swithun, Winchester, and the rest of the premises in (ii) above in Henton Dawbney and Henton Hormere in Katherington; (3) lands called Colloughton Rydinge in Sheynton (*described with tenant's name*) and lands called Amners Grounde in Wenlock and Sheynton, co. Salop, (now or late in the tenure of Thomas Havarde *alias* Haywarde), all once of the monastery of Wenlocke; (4) a tenement or grange called Courte Carney Graunge in Llandilo, the tithes of corn and other tithes of the same, the tithes of lands and wool and other tithes of lands at Blaynant, Gonvayne and Courte Carney called Abbottes Landes (once in the tenures of Philip Williams and William Morgan ap Rice Lloyd) and lands (*named with tenants' names*) in Llandilo and Llanruddion, all within the manor of Gower, co. Glamorgan, and once of the monastery of Neathe, co. Glamorgan; (5) the premises in (iv) above in Plymouthe; (6) the portion of tithes in Beckton   [*m.* 22]
in (v) above; (7) the premises in Claworthe *alias* Keyworthe in (vi) above; and (8) the manors of Busbye, Facebye and Carleton, co. York, parcels of the duchy of York, the premises in Great Busbye in (viii) above and all lands in Busbye, Facebye and Carleton being parcels of the duchy.

---

[1] Preceding this recital, the patent recites a lease by patent, 30 July, 10 Eliz., to William Morgan ap Res Lloyd *inter alia* of the tithes of lands called Abbottes Landes, co. Glamorgan, late of the monastery of Neathe, for 21 years at a yearly rent for the same, together with the rectory of Llandilo, of £7 6*s.* 8*d.*

Bells and lead, except lead in gutters and windows, reserved. To hold as of the manor of Estgrenewiche, co. Kent, in socage and by yearly rents of (1) £5 14s. 9d., (2) £7 3s. 10d., (3) 4s. for Colloughton Riddinge   [*m.* 23] and 22s. for the premises in Wenlocke, (4) 55s. 2d., (5) 40s., (6) 6s. 8d., (7) 29s. 10d. and (8) £29 17s. Issues from Michaelmas last.

For the service of Henry Broke *alias* Cobham, knight, and at his suit.   By Q.

675.)   13 *Feb.* 1576.   Lease for 21 years to Henry Hawthorne, the Queen's servant, of (1) a coney warren at Ampthill, co. Bedford, parcel of the lordship of Ampthill, (2) lands called Kingesmeade next Wallingforde   [*m.* 24] castle, co. Berks, parcel of the castle and manor of Wallingforde and of the honour of Ewelme, (3) the herbage and agistment of Woodhall park in the lordship of Midleham, co. York, (4) lands (*named*) in Thoralbye in the archdeaconry of Richmond, co. York, parcel of the lordship of Middelham and Richmond, (5) lands in Bradley in the said archdeaconry, parcel of the lordship of Middelham, (6) lands (*named with tenant's name*) in Combes, co. Oxford, parcel of lands once purchased from Richard Andrewes and others, and (7) lands (*named*) in Mere, co. Wilts, parcel of the manor of Mere, granted to Thomas Chafyn and Edward and Leonard Chafyn, his elder sons, for life by copy of court roll, parcel of the duchy of Cornwall; with reservations, including pasture for the deer and wild beasts in Woodhall park in both winter and summer; (1) from Lady Day 1587, having been leased

[*m.* 25]

by patent, 12 July, 8 Eliz., to John Whitbroke for 21 years from Lady Day then last at a yearly rent of £6; (2) from Lady Day 1589, having been leased by patent, 2 July, 10 Eliz., to the mayor, burgesses and commonalty of the borough of Wallingforde for 21 years at a yearly rent of £7 2s.; (3) from the termination of a lease thereof *inter alia* by patent, 2 April, 16 Eliz., to Mary Hogan, widow, at a yearly rent of 40s. for 21 years from the death of Christopher Metcalfe, knight, to whom by patent, 27 July, 25 Hen. VIII, it was granted for life; (4) from 17 May 1596, having been leased by patent of the Exchequer, 17 May, 17 Eliz., to William Gowerley for 21 years from that date at a yearly rent of 40s. 6d.; (5) from Michaelmas 1594, having been leased by patent 25 Feb., 13 Eliz., to Robert Game *inter alia* for 21 years from Michaelmas 1573 at a yearly rent of 40s.; (6) from Michaelmas next or the termination of any lease or grant thereof for life or years enduring after that date; (7) from the death or termination of the interest of the said Thomas, Edward and Leonard Chafyn and the wives of any of them having an estate of widowhood therein by custom of the manor of Mere; yearly rents (1) £6, (2) £7 2s., (3) 40s., (4) 40s. 6d., (5) 40s., (6) 20s. and (7) 22s. 7½d. (*detailed*).   [*m.* 26] For his service.

676.)   9 *March* 1576.   Lease for 21 years to Stephen Foxe, late a yeoman usher of the chamber, of (1) lands (*tenant named*) in Great Bloxwiche, co. Stafford, late of the chantry of Blowiche, (2) lands (*tenant named*) in Walsall, co. Stafford, and (3) lands (*tenant named*) in Caldemore, co.   [*m.* 27] Stafford, which premises in Walsall and Caldemore belonged to the second chantry of the foundation of Thomas Aston, knight, in Walsall, (4) lands (*named with tenant's name*) in Knighton, co. Radnor, parcel of the manor or borough of Knighton, (5) lands (*tenant named*) in Seginhales, co. Radnor, parcel of the manor of Knighton, (6) lands (*named with tenants' names*) in Kevensweran, parcel of the manor of Southruralth, co. Radnor, and (7) lands (*named with tenant's name*) in Preston, co. Radnor, parcel of the manor of Preston, which premises in the county of Radnor belonged to the late earl of March, (8) lands (*tenant named*) in Picall, co. York, late of St John the Baptist's chantry in Wathe church, co. York, (9) lands (*named*), including the mansion house of the rectory, in Bradborne, co. Derby, once of the

monastery of Dunstable, co. Bedford, (10) lands (*named with tenants' names*) in Llanedwyn in the commote of Ardudwy Issartro, co. Merioneth, parcel of the principality of North Wales, (11) the tithes of corn, hay,   [*m.* 28]
flax and hemp in Hemyngton and lands (*described with tenant's name*) in Lockington, co. Leicester, and (12) lands (*named with tenant's name*), parcel of the manor of Barrowe, co. Lincoln, and (13) lands (*tenant named*) in Wotton, co. Lincoln, parcel of the manor of Wooton, which premises in the county of Lincoln belonged to Thornton college, co. Lincoln; with reservations, including lands etc. (*specified*) in Bradborne; (1), (2) and (3) from Lady Day 1583, having been leased (1) by patent of the Exchequer, 18 May, 4 Eliz., to Robert Caldwell *inter alia* for 21 years from Lady Day then last at a yearly rent of 15*s.* and (2) and (3) by another patent of the Exchequer of the same date to the said Caldwell for 21 years from Lady Day then last at yearly rents of (2) 16*s.* and (3) 40*s.*; (4), (5), (6) and (7) from Lady Day 1584, having been leased by patent of the Exchequer, 22 May, 5 Eliz., to Edward Pryce—(4) being then late found to have been concealed—for 21 years from Lady Day then last at yearly rents of (4) 11*s.* 10*d.* (*detailed*), (5) 7*s.*, (6) 3*s.* 5*d.* (*detailed*) and (7) 14*d.*; (8) from Lady Day 1589, having been leased by patent of the Exchequer, 24 June, 10 Eliz., to George Fothergill *inter alia* for 21 years from Lady Day then last at a yearly rent of 26*s.* 8*d.*; (9) from Michaelmas 1592 [*sic*], having been leased by patent, 10 Dec., 5 Eliz., to George Lorte *inter alia* at a yearly rent   [*m.* 29]
of 73*s.* 4*d.* for 21 years from Lady Day 1571 or the termination of a lease thereof by conventual indenture, 10 Aug. 1531, to George Buxstons for 40 years from the eve of Lady Day then last at the same rent; (10) from Michaelmas next or the termination of any lease or grant thereof for life or years lawfully enduring after that date; (11) from the termination of a lease thereof by John, abbot, and the convent of the monastery of Pré, Leicester, by indenture, 10 Nov., 26 Hen. VIII, to William Milnegate of Lockington, 'yoman', for 70 years from Michaelmas then last at a yearly rent of £6 6*s.*; (12) and (13) from Michaelmas 1589, having been leased by patent of the Exchequer, 7 Dec., 11 Eliz., to Benet Serjante for 21 years from Michaelmas then next at yearly rents of (12) 23*s.* 4*d.* and (13) 56*s.* 3*d.*; yearly rents (1) 15*s.*, (2) 16*s.*, (3) 40*s.*, (4)–(7) 23*s.* 5*d.*, (8) 26*s.* 8*d.*, (9) 73*s.* 4*d.*, (10) 8*s.* 10*d.*, (11) £6 6*s.*, (12) 23*s.* 4*d.* and (13) 56*s.* 3*d.*   [*m.* 30]
For his service.   By p.s.

677.) 9 *March* 1576.   Lease for 21 years to Margaret Benson, widow, of (1) lands (*named*), parcel of the demesne lands of the monastery of Holme Coltram, co. Cumberland, (2) a watermill called Dubbmill in Westwaver in the lordship of Holme Coltrame, (3) a tenement in Millhill in Westwaver in the said lordship and (4) a tenement in Dubbmill in Westwaver, in the said lordship, all once of the said monastery; with reservations; from Michaelmas last; yearly rents (1) 14*s.* 10*d.* (*detailed*), (2)   [*m.* 31]
£6, (3) 6*s.* 8*d.* and (4) 6*s.* 9*d.*; the lessee to pay out of the said two small tenements in Westwaver every tenth year a gersum according to the custom of the said manor and do all other services appertaining to such tenements as the rest of the tenants of the manor do; also to occupy the premises by a sufficient man or men, to serve with horse and arms in the North when commanded in the Queen's name by the warden or lieutenant of the marches there, to bear and do all other services and charges touching the Queen's service according to the custom of the country, and to fence the premises as ordered by the Queen's steward, understeward or other commissioners there. In consideration of the surrender by the said Margaret in Chancery of a patent, 2 March, 7 Eliz., leasing the premises to William Edmondes for 21 years from Michaelmas then last at the same rents; and for a fine of £14 16*s.* 6*d.* paid at the Exchequer.   By the commissioners by virtue of the Queen's warrant.

678.) 24 *March* 1576.   *Gorhambury.*   Grant in fee simple to Thomas Cranmere of—the

reversion and rent of the site of Arthington priory, co. York, and lands (*named with tenants' names*) in the parishes of Harwood and Adeley, co. York, all once of the said priory and leased by patent, 18 May, 16 Eliz., to Thomas Nevyson *inter alia* for 21 years from Lady Day then last at a   [*m.* 32]
yearly rent of 6*s.* 6*d.*; and the site and house of the said priory, lands (*named*) parcel of the demesne lands of Arthington and all appurtenances of the premises in Arthington, Adley and Harwood. Advowsons, bells and lead, except lead in gutters and windows, reserved. To hold as of the manor of Estgrenewiche, co. Kent, in socage. Issues from Michaelmas last.

[*m.* 33]
The grantee not discharged of charges by reason of the gift made of the premises *inter alia* to Thomas Cranmere, late archbishop of Canterbury, by patent, 6 June, 1 Edw. VI.
    For £108 6*s.* 8*d.* paid at the Exchequer to Robert Freke, a teller there.   By p.s.

679.)   26 *March* 1576.   *Gorhambury.*   Incorporation of the town or borough of Daventre, co. Northampton, as a free borough with a bailiff, 14 burgesses and 20 of the commonalty, by the name of the bailiff, burgesses and commonalty of the borough of Daventre; the borough to have the same bounds as accustomed from time immemorial, and the bailiff, burgesses and commonalty may make perambulations of the same as often as shall seem necessary. Grant to the bailiff, burgesses and commonalty of liberties as follows— There shall be 14 of the more discreet men of the borough assisting the bailiff, who shall be called the principal burgesses and shall be the common council for the making of ordinances for the borough. There shall be 20 other men   [*m.* 34]
of the residue of the inhabitants who shall be the full number of the commonalty below the burgesses, and, whenever one of them shall die or for reasonable cause be removed, the bailiff and the recorder may elect and admit to the commonalty another of the inhabitants. Power by the bailiff and the recorder and by the common council or a majority of them of whom the recorder shall be one to make ordinances for the government and victualling of the borough; so that they be not repugnant to the laws of the realm or the prerogative of the Crown. There shall be a recorder. The bailiff may during his time of office appoint two serjeants at mace, who shall be able to bear by the bailiff's command two silver maces inscribed with the Queen's arms within the precinct of the borough and shall make proclamations and executions and perform all other things appertaining to the office of serjeant at mace as the serjeants at mace do in the city of London; every person appointed to the office of serjeant at mace shall be sworn before the bailiff. The bailiff to be clerk of the market, to do all things appertaining to that office as clerks of the market of the household do; no other clerk of the market to intermeddle there. Appointment of John Savage to be the first and present bailiff, to perform the office on his oath until Michaelmas next and thereafter until another be sworn and appointed. Appointment of Lawrence Eaton, Thomas Andrewe, John Symmes, William Salter, Henry Roper, William Symons, John Savage, Richard Allen, Nicholas Smythe, William Hollowell, William Farmer, Richard Farmer, John Jesson and John Godbye to be the first and present 14 principal burgesses, to be, on their oath taken before the bailiff, the common council of the borough together with him. Appointment of John Daffarne to be recorder for life, to exercise there on his oath justice by himself or a sufficient deputy. The bailiff and the recorder to be justices of the peace of the borough. Every bailiff in the year following the end of his office of bailiff shall exercise in the borough for one year the office of coroner, being sworn before the bailiff for the time being. There shall be—in addition to the market every Wednesday and the yearly fair on St. Austin's Day, which the inhabitants have enjoyed from time immemorial—two other yearly fairs, one on Tuesday after Easter and the two days following and the other on St. Matthew's Day and the two days following. The house there called 'le Moote Hall' shall be the common hall of the bailiff, burgesses and commonalty. Yearly on Michaelmas Day

between 9 and 12 in the morning the bailiffs, burgesses and commonalty may in 'le Moote Hawle' or any convenient place in the borough elect two of the principal burgesses before the other inhabitants that the inhabitants there and then present may elect one of them to the office of bailiff,   [*m.* 35]
who shall after being duly sworn exercise the office for a year; if anyone after notice of his election to be bailiff shall refuse to take the office upon him without reasonable cause, the bailiff and the rest of the 14 chief burgesses may commit him to gaol until he will exercise it or may impose a competent fine upon him and keep him in prison until he will pay it; the bailiff elect shall be sworn before his predecessor if the same be alive and present, and, if his predecessor be dead or absent, before the recorder and the other principal burgesses; and, if a bailiff shall die or be removed during his time of office, the burgesses may assemble as aforesaid on an appointed day within eight days of his death or removal and nominate two persons of whom one shall be elected bailiff in the manner aforesaid until Michaelmas following and thereafter until another be elected and sworn, and the person elected shall be sworn before the recorder or his deputy and the other chief burgesses. Whenever a burgess shall die, dwell outside the borough or be removed from office, the bailiff and burgesses may within eight days assemble and elect another of the inhabitants to be burgess for life or otherwise if it shall seem good to the bailiff and other burgesses; and the burgess elect shall be sworn before the bailiff. Whenever the recorder shall die or be removed, the bailiff and burgesses may within eight days assemble and elect another suitable person to be recorder for life or otherwise as it shall seem good to the bailiff and burgesses; and the recorder elect shall be sworn before the bailiff. The bailiff, burgesses and commonalty shall have a court of record before the bailiff and the recorder in 'le Moote Hawle' or another more convenient place in the borough on Thursday in every second week except in the weeks of Easter, Whitsun, and Christmas; power for the bailiff and recorder or the deputy recorder with the bailiff to hear and decide pleas arising within the borough not exceeding £50 in value; and the bailiff and recorder or either of them may direct the serjeants at mace to bring defendants to answer pleas by summonses, attachments and distraints according to the custom in the city of London, and actions shall be tried as in the said city. Anyone of the borough who shall be disobedient to the ordinances made for the same shall straightway be punished by the bailiff according to the law and custom of the realm. None of the inhabitants to be put on any assize or jury outside the borough; nor shall any stranger be put on any assizes or juries with any inhabitants within the borough to try any issue there arising unless the Crown itself be a party. Licence to acquire lands of the   [*m.* 36]
yearly value of £40 not held of the Crown in chief or by knight service. The bailiff, burgesses and commonalty to have all franchises and privileges heretofore enjoyed by the inhabitants, rendering to the Crown yearly for the fairs above granted a rent of 6s. 8d. at Michaelmas.

At the suit of the inhabitants: the town is an ancient borough and parcel of the duchy of Lancaster and the inhabitants have from time immemorial enjoyed divers liberties by grants of the Queen's progenitors to dukes of Lancaster and the inhabitants and by prescription, which have for many years past been little used.   By p.s.

680.)   16 *April* 1576.   Lease for 21 years to Christopher Preston of (1) the site of the manor of Cartemeale, co. Lancaster, and lands (*named*), parcel of the said manor, and (2) lands (*named*) within the site of Cartemeale priory or parcel of the demesne lands thereof, all once of the said   [*m.* 37]
priory and afterwards parcels of the possessions of Thomas Holcrofte, knight, exchanged with Henry VIII; with reservations; from Lady Day last; yearly rents (1) £8 13s. 4d. and (2) £6 8s. 4d.; the lessee to find two sufficient men to serve the Crown in the North when necessary. In consideration of his surrender of a patent, 9 April, 10 Eliz., leasing to Christopher Preston the premises (1) above for 21 years from Lady Day then last at the same

rent and a patent, 4 Feb., 11 Eliz., leasing to the same Christopher the premises (2) above for 21 years from Michaelmas then last at the same rent; and for a fine of £30 3s. 4d. paid at the Exchequer within a sum of £38 14s. By p.s.

681.) 6 *April* 1576. *Gorhambury.* Lease for 21 years to Edward Holte of (1) the rectory of Bromewiche *alias* Westbromewiche, co. Stafford, once of Sandall *alias* Sandwall priory, co. Lincoln [*sic*], (2) lands in Bromewich [*m.* 38] aforesaid, late of the new college of chanters in Lichfield, and (3) the rectory of Bulkington, the tithes of grain in Bulkington, Weston, Marston, Bramecote, Welbeckhill *alias* Wolver-hill, Ryton and Barvangle *alias* Barnangle, co. Warwick, and the tithes of hay and wood belonging to the said rectory, once of the monastery of Pré, Leicestr', co. Leicester; with reservations; (1) and (2) from Michaelmas 1583, having been leased by patent, 3 March, 5 Eliz., to Robert Cawdwell for 21 years from Michaelmas then last at a yearly rent £9 9s., to wit, for (1) £9 and (2) 9s.; (3) from Michaelmas 1592, having been leased by patent, 10 Nov., 13 Eliz., to Richard Over for 21 years from Michaelmas then last at a yearly rent of £17; same rents. For a fine of £52 18s. paid at the Exchequer. By p.s.

682.) 9 *May* 1576. Lease for 47 years to Paul Wood of lands (*tenants named*) in (1) Northampton, co. Northampton, late of St. Mary's guild, Holy Trinity guild in All Saints church, Corpus Christi guild, Bowghtons chantry, [*m.* 39] St. Clement's guild, SS. John Baptist and Catherine's guild or brotherhood (*described*) and All Saints college, Northampton, and (2) Northampton (*described*) and Spellowe hundred, co. Northampton, given for obits and the like in towns in the said hundred; from Michaelmas last; yearly rent £39 10s. 10d.; the lessee to have made a particular terrier and rental of the premises and deliver it written in parchment every tenth year to the surveyor of the county; he is also to have a yearly allowance of 66s. 8d. deducted from the rent, to wit, [*m.* 40] at Lady Day 33s. 4d. and at Michaelmas 33s. 4d., to buy timber for repairs. In consideration of the surrender in Chancery by Wood of a patent, 30 March, 5 Eliz., leasing the premises to Thomas Moone, now deceased, for 60 years from Michaelmas then last at a yearly rent of £40 3s. 10d. By p.s.

683.) 12 *March* 1576. Lease for 21 years to James More of the manors of Poughill and Treglaston and all lands in Poughill and Treglaston, co. Cornwall, once of the monastery of Clyve, co. Somerset; with reservations, including wards, marriages and advowson of vicarages; from Lady Day next; yearly rent from the time when he shall obtain possession £46. In consideration that he offers at his own costs to prove void in law a pretended lease thereof to Thomas Cole by conventual deed for 47 years and more still to run. By p.s.

684.) 19 *May* 1576. Manumission of William Puntyng of Waldrenfeld, co. [*m.* 41] Suffolk, 'husbondman', villein (*nativus*) regardant to the manor of Walton with Tremley, co. Suffolk, William Puntyng, his son, and Alice Puntyng, his daughter, and their issue. At the suit of Henry Lee *alias* Lea, knight, the Queen's servant, according to a warrant made to him by patent, 17 Jan., 17 Eliz.

By the keeper of the great seal by virtue of the Queen's warrant.

The like of the following:—
685.) 2 *June* 1576. John Ingolf *alias* Ingle of Stradbrooke, co. Suffolk, 'husbondman', villein regardant to the manor of Stradbrooke, and John, Lionel and Benjamin Ingolf *alias* Ingle, his sons.
686.) 20 *Feb.* 1576. William Charke of Rillaton in the parish of Lankyhorne, co.

Cornwall, son of Richard Charke, villein regardant to[—], and Edward, John, William and Stephen Charke, sons of the said William, and Sybil, Anne, Julian, Joan and Isabel Charke, his daughters.

687.)   14 *Nov.* 1576.   Sampson Munke of Stokesclymesland, co. Cornwall, 'husbandman', villein regardant to the manor of Stokesclymesland, and Edmund Munke, his son, and Flora, Thomasina, Margery and Mary Munke, his daughters.

688.)   14 *Nov.* 1576.   Robert Powle of Thacham, co. Berks, villein regardant to the manor of Leompster, co. Hereford, John Powle, his son, and Jane Powle, his daughter.

689.)   14 *Nov.* 1576.   William Powle of Chorlestre, co. Hereford, 'husbondman', villein regardant to the manor of Leompster, co. Hereford.

690.)   14 *Nov.* 1576.   Henry Wall of Sutton in the parish of Marden, co. Hereford, villein regardant to the manor of Leompster, John Wall, his son, and Jane and Joan Wall, his daughters.

691.)   14 *Nov.* 1576.   William Powle of Leompster, co Hereford, villein regardant to the manor of Leompster, Richard, William, John and Robert Powle, his sons, and Joan Powle, wife of William Hunt, Anne Powle, wife of Thomas Wall, Maud, Lucy, Elizabeth, Margaret and Eleanor Powle, his daughters.

692.)   14 *Nov.* 1576.   Henry Munke of Stokesclymesland, co. Cornwall, villein regardant to the manor of Stokesclymesland, John, Ralph and Henry Munke, his sons, and Mary, Joan and Agatha Munke, his daughters.

693.)   15 *Nov.* 1576.   Roger Skyner of Saint Stevens, co. Cornwall, villein regardant to the manor of Trem[aton][1], co. Cornwall, Richard and Walter Skyner, his sons, and Margaret Skyner, wife of John Knebon, his daughter.

694.)   15 *Nov.* 1576.   John Knyght of Stokesclymesland, co. Cornwall, villein   [*m.* 42] regardant to the manor of Stokesclymesland, Henry and Robert Knight, his sons, and Alison, Margaret, Elizabeth and Joan Knight, his daughters.

695.)   8 *Nov.* 1576.   Mark Harman of Sudborne, co. Suffolk, 'husbondman', villein regardant to the manors of Walton with Tremley, Felixstowe or Fakenham, and Alice and Mary Harman, his daughters.

696.)   10 *Nov.* 1576.   Henry Waklen of Hannyshe Clyfforde, co. Hereford, 'husbondman', villein regardant to the manor of Leompster, co. Hereford.

697.)   10 *Nov.* 1576.   William Bache of Leompster, co. Hereford, 'husbondman', villein regardant to the manor of Leompster, and William, Richard, John and George Bache, his sons.

698.)   10 *Nov.* 1576.   Richard Wanklen of Stockton, co. Hereford, 'husbondman', villein regardant to the manor of Leompster, and Richard Wanklen, his son.

699.)   10 *Nov.* 1576.   William Wanklen of Kymbalton, co. Hereford, 'husbondman', villein regardant to the manor of Leompster, and Hugh and Thomas Wanklen, his sons.

700.)   10 *Nov.* 1576.   Richard Bache of Stockton, co. Hereford, 'husbondman', villein regardant to the manor of Leompster, William Bache, his son, and Anne Bache, his daughter.

701.)   10 *Nov.* 1576.   Walter Wanklen of Kymbalton, co. Hereford, 'husbondman', villein regardant to the manor of Leompster, and William and John Wanklen, his sons.

702.)   15 *Nov.* 1576.   John Wall of Hope under Dimorehill, co. Hereford, villein regardant to the manor of Leompster, Thomas Wall, his son, and Margery, Margaret and Eleanor Wall, his daughters.

703.)   15 *Nov.* 1576.   Nicholas Bonde of the parish of St. Stephen in the manor of Trematon, co. Cornwall, villein regardant to the manor of Trematon, Richard Bonde, his son, and Elizabeth Bonde, his daughter.

---

[1] The roll is rubbed at this point.

704.) 15 *Nov.* 1576. Thomas Skory of the parish of St. Stephen, co. Cornwall, villein regardant to the manor of Kalstocke, co. Cornwall, Roger, William, Richard and John Skory, his sons, and Eleanor, Thomasina, Joan, Mary and Frances Skory, his daughters.

705.) 12 *May* 1576. William Dun *alias* Dunne, M.A., fellow of Exeter college, Oxford, son of Robert Dun *alias* Dunne, late of the parish of St. Botolph without Aldersgate, London, villein regardant to the honour of Eye, co. Suffolk.

706.) 12 *May* 1576. Daniel Dun *alias* Dunne, B.C.L., fellow of All Souls College, Oxford, son of Robert Dun *alias* Dunne, late of the parish of St. Botolph without Aldersgate, London, villein regardant to the honour of Eye.

707.) 29 *May* 1576. Thomas Puntynge of Hemley, co. Suffolk, 'husbondman', villein regardant to the manor of Walton with Tremley, co. Suffolk, William Puntinge, his son, and Elizabeth Puntinge, his daughter.

708.) 26 *May* 1576. John Munke of Stokesclymesland, co. Cornwall, the younger, villein regardant to the manor of Stokeclymesland, Michael and James Munke, his sons, and Joan, Thomasina, Elsbia and Susan Munke, his daughters.

709.) 7 *July* 1576. Martin Style of Eastdereham, co. Norfolk, villein regardant to the manor of Eastdereham.

710.) 30 *Jan.* 1576. William Dunne *alias* Donne of Mendlesam, co. Suffolk, 'smyth', the Queen's villein, Richard Dunne *alias* Donne of Dickleborough, 'smyth', Robert Dunne *alias* Donne of Laiestofte, living with Ambrose Kyng, Thomas Donne *alias* Dunne of Mendlesam and John Dunne *alias* Donne of Mendlesam, sons of William, and Margaret now the wife of Roger Powlinge of Laiestofte, Grace now the wife of George Fyfeelde of Laiestofte, Elizabeth Dunne *alias* Donne, Catherine Dunne *alias* Donne and Joan Dunne *alias* Donne, his daughters.

711.) 30 *Jan.* 1576. Roger Annout *alias* Annot of Heymesby, co. Norfolk, the Queen's villein, and Alice now the wife of John Peke of Heymesby and Helen now the wife of John Custons of Heymesby, his daughters.

712.) 30 *Jan.* 1576. William Dunne *alias* Donne of Cossey, co. Suffolk, 'smyth', the Queen's villein, and Thomas Dunne *alias* Donne, his son.

713.) 9 *Feb.* 1576. Ralph Kyng of Swanborne, co. Buckingham, the Queen's villein, and William, Thomas and John Kyng, his sons.

714.) 14 *Oct.* 1576. John Stevens of Westpennard, co. Somerset, villein regardant to the manor of Glastowne, co. Somerset, John, Thomas, Richard and Edward Stevens, his sons, and Joan and Agnes Stevens, his daughters.

715.) 10 *March* 1576. Denization for Peter Johnson, born a Spanish　　[*m.* 43] subject; to pay customs as an alien; and not to dwell in Berwicke or Portesmouth without special licence. For 13*s.* 4*d.* in the hanaper.

　　　By the keeper of the great seal by virtue of the Queen's warrant.

The like for the following, for the fines in the hanaper specified, viz.—

716.)	10 *March* 1576.	Jasper Dissert, French subject.	6*s.* 8*d.*
717.)	14 *March* 1576.	Christopher Cunan, subject of the bishop of Cologne	10*s.*
718.)	14 *March* 1576.	John Garrettes, Spanish subject.	6*s.* 8*d.*
719.)	20 *Nov.* 1575.	Luke Reynoldes, subject of [—]	6*s.* 8*d.*
720.)	11 *July* 1576.	William Ryskyns, subject of the duke of Cleves.	10*s.*
721.)	9 *May* 1576,	Francis Rozeaw *alias* Deblock, Spanish subject.	10*s.*
722.)	9 *March* 1576.	William Dulong, French subject born in Normandy.	6*s.* 8*d.*
723.)	4 *June* 1576.	William Flemyn, Scottish subject.	6*s.* 8*d.*
724.)	7 *Feb.* 1576.	Lawrence Sheriff, subject of the duke of Cleves.	6*s.* 8*d.*
725.)	9 *Feb.* 1576.	Peter Clarke, subject of the duke of Guelders.	6*s.* 8*d.*

726.)	14 *Feb.* 1576.	Simon Allame, Spanish subject.	6s. 8d.
727.)	14 *Feb.* 1576.	William Brycott, Spanish subject.	6s. 8d.
728.)	17 *Feb.* 1576.	Geoffrey Myller, subject of the duke of Cleves.	6s. 8d.
729.)	20 *Feb.* 1576.	Levelin Bryand, Spanish subject.	6s. 8d.
730.)	20 *May* 1576.	Conrad Meughen, subject of the bishop of Cologne.	10s.
731.)	21 *May* 1576.	Henry Starkey, subject of the Emperor.	6s. 8d.
732.)	15 *May* 1576.	Francis Curdere, Spanish subject.	10s.
733.)	9 *Feb.* 1576.	William Mytchell, Scottish subject, born in St. Johnstons.	6s. 8d.
734.)	5 *March* 1576.	Nicholas Bornory, Spanish subject.	6s. 8d.
735.)	19 *March* 1576.	Daniel Copeians, Spanish subject.	6s. 8d.
736.)	19 *March* 1576.	Garrett Hollander, subject of the duke of Cleves.	6s. 8d.
737.)	2 *June* 1576.	Giles Blunden, French subject.	6s. 8d.
738.)	2 *June* 1576.	Nicholas Ryse, subject of the duke of Cleves.	10s.
739.)	2 *June* 1576.	Peter Watnes, Spanish subject.	6s. 8d.
740.)	2 *July* 1576.	Alert Faryngyowe, Spanish subject.	13s. 4d.
741.)	4 *July* 1576.	John Lyon, subject of the Emperor.	6s. 8d.
742.)	4 *July* 1576.	Matthew Reyners, subject of the Emperor.	6s. 8d.
743.)	4 *July* 1576.	William Mullens, Spanish subject.	6s. 8d.[1]
744.)	4 *July* 1576.	John Bowteron, French subject.	6s. 8d.

[*m.* 44]

745.)	22 *June* 1576.	Martin Slypen, subject of the Emperor.	10s.
746.)	18 *June* 1576.	Albert Gilbert, Spanish subject.	6s. 8d.
747.)	10 *March* 1576.	Peter Johnson, Spanish subject.	13s. 4d.
748.)	19 *March* 1576.	Galen Beyke, subject of [—]	20s.
749.)	23 *March* 1576.	*Gorhambury.* Nicholas Bowcher, French subject.	
750.)	23 *March* 1576.	*Gorhambury.* John Heyns, subject of the bishop of Cologne.	10s.
751.)	23 *March* 1576.	*Gorhambury.* Edward Bresse, Spanish subject.	6s. 8d.
752.)	26 *March* 1576.	*Gorhambury.* George de Bucker, Spanish subject.	6s. 8d.
753.)	6 *April* 1576.	*Gorhambury.* Lewis Moll, subject of the duke of Cleves.	6s. 8d.
754.)	20 *April* 1576.	*Gorhambury.* James Gilbert, subject of the duke of Cleves.	6s. 8d.
755.)	20 *April* 1576.	*Gorhambury.* Leonard Bumer, subject of the duke of Cleves.	6s. 8d.
756.)	11 *Feb.* 1576.	Harmon Cuppleman, Spanish subject.	6s. 8d.
757.)	28 *May* 1576.	James Janse, French subject.	6s. 8d.
758.)	10 *March* 1576.	William Lagraunce, Spanish subject.	10s.
759.)	22 *June* 1576.	John Grosse, Spanish subject.	10s.
760.)	2 *June* 1576.	John Lambertes, Spanish subject.	6s. 8d.
761.)	10 *March* 1576.	John Pyngen, subject of the duke of Cleves.	6s. 8d.
762.)	2 *Feb.* 1576.	Henry Swyer, subject of the duke of Cleves.	6s. 8d.
763.)	10 *March* 1576.	William Keye, Spanish subject.	6s. 8d.
764.)	3 *Feb.* 1576.	Paul Tybawe, French subject.	6s. 8d.
765.)	11 *Feb.* 1576.	Peter Savage, subject of the Emperor.	6s. 8d.
766.)	11 *Feb.* 1576.	Oliver Stadd, subject of the duke of Cleves.	6s. 8d.

---

[1] From this point the roll is partially illegible, and the readings of nos. 744–810 have in several cases been taken from the enrolment of the same patents on Exchequer, Lord Treasurer's Remembrancer, Originalia Roll (E.371) 470, *ms.* cli–clviii.

767.) 11 *Feb.* 1576. John Pettes, subject of the duke of Cleves. 6*s.* 8*d.*
768.) 11 *Feb.* 1576. William Batter, Spanish subject. 6*s.* 8*d.*
769.) 11 *Feb.* 1576. Allerd Laniell, Spanish subject. 6*s.* 8*d.*
770.) 12 *Feb.* 1576. Lewis Beyt, Spanish subject.
771.) 11 *Feb.* 1576. James Novar, Spanish subject. 6*s.* 8*d.*
772.) 8 *Feb.* 1576. Garrett Waters, Spanish subject. 6*s.* 8*d.*
773.) 1 *March* 1576. Benet le Sagey, Spanish subject. 6*s.* 8*d.*
774.) 3 *March* 1576. Ferdinand Buttoney, Spanish subject. 10*s.*
775.) 7 *March* 1576. Stacy van den Starre, subject of the Emperor. 10*s.*
776.) 7 *March* 1576. Peter Barre, French subject. 6*s.* 8*d.*
777.) 11 *Feb.* 1576. James Byzon, Spanish subject. 6*s.* 8*d.*
778.) 14 *Feb.* 1576. Gilbert Toulemond, Spanish subject. 6*s.* 8*d.*
779.) 11 *Feb.* 1576. John Vanderspike, Spanish subject. 6*s.* 8*d.*
780.) 4 *Feb.* 1576. John Spinosa, Spanish subject. 6*s.* 8*d.*
781.) 11 *Feb.* 1576. Oliver Cleven, subject of the bishop of Cologne. 6*s.* 8*d.*
782.) 5 *March* 1576. Lewis Vallee, French subject. 6*s.* 8*d.*
783.) 11 *Feb.* 1576. Henry Leonardes, subject of the Emperor. 6*s.* 8*d.*
784.) 3 *March* 1576. Peter Barmeston, subject of the Emperor. 6*s.* 8*d.*
785.) 1 *March* 1576. Matthew Delacambre, Spanish subject. 6*s.* 8*d.*
786.) 3 *March* 1576. Balthazar Pygen, subject of the duke of Cleves. 6*s.* 8*d.*
787.) 23 *Feb.* 1576. Harman Buckhold, Spanish subject. 6*s.* 8*d.*
788.) 12 *Feb.* 1576. Peter Bayly, Spanish subject. 6*s.* 8*d.*
789.) 12 *Feb.* 1576. Martin St. Legier, Spanish subject. 10*s.* [*m.* 45]
790.) 12 *Feb.* 1576. Fiacre Hocede, Spanish subject. 6*s.* 8*d.*
791.) 12 *Feb.* 1576. John Doreyne, Spanish subject. 6*s.* 8*d.*
792.) 12 *Feb.* 1576. Michael du Crope, Spanish subject. 6*s.* 8*d.*
793.) 11 *Feb.* 1576. Alexandrin du Coon, Spanish subject. 6*s.* 8*d.*
794.) 11 *Feb.* 1576. Arnold Goodawe, Spanish subject. 6*s.* 8*d.*
795.) 15 *Feb.* 1576. Bastrian Cobryse, Spanish subject. 6*s.* 8*d.*
796.) 11 *Feb.* 1576. John Lawney, clerk, French subject. 20*s.*
797.) 11 *Feb.* 1576. Jerman Honyon, Spanish subject. 6*s.* 8*d.*
798.) 11 *Feb.* 1576. John Ifeler, subject of the duke of Cleves. 6*s.* 8*d.*
799.) 11 *Feb.* 1576. Philip Ruttey, Spanish subject. 6*s.* 8*d.*
800.) 11 *Feb.* 1576. Bonus Raperlye, Spanish subject. 6*s.* 8*d.*
801.) 11 *Feb.* 1576. Lambert Leonardes, subject of the Emperor. 6*s.* 8*d.*
802.) 20 *March* 1576. Dominic Bowscher, Spanish subject. 10*s.*
803.) 3 *Nov.* 1576. Giles Scoltons, Spanish subject. 6*s.* 8*d.*
804.) 14 *Sept.* 1576. *Gorhambury.* Stephen Johnson, subject of [—]. 6*s.* 8*d.*
805.) 16 *Nov.* 1576. Michael Durrant, French subject. 10*s.*
806.) 15 *Nov.* 1576. Nicholas Leonarde, Spanish subject. 16*s.*
807.) 6 *Nov.* 1576. Peter Dixsonn, Scottish subject. 10*s.*
808.) 5 *Nov.* 1576. Peter Bungard, French subject. 6*s.* 8*d.*
809.) 12 *Nov.* 1576. John Thomas, Spanish subject. 46*s.* 8*d.*
810.) 12 *Nov.* 1576. Willielma Thomas, wife of John Thomas, Spanish subject. 10*s.*

811.) 5 *Oct.* 1576. *Gorhambury.* Pardon for Robert Smyth late of London. It is reported by a tenor of the record of Robert Hogeson, coroner of the city, that in the parish of St. Bride in Fletestrete in Farringden Without ward, London, on 30 August, 18 Eliz., he wounded Nicholas Jones, 'yoman', in self defence so that he died on the same day in the parish of St. Andrew in Holborne in the ward aforesaid (*details given*).

(*The dorse of this roll is blank.*)

PART VIII

C. 66/1144

812.)   18 *Nov.* 1575.   Lease for 21 years to Giles Durdray of London   [*m.* 1]
of (1) lands (*named with tenants' names*), parcel of Glyn park next Wrexham, in Estlusham, co.
Denbigh, parcel of the lordship of Bromefield and late of William Stanley, knight, attainted,
(2) lands (*named with tenants' names*) in Glynne park, parcel of the lordships of Bromfeld and
Yale, co. Denbigh, late of Stanley aforesaid, (3) lands (*named*) in Glyn park in the charge of
the bailiff of Estlusham, parcel of the lordships of Bromfeld and Yale, late of Stanley
aforesaid, (4) the tithes of corn in Lenton and Radford or elsewhere, co. Nottingham,
belonging to the rectories of Lenton and Radford, late of the monastery of Lenton, (5) the
site of the manor of Cardeston and lands (*named*) in Cardeston and Riffehame, co. Norfolk,
(6) lands (*named*) in Cardeston and Riffehame, (7) lands (*named*) in Cawston, co. Norfolk, late
of James   [*m.* 2]
Bulleyn, knight, (8) lands called 'lez demeasne' of the lordship of Kilgaron, co. Pembroke,
and herbage of the forest there, (9) lands (*named*) in Horsington More, parcel of the manor of
Norton Ferrers, co. Somerset, and late of Charles, lord Stourton, attainted of murder, (10)
lands (*named with tenants' names*) in the manor of Mere, co. Wilts, parcel of the duchy of
Cornwall, and (11) lands (*named with tenants' names*), parcels of the manor of Prestbury, co.
Gloucester, and leased severally by indentures of John, late bishop of Hereford, for terms of
years; (1) and (2) from Lady Day 1585, having   [*m.* 3]
been leased by patents of the Exchequer, (1) 21 May, 6 Eliz., to John Sonlley *alias* Sontlley
inter alia for 21 years from Lady Day then last at a yearly rent of 28s. and (2) 5 July, 6 Eliz., to
Edward Gittins *inter alia* for 21 years from Lady Day then last at a yearly rent of 27s. 8d.; (3)
from Lady Day 1586, having been leased by patent of the Exchequer, 13 July, 7 Eliz., to
Francis Gittins *inter alia* for 21 years from Lady Day then last at a yearly rent of 24s.; (4) from
Michaelmas 1582, having been leased by patent, 12 March, 4 Eliz., to Edward Southworth
for 21 years from Michaelmas then last at a yearly rent of £11; (5), (6) and (7) from Lady Day
1583, having been leased by patent, 21 Nov., 5 Eliz., to Thomas Payne for 21 years from
Lady Day then last at yearly rents of (5) 66s. 8d., (6) 7s. and (7) £10; (8) from Michaelmas
1598, having been leased by patent, 26 June, 4 & 5 Ph. & Mary, to Thomas Phaire for 40
years from Michaelmas then next at a yearly rent of £4 16d.; (9) from the termination of a
lease therof by patent, 16 July, 16 Eliz., to Thomas Wolfe, Gervase Bazden, William Mercer
and Mathew Twyford *inter alia* at a yearly rent of 6s. 8d. for 21 years from the death,
surrender or forfeiture of the interest therein of Agnes Rise, now wife of Edward Baynton;
(10) from Michaelmas next or the termination of any lease or grant thereof by copy of court
roll for life or years or estate of widowhood according to the custom of the manor enduring
after that date; (11) from   [*m.* 4]
Michaelmas 1591; yearly rents (1) 28s., (2) 27s. 8d. (3) 24s., (4) £11, (5), (6) and (7)
£13 13s. 8d., (8) £4 16d., (9) 6s. 8d., (10) 6s. 1d. and (11) 34s. 10d. (*detailed*). For the service and
at the suit of Ralph Lane, an equerry of the stable.   By p.s.

813.)   1 *Dec.* 1575.   *Inspeximus* and confirmation for the mayor, bailiffs and citizens of
Corke in Ireland of a patent of confirmation, 9 May, 3 Edw. VI,   [*m.* 5]
inspecting and confirming—(1) a patent of confirmation, 24 Feb., 1 Hen. VIII, inspecting
and confirming a patent, 1 Aug., 15 Hen. VII, [*Calendar of Patent Rolls*, 1494-1509, p. 204]

inspecting and confirming, with grant of additional liberties, a patent, 12 Feb., 5 Ric. II,
inspecting and confirming a   [*m.* 6]
charter of confirmation, 15 July, 4 Edw. III [*Calendar of Charter Rolls*, Vol. IV, p. 180]
inspecting and confirming, with grant of an additional liberty, a charter of confirmation, 20
July, 12 Edw. II [*Calendar of Charter Rolls*, Vol. III, p. 390] inspecting and confirming, with
grant of additional   [*m.* 7]
liberties, a charter of confirmation, 12 June, 19 Edw. I, inspecting and confirming a charter,
2 Jan., 26 Hen. III [*Calendar of Charter Rolls*, Vol. I, p. 266] granting to the citizens the said
city at fee farm with divers liberties; (2) a patent, 11 March, 28 Hen. VIII [*Letters and Papers,
Henry VIII*, Vol. XII, Part I, no. 795 (21)] granting liberties to the mayor, bailiffs and
commonalty of the said city; and (3) a patent of confirmation, 17 July, 4 Edw. III [*Calendar of
Patent Rolls*, 1327–1330, p. 54] inspecting and confirming a patent under the seal used in
Ireland, 20 Jan., 11 Edw. II, granting liberties to the said mayor, bailiffs and commonalty.

Also grant to them of liberties as follows:— The mayor, recorder and bailiffs for the time
being and the four senior aldermen who have been mayor as long as they remain aldermen to
be keepers of the peace in the city and the liberties and suburbs thereof by land and by water;
the same (or three of them, the mayor or the recorder being one) to be justices to inquire
touching all offences appertaining to justices of the peace; the same (or three of them, the
mayor or the recorder being one)   [*m.* 8]
also to be justices of gaol delivery, and to have gallows within the liberties of the city for the
lawful putting to death of malefactors according to the law of the land. To have all fines,
redemptions and amercements for offences committed there, all penalties and forfeitures of
the citizens and residents there for the peace and otherwise, and all issues, fines, redemptions
and amercements of the citizens and residents forfeited before any of the justices,
commissioners or officers of the Crown; to be levied by the bailiffs to the use of the mayor,
bailiffs and citizens. To have all goods of felons and outlaws, deodands and other forfeitures
concerning all citizens resident and non-resident there and all others found there and for any
offence in whatever court justice ought to be done concerning it; to be taken by the bailiffs or
others in their name to the use of the mayor, bailiffs and citizens, although first seized by the
Crown or its ministers. Licence to acquire lands to the yearly value of £40, for the
maintenance of the churches of Holy Trinity and St. Peter in the said city, to wit, £20 to the
use of each church.

At their suit.   By p.s.

814.) 7 *Feb.* 1576.   Pardon of outlawry for John Jackson late of Walden, co. Essex, the
younger, 'yoman', who was put in exigent in the county of Cambridge for non-appearance
in the Common Pleas to answer John Fokes *alias* Fowkes of Bottesham, co. Cambridge, in a
plea of debt of £200 and has now surrendered himself to the Fleet prison.

815.) 9 *Dec.* 1575.   The like for Thomas Boreham late of London, 'yoman', *alias* of
Matching, co. Essex, 'singleman', who was put in exigent in the husting of London for
non-appearance in the Common Pleas to answer   [*m.* 9]
Thomas Jonson of London, 'husbandman', in a plea for payment of £10 and has now
surrendered himself to the Fleet prison.

816.) 1 *Dec.* 1575.   The like for Richard Smytheson late of London, 'yoman', *alias* of
Rumbalde, co. York, who was put in exigent in the husting of London for non-appearance
in the Common Pleas to answer Robert Temple, Alice his wife and James Temple, his son,
in a plea of debt of £10 and has now surrendered himself to the Fleet prison.

817.) 1 *Dec.* 1575.   The like for Jenkin David of Kellaunn, co. Cardigan, *alias* Jenkin

David Lloid of the parish of Gellan, co. Cardigan, 'yoman', and Morgan ap Jevan *alias* Morgan Abevan Morgan Price of Llandewy Brevy, co. Cardigan, 'yeoman', who were put in exigent in the county of Cardigan for non-appearance at the great session in the said county at Cardigan to satisfy Edward Myddleton of Carmarthen, merchant, in respect of a debt of 42s., and 16s. damages, recovered in the same court and have now surrendered themselves to Cardigan gaol (as certified by George Fetyplace, justice of the great session in the said county).

818.)   24 *Nov.* 1575.   The like for William Knyght late of Atherston, co. Warwick, 'yoman', administrator of Joyce Hyll, widow, who died intestate, *alias* administratrix of Amias Hyll, who died intestate, which Knyght was put in exigent in the county of Warwick for non-appearance in the Common Pleas to answer William Hodgekyns of Atherston, 'glover', and Richard Brookes of Bentley, co. Warwick, 'husbandman', in a plea of debt of £30 and has now surrendered himself to the Fleet prison.

819.)   17 *Feb.* 1576.   Lease for 30 years to Thomas Nevinson of (1) the site of the manor or 'le manour place' of Wingham, co. Kent, demesne lands (*named*) there and the profits of the fairs at Godneston, co. Kent, and   [*m.* 10]
(2) lands (*named with tenant's name*) adjoining the premises, all parcels of the manor of Wingham and of the possessions of the late archbishop of Canterbury in the Queen's hands by exchange and now in the tenure of the said Thomas Nevinson and his assigns; with reservations; from Michaelmas 1590, having been leased by indenture, 3 July, 1 Edw. VI, by Thomas, once archbishop of Canterbury, to Christopher Nevinson and Anne his wife at a yearly rent of £27 3s. 4d. for 21 years from Michaelmas 1569, the premises in (1) having been leased by the same archbishop by indenture, 1 March, 27 Hen. VIII, to Henry Bingham, then his servant, and Jane his wife for 30 years from Michaelmas 1539 at a yearly rent of £24 13s. 4d. (the interest of which Henry and Jane having been obtained by the said Christopher and Anne was by the said indenture of 3 July, 1 Edw. VI, confirmed to them); yearly rent £27 3s. 4d.; the lessee to provide entertainment at the manor for the Queen's steward, surveyor and bailiff coming to hold courts or make a survey. For the service and at the suit of Thomas Windebancke, a clerk of the signet.   By p.s.

820.)   17 *Feb.* 1576.   Lease for 21 years to Hugh Lloyd of the late college and collegiate church of Caercubie *alias* Hollyhead, the chapel of   [*m.* 11]
Eccloyse y Bedd *alias* Egloys y Bedd within the graveyard of the said church and the churches or chapels of Boderocke *alias* Bodwrocke, Bodederne and Llandrigarne, co. Anglesey, annexed to the same college; with reservations; from Michaelmas last or the termination of any former lease sufficient in law of the same or any parcel thereof enduring after that date; yearly rent £25 20d.; the lessee to find three sufficient chaplains or curates for the churches and chapels of Bodederne, Boderocke, Bodwrocke and Llandringarne; also to pay yearly 100s. for the stipend of the vicar of Hollyhead, 22s. 10d. for proxies and synodals to the bishop of Bangor and 6s. 2d. for proxies and synodals to the archdeacon of Anglesey. In   [*m.* 12]
consideration of the surrender in Chancery by Lloyd of a patent, 14 Feb., 12 Eliz., leasing the premises to him at a yearly rent of £25 20d. for 21 years from the termination of a lease thereof by patent, 20 Dec., 7 Eliz., to Owen Woodde for 21 years from Michaelmas then last at a yearly rent of £23 12s. 8d.; also because it is doubtful whether the patents aforesaid made to Woodde and Lloyd were sufficient in law.   By p.s.

821.)   6 *March* 1576.   Lease for 21 years (1) to John Nettleton of the rectory of Hotton

Crancewicke, co. York, the tithes of corn of the glebe land of the same rectory and the tithes
of corn in the parish of Hooton Crancewick,   [m. 13]
all late of the monastery of Watton, co. York, and (2) to Edward Nettleton of the rectory of
Skerne, co. York, late of the said monastery; with reservations; from Lady Day next; yearly
rents (1) £8 for the rectory and £26 13s. 4d. for the tithes of corn in the parish and (2) £8; the
lessee to pay to the vicar of Hootton Cranswick a yearly stipend of £16. On surrender by the
said John and Edward of patents, (a) 11 Jan., 5 Eliz., leasing to William Forster the tithes of
corn in the parish of Hooton Crancewicke, except the tithes of the glebe land there, for 21
years from Michaelmas then last at a yearly rent of £26 13s. 4d., (b) 16 Feb., 8 Eliz., to Jane
Nettleton, widow, of the rectory of Hooton Crancewick (the tithes of corn in the parish,
except those on the glebe lands of the rectory, reserved) for 21 years from Michaelmas then
last at a yearly rent of £8 and (c) 16 Feb., 8 Eliz., to the said Jane of the rectory of Skerne for
21 years from Michaelmas then last at a yearly rent of £8. For a fine of £66 13s. 4d. paid at the
Exchequer.

                              By the commissioners by virtue of the Queen's warrant.

822.)   14 *May* 1576.   Lease for 21 years to William Hunys, master of the children of the
Queen's chapel, of (1) a tenement in Westminster, co. Middlesex, (to the South of 'le Longe
Wolstaple' abutting towards the   [m. 14]
North on a tenement belonging to the late brotherhood of Our Lady in St. Margaret's
church there, towards the royal palace in the South, on a tenement of the dean and canons
there once in the tenure of John Allyn in the East and on 'le Longe Wolstaple' in the North),
once inhabited by Richard Heton and belonging to the late college or free chapel of St.
Stephen, Westminster, (2) the church of Fourde, co. Salop, and a tenement (*tenant named*)
there, once of the late college of Battlefeild, co. Salop, (3) the rectory, chapel or church of
Dalley (*alias* Dawley), co. Salop, once of Battlefeild college, (4) a mill (*named with tenants'
names*) in Over Elvell in the lordship of Elvell in the commote of Colion, co. Radnor,
belonging to the late earl of March, (5) the rectory of Dodington, co. Northampton, once of
the monastery of Delepraye, co. Northampton,   [m. 15]
and (6) the tithes of corn and hay in Nunley and (7) all the tithes in Bagley *alias* Bagbie, which
tithes (*tenants named*) in Nunley and Bagley are parcels of the rectory of Basechurche, co.
Salop, and were once of the monastery of SS. Peter and Paul, Shrewsbury, co. Salop; with
reservations; (1) from Michaelmas 1585, having been leased by patent of the Exchequer, 15
Jan., 7 Eliz., to Richard Lewes, the Queen's servant, for 21 years from Michaelmas then last
at a yearly rent of 66s. 8d.; (2) and (3) from Michaelmas 1583, having been leased by two
several patents of the Exchequer, 9 March, 5 Eliz., to John Jackson for 21 years from
Michaelmas then last at yearly rents of (2) 66s. 8d. and (3) 66s. 8d.; (4) from Lady Day 1582,
having been leased by patent of the Exchequer, 21 June, 3 Eliz., to John Vaughan for 21
years from Lady Day then last at a yearly rent of 10s.; (5) from Michaelmas next or the
termination of any former lease or grant thereof for life or years enduring after that date; (6)
and (7) from Midsummer next or the termination of any former lease or grant thereof for life
or years enduring after that date; yearly rents (1) 66s. 8d., (2) 66s. 8d., (3) 66s. 8d., (4) 10s., (5)
£10, (6) 15s. and (7) 20s.   [m. 16]
    For his service.   By Q.

823.)   20 *Feb.* 1576.   Lease for 21 years, if they or either of them shall so long live, to Peter
Gye, the Queen's servant, and Isabel his wife of lands in Eastgrenewich, co. Kent, (1) West
of the Queen's park and (2) (*former tenant named*) South of the Queen's garden, all now or late
in the tenure of Gye and once of Shene priory, co. Surrey; with reservations; (1) from the
death of George Haward, knight, or the termination of a grant by patent, 28 Oct., 14 Eliz.,
to him for life of the offices of steward of the lordships and manors of Lewisham,

Sayescourte, Westgrenewich, Estgrenewich, Le Shrofolde and Bankers, co. Kent, chief steward of the lordship and manor and town of Depford and Stronde, co. Kent, and bailiff of the manor of Sayescourte and (2) from Lady Day next; yearly rents   [*m.* 17] (1) 13*s.* 4*d.* and (2) 6*s.* 8*d.*   By p.s.

824.)   20 *Feb.* 1576.   Lease for 21 years to John Taylour of the site of the manor of Wetwange, co. York, and lands there (*named*), parcels of the manor of Wetwange and of possessions of the archbishop of York, exchanged; with reservations; including a sheep pasture (*named with tenants' names*); from Lady Day next; yearly rent £11. In consideration of the surrender by Taylour of the interest therein of William Lepington of Wetwange on le Woolde, 'yoman', to whom Edward, archbishop of York, by indenture, 21 Feb., 31 Hen. VIII, leased *inter alia* the premises, then in Lepington tenure, for 41 years from Michaelmas then next at the same rent; and for a fine of £11 paid at the Exchequer.
By the commissioners by virtue of the Queen's warrant.

825.)   24 *Feb.* 1576.   Lease for 21 years to William Knowles and Jane his wife of a capital messuage called 'le Hall Garth' and lands belonging thereto in Withorne Wicke, co. York, parcel of lands late of Richard Gresham, knight, exchanged; with reservations; from Lady Day next;   [*m.* 18] yearly rent £7 6*s.* 8*d.* In consideration of the surrender by the said William and Jane of a patent, 3 July, 3 & 4 Ph. & Mary, leasing the premises to William Bolton for 31 years from Lady Day then last at the same rent; and for a fine of £12 paid at the Exchequer.
By the commissioners by virtue of the Queen's warrant.

826.)   9 *May* 1576.   Lease for 21 years to William Swayne of the coal mines and 'le vaynes' of coal called 'pittcole', 'store cole' or 'sea cole' in a close or field called Morefeild *alias* Moresfeld *alias* Moricefeild in the parish of Wickeham in the bishopric of Durham; from Lady Day last; yearly rent £20, if the mine and 'le vaynes' last so long; licence to dig and make pits and ditches called 'le sowghes' to carry off water from the mines   [*m.* 19] and to use 'le sowghes' heretofore made; also licence to carry coals won through lands of the parish to the Tyne or elsewhere; also to have wood in adjoining woods of the bishopric for the maintenance of the pits; the pits and 'le sowghes' are to be closed over as soon as they are completed and not left open, and the earth dug out is to be scattered. In consideration that John Heath, Robert Swyfte, LL.B., Gregory Butler, John Bathe and John Clopton, receiver general in the bishopric, commissioners by virtue of a commission out of the Exchequer to survey certain lands in the bishopric, have reported that the said close (*described*) (44ac.) probably contains a mine of 'pittecoles' worth £20 yearly for leasing, and Swayne offers to pay the said rent.   By p.s.

827.)   24 *Feb.* 1576.   Lease for 21 years to John Dodington of woods (*named*) in the manor of Salford, co. Warwick; with reservations; from Michaelmas last; yearly rent from the time when he shall enjoy possession £8 16*s.* 9*d.*; the lessee to make two cuttings only of the woods and at suitable times, to enclose the woods after cutting and preserve 'lez springes' from damage by animals during the term limited by statute, to leave sufficient 'lez staddelles' in every acre according to statute, and to cause this patent to be enrolled before the auditor of the county for charging of the rent and before the surveyor of woods this side of Trent for survey of the performance of the said covenants before any cutting be made. In consideration that he will undertake the charges of enclosure of the woods, which must be enclosed for seven years after cutting as is certified by the surveyor aforesaid.   [*m.* 20]
By the commissioners by virtue of the Queen's warrant.

828.)   23 *March* 1576.   *Gorhambury*.   Lease for 21 years to William Kendall of Braunce-peth, 'yoman', of lands (*named*) in Cottingham, co. York, parcels of the lordship of Cottingham and of lands late had in exchange from Charles, late earl of Westmorland; with reservations; from Michaelmas last; yearly rent 106*s*. 8*d*. In consideration of the surrender of an indenture, 2 Oct., 4 Eliz., whereby Henry, earl of Westmorland, leased to Kendall, then his servant, *inter alia* the said lands, then or late in Kendall's tenure, for 21 years from Candlemas then next at a yearly rent for them and other lands specified in the indenture of £11 6*s*. 8*d*.; and for a fine of £10 13*s*. 4*d*. paid at the Exchequer within a sum of £22 13*s*. 4*d*.
By the commissioners by virtue of the Queen's warrant.

829.)   14 *July* 1576.   Lease for 21 years to Lawrence Wagstaffe, John Strete and John Wheeler, the Queen's servants, of (1) a moiety of the demesne lands of the manor of Northborne, co. Kent, of buildings belonging to the manor once parcel of the possessions of the archbishop of Canterbury, to wit, the mansion house of the manor and a house called 'le myllehouse', 'le kylnehouse' and 'le brewhouse', late parcel of 'the Abbottes Howse' there, and of lands etc. (*named*) some parcel of the demesne lands, with the tithes of corn of the premises and a moiety of all other tithes anciently payable to the farmer of the site of the manor out of divers lands parcel of the manor and a moiety of the customs of white salt and of 'le shares' (*vomer*') belonging to the said farmer, (2) lands (*named with tenants' names*) in Northborne and Sholden, co. Kent, parcels of the manor of Northborne, (3) lands (*named with tenants' names*) in Northborne, parcels of the said manor, and (4) the manor called Brokas in Cluer, co. Berks, late purchased from lord Sandes; with reservations, including 'le Abbottes Howse', the other moiety of the demesne lands of the manor aforesaid and the tithes thereof now in the tenure of Miles Pendreth, the other moiety of the tithes payable to the farmer of the site of the manor, also the rents of assize, rents of cocks, hens and eggs and all other like rents and profits which the beadle of Northborne used to collect yearly, also the rents of the manors of Rypley and Langdon, also all marshes, lands, rivers and 'lez brookes' belonging to the manor of Northborne (except those leased hereby), rents called 'le Holycrosse rent', 'grasse silver', 'potte sylver', quit rents in the weald, straw, reeds and 'rushberdes' on the lands of the said manor, and 534 'le helme seames' on the lands of the manor of Northborne to be collected yearly to the use of the Crown, also the moiety of 'le kylhowse', 'the mylhouse' and 'the brwehouse' now or late in the tenure of Pendreth, and the rents of   [*m. 21*]
assize of free tenants parcel of the manor of Brokas amounting to 53*s*. 11*d*.; (1) from Michaelmas 1588, the farm of the manor of Northborne, the tithes of the lands of the same, 33 ac. of marsh and brooks (*brosc*') and the custom of white salt and of 'le shares' belonging to the farm of the manor, parcels of possessions of the late archbishop of Canterbury in the Queen's hands by act of Parliament, having been leased by patent, 5 July[1], 7 Eliz., to Henry Leigh, avener of the stable, as to one moiety and Peter Atkinson and Margery his wife, a daughter of Anne Penreth, deceased, late the Queen's nurse, as to the other moiety for 30 years from Michaelmas 1567 or the termination of the interest therein of   [*m. 22*]
Robert and Henry Poysshe at a yearly rent of £18 18*s*. 9*d*.; (2) from Michaelmas 1587, having been leased by patent of the Exchequer, 29 Oct., 8 Eliz., to Thomas Manneringe for 21 years at a yearly rent of £4 8*s*. 8*d*. (*detailed*); (3) from Michaelmas 1594, having been leased by patent, 28 Nov., 16 Eliz., to Thomas Fowrde for 21 years from Michaelmas then last at a yearly rent of 12*s*. 8*d*. (*detailed*); (4) from the termination of the interest of John Durdaunte, to whom the manor was leased by Thomas, lord Sandes, by indenture, 2 Dec., 35 Hen. VIII, for 50 years from Michaelmas then next at a yearly rent of £7; yearly rents (1) £18 18*s*. 9*d*., (2) £4 8*s*. 8*d*., (3) 12*s*. 8*d*. and (4) £6 12*s*. 4½*d*.; the lessees to discharge the Crown from the yearly

---

[1] The enrolment of this patent (*Calendar*, 1563–66 no. 1105) gives its date as '7 July'.

payment of 6s. 8d. out of (4) once payable to the monastery of Busclesham, 29s. 9½d. to the castle of Wyndesore for rent of assarts and purprestures and 2s. 4d. at the said castle for rent called 'lostfeild sylver'; the lessees may use in common with the farmer of the other moiety of the site and demesne lands of the manor of Northborne 'le yarde' or close before the said site, 'le Abbottes House' and the stables and access to or from the water or river there, as accustomed; the lessees to provide a moiety of the entertainment for the Queen's steward, surveyor and beadle at the manor coming to hold courts or make a survey; licence also to take estovers both in the premises and in the Queen's woods called   [m. 23] Betteshanger and Hedlinge in the parish of Waldershire, co. Kent. For their service.

By p.s.

830.)   12 *July* 1576.   Lease for 80 years to William Fyssher of (1) a capital messuage in Fencote in the halimote of Stoke, co. Hereford, a tenement (*tenant named*) there and a hereditament called Westwoode *alias* Westwoode Parke (*tenant named*), once of Leompster Priory, co. Hereford, (2) the   [m. 24] herbage and pannage of Rockingham park, with the office of keeper of the deer and wild beasts in Rockingham park and in Corby Woodes within Rockingham forest, co. Northampton, (3) all lands in Kington Maundfelde *alias* Knighton Maundesfeild, Estlydforde and Babcary, co. Somerset, once of the late priory or hospital of St. John, Bridgwater, (4) lands (*named*) parcel of Glynne Parke next Wrexham, parcel of the lordship of Bromfelde, co. Denbigh, and late of William Stanley, knight, attainted of treason, (5) lands (*named with tenants' names*) in Glynne park, parcel of the lordships of Bromefelde and Yale, co. Denbigh, (6) lands (*named*) in Glynne park, parcel of lands in the charge of the bailiff of   [m. 25] Estlusham, parcel of the lordships of Bromefeld and Yale, late of Stanley aforesaid, (7) a moiety of the site of the rectory of Erlingham, co. Gloucester, of the tithes of corn and hay, of the tithes of fish taken in Garronwere and Rodleyswere and of all other fruits and emoluments belonging to the rectory, (8) lands in Lymby *alias* Lynby, co. Nottingham, once of Jasper, duke of Bedford, (9) lands (*named with tenants' names*) in Staunton under Bardon in the parish of Thorneton and elsewhere,   [m. 26] co. Leicester, parcel of the manor of Whitwick and late of the late duke of Suffolk, attainted, (10) lands (*named with tenant's name*), parcel of the said manor of Whitwick, (11) lands (*named with tenant's name*), parcel of the said manor of Whitwicke, (12) mines and 'le vaynes' of coal called 'pitcole', 'stonecole' or 'seacole' in Lenton and Radforde, Stapleforde, Brampecote and Briston, co. Nottingham, (13) the site of the manor and the capital messuage, farm or hereditament of Thickwood, co. Wilts, once of the monastery of Malmesbury, co. Wilts, (14) lands (*tenant named*) in the manor and borough of Honyton and the parish of Offewell, co. Devon, late of Henry, late duke of Suffolk, (15) lands (*tenant named*) in Goteham, co. Nottingham, once of the monastery of Durham, and all appurtenances thereof including 'lez playster', (16) the towns of Bodverryn and Penllegh in the commote of Kemytmayne, co. Carnarvon, parcel of the principality of North Wales, and (17) lands called Norwoode Parke, once of the monastery of Glaston and late of Edward, late duke of Somerset, and all appurtenances thereof in Glaston and elsewhere, co. Somerset; with reservations; (1), (9) and (12) from Michaelmas 1596, having been leased (1) by patent, 20 Jan., 18 Eliz., to Thomas Harrys for 21 years from Michaelmas then last at a yearly rent of 50s. 4d., (9) by patent of the Exchequer, 17 May, 17 Eliz., to William Raven for 21 years from Lady Day then last at a yearly rent of 24s. and (12) by patent, 6 March, 18 Eliz., to Edward, earl of Rutland, for 21 years from Michaelmas then last at a yearly rent of 10s.; (2) from the termination of a lease thereof by patent, 24 Dec., 14 Eliz.,   [m. 27] to lady Dorothy Stafforde *inter alia* at a yearly rent of £4 for 31 years from the termination of a lease thereof by the Crown dated 10 April, 1 & 2 Ph. & Mary, to Edward Watson for 30 years from Lady Day then next, and without the fee of £3 6s. 8d. and any other payments formerly allowed for the office of keeper aforesaid; (3), (8), (10), (11) and (15) from Michaelmas 1591, having been leased (3) by patent, 18 July, 12 Eliz., to Richard Barnard for 21 years from Lady Day then last at a yearly rent of 109s. 8d., (8) by patent, 4 Dec., 13 Eliz., to Thomas Staveley for 21 years from Michaelmas then last at a yearly rent of £7 2s. 6½d., (10) by patent, 10 May, 12 Eliz., to Thomas Woode *inter alia* for 21 years from Lady Day then last at a yearly rent of 60s., (11) by patent of the Exchequer, 3 Dec., 14 Eliz., to John Cholmley for 21 years from Michaelmas then last at a yearly rent of 41s. 6d. and (15) by patent of the Exchequer, 4 April, 11 Eliz., to Henry Wright for 21 years at a yearly rent of 64s. 6d. (*detailed*); (4), (5) and (6) from Lady Day 1606, having been leased by patent, 18 Nov., 18 Eliz., to Giles Durdray *inter alia* for 21 years from (4) and (5) Lady Day 1585 and (6) Lady Day 1586 at yearly rents of (4) 28s., (5) 27s. 8d. and (6) 24s.; (7) from Michaelmas 1582, having been leased by patent of the court of Augmentations, 21 Feb., 7 Edw. VI, to John Smyth, the king's servant, *inter alia* (the same having been leased by William, late abbot, and the convent of the monastery of St. Peter, Gloucester, and John Rodley, late prior of Stanley St. Leonard, by indenture, 1 July, 23 Hen. VIII, to Richard Longney, Walter his son, Agnes wife of Walter and Richard and Robert sons of Walter and Agnes for 50 years if they or any of them should so long live), with reservations of the portion of the vicar of Erlingham and all lands belonging to the rectory, for 30 years from Michaelmas then last at a yearly rent of £7 10s.; (13) and (14) from Michaelmas next or the termination of any former lease or grant thereof for life or years enduring after that date; (17) from the termination of a lease thereof by patent, 7 April, 5 Eliz., to Maurice Barkeley, knight, for 40 years from Lady Day then last at a yearly rent of £6 13s. 4d.; (16) from Lady Day 1603, having been leased by patent, 28 May, 10 Eliz., to Edward, earl of Lincoln, councillor, by the name of Edward Fynes, K.G., lord Clynton and Saye, *inter alia* at a yearly rent of £6 2s. 4d. for 30 years from the termination of a lease thereof by patent, 29 March, 6 Edw. VI, to John Boddye for 21 years from Michaelmas then next; yearly rents (1) 50s. 4d., (2) £4,

[*m.* 28]

(3) £5 9s. 8d., (4), (5) and (6) 79s. 8d., (7) £7 10s., (8) £7 2s. 6½d., (9) 24s., (10) 60s., (11) 41s. 6d., (12) 10s., (13) 106s. 8d., (14) 26s., (15) 64s. 6d. (*detailed*), (16) £6 2s. 4d. and (17) £6 13s. 4d.; the lessee may take yearly in Rockingham park and Corbye Woodes six wild beasts and six deer and dispose of them at his discretion to inhabitants thereby, for the better preservation of the deer and wild beasts there; the lessee shall preserve yearly 300 wild beasts and deer in Norwoode park and distribute the same at the Queen's pleasure; he shall also at his own charges maintain the lodge and the pale of Norwoode park and the sewers and 'lez water draynes' and 'lez rayles' therein. In consideration of the service of Alphonso de Ferrabosco, a gentleman of the privy chamber, and of the surrender of an annuity of £50, parcel of £100 granted him by the Queen for life; and at the same Alphonso's suit.

By Q.

831.)   20 *July* 1576.   *Gorhambury.*   Grant to John Farneham, a gentleman pensioner, his heirs and assigns of—(1) the hospital of St. Thomas the Martyr of Eastbridge in Canterbury and all its possessions in Canterbury and elsewhere; (2) land in the parish of St. Andrew in Canterbury, given for obits in the church of St. Andrew aforesaid; (3) the hospital of St. Thomas the Martyr of Boulton and all its possessions in Boulton and elsewhere, co. Northumberland; (4) the hospital of St. Bartholomew in Newberye, co. Berks, and all lands and the fairs in Newberye belonging thereto; (5) lands in Ledcombe Regis and Hannye, co. Berks, given for priests and the like in the church of Wantage, co. Berks; (6) the rectory of Wyssett, co. Suffolk, now or late in the tenure of Christian Wharton, widow, and land and all other possessions belonging thereto, late of Thomas, late duke of Norfolk, attainted of treason; (7) a tenement called 'Saynt Johns Hospytall' in Bedford, co. Bedford, and all

possessions of the same hospital; (8) all lands in Lechelade, co. Gloucester, now or late in the tenure of the churchwardens there given for lights and other superstitious uses in Lechelade church; (9) all lands in Moreton Henmarshe, co. Gloucester, now or late in the tenure of the churchwardens there given for lights and other superstitious uses in Moreton Henmarshe church; (10) lands in Wolston and Goderton *alias* Godrington, co. Gloucester, given for prayer for the departed in Wolston church; (11) tithes and lands (*named,* including 'the Churche House') in Haresfeld and Harescombe, cos. Gloucester and city of Gloucester, given for a clerk saying mass and the distribution of holy bread and water in Haresfeld church; (12) land (*named with tenant's name*)   [*m. 29*]
in Standishe, co. Gloucester, given for a lamp in the church of Harescombe, co. city of Gloucester; (13) lands (*named with tenants' names*) in Quedesley *alias* Quoddesley, co. Gloucester, given for a light on the altar and before St. James's image in Quedesley church; (14) land in Estington by Northelache and in Northelache, co. Gloucester, given for a chaplain in a chapel in Estington; (15) lands (*named*) in Payneswicke, co. Gloucester, given to a chaplain celebrating mass before St. Mary's image in St. Mary's chapel in Payneswicke church; (16) lands (*named with tenants' names*) in Stynchecombe, co. Gloucester, given for superstitious uses in the church there and elsewhere in the county; (17) two ruinous tenements in the parish of St. Martin Outwiche in London, which Joan Yarrowe, widow, held for life by grant of Henry VIII and which she is reported to have alienated on 1 Dec. last to Catherine Yarrow, her daughter, and her heirs to the disinheriting of the Queen; (18) waste ground partly built on, once a tenement, in Lymestreate in the parish of St. Dionis Backchurche in London, now or late in the tenure of Benjamin Digbye, once of the late chantry, almshouse or college of the Holy Trinity called 'Knolles Almeshowse' in Pontefract, co. York; (19) two messuages one in Woodstreate in the parish of St. Peter Westchepe in London and the other in the parish of St. Mary Magdalen in Milkestrete, London, now or late in the tenures of Richard Fulkes and William Warden, given for priests or the like; (20) a tenement in Terringe *alias* Taringe, (21) the advowson of the rectory of Terringe aforesaid, co. Sussex, and (22) lands (*tenants named*) in Compton, co. Sussex, in the Queen's hands by exchange between Henry VIII and Thomas, late lord la Ware; (23) two tenements and (24) the advowson of the rectory of Chalton *alias* Chaweton, co. Southampton, once of the monastery of Nuneton, co. Warwick; (25) lands (*named with tenant's name*) in Cadington, co. Hertford, once of Sannyngfelde priory; (26) woodland called 'Churche Landes' (*tenant named*) in Beconsfeld, co. Buckingham; (27) a ruinous chapel in the graveyard of Beconsfeld; (28) three cottages with gardens adjoining next 'Lez Minories' in the parish of St. Botolph without Algate, London, within the liberties of London and in the county of Middlesex, now or late in the several tenures of Richard Levesham, William Ketlewood, Richard Adamson and widow Clerke, (between a tenement now or late of Martin Bowes, late alderman of London, on the South, land late of the monastery of Graces on the North, the highway on the West and a great garden there on the East), given for priests or the like in the church of St. Mary Athill; (29) a parcel of waste land in the parish of St. Giles in the Fields, co. Middlesex, in the high street (200 ft. long on the East and West and 20 ft. wide on the North and South); (30) all lands now or late called 'le Owte Groundes', 'Twelve Acres' and 'le Estbreache' in the marshes of Popeler and Stebenhithe and in marshes there now or late called 'the Wete Marshes' *alias* 'le Owte Groundes' in Popeler Marshe and Stebenhithe Marshe in Stibenhithe or elsewhere, co. Middlesex, once, it is said, flooded, late of the priory of Graces by the Tower of London, co. Middlesex, leased by the same to Richard, once bishop of London, for a term of years and afterwards by lease of the said bishop in the tenure of Thomas Knighte of London, 'bruer', Edmund and Robert, his sons, and James Marshe; (31) land now used for a garden ($\frac{1}{2}$ac. more or less) adjoining Roper Lane on the North, in the tenure once of Robert Coke, afterwards of Robert Wilson and now of John Miller and others, in the parish of St. Mary Magdalen of

Bermondsey, co. Surrey, late of the monastery of Bermondsey; (32) land (extending from the West gate of the said monastery towards St. George's church Westwards containing in length 40 'lez roodes' more or less and in width at the West end 3 rods more or less and at the East end extending from the said gate towards Barmondsey Graunge 10 rods more or less) with two small cottages   [*m.* 30]
built thereon, now or late in the tenure of Hugh Full, in the said parish of St. Mary Magdalen, late of the said monastery of Bermondsey; (33) a messuage in Saynt Michaells Lane in the parish of St. Michael in Croked Lane by Candellwickestrete, London, in the tenure late of [—] Rawlyns and now or late of James Jackson, and two tenements in Estchepe, London, in the parish of St. Clement by Estchepe, late in the tenure of George Henrye, one of them called 'le Signe of the Horse Shoe', now or late in the tenure of Henry Lewes, and the other called 'le Signe of the Horsehed', now or late in the tenure of James Ilye, once of Benet Jackson, citizen and butcher of London, and William, his bastard son, and in the Queen's hands as in right of the Crown of England and by divers acts of Parliament; (34) two parcels of land called 'Dryvinges Wales', whereof one extends from Bermondsey grange to 'Priestes Marshe' and the other from the same grange to Rederhithe *alias* Reddriffe, with the herbage or pasture of the said walls in the parishes of Redderhithe and St. Mary Magdalen, co. Surrey, now or late in the tenure of Robert Trappes and Thomas Shepard, late of Bermondsey abbey; (35) the tithes of lands (*named with tenant's name*) within Beverlacye park in Beverley, co. York, late parcel of possessions of the archbishop of York, exchanged and parcel of the church of St. John of Beverlacye; (36) fisheries etc. (*named with tenant's name*) in Rowthe, co. York, late of the monastery of Meux, co. York; (37) lands (*tenant named*) in Raventhorpe, co. York, late of the monastery of Meux; (38) lands (*tenant named*) in Eston next Bridlington, co. York, late of Merrycke priory, co. York; (39) lands (*tenants named*) in Folyflatt, co. York, once of the monastery of Newborroughe, co. York; (40) the tithes of turves (*tenants named*) in Kylnewicke, co. York, once of the monastery of Watton, co. York; (41) the tithes of lands (*named*) within the manor of Beverley, co. York, (*tenant named*), late of the collegiate church of St. John Beverlacye in Beverley; (42) the tithes of hay in Beswicke, co. York, late of the monastery of Watton, co. York; (43) the tithes of two wind mills in Kynewicke, co. York, (*tenant named*), once of the said monastery of Watton; (44) 'a chapell howse' in Molles Crofte, co. York, once of St. Mary the Virgin's chantry in Mollescrofte; (45) land (*named with tenant's name*) in Ruston, co. York, once of the late provostry of St. John Beverlacye, co. York; (46) land (*named with tenant's name*) in Lowthorpe, co. York, belonging to the said late provostry; (47) lands (*named*) in Affordbye, co. Leicester, given for lights or lamps in Affordbye church; (48) lands (*named with tenants' names*) in the parish of Bettus, co. Glamorgan; (49) cottages (*described with tenants' names*) in Cardiffe, co. Glamorgan; (50) lands (*named with tenants' names*) in the parish of St. Michael in St. Albans, co. Hertford, in St. Albans and in the parish of St. Peter in St. Albans,

                                                                              [*m.* 31]
all late of the monastery of St. Albans or given for obits and the like there; (51) lands (*named with tenants' names*) in Fromeselwood, co. Somerset, given severally for a lamp in the church there, for obits and the like in the same church and for divers superstitious uses; (52) lands (*named with tenants' names*) in Maston *alias* Marston, co. Somerset, given for superstitious uses; (53) land (*tenant named*) in Maston; (54) land (*described with tenant's name*) in Fromeselwood; (55) lands (*tenants named*) in Melles, co. Somerset, given for masses, lights and other ceremonies in Melles; (56) three chambers in the parish of St. Olave in Old Jewry in London, now or late in the tenures of William Bucknell, Thomas Garnett and Thomas Molte, given for obits and the like by Thomas Musted; (57) a messuage in Peter Lane next Pawles Wharfe in London, now or late in the tenure of Robert Cosynne, late of the monastery of St. Mary next the walls of York; (58) a tenement in the parish of St. Mary Somerset in London, now or late in the tenure of Anthony Abbott, given for superstitious

uses in the church of St. Mary Somerset; (59) two tenements, now or late in the tenures of William Lucas and John Pett in the parish of St. Margaret Patentes in London, given for an obit in the church of St. Margaret aforesaid by William Turnor; (60) a messuage and garden called Gossarde *alias* Austins in the parish of St. Leonard by Shordiche, co. Middlesex, now or late in the tenure of John Smythe and Elizabeth his wife, given for a chantry in the church of St. Leonard aforesaid; (61) a messuage with a garden called 'the Priestes House', now or late in the tenure of William Wallys, in the parish of St. Leonard by Shordiche, given for the dwelling of divers priests saying mass daily in Hallywell chapel for the soul of Thomas Lovell, knight; (62) tenements (*named with tenant's name*) in St. Albans, co. Hertford, once of the monastery of St. Albans; (63) lands (*named with tenants' names*) in Spaldinge, co. Lincoln; (64) lands   [*m.* 32]
(*tenants named*) in Quadringe, co. Lincoln, given to St. John's chantry in the church there; (65) lands (*tenants named*) in Osbornebye, co. Lincoln, given (*a*) for a light before an image in Osbornebye church and (*b*) by Richard Pell to distribute bread for the souls of him and others his ancestors, called 'Richard Pelles obitte'; (66) lands (*tenant named*) in Osbornebye, late of the monasteries of Kyme and Sempringham, co. Lincoln; (67) lands (*named with tenant's name*) in Osbornebye and Willoughbye *alias* Water Willoughbye, co. Lincoln, given for lights on the altar and other superstitious uses in the church there; (68) land (*named with tenant's name*) in Dowsbye, co. Lincoln, late of the monastery of Crowland, co. Lincoln; (69) lands (*named*) at Spitle, co. Lincoln, given for lights and the like; (70) lands (*tenant named*) in the parish of Hemswell, co. Lincoln, given for lights and the like; (71) a chapel called 'the Chappell House' and lands (*tenants named*) in Hemswell, given for lights and the like; (72) 'the Spittle on Street chauntrye' and all its possessions in Spittle on Streete and elsewhere, co. Lincoln, now or late in the tenure of Robert Wraye, clerk; (73) the rectory of Skellingthorpe, co. Lincoln, late of Spitle on Streete chantry; (74) tenements (*tenant named*) in Lincoln, once of Spittle on Streete chantry; (75) a toft (*tenant named*) in Corringham Magna, co. Lincoln; (76) a tenement (*tenants named*) in Springthorpe, co. Lincoln, given for St. George's brotherhood there; (77) 'a guildhall' in Upton, co. Lincoln, given for brotherhoods and the like; (78) a chapel called 'the Easte Chappell' and lands (*tenant named*) in Glamford Brigges and in Brigge and Wrawbye, co. Lincoln, given for a priest celebrating in the same chapel for its founders; (79) lands (*tenant named*) in Belton, co. Lincoln, given for lights and the like; (80) a chantry and ruinous chapel in Barton on Humber, co. Lincoln, and all the chantry's possessions there; (81) lands (*named including* 'the Churche House'), now or late in the several tenures of John Newland, vicar of Haxey, and others (*named*), in Haxey in the isle of Axholme, co. Lincoln, given for obits and the like; (82) all lands and other hereditaments in Haxey aforesaid and adjacent towns, co. Lincoln, late of Newsted Priory, co. Lincoln; (83) lands (*named with tenants' names*)   [*m.* 33]
in Epworth in the isle of Axholme, given for obits and the like; (84) 'the Churchclose' in Willerton, co. Lincoln, now or late in the tenure of John Farmerye, clerk; (85) lands (*named with tenants' names*) in Willerton, now or late in the tenure of the provost of St. Mary's guild of Tydde St. Giles, co. Lincoln, given for guilds and the like; (86) lands (*named with tenants' name*) in Grimesbye and Wellowe, co. Lincoln, late of the monastery of Wellowe; (87) cottages etc. in the parish of St. Giles, co. Middlesex, now or late in the several tenures of John Battersbye, Henry Barnes, John Garford, John Yonge, William Burnam, John Hollinbrigge, Thomas Manlye, John Griffithe, William Whetcrofte, Peter Foxe, Alan Fowlkes, Thomas Cole, Robert Clere, James Thomas, William Strowde, William Alesburye, William Burde, William Allen, Henry Marshall, Henry Heron, Burquot Craniche   [*m.* 34]
and William Whetcrofte, and (88) cottages etc. in the parish of St. Sepulchre without Newgate in the suburbs of London, now or late in the several tenures of John Sexbye, Christopher Kellett, David Powell, Richard Marcye *alias* Grene and Thomas Bright, all

once of John, late duke of Northumberland, attainted of treason; lands (*named with tenants' names*) in (89) Bykeleswade, (90) Sutton, (91) Bykelswade, (92) Sharnebrooke, (93) Bickeleswade, (94) Calcote *alias* Caldecote in Northiell *alias* Norrell, (95) Beston *alias* Beson in Sondey and Northiell, (96) Bykeleswade, (97) Old Warden, (98) Sondey, (99) Blunham, (100) Byddenham and (101) Milton Harneys, co. Bedford; (102) lands (*named with tenant's name*) in Rocliffe, co. York, and (103) the court baron of the manor of Rocliffe and the leet and view of frankpledge with all profits belonging to the manor, once of the monastery of Selbye, co. York; and (104) the site of the manor of Pebworth, co. Gloucester   [*m.* 35] once of Thomas Cromwell, knight, late earl of Essex, attainted of treason. Which premises were all concealed from the Queen or from Henry VIII, Edward VI or Queen Mary, and are in all according to the several particulars thereof of the yearly value of £17 4s. 10½d. To hold as of the manor of Estgrenewiche, co. Kent, in socage and by yearly rents of (1) 53s. 4d., (2) 12d., (3) 33s. 4d., (4) 33s. 4d., (5) 6s. 8d., (6) 6s. 8d., (7) 6s. 8d., (8) 3s. 4d., (9) 5s., (10) 2s. 6d., (11) 12d., (12) 4d., (13) 4d., (14) 20d., (15) 20d., (16) 16d., (17) 5s., (18) 4d., (19) 3s. 4d., (20) 12d., (22) 3s. 4d., (23) 20d., (24) 20d., (25) 12d., (26) 17d., (27) 1d., (28) 5s., (29) 6d., (30) 20s., (31) 2s., (32) 3s. 4d., (33) 16s., (34) 3s. 4d., (35) 7s. 6d., (36) 20d., (37) 2s. 6d., (38) 20d., (39) 12d., (40) 4d., (41) 2s. 6d.,   [*m.* 36] (42) 12d., (43) 3d., (44) 2d., (45) 3d., (46) 1d., (47) 12 d., (48) 30d. (*detailed*), (49) 10d. (*detailed*), (50) 9s. 10d. (*detailed*), (51) 3s. 4d. (*detailed*), (52) 21d. (*detailed*), (53) 4d., (54) 4d., (55) 16d., (56) 12d., (57) 2s. 6d., (58) 2s. 6d., (59) 2s., (60) 20d., (61) 12d., (62) 16d. (*detailed*), (63) 2s. 8d. (*detailed*), (64) 8d., (65) 2s. 6d., (66) 16d., (67) 18d., (68) 8d., (69) 12d., (70) 12d., (71) 6d., (72) 3s. 4d., (73) 3s. 4d., (74) 6d., (75) 2d., (76) 2d., (77) 2d., (78) 8d., (79) 6d., (80) 12d., (81) 2s. 6d., (82) 8d., (83) 20d., (84) 2d., (85) 12d., (86) 12d., (87) 7s. 10d. (*detailed*), (88) 22d. (*detailed*), (89) 1½d. (*detailed*), (90) 3d., (91) 1d.,   [*m.* 37] (92) 1d., (93) 32d. (*detailed*), (94) 13d. (*detailed*), (95) 4d., (96) 1d., (97) 4d., (98) 4d., (99) 12d. (*detailed*), (100) 4d., (101) 2d., (102) 12d., (103) 12d. and (104) 20s. Issues from the time when the premises should have come to the Crown's hands. Power for the grantee in the Crown's name to prosecute in the Exchequer for the concealment of the   [*m.* 38] premises and the levying of the rents and arrears thereof. If any of the premises shall hereafter be recovered from the grantee's possession, he shall have from the Crown other concealed lands of the same value as those recovered and at a like rent. The grant to be void in respect of any parcel of the premises which was not concealed before the taking of the first inquisition or before the first certifying of the premises.

    For his service.   By Q.

832.)   16 *July* 1576.   Lease for 21 years to John Flymynge *alias* Flemynge, master gunner of the town of Berwick on Tweed, of (1) the manor of Wikeburnell, co. Worcester, late of John, late duke of Northumberland, attainted of treason, (2) lands (*named with tenants' names*) in Adle, co. York, once of the monastery of Kirkestall, co. York, and (3) lands   [*m.* 39] (*named with tenants' names*) in Spitty Riwiscoith and Stratmericke, co. Cardigan, parcels of the new escheats in the same county and of the principality of South Wales; with reservations; (1) from Lady Day 1596, having been leased by patent, 29 July, 3 & 4 Ph. & Mary, to William Babington and Elizabeth his wife *inter alia* for 40 years from Lady Day then last at a yearly rent of £15 6d.; (2) from Lady Day 1585, having been leased by patent of the Exchequer, 23 June, 6 Eliz., some to John Browne at a yearly rent of 36s. 10d. and the rest to Adam Speight and Robert Speight at a yearly rent of 25s. 10d. for 21 years from Lady Day then last; (3) from Lady Day 1582, having been leased by patent, 3 June, 3 Eliz., to Morgan ap Jevan ap Morrice, Thomas ap Morrice Goz, David ap Res ap Hoell, David Lloid ap Thomas ap Mered and Thomas ap Llewelin Moyle for 21 years at yearly rents amounting to 30s.; yearly rents (1) £15 6d., (2) 62s. 8d. and (3) 30s.; the lessee to discharge the Crown of all   [*m.* 40] payments out of (1). For his service.   By p.s.

833.)   20 *July* 1576.   *Gorhambury.*   Lease for 21 years to William Seres of underwoods called Drayton Wood, parcel of the manor of Drayton, co. Somerset, and late of the late duke of Somerset; with reservations; from Michaelmas next; yearly rent £10; the lessee to cut the underwoods only at times suitable for cutting, to enclose them after cutting for the statutory term, to leave sufficient 'lez staddelles' in every acre according to statute, and to sell them when cut to the tenants of the manor, if they wish, at a reasonable price; any dispute between the lessee and the tenants to be determined by the treasurer and the chancellor of the Exchequer; the lessee to cause the patent to be enrolled before the auditor of the county for charging of the rent within one year and before the surveyor of woods this side Trent for survey of the performance of covenants before any cutting is made. In consideration that the woods must be enclosed for seven years after cutting for better preservation of 'lez springes' thereof, as appears by certificate of the said surveyor of woods, the charges of which enclosures Seres offers to undertake.

By the commissioners by virtue of the Queen's warrant.

Vacated because surrendered 6 *Nov.*, 21 *Eliz.*; *signed*: Wyll'm Cordell; Will'm Seres; *with a note'*. . . . Metcalf cogn' part.'[1]

(*The dorse of this roll is blank.*)

---

[1] The roll is rubbed and partially illegible at this point.

PART IX

C. 66/1145

834.) 1 *June* 1576.   Licence for William Parker, Andrew Grey and   [*m.* 1]
Robert Dyckynson to alienate the manor of Duckettes and all its appurtenances in
Tottenham and elsewhere, co. Middlesex, to William Cordell, knight, master of the rolls,
William Glasier, John Gardyner, Richard Bowland, Robert Freke and Edmund Downynge.
For £3 6s. 8d. paid to the Queen's farmer.

835.) 10 *July* 1576.   Pardon of alienation for Nicholas Webbe and Robert Webbe: by
indenture, 30 March, 18 Eliz., they acquired from Richard Dennys lands (*named with tenants'
names*) in Aleston *alias* Alweston *alias* Alveston, co. Gloucester; and in Trinity term, 18 Eliz.,
by fine in the Common Pleas the premises, by the name of lands in Aleston and Ercott, co.
Gloucester, were for better assurance conveyed to them by Dennis. For 40s. paid to the
Queen's farmer.

836.) 28 *May* 1576.   Licence for John Vaughan, Anne his wife and Francis Vaughan,
their son, to alienate the manors of Huntington *alias* Huntingdon Englyshe and Huntington
alias Huntingdon Welshe, lands in Huntingdon Englyshe, Huntingdon Walshe, Rosshock
and Barton and free fishery in the waters   [*m.* 2]
of Ariowe, Beled, Llandouenog and Waythell, co. Hereford, to Roger Vaughan and Miles
Whitney and the heirs and assigns of Roger; and for them to convey the premises back to the
said John and Anne for life in survivorship, with successive remainders to Francis in tail
male and to the right heirs of Anne. For £16 7s. 8d. paid to the Queen's farmer.

837.) 12 *July* 1576.   Pardon of alienation: John Jackson in Hilary term, 18 Eliz., by fine in
the Common Pleas acquired from Ambrose, earl of Warwick, and Anne his wife the manors
of Bedall *alias* Bedell and Ascugh, lands in Bedall, Ascugh, Burrell, Ferby, Lymynge Magna,
Lymynge Parva, Cracoll Magna, Newton, Morcar, Therne Watloose, Thorneton Watloose,
Melsonby, Kyplyn, Northcowton, Wensley, Labron, Northleys and Morton and the
advowson of Bedall church, co. York. For 40s. paid to the Queen's farmer.

838.) 22 *June* 1576.   The like: John Dalton in Easter term, 18 Eliz., by fine in the
Common Pleas acquired from Thomas Sawyer and Margaret his wife lands in Pulboroughe,
co. Sussex. For 22s. 4d.

839.) 28 *May* 1576.   Licence for Thomas Gryffyn and Agnes his wife to alienate lands in
Butlers Marston, co. Warwick, to Robert Clarke and Isabel his wife and the heirs and assigns
of Robert. For 17s. 3d. paid to the Queen's farmer.

840.) 6 *July* 1576.   Pardon of alienation for Alice Conye, Catherine Baber and Winefrid
Bond: they acquired from Richard Catesby and Isabel Leigh, now his wife, a capital
messuage in or by Old Jewry, London, late in the tenure of Thomas Leigh, knight, and three
messuages, once divided into six several tenements, in Old Jewry, late in the several tenures
of Thomas Nycholles, Austin Foulke and William Cutte, to hold one third part unto each of
the said Alice, Catherine and Winefrid; afterwards in the   [*m.* 3]

quinzaine of Easter, 18 Eliz., for better assurance by fine in the Common Pleas the said Richard and Isabel for them and the heirs of Isabel conveyed to Alice, Catherine and Winefrid and the heirs of Alice the premises by the name of seven messuages in the parishes of St. Olave in Old Jewry and St. Mary Colchurch in London. For 44s. 6d. paid to the Queen's farmer.

841.)   10 *May* 1576.   Licence for Henry Woodhowse, Roger Towneshend and Jane his wife to alienate the manor of West Somerton Butleye *alias* Westsomerton and lands in West Somerton Butleye, East Somerton, Wynterton, Bastwick, Reppys, Hemsbye and Martham, co. Norfolk, to Edward Bacon, clerk and officer of licences and pardons for alienations, and John Osborne, a servant of Nicholas Bacon, knight, keeper of the great seal, and the heirs and assigns of Edward.

842.)   21 *May* 1576.   Licence for William Jackson and Joan his wife to alienate a messuage called 'le Blacke Lyon' in the parish of St. Mary the Virgin in Abchurch in Candellwicke Streat, London, now in William's tenure, to James Tappynge and Elizabeth his wife and the heirs and assigns of James. For 20s. paid to the Queen's farmer.

843.)   12 *April* 1576.   The like for John Haselop to alienate the   [*m.* 4]
site of the house of Gilbertine or white canons in or by Cambridge, co. Cambridge, to John Hatcher. For 6s. 8d.

844.)   20 *May* 1576.   Pardon of alienation: Richard Paramore in Easter term, 17 Eliz., by fine in the Common Pleas acquired from Thomas Robynson the manor of Alvecote *alias* Avecote, land in Alvecote, Shittynton and Awstrye *alias* Alstwye, the rectories of Shyttynton and Awstrye and the advowson of the vicarage of Awstrye, co. Warwick. For £21 paid to the Queen's farmer.

845.)   20 *April* 1576.   Licence for Nicholas Lestrange, knight, and Hamond Lestrange to alienate the manor of Chosell *alias* Chosellee, all appurtenances thereof in Chosell, Hunworth, Studye, Burnyngham, Brynton, Holkham and Borowghe, co. Norfolk, late of the house or hospital of Burton St. Lazar of Jerusalem in England, co. Lincoln [*sic*], and all their lands in Chosell (lands, parcel of the manor, in Kynges Lynne excepted) to Thomas Reade. For 33s. 4d. in the hanaper.

846.)   2 *May* 1576.   The like for Thomas Myldemaye, knight, to alienate the manor of Bysshopps Leighes, all appurtenances thereof in Bysshoppes Leighes, Moche Leighes, Terlynge, Fayrested, Littell Leighes, Chateley, Boreham or elsewhere, co. Essex, and the reversions and rents arising on leases by Henry Myldmaye by indentures, 10 Oct., 16 Eliz., of parcels   [*m.* 5]
of the premises (*lessees named*) to Thomas Shaa. For 22s.

847.)   26 *May* 1576.   Licence for Lewis Mordante, knight, lord Mordante, Elizabeth his wife, Henry Darcy, knight, and Catherine his wife to alienate lands in Brymbem *alias* Brymham, Bollershaw, Felbecke and Lareton, co. York, to James Brathwayte. For £4 10s. paid to the Queen's farmer.

848.)   28 *May* 1576.   The like for Henry Nye and Elizabeth his wife to alienate the manors of Polynge and Knepp *alias* Knapp *alias* 'le Holye Mote' of Knepp and lands in Polynge, East Angmerynge, West Angmerynge, East Preston, West Preston, Lymyster, Pepperinge, Hampton Parva, Burfham, Barfham, Arundell, Warnehame, Hame, Northstocke, Polynge

St. John, Horsham, West Grensted, Steanynge, Shypley, Nuthurst, Wasshington, Asshington, Cowfold and Balcombe, co. Sussex, to Edward Caryll. For £6 13s. 4d.

849.)   26 *May* 1576.   The like for Lewis Mordaunte, knight, lord Mordaunte, Elizabeth his wife, Henry Darcye, knight, and Catherine his wife to alienate lands in Wynesley and Lareton, co. York, to John Syngleton.   [*m.* 6]
For 8s. 1d.

850.)   5 *July* 1576.   The like for Walter Talbott to alienate lands called Cassyes *alias* Cassies Ferme in Elingbridge, co. Worcester, to John Talbot of Grafton, co. Worcester, and Robert Caldwall of Upton Warren to the use of John Talbot, elder son of Walter, in tail male, with successive remainders to Thomas Talbott, another son of Walter, in tail male, and to John Talbot, son and heir of the said John Talbot of Grafton, in fee simple. For 40s.

851.)   26 *May* 1576.   The like for John Felton and Elizabeth his wife to alienate lands in Cavendyshe, co. Suffolk, to George Colte. For 22s. 3d.

852.)   28 *May* 1576.   The like for John Wogan to alienate a chapel or tenement called Cryswell, with all profits of ferries and liberties both by water and by land belonging thereto, and the rectory of Martiltwy, with the patronage of the vicarage of the same, co. Pembroke, to John Barlo. For £6 6s.

853.)   26 *May* 1576.   The like for Lewis Mordante, knight, lord Mordante, Elizabeth his wife, Henry Darcye, knight, and Catherine his wife to alienate lands in Wenesley, Hartwith, Felbecke and Lareton, co. York,   [*m.* 7]
to John Smyth. For 28s. 8d.

854.)   11 *July* 1576.   Pardon of alienation for Alice Gawen, widow, and Thomas Gawen: they acquired by indenture, 21 April, 18 Eliz., from Robert Ludlowe the manors of Horsington and South Cherton *alias* Cheryton, lands in the said places and elsewhere, co. Somerset, and the advowson of the vicarage of Horsington; and in Trinity term, 18 Eliz., for better assurance Ludlowe and Dorothy his wife by fine in the Common Pleas, for them and the heirs of Ludlowe, conveyed the premises, by the name of the manors of Horsington and South Cherton *alias* Cheryton, lands in Horsington, South Cherton, Templecombe and Wyncaulton *alias* Wyncawnton and the advowson of Horsington church, co. Somerset, to Alice and Thomas and the heirs of Thomas. For £8 17s. 10d. paid to the Queen's farmer.

855.)   4 *July* 1576.   Licence for John Arundell, knight, and Anne his wife to alienate a fourth part of the manor of Overourton *alias* Overworton and of lands in Overworton, co. Oxford, to Felix Hollway and John Myes. For 17s. 11d. paid to the Queen's farmer.

856.)   26 *May* 1576.   The like for Richard Bostock to alienate lands in Newyngton and Stretham, co. Surrey, to Thomas Mylles and John Mylles   [*m.* 8]
and the heirs and assigns of Thomas. For 29s. 7d.

857.)   6 *July* 1576.   Pardon of alienation: George Pygott, second son of Thomas Pygott, who acquired by indenture, 1 Sept., 16 Eliz., from his said father a pasture and meadow called 'Gorefeld', co. Buckingham to the use of Thomas for life, with successive remainders to George in tail[1] and to the right heirs of Thomas. For 46s. 8d. paid to the Queen's farmer.

---

[1] Given elsewhere in the patent as 'tail male'.

858.)   6 *June* 1576.   The like: Christopher Hatton, gentleman of the privy chamber and captain of the yeomen of the guard, and William Saunders, in Easter term, 18 Eliz., by fine in the Common Pleas acquired unto them and the heirs and assigns of Hatton from John Stafford and Bridget his wife the manor of Kyrkebye *alias* Kyrbye and lands in Kyrbye, Harringworth, Great Weldon, Little Weldon, Corbye and Gretton, co. Northampton. For 43*s.* 8*d.*

859.)   26 *May* 1576.   Licence for John Dolman and Mary his wife to alienate a third part of the manor of Staunton, of lands in Staunton and of the advowson of the church of Staunton and free chapel of Swowshill, co. Gloucester, to Matthias Dolman. For £3 1*s.* 2*d.* paid to the Queen's farmer.

860.)   26 *March* 1576.   *Gorhambury.*   Licence for John Mabbe the elder, citizen and goldsmith of London, to alienate the rectory of Chalke,   [*m.* 9] co. Kent, to William Slywryght and Joan his wife and the heirs and assigns of William. For £4 17*s.* in the hanaper.

861.)   1 *June* 1576.   Licence for Alban Butler and George Butler to alienate lands (*tenants named*) in Nether Bodyngton, co. Northampton, (as held by John Dudley, knight *inter alia* by grant of Henry VIII by patent, 26 March, 32 Hen. VIII, and as held by John Butler, Alban's father, *inter alia* by grant of Dudley by indenture, 30 March, 32 Hen. VIII) to Robert Cleyver. For 8*s.* 11*d.* paid to the Queen's farmer.

862.)   1 *June* 1576.   The like for the same to alienate lands (*tenants named*) in Nether Bodyngton (as held by John Dudley, knight, and John Butler as aforesaid) to Henry Buckerfeld. For 4*s.* 6*d.*

863.)   1 *June* 1576.   The like for the same to alienate lands (*tenants named*) in Nether Bodington (as held by John Dudley, knight, and John Butler as   [*m.* 10] aforesaid) to Thomas Cosens. For 11*s.* 2*d.*

864.)   1 *June* 1576.   The like for the same to alienate lands (*tenants named*) in Nether Bodington (as held by John Dudley, knight, and John Butler as aforesaid) to William Cottysbroke. For 4*s.* 6*d.*

865.)   8 *June* 1576.   The like for Richard Rosseter to alienate lands in Hunsley, Wedeley and Cave, co. York, to John Hotham. For £4.

866.)   26 *May* 1576.   The like for Francis Uvedall to alienate lands in Horton, Knolton and Henton Martell and the rectory of Horton, co. Dorset, to Henry Uvedall and Richard Badger and the heirs and assigns of Henry to the use of Francis. For 40*s.*   [*m.* 11]

867.)   26 *May* 1576.   The like for Simon Codrington, Agnes his wife, Richard Sperte and Grisel his wife to alienate lands in Kyngeswood, co. Wilts, to Richard Salte and Philip Clyff. For £7 11*s.* 2*d.*

868.)   22 *May* 1576.   The like for Michael Forster to alienate lands (*named*) in Westbromwiche, co. Stafford, to Thomas Dudley. For 13*s.*

869.)   26 *May* 1576.   The like for Henry Cheeke to alienate the manor of Fresheford

Woodwyk *alias* Fresheford Wudwyckes and lands in Fresheford *alias* Fresheford Wood-
wyck, Henton, Phillips Norton and Combe, co. Somerset, to William Appryce. For 25*s.* 6*d.*

870.)   26 *May* 1576.   The like for Lewis Mordante, knight, Lord Mordante, Elizabeth his
wife, Henry Darcy, knight, and Catherine his wife to alienate lands in Hartwith, Wynnesley,
Dacre, Hayshaye, Dereynge, Dykeyaites, Baudgerhouses and Lareton, co. York, to William
Ingleby, knight, and William Ingleby. For £9 6*s.* 9*d.*   [*m.* 12]

871.)   1 *June* 1576.   The like for Alban Butler and George Butler to alienate lands (*tenants
named*) in Nether Bodington, co. Northampton, (as held by John Dudley, knight, *inter alia*
by grant of Henry VIII by patent, 26 March, 32 Hen. VIII, and as held by John Butler,
Alban's father, *inter alia* by grant of Dudley by indenture, 30 March, 32 Hen. VIII) to
William Myller. For 13*s.* 4*d.*

872.)   26 *May* 1576.   The like for Henry Darcy, knight, and Nicholas Darcy, John Darcy
and Francis Darcy, his brothers, to alienate the manor of Almondesbury *alias* Almesbury
and lands in Almondesbury, Thornebury, Oldbury, Tockington and Olstone, co.
Gloucester, to Thomas Chester. For £26 12*d.*

873.)   26 *May* 1576.   The like for Thomas Suter *alias* Merser to alienate lands in Odyham,
co. Southampton, to Hugh Darvall and Thomas Darvale and the heirs and assigns of
Thomas Darvall. For 26*s.* 8*d.*

874.)   12 *April* 1576.   Licence for Catherine Throkmerton, widow, and Job Throkmerton to alienate lands in Claredon and Rowington, co.   [*m.* 13]
Warwick, to John Robyns. For 40*s.* in the hanaper.

875.)   3 *May* 1576.   Pardon of alienation: John Large the younger, in Michaelmas term,
16 Eliz., by fine in the Common Pleas acquired from James Corye and Charity his wife lands
in Overeston *alias* Overston and in the hundred of Barton Regis, co. Gloucester. For £4 13*s.*
4*d.* in the hanaper.

876.)   1 *June* 1576.   Pardon of alienation: William Cordell, knight, Edward Saunders,
knight, chief baron of the Exchequer, and Christopher Hatton, in Hilary term, 17 Eliz., by
fine in the Common Pleas, acquired unto them and the heirs of Cordell from Vincent
Curson, Elizabeth his wife and Francis Curson *inter alia* the advowson of Addington church,
co. Buckingham. For £4 5*s.* 6*d.* paid to the Queen's farmer.

877.)   2 *Jan.* 1576.   Licence for Anthony Martyn, Anne his wife and Henry Martyn, his
son and heir apparent, to alienate lands in West Compton, co. Berks, to John Stampe. For
24*s.* 7*d.* in the hanaper.

878.)   26 *May* 1576.   Licence for Roger Roser to alienate the manor of Blomvyles in
Hacheston, Parham and Eston, co. Suffolk, to Charles Radclyffe and Ralph Damphorde. For
33*s.* 4*d.* paid to the Queen's farmer.   [*m.* 14]

879.)   6 *June* 1576.   Pardon of alienation: William Holden, Robert Goodwyn and Edward
Vicars, in Easter term, 18 Eliz., by fine in the Common Pleas acquired from Thomas
Gressham, knight, and Anne his wife lands in Fynderne and Little Over in the parish of
Great Over *alias* Myckell Over, co. Derby. For 17*s.* 8*d.* paid to the Queen's farmer.

880.)   6 June 1576.   The like: Thomas Ramsey, alderman of London, and Alice his wife by fine in the Common Pleas in the quinzaine of Hilary, 17 Eliz., conveyed for them and the heirs of Ramsey to Thomas Tirrell and Edward Holmeden and the heirs of Tirrell the site of the manor of Hexted and lands in Lingfeild and Lynsfeld, co. Surrey, and they by the same fine conveyed them back to Ramsey and Alice and the heirs and assigns of Ramsey. For £13 6s. 8d.

881.)   22 May 1576.   The like: Marmaduke Claver by writing, 12 April, 13 Eliz., acquired from Thomas Myller of Stukeley, co. Buckingham, 'yoman', lands (named with tenants' names) in Stukeley. For £5.

882.)   21 May 1576.   The like: Anthony Copleston the younger in Hilary term, 18 Eliz., by fine in the Common Pleas acquired from Thomas   [m. 15]
Hunt a fourth part of lands in Rollesclyffe and Brodeclyste, co. Devon. For 13s. 4d.

883.)   26 June 1576.   The like: William Malyn in Easter term, 18 Eliz., by fine in the Common Pleas acquired from Thomas Essex lands in Badburye, co. Wilts. For 14s.

884.)   24 May 1576.   The like: Richard Dene and Roger Dene by indenture, 22 Oct., 15 Eliz., acquired from Matthew Gravys, 'yoman', his part and pourparty of a third part of the manor of Frystock alias Frythelstock, co. Devon, which third part Gravys, John Hockinge and John Tetherby jointly purchased from Arthur Bassett. For 55s.

885.)   20 May 1576.   The like: Edward Charde and William Hassard by indenture, 20 Jan., 17 Eliz., acquired from Thomas Charde of Birpott, co. Dorset, lands (named with tenants' names) in Brappole, co. Dorset, to the use of the same Thomas Charde for life and thereafter to the use of Thomas Charde, son of the said Edward. For 32s.

886.)   5 July 1576.   The like: John Cresby in Easter term, 18 Eliz., by fine in the Common Pleas acquired from Thomas Essex   [m. 16]
lands in Badburye, co. Wilts. For 20s.

887.)   5 July 1576.   The like: William Dalyson in Easter term, 15 Eliz., by fine in the Common Pleas acquired from Edward Skypwith the manor of Kyrnyngton and lands in Kyrnyngton, co. Lincoln. For £5.

888.)   5 July 1576.   The like: William Shakylton the elder and William Shakylton the younger by indenture, 15 April, 15 Eliz., acquired unto them and the heirs of William the elder from Samuel Howell, brother of George Howell of London, all the messuages late of John Howell, Samuel's father, in Phillippe Lane in the parish of St. Alphege within Crepulgate, London, which messuages descended after John's death to George as his son and heir and after George's death to Samuel as his brother and heir. For 40s.

889.)   5 July 1576.   The like: William Dalyson and Marmaduke Tyrwhytt in Michaelmas term, 17 Eliz., by fine in the Common Pleas acquired unto them and the heirs of Dalison from Robert Mounson, a justice of the Common Pleas, Elizabeth his wife, John Mounson, Jane his wife and George Mounson inter alia the manors of Carlton Pannell alias South Carleton, Keelbye, Owersbye Newhall alias Owersbye Mounson, Owersby Thornton and North Carlton and lands in Carlton Pannell, Rysam, Repham, Cheryburton, Kexby, Newton, Marten, Gaitburton, Spittell, Braughton, Keelby, Stallingburghe, Roxton, Lyttell

Limburghe, Wotton, Colsehill, Owersby, Osgodby, Uselby, Claxby, North Carlton and Barton, co. Lincoln. For £13 6s. 8d.

890.)   6 *June* 1576.   The like: Roger Lygon in Easter term, 18 Eliz., by fine in the Common Pleas acquired from Dennis Toppes and Dorothy   [*m.* 17] his wife the manor of Lachelade and lands in Lachelade, co. Gloucester. For £10.

891.)   26 *June* 1576.   The like: Thomas Morton and Warbary his wife by indenture, 20 Aug., 17 Eliz., acquired from John Wyllyams of Heryngton, co. Dorset, a third part of the manor of Lalee and of all lands belonging thereto in Lalee, Mylton and Whitechurche, co. Dorset. For £4 6s. 6d.

892.)   2 *July* 1576.   The like: by fine in the Common Pleas on the morrow of Ascension and afterwards on the morrow of Trinity, 16 Eliz., Alexander Colepepir, knight, and Mary his wife, for them and the heirs of Alexander, conveyed to William Allanbie and Charles Sterry and the heirs of Allanbie the manor of Comewell and lands in Comewell, Gountherst and Tyseherst, co. Kent, and they by the same fine conveyed them back to Alexander. For £13.

893.)   26 *May* 1576.   Licence for Joyce Stanley, widow, Thomas Wilford and Mary his wife to alienate the manor of Loveherst *alias* Loffeherst *alias* Loweherst, lands in Loweherst and all the tithes in Loweherst, co. Kent, to John Popham, Edward Drinkell and Thomas Nycholson. For £17 6s. 8d. paid   [*m.* 18] to the Queen's farmer.

894.)   22 *June* 1576.   Pardon of alienation: Aden Beresford in Easter term, 18 Eliz., by fine in the Common Pleas acquired from Edward Bentley a moiety of a messuage called Newton grange and of lands in Asshborne, Allsoppe in le Dale, Tysington, Penwiche and Thorpe, co. Derby. For 22s. 4d. paid to the Queen's farmer.

895.)   26 *May* 1576.   Licence for Ralph Wysteler to alienate lands in Aston Turrold, co. Berks, to Richard Lewenden. For 20s. 3d. paid to the Queen's farmer.

896.)   1 *Jan.* 1576.   Licence for Henry Browne and Alice his wife, daughter and co-heir of Nicholas Trappes late of London, to alienate the manor and farm called Fryers Grange and lands in Eythrop Roodinge, High Roodynge, High Ester and Leaden Roodinge, co. Essex, to Thomas Stokes. For £3 in the hanaper.

897.)   22 *May* 1576.   Licence for Henry Goodere, Frances his wife, Thomas Goodere, William Goodere, William Foster, Anne his wife, William Shether, Anne his wife, George Herde and Elizabeth his wife to   [*m.* 19] alienate the manor of Thedingworth, lands in Thedingworth, the rectory of Thedingworth, the advowson of the vicarage there and a yearly rent of 13s. 4d. out of the same vicarage, cos. Leicester and Northampton, to Williams Brocas. For £12 paid to the Queen's farmer.

898.)   26 *May* 1576.   The like for John Tufton, Christian his wife, Thomas Wilford, Mary his wife and Catherine Browne to alienate eleven twelfth parts of the rectory of Manewden, of lands in Manewden and Barden *alias* Berden and of the advowson of the vicarage of Manewden, co. Essex, to Robert Bell and Stephen Thymylbye and the heirs and assigns of Bell. For £8 4s.

899.)   20 *May* 1576.   Pardon of alienation: William Waldgrave, John Higham, Thomas

Jermyn and George Higham by indenture, 12 Jan., 14 Eliz., acquired from Edmund Jermyn the manor of Swyftes, co. Suffolk, and all appurtenances thereof in Preston, Thorpe Morieux and Ketlebeston or adjacent towns, to the use of the said Edmund and his heirs until during his life John Jermyn, his brother, should pay him 12d., and thereafter to the use of the said John Jermyn. For £13 6s. 8d. paid to the Queen's farmer.

900.)   24 May 1576.   Licence for George Horsey to alienate the manor of Norton Dawney with free fishery in the water of Puddesworthye, all appurtenances of the said manor in Townestall and elsewhere, co. Devon, lands (*tenants named*) in Townestall once of Joan wife of John Fynton and all other lands in Norton Dawney, Puddesworthie, Puddesforthe, Townestall or Dartmouth to Hugh Culme and Mary his wife and the heirs and assigns of
[*m. 20*]
Hugh. For £11 1s. 6d. paid to the Queen's farmer.

901.)   3 May 1576.   Pardon of alienation: John Marrys of Northkelsey, co. Lincoln, 'yoman', by writing, 4 Jan., 17 Eliz., acquired from Thomas Grene of Rothewell, 'yoman', the manor of Rothewell, lands (*named with tenants' names*) in Rothewell and all his lands in Rothewell or elsewhere, co. Lincoln. For 30s. in the hanaper.

902.)   3 May 1576.   The like: William Rysley in Hilary term, 16 Eliz., by fine in the Common Pleas acquired from Isabel Weynman, widow, and Thomas Heath the manor of Fryngford *alias* Fringeford, lands in Fringford and the advowson of Fryngford church, co. Oxford. For £5 10s.

903.)   17 April 1576.   *Gorhambury.*   The like: Rice Miricke by indenture, 15 Sept., 17 Eliz., acquired from William Bassett of Bewper, co. Glamorgan, the manor of Boulston *alias* Bonvillston and lands (*named with tenants' names*) belonging thereto in Bolston, St. Nicholas, Pendoylon, Wenvoe and   [*m. 21*]
Lancarvan, co. Glamorgan. For £11 7s. 8d.

904.)   3 April 1576.   Licence for John Knyghton the elder of Bayforde, co. Hertford, to alienate the manor of Amwellburye *alias* Rushen *alias* Lyttle Amwelburye, co. Hertford, late of the monastery of Waltham, co. Essex, all appurtenances of the said manor in Amwell and Lyttle Amwell and in Russhen and elsewhere, co. Hertford, and the tithes thereon to John Knyghton, son of George Knighton, in tail male with remainder to George and his heirs. For £3 9s. in the hanaper.

905.)   1 June 1576.   Licence for Charles Stutvyle and Catherine his wife to alienate two third parts of a capital messuage in Fyldallynge called Saveney *alias* Mountgrace and of lands in Bathell, Sheryngton and Fyldallynge, co. Norfolk, now in the tenure of Giles Mabbes, to Gregory Pagrave   [*m. 22*]
and Robert Paygrave the younger. For £3 2s. 4d. paid to the Queen's farmer.

906.)   1 June 1576.   The like for the same to alienate a third part of the same capital messuage and lands to Thomas Hastinges. For 31s. 2d.

907.)   10 April 1576.   Licence for Thomas Whetnall, Dorothy his wife, Fulk Onslowe and Mary his wife to alienate the manor of Walburye and lands in Halyngbury Magna, Halingburye Parva, Halingburye Morley and Halingburye Bowsers, co. Essex, to Thomas Meade, serjeant at law. For £6 13s. 4d. in the hanaper.

908.)   2 *Jan.* 1576.   The like for Robert Riche, knight, lord Ryche, Elizabeth his wife and Edmund Thorneton to alienate the manor of Butlars, lands in Shopland, Sutton, Pryttelwell, Lighe, Hadleigh, Wakeringe Magna, Wakering Parva, Showberye, Rocheford, Hackwell, Rawreth and Cryksyheth and a moiety of the manor of Shoplande Hall in Shoplande, co. Essex, to William Bendlowes, serjeant at law, and for him by the same fine to convey them back to Robert and Elizabeth and the heirs of Elizabeth.   [*m.* 23] For £10.

909.)   3 *May* 1576.   Pardon of alienation: Adam Sutclyff, younger son of William Sutclyff, by writing, 17 Dec., 18 Eliz., acquired from the said William lands etc. (*named with tenants' names*) in Ayrenden, co. York. For 40*s.* in the hanaper.

910.)   20 *April* 1576.   The like: William Wolloughbie by indenture, 24 April, 16 Eliz., acquired from William Stoke a farm or grange called Wolvey Grange and lands (*named with tenants' names*) in Wolvey, co. Warwick, and all other lands there which Stoke and Anne his wife purchased from John Marrowe of London or wherein Stoke had an estate of inheritance. For 66*s.* 8*d.*

911.)   9 *March* 1576.   Licence for Anthony Cooke, knight, to alienate a moiety of lands in Dorsett *alias* Chippynge Dorsett and Hardwyck, co. Warwick, late of Balsall preceptory, co. Warwick, to Francis Ramme, Robert Badbye and George Toone, 'yoman', to the use of Cooke.   [*m.* 24] For 22*s.* 4*d.* in the hanaper.

912.)   12 *April* 1576.   The like for Job Throckmerton to alienate the manor of Wolverdyngton and lands in Warwick, Smytterfeld, Wolverdington and Claredon, co. Warwick, to William Baylyes and Thomas Staunton the younger. For £3 10*s.* 8*d.*

913.)   3 *April* 1576.   The like for John Lawrence of Bredge, co. Kent, to alienate lands (*named with tenants' names*) in Bredge, parcels of the lordship of Langport, co. Kent, late of the monastery of St. Augustine by Canterbury, to William Partheriche. For 21*s.* 10*d.*

914.)   26 *March* 1576.   *Gorhambury.*   The like for Thomas Barnes *alias* Baron and Mary his wife to alienate a tenement called Donce Hall in   [*m.* 25] Barkinge, co. Essex, now in the tenure of John Gefferey, to Gefferey. For 6*s.* 8*d.*

915.)   12 *Feb.* 1576.   The like for Martin Bowes to alienate lands (*tenants named*) in Plumsted, co. Kent, once of Martin Bowes, knight, deceased, and late of Thomas Bowes, his son and heir, and bargained and sold by Thomas *inter alia* to Martin Bowes his brother, father of Martin the licensee, to whom they descended *inter alia* by right of inheritance, to Thomas Smyth. For 44*s.* 6*d.*

916.)   26 *May* 1576.   Licence for John Tufton, Christian his wife, Thomas Wilford, Mary his wife and Catherine Browne to alienate the manor of Dryfeild and lands in Dryfeild, co. Gloucester, to Robert Bell and Stephen Thymylbye and the heirs and assigns of Bell to the use of Thomas and Mary and the heirs and assigns of Mary. For £7 2*s.* paid to the Queen's farmer.

917.)   23 *Jan.* 1576.   Pardon of alienation for Robert Hodgeson of London, to whom Richard Hodgeson late of London by indenture, 1 May, 17 Eliz., bargained and sold *inter alia* lands (*named*) in the parishes of Scalford and Walton, co. Leicester, parcels of

Goldsmythes Grange *alias* Rynglethorpe Grange, co. Leicester, and the reversion thereof, by the name of all his lands in the counties of Middlesex, Essex, Leicester and Huntingdon

[*m.* 26]

or elsewhere in England. For £20 in the hanaper.

918.)   26 *May* 1576.   Licence for Lewis Mordante, knight, lord Mordante, Elizabeth his wife, Henry Darcye, knight, and Catherine his wife to alienate lands in Wynnesley, Hartwith, Dacre, Hayshaye, Baudgerhouses, Dykeyaites, Newehowse and Lareton, co. York, to William Ingleby, knight, and William Ingleby. For £4 13*s.* 4*d.* paid to the Queen's farmer.

919.)   12 *April* 1576.   Licence for Thomas Essex to alienate lands in Badburye, Chysylden and Hodeson, co. Wilts, to Thomas Keblewhitt. For £4 3*s.* 8*d.* in the hanaper.

920.)   26 *May* 1576.   Licence for John Tufton, Christian his wife, Thomas Wylford and Mary his wife to alienate two third parts of (1) the manor of Lockington, lands in Lockington and Mychelholme, the tithes of   [*m.* 27]
corn, hay, flax and hemp in Lockington and Mychelholme, a rent of 53*s.* 4*d.* yearly out of the vicarage of Lockington, free fishery in the water of Trente and the vicarage of Lockington, co. Leicester, and (2) a third part of the manor of Hokenhanger and Kympton and lands in Hokenhanger, Kympton, Barkelowe and Redborne, co. Hertford, to Robert Bell and Stephen Thymylbye and the heirs and assigns of Bell to the use of John and Christian and the heirs and assigns of John. For £11 11*s.* 5*d.* paid to the Queen's farmer.

921.)   12 *July* 1576.   Pardon of alienation: John Jackson and Asculph Clesby by indenture, 20 July, 14 Eliz., acquired from Anthony Kempe *inter alia* a third part of (1) the manors of Skelton, Morton, Langbargh, Marske, Brotton, Newton and Yarme and lands in Skelton, Morton, Apleton, Langbargh, Marske, Brotton, Langthorne, Westbrompton, Eryethorne, Eastbrompton, Westapleton, Newton Morker, Constable Burton, Little Crakell, Upplethom, Redcar, Yarme, Tunstall, Aldewarke, Easton, Hackfourth, Tampton, Wharleton, Northallerton and Longe Newton, co. York, (2) the manor of Belfourde and Wuller *alias* Wolmer, co. Northumberland, and (3) the manor of Kyrbye Nesfeld *alias* Kirkebye in Ashefeld, co. Nottingham, and of all lands parcel thereof in which Anthony or Anne once his wife had any estate of inheritance. For £28 paid to the Queen's farmer.

922.)   26 *May* 1576.   Licence for John Staynesbye to alienate the manor of West Tytherley, co. Southampton, and the patronage of the rectory of West Tytherley to John Thystelthwayte, Alexander Thystelthwayte and Richard Aysheley to the use of Staynesbye and Dorothy Thistelthwayte, daughter of John Thystelthwayte aforesaid. For 38*s.* 2*d.* paid to the Queen's farmer.

923.)   6 *Nov.* 1576.   Pardon of alienation: William Bond, late alderman of London, by his will, 30 May, 18 Eliz., bequeathed a great capital   [*m.* 28]
messuage called Crosbye Place in the parish of St. Helen within Bisshopps Gate, London, successively (1) to Margaret then his wife for her dower so long as she should live unmarried, (2) on her marriage, to William Bond, his second son, for life paying to each of the testator's sons, Nicholas Bond and Martin Bond, an annuity of £13 13*s.* 4*d.*, (3) on William's death, to Nicholas for life paying to Martin an annuity of £20 and (4) on Nicholas's death, to Martin for life; after the death of the testator seised of the messuage, Margaret entered it. For £5 paid to the Queen's farmer.

924.)   21 *Sept.* 1576.   Licence for Adam Martyne and Robert Pytt *alias* Pytman to alienate a fourth part of the manor or farm of Lwyde and of lands in Yevell, co. Somerset, to Broom (*Bromas*) Joneson. For 16*s.* 8*d.* paid to the Queen's farmer.

925.)   1 *Oct.* 1576.   The like for Edward Honynge, Ursula his wife and William Honynge to alienate the manor of Mantons and lands in Hitcham, Ketlebarston and Billston, co. Suffolk, to Edmund Wythypoll. for £3 6*s.* 8*d.*

926.)   1 *Oct.* 1576.   Pardon of alienation: by indenture, 20 May, 16 Eliz., it was covenanted *inter alia* between Richard Chocke and Thomas Webbe that Webbe and Margaret his wife should by fine convey to Chocke and Thomas Raynes the manor of Westbury under le Playne, a fourth part of the hundred of Westbury and divers other lands in Westbury under le Playne, co. Wilts, (which premises had been purchased by Webbe and Margaret from John Stowell, now knight, and Richard Bamfild unto them and the heirs of Webbe) to the use of Webbe and Margaret and the heirs of Webbe until the marriage of Alexander Chocke, the said Richard's son and heir apparent, and Joan Webbe, a daughter and co-heir apparent of the said Thomas Webbe, and after such marriage, as to one moiety of the premises to the use of Alexander and Joan for life in survivorship and then of Joan's heirs by him, with successive remainders to the heirs of Joan by any other husband, to Elizabeth Webbe, then wife of Robert Webbe, another daughter of the said Thomas Webbe, in tail and to the right heirs of the said Thomas, and, as to the other moiety, to the use of the said Thomas Webbe and Margaret for life in survivorship with successive remainders to Alexander and Joan for life in survivorship, to Joan's heirs by Alexander, to Joan's heirs by any other husband, to the said Elizabeth in tail and to the right heirs of the said Thomas; in Trinity term, 16 Eliz.,   [*m.* 29]
by fine in the Common Pleas the premises, by the name of the manor of Westburye under le Playne, lands in Westburye under le Playne, Bratton, Edington, Culstone, Stepleashton, Imber, Warmer, Northe Bradley, Haywood, Hanbridge, Brooke, Lee, Dylton, Shortstreate and Skidemores Upton and a fourth part of the hundred of Westbury under le Playne, co. Wilts, were conveyed by the said Thomas Webbe and Margaret to the said Richard Chocke and Raynes and the heirs of Richard to the uses covenanted; afterwards the marriage between Alexander and Joan was solemnised as agreed. For £15 paid to the Queen's farmer.

927.)   1 *Oct.* 1576.   Licence for Henry, earl of Arundell, John Lumley, knight, lord Lumley, and Jane his wife to alienate the manor of Pynckhurst and lands in Slyndefold, Byllyngeshurst, Hitchingfyeld and Chiltington, co. Sussex, to John Apsley. For £3 8*d.* paid to the Queen's farmer.

928.)   2 *July* 1576.   The like for John Dynham to alienate 'le Newe Parke' in the lordship or parish of Borstall, co. Buckingham, and lands (*named with tenant's name*) in the said park to Alexander Denton. For   [*m.* 30]
£3 6*s.* 8*d.*

929.)   1 *Oct.* 1576.   Pardon of alienation: by indenture, 20 May, 16 Eliz., it was covenanted *inter alia* between Richard Chock and Thomas Webbe that Chock and Elizabeth his wife should by fine convey to the said Thomas and Nicholas Webb *inter alia* the manor and farm of Avington, co. Berks, and the advowson of Avington church to the use of the said Richard until the marriage of Alexander Chock, Richard's son and heir apparent, and Joan a daughter and co-heir apparent of the said Thomas, and after such marriage to the use of the said Richard for life and after his death to the use of Alexander and the heirs male of his body by Joan, with successive remainders to the heirs male of Alexander's body by another wife, to the heirs male of the said Richard's body, to Francis Chock, Richard's brother, in tail male, to John Chock of Shalborne, cos. Berks and Wilts, in tail male, to the heirs female of Richard's body and to Richard's right heirs; in Trinity term, 16 Eliz., by fine in the Common Pleas the premises *inter alia*, by the name of the manors of Denford, Shalborne, Avington and Radley, lands in Denford, Kinbery, Avington, Radley, Shalborne, Inckpen, Hungerford and Bagshote and the advowson of Avington church, co. Berks, were conveyed by the said Richard and Elizabeth for them and the heirs of Richard to the said Thomas and Nicholas and the heirs of Thomas to the uses covenanted; afterwards the marriage between Alexander and Joan was solemnised as agreed, and Elizabeth has died. For £5 10s. paid to the Queen's farmer.

930.)   1 *Oct.* 1576.   Licence for William Courtney, knight, to alienate (1) the manors of Boltbery, Beacham, Mylton Damarell, Moreton *alias* Moreton Hamstede, Cadley *alias* Cadleighe and Honyton, the boroughs of Honyton and Moreton Hamstede, Cadley park, view of frankpledge in Honyton, Moreton Hamstede, Cadley, Cadbury and Milton Damarell, the advowsons of the churches of Honyton, Moreton and Cadley and all his other lands in Boltebery, Beacham, Mylton Damarell, Moreton Hamstede, Cadley, Cadbery, Rudge, Popton, North Molton, Honyton, Combe Coffyn and Combe Raleigh,   [*m.* 31] co. Devon, (2) the manor of Steveley *alias* Steveleigh and lands in Steveley, Curryevill, Bere Crokum, Abbotsille, Ilton, Bradwey, Asshell *alias* Ayshill and the forest of Roche, co. Somerset, and (3) the manor of Brodewynsere, the hundred of Brodwynsere and lands in Brodewynsere, Drempton, Chilehay and Adysham *alias* Atsan, co. Dorset, to Thomas Manners, knight, Roger Manners and John Manners and the heirs and assigns of Thomas to the use of Courtney and Elizabeth his wife in tail male, with successive remainder to the heirs male of the body of Courtney and to the right heirs of Courtney. For £50 paid to the Queen's farmer.

931.)   22 *June* 1576.   The like for George Peckham, knight, to alienate the site of the monastery of Bytelsden, co. Buckingham, lands (*named*) there and in Wapenam, co. Northampton, and all other lands in Bytlesden, Dodford or Stowe, co. Buckingham, formerly of Edmund Peckham, knight, George's father, Robert Peckham, knight, George's brother, or George with reservations (*specified*), to Arthur Grey, knight, lord Grey of
[*m.* 32]
Wylton. For £9 15s. 8d.

932.)   4 *Sept.* 1576.   *Gorhambury.*   The like for William Payne to alienate a messuage called 'le Owter Dagger', now in the tenure of Thomas Bonner the elder, and a messuage called 'le Inner Dagger', in the tenure late of Thomas Edmondes and now of William Jones of London, 'mercer', both in Westcheape *alias* Cheapside in the parish of St. Mary de Arcubus, London, to the said Thomas Bonner, citizen and 'clotheworker' of London, Agnes his wife, Thomas Bonner the younger of London, 'clothworker', and William Bonner, citizen and scrivener of London, to hold 'le Owter Dagger' unto Thomas the elder and Agnes for life in survivorship and thereafter to Thomas the younger and 'le Inner dagger' to Thomas the elder and Agnes for life in survivorship and thereafter to William Bonner aforesaid. For £4 5s.

933.)   7 *Nov.* 1576.   Pardon of alienation: by fine in the Common Pleas in the octave of Trinity, 18 Eliz., Edward Nugent and James Cadell acquired from Christopher, viscount Gormanston, Catherine his wife, Henry Gorland and James Donne *inter alia* a fourth part of the manor of Northwell *alias* Norrell *alias* Northvell, of lands in Bedlowe, Northwell, Clophill, Maldon, Syleshe, Polloxhill *alias* Pulloxhill, Caldecote and Thornecote, of the rectory of Northwell and of the advowsons of Clophill church and the vicarage of Northwell, co. Bedford; and they by the same fine conveyed the same *inter alia* back to the viscount, Gorland and Donne and the heirs of the viscount. For £10 paid to the Queen's farmer.

934.)   8 *Nov.* 1576.   The like: Robert Catlyn, knight, deceased, by charter, 14 Sept., 16 Eliz., enfeoffed John Burgoyne, James Byll, rector of Sutton, Robert Burgoyne, Robert Temple, Robert Hatley, Richard   [*m.* 33]
Johnson, William Langhorne and Richard Grey of the manor of Sondey, the warren of Sondey and all other lands in Sondey, Beaston, Blonham, Temisford and Mogerhanger, co. Bedford, to uses specified in an indenture, 14 Sept., 16 Eliz., annexed to the said charter of feoffment, by which indenture it was declared that Burgoyne and the rest of the co-feoffees should stand seised of the premises to the use successively of the said Robert Catlyn and lady Anne his wife (who still survives) for life in survivorship, of Mary Spencer, Robert's daughter, then wife of John Spencer, for life, of Robert Spencer, son and heir apparent of the said John and Mary, for life, and of the elder son and heir male of the body of the said Robert Spencer in tail male, with successive remainders to the second, third, fourth, fifth, sixth, seventh, eighth, ninth and tenth sons of the said Robert Spencer in tail male, with remainder to the heirs male of the body of Thomas Catelin, the feoffer's father, in tail male, with remainder to the heirs male of Robert Catelin late of Rawodes, co. Northampton, deceased, the feoffer's uncle, in tail male, with remainder to the right heirs of the feoffer; afterwards seisin was delivered of the premises according to the form of the charter. For £20.

935.)   8 *Nov.* 1576.   The like: Thomas Tyryngham of Tiringham, co. Buckingham, and Thomas Tyryngham, his son, by indenture, 11 Nov., 17 Eliz.,   [*m.* 34]
acquired from Jerome Weston a farm, messuage and hereditament called Wynchenden, the site and capital messuage of the manor of Nether Wynchenden *alias* Nether Wynchendon *alias* Netherwynchenham, a warren and water mill with all lands late in the tenure of John Dauntsey, knight, deceased, in Nether Wynchenden, co. Buckingham, late of the monastery of Noteley, and the tithes of the premises, late of the said monastery and late in the tenure of Dauntsey. For £8.

936.)   11 *June* 1576.   Licence for Henry Norrys, knight, lord Norrys of Rycott, and Margery his wife to alienate (1) the manors of Comnor, Yeatenden, Hampsted Norrys and Goshey and lands there and the manor of Sugworth, lands in Sugworth and Radley and the tithes of fleeces and lambs in Radley and Barton, co. Berks, and (2) the manor of Stokenchurche and lands there and the manors of Lewkenor and Weston in le Grene and lands there, co. Oxford, to Francis, earl of Bedford, Charles Moryson and Robert Creswell and the heirs and assigns of the earl. For £30 8s. 11d. paid to the Queen's farmer.

937.)   28 *May* 1576.   The like for Robert Longe and Barbara his wife to alienate the manors of Tuderington Keylweys, Tuderington Lucas and Sutton Benger, lands in the said places and Chipnam and Calne and the advowson of Tuderington Kelweys church, co. Wilts, to Edward Hungerford and Henry Blanchard and the heirs and assigns of Hungerford. For £22 13s. 4d.

938.)   1 *Oct.* 1576.   The like for Lewis Stuckley and John Stuckley, his son and heir, and Frances his wife to alienate the manor of Beylesford and all appurtenances thereof in Baylesford, Hurburnford, Leighederet *alias* Leighderant, Washeborne, Kyngesbridge, Dodbroke and Shilston or elsewhere, co. Devon, to John Gyles. For 37s. 6d.

939.)   4 *June* 1576.   The like for Christopher, viscount Gormanston,   [*m. 35*]
Catherine his wife, Henry Gorland and James Donne to alienate (1) a third part of the
manors of Higheclere and Burghclere *alias* Burroughclere, of lands in the said places and of
the advowsons of the churches there, co. Southampton, and (2) a fourth part of the manor of
Bedelowe, of lands and of the rectory of Chiphill, co. Bedford, to Edward Nugent and
James Cadall and the heirs and assigns of Cadall; and for them by the same fine to convey the
premises back to the said viscount, Gorland and Donne and the heirs and assigns of the
viscount. For £5 6s. 8d.

940.)   1 *Oct.* 1576.   The like for John Sturtyvaunt of Newark on Trent, co. Nottingham,
'grocer', and John Smyth to alienate a mansion house called 'le Graunge' late of the
monastery of Tupholme in the parish of St. Peter in Mydle Rason, with lands and the tithe
hay belonging to the said grange in Mydle Rason and Lyssenley, late of the same monastery,
and lands (*tenants named*) in the said parish and the parish of All Saints in Mydle Rasen, co.
Lincoln, to John Lambert. For 44s. 6d.

941.)   27 *Sept.* 1576.   *Gorhambury.*   The like for Rooke (*Rochus*) Grene and William
Grene to alienate the manor of Coggeshall in Ixnyng *alias* the manor of Ixnyng Coggeshall
in Ixnyng, cos. Suffolk and Cambridge, and all their lands in Ixnyng, Burwell, Lanwode and
Newmarkett, cos. Suffolk and Cambridge, or elsewhere, to Anthony Cage, citizen and
'salter' of London, and   [*m. 36*]
Anthony Cage of Longeslowe, co. Cambridge. For £9 10s.

942.)   12 *July* 1576.   The like for Warham Sentleger, knight, and Anthony Sentleger to
alienate a messuage (*tenants named*) in Lewdsham, co. Kent, to George Fletcher. For 13s. 4d.

943.)   12 *July* 1576.   The like for Richard Grenevile to alienate a capital messuage called
'Saint Austens *alias* Sentleger House' (between 'le Bridghouse' of London there to the East,
'le Wood Wharff' in the tenure of John Selby and a tenement there called 'le Drapers Rentes'
to the West, the river Thames to the North and a lane leading to the said capital messuage
and 'le Bridghouse' to the South) in the parish of St. Olave in Southwarke, co. Surrey, late in
the tenure of Warham Sentleger, knight, and now in that of Grenevyl, and a yearly rent of
20s. out of 'le Drapers Rentes' to George Fletcher. For 10s.

944.)   1 *Oct.* 1576.   The like for Thomas Warne and John Warne to   [*m. 37*]
alienate lands in Myth *alias* Muyth, Muyth Hoocke, Tewxburye and Twynnynge, co. [—],
and the tithes of corn, hay, wool and lambs thereof to William Wakeman and John
Wakeman. For £4 3s.

945.)   4 *Sept.* 1576.   *Gorhambury.*   The like for John Wattes and Elizabeth his wife to
alienate the manor of Swanborne, co. Buckingham, and a capital messuage and all lands in
Swanborne now or late in the tenure of Wattes to Henry Shepharde. For 44s. 6d.

946.)   1 *Oct.* 1576.   The like for John Apseley to alienate the site and demesne lands of the
manor of Pynckhurst and all lands, parcel of the manor, late occupied by William Weller,
late leased by Apseley for a term of years to John Thorneden and now in the tenure of Henry
Thorneden, and lands (*tenants named*) of the manor (copyhold lands excepted) to the same
John and Henry Thorneden. For 6s. 8d.

947.)   1 *Oct.* 1576.   The like for Richard Kyng, Joan his wife, Thomas Lodge, Edith his
wife, Walter Whyte, Agnes his wife, Thomas Hycheborne, Helen his wife and Margery

Pulvertoft to alienate lands in Iwerne   [m. 38]
Mynster and Catley, co. Dorset, to John Were. For 10s.

948.)   7 Nov. 1576.   Pardon of alienation: Thomas Huyck, LL.D., a master in Chancery,
now deceased, by his will, 15 Aug., 15 Eliz., bequeathed a messuage called 'le Swanne' in the
parish of St. Martin in the Fields by Charinge Crosse, co. Middlesex, to his niece, Anne wife
of Mark Styward, and the heirs of her body by Mark with remainder to his brother, Dr.
Huyck; afterwards Mark and Anne as in right of Anne under the said will entered the
premises. For 46s. 8d. paid to the Queen's farmer.

949.)   1 Oct. 1576.   Licence for Edward, earl of Oxford, to alienate lands in Thornecombe, co. Devon, to William Bragg. For 60s. 7d. paid to the Queen's farmer.

950.)   1 Oct. 1576.   The like for John Waddesworthe the elder to alienate lands (named with
tenants' names) in Armyn, Smeth and Sneth and in Great Crowe Parke, Little Crowe Parke
and Hall Garthe, co. York, to John Waddesworth the younger. For £3 6s. 8d.

951.)   1 Oct. 1576.   The like for John Wynn ap Meredith, Maud his wife and Hugh ap
John Wynn to alienate lands in Porkington alias Porkinton   [m. 39]
and Whittingdon alias Whittington, co. Salop, to Roger Kynaston and Richard Lloyd and
the heirs and assigns of Kynaston. For 20s.

952.)   1 Oct. 1576.   The like for Henry Knyvett, knight, and Elizabeth his wife to alienate
lands in Brokenborowe and Foxley, co. Wilts, to John Stumpe and William Stumpe and the
heirs and assigns of John, and for them by the same fine to convey the premises back to the
said Henry and Elizabeth in tail, with remainder to the heirs of the body of Elizabeth, with
remainder to her right heirs. For 40s.

953.)   1 Oct. 1576.   The like for Innocent Rede to alienate lands (named, including 'Saint
Amfabelles Chappell', with tenants' names) in Redborne, co. Hertford, some late of the priory
there, to Richard Wright and Thomas Bayland. For 6s. 8d.

954.)   1 Oct. 1576.   The like for Robert Wyngfeild, knight, and Bridget his wife to
alienate a moiety of (1) the manor of Saxton in Saxton, Dytton, Cheveleighe, Cartling and
Newmarkett, co. Cambridge, (2) the manor of Calverton and Stonystratford in Calverton,
Stonystratford, Denshanger, Wolverton and Parsenham, co. Buckingham, and (3) the
manor of Kenzington in Kenzington, Chelsey, Fullham, Cheswick, Hamersmyth and
Acton, co. Middlesex, to Richard Wingefeilde and Anthony Wingfyeld to the use of the said
                                                                            [m. 40]
Robert for life, and thereafter to the use of Anthony Wingfyeld, Robert's son, in tail, with
remainder to the right heirs of Robert. For £10 13s. 4d.

955.)   7 Nov. 1576.   Pardon of alienation: Anne Wilbraham, widow, by indenture, 17
May, 16 Eliz., acquired from Thomas Alldersey, citizen and 'haberdassher' of London, and
Richard Wylbraham a great messuage, late acquired by Ralph Davenaunte from Francis
Lovell, knight, and Thomas Lovell by indenture, 2 Aug., 2 Edw. VI, in Edelmeton alias
Edminton, co. Middlesex, and lands (named) there. For 100s. paid to the Queen's farmer.

956.)   7 Nov. 1576.   The like: Frances Ratclyff, widow, and John Townley in Trinity
term, 14 Eliz., by fine in the Common Pleas acquired unto them and the heirs of Frances
from William Stanley, lord Mounteagle, and Gregory More a third part of the manors of

Alington, Waterwilloughbie *alias* Waterwillowbie and Osburnebye *alias* Osburnbie and of lands in Alington, Waterwilloughbie, Osburneby, Hinglebye *alias* Inglebie, Stirton, Cotes and Nanbye *alias* Naunbye, co. Lincoln. For 40*s.*

957.)   1 *Oct.* 1576.   The like: Arthur Lee and Margaret his wife by indenture, 14 July, 17 Eliz., acquired from John Bales, citizen and 'tallowchandler' of London, three gardens, now made into two, in 'le Horse Alley' in the parish of St. Stephen in Coleman Strete in London, late in the tenure of Bales and now in the several tenures of the said Arthur and James Turwin, late of the monastry de Regali Loco called Rowley, (abutting on 'le Horse Alley' towards the North, on gardens late of Thomas Cole, 'grocer', and Robert Essington towards the South, on a garden of William Lambe, late in the tenure of John Malliard, towards the West and on the garden of the said Cole towards the East, in length from East to West 109 feet and in width from South to North on the West side 37 feet) unto them and the heirs and assigns of Arthur to the use of Arthur and Margaret for life in survivorship, with remainder to Cuthbert, their younger son, in tail, with remainder to the right heirs of Arthur. For 15*s.*   [*m.* 41]

958.)   1 *Sept.* 1576.   The like: Thomas Repington, Thomas Dabridgecourte, Stephen Varney and Richard Repington in Easter term, 16 Eliz., by fine in the Common Pleas acquired unto them and the heirs and assigns of Thomas Repington from Clement Fyssher and Mary his wife the manors of Packington Magna and Hill Bicknell *alias* Byckenhull [and] Midle Bicknell *alias* Bickenhull, lands in the said places, the advowson of the vicarage of Packington Magna and view of frankpledge in Packington, co. Warwick. For £10.

959.)   9 *Nov.* 1576.   The like: Robert Brett, citizen and merchant taylor of London, by indenture, 28 Sept., 17 Eliz., acquired from Anne Wilbraham, widow, a great messuage late acquired by Ralph Davenaunte from Francis Lovell, knight, and Thomas Lovell by indenture, 2 Aug., 2 Edw. VI, in Edelmeton *alias* Edminton, co. Middlesex, and lands (*named*) there. For 100*s.*

960.)   1 *Oct.* 1576.   Licence for Robert Sutton to alienate two parts of a capital messuage called 'le Comaundry of Wyllerton' and of lands in Willerton *alias* Willoughton, co. Lincoln, to Nicholas Sutton. For £3 6*s.* 8*d.* paid to the Queen's farmer.

961.)   1 *Oct.* 1576.   The like for Francis Sandes to alienate a third part of the site of the priory of Fallington *alias* Bullington and of lands   [*m.* 42] in Ballington, Fulnetbye, Apley, Golthowe and Newbell, co. Lincoln, to Charles Dymmocke. For 26*s.* 8*d.*

962.)   8 *Oct.* 1576.   Pardon of alienation: Nicholas Wylkynson by indenture, 24 Feb., 17 Eliz., acquired from James FitzJames, knight, and William Cooke a moiety of the manors of Pytcombe *alias* Pidcombe and Cole and of all appurtenances thereof in Brewton, Castell Carye, Almesforde and Shepton Mountague, co. Somerset, or elsewhere. For £3 paid to the Queen's farmer.

963.)   8 *July* 1576.   Licence for George Tuchett *alias* Tutchett, lord Awedley, Lucy his wife and James Tuchett *alias* Awdeley to alienate the manor of Tunstall and lands in Tunstall, Chesterton and Awdeley, co. Stafford, to Ralph Sneyde. For £8 18*s.* 8*d.* paid to the Queen's farmer.

964.) 1 *Oct.* 1576.   The like for Thomas Wakeman and Jane his wife to alienate lands in Southwyck and Tewkesburye, co. Gloucester, and the tithes of lands (*named*) there to John Woodward *alias* Smyth. For 4*s.* 8*d.*

965.) 1 *Oct.* 1576.   The like for Thomas Robynson to alienate the manors   [*m.* 43] of Alvecote *alias* Avecote and Shittington, lands in Alvecote, Shittington and Awstrye *alias* Alstrye, the rectories of Shittington and Awstrie and the advowson of the vicarage of Awstrie, co. Warwick, to Thomas Fortescue and Walter Fyshe and the heirs and assigns of Fortescue. For £7.

966.) 1 *Oct.* 1576.   Pardon of alienation: Robert Savyle in Trinity term, 17 Eliz., by fine in the Common Pleas acquired from Thomas Foster, Elizabeth his wife, one of the daughters and co-heirs of John Freman, Richard Howe, citizen and goldsmith of London, William Badby and Mary his wife, the other daughter and co-heir of Freman, the part and pourparty of Elizabeth and Mary of the site of the monastery of Hagnaby *alias* Hawnbye, of lands in Hagnaby, Trustopp, Mayden Well, Anderby, Stepinge, Markeby, Heytoft, Albye, Sutton in the Marsh, Farffurth and Aleford *alias* Awforth and of the rectory of Hagnaby, co. Lincoln. For £16 paid to the Queen's farmer.

967.) 1 *Oct.* 1576.   Licence for Thomas White and Anne his wife to alienate the rectory of Whitechurche *alias* Winterburne Whitechurche, co. Dorset, late of the late college of St. Edmund in Salisbury, the advowson of the vicarage there, late of the said college, and lands there to Nicholas Turbervile. For 36*s.* paid to the Queen's farmer.

968.) 1 *Oct.* 1576.   The like for William Stumpe to alienate the site of the manor of Thornehill and lands in Thornehill, Bourton, Malmesburie and Westporte, co. Wilts, to William Grymer. For 33*s.* 4*d.*   [*m.* 44]

969.) 1 *Oct.* 1576.   The like for Thomas Gressham, knight, and Anne his wife to alienate lands in Little Walsingham, Great Walsingham and Houghton by Walsingham, parcel of the manor of Little Walsingham, co. Norfolk, to Henry Sydney and George Wenne to the use of Thomas Sydney and Barbara his wife and the heirs and assigns of the same Thomas Sydney. For 26*s.* 8*d.*

970.) 1 *Oct.* 1576.   The like for Henry Knyvett and Elizabeth his wife to alienate the manor of Brinkworth and lands in Brynkworth, co. Wilts, to Robert Halton. For £18 15*s.* 9*d.*

971.) 1 *Oct.* 1576.   The like for John Warneforde to alienate the manor of Clotebye and lands in Hanckerton, Cloteby, Charleton, Escott and Crudwell, co. Wilts, to William Bruncker, John Cotton and John Dutton to the use of Warneforde and Anne his wife and the heirs male of the body of Warneforde, with remainder to Warneforde's right heirs. For £4 8*s.* 11*d.*

972.) 1 *Oct.* 1576.   The like for Thomas Denys and Elizabeth his wife to alienate lands (*named*) in Bartonstrete, Battesdon, Trywarth and   [*m.* 45] Hamsted in the city of Gloucester to John Smyth and Joan his wife and the heirs and assigns of John. For 9*s.*

973.) 10 *Sept.* 1576.   The like for Lancelot Cramlington to alienate the manor of Newsam and lands in Newsam and Blythes Nooke, co. Northumberland, to James Ogle, Robert

Mydleton, Gerrard Lawson and John Fenwicke and the heirs and assigns of Ogle. For £4 13s. 4d.

974.)   2 *July* 1576.   Pardon for Richard Clarke of Offham, co. Kent. It was found by an inquisition taken before William Webbe, a coroner in the county, on 5 March, 18 Eliz., on the body of Stephen Ongeley late of Igham, co. Kent, 'blacksmythe', at Offham, that on 28 Feb., 18 Eliz., Ongeley, at Offham in the company of Richard Johnson of Igham, 'sawyer', and Agnes his wife, assaulted Clarke, who by misadventure wounded him so that he died on 3 March in the house of Thomas Wylkyns there (*details given*).

975.)   25 *May* 1576.   Pardon of outlawry for Humphrey Kendall of London, who was put in exigent in the husting of London for non-appearance in the Common Pleas to answer a plea of debt of £20 brought by Henry Kendall of Awestride, co. Warwick, and has now surrendered himself to the Fleet prison.

976.)   9 *July* 1576.   Pardon for William Busshell late of Tamworthe, co. Warwick, tailor (? *vestiarius*). It was found by an inquisition taken before Robert Higgynson, a coroner of the county, on 17 Jan., 18 Eliz., on the body of Richard Wolley late of Tamworthe, 'laborer',

[*m.* 46]

at Tamworthe that Busshell killed Wolley there on 15 Jan., 18 Eliz., in self defence (*details given*).

977.)   1 *Oct.* 1576.   Licence for Thomas Gresham, knight, and Anne his wife to alienate lands in Wedmore, Marcke, Wookey, Meare, Stokegyfford, Chelton, Panboroughe, Blackeford, Allerton and Sonde and common of pasture in moors (*named*) there, co. Somerset, to Thomas Hodgys. For 13s. 4d. paid to the Queen's farmer.

978.)   7 *July* 1576.   Pardon for John Aston late of Hereford, co. Hereford. It was found by an inquisition taken at Worcester castle, co. Worcester, before Edmund Gower, a coroner in the county, on 6 June, 18 Eliz., on the body of Matthew Mynton that Aston killed Mynton by misadventure on 14 May, 18 Eliz., at Bolles Grene by Worcester (*details given*); which inquisition was certified into the Queen's Bench and Aston was committed to the prison of the marshalsea of the said court to await the Queen's grace, as appears by a tenor of the inquisition sent into Chancery by Christopher Wraye, knight, chief justice of the Queen's Bench.

979.)   7 *July* 1576.   Pardon for Richard Bunell *alias* Tincker late of Dorchester, co. Dorset, 'tyncker'. He was indicted by an inquisition taken at Dorchester before George Robynson, coroner of the borough, on the body of William Moore on 10 Jan., 18 Eliz., for that he

[*m.* 47]

killed Moore in self defence on 9 Jan., 18 Eliz., at Wolveton, co. Dorset, (*details given*); as appears by a tenor thereof on the Chancery files certified by Roger Manwood, a justice of the Common Pleas, and John Jefferay, a justice of the Queen's Bench, justices of gaol delivery of Dorchester.

980.)   2 *July* 1576.   Pardon of outlawry for Robert Hyllary, who was put in exigent in the county of Suffolk (and twice outlawed) for non-appearance in the Queen's Bench to answer an indictment for various trespasses, contempts and extortions and has now surrendered himself to the Marshalsea prison.

981.)   8 *Nov.* 1576.   The like for John Bowyer of Bray, co. Berks, 'yoman', who was put in exigent in the husting of London for non-appearance in the Common Pleas to answer a plea of trespass brought by Silvester Cowper and has now surrendered himself to the Fleet prison.

982.)   5 *March* 1576.   The like for William Porter late of Grantham, co. Lincoln, who was put in exigent in the husting of London for non-appearance in the Common Pleas to satisfy William Gumersall *alias* Gombersoull of London, 'yoman', touching a debt of £10, and 30*s.* damages, recovered in the said court and has now surrendered himself to the Fleet prison.

983.)   14 *Nov.* 1576.   The like for Adrian Gilbert late of Stoke Gabriell, co. Devon, who was put in exigent in the county of the city of Exeter for non-appearance in the Common Pleas to satisfy Hugh Wylsdon touching a debt of £11 3*s.* 7*d.*, and 20*s.* damages recovered in the said court and has now surrendered himself to the Fleet prison.

984.)   10 *May* 1576.   Presentation of John Gouldsmyth, B.A., to the   [*m.* 48] vicarage of Seynt Kewe, Exeter dioc.

    The like for the following clerks, viz.—

985.)   9 *June* 1576.   *Gorhambury.*   William Whalley to the vicarage of Hardingestorne, Peterborough dioc.

986.)   24 *Feb.* 1576.   Thomas Gyles to the vicarage of Eburton, Gloucester dioc.

987.)   13 *June* 1576.   *Gorhambury.*   James Saer to the rectory of Harston, Lincoln dioc.

988.)   24 *Feb.* 1576.   Anthony Fletcher to the vicarage of Holy Trinity, Coventry, Coventry and Lichfield dioc.

989.)   20 *Feb.* 1576.   Walter Stephens to the vicarage of Busshoppes Castell, Hereford dioc.

990.)   9 *Feb.* 1576.   Peter Tye to the vicarage of Wycheford in the isle of Ely, Ely dioc.

991.)   9 *Feb.* 1576.   William Gunter to the vicarage of Tonskall with the chapel of St. Saviour, Exeter dioc.

992.)   9 *April* 1576.   *Gorhambury.*   William Dyke to the rectory of Waterstock, Oxford dioc.

993.)   27 *April* 1576.   *Gorhambury.*   John Penven to the vicarage of Stanes, London dioc.

994.)   24 *Feb.* 1576.   Thomas Mawdesley to the rectory of Wynterslowe, Salisbury dioc.

995.)   14 *April* 1576.   *Gorhambury.*   Thomas Cowper to the rectory of Farnedon, Peterborough dioc.

996.)   4 *June* 1576.   William Bilduck to the vicarage of Baburham, Ely dioc.

997.)   4 *June* 1576.   Gawain Conaut to the vicarage of St. Clement, Cornwall, Exeter dioc.

998.)   4 *June* 1576.   Philip Jones to the vicarage of Llaniwarowe, Llandaff dioc.

999.)   2 *July* 1576.   John Paule, B.A., to the rectory of St. Ebbe, Oxford dioc.

1000.)   28 *June* 1576.   Nicholas Eccleston to the rectory of Stradgehull, Norwich dioc.

1001.)   2 *March* 1576.   Thomas Pylkyngton to the rectory of Newton in the deanery of Grimmesbie, Lincoln dioc.

1002.)   9 *March* 1576.   James Byrttles to the rectory of Fynmere, Oxford dioc.

1003.)   9 *March* 1576.   John Swone, M.A., to the rectory of Mylton in the deanery of Rochester, Rochester dioc.

1004.)   15 *Feb.* 1576.   Anthony Garforthe to the rectory of Whesshington, Durham dioc.

1005.)   9 *March* 1576.   Thomas Gyllyngham, M.A., to the vicarage of Dartford, Rochester dioc.

1006.)   17 *Feb.* 1576.   John Kynge, M.A., to the rectory of Crawmershe Gyfford, Oxford dioc.

1007.)   17 *Feb.* 1576.   Thomas Spratt to the rectory of All Saints of Hope, Canterbury dioc.

1008.)   29 *Feb.* 1576.   Francis Shakelton to the rectory of St. Mildred le Poultrie, London, London dioc.

1009.)   2 *March* 1576.   Richard Carter to the rectory of St. Margaret of Lothbury, London, London dioc.

1010.)   4 *April* 1576.   *Gorhambury.*   John Browne, M.A., to the vicarage of Dertford,
[*m.* 49]
Rochester dioc.

1011.)   30 *May* 1576.   William Bolton, M.A., to the rectory of Truswell, York dioc.

1012.)   22 *May* 1576.   Thomas Thomson to the rectory of Sutton, York dioc.

1013.)   25 *June* 1576.   Robert Buller to the rectory of Stokeley Inglishe, Exeter dioc.

1014.)   25 *June* 1576.   Oliver Sarson to the rectory of Ledgate, Norwich dioc.

1015.)   9 *March* 1576.   Thomas Colman to the vicarage of St. Philip in Bristoll, Bristol dioc.

1016.)   30 *May* 1576.   Robert Jackson to the vicarage of Lenge *alias* Westlenge, Bath and Wells dioc.

1017.)   30 *May* 1576.   John Whyte to the vicarage of Bladyngton, Gloucester dioc.

1018.)   30 *May* 1576.   William Metcalfe to the rectory of Chetington, Lincoln dioc.

1019.)   21 *May* 1576.   Lawrence Huslock to the vicarage of Wykewan, Gloucester dioc.

1020.)   2 *April* 1576.   *Gorhambury.*   Robert Browne to the vicarage of Burton in the deanery of Dykeringe, York dioc.

1021.)   19 *May* 1576.   Thomas Petty to the rectory of Wynthorpe, York dioc.

1022.)   10 *May* 1576.   Alexander Shepard to the vicarage of Whytchurche, Lincoln dioc.

1023.)   15 *May* 1576.   Francis Yate to the rectory of Blendworthe, Winchester dioc.

1024.)   15 *May* 1576.   Robert Jones to the vicarage of Crosse, Gloucester dioc.

1025.)   15 *May* 1576.   Stephen Streate, B.A., to the rectory of Wynferthing, Norwich dioc.

1026.)   19 *May* 1576.   William Brode to the rectory of Rancombe, Gloucester dioc.

1027.)   6 *April* 1576.   *Gorhambury.*   Henry Fyssher to the rectory of St. Michael in York, York dioc.

1028.)   21 *May* 1576.   John Hunter to the rectory of All Saints on the Pavement of York, York dioc.

1029.)   16 *May* 1576.   Richard Marcam to the rectory of St. Michael in Wareham, Salisbury dioc.

1030.)   7 *July* 1576.   James Sayer to the rectory of Saxby, Lincoln dioc.

1031.)   7 *July* 1576.   Robert Fludd to the vicarage of Cerne, Bristol dioc.

1032.)   24 *Feb.* 1576.   Thomas Mawdesley to the rectory of Wynterslowe, Salisbury dioc.

1033.)   18 *March* 1576.   John Williams to the rectory of Llangeby, Llandaff dioc.

1034.)   10 *March* 1576.   Gilbert Otes to the vicarage of Kyrkblyfletham, Chester dioc.

1035.)   22 *May* 1576.   Thomas Walkington to the vicarage of Thorneton, Lincoln dioc.

1036.)   7 *July* 1576.   David Rice, B.A., to the vicarage of Bybay with the chapel of Wynston, Gloucester dioc.

1037.)   15 *June* 1576.   *Gorhambury.*   Robert Sendell, M.A., to the rectory of Cheveley, Norwich dioc.

1038.)   5 *June* 1576.   Thomas Pyckerynge to the vicarage of Hatherleghe, Exeter dioc.

1039.)   14 *June* 1576.   *Gorhambury.*   Thomas Humbleton to the rectory   [*m.* 50] of Alington, Lincoln dioc.

1040.)   4 *July* 1576.   John Glasse to the vicarage of Roydon, London dioc.

1041.)   16 *March* 1576.   Thomas Pepper to the vicarage of Mevy *alias* Mewy, Exeter dioc.

1042.)   16 *March* 1576.   Roger ap Howell to the vicarage of Norton, Hereford dioc.

1043.)   16 *March* 1576.   Edmund Pryse, M.A., to the rectory of Ludlowe, Hereford dioc.

1044.)   16 *March* 1576.   Nicholas Hayle to the rectory of Spekeshall, Norwich dioc.

1045.)   16 *March* 1576.   William Hewett to the rectory of Asheley, Winchester dioc.

1046.)   3 *Nov.* 1576.   Hugh Hargraves to the vicarage of Bardewell, Norwich dioc.

1047.)   8 *Nov.* 1576.   John Ambler to the vicarage of Lydbury, Hereford dioc.

1048.)   9 *Nov.* 1576.   Robert Humpston to the vicarage of Ratclyff, Lincoln dioc.

1049.)   8 *Nov.* 1576.   Roger Spencer to the vicarage of Overton under Ardern, Lincoln dioc.

1050.)   3 *Nov.* 1576.   Thomas Wyllyamson, M.A., to the vicarage of Eccles, Chester dioc.

1051.)   12 *Nov.* 1576.   John Longlond, M.A., to the rectory of Tingewick, Lincoln dioc.

1052.)   12 *Nov.* 1576.   George Cawood to the rectory of All Saints in Northstreate, York dioc.

1053.)   12 *Nov.* 1576.   John Lever, M.A., to the rectory of Whessington, York dioc.

1054.)   20 *July* 1576.   *Gorhambury.*   John Symondes to the vicarage of Overton under Ardern, Lincoln dioc.

1055.)   24 *July* 1576.   *Gorhambury.*   Ralph Williams to the vicarage of Sowthorpe, Gloucester dioc.

1056.)   16 *July* 1576.   Morgan Pryce to the vicarage of Garton, York dioc.

1057.)   17 *Sept.* 1576.   *Gorhambury.*   John Rathburne to the rectory of Chale, Winchester dioc.

1058.)   17 *Sept.* 1576.   *Gorhambury.*   Thomas Crosse to the rectory of Hilborgh, Norwich dioc.

1059.)   3 *Sept.* 1576.   *Gorhambury.*   Hopkin Davie to the vicarage of Newcastle, Llandaff dioc.

1060.)   12 *Sept.* 1576.   *Gorhambury.*   William Barkesdale to the vicarage of Marston, Peterborough dioc.

1061.)   7 *Sept.* 1576.   *Gorhambury.*   Thomas Stonyng to the rectory of Purley, Salisbury dioc.

1062.)   27 *Aug.* 1576.   *Gorhambury.*   Jasper Meryck *alias* Owen to the vicarage of Great Barrington, Gloucester dioc.

1063.)   3 *Sept.* 1576.   *Gorhambury.*   Andrew Castelton, M.A., to the rectory of St. Martin in Iremonger Lane, London dioc.

1064.)   6 *Aug.* 1576.   *Gorhambury.*   Nicholas Haygh to the rectory of Wynthorpe, York dioc.

1065.)   1 *Aug.* 1576.   *Gorhambury.*   Richard Gouge, clerk, to the vicarage of Quersted, Norwich dioc.

1066.)   9 *Aug.* 1576.   *Gorhambury.*   Robert Hobson to the rectory of Padeworth, Salisbury dioc.

1067.)   16 *July* 1576.   Patrick Blare to the vicarage of Lapford, Exeter dioc.

1068.)   8 *Aug.* 1576.   *Gorhambury.*   Robert Taylor to the rectory of Somerby, Lincoln dioc.

1069.)   6 *Aug.* 1576.   *Gorhambury.*   Thomas Puckering, B.A., to the rectory   [*m.* 51] of St. Mary in Grymesby, Lincoln dioc.

1070.)   3 *Aug.* 1576.   *Gorhambury.*   John Barnes to the vicarage of Shapwick, Bristol dioc.

1071.)   29 *Aug.* 1576.   *Gorhambury.*   George Boston to the vicarage of Little Wakering, London dioc.

1072.)   28 *June* 1576.   *Gorhambury.*   Christopher Lowther to the rectory of Kirkanders, Carlisle dioc.

1073.)   14 *Aug.* 1576.   *Gorhambury.*   William Stone, M.A., to the rectory of Marseham, Norwich dioc.

1074.)   16 *July* 1576.   *Gorhambury*.   Hugh Jones to the rectory of Idelstre, London dioc.

1075.)   3 *Sept*. 1576.   *Gorhambury*.   William Atkynson to the vicarage of Kirkeby on the Moor, Chester dioc.

1076.)   12 *Oct*. 1576.   *Gorhambury*.   Philip Meteyarde to the vicarage of Culme Ayelewyn, Gloucester dioc.

1077.)   19 *Oct*. 1576.   *Gorhambury*.   Christopher Bayles to the rectory of Nunnyngton, York dioc.

1078.)   26 *July* 1576.   *Gorhambury*.   Robert Sutton to the vicarage of Mylton Harnyeis, Lincoln dioc.

1079.)   25 *July* 1576.   *Gorhambury*.   Julius Watson to the vicarage of Abkettilby, Lincoln dioc.

1080.)   5 *Dec*. 1575.   *Gorhambury*.   Owen Jones, M.A., to the rectory of Marston Sicca, Gloucester dioc.

1081.)   18 *July* 1576.   *Gorhambury*.   William Tabor, S.T.B., to the rectory of Willingale Spayne, London dioc.

1082.)   30 *July* 1576.   *Gorhambury*.   Michael Nicholsonne to the rectory of Geldeston, Norwich dioc.

1083.)   30 *July* 1576.   *Gorhambury*.   John Allrick, B.A., to the rectory of Holbroke, Norwich dioc.

1084.)   31 *July* 1576.   *Gorhambury*.   William Whiteacre, M.A., to the rectory of St. Florence, St. Davids dioc.

1085.)   20 *Sept*. 1576.   *Gorhambury*.   Henry Ledsham, M.A., to the rectory of Wallington, Lincoln dioc.

1086.)   20 *Sept*. 1576.   *Gorhambury*.   John Foxe, B.A., to the vicarage of Holy Trinity in Cambridge, Ely dioc.

1087.)   20 *Sept*. 1576.   *Gorhambury*.   David Georges to the vicarage of Stratfeld Mortimer, Salisbury dioc.

1088.)   13 *Aug*. 1576.   *Gorhambury*.   Thomas Stevens, M.A., to the rectory of Bicklegh, Exeter dioc.

1089.)   3 *Sept*. 1576.   *Gorhambury*.   George Mutley to the vicarage of Shustock, Coventry and Lichfield dioc.

1090.)   26 *Sept*. 1576.   *Gorhambury*.   Edmund Pryce, M.A., to the archdeaconry of Merioneth, Bangor dioc.

1091.)   30 *Sept*. 1576.   *Gorhambury*.   John Mowyer to the rectory of Bagendon, Gloucester dioc.

1092.)   30 *Sept*. 1576.   *Gorhambury*.   Richard Maynerd to the vicarage of Tallan, Exeter dioc.

1093.)   1 *Oct*. 1576.   Jenkin Walter to the rectory of Crawmershe Gyfford, Oxford dioc.

1094.)   13 *July* 1576.   Thomas Leache to the rectory of Saxbye, Lincoln dioc.

1095.)   13 *July* 1576.   William Dixon to the vicarage of Thundriche, London dioc.

1096.)   13 *July* 1576.   Bartholomew Andrewe to the vicarage of Brancktre, London dioc.

1097.)   28 *June* 1576.   Alexander Smythe to the vicarage of Eccles, Chester dioc.

1098.)   13 *Nov*. 1576.   Thomas Watkyns to the rectory of Shawe, Salisbury   [*m.* 52] dioc.

1099.)   26 *Oct*. 1576.   *Gorhambury*.   Hugh Barlowe to the rectory of Braden, Peterborough dioc.

1100.)   14 *Nov*. 1576.   David Rice to the rectory of Westwell, Oxford dioc.

1101.)   17 *Nov*. 1576.[1]   Lancelot Sympson to the vicarage of Estmalling, Canterbury dioc.

---

[1] Entry stated to be of the year 19 Eliz.

1102.)   24 *July* 1576.   *Gorhambury.*   Ralph Williams to the vicarage of Sowthorpe, Gloucester dioc.

1103.)   24 *Sept.* 1576.   *Gorhambury.*   Grant for life to John Duncombe, student of civil law, of the canonry or prebend of Gevindall in York cathedral, void by death and in the Queen's gift *sede vacante.*   By the keeper of the great seal.

1104.)   6 *Aug.* 1576.   *Gorhambury.*   Grant for life to Thomas Woodland, clerk, of the office of warden or master of the hospital of St. John the Evangelist in Cirencester, co. Gloucester, void by death.   By the keeper of the great seal.
    Vacated, because surrendered 30 *June,* 20 *Eliz.; signed:* Thomas Woodland.

1105.)   6 *Aug.* 1576.   *Gorhambury.*   Grant for life to William Undern, clerk, of the canonry or prebend of Halughton in the college of Southwell, York dioc., void by the resignation of William Mowse, LL.D.   By the keeper of the great seal.

1106.)   26 *June* 1576.   Grant for life to Humphrey Fowler, clerk, of the canonry or prebend of Woodburye in the cathedral church [*sic*] of Sowthwell, void by death.
                    By the keeper of the great seal.

1107.)   28 *Sept.* 1576.   *Gorhambury.*   Presentation of Richard Adamson, clerk, to the rectory of Bynbroke St. Mary, Lincoln dioc.

(*The dorse of the roll is blank.*)

PART X

C. 66/1146

1108.)   11 *Nov.* 1576.   Licence for Robert Hyll, son and heir of   [*m.* 1]
Amias Hyll, to enter upon his lands; issues from the time when he   [*m.* 2]
attained the age of 21.   By bill of the court of Wards.

1109.)   13 *July* 1576.   The like for Thomas Stydolfe, son and heir of John Stydolfe; issues
from John's death.   [*m.* 3]
                                                By bill of the court of Wards.

1110.)   2 *July* 1576.   The like for Thomas Essex, son and heir of Thomas Essex; issues
from Thomas the father's death.   [*mm.* 4,5]
                                                By bill of the court of Wards.

1111.)   2 *March* 1576.   The like for Jerome Stanshalle, Mary his wife, William Davison
and Elizabeth his wife, as in right of the same Mary   [*m.* 6]
and Elizabeth, sisters and co-heirs of William Kydwelley; issues from Kidwelly's death.
                                                By bill of the court of Wards.

1112.)   4 *Feb.* 1576.   The like for Arthur Asscote, son and heir of John Asscote late of
Tetcote, co. Devon; issues from the time when he   [*m.* 7]
attained the age of 21.   By bill of the court of Wards.

1113.)   2 *May* 1576.   The like for John Stratforde, son and heir of Henry Stretforde late of
[—], co. Gloucester; issues from the time   [*mm.* 8,9]
when he attained the age of 21.   By bill of the court of Wards.

1114.)   13 *July* 1576.   Licence for life for John, bishop of Rochester, to hold *in commendam*
the deanery of Salisbury, which he now possesses.

1115.)   12 *May* 1576.   Licence for Henry Shelley, kinsman and heir of   [*mm.* 10,11]
Edward Shelley, to wit, the son of Henry Shelley, late the son and heir apparent of the said
Edward, to enter upon his lands; issues from the time when he attained the age of 21.
                                                By bill of the court of Wards.

1116.)   18 *May* 1576.   The like for Robert Moore, son and heir of   [*m.* 12]
Thomas Moore; issues from Thomas's death.
                                                By bill of the court of Wards.

1117.)   28 *May* 1576.   The like for Vincent Grantham, son and heir of Thomas Grantham;
issues from the time when he attained the age   [*mm.* 13,14]
of 21.   By bill of the court of Wards.

1118.)   5 *June* 1576.   The like for John Dolman, son and heir of Thomas Dolman late of
Newbery, co. Berks; issues from Thomas's   [*m.* 15]
death.
                                                By bill of the court of Wards.

1119.)   8 *June* 1576.   *Gorhambury.*   The like for Martin Barneham, son and heir of Francis Barneham, late alderman of London; issues from Francis's death.   [*m.* 16]
By bill of the court of Wards.

1120.)   30 *June* 1576.   The like for John Acclome, son and heir of William Acclome late of Moreby, co. York; issues from the time when he attained the age of 21.   [*m.* 17]
By bill of the court of Wards.

1121.)   12 *July* 1576.   The like for Peter Colles, son and heir of   [*mm.* 18, 19]
Richard Colles; issues from Richard's death.
By bill of the court of Wards.

1122.)   17 *July* 1576.   The like for Philip Boteler, son and heir of John Boteler, knight; issues from John's death.   [*m.* 20]
By bill of the court of Wards.

1123.)   14 *Nov.* 1576.   Pardon of outlawry for William Burges late of Barnesley, co. York, 'lynnen draper', who was put in exigent in the said county for non-appearance in the Common Pleas to answer Thomas Thompson in a plea of debt of 40*s.* and has now surrendered himself to the Fleet prison.

1124.)   2 *July* 1576.   The like for Thomas Tarne late of Penreth,   [*m.* 21]
co. Cumberland, 'yoman', who was put in exigent in the husting of London for non-appearance in the Common Pleas to answer Martin Gylpyn, godson and sole executor of Richard Gylpyn, in a plea for payment of £6 13*s.* 4*d.* and has now surrendered himself to the Fleet prison.

1125.)   24 *Nov.* 1575.   Licence for Anthony Bourne, son and heir of   [*m.* 22]
John Bourne, knight, to enter upon his lands; issues from John's death.   [*m.* 23]
By bill of the court of Wards.

1126.)   25 *Nov.* 1575.   The like for Robert Wrothe, son and heir of Thomas Wrothe, knight; issues from Thomas's death.
By bill of the court of Wards.

1127.)   1 *Feb.* 1576.   The like for Thomas Neale, son and heir of   [*m.* 24]
Richard Neale late of Deane, co. Bedford; issues from Richard's death.
By bill of the court of Wards.

1128.)   11 *Feb.* 1576.   The like for Robert Dormer, son and heir of William Dormer, knight; issues from William's death.   [*m.* 25]
By bill of the court of Wards.

1129.)   7 *Feb.* 1576.   The like for Hugh Smythe, son and heir of Thomas Smythe; issues from Thomas's death.   [*m.* 26]
By bill of the court of Wards.

1130.)   28 *May* 1576.   The like for Thomas Rolte, son and heir of Richard Rolte; issues from Richard's death.
By bill of the court of Wards. [*m.* 27]

1131.)   12 *May* 1576.   The like for Henry Warner, son and heir of   [*m.* 28]
Robert Warner; issues from Robert's death.

By bill of the court of Wards.

1132.)   12 *May* 1576.   The like for Philip Constable, son and heir of Marmaduke
Constable, knight; issues from Marmaduke's death.   [*m.* 29]

By bill of the court of Wards.

1133.)   6 *April* 1576.   *Gorhambury.*   Licence for the dean and chapter of Rochester
cathedral to elect a bishop to that church, void by translation.   By p.s.

1134.)   12 *April* 1576.   *Gorhambury.*   Signification to Edmund, archbishop of Canterbury, and all other bishops whom it shall concern of the royal assent to the election of John
Peerse, S.T.P., to the bishopric of Rochester, void by translation; and order to confirm the
election and to do all other things incumbent on them herein according to statute.

By p.s. [*m.* 30]

1135.)   11 *May* 1576.   Writ to the escheator in the county of Kent to deliver to John
Pearse, S.T.P., bishop elect of Rochester, the temporalities of his see, except any lands now
in the Queen's hands by stat. 1 Eliz.; the Queen having received his fealty and restored them
to him hereby; issues from Michaelmas last.   By p.s.

1136.)   11 *May* 1576.   The like to the escheators in the following counties—Norfolk;
Suffolk; Northampton.

1137.)   11 *May* 1576.   Order to the tenants of the see to be intendant accordingly.

1138.)   13 *April* 1576.   *Gorhambury.*   Signification to Edmund, archbishop of Canterbury, and all other bishops whom it shall concern of the royal assent to the nomination of
John Meric, M.A., to the bishopric in the isle of Man by Henry, earl of Derby, patron by
ancient right of the said see, void by the death of John Salesburye; and order to confirm the
nomination, consecrate him, invest him and do all other things incumbent on them herein
according to statute.   By p.s.

1139.)   12 *July* 1576.   Licence for Edmund Lucy, son and heir of George Lucy, to enter
upon his lands; issues from the time when he attained the age of 21.   [*m.* 31]

By bill of the court of Wards.

1140.)   26 *June* 1576.   The like for Henry Quintyn, son and heir of   [*m.* 32]
Michael Quyntyn; issues from Michael's death.

By bill of the court of Wards. [*m.* 33]

1141.)   14 *July* 1576.   The like for Henry Vanwilder, son and heir of Philip Vanwilder and
Frances his wife; issues from Philip's death.   [*m.* 34]

By bill of the court of Wards.

1142.)   16 *Nov.* 1576.   The like for Humphrey Ferrers, son and heir of John Ferrers;
issues from John's death.

By bill of the court of Wards. [*m.* 35]

1143.)   30 *Oct.* 1576.   The like for Thomas Robinson, son and heir of William Robinson; issues from the time when he attained the age of 21.   [*mm*. 36,37]
By bill of the court of Wards.

1144.)   18 *Nov.* 1575.   The like for George Salkelde and Barbary   [*m*. 38]
his wife, as in right of the same Barbary, daughter and sole heir of Richard Salkeld; issues
from Richard's death.   [*m*. 39]
By bill of the court of Wards.

1145.)   3 *Jan.* 1576.   The like for William Powlett, son and heir of Chidiock Powlett *alias*
lord Chidiock Powlett; issues from   [*m*. 40]
the time when he attained the age of 21.
By bill of the court of Wards.

1146.)   4 *Feb.* 1576.   The like for Anthony Fawnte, brother and heir of William Fawnte;
issues from William's death   [*mm*. 41,42]
By bill of the court of Wards.

1147.)   11 *Feb.* 1576.   The like for William Sellewood, son and heir of Thomas
Sellewood; issues from the time when he attained the age of 21.   [*m*. 43]
By bill of the court of Wards.

1148.)   4 *Feb.* 1576.   The like for Andrew Wyndsor, son and heir of Mary Wyndsor,
widow, late the wife of Thomas Wyndsor; issues from Mary's death.   [*m*. 44]
By bill of the court of Wards.

1149.)   10 *July* 1576.   The like for Thomas Lucy and Dorothy his wife,   [*m*. 45]
as in right of the same Dorothy, daughter and heir of Rowland Arnolde; issues from the time
when she attained the age of 16.   [*m*. 46]
By bill of the court of Wards.

1150.)   2 *June* 1576.   The like for Robert Awdeley, son and heir of Thomas Awdeley late
of Berechurche, co. Essex; issues from the time he attained the age of 21.   [*m*. 47]
By bill of the court of Wards.

1151.)   4 *July* 1576.   The like for Asheton Ayleworthe, son and heir of John Ayleworthe
and Elizabeth Ayleworthe; issues from the death of John and Elizabeth.   [*m*. 48]
By bill of the court of Wards.

1152.)   26 *May* 1576.   The like for Francis Throckmerton, son and heir of Michael
Throckmerton; issues from the time when he attained the age of 21.   [*m*. 49]
By bill of the court of Wards.

1153.)   29 *Dec.* 1575.   Licence for the dean and chapter of Canterbury   [*m*. 50]
cathedral to elect an archbishop to that church, void by death.   By p.s.

1154.)   14 *Feb.* 1576.   Signification to Edwin, bishop of London, Robert, bishop of
Winchester, Richard, bishop of Ely, John, bishop of Hereford, Richard, bishop of St.
Davids, and Edmund, bishop of Salisbury, of the royal assent to the election of Edmund,
archbishop of York, to the archbishopric of Canterbury, void by the death of Matthew
Parker; and order to them (or four at least of them) to confirm the election and do all other
things incumbent on them herein according to statute.   By p.s.

1155.)   23 *April* 1576.   *Gorhambury*.   Writ to the escheator in the county of Kent to deliver to Edmund, archbishop of York, archbishop elect of Canterbury, the temporalities of his see, except any lands now in the queen's hands by stat. 1 Eliz.; the Queen having received his fealty and restored them to him; issues from Michaelmas last.   By p.s.

1156.)   23 *April* 1576.   *Gorhambury*. The like to the following escheators—co. Middlesex; cos. Surrey and Sussex; cos. Oxford and Berks; co. York; co. Buckingham; cos. Essex and Hertford; cos. Norfolk and Suffolk; co. palatine of Lancaster (the chancellor therein); London (Ambrose Nicholas, knight, mayor of the city and escheator therein); Canterbury (the mayor of the city and escheator therein).

1157.)   23 *April* 1576.   *Gorhambury*. Order to the tenants of the see to be intendant accordingly.

1158.)   19 *June* 1576.   Order to all sheriffs etc. to permit the men and tenants of the salt pits in the town of Wych, co. Worcester, to be quit, according to custom, as tenants in ancient demesne, of toll and other dues (*named*), of contributions to expenses of knights of Parliament and of juries etc. outside the court of the town. They are found to be tenants in ancient demesne by a certificate sent into Chancery by the treasurer and chamberlains of the Exchequer.

1159.)   16 *May* 1576.   The like letters executory for the men and tenants of the towns of Bloxham and Adderbury, co. Oxford, who are found to be tenants in ancient demesne by a like certificate.

1160.)   14 *Feb.* 1576.   Order to William Dawtreye, Thomas Lewkenor and Edward Gage to make a perambulation between the land of Henry, earl of Arrundell, of his manor of Avenelles and the land of William Shelley of his manor of Patchinge, by a jury of the county of Sussex.

1161.)   23 *Jan.* 1576.   Licence for John Markham, kinsman and heir   [*m.* 51] of Richard Markham late of Segebroke, co. Lincoln, to enter upon his lands; issues from Richard's death.

1162.)   6 *Feb.* 1576.   The like for John Maye, son and heir of Robert Maye late of Charterhouse Hydon, co. Somerset; issues from   [*m.* 52] the time when he attained the age of 21.

1163.)   1 *Dec.* 1575.   The like for William Clerke, son and heir of Henry Clerke; issues from Henry's death.   [*m.* 53]

(*Ms.* 1*d.* to 8*d.* are blank.)

1164.)   9 *Nov.* 1576.   Admission of John Wade as mayor, and Robert   [*m.* 9*d.*] Saxey and John Prewett as constables, of the staple of wool, hides, woolfells and lead at Bristol. They have been elected to the said offices for one year, as the mayor, constables and commonalty of merchants of the said staple have certified into Chancery.

(*The rest of the dorse is blank.*)

PART XI

C. 66/1147

1165.)   20 *Dec.* 1575.   Licence for Richard Bellamy to alienate   [*m.* 1]
the manor of Southall and lands in Rayneham, Wennyngton, Alveley, Upmynstre and
Okyngton, co. Essex, to Anthony Radclyf, citizen and merchant taylor of London. For £8
18*s.* in the hanaper.

1166.)   29 *Nov.* 1575.   The like for John Keynes of Compton Pauncefote, co. Somerset, to
alienate the manor of Puryton and all appurtenances thereof in Puryton, Woollavington,
Hunspill, Powlett, Bawdripp, Bridgewater, Wembdon, Spaxton, Canyngton, Otterhamp-
ton, Stockland and Stogussey, co. Somerset, to William Lottisham. For £7 8*s.* 2*d.*

1167.)   2 *Jan.* 1576.   The like for Francis Darcye to alienate lands in Arden *alias* Noune
Arden and Halnebye and free fishery in the water of Rye there, co. York, to Ralph Tankerd
and Mary his wife and the heirs and assigns of Ralph. For 57*s.* 10*d.*

1168.)   2 *Jan.* 1576.   The like for Robert Losse and Hester his wife to alienate two
messuages, a stable and two gardens in the parish of St. Peter by Pawles Wharff, London,
called 'le Abbot of Saynt Mary of Yorkes Place' to Thomas Randolphe. For 13*s.* 4*d.*

1169.)   2 *Jan.* 1576.   The like for John Browne to alienate land (*tenants named*) in Longe
Ludforth and Tevilbye, co. Lincoln, to John Huggon. For 6*s.*   [*m.* 2]

1170.)   2 *Jan.* 1576.   The like for Thomas Taylor to alienate lands (*named with tenants'
names*) in Estbarnett, co. Hertford, to John Warren. For 26*s.* 8*d.*

1171.)   2 *Jan.* 1576.   The like for Gabriel Grymston to alienate the manor of Depehams
and lands in Edelmeton, co. Middlesex, to John Best and Giles Lloyd to the use of Gabriel
and Emma his wife and the heirs and assigns of Gabriel. For £7 13*s.* 4*d.*.

1172.)   2 *Jan.* 1576.   The like for George Peckham, knight, to alienate lands (*named*) in
Syresham, co. Northampton, with the tithes of corn, hay, wool and lambs thereof, late of the
monastery of Bytlesdon, co. Buckingham, to Edmund Mannynge. For 8*s.*

1173.)   2 *Jan.* 1576.   The like for Thomasina Paynell, widow, to alienate lands in Tunstede
and Scoruston, a moiety of the tithes and other profits of the rectory of Scoruston and
Tunstede and a moiety of the advowson of the vicarage of Tunsted and Scoruston, late of
the monastery of Campessey, co. Suffolk, to Thomas Pettus. For 10*s.*   [*m.* 3]

1174.)   2 *Jan.* 1576.   The like for Richard Norton, knight, Catherine his wife and Richard
Norton to alienate the manor of Nutley, co. Southampton, to Henry Becher and Fane
(*Phanus*) Becher and the heirs and assigns of Henry. For £4 2*s.* 4*d.*

1175.)   2 *Jan.* 1576.   The like for Edward Carleton and Mary his wife to alienate the manor
of Est Clandon, lands in Est Clandon, West Clandon, West Horseley and Sende and free

warren and view of frankpledge in Est Clandon, co. Surrey, to Lawrence Hollys and Walter Cope and the heirs and assigns of Hollys. For £6 13s. 4d.

1176.)   2 Jan. 1576.   The like for Richard Howe to alienate five messuages in the parish of St. Nicholas Goldeabbey *alias* Goldenabbey, London, to Robert Howe to the use of Richard. For 66s. 8d..

1177.)   2 Jan. 1576.   The like for Alan Chapman, Elizabeth Calton, widow, John Synderton and Margaret his wife to alienate the manor of Badburham *alias* Babram called 'Brusierd Mannor' and lands etc. (*named*) in Badburham, Pampisforde, Sawston, Abington Magna and Abington Parva, co. Cambridge, parcel of the same manor, now or late   [m. 4] in the tenure of John Pott, to Robert Taylor. For £4 10s. 8d.

1178.)   2 Jan. 1576.   The like for Thomas Throckmarton and Margaret his wife to alienate lands in Stoterton *alias* Stotysdon, co. Salop, to John Goodwyn, knight, and Ralph Sheldon and the heirs and assigns of Sheldon. For 6s. 4d.

1179.)   19 Dec. 1575.   The like for Thomas Nasshe and Anne his wife to alienate the manor of Netherworton *alias* Nether Orton, co. Oxford, a capital messuage in Nether Worton and a messuage called Rymettes Farme there to Richard Purefey. For £3.

1180.)   13 Dec. 1575.   The like for Richard Knyght to alienate lands called 'le More' in Tymbersburye, co. Southampton, with a watercourse and fishery there and all his swans in the said county to Richard Worseley. For 26s. 8d.   [m. 5]

1181.)   13 Dec. 1575.   Pardon of alienation: Rose Trott, widow, being seised of a tenement called 'le Stane' in Westchepe in the parish of St. Mary of Colchurche, London, late in the tenure of George Dyamond, by her will, 20 Jan. 1573 [74], bequeathed to her son Martin Trott the said messuage, described as 'the Starre' wherein John Trott, her son, dwelt in Westcheape; after her death Martin entered the same. For £3 6s. 8d. in the hanaper.

1182.)   2 Jan. 1576.   Licence for Edmund Gibbons to alienate the manor of Hensington and all his lands in Hensington, co. Oxford, to Thomas Gibbons and Robert Gibbons and the heirs and assigns of Robert. For 27s. 8d. in the hanaper.

1183.)   2 Jan. 1576.   The like for William Pawlett to alienate the manors of Wade and Totton *alias* Lopperworthe *alias* Lopworth and lands in Wade, Romsey, Lee *alias* Leyghe, Ore, Elinge, Totton and Lopperworth, co. Southampton, to Thomas Braban and Thomas Sayntebarbe and the heirs and assigns of Braban to the use of Pawlett. For £11 13s. 4d.

1184.)   23 Jan. 1576.   The like for William Skipwith and Frances his wife to alienate the manor of Newneham, lands in Newneham, Caldecott, Radwell, Hynckesworthe and Asshewell, the rectory of Newneham and the advowson of the vicarage of Newneham, co. Hertford, to James Dawman and Joan his wife and the heirs and assigns of James. For £5 6s. 8d.   [m. 6]

1185.)   2 Jan. 1576.   The like for Matthew Arondell, knight, and Margaret his wife to alienate lands in Shafton *alias* Shaston *alias* Shaftysburye, Alyncester *alias* Alcester, Hynton Marie, Margaret Marshe and Marnehull *alias* Marnell, co. Dorset, to William Grove and James Sharrock and the heirs and assigns of Grove. For 31s. 2d.

1186.)   20 *Nov.* 1575.   The like for Anthony Barber, Thomas Goodwyn and Nicholas Smythe to alienate lands (*named*) in Bockinges, Gosfelde and Stystede, co. Essex, to Oswald Fytche. For 13*s.* 4*d.*

1187.)   8 *Dec.* 1575.   The like for Thomas Ryley to alienate the house and site of the Carthusian priory by Coventry to Sampson Baker. For 33*s.* 4*d.*

1188.)   21 *May* 1576.   Licence for Thomas Salmon and Alice his wife to alienate the manor of Hunton and lands in Hunton and Crawley, co. Southampton, to John Hunte. For £4 15*s.* paid to the Queen's farmer.   [*m.* 7]

1189.)   21 *May* 1576.   The like for Richard Yate the elder to alienate the manor of Worthe in Longworthe and all his other lands in Longworth, co. Berks, to John Fysssher. For 33*s.* 4*d.*

1190.)   21 *May* 1576.   The like for Christopher Robyns to alienate lands (*described with tenants' names*) in Ravensthorpe, co. Northampton, and all other lands late of William Jenowaye which should after his death have descended to his son, Richard Jenowaye, to the said Richard. For 8*s.* 8*d.*

1191.)   21 *May* 1576.   The like for Robert Longe and Barbary his wife to alienate the manor and hundred of Barton Sacye and lands in Barton Sacye and Newton Sacye, co. Southampton, to John Henton. For £10.

1192.)   21 *May* 1576.   The like for Robert Richers and Elizabeth his wife to alienate a moiety of the manor of Peverells and of the advowson of All Saints church in Melton with all appurtenances thereof in Melton Magna, Agasthorpe, Melton Parva, Colney, Hethesett, Ketryngham, Wymondham, Barforde, Carleton and Wramplyngham, co. Norfolk, to Robert Downes. For 40*s.*

1193.)   20 *March* 1576.   *Gorhambury.*   Licence for Robert Losse to alienate two tenements, late one messuage, once in the tenure of John Burneham and now in the several tenures of Nicholas Killingworthe and William Marryn, in the parish of St. Michael Bassinges Hall, London, late of Elzynge Spittell priory, (as they descended to the said Robert by the death of Hugh Losse, his father, and in as ample manner as they were granted to the said Hugh and William Bocher by patent, 10 May, 35 Hen. VIII) to Mary Barnes, daughter of Thomas Barnes, citizen   [*m.* 8] and 'currier' of London. For 6*s.* 8*d.* in the hanaper.

1194.)   24 *May* 1576.   Licence for Robert Whyte to alienate lands (*named with tenants' names*) in Burnesall, Overbordeley, Netherbordeley, Hetton, Kyrkbye and Malham, co. York, to John Kydd, John Waylock and John Tenaunte. For £6 8*s.* 4*d.* paid to the Queen's farmer.

1195.)   1 *Feb.* 1576.   Licence for George Harryson of Grays Inne, co. Middlesex, to alienate eight tenements in the parish of St. Giles in the Fields, co. Middlesex, now or late in the several tenures of him, Thomas Tirrie, William Cotton, John Byll, Alexander Runckhorne, William Weston, Thomas Leigh and [—] Webbe, to Robert Staunton and Michael Higbedd to the use of Harryson and Elizabeth his wife and the survivor of them, with remainder to the right heirs of Harryson. For   [*m.* 9] 20*s.* 8*d.* in the hanaper.

1196.)   10 *April* 1576.   *Gorhambury.*   The like for William Burgh, knight, lord Burgh, and Catherine his wife to alienate the manor of Kinges Walden *alias* Walden Regis and lands in Kinges Walden, Powles Walden and Follett, co. Hertford, to Richard Hale. For £10.

1197.)   24 *April* 1576.   The like for Richard Warner to alienate a messuage in the parish and ward of St. Olave in Oldfyshstrete, London, now or late in the tenure of John Ventrise, to Ventrise. For 9s.

1198.)   4 *April* 1576.   *Gorhambury.*   The like for Christopher Hatton, a gentleman of the privy chamber, captain of the guard, to alienate the manor of Upton Episcopi, co. Hereford, late of the bishopric of Hereford, and the advowson of the rectory of Upton Episcopi to William Dodington and Christian his wife and the heirs and assigns of Dodington. For £7 6s.

1199.)   24 *May* 1576.   Licence for John Dynham to alienate a hide   [*m.* 10] of land in Borstall, co. Buckingham, called 'Deare Hide', with 'le housebote', 'hey bote' and 'firebote' belonging thereto, the bailiwick, keepership and stewardship of the forest of Barnewood, co. Buckingham, and the bailiwicks or 'lez walkes' called Heckeshulte and Leadwynslade *alias* Ickeshilt and Leatherslade, Pauncill, Malcombe and Le Frythe in the said forest to Alexander Denton. For 33s. 4d. paid to the Queen's farmer.

1200.)   6 *June* 1576.   Pardon of alienation: Matthew Smythe in Easter term, 18 Eliz., by fine in the Common Pleas acquired from Thomas Kempe, Dorothy his wife, Nicholas Sentleger and Catherine his wife the manor of Kyngweston *alias* Kyngwardeston, lands in Kingweston and the advowson of Kyngweston church, co. Somerset. For £4 4s. 8d. paid to the Queen's farmer.

1201.)   9 *March* 1576.   Licence for Robert Chamberlayne, citizen and 'iremonger' of London, to alienate two messuages, once in the tenure of Thomas Barrett, afterwards leased to Robert Downe and now in the several tenures of Nicholas Chapman and Joan Craicall, widow, in the parish of St. Mary Colchurche, London, late of the late house or college of Acon, London, to William Chapman, citizen and 'iremonger' of London, and Joan his wife and the heirs and assigns of William. For 31s. 2d. in the hanaper.

1202.)   6 *June* 1576.   Pardon of alienation: Edmund Smythe in Easter term, 18 Eliz., by fine in the Common Pleas acquired from Marmaduke Claver and Elizabeth his wife lands in Stukeley, co. Buckingham. For 33s. 4d. paid to the Queen's farmer.

1203.)   6 *June* 1576.   The like: Robert Hepworthe in Easter term, 18 Eliz., acquired from Thomas Storthes lands (*named with*   [*m.* 11] *tenants' names*) in Thurstonlande, co. York. For 8s. 8d.

1204.)   6 *June* 1576.   The like: Jerome Weston in Easter term, 18 Eliz., by fine in the Common Pleas acquired from Richard Cooke and Stanfild Cooke the manor of Barkebye *alias* Barkebie, Thorpe Barkeby and Hamelton, lands in the said places and the rectory and the advowson of the vicarage of Barkeby, co. Leicester. For £11 6s. 8d.

1205.)   6 *June* 1576.   The like: Marmaduke Claver in Easter term, 18 Eliz., by fine in the Common Pleas acquired from Edmund Smythe a third part of the manor of Foscott *alias* Foxcott and of lands and free fishery in the water of Owse in Foscott, Lechamstede *alias*

Lekhamstede and Thorneton and the advowson of a third part of Foscott church, co. Buckingham. For 33s. 4d.

1206.)   6 *June* 1576.   The like: William Parker in Easter term, 18 Eliz., by fine in the Common Pleas acquired from Catherine Throckmarton, widow, and Job Throckmerton the manor of Kyngton and lands in Claverdon *alias* Claredon and Preston Bagott, co. Warwick. For 33s. 4d.

1207.)   6 *June* 1576.   The like: William Box the younger, son of William Box the elder, alderman of London, in Easter term, 18 Eliz., by fine in the Common Pleas acquired from the said William the elder and Anne his wife the manors of Marcham and Garford and lands in Marcham, Freford and Garford, co. Berks. For £19 6s. 8d.

1208.)   21 *May* 1576.   The like: William Bonde in Easter term, 17 Eliz., by fine in the Common Pleas acquired from Daniel Snowe, Thomas Goddard and William Goddard the manor and priory of Ascott, lands in Ascott and Shipton and all tithes there, co. Oxford. For £3.

1209.)   6 *June* 1576.   The like: Lawrence Danson in Easter term,   [*m.* 12] 18 Eliz., by fine in the Common Pleas acquired from Lewis Mordaunt, knight, lord Mordaunt, Elizabeth his wife, Henry Darcye, knight, and Catherine his wife lands in Wenysley and Lareton, co. York. For 10s.

1210.)   6 *June* 1576.   The like: Robert Longe in Easter term, 18 Eliz., by fine in the Common Pleas acquired from the said lord Mordaunt, Elizabeth his wife, Henry Darcye, knight, and Catherine his wife lands in Wynesley, Hartwithe and Laireton, co. York. For 29s. 4d.

1211.)   6 *June* 1576.   The like: Robert Skayff, in Easter term, 18 Eliz., by fine in the Common Pleas acquired from the said lord Mordaunt, Elizabeth his wife, Henry Darcye, knight, and Catherine his wife lands in Wynesley, Hartwirth and Lareton, co. York. For 9s.

1212.)   6 *June* 1576.   The like: Roger Ratclyff and Joan his wife in Easter term, 18 Eliz., by fine in the Common Pleas acquired unto them and the heirs and assigns of Ratclyff from the said lord Mordaunt, Elizabeth his wife, Henry Darcye, knight, and Catherine his wife lands in Felbeck, Brymbem *alias* Brymham and Lareton, co. York. For 4s. 4d.

1213.)   6 *June* 1576.   The like: Miles Hardcastell in Easter term, 18 Eliz., by fine in the Common Pleas acquired from the said lord Mordaunte, Elizabeth his wife, Henry Darcye, knight, and Catherine his wife lands in Hartwith, Dacre, Hayshaye and Lareton, co. York. For 10s.

1214.)   6 *June* 1576.   The like: Robert Haxebye in Easter term, 18 Eliz., by fine in the Common Pleas acquired from the said lord Mordaunte,   [*m.* 13] Elizabeth his wife, Henry Darcye, knight, and Catherine his wife lands in Hartwith and Lareton, co. York. For 10s.

1215.)   6 *June* 1576.   The like: Robert Horseman in Easter term, 18 Eliz., by fine in the Common Pleas acquired from the said lord Mordaunt, Elizabeth his wife, Henry Darcye, knight, and Catherine his wife lands in Hartwith and Lareton, co. York. For 6s.

1216.) 6 *June* 1576. The like: William Byrnand in Easter term, 18 Eliz., by fine in the Common Pleas acquired from the said lord Mordaunt, Elizabeth his wife, Henry Darcye, knight, and Catherine his wife lands in Brymbem *alias* Brymham, Northe Pasture and Lareton, co. York. For 58s. 6d.

1217.) 6 *June* 1576. The like: Richard Baylye in Easter term, 18 Eliz., by fine in the Common Pleas acquired from the said lord Mordaunte, Elizabeth his wife, Henry Darcye, knight, and Catherine his wife lands in Hartwith, Dacre and Lareton, co. York. For 26s. 8d.

1218.) 5 *July* 1576. The like: Robert Kemys in Trinity term, 13 Eliz., by fine in the Common Pleas acquired from Charles Zouche a moiety of the manors of Wyncaunton *alias* Wyncalton, Marshe, Pytcombe and Coole and lands in the said places, co. Somerset. For £15.

1219.) 26 *June* 1576. The like: Thomas Guldeford, knight, and Edward Barrowe in Hilary term, 16 Eliz., by fine in the Common Pleas acquired unto them and the heirs of Guldeforde from Richard Rogers and Andrew Rogers the manor of Bryanston, lands in Bryanston and the advowson of Bryanston church, co. Dorset, to hold to the use of the said Richard and Mary now his wife and the heirs and assigns of Richard. For £20.   [*m.* 14]

1220.) 20 *June* 1576. The like: William Stone in Easter term, 18 Eliz., by fine in the Common Pleas acquired from Agnes Franke, widow, Benet Barefote and Elizabeth his wife a brewhouse called 'le Three Kinges' in Estsmythfelde in the parish of St. Botolph in Estsmythefelde, co. Middlesex, 'le wharff' belonging thereto and a granary house attaching thereto, now or late in the tenure of William Woode. For £4.

1221.) 6 *June* 1576. The like: Ranulph Elveston, Thomas Jackson and Ralph Hardye in Easter term, 18 Eliz., by fine in the Common Pleas acquired from Thomas Gresham, knight, and Anne his wife lands in Great Over *alias* Mickell Over, co. Derby. For 12s. 4d.

1222.) 6 *June* 1576. The like: John Shardlowe, William Carter *alias* Shepperd and William Twigge in Easter term, 18 Eliz., by fine in the Common Pleas acquired from Thomas Gresham, knight, and Anne his wife lands in Little Over in Great Over *alias* Mickell Over, co. Derby. For 11s. 4d.

1223.) 6 *June* 1576. The like: Richard Pecocke in Michaelmas term, 12 Eliz., by fine in the Common Pleas acquired from Henry Bellamy and Elea his wife lands in East Barnett, co. Hertford. For £6.

1224.) 3 *May* 1576. Pardon of alienation: William Muschamp in Michaelmas term, 16 Eliz., by fine in the Common Pleas acquired from Ralph Frythe and Joan his wife the manor of Bowells *alias* Cock a Bowells and lands in Southweld, co. Essex. For £3 in the hanaper.

1225.) 6 *June* 1576. Pardon of alienation: Richard Thomson and Bridget his wife in Easter term, 18 Eliz., by fine in the Common Pleas acquired from Lewis Mordaunte, knight, lord Mordaunte, Elizabeth his wife, Henry Darcye, knight, and Catherine his wife lands in

[*m.* 15]

Hartwith and Layrton, co. York. For 26s. 8d. paid to the Queen's farmer.

1226.) 6 *June* 1576. The like: Richard Rossater in Easter term, 18 Eliz., by fine in the

Common Pleas acquired from Edward Rosseter and George Rosseter lands in Hunsley, Wedeley and Cave, co. York. For £4.

1227.)   26 *June* 1576.   The like: William Mallowes and George Hagarth in Michaelmas term, 16 Eliz., by fine in the Common Pleas acquired unto them and the heirs of Mallowes from Richard Skipwith the manor of Bechewood *alias* Saynt Gyles in le Wood and lands in Flamsteade, co. Hertford. For £10.

1228.)   28 *June* 1576.   The like: Edward Baynton, knight, in Hilary term, 18 Eliz., by fine in the Common Pleas acquired from Henry Baynton of Bromeham and Anne his wife lands in Loxwell, Stanley and Chypenham, co. Wilts. For £21.

1229.)   26 *June* 1576.   The like: Paul Pope in Easter term, 15 Eliz., by fine in the Common Pleas acquired from Richard Skipwyth, son and heir apparent of William Skipwith, knight, the manor of Beachewoode *alias* Saynte Gyles in the Wood and lands in Bechewood *alias* Saynt Gyles in the Wood, co. Hertford. For £10.

1230.)   25 *June* 1576.   The like: John Hale by indenture, 25 Oct., 15 Eliz., acquired from Thomas Chester of Bristoll, merchant, a wood called Highewood late enclosed out of the common wood called Kyngeswood, co. Wilts. For £3 6s. 8d.

1231.)   6 *June* 1576.   The like: Robert Brabon in Easter term, 18 Eliz., by fine in the Common Pleas acquired from Henry Peck and Joan Farrar, widow, the manor of the hospital of St. Bartholomew *alias* Playden and lands in Rye, Playden, Iden, Pesemershe, Beckley and Northeam,   [*m.* 16]
co. Sussex, to hold to the use of the said Joan and Robert Osmanton. For 40s.

1232.)   26 *May* 1576.   Licence for Philip Awdeley, Margaret his wife, John Wyngfelde, Anne his wife, Arthur Downynge, Susan his wife, Barnard Whitston and Elizabeth his wife to alienate the manor of Westlexham, co. Norfolk, to Robert Downes, Anthony Hogan and James Awdley to the use of Dowynge and Susan his wife and the heirs and assigns of Dowynge. For £5 paid to the Queen's farmer.

1233.)   4 *June* 1576.   The like for John Mychell and Marion his wife, one of the kin and co-heirs of Thomas Hale, to alienate a third part of a third part of (1) the manor of Donyngton and lands in Donyngton, co. Gloucester, late of the monastery of Evesham, co. Worcester, and (2) a portion of the tithes of corn and hay in Donyngton aforesaid in the parishes of Bradwell and Stowe, co. Gloucester, late of the same monastery and late in the tenure of Thomas Harrys, to Richard Ockeholde. For 8s. 11d.

1234.)   12 *April* 1576.   Licence for Henry Cotterell to alienate lands (*named with tenant's name*) in Upton on Severn, co. Worcester, to his younger son, Francis Cotterell. For 5s. 4d. in the hanaper.

1235.)   26 *March* 1576.   *Gorhambury.*   The like for George Willoughbye of Coventry to alienate a capital messuage called 'le Castell' in Holborne in the parish of St. Andrew in the suburbs of London,   [*m.*17]
late of the monastery of Malmesburye, co. Wilts, and the appurtenances thereof, now in the several tenures of Ralph Barton, David Applethyn, James Rauf, John Gregorye, William Deathe, Thomas Chalfonte, Nicholas Broket, Richard Flower, James Perye, John Oker and Hammond Parke, to Richard Stonley. For 32s.

1236.)   12 *April* 1576.   The like for Richard Becke to alienate lands in Friesley, co. Warwick, to William Cookes and Thomas Reve to his use. For 33*s.* 4*d.*

1237.)   22 *May* 1576.   Licence for Thomas Francke and Mary his wife to alienate lands (*named with tenant's name*) by Maldon, co. Essex, late of the monastery of Byleigh, co. Essex, to Robert Caunnocke. For 23*s.* 4*d.* paid to the Queen's farmer.

1238.)   26 *May* 1576.   The like for John Dolman and Mary his wife to alienate a third part of the manors of Shawe and Colthropp, of lands in Shawe, Colthropp, Mygeham, Thacham, Newberye, Donyngton and Woodspene, of two fisheries in the waters of Shawe and Colthropp and of the advowson of Shawe church, co. Berks, to Thomas Dolman. For £5 1*s.* 4*d.*

1239.)   1 *June* 1576.   The like for John, marquess of Winchester, to alienate the manor of Estpennard, all appurtenances thereof in Estpennarde, Lyttlepennarde, Easten, Henbridge, Wythyll, Huckesham,   [*m.* 18]
Bradley, Bradleyend and Pyll or elsewhere, co. Somerset, and all his other lands in the said places to Thomas Smythe. For £11 6*s.* 8*d.*

1240.)   20 *June* 1576.   The like for Thomas Cockes the elder to alienate lands (*named with tenants' names*), parcel of a grange called Swynstede Grange *alias* Pyckeringe Grange, in Ibstock *alias* Ivestocke, co. Leicester, late of the monastery of Garryngton, co. Leicester, to Gregory Cockes and John Cockes. For 20*s.*

1241.)   22 *May* 1576.   The like for Henry Coxhed, Margaret his wife, Oliver Coxhed and James Coxhed to alienate lands in Lockinge *alias* Lockyndge and the tithes in Bitterton *alias* Betterton, co. Berks, to John Clerke, Edward Keet, and William Cater and the heirs and assigns of Clerke. For 40*s.*

1242.)   20 *June* 1576.   The like for John Henton to alienate the manor and hundred of Barton Sacye and lands in Barton Sacye and Newton Sacye, co. Southampton, to Richard Lee and Thomas Sayntbarbe to the use of Thomas Salmon the elder, Alice his wife and Thomas Salmon the younger and the heirs and assigns of Thomas the elder. For £10.

1243.)   21 *May* 1576.   The like for Thomas Dearinge and Winifrid his wife to alienate lands in Beryton, Petersfeld and Nustede, co. Southampton, to William Bolde. For 37*s.* 4*d.*
                                                                                      [*m.* 19]

1244.)   26 *May* 1576.   The like for Andrew Studley to alienate lands in the parish of St. Lawrence in Southampton to Alice Grosse, widow, and John Alie. For 26*s.* 8*d.*

1245.)   26 *May* 1576.   The like for John Savage to alienate lands (*tenant named*) in Butlers Merston, co. Warwick, to William Commaunder. For 20*s.* 8*d.*

1246.)   4 *Sept.* 1576.   *Gorhambury.*   The like for John Spencer and Mary his wife to alienate the manors of Barne *alias* Berne and Morecomblake and lands and view of frankpledge in Berne, Morecomblake, Orcharde, Marshewoodvale and Whitchurche, co. Dorset, to Paul Pope. For £10 17*s.* 4*d.*

1247.)   12 *July* 1576.   Pardon of alienation: Ambrose Smythe, Thomas Cave and Thomas Skevington in Easter term, 17 Eliz., by fine in the Common Pleas acquired unto them and the heirs of Ambrose from Roger Smythe the manor of Withecoke and Whitcoke *alias* Withcoke, lands in Withecoke and the advowson of Withecoke church, co. Leicester. For 60s. paid to the Queen's farmer.

1248.)   13 *Aug.* 1576.   *Gorhambury.*   Licence for Simon Welberye to alienate the manor of Castell Edem in the bishopric of Durham and all his other lands in Castell Edem, certain lands (*tenants named*) excepted, to Ralph Hedworthe and William Perkynson and the heirs and assigns of Perkynson to the use of the said Simon and Anthony Welberye and the heirs and assigns of Anthony. For £9 6s. 4d. paid to the Queen's   [*m.* 20] farmer.

1249.)   12 *July* 1576.   Pardon of alienation: Richard Greneville in Michaelmas term, 17 Eliz., by fine in the Common Pleas acquired from Warham Seyntleger, knight, and Anthony Seyntleger a messuage, two curtilages, two tofts, two gardens and 30s. worth of rent in the parish of St. Olave in Southwarke, co. Surrey. For 30s. paid to the Queen's farmer.

1250.)   1 *June* 1576.   Licence for Arthur Breame, James Platte and Bridget his wife to alienate lands in Estham and Westham, co. Essex, to Richard Stoneley. For £3 6s. 8d. paid to the Queen's farmer.

1251.)   1 *Oct.* 1576.   Pardon of alienation: Thomas Seyntpoll in Hilary term, 17 Eliz., by fine in the Common Pleas acquired from Richard Candyshe and Austin Candyshe the manor of Melwood *alias* Wood *alias* Charterhouse and lands in Melwood, Owston, Axey and Upperbournham, co. Lincoln. For £3 7s. paid to the Queen's farmer.

1252.)   1 *Oct.* 1576.   The like: Henry Harvye in Hilary term, 17 Eliz., by fine in the Common Pleas acquired from William Richebell the manor of Freren and lands in Freren, co. Surrey. For £5.

1253.)   1 *Oct.* 1576.   The like: Richard Purefey in Easter term, 18 Eliz., by fine in the Common Pleas acquired from Thomas Nashe, Anne his wife, Edmund Mannynge and Mary his wife the manor of Netherworton *alias* Netherorton and lands in Netherworton, co. Oxford. For £3.

1254.)   1 *Oct.* 1576.   The like: William Graye in Trinity term, 17 Eliz., by fine in the Common Pleas acquired from Robert Wolley, Joan his wife and Thomas Wolley, his son and heir apparent, the manor of Kermonde in le Myre   [*m.* 21] and lands in Kermond, Cumbenworth and Tevelbye, co. Lincoln. For 54s.

1255.)   8 *July* 1576.   Licence for George Tucket *alias* Tutchett, lord Awdeley, and James Tuchett *alias* Tutchett *alias* Awdeley to alienate lands in Awdley, Bettley and Balterley, co. Stafford, to Ralph Edgerton. For 16s. 4d. paid to the Queen's farmer.

1256.)   1 *Oct.* 1576.   The like for Ferdinand Parrys to alienate the rectories of Abington *alias* Abington Magna and Abington *alias* Abington Parva and the advowsons of the vicarages of Abington Magna and Abington Parva, co. Cambridge, to Thomas Dalton. For 40s.

1257.)   8 *Nov.* 1576.   Pardon of alienation: Charles Foxe, John Seborne the younger, Edmund Foxe and Edmund Scrope by indenture, 14 Aug., 17 Eliz., had from Richard Harford the manor of Cannon Frome, co. Hereford. For £7 paid to the Queen's farmer.

1258.)   1 *Oct.* 1576.   Licence for Stephen Hadnoll and Margaret his wife to alienate lands (*tenants named*) in Benthall, Posenhall and Wyke, co. Salop, to Lawrence Benthall. For 5*s.* 2*d.* paid to the Queen's farmer.

1259.)   9 *July* 1576.   The like for William, lord Burghley, treasurer, Walter Myldmaye, knight, chancellor of the Exchequer, William Cordell, knight, master of the rolls, James Dyer, knight, chief justice of the Common Pleas, and Roger Manwood, a justice of the Common Pleas, to alienate the manor and the rectory of Lenham and lands in Lenham, Heresham, Boulton Malherbie, Charinge, Wytchlynge, Royton and   [*m.* 22] Egerton, co. Kent, to Stephen Themylbie, Thomas Horseman and Edward Eyre. For £20.

1260.)   1 *Oct.* 1576.   The like for John Jefferay, a justice of the Queen's Bench, to alienate by fine in the Common Pleas a moiety of the manor of Mydleton, co. Sussex, of lands in Mydleton, Westmeston, Streate, Chayleyghe *alias* Chayley, Westhothleyghe and Wyvesfelde *alias* Wylsfelde and of free warren and liberty of park in the said manor and tenements to Henry, earl of Derby, K.G., Margaret his wife, Henry, earl of Kent, Mary his wife, Thomas Stanley, knight, and Edward Stanley, knight, and the heirs of Derby; and for them by the said fine to convey the same back to Jefferey in tail, with remainder to the heirs of the body of his grandfather, John Jefferey, deceased. For 46*s.* 8*d.*

1261.)   1 *Oct.* 1576.   Pardon of alienation: William Fulwere *alias* Fuller and Nathaniel Fuller, his son by indenture, 16 Feb., 16 Eliz., acquired from John Clarke, citizen and 'inholder' of London, the reversion of a messuage and garden in or near the graveyard of the monastery of 'le Charterhouse' in the parish of St. Botolph without Aldersgate, London, formerly of the said monastery and leased to Nicholas Sedley by William Dauntsey by indenture, 3 Dec., 11 Eliz., at a yearly rent of 13*s.* 4*d.* For 13*s.* 4*d.* paid to the Queen's farmer.

1262.)   1 *Oct.* 1576.   Licence for John Wakeman and William Wakeman to alienate a capital messuage in Le Muyth near Tewxburne and adjoining   [*m.* 23] the late chapel there and lands and tithes (*named with tenants' names*)—except certain tithes heretofore leased by the monastery of Tewxburie—and all hereditaments heretofore leased by the monastery by indenture, 10 Oct., 26 Hen. VIII, to Richard Wakeman, deceased, father of the undermentioned Richard, as the said John and William late acquired the premises from Thomas Warne of Snowshill, co. Gloucester, to Richard Wakeman. For 23*s.* 4*d.* paid to the Queen's farmer.

1263.)   1 *Oct.* 1576.   The like for George Rotheram and Jane his wife to alienate the manor of Kempston *alias* Kempstone Hardwick *alias* Hardwicke and lands and free fishery in the waters of Ose, Olde Raye and Newe Raye in Kempston, Wotton, Estow, Byddenham and Bedford, co. Bedford, to Humphrey Fitzwilliams. For £4 9*s.*

1264.)   7 *Nov.* 1576.   Pardon of alienation: John Warne and Thomas Warne, 'yomen', by indenture, 17 Feb., 18 Eliz., acquired from Miles Sandes, John Popham, George Fetyplace and Matthew Smythe the manor of Snowshill, co. Gloucester, late of the monastery of Wynchecombe, co. Gloucester, formerly conveyed by John, late earl of Warwick, to George Willoughbie and Anne his wife and afterwards by fine in the Common Pleas in Hilary term, 14 Eliz., by Henry Willoughby and Thomas Willoughbie,   [*m.* 24] sons of the said George and Anne, conveyed to Popham, Fetyplace and Smythe and the heirs of Popham, except (1) lands (*named*) sold by the said Henry to Anthony Alborough, (2) all lands which were late customable lands demisable by copy of court roll and (3) all lands bargained and sold by Sandes, Popham, Fetyplace and Smythe by indenture, 21 June, 17

Eliz., to Rowland Baugh, Nicholas Tyckeridge, Thomas Tickeridge, his son, Thomas Sauvage, Ralph Savage, John Haddocke, John Cotterell, James Davyes, John Wyett and Thomas Brevall the younger. For £20 paid to the Queen's farmer.

1265.) 1 *Oct.* 1576.   The like: Everard Digby, son and heir apparent of Kenelm Digbye, in Hilary term, 16 Eliz., by fine in the Common Pleas acquired from Kenelm aforesaid and John Burton *inter alia* the advowson of Stoke Drye *alias* Drystocke church, co. Rutland. For 30s.

1266.) 1 *Oct.* 1576.   Licence for Christopher, viscount Gormanston, to alienate a third part of the manor of Highclere and Burghclere *alias* Burroughclere, of lands in Highclere and Burghclere and of the advowsons of Highclere and Burghclere churches, co. Southampton, to Richard Kingesmyll, attorney of the court of Wards, William Kingesmyll, knight, John Kingesmyll and George Kingesmyll and the heirs and assigns of Richard. For £7 15s. 7d. paid to the Queen's farmer.

1267.) 1 *Oct.* 1576.   The like for John Kydd, John Wallocke and John Tenaunte to alienate lands in Cowgilhouses, Hetton, Over Bordley, Nether Bordley and Malham, co. York, to Margaret Thomson, widow, and Isabel Thomson and the heirs and assigns of Margaret. For 2s. 8d.

1268.) 1 *Oct.* 1576.   The like for the same to alienate lands in   [*m.* 25] Hetton, Over Bordley, Nether Bordley and Malhame, co. York, to John Thomson and Henry Thomson and the heirs and assigns of John. For 5s. 4d.

1269.) 1 *Oct.* 1576.   The like for the same to alienate lands in Cowgillhouses, Hetton, Over Bordley, Nether Bordley and Malham, co. York, to William Thomson the elder. For 4s. 4d.

1270.) 1 *Oct.* 1576.   The like for the same to alienate lands in Hetton, Over Bordley, Nether Bordley and Malham, co. York, to Robert Airton. For 6s. 2d.

1271.) 1 *Oct.* 1576.   The like for the same to alienate lands in Hetton, Over Bordley, Nether Bordley and Malham, co. York, to Christopher   [*m.* 26] Thomson and William Thomson the younger and the heirs and assigns of Christopher. For 14s. 8d..

1272.) 1 *Oct.* 1576.   The like for the same to alienate lands in Hetton, Over Bordley, Nether Bordley and Malhame, co. York, to Roger Wallocke and Henry Tenaunte and the heirs and assigns of Roger. For 12s. 8d.

1273.) 1 *Oct.* 1576.   The like for the same to alienate lands in Hetton, Over Bordley, Nether Bordley and Malhame, co. York, to Richard Ayrton. For 4s.

1274.) 1 *Oct.* 1576.   The like for the same to alienate lands in Hetton, Over Bordley, Nether Bordley and Malhame, co. York, to Edward Thomson. For 10s. 8d.   [*m.* 27]

1275.) 1 *Oct.* 1576.   The like for the same to alienate lands in Hetton, Over Bordley, Nether Bordley and Malhame, co. York, to Anthony Procter. For 13s. 4d.

1276.)   1 *Oct.* 1576.   The like for the same to alienate lands in Hetton, Over Bordley, Nether Bordley and Malhame, co. York, to Christopher Wilkinson. For 12*s.*

1277.)   28 *May* 1576.   The like for Francis Keilwaye, Thomas Keilwaye and Ambrose Keilwaye to alienate (1) the manors of Rogebourne *alias* Rockborne, Rockestede *alias* Rockesythe and Alwynes, lands in Rogebourne, Rockestede, Alwynes, Dunwaye, Brem- mer, Burgate and Byckton and free warren and view of frankpledge in Rogebourne, Rockestede and Alwynes, co. Southampton, and (2) the manor of Combe Bissett and lands in Combe, Bissett and Whiteparishe, co. Wilts, to John Baylie and William Grygge and the heirs and assigns of Baylie. For £17 13*s.* 4*d.*

1278.)   1 *Oct.* 1576.   The like for Humphrey Ferrers *alias* Ferys to alienate three mes- suages, three cottages and a garden in the parish of St. Botolph without Aldersgate in Aldersgate ward, London, to   [*m.* 28] George Dacars. For 26*s.* 8*d.*

1279.)   1 *Oct.* 1576.   The like for William Norrys, Mary his wife, Joyce Avelyn, widow, and Edward Avelyn to alienate lands in Wallingford and Clopcote, co. Berks, and Ewelme and Soncombe, co. Oxford, to Richard Hyde and Elizabeth his wife and the heirs and assigns of Richard. For £4.

1280.)   7 *Nov.* 1576.   Pardon of alienation: George Burgoyne in Trinity term, 14 Eliz., by fine in the Common Pleas acquired from Henry Berkley, knight, lord Berkley of Mowbray, Segrave and Bruce, the manor of Weston *alias* Weston by Baldock and lands in Weston, co. Hertford. For £30 paid to the Queen's farmer.

1281.)   1 *Oct.* 1576.   The like: John Clarke, citizen and 'inholder' of London, by inden- ture, 30 April, 15 Eliz., acquired from Robert Tayler two messuages, six cottages and the gardens and other hereditaments belonging thereto, once in the tenure of Philip Connowaye and now or late in the several tenures of Nicholas Brome *alias* Browne, Catherine Quene, Thomas Clarke, William Donne, Thomas Crill and Francis Harvye, in Whitecrosstrete *alias* Whitecrowchestrete in the parish of St. Giles without Creplegate, London, and a messuage and garden, once in the tenure of Thomas Carkett and afterwards in that of Nicholas Sedley, in or by the graveyard of the monastery of 'le Charterhowse' by London in the parish of St. Botolph without Aldersgate in the suburbs of London, co. Middlesex, (except certain lands now in the tenure of Andrew Mayniesborowe *alias* Sare, whereof Robert Taylour remitted his interest to the said Maynesborowe *alias* Sare). For £8.

1282.)   1 *Oct.* 1576.   Licence for John Rede and Elizabeth his wife to alienate the manors of Tanrugge *alias* Tanridge *alias* Northall *alias* Le Priorie and Oxstede *alias* Berstede *alias* Burstede in Oxstede,   [*m.* 29] the site of the monastery of Tanrigge lands in Tanrigge, Oxstede, Horne, Blechingleigh, Crowherst, Welcombstede *alias* Godstone, Chelshame, Warlingham and Waldingham, co. Surrey, Seale, Chydingstone and Stonbridge, co. Kent, and Longe Sutton, co. Southamp- ton, the rectory of Tanridge and Crowherst, a moiety of the rectory of Welcombstede *alias* Godstone and the advowson of the vicarage of Welcombstede *alias* Godstone, co. Surrey, to Richard Bostocke. For £16 13*s.* 4*d.* paid to the Queen's farmer.

1283.)   7 *Oct.* 1576.   The like for Matthew Smythe, Edith his wife, John Smythe, son and heir apparent of the said Matthew, John Archer and Magdalen his wife to alienate six messuages and four gardens in Southwark, co. Surrey, to William Emes. For 21*s.* 8*d.*

1284.)   1 *Oct.* 1576.   The like for William Hannam, 'yoman', to alienate lands (*named*) in Horsington, co. Somerset, now or late in the tenure of William Hobbes. For 3*s.* 11*d.*

1285.)   1 *Oct.* 1576.   Pardon of alienation: Thomas Haywarde and Thomas Armiger in Michaelmas term, 17 & 18 Eliz., by fine in the Common Pleas acquired unto them and the heirs and assigns of Haywarde from James Bourne and Ursula his wife the manor of Fildallynge *alias* Feldallynge and lands in Fildallynge, Batheley, Saxlinham, Sharington and Langham, co. Norfolk. For £13 6*s.* 8*d.* paid to the Queen's farmer.

1286.)   28 *Oct.* 1576.   Licence for David Wylkyns, Robert Honywood   [*m.* 30] of Grayes Inne and Roger Manwood of the Inner Temple to alienate lands, parcel of the manor of Tonge, co. Kent, to Edward Lucas, Thomas Willowes and Agnes Thompson. For £4 paid to the Queen's farmer.

1287.)   1 *Oct.* 1576.   Pardon of alienation: by fine in the Common Pleas on the morrow of Candlemas, 17 Eliz., Robert Petre and Edmund Dowynge acquired from Walter Myldmaye, knight, the manors of Seyntcler and Herons, lands in Danburye, Sandon, Great Baddowe and Little Baddowe, and the advowson of Danburye church, co. Essex, and by the same fine conveyed them back to Myldmaye. For 5*s.* 2*d.* paid to the Queen's farmer.

1288.)   1 *Oct.* 1576.   Licence for John Tufton and Christian his wife to alienate the manor of Lockington, lands and free fishery in the water of Trent in Lockington and Michelholme, the tithes of corn, hay, flax and hemp in Lockington and Michelholme, a yearly pension of 53*s.* 4*d.* out of the vicarage of Lockington and the advowson of the said vicarage, co. Leicester, to William Baynbrige. For £15 12*s.* paid to the Queen's farmer.

1289.)   1 *Oct.* 1576.   The like for Richard Turnour to alienate lands (*tenants named*) in Bromptone, co. Hereford, to Walter Nurs. For 5*s.* 2*d.*   [*m.* 31]

1290.)   7 *Nov.* 1576.   Pardon of alienation: Stephen Slany, citizen and 'skyner' of London, by indenture, 10 May, 13 Eliz., acquired from William Widnell, citizen and merchant taylor of London, *inter alia* a moiety of the manor of Stanton *alias* Stenton, co. Lincoln. For £9 paid to the Queen's farmer.

1291.)   4 *Nov.* 1576.   Licence for Henry Cheyne, knight, lord Cheyne, to alienate Holy Trinity chantry in Reculver church and appurtenances (*tenants named*) thereof in Reculver, Herne, Heth, Chystlett, Swalclyff and Whitstable or elsewhere, co. Kent, called 'le chauntry landes' of Reculver, to George Meycott and Caviller Meycott, his son. For £4 paid to the Queen's farmer.

1292.)   7 *Nov.* 1576.   The like for Thomas Brande the elder, 'yoman', and John Brande, Edward Brande and George Brande, his sons, to alienate the rectory of Hormeade Magna, co. Hertford, with the advowson of the vicarage there, the parsonage house and all appurtenances of the rectory—except lands (*named*) in Hormeade Magna and Burnt Pellam, co. Hertford, reserved to the said Thomas and Michael Brande, his son, and the heirs of Michael—to Francis Wood and Henry Edmondes to the use of the said Thomas for life and thereafter of the said John, Edward and George. For £3.

1293.)   7 *Nov.* 1576.   Pardon of alienation: William Gybbyns, 'salter', Alexander Avenor the younger, 'iremonger', and Nicholas Warner, 'skyner', citizens of London, by indenture, 30 Oct., 15 Eliz., acquired from Edmund Skarnynge the rectory of Cotton *alias* Potters

Cotton *alias* Coyton and all appurtenances thereof in Potters Cotton, Chilvers Coton, Griff, Griff Poole, Atlebarowe, Stockenforde, Annesley, Astley, Bedworthe,   [*m.* 32] Burton Hastynges and Marson, co. Warwick, formerly conveyed to Skarnynge by John Younge late of London and Robert Browne of London, goldsmith, by indenture, 11 Aug., 38 Hen. VIII, (except the herbage of the little park of Astley, co. Warwick, and the tithes and all other profits in the said park reserved to Skarnynge) and lands (*named with tenant's name*) in Potters Cotton. For 100s. paid to the Queen's farmer.

1294.)   7 *Nov.* 1576.   Licence for Thomas Brande the elder, 'yoman', and Michael his son to alienate lands (*named*) in Hormeade Magna and Burnt Pellam, co. Hertford, parcel of the rectory of Hormeade Magna, to Francis Wood and Henry Edmondes, 'yoman', to the use of the said Thomas for life and thereafter of Michael. For 10s. paid to the Queen's farmer.

1295.)   1 *Oct.* 1576.   The like for Richard Guldeford to alienate the manor of Kenaston *alias* Kenardington and the advowson of Kenarton church, co. Kent, to John Shelley and Walter Moyle and the heirs and assigns of Shelley. For £3 6s. 8d.

1296.)   4 *Oct.* 1576.   *Gorhambury.*   Pardon of alienation: John Sotherton and Mary his wife in Michaelmas term, 15 Eliz., acquired unto them and the heirs of John from James Frost, Joan his wife, Simon Suckerman, Richard Rolfe, Catherine his wife and William Hagon three fourth parts of a messuage, a curtilage and a garden in the parish of St. Botolph without Aldrichegate *alias* Aldresgate, London. For 30s. paid to the Queen's farmer.

1297.)   1 *Sept.* 1576.   Licence for William Knyveton to alienate the manor of Osmaston next Derby, co. Derby, to Thomas Trentham and   [*m.* 33] John Flackett to the use of Knyveton. For £4 2s. 6d. paid to the Queen's farmer.

1298.)   8 *Oct.* 1576.   *Gorhambury.*   Pardon of alienation: Robert Gybbes in Easter term, 18 Eliz., by fine in the Common Pleas acquired from Thomas Essex lands in Badburye, co. Wilts. For 24s. 6d. paid to the Queen's farmer.

1299.)   8 *Oct.* 1576.   *Gorhambury.*   The like: Robert Hedges by fine as above acquired from Thomas Essex lands in Badburye, co. Wilts. For 12s.

1300.)   8 *Nov.* [*sic*] 1576.   *Gorhambury.*   The like: William Looker by fine as above acquired from Thomas Essex lands in Badburye, co. Wilts. For 22s. 2d.

1301.)   8 *Oct.* 1576.   *Gorhambury.*   The like: William Collett by fine as above acquired from Thomas Essex lands in Badburye, co. Wilts. For 19s. 8d.

1302.)   8 *Oct.* 1576.   *Gorhambury.*   The like: Thomas Combe by fine as above acquired from Thomas Essex lands in Badburye, co. Wilts. For 14s.

1303.)   8 *Oct.* 1576.   *Gorhambury.*   The like: Thomas Hardynge by fine as above acquired from Thomas Essex lands in Badburye, co. Wilts.   [*m.* 34] For 25s. 4d.

1304.)   8 *Oct.* 1576.   *Gorhambury.*   The like: Nicholas Wixie by fine as above acquired from Thomas Essex lands in Badburye, co. Wilts. For 20s.

1305.)   8 *Oct.* 1576.   *Gorhambury.*   The like: John Smythe by fine as above acquired from Thomas Essex lands in Badburye, co. Wilts. For 23s. 6d.

1306.)   12 *June* 1576.   Licence for William Payne, Jane his wife, Thomas Payne and George Payne to alienate two messuages in the parish of St. Mary de Arcubus, London, to Robert Mounson, a justice of the Common Pleas, John Calton and Thomas Dryland to the use of the said William. For £4 paid to the Queen's farmer.

1307.)   1 *Oct.* 1576.   The like for Robert Lane, knight, Mary his wife and William Lane, his son and heir apparent to alienate lands (*named*) in Hogshowe, common of pasture for 320 sheep in Coppesley Hills, Estcleydon and Bottlecleydon and the tithes of the lands in Hogshowe, co. Buckingham, to Paul Wentworthe and Helen his wife and the heirs and assigns of Paul. For 49s.

1308.)   1 *Aug.* 1576.   *Gorhambury*.   Pardon of alienation: William Rooper and William Dawtre in Michaelmas term, 14 Eliz., by fine in the Common Pleas acquired unto them and the heirs of Rooper from Thomas Quadringe and Anne his wife lands in Burgh *alias* Burrowe   [*m.* 35]
and common of pasture in Scalstrete in Burgh, co. Lincoln. For £20 paid to the Queen's farmer.

1309.)   7 *Nov.* 1576.   The like: Frances Ratcliff, widow, in Trinity term, 14 Eliz., by fine in the Common Pleas acquired from William Stanley, knight, lord Mountegle, and Gregory More a third part of the manor of Nocton Parke, of lands in Nocton and Dunston, of view of frankpledge and other liberties in Nocton and Dunston and of the rectory of Nocton, co. Lincoln. For 40s.

1310.)   1 *Oct.* 1576.   Licence for Thomas Dearynge and Winifrid his wife to alienate lands in Burton, co. Southampton, to John Trybe. For 8s. 8d. paid to the Queen's farmer.

1311.)   1 *Oct.* 1576.   Pardon of alienation: Thomas Birde in Hilary term, 17 Eliz., by fine in the Common Pleas acquired from Thomas Lodge, knight, and Anne his wife *inter alia* the free chapel in Nayland and the advowson thereof, co. Suffolk. For £10 paid to the Queen's farmer.

1312.)   1 *Oct.* 1576.   Licence for Edward, earl of Oxford, to alienate lands in Thornecombe, co. Devon, to William Downe. For 24s. 5d. paid to the Queen's farmer.

1313.)   1 *Oct.* 1576.   The like for Thomas Philpott and George Philpott to alienate the manor of Sowthbaddesley and Shurpryckes, lands   [*m.* 36]
in Woodhouse and the keepership of Chutt park, cos. Southampton and Wilts, to Richard Whyte and John Paynter and the heirs and assigns of Whyte. For 28s. 2d.

1314.)   1 *Oct.* 1576.   The like for Thomas Chester, Catherine his wife and Edward Chester to alienate lands in Westerley and Pucklechurche, co. Gloucester, to John Robertes. For £4.

1315.)   1 *Oct.* 1576.   The like for Edward, earl of Oxford, to alienate lands in Thornecombe, co. Devon, to Leonard Tucker *alias* Penyngton. For 14s. 10d.

1316.)   1 *Oct.* 1576.   Pardon of alienation: Henry Haydon in Trinity term, 17 Eliz., by fine in the Common Pleas acquired from James Bourne *alias* Burne and Ursula his wife lands in Faldalinge *alias* Feldallinge, the rectory of Felddallinge and the advowson of Felddallinge church, co. Norfolk. For £5 paid to the Queen's farmer.

1317.) 1 *Aug.* 1576. *Gorhambury.* Licence for Christopher, viscount Gormanston, to alienate a fourth part of St. Mary's college in the church of Northwell *alias* Norrell *alias* Northvell and of the manor of Northwell with all its appurtenances in Caldecotes, Ickwell, Hatche, Northwell, Nether Calcot, Overcalcot, Thornecot and Bexston, co. Bedford, to Thomas Browne, knight. For £3 6s. 8d. paid to the Queen's farmer.

1318.) 1 *Oct.* 1576. Pardon of alienation: Robert Tayler in Hilary term, 18 Eliz., by fine in the Common Pleas acquired from Alan Chapman, Elizabeth Calton, widow, John Sinderton and Margaret his wife *inter alia* the manor of Mountpellers in Badburgham, Sawston, Pampisford   [*m.* 37] and Abbington, co. Cambridge. For £8 paid to the Queen's farmer.

1319.) 7 *Nov.* 1576. The like: Henry Mervyn and Robert Hill in Hilary term, 14 Eliz., by fine in the Common Pleas acquired unto them and the heirs of the same Henry from James Mervyn *inter alia* the manor of Compton Basset and lands in Compton Bassett and Calne, co. Wilts. For £12 10s. 10d.

1320.) 1 *Oct.* 1576. The like: Gerard Suthill in Trinity term, 18 Eliz., by fine in the Common Pleas acquired from Silvester Bellowe the rectory of Hybaulstowe and a moiety of the tithes of corn and hay in Hybaulstowe, co. Lincoln. For 40s.

1321.) 1 *Oct.* 1576. The like: John Conyers of London in Michaelmas term, 17 Eliz., by fine in the Common Pleas acquired from John Conyers of Sokebourne the manors of Carleton Magna, Carleton Parva and Castell Carleton, lands in Carleton Magna, Carleton Parva and Castell Carleton and the advowsons of Castell Carleton and Carleton Magna churches, co. Lincoln. For £4.

1322.) 7 *Nov.* 1576. The like: William Whittingham, clerk, dean of Durham cathedral, in Easter term, 16 Eliz., by fine in the Common Pleas acquired from Roger Menell and Joan his wife the manor of Baulke by Sutton and lands in Baulke, Bagbye and Kirkbye Knowles by Sutton, co. York. For £8.

1323.) 7 *Nov.* 1576. The like: Robert Rice by indenture, 1 Nov., 17 Eliz., acquired from Robert Sprynge the tithes belonging to the rectory of Preston, co. Suffolk, late of Holy Trinity Priory in Ipswiche, co. Suffolk, the advowson of the vicarage of Preston, late of the said priory, and lands (*named*) in Preston. For £5.   [*m.* 38]

1324.) 8 *Oct.* 1576. The like: William Lamborne in Easter term, 18 Eliz., by fine in the Common Pleas acquired from Thomas Essex lands in Badburye, co. Wilts. For 19s.

1325.) 7 *Nov.* 1576. The like: Edmund Hassellwood by indenture, 4 July, 18 Eliz., acquired from Kenelm Digbye and Francis Cave *inter alia* the manor of Kerkbye Underwood and all their lands in Kerkbye Underwood, Bulbye, Yernham, Keisbye (in Laughton) and Hawthropp, co. Lincoln, whereof divers lands (*named*), late of the monastery of Sempryngham, are held of the Crown in chief, as appears by process out of the Exchequer. For £6 13s. 4d.

1326.) 4 *Oct.* 1576. Licence for William Gent to alienate the manor of Norton by Daventre *alias* Mantells Manner in Norton, co. Northampton, to William Baldwyn and James Chamberlen. For £8 6s. 8d. paid to the Queen's farmer.

1327.)   1 *Oct.* 1576.   The like for Matthew Packnam to alienate the manor of Burdfeilde *alias* Boardfeilde and all appurtenances thereof in Burdefeilde, Otterden and Witchlinge or elsewhere, co. Kent, to John Baker. For 28*s.*

1328.)   1 *Oct.* 1576.   The like for John Bacon to alienate a moiety of the manor of Esthorppe, of the advowson of the rectory of Esthorppe and of lands in Birche or elsewhere, co. Essex, to   [*m.* 39]
Henry Goldynge. For £3 6*s.* 11*d.*

1329.)   1 *Oct.* 1576.   The like for Thomas Everarde the elder and Dorothy his wife to alienate the manors of Aston Tyrold and Aston Tyroll and lands in Aston Tyrold, co. Berks, to Edward Unton, knight, John Fetyplace, knight, William Hyed, Francis Yate, George Evelyn and Richard Hatton and the heirs and assigns of Unton. For 37*s.* 4*d.*

1330.)   1 *Oct.* 1576.   The like for Thomas Cassone, William Marshall, Robert Killing-beck, William Fladder and Thomas Thwaytes to alienate lands (*named with tenants' names*) in Chappelallerton and in the manor of Chappellallerton, co. York, and all profits of the said manor to Thomas Whalley. For 13*s.* 6*d.*

1331.)   1 *Oct.* 1576.   The like for Humphrey Columbell and Margaret his wife to alienate lands in Palterton, Scarclyff *alias* Scardeclyff, Ulkarthorpe and Ryley and a moiety of the manor of Pallerton, co. Derby, to Francis Leeke, knight. For 35*s.* 8*d.*

1332.)   1 *Oct.* 1576.   Pardon of alienation: George Sayer   [*m.* 40]
the younger and John Spencer in Easter term, 18 Eliz., by fine in the Common Pleas acquired *inter alia* from Richard Sayer and Alice his wife lands in Markeshall, co. Essex, to hold unto the same George and John and the heirs and assigns of George to the use of Richard and Alice and the heirs and assigns of Alice. For 21*s.* 8*d.* paid to the Queen's farmer.

1333.)   1 *Oct.* 1576.   The like: William Tanckard by indenture, 14 Sept., 16 Eliz., acquired from Ralph Tanckarde *inter alia* the site of the nunnery of Nunarden and Kexbye with lands in Nunarden and Kexbie, co. York. For £5.

1334.)   7 *Nov.* 1576.   The like: John Turner by indenture, 20 April, 15 Eliz., acquired from Robert, earl of Leicester, the manor of Atherston on Stowre, co. Warwick, late acquired by the said earl of John Lidcott of Swallofeilde, co. Berks. For £16.

1335.)   8 *Oct.* 1576.   The like: Thomas Morse in Easter term, 18 Eliz., by fine in the Common Pleas acquired from Thomas Essex lands in Badburye, co. Wilts. For 46*s.* 8*d.*

1336.)   1 *Oct.* 1576.   Licence for William Waldegrave, knight, and Elizabeth his wife to alienate the site of the manor of Gladfenhall and lands in Haulstede, co. Essex, to Arthur Breame. For £3 6*s.* 8*d.* paid to the Queen's farmer.

(*The dorse of this roll is blank.*)

PART XII

C. 66/1148

1337.)   26 *Nov.* 1575.   Grant in fee simple to Henry, earl of Huntingdon,   [*m.* 1]
of the reversions and rents of lands (*named with tenants' names*) in Loughborough, parcel of
the manor of Loughborough, leased for 21 years as follows—

   (i) By patent of the Exchequer, 3 July, 1 & 2 Ph. & Mary, to Nicholas Jenkynson and
Thomas Hebbe, from Lady Day then last at a yearly rent of 36s.

   (ii) By patent, 1 May, 1 & 2 Ph. & Mary, to Isabel Gybson, from Lady Day then last at a
yearly rent of £22.

   (iii) By patent, 9 March, 1 & 2 Ph. & Mary, to William Warde *alias* Fermer *inter alia*,
from Lady Day then next at a yearly rest of 54s. 8d. (*detailed*).

   (iv) By patent of the Exchequer, 2 May, 1 & 2 Ph. & Mary, to William Warde *alias*
Fermer *inter alia*, from Lady Day then last at a yearly rent of 11s. 8d. (*detailed*).

   (v) By patent of the Exchequer, 3 July, 1 & 2 Ph. & Mary, to George Swillington, from
Michaelmas then next at a yearly rent of 24s.

   (vi) By patent of the Exchequer, 18 June, 1 & 2 Ph. & Mary, to   [*m.* 2]
Geoffrey Wulphett, from Lady Day then last at a yearly rent of 22s.

   (vii) By patent of the Exchequer, 7 April, 1 & 2 Ph. & Mary, to Edward Charde, from
Lady Day then last at a yearly rent of 18s.

   (viii) By patent of the Exchequer, 26 Sept., 1 & 2 Ph. & Mary, to Peter Ithell, from
Michaelmas then next at a yearly rent of 24s.

   (ix) By patent of the Exchequer, 26 Sept., 1 & 2 Ph. & Mary, to George Medley, from
Michaelmas then next at a yearly rent of 32s.   [*m.* 3]
(*detailed*).

   Also grant of the lordship and manor of Loughborowe *alias*   [*m.* 4]
Loughborough, the parks of Loughborough and Burley, a coney warren in Loughborough
and the advowson of the rectory of Loughborough, co. Leicester, late of Henry, late duke of
Suffolk, attainted of treason.

   Reserving to the Crown the rent reserved under a grant of the premises by patent, 25
April, 11 Eliz., [*Calendar*, 1566–1569, *no.* 2109]   [*m.* 5]
to the said earl of Huntingdon, in tail male in reversion—having been granted by patent, 21
March, 4 & 5 Ph. & Mary, to Edward Hastinges, knight, lord Hastinges of Loughborough,
in tail male—to hold by service of the fortieth part of a knight's fee and by a yearly rent of
£115 16s. 6d.   [*m.* 6]
To hold by service of the fortieth part of a knight's fee and by a rent from the time when the
said earl of Huntingdon shall die without an heir male of his body of £115 16s. 6d.

   The said lord Hastinges is dead without an heir male of his body.   By p.s.

1338.)   24 *Nov.* 1575.   Lease for 21 years to Thomas Parkinson of lands   [*m.* 7]
(*named*) in Burneston, co. York, and the tithes of hay (*tenants named*) in Allethorpe,
Gatenbye, Newton, Lemynge and Exillbye, co. York, parcels of the manor of Burneston
and late of the monastery of St. Mary by the walls of York; with reservations; from
Michaelmas last; yearly rent £12. For a fine of £24 paid at the Exchequer.

   By the commissioners by virtue of the Queen's warrant.

1339.)   5 *Dec.* 1575.   Commitment for 31 years (by mainprise before [—]) to John Lee of the custody of a tenement in the parish of St. Stephen in Walbroke, London, late in the tenure of Thomas Maugham and in the Queen's hands by his death without lawful issue; from Michaelmas last; yearly rent 40*s.*; provided that, if any other will give more of increase yearly for the said custody without fraud, Lee shall be bound to pay so much if he wishes to have it.   By bill of the treasurer.

1340.)   19 *Nov.* 1575.   Grant in fee simple to Peter Edgcombe, an esquire for the body, lord of the manor and town of Stonehowse, co. Devon, that he may have a market every Wednesday in the said town and two fairs yearly, one at midday on the eve of the feast of St. Lambert until midday on the morrow of the same feast and the other at midday on the eve of the Ascension until midday on the morrow of the same feast. At his suit, for the convenience of the inhabitants of the said town and other the Queen's subjects coming thither.   By p.s.

1341.)   30 *Dec.* 1575.   Lease for 21 years to Humphrey Mychell, clerk of the castle and honour of Wyndesore, of (1) the site of the manor,   [*m.* 8] lordship and rectory of New and Old Wyndesore and all lands and tithes belonging thereto, parcel of the honour of Wyndesor, co. Berks,   [*m.* 9] (2) lands (*named*) in New Wyndesore and Wyndesore Underore, co. Berks, (3) lands (*named*) in Old Wyndesore, (4) a messuage or capital mansion   [*m.* 10] called Frogmore and lands (*named*), late in the tenure of Walter Chaltecote, in New Wyndesore, (5) lands (*tenants named*) in Old Wyndesore and (6) a messuage (*named with tenants' names*) in Old Wyndesore; with reservations; (1) from Lady Day 1585, having been leased by patent, 19 June, 6 Eliz., to Humphrey Mychell for 21 years from Lady Day then last at a yearly rent of £17; (2) from the termination of a lease thereof by patent, 17 April, 10 Eliz., to Robert Rampston and Freman Yonge *inter alia* at a yearly rent of 38*s.* 4*d.* for 21 years from the termination of a lease thereof by patent of the Exchequer, 15 May, 9 Eliz., to the said Mychell *inter alia* for 21 years from Lady Day then last at the same rent; (3) from Lady Day 1588, having been leased by the said patent, 15 May, 9 Eliz., to Mychell *inter alia* for 21 years from Lady Day then last at a yearly rent of 37*s.* 6*d.*; (4) from Michaelmas 1586, having been leased by patent, 16 Feb., 8 Eliz., to the said Mychell for 21 years from Michaelmas then last at a yearly rent of £12 20*d.*; (5) from Lady Day 1587, having been leased by patent, 14 Feb., 4 & 5 Ph. & Mary, to Dorothy Wright *inter alia* for 30 years from Lady Day then last at a yearly rent of £10; (6) from the termination of a lease thereof by the said patent, 17 April, 10 Eliz., to Rampston and Yonge *inter alia* at a yearly rent of £4 for 21 years from the termination of a lease thereof by the said patent, 14 Feb., 4 & 5 Ph. & Mary, to Dorothy Wright aforesaid *inter alia* for 30 years from Lady Day then last at the same rent; same rents. For his service   [*m.* 11] and for a fine of £80 paid at the Exchequer.   By p.s.

1342.)   16 *Dec.* 1575.   Lease for 30 years to Henry Harvye, a gentleman pensioner, of (1) lands (*named*), including a third part of the demesne lands, parcel of the manor of Clyfforde, co. Hereford, late of the late earl of March, (2) the residue of the said demesne lands, (3) agistment of the park of Clyfforde aforesaid and pannage of swine in the said park, late of   [*m.* 12] the earl of March, (4) the town of Eskyveoke in the commote of Meney, co. Anglesey, parcel of the principality of North Wales, and the coal mines in the said town, (5) lands (*named*) in the manor of Brampton, co. Huntingdon, (6) the tithes in Workington *alias* Worthington, Newbolde, Staunton and Wilson, co. Leicester, parcel of the rectory of Bredon, co. Leicester, late of the cell of Bredon, and (7) the chapel of Llanyhangell Cum De *alias*

Llanyhangell Cuney, co. Brecon, once of Brecknock priory; with reservations; (1) from Michaelmas 1590 or the termination of a lease by patent of the Exchequer, 21 Feb., 12 Eliz., to William Whitney of the same, then formerly in the tenure of Robert Whitney, for 21 years from   [*m.* 13]
Michaelmas then last at a yearly rent of 64*s.* 8*d.*; (2) and (3) from the termination of a lease by Anthony Bourchire by indenture, 5 May, 2 Edw. VI, to Richard Trotman of Utton under Hedge, co. Gloucester, 'yoman', of lands (*named*) in Clyfford commonly called 'lez demeasne landes' of the manor of Clyfforde, then or late held by Robert Whitney for a term of years then unexpired, for 60 years from Michaelmas 1558, or, if Trotman should so elect, from Michaelmas following the termination of the interest of the said Robert, at the same rent as paid by Robert (by indenture, 20 Feb., 12 Hen. VIII, Arthur, prince of Wales, leased to James Whitney the demesne lands of Clyfforde and the park there for 60 years from Michaelmas then last at a yearly rents of £5 13*s.* 8*d.* for the demesne lands and 13*s.* 8*d.* for the park with 10*s.* beyond of increase); (4) from Michaelmas 1596, having been leased by patent, 1 July, 7 Eliz., to Nicholas Bagnall, knight, *inter alia* at a yearly rent of £7 8*s.* 8*d.* for 25 years from Michaelmas 1571 or the termination of a lease thereof by patent, 13 Sept., 23 Hen. VIII, to William Sackevyle for 40 years from Michaelmas then last; (5) from Lady Day 1584, having been leased by patent of the Exchequer, 21 June, 5 Eliz., to Thomas Slade for 21 years from Lady Day then last at a yearly rent of £4 10*s.*; (6) and (7) from Michaelmas 1581, having been leased (6) by patent, 17 Feb., 3 Eliz., to Francis Shirley for 21 years from Michaelmas then last at a yearly rent of £9 6*s.* 8*d.* and (7) by patent, 18 June, 3 Eliz., to William Phillipps for 21 years from Michaelmas then last at a yearly rent of 20*s.*; yearly rents (1) 64*s.* 8*d.*, (2) £6 3*s.* 8*d.*, (3) 13*s.* 8*d.*, (4) £7 8*s.* 8*d.*, (5) £4 10*s.*, (6) £9 6*s.* 8*d.* and (7) 20*s.*; the lessee to pay yearly out of (6) 40*s.* for the salaries of two priests in Staunton and Workington churches. For his service.   By p.s.

1343.)   19 *Dec.* 1575.   Lease for 21 years to Miles Pendreth of (1) a moiety of the demesne lands of the manor of Northborne, co. Kent, to wit, lands etc. (*named*), the tithes of corn of the premises, a moiety of all other tithes anciently   [*m.* 14]
payable to the farmer of the site of the manor out of divers lands parcel of the manor, a moiety of marshes (*named*) and a moiety of the custom of white salt and of 'le shares' (*vomer*) belonging to the said farmer, now or late in the tenure of the said Miles, and (2) the principal mansion called 'le Abbottes House' and a garden and the croft annexed to the same principal messuage where plum trees were lately planted in Northborne, all once of the archbishop of Canterbury; with reservations, including the rents of assize, rents of cocks, hens and eggs and all like rents and profits which the beadle of Northborne used to collect yearly, the rents of the manors of Ripley and Langdon, all marshes, lands, rivers and 'lez brookes' belonging to the manor other than those leased hereby, the rent called 'le Hollye Crosse rent', 'grasse sylver', 'potsylver', quit rents in the weald, straw, reeds and 'rusheberdes' on the lands of the manor, 534 'le helmesemes' on the lands of the manor to be collected yearly to the use of the Crown, and a moiety of 'the kilhouse, milhouse and brewhouse' now or late in the tenure of Peter Atkinson, farmer of the other moiety   [*m.* 15]
of the site and demesne lands of the manor; (1) from Michaelmas 1588, being the termination of a lease by patent, 5 July[1], 7 Eliz., of the farm of the said manor, the tithes of the lands thereof, also 33 ac. of marsh and brooks and the custom of white salt and of 'le shares' belonging to the farm to Henry Leighe, as to one moiety, and Peter Atkynson and Margery his wife, as to the other moiety, at a yearly rent of £18 18*s.* 9*d.* for each moiety for 21 years from Michaelmas 1567 or the termination of a lease thereof by the monastery of St. Augustine by the walls of Canterbury by indenture, 8 March, 29 Hen. VIII, to Robert

---

[1] The enrolment of this patent (*Calendar*, 1563–1566, *no.* 1105) gives its date as '7 July'.

Paysshe and Henry Paysshe for 30 years from Michaelmas then last; (2) from Michaelmas 1587, being the termination of a lease thereof by patent of the Exchequer, 8 Nov., 8 Eliz., to the said Leigh and Atkynson for 21 years from Michaelmas then last at a yearly rent of 20s.; yearly rents (1) £18 18s. 9d. and (2) 20s.; the lessee may use in common with the farmer of the other moiety of the site and demesne lands the yard or close before the said site, 'le Abbottes Howse' and the stables and access to and from the river there and to and from the farm, stable and the rest of the premises over 'le yarde' and over the other moiety of the demesne lands as accustomed, and shall suffer the farmer of the other moiety to have the like liberty; also to provide a moiety of the entertainment of the Queen's steward, surveyor and beadle at the manor coming to hold courts or make a survey; licence to take estovers both in the premises and in the Queen's woods called Betteshanger and Hedlynge in the parish of Waldershyre, co. Kent.   By p.s.

1344.)   16 *Dec.* 1575.   Lease for 21 years to Edward Wotton and Hester his wife of lands (*tenants named*) in the county of York as follows—   [*m.* 16] (1) in Oldebylande, (2) in Oldsteade, (3) in Wasse and (4) in Oswalkirke (*named*), all late of the monastery of Bylande, co. York, (5) in Oswalkirke, late of the monastery of Ryvalles, co. York, and (6) in Oswalkirke, late of the house of Austin friars in York; with reservations; from Michaelmas   [*m.* 17] last; yearly rent £13 16s. 11d. In consideration of the surrender by Wotton of the interest in (1), (2), (5) and (6) of William Pickeringe, knight, deceased, to whom they were leased *inter alia* by patent, 4 May, 4 Eliz., for 21 years from Michaelmas then last at yearly rents of (1) £7 12s. 5d. (*detailed*), (2) £2 8s. 8d. (*detailed*), (5) 13s. 4d. and (6) 24s.; and for a fine of £41 10s. 9d. paid at the Exchequer by Wotton and Hester.   By p.s.

1345.)   2 *Jan.* 1576.   Lease for 21 years to Richard Coningsbye of the following (*tenants named*) in the county of Warwick, once of the late   [*m.* 18] college or chantry of Stratforde on Avon—tenements (*described*) in Stratforde on Avon, a tenement in Oldstratforde, lands in Drayton, lands in Southill, lands in Bridgetowne Feilde in Stratforde, lands in Bynton, lands (*named*) at Wyncote, a rent of 17s. 3d. in Stratforde, tithes in Shotterey, tithes in Burgetowne and Ryvenclyfforde *alias* Ryen Clyfford, [*m.* 19] tithes in Lodington, tithes in Drayton, tithes in Clopton, tithes of Shotterey Meadowe, tithes of the mill of Stratforde, tithes of a meadow called Brodemeadowe, tithes of Bushewoodhall and Bushewood, tithes of fisheries of the waters of Avon and tithes of the mill of Ryen Clyfford; with reservations; from Michaelmas last; yearly rent £64 8s. 5d.; the Crown to discharge the lessee from 17s. 3d. payable yearly out of lands in Stratforde to the bishop of Worcester and all other charges except the rent hereby reserved; the lessee to make two cuttings only of the woods and at fitting seasons, to enclose the young growth and 'lez springes' thereof for nine years after cutting and to leave 12 'lez staddelles' in every acre of the woods according to statute. In consideration of his surrender of a patent, 13 Dec., 17 Eliz., leasing to him the late college of Stratforde on Avon and all its possessions for 21 years from Lady Day then last at a yearly rent of £63 9s. 7d.   By p.s.

1346.)   12 *Dec.* 1575.   Lease for 21 years to John Aslaby of the rectory and mansion house of Kyrkby in Grindalith, co. York, once of Kyrkham priory, co. York, and all hereditaments heretofore leased with the said rectory in   [*m.* 20] Kirkbye in Grindalith; with reservations, including all courts baron and profits thereof, free rents and all tithes of wool and lambs in Kirkbye belonging to the rectory, and a wind mill with a sheep pasture there;   [*m.* 21] from Lady Day next; yearly rent £32 4s. 4d.; the lessee to discharge the Crown from the stipend payable yearly to the curate there, and to pay the Crown 13s. 4d. yearly for 'thraves'.

In consideration of the surrender by Aslaby of (a) an indenture, 7 March, 27 Hen. VIII, whereby John, prior, and the convent of the said priory leased the premises to Nicholas Simpson, a groom of the King's privy chamber, with like reservations, for 40 years from the feast of St Thomas the Martyr 1537 at a yearly rent of 30 quarters of wheat, 120 quarters of barley malt, 16 pigs (worth 4s. each), 25 geese (13 worth 4d. at least and the other 12 worth 2d. each at least) and 12 capons (worth 4d. each at least) and (b) a patent, 3 March, 3 Eliz., leasing to William Brakenbury the said rents in kind payable by the farmer of the manor of Kirkbye in Grindalith and of the tithes of sheaves of the rectory of Kyrkbye in Grindalith at a yearly rent of £32 4s. 4d. for 30 years from Pentecost 1565 or the termination of a lease thereof by indenture of the court of Augmentations, 26 March, 35 Hen. VIII, to James Sympson and William Savage *inter alia* for 21 years from Pentecost then next at the same rent; and for a certain sum paid at the Exchequer by Aslaby.   By p.s.

1347.)   30 *Jan.* 1576.   Grant in fee simple to John Duddeley and John Ayscough of the reversions and rents of the lands comprised in leases as follows—

(i) By patent, 14 Feb., 10 Eliz., to Simon Leper *inter alia* of lands (*named with tenant's name*) in Houghton Conquest and Hawnes and in Maldon, co. Bedford, late of the monastery of Wardon, co. Bedford, for 21 years from Michaelmas last at a yearly rent of 15s., parcel of a rent for them and other lands of £4 11s. 4d.

(ii) By patent, 16 Jan., 15 Eliz., to John Lewell *inter alia* of (a) the site of the mill of Llanvaies (*tenants named*) in the suburbs of Brecon, late of Brecknock priory, and (b) land (*tenant named*) in Brentles, co. Brecon, late of Clyfforde priory, co. Hereford, for 21 years from Michaelmas then last at yearly rents of (a) 7s. 6d. and (b) 20d.

(iii) By patent of the Exchequer, 14 June, 15 Eliz., to Nicholas Preston *inter alia* of the tithes of corn and hay (*tenants named*) in Kyllerbye in the lordship of Cattarick, co. York, late of the monastery of St. Mary by the walls of York, for 21 years from Lady Day then last at a yearly rent of 10s., parcel of a rent for them and other things of 43s. 4d..

(iv) By patent, 13 Feb., 10 Eliz., to Ellis Wynne *inter alia* of lands (*tenants named*) in (a) Dilwyn, co. Hereford, once of Wormesley priory, co. Hereford, and (b) Holme in Dilwyn, once of St. Mary's chantry in Dilwyn Parva, co. Hereford, for 21 years from Michaelmas then last at yearly rents of (a) 5s. and (b) 3s.

(v) By patent, 26 May, 14 Eliz., to Agnes Morgan, widow, *inter alia* of   [*m.* 22] the premises in (iv) above for 21 years from Michaelmas 1588 at the same rents.

(vi) By patent, 13 May, 16 Eliz., to John Lewcas of a house called 'le Brewehouse', 'le Storehouse' and 'le Milhouse' with 'le Backhouse' in Dover, co. Kent, with a well and 'le putt gallye', gutters and leads in the parish of St. Mary, Dover, under 'le Cliffe' and next 'le Peere' (*tenants named*), late parcel of a tenement built on 'le Peere' and under 'le Cliffe', for 21 years from Lady Day then last at a yearly rent of 3s. 4d.

(vii) By patent, 14 May, 4 Eliz., to John Johnson *alias* John Anthonye of a sheep pasture called 'Braddon' in Dover *alias* in the liberty of Dover next Braddeston in the parish of Hugham, co. Kent, for 21 years from Lady Day then last at a yearly rent of 20s.

(viii) By patent, 4 May, 10 Eliz., to Philip Conwaye *inter alia* of a pasture and lands called 'Braddon' in Dover, late in the tenure of John Anthonye, for 21 years from Lady Day then last or the termination of any lease or grant for life or years enduring after that date at a yearly rent of 20s.

(ix) By patent of the Exchequer, 6 July, 7 Eliz., to Richard Portington of all lands in Sawcliff in Reisbye and a coney warren within the walls of Reisbye and Saynton, co. Lincoln, late in the tenure of Thomas Portington, once of the monastery of Thorneholme, co. Lincoln, for 21 years from Lady Day then last at a yearly rent of 23s. 4d.

(x) By patent, 12 Feb., 14 Eliz., to Henry Burton of lands (*tenants named*) in

Buckemynster, co. Leicester, for 21 years from Michaelmas then last at a   [*m.* 23] yearly rent of 29*s.* (*detailed*).

(xi) By patent, 19 Dec., 10 Eliz., to William Gunbye of lands (*tenant named*) in Sewesterne, co. Leicester, for 21 years from Michaelmas then last at a yearly rent of 10*s.*

(xii) By patent, 29 May, 5 Eliz., to Henry Allen *inter alia* of lands (*tenant named*) in Sewsterne, co. Leicester, for 21 years from Lady Day then last at a yearly rent of 10*s.*

(xiii) By patent, 13 June, 15 Eliz., to Henry Bate *inter alia* of lands (*tenant named*) in Sewesterne, co. Leicester, for 21 years from Lady Day then last at a yearly rent of 4*s.*, parcel of a rent for them and other lands of 40*s.*

(xiv) By patent, 23 May, 15 Eliz., to Robert Power, an equerry of the stable *inter alia* of   [*m.* 24]
the rectory of Lingwood, co. Norfolk, at a yearly rent of 5*s.* for 21 years from the termination of a lease thereof by patent, 26 June, 10 Eliz., to Thomas Ormesbye, Anthony Reynolde, John Reynolde, Nicholas Rysyn, Robert Smythe and John Budyfant for 21 years from Lady Day then last at the same rent.

(xv) By patent, 27 Feb., 16 Eliz., to Margaret Dane, widow, of the tithes (*tenants named*) of hay in Bassechurche and of corn in Birche and the farm of Fynymer *alias* Lynches, parcels of the rectory of Bassechurche, co. Salop, for 21 years from Lady Day then next at a yearly rent of 8*s.* 4*d.*

(xvi) By patent, 15 May, 6 Eliz., to John Hawarde *inter alia* of the tithes of wool, lambs and hemp and the tithes of corn of land (*named*) with the profits of the Easter book belonging to the parish church of St. Mary Magdalen in Bridgenorthe, co. Salop, then or late in the tenure of the vicars choral there, for 21 years from Lady Day then last at a yearly rent of £8.

(xvii) By patent, 17 May, 10 Eliz., to Anthony Rotsey *inter alia* of lands (*tenant named*) in Hinlope, co. Worcester, given for a light in Hinloppe church, for 21 years from Michaelmas then last at a yearly rent of 6*s.* 4*d.*

(xviii) By patent of the Exchequer, 29 June, 6 Eliz., to Henry Hodgekyns the elder, Anthony Hodgekyns and Henry Hodgekyns the younger of the rectory of Hailes and Didbroke, co. Gloucester, the tithes (*tenant named*) belonging to the said rectory, the small tithes, altarages and oblations belonging to Hailes chapel, the tithes of lands (*named with tenant's name*) in Didbroke and a portion of tithes of a meadow (*named with tenant's name*), once of the monastery of Hailes, for life in succession from Lady Day then last at a yearly rent of 17*s.* 4*d.*

(xix) By patent, 10 Jan., 14 Eliz., to William Gorge *inter alia* of the premises in (xviii) above for 30 years in reversion at the same rent.   [*m.* 25]

(xx) By patent of the Exchequer, 20 July, 13 Eliz., to Thomas Hanburye *inter alia* of (*a*) a fishery in the water of Avon (*tenants named*) before the lordship of Corston, co. Somerset, and (*b*) lands (*named with tenants' names*) in the lordship of Weston and tithing of Walcottes, co. Somerset, late of the monastery of Bathe, for 21 years from Lady Day then last at yearly rents of (*a*) 6*d.* and (*b*) 6*s.* 8*d.*

(xxi) By patent, 16 May, 2 & 3 Ph. & Mary, to William Petre, knight, *inter alia* of lands (*named*) in Stoke, included in a grant of the site of Mountague priory, the borough, and the manors of Mountague Forinseca and Tintenhull, co. Somerset, late of the said priory, for 40 years from Michaelmas or Lady Day next after the death of Elizabeth Strowde, then wife of Robert Strowde, at a yearly rent of 5*s.*, parcel of a rent of £128 7*s.* 11¾*d.*

(xxii) By patent, 27 June, 9 Eliz., to John Cleves *inter alia* of lands (*named with tenant's name*) in Yevell, co. Somerset, for 21 years from Lady Day then last at a yearly rent of 10*s.*

(xxiii) By patent of the Exchequer, 28 Feb., 13 Eliz., to Hugh Sexey *inter alia* of land (*tenant named*) in Drayton, co. Somerset, late of Henry, late duke of Suffolk, for 21 years from Lady Day then last at a yearly rent of 13*s.* 4*d.*

(xxiv) By patent, 11 May, 13 Eliz., to John Bryton *inter alia* of a tenement (*tenant named*) on Seynt Augustynes Grene in the county of the city of Bristol for 21 years from Lady Day then last at a a yearly rent of 5s.

(xxv) By patent of the Exchequer, [—] June, 5 Eliz., to Robert Armonde *inter alia* of land in Baydon, co. Wilts, for 21 years from Lady Day then last at a yearly rent of 3s. 4d.

Also grant of—the premises in (i) above; the premises in (ii) above; the premises in (iii) above; the premises in (iv) and (v) above; the   [*m.* 26] premises in (vi) above; the premises in (vii) and (viii), described as lands called Braddon *alias* Brydon Downe to the South of Dover, parcel of the lordship or preceptory of Swynsfeilde, co. Kent, belonging to the hospital of St. John of Jerusalem; the premises in (ix) above, described as lands in Sawcleiffe *alias* Sawchieff in Reisbye, a coney warren within the moors of Reisbye and Saynton *alias* Stainton and all moors and lands in Sawclieff, Reisbye and Saynton called 'the warren'; the premises in (x), (xi), (xii) and (xiii) above, late of Kyrkebybellers priory, co. Leicester; the premises in (xiv) above, once of Waybridge priory, co. Norfolk; the premises in (xv) above, once of the monastery of SS. Peter and Paul in Shrewsbury; the premises in (xvi) above; the premises in (xvii) above;   [*m.* 27] the premises in (xviii) and (xix) above, by the name of the rectory and chapel of Hailes and Didbroke, all tithes in Hailes and Didbroke belonging to the said rectory and chapel, the small tithes, altarages and oblations belonging to Hayles chapel, the tithes of lands (*named*) in Didbroke and a portion of tithes of a meadow (*named*); lands (*named*) in Didbroke, once of the monastery of Hailes and leased by patent, 28 Feb., 3 Eliz., to Henry Hodgkyns *inter alia* for 21 years from Michaelmas then last at a yearly rent of 6s. 8d.; the premises in (xx) above; the premises in (xxi) above; the premises in (xxii) above, parcel of the Name of Jesus chantry commonly called 'Jesus chauntrie' in Yevell; the premises in (xxiii) above; the premises in (xxiv) above, by the name of a tenement on Saynt Augustynes Back and Saynt Augustynes Grene or either of them in the county of the city of Bristoll, once of the monastery of Nethe; the premises in (xxv) above, given at 'lez strowdes' or 'lez   [*m.* 28] shrowdes' or the like for prayer every Sunday, parcel of lands late concealed; lands (*tenant named*) in Marshefeilde, co. Gloucester, once of St. Clement's chantry in Marshfeilde church and leased by patent, 13 Dec., 14 Eliz., to George Whyte *inter alia* for 21 years from Michaelmas then last at a yearly rent of 3s. 4d.; and a tenement or late chapel of St. Rombald in Dorchester, co. Dorset, and all its appurtenances.

Also grant of—lands (*named*) in Riswarpe,   [*m.* 29] co. York, late of the monastery of Whytbye, co. York, and leased by patent, 2 June, 3 & 4 Ph. & Mary, to John Pacocke and George Newton *inter alia* for 21 years from Lady Day then last at a yearly rent of 21s. 8d.; lands (*tenant named*) in Kynnersley, co. Hereford, late of Leomynster priory, co. Hereford, cell of the monastery of Readinge, co. Berks, and leased by patent of the Exchequer, 4 Jan., 14 Eliz., to Hugh Towers for 21 years from Michaelmas then last at a yearly rent of 33s. 4d.; lands (*named*) in Footiscrey, co. Kent, given for an obit there and leased *inter alia* by patent, 20 June, 6 Eliz., to Humphrey Ryman for 21 years from Lady Day then last at a yearly rent of 4s. 5¼d.; lands (*named with tenants' names*) in Grymston, co. Leicester, given for (*a*) lights before the Trinity there and (*b*) for a lamp there, late of Kirkebibelers priory, and in Thurcaston, Briscall and (given for a lamp there) Quenebor-ough, co. Leicester, late of the hospital of St. John of Jerusalem, all leased *inter alia* by patent, 16 Feb., 8 Eliz., to Richard Hodgeson for 21 years at several rents of 8d., 8d., 2s. 6d. and 2s.; lands in Scalforde, co. Leicester, once of the monastery of Pré, Leicester, and leased *inter alia* by patent, 8 Aug., 3 Eliz., to the said Richard Hodgeson for 21 years from Lady Day then last at a yearly rent of 5s.; lands etc. in Staunton under Bardon, co. Leicester, late of the hospital of St. John of Jerusalem and leased (*a*) by patent, 7 June, 6 Eliz., for 21 years at a yearly rent of 7s. 4d. to William Baynham and (*b*) *inter alia* by patent of the Exchequer, 17 May, 17 Eliz., for 21 years at the same rent to William Raven; lands (*tenants named*) in

Affordbye *alias* Ashfordby, co. Leicester, late of Kirkebybellers priory and leased *inter alia* by patent, 16 Feb., 8 Eliz., for 21 years from Michaelmas then last at a yearly rent of 16s. to Richard Hodgeson aforesaid; lands (*tenant named*) in Affordbye, late of Kirkebybellers priory and leased *inter alia* by patent of the Exchequer, 2 May, 6 Eliz., for 21 years at a yearly rent of 4s. to Thomas Martyn; lands (*tenants named*) in Twyforde, co. Leicester, late of the hospital of St. John of Jerusalem, (yearly value 20s.); woods (*named with tenant's name*) in Cosgrave, co. Northampton, parcel of lands purchased from John Heneage and leased by patent, 27 Nov., 11 Eliz., for 21 years from Michaelmas then last at a yearly rent of 8s. to Thomas Furtho; lands (*tenant named*) in Bingham, co. Nottingham, late of St. Mary's guild there and leased by patent, 13 July, 5 Eliz., for 21 years from Lady Day then last at a

[*m.* 30]

a yearly rent of 32s. to Hugh Davyes; the house of the late chantry of Ruddington, co. Nottingham, leased *inter alia* by patent, 27 Feb., 10 Eliz., for 21 years at a yearly rent of 5s. to Lawrence Brodebent; lands in Curryryvell, co. Somerset, in the Crown's hands by the statute for the dissolution of chantries and the like and leased *inter alia* by patent, 28 June, 9 Eliz., for 21 years from Lady Day then next at a yearly rent of 5s. to William Stonynge; a messuage (*tenant named*) in Blackeforde, co. Somerset, late of the monastery of Cleve and leased by patent, 18 Dec., 10 Eliz., for 21 years from Michaelmas then last at a yearly rent of 13s. 4d. to John Cortier; a chapel or tenement in Ilchestre, co. Somerset, called Michelles Bowe and lands in Ilchester; the two late free chapels of Upton and Knolle in Martock, co. Somerset; lands (*named*) in Langforde Budvyle, co. Somerset, given for lights in the church there and leased *inter alia* by patent, 28 June, 9 Eliz., for 21 years from Lady Day then last at a yearly rent of 3s. to William Stonynge aforesaid; a messuage (*tenant named*) in Roode, co. Somerset, given for a lamp in Roode church and leased *inter alia* by patent, 23 Jan., 10 Eliz., for 21 years from Michaelmas then last at a yearly rent of 2s. to Ellis Wynne; lands (*tenant named*) in Milborne Porte, co. Somerset, late of the brotherhood of St. John the Evangelist there and leased *inter alia* by patent, 28 June, 9 Eliz., for 21 years from Lady Day then last at a yearly rent of 2s. to William Stonynge aforesaid; two third parts of lands in St. Mary Magdalen's parish, Barmondsey, co. Surrey, late of John Kittow *alias* Gittow of Southwerke, deceased, which Elizabeth once his wife, afterwards the wife of William Adlington and late the wife of George Tottye, had for life and which after her death escheated to the Crown, leased by patent, 29 June, 15 Eliz., *inter alia* to Christopher Edmundes.

Grant also of—the manor or grange of Sibdon Lye, co. Buckingham, late of the monastery of Thame, co. Oxford; lands (*named with tenants' names*) in Langton in Purbeck, co. Dorset, late of Thomas, lord Seymour of Sudley, attainted; lands (*tenants named*) in Bridport, co. Dorset, parcel of Mundeynes chantry there; woods (*named*) in Mynterne, co. Dorset, late of the monastery of Cerne, co. Dorset; the advowson of the rectory of Mynterne;   [*m.* 31]

lands (*named with tenants' names*) in Collyton or elsewhere, co. Devon, once of the chantry of Collyforde in Collyton of the earl of Devon's foundation; lands (*named with tenants' names*) in Wormesley *alias* Overwormesley, co. Hereford, once of Wormesley priory; a parcel of ground and 'a brickwall', now in the tenure of Lewis Stockett, between Temple Lane, leading from Fletestrete, London, towards Templebridge, on the East and the messuage, curtilage and garden of the said Stockett by the bars of the New Temple on the West, the South head thereof abutting on the garden of the Middle Temple and the North head on a kitchen or house now occupied by Florence Bellowes, widow, (containing in length 119 feet and in width between the Lane and Stockett's messuage by the length of the messuage from the said kitchen to Stockett's curtilage 10 feet and between Stockett's curtilage and garden and the Lane by the length of the curtilage and garden 12 feet), late of the hospital of St. John of Jerusalem; a piece of land inclosed in the parish of St. Clement Danes without the bars of the New Temple, London, adjoining a house once of Richard Hersey and formerly of Walter Barbour and Joan his wife on the West and a small lane about 40½ feet long on the East, one head whereof containing about 25½ feet abbuts on the high street towards the South and the other head containing 24½ feet abbuts on Holewaye Lane towards the North (the said piece of land containing in width from the house to the small lane 25½ feet and in length from the high street to Holewaye Lane 43½ feet), the custody of which was committed by patent, 8 May, 9 Hen. V, to Nicholas Burye and Richard Hercye from Michaelmas then last as long it should remain in the Crown's hands at a yearly rent of 3s. 4d.; a tenement (*tenant named*) in Rempeston, co. Nottingham, late of the monastery of Lenton; woods (*named with tenant's name*) in Wanstrowe *alias* Churchwanstrowe, co. Somerset, late of Charles, lord Stourton, attainted of murder; a messuage called 'the Moteplace' (*described*) in Rederithe, co. Surrey, acquired by exchange from Henry Polsted; lands (*tenants named*) in Acton Woodhouse, Mounslowe, Hungerforde, Carston and Hopeshaye, co. Salop, late of St. John of Jerusalem; lands (*tenant named*) in Eccleshall, co. Stafford, once of Ronton priory, co. Stafford, and leased *inter alia* by patent, 17 July, 16 Eliz., for 21 years at a yearly rent of 18s. to John Stanley, and the advowsons of the rectories of St. Michael, Stamforde *alias* Staunforde, co. Lincoln, and Barkampstede Parva, co. Hertford.

Grant also of—the reversion and rent of lands in Romaldkirke, co. York, late of William, late marquess of Northampton, deceased, and leased *inter alia* by patent of the Exchequer, 5 Dec., 15 Eliz., to Thomas Mullyneux for 21 years from Michaelmas then last at a yearly rent of 45s.; lands (*tenants named*)   [*m.* 32] in Romaldkirk; and the advowson of the rectory of Romaldkirk.

Grant also of—the reversion and rent of the manor of Estington, co. Dorset, late of Edward, duke of Somerset, formerly of Christchurch Twynam priory, co. Southampton, and leased by patent, 18 Jan., 13 Eliz., to Robert Hopton at a yearly rent of £9 14s. 2d. for 30 years from the termination of a lease thereof by conventual indenture, 7 July, 29 Hen. VIII, for 60 years from Michaelmas then next to William Haveland, Frances his wife and John his son at the same rent; the said manor; and lands (*named with tenant's name*) in Estington, late of the same duke, formerly of the same monastery.

Grant also of—the reversion and rents of lands (*tenants named*) in (*a*) Playnesfelde, (*b*) Asshehill (*named*), (*c*) Padnaller in Spaxton (*named*),   [*m.* 33] (*d*) Wormeston in Burneham (*named*), (*e*) Wormeston and Burneham and (*f*) Taunton, co. Somerset, leased by patent, 23 June, 10 Eliz., *inter alia* to Edward Martyn and Humphrey Sandforde for 21 years from Michaelmas then next at a yearly rent of £5 9d., to wit, for (*a*) 15s. 8d., (*b*) 24s., (*c*) 2s. 8d., (*d*) 27s., (*e*) 31s.. 4d. and (*f*) 1d; and the said lands, late of Nicholas Williams, deceased.

Grant also of the reversions and rents of the lands comprised in leases as follows—

(i) By patent of the Exchequer, 12 July, 8 Eliz., to Thomas Wymberley *inter alia* of lands (*named with tenant's name*) in Southwitham, co. Lincoln, late of Templebruer preceptory, for 21 years from Lady Day then last at a yearly rent of 20s. 4d., parcel of a rent for them and other lands of £4 17s. 5½d.

(ii) By another patent of the Exchequer, 12 July, 8 Eliz., to the   [*m.* 34] same Wymberley *inter alia* of lands (*named*) in Southwitham, late of Templebruer preceptory, for 21 years from Lady Day then last at a yearly rent of 9s. 8d., parcel of a rent for them and other lands of 19s. 8d.

(iii) By patent, 22 May, 13 Eliz., to George Tailour *inter alia* of lands (*named*) in Southstoke, co. Lincoln, parcel of the jointure of Jane, once Queen of England, for 21 years from Michaelmas then last at a yearly rent of 2s., parcel of a rent for them and other lands of 16s. 6d.[1]

---

[1] Given elsewhere in this enrolment as '17s. 6d.'; but the enrolment of Tailour's lease in Exchequer, Augmentations, Enrolments of Leases (E.309), 13 Eliz., roll 8, no. 4, reads '16s. 6d.'

Grant also of the lands aforesaid in Southwitham and Southstoke.

Grant also, for further security, of—the reversion and rent of lands (*named*) in Moresley, co. Buckingham, leased (i) by patent of the Exchequer, 26 July, 4 & 5 Ph. & Mary, to Thomas Stafford—having been formerly leased by Hugh, prior, and the convent of the monastery of Snelleshall, co. Buckingham, by indenture, 20 March, 11 Hen. VIII, to John Cooke—for 31 years from Lady Day then last at a yearly rent of 53s. 4d. and (ii) by patent, 11 Aug., 16 Eliz., to Robert Nycolles for 21 years from Lady Day 1588 at the same rent; and the said lands in Muresley, which by patent,   [*m.* 35] 29 Jan., 17 Eliz., were granted to Duddeley and Ayscough *inter alia* in fee simple. In which patent made to Duddeley and Ayscough the recitation of Nicolles's patent was omitted, and therefore it is invalid, it is said, in respect of these lands.

Grant also of lands (*named with tenant's name*) in Brayles, co. Warwick, parcel of the late guild there and leased by patent, [—] Feb., 10 Eliz., to Thomas Bisshop and John Bisshop *inter alia* for 21 years at a yearly rent of 14s. 4d.

Grant also of—the reversion and rents of lands (*tenants named*) in (*a*) Greneborough *alias* Granborough and (*b*) Walcote, co. Warwick, leased by patent, 2 May, 17 Eliz., to William Towne *inter alia* for 21 years from Lady Day then last at yearly rents of (*a*) 9s. (*detailed*) and (*b*) 23d.; and the said lands and other lands (*tenant named*) in Walcote *alias* Wollescott aforesaid, all once of the monastery of Ronton.

Reserving to the Crown lands (*named*) in Sybdon Lye, which were   [*m.* 36] usually leased and were conveyed to Christopher Carewe, and were afterwards leased to Peter Dormer and Agnes his wife by the abbot and convent of Thame by indenture, 28 Sept., 26 Hen. VIII, for 99 years at yearly rents of £8 8s. 2d. and 40s. To hold as of the manor of Estgrenewiche, co.   [*m.* 37] Kent, in socage. Issues from Michaelmas, 16 Eliz. The grantees charged with the yearly payment of—£7 6s. 8d. out of the premises in Bridgenorthe to divers persons celebrating, preaching or serving in the parish church of Bridgenorth aforesaid; 11s. out of the premises in Eccleshall to the bishop of Coventry as in right of the monastery of Ronton; 18¾d. out of the premises in Footiscre to John Carewe, knight, and his heirs; 17s. 9d. out of the rectory of Didbroke and the rest of the premises in Didbroke to the bishop of Worcester for proxies and visitations, by virtue of a decree, 31 May, 1 Edw. VI, of the court of Augmentations; and a rent of 27s. 8d. out of the premises in Brayles payable to Mr. Wynbiche.

In consideration of lands in the isle of Scapeie *alias* Chepei, co. Kent, bargained and sold to the Crown by Henry Cheyne, knight, lord Cheyne; and at his request.   By Q.

1348.)   3 *March* 1576.   Grant to Francis Wolsingham, one of the principal secretaries, his heirs and assigns of the reversions and rents of the lands comprised in leases for 21 years by patents of the dates specified as follows—

(i) 5 April, 13 Eliz., to Henry, earl of Pembroke, *inter alia* of the manor of Bradforde, lands and woods called Togarlewe in Bradforde and all other appurtenances of the said manor in Bradforde, Atworthe, Troile, Stoke, Leigh, Wraxall, Holte and Wynnesleigh or elsewhere, co. Wilts, with reservations including the site and demesne lands of the manor of Bradforde and the capital messuage or farm of Atworth *alias* Atforde, parcel of the said manor, from Lady Day then last at a yearly rent of £76 4s. 2½d., parcel of a rent of £93 16s. 1d. for the whole manor.

(ii) 9 Jan., 10 Eliz., to Henry, lord Harbert, of (*a*) the site of the manor of Bradforde and lands (*named*) belonging to the said site and (b) the site and capital messuage of Atworthe *alias* Atforde, co. Wilts, and lands (*named*) belonging thereto, parcels of the manor of Bradforde, co. Wilts, from Michaelmas then last at a yearly rents of (*a*) £22 18d. [*m.* 38] and (*b*) £4 16s. 8d..

(iii) 22 May, 16 Eliz., to Stephen Blauncherde *alias* Sanshewe of the premises in (ii) above (leased to the said Henry, earl of Pembroke, by the name of Henry, lord Harbert) from Michaelmas 1588 at the same rents.

(iv) 16 Dec., 15 Eliz., to Henry, earl of Pembroke, of woods called Bradforde Wood in the manor of Bradforde, co. Wilts, from Michaelmas then last at a yearly rent of £8 4s.

[m. 39]

Grant also of (1) the said manor, site of the manor, capital messuage and woods, once of the monastery of Shaston, co. Dorset, and (2) the hundred of Bradforde, co. Wilts.

As formerly held by any abbot, abbess, prior or prioress of Shaston or Edward Bellingham. To hold by service of the fortieth part of a knight's   [m. 40] fee and by a yearly rent of £13 16s.8½d. Issues from Michaelmas last. The grantee to pay yearly 26s. 8d. to the bailiff of the said hundred.

For his service.   By Q.

1349.)   27 Feb. 1576.   Lease for 21 years to Marmaduke Langdale and William Hallylonde of the oblations and privy tithes in both the collegiate church of St John, Beverley, co. York, and St. Mary the Virgin's church there, which oblations and tithes were late in the collection or tenure of John Levett, clerk, and were parcel of the late collegiate church of Beverley; from Lady Day next; yearly rent £11.

By the commissioners by virtue of the Queen's warrant.

(*The dorse of this roll is blank.*)

PART XIII

C. 66/1149

1350.) 3 *April* 1576. *Gorhambury.* Grant in fee simple to Christopher   [*m.* 1]
Hatton, a gentleman of the privy chamber and captain of the guard, of—the reversions and
several rents of £12 8 *s.*, 26*s.* 8*d.*, 29*s.*, £6 13*s.* 4*d.* and 6*s.* 8*d.* of the site and capital messuage
of the manor of Stangrounde, co. Huntingdon, lands (*named*) in Stangrounde, marshes
(*named*) in Stangrounde and Witlessey or elsewhere, cos. Huntingdon and Cambridge, lands
(*named with tenants' names*) in Stangrounde, the messuage or tenement of a grange or farm
called Horsey with a ferry, waters and other appurtenances (*described*) of the said messuage in
Stangrounde or elsewhere, co. Huntingdon, lands in Witlessey Boundes, co. Cambridge,
parcel of the said grange or farm, with appurtenances thereof in Witlessey, and lands (*named
with tenants' names*) in Northey next Muscote, cos. Cambridge and Huntingdon, included in a
lease by patent, 25 Aug., 4 Eliz., to Walter Mildmay, knight, of the manor and the rectory of
Stangrounde, waters etc. in Peterborough, Stangrounde and Witlessey, cos. Huntingdon,
Cambridge and Northampton, 'the Horsey' and the ferry there and tithes etc. in
Stangrounde, in Northey in Witlessey and in Stangrounde and Farcett, co. Huntingdon,
and a rent payable by the tenants of Fletton, co. Huntingdon, all once of the monastery of
Thorney, co. Cambridge, for 60 years from Michaelmas then next at a yearly rent of £73 6*s.*
7*d.*; and the said   [*m.* 2]
capital messuage and site, the said messuage, grange and farm, the lands etc. aforesaid and
the tithes thereof.

   Grant also of—the reversion and rent of demesne lands (*named*)   [*m.* 3]
of the manor of Bysshoppes Castell, co. Salop, leased by John, bishop of Hereford, by
indenture, 9 March, 36 Hen. VIII, under the seal of the dean and chapter of Hereford
cathedral, to Lewis Jones, Richard Willison and John Harford for 60 years at a yearly rent of
26*s.* 8*d.*; lands (*named with tenants' names*) in Bysshoppes Castell, including the said demesne
lands, once of the bishopric of Hereford; lands (*named with tenants' names*) in Shrewsbury, co.
Salop, once of Dynmore preceptory and parcel of the possessions of the hospital of St. John
of Clarkenwell, co. Middlesex; and a farm and tenement called the farm of Lydburye *alias*
Lydburye Northe, co. Salop, and lands (*named with tenant's name*) belonging thereto, late of
the bishopric of Hereford, and the reversion and yearly rent of £4 thereof.

   Grant also of —lands (*named with tenants' names*) in Mountague, Tyntenhull and
Babcarye, co. Somerset, once of Mountague priory; lands   [*m.* 4]
(*named with tenant's name*) in Sturmyster *alias* Sturmyster Newton Castell,   [*m.* 5]
co. Dorset, once of the monastery of Glaston; lands (*named with tenants' names*) in Ilton, co.
Somerset, once of the monastery of Athelney; lands (*named with tenants' names*) in Chiwe *alias*
Chewe, co. Somerset, and the reversion thereof and a yearly rent of 64*s.* 11*d.*, parcel of a rent
for the same *inter alia* of £101 15*s.* 5½*d.*, late of Edward, late duke of Somerset, attainted of
felony; lands (*named with tenants' names*) in Yevelchester, co. Somerset, once of the late free
chapel of Whitehall there; lands (*named with tenants' names*) in Glaston, co. Somerset, late of
Edward, late duke of Somerset, attainted, and formerly   [*m.* 6]
of the monastery of Glaston; lands (*named with tenants' names*) in Brewton, co. Somerset, once
of the monastery of Taunton; lands (*named with tenants' names*) in Wellington, co. Somerset,
and the reversion thereof and a yearly rent of £6 18*s.* 5¾*d.* , parcel of a rent for the same *inter
alia* of £102 13*s.* 4*d.*, late of John, duke of Northumberland, attainted of treason; lands

(*named with tenant's name*) in Beresbye and Crowson, co. Leicester, once of the hospital of St. John of Jerusalem; lands (*named with tenant's name*) in Benorthdowne and Frodington *alias* Fourdington or elsewhere, co. Southampton, once   [*m.* 7] of the late hospital of St. Nicholas in Portesmouthe, lands (*named with tenant's name*) in Segenho, co. Bedford, late of the earl of Kent and afterwards annexed to the honour of Ampthill; lands (*named with tenants' names*) in Bengeworthe, co. Worcester, once of the monastery of Evesham, co. Worcester; the site of the manor of Lieghe, co. Worcester, and lands etc. (*tenants named*) thereon, once of the monastery of Pershore, co. Worcester; the tithes in Samborne in Coughton and in Coughton, co. Warwick, a yearly rent of £10 out of the vicarage of Coughton, and the rectory of Coughton, all once of Studley priory, co. Warwick, and the advowson of the said vicarage; lands etc. (*tenant named*) in Kington Magna and Kington Parve, co. Warwick, once of the monastery of Kenelworthe; lands (*named with tenants' names*) in Trefmorva, co. Carnarvon, parcel of the manor of Ultradaron once of the monastery of Bardsey; a grange called Ymanaughtie and other lands (*tenant named*) in Corneweye, cos. Carnarvon and Anglesey, once of the monastery of Conwaye; lands (*tenant named*) in Bangor, co. Carnarvon, given for an obit there; lands (*tenant named*) in Come, co. Carnarvon, once of the monastery of Conweye; lands (*tenant named*) in St. Bride *alias* St. Brydes, co. Monmouth, once of Chepstowe *alias* Strugull   [*m.* 8] priory; and lands (*named with tenants' names*) in Ludgareshall *alias* Lurgeshall and Tillington or elsewhere, co. Sussex, now or late parcel of the manor of Ryver *alias* Rever, co. Sussex, and once annexed to the honour of Petworthe.

Grant also of—woods (*named with tenants' names*) in Plympton Morrice,   [*m.* 9] co. Devon, once of Plympton priory; and messuages (*tenants named*) in the parish of St. Mary Arches in Exeter, given (*a*) for a mass in St. Mary Arches church in the name of St. Mary every Saturday and (*b*) for an obit in the said church, and yearly rents of 9s. 4d. and 4s. 3d. for the same.

Grant also of—a capital messuage and farm and 'lez demesne landes' in Pamington by Ashechurche, co. Gloucester, now or late in the tenure of William Higgons, once of the monastery of Tewkesburye; lands (*tenants named*) in Brokehampton, Sowtham and Clive, called Whomedowne *alias* Hamondowne (in the tenure of tenants of Ashechurche) and in Tewkesburye (*named*, in the tenure of tenants of Northey), co. Gloucester, parcels of the manor of Tewkesburye and once of Thomas, lord Seymour of Sudeley, attainted; lands (*described with tenants' names*) in Cirencester, co. Gloucester, late of the monastery of Cirencester; lands (*named with tenants' names*) in Presburye, Sevenhampton, Brokehampton, Clopley and Swyndon, co. Gloucester, late of the bishopric of Hereford and in the Queen's hands by exchange; lands (*named with tenant's name*), parcel of   [*m.* 10] the manor of Clive Episcopi, co. Gloucester, late of the bishopric of Worcester and in the Queen's hands by exchange; lands (*named with tenant's names*) in Stanley Regis *alias* Kingstanley, co. Gloucester, some parcel of the demesne lands of the manor there, once of Henry, earl of Arundel; woods (*named with tenants' name*) in Etton, co. York, once of Holy Trinity preceptory in Beverley in the East Riding, co. York; lands in Heslington near York in the East Riding, now in the tenure of Thomas Eynns, farmer of the manor or grange of Heslington, late of St. Leonard's hospital, York, with the ground whereon Eynns new built the mansion house of the manor or grange; and lands (*tenant named*) in Doddeworth, co. York, once of the monastery of Pontefract.

Grant also of—land (*described with tenant's name*) in Mortlack, co. Surrey, and the mansion house of the manor of Wimbledon, co. Surrey, and all appurtenances thereof, now or late in the tenure of John Chylde, all late of Thomas Crumwell, knight, late earl of Essex, attainted of treason, and afterwards assigned to cardinal Poole for life, and the reversions and yearly rents of 53s. 4d. and £21 of the same; lands (*named with tenants' names*) in the parish of St. Michael in the county of the city of Coventry and in Foxhull in the county of the said city, all once of St. Mary's priory in Coventry; woods (*named with tenant's name*) in Brackley *alias* Olde Brackley or elsewhere, co. Northampton, once of the monastery of Pré, Leicester; lands (*named with tenants' names*) in Wendlingborough *alias* Wellingborough,   [*m.* 11] co. Northampton, once of the monastery of Crowlande and afterwards   [*m.* 12] annexed to the honour of Grafton; and lands (*tenant named*) in Hacculton in Peddington, co. Northampton, once of the monastery of St. Andrew in Northampton.

Grant also of the manor of Upton Episcopi, co. Hereford, late of the bishopric of Hereford, and the advowson of the rectory of Upton Episcopi.

To hold the manor of Upton Episcopi and the premises in Wimbledon by service of the hundredth part of a knight's fee, and the rest as of the manor of Est Grenewiche, co. Kent, in socage. Issues from Michaelmas   [*m.* 13] last. The grantee to pay yearly £10 to the vicar of Coughton for his stipend and 27*s.* 4*d.* out of the manor of Upton Episcopi to the bailiff thereof for his fee.

In consideration of the manor of Bremor *alias* Bulbarne Bremor and the site of the monastery of Bremor, co. Southampton, and the manor of Marston *alias* Marston Bygod, co. Somerset, bargained and sold to the Crown by Hatton.   By Q.

1351.)   9 *May* 1576.   Grant in fee simple to Walter, earl of Essex and Ewe, of the lordships and territories called Ferney *alias* Hiffearne and Macguyes Ilande within 'the provynce or erledome of Ulster' in Ireland, with all lands and hereditaments both spiritual and temporal in Ferney *alias* Hiffarne, Downe Mayne and Clankevile and Macguyes Iland heretofore under the government of any captain or chieftain (*prepositus*) of Ferney or any captain of Macguyes Iland; reserving to the Crown all ports, customs and subsidies and demands due for any wares; to hold Ferney in socage as of Dublin castle by fealty and a yearly rent of one horse or £13 6*s.* 8*d.* Irish at Michaelmas, and Macguyes Island as of Knockfergus castle by fealty and a yearly rent of a falcon at Michaelmas. Licence for the grantee to alienate any of the premises, to hold of him by such services, customs and rents as he pleases. Power also during the next 20 years   [*m.* 14] to appoint views of frankpledge and leets, fairs and markets in any place comprised in the grant as to him shall seem fitting; and grant for ever of the right to hold courts before his steward in personal pleas and amounts of not more than 40*s.*, and all suits tenable before a court baron according to the law of England or Ireland; also that he may have his court to hold pleas in the lordship and territory of Ferney and the rest of the premises before his steward or deputy steward for all pleas except pleas of the Crown, and to have in the premises by his bailiffs the return of writs and the like out of courts of the Crown in Ireland or the Exchequer of Ireland and the return of juries in all causes in courts of the Crown in Ireland except in causes touching the Crown; also to have all profits arising in the said court and in the views of frankpledge, leets, fairs and markets aforesaid. The grantee and all tenants and others resident in the premises to have exemption from all taxes, 'bohaghties' and customs called 'cesse', 'cogne', 'lyverie' and other Irish charges except taxes imposed after seven years by the Parliament of Ireland. Grant also of goods of felons and outlaws, wreck of the sea, deodands and the like in the premises. Also to have   [*m.* 15] free warren, free chase and liberty of park there. Licence also for 20 years for him, his heirs and assigns remaining in loyalty towards the Crown to repair and rebuild castles and fortresses within the territories comprised in the grant and place arms and garrisons therein. Licence also for him and the tenants and residents in the premises to repel by armed force attacks by Irish, Scottish, rebels, outlaws or enemies of the Crown.

Also—that no doubt may arise as to the boundaries of the premises—the deputy of Ireland shall, at the grantee's request, direct commissions to be issued to survey the same, to be certified to the Chancery of Ireland to be enrolled of record.

For the earl's service in the wars against rebels in Ireland.   By Q.

1352.) 9 *May* 1576. Grant for life to Walter, earl of Essex, of the   [*m.* 16] office and title of earl marshal of Ireland; with all such offices, profits and appurtenances belonging to the same in Ireland as belong in England to the office of earl marshal of England. Grant also that the office of marshal of the army in Ireland shall when void by the death, forfeiture or surrender of Nicholas Bagnall, knight, who now holds it, remain to the earl during his life, with power to exercise the same by himself or by deputy. He may freely grant all other offices belonging to the office of earl marshal, notwithstanding any customs or patents to the contrary. He and any his deputy may bear in Ireland, both in the presence and in the absence of the Sovereign, a gold stick ringed with black at both ends, adorned with the royal arms at the upper end and with the earl's arms at the lower end. He shall have a place and voice in the Parliament of Ireland as one of the magnates and lords of Ireland, and he shall be assigned in Parliament the place next to the treasurer of Ireland being one of the magnates and lords.

For his service in Ireland.   By Q.

1353.) 27 *April* 1576. *Gorhambury.* Grant to Roger Manners, an esquire for the body, and his heirs and assigns of—(1) the rectory of Grandbye, co. Nottingham, once of the monastery of Thurgarton, co. Nottingham; (2) the rectory of Bonney, co. Nottingham, once of Olvescrofte priory, co. Leicester; (3) the rectory of Annesley, co. Nottingham, late of William Bolles, exchanged; (4) the rectory of Kirkeby Bedon, co. Norfolk, once of Langley priory, co. Norfolk; (5) tithes of hay (*named with tenants' names*) in Severneham, co. Gloucester, once of the monastery of Tewkesberye, co. Gloucester; (6) the rectory of Estchynnock, co.   [*m.* 17] Somerset, once of Mountague priory, co. Somerset; (7) all lands in Wells, Southover, Estwalles, Portwaye and Wookaye and elsewhere in the parish of Wokaye and St. Cuthbert, Wells, or elsewhere, co. Somerset, late leased to John Ayleworthe, once of the hospital of St. John, Wells, and afterwards of the bishopric of Bath and Wells; (8) the rectory of Wincaunton, co. Somerset, formerly in the tenure of John FitzJames, knight, and lady Elizabeth his wife and now or late in that of John Wadham, once of the monastery of Taunton and late of Charles, late lord Stourton, attainted of murder; (9) the rectory of Chewton under Mendipe, co. Somerset, late of the monastery of Shene, co. Surrey; (10) the advowson of the vicarage of Chewton aforesaid with the chapel annexed; (11) all lands in Stoke Abbott, Bechinstoke and Chewe or elsewhere, co. Somerset, once in the tenure of John Seyntlowe, knight, and now or late in that of Edmund Downyng, once of the monastery of Keynesham, co. Somerset; (12) the rectory of Mikelton *alias* Micleton, co. Gloucester, once of the monastery of Eynesham, the mansion house of the rectory, late in the tenure of Edmund Porter, the tithes of corn, wool and lambs in Mikelton, Clopton and Hitcote *alias* Hidcote, 'le gyldable tythes' in Queynton, co. Gloucester, and all appurtenances of the said rectory; (13) the rectory of St. George of Tomelonde in Norwich, co. Norfolk, now or late in the tenure of Ellis Jermyn, once of the late college or chapel in the fields near Norwich; (14) the tithes of corn and hay in Stapleton, co. York, now or late in the tenure of Nicholas Hothome, once of the monastery of St. Mary next the walls of York; (15) lands (*named with tenant's name*) in the parish of Manfeilde, co. York, once of William, late marquess of Northampton; (16) lands (*described with tenants' names*) in Pontefract and Preston Jaclyn, co. York, once of   [*m.* 18] the monastery of St. Oswald, co. York; (17) lands and tithes (*named with tenants' names*) in Sheffeilde, co. York, once of the monastery of Workesopp, co. Nottingham; (18) lands (*named with tenant's name*) in Stannoue, co. York, once of Mount St. John preceptory, co. York; (19) lands (*tenants named*) in Hannesworthe Woodhouse, co. York, once of the monastery of Wallingwelles, co. Nottingham; (20) lands (*tenants named*) in Cossall, co. Nottingham, once of the monastery of Newstedd; (21) lands (*tenant named*) in Bradmere, co.

Nottingham, once of the monastery of Lenton, co. Nottingham; (22) lands (*tenants named*) in Slosewick in the parish of Workesopp, co. Nottingham, once of the monastery of Workesopp; (23) a mill (*tenant named*) in Shifnall, co. Salop, once of the monastery of Womebridge, co. Salop; (24) lands (*tenant named*) in Brackley, co. Northampton, once of the monastery of Pré, Leicester; (25) lands (*named with tenant's name*) in Scotfeilde *alias* Stotfielde, co. Stafford, once of the monastery of Pollesworthe, co. Warwick; (26) lands (*named with tenants' names*) in Lingfielde, co. Surrey; (27) lands (*tenant named*)   [*m.* 19] in Combes, co. Oxford, late purchased from Richard Andrewes; (28) lands (*tenant named*) in Weston, Ipwell and Kingham *alias* Kenkham, co. Oxford, once of the brotherhood or guild of Brayles, co. Warwick; (29) lands in Fresheforde (*named*), given for salt for holy water in Fresheforde church, in the manor of Dichegate (*tenant named*), given for a lamp in the church there, in Wincaunton (*named with tenants' names*) given for mass for the souls of Thomas Brame and his parents in Wyncaunton church, and in Riding in the parish of Wrington, given for a light in the church there, all in the county of Somerset and in the Crown's hands by stat. 1 Edw. VI for the dissolution of chantries and the like; (30) lands (*named with tenants' names*) in Dowbridge, co. Derby, and Uttoxater, co. Stafford, once of Dowbridge chantry; (31) a tenement in Seynt Stephens Alley in Westminster, co. Middlesex, late in the tenure of John Ragge and now or late in that of William Man, once of the late college of SS. Mary and Stephen in the palace of Westminster; (32) certs and casuals arising yearly in towns within the honour of Gloucester in the county Northampton now amounting to 15s. 8d., the common fines of the said towns now of the yearly value of 2s. and all courts, liberties and profits belonging to the said honour, leased to John Marshe by patent, 28 Feb., 8 Eliz., for 21 years at a yearly rent of 31s.; (33) a fee or hereditament called Gloucester Fee, all yearly payments in Woodforde (co. Northampton) in right of the same fee, all courts of the tenants and residents in Woodforde and all appurtenances of the said fee, leased to Simon Mallerye by patent, 24 Nov., 7 Eliz., for 21 years at a yearly rent of 2s. 6d.; (34) lands (*named with tenants' names*) in Estecote, Asshecote and Pateshull, co.   [*m.* 20] Northampton, once of the monastery of St. James next Northampton and late annexed to the honour of Grafton; (35) lands (*tenant named*) in Asshebye, co. Lincoln, once of Willoughton preceptory; (36) lands (*named with tenant's name*) in Mortelake, co. Surrey, and (37) lands (*named with tenant's name*) in Puttenhethe, co. Surrey, now or late parcel of the manor of Wimbledon, co. Surrey, once of Thomas Cromwell, knight, late earl of Essex, attainted of treason, and afterwards assigned to cardinal Poole for life; (38) all lands called Burlion Fee in Gedney, co. Lincoln, rents of assize amounting to 8s. 1¼d., in Gedney and all lands, courts, liberties and profits there belonging to the said Fee, once of the monastery of Crowlande, co. Lincoln; and (39) lands (*named with tenants' names*) in Weston, co. Lincoln, and (40) lands (*tenants named*) in Pynchebeck, co. Lincoln, all once of the monastery of Spalding, co. Lincoln. Yearly value £200 4s. 11d. Bells and   [*m.* 21] lead, except lead in gutters and windows, reserved. To hold as of the manor of Estgrenewiche, co. Kent, in socage and by yearly rents of (1) £12, (2) £13 6s. 8d., (3) 53s. 4d., (4) 20s., (5) 11s. 10d., (6) £6, (7) £19 15s. 8d., (8) £8, (9) £20, (11) £10, (12) £4, (13) 3s. 4d., (14) 26s. 8d., (15) £8 13s. 4d., (16) £4 9s. 10d., (17) 68s. 2d. (*detailed*), (18) £4, (19) 32s. 2d. (*detailed*), (20) 57s. 8d., (21) 63s. 4d., (22) £4 8s., (23) 40s., (24) 32s., (25) 10s.,   [*m.* 22] (26) 20d., (27) 12s. 2d., (28) 30s., (29) 16s. 8d., (30) £8 9s. 11¼d., (31) 16s. 8d., (32) 31s., (33) 2s. 6d. (34) 76s. (*detailed*), (35) 10s., (36) 53s. 4d., (37) 16s., (38) £15 6s. 1⅝d., (39) £23 17s. (*detailed*) and (40) 73s. (*detailed*). Issues from Lady Day last. The grantee—to find a priest or curate in Bonney; to pay yearly 53s. 4d. out of the rectory of Annesley to the vicar there for stipend; to find a priest or curate in Kyrkybedon and another in Wincaunton; to pay yearly out of the rectory of Micleton 13s. 4d. to the bishop of Worcester for pension, 9s. to the archdeacon of Gloucester for proxies and synodals and 53s. 4d. to the vicar there; to find a priest or curate in the parish or St. George in Tombland in Norwich; and to pay yearly 7s. 4½d. out

of the premises in Dowbridge and Uttoxater and 40s. out ot the same to be distributed to the poor   [m. 23]
there.

    In consideration of the manor of Cottam Conyers, co. Durham, bargained and sold to the Crown by Manners; and for his service.   By p.s.

1354.)   12 *May* 1576.   Lease for 21 years to William Fyshe of (1) a house in 'le markett place', lands (*named with tenants' names*), a fishery, the toll of the market and fairs and all shops and 'lez stalles' in 'le markett place' in Bickleswade, co. Bedford, all parcels of the demesne lands of the manor of Bickleswade and late of the bishopric of Lincoln, (2) lands (*named with tenants' names*) in Norrell and Ouldwardon, co. Bedford, once of the bishop of Lincoln, and (3) the toll and profits of two fairs in Bicleswade, to wit, on Monday and Tuesday in the week of Pentecost and on Candlemas Day, and all profits and hereditaments in Bickleswade and Ouldwardon reputed parcels of the manor of Bickleswade and late of the bishopric of Lincoln; with reservations, including a   [m. 25]
chamber or hall (60 feet long and 24 feet wide), parcel of the house aforesaid, which should be reserved for the justices, commissioners and officers of the Crown whenever they come to hold assizes, courts or other business in the town and county aforesaid, and 'a stockhouse', parcel of the house aforesaid, for the detention of malefactors; from Michaelmas next; yearly rent £10 16s. 8d. In consideration of the surrender by Fyshe in respect of the premises of (a) a patent, 3 Feb., 7 Eliz., leasing (1) to William Stewarde *inter alia* for 21 years from Michaelmas then last at a yearly rent of £9 10s. and (b) a patent of the Exchequer, 14 June, 15 Eliz., leasing (2) and (3) to Robert Thorpe *inter alia* for 21 years from Lady Day then last at a yearly rent of 26s. 8d.; and for a fine of £20 6s. 8d. paid at the Exchequer.
                        By the commissioners by virtue of the Queen's warrant.

1355A.)   22 *July* 1576.   *Gorhambury.*   Grant in fee simple to Thomas Hennage, treasurer of the chamber, Michael Hennage, William Poyntz and Miles Grey of—lands (*tenants named*) in Sibsey, co. Lincoln, once of the hospital of St. John of Jerusalem; lands (*tenants named*) in Grantham, Barkeston and Harlaxston, co. Lincoln, parcel of the jointure of Jane, once Queen of England; lands etc. in Ludforde, including all fairs and the fair called 'Lammas faier' there and all strays and waifs in the lordship and parish of Ludford, and lands (*tenant named*) in Estrayson, co. Lincoln, once of the monastery of Sixhill, co. Lincoln; the rectory of Kirmond, co. Lincoln, once of Robert Constable, knight; lands (*tenants named*) in Dunscrope   [m. 26]
(*named*), Willoughbye and Waterwilloughby, co. Lincoln, given for chantries, guilds and lamps; lands (*named with tenants' names*) in Barkesten, co. Lincoln, once of the monastery of Halamprice; lands (*tenants named*) in Coldeashebye, co. Northampton, once of the monastery of Sowlbye; the manor of Brightlingsey, co. Essex, assigned to Queen Mary before her accession and formerly of St. John's monastery near Colchester, with rents and 'le mannor place' called 'le Brightlingsey Hall', the tithes of 'le mannor place' and demesne lands and the rents of 'le borde landes' in Brightlingsey outside the charge of the collector of the manor, once of the said monastery; lands and marshes in Brightlingsey and Terington, co. Essex, once of the said monastery of St. John; the manor of Brettes, co. Essex, late granted to Peter Mewtis, knight, and Jane his wife for life, once of Margaret, countess of Salisbury, attained of treason; lands (*tenants named*) in Westham (*named*) and Flatwick, co. Essex; and the manor of Fifhedd, co. Somerset, once of Edward, late duke of Somerset. To   [m. 27]
hold the manors of Brightlingsey and Brettes and the other premises in Brightlingsey, Brettes and Westham by service of the fortieth part of a knight's fee, and the rest as of the manor of Estgrenewiche, co. Kent, on socage. Issues from Lady Day last. The grantees to

pay 25*s.* yearly out of the manor of Brightlingsey to John Baker, bailiff of the manor, for his fee, and 3*s.* 7*d.* out of the said manor.

Grant also for 60 years to Thomas Hennage of an annuity of £28 16*s.* 9½*d.* payable at the Exchequer, if lady Jane Mewtis, late the wife of Peter Mewtis, knight, lives so long; provided that the grant be void after the   [*m.* 28] expiry of a lease of the manor of Brettes for 21 years to the said Jane and Frances Mewtis by patent, 15 Dec., 8 Eliz.

In consideration of the manor of Kellithorpe and other lands in Kellithorpe, Dryfeild Magna, Dryfeilde Parva and Elmeswell, co. York, bargained and sold to the Crown by the said Thomas Hennage.   By Q.

1355B.)   19 *March* 1576.   Lease for 21 years to John Grescrofte of a capital messuage in Ottringham Marche *alias* Ottringham Marsh in Holdernes, co. York, parcel of the manor of Ottringham, once of Thorneton college, co. Lincoln; with reservations; from Lady Day next; yearly rent £10; the lessee to repair sea walls, 'lez Humberbanckes' and all other waterworks. In consideration of the surrender by Grescrofte in Chancery of a lease thereof by patent, 13 May, 6 Eliz., to Richard Barnarde for 21 years from Lady Day then last at the same rent; and for a fine of £20 paid at the Exchequer.
                    By the commissioners by virtue of the Queen's warrant.

1356.)   15 *March* 1576.   Lease for 21 years to Rose Holforde, widow, late the wife of Richard Holforde, and Henry Holforde, their son, of the rectory of   [*m.* 29] Armington *alias* Ermington, co. Devon, once of the monastery of Mountague, co. Somerset; with reservations; from Lady Day next; yearly rent £15 15*s.* 10*d.* In consideration of the surrender by Rose and Henry in respect of the premises of a patent, 16 June, 3 Eliz., leasing the same *inter alia* to Richard for 21 years from Lady Day then last at a yearly rent of £18; and for a fine of £33 6*s.* 8*d.* paid at the Exchequer.   By p.s.

1357.)   26 *March* 1576.   *Gorhambury.*   Lease for 21 years to Robert, earl of Leicester, baron of Denbigh, councillor, K.G., knight of St. Michael, of the demesne and other lands in the lordship of Grafton, co. Northampton,   [*m.* 30] parcel of the honour of Grafton; with reservations, including Grafton park, the wild beasts therein and certain lands (*tenants named*) enclosed therein; from Michaelmas last; yearly rent £42 12*s.* 11*d.*; the lessee to collect the issues of courts within the lordship and pay them to the receiver general of the county. In consideration of the surrender by the said earl by deed, 28 June, 17 Eliz., enrolled in Chancery, of a lease thereof by patent, 24 Jan., 4 Eliz., to William, baron of Burghley, treasurer, by the name of William Cecill, knight, principal secretary, for 21 years from Michaelmas then last at the same rent; and for a fine of 100 marks paid at the Exchequer.   By p.s.

1358.)   16 *May* 1576.   Lease for 21 years to Robert Dudley of eight tenements (*tenants named*) in Willington, co. Northumberland, once of the monastery of Durham; with reservations; from Lady Day last; yearly rent 33*s.* 4*d.* for each tenement; the lessee to inhabit the   [*m.* 31] premises by himself or sufficient men, to cultivate the lands, to find a man or men to serve with horse and arms when summoned by the warden or lieutenant of the marches there, and to fence the premises as ordered by the steward of the Queen's courts or other her officers there. On surrender by Dudley of a patent, 8 July, 8 Eliz., leasing the premises to Robert Brandlinge, knight, for 21 years from Lady Day then last at the same rent. For a fine of £26 13*s.* 4*d.* paid at the Exchequer.   By the commissioners by virtue of the Queen's warrant.

1359.)   24 *Feb.* 1576.   Lease for 21 years to Richard Plewman (or Plowman) *alias* Love of

(1) lands (*tenants named*) in Clifton, co. York, parcels   [*m. 32*] of the manor of Clifton, and (2) lands (*named with tenants' names*) in Northill and within the lordship of Estcottingwith, parcels of the manor of Estcottingwith, co. York, all late of the monastery of St. Mary next the walls of York; with reservations; from Lady Day next; yearly rents (1) 36s. 7d. and 22s. and (2) 27s. 10½d. and 29s. 4d., also rendering yearly for each of the two tenements in (1) 2 hens and 20 eggs as accustomed; the lease to be void in respect of any parcel of the premises if the lessee shall expel the present tenants therefrom or if he shall not before Michaelmas next make them leases thereof for the whole term and at the same rent provided that they pay him among themselves his costs about obtaining this patent. In consideration of the surrender by Plowman of (*a*) a patent of the Exchequer, 15 Jan., 3 Eliz., leasing to Thomas Reve *inter alia* the premises (2) above and certain of the premises in (1) for 21 years from Michaelmas then last at yearly rents of 15s. for the premises in (1) and 27s. 10½d. and 29s. 4d. for the premises in (2) and (*b*) a patent of the Exchequer, [—] July, 3 Eliz., leasing to John Atkynson, Agnes Love and Plowman the rest of the premises in (1) for 21 years from Lady Day then last at yearly rents of 22s., 13s. 7d. and 8s. and rents of hens and eggs as aforesaid; and for a fine of £11 11s. 7d. paid at the Exchequer.

           By the commissioners by virtue of the Queen's warrant.

1360.)   17 *May* 1576.   Lease for 21 years to John Forde of (1) demesne lands (*tenants named*) of the manor of Bydlington in Bramber, Staynynge,   [*m. 33*] Sompertinge and Anmingdon, co. Sussex, and (2) a tenement (*named with tenant's name*) in Asshehurste, co. Sussex; with reservations; from Lady Day last; yearly rents, from the time when he shall enjoy possession, (1) £6 and (2) 3s. In consideration that the premises have been concealed, but Forde offers to recover them for the Crown and thereafter pay the rents aforesaid.   By the commissioners by virtue of the Queen's warrant.

1361.)   4 *May* 1576.   *Gorhambury*. Lease for 21 years to Adam Trigge of (1) the rectory of Missen, co. Nottingham, the tithes of corn belonging thereto and a meadow (*named*) belonging thereto and (2) Missen grange, all once of Mattersey abbey, co. Nottingham; with reservations; from   [*m. 34*] Lady Day last; yearly rents, from the time when he shall enjoy possession, (1) £7 18s. 4d. and (2) 21s. In consideration that Trigge will endeavour at his costs to make void in law pretended leases for 60 years of the rectory by indenture 12 Nov., 27 Hen. VIII, to William Brian and Agnes his wife and the grange by indenture, 11 Nov., 27 Hen. VIII, to William Legate and Isabel his wife; and for a fine of £7 2s. paid at the Exchequer.

           By the commissioners by virtue of the Queen's warrant.

1362.)   13 *April* 1576.   *Gorhambury*   Lease for 21 years to Robert Syssesson of (1) lands (*named*) in Anlabye in the county of the town of Kingston on Hull, once of the monastery of Haltemprice, co. York, and (2) lands (*named*) in the lordship of Cottingham, co. York, parcel of the said lordship and of lands exchanged with Charles, late earl of Westmorland; with reservations; from Lady Day last; yearly rents (1) £5 13s. 4d. and (2) £6 13s. 4d. In consideration of the surrender by the said Robert of (*a*) a patent, 4 June, 3 & 4 Ph. & Mary, leasing (1) to Robert Syssatson for 21 years from Michaelmas then next at the same rent and (*b*) an indenture, 15 Aug., 1 & 2 Ph. & Mary, whereby Henry, late earl of Westmorland, leased (2) to John Sissotson and Robert Sissotson, his son, the present lessee, for 30 years from   [*m. 35*] Candlemas then next at the same rent; and for a fine of £24 13s. 4d. paid at the Exchequer.

           By the commissioners by virtue of the Queen's warrant.

1363.)   27 *Feb.* 1576.   Lease for 21 years to Margaret Stricklande, widow, of lands (*tenants named*) in (1) Yowlethorpe, co. York, and (2) Meltinbye, co. York, once of Wilberfosse priory, co. York, and (3) Sutton, co. York, once of the monastery of Meux, co. York; with reservations; from Lady Day next; yearly rents (1) 66*s.* 4*d.*, (2) 42*s.* 8*d.* and (3) 6*s.* In consideration of the surrender of a patent, 5 Nov.[1], 4 Eliz., leasing (1) and (2) to her for 21 years from Michaelmas then last at the same rents; and for a fine of £5 15*s.* paid at the Exchequer.   By the commissioners by virtue of the Queen's warrant.

1364.)   13 *April* 1576.   *Gorhambury*   Lease for 21 years to Alice Weston, widow, late the wife of Robert Weston, LL.D., late chancellor of   [*m.* 36] Ireland, of the rectory of Skestlinge *alias* Skeflinge called Bristoll Garthe *alias* Burstall Garthe and all appurtenances thereof in Skestlinge in Holdernes or elsewhere, co. York, and the tithes of corn, hay, wood, wool, flax and lambs in Risome in Holdernes, co. York, all once of the monastery of Kirkestall, co. York; with reservations; from Lady Day 1584, having been leased by patent, 25 May, 5 Eliz., to Henry Vavasor for 21 years from Lady Day then last at a yearly rent of £39 13*s.* 4*d.*; same rent; the lease to be void if she shall not within six weeks of entry on the premises surrender or cancel a patent, 21 May, 16 Eliz., granting her an annuity of £20 during her widowhood.   By Q.

1365.)   15 *March* 1576.   Lease for 21 years to Hugh Bethell of lands (*named with tenants' names*) in Belthorpe and Fangfosse, parcels of   [*m.* 37] the manor of Belthorpe, co. York, late of Thomas Hennage, knight, exchanged; with reservations; from Lady Day next; yearly rent £18 10*s.* In consideration of the surrender by Bethell of (*a*) a patent, 15 March[2], 5 Eliz., leasing part of the premises at a yearly rent of £12 3*s.* 4*d.* and (*b*) a patent, 30 Nov.[2], 5 Eliz., leasing the rest at a yearly rent of £6 6*s.* 8*d.* in both cases to John Dawson for 21 years from Michaelmas then last; and for a fine of £18 10*s.* paid at the Exchequer.   By p.s.

1366.)   12 *March* 1576.   Lease for 21 years to Francis Metham of the rectory of Kirkedale, co. York, once of the monastery of Newborough, co. York; with reservations; from Lady Day next; yearly rent   [*m.* 38] £26 8*s.*; the lessee to bear all charges ordinary and extraordinary. In consideration of the surrender by Methan of the interest in the rectory of John Heynes, to whom it was leased *inter alia* by patent, 28 Nov., 7 Eliz., for 21 years from Michaelmas then last at the same rent; and for a fine of £52 15*s.* paid to the Queen's use by Metham to Richard Hebborne by way of reward for his charges about her works at Sherifhutton castle, co. York, over the past three summers having no allowance for the same, as appears by the particular book of the same works remaining with the auditor of the county, and as reported by Henry, earl of Huntingdon, president of the council in the North.   By p.s.

1367.)   28 *March* 1576.   *Gorhambury.*   Lease for 21 years to Christopher Legerd of the rectory of Heasill *alias* Hesill in the county of Kingeston on Hull, late of the monastery [*sic*] of Gisbroughe and Watton; with reservations; from Lady Day last; yearly rent £18 4*s.* In consideration of the surrender in Chancery of a patent, 6 Dec., 6 Eliz., leasing the rectory to him for 21 years from Michaelmas then last at the same rent; and for a fine of £36 8*s.* at the Exchequer.   By p.s.

---

[1] The enrolment of the surrendered patent (*cf Calendar* 1560-1563, p.249) gives its date as 25 Nov.
[2] The enrolments of the surrendered patents (*cf Calendar* 1560-1563, pp. 515 and 532) give their dates as (*a*) 30 Nov and (*b*) 15 March.

1368.)   19 *March* 1576.   Lease for 21 years to William Gardiner of a tenement or grange by
the late monastery of Barmondsey, co. Surrey;   [*m.* 39]
with reservations; from the termination of a lease thereof by indenture, 21 May 1534, by
Robert, abbot, and the convent of the said monastery to Ralph Wryne and Helen his wife, as
then formerly held by William Barkyvith or Robert Oggan, for 60 years from that date at a
yearly rent of £48 for the said grange and the tithes thereof; same rent; the lessee at his own
expense to scour and maintain 'a sewer' from the bridge of St. Thomas a Wateringes to 'le
sluce' this side of Rederith, co. Surrey. For a fine of £166 13s. 4d. paid at the Exchequer.

By p.s.

1369.)   15 *March.* 1576.   Lease for 21 years to Thomas Holgate of Stapleton, co. York, of
the rectory of North Dalton, co. York, late of the monastery of Watton, co. York; with
reservations; from Michaelmas next; yearly rent £20; the lessee to provide a chaplain or
minister in North Dalton church. On surrender by the said Thomas of the interest in the
rectory of Thomas Reynoldes, Elizabeth his wife, Thomas Holgaite,   [*m.* 40]
William Holgaite and Jane Bradforde, to whom it was leased *inter alia* by Robert, prior
commendatory, and the convent of the said monastery by indenture, 13 Jan., 30 Hen. VIII,
for 40 years from the feast of St. Mark 1540 at the same rent. For a fine of £6 13s. 4d. paid at
the Exchequer.   By p.s.

1370.)   9 *May* 1576.   Lease for 21 years to Walter Games of the rectory of Devynnocke,
co. Brecon, once of Brecknock priory; with reservations; from Lady Day last; yearly rent
£15; the lessee to pay to the archdeacon of Brecknock all yearly proxies and synodals. In
consideration of the surrender by Games of a patent, 24 Feb., 3 Eliz., leasing the rectory to
Valentine Dale, LL.D., for 21 years from Michaelmas then last at a yearly rent of £14 15s.
3d.; and for a fine of £15 paid at the Exchequer.   By p.s

(The dorse of this roll is blank.)

PART XIV

C. 66/1150

1371.)   14 *July* 1576.   Lease for life to Blaise Radberde, with   [*m.* 1]
remainder to Marmaduke More and George More for life in survivorship, of all buildings
belonging to the grange or farm of Westover and lands (*named with tenants' names*) in Drayton
and Westover or elsewhere, co. Somerset, late of Edward, late duke of Somerset, and once
of the monastery of Mochelmer, co. Somerset; with reservations; from the present date;
yearly rent £14 4s. and heriot the best beast. For a fine of £20 paid at the Exchequer by
Radberde.   By p.s.

1372.)   14 *July* 1576.   Lease for 21 years to Charles Russell of a tenement called 'the
mannour of Forde' and other lands late of Catherine, countess of Bridgewater, by royal gift
for life, and once of Rice Griffith, attainted of treason; with reservations, including courts
and the like; from Lady Day last; yearly rent £6. In consideration of the surrender by Russell
of the interest of John Parrott, knight, to whom the premises were leased by patent, 14
April, 4 Eliz., *inter alia* for 21 years from Lady Day then last at the same rent; and for a fine of
£6 paid at the Exchequer.   [*m.* 2]
                    By the commissioners by virtue of the Queen's warrant.

1373.)   12 *July* 1576.   Lease for 21 years to Richard Aston of Aston, co. Chester, of lands
called 'Byrdesperke Closes', parcel of the demesne lands within the lordship of Kendall, co.
Westmorland, parcel of lands assigned by the Queen to Eleanor, marchioness of
Northampton, for her jointure and now in the Queen's hands by exchange between her and
the marchioness; with reservations; from Lady Day last; yearly rent £15. In consideration of
the surrender of an indenture, 20 Nov., 15 Eliz., whereby the marchioness leased to Aston
the premises, then described as within 'the parke of Kendall', then in the tenure of the same
Aston and parcel of the demesne lands belonging to Kendall castle, for 21 years from
Martinmas then last at the same rent; and for a fine of £10 paid at the Exchequer.
                                                                                     By p.s.

1374.)   12 *July* 1576.   Lease for 40 years to Robert Zinzano *alias* Alexander, an equerry of
the stable, of a water mill called 'le Abbey Mill' with a tenement adjoining in St. Albans
within the parish of St. Alban, co. Hertford,   [*m.* 3]
late of Richard Lee, knight, exchanged and formerly of the monastery of St. Albans; from
Lady Day last; yearly rent £16 13s. 4d.. In consideration of the surrender by Zinzano of the
interest of John Seale, to whom Lee by the name of Richard Lee of Sopwell in St. Albans,
knight, by indenture, 1 May, 4 Edw. VI, leased the premises, then in Seale's tenure, for 31
years from Michaelmas then next at the same rent; and because the Crown has been charged
with the repairs, which Zinzano has undertaken to do.   By p.s.

1375.)   14 *July* 1576.   Lease for 21 years to Nicholas Bacon, son and heir apparent of
Nicholas Bacon, knight, councillor, keeper of the great seal, of (1) the site and capital
messuage of the manor of Dullingham in Burwell and lands (*named*) in Burwell, co.

Cambridge, parcel of lands exchanged with Edward Northe, knight, lord North, (2) the tithes of corn of lands in Myldenhall, co. Suffolk, parcel of the rectory there and of possessions assigned to Queen Mary before her accession, formerly of the monastery of Burye, co Suffolk, and (3) the tithes of hay of lands of the tenants of the manor of Myldenhall, which by ancient custom were sold yearly to divers persons there, parcel of the rectory and of the possessions aforesaid; with reservations; from Michaelmas next; yearly rents (1) £7 13s. 4d.,   [m. 4]
(2) £11 15s. and (3) 26s. 8d. In consideration of the surrender by Nicholas the father of a patent, 2 May[1], 3 Eliz., leasing the premises to him for 21 years from Michaelmas then last at the same rents; and for a fine of £30 paid at the Exchequer by Nicholas the son. By p.s.

1376.)   14 July 1576.   Lease for 21 years to Francis Rogers of the manor of Dertforde *alias* Temples in Dertforde, co. Kent, late of the hospital of St. John of Jerusalem; with reservations of oaks and elms 60 years and more old growing on the premises, and a moiety of reliefs and escheats above the value of 40s.; from Lady Day last; yearly rent £20 7s. 9d. In consideration of the surrender by Rogers by deed, [—] July, 18 Eliz., enrolled in Chancery, of the interest of Nicholas Stathome, late citizen of London, who   [m. 5]
held the manor by virtue of a conventual indenture, 30 May, 28 Hen. VIII, with like reservations, for 65 years from Michaelmas then next at a yearly rent for it and other things granted therewith of £27 16s. 8d.; and for a fine of £10 paid at the Exchequer.   By p.s.

1377.)   10 July 1576.   Lease for 21 years to Thomas Elwalde of lands (*named*) in Cottingham, co. York, parcels of the manor of Cottingham, (1) late of the late earl of Richmond and (2) parcel of the late duchy of York; with reservations; from Lady Day last; yearly rents (*detailed*) (1) £13 13s. 6d.. and (2) £7 8s. 4d.; the lessee may have allowances of wood (*specified*) to be assigned by the bailiff or woodward of Cottingham, rendering 3s. for every hundred of faggots or such sum as other the Queen's tenants there pay. In consideration of the surrender by Elwalde by   [m. 6]
deed, 8 May last, enrolled in Chancery, of his interest under a patent, 20 May, 11 Eliz., whereby the premises were leased to him for 21 years from Lady Day then last at the same rents; and for a sum within a sum of £20 paid at the Exchequer by him and Thomas Hellarde.

                                                                              By p.s.

1378.)   16 July 1576.   Lease for 21 years to John Morley of the rectories of (1) Dylham and (2) Honynge, co. Norfolk, once of Bromeholme priory, co. Norfolk; with reservations; from Michaelmas next; yearly rents (1) £6 13s. 4d. and (2) £6 13s. 4d. In consideration of the surrender by Morley of (*a*) a patent, 30 April, 9 Eliz., leasing (1) to him and (*b*) a patent, 27 June, 9 Eliz., leasing (2) to him and Richard Hodgson, in both cases for 21 years from Lady Day then last at the same rent; and for his service in divers affairs of the Queen.
                              By the commissioners by virtue of the Queen's warrant.

1379).   16 July 1576.   Lease for 21 years to Edward Fenton of tenements etc. (*described with tenants' names*), late of the brother-   [m. 7]
hood of St. John Baptist *alias* of tailors (*sutor' vestiar'*) in the parish of St. Ewen in Bristoll; from Lady Day last; yearly rent £16 16s. 10½d.; the lessee to pay yearly rents amounting to 47s. 5½d., to wit, to the chamberlain of the city 2s., for rent resolute called 'langable' 3s. 3½d.,

---

[1] The enrolment of the surrendered patent (*cf. Calendar*, 1560–1563, p. 213) gives its date as 2 March.

to the late house of the Magdalen 18s. 8d., to Bristoll cathedral 16s. and out of certain of the premises to Christchurch, Bristoll, 7s. 6d. For a fine of £16 16s. 10½d. paid at the Exchequer.

By p.s.

1380.)   14 *July* 1576.   Licence for Thomas Gressham, William Allen and Lionel Duckett, knights, Richard Barnes, Matthew Fielde, Thomas Heaton, John Gressham, Thomas Colshill, John Brampston and John Issham, citizens and mercers of London, or the survivors of them to alienate to the wardens and commonalty of the mistery of mercers of London lands in Stebbunhuth *alias* Stepney, Spilmanstrete, Churchestrete, Clevestreate *alias* Whitehartestreate, Southstreate, Shadwell Fielde, London Fieldes, Ratcliff, Lymehouse, Popeler, Myle Ende Grene and Whitechappell, co. Middlesex, which were customary lands, parcel of the manor of Stepney and once in the tenure of John Collett, deceased, late dean of St Paul's cathedral, London, and given by him for the erection of a school; licence also for the said wardens and commonalty to acquire lands in mortmain to the yearly value of £100 not   [*m.* 8]
held of the Crown immediately in chief by knight service or otherwise by knight service. In consideration of Collett's purpose in building the said school in the churchyard of St. Paul's and for the better support of a master and an usher or two ushers and other necessary things there.   By p.s.

1381.)   16 *July* 1576.   Lease for 21 years to Richard Bernarde of 'les loppes, toppes and shreddinges' of 4,147 oaks in Kendall park, co. Westmoreland, heretofore lopped and shredded for 'lez browse' for the deer and wild beasts there, and of 440 oaks called 'doterdes' unsuitable for timber in the said park, parcel of the possessions of William, late marquess of Northampton, afterwards assigned for the jointure of Helen, now marchioness of Northampton, and in the Queen's hands by exchange with her; with reservations; from Lady Day last; yearly rent £8; the lessee shall not make more than two cuttings of the trees, and shall cause this patent to be enrolled before the auditor of the county within one year for charging of the rent and before the surveyor of woods beyond that before any cutting be made.   By the commissioners by virtue of the Queen's warrant.

1382.)   9 *March* 1576.   Lease for 21 years to Richard Farewell of the chapel of Hull Episcopi, co. Somerset, once of the monastery of Taunton, co. Somerset; with reservations; from Lady Day next; yearly rent   [*m.* 9]
£11 6s. 8d.; the lessee to pay a yearly stipend of £6 6s. 8d. to a priest or chaplain there. In consideration of the surrender by Farewell of a patent, 26 June, 3 Eliz., leasing the same to Nicholas Pawlett for 21 years from Lady Day then last at a yearly rent of £11 6s. 4d.; and for a fine of £22 13s. 4d. paid at the Exchequer.
By the commissioners by virtue of the Queen's warrant.

1383.)   16 *May* 1576.   Lease for 21 years to Henry ap Harry of a corn mill in the county of Flint within the bishopric of St. Asaph, once of the monastery of Basingwark in the said bishopric; from Lady Day last; yearly rent 106s. 8d.. In consideration of the surrender in Chancery by the said Henry of a patent, 27 July, 4 & 5 Ph. & Mary, leasing the same to Nicholas Griffith for 21 years from Lady Day then last at the same rent; and for a fine of £21 6s. 8d. paid at the Exchequer.   By the commissioners by virtue of the Queen's warrant.

1384.)   13 *April* 1576.   *Gorhambury.*   Lease for 21 years to Robert   [*m.* 10]
Browne, Peter Chare and Thomas Harrys of lands (*named with tenants' names*) in the parishes of (1) Cowffelde, and (2) Seale, co. Sussex; with reservations; from Lady Day last; yearly rents from the time when they shall obtain possession (1) 66s. 8d. and (2) 66s. 8d. In

consideration that the premises have been concealed, but Browne, Chare and Harrys offer to take them at farm, and, after recovery thereof to the Queen's use, to pay the said rents.

By the commissioners by virtue of the Queen's warrant.

1385.)   23 *March* 1576.   *Gorhambury*. Lease for 21 years, if they shall so long remain in the hands of the Crown, to Christopher Bancrofte of the rectories of Overton and Twycrosse, co. Leicester, late of the bishopric of Oxford and now or late in his tenure; with reservations; from Michaelmas last; yearly rent £28 2s. 2d.; the lessee to pay yearly out of the rectory of Overton 40s. to the vicar of Overton for pension and £10 for the stipend of a curate in Twycrosse and Gopshill churches.   By p.s.

1386.)   16 *April* 1576.   *Gorhambury*.   Lease for 21 years to John Bowsewell of (1) lands in Borley, Foxearth and Lyston, co. Essex, given by William Clopton, knight, for 99 years for 'Our Ladye priest' in Melforde church, co. Suffolk, to pray for the souls of him and others, and (2) the manor of Bowrehall in Pentelowe, co. Essex, given by John Hill of Melforde for 99 years for a stipendiary priest in   [*m*. 11]
Melforde church to pray for the souls of him and others; with reservations; from Lady Day last; yearly rents from the time when he shall enjoy possession (1) £5 5s. 4d. and (2) £6 5s. 11d. In consideration that the premises have been concealed, as appears by a certificate in the Exchequer by the Queen's commissioners in this behalf, and Bowsewell offers to take them at farm and, after obtaining possession, pay the said rents.

By the commissioners by virtue of the Queen's warrant.

1387.)   28 *March* 1576.   *Gorhambury*.   Lease for 21 years to Anthony Roue of lands called 'le South Parke' within the lordship of Cottingham, co. York, late had in exchange from Charles, late earl of Westmorland; with reservations; from Lady Day last; yearly rent £6. In consideration of the surrender by Roue of the interest of William Kendall, to whom by indenture, 2 Oct., 4 Eliz., Henry, earl of Westmorland, leased, by the name of William Kendall of Brauncepeth, 'yoman', then servant to the said earl, *inter alia* the premises, then in Kendall's tenure, for 21 years from Candlemas then next at a yearly rent for them and other lands in Cottingham of £11 6s. 8d.; and for a fine of £12 paid at the Exchequer within a sum of £22 13s. 4d.   By the commissioners by virtue of the Queen's warrant.

1388.)   6 *April* 1576.   *Gorhambury*.   Lease for 21 years to Maurice   [*m*. 12]
Barkeley, knight, of a farm called Ridding Court, parcel of the lordship of Datchett, co. Buckingham, and of the possessions of the honour and castle of Windesore, co. Berks; with reservations; from Lady Day last; yearly rent £12 8s. 4d. In consideration of his surrender of a patent, 14 Nov., 4 & 5 Ph. & Mary, leasing the same to him for 21 years from Michaelmas 1567 at the same rent; and for a fine of £15 paid at the Exchequer.

By the commissioners by virtue of the Queen's warrant.

1389.)   9 *March* 1576.   Lease for 21 years to John Perrott, knight, of all the possessions in the counties of Carmarthen, Cardigan and Radnor of Slebeche preceptory; with reservations; from Michaelmas last; yearly rent £40. In consideration of the surrender by Perrott of a patent, 6 July,   [*m*. 13]
5 Eliz., leasing the same to John Barlowe for 21 years from Lady Day then last at the same rent; and for a fine of £60 paid at the Exchequer.   By p.s.

1390.)   16 *April* 1576.   *Gorhambury*.   Lease for 21 years to Stephen Geere and William Hardye of lands, in the several tenures (1) once of Robert Hardye and now of Geere and (2) once of John Hardye and now of the said William, in the parish of Bayneton, co. York, formerly of Francis Bygott, knight, attainted; from Lady Day last; yearly rents (1) £7 8s. 4d. and (2) 70s. For a fine of £12 paid at the Exchequer by Geere, John Ottley and the said William within a sum of £17 12s. 8d.

By the commissioners by virtue of the Queen's warrant.

1391.)   9 *March* 1576.   Lease for 40 years, if Jaconinus Fregoze shall so long live, to John Coryatt of two corn mills on the river Aven within the manor of Sopley, co. Southampton; from Lady Day next; yearly rent 40s. In consideration that—Fregoze holds the said mills for life by grant of John Barkeley, knight, and Frances his wife by indenture at a yearly rent of £10; he is an alien born in Italy, a subject of the Emperor, and has not obtained a licence to acquire lands nor has any power so to do; he was found by inquisition taken at Forttingbridge, co. Southampton, on 18 Jan. last returned in the Exchequer to be alive and therefore the premises have come into the Queen's hands; Coryatt caused the said inquisition to be made at his own costs and offers to pay a yearly rent of 40s. over and above the £10 payable to   [*m.* 14]
Berkeley and his wife and their heirs.

By the commissioners by virtue of the Queen's warrant.

Vacated because surrendered, 20 *May,* 19 *Eliz.; signed*: Wyll'm Cordell; John Coryat; *with a note* Egedius Estcourt cogn' partem.

1392.)   6 *April* 1576.   *Gorhambury.*   Lease for 21 years to William Hollicombe, a yeoman of the guard, of the rectory of Dewestowe and the tithes of corn in Dewestowe or elsewhere, co. Cornwall, belonging thereto, once of the hospital or priory of St. John, Bridgwater, co. Somerset; with reservations; from Lady Day last; yearly rent £7.

By the commissioners by virtue of the Queen's warrant.

1393.)   20 *April* 1576.   *Gorhambury.*   Lease for 21 years to lady Joyce Gamage, widow, of all lands in Llanvineth, Llangathen, Llanegwade, Llannyherden, Kethinnock, Kylsaen, Llantharock, Llannertheneye, Llanvyangell Aberbuthick, Abergwllye, Carmerthen, Elvett, Seyntclere, Dursloyne and Althegare and elsewhere, co. Carmarthen, late of lady Catherine Edgcombe for her life, formerly of Rice Gryffith, attainted of treason; with reservations; from Michaelmas next; yearly rent £25 7s. For a fine of £50 14s. paid   [*m.* 15]
at the Exchequer.   By p.s.

1394.)   17 *Feb.* 1576.   Commitment for 21 years (by mainprise of Richard Burton of the parish of St. Botolph without Aldersgate, London, and John Smythe of the parish of St. Sepulchre without Newgate, London, found in [—]) to Richard Burtone of the custody of lands in Sowthe Clyfton, co. Nottingham; from Michaelmas last; yearly rent 8s. 8d. as heretofore answered and 8d. beyond of increase; provided that, if anyone will give more of increase yearly without fraud, Burtone shall pay so much if he wishes to have the custody.

By treasurer's bill.

1395.)   11 *Feb.* 1576.   Licence for Walter Aston, knight, his heirs and assigns to enclose and impark 500 ac. of land in Tixall, co. Stafford, and to have free warren and liberty of park there and in Birchwood Parke in the parish of Leigh, co. Stafford; no one to enter to hunt there without leave of the licensee under forfeiture to the Queen of £10; so long as the lands are not within the bounds of the Queen's forest.   By p.s.

1396.)   16 *July* 1576.   Licence for Edward Clere, the Queen's servant, to erect within the lordship of Thetford a grammar school and a house or hospital for four poor and all other buildings necessary for a schoolmaster, an usher, a preacher and other ministers to be called the Domus Dei built in accomplishment of the will of Richard Fulmerston, knight; and foundation of the said house and school with one preacher, one schoolmaster, one usher and four or more poor. There shall be seven governors of the Domus Dei; and appointment of Roger, lord North, Christopher Wraye, knight, the Queen's chief justice, William Cordell, knight, master of the rolls, Robert Wyngfelde, knight, Gilbert Gerrard, attorney [*m.* 16] general, Thomas Sackeforde, a master of the court of Requests, and Clere to be the first and present wardens and governors for life. Incorporation of the wardens and governors. Whenever a governor shall die, the survivors may elect another in his place; and, if they refuse or fail so to do for seven months after his death, the bishop of Norwich may appoint another in his place. Power for Clere during his life to appoint the preacher, the schoolmaster, the usher and the four or more poor, and to make ordinances for the Domus Dei. After Clere's death the governors may make the said appointments; and, if they fail so to do within one month of a place becoming void, the bishop of Norwich may appoint. The governors may also after Clere's death make ordinances, with the advice and consent of his heirs being of full age and of the bishop of Norwich; so that they be not contrary to the ordinances made by Clere. Licence for the wardens and governors to hold and acquire lands, over and above those assigned by the will aforesaid, to the yearly value of £60 not held of the Crown immediately in chief or otherwise by   [*m.* 17] knight service, for the maintenance of the Domus Dei and to the other uses above specified and to be declared in Clere's lifetime.

At the suit of Clere: Fulmerston by his will, 23 June 1566, desired that there should be by his foundation a preacher to preach in the church of St. Mary, Thetforde, at four times of the year, and that lands called Trynytie Churche Yarde and Fryers Yarde in Thetford, three tenements in the parish of St. Mary there (in one of which Robert Hargrave then dwelt) and another tenement in the said parish late purchased from Robert Critofte of Lavenham, co. Suffolk, inhabited by poor persons should be assigned for the erection of a grammar school, subject to the Queen's licence being procured for the erection of the same, and further for the better provision of the preacher's stipend and the perpetual maintenance of four poor he appointed that lands should be acquired to the yearly value of £35 besides the lands above recited, and he also bequeathed a portion out of lands in Faresfelde, co. Norfolk, for the relief of poor and prisoners in the counties of Norfolk and Suffolk; he nominated as his executors Thomas, late duke of Norfolk, Osbert Moundforde, John Blenerhassett and Edward Pecocke; they renounced the executorship, and full administration of Fulmerston's estate was committed by Matthew, late archbishop of Canterbury, to Clere and Frances his wife, Fulmerston's sole daughter and heir, as appears by letters of administration dated at London, 21 Nov. 1567; nevertheless Clere, minded to give effect to the will and erect anew a grammar school in the lordship and town of Thetforde over the water towards Suffolk for the education of youth of the said town and other places in the counties of Norfolk and Suffolk, has built a house for teaching the scholars there and at his very great charges a house for the schoolmaster, and also intends to repair a tenement for the inhabitation of four poor and to carry out other works of piety.   By p.s.

1397.)   12 *July* 1576.   Foundation of the grammar school of Queen Elizabeth in Alforde, co. Lincoln, of the foundation of William, lord Burghley, and Thomas Cecill, knight, his son; with a master and an usher. Grant that there shall be 10 governors of the school; and appointment of John Tothebye, Robert Giseynge, 'mercer', John Brokebancke, 'draper', Ralph Richardson, 'glover', and Richard Wyatt, William Hawley, James Turtell, Simon Birkett, Henry Cooke and Richard Dickson, all 'yomen', to be the first and present wardens and governors for life. Incorporation of the governors. Whenever a governor shall die or dwell elsewhere, the survivors may elect in his place another inhabitant of Alforde. Power for the governors to appoint the master and usher and to make ordinances for the school. Licence for the governors to acquire lands to the yearly   [*m.* 18] value of £40 in England or elsewhere within the Queen's dominions not held of the Crown in chief or by knight service, and to have the same without fine or fee for the Queen's licence in this behalf, and without suing any writ of *ad quod dampnum* or making of an inquisition.

At the suit of the said William Cecill, K.G., lord Burghley, treasurer, councillor.

By p.s.

1398.)   20 *July* 1576.   Grant to Ambrose, earl of Warwick, K.G., one of the Privy Council, and Anne his wife and his heirs and assigns of (1) the manor of Northawe, the site and capital messuage and 'lez demeane landes' of the said manor and lands (*named with tenants' names*) in Northawe and elsewhere, co. Hertford, once of William Cavendishe, knight, deceased, (2) lands (*named with tenants' names*) in Cuffley and Northawe, (3) the rectory of Northawe, late of Cavendishe aforesaid, and all appurtenances thereof in Northawe and Cuffley or elsewhere, co. Hertford, and (4) woods (*named*) in Northawe; to hold (3) as of the manor of Est Grenewiche, co.   [*m.* 19] Kent, in socage and the rest by service of the fortieth part of a knight's fee, and by a yearly rent for all the premises of £33 7s. 2½d.; issues from Lady Day last; the grantees to pay yearly 66s. 8d. to William Clarke as bailiff, steward and woodward of the manor; the earl, his heirs, executors and assigns may sue in the name either of the earl, his executors and administrators or of the Crown concerning all covenants and the like touching the premises made or acknowledged by Cavendishe to Edward VI or the Queen. In consideration of the manor and site of Rosedale priory and the demesne lands of the said priory, co. York, bargained and sold by the earl to the Crown.   By Q.

1399.)   3 *Nov.* 1576.   Lease for 21 years to Henry Awdley of the   [*m.* 20] manor of Wordelham *alias* Estwordelham and Westwordelham, co. Southampton; with reservations of the oats called 'rente otes' in Hedley, Greatham, Benstede and Kingesley belonging to the said manor and the 'rente hennes' in Bensted and Kingesley also belonging thereto; from the death, forfeiture or surrender of William, marquess of Winchester, councillor, and John Pawlett, lord Seynt John, to whom the manor was granted *inter alia* by patent, 29 Jan., 3 Eliz., for life in survivorship; yearly rent £31 2s. 11d. For a fine of £124 11s. 8d. paid at the Exchequer.   By Q.

1400.)   10 *Aug.* 1576.   *Gorhambury.*   Lease for 21 years to Thomas Marshe, clerk to the Council in the court of Star Chamber, of the manor of Stanmer Magna, the advowson of the rectory of Stanmer Magna, all appurtenances of the said manor in Stanmer Magna or elsewhere, co. Middlesex, and all   [*m.* 21] other lands in Stanmer Magna and Harrowe on the Hill, co. Middlesex, once of Geoffrey Chamber or his wife; from the termination of a lease thereof by patent, 22 April, 5 Eliz., to lady Dorothy Blage at a yearly rent of £64 2s. 2d. for 21 years from the termination of a lease thereof by patent of the court of Augmentations, 22 April, 4 Edw. VI, to George Blage, knight, for 21 years from Michaelmas then last at a yearly rent of £68 2s. 2d. (reduced by decree of the court of Augmentations, 12 Feb., 7 Edw. VI, to £64 2s. 2d.); yearly rent £64 2s. 2d..; the lessee charged with the payment of a yearly rent of 20s. out of part of the premises to Anne Borough. For his service; and for a fine of £100 paid at the Exchequer.   By p.s.

1401.)   10 *Aug.* 1576.   *Gorhambury.*   Lease for 21 years to William Pynchebeck of the rectory of Chepingwicombe *alias* Chepingwickham and all appurtenances thereof in Chepingwicombe and elsewhere, co. Buckingham, once of the monastery of Godestowe, co. Oxford, and late in the tenure of William   [*m.* 22]

Grene; with reservations; from Michaelmas next; yearly rent £30, to wit, for the rectory £16 13*s*. 4*d*., for a rent once payable out of the rectory to two chanters called 'Charnell preistes' £8 and for a rent once payable out of the rectory to a priest called 'le Bower preist' £5 6*s*. 8*d*. In consideration of the surrender in Chancery of a patent, 24 March, 16 Eliz., leasing the same to Pinchebecke for 21 years from Michaelmas then last at the same rent.

By the commissioners by virtue of the Queen's warrant.

1402.)   8 *Aug.* 1576.   *Gorhambury.*   Lease for 31 years to Richard Oseley, a clerk of the privy seal, of the manor of Courtenhall, co. Northampton, once of the monastery of Lenton, co. Nottingham, and the rents and reversions of lands in Courtenhall, parcels of the said manor, leased severally by three patents of the Exchequer, 19 Feb., 11 Eliz., for 21 years from Michaelmas then last (*a*) to Margaret Clarke, widow, at a yearly rent of 43*s*. 4*d*. (on surrender of her interest in the same, now or late in the tenure of Robert Clarke), (*b*) (*named*) to John Clarke at a yearly rent   [*m*. 23]
of 45*s*. 6*d*. (on surrender of his interest in the same) and (*c*) to William Clerke at a yearly rent of 45*s*. 6*d*. (on surrender of his interest in the same); with reservations, including the advowson of Courtenhall church; from the termination of a lease by patent of the court of Augmentations, 19 March, 5 Edw. VI, to Reginald Conyers of the said manor and all lands of the Crown in Courtnall at a yearly rent of £30 for 21 years from the termination of a lease thereof by conventual indenture, 6 Jan., 20 Hen. VIII, to Edmund Max for 30 years from Martinmas then next;   [*m*. 24]
yearly rent £30.

Also grant for the same term of the office of collector of the rents of all portions and pensions in the county of Northampton late of the monastery of Lenton, with a yearly fee of 40*s*., payable out of the rents and revenues of the said portions and pensions; the grantee to render account before the auditor appointed and to pay the moneys arising to the receiver general of the county according to the form of stat. 7 Edw. VI.

For Oseley's service; also in consideration of his surrender in Chancery of his interest under a patent, 16 March, 13 Eliz., leasing to him the said manor for 31 years from the termination of Conyers's lease at the same rent; and in consideration of the payment of £60 at the Exchequer for the said surrendered lease.   By p.s.

1403.)   27 *July* 1576.   *Gorhambury.*   Lease for life to William Wynter, with remainder to Mary Wynter, his wife, and William Wynter, their son, for life in survivorship, of the site of the manor of Frodington *alias* Fraudinton, co. Southampton, lands (*named*) and all appurtenances of the said site, parcels of the said manor and late of St. Nicholas's hospital in Portesmouthe; with reservations, including a wind mill (*named*); from the present date; yearly rent £18 9*s*. and heriot the best beast. In consideration of the surrender by William the father, now farmer   [*m*. 25]
of the premises, of a patent, 11 March, 10 Eliz., leasing the same to Richard Bynstede for 21 years from Michaelmas then last at the same rent; and for a fitting sum paid at the Exchequer by way of fine.   By p.s.

1404.)   14 *Sept.* 1576.   *Gorhambury.*   Lease for 30 years to Edward Weldon, a gentleman at arms, and William Sparke of (1) lands in Wandlesworth, co. Surrey, (2) the rectory of Ancastre, co. Lincoln, once of the   [*m*. 26]
monastery of Malton, (3) lands (*tenants named*) in Moulton, co. Northampton, parcel of the manor of Moulton and of 'Warwickes and Spencers landes', (4) the site and demesne lands of the manor of Yartcombe, co. Devon, once of the monastery of Syon, co. Middlesex, and (5) a capital messuage or grange in Grimston, co. York, late of St. Clement's priory near York; with reservations; (1) from Michaelmas 1587, having been leased by patent of the

Exchequer, 10 July, 3 & 5 Ph. & Mary, to Thomas Bradshawe, then occupier, for 30 years from Michaelmas then next at a yearly rent of £4 6s. 8d. (*detailed*); (2) from Lady Day 1589, having been leased by patent of the Exchequer, 30 May, 10 Eliz, to Nicholas Gedney, being then late in the tenure of Thomas Wakefelde, for 21 years from Lady Day then last at a yearly rent of 55s.; (3) from Michaelmas 1589, having been leased by patent, 4 Dec., 11 Eliz., to Richard Catesbye for 21 years from Michaelmas then last at a yearly rent of 38s. 4d.; (4) from Lady Day 1583, having been leased by patent, 17 June, 4 Eliz., *inter alia* to John Haydon; (5) from Lady Day 1588, having been leased by patent, 8 July, 4 & 5 Ph. & Mary, to Thomas Bustarde for 30 years from Lady Day then last at a yearly rent of £5 6s. 8d.; yearly rents (1) £4 6s. 8d., (2) 55s., (3) 38s. 4d., (4) 56s. and (5) £5 6s. 8d.; the lessees to pay yearly out of (2) 25s. to the archdeacon of Lincoln   [*m.* 27]
for proxies and synodals. For Weldon's service.   By p.s.

1405.)   3 *Sept.* 1576.   *Gorhambury.*   Lease for 21 years to John Marshall the elder of the rectory of Wolborough, co. Devon, once of the monastery of Torre, co. Devon; with reservations; from Lady Day last; yearly rent £11 9d.; the lessee to pay yearly £6 13s. 4d. to the vicar of Wolborough or the chaplain there. In consideration of the surrender by Marshall of a patent, 9 Jan., 3 Eliz., to Robert Gyles for 21 years from Michaelmas then last at the same rent; and for a fine of £22 18d. paid at the Exchequer.
                          By the commissioners by virtue of the Queen's warrant.

1406.)   27 *July* 1576.   *Gorhambury.*   Lease for 21 years to Thomas Fanshawe, remembrancer of the Exchequer, of (1) the rectory of Dronsfeilde *alias* Dronefeilde, co. Derby, the grange of Dronsfeilde, the profits of the Easter roll, a tithe barn and all hereditaments in Dronsfeilde, Ounston, Hownesfeilde *alias* Holmesfeilde, Woodhowse, Totley, Dore, Hundale, Somerley, Apperknolle, Poudye *alias* Powvey or elsewhere in the parish of Dronsfeilde belonging to the said rectory and (2) the tithes of corn and all other tithes in Coldaston *alias* Coleaston, Hallowmershe, Stubley and Birchett and a croft in Birchett, parcels of the said rectory, all once of the monastery of   [*m.* 28]
Beauchiff, co. Derby; with reservations; from Lady Day last; yearly rents (1) £20 11s. 2d. and (2) £7 16s.; the lessee to pay yearly £10 to the vicar or curate of Dronsfeilde for stipend, 13s. 4d. to the archdeacon of Derby for pension and 13s. 4d. to the bishop of Coventry and Lichfield. In consideration of the surrender in Chancery by the said Thomas of (*a*) a patent, 10 July, 8 Eliz., leasing (1) to Henry Fanshawe for 21 years from Lady Day last at the same rent and (*b*) a patent of the court of Augmentations, 19 April, 7 Edw. VI, leasing (2) to James Canciller, the King's servant, *inter alia* at the same rent for 21 years from the termination of a lease thereof by indenture of the said court, 21 Aug., 38 Hen. VIII, to John Parker for 21 years from Lady Day then last; and for a fine of £28 7s. 2d. paid at the Exchequer.   By p.s.

1407.)   30 *July* 1576.   *Gorhambury.*   Lease for 21 years to John Hall of   [*m.* 29]
Royston of a house, free chapel and hospital in Royston, co. Hertford, and lands (*tenants named*) in Royston, in Barley, co. Hertford, in Tharesfeilde, co. Hertford, and in Knesworthe and Melborne, co. Cambridge, and Chesell, co. Essex, all (*rents detailed*) once of the late free chapel or hospital of SS. John and James in Royston; with reservations; from Lady Day last; yearly rent £6 14s. 6d.; the lessee to pay yearly to the lord of the manor of Royston three grains of incense out of the house of the hospital and rents of 5s. and 6d. out of the lands (*described*) in Royston. In consideration of the surrender by Edward Chester of a patent, 22 Jan., 8 Eliz., leasing the premises to him for 21 years from Michaelmas then last at the same rent.   By the commissioners by virtue of the Queen's warrant.

1408.)   30 *July* 1576.   *Gorhambury*.   Lease for 21 years to Edmund Ashton of the rectory of Frampton, co. Lincoln, and the mansion house belonging thereto, once of the late college of Durham; with reservations;   [*m*. 30]
from Michaelmas next; yearly rent £27 13*s*. 4*d*.; the lessee to pay a yearly pension of 13*s*. 4*d*. to the dean and chapter of Lincoln cathedral, and to discharge the Crown from all other payments due to the vicar of Frampton or others. In consideration of the surrender by Asheton of a patent, 8 July, 4 Eliz., leasing the premises to him for 21 years from Lady Day then last at the same rent; and for a fine of £55 6*s*. 8*d*. paid at the Exchequer.   By p.s.

1409.)   20 *July* 1576.   Lease for 21 years to John Vaughan of the following (of the yearly rents specified and now or late in the tenure of the persons named) in the town of Westminster, late exchanged with Francis Inglefelde, knight,—a messuage with a garden and two stables adjoining (John Vaughan, £9), a small tenement (George Holland, 6*s*. 8*d*.), a small tenement (John Androwes, 6*s*. 8*d*.), a small tenement (Thomas Dognell, 6*s*. 8*d*.), a tenement (John Berde, 6*s*. 8*d*.), a tenement (John Evans, 6*s*. 8*d*.), a tenement (Henry Johnson, 13*s*. 4*d*.) and a tenement (Margaret Trayforde, 10*s*.); from Lady Day last; yearly rent £11 16*s*. 8*d*.   By the commissioners by virtue of the Queen's warrant.

1410.)   17 *July* 1576.   Grant in fee simple to Thomas Aldersey, citizen   [*m*. 31] and 'haberdasher' of London, of —the reversion and rent of the tithes of corn and hay, the small tithes (called 'the white tiethes'), the tithes of wool and lambs, the oblations and profits of the four yearly feast days called 'the fower offringe dayes' (or 'the fower festivall dayes'), the mortuaries and profits of mortuaries and the tithes, profits and moneys arising yearly from the Easter book called 'the Lentroll' at the seasons of Lent and Easter in Bumbery *alias* Bunbury, Alpeckeham, Beston, Tarton, Calveley, Wardell, Taleston, Haughton, Spurstall, Rideley, Peckserton *alias* Peckforton and Boresley, co. Chester, late of the late college and rectory of Bunbery and leased by patent, 10 July, 3 Eliz., to John Walgrave for 21 years from Michaelmas 1569 or the termination of the interest of Richard Collye at a yearly rent of £27 18*s*.; and the rectory of Bunbury, once of the late college of Bunbery, and all its appurtenances aforesaid. To hold in socage as of the manor of   [*m*. 32] Estgrenewiche, co. Kent. Issues from Lady Day last. The grantee to find a priest or curate and vicar in Bumberye church and an assistant priest therein; also to pay yearly 10*s*. to the bishop of Chester, 16*s*. 8*d*. to the archdeacon of Chester for synodals and proxies, 3*s*. 4*d*. to the same archdeacon for a rent and 4*s*. to the dean and chapter of Lichfield for a pension.

    Grant also of power to disappropriate the said rectory and make presentations thereto; clerks presented shall be discharged against the Crown of all payments for first fruits and tenths and all other charges. Power also to amortise and convey in mortmain for the maintenance of a schoolmaster, who shall teach free a grammar school in Bumbury, any parcel of the premises up to the yearly value of £20; also to amortise and convey in mortmain the advowson of the rectory when it has been disappropriated. For £697 10*s*. paid at the Exchequer.   By p.s.

1411.)   14 *July* 1576.   Foundation of the free grammar school of Queen Elizabeth in Faversham, co. Kent; with a master. The mayor, jurats and commonalty of the town of Faversham to be governors of the school;   [*m*. 33] incorporation of the governors. Power for the warden of All Souls college, Oxford, or when that office is void or in his absence the subwarden of the college, and six seniors of the college to appoint and remove the master; and for the same warden or subwarden and seniors with the mayor, jurats and commonalty to make ordinances for the school; whenever the office of master shall be void and another master shall not within two months be appointed or named to the mayor, jurats and commonalty, the archbishop of Canterbury may appoint to the office.

Also—in consideration that the mayor, jurats and commonalty, governors of the school, will pay to the master £20 yearly—grant to them of—(1) lands (*named with tenants' names*) in Faversham, once of the monastery of Faversham, and the reversion and rent of the same, which were leased by patent, 30 Oct., 4 Eliz., to Robert Fagg and Edward Fagg for 21 years from Lady Day then last at a yearly rent of £6 6s. 11¾d..;   [*m.* 34]
(2) a third part of a manor or tenement called Ewell and of lands (*named*) in Faversham and Goodwynston by Faversham, once of the said monastery, which third part was held by the said Robert Fagg at the time of his death at a yearly rent to the Crown of £5 14s. 8¾d. and is now held by his executors or assigns at the said rent; and (3) lands in Leysdowne in the isle of Shepey and in Hearonhill (*named with tenant's name*), co. Kent, once of the said monastery and after the dissolution thereof concealed. To hold as of the manor of Estgrenewyche, co. Kent, in socage. Issues of (1) and (2) from Lady Day last and (3) from the time when they should have come to the Crown's hands. Power to sue in the Crown's name the occupiers of (3) as the Crown could have done for the levying of arrears of rent. The patent to be void in respect of the lands in (3) if they were not concealed.

Also licence for the governors to acquire, for the better maintenance of the school, lands to the yearly value of £20 not held of the Crown immediately in chief or otherwise by knight service.   [*m.* 35]

At the suit of the inhabitants of Faversham: it appears by evidences shown to Queen's counsel that—John Cole, clerk, on 10 Dec., 18 Hen. VIII, with the King's licence conveyed lands (*named with tenants' names*) in Leysdowne, Hearonhill, Faversham and Gooddenston by Faversham, then appraised at a yearly value of £14, to John, abbot, and the convent of the monastery aforesaid for the maintenance of a grammar school there; by indenture tripartite, 10 Dec., 18 Hen. VIII, between the abbot and convent, Cole and the warden and fellows of All Souls college, the abbot and convent granted *inter alia* that the warden and fellows should appoint the master of the school and the abbot and convent should give the master wages of £10 a year and living and vesture, to wit, a gown, a chamber and three cart loads of fuel (in default whereof the warden and fellows could distrain at the rate of £5 for any default made in any month on the monastery's possessions); the school was maintained thenceforth until the dissolution of the monastery, but not thereafter; and divers parcels of the said lands are now or ought to be in the Crown's hands.   By Q.

1412.)   17 *July* 1576.   Grant to Christopher Hatton, captain of the guard, and his heirs, lords of the castle, lordship and manor of Corff in the   [*m.* 36]
isle of Purbeck, co. Dorset, that they may have within the said castle, lordship and manor, within the borough of Corff and within the said isle and the liberty thereof all such lawful customs, privileges and jurisdictions as any constable or warden of the said castle has heretofore had by reason of any grant of the Queen or her predecessors or any other lawful custom or title; also that the said isle and the precinct thereof shall have the same boundaries as heretofore from time immemorial or at any time before the present date, and that the grantee, his bailiffs and other ministers and the tenants and residents within the isle may perambulate and mark the same as heretofore at their pleasure. Also that the said castle, lordship and manor and the isle may be exempt from the jurisdiction of the admiral of England; and that Hatton and his heirs holding the said castle and lordship may be admirals within the castle, lordship, manor and isle and the liberties thereof, and exercise before them, their bailiffs or deputies the jurisdiction appertaining to the office of admiralty for all causes arising there. Also that Hatton, his heirs and assigns, lords of the said castle, lordship and manor, may be quit throughout the Queen's power from all tolls and other imposts for all things brought within the isle for the provision and defence of the said castle; and grant

to Hatton for life of the wardenship and governorship   [m. 37]
of the castle or fortress of Bronkehesey, co. Dorset. Also that Hatton or his heirs or their
deputies may have power to take musters of the inhabitants within the borough and isle
aforesaid; no commissioners of musters shall enter the isle to execute their office; and no
armour or weapons of war shall be taken outside the isle, but all shall remain there solely for
the defence of the isle.

Also—in consideration of the service which the mayor and barons and other inhabitants
of the borough of Corff have heretofore done in defence of the castle and isle aforesaid, and
which at present by tenure of their lands they are bound to do at their own costs whenever
necessary—grant to the said mayor and barons and inhabitants that they may have all such
lawful customs, privileges and jurisdictions as they have heretofore lawfully had by any
name or incorporation whatsoever by reason of any grant of the Queen or her predecessors
or any other lawful custom or title; and that the mayor and barons of Corff and the
inhabitants of the parish of Corff may have all such liberties and exemptions as the
inhabitants in any of the Cinque Ports lawfully have. Also protection for the said inhabitants
of the borough and the isle of Purbeck and grant that of their victuals or goods within the
isle nothing shall be taken outside the isle to the use of the Crown or others; and no bailiff,
minister or purveyor of victuals of the Queen's household or other minister of the Crown
shall intermeddle there to take anything. Also grant to the same mayor, barons and
inhabitants of the isle and the precinct thereof that they be not put on assizes, juries and the
like before any justices or other ministers of the Crown by reason of any foreign lands,
trespasses or other matters, save only on assizes, juries and the like touching lands in the isle
or trespasses and other matters arising in the isle, if they have not lands or rents outside the
isle for which they ought rightly to be put thereon.

At the suit of Hatton and the said mayor and barons and inhabitants; by information of
divers trustworthy persons; and for Hatton's service. Hatton lately had unto him and his
heirs *inter alia* by the Queen's grant the castle of Corff and the lordship or manor of Corff,
which castle is an ancient one and conveniently sited for the defence of the isle against
foreign enemies; and the warden or constable of the castle, the mayor and barons of the
borough and the inhabitants of the isle have from time immemorial severally had divers
rights and exemptions; and, because the charters and grants of the said liberties have for
many years past not been allowed and confirmed by the Queen or her predecessors, the
constable, the mayor and barons and the inhabitants have often been interrupted in the
enjoyment of the same.   By p.s.

1413.)   17 *July* 1576.   Lease for life to Thomas Docton, with remainder to Alice Docton,
his wife, and Nicholas Docton, their son, for life in survivorship, of the tithes of corn and all
tithes and oblations   [m. 38]
whatsoever belonging to the parish church and the rectory of Woldesworthye and all other
tithes, a house called 'the Preistes Howse' and all other hereditaments belonging thereto in
Woldesworthye, co. Devon, once of the monastery of Hartland, co. Devon; with reservations; from Lady Day last; yearly rent £12 18s. 7d.; the lessees to pay yearly 8s. 1d. for
synodals and proxies to the archdeacon of Salisbury, 6s. 8d. for bread, wine and wax and £6
6s. 8d. for stipend to a chaplain serving there. In consideration of the surrender by the said
Thomas of a lease by Thomas Pope, abbot, and the convent of the said monastery by
indenture, 31 Jan., 38 Hen. VIII, to Thomas Cole of the premises, once in the tenure of
Richard Preiste, for 50 years from Candlemas then next at a yearly rent of £20; and for a fine
of £25 17s. 2d. paid at the Exchequer.
                    By the commissioners by virtue of the Queen's warrant.

1414.)   20 *July* 1576.   *Gorhambury*.   Lease for 21 years to Stephen Marche of the site of the

manor or the farm of Thorney in the isle of Wight, co. Southampton, and all lands, coney warrens and other hereditaments belonging thereto; with reservations; from Lady Day last; yearly rent £8 1s. 8d. In consideration of the surrender in Chancery by Marche of a patent, 12 July,   [*m.* 39]
3 & 5 Ph. & Mary, leasing to Robert Raymond, now deceased, the site or farm of the said manor and the rest of the premises for 30 years from Lady Day then last at the same rent; and for a fine of £16 3s. 4d. paid at the Exchequer.

By the commissioners by virtue of the Queen's warrant.

1415.)   20 *July* 1576.   *Gorhambury.*   Lease for 21 years to Matthew Cooke of the rectory of Tymberland, co. Lincoln, all lands, turbary and commons within 'le fennes' there belonging to the rectory, the tithes of wool and lambs, corn and hay in the parish and hamlets of Tymberland and two parts of 'le mortuaries' arising there (against one part due to the vicar of Tymberland by order of a statute), all late of the monastery of Thurgarton, co. Lincoln; with reservations; from Easter 1587, having been leased by conventual indenture, 2 Jan., 26 Hen. VIII, to George Dakyn *inter alia* for 41 years from the feast of SS. Philip and James 1546 at a yearly rent of £13 6s. 8d.; same rent. For a fine of £53 6s. 8d. paid at the Exchequer.   By p.s.

1416.)   20 *July* 1576.   *Gorhambury.*   Lease for 21 years to Thomas Wilson   [*m.* 40]
of a capital messuage called 'le Brewhouse' and all tenements, wharfs and other heredita- ments in the parish of St Martin in the Fields by Charingcrosse, co. Middlesex, now or late in the several tenures of Alice Stockwood, Anthony Lowe, Anthony Mytton (*alias* Mylton) and Elizabeth his wife and Robert Penythorne, Thomas Condicote, Richard Hamden and William Stephenson, late had of Henry Polstede by exchange and once of the monastery of St. John of Jerusalem in England; from Lady Day 1590, having been leased by patent, 7 May, 11 Eliz., to James Gerrarde for 21 years from Lady Day then last at a yearly rent of £37 17s. 4d.; same rent. In consideration of the heavy charges of Wilson, now tenant, about the repair of the premises; and for a fine of £100 paid at the Exchequer.   By p.s.

1417.)   23 *July* 1576.   *Gorhambury.*   Lease for 21 years to John Griffith of the town of Cayrus *alias* Kayrus, co. Flint, a mill in Cayrus, all rents, perquisites of court, tolls, markets and fairs in the said town and all other casual profits belonging thereto, now or late in the tenure of George Salisburye, formerly of the late earl of Chester; with reservations; from Lady Day last; yearly rent £7 2s. 4d. and for escheat lands there 4s. 2d. beyond. For a fine of £5 6s. paid at the Exchequer.   By the commissioners by virtue of the Queen's warrant.

1418.)   7 *Sept.* 1576.   *Gorhambury.*   Lease for 21 years to Roger Keyrchevor of the courts in the manor of Burwell, co. Cambridge, late had by exchange from Edward Northe, knight, and all profits and hereditaments arising by reason thereof; goods of felons, fugitives and outlaws in the manor reserved; from Lady Day last; yearly rent £4 7s. 10d. For a fine of £8 15s. 8d. paid at the Exchequer.   By the commissioners by virtue of the Queen's warrant.

(*The dorse of this roll is blank.*)

19 ELIZABETH I
17 November 1576–16 November 1577
PART I
C. 66/1151

1419.)   27 *June* 1577.   Lease for 21 years to John Dente of lands   [*m.* 1]
(*named with former tenants' names*), now in his tenure, in Percebrigge in the bishopric of
Durham, parcel of the manor of Gayneford and of the lordship of Barnard Castell; with
reservations; from Lady Day last; yearly rent £6 3s. 1d.; the lessee to pay suit of court, to
serve by himself or sufficient men with horse and arms when summoned by the warden of
the East marches, to occupy the premises by himself or sufficient men and cultivate the same,
and to fence them as ordered by the steward of the Queen's courts there. In consideration of
the surrender by Dente of the interest in certain of the premises of Henry Brakenburye, to
whom they were leased by patent, 14 July, 7 Eliz., *inter alia* for 21 years from Lady Day then
last at a yearly rent of £5; and for a fine of £12 6s. 2d. paid at the Exchequer.

By warrant of the commissioners.

1420.)   28 *June* 1577.   Lease for 21 years to John Mason of (1) all lands in Appleton in le
Streate, co. York, parcel of the lordship of Sherifhoton, co. York, (2) lands (*tenant named*) in
Appleton aforesaid, parcel of   [*m.* 2]
a chantry in the parish church there, and (3) lands (*named with tenant's name*) in Appleton
aforesaid, parcel of the manor of Malton, co. York, and once of the monastery of Malton;
with reservations; from Lady Day last; yearly rents (1) £11 5s. 5½d., (2) 33s. 4d. and (3) 30s.;
the lease to be void, if the lessee shall not before Michaelmas next make leases to the tenants
of the several parcels of the premises in their tenures for his whole term and at the rents
heretofore payable, so long as they pay him among themselves his costs about obtaining this
patent. In consideration of the surrender by Mason of a patent, 28 Nov., 7 Eliz., leasing the
premises to Anthony Thorpe for 21 years from Michaelmas then last at the same rents,
together with an indenture, 20 Aug., 10 Eliz., whereby Thorpe assigned his interest to
Mason; and for a fine of £28 17s. 7d. paid at the Exchequer.   By p.s.

1421.)   25 *June* 1577.   Licence for 20 years for Hector Nunez, doctor of physic, born a
subject of the King of Portugal, or his factors or deputies appointed in writing, to buy in
Spain and Navarre or other dominions of the King of Spain and import Spanish wrought
and unwrought wool fit for the making of hats or felts; from the present date; provided that
he shall receive   [*m.* 3]
upon sale of the same for the rove (that is to say 25lb. weight) of the growth of Mancha,
which is the finer sort, not above 33s. 4d. and for the coarser sort called Biskey wool not
above 30s. the rove; provided also that he shall pay for the customs and subsidies of every
hundred weight imported 4s. 2d., which is double the duty which he and other merchants
strangers commonly before the year 11 Eliz. paid; the treasurer and barons of the Exchequer
shall at the licensee's request direct writs close or patent to customers, collectors and
controllers in the city and port of London or other places in England commanding them not
to receive any payment, make any entry in their books or make any agreement for duties for

any the wools aforesaid except in the name and by the consent of the licensee; no other persons to attempt the importation of any of the said Spanish wools or do anything to the prejudice of the licensee, on pain of forfeiture of the wool, whereof one moiety shall go to the Crown and the other to Christ's hospital in London for the relief of the poor children and infants there; customers,   [m. 4]
searchers and other officers in any port of England and Wales shall upon request made by the licensee search any ship and take note of all the wools before mentioned as shall there be found, giving the licensee notice thereof without delay, and, if they refuse or neglect to do so, the licensee may lawfully make search. Nunez in the time of Queen Mary devised and has hitherto used the trade of bringing in the wools aforesaid which serve only for the making of felts, by reason whereof there has been greater plenty of felts and of finer sort and better fashion made in England than in any other country; which has been very commodious for the setting on work of many of the Queen's subjects and the profit of her subjects and country; he has been at great charges about the same and has as yet (it is reported) received small profit thereby, but is willing to continue the trade and pay the duty above mentioned.
English.   By Q.

1422.)   27 *June* 1577.   Lease for 21 years to Edward Stanhope of (1) the site of the manor of Thorneton by Humber called Westhall, lands etc. (*named*) in Thorneton and Wutton, co. Lincoln, tithes of corn in   [m. 5]
Thorneton and lands (*named*) in Gouxhill and Barrowe, co. Lincoln, once of the monastery or college of Thorneton upon Humber, and (2) a moiety of the rectory of Gouxhill, co. Lincoln, late of John Bellowe; with reservations; from Michaelmas next; yearly rents (1) £16 4s. 8d. and (2) £24 13s. 4d.; the lessee to pay yearly out of (2) 66s. 8d. for the stipend of the vicar of Gouxhill. In consideration of the surrender by Stanhope by deed, [—] June, 19 Eliz., enrolled in Chancery, of (a) an indenture, 4 Feb., 24 Hen. VIII, whereby John Moore, abbot, and the convent of the monastery of Thorneton leased (1) to Thomas Donne of Bishopburton, co. York, as formerly held by Thomas Kirby, for 60 years from the Invention of Holy Cross then next at a yearly rent of 40 quarters of wheat, 80 quarters of barley, 1 quarter of beans or pease, 10 capons and one boar (to be delivered at times and places *specified*), with cartage at haymaking time for 12 days, (b) an indenture, 23 March, 5 Edw. VI, whereby Bellowe, by the name of John Bellowe of Newstede upon Ankonne, co. Lincoln, leased (2) to Thomas Wentworthe, then of Gouxhill, son of John Wentworthe, knight, (with reservations including rents late belonging to the office of bursar of the monastery of Bridlington) at a yearly rent of £28 for 21 years from the termination of a lease by patent of the court of Augmentations, 18 July, 33 Hen. VIII, to the said John Wentworthe of the entire rectory of Gousle, late of the monastery of Bridlington, for 21 years at a yearly rent of £14 13s. 4d. and 20s. beyond of increase (the fee simple of which rectory was acquired from Edward VI by Bellowe and John Broxholme, and Bellowe's moiety now belongs to the Crown) and (c) a lease by the dean and chapter of the cathedral [*sic*]   [m. 6]
church of Thorneton by indenture, 6 July, 35 Hen. VIII, to Robert Tirwhit of the rents in kind aforesaid, reserved under the lease to Donne, for 40 years from Michaelmas 1545 at a yearly rent of £16 4s. 8d.   By p.s.

1423.)   28 *June* 1577.   Lease for 21 years, if Thomas Bisshoppe shall so long live, to Margaret Bisshoppe of (1) the manor of Pocklington, co. York, and (2) the toll of the market there, and all other appurtenances of the said manor, late of the said Thomas, attainted; with reservations, including wards, marriages and advowsons; from Lady Day last; yearly rents (1) £23 6s. 8d. and (2), from the termination of a lease thereof to Hugh Longworthe for seven years unexpired, £6 13s. 4d.; the lessee on payment of the rent for (1) shall have allowance yearly of £13 6s. 8d. for an annuity which she shall pay to Cecily Bisshoppe, wife of the said Thomas, during the Queen's pleasure; the lessee to make two cuttings only of the woods in the manor and at fitting seasons, to enclose 'lez springes' for   [m. 7] seven years after cutting and to leave sufficient 'lez staddelles' in every acre according to statute. In consideration of the surrender by Margaret of a lease by the said Thomas by indenture, 1 May, 4 & 5 Ph. & Mary, to William, lord Pagett of Beawdesert, K.G., then keeper of the privy seal, of the said manor, then late of Henry, late earl of Northumberland, for 21 years from that date at a yearly rent of £44 2s. 2d.; and for a fine of £10 paid at the Exchequer.   By p.s.

1424.)   20 *June* 1577.   Grant in fee simple to Henry Knyvet, knight, the Queen's servant, of (1) the manor of Great Houghton, co. York, late of Edward Dacre, attainted of treason, (2) all lands in Moreton upon Swale and Potterton in Barwicke, co. York, late of the said Dacre, and (3) yearly rents of 7s. 2d. and service payable by free tenants and yearly rents of 3s. 8d. and service payable by customary tenants in Kirke Oswald, late of Dacre, and all lands in Kirkeoswald, Netherdenton, Hedsnewke, Castle Carrocke *alias* Casel Carrocke, Litlecrokeby and Lasenbye, co. Cumberland, late of Dacre, with all appurtenances thereof in Houghton and Billingley, co. York, and the other places named or elsewhere; to hold (1) by service of the fortieth part of a knight's fee and (2) and (3) as of the manor of Estgrenewiche, co. Kent, in socage; issues from Michaelmas, 12 Eliz. For his service; [m. 8] and for £240 4s. 4½d. paid at the Exchequer.   By p.s.

1425.)   22 *June* 1577.   Lease for 21 years to William Thwaytes of the tithes of hay, wool and lambs and other tithes great and small and the oblations and other profits in Sylkeston, Barnesley and Calthorne, co. York, and the tallages and tolls of two fairs called 'Saynte Paule feyre' and 'Saynte Ellyn feyre' at Barnesley, once of the monastery of Pontefract, co. York; with reservations of the tithes of corn of Sylkeston, Barnesley and Calthorne, the tithes of corn, hay, wool, lambs, calves, oblations, obventions and other small tithes in Dodworthe in Silkeston and the tithes of wool, lambs, calves, oblations and obventions and all other small tithes in Staynburgh in Silkeston; from Lady Day last; yearly rent £8 12s.; the lessee to pay a yearly pension of £13 6s. 8d. to the vicar of Silkestone, to appoint curates in the churches of Barnesley and Cathorne and provide for them yearly stipends of £5 and £4 13s. 4d.   [m. 9] respectively, to pay yearly 11s. for proxies and 7s. 6d. for synodals, and to bear all other charges payable by the farmer of the premises. In consideration of the surrender by the said William of a patent, 5 May, 17 Eliz., leasing the premises *inter alia* to Robert Thwyates, his father, for 21 years from Lady Day then last at a yearly rent for the premises and other hereditaments of £12 12s.; and for a fine of £5 paid at the Exchequer.

         By warrant of the commissioner.

1426.)   22 *June* 1577.   Lease for 21 years to James Middleton of lands in Middleton *alias* Middleton on Leven, co. York, (1) now or late in the tenure of James Middleton, assign of Thomas Middleton, and (2) now or late in the tenure of the said James, late of Leonard Dacres, attainted of treason; with reservations; from Lady Day last; yearly rents (1) £6 14s. 9d. and (2) 13s. 4d.; the lease to be void if the lessee shall expel Edmund Ingledays from any parcel of the premises in his possession within the past 12 months and shall not before Michaelmas next make him sufficient leases thereof by deed at the accustomed rent and for the period of the present lease without any fine or gersum besides that paid for the present lease as below, or if he shall expel any other tenants, so long as they pay him among themselves the fines, gersums and rents accustomed. For a fine of £14 16s. 2d. paid at the Exchequer by Engledaye.   By warrant of the commissioners.

1427.)   22 *June* 1577.   Licence for Nicholas Bacon, knight, keeper of the great seal, councillor, William, lord Burghley, K.G., treasurer, councillor, Henry, earl of Huntingdon, Walter Mildmaye, knight, chancellor of the Exchequer, Ralph Sadler, knight, chancellor of the duchy of Lancaster, Alexander Nowell, dean of St. Paul's cathedral, London, Thomas Bromley, solicitor general, William Fleetewood, recorder of London, Adrian Stokes, Henry Knollys the elder, John Harrington, Edward Elrington, John Hastinges, George Carleton, Robert Creswell, Richard Hurleston and Thomas Norton to alienate the manors of Bylande and Oswaldekirke, co. York, and all the manors and lands late of William Pikeringe, knight, deceased, in the   [*m.* 10]
county of York and the city of London, except the manor of Olde Bylande, co. York, to Hester now wife of Edward Wotton, knight, in tail, with remainder of the manor of Bylande to the chancellor, masters and scholars of Cambridge University, and of the manor of Oswaldekirke and the rest of the premises to the chancellor, masters and scholars of Oxford university; the statute of mortmain notwithstanding.   By Q.

1428.)   26 *June* 1577.   Lease for 21 years to Robert Wright of the capital messuage or site of the manor of Welwick, co. York, lands (*named*) belonging to the same site and the rectory of Welwicke, late of the preceptory [*sic*]   [*m.* 11]
of St. John of Beverley; with reservations; from Lady Day last; yearly rent £37; the lessee at the end of the term to leave sown (at the price of 5*s.* an acre) 40 ac. of wheat, 40 ac. of pease, drage and oats and 20 ac. of barley and all other arable land ploughed, to wit 'falowed', as shall seem good to four good men to be appointed by the Crown. On surrender by the said Robert of an indenture whereby Thomas Winter, clerk, provost of the collegiate church of St. John, Beverley, leased the manor of Welwick in Holdernes and the rest of the premises to John Wright for 52 years from the feast of St. Mark then next at the same rent. For a fine of £50 paid at the Exchequer by Robert within a sum of £80 paid in the name of Christopher Babham, as appears by a tally levied 21 May last.   By p.s.

1429.)   26 *June* 1577.   Lease for 21 years to John Heathe of a fishery of the waters of the town of Berwick, called 'the King's Water of Twede', co. Northumberland, parcel of possessions late assigned for the payment of the wages of the captain and soldiers of Berwick on Tweed; with reservation of the commodities of the same waters customarily belonging to Berwick castle and the officers there; from Lady Day last; yearly rent £52 15*s.* In consideration of the surrender by Heathe of a patent, 5 Nov., 10 Eliz., leasing the fishery to Edmund Eynns and George Beverley for 21 years from Michaelmas then last at the same rent; and for a fine of £66 13*s.* 4*d.* paid at the Exchequer.   By p.s.

1430.)   20 *June* 1577.   Lease for 21 years to William Wightman of lands (*named with tenants' names*) in Anastaslade, Tyreholme and the lordship   [*m.* 12]
of Haverford, co. Pembroke, all parcels of the rents of customary tenants in Lewelston, co. Pembroke, late of Jasper, late duke of Bedford; with reservations; from Lady Day last; yearly rent 106*s.* 8*d.*. In consideration of the surrender in Chancery by Wightman of a patent, 21 July, 5 Eliz., leasing the premises to Robert Pursell for 21 years from Lady Day then last at the same rent; and for a fine of £10 13*s.* 4*d.* paid at the Exchequer.
                                                      By warrant of the commissioners.

1431.)   28 *June* 1577.   Lease for 21 years to Robert Thriske, John Thriske and Nicholas Jeffrason of the demesne lands of the manor of Skydby, co. York, late acquired from Robert, earl of Leicester, by exchange; with reservations; from Lady Day last; yearly rent £9 7*s.* On surrender by the said Robert and John Thriske and Jeffrason of the interest of Simon

Musgrave, knight, to whom, by the name of Simon Musgrave, esquire, Robert, earl of
Leicester, by indenture,   [*m.* 13]
26 March, 9 Eliz., leased the premises *inter alia* for 21 years from that date at the same rent.
For a fine of £18 14*s*. paid at the Exchequer.   By warrant of the commissioners.

1432.)   20 *June* 1577.   Lease for 21 years to Alexander Kinge of (1) lands in Mobberley, co.
Chester, now or late in the tenure of John Leighe, knight, lands (*named*) in the lordship of
Middlewich, the ferry of Seacon and a fourth part and a sixth part of another fourth part of
the said ferry, the ferry of Donnyngton with Lanceton *alias* Langton Lidiate, and the fines
and other profits arising yearly in the hundred and forest of Macclesfielde, all in the county
of Chester and once of the earl of Chester, and (2) lands in Mobberley, now or late in the
tenure of John Leighe, knight, in the Queen's hands by the statute concerning chantries and
the like; with reservations; from Lady Day last; yearly rents (1) 72*s*. 4*d*. and (2) 39*s*. 8*d*. For a
fine of £14 9*s*. 4*d*. paid at the Exchequer.   By warrant of the commissioners.

1433.)   26 *June* 1577.   Lease for 21 years to John Heathe of fisheries in the water of
Tweade called Brode and Orett, parcel of the manor of   [*m.* 14]
Etall, co. Northumberland, late of Thomas, earl of Rutland, exchanged; with reservations;
from Lady Day last; yearly rent £10. In consideration of the surrender by Heathe of a patent,
14 Dec., 7 Eliz., leasing the same to Robert Carre for 21 years from Michaelmas then last at
the same rent; and for a fine of £20 paid at the Exchequer.
                                                By warrant of the commissioners.

1434.)   27 *June* 1577.   Pardon for Jenkin Llewellyn late of Glyncorucke, co. Glamorgan,
indicted for the manslaughter of Jenkin ap Morgan late of Llanyltid, co. Glamorgan, on 9
Sept., 18 Eliz., at Llannyltid (*details given*).   By Q.

1435.)   29 *June* 1577.   Pardon for Thomas Bellingham late of London, 'yoman', for all
offences committed before 1 May, 19 Eliz. He was indicted at the gaol delivery of Newgate
held in 'le Justice Hall' in 'le Olde Baylie' in the parish of St. Sepulchre without Newgate in
the suburbs of London on 14 Feb., 19 Eliz., before John Langley, mayor of the city, John
Southcot, a justice of the Queen's Bench, Roger Manwood, a justice of the Common Pleas,
Thomas Sackford, a master of the court of Requests, William Damsell, knight, Owen
Hopton, knight, and their fellows, justices of gaol delivery in the city, for that he burgled the
house of Thomas Barrowe, goldsmith, in the parish of St. John Zakerye in Aldrichgate
ward, London, on 10 Feb., 19 Eliz.,   [*m.* 15]
and stole plate (*described*) belonging to him.   By Q.

1436.)   20 *June* 1577.   Pardon for—Edward Skynner late of Colchester, co. Essex,
'laborer', indicted for that he broke and entered the close of Edward Colman at
Waldingfelde Magna, co. Suffolk, by night on 7 Jan., 19 Eliz., and stole cloth (*described*)
belonging to him; and Erasmus Folkard late of Dynyngton, co. Suffolk, 'tayler', indicted for
that he broke and entered the close of Thomas Watlynge at Brampfelde, co. Suffolk, by
night on 22 Jan., 19 Eliz., and stole a gelding belonging to him.   By Q.

1437.)   27 *June* 1577.   Grant to George Bolton of Great Woolford, co. Warwick, his heirs
and assigns of the gift of the canonry or prebend in Worcester cathedral which shall next be
void for one vacancy only; so that he may present thereto John Langworth, M.A., and no
other.   By p.s.

1438.)   4 *Nov.* 1577.   *Windsor Castle.*   Lease for 31 years to Thomas   [*m.* 16]

Manners, knight, of the late chapel of St. Mary and the Holy Angels called 'Sepulchres Chappell' by York cathedral, all possessions of the same chapel in Calverley, Bradsey, Collingham, Thorpe Arche, Hoton Panell and Oteley, co. York, and Sutton Lounde, Scrooby, Everton, Haiton, Clareborough, Eringley, Wellome, Bollome, Tilne and Retfourth, co. Nottingham, and the tithes of mills in Retfourth, late of the chapel; with reservations; from Michaelmas 1592, being the termination of a lease thereof by patent, 3 April, 4 Eliz., to George Webster for 31 years from Michaelmas then last at a yearly rent of £137 19s. 2½d.; same rent; the lessee to pay yearly to the poor in alms 46s. 8d. on Maundy Thursday in York, 26s. 8d. in Thorpe Arche, 26s. 8d. in Collingham, 40s. in Bradsey, 106s. 8d. in Oteley, £4 in Calverley, 26s. 8d. in Hoton Pannell, 53s. 4d. in Sutton, 66s. 8d. in Clarebrough, 26s. 8d. in Retfourth and 40s. in Everton, as accustomed. For a fine of £100 paid at the Exchequer; and for his service.   By Q.

1439.)   2 Nov. 1577.   Windsor Castle.   Lease to William Wightman, receiver general of South Wales, of (1) the grange of Gregerith, co. Cardigan, (2) the grange of Terenewith, co. Cardigan, (3) the grange of Rowlandevy, co. Cardigan, and (4) the tithes, oblations and other profits of the church of Llandisilio in the commote of Karwedros, co. Cardigan, all late of the monastery of Whitland, co. Carmarthen; with reservations; (1), (2)   [m. 17] and (3) for 60 years from Lady Day last; and (4) for 21 years from Lady Day last; yearly rents (1) £20 13s. 10½d., (2) £17 2s. 5½d., (3) £16 18s. 7d. and (4) 46s. 8d. In consideration of the surrender in Chancery by Wightman of a patent, 3 Aug., 5 Eliz., leasing (1), (2) and (3) to Gilbert Gerrard, attorney general, for 21 years from Lady Day then last at yearly rents of (1) £23 6½d., (2) £17 2s. 5½d. and (3) £18 5s. 3d.; and for a fine of £260 paid at the Exchequer.   By p.s.

1440.)   29 Oct. 1577.   Windsor Castle.   Grant to Ambrose Smythe, citizen and mercer of London, and Henry Smythe, his son, their heirs and assigns of—(1) the manor of Netherlymington, co. Gloucester, once of the monastery of Tewkesburie; (2) the manor of Lepington and all other lands in Lepington and elsewhere, co. York, late of cardinal Wolsey, leased by patent, 3 Dec., 8 Eliz., to Leonard Chamberleyn for 21 years at a yearly rent of £25 9s. 7d.; (3) lands (named with tenants' names), parcel of the grange of Whittington, co. Leicester, once of Henry, late duke of Suffolk, attainted; (4) the tithes of corn of the demesne lands of the manor of Hope and the tithes of corn and flax in Hope, Hampton and Wynnesley, co. Hereford, and all other   [m. 18] tithes there late leased to John Wall at a yearly rent of £5, late of the priory or cell of Leompster, co. Hereford; (5) lands (described with tenant's name) in Hereford, once of the monastery of Dore; (6) the tithes of corn (tenant named) in Colton (alias Calton), co. York, late of the monastery of Newbroughe, co. York; (7) the tithes of corn and hay in Overton, co. York, late leased to Elizabeth Herbert by patent and late of the monastery of St. Mary next the walls of York; (8) lands (named with tenants' names) in Riswarpe in the parish of Whitbye and in Whitbye, co. York, once of the monastery of Whitbye; (9) lands (named with tenant's name) in Horseley, co. Derby, once of the monastery of Darley; (10) a burgage (tenant named) in Taunton, co. Somerset, late of Henry, late duke of Suffolk, attainted of treason; (11) lands (named with tenants' names) in Hartland, co. Devon, once of the monastery of Hartland; (12) lands (named with tenants' names, some in East Eckworthie and Thornewiger) in Vielston or elsewhere, co. Devon, once of Edward, late earl of Devon; (13) the tithes of corn, hay, salt, flax, wool, hemp and lambs and all other tithes, oblations and the like in Walhampton, Sharprickes, Baddesley, Pylley, Bolder, Penyton and Lymington, co. Southampton, once of Christchurche Twyneham priory, co. Southampton; (14) lands (tenant named) in Langley Buriell, co. Wilts, late of the monastery of Bradenstoke; and (15) a tenement in Imshett alias Jambassett, co. Southampton, once of the monastery of Godstowe, co.   [m. 19]

Oxford. Bells and lead, except lead in gutters and windows, reserved. To hold (2) by service of the twentieth part of a knight's fee and the rest as of the manor of Eastgrenewiche, co. Kent, in socage, and by yearly rents of (1) £3 17s. 4d., (2) £25 9s. 7d., (3) 10s., (4) £5, (5) 5s., (6) 33s. 4d., (7) 40s., (8) 16s. (*detailed*), (9) 40s., (10) 13s. 4d., (11) £4 7s. 7d. (*detailed*), (12) 22s. 8d. (*detailed*), (13) 45s. 8d., (14) 4s. and (15) 4s. Issues from Lady Day last. The grantees to
[*m.* 20]
pay yearly a stipend of £8 13s. 4d. to the curate, chaplain or vicar of Holnest, in default of which payment the Crown may repossess (13) until it be paid.

In consideration of the surrender of the manor of Meriott, co. Somerset, and the reversion thereof late granted by the Queen to Jerome Bowes, knight, her servant, for 2,000 years; for the service of Bowes; and at his suit.   By p.s.

1441.)   28 *Oct.* 1577.   *Windsor Castle.*   Grant to the dean and chapter of Winchester cathedral of—the manor and manors of Bechinstoke and Botwell, co. Wilts, once of the monastery of St. Swithun, Winchester, co. Southampton, and all lands in Bechinstoke and Botwell or elsewhere, co. Wilts, late of Anne Fortescu, a kinswoman of Joan Ingaldesthropp; and the manor of Alton *alias* Alton Parva, co. Wilts, once of the monastery of Ambresbury.   [*m.* 21]
To hold in frankalmoign. Issues from 1 May, 33 Hen. VIII.

By patent, 1 May, 33 Hen. VIII, divers manors and hereditaments therein specified were granted to the dean and chapter, and the King intended thereby to assure to them the premises in Bechinstoke and Botwell, as appears by the particular thereof signed by Richard Riche, knight, then chancellor of the court of Augmentations, and other officers of the same court, and also the premises in Alton; all which the dean and chapter have enjoyed from the making of the said patent, but without lawful assurance, because they were omitted through the writer's negligence from the warrant signed by the King.   By p.s.

1442.)   25 *Oct.* 1577.   *Windsor Castle.*   Grant for life to William Whitakers, M.A., of the sixth canonry or prebend in Norwich cathedral, void by the resignation of Griffith Toy.
By p.s.

1443.)   15 *Nov.* 1577.   Grant to Francis Goldsmythe of the wardship and   [*m.* 22]
marriage of Parnel Hunwicke, a sister and heir of William Hunwicke, deceased under age; with an annuity of £5 from 23 Dec., 19 Eliz., when William died. Yearly value of the inheritance £12 17s. 4d.   By Q.

1444.)   15 *Nov.* 1577.   Grant to Joan Darte, widow, and George Wyotte of the wardship and marriage of Lewis Darte, son and heir of John Darte; with an annuity of £6 13s. 4d. from 5 Oct., 18 Eliz., when John died.   By Q.

1445.)   7 *Nov.* 1577.   *Windsor Castle.*   Grant to Thomas Wale of the wardship and marriage of James Tebold, son and heir of Richard Tebold; with an annuity of £3 6s. 8d. from 13 Feb., 12 Eliz., when Richard died.   [*m.* 23]
By Q.

1446.)   18 *Oct.* 1577.   *Windsor Castle.*   Protection for one year for Edmund Robertes of Hawkehurste, co. Kent.   *English.*

1447.)   4 *Nov.* 1577.   *Windsor Castle.*   Grant to Edward More, a gentleman pensioner, of the wardship and marriage of Alexander Sheppard, son and heir of Robert Sheppard; with an annuity of £6 13s. 4d. from 9 Nov.,   [*m.* 24]
17 Eliz., when Robert died.   By p.s.

1448.)   18 *Oct.* 1577.   *Windsor Castle.*   Protection for one year for George Southake of London, merchant. Because he has suffered many losses overseas.   By p.s.

1449.)   19 *Oct.* 1577.   *Windsor Castle.*   Grant for life to Thomas Knyvet, a groom of the privy chamber, of the office of steward of the manors of Penreth Castell, Souresby, Scottby, Gamlesby and Queneshames, co. Cumberland, and clerk of the courts of the same manors; with a yearly fee of 100*s.*; as formerly held by [—] Wentworth, Anthony Barwes, John Vaghan or Edward Eglyonbye. On the termination hereby of a grant of the said office of steward during pleasure to John Dudley by patent of the Exchequer, 5 July last. For Knyvet's service.   By p.s.

1450.)   4 *Nov.* 1577.   *Windsor Castle.*   Lease for life in survivorship   [*m.* 25] to Anthony Roue and Audrey his wife, with remainder to Edward Roue, their son, for life, of (1) lands (*named*) in the lordship of Cottingham, co. York, parcel of the duchy of York or of lands once assigned by statute for payment of the wages of the captain, soldiers and others in the town and castle of Berwick, (2) lands (*named*) in the lordship of Cottingham, had in exchange from Charles, late earl of Westmorland, and (3) lands (*named*) and the tithes of corn in Hatton in Bedfount, co. Middlesex, once of the priory or house of friars of Hundesloo *alias* Howneslowe, co. Middlesex; with reservations; from the present date; yearly rents (1) £19 10*s.*, (2) £6 and (3) £4. On Anthony's surrender of leases of the premises to him (1) by patent, 22 March, 16 Eliz., for 21 years from   [*m.* 26] Lady Day then next, (2) by patent, 28 March, 18 Eliz., for 21 years from Lady Day then last and (3) by patent of the Exchequer, 19 Feb., 13 Eliz., for 21 years from Michaelmas then last, at the same rent in each case. For a fine of £29 paid at the Exchequer.   By p.s.

1451.)   28 *June* 1577.   Grant that an almshouse late erected in Stoneley, co. Warwick, by Thomas Leighe, knight, late alderman of London, deceased, and Alice Leighe, widow, his executrix and late his wife, may remain in perpetuity; with two wardens and five poor men and five poor women. The wardens of the parish church of Stonely so long as they shall be in office shall be wardens of the almshouse. Thomas Knight, Henry Meeres, John Fallowes, Richard Dolland and Robert Towneson shall be the present five poor men; and Agnes Martyn, Margaret Blicke, Margery Gressingham, Agnes Taylor and Agnes Squyer, widows, the present five poor women. Incorporation of the wardens and poor of the said almshouse, to be called the almshouse of Thomas Leighe, knight, and Alice his wife. Licence for the wardens and poor to hold lands to the yearly value of £40; licence also for them to acquire in mortmain from Alice the almshouse and the garden and orchard adjoining enclosed with palings, now occupied by the present poor, and a yearly rent of £29 out of the grange of Milborne, co. Warwick; and licence for Alice to grant to them the said rent. Grant to Alice for her life, and thereafter to Thomas Leighe of Stoneley, son of Thomas Leighe, knight, and Alice, and the heirs of his body, and in default of such heirs to William Leigh, another of their sons, and the heirs of his body, and in default of such heirs to Rowland Leighe, another of their sons, and his heirs, that they may be   [*m.* 27] surveyors and visitors of the almshouse and the wardens and poor and, whenever any of the poor shall die, depart or be lawfully removed by visitation of the ordinary of the place or otherwise, they may place others there up to the number aforesaid and no more within three months; in default whereof the ordinary of the place shall be surveyor and visitor and place poor in the almshouse within three months; in default whereof the mayor of Coventry shall be surveyor and visitor and place poor there within three months. Order that from Lady Day 1578:— the possessor of Milborne grange shall pay yearly to each of the poor 52*s.*, which sums amount to £26 a year; the wardens shall provide a learned preacher to preach in the parish church quarterly on a Sunday at the time of morning prayer before noon, and the ten poor shall be present, unless there be reasonable cause to the contrary; and the preacher shall have for every such preaching 6s. 8d. from the wardens out of the revenues of the almshouse; the wardens shall spend yearly out of the said revenue 10s. about the repair of the parish church; each of the wardens shall have 6s. 8d. out of the said revenues yearly at Michaelmas for his survey and provision; each of the poor shall every Sabbath day and feast day come to the parish church to service, unless there be reasonable cause to the contrary; and the mayor of Coventry shall have 10s. out of the said revenues yearly at Michaelmas for the performance of such of the premises as are appointed to be done by him. If any of the wardens and poor consent to the alienation of any of the hereditaments which they hold in right of the almshouse or the conversion thereof to uses other than those appointed in this patent or in ordinances of the same house to be established by Alice, he shall *ipso facto* cease to be one of the corporation as if dead and be expelled and deprived. No poor man or woman shall be placed in the almshouse unless sole and unmarried, and shall not thereafter marry under pain of deprivation.

At Alice's suit: she has according to the purpose of her husband and herself during his life erected the said almshouse and has placed therein the five poor men and five poor women above named.

1452.)   19 *Oct.* 1577.   *Windsor Castle.*   Grant for life to Henry Knyvet, knight, the Queen's servant, of the office of steward of the forest of Galtries and the lawns therein, the office of the game of wild beasts therein and the herbage, pannage and breakings of wood called 'wyndfall trees' and 'browsinges' therein, which office John Vaughan, deceased, held; as formerly held by John Nevell, lord Latimer, Henry, earl of Westmorland or Vaughan. For his service.   By p.s.
     Vacated because surrendered, 20 *Aug.*, 31 *Eliz.*; *signed*: G. Gerrard [M.R.]; J. Knyvett.

1453.)   12 *June* 1577.   Pardon for Thomas Nicholson late of Cartynton, co. Northumberland, 'yeoman', indicted for the murder of Thomas Hobkirke   [*m.* 28] at Cartynton on 10 Oct., 6 Eliz. (*details given*).   By Q.

1454.)   4 *Feb.* 1577.   Lease for 21 years to Edward Holme of (1) a   [*m.* 29] tithe barn and the tithes of corn and hay belonging to the late chapel of Thornegombalde, lands (*named*) and the tithes of corn in Camerton, parcels of the rectory of Paule, co. York, and (2) the tithes of lambs in Withornsey, Holeym, Paule, Pauleflete, Pauleholme, Litle Humbre, Thorneycroftes, Camerton, Thorngombalde and parcel of Brustwick, co. York, all once of the monastery of Kirkestall, co. York; with reservations; from Michaelmas last; yearly rents (1) £14 and (2) 41s. In consideration of the surrender by Holme of an indenture, 6 April, 24 Hen. VIII, whereby John, abbot, and the convent of the said monastery leased (1) to Catherine Holme, widow, for 48 years from the feast of St. Mark then last at the same rent and an indenture, 4 April, 26 Hen. VIII, whereby the same abbot and convent leased (2) to her for 47 years from that date at the same rent; and for a fine of £32 2s. paid at the Exchequer.   By p.s.

1455.)   1 *Dec.* 1576.   Lease for 21 years to Humphrey Bradshawe of lands (*named with tenants' names*) in Whaplod, co. Lincoln, once of the monastery of Crowland, co. Lincoln; with reservations; from Michaelmas last; yearly rent £5 15s. 8d. (*detailed*); the lease to be void if the lessee shall   [*m.* 30] expel any of the present tenants from the parcels of the premises in their several tenures or shall not before Easter next make them leases thereof by deed for the whole term and at the same rents, so long as they pay him among themselves his costs about obtaining this patent. For a fine of £23 2s. 8d. paid at the Exchequer.   By warrant of the commissioners.

1456.)   1 *Dec.* 1576.   Lease for life in succession to John Piers the elder and Mark Piers and John Piers the younger, his sons, of the rectory of Holme *alias* Holl, co. Devon, the tithes of corn in Holme and a barn and a garden adjoining there, all once of St. John's priory, Exeter; the advowson of the vicarage reserved; from Michaelmas last; yearly rent £6. In consideration of the surrender by John the elder of a patent, 14 Feb., 3 Eliz., leasing the premises to his father, Thomas Piars, for 21 years from Michaelmas then last at the same rent; and for a fine of £18 paid at the Exchequer.   By warrant of the commissioners.

1457.)   24 *Nov.* 1576.   Lease for 21 years to Rowland Pulleston, son of John Pulleston, knight, of two water mills within the franchise of   [*m.* 31] the town of Caernarvan, co. Carnarvon, and three weirs called Kendallen on the water of Sainte near Caernarvan, parcels of the principality of North Wales; with reservations; from Michaelmas last; yearly rent £13 2s. 4d.. In consideration of the surrender by the said Rowland of the interest in the premises of William Warde, Lewis Lloyde and William Edwardes, to whom they were leased *inter alia* by patent, 12 April, 8 Eliz., at the same rent for 21 years from Michaelmas 1571 or the termination of the interest of the said John Pulleston, then late deceased; and for a fine of 100s. paid at the Exchequer.
                                                            By warrant of the commissioners.

1458.)   4 *Feb.* 1577.   Lease for 21 years to Edward Mountague, knight, of the site of the manor of the rectory of Brigstock and the said rectory, co. Northampton, once of the monastery of Cirencestre, co. Gloucester; with reservations; from Michaelmas last; yearly rent £10 2s. 2d.; the lessee to pay a yearly pension of 21s. 8d. to the vicar of Brigstock as
                                                                                       [*m.* 32] accustomed. In consideration of his surrender of a patent, 7 Dec., 5 Eliz., leasing the premises to him, by the name of Edward Mountague, esquire, for 21 years from Michaelmas then last at the same rent; and for a fine of £20 4s. 4d. paid at the Exchequer.
                                                            By warrant of the commissioners.

1459.)   4 *Feb.* 1577.   Lease for 21 years to Robert Hallywell of the rectory of St. Botolph without Aldgate in the county of the city of London, once of Christ Church priory, London; from Michaelmas last; yearly rent £22; the lessee to find a suitable priest or curate in St. Botolph's church, to find bread, wine and other necessaries to be expended there, and to pay the increase of the stipend of the said curate as shall hereafter be ordered. In consideration of his surrender of a patent, 12 Feb., 6 Eliz., leasing the rectory to him for 21 years from Michaelmas then last at the same rent; and for a fine of £23 paid at the Exchequer.
                                                                                        By p.s.

1460.)   17 *Nov.* 1576.   Lease for 21 years to John Lawrence of the   [*m.* 33] demesne lands of the monastery of SS. Mary the Virgin and Thomas the Martyr of Langdon, co. Kent, the yearly farm of lands late leased to Ralph Blunston, clerk, vicar of Ewell, and William Bolly and the tithes of corn and pasture arising from lands within 'le wicket' and circuit of the said monastery; with reservations, including lands (*named*); from Lady Day next; yearly rent £20; the lessee to provide entertainment for the Queen's steward and surveyor coming to the manor there to hold courts or survey the premises. In consideration of the surrender in Chancery by Lawrence of a patent, 16 May, 13 Eliz., leasing the premises to William Partriche for 21 years from Lady Day then last at the same rent; and for a fine of £20 paid at the Exchequer.   By p.s.

1461.)   4 *Feb.* 1577.   Lease for 21 years to Thomas Smythe of the rectory of Cosseham, co. Wilts, once of the monastery of Syon, co. Middlesex; with reservations, including escheats; from Michaelmas last; yearly rent £26 13*s.* 8*d.* [*sic*].   [*m.* 34]

In consideration of the surrender by Smythe of a patent, 10 Dec., 5 Eliz., leasing the rectory *inter alia* to George Nedeham for 21 years from Michaelmas then last at a yearly rent of £26 13*s.* 4*d.*; and for a fine of £53 6*s.* 8*d.* paid to the Queen's use, namely £19 6*s.* 8*d.* at the Exchequer and £34 to Robert George, in satisfaction of a like sum paid by the said Robert for the price of a lease of the manor of Tileshead, co. Wilts, which was not granted to him, the greater part of the manor being already leased to Robert Gamme in the year 13 Eliz., as appears by a bill signed by Christopher Smythe, clerk of the pipe, and annexed to the particular on which this patent has issued.   By p.s.

1462.)   28 *Nov.* 1576.   Lease for 21 years to Ellis Williams of lands (*named*) within the franchise of the town of Rutherland, co. Flint, parcel of lands of the late earl of Chester; with reservations; from the present date; yearly rent 106*s.* 8*d.* In consideration of the surrender in Chancery by Williams of the interest in the premises of Hugh Lloyd and William Hollycombe, to whom they, by the name of lands (*named*) parcel of the demesne lands of Ruthland castle, were leased *inter alia* by patent, 22 June, 6 Eliz., at the same rent for 21 years from Michaelmas 1575 or the termination of the interest of Thomas Marshe, to whom they were leased by patent, 28 March, 4 Edw. VI; and for a fine of 66*s.* 8*d.* paid at the Exchequer.
                              By warrant of the commissioners.

1463.)   24 *Nov.* 1576.   Pardon for Thomas ap Hoell David late of Llanvihangell Cumduy, co. Brecon, 'yeoman'. It was found by an inquisition taken before William Goz, a coroner in the county, on 10 April, 18 Eliz., on the body of William Jenkyn at Llanvihangell Kumdye (*jury named*), and by indictment, that the said Thomas feloniously killed Jenkyn by wounding him at   [*m.* 35]
Llanvihangell Kumduy on 3 April, 18 Eliz., so that he died there on 9 (or 7) April (*details given*). At the suit of Rice Thomas.   By p.s.

1464.)   24 *Nov.* 1576.   Pardon for Christian Lyncoln late of Norwich, 'spynster', indicted at the sessions of the peace held at the guildhall of Norwich on 19 July, 18 Eliz., before Thomas Layor, mayor of the city, Francis Windam, recorder, and their fellows, justices of the peace and of oyer and   [*m.* 36]
terminer in the county of the said city, for the theft of £30 in a purse belonging to John Andrewes at Norwich on 11 June, 18 Eliz.   By Q.

1465.)   29 *Nov.* 1576.   Appointment for life in survivorship of James Pryce and Edward Pryce to be attorneys for the Crown and for plaintiffs only in the county court within the county of Hereford; with a fee of 4*d.* for every action at every several county court so long as it remains undetermined; the sheriffs of the county and others to admit them to the said office, and no other person to intermeddle with the practice of any attorneyship on behalf of any plaintiff in the county court; the sheriff's clerks are to give them access to all records; and they are to put in sufficient sureties before the council in the marches of Wales before entering office for the true exercising thereof and for the payment of sums awarded by the court to any persons or so much thereof as the appointees shall receive from any bailiffs of hundreds of the county to any person's use. By stat. 1 Hen. V it was ordained that no undersheriff, sheriff's clerk, receiver or sheriff's bailiff should be attorney in any the King's courts during the time that he should be in office with any such sheriff; but it is reported that the free suitors, clerks and bailiffs of the sheriffs of the county of Hereford for long time past have usurped the office of attorneys in the county court held monthly in Hereford castle, contrary to the statute; and the Queen is minded that henceforth the office of attorney in the said court shall be supplied with apt persons. *English.*　　　　By p.s.

1466.)　30 *Nov.* 1576.　Grant to William Roche of the wardship and marriage of William Watham, son and heir of Jasper Watham; with an annuity of 26s. 8d. from 1 Aug., 14 Eliz., when Jasper died. Yearly value of the　　　　[*m.* 37] inheritance £3 6s. 8d.　　　　By Q.

1467.)　19 *Nov.* 1576.　Pardon for Thomas Wallis late of Blewberry, co. Berks, 'yeoman', for all offences. He is indicted for the theft of two horses belonging to Henry Slade at Bedford, co. Bedford, on 8 Aug., 18 Eliz. (*details given*). On information of Thomas Snagge, recorder of Bedford.　　　　By p.s.

1468.)　30 *Nov.* 1576.　Grant to Thomas Wright of the wardship and marriage of Thomas Bountayne, son and heir of Francis Bountayne; with an annuity of 33s. 4d. from 15 Dec., 15 Eliz., when Francis died. Yearly value　　　　[*m.* 38] of the inheritance £8.　　　　By Q.

1469.)　23 *Nov.* 1576.　Pardon for Richard Morreyn late of Gravesende, co. Kent, 'yoman', indicted for that in the highway at Aylesforde, co. Kent, on 22 Sept., 17 Eliz., he robbed John Albrighte of cloth belonging to (1) Jocase Vaunderplanken and (2) John Dobbes (*details given*).　　　　By Q.

1470.)　5 *Feb.* 1577.　Grant to Anne Luke, widow, of the wardship and marriage of Thomas Luke, son and heir of John Luke; with an annuity of 26s. 8d. from 3 Oct., 17 Eliz., when John died. Yearly value of the inheritance 46s. 8d.　　　　By Q.

1471.)　4 *Feb.* 1577.　Grant to Thomas Sackforde, master of the court of Requests, and Henry Sackford of the wardship and marriage of John Bull, kinsman and heir of Thomas Bull of Hacheston, co. Suffolk, and John　　　　[*m.* 39] Bull of Hacheston, father of the said Thomas Bull; with an annuity of £6 13s. 4d. from 5 April, 16 Eliz., when Thomas died.　　　　By Q.

1472.)　5 *Feb.* 1577.　Grant to George Carleton and Joyce Carleton, widow, of the wardship and marriage of George Carleton, son and heir of Anthony Carleton; with an annuity of £6 13s. 4d. from 18 Jan., 18 Eliz., when Anthony died.　　　　By Q.

1473.)　22 *June* 1577.　Protection for one year for Thurstan Tildisley.　　　　[*m.* 40]
　　　　By Q.

1474.)　28 *June* 1577.　Pardon for Matthew Farmer late of Leeke, co. Stafford, 'yoman', indicted at the gaol delivery of the county of Leicester held at Leicester on Tuesday in the third week of Lent, 19 Eliz., before James Dyer, knight, chief justice of the Common Pleas, and Nicholas Barham, one of the Queen's serjeants at law, justices of gaol delivery, for that he burgled the house of William Blunt at Osberton, co. Leicester, on 26 Jan., 19 Eliz., and stole a gelding belonging to Blunt (*details given*).　　　　By p.s.

1475.)　22 *June* 1577.　Lease for 21 years to John Lunde of a capital messuage and lands in Redenes, co. York, now in his tenure and late in that of Robert Lunde, once of the monastery of St. Mary near the walls of York;　　　　[*m.* 41] with reservations; from Lady Day last; yearly rent £7. In consideration of the great yearly costs of keeping the premises in repair on account of floods, as appears by certificate of the auditor of the county; and for a fine of £14 paid at the Exchequer.

By warrant of the commissioners.

1476.)   22 *June* 1577.   Presentation of Anthony Hyggyns, preacher and minister of God's Word, to the sixth canonry or prebend in Gloucester cathedral, void by death.   By p.s.

1477.)   22 *June* 1577.   Pardon for Rowland Cole late of Northwey, co. Gloucester, for all offences committed before 20 Dec. last. At the suit of Richard Baylies of Ludlowe, co. Salop, mercer: he was by Cole and others feloniously and burglariously despoiled of goods to the value of 400 marks, to the utter impoverishment of him, his wife and 10 children, as appears by a bill signed by the vice-president and others of the council in the marches of Wales; and the parents and friends of Cole are prepared to make restitution of the greater part of the goods, if Cole is pardoned.   By Q.

1478.)   22 *June* 1577.   Lease for 21 years to Richard Masselyn of lands (*named*, including Rumney Meade, *with tenants' names*) in New Wyndsore,   [*m.* 42] co. Berks, same called 'master Bosces landes', others acquired by Henry VIII from Eaton college near Windsore; now annexed to the honour of Windsore; with reservations, including money due yearly for horses drawing 'lez barges' in Rumney Meade; from Michaelmas last; yearly rent £13 15s. 4d. In consideration of the surrender by Masselyn of a patent, 13 Dec., 11 Eliz., leasing the premises to Roger Langforde for 21 years from Michaelmas then last at the same rent; and for a sum paid at the Exchequer by way of fine.

By p.s.

1479.)   27 *June* 1577.   Lease for 21 years to Anthony Dawson of the tithes of corn and hay of Scorton in the parish of Catterick, co. York, once of the monastery of St. Mary next the walls of York; from Lady Day last; yearly rent £8. On surrender by Dawson of a lease of the premises by conventual   [*m.* 43] indenture, 10 Oct., 30 Hen. VIII, *inter alia* to Leonard Warcopp of Eastanfeild, co. York, for 41 years from that date at the same rent. For a fine of £24 paid at the Exchequer.

By warrant of the commissioners.

1480.)   24 *June* 1577.   Pardon for Matthew van Breamen, servant and factor to Magnus Spencehorne and David Clame, merchants of Hambroughe, for shipping money out of the realm; and restitution of the money forfeited. A ship *The Rose* of Hambroughe came aground in the Downes on the Goodwyn sands by reason of great winds about 23 April last, whereupon van Breamen and the crew left the ship in the ship's boat, van Breamen carrying with him 394 dollars, brought from Hambroughe for the provision of merchandise in Spain, whither the ship was bound; he came to Sandwiche, where he was within a small time advertised that the ship was found floating and was carried into the haven of Newporte in Flanders; whereupon he embarked in a ship of Sandwich with the dollars to go to Newporte, and before he passed out of the haven of Sandwich he was searched by the Queen's searcher there and the dollars were seized as forfeit; he is a stranger born and has transgressed the laws of the realm only through ignorance. *English.*   By p.s.

1481.)   27 *June* 1577.   Grant to Eleanor Stockdall, widow, of the wardship and marriage of Christopher Stockdall, brother and heir of William Stockdall; with an annuity of £3 from 1 Dec., 17 Eliz., when William died. Yearly   [*m.* 44] value of the inheritance £10 2s. 6d.   By Q.

1482.)   27 *June* 1577. Lease for 21 years to Richard Awdeley of woods parcel of the demesne woods of Melchett forest, co. Wilts; with reservations; including 'rootefall trees' and pannage of the forest; from Lady Day last; yearly rent £12; the lessee to make two cuttings only of the woods growing in or on 'le straightes' and at suitable seasons, to enclose and preserve 'lez springes' thereof according to statute, and to enclose 'le straightes' of 'le outering' of the forest; he may have from the forest 40 oaks for the paling of 'le straightes' and 'le outeringe'; the patent to be enrolled before the auditor of the county within one year for the charging of the rent and before the surveyor of woods this side Trent for performance of the covenants. In consideration that Awdeley will undertake the charges of enclosing the woods, which must be enclosed for nine years after cutting, and will pay the said rent.   By warrant of the commissioners.

1483.)   26 *June* 1577.   Lease for 21 years to William Griffith of lands (*named*) within the franchise of the town of Ruthland, co. Flint, formerly of the late earl of Chester; from Michaelmas next; yearly rent 106s. 8d. For a fine of 106s. 8d. paid at the Exchequer.
                                      By warrant of the commissioners.

(The dorse of this roll is blank.)

PART II

C. 66/1152

1484.)   8 *May* 1577.   Pardon for John Inskepe late of Rodmyll, co.   [*m.* 1]
Sussex, Richard Yonge late of Pedingho, co. Sussex, and John Downer late of Pedingho,
'husbandmen', for manslaughter. Inskepe and Yonge are indicted for that at Telscom, co.
Sussex, on 2 June, 18 Eliz., they assaulted John Barneden so that he died at Telscom on 8
June (*details given*), and Downer is indicted for that he was present aiding and abetting them.
                                                                              By Q.

1485.)   8 *May* 1577.   Pardon for Grace Ludgar, wife of Stephen Ludgar of Southe
Courtoll, co. Cornwall, 'husbandman'. She was indicted at the gaol delivery held at
Launceston castle, co. Cornwall, before John Jefferay, a justice of the Queen's Bench, and
his fellows, justices of gaol   [*m.* 2]
delivery of the castle, on Monday in the fifth week of Lent, 19 Eliz., by an inquisition taken
before John Tubb, a coroner in the county, for the manslaughter of William Thorne at
Southe Courtall on 15 Dec., 19 Eliz., (*details given*). At the suit of her said husband. By Q.

1486.)   10 *May* 1577.   Pardon for John Mychell late of Stowe, co. Norfolk, 'laborer'.
Bartholomew Hawkyns late of Bexwell, co. Norfolk, 'clothier', Stephen Woodcock late of
Wymersham, co. Norfolk, 'laborer', Mychell, Nicholas Barnes late of Newton. co. Suffolk,
'laborer', and John Barnes of Eye, co. Suffolk, 'weaver', are indicted for that they burgled
the close and house of Richard Backler at Redlingfeild, co. Suffolk, on 16 Nov., 18 Eliz., put
him and Sybil his wife in fear, bound him and stole goods (*described*) and 8s. 9d. belonging to
him.   By Q.

1487.)   8 *May* 1577.   Grant to David Lewes, LL.D., judge of the court of Admiralty, of
the next presentation to the rectory of Nearberthe with the chapel of Robarston annexed, co.
Pembroke, for this turn only.   By p.s.

1488.)   13 *May* 1577.   Protection for one year for William Hearle of London, the Queen's
servant, about to go to Scotland on business of the realm not to be revealed or hindered.
                                                                              By p.s.

1489.)   11 *May* 1577.   Pardon for Ralph Johnston late of Thorneton on   [*m.* 3]
the Hill in the North Riding, co. York, 'yoman', for all offences committed concerning the
felonious buying, receiving and carrying away of nine cattle and a mare.   By p.s.

1490.)   13 *May* 1577.   Grant to Mary Seymer, widow, of the wardship and marriage of
John Woodhull, son and heir of Leonard Woodhull; with an annuity of £3 from 11 April, 17
Eliz., when Leonard died. Yearly value of the inheritance £5 7s. 8d.   By Q.

1491.)   11 *May* 1577.   Grant to the mayor and burgesses of the town of Kyngeston on
Hull that no stranger or foreigner to the liberty of the town shall trade there with any other
stranger or foreigner in any wares save at the time of markets and fairs held there, salt and
fish excepted, on pain of forfeiture of the wares to the use of the mayor and burgesses.
                                                                              [*m.* 4]

Grant also to the burgesses merchants of the town of incorporation as the governor, assistants and fellowship of merchants inhabiting in Kingston on Hull. The governor, assistants and fellowship to have a hall or council house and power to make ordinances there consonant with the laws of the realm and reason for their government. Also power according to their ordinances to elect from the burgesses and merchants a governor and six assistants with power to appoint to and remove from the fellowship whom they will. Also power to acquire in mortmain lands not held of the Crown in chief or by knight service to the yearly value of £30. Also—for the better support of the freemen of the fellowship, for the better maintenance of the fleet and navy of the realm according to the intention of an article of stat. 5 Eliz., also that the town and the inhabitants and burgesses may be better maintained by commerce and merchandise, and in consideration of the poverty and decay of the said merchants by many misfortunes of the sea and pirates—grant that no burgess or inhabitant of the town not being or willing to be a freeman of the fellowship shall carry wares or trade between the town or port and parts overseas or Scotland, or be admitted to any of the privileges hereby granted save at the will of the governor, assistants and fellowship, under pain of forfeiture of such wares to the use of the governor, assistants and fellowship; provided that, if any burgess of Kingston on Hull exercising any occupation of merchandise desires to be admitted   [m. 5]
to the fellowship and to follow the business of merchant only and observe the ordinances of the fellowship, the governor, assistants and fellowship shall admit him during the time that he shall exercise no other occupation. Provided that by reason of this grant treaties between the Queen and other princes be in no way infringed, but that the subjects of other princes may trade as freely in the said town as in other towns of the realm according to the form of the treaties.

That they may be assisted to overcome the damage done to the town and its port by the water of Humber, which is a branch of the sea, flooding over the walls and ditches erected for their defence; and in consideration of the services of the mayor and burgesses, especially in the last rebellion in the North, and their great labour and charges about the defence of the port and the Queen's castle and fortifications there.   By p.s.

1492.)   17 *May* 1577.   *Gorhambury.*   Lease for 21 years to John Appleyarde of a capital messuage called 'the Mannor Place' in Frothingham, co. York, the tithes of corn and hay belonging to the said messuage and to the town of Frothingham, liberty of fowling, hunting and fishing in the manor of Frothingham and lands etc. (*named with tenants' names*) in Frothingham, all parcels of the said manor and once belonging to the monastery of Thornton, co. Lincoln; with reservations, including a pasture (*described*); from Lady Day last; yearly rent £31; the lessee to leave to the use of   [m. 6]
the Crown the tithes of corn of the arable land in whatsoever manner they shall chance to be sown at the end of the term; also to provide entertainment for the Queen's steward and surveyor coming to the manor to hold courts or make a survey. In consideration of his surrender of his interest under a patent, 16 Feb., 8 Eliz., leasing the premises to him for 21 years from Michaelmas then last at the same rent; and for a fine of £50 paid at the Exchequer.
                                                                           By p.s.

1493.)   17 *May* 1577.   *Gorhambury.*   Grant for life to John Styll, S.T.D., of the office of master or president of Trinity college, Cambridge, void by the resignation of John Whitegifte.   By p.s.

1494.)   22 *May* 1577.   *Gorhambury.*   Assignment to John Hampshere of Chalfunt, co. Buckingham, 'yeoman', the Queen's servant, of a lease to the Queen by Robert, bishop of Winchester, by indenture, 18 April,   [m. 7]

19 Eliz., of (1) a capital messuage called Curbridge Farme and lands in the tithing of Haylinge within the manor of Wytney, co. Oxford, at a yearly rent of £3 18s. 8d. for 60 years from Michaelmas 1593 or the termination of a lease thereof by Stephen, late bishop of Winchester, by indenture, 20 April, 1 Mary, to David Lawley (having been once leased to Thomas Lawley, deceased, by copy of court roll) for 40 years from Michaelmas then last and (2) lands (*named with tenants' names*) in Crawley in the said lordship of Wytney at a yearly rent of 13s. 4d. for 60 years from Michaelmas 1597 or the termination of a lease thereof by the said present bishop by indenture, 15 Sept., 8 [*sic*] Eliz., to William Hobby for 21 years from Michaelmas then next.   By p.s.

1495.)   22 *May* 1577.   *Gorhambury.*   Lease for 40 years, if Jacominus Fregoze shall so long live, to John Coryatt of two corn mills on the river Aven within the manor of Sopley, co. Southampton; from Lady Day last; yearly rent 40s., besides £10 payable to the chief lord of premises. In consideration that Fregoze, an alien born subject of the Emperor in Italy, holds the premises for life by grant of John Barkeley, knight, and lady Frances his wife for a yearly rent of £10, without having any licence to acquire lands or capacity to hold them, wherefore his interest has come to the Crown, and he was alive on 18 Jan., 18 Eliz., as appears by an inquisition taken at Forthingbridge, co. Southampton, on the said date and returned into the Exchequer, which was procured by Coryatt at his own costs; and because Coryatt offers to pay the said rent of 40s. beyond the rent of £10 payable to Barkeley and his wife and their heirs.   By warrant of the commissioners.

1496.)   22 *May* 1577.   *Gorhambury.*   Lease for 21 years to John Thweinge of lands (*tenants named*) in Tybthorpe, co. York, late of Robert Constable, knight, attainted; with reservations; from Lady Day last; yearly   [*m.* 8] rent £9 5s. 2d. (*detailed*). For a fine of £27 15s. 6d. paid at the Exchequer.
                                                              By warrant of the commissioners.

1497.)   22 *May* 1577.   *Gorhambury.*   Lease for 21 years to Edward Musgrave of Sandenhouse grange and lands (*named with tenants' names*) in   [*m.* 9] Sandenhouse and Holme Cultram or elsewhere, co. Cumberland, once of the monastery of Holme Cultram; with reservations; from Lady Day last; yearly rent £6 8s. 3d.; the lessee to inhabit the premises by himself and by so many sufficient men as inhabited them before the making of a former lease thereof to Ralph Bagnall, to cultivate the same, to find so many sufficient men with arms in the North when he is ordered, to bear all other charges touching the Queen's service according to the custom of the country, and to fence the premises as ordered by the steward or understeward of the Queen's court or other her officers there. In consideration of his surrender of a patent, 25 June, 5 Eliz., leasing the premises to him for 21 years from Lady Day then last at the same rent; and for a fine of £12 16s. 6d. paid at the Exchequer.   By warrant of the commissioners.

1498.)   6 *May* 1577.   Lease for 21 years to lady Isabel Ellerker, late the wife of Christopher Eastofte, of tithes (*tenants named*) in Kilnewick, co. York, once of the monastery of Watton, co. York; from Lady Day last; yearly rent £10. In consideration of her surrender of the interest   [*m.* 10] of William Forster, to whom by patent, 11 Jan., 5 Eliz., the said tithes were leased *inter alia* for 21 years from Michaelmas then last at the same rent; and for a fine of £20 within a sum of £67 13s. 4d. paid at the Exchequer.   By warrant of the commissioners.

1499.)   24 *May* 1577.   *Gorhambury.*   Grant in fee simple to Lewis Dyve of Bromeham, co. Bedford, and John Dyve, his son and heir apparent, of the rectory of Stevington, co.

Bedford, once of Harrold priory, co. Bedford, and the advowson of the vicarage of Stevington; bells and lead, except lead in gutters and windows, reserved; to hold as of the manor of Eastgrenewich,   [*m.* 11]
co. Kent, in socage; issues from Lady Day last; the grantees to pay yearly out of the rectory 6s. 8d. for hiring (*locacione*), 15s. to the archdeacon of Bedford for proxy and synodals, and 2s. 6d. for visitation. For £364 12d. paid at the Exchequer by Lewis.   By p.s.

1500.)   4 *May* 1577.   Lease for life in succession to George Turbervile, Troilus Turbervile, son of Nicholas Turbervile, and Robert Freke the   [*m.* 12]
younger, son of Robert Freake of Iwerne Corteney, co. Dorset, of the rectory of Shapwicke, co. Dorset, late of the great chantry in the late college of Wymborne called 'Bremberies chauntrie', co. Dorset; with reservations; from Michaelmas last; yearly rent £15 15s. 4d. and heriot the best beast. On surrender by the said George by deed, 9 Feb. last, enrolled in Chancery, of the interest of James Moore, to whom the rectory was leased *inter alia* by patent of the court of Augmentations, 31 March, 5 Edw. VI, at the same rent for 21 years from the termination of a lease thereof to Thomas Clawghton for 30 years then unexpired. For a fine of £20 paid at the Exchequer by George.   By p.s.

1501.)   4 *May* 1577.   Lease for 21 years to Robert Cuffe of (1) the   [*m.* 13]
tithes from twelve mills of the bishop of Winchester in Taunton hundred, co. Somerset, once of the monastery of Taunton, and (2) the rectory of Mychell Creche, co. Somerset; late of the monastery of Mountague, co. Somerset; with reservations; (1) from Lady Day 1586, having been leased by patent of the Exchequer, 20 May, 7 Eliz., to the said Robert (being then or late in the tenure of Ralph Lambe) for 21 years from Lady Day then last at a yearly rent of 40s. and (2) from the said Robert's death, the rectory having been leased by indenture, 17 Nov., 27 Hen. VIII, by Robert Shirborne, prior, and the convent of the monastery of Montague to John Cuffe of Criche, Joan his wife and Robert their son for life in survivorship at a yearly rent of £8 6s. 8d.; same rents. At the suit of William Stowe, the Queen's servant, and for his service; and for a fine of £20 13s. 4d. paid at the Exchequer by the said Robert.   By p.s.

1502.)   6 *May* 1577.   Lease for 21 years to Lady Isabel Ellerker, late the wife of Christopher Estofte, of the tithes and other profits in Saltmershe, Cotnes, Metham and Yokeflete *alias* Yowkeflete or elsewhere, co. York, once belonging to Saltemershe prebend in the collegiate church of Howden, co. York; from Lady Day last; yearly rent   [*m.* 14]
£18 6s. 8d. In consideration of her surrender of a patent, 6 July, 8 Eliz., leasing the premises to her for 19 years from Lady Day then last at the same rent; and for a fine of £36 13s. 4d. within a sum of £67 13s. 4d. paid at the Exchequer.   By p.s.

1503.)   7 *May* 1577.   Lease to Robert Power, an equerry of the stable, of—the reversion and rent of (1) the site of the manor of Mulshoo *alias* Mulso, co. Buckingham, and lands belonging thereto and (2) lands (*named with tenants' names*) in Mulshoo, all assigned to the present Queen before her accession, having been acquired by Henry VIII from John Marshe in exchange and annexed to the honour of Ampthill, and leased by patent, 29 May, 12 Eliz., to Richard Stonely for 21 years from Michaelmas then next at yearly rents of (1) £8 and (2) £16 17s. 8d.; the reversion and rent of (3) the prebend   [*m.* 15]
of Crowpredy, co. Oxford, late of John, late earl of Warwick, and afterwards assigned to cardinal Pole and the clergy of England by act of Parliament, leased by patent, 17 June, 10 Eliz., to Power with the reversion and rent thereof (the prebend having been leased by patent of the court of Augmentations, 22 May, 7 Edw. VI, to William Gyffard at a yearly rent of £50 for 21 years from the termination of a lease thereof by indenture to the said

William and George Gyffarde) from that date for Power's life and after his death to him, his executors and assigns until the expiry of the said William's lease, with remainder thereafter for 21 years, at a yearly rent of a red rose at Midsummer (if sought) during Power's life and thereafter of £50; and the premises (1), (2) [m. 16] and (3) above. With reservations. From the present date for Power's life and after his death (1) and (2) to him, his executors and assigns until the expiry of Stoneley's lease, with remainder thereafter for 45 years, and (3) to him, his executors and assigns until the expiry of William Gyffard's lease, with remainder thereafter for 29 years. Yearly rents (1) and (2) a red rose at Midsummer (if it be sought) during Power's life and thereafter £8 and £16 17s. 8d. respectively, and (3) a red rose at Midsummer (if it be sought) during his life and thereafter £50. Issues of (1) and (2) from Lady Day last. The lessee [m. 17] to pay yearly, after the termination of the said several terms of 21 years, to the dean and chapter of Lincoln cathedral out of (3) a pension or rent called 'a sepdyme' and all other ordinary charges accustomed to be paid to the same dean and chapter.

For his service. By p.s.

1504.) 6 *May* 1577. Grant for life to Griffith Floide (*alias* Lloyd), doctor of law and student in the university of Oxford, (and his sufficient substitute allowed by the chancellor of the university) of the office of 'readinge of our civil lecture' in the said university; with a yearly fee of £40, payable at the Exchequer from Lady Day last, and all other [m. 18] fees incident to the said office 'for proceadinges due by the laudable custome of the said universitie'. On surrender in Chancery by Robert Lougher of a patent, 10 Jan., 8 Eliz., granting him the office for life. *English*. By p.s.

1505.) 25 *Feb.* 1577. Grant for seven years to Ralph Lane, the Queen's servant, of all forfeitures due to the Crown in respect of offences against stat. 5 & 6 Edw. VI concerning the exchange of money current in the realm, and the Crown's moiety of all such forfeitures as shall be recovered by any other person. Licence also to inquire into such offences by juries of twelve or more, by corporal oaths administered lawfully to suspects or by other lawful means in England and Wales; this patent or the duplicate or enrolment thereof to be sufficient warrant for the issue of [m. 19] commissions to Lane, his assigns and deputies or any of them with such other persons as the keeper of the great seal, the treasurer or the chancellor or barons of the Exchequer shall appoint for the executing of the premises. Also licence to search the houses and accounts of suspected offenders and to arrest and sue such suspects in the name of the Crown or of the licensee. No others to make composition with any person or otherwise intermeddle with the premises. Any forfeitures paid into the Exchequer or to any the Queen's officers shall on the licensee's request be delivered over to him. Power to compound with offenders giving [m. 20] them acquittance by writing sealed; which acquittance shall be sufficient warrant for passing under the great seal pardons general or special for offenders, without fine or fee other than ordinary fees payable in Chancery for pardons of course. The grant to be void if the licensee shall compound with any persons for an offence before it be committed. *English*. By p.s.

1506.) 26 *Feb.* 1577. Grant for life in survivorship to Henry Jordan and Edmund Martyn of the keeping of the bulwark or blockhouse of Estmersey, co. Essex; with a fee of 8d. a day, payable at the Exchequer. At suit made on behalf of Jordan, it appears by warrant, 9 March, 4 Eliz., under the privy seal, remaining in the Exchequer, that he, having the charge of keeping the said bulwark or blockhouse, has been allowed wages of 8d. a day, payable at the Exchequer. For the service of Jordan and Martyn in the wars of Henry VIII, Edward VI and Queen Mary and to the present Queen. *English.*   By p.s.

1507.)   20 *Feb.* 1577.   Pardon for Cuthbert Wytham late of Bretonbye, co. York, indicted by an inquisition taken at York castle, co. York, on 20 March, 12 Eliz., before Thomas, earl of Sussex, president of the council in the North, John, lord Darcye, William, lord Ewre, Henry, lord of Hunsden, warden of the East marches towards Scotland, Gilbert Gerrarde, attorney general, Thomas Bromeley, solicitor general, Thomas Gargrave, knight, George Bowes, knight, and their fellows, justices of oyer and terminer   [*m.* 21] concerning divers treasons and other offences, for acts of rebellion committed at Topcliff, co. York, on 1 Sept., 11 Eliz., at Ryppon, co. York, on 16 Nov., 11 Eliz., and from 16 to 26 Nov., 11 Eliz., at Ryppon, Buroughbridge, Wetherbye, Northallerton and Richemonde, co. York (*details given*).   By Q.

1508.)   9 *Feb.* 1577.   Grant for life in reversion to Fulk Grevill, the Queen's servant, of the offices of (1) clerk of the council in the   [*m.* 22] principality of South Wales and North Wales and in the counties of Salop, Hereford, Gloucester, Worcester, Chester and Flint and the marches of Wales thereto adjoining, now held by Charles Fox, (2) clerk of the signet for business in the said principality, counties and marches before the Queen's councillors or commissioners there, now held by Charles Fox aforesaid, and (3) clerk of the signet for all writs and process touching suits in the said principality, counties and marches before the Queen's councillors or commissioners there. By patent, 29 Dec., 29 Hen. VIII, Edmund Fox and the said Charles Fox were appointed to (1) and (2) for life in survivorship in reversion; by patent, 2 July, 7 Eliz., (3) was granted to John Duddeley for life; and by patent, 10 Oct., 9 Eliz., (1) was granted to George Brooke *alias* Cobham, now deceased, and Gilbert   [*m.* 23] Duke, still surviving, for life in survivorship in reversion.   By Q.

1509.)   27 *Feb.* 1577.   Lease for 21 years to James Conyers of the rectory of Southmymes, co. Middlesex, late of William Cavendishe, knight; with reservations; from Lady Day next; yearly rent £21 16s.   By p.s.

1510.)   27 *Feb.* 1577.   Lease for 21 years to Henry Powle of a moiety of the manor of Walton Cardiff, co. Gloucester, late of Thomas   [*m.* 24] Hennage, knight, and all appurtenances of said moiety, once in the tenure of Charles Herbert; with reservations; from Michaelmas last; yearly rent £21 10s.   By p.s.

1511.)   22 *May* 1577.   *Gorhambury.*   Presentation of Francis Nevell, clerk, M.A., to the rectory of Benefeilde *alias* Benyngfeilde, Peterborough dioc.   By Q.

1512.)   17 *May* 1577.   *Gorhambury.*   Presentation of William Cole, S.T.D., to the archdeaconry of Lincoln in Lincoln cathedral, void by the promotion of John Aylmer, S.T.D., to the bishopric of London.   By p.s.

1513.)   23 *May* 1577.   *Gorhambury.*   Presentation of Anthony Heywood, B.A., chaplain of the household, to the rectory of Stokesley, York dioc., void by the translation of Richard Barnes, late bishop of Carlisle, who held it *in commendam*, to the bishopric of Durham.   By p.s.

1514.)   22 *May* 1577.   *Gorhambury.*   Grant to Edward Cheeke of a bond, 7 March, 19 Eliz., wherein Edward Bevell of the city of Wells is bound to the Crown in £200 for performance of an order and decree of Edmund, archbishop of Canterbury, and others, commissioners for ecclesiastical　　　　　　　　　　　　　　　　　　　　　　　　　[*m*. 25]

causes, annexed to the bond, as appears by the same bond remaining in the keeping of the Queen's remembrancer of the Exchequer; with power to sue in the Queen's name or his own in the Exchequer for the said £200.　　　　　　　　　　　　　　　　　　　　　　By p.s.

1515.)　1 *Nov.* 1577.　*Windsor Castle.*　Grant to John Lovyson, master worker of the moneys in the Tower of London and elsewhere in England, of power to coin of such gold agreeable to the standard of 23 carats 3½ grains of fine gold and ½ grain of alloy as shall be delivered to him by Richard Martyn, warden of the mint, two manner of moneys of gold as follows—one piece to be called 'the soveraigne', running for 30*s.*, and there shall be 24 of those sovereigns in every pound weight troy, and another piece to be called 'the royall half of a soveraigne', running for 15*s.*, and there shall be of those royals 48 in every pound weight troy; every pound weight troy of the said moneys shall hold in number and be in value £36 sterling, and shall be in fineness 23 carats 3½ grains of fine gold and ½ grain of alloy, which is the old right standard of gold of England. If the moneys be found at the assay before the deliverance to be too strong or too feeble by too much or too little in weight or in fineness or in both by more than ⅛ carat (which ⅛ carat shall be called 'remedye' for the said master that such money be delivered for good, so as the same default happen by casualty, otherwise not), the deliverance shall cease and the moneys shall be challenged by the warden for less than good and be new molten at the costs of the master till they be put to point as money deliverable as aforesaid. The warden of the mint, his deputy or deputies shall take up for the Queen's use of every pound of the said gold standard so coined 4*s.*, of which he shall pay to Lovison for his charges 3*s.* 6*d.* and shall retain the residue to the Queen's use. The warden or such sufficient deputy as he shall thereunto appoint shall have joint custody and the view and oversight of the rating, melting and making of the said gold from time to time from the first deliverance of the same until it be made into coined moneys, so as it be plainly entered into the Queen's ledger and melting book kept in the mint in the Tower and the Queen be also informed at her pleasure how the said moneys in the making thereof agree with the true old standard aforesaid. The grantee to make speedy coinage of all such gold as the warden shall deliver and the same to deliver again to the warden by weight according to the just value of that he shall bring in (one piece to be taken of every melting for the pixing only except).

By indentures, 19 April, 13 Eliz., between the Queen and Lovyson, by the name of John Lovyson, citizen and goldsmith of London, he was authorised to make three manner of gold moneys of the standard aforesaid, and now the Queen is minded to have two others.　*English.*

1516.)　11 *March* 1577.　*Gorhambury.*　Grant for life to Richard Stafferton of Warfeild, co. Berks, son of Richard Stafferton, a gentleman pensioner, lately deceased, of (1) the office of woodward or keeper of the woods in the　　　　　　　　　　　　　　　　[*m*. 26]

lordships of Cokeham and Braye, co. Berks, and warrener in the same, held by John Norres, deceased, with wages of 2*d.* a day, payable out of the issues of the lordships, and all 'windfalles' and 'fee trees' in the said woods, and (2) the office of keeper of the house called 'le Newe Lodge' with a close adjoining in Craneborn in Windesor forest in the bailiwick of Battusbayly *alias* the office of a forester in the said forest, with wages of 4*d.* a day, payable out of the revenues of Windesor castle from the death of the said Norres, and herbage and pannage and the wood arising from 'browsinge' there and all manner of pannage and trees dead and felled by the wind there.　　　　　　　　　　　　　　　　　　　　　　By Q.

1517.)　11 *March* 1577.　*Gorhambury.*　Pardon for Thomas Pottell late of Modbery, co.

Devon, 'inholder'. At the general gaol delivery of Exeter castle, co. Devon, made there on 10 Sept., 18 Eliz., before Roger Manwood, a justice of the Common Pleas, and John Jeffrey, a justice of the Queen's Bench, and their fellows, justices of gaol delivery, Rowland Cole late of Ashechurche, co. Gloucester, was indicted for the theft of cloth (*described*) belonging to William Turney at Modbury, co. Devon, on the night of 30 April, 18 Eliz., and Pottell with others was indicted for receiving and abetting him on 4 May, 18 Eliz.; Pottell pleaded not guilty, was convicted, and for divers reasons was committed back to gaol. On confirmation of the justices above-named.   By p.s.

1518.)   11 *March* 1577.   *Gorhambury.*   Presentation of Robert Downes, clerk, M.A., to the fourth canonry and prebend in Norwich cathedral.   [*m.* 27]
                                                                              By p.s.

1519.)   20 *March* 1577.   *Gorhambury.*   Lease for 21 years to Henry Johnes, knight, of (1) a grange called Brekagothi, co. Carmarthen, (2) granges called Aberporth and Blaynannerth, cos. Cardigan and Carmarthen, (3) 160 'lez stackes' of oats out of the granges of Laynecrose, Trasnelgan, Kevenglith, Gothegrigg and Custa *alias* Custoda yearly by way of rent, (4) 262 'daye workes' yearly in the same granges of Llaynecrose, Trasnelgan, Kevenglith, Gothgrige and Custa, (5) the rectory of Talley and (6) the rectory of Llansadurn and chapel of Llanurda, co. Carmarthen, once of the monastery of Talley; with reservations; from Michaelmas last; yearly rents (1) 77*s*. 9*d*., (2) 20*s*., (3) 40*s*., (4) 21*s*. 10*d*., (5) £13 6*s*. 8*d*. and (6) £15 11*s*. 6*d*.; the Crown to discharge the lessee from the stipend of a chaplain in Tally church and all other charges. In consideration of his surrender of a patent,   [*m.* 28] 9 Nov., 1 Eliz., leasing the premises to him *inter alia* for 24 years from Lady Day then last at the same rents; and for a fine of £73 15*s*. 6*d*. paid at the Exchequer.   By p.s.

1520.)   11 *March* 1577.   *Gorhambury.*   Lease for 21 years to Richard George of (1) a yearly rent of 5*s*. out of a tenement (*tenant named*) in Stowe, or Swel or elsewhere, co. Gloucester, given for an obit there, and (2) lands (*tenants named*) in Stowe or Swell or elsewhere, co. Gloucester, given for an obit and for the Holy Trinity service in the church of Stowe or Suell; with reservations; from Michaelmas last; yearly rent £5 10*s*. 8*d*. In consideration of the surrender by George of a patent, 17 May, 6 Eliz., leasing to John Jenever the premises (therein described as in Stowe) for 21 years from Lady Day then last at yearly rents of (1) 5*s*. and (2) 105*s*. 8*d*.   By warrant of the commissioners.

1521.)   13 *March* 1577.   *Gorhambury.*   Lease for 21 years to Roger Tanner of (1) lands in Colsterworth *alias* Colesworth, co. Lincoln, (2) lands in   [*m.* 29] Somerbye, co. Lincoln, parcel of the manor of Costerworth, (3) woods (*named*) in Somerbye and (4) woods (*named*) in Colsterworth, all once of Fodringhay college, co. Northampton; with reservations; from Lady Day 1588, having been leased by patent, 3 July, 9 Eliz., for 21 years from Lady Day then last to Gilbert Bury; yearly rents (1) £9 13*s*. 4¾*d*., (2) 63*s*. 9*d*., (3) 40*s*. 6*d*. and (4) 10*s*. 6*d*.; the lessee to discharge the Crown of all charges; the lessee to make two   [*m.* 30] cuttings only of the woods and at fitting seasons; to enclose 'lez springes' thereof after cutting, to leave 12 'lez staddelles' in every acre according to statute, and to permit the tenants of the lordship of Colsterworth to have in (4) thorn and other 'le smale ryce' for making 'le pinfold' in Colsterworth. For his service.   By p.s.

1522.)   13 *March* 1577.   *Gorhambury.*   Protection for Thomas Herne *alias* Heron; provided that during the term (*not specified*) of this protection he behaves well towards the Queen, her realm and subjects. For his service.   By p.s.

1523.)   13 *March* 1577.   *Gorhambury*.   Pardon for Richard Rogers late of Eye, co. Suffolk, 'yeoman', for all offences committed between 1 Jan., 17 Eliz., and 1 Jan., 19 Eliz. At the suit of his wife.   By p.s.

1524.)   15 *March* 1577.   *Gorhambury*.   Presentation of Thomas Geffreys, S.T.B., to the rectory of Asprington, Exeter dioc.   By p.s.

1525.)   15 *March* 1577.   *Gorhambury*.   Lease for 21 years to George Alington of lands (*tenants named*) in (1) Walcote, (2) Burringham, (3) Gayton, (4) Grymolbye, (5) Ashebye *alias* Askebye, (6) Navenbye, (7) Wellenger, (8) Baughton, (9) Corringham, (10) Herbye *alias* Harebye, (11) Lasbye,   [*m.* 31]
(12) Little Lymber, (13) Epworthe, (14) Belton, (15) Scawpwyke, (16) Mariscom Blankney and (17) Deryngton, co. Lincoln, late of the hospital of St. John of Jerusalem; with reservations; from Lady   [*m.* 32]
Day next; yearly rents (1) 11s., (2) 10s. 6d. (*detailed*), (3) 3s. 4d., (4) 12d., (5) 16s. 4d. (*detailed*), (6) 6s. 8d., (7) 3s. 4d., (8) 4s. 4d., (9) 20d., (10) 56s. 11d. (*detailed*), (11) 9s., (12) 4d., (13) 2s. 8d., (14) 2s., (15) 4s. 4d. (*detailed*), (16) 3s. 4d. and (17) 7s. For a fine of £28 11s. paid at the Exchequer.   By warrant of the commissioners.
   Vacated because surrendered, 22 Feb., 21 *Eliz.*; *signed*: Wyllm' Cordell; Geo. Alington.

1526.)   15 *March* 1577.   *Gorhambury*.   Grant for life to Edward Brereton of an annuity of 2s. 6d. a day from Christmas last, payable at the Exchequer. For his service in military expeditions in Ireland and elsewhere.   By p.s.

1527.)   15 *March* 1577.   *Gorhambury*.   Lease for 21 years to Leonard Moyle, one of 'lez sewers' of the chamber, of the tithes of grain in Nottingham and Sneynton, co. Nottingham, late in the tenure of Thomas Shelton and now or late in that of Henry Newton, once of the monastery of Lenton, co. Nottingham; from Lady Day 1582, having been leased by patent, 20 Jan., 3 Eliz., to the said Shelton and Joan Willoughbye, his wife, *inter alia* for 21 years from Lady Day then next at a yearly rent for the said tithes *inter alia* of £22; yearly rent £20. For his service.   By p.s.

1528.)   15 *March* 1577.   *Gorhambury*.   Lease for life in survivorship to William Swayne, Mary Willinghale and John Morley of the rectory of Ayton in Clevelande, co. York, once of the monastery of Whitbye;   [*m.* 33]
with reservations; from Michaelmas last; yearly rent £10; the lessees to provide a curate to serve in Ayton church. In consideration of the surrender by Swayne of a patent, 23 Nov., 14 Eliz., leasing the rectory to him for 21 years from Michaelmas then last at the same rent; and for a fine of £10 paid at the Exchequer by him.   By warrant of the commissioners.

1529.)   15 *March* 1577.   *Gorhambury*.   Protection for one year for Thomas Steynton of London, mercer, and the sureties standing bound with or for him for his debt or cause. *English*.   By p.s.

1530.)   15 *March* 1577.   *Gorhambury*.   Lease for 21 years to Richard   [*m.* 34]
Oseley, a clerk of the privy seal, of the manor of Courtenhall *alias*   [*m.* 35]
Courtnall, co. Northampton, late of the monastery of Lenton, co. Nottingham, and the reversions and rents of lands (*named*), parcel of the said manor, severally leased by three patents of the Exchequer, 19 Feb., 11 Eliz., to Margaret Clarke, widow, John Clerke and William Clerke for 21 years from Michaelmas then next at yearly rents of 43s. 4d., 45s. 6d. and 45s. 6d. respectively; woods, wards, marriages, mines and quarries and the advowson of

Courtnall church reserved; yearly rent £30; the lessee discharged from all other payments.

Grant also for 21 years to Oseley of the office of bailiff and collector of all portions and pensions late of the monastery of Lenton in the county of Northampton; with a yearly fee of 40*s.*, payable out of the said revenue by himself or by the receiver in the county; [*m.* 36] the grantee to render account to the auditor hereunto assigned, and to answer for the moneys arising to the receiver general of the county according to stat. 7 Edw. VI.

From Martinmas 1611, the manor and the office having been respectively leased at the same rent and granted to Oseley by patent, 8 Aug., 18 Eliz., for 31 years from the termination of a lease by patent of the court of Augmentations, 19 March, 5 Edw. VI., to Reginald Conyers of the said manor for 21 years from the termination of a lease thereof by conventual indenture, 6 Jan., 20 Hen. VIII, to Edmund Maxe for 30 years from Martinmas then next.

For his service.   By p.s.

1531.)   27 *July* 1577.   *Gorhambury.*   Dispensation, pardon and re-admission to the fellowship of merchants adventurers of England for George Gylpyn, citizen and draper of London, who has been *ipso facto* disfranchised from the fellowship, pursuant to a patent, 18 July, 6 Eliz., through his marriage to Jane Hellen, daughter of John Hellen of Cortrick in the county of Flanders, merchant, which Jane was also born in the said county beyond the seas, and through his acquisition of lands in the said county as in her right; and licence for the governor or deputy governor, assistants and fellowship of the merchants adventurers to re-admit   [*m.* 37] him; the patent to be void if he shall not within a time to be appointed by the governor, assistants and fellowship sell the said lands, and if he shall not keep his wife and family resident in England unless some necessary occasion to be allowed by the governor, his deputy and assistants shall enforce him to the contrary. The governor and fellowship are contented that he should be re-admitted, the Queen's assent and licence being first obtained.   *English.*   By p.s.

1532.)   9 *Aug.* 1577.   *Gorhambury.*   Grant for life in survivorship to Christopher Russell and Gerald Dyllon, both of Swerde, co. Dublin, of the offices of (1) clerk of the crown in the Queen's Bench (*coram nobis in capitali placea nostra*) in Ireland and (2) clerk of the common pleas and keeper of the writs and rolls in the said Queen's Bench (*in capitali placea nostra predicta*); after the offices shall become void by the death, forfeiture or surrender of Bartholomew Russell, to whom they were granted by patent [under the great seal of Ireland[1]], 23 Oct., 35 Hen. VIII, for life; with fees as received by the said Bartholomew, payable at the Exchequer of Ireland.   By p.s.

1533.)   12 *Aug.* 1577.   *Gorhambury.*   Grant to Hugh Castelton, S.T.B., of a canonry or prebend in the collegiate church or free chapel of Holy Trinity, Norwich, void by the death of William Fenton.   By p.s.

1534.)   29 *July* 1577.   *Gorhambury.*   Presentation of William Rustat, clerk, to the mastership or wardenship of the hospital of St. John at Litterworthe, Lincoln dioc.
                                                                                  By p.s.

1535.)   18 *Sept.* 1577.   *Gorhambury.*   Grant to life to William Spencer, third son of John Spencer of Althropp, co. Northampton, knight, of the office of one of the seven auditors of the Exchequer which shall next   [*m.* 38]

---

[1] *Cf. Calendar of Patent and Close Rolls of Chancery in Ireland, Henry VIII–Elizabeth*, Vol. I, p. 102.

be void; with a yearly fee of £20, payable at the Exchequer. Francis Southwell, John Thompson, Thomas Neale, William Fuller, William Neale, Robert Multon and Henry Dynne, the present auditors, hold their offices for life by patents severally made to them thereof, and Anthony Roue was granted the reversion of Southwell's office by patent, 5 Nov., 5 & 6 Ph. & Mary, for life.   By p.s.

1536.)   13 *Sept.* 1577.   *Gorhambury.*   Lease for 40 years to Arthur Champernowne, knight, the Queen's servant, of the rectory of Brodecliste, co. Devon, and the advowson of the vicarage of Brodecliste; with reservations, including the manor of Brodecliste and all lands   [*m.* 39]
called Loxebroke, Stilesham, Farthinges and Priers Courte, once leased to Thomas Arundell, knight, with the rectory; from Michaelmas 1593, the rectory having been leased by patent, 26 July, 9 Eliz., to Arthur Champernowne, knight, (the advowson of the vicarage reserved) for 21 years from Michaelmas 1572 at a yearly rent of £47 3s. 6d.; same rent; the lessee discharged from all other charges. For his service.   By p.s.

1537.)   26 *Aug.* 1577.   *Gorhambury.*   Licence for life in survivorship for John Daye, citizen and stationer of London, and Richard Daye, his son, to print the Psalms of David in English metre, with notes to sing them, the A.B.C. with the Little Catechism appointed by the Queen's injunctions for the instruction of children, the Catechism in English and Latin compiled by Alexander Nowell, now dean of St. Paul's, with all other books in English or Latin which the said Nowell has made or shall make, write or translate, and has appointed or shall appoint to be printed by them, and also all other books compiled, translated and set out by any learned man at their procurement and charges, so that no such book be repugnant to the Holy Scripture or the laws or order of the realm; provided that none of the said other books be for any copies now belonging to any of the Queen's subjects by express and special privilege heretofore granted by the Queen, Henry VIII, Edward VI or Queen Mary, and that every book printed by virtue of this privilege be perused and allowed before it be put in print as ordered by the Queen's injunction or otherwise to be forfeited; no other person to print any books that the licensees have hereby licence to print, nor bring them into England or there sell or bind them on pain of the Queen's high indignation; every offender to forfeit to the Queen's use 40s. for every book printed, brought in, sold or bound contrary to this licence, besides every such book to be forfeited to such person as shall seize the same and give information   [*m.* 40]
of the said forfeiture of 40s., and to abide such penalties and order of bond as by the decrees (which upon motion of the Queen's commissioners in causes ecclesiastical have been by the Privy Council at the Star Chamber at Westminster, 29 June, 8 Eliz., appointed to be observed for the reformation of divers disorders in printing and uttering of books) is appointed for the correction of persons so offending contrary to any law or ordinance; the said commissioners duly to execute the said ordinances against such person as upon information or complaint by the licensees shall be found meet to be bound, and the sight of this patent or the exemplification thereof under the great seal shall be sufficient warrant to the commissioners; the master and wardens of the mistery of stationers of London and all other the Queen's ministers to assist the licensees in the execution of this licence.   *English.*
                                                                                                             By p.s.

1538.)   6 *Sept.* 1577.   *Gorhambury.*   Pardon for Thomas White late of Tenbye, co. Pembroke, 'mariner', indicated by two indictments for piracy in that he with many others on 1 April, 18 Eliz., boarded 'a pynnesse' belonging to Walter Meriell of Ipswich, co. Suffolk, merchant, lying at anchor in Oxforde (*alias* Oxeforde) river within the jurisdiction of the Admiralty, assaulted Thomas Collins, master thereof, and Thomas Padley, mariner, and

stole (1) goods (*described*) severally belonging to Peter Merrimounte of Ipswich, stranger, Bastian Man of Ipswich, merchant, and Thomas Kildermershe of Ipswich, 'merchant', and (2) goods (*described*) and 'lez pynnesse' aforesaid belonging to Merriell. Upon information of Thomas Gawdye, a justice of the Queen's Bench, William Paston, Henry Woodhouse, vice-admiral in the counties of Norfolk and Suffolk, Francis Windam and William Heydon, justices of the peace of the county of Norfolk.   [*m.* 41]
                                                                                                   By p.s.

1539.)   13 *Nov.* 1577.   *Windsor Castle.*   Grant for life to Thomas West, lord Delawarre, of the manor of Wordelham *alias* East Wordelham and West Wordelham, co. Southampton, together with the reversion and rent of the same manor, which was leased by patent, 3 Nov., 18 Eliz., to Henry Audeley at a yearly rent of £31 2s. 11d. for 21 years from the death, forfeiture or surrender of William, marquess of Winchester, and John Pawlett, lord St. John, late marquess of Winchester, both now deceased, to whom it was granted *inter alia* by patent, 29 Jan., 3 Eliz., for life in survivorship; that the grantee may pay the fees and stipends of the foresters, keepers and ministers of the forests and chases below specified.
     Grant also for life of the office of lieutenant or keeper of the forests or chases of Aylyshott and Wolmer, co. Southampton; with power to appoint a deputy or deputies at pleasure, and such foresters and keepers as have hitherto been there; also to have all attachments of animals in the forests, all woods felled by the wind or dead, the boughs and leaves of all trees cut down, wood called 'houseboote' and 'fireboote' for himself and the foresters and keepers, 'waief' and 'straif', honey and wax found there, pasture in the lands of the Crown there for two horses of himself and his deputies and for one horse of each forester and keeper, and liberty of fishing in the Crown's waters there; also grant of 15 quarters of oats yearly from the tenants of Alton Eastbrooke and Alton Westbrooke; also grant of oats called 'rent otes' in Hedley, Greateham, Benstede and Kingesley and hens   [*m.* 42] called 'rent hennes' in Benstede and Kingesley, belonging to the said manor of Wordleham and reserved to the Crown under the lease to Audeley; also power to hold before him or his lieutenant every sixth week 'a woode courte', to have the issues thereof and to keep the 'nombles' and the 'suytes' of wild beasts killed in the forests; also that he may take there yearly in summer one stag and one hind and in winter one young stag and one young hind.
     For his service.   By p.s.

1540.)   20 *July* 1577.   *Gorhambury.*   Pardon for Anthony Caverley *alias* Gye, late of London, 'yeoman', for the theft of clothing (*described*) belonging to Thomas Rosse at Westminster, co. Middlesex, on 6 April, 19 Eliz., whereof he is indicted, and all other offences. At the suit of Elizabeth Caverley, his mother.

1541.)   8 *July* 1577.   *Gorhambury.*   Commitment for 21 years to Chidiock Wardoure of the custody or farm of (1) lands in Cheriell *alias* Cherell, co. Wilts, late leased to Richard Grafton in the year 29 Hen. VIII for 20 years, and (2) wastes in the forest of Chiute and the forest of Savernak, co. Wilts, leased to William Sturmy, knight, in the year 5 Hen. IV for 100 years; from Lady Day last; yearly rent 32s. 8d., to wit, for (1) 8s. 4d. and (2) 24s. 4d. and 4d. beyond of increase. Because he has found security before the barons of the Exchequer.
                                                       By warrant of the commissioners.

1542.)   17 *June* 1577.   Lease for 21 years to John Rade, one of the   [*m.* 43] Queen's footmen, of (1) lands (*named*) in Wenington, co. Essex, once of Shene priory, co. Surrey, and (2) the demesne lands of the manor of Estderham, co. Norfolk, late of the bishopric of Ely and in the Queen's hands by act of Parliament; with reservations; (1) from Michaelmas last and (2) from Lady Day last or the termination of any existing lease or grant thereof for life or years enduring after that date; yearly rents (1) 46s. 8d. and (2) £13 13s. 2d. For his service.   By p.s.

(The dorse of this roll is blank.)

PART III

C. 66/1153

1543.)   20 *Dec.* 1576.   Licence for Roger Ligon and Catherine his   [*m.* 1]
wife to alienate the manor of Fayrford *alias* Ferford, lands in Fayreford and a fishery in the
water of Fairyford, Coowne and Byberrye, co. Gloucester, to John Hungerford, knight,
and Thomas Boowrcher to the use of Roger and Catherine for life in survivorship, with
successive remainders to the executors and administrators of the survivor of them for one
year, to Walter Dennys and Margaret his wife and the heirs male of the body of Walter and
to the right heirs of Catherine. For £13 6s. 8d. paid to the Queen's farmer.

1544.)   3 *Jan.* 1577.   The like for William Carowe, citizen and draper of London, and
Anne his wife to alienate lands (*tenants named*) in Stone, Darrent and Dratford, co. Kent, to
Edward Mannynge of Grayes Inne. For 23s. 8d.

1545.)   3 *Jan.* 1577.   The like for Thomas Lorde to alienate lands in Ullestthorpe and
Cleybrooke, co. Leicester, to Thomas Payne. For 9s. 4d.

1546.)   3 *Jan.* 1577.   The like for Hugh Hare, Innocent Rede and Elizabeth his wife to
alienate a third part of the manors of Highclere and Burghclere *alias* Burroughclere, of lands
in Highclere and Burghclere and of the advowsons of Highclere and Burghclere churches,
co. Southampton, to Richard Kingesmyll, attorney of the court of Wards, William
Kingesmyll, knight, John Kingesmyll and George Kingesmyll and the heirs and assigns of
Richard. For £7 15s. 7d.

1547.)   3 *Jan.* 1577.   Pardon of alienation: William Savyle by   [*m.* 2]
indenture, 18 Jan., 16 Eliz., acquired from George Barwell and William Barwell the manor
or capital messuage of Saperton, co. Lincoln. For £3 6s. 8d. paid to the Queen's farmer.

1548.)   3 *Jan.* 1577.   The like: John Savyle in Trinity term by fine in the Common Pleas
acquired from William Poulett, knight, lord St. John, and Agnes his wife the manor of
Thorplangton and lands in Thorplangton, Churchelangton, Tyrlangton, Eastlangton and
Westlangton, co. Leicester. For 60s.

1549.)   3 *Jan.* 1577.   Licence for William Godfrey *alias* Cowper, 'yoman', to alienate a
third part of lands (*named*) in Lecheworth, Langley and Hytchen, co. Hertford, to Francis
Godfrey *alias* Cowper. For 10s. 8d. paid to the Queen's farmer.

1550.)   23 *Jan.* 1577.   The like for John Crispe, son and heir of William Crispe, to alienate
a manor or messuage called Lambertestand and all its appurtenances in Hernehill and
Sesalter, co. Kent, to Richard Hartuse, 'yeoman'. For £5.

1551.)   3 *Jan.* 1577.   Pardon of alienation: William Davyson, citizen and 'glasier' of
London, and Elizabeth his wife by writing, 7 Nov., 17 Eliz., acquired unto them and the
heirs of their bodies, with remainder to the right heirs of the said William, from William
Armorer, son and heir of George Armorer, late citizen and 'clothworker' of London, a

messuage, in the tenure of Humphrey Smythe of London, joiner, in Longelane in the parish of St. Sepulchre, London. For 40s. paid to the Queen's farmer.   [m. 3]

1552.)   3 *Jan.* 1577.   Licence for Richard Mergittes, 'yeoman', to alienate lands (*named*) in Bredfeld, co. Suffolk, to John Soone. For 13s. 4d. paid to the Queen's farmer.

1553.)   2 *Jan.* 1577.   The like for Giles Duncombe to alienate lands in Great Brickhill, co. Buckingham, to Thomas Duncumbe the elder. For 9s.

1554.)   10 *Dec.* 1576.   The like for Francis Jermye and Elizabeth his wife to alienate a fourth part of the manor of Norrell *alias* Northwell *alias* Northeyvell, of lands in Norrell, Overcaldecote, Nether Caldecote, Ikewell, Beiston, Hatche and Thornecote and of the rectory of Norrell, co. Bedford, to Thomas Browne, knight. For £3 6s. 8d.

1555.)   20 *Dec.* 1576.   The like for Anne Goodwyn, widow, and John Wighell to alienate the manor or capital messuage of Muswell *alias* Muswell Chapell, a messuage or farm called Muswell Fearme and all lands in Muswell, Haringey *alias* Hernsey, Fyncheley and Clarkenwell, co. Middlesex, late of John Goodwyn, deceased, to William Rowe, citizen of London. For 36s. 8d.

1556.)   3 *Jan.* 1577.   The like for Richard Cooke to alienate the   [m. 4] rectory of Dorsett *alias* Dassett *alias* Byrton Dassett *alias* Dassett Magna, the tithes there and a third part of the manor of Dorsett aforesaid and of lands there, co. Warwick, to Francis Raumme and Robert Badby. For £26 13s. 4d.

1557.)   3 *Jan.* 1577.   Pardon of alienation: Thomas Thetford by writing, 18 Oct., 16 Eliz., acquired from John Revett and Thomas Revett, his brother, 'yeoman', the manor of Aslecton Priorye, with the appropriated rectory of Aslecton, and lands in Aslacton, Moulton St. Michael, Moulton All Saints, Tybenham, Waketon and Fornsett or elsewhere, co. Norfolk. For £10 paid to the Queen's farmer.

1558.)   3 *Jan.* 1577.   Licence for Richard Martyn and Margaret his wife to alienate a moiety of the manor of Chilcombe and of lands in Chilcombe, co. Dorset, to John Bisshoppe and Humphrey Bisshoppe, his son and heir apparent, and the heirs and assigns of Humphrey. For 46s. 8d. paid to the Queen's farmer.

1559.)   12 *Dec.* 1576.   The like for Thomas Birde and Elizabeth his wife to alienate lands in Great Horsey, co. Essex, and lands, a free chapel and the advowson of the chapel in Naylande, co. Suffolk, to Thomas Lodge, knight, and Anne his wife and the heirs and assigns of Anne. For £3 6s. 8d..

1560.)   2 *Jan.* 1577.   The like for John Scudamore and Mary his wife to alienate the park of Blagedon *alias* Cranborne *alias* Cramborne   [m. 5] and lands in Blagedon and Cranborne, co. Dorset, to Henry, earl of Pembroke. For £6 2s. 6d.

1561.)   3 *Jan.* 1577.   The like for Edmund Gybbons to alienate the manor of Hensington and all his lands in Hensington, co. Oxford, to George Whitton. For 27s. 8d.

1562.)   3 *Jan.* 1577.   The like for William Merston to alienate the manor of Woodhall in Hempsted *alias* Hemelhempsted and lands in Hemelhempsted, co. Hertford, to Francis Merston. For 26s. 8d.

1563.)   3 *Jan.* 1577.   The like for Thomas Holgate of Pountfrett, merchant, and Thomas Holgate, his son, to alienate lands in Yeddingham, co. York, to Robert Singleton and Bartholomew Laikyn, 'yeoman'. For £3 6s. 8d.

1564.)   3 *Jan.* 1577.   Pardon of alienation: Henry Elmeley in Easter term, 16 Eliz., by fine in the Common Pleas acquired from William Darke and Margery his wife lands in Pouclechurche, co. Gloucester. For 21s. paid to the Queen's farmer.   [*m.* 6]

1565.)   3 *Jan.* 1577.   The like: Anthony Martyn by fine in the Common Pleas in Michaelmas term, 17 Eliz., acquired from John Parsmyth *alias* Cheyney the younger and Mary his wife for the life of Mary the rectory of Manewden, lands in Manewden and the advowson of the vicarage of Manewden, co. Essex. For £20.

1566.)   3 *Jan.* 1577.   Licence for Francis Jermye and Elizabeth his wife to alienate a third part of the manors of Highclere and Burghclere *alias* Burroughclere, of lands in Highclere and Burghclere and of the advowsons of Highclere and Burghclere churches, co. Southampton, to Richard Kingesmyll, attorney of the court of Wards, John Thornborough and George Kingesmyll and the heirs and assigns of Richard. For £7 15s. 7d. paid to the Queen's farmer.

1567.)   2 *Jan.* 1577.   The like for Robert Hayes and Alice his wife to alienate lands in Sherston, co. Wilts, to Edward, earl of Hertford, during the life of Alice. For £3.

1568.)   2 *Jan.* 1577.   The like for Francis, earl of Bedford, to alienate the manor of Borington and lands in Borington, co. Devon, to Lewis Stucley and John Stucley and the heirs and assigns of Lewis. For £4 10s. 6d.

1569.)   2 *Jan.* 1577.   The like for John Petty to alienate the manor of Wivold Courte and the site or farm thereof in Chekindon, Pyperd and   [*m.* 7] Rotherveld, co. Oxford, to Robert Petty of Lincolns Inne, co. Middlesex. For 33s. 4d.

1570.)   3 *Jan.* 1577.   Pardon of alienation: Thomas Carewe of Haccombe, co. Devon, and Humphrey Aleigh had by feoffment, 2 Jan., 18 Eliz., from Thomas Walton the elder the manor of Shapwicke, co. Somerset, and all his other lands in Shapwicke to hold to the use of Thomas Walton the younger, son and heir of the said Thomas Walton the elder, and Mary his wife for life in survivorship, with remainder to the heirs and assigns of Thomas the younger. For £3 18s. 8d. paid to the Queen's farmer.

1571.)   3 *Jan.* 1577.   The like: Gregory Moore and Peter Kempe in Michaelmas term, 13 Eliz., by fine in the Common Pleas acquired unto them and the heirs of Moore from William Stanley, knight, lord Mountegle, a third part of the site of the monastery of Valdy, of lands in Valdy, of the manors of Edenham, Scotelthorpp, Ingoldesby, Welby, Birton *alias* Burton and Willesforde, of lands in Edenham, Scotelthorpp, Ingoldsby, Welby, Burton, Willesforde, Langton *alias* Lavington, Little Humby, Belton, Farhumby, Gunwarby, Waterwilloughby, Hether *alias* Hethorne, Lunderthorpe *alias* Lundunthorpe, Rappesley, Sapperton *alias* Saperton, Puckworth *alias* Pickwith, Bilchfeld *alias* Bichefeld, Steneby, Corby, Eston, Westby, Skillington, Casson *alias* Colson, Swayfeld, Colsworth *alias* Colserworth, Grauntham, Sowthstocke, Grymsthorpe, Witham, Toft, Manthorpe, Bytham, Careby, Creton, Swynsted, Irneham, Bulby, Pinchbecke, Caxby *alias* Kelsby, Ankoster, Norththickham, Haddington and Lowthe Parke and of the advowson of Fullestowe church, co. Lincoln, and of lands in the city of Lincoln. For 40s.

1572.) 3 *Jan.* 1577.   The like: Gregory Moore and Peter Kempe in Easter term, 14 Eliz., by fine in the Common Pleas acquired unto them and the heirs of Moore from William Stanley, knight, lord Montegle, a third part of lands in Bowrne and Snafforde and of the rectory of Fullestowe, co. Lincoln. For 13s. 4d.

1573.) 3 *Jan.* 1577.   The like: Gregory Moore in Michaelmas term, 14 Eliz., acquired from William Stanley, knight, lord Mountegle, a third part of the manor of Abye and of lands in Abye, Saleley,   [*m.* 8]
Wythern and Tothill, co. Lincoln. For 13s. 4d.

1574.) 3 *Jan.* 1577.   The like: Jasper Moore by writing, 24 July, 16 Eliz., acquired from Thomas Moore a moiety of the manor of Wythyes and all appurtenances thereof in Hunspill and Shoppwick or elsewhere, co. Somerset. For £6 13s. 4d.

1575.) 8 *Dec.* 1576.   Licence for William Vincent to alienate the manor of Potters Marston and all his lands in Potters Marston, Banwell and Stanton, co. Leicester, to John Ploumbe. For £4 9s. paid to the Queen's farmer.

1576.) 3 *Jan.* 1577.   The like for Henry, earl of Derby, and Margaret his wife to alienate (1) a moiety of the manors of Brighthelmyston, Meechinge, Allington and Seaford, of lands in Brighthelmyston, Mechinge, Pedinghoo, Telscombe, Southeese, Seaforde, Iforde, Chayleigh, Newicke, Barcombe, Southover, Ovindene, Rottingdene, Denton, Torringe and St. Johns under the castle of Lewes, of free warren in Mechinge, Pedinghoo, Telscombe and Southeese and of free fishery in the water of Barcombe, Hamsey, St. Johns under the castle of Lewis, Lewes, Southover, Iforde, Radmell, Southeese, Telscombe, Pedinghoo and Meechinge and (2) a fourth part of the barony of Lewes, of the borough of Lewis, of the hundred of Lewis, of the barony and manor of Lewes *alias* Lewes Burgus, of lands in Lewes and Erthinglye and of the hundred and view of frankpledge of Lewes, Strete, Buttinghill, Barcombe, Swanborugh *alias* Swanburgh, Holmestowe, Yowensmare *alias* Yonesmare, Whalesbone, Fishers Gate and Poonynges *alias* Poyninges, co. Sussex, to Thomas Sackvile, knight, lord Buckherst. For £20.

1577.) 3 *Jan.* 1577.   Pardon of alienation: Thomas Hennage, treasurer of the chamber, and Moyle (*Moilus*) Fynche in Michaelmas term, 17 Eliz., by fine in the Common Pleas acquire unto them and the heirs of Fynche from Nicholas Seyntleger and Catherine his wife *inter alia* the manors of Estwell, Seaton and Willnington *alias* Wilmingdon, the park of Estwell and the advowson of Estewell, co. Kent. For £8 paid to the Queen's farmer.

[*m.* 9]

1578.) 3 *Dec.* 1576.   The like: Thomas Hedges by indenture, 2 Sept., 17 Eliz., demised to Anne Woodward, widow, then the relict of John Woodward afterwards wife of the said Hedges, deceased, for life *inter alia* the manors of Shipton Moyne and Shipton Dovell and all his lands in Shipton Moyne and Shipton Dovell, co. Gloucester, and the manor of Eston Grey and all his lands in Eston Grey, co. Wilts. For £26 2s. 2d.

1579.) 2 *Jan.* 1577.   Licence for John Trye and Margaret his wife to alienate lands in Revesby *alias* Resby, St. Sythes and Wildemore, co. Lincoln, to Thomas Cecill, knight. For 46s. 8d. paid to the Queen's farmer.

1580.) 3 *Jan.* 1577.   The like for John Curteis and Anne his wife to alienate lands in

Christen Malford, co. Wilts, to William Button and Ambrose Button and the heirs and assigns of William. For 23*s.*

1581.)   3 *Jan.* 1577.   The like for Richard Jenowaye to alienate lands (*described with tenants' names*) in Ravensthorpe, co. Northampton, and all lands which ought to descend to him by the death of William Jenowaye, his father, in Ravensthorpe to William Jenowaye the elder, Richard's brother. For 8*s.* 8*d.*

1582.)   3 *Jan.* 1577.   The like for Thomas Walkeden to alienate woods (*described with tenants' names*) (1) called Loddynges Grove, (2) called Darkesallys *alias* Darksalles, (3) called Lachynges Grove, (4) near a wood called Minchenwood (5) in a   [*m.* 10] wood called Hasilhaught, (6) between Canfeldes and lands of the lord of Edmonton, (7) called Peverelles, (8) between Lingate or Libroke and land called Cockestones, (9) called Bachelers Grove and (10) called Priors Grove near Wynsmore Hill, and a pasture called Peverelles Pasture (*described*), co. Middlesex, to Thomas Hoo the elder and Nicholas Brokett to the use of Walkeden and Jane his wife and his heirs male by her, with remainder to Walkeden. For 22*s.*

1583.)   3 *Jan.* 1577.   The like for William Porter *alias* Purcas to alienate land (*named*) in Braxsted Magna, co. Essex, to Brian Darcy. For 13*s.* 4*d.*

1584.)   2 *Jan.* 1577.   The like for John Chamberlayne and Elizabeth his wife to alienate the manor of Cuttyslowe *alias* Cuddislowe and lands in Cuttyslowe, Twyslowe and Wolvercote, co. Oxford, to Anthony Bourne and Elizabeth his wife and the heirs and assigns of Anthony. For £4.   [*m.* 11]

1585.)   3 *Jan.* 1577.   Pardon of alienation: William Harrys by writing, 20 July, 14 Eliz., acquired from John Scott, 'yoman', a tenement in Calston Wylie in Calne, co. Wilts. For 5*s.* paid to the Queen's farmer.

1586.)   3 *Jan.* 1577.   The like: Richard Westcombe in Easter term, 16 Eliz., by fine in the Common Pleas acquired from John Parker and Elizabeth his wife lands in Hillfarrans and Nynhed and the tithes of hay in the manor of Pixton belonging to the farm of Pixton in Nynhed, co. Somerset. For £7 6*s.*

1587.)   2 *Jan.* 1577.   Licence for Elizabeth Grey to alienate her part or pourparty of lands in Lissington, co. Lincoln, to Gregory Ustwoode. For 4*s.* paid to the Queen's farmer.

1588.)   12 *Dec.* 1576.   The like for Thomas Dearinge, Winifred his wife, Thomas Carson, Nicholas Langrishe, William Penne, Nicholas Hedger and Ralph Hedger to alienate lands in Beryton, co. Southampton, to Richard Penne and John Westbrooke and the heirs and assigns of Richard. For 20*s.*

1589.)   3 *Jan.* 1577.   The like for Walter Beconsawe and Anne his wife to alienate lands and free pasture [*sic*] in the water of Lodon in Shirfeld, co. Southampton, to Fane (*Phanus*) Becher, Henry Beacher, Edward Becher and Chidiock Warder and the heirs and assigns of Fane. For 15*s.* 7*d.*   [*m.* 12]

1590.)   2 *Jan.* 1577.   The like for Thomas Wotton to alienate a third part of the manor of Stokingford and all other lands which after the death of his father, Edward Wotton, knight, or by descent, purchase, partition or otherwise came to the said Thomas in Stokingford,

Lutmans End, Bowles, Overend, Attilborowe and Cotton, co. Warwick, to Richard Cooke. For £3 6s. 8d.

1591.) 2 Jan. 1577.   The like for William Plompton to alienate the manor of Sacombe and all his other lands in Sacombe, Standon, Wadesmyll, Watton and Stapleforde, co. Hertford, to Edmund Thurland and Anthony Latham. For £8 6s. 8d.

1592.) 3 Jan. 1577.   Pardon of alienation: Matthew Smyth in Michaelmas term, 17 Eliz., by fine in the Common Pleas acquired from John Bonham and Mabel his wife lands in Boxx, Ridlowe, Wades, Wike, Aisheley and Hasilbury, the rectory of Boxx and the tithes belonging thereto in the said places and the advowson of the vicarage of Boxx, co. Wilts. For £6 10s. paid to the Queen's farmer.

1593.) 3 Jan. 1577.   The like: Richard Patricke, citizen and 'haberdasher' of London, and George Utlaye and William Bennett, 'drapers' of London, acquired by feoffment, 9 July, 16 Eliz., of Francis Barnham, alderman of London, the following in London—(1) a messuage in St. Clementes Lane in the parish of St. Clement in Lanborne ward, now in his tenure, acquired by him from Rowland Hayward, knight, alderman of London, George Basforde, citizen and 'letherseller' of London, and Francis Boyer of London, 'grocer', by indenture, 14 Jan., 3 Eliz., (2) another messuage in St. Clement's Lane, in his tenure, purchased by him from Roger Jorden, 'clothworker' of London, by indenture, 26 March, 9 Eliz., (3) a great messuage in St. Botolph's Lane in the parish of St. George by Eschepe and in Love Lane in the parish of St. Marie Hill, purchased by him from Henry, earl of Arundel, by indenture, 18 Nov., 3 [sic] Ph. & Mary, and (4) five messuages, now or late in the several tenures of William Hobson, James Presse, Henry Richardson, Andrew Nullon and Ralph Westwood, in 'le Powltrie' in Chepe ward (between   [m. 13]
a tenement now or late inhabited by Westwood and a tenement late of Chockston priory called 'le Blacke Bull', now or late in the tenure of Nullon), two messuages, now or late in the tenure of William Perrye and Margaret his wife, in the parish of St. Mildred in 'le Powltrie', two messuages in the parish of St. Mary Colchurche, now or late in the several tenures of John Hursell and Elizabeth Grene, a capital messuage called 'le Rosse' in 'le Olde Jurye', now or late in the tenure of William Perrie and Martin Perrye, a messuage in Old Jewry, now or late in the tenure of Richard Blacke, a messuage in Old Jewry in the parish of St. Olave, now or late in the tenure of William Hardinge, a messuage, now or late in the tenure of Ralph Westwood, and two adjoining shops leased therewith to Westwood on Conyhopelane in the parish of St. Mildred aforesaid and a messuage, now or late in the tenure of Henry Skynner, and two adjoining shops leased therewith to Skynner in the said parish of St. Mildred, all purchased by the said Francis Barnham from John Brooke, citizen and 'draper' of London, by indenture, 16 July, 2 Eliz., and all other lands of the said Francis in the said places, to hold (1) and (2) to the use of Francis for life, with successive remainders to Alice Barneham, his wife, so long as she should live unmarried, to Stephen Barnham and Anne Patrick and the heirs of the body of Stephen, to Benet Barnham, Francis's younger son, in tail and to the right heirs of Francis, and to hold the rest to the use of Francis for life, with successive remainders to the said Stephen and Anne and the heirs of the body of Stephen, to the said Benet in tail and to the right heirs of Francis. For £20.

1594.) 2 Jan. 1577.   Licence for William Ascoughe to alienate the manors of Stalling-burgh [and] Caster, the soke of Caster, lands to Stallingburgh [and] Castor, the yearly fair of Castor and the market of Castor, co. Lincoln, to Francis Manbye, Vincent Grantham and Thomas Hatcliffe and the heirs and assigns of Manbye. For £12 paid to the Queen's farmer.

1595.) 1 *Dec.* 1576.   The like for William Hodgeson, citizen and merchant taylor of London, to alienate a garden, late in the tenure of   [*m.* 14] Gregory Isham and now in that of Hodgeson, by Mille Alley in the parish of St. Stephen in Colmanstreate, London, late of the monastery of Ruley, to Ambrose Smyth, citizen and mercer of London. For 3*s.* 8*d.*

1596.) 3 *Jan.* 1577.   The like for William Underhill of Newbold Rivell, co. Warwick, to alienate the manor of Loxley and lands in Loxley and Barford, co. Warwick, to Thomas Underhill of Lincolns Inne. For £3 10*s.*

1597.) 3 *Jan.* 1577.   The like for Edward Ayscoghe and Hester his wife to alienate the manor of Swynhop, co. Lincoln, to Hugh Alington and George Alington. For £5 8*s.* 2*d.*

1598.) 11 *Feb.* 1577.   Pardon for Lawrence Mowle late of London, 'lymeman'. It was found by an inquisition taken before Robert Hodgeson, coroner of the city, on 16 Jan. on the body of John Harvye late of London, 'lymeman', in the parish of St. Mary Somersett in Quenshithe ward, London, that Mowle killed Harvye by misadventure in the said parish on 15 Jan., 19 Eliz. (*details given*).

1599.) 12 *Feb.* 1577.   Pardon of outlawry for Gregory Sprint late of London, draper, who was put in exigent in the husting of London for non-appearance in the Common Pleas to answer Edmund Huggan, citizen and merchant of London, in a plea of debt of £100 and has now surrendered himself to the Fleet prison.

1600.) 7 *Feb.* 1577.   Pardon for William Tappe of Fylley, co. Cornwall, 'servyngman'. It was found by an inquisition taken at Lostwythyell,   [*m.* 15] co. Cornwall, before Thomas Trenance, a coroner in the county, on 21 March on the body of Lewis Brodley late of Lostwythyell, 'taylder', that Tappe wounded Brodley in self defence on 7 Dec., 18 Eliz., at 'Saincte Nicholas' chapel in Bodmyn, co. Cornwall, (*details given*), so that he died on 20 March at Lostwythyell.

1601.) 26 *Jan.* 1577.   Pardon for Putnam Woodes. It was found by an inquisition taken at Heston, co. Middlesex, before Robert Cooke, a coroner of the county, on Monday 7 [*recte* 27] Aug., 18 Eliz., on the body of Thomas Stockdoune late of Heston, 'yeoman', that Woodes, being engaged with Stockdoune and others (*named*) at archery on 26 Aug., 18 Eliz., at Heston by misadventure shot and killed Stockdoune (*details given*).

1602.) 28 *Jan.* 1577.   Pardon of outlawry for Henry Mordaunte of London *alias* of the Middle Temple, London, who was put in exigent in the husting of London for non-appearance in the Common Pleas to satisfy James Taylor, citizen and grocer of London, touching a debt of £30, and 33*s.* 4*d.* damages, recovered in the same court and has now surrendered himself to the Fleet prison.

1603.) 19 *Jan.* 1577.   The like for Richard Nychollettes, son of William Nycollettes, *alias* Richard Nicollettes of Wyketon, co. Hereford, who was put in exigent in the husting of London for non-appearance in the Common Pleas to answer Richard Nycollettes, son of James Nichollettes, in a plea of debt of £40 and has now surrendered himself to the Fleet prison.

1604.) 22 *Jan.* 1577.   Pardon for James Redye *alias* Gardiner late of Brington, co. Northampton, 'yoman'. He was indicted before William   [*m.* 16]

Vaus, lord Harrowdon, John Spencer, knight, Thomas Spencer, Francis Saunders and their fellows, keepers of the peace and justices of oyer and terminer in the county, on Tuesday after Trinity, 18 Eliz., at the session of the peace held at Northampton castle for the death of Ralph Fyn late of Northampton, 'yoman', by wounding him in self defence outside the house of John Lowycke in the parish of All Saints in the liberty of the town of Northampton on 28 March, 18 Eliz., so that he died in Northampton on the following day (*details given*); the indictment was removed into the Queen's Bench; Redy pleaded not guilty and it was found that he killed Fyn in self defence, as appears by the record of Christopher Wray, knight, chief justice of the Queen's Bench, sent into Chancery.

1605.)   19 *Nov.* 1576.   Pardon of outlawry for Edward Taylor late of London, 'merchaunttaylor', who was put in exigent in the husting of London for non-appearance in the Common Pleas to answer Robert Milburne of Westminster, co. Middlesex, 'yoman', in a plea of debt of £20 and has now surrendered himself to the Fleet prison.

1606.)   22 *Nov.* 1576.   Pardon for George Towres *alias* Stowres, late of Langporte, co. Somerset, 'yoman'. It was found by an inquisition taken before Francis Sandes, a coroner of the county, that Towres feloniously wounded Stephen Harrys at Langporte on 9 July, 18 Eliz., so that he died there on 16 July following (*details given*); afterwards at a session held at Charde, co. Somerset, on 5 Sept., 18 Eliz., before Roger Manwood, a justice of the Common Pleas, and John Jefferay, a justice of the Queen's Bench, justices of gaol delivery of Yvelchester, he pleaded not guilty and it was found that he killed Harrys in self defence.

1607.)   28 *Nov.* 1576.   Pardon for John Hoy of Tunstall, co. Kent,   [*m.* 17] 'yoman'. It was found by an inquisition taken at Syttingborne, co. Kent, before John Fremlyn, a coroner of the county, on 4 Oct., 18 Eliz., on the body of Thomas Hendley, servant of George Fynche of Norton, co. Kent, that Hoy wounded Hendley at Syttingborne on 29 Sept., 18 Eliz., in self defence so that he died there on 30 Sept. (*details given*); the indictment was removed into the Queen's Bench and on Tuesday after the octave of Martinmas in Michaelmas term, 18 & 19 Eliz., Hoy came before the said court and surrendered himself to the Marshalsea prison.

1608.)   11 *Feb.* 1577.   Pardon of outlawry for Robert Baylie late of Glastenbury, co. Somerset, 'husbandman', who was put in exigent in the county of Somerset for non-appearance in the Common Pleas to answer John Stevans of Egersley, co. Somerset, 'husbandman', in a plea of debt of £5 12s. and has now surrendered himself to the Fleet prison.

1609.)   20 *Dec.* 1576.   The like for Robert Bourman late of London, 'hosyer', who was put in exigent in the county of Salop for non-appearance in the Common Pleas to answer Hugh Phillippes the younger, administrator of Richard Phillippes, who died intestate, in a plea for restitution of a gold ring (price £10) and has now surrendered himself to the Fleet prison.

1610.)   20 *Nov.* 1576.   Pardon for Ralph Colston late of Grayes Inne, co. Middlesex. It was found by an inquisition taken at High Holborne in the parish of St. Andrew, co. Middlesex, before Richard Vale, a coroner in the county, on 3 Oct. on the body of Richard Baker late of London   [*m.* 18] that Colston wounded Baker on 27 Sept., 18 Eliz., in Grayes Inne Feildes in the said parish in self defence, so that he died on 3 Oct. at Highe Holborne (*details given*).

1611.)   15 *Feb.* 1577.   Pardon for George Price. It was found by an inquisition (*jury named*) taken at Derby, co. Derby, before Thomas Fowcher, coroner in the said town, on 16 July on the body of William Taylor, a vagabond and sturdy beggar, that Price wounded Taylor in self defence at Derby on 23 June, 18 Eliz., so that he died there on 4 July (*details given*).

1612.)   7 *Feb.* 1577.   Pardon for Roger Brinscombe late of Cameley, co. Somerset, 'yeoman'. It was found by an inquisition (*jury named*) taken at Cameley before John Coward, a coroner in the county, on 19 June on the body of John Hynenam, aged 11 years, that Brinscombe shot Hynenam by misadventure with 'a dagge' on 7 June, 18 Eliz., in the house of Mary Hyppesley, widow, so that he died there on 8 June (*details given*).

1613.)   6 *March* 1577.   Pardon of outlawry for Thomas Ibyll late of Upton Episcopi, co. Hereford, 'yeoman', who was put in exigent in the county of Hereford for non-appearance in the Common Pleas to answer Thomas Maylard of Hereford, co. Hereford, 'capper', in a plea of debt of £20 and has now surrendered himself to the Fleet prison.   [*m.* 19]

1614.)   8 *Feb.* 1577.   Pardon for Edward Cornewallis late of Fyncham, co. Norfolk. It was found by an inquisition (*jury named*) taken at Norwich in 'le Sherehowse', co. Norfolk, before Christopher Heydon, knight, William Paston, Drew Drewrye, Richard Shelton, Henry Doiley, William Heydon and others, justices of the peace and of oyer and terminer in the county, on 2 Oct. that Cornewallis wounded Thomas Haynsworth late of Fyncham, 'yeoman', in self defence on 25 Aug., 18 Eliz., at Fyncham so that he died there on 29 Aug. (*details given*).

1615.)   *Undated.*   Pardon for John Tarlton *alias* Thorneton late of Estsmythfield, co. Middlesex, 'yeoman'. It was found by an inquisition taken at Eastsmythfeild before Robert Cooke, a coroner in the county, on 12 March, 19 Eliz., on the body of Richard Blunt late of London, 'yeoman', that Tarlton killed Blunt at Well Close in Eastsmythefeyld on 11 March, 19 Eliz., in self defence (*details given*).

1616.)   12 *March* 1577.   Licence for Edmund Slyfeilde to alienate lands in Chertsey, co. Surrey, to Dorothy Gravett and Frances Gravett. For 7s. 10d. paid to the Queen's farmer.
                                                                                                          [*m.* 20].

1617)   4 *Feb.* 1577.   Pardon of alienation: Thomas Rawlens in Trinity term, 18 Eliz., by fine in the Common Pleas acquired from Henry Compton, knight, lord Compton, a messuage in the parish of St. Faith, London. For 26s. 8d. paid to the Queen's farmer.

1618.)   2 *Jan.* 1577.   Licence for Robert Hare, Hugh Hare and Richard Wykes to alienate lands in Staines, co. Middlesex, to William Cocke, Elizabeth his wife, William Gurney, Frances his wife, Lionel Duckett and Anne his wife and the heirs of Cocke, and for them by the same fine to convey back the premises to the said Robert Hare. For 8s. 11d. paid to the Queen's farmer.

1619.)   2 *Jan.* 1577.   The like for Edward, earl of Oxford, to alienate lands (*named with tenant's name*) in Thornecombe, co. Devon, to John Parrys *alias* Corte. For 26s. 8d.

1620.)   2 *Jan.* 1577.   The like for Edward, earl of Oxford, to alienate lands (*named with tenant's name*) in Musburye, co. Devon, to Bernard Drake. For 10s.   [*m.* 21]

1621.)   2 *Jan.* 1577.   The like for Edward, earl of Oxford, to alienate lands (*named with tenant's names*) in Thornecombe, co. Devon, to John Edgar *alias* Barefoote the younger. For 17*s.*

1622.) 2 *Jan.* 1577.   The like for Edward Chester, Bridget his wife and Thomas Chester to alienate lands in Rodford and Westerley, co. Gloucester, to John Robertes. For £3 6*s.* 8*d.*

1623.) 2 *Jan.* 1577.   The like for John Chitham to alienate lands in Wormegaye *alias* Wrongaye and Totnell, co. Norfolk, to Thomas Aldham. For £3.

1624.) 31 *Dec.* 1576.   Pardon of alienation: Richard Fowkes, citizen and grocer of London, by indenture, 26 May, 16 Eliz., acquired from Edward Lutwich and James Slape, citizen and grocer of London, a messuage called 'le Lambe' in the parish of St. Dunstan in the West, London, now in the tenure of Fowkes or late in that of Slape, (adjoining a tenement in the tenure of Gabriel Levesey, grocer, on the East side, parcel of a tenement occupied by Thomas Nogay *alias* Ager on the North, a tenement late in the tenure of John Rundell on the West and Fleatestrete on the South). For 33*s.* 4*d.* paid to the Queen's farmer.

[*m.* 22]

1625.) 2 *Jan.* 1577.   Licence for Benet Wynchecombe to alienate the manor of Halton and Bradshawes Mannor in Wendover and lands in Halton, Wendover, Wendover Foreign and Marshe, co. Buckingham, to Thomas Fermor and Bridget his wife and the heirs and assigns of Bridget. For £5 3*s.* 4*d.* paid to the Queen's farmer.

1626.) 2 *Jan.* 1577.   The like for John Gage, Thomas Gage, George Gage, Edward Gage, Robert [Gage?] and Richard Gage to alienate the manor of Dichenynge Garden *alias* Dichelinge Garden and lands in Dichenynge *alias* Dichelinge, Cookefeild, Bolney, Twynham, Hourstperpownd, Chyltington, Chayleigh and Woodmancote, co. Sussex, to Simon Fenell to the use of the said Thomas Gage. For £7.

1627.) 2 *Jan.* 1577.   The like for Thomas Fermor and Bridget his wife to alienate the manor of Langhull in Chalgrave, lands in Chalgrave, a third part of the manor of Noke and a third part of lands in Noke, Islipp and Beckley and of free fishery in the water of Charwell, co. Oxford, to Benet Wynchecombe. For 55*s.* 4*d.*

1628.) 20 *Feb.* 1577.   The like for Agnes Francke, widow, Benet Barefoote and Elizabeth his wife to alienate a messuage and brewhouse called 'le Three Kynges' in Est Smythfeilde, co. Middlesex, in the parish   [*m.* 23]
of St. Botolph without Algate, with the wharf belonging thereto and a grain house adjoining the wharf, occupied by John Taylor and Christopher Stanley, a messuage in East Smythfeild, now or late occupied by William Wood, and another messuage in East Smythfeild in the said parish, now or late occupied by Anthony Duffeld, to John Taylor, citizen and draper of London. For £4.

1629.) 21 *Feb.* 1577.   The like for William Gage and Joan his wife to alienate the manor of Attingham *alias* Acham, lands in Attingham, the rectory of Attingham, the tithes of corn in Attingham, Uckington, Barwicke, Ernstre, Chilton and Crouckhill and the advowson of the vicarage of Attingham, co. Salop, to John Byest. For £4.

1630.) 28 *Sept.* 1577.   The like for Edward, earl of Lincoln, and Elizabeth his wife to alienate lands in Shertsey, co. Surrey, to Edmund Slyfelde. For 7*s.* 10*d.*

1631.)   14 *June* 1577.   The like for Henry, earl of Huntingdon, Anne, countess of Pembroke, widow, and Henry Compton, knight, lord Compton, to alienate the manor of Fyncheley and lands in Fyncheley and Hendon, co. Middlesex, to John Payne and William Atkinson and the heirs   [*m.* 24] and assigns of Payne to the use of the said countess for life, with successive remainders to Thomas Compton, second son of the said lord Compton, for life, to such wife as Thomas might have at his death for her life (if he should so appoint by will), to the heirs male of Thomas's body, to lord Compton in tail and to the right heirs of lord Compton, and, if Thomas should not at his death have a wife or having one should not limit the premises to her, then with successive remainders after his decease to the heirs of his body, to the heirs of the body of lord Compton and to the right heirs of lord Compton. For £10.

1632.)   1 *Feb.* 1577.   The like for George Chambre, merchant of the staple, and William Weale to alienate a moiety of lands (*named*) in Haberley, Mynsterley, Weatbury, Shelve, Worthyn, Westley, Ponsburye and the forest of Hoggestowe, co. Salop, to John Thynne, knight. For 33s. 6d.

1633.)   2 *Jan.* 1577.   The like for Anthony Bourne and Elizabeth his wife to alienate the manor of Battenhall and lands in Battenhall, Kympsey, Whytington, Barnes by Worcester, Tymberden, Norton, Newland and the city of Worcester, co. Worcester, to Thomas Bromeley, solicitor general, and Thomas Fortescue and the heirs and assigns of Bromeley. For £11 13s. 4d.

1634.)   2 *Jan.* 1577.   The like for Edward, earl of Oxford, to alienate the manor of Thornecombe, lands in Thornecombe and Axmyster, the tithes of corn and hay of lands in Thornecombe and the advowson of Thornecombe church, co. Devon, to John Franke and Matthew Bragge and the heirs and assigns of Freake. For £3 16s. 8d.   [*m.* 25]

1635.)   3 *Jan.* 1577.   Pardon of alienation: William Pyckringe, knight, by indenture, 27 Dec., 17 Eliz., granted to Nicholas Bacon, knight, keeper of the great seal, William, lord Burghley, treasurer, Henry, earl of Huntingdon, Walter Myldmey, knight, chancellor of the Exchequer, Ralph Sadler, knight, chancellor of the duchy of Lancaster, Alexander Nowell, dean of St. Paul's cathedral, London, Thomas Bromelye, solicitor general, William Fletewood, recorder of London, Adrian Stokes, Henry Knolles the elder, John Harrington, Edward Elrington, John Hastinges, George Carleton, Robert Creswell, Richard Harleston and Thomas Norton *inter alia* the manors of Bylande and Oldbylande and all his lands in Southborne, co. York, and all his lands in the city of London. For 100 marks paid to the Queen's farmer.

1636.)   1 *May* 1577.   Licence for Henry Woodhouse, Anne his wife, Roger Townesend, Jane his wife and John Osborne to alienate the manor of West Somerton, lands in West Somerton, Butley, Est Somerton, Wynterton, Bastewyke, Reppys, Hemesbye and Martham and free fishery in the water of Weste Somerton, Bastwicke, Reppys, Hemesby and Martham, co. Norfolk, to Thomas Revett. For £10 paid to the Queen's farmer.

1637.)   20 *June* 1577.   Pardon of alienation: Francis Rodes in Easter term, 13 Eliz., by fine in the Common Pleas acquired from Edmund West the manor of Handley and lands in Staveley, Handley and Dranfeld, co. Derby. For £10 paid to the Queen's farmer.

1638.)   20 *June* 1577.   The like: George Brodley by writing, 23 Jan., 19 Eliz., acquired

from Isabel Fowrnes and Elizabeth Fowrnes, daughters   [*m. 26*]
of Thomas Fowrnes, lands (*tenant named*) in Aringdem Parke, co. York. For 20*s.*

1639.)   20 *June* 1577.   The like: John Burre and James Farmer in Trinity term, 14 Eliz., by
fine in the Common Pleas acquired unto them and the heirs of the said James from John
Burlace and Thomas Farmer four fifth parts of lands in Great Marlowe, co. Buckingham.
For 20*s.*

1640.)   1 *May* 1577.   Licence for Gregory Fynes, lord Dacre, and Anne his wife to alienate
the manor of Wollefynes *alias* Wolleverfynes and lands in White Waltham, Cokeham and
Hurley, co. Berks, to William Chapman. For £4 paid to the Queen's farmer.

1641.)   1 *May* 1577.   The like for Richard Knyghtley, knight, and Valentine Knyghtley to
alienate the manor of Upton and lands in Upton, co. Northampton, to John Fetyplace,
knight, Thomas Andrewes, George Fermer, Griffin Hampden, John Croke and James
Braybrooke. For £13 6*s.* 8*d.*

1642.)   1 *May* 1577.   The like for William Sandys, lord Sandys, and Walter Sandys to
alienate the manors of Estdeane, Elden, Longestoke, Somborne Regis, Andevor, Enham
Militis and Appleshawe, lands in Eastdeane, Elden, Eldenmarshe, Longestoke, Somborne
Regis, Andevor, Enham Militis, Appleshawe, Enham Regis, Faccombe, Sholworton,
Somborne Parva, Stockbridge, Elinge, Compton, Brooke, Lockerley, Bentley, Butter-
meare, Fyfehead, Kympton, Woodcott, Upton, Durley, Charleton, Netherdeane, Hether-
deane, Reddenham, Mottes-   [*m. 27*]
founte, Cadbury, Tymmesburye *alias* Tymberburye, Upclatford, Longestoke Harrington,
Le Vyne, Shirborne St. John, Romsey, the town of Southampton and the city of
Winchester, common of pasture in the New Forest and Cawemore, free fishery in the water
of Teerste, free warren in the New Forest, view of frankpledge in Lonstoke, Durley,
Mottesfount, Tymmesbury and Shirborne St. John, the rectories of Elinge, Longestoke,
Compton, Somborne Regis, Somborne Parva and Stockbridge, the advowsons of the
churches of Faccombe, Kympton and Shirborne St. John and the advowsons of the
vicarages of Longstoke, Elinge, Somborne Regis and Asheley, co. Southampton, to
Thomas Farmer and Matthew Smyth and the heirs and assigns of Farmer. For £21 15*s.* 1*d.*

1643.)   1 *June* 1577.   The like for John Sentleger, knight, and Catherine his wife to
alienate the honour or manor of Kylpecke, the manors of Kyvernoe and Trenell and lands in
Kylpecke, Kyvernowe, Trenell, Brodeocke, Dewchurche, Hereforde, Throxton, Saincte
Deverox, Gracedene, Didleywormen, Brompton, Whynehall, Mynde and Woodwarde, co.
Hereford, to Reginald Hygate. For £16 13*s.* 4*d.*

1644.)   1 *May* 1577.   The like for Henry Compton, knight, lord Compton, to alienate ten
messuages and two gardens in the parish of St. Faith, London, to John Payne. For £3 6*s.* 8*d.*

1645.)   22 *June* 1577.   The like for Richard Taverner to alienate a third part of a messuage
in Hartington, co. Surrey, to Peter Taverner. For 33*s.* 4*d.*

1646.)   1 *May* 1577.   The like for Thomas Sackvile, knight, lord   [*m. 28*]
Buckhurst, and Cecily his wife to alienate the manor of South *alias* Southborough in
Tunbridge, Spelhurst, Tudeley, Capell and Pepingberie *alias* Pemberue, co. Kent, to
Thomas Smythe. For £6 13*s.* 4*d.*

1647.)   16 *June* 1577.   Pardon of alienation: George Goringe in Hilary term, 14 Eliz., by fine in the Common Pleas acquired from Francis Carewe the manor of Bercombe *alias* Barcombe and lands in Barcomb, Hamsey and Newicke, co. Sussex. For £20 paid to the Queen's farmer.

1648.)   20 *June* 1577.   The like: Henry Goringe, George Goring and William Goringe in Michaelmas term, 17 Eliz., by fine in the Common Pleas acquired unto them and the heirs of Henry from John Selwyn and Beatrice his wife *inter alia* lands (*named*) in Pevensey, co. Sussex. For 20*s.*

1649.)   22 *June* 1577.   The like: Henry Goring and William Goringe in Hilary term, 18 Eliz., recovered against George Gorynge the manor of Bercombe *alias* Barcombe and lands in Barcombe, Hampsey and Newicke, co. Sussex, which recovery was to the use of George, as appears by an indenture, 10 Jan., 18 Eliz., between the said parties. For £20.

1650.)   21 *June* 1577.   The like: Henry Goringe, George Gorynge and William Goringe in Michaelmas term, 17 Eliz., acquired unto them and the heirs of Henry from John Selwyn and Beatrice his wife the manor of Eastborne and lands, view of frankpledge, the hundred of Eastborne and wreck of the sea in Easteborne and Willingdon, co. Sussex. For £20. [*m.* 29]

1651.)   26 *Sept.* 1577.   *Gorhambury.*   Licence for Henry Jernegan, son and heir of Henry Jernegan, knight, deceased, to alienate his reversion in the manor of Sileham and a water mill called Sileham Mill, co. Suffolk, to Thomas Barrowe. For £13 13*s.* 5*d.* paid to the Queen's farmer.

1652.)   22 *June* 1577.   The like for Richard Taverner to alienate a third part of the manor of Sowndes, co. Oxford, to Edmund Taverner. For 33*s.* 4*d.*

1653.)   20 *June* 1577.   Pardon of alienation: Richard Taverner of Woodeton, co. Oxford, being seised of the manor of Woodeton *alias* Woodeton Mylton and the manor of Soundes, co. Oxford, and lands in Kingeston on Thames, co. Surrey, called Hartington, by his will, 15 June, 17 Eliz., bequeathed to his sons, Peter Taverner and Edmund Taverner, a third part each of all his lands; after Richard's death Edmund entered upon a third part of the premises. For £3 6*s.* 8*d.* paid to the Queen's farmer.

1654.)   20 *June* 1577.   The like: Richard Taverner of Woodeton being seised as above (*no.* 1653) bequeathed to his sons, Peter Taverner and Edmund Taverner, a third part each of all his lands; after Richard's death Peter entered upon a third part of the premises. For £3 6*s.* 8*d.* [*m.* 30]

1655.)   22 *June* 1577.   Licence for Edmund Taverner to alienate a third part of lands in Hartington, co. Surrey, to Peter Taverner. For 33*s.* 4*d.* paid to the Queen's farmer.

1656.)   22 *June* 1577.   The like for Peter Taverner to alienate a third part of the manor of Sowndes, co. Oxford, to Edmund Taverner. For 33*s.* 4*d.*

1657.)   13 *Nov.* 1577.   Pardon of alienation: Thomas Dolman the elder of Newbery, co. Berks, 'clothier', being seised of the manors of Colthrope and Shawe, the advowson of Shawe church and lands in Shawe and Colthrope, co. Berks, by his will, 8 Jan., 14 Eliz., bequeathed to his son Thomas the manors of Colthrope and Shawe and the house wherein the testator then dwelt; he died on 19 Nov., 18 Eliz., and the said Thomas Dolman the younger entered upon the premises. For £7 18s. 2d. paid to the Queen's farmer.

1658.)   13 *Nov.* 1577.   The like: Richard Smythe and Peter Smythe, his son, by indenture, 1 Feb., 19 Eliz., acquired from Robert Craven land   [*m.* 31] (*named with tenants' names*) in Horsforth, co. York. For 9s.

1659.)   13 *Nov.* 1577.   The like: William Deane by indenture, 1 Feb., 19 Eliz., acquired from Richard Pollarde and James Lister lands (*named with tenants' names*) in Horsfurth, co. York. For 6s. 8d.

1660.)   25 *June* 1577.   The like: Francis Brooke in Easter term, 14 Eliz., by fine in the Commons Pleas acquired from John Russell lands in Brode Campden, co. Gloucester. For £4.

1661.)   13 *Nov.* 1577.   The like: James Whitehead and Richard Whitehead, his son, by indenture, 28 Jan., 19 Eliz., acquired from Robert Oglethorpe lands etc. (*named with tenants' names* including two 'setes' in Horsforthe chapel) in Horsfourth, co. York. For 10s. 5¼d.

1662.)   13 *Nov.* 1577.   The like: Thomas Hill the elder by indenture, 18 Jan., 14 Eliz., enfeoffed Francis Brooke and Ralph Borfeild of lands in Longefeilde *alias* Longvelde in the parish of Eaton *alias* Eyton, co. Salop, and the tithes of corn thereof to the use of the said Thomas for life, with successive remainders to Thomas Hill, his son, in tail, to Ralph Hill, his younger son, in tail and to the right heirs of the feoffor. For 14s.

1663.)   16 *Nov.* 1577.   Pardon of outlawry for Matthew Welburne of   [*m.* 32] Mowthorpe, co. York, 'husbandman', who was put in exigent in the county of York for non-appearance in the Common Pleas to answer Giles Taylor of York, 'yoman', in a plea for payment of £10 and has now surrendered himself to the Fleet prison.

1664.)   13 *Nov.* 1577.   Pardon of alienation: George Hill by indenture, 1 Feb., 19 Eliz., acquired from Robert Craven lands (*named with tenants' names*) in Horsforth, co. York. For 16s. 1¾d. paid to the Queen's farmer.

1665.)   13 *Nov.* 1577.   The like: John Hobson by indenture, 1 Feb., 19 Eliz., acquired from Gabriel Grene lands (*named with tenants' names*) in Horsforth, co. York. For 5s. 10½d.

1666.)   13 *Nov.* 1577.   The like: John Browne and Robert Adamson by indenture, 1 Feb., 19 Eliz., acquired from Robert Oglethorpe lands (*named with*   [*m.* 33] *tenants' names*) in Horsforth, co. York. For 9s. 3d.

1667.)   13 *Nov.* 1577.   The like: Thomas Womersley, 'clothier', by indenture, 1 Feb., 19 Eliz., acquired from Gabriel Greene lands (*named with tenants' names*) in Horsfourth, co. York. For 12s. 4d.

1668.)   1 *Oct.* 1577.   Licence for Henry Cheyne, knight, lord Cheyne of Toddington, to alienate lands in Eastchurch and Mynster in the isle of Sheppey (*Scapei alias Shepei*), co. Kent, to John Swallman, 'yoman'. For 40s. paid to the Queen's farmer.

1669.)   1 *Oct.* 1577.   The like for Henry Richeman and Agnes his wife to alienate lands and the tithes of the demesne lands of the manor of Byncknoll *alias* Bynold in Broddhinton,

Lydyard Tregose, Chadington and Bincknoll *alias* Bynoll *alias* Brincknoll, common of pasture for six oxen in Lynton and common of pasture for all manner of beasts in Westmersh, co. Wilts, to Richard Francklyn and Catherine Francklyn, his daughter. For 13*s.* 4*d.*

1670.)   1 *Oct.* 1577.   The like for William Dorrell to alienate the   [*m.* 34] manor of Wynterbourne Muncton and lands in Wynterbourne Mouncton, co. Wilts, to James Harvye, alderman of London. For £7 13*s.* 4*d.*

1671.)   1 *Oct.* 1577.   The like for Edward Cary and William Doddyngton to alienate the manor of Burton Hyll, co. Wilts, late of the monastery of Malmesbury, co. Wilts, and all other lands in Burton Hill to Adam Archerd, 'clothyer', and Thomas Hall, 'yeoman'. For £7 3*s.* 4*d.*

1672.)   1 *Oct.* 1577.   The like for Anthony Procter to alienate lands in Hetten, Overbordley, Netherbordley and Malham, co. York, to Thomas Procter. For 5*s.* 4*d.*

1673.)   1 *May* 1577.   The like for William Burgh, knight, lord Burgh, and Catherine his wife to alienate the manor of Ocksted *alias* Oxsted and lands in Ocksted, Lyngfeild, Croherst, Tanridge, Lymposfeild, Horne, Godstone, Tytsey, Bletchyngley and Waldyng- ham, co. Surrey, to John Rede and Elizabeth his wife and the heirs and assigns of John. For £8 14*s.* 5*d.*

1674.)   13 *Nov.* 1577.   Pardon of alienation: Richard Harford by indenture, 14 Aug., 17 Eliz., enfeoffed Charles Foxe, John Seyborne,   [*m.* 35] Edmund Foxe and Edmund Scrope *inter alia* of the manor of Canon Frome, co. Hereford, and all other lands there to the use of the said Richard and Martha his wife and the heirs of his body by her, with successive remainders to Nathaniel Harford, his brother, in tail male, to Henry Harford, another of his brothers, in tail male, to Anthony Harford, another of his brothers, in tail male and to the right heirs of Richard. For £7 paid to the Queen's farmer.

1675.)   13 *Nov.* 1577.   The like: Charles Hall by indenture, 8 May, 18 Eliz., acquired from John, marquess of Winchester, lands (*named with tenants' names*) in Knowke *alias* Knooke in the parishes of Upton Lowell or Haytesbury, co. Wilts, and all his other lands in Knooke or elsewhere, co. Wilts. For £5.

1676.)   1 *Oct.* 1577.   Licence for Robert Ball to alienate a great messuage called 'le Pryory' of Little Horkesleigh and lands (*named*) in Little Horkesleigh and Great Horkesleigh, co. Essex, to John Ball the elder and John Ball the younger. For 53*s.* 4*d.* paid to the Queen's farmer.

1677.)   1 *Oct.* 1577.   The like for Richard Jannaway the elder and Richard Jenawaye the younger to alienate lands in Westhalden, co.   [*m.* 36] Northampton, to Edward Andrewe. For 16*s.* 8*d.*

1678.)   1 *Oct.* 1577.   The like for Thomas Gresham, knight, and Anne his wife to alienate lands in Great Walsyngham, Little Walsyngham and Egmer, co. Norfolk, to Thomas Sydney. For 40*s.*

1679.)   1 *Oct.* 1577.   The like for Innocent Reade and John Rede to alienate a fourth part of the manor of Upper Walloppe *alias* Walloppe Moyles and of lands in Walloppe *alias*

Walloppe Moyles, co. Southampton, to Nicholas Rede and Alexander Rede and the heirs and assigns of Nicholas. For 20s.

1680.)   1 Oct. 1577.   The like for Robert Halton to alienate the manor of Brynkworth and lands in Brynkworth, co. Wilts, to Henry Knyvett, knight, and Elizabeth his wife and the heirs and assigns of Henry to the use of Henry and Elizabeth for life in survivorship, with successive remainders to Henry and the heirs of his body by Elizabeth, to Elizabeth in tail and to the right heirs of Henry. For £18 15s. 9d.

1681.)   1 Oct. 1577.   The like for John Grey and Jane his wife to alienate the manor or grange of Wythebroke, once of the monastery of Combe, co. Warwick, in Wythebroke and Hoppesford alias Happesford, co. Warwick, and all other lands there belonging to the said monastery to Edward Boughton. For 50s. 4d.

1682.)   1 Oct. 1577.   The like for Thomas Wyberd and Anne his wife to alienate lands in Westham, co. Essex, to John Collyn. For   [m. 37]
£3 6s. 8d.

1683.)   1 Oct. 1577.   The like for Arthur, lord Grey, and Jane Sibell his wife to alienate lands in Wylton, Brydstowe and Peterstowe alias Pytstowe, co. Hereford, to Nicholas Wright. For 13s. 4d.

1684.)   1 Oct. 1577.   The like for Thomas Knyvett, knight, to alienate the manor of Thurnynge and lands in Thurnynge (except the advowson of Thurnynge church), co. Huntingdon, and the manor of Thurnyng and lands in Thurnynge, Hennyngton and Luddyngton (except the advowson of Thurnynge church), co. Northampton, to Robert Byworth, Robert Smyth, Nicholas Smyth and Silvester Colly and the heirs and assigns of Colly. For 46s. 8d.

1685.)   5 Nov. 1577.   The like for Edward, earl of Oxford, to alienate the manor of Great Abyngdon alias Great Abyngton and lands in Great Abyngdon, Hyldersham, Abyngdon Parva alias Abyngton Parva, Pampysford and Badburham, co. Cambridge, to Robert Tayllor. For 46s. 8d.

1686.)   26 March 1577.   Denization for Robert Ittles, born a Spanish   [m. 38]
subject; provided that he shall not dwell in Barwyck or Portesmouthe without special licence. For a fine of 6s. 8d.

The like for the following, for the fines specified,—

1687.)   2 Nov. 1577.   Charles van Poele, Spanish subject; 6s. 8d.
1688.)   14 May 1577.   Nicholas Illero, French subject; 10s.
1689.)   14 June 1577.   Peter Wanrowe, Spanish subject; 6s. 8d.
1690.)   25 June 1577.   Peter Hubberd, Spanish subject; 13s. 4d.
1691.)   20 June 1577.   Philip Johnson, Spanish subject; 10s.
1692.)   19 June 1577.   James del Cappell, Spanish subject; 10s.
1693.)   19 June 1577.   John Hofman, subject of the Emperor; 13s. 4d.
1694.)   11 Feb. 1577.   Garrett Juyst, Spanish subject; 13s. 4d.
1695.)   10 May 1577.   William Davyson, Scottish subject; 10s.
1696.)   13 May 1577.   Ellis Brune, French subject; 10s.
1697.)   13 May 1577.   Paul de la Hay, Spanish subject; 10s.
1698.)   3 May 1577.   Nicholas Andrewe, subject of the bishop of Liège; 10s.

1699.)   3 *May* 1577.   Richard Clowghe, Spanish subject; 6s. 8d.

1700.)   26 *Oct.* 1577.   *Gorhambury.*   Francis Guylliker, subject of the duke of Cleves; 6s. 8d.

1701.)   4 *May* 1577.   John Kynge, subject of the duke of Cleves; 10s.

1702.)   6 *May* 1577.   Nicholas Castell, Spanish subject; 13s. 4d.

1703.)   6 *May* 1577.   Peter Cilly the younger, French subject; 13s. 4d.

1704.)   11 *Feb.* 1577.   Francis Allard, Spanish subject; 6s. 8d.

1705.)   17 *Nov.* 1576.   Luke Johnson, subject of the bishop of Liège; 6s. 8d.

1706.)   4 *Feb.* 1577.   Adrian Deblaughe, French subject; 6s. 8d.

1707.)   6 *Feb.* 1577.   Peter Craft, Spanish subject; [*no fine specified*].

1708.)   2 *July* 1577.   Cornelius Kersken, 'joyner', subject of the bishop of Cologne; 6s. 8d.

1709.)   2 *July* 1577.   Giles Porter, Spanish subject; 6s. 8d.

1710.)   23 *Jan.* 1577.   Cornelius van Essen, Spanish subject; 10s.

1711.)   26 *Nov.* 1576.   John Gerraddes, subject of the Emperor; 6s. 8d.

1712.)   28 *Jan.* 1577.   Nicholas Emerson, subject of the Emperor; 10s.

1713.)   31 *Jan.* 1577.   John Hixkyns, subject of the duke of Cleves; 6s. 8d.

1714.)   11 *Feb.* 1577.   Hermo Cuppleman, Spanish subject; 6s. 8d.

1715.)   26 *Nov.* 1576.   James Verselyne, subject of the duke of Venice; 10s.

1716.)   23 *Jan.* 1577.   John Chevalier, Spanish subject; 6s. 8d.

1717.)   28 *Jan.* 1577.   Michael Whight, Spanish subject; 6s. 8d.

1718.)   8 *Dec.* 1576.   John Duman, Spanish subject; 13s. 4d.

1719.)   10 *June* 1577.   John de Beustele, French subject; [*no fine specified*].   [*m.* 39]

1720.)   22 *Jan.* 1577.   Roger Shobye, French subject; 6s. 8d.

1721.)   20 *Nov.* 1576.   Tilman Cooke, subject of the duke of Cleves; 10s.

1722.)   16 *Dec.* 1576.   John Yonge, subject of the duke of Cleves; 13s. 4d.

1723.)   16 *Dec.* 1576.   Ghevert Ghelynx, Spanish subject; 6s. 8d.

1724.)   6 *Dec.* 1576.   John Peter, Spanish subject; 13s. 4d.

1725.)   29 *Jan.* 1577.   Peter le Catte, Spanish subject; 6s. 8d.

1726.)   6 *Feb.* 1577.   Peter Crafte, Spanish subject; 6s. 8d.

1727.)   2 *Feb.* 1577.   Nicholas Toylyard, French subject; 6s. 8d.

1728.)   7 *Feb.* 1577.   John Buck, subject of the duke of Cleves; 6s. 8d.

1729.)   7 *Feb.* 1577.   James Boaught, Spanish subject; 13s. 4d.

1730.)   20 *March* 1577.   *Gorhambury.*   Henry Clerkes, subject of the bishop of Liège; 6s. 8d.

1731.)   26 *March* 1577.   George Smythe, Scottish subject; 6s. 8d.

1732.)   2 *Aug.* 1577.   *Gorhambury.*   Vincent Jacre, Spanish subject; 6s. 8d.

1733.)   14 *Nov.* 1577.   John Hewett, French subject; 10s.

1734.)   11 *Feb.* 1577.   Gosen Smyth, subject of the duke of Cleves; 6s. 8d.

1735.)   14 *Feb.* 1577.   Isebrand Hulparke, Spanish subject; [*no fine specified*].

1736.)   14 *Nov.* 1577.   Anthony Chorys, subject of the Emperor; 10s.

1737.)   29 *April* 1577.   Presentation of Hugh Boothe, S.T.B., to the third prebend in Ely cathedral, void by the promotion of John Whytgyfte, S.T.P., to the bishopric of Worcester.

The like of the following clerks, viz.,—

1738.)   19 *April* 1577.   Zachary Babyngton to the vicarage of Chilmarke, Salisbury dioc.

1739.)   28 *April* 1577.   Evan Powell to the rectory of Chervylde, Gloucester dioc.

1740.)   28 *April* 1577.   Henry Mason to the vicarage of Snape, Norwich dioc.

1741.)   28 *April* 1577.   Christopher Dugdayll to the rectory of Pollesholte, Salisbury dioc., void by resignation.

1742.)   28 *April* 1577.   Richard Sutton to the rectory of Wilbye, Peterborough dioc.

1743.)   29 *April* 1577.   William Bradley, M.A., to the rectory of Lasbe, Lincoln dioc.

1744.)   6 *April* 1577.   *Gorhambury.*   Hugh Boothe, S.T.P., to the rectory of Cosyngton, Lincoln dioc.

1745.)   6 *May* 1577.   William Slack to the rectory of Edlyngton, Lincoln dioc., void by resignation.

1746.)   2 *May* 1577.   John Gamon to the vicarage of Kyrkby Greene, Lincoln dioc., void by resignation.

1747.)   4 *May* 1577.   William Rogers to the rectory of Hubbertyston, St. Davids dioc.

1748.)   4 *May* 1577.   Nicholas Watkyns to the vicarage of Clarebrough, York dioc., void by death.

1749.)   4 *May* 1577.   Thomas Dyggones to the rectory of Gates, Chichester dioc.

1750.)   11 *May* 1577.   Anthony Goodwyn, B. A., to the rectory of Rawmershe, York dioc., void by death.

1751.)   9 *May* 1577.   John Hardy to the rectory of Kyrkeborne, York dioc.

1752.)   27 *June* 1577.   John Markes, B.A., to the vicarage of Pattyshull of the one part, Peterborough dioc., void by resignation.

1753.)   28 *June* 1577.   John Sprynte, S.T.P., to the rectory of Allyngton *alias* Adlyngton, Canterbury dioc.

1754.)   25 *June* 1577.   Christopher Greene to the rectory of Westwoughton, York dioc.

1755.)   27 *June* 1577.   William Underwood to the prebend of Gorwall in Hereford cathedral, void of right or by lapse.

1756.)   12 *July* 1577.   *Gorhambury.*   John Morris to the vicarage of Bardesay, York dioc., void by death.

1757.)   23 *May* 1577.   *Gorhambury.*   Richard Stokes to the rectory of Banham, Norwich dioc., void by resignation.

1758.)   13 *June* 1577.   John Pyldrem to the rectory of Wynterslowe, Salisbury dioc., void by lapse.

1759.)   15 *June* 1577.   Robert Boothe, M. A., to the rectory of Wenham Combust, Norwich dioc., void by resignation.

1760.)   15 *June* 1577.   Samuel Otes, B.A., to the rectory of Marseham,   [*m.* 40] Norwich dioc., void by resignation.

1761.)   13 *May* 1577.   John Shapearrowe to the rectory of Shamborne, Norwich dioc.

1762.)   12 *April* 1577.   *Gorhambury.*   Thomas Philyppes to the vicarage of Ravensden, Lincoln dioc., void by death.

1763.)   9 *April* 1577.   *Gorhambury.*   Thomas Collyns to the rectory of Mylton Bryon, Lincoln dioc., void by resignation.

1764.)   29 *May* 1577.   Richard Harrys, M.A., to the rectory of Bladon with the chapel of Woodstock, Oxford dioc., void by resignation.

1765.)   29 *March* 1577.   William Bolton to the rectory of Pryston, Bath and Wells dioc.

1766.)   1 *April* 1577.   Robert Blunt to the rectory of Thorpe by Newarke, York dioc., void by death.

1767.)   21 *Feb.* 1577.   George Morris to the rectory of Cluddesdeane, Winchester dioc., void by lapse.

1768.)   21 *Feb.* 1577.   Bartholomew Bowsfell to the vicarage of Cuxham, Oxford dioc.

1769.)   21 *Feb.* 1577.   William Rhodes to the rectory of St. Michael in Lewes, Chichester dioc.

1770.)   13 *March* 1577.   *Gorhambury.*   Lawrence Bankes to the vicarage of Downefeild, Coventry and Lichfield dioc.

1771.)   8 *March* 1577.   Christopher Bannyster to the rectory of St. Peter, Lincoln dioc.

1772.)   15 *March* 1577.   *Gorhambury.*   Mark Saunders to the vicarage of Monketon, Canterbury dioc., void by lapse.

1773.)   13 *March* 1577.   *Gorhambury*.   Herbert Westfalyng, S.T.D., to the rectory of Butwell, Oxford dioc.

1774.)   3 *May* 1577.   Stephen Cathilyn to the rectory of Longdytton, Winchester dioc.

1775.)   3 *May* 1577.   Thomas Pryce to the rectory of Herbrandeston, St. Davids dioc., void by resignation.

1776.)   3 *May* 1577.   James Stephenson to the rectory of Addilthorpe, Lincoln dioc., void by death.

1777.)   11 *March* 1577.   *Gorhambury*.   Hugh Smyth to the rectory of St. Peter in Sandwich, Canterbury dioc., void by death.

1778.)   19 *Nov.* 1576.   Ralph Wray to the rectory of Pylham, Lincoln dioc., void by resignation.

1779.)   19 *Nov.* 1576.   Reginald Brooke to the vicarage of Haselor, Worcester dioc.

1780.)   21 *Nov.* 1576.   Boniface Martyn to the rectory of Spryngthorpe, Lincoln dioc., void by resignation.

1781.)   29 *Jan.* 1577.   William Saunders to the vicarage of Chesham Leicestr', Lincoln dioc.

1782.)   7 *Feb.* 1577.   John Nutter to the rectory of Aghton, Chester dioc.

1783.)   26 *Jan.* 1577.   William Cheston, M.A., to the rectory of Llangela, St. Davids dioc., void by death.

1784.)   23 *Jan.* 1577.   William Smyth to the vicarage of Beninden, Canterbury dioc.

1785.)   26 *Jan.* 1577.   William Davyd to the rectory of Ketheddyn, St. Davids dioc., void by death.

1786A.)   23 *Jan.* 1577.   David Meyricke to the vicarage of Kynlett, Hereford dioc., void by death.

1786B.)   23 *Jan.* 1577.   Robert Cottesforde, M.A., to the rectory of Stower Provys, Canterbury dioc.

1787A.)   3 *Jan.* 1577.   Edward Hoome to the vicarage of Lidbury, Hereford dioc.

1787B.)   18 *Jan.* 1577.   George Shawe to the vicarage of Bayton, Worcester dioc., void by death.

1788A.)   18 *Jan.* 1577.   John Bradford to the vicarage of Newton St. Cyres (*Sancti Cirini*), Exeter dioc.

1788B.)   6 *Dec.* 1576.   *Gorhambury*.   Giles Crede to the vicarage of Mynfrey, Exeter dioc., void by resignation.

1789.)   14 *Dec.* 1576.   Richard Rychardson, M.A., to the rectory of Saxby, Lincoln dioc., void by death.

1790.)   14 *Dec.* 1576.   John Powell to the vicarage of Scottesdon, Hereford dioc.

1791.)   14 *Dec.* 1576.   David Pryce to the rectory of Wrastlyngworth, Lincoln dioc., void by death.

1792.)   14 *Dec.* 1576.   Arthur Willyams, M.A., to the vicarage of Madyngley, Ely dioc., void by lapse.

1793.)   14 *Dec.* 1576.   Anthony Batten, M.A., to the vicarage of Newenton, Canterbury dioc.

1794.)   17 *April* 1577.   William Browne to the rectory of St. Peter, Norwich dioc., void by deprivation.

1795.)   26 *Jan.* 1577.   William Cheston, M.A., to the free portion of Llanthewydelfre, St. Davids dioc., void by death.

1796.)   19 *Nov.* 1576.   William Banner to the vicarage of New Wyndsor, Salisbury dioc.

1797.)   1 *Dec.* 1576.   Thomas Willyams to the vicarage of Eye, Norwich dioc., void by death.

1798.)   1 *Dec.* 1576.   Evan Robertes to the rectory of Crawmershe Gyfford, Oxford dioc., void by death.

1799.)   1 *Dec.* 1576.   William Dawnsey to the vicarage of Plynt *alias* Pylynt, Exeter dioc.

1800.)   22 *March* 1577.   Walter Selwenne to the rectory of Blendworth, Winchester dioc., void by resignation.

1801.)   18 *March* 1577.   *Gorhambury.*   Walter Davyes to the vicarage of Brecon, St. Davids dioc., void by resignation.

1802.)   5 *June* 1577.   Edmund Mentell to the vicarage of Great Eversden,   [*m.* 41] Ely dioc.

1803.)   18 *March* 1577.   *Gorhambury.*   Francis Yate, M.A., to the rectory of Wykeware, Gloucester dioc.

1804.)   18 *March* 1577.   *Gorhambury.*   James Yerothe, B.A., to the rectory of Wareham Holy Trinity, Canterbury dioc.

1805.)   13 *March* 1577.   *Gorhambury.*   Herbert Westfalyng, S.T.P., to the rectory of Brytewell, Oxford dioc., void by lapse.

1806.)   20 *June* 1577.   Richard Griffyn to the vicarage of Cerne, Canterbury dioc., void by death.

1807.)   20 *June* 1577.   Philemon Whale to the rectory of Chickney, London dioc.

1808.)   22 *June* 1577.   William Barbar to the rectory of Denton, Canterbury dioc., void by lapse.

1809.)   7 *June* 1577.   Francis Hodgekyn to the rectory of Gratewyche, Coventry and Lichfield dioc., void by lapse.

1810.)   25 *May* 1577.   *Gorhambury.*   George Morris to the rectory of Wotton Courtney, Bath and Wells dioc.

1811.)   24 *May* 1577.   *Gorhambury.*   John Thomas to the vicarage of Stebynheathe, London dioc. void by lapse.

1812.)   8 *July* 1577.   *Gorhambury.*   John Smyth to the rectory of Hargrave, Peterborough dioc.

1813.)   17 *July* 1577.   *Gorhambury.*   John Wylson, M.A., to the rectory of Barton in Fabis, York dioc., void by death.

1814.)   11 *Oct.* 1577.   *Windsor.*   George Brooke to the vicarage of Humbleton, York dioc., void by death.

1815.)   13 *June* 1577.   Richard Gregorye to the rectory of Worte, Lincoln dioc., void by death.

1816.)   20 *Aug.* 1577.   *Gorhambury.*   John Wylson, M.A., to the vicarage of Spondon, Coventry and Lichfield dioc., void by death.

1817.)   6 *Dec.* 1576.   *Gorhambury.*   Robert Norgate, S.T.B., to the prebend of Decem Librarum in Lincoln cathedral.

1818.)   4 *Oct.* 1577.   *Gorhambury.*   John Hall to the rectory of Brisley, Norwich dioc.

1819.)   4 *Oct.* 1577.   *Gorhambury.*   James Lockey to the vicarage of Usborne Magna, Chester dioc., void by death.

1820.)   25 *Oct.* 1577.   *Windsor.*   John Walker to the vicarage of Mavagegye, Exeter dioc.

1821.)   25 *Oct.* 1577.   *Windsor.*   Richard Peake to the rectory of Rusheden, Peterborough dioc., void by resignation.

1822.)   5 *Aug.* 1577.   *Gorhambury.*   Zachary Hunte to the rectory of Collyweston, Peterborough dioc., void by resignation.

1823.)   5 *Aug.* 1577.   *Gorhambury.*   John Davyes to the vicarage of Lye, Gloucester dioc., void by death.

1824.)   9 *Aug.* 1577.   *Gorhambury.*   Henry Donne to the vicarage of Tedrynton, Gloucester dioc., void by resignation.

1825.)   9 *Aug.* 1577.   *Gorhambury.*   John Harle to the rectory of Talsthorpe, Lincoln dioc., void by lapse.

1826.)   24 *July* 1577.   *Gorhambury.*   Robert Dobson to the rectory of Wrote, Lincoln dioc., void by death.

1827.) 26 *July* 1577. *Gorhambury*. Lawrence Robynson to the vicarage of Steynton, St. Davids dioc., void by death.

1828.) 30 *Aug.* 1577. *Gorhambury*. Henry Waddyngton, M.A., to the rectory of Rychmond, Chester dioc., void by resignation.

1829.) 26 *Aug.* 1577. *Gorhambury*. Robert Rychardson to the rectory of Cluddesdeane, Winchester dioc., void by lapse.

1830.) 26 *Aug.* 1577. *Gorhambury*. Thomas Morley to the vicarage of Hekyngton, Lincoln dioc., void by resignation.

1831.) 26 *Aug.* 1577. *Gorhambury*. Thomas Arrundell to the rectory of Bagborough, Bath and Wells dioc., void by lapse.

1832.) 26 *Aug.* 1577. *Gorhambury*. Thomas Thorneton, B.A., to the vicarage of Wyggeston, Lincoln dioc., void by death.

1833.) 18 *March* 1577. *Gorhambury*. Owen Davyes, M.A., to the rectory of Llan Bedyr in the deanery of Issaphe Nanconwey Cruthin, Bangor dioc., void by lapse.

1834.) 9 *Feb.* 1577. Commission to Robert Newdgate, Lewis Dyve,   [*m. 1d*] William Chauncye, John Dryden, Robert Hatley and George Wyngate, feodary of the county, (or two of them, the feodary being one) to inquire in the county of Bedford *post mortem* Robert Catlyn, knight.

The like to the following in the counties named, viz.—

1835.) 22 *Jan.* 1577. Nicholas Beamond, George Vyllers, Henry Poole and Robert Braham, feodary of the county of Leicester, (or two of them, the feodary being one); *p.m.* William Hawford, 'yoman'.

1836.) 11 *Feb.* 1577. Roger Prydeaux, Robert Chaffe, mayor of the city of Exeter, John Eveleygh, feodary of the same city, and John Perryman (or two of them, the feodary being one); *p.m.* Thomas Prestwood.

1837.) 11 *Feb.* 1577. Henry Owtred, Thomas West, John Crooke and Richard Hoore, feodary of the town of Southampton, (or two of them, the feodary being one); *p.m.* lady Elizabeth Dawtrey, late the wife of Francis Dawtrey, knight, deceased.

1838.) 9 *Feb.* 1577. John Boyle, John Parry, deputy feodary of the county of Hereford, James Garnons, Edward Trovell and Richard Trovell (or two of them, Parry being one); *p.m.* Richard Harford.

1839.) 9 *Feb.* 1577. William Sutton, Robert Staunton, Robert Fletcher and Ralph Barton, feodary of the county of Nottingham, (or two of them, the feodary being one); *p.m.* Thomas Huett.

1840.) 11 *Feb.* 1577. Thomas Andrewes, feodary of the county of Suffolk, Anthony Rushe and George Chittynge (or two of them, the feodary being one); *p.m.* William Latton.

1841.) 11 *Feb.* 1577. John Lee, Robert Grenewood, Henry Farrowe, John Ellys and Brian Hamond, feodary of the West Riding, co. York, (or two of them, the feodary being one); *p.m.* Walter Passelowe.

1842.) 9 *Feb.* 1577. Nicholas Powtrell, serjeant at law, Thomas Markeham, Ralph Barton, feodary of the county of Nottingham, and Charles Fytzwilliams (or two of them, the feodary being one); *p.m.* Edward Thurland.

1843.) 5 *Feb.* 1577. Thomas Morgan, William Garnons and John Apparry, deputy feodary of the county of Hereford, (or two of them, the feodary [*sic*] being one); *p.m.* James Baskervyle, knight.

1844.) 5 *Feb.* 1577. Christopher Preston, George Myddleton, Christopher Carus, Thomas Brethwayte, deputy feodary of the county of Westmorland, and William Atkynson (or two of them, the deputy feodary or Atkynson being one); *p.m.* John Preston.

1845.) 4 *Feb.* 1577. John Gyfford, Thomas Warynge, Richard Rypyngton, feodary of the county of Stafford, and Francis Congreve (or two of them, the feodary being one); *p.m.* John Lane.

1846.)   5 *Feb.* 1577.   William Chylde, feodary of the county of Worcester, George Pytcher and William Evett (or two of them, the feodary being one); *p.m.* John Garwaye.

1847.)   2 *Feb.* 1577.   William Tooke, auditor general of the court of Wards, Thomas Lodge, Richard Gadburye and William Necton, feodary of the city of London, (or two of them, the feodary being one); *p.m.* Thomas Archer.

1848.)   1 *Feb.* 1577.   Thomas Baryngton, knight, George Bromley, attorney of the duchy of Lancaster, William Tooke, auditor of the court of Wards, George Fetyplace, Francis Beamount and John Glascock, feodary of the county of Essex, (or two of them, the feodary being one); *p.m.* Walter, earl of Essex.

1849.)   29 *Jan.* 1577.   George Turpyn, knight, Robert Barham, feodary of the county of Leicester, William Raven and Geoffrey Ithell (or two of them, the feodary being one); *p.m.* Richard Hodgeson.

1850.)   29 *Jan.* 1577.   John Coles, feodary of the county of Somerset, Thomas Phillyppes, Humphrey Worthe and James Ashe (or two of them, the feodary being one); *p.m.* Thomas Somer.

1851.)   28 *Jan.* 1577. Thomas Lewkoner, Richard Lewkoner, John Comber, John Knyght and Edward Myddleton, feodary of the county of Sussex, (or two of them, the feodary being one); *p.m.* Thomas Harryson *alias* Hall.

1852.)   4 *Jan.* 1577.   Robert Crane, Francis Claxton, Robert Gordon and Thomas Andrewes, feodary of the county of Suffolk, (or two of them, the feodary being one); *p.m.* John Wyncoll.

1853.)   24 *Jan.* 1577.   Nicholas West, William Hawtrey, Paul Dorrell and Peter Palmer, feodary of the county of Buckingham, (or two of them, the feodary being one); *p.m.* Alexander Denton.

1854.)   14 *Jan.* 1577.   John Fortescue of Spridelston, John Fortescue of Valapytt, Christopher Harrys and John Eveleygh, feodary of the county of Devon, (or two of them, the feodary being one); *p.m.* John Blake,   [*m. 2d.*] 'yeoman'.

1855.)   22 *Jan.* 1577.   Francis Hastynges, Adrian Stokes, George Vyllers and Robert Braham, feodary of the county of Leicester, (or two of them, the feodary being one); *p.m.* William Hawford.

1856.)   20 *Dec.* 1576.   Lewis Dyve, Oliver Saynt John, John Thompson, Thomas Snagge and Peter Gray (or two of them, Thompson, Snagge or Gray being one); *p.m.* Richard Faldoo.

1857.)   21 *Feb.* 1577.   Thomas Willyamson, feodary of the North Riding, co. York, Anthony Smethley, feodary of the East Riding, co. York, Thomas Layton and Roger Dalton (or two of them, Williamson being one); *p.m.* William Webster.

1858.)   16 *Feb.* 1577.   Henry Nevill, knight, Richard Lovelace, Thomas Fortescue and Thomas Noke, feodary of the county of Berks, (or two of them, the feodary being one); *p.m.* John Norrys.

1859.)   21 *Feb.* 1577.   Roger Prydeaux, John Chaffe, mayor of Exeter, John Evellygh, feodary of the county of Devon, and John Peryam (or two of them, the feodary being one); *p.m.* Thomas Prestwood.

1860.)   20 *Feb.* 1577.   John Hubband, knight, Richard Seyborne, John Kyghley, Thomas Baskervyle and George Wylkes (or two of them, Seyborn being one); *p.m.* Richard Browne.

1861.)   7 *Dec.* 1576.   Jasper Leake, John Boys, Andrew Ryccarde and Michael Berysford, feodary of the county of Kent, (or two of them, the feodary being one); *p.m.* lady Elizabeth Dennys.

1862.)   7 *Dec.* 1576.   Roger Yonge, Thomas Bullock, Richard Warde and Thomas Noke, feodary of the county of Berks, (or two of them, the feodary being one); *p.m.* William Gray.

1863.)   10 *Dec.* 1576.   Henry Gates, knight, Marmaduke Lucye, Thomas Williamson, feodary of the North Riding, co. York, and William Wyvell (or two of them, the feodary being one); *p.m.* Ralph Raysyng.

1864.)   10 *Dec.* 1576.   Francis Cave, Brian Cave, Francis Saunders, Francis Harryngton and Robert Braham, feodary of the county of Leicester, (or two of them, the feodary being one); *p.m.* Thomas Neale.

1865.)   11 *Dec.* 1576.   William Dyxe, Alexander Whytehed and Eustace Webbe, deputy feodary of the county of Surrey, (or two of them, Webbe being one); *p.m.* William Note.

1866.)   12 *Feb.* 1577.   John Lawson, feodary of the county of Northumberland, Robert Roddan, Ralph Botteflower and Cuthbert Rydley (or two of them, the feodary being one); *p.m.* Richard Newton.

1867.)   14 *Feb.* 1577.   Henry Gates, knight, Francis Wortley, Thomas Pagytt, John Savyle and Thomas Williamson, feodary of the North Riding, co. York, (or two of them, the feodary being one); *p.m.* Andrew Oglethorpe.

1868.)   12 *Feb.* 1577.   Henry Gates, knight, Thomas Williamson, feodary of the North Riding, co. York, and Brian Hamond, feodary of the West Riding, co. York, (or two of them, Williamson being one); *p.m.* John Harwood.

1869.)   14 *Feb.* 1577.   Henry Gates, knight, Francis Wortley, Thomas Pagytt, John Savyle and Brian Hamond, feodary of the West Riding, co. York, (or two of them, the feodary being one); *p.m.* Richard Welbore.

1870.)   14 *Feb.* 1577.   Richard Seyborn, John Kyghley, Thomas Baskervyle and George Wykes (or two of them, Seyborn being one); *p.m.* John Browne.

1871.)   12 *Feb.* 1577.   Ralph Barton, feodary of the county of Nottingham, Anthony Brakenbury and Edward Northe (or two of them, the feodary being one); *p.m.* John Williamson.

1872.)   12 *Feb.* 1577.   Francis Metham, William Thorneton, Thomas Savell and Thomas Williamson, feodary of the North Riding, co. York, (or two of them, the feodary being one); *p.m.* John Atherton.

1873.)   9 *Feb.* 1577.   Henry Weston, knight, Thomas Heward, Henry Hunston and Christopher Dawbney, feodary of the county of Norfolk, (or two of them, the feodary being one); *p.m.* Thomas Adamson, 'yeoman'.

1874.)   11 *Feb.* 1577.   Thomas Tresham, knight, Thomas Brooke, Edward Watson and William Rudd, deputy feodary of the county of Northampton, (or two of them, the deputy feodary being one); *p.m.* William Hawford.

1875.)   5 *Feb.* 1577.   John Eveleygh, feodary of the county of Devon, Richard Reynell, Richard Fowell and Christopher Martyn (or two of them, the feodary being one); *p.m.* John Rowse.

1876.)   5 *Feb.* 1577.   William Grove, feodary of the county of Wilts, Gerard Eryngton, Edward Langford and John Mychell (or two of them, the feodary being one); *p.m.* Stephen Wheteacre.

1877.)   5 *Feb.* 1577.   James Boyle, William Garnons, John Apparry, deputy feodary of the county of Hereford, and John Lygon (or two of them, Parry being one); *p.m.* Richard Cave.

1878.)   6 *Feb.* 1577.   Benjamin Tytcheborne, Roger Corham, William Bagger and Richard Hore, feodary of the county of Southampton, (or two of them, the feodary being one); *p.m.* James Rythe.

1879.)   9 *Feb.* 1577.   Commission to Nicholas Beamond, George Vyllers, Henry Poole and Robert Braham, feodary of the county, (or two of them, the feodary being one) to inquire in the county of Leicester touching the lunacy of Francis Sherrard.   [*m. 3d.*]

1880.)   28 *Jan.* 1577.   Commission to John Popham, Edward Flowerdue, Jasper Fysher and William Necton, feodary of the city, (or two of them, the feodary being one) to inquire in the city of London touching the lunacy of Thomas Machell.

1881.)   12 *Feb.* 1577.   Commission to Henry Gates, knight, Ralph Rookebye, Richard Franckland and Thomas Williamson, feodary of the North Riding, co. York, (or two of them, the feodary being one) to inquire in the county of York touching the idiocy of William Coverdale.

1882.)   25 *June* 1577.   Commission to William Ingleby, Marmaduke Constable, William Danyell and Anthony Smethley, feodary of the East Riding, co. York, (or two of them, the feodary being one) to inquire in the county of York *post mortem* Tristram Swanedale.

The like to the following in the counties named, viz.—

1883.)   25 *June* 1577.   William Grove, John Skerne and James Sherrock, feodary of the county of Dorset, (or two of them, the feodary being one); *p.m.* Thomas Yong the elder.

1884.)   25 *June* 1577.   William Inglebye, Marmaduke Constable, William Danyell and Anthony Smethley, feodary of the East Riding, co. York, (or two of them, the feodary being one); *p.m.* Anthony Langdale.

1885.)   25 *June* 1577.   The same; *p.m.* John Gybson.

1886.)   28 *June* 1577.   William Fayrfaxe, knight, William Babthorpe, knight, Francis Rodes and Thomas Willyamson, feodary of the North Riding, co. York, (or two of them, the feodary being one); *p.m.* John Nevell, knight, lord Latymer.

1887.)   28 *June* 1577.   Christopher Haydon, knight, Henry Woodhouse, Thomas Townsend, Francis Wyndam, William Paston and Christopher Dawbney, feodary of the county of Norfolk, (or two of them, the feodary being one); *p.m.* the same.

1888.)   28 *June* 1577.   Lewis Dyve, Thomas Ratclyffe, Robert Newdygate, Thomas Pyggot and George Wyngate, feodary of the county of Bedford, (or two of them, the feodary being one); *p.m.* the same.

1889.)   28 *June* 1577.   Edward Mountague, knight, Edmund Brudenell, knight, Edmund Watson, Michael Lewes and William Rudd, deputy feodary of the county of Northampton, (or two of them, Rudd being one); *p.m.* the same.

1890.)   20 *June* 1577.   George Grenefeild, Thomas Browne, feodary   [*m.* 4*d.*] of the county of Cornwall, and William Samuell (or two of them, the feodary being one); *p.m.* John Tryvylion.

1891.)   21 *June* 1577.   William Tooke, auditor general of the court of Wards, Robert Worthe, William Necton, feodary of the county of Middlesex, and Robert Hayes (or two of them, the feodary being one); *p.m.* John Sheppard.

1892.)   21 *June* 1577.   Thomas Warynges, Richard Repyngton, feodary of the county of Stafford, and William Cockayne (or two of them, the feodary being one); *p.m.* Hugh Lee.

1893.)   18 *June* 1577.   William Heydon, John Jernyngham, Charles Cutler, Richard Godfrey and Christopher Dawbney, feodary of the county of Norfolk, (or two of them, the feodary being one); *p.m.* Edward Spanye.

1894.)   20 *June* 1577.   George Danvers, Thomas Panystone, Vincent Curson, George Throgmerton and Thomas Ryccardes, feodary of the county[1], (or two of them, the feodary being one); *p.m.* Gerard Crocker, knight.

1895.)   20 *June* 1577.   The same; *p.m.* Edmund Hampden.

1896.)   20 *June* 1577.   William Cavendyshe, Thomas Knyveton, Anthony Gell, feodary of the county of Derby, and Richard Cooke (or two of them, the feodary being one); *p.m.* Thomas Eyre.

1897.)   20 *June* 1577.   George Grenefeild, Thomas Browne, feodary of the county of Cornwall, and William Samuel (or two of them, the feodary being one); *p.m.* John Trevylyon.

---

[1] Inquisition not found; apparently co. Oxford.

1898.)   21 *June* 1577.   Christopher Heydon, knight, William Yelverton and Christopher Dawbney, feodary of the county of Norfolk, (or two of them, the feodary being one); *p.m.* Edmund Brand.

1899.)   22 *June* 1577.   Gilbert Talbott, Thomas Knyveton and Anthony Gell, feodary of the county of Derby, (or two of them, the feodary being one); *p.m.* Christopher Eyre.

1900.)   10 *June* 1577.   John Strowde, John Skearne, Giles Penney and James Sharrock, feodary of the county of Dorset, (or two of them, the feodary being one); *p.m.* Anthony Cullyford.

1901.)   11 *May* 1577.   Thomas Baryngton, knight, William Ayloff, John Wentworth and John Glascocke, feodary of the county of Essex, (or two of them, the feodary being one); *p.m.* Edward Capell, knight.

1902.)   20 *May* 1577.   John Spylman, Edmund Awdeley, Robert Downes and Christopher Dawbney, feodary of the county of Norfolk, (or two of them, the feodary being one); *p.m.* Thomas Derham.

1903.)   20 *May* 1577.   Edward Denton, William Buttle, Thomas Ryccardes, feodary of the county of Oxford, (or two of them, the feodary being one); *p.m.* Thomas Moore.

1904.)   *Undated.*   The same; as above.

1905.)   22 *May* 1577.   John Salisbury, John Edwardes, Robert Puleston, William Almer and John Bellott, feodary of the county of Denbigh, (or two of them, the feodary being one); *p.m.* John Yardeley.

1906.)   14 *May* 1577.   John Eveleygh, feodary of the county of Devon, Thomas Mouncke, George Rolle and Richard Gylbert (or two of them, the feodary being one); *p.m.* Robert Mallett.

1907.)   14 *May* 1577.   Ralph Barton, feodary of the county of Nottingham, Robert Bradford, Charles Wawyn, Francis Power and Thomas Bullocke (or two of them, the feodary being one); *p.m.* John Williamson.

1908.)   29 *April* 1577.   Hamond Upton, Anthony Kyme, feodary of the county of Lincoln, George Hartgrave and Henry Wynckfeild (or two of them, the feodary being one); *p.m.* James Enderby.

1909.)   29 *April* 1577.   Anthony Smethley, feodary of the East Riding, co. York, William Inglebye, Marmaduke Constable and William Danyell (or two of them, the feodary being one); *p.m.* Gabriel St. Quyntyn.

1910.)   6 *May* 1577.   Edward Abarrowe, Ambrose Kelwey and Richard Hore, feodary of the county of Southampton, (or two of them, the feodary being one); *p.m.* Thomas Carewe.

1911.)   6 *May* 1577.   Christopher Wyvell, Ralph Lawson, Nicholas Gyrlyngton the younger and Thomas Williamson, feodary of the North Riding, co. York, (or two of them, the feodary being one); *p.m.* James Conyers.

1912.)   27 *April* 1577.   John Zouche, knight, Ralph Sacheverell, John Harper and Anthony Gell, feodary of the county of Derby, (or two of them, the feodary being one); *p.m.* Christopher Eyre.

1913.)   17 *April* 1577.   William Tooke, auditor general of the court of Wards, John Brockett, Henry Conysbye and Walter Tooke, deputy feodary of the county of Hertford, (or two of them, William or Walter Tooke being one); *p.m.* George Grubbe.

1914.)   17 *April* 1577.   Thomas Scott, knight, Edward Boyse, Francis Wylforde and Michael Berysford, feodary of the county of Kent, (or two of them, the feodary being one); *p.m.* Christopher Dygges.

1915.)   30 *April* 1577.   William St. John, John Fysher and Richard Hore, feodary of the county of Southampton, (or two of them, the feodary being one); *p.m.* Nicholas Knyght.

1916.)   30 *April* 1577.   George Zouche, Christopher George, feodary of the county of Gloucester, John Maddock and James Bucke (or two of them, the feodary being one); *p.m.* Maurice Smyth.

1917.) 2 *May* 1577. William Brouncker, John Dauntesey, Richard Goore and William Grove, feodary of the county of Wilts, (or two of them, the feodary being one); *p.m.* Nicholas Snell.

1918.) 29 *June* 1577. Thomas Grey, knight, Cuthbert Collyngwood, knight, Henry Woodryngton, William Fenwycke, James Ogle and Henry Haggarston (or four of them); *p.m.* John Fenwyck.[1]

1919.) 29 *June* 1577. Edward Carrell, Francis Sherley, Richard Shelley and Edward Myddleton, feodary of the county of Sussex, (or two of them, the feodary being one); *p.m.* Henry Catley.

1920.) 14 *June* 1577. Fulk Grevyll, knight, George Curson, Edward Eglonby, Richard Eglenbye and Arthur Gregorye, feodary of the county of Warwick, (or two of them, the feodary being one); *p.m.* Thomas Massyn.

1921.) 15 *June* 1577. Giles Escourte, Henry Clyfforde, Gerard Eryngton and William Grove, feodary of the county of Wilts, (or two of them, the feodary being one); *p.m.* Henry Clyfton.

1922.) 15 *June* 1577. Ralph Sheldon, William Chylde, feodary of the county of Worcester, William Bell, Thomas Graunte and John Wolmer (or two of them, the feodary being one); *p.m.* William Hunt.   [*m. 5d.*]

1923.) 15 *June* 1577. Ralph Shelton, Thomas Huggon, Edmund Awdeley and Christopher Dawbney, feodary of the county of Norfolk, (or two of them, the feodary being one); *p.m.* Thomas Dereham.

1924.) 26 *June* 1577. Henry Conysbye, Rowland Lytton, Nicholas Bristowe, Walter Tooke, deputy feodary of the county of Hertford, and Thomas Newce (or two of them, Tooke being one); *p.m.* Henry Fortescue.

1925.) 26 *June* 1577. Brian Hamond, feodary of the county of York, John Ramsden and Thomas Norclyfe (or two of them, the feodary being one); *p.m.* Ranulf Fernley.

1926.) 26 *June* 1577. George Carye, Richard Reynoldes and John Eveleygh, feodary of the county of Devon, (or two of them, the feodary being one); *p.m.* Margaret Parke, widow.

1927.) 26 *June* 1577. George Carye, John Coffyn, Thomas Rudgeway and John Eveleygh, feodary of the county of Devon, (or two of them, the feodary being one); *p.m.* Richard Byssett.

1928.) 26 *June* 1577. Richard Seyborne, Roger Boddenham, Gregory Pryce and John Parry, deputy feodary of the county of Hereford, (or two of them, Perry being one); *p.m.* Elizabeth Hopton.

1929.) 26 *June* 1577. Thomas Hannam, Lawrence Huyde, William Grove and James Sharrock, feodary of the county of Dorset, (or two of them, the feodary being one); *p.m.* Ralph Scroope.

1930.) 15 *March* 1577. John Pellam, knight, William Morley, John Lunsforde, Edward Gage and Edward Myddleton, feodary of the county of Sussex, (or two of them, the feodary being one); *p.m.* John Bellyngham.

1931.) 15 *April* 1577. Nicholas Barham, one of the Queen's serjeants at law, Nicholas St. Leger, Thomas Barham, William Aucher and Michael Berysford, feodary of the county of Kent, (or three of them, Nicholas Barham and Berysford being two); *p.m.* William Lovelace, serjeant at law.

1932.) 1 *April* 1577. Henry Archer, Robert Stepneth, Richard Browne, John Glascock, feodary of the county of Essex, Thomas Brydges and Robert Byddell (or two of them, the feodary being one); *p.m.* John Welborne and John Turner.

1933.) 1 *April* 1577. George Asheby, William Necton, feodary of the county of

---

[1] No inquisition found; apparently co. Northumberland.

Middlesex, Robert Stepneth, Richard Browne and Robert Byddell (or two of them, the feodary being one); *p.m.* Thomas Deane.

1934.)   1 *April* 1577.   Henry Archer, Robert Stepneth, Richard Brown, John Glascocke, feodary of the county of Essex, Thomas Brydges and Robert Byddell (or two of them, the feodary being one); *p.m.* Edmund Arblaster.

1935.)   1 *April* 1577.   Henry Weston, knight, Christopher Dawbney, feodary of the county of Norfolk, Thomas Hewarde and Henry Hunston (or two of them, the feodary being one); *p.m.* John Delahey.

1936.)   1 *March* 1577.   Anthony Maxye, John Glascock, feodary of the county of Essex, and William Twydey (or two of them, the feodary being one); *p.m.* Henry Fortescue.

1937.)   1 *March* 1577.   Richard Seborne, Roger Boddenham, Gregory Pryce and John Parry, deputy feodary of the county of Hereford, (or two of them, Parry being one); *p.m.* Elizabeth Hopton, widow.

1938.)   20 *March* 1577.   Ralph Lawson, Thomas Williamson, feodary of the North Riding, co. York, Marmaduke Slyngesbye and Henry Norton (or two of them, the feodary being one); *p.m.* John Conyers.

1939.)   29 *June* 1577.   Thomas Lewkenor, Richard Lewkenor, Lawrence Stoughton and Edward Myddleton, feodary of the county of Sussex, (or two of them, the feodary being one); *p.m.* Richard Myll *alias* Mylles.

1940.)   9 *May* 1577.   John Moyle, Robert Smythe and Thomas Browne, feodary of the county of Cornwall, (or two of them, the feodary being one); *p.m.* John Ellyott.

1941.)   24 *May* 1577.   Commission to Thomas Gawdye and John Jeffereys, justices of the Queen's Bench, to hear at the guildhall of London an appeal of error in (1) the record and process of a precept of *scire facias* before the mayor and aldermen of London in the chamber of the guildhall in a suit by John Powlett of Frefock, co. Southampton, against George Puttenham for 100 marks recovered by virtue of an original bill touching a plea of debt of 1,000 marks brought in the said court before Ambrose Nicholas, late mayor, and the aldermen by Puttenham against Pawlett and (2) the judgment on the said precept before the present mayor and aldermen. At the suit of Puttenham.

1942.)   11 *March* 1577.   *Gorhambury.*   Appointment of David Lewes, LL.D., judge and lieutenant of the court of Admiralty, Valentine Dale, LL.D., master of the Requests, William Awbrey, LL.D., and John Hamond, LL.D., to be commissioners, recoverors and judges delegate on the Queen's part in pursuance of the treaty lately made between her and the King of Portugal for the mutual restitution of goods, moneys, debts and ships of the subjects of either party which had been detained and sequestrated in their dominions by the said princes' authority; with power of treating, defining and determining concerning the said mutual restitution and compensation, of valuing wares sold or alienated, of giving compensation out of arrested goods, of judging or arbitrating touching the just price of wares sold, the valuation of money or the recovery of interest on debts, taking advice if necessary, by mutual consent, of skilled merchants, also of hearing, judging and determining touching goods, moneys and debts suppressed or alienated by the subjects of either realm or by authority of either prince, and of proceeding with every remedy of law against offenders in   [*m. 6d.*]
this behalf. By the said treaty it was agreed that within six months after 15 Nov. following there should be a mutual restitution of goods and the like detained in either party's dominions from the year 1568 to the said 15 Nov., each party to appoint four men of fitting standing with power within three months after the said 15 Nov. to treat and determine as aforesaid.   By Q.

1943.)   11 *March* 1577.   *Gorhambury.*   Appointment during pleasure of David Lewes, LL.D., judge and president of the court of Admiralty, Valentine Dale, LL.D., master of the Requests, William Awbrey, LL.D., and Robert Forth, LL.D., (or two of them, Lewes or Dale being one) to be commissioners and judges delegate to hear, judge and determine, without appeal, complaints of piracy committed by the Queen's subjects against subjects of the Most Christian King; no other person having jurisdiction in the said causes to hear or judge the same during this commission. The said King, moved by constant representations of the Queen's ambassadors and complaints of her subjects concerning piratical attacks by his subjects, has appointed certain commissioners and judges to hear such causes; and the Queen, though she has heretofore appointed judges with the fullest power to this end, wishes to leave nothing undone to suppress piracies.   By Q.

1944.)   11 *Oct.* 1577.   Commission to John Southcott, a justice of the Queen's Bench, and Roger Manwood, a justice of the Common Pleas, to hear at the guildhall of London an appeal of error in (1) the record and process of a suit before James Harvye, alderman, late a sheriff of London, in the city court brought by Henry Lane, skinner, against Richard Procter, grocer, touching a trespass on the case and afterwards, at Procter's instance, removed before John Ryvers, knight, then mayor, and the then aldermen of the city in the chamber of the guildhall and (2) the judgment of the same suit before Ambrose Nycholas, knight, late mayor, and the aldermen in the chamber of the guildhall. At the suit of Procter.

1945.)   14 *Oct.* 1577.   *Windsor.*   Commission to John Hugham, Robert Ashefeild, Thomas Badby and Thomas Andrews, feodary of the county, (or two of them, the feodary being one) to inquire *post mortem* [———] Dobbes in the county of Suffolk.

The like to the following in the counties named, viz.—   [*m. 7d.*]

1946.)   14 *Oct.* 1577.   *Windsor.*   Ralph Shelton, Thomas Barrowe, Robert Kempe and [———] Dawbney, feodary of the county of Norfolk, (or two of them, the feodary being one); *p.m.* as above.

1947.)   17 *July* 1577.   *Gorhambury.*   William Walgrave, knight, Edward Grymston, William Cardynall and Thomas Andrewes, feodary of the county of Suffolk, (or two of them, the feodary being one); *p.m.* William Veisey.

1948.)   17 *July* 1577.   *Gorhambury.*   Hugh Cholmeley, knight, John Mosterton, Hugh Bromley and John Warde, feodary of the county palatine of Chester, (or two of them, the feodary being one); *p.m.* William Sheriff.

1949.)   21 *Aug.* 1577.   Thomas Tresham, knight, William Saunders, John Lane, Edward Watson and William Rudde, deputy feodary of the county of Northampton, (or two of them, Rudd being one); *p.m.* Ralph Leicester, knight.

1950.)   20 *July* 1577.   *Gorhambury.*   Thomas Lucas, knight, Edmund Pyrton, Thomas Teye and John Glascocke, feodary of the county of Essex, (or three of them, the feodary being one); *p.m.* Edmund Wylson.

1951.)   6 *Oct.* 1577.   *Gorhambury.*   Edmund Ashefeyld, knight, James Braybrook, William Mercer and John Capper, feodary of the county of Oxford, (or two of them, the feodary being one); *p.m.* Edward Whysteler.

1952.)   27 *Sept.* 1577.   *Windsor.*   George Peckham, knight, Michael Blunte, Miles Sandes and Peter Palmer, feodary of the county of Buckingham, (or two of them, the feodary being one); *p.m.* Robert Drury, knight.

1953.)   20 *Sept.* 1577.   *Gorhambury.*   Francis Wylloughbye, knight, George Wylloughby, Edward Eglyanby, Clement Fysher and Arthur Gregorye, feodary of the county of the city of Coventry, (or two of them, the feodary being one); *p.m.* William Starkey.

1954.)   20 *Sept.* 1577.   *Gorhambury.*   The same; *p.m.* Thomas Hyll.

1955.)   6 *Sept.* 1577.   *Gorhambury.*   Thomas Hoogan, Edward Flowerdue, Thomas

Barrowe, Thomas Heywar and Christopher Dawbney, feodary of the county of Norfolk, (or two of them, the feodary being one); *p.m.* Robert Bell, knight, late chief baron of the Exchequer.

1956.)   6 *Sept.* 1577.   *Gorhambury.*   John Abrahall, Philip Scudamore, James Boyle and John Parry, feodary of the county of Hereford, (or three of them, the feodary being one); *p.m.* Thomas Kyrll.

1957.)   20 *Sept.* 1577.   *Gorhambury.*   John Spencer, knight, Thomas Lucy, knight, Edward Boughton, Edward Eglionby and Arthur Gregorye, feodary of the county of Warwick, (or three of them, the feodary being one); *p.m.* Robert Wilkes.

1958.)   20 *Sept.* 1577.   *Gorhambury.*   Francis Wilford, Nicholas Sayntleger, Thomas Barham, William Aucher and Michael Berisford, feodary of the county of Kent, (or two of them, the feodary being one); *p.m.* William Lovelace, serjeant at law.

1959.)   20 *Sept.* 1577.   *Gorhambury.*   Edmund Ashefeyld, knight, Richard Blunte, Thomas Ryccardes, feodary of the county of Oxford, William Mercer and Ralph Warcoppe (or two of them, the feodary being one); *p.m.* Edward Whisteler.

1960.)   11 *Sept.* 1577.   *Gorhambury.*   Nicholas Poyntes, knight, Thomas Throgmerton, William Reade and Christopher George, feodary of the county of Gloucester, (or two of them, the feodary being one); *p.m.* Edward Veale.

1961.)   11 *Sept.* 1577.   *Gorhambury.*   Francis Leeke, knight, Godfrey Bossevyle, Francis Curson, Henry Foljambe and Anthony Gell, feodary of the county of Derby, (or two of them, the feodary being one); *p.m.* George Selyock.

1962.)   5 *June* 1577.   *Gorhambury.*   William Babthorpe, knight, Thomas Metham, Anthony Smethley, feodary of the East Riding, co. York, and Thomas Dunne (or two of them, the feodary being one); *p.m.* William Stephenson.

1963.)   8 *June* 1577.   Geoffrey Ithell, Robert Braham, feodary of the county of Leicester, William Raven, John Segrave and John Clement (or two of them, the feodary being one); *p.m.* Robert Hodgeson.

1964.)   14 *Oct.* 1577.   *Windsor.*   William Heydon, Richard Godfrey, Charles Cutler and Christopher Dawbney, feodary of the county of Norfolk, (or two of them, the feodary being one); *p.m.* Anthony Bates.

1965.)   6 *Sept.* 1577.   *Gorhambury.*   John Clopton, Christopher Chator, Christopher Rookeley and Thomas Willyamson, feodary of the North Riding, co. York, (or two of them, the feodary being one); *p.m.* Richard Metricke.

1966.)   11 *June* 1577.   Edward Bashe, William Tooke, auditor general of the court of Wards, Robert Wrothe, William Necton, feodary of the county of Middlesex, and Robert Hayes (or two of them, the feodary being one); *p.m.* Henry Hunsdon.

1967.)   13 *June* 1577.   John Higham, Robert Ashefeild, Robert Gurden and Thomas Andrewes, feodary of the county of Norfolk, (or two of them, the feodary being one); *p.m.* Ambrose Jermyn, knight.

1968.)   24 *May* 1577.   *Gorhambury.*   John Purvey, Thomas Sadler, Henry Sadler, George Horsey, Thomas Leventhorpe and Walter Tooke, deputy feodary of the county of Hertford, (or two of them, Purvey or Tooke being one); *p.m.* William Franckland.

1969.)   21 *Oct.* 1577.   *Windsor.*   Giles Poole, knight, John Hungerford, knight, Roger Lyggon and Christopher George, feodary of the county of Gloucester, (or two of them, the feodary being one); *p.m.* George Fetyplace.

1970.)   21 *Oct.* 1577.   *Windsor.*   John Hygford, Christopher George, feodary of the county of Gloucester, and Kenard Delabere (or two of them, the feodary being one); *p.m.* William Harwarde.

1971.)   21 *Oct.* 1577.   *Windsor.*   Henry Lee, knight, Hercules Raynsford, Thomas Penyston and Thomas Ryccardes (or two of them, the said feodary [*sic*] being one); *p.m.* Richard Crowley.

1972.)   9 *Nov.* 1577.   *Windsor.*   Ralph Shelton, William Heydon, Robert Kempe and

Christopher Dawbney, feodary of the county of Norfolk, (or two of them, the feodary being one); *p.m.* John Dobbes.   [*m. 8d.*]

1973.)   28 *Oct.* 1577.   *Windsor.*   Thomas Terryngham, Paul Darrell, Nicholas Colles and Peter Palmer, feodary of the county of Buckingham, (or two of them, the feodary being one); *p.m.* Elizabeth Weston.

1974.)   *Undated.*   William Tooke, Richard Alexander, Francis Heydon and Walter Tooke, deputy feodary of the county of Hertford, (or two of them, William Tooke or Walter Tooke being one); *p.m.* Thomas Johnson.

1975.)   1 *July* 1577.   Richard, bishop of St. Davids, Henry Jones, knight, Erasmus Saunders, feodary of the county of Carmarthen, and John Davyes, (or two of them, the feodary being one); *p.m.* David William Reade.

1976.)   1 *July* 1577.   The same; *p.m.* John Morris ap Owen.

1977.)   1 *July* 1577.   The same; *p.m.* Rethergh David Price.

1978.)   11 *July* 1577.   John Hubband, knight, Gregory Pryce and Thomas Hackluytt (or two of them, Hubband being one); *p.m.* Thomas Browne.

1979.)   11 *July* 1577.   Thomas Boynton, Christopher Helyard, Cotton Gargrave and Anthony Smethley, feodary of the East Riding, co. York, (or two of them, the feodary being one); *p.m.* John Vaughan.

1980.)   11 *July* 1577.   *Gorhambury.*   John, bishop of Hereford, John Lyggyns and George Wykes (or two of them, Wykes being one); *p.m.* John Browne.

1981.)   15 *Nov.* 1577.   Christopher Browne, knight, John Cupper, John Chylde and Thomas Ryccardes, feodary of the county of Oxford, (or two of them, the feodary being one); *p.m.* William Babyngton, knight.

1982.)   15 *Nov.* 1577.   Nicholas Debden, William Baggott and William Chylde, feodary of the county of Worcester, (or two of them, the feodary being one); *p.m.* Peter Romney.

1983.)   14 *Oct.* 1577.   *Windsor.*   John Higham, Robert Ashefeyld, Thomas Badby and Thomas Andrews, feodary of the county of Suffolk, (or two of them, the feodary being one); *p.m.* [——] Dobbes.

1984.)   14 *Oct.* 1577.   *Windsor.*   Ralph Shelton, Thomas Barrowe, Robert Kempe and [——] Dawbney, feodary of the county of Norfolk, (or two of them, the feodary being one); *p.m.* the same.

1985.)   4 *Nov.* 1577.   *Windsor.*   Henry Goodier, Thomas Bewfeild, William Hudson and Arthur Gregorye, feodary of the county of Warwick, (or two of them, the feodary being one); *p.m.* John Yardeley.

1986.)   11 *Nov.* 1577.   *Windsor.*   James Lewes, Thomas Griffyth, John Stedman, Maurice ap Rychard and Geoffrey Lloyd, LL.D., (or three of them); *p.m.* Hugh ap Llewelyn Lloyd.

1987.)   7 *Nov.* 1577.   *Windsor.*   Thomas Southcott, John Eveleigh, feodary of the county of Devon, John Courtney and Richard Channon (or two of them, the feodary being one); *p.m.* Christian Cary, widow.

1988.)   18 *Oct.* 1577.   *Windsor.*   William Heydon, Richard Godfrey, Charles Cutler and Christopher Dawbney, feodary of the county of Norfolk, (or two of them, the feodary being one); *p.m.* Anthony Bates.

1989.)   8 *June* 1577.   Geoffrey Ithell, Robert Braham, feodary of the county of Leicester, William Raven, John Segrave and John Clement (or two of them, the feodary being one); *p.m.* Robert Hodgeson.

1990.)   5 *June* 1577.   *Gorhambury.*   William Babthorpe, knight, Thomas Metham, Anthony Smethley, feodary of the East Riding, co. York, and Thomas Dunne (or two of them, the feodary being one); *p.m.* William Stephenson.

1991.)   11 *Oct.* 1577.   Commission to John Southcott, a justice of the Queen's Bench, and Roger Manwood, a justice of the Common Pleas, to hear an appeal of error as above (no. 1944).

(The rest of the dorse is blank.)

PART IV

C. 66/1154

1992.)   26 *March* 1577.   Licence for Richard Coxe and Sibyl his   [*m.* 1]
wife to alienate lands in Balingham *alias* Balynam *alias* Balingeham, co. Hereford, to Hugh
Smyth. For 2*s.* 8*d.* paid to the Queen's farmer.

1993.)   26 *March* 1577.   The like for Amyas Powlett, knight, and Margaret his wife to
alienate the manors of Monckenzeale *alias* Zeale Monacorum and Losebeare, lands in
Monckenzeale, Losebeare, Lapford and Bowe, free warren and view of frankpledge in
Monckenzeale and Losebere and the advowson of Monckenzeale church, co. Devon, to
Edward Seymore, knight, lord Seymore. For £7 8*s.* 4*d.*.

1994.)   26 *March* 1577.   The like for Helen Burton, widow, late the wife of Ralph Burton,
citizen and draper of London, to alienate a messuage called Rydegate and all her other lands
in Est Smythfeld by the Tower of London in the parish of St. Botolph without Algate,
London, late of the monastery of Coggeshall *alias* Coxhall, co. Essex, which premises she
held jointly with her said husband after the death of Walter Myers, citizen and
'waxechaundelor' of London, and Marion his wife, deceased, by charter of Walter dated 29
April 1557, to Christoper Myers. For 43*s.* 4*d.*

1995.)   1 *May* 1577.   The like for John Thynne, knight, and Dorothy his wife to alienate
(1) a moiety of the manor of Nonekeeling, of lands in Nonekeelinge, Keelynge, Bewholme,
Benyngholme, Cattewyke and Waghen and of the advowson of Nonekeelynge church, co.
York, (2) the manors of Yarton *alias* Yardington and Walton and lands in Bridgenorthe,
Walton, Yarton, Quatford and Morvyle, co. Salop, (3) lands in Frome Selwood,
Horringdon and Wells, co. Somerset, (4) lands and the bailiwick of keeper of Selwood forest
alias 'Wilts Ballywycke' in Corseley, Warmyster, Westbury, Heytredesburye *alias* Hatche-
burie, Asheton, Seles, Southwick, Slogrowe, Wingfeld, Stowrton, Bradleighe, Meere,
Knylmyngton and Knoyle, co. Wilts, and (5) the manors of Bucland and Laverton and lands
in   [*m.* 2]
Bucland, Laverton, Wornyngton Lees *alias* Wornyngton and Didbroke, co. Gloucester, to
Robert Creswell and John Lacy and the heirs and assigns of Creswell. For £49 12*s.* 3*d.*

1996.)   1 *May* 1577.   The like for Thomas Poly to alienate the manor of Aspalles in
Myldenhall, co. Suffolk, to Roger, lord Northe, baron of Kirtelinge, to the use of Poly and
Julian his wife for life in survivorship and thereafter of the said lord Northe. For 53*s.* 4*d.*

1997.)   1 *May* 1577.   The like for George Bradshawe to alienate the manor of Morebarne
and lands in Orton *alias* Overton under Arderne *alias* Overton on the Hill, Morebarne and
Meryvale, co. Leicester, to Robert Bradshawe. For £4 8*s.*

1998.)   26 *March* 1577.   The like for Humphrey Conyngesby and Mary his wife to alienate
lands in Beckeford, Grafton, Ashton under Hill and Aston on Currant and the tithes of corn
and hay of lands in Beckeford and in Bengrove in Beckeford, co. Gloucester, to John Kettle
and Robert Wheathill and the heirs and assigns of Kettle to the use of Humphrey for life and
thereafter of Mary. For £3 6*s.* 8*d.*   [*m.* 3]

1999.)   8 *May* 1577.   The like for John Abrahall the elder and Blanche his wife to alienate lands in Brompton *alias* Brompton Abbottes, co. Hereford, to Rowland Hunt. For £3 2s. 5d.

2000.)   1 *May* 1577.   The like for Richard Speight the elder, 'yoman', to alienate lands (*named with tenant's name*) in Ossett Sandes next Heaton in the parish of Dewesbury, late of the monastery of Kirkstall, co. York, to Richard Speight the younger and Elizabeth his wife for life in survivorship, with remainder to the right heirs of Richard the younger. For 6s. 8d.

2001.)   1 *May* 1577.   The like for George Frevyle, a baron of the Exchequer, Jane his wife and Robert Frevyle the elder to alienate the manor of Shelford Parva and lands in Shelford Parva, Hawkeston, Harston, Wiclesforde, Stapleforde, Newton and Sheprithe, co. Cambridge, to John Banckes. For £6 13s. 4d.

2002.)   1 *May* 1577.   The like for Christopher Berisford to alienate the manors of Ledenham and Fulbecke, the rectories of Ledenham and Fulbecke and lands in Ledenham and Fulbecke aforesaid, Tattersall and Tattersall Thorpe with the rectory thereto belonging and in Swyne, Bouth, Armetree, Corner and Wildmore in the parish of Cunsby, co. Lincoln, to   [*m.* 4]
George Metham, Michael Berisford and Lawrence Blundeston. For £5 11s. 10d.

2003.)   1 *May* 1577. The like for Thomas Taverner to alienate lands in Lamborne, co. Essex, to Charles Newcombe and Thomas Parker and the heirs and assigns of Newcombe. For 10s.

2004.)   11 *June* 1577.   Pardon of alienation: William Forster of Aldermaston, co. Berks, by his will, 28 Dec. 1573, devised to William Forster, his son, in tail male the manor of Grange and lands in Currage, Shawe and Chevely, co. Berks, late purchased of lord Mountague, and after his death William the son entered the same. For 36s. 8d. paid to the Queen's farmer.

2005.)   11 *June* 1577. The like: Robert Mydgeley and John Mydgeley, his son, by indenture, 1 Feb., 19 Eliz., acquired from Richard Pollard and James Lyster lands (*named with tenants' names*) in Horsfurth, co. York. For 28s. 11¾d.

2006.) 1 *May* 1577.   Licence for Henry Bridges and Anne his wife to alienate the manor of Keynesham, co. Somerset, all the said Henry's lands in Keynesham and Westhannam, co. Gloucester, and the grange of Tyngley with all his lands in Tingley, Brewere and Fyfeild, co. Oxford, to Humphrey Fitzwilliam and Nicholas Bodenham. For £17 4s. paid to   [*m.* 5] the Queen's farmer.

2007.)   1 *May* 1577.   The like for Edward Denny to alienate the rectory and the advowson of the vicarage of Amwell, co. Hertford, to John Skynner and Thomas Skynner. For £3 6s. 8d.

2008.)   1 *May* 1577.   The like for Henry Sheppard and Mary his wife to alienate lands in Swanborne, co. Buckingham, to Christopher Barnaby. For 44s. 5½d.

2009.)   1 *May* 1577.   The like for Hugh Parlor to alienate lands in Wyckham *alias* Estwickham, co. Kent, to William Billesbye, John Madockes and Maurice Pickringe and the heirs and assigns of the said William to the use of Parlor and Margaret Billesbye and the heirs of their bodies begotten between them, with remainder to the right heirs of Parlor. For 33s. 4d.

2010.)   1 *June* 1577.   The like for John Vaghan to alienate the manor of Glasburye, co. Radnor, to Blanche Parry, a gentlewoman of the privy chamber. For £6 13s. 4d.

2011.)   8 *May* 1577.   Pardon of alienation: Alexander Sydenham and Anne his wife in Easter term, 18 Eliz., by fine in the Common Pleas acquired unto them and Alexander's heirs from James Cappes and Nicholas Cappes a moiety of the manor of Huyschampflower, of lands in Huyschampflower   [*m.* 6] and of the advowson of the rectory of Huyschampflower, co. Somerset. For 43s. 2½d. paid to the Queen's farmer.

2012.)   1 *May* 1577.   Licence for Giles Bridges, knight, lord Chandos, to alienate lands in Norton and Malmesburye, co. Wilts, to Thomas Best and Anthony Bonner. For 66s. 8d. paid to the Queen's farmer.

2013.)   21 *May* 1577.   Pardon of alienation: John Cooke by indenture, 7 Nov., 15 Eliz., acquired from John Conyers and Francis Manby lands (*tenants named*) in Scamolsbye, co. Lincoln. For £3 12s. 4d. paid to the Queen's farmer.

2014.)   1 *June* 1577.   Licence for Francis Egglesfyeld and Joan his wife to alienate lands in Wolwiche, co. Kent, and Est Ham, co. Essex, to Nicholas Bacon, knight, councillor, keeper of the great seal, and John Osborne, a servant of Bacon, and the heirs and assigns of Bacon.

2015.)   1 *May* 1577.   The like for Nicholas Turbervile to alienate the rectory and the advowson of the vicarage of Whitechurche *alias* Wynterburne Whitechurche, co. Dorset, late of St. Edmund's college, Salisbury,   [*m.* 7] and lands there to Stephen Humber. For 36s. paid to the Queen's farmer.

2016.)   11 *June* 1577.   Pardon of alienation: Thomas Killingbecke by indenture, 5 Jan., 19 Eliz., acquired from John Stanworth lands (*named with tenants' names*) in Horsfurth, co. York. For 12s. 9d. paid to the Queen's farmer.

2017.)   12 *June* 1577.   The like: William Hobby, William Sheldon, Edmund Lachemere, Bartholomew Kightley and Humphrey Dyke the younger in Trinity term, 17 Eliz., by fine in the Common Pleas acquired unto them and the heirs of Hobby from Henry Dyneley the manors of Peddington, Avenons Courte and Wicke and lands in Peddington, Avenons Courte, Wicke and Barckley, co. Gloucester, For £16.

2018.)   21 *May* 1577.   Licence for Ralph Huggons to alienate land (*described*) in the city of Gloucester to Walter Nurse. For 33s. 4d. paid to the Queen's farmer.

2019.)   12 *June* 1577.   Pardon of alienation: Daniel Dysney in Michaelmas term, 15 Eliz., by fine in the Common Pleas acquired from John Hussey and Elizabeth his wife the manor of Hollywell and lands in Holliwell,   [*m.* 8] co. Lincoln. For £5 paid to the Queen's farmer.

2020.)   1 *May* 1577.   Licence for John Coke and Dorothy his wife to alienate lands in Rudge, Froxfeld, Little Bedwyn and Chesburie, co. Wilts, to John Organ *alias* Taylor the elder, Richard Organ *alias* Taylor and John Organ *alias* Taylor the younger and the heirs and assigns of the same John Organ the elder. For 29s. 8d. paid to the Queen's farmer.

2021.) 1 *May* 1577. The like for Thomas Saunders *alias* Mylles, 'yoman', to alienate the manor of Barwicke Bassett and lands in Barwicke Bassett and Ricardston, co. Wilts, to Alexander Staples and George Staples, his son, and the heirs and assigns of Alexander. For 50s.

2022.) 1 *May* 1577. The like for William Day, clerk, to alienate the manor, the rectory and the advowson of the vicarage of Shulton, late of the monastery of Beaulieu (*Bello Loco*), co. Southampton, and all appurtenances of the said manor and rectory in Shulton in the hundred of Faringdon, co. Berks, to William Daye the younger and Richard Daye, son of the said William Daye, clerk. For £6.

2023.) 1 *May* 1577. Pardon of alienation: Thomas Blake by indenture, 24 March, 15 Eliz., acquired from James Clarke and Matthew Stradlynge the manor of Tuxwell with Radlett, co. Somerset, with all their lands in   [*m.* 9] Spaxton, Overstowye and Netherstowye, co. Somerset. For £6 11s. 4d. paid to the Queen's farmer.

2024.) 1 *May* 1577. Licence for Francis, earl of Bedford, to alienate lands in Denbery, co. Devon, to Edward Seymor, knight, lord Seymor. For 7s. 2d. paid to the Queen's farmer.

2025.) 12 *June* 1577. Pardon of alienation: John Browne in Easter term, 17 Eliz., by fine in the Common Pleas acquired from Richard Sydenham, Jane his wife and John Samwayes lands in Tollor Porcorum, co. Dorset. For £4 paid to the Queen's farmer.

2026.) 1 *May* 1577. The like: Anthony Roue and Audrey his wife in Michaelmas term, 15 Eliz., by fine in the Common Pleas acquired unto them and the heirs of Anthony from James Frost, Joan his wife, Simon Suckerman, Richard Rolfe, Catherine his wife and William Fysher three fourth parts of a capital messuage called 'lez Wrastlers', a curtilage, two barns, a garden and 10s. rent in the parish of St. Botolph without Aldrichgate *alias* Aldersgate, London. For 50s.

2027.) 1 *June* 1577. Licence for Thomas Blake to alienate the manor of Tuxwell with Radlett with all his lands appertaining thereto in Spaxton, Overstowey and Netherstowey, co. Somerset, to Robert Blake of Bridgewater, merchant. For 43s. 6d. paid to the queen's farmer.

2028.) 1 *May* 1577. The like for Bartholomew Hales and Mary his wife to alienate lands in Bearley, Wottons Wawen and Snyterfeild, co.   [*m.* 10] Warwick, to Thomas Stringer and John Stringer and the heirs and assigns of Thomas. For 27s. 6d.

2029.) 1 *May* 1577. The like for William Beswicke, Mary his wife, Robert Thomson, Catherine his wife, Robert Seaton and Elizabeth his wife, to alienate the manor of Salford Abbottes *alias* Salford Abbatis, lands in Priors Salford and Abbottes Salford and the tithes of corn and hay in Abbotts Salford, co. Warwick, to John Alderford. For 44s. 6d.

2030.) 15 *April* 1577. The like for Henry Knowlls and Edward Williams to alienate the manor of Knighton, co. Leicester, to George Turpyn, knight, and Matthew Farnham. For £7 3s. ½d.

2031.) 26 *March* 1577. The like for John Arrundell and Anne his wife to alienate a fourth part of the manors of Colyton and Whiteforde, of the manor and borough of Colyforde, of the hundred of Colyton, of lands in Colyton, Colyford and Whiteforde and of free fishery in the waters of Esse, Yeartye, Colye and Axe, co. Devon, to William Poole. For £6 13s. 4d.

2032.)   26 *March* 1577.   The like for Richard Knight to alienate   [*m.* 11] the tithes belonging to the rectories of Crokeham and Greneham in the parish of Thacham, co. Berks, late of the monastery of Redinge, co. Berks, to John Knight, his brother.

2033.)   23 *April* 1577.   The like for William Gratewood, Mary his wife and Alice Corbett, widow, to alienate the manor of Adderley, lands in Adderley, Morrey, Speneley, Betton Underlyne, Shavington and Calverhall and the advowson of Adderley church, co. Salop, to Robert Nedham and Rowland Barker to the use of Gratewood and Mary his wife for life in survivorship, with successive remainders to Gratewood's wife at the time of his death for life and to the said Alice. For £26 13s. 4d.

2034.)   26 *March* 1577.   The like for Richard Denys to alienate his interest in lands (*tenants named*) in Allaston *alias* Alveston and Ircote, co. Gloucester, to Maurice Shipward. For 4d.

2035.)   26 *March* 1577.   The like for George Ratclyff, knight, to alienate the manor of Devilston *alias* Dylston and lands in Devilston *alias* Dylston, co. Northumberland, to Cuthbert, lord Ogle, Thomas Grey, knight, Ralph Grey and Cuthbert Carnaby and the heirs and assigns   [*m.* 12] of lord Ogle. For £8.

2036.)   26 *March* 1577.   The like for William Thornebery and Christopher Daunce to alienate lands (*described with tenants' names*) in Tewkesberye, co. Gloucester, to Thomas Wyllys and Anne Clynton, widow, and the heirs and assigns of Wyllys to the use of him and Anne and their heirs and assigns. For 6s. 8d.

2037.)   26 *March* 1577.   The like for Thomas Gressham, knight, to alienate lands in Myleham and Beston near Myleham, co. Norfolk, to Christopher Crowe. For 60s.

2038.)   1 *May* 1577.   Pardon of alienation: Robert Straunge and Christopher Gorge in Michaelmas term, 15 Eliz., by fine in the Common Pleas acquired unto them and the heirs and assigns of Straunge from Roger Lygon and George Lygon the manor of Calmesdon and lands in Calmesdon, Oldgore and North Cerney, co. Gloucester. For £4 paid to the Queen's farmer.

2039.)   26 *March* 1577.   Licence for Edward Manley to alienate the rectory of Sprotton, late of the monastery of St. James by Northampton, the advowson of the vicarage of Sprotton and lands in Sprotton and Credon *alias* Creton, co. Northampton, to Robert Manley and Edmund Manley and the heirs and assigns of Robert. For £5 1s. 4d. paid to the Queen's farmer.   [*m.* 13]

2040.)   2 *May* 1577.   Pardon of alienation: Thomas Cecill, knight, in Michaelmas term, 17 Eliz., by fine in the Common Pleas acquired from Philip Tylney the manor of Langton and lands in Langton, Mareten, Hornecastle, Thymelby, Whitehall, Thorneton and Woodall, co. Lincoln. For £5 8s. paid to the Queen's farmer.

2041.)   2 *May* 1577.   The like: Thomas Cecill, knight, in Hilary term, 17 Eliz., by fine in the Common Pleas acquired from John Carsey, Francis Carsey, his son and heir apparent, and Anne wife of Francis the manors of Revesby, Wilkesbie and Woodenderbie, lands in Revesbye, Wylkesbye and Woodenderbye and a moiety of the rectory of Revesbie, co. Lincoln. For 33s. 4d.

2042.)   1 *May* 1577.   Licence for John Felton and Catherine his wife to alienate lands in Cavendishe, co. Suffolk, to John Frenche. For 26s. 8d. paid to the Queen's farmer.

2043.)   7 *May* 1577.   The like for Walter Hastinges to alienate the rectory of Wheston *alias* Weston, 6s. 8d. rent in Wheston and the advowson of Wheston church, co. Leicester, to John Browne and Stephen Harvey to the use of Hastinges. For 44s. 6d.

2044.)   26 *March* 1577.   The like for Lewis Mordaunte, knight, lord Mordaunt, to alienate a third part of the manors of Warmyster, Boram, Westbury *alias* Mawdittes, Fyffehed Verdon *alias* Fydington and   [*m.* 14]
Dytheriche *alias* Dycherich, of lands in the said places, Estlavington and Westlavington, of the hundred of Warmyster and of a moiety of the advowson of Dytheriche church, co. Wilts, to George Tuchett, lord Awdley, and James Mervyn, knight, and the heirs and assigns of lord Awdley. For £11 13s. 9d.

2045.)   23 *April* 1577.   The like for Edward Mytton to alienate the manor of Haulston and lands in Haulston, Kynsill and Whittington, co. Salop, to George Prowde and Humphrey Mytton to the use of Edward and Anne his wife and his heirs and assigns [*sic*] by her, with successive remainders to the heirs male of the body of the said Edward, to the heirs male of the body of Edward Mytton, deceased, his father, to the heirs male of the body of Richard Mytton, grandfather of the said Edward the son, now surviving, and to the right heirs of Richard. For £6 13s. 4d.

2046.)   1 *May* 1577.   The like for Henry Langholme, Jane his wife, George Pormorte and Elizabeth his wife to alienate lands in Kennyngton *alias* Keddington, co. Lincoln, to Martin Brighouse and Roger Norton. For 33s. 4d.

2047.)   26 *March* 1577.   The like for William Wilson the elder and William Wilson the younger to alienate lands (*tenants named*) in   [*m.* 15]
Hickelton, co. York, some late of St. Catherine's chantry in Athewick Strete, co. York, and a moiety of the tithes of hay in Hickelton and Golthorpe, co. York, and in lands (*named*) in Bolton on Dearne, co. York, to William Rokeby and Mary his wife and the heirs and assigns of Rokeby. For 24s. 6d.

2048.)   26 *March* 1577.   The like for Robert Bowes and Percival Gunston to alienate lands in Estharlesey, co. York, to Thomas Grange the elder and Thomas Grange the younger. For 33s. 5d.

2049.)   26 *April* 1577.   The like for Thomas Goodere and William Goodere to alienate the rectory of Wheston *alias* Weston, 6s. 8d. rent in Wheston and the advowson of Wheston church, co. Leicester, to Walter Hastinges. For 44s. 6d.

2050.)   1 *May* 1577.   Pardon of alienation: Philip Parker in Michaelmas term, 16 Eliz., by fine in the Common Pleas acquired from Drew Drurye and Elizabeth his wife *inter alia* the manor of Erwarton, lands in Erwarton and the advowson of Erwarton, co. Suffolk, and the reversion of the premises. For £6 13s. 4d. paid to the Queen's farmer.

2051.)   1 *May* 1577.   The like: William Goodere, by indenture, 25 May, 18 Eliz., acquired from Thomas Goodere the rectory of Weston, co. Leicester, the advowson of the vicarage of Weston, a yearly rent of 6s. 8d. out of lands (*named*) in Weston and all lands there of the said Thomas conveyed to him by Ralph Rowlett, knight, deceased, or of his assigns. For £6 13s. 4d.   [*m.* 16]

2052.)   11 *June* 1577.   The like: Thomas Killingbecke by indenture, 20 Jan., 19 Eliz., acquired from Richard Pollarde and James Lyster lands (*named with tenants' names*) in Horsfurth, co. York. For 5s. 9d.

2053.)   26 *March* 1577.   Licence for William, lord Sandes, and Walter Sandes to alienate lands in Elsefeld *alias* Ellesfeld *alias* Ellysfyld *alias* Ulsefeld St. Martin *alias* Ulsefeld All Saints, co. Southampton, to Henry Walloppe, knight. For 18s. paid to the Queen's farmer.

2054.)   1 *May* 1577.   The like for Giles, lord Chaundos, to alienate the castle and manor of Sudeley, with the rectory and park there, the house and site of the monastery of Winchombe and lands in Sudeley, Winchombe, Cornden, Greete, Gretton, Potteslippe, Rowell, Carleton Abbottes and Langley, co. Gloucester, and lands in Noneaton *alias* Westeaton and Brodeblonsden, co. Wilts, to Thomas Clynton and Thomas Gorge to the use of the said lord Chaundos. For £54.

2055.)   1 *April* 1577. The like for Edmund Dighton and Thomas Dighton, his son and heir apparent, to alienate the manor of Sotby and lands in Sotbye and Panton, co. Lincoln, to Richard Goodericke. For £12.   [*m.* 17]

2056.)   1 *April* 1577.   The like for Robert Jermyn, Edmund Dighton and Thomas Dighton, son and heir apparent of Edmund, to alienate the rectory of Bamburgh *alias* Bambrugh, co. Lincoln, to Richard Goodericke. For 44s. 6d.

2057.)   26 *March* 1577.   The like for Francis Sandes to alienate the remainder and reversion of a grange called 'Yngham Grange' and all lands so called in Ingham, co. Lincoln, late of Bullington priory, co. Lincoln, to Christopher Stowe. For 10s. 5d.

2058.)   1 *May* 1577.   The like for Thomas Smyth to alienate a fourth part of the manor of Campden and of lands in Campden, Chepinge Campden, Broade Campden, Burington and Westlington, co. Gloucester, to Thomas Farmer and Robert Atkinson. For £5.

2059.)   1 *May* 1577.   The like for Thomas, lord Poulett, Anne his wife, John Wattes, Elizabeth his wife and Thomas Broughton to alienate the manor of Little Henton *alias* Stanbridge, lands in Little Henton *alias* Stanbridge and the advowson of the church there, co. Dorset, to Edward Poulett, Richard Walton and John Macham and the heirs and assigns of Edward. For 33s. 4d.   [*m.* 18]

2060.)   1 *May* 1577.   The like for Thomas Seckford to alienate the manor of Crepinge Hall and lands in Stutton, co. Suffolk, to Humphrey Wingefeld. For 46s. 8d.

2061.)   1 *June* 1577.   Pardon of alienation: Stephen Barnam, citizen and 'draper' of London, by indenture, 9 July, 16 Eliz., acquired from Richard Patricke, citizen and 'haberdasher' of London, all manors and lands of the said Patricke in Snawe, Ivechurche, Brockland and Romley Mershe, co. Kent. For £26 13s. 4d. paid to the Queen's farmer.

2062.)   1 *April* 1577.   Licence for Edward Honyng and Ursula his wife to alienate the site of the manor of Carleton, lands in Carleton and the advowson of Carleton church, co. Suffolk, to John Guybon. For 26s. 8d. paid to the Queen's farmer.

2063.)   11 *June* 1577.   Pardon of alienation: Stephen Saxtone by indenture, 1 Feb., 19 Eliz., acquired from Robert Craven lands (*named with tenants' names*) in Horsfurth, co. York. For 34s. ¾d. paid to the Queen's farmer.   [*m.* 19]

2064.)   1 *May* 1577.   Licence for William Hobby to alienate the manors of Rowell and Cottesden and lands in Rowell and Cottesden, co. Gloucester, to Austin Dyke, Anthony Hodgekyns and George Townsend and the heirs and assigns of Dyke. For £9 15s. 7d. paid to the Queen's farmer.

2065.)   26 *April* 1577.   Pardon of alienation: William Lovedaye and William Jackman in Easter term, 14 Eliz., by common recovery acquired from James Clarke and Matthew Stradlinge the manor of Tuxwell *alias* Radlett and lands in Spaxton, Netherstowey and Overstowey, co. Somerset, to the use of Clarke and Stradlinge, as appears by an indenture, 20 April, 14 Eliz., between Thomas Blake of the one part and Clarke and Stradlinge of the other. For £6 11s. 4d. paid to the Queen's farmer.

2066.)   1 *May* 1577.   Licence for Francis Roodes and Mary his wife to alienate the manor and rectory of West Burton and all appurtenances thereof in West Burton and Stourton, co. Nottingham, to Robert Williamsone. For £4 6s. 8d. paid to the Queen's farmer.

2067.)   23 *April* 1577.   Pardon of alienation: William Whittington by indenture, 23 Nov., 19 Eliz., acquired from Thomas Hanford and Kenard Delaber the capital house of the manor of Erdisland *alias* Earsland, co. Hereford, and the site and demesne lands of the said manor, now in   [*m.* 20]
the tenure of John Wever by an indenture of lease of Queen Mary for certain years still to run, (with reservations to Hanford and Delaber of entry to 'le Old Hall Howse' in Erdisland for the keeping of courts leet or baron there twice yearly and the issues of the said courts). For 40s. paid to the Queen's farmer.

2068.)   26 *March* 1577.   Licence for Edmund Hampden to alienate the manor of Lytleton and lands in Lytleton on Severne, co. Gloucester, and lands in Newe Woodstock, Old Woodstock, Bladon and Wotton, co. Oxford, to John Bonner and Thomas Duffyld to the use of Hampden and Isabel now his wife for life in survivorship, with successive remainders to John Croker and Elizabeth his wife and the heirs of Elizabeth's body by John, to the heirs of the body of Elizabeth and to the right heirs of Hampden. For £9 paid to the Queen's farmer.

2069.)   5 *June* 1577.   Pardon of alienation: Nicholas Lesse of London, draper, by indenture, 25 Nov., 17 Eliz., granted to Simon Burton, 'waxchaundeler', Richard Allen, mercer, and Mark Warner, draper, citizens of London, William Tucker of Bristol, draper, and George Snegge of the same, merchant, a house in the parish of St. Catherine Christchurche commonly called Creechurche within Algate, London, with a garden, a shop and all other appurtenances therof (abutting to the East on lands of the fishmongers of London, to the West on lands of the late prior of Halliwell, to the North on the highway and to the South on lands of the late abbot of Eyvesham), now in the tenure of Lesse, having been purchased by him from Francis Taverner of Writtle, co. Essex, son and heir of Nicholas Taverner late of Writtle, to hold unto the said grantees to the use of Lesse and

Agnes his wife for life in survivorship, with remainder to the heirs and assigns of the survivor. For 40*s.* paid to the Queen's farmer.

2070.)   26 *March* 1577.   Licence for Thomas Catesbie to alienate a messuage called 'Launde Halle' in Arthingworth *alias* Ardingworth and lands (*named*) in Ardingworth, parcel of the late monastery of St. [*m.* 21] James by Northampton, co. Northampton, to Edward Heselrige. For 33*s.* 4*d.* paid to the Queen's farmer.

2071.)   4 *Jan.* 1577.   Pardon of alienation: William Cloterboke, William Parsons, Edward Wilkins and Thomas Brewer in Michaelmas term, 15 Eliz., by fine in the Common Pleas acquired unto them and the heirs of William Cloterboke from Richard Cloterboke and Elizabeth his wife lands in Kingestanley, co. Gloucester, to the use of the said William Cloterboke. For £7 paid to the Queen's farmer.

2072.)   10 *May* 1577.   The like: Elizabeth Bassak, widow, late the wife of Robert Bassak, late citizen and grocer of London, by her will, 16 June 1576, bequeathed a messuage called 'the Shipp' in the parish of St. Gabriel Fanchurche, London, to John Mullet, who after her death entered the same. For 20*s.* 6*d.*

2073.)   1 *April* 1577.   Licence for John Lacy and Helen his wife to alienate lands in Waddingworthe, co. Lincoln, to Dorothy Jermyn, widow. For 31*s.* 2*d.* paid to the Queen's farmer.

2074.)   1 *April* 1577.   The like for Henry Norreis, knight, lord Norreis of Rycott, and Margery his wife to alienate lands and the tithes of corn and hay in Sowthynxsey in the parish of Comnor, co. Berks, to John Norries and Edward Norries and the heirs and assigns of John, and for them by the same fine to grant the premises back to Henry and Margery and [*m.* 22] the heirs and assigns of Margery. For £3 11*s.* 4*d.*

2075.)   26 *March* 1577.   The like for Francis, earl of Bedford, to alienate lands in Odelhill *alias* Grenehill, West Downe, Higher Burne, Seale, Buckeridge, Shute, Downe in Towne and Denberye and common of pasture in Odelhill and Holywell in Denberye, co. Devon, to William Peryam and John Glanfyld and the heirs and assigns of Peryam, and for them by the same fine to grant the premises back to the said earl. For 56*s.* 8*d.*

2076.)   26 *March* 1577.   The like for George Page, Isabel his wife, Thomas A Courte *alias* Gardener and Margaret his wife to alienate lands in Shorne and Harteley, co. Kent, to Michael Berisford and George Berisford and the heirs and assigns of Michael. For 17*s.* 10*d.*

2077.)   26 *March* 1577.   The like for John Ewe to alienate the manor of Great Somerford, co. Wilts, with all lands in Somerford Matrevers *alias* Brode Somerford, co. Wilts, late of the monastery of Kyngton, co. Wilts, together with all lands in Seivyngton *alias* Lyghe Dalamere, Malmesburye and Boytoon *alias* Boyton, co. Wilts, and in Stowre Payne, co. Dorset, to John Thynn, knight. For 31*s.* 11*d.* [*m.* 23]

2078.)   23 *April* 1577.   Pardon of alienation: James Fitzjames, knight, and William Cooke by indenture, 27 Oct., 13 Eliz., acquired unto them and the heirs of Cooke from Charles Zouche and Robert Keymis a moiety of the manors of Pitcombe *alias* Pidcombe and Coll and of all appurtenances of the said manors in Pitcombe and Coll and in the parish of Brewton, co. Somerset. For £3 paid to the Queen's farmer.

2079.)   29 *April* 1577.   The like: George Trigg and Edward Burton in Michaelmas term, 17 Eliz., by fine in the Common Pleas acquired unto them and the heirs of Trigg from William Burton and Alice his wife the manor of Braunston and lands in Braunston and Ockham, co. Rutland. For £4 6s. 8d.

2080.)   26 *March* 1577.   Licence for Henry Heydon to alienate the rectory of Feldallinge *alias* Fildallinge, co. Norfolk, to William Paston and Miles Corbett. For £4 2s. 3d. paid to the Queen's farmer.

2081.)   16 *March* 1577.   Licence for Walter Waller, knight, and Elizabeth Fane, widow, to alienate lands in Lydde *alias* Lyde, co. Kent, to Nicholas Bacon, knight, councillor, keeper of the great seal, and John Osborne, a servant of Bacon, and the heirs and assigns of Bacon.

2082.)   26 *March* 1577.   Licence for William Bruncker, Henry Bruncker, Richard Coker and Anne his wife to alienate the manor of Chadelworthe,   [*m.* 24] lands in Chadelworthe, Bright Walton, Leckhamsted, Est Shefford, West Shefford, Great Fallay, Little Falley and Boxworth and view of frankpledge in Chadelworth, co. Berks, to William Nelson, Michael Moseley and Thomas Nelson and the heirs and assigns of William Nelson. For £4 5s. 4d. paid to the Queen's farmer.

2083.)   26 *March* 1577.   The like for George Whyte and Catherine his wife to alienate lands in Hockley Magna and Hockley Parva, co. Essex, to Richard Boilland. For 48s. 11d.

2084.)   23 *April* 1577.   Pardon of alienation: Thomas Reynoldes by indenture, 4 Sept., 13 Eliz., acquired from John Pope the manor and rectory of Llantrissen, co. Monmouth, once of the monastery of Llanthony by Gloucester, 'le tythinge grange' and the tithes of corn and hay in Llantrissen, now or late in the tenure of Thomas ap Philippe, clerk, once of the said monastery, and all lands and the advowson of the vicarage there belonging to the said monastery. For £4 10s. paid to the Queen's farmer.

2085.)   1 *April* 1577.   Licence for John Broke to alienate lands in Madeley and Badger, co. Salop, to Francis Lawley, Thomas Hord and Humphrey Nycolles, 'yeoman', and the heirs and assigns of Lawley to the use of Broke and Anne his wife and the heirs of the body of Broke, with remainder to his right heirs. For £5 13s. 4d. paid to the Queen's farmer.

[*m.* 25]

2086.)   18 *March* 1577.   The like for Richard Beverley and Anne his wife to alienate lands in Haconby and Steanewheate, co. Lincoln, to Richard Thorolde and John Thorolde and the heirs and assigns of Richard Thorolde. For 17s. 4d.

2087.)   26 *March* 1577.   The like for Edward Rokewood and Elizabeth his wife to alienate the manor of Stantons and lands in Knettishall, Conneston *alias* Cunston, Hopton, Garsthorpe, Reddlesworth and Rowsworth *alias* Rowshforde, co. Suffolk, to Thomas Lovell. For 53s. 4d.

2088.)   15 *May* 1577.   Pardon of alienation: Clement Newce in Michaelmas term, 18 Eliz., by fine in the Common Pleas acquired from John Mounson and Margaret Thoralde, widow, a twentieth part of the manors of Byggyns and Barwickes and of lands in Hadham Magna and Standon, co. Hertford. For 3s. 4d. paid to the Queen's farmer.

2089.)   26 *March* 1577.   Licence for Christopher Jackson to alienate the site of the late farm called 'le Grey Fryers' *alias* 'le Freers Minors' and lands in Castelgait in the city of York to William Hewytsone. For 9s. paid to the Queen's farmer.

2090.)   26 *March* 1577.   The like for Edward Clyfton and Alice his wife to alienate a messuage and two gardens in the parish of St.   [*m*. 26]
Dunstan in the West, co. Middlesex, to John Dalton and Richard Holland and the heirs of Dalton. For 4s. 6d.

2091.)   26 *March* 1577.   The like for Robert Crane to alienate the manor of Cretinge St. Olave *alias* Wolnehall *alias* Woonhall and the farm or manor of Myneottes *alias* Mynettes and lands in Cretinge St. Olave, Cretinge St. Mary, Cretinge All Saints, Myckfeild, Brettenham, Bayleham, Stoneham Aspall, Cuddenham and Crowfeild, co. Suffolk, to William Waldgrave, knight, William Clopton of the parish of St. Botolph without Aldersgate, London, and William Beale to the use of Henry Crane and Anne his wife and the heirs and assigns of Henry. For £12.

2092.)   1 *May* 1577.   Pardon of alienation: William Olney by indenture, 12 Dec., 14 Eliz., acquired from William Morecott a close of pasture called 'le Hethe Cotte' in Warwick, co. Warwick, now or late in the tenure of Henry Morecotte. For £5 6s. 8d. paid to the Queen's farmer.

2093.)   3 *Jan.* 1577.   The like: Anthony Kempe in Trinity term, 17 Eliz., by fine in the Common Pleas acquired from William Waller and John Waller the manor of Shalfleete, lands in Shalflete in the Isle of Wight and the advowson of Shalflete church, co. Southampton. For £10.

2094.)   11 *May* 1577.   The like: Henry Palmer in Trinity term, 18 Eliz., by fine in the Common Pleas acquired from William Awcher, Alice his wife, William Rickthorne, Anne his wife and Gregory Bradshawe the   [*m*. 27]
manor of Kingeston, lands in Kingston and the advowson of Kingston church, co. Kent. For £4.

2095.)   1 *May* 1577.   The like: John Adys in Michaelmas term, 16 Eliz., by fine in the Common Pleas acquired from Richard Pecocke and Anne his wife a fifth part of a third part of lands in Lushecott, Longvile *alias* Longveld and Eton, co. Salop. For 4s.

2096.)   1 *May* 1577.   The like: John Adys by indenture, 11 Nov., 15 Eliz., acquired from Richard Thomas a fifth part of lands in Lushecott and Longvile in the parish of Eaton, co. Salop. For 4s.

2097.)   26 *March* 1577.   Licence for Robert Longe to alienate lands in Hartwith in the parish of Kyrkeby Malsert, co. York, to Richard Ellesworth and Robert Ellesworth and the heirs and assigns of Richard. For 16s. 4d. paid to the Queen's farmer.

2098.)   1 *April* 1577.   The like for Stephen Hadnall and Margaret his wife to alienate lands in Cleoberye Barnes and Cleoberye Mortymer, co. Salop, to Thomas Thorneton. for 36s. 6d.   [*m*. 28]

2099.)   26 *March* 1577.   The like for Nicholas Cudworth and Frances his wife to alienate lands in Dodworth, co. York, to John Hobson, Anne his wife, Richard Hobson and Robert Hobson and the heirs and assigns of John. For 5s. 8d.

2100.)   26 *March* 1577.   The like for Anthony Bourne and Elizabeth his wife to alienate the manor of Willarsey *alias* Willersey, lands, view of frankpledge and free warren in Willarsey and the advowson of Willarsey church, co. Gloucester, to Richard Hobby and Elizabeth his wife and the heirs and assigns of Richard. For £3 16s. 8d.

2101.)   26 *March* 1577.   The like for Robert Tempest to alienate lands (*tenant named*) and the tithes of corn in Tonge, co. York, late of the monastery of St. Oswald of Nostell, co. York, to Robert Popeley. For £3 11s. 4d.

2102.)   1 *April* 1577.   The like for William Fryer to alienate the manor of Garnons in Bunsted ad Turrim *alias* Steple Bumsted, co. Essex, to   [*m.* 29]
Thomas Croftes, John Southwell and Charles Croftes and the heirs and assigns of Charles. For 53s. 4d.

2103.)   26 *March* 1577.   The like for Richard Rolles to alienate the rectory of Waddesworth, lands and all tithes, oblations and obventions in Waddisworth and the advowson of the vicarage of Waddesworth, co. York, to John Cockson. For £6 13s. 4d.

2104.)   26 *March* 1577.   The like for John Brigge to alienate tithes called 'Gilderston tythe' in the parish of Batley, co. York, to Thomas Norclyff. For 46s. 8d.

2105.)   26 *March* 1577.   The like for Edmund Colthruste to alienate woods in Charterhouse Henton and Henton, co. Somerset, to Walter Hungerford, knight. For 13s. 4d.

2106.)   26 *March* 1577.   The like for William Sparowe to alienate lands (*named*) in Ovesden, co. Suffolk, to Richard Sparowe. For 13s. 4d.   [*m.* 30]

2107.)   26 *March* 1577.   The like for Robert Springe to alienate a messuage late called the priory and house of the rectory of Preston, late of Preston Priory, co. Suffolk, to Robert Jermyn. For 40s.

2108.)   26 *March* 1577.   The like for Thomas Heyward and Thomas Armiger to alienate the manor of Fildallinge *alias* Feldallinge and lands in Fildallinge, Bathley, Saxlingham, Sharington and Langham, co. Norfolk, to William Paston and Miles Corbett. For £4 9s.

2109.)   26 *March* 1577.   The like for John Wythe to alienate a moiety of St. Peter's farm and the rectory of St. Peter's church in Witton near Wyche, co. Worcester, to Richard Bartelett. For 8s. 11d.

2110.)   19 *April* 1577.   The like for Edward Cary and William Dodington to alienate lands (*named*) in Burton Hill and Radburne, co. Wilts, now in the tenure of Thomas Coppley the elder, to Thomas Coppley the   [*m.* 31]
younger. For 16s. ½d.

2111.)   26 *March* 1577.   The like for William Barwell to alienate lands called 'le Greyfryers' in Grymsby, co. Lincoln, to Richard Thymbleby. For 13s. 4d.

2112.)   26 *March* 1577.   The like for Gerard Croker, knight, to alienate the manor of Watereaton and lands in Watereaton, co. Oxford, to Walter Curson and Edward Palmer to the use of the said Gerard and his heirs until Michaelmas 1580, and thereafter to the use successively of John Croker, Gerard's son and heir apparent, and Elizabeth his wife and the heirs male of John's body by her, of John in tail male and of Gerard and his heirs. For £8 13s. 4d.

2113.)   26 *March* 1577.   The like for George Penruddock, knight, and Anne his wife to alienate lands in Compton Chamberlayne, co. Wilts, to George Elrington and Thomas Latheburie and the heirs and assigns of Elrington, and for them by the same fine to convey them back to Penruddock. For 36s. 8d.

2114.)   26 *March* 1577.   The like for William Keyme and Elizabeth his   [*m.* 32]
wife to alienate lands in the suburbs of Coventre to George Kenett. For 33s. 4d.

2115.)   13 *May* 1577.   Pardon of alienation: John Smythe, John Knolles, Christopher Garbray and Brian Headon in Trinity term, 18 Eliz., acquired unto them and the heirs and assigns of Smythe by fine in the Common Pleas from John Wighell, Elizabeth his wife and William Goodwen the manor of Muswell *alias* Muswell Chappell and lands in Muswell *alias* Muswell Chappell, co. Middlesex. For £5 10s. paid to the Queen's farmer.

2116.)   2 *May* 1577. The like: Thomas Cecyll, knight, by indenture, 23 April, 18 Eliz., acquired from Christopher Hatton, a gentleman of the privy chamber and captain of the guard, the mansion house of the manor of Wymbledon in Wymbledon, co. Surrey, and all lands occupied therewith, now or late in the tenure of John Chylde, and the reversion and rent of the premises, late of Thomas Cromwell, knight, earl of Essex, and afterwards assigned to cardinal Poole for life. For £4 10s.

2117.)   1 *May* 1577.   Licence for Rowland Hayward, knight, and Joan his wife to alienate the manor of Cause *alias* Caurs *alias* Cause   [*m.* 33]
Castell, lands in Cause *alias* Cause Castell, Bromhill, Walloppe, Lowe, Hoggeston, Mynsterley, Adderstone and Wentnore and the rectory of Wentnore, co. Salop, to Robert Creswell and John Lacy and the heirs and assigns of Creswell. For £8 7s. 8d. paid to the Queen's farmer.

2118.)   26 *March* 1577.   The like for Anthony Wekes *alias* Mason and Elizabeth his wife to alienate lands in Wynchfyld and common of pasture in Wynchefeyld and Odyham, co. Southampton, to Richard Davyes and Henry Permyter and the heirs and assigns of Davyes. For 49s.

2119.)   1 *May* 1577.   Pardon of alienation: Joan Nutte late had by feoffment, 16 Nov., 17 Eliz., of Thomas Nutte, 'yoman', lands in Stokelacye, co. Hereford. For 10s. 6d. paid to the Queen's farmer.

2120.)   3 *Jan.* 1577.   The like: John Cooke in Michaelmas term, 18 Eliz., by fine in the Common Pleas acquired from William Stumpe and Mary his wife the chapel of Chesburie, lands in Chesburye and the tithes of lands in Little Bedwyn and Chesburye, co. Wilts. For 53s. 4d.

2121.)   20 *June* 1577.   The like: Thomas Dolman of Newberye, co. Berks, 'clothier', being seised of the manor of Staunton and the advowson of the church of Staunton and free chapel of Snowshill,   [*m.* 34]
co. Gloucester, by his will, 8 Jan., 14 Eliz., bequeathed to his son, Matthias Dolman, the same, by the name of the manor of Staunton and all his other lands in Staunton, and after Thomas's death Matthias entered upon two parts of the premises. For £6 2s. 6d.

2122.)   26 *March* 1577.   Licence for Lewis Grevyll and Thomasine his wife to alienate lands in Welneford *alias* Welford, co. Gloucester, to Walter Robertes. For 8*s*. 1*d*. paid to the Queen's farmer.

2123.)   26 *March* 1577.   The like for Francis, earl of Bedford, to alienate lands in Denbury and common of pasture in Odehill, co. Devon, to Robert Cole and John Cole and the heirs and assigns of Robert. For 4*s*. 5*d*.

2124.)   26 *March* 1577.   The like for Francis, earl of Bedford, to alienate lands in Denbury and common of pasture in Odehill, co. Devon, to John Stephyn. For 15*s*.

2125.)   22 *June* 1577.   Pardon of alienation: Robert Carr and Anthony Thorold in Hilary term, 18 Eliz., by fine in the Common Pleas acquired unto them and the heirs of Thorold from Christopher Kelke, Elizabeth his wife, late the wife of William Faireffax, and Elizabeth Fairefax, daughter and heir of the bodies of William and Elizabeth, the   [*m*. 35] rectory of Metheringham, lands in Metheringham and Blankney and the advowson of Metheringham church, co. Lincoln. For £7 paid to the Queen's farmer.

2126.)   1 *May* 1577.   The like: Henry Blanchard and Matthew Haylocke in Trinity term, 17 Eliz., by fine in the Common Pleas acquired unto them and the heirs of Blanchard from William Forster and John Forster the manor of Shawe and lands in Shawe, Chevely and Hampstead Norrys, co. Berks. For 110*s*.

2127.)   1 *April* 1577.   Licence for Bartholomew Lane to alienate lands in Langley, Mynseden and Hitchin, co. Hertford, to John Brockett. For 20*s*. paid to the Queen's farmer.

2128.)   12 *Feb*. 1577.   Pardon of alienation: Walter Denys in Hilary term, 18 Eliz., by fine in the Common Pleas acquired from Giles Cotherington and Isabel his wife the manor of Pucklechurch, 3*s*. 4*d*. rent and view of frankpledge in Pucklechurch and the hundred of Pucklechurche, co. Gloucester. For £10 paid to the Queen's farmer.

2129.)   26 *March* 1577.   Licence for Francis, earl of Bedford, to alienate lands in Denbury and common of pasture in Odehill, co. Devon, to James Lache and Thomas Lache and the heirs and assigns of James. For 15*s*. 6*d*. paid to the Queen's farmer.

2130.)   8 *Feb*. 1577.   Pardon of alienation: John Slape in Easter term, 15 Eliz., by fine in the Common Pleas acquired from George Hill and Elizabeth his wife lands in Broomefeilde, co. Somerset. For 17*s*. paid to the Queen's farmer.   [*m*. 36]

2131.)   4 *Feb*. 1577.   The like: Richard Lowther, Edward Lewkenor, Gerrard Lowther, Thomas Wroth, Thomas Rogers and John Alsoppe in Trinity term, 16 Eliz., by fine in the Common Pleas acquired unto them and the heirs of Richard from Henry Goodere and Frances his wife the manor of Pollesworth and lands in Pollesworth, Warton, Pooley, Dordon, Hallende, Freseley and Baddesley, co. Warwick, to hold to the use of Goodere. For £13 6*s*. 8*d*.

2132.)   26 *March* 1577.   Licence for John Bragg, son and heir of Robert Bragg, to alienate lands (*named*) in Bulmer, co. Essex, to Thomas Eden. For 33*s*. 4*d*. paid to the Queen's farmer.

2133.)   26 *March* 1577.   The like for Lewis Grevyll and Thomasine his wife to alienate lands in Wellneford *alias* Welford, co. Gloucester, to Gregory Cannynge. For 8s. 6d.

2134.)   26 *March* 1577.   The like for Lewis Grevill and Thomasine his wife to alienate lands in Wellneford *alias* Welford, co. Gloucester,   [*m.* 37] to William Robertes. For 5s. 11d.

2135.)   26 *March* 1577. The like for Mary Guldeford, widow, late the wife of John Guldeford, knight, to alienate the manor of Townland *alias* Towland in Woodchurche, co. Kent, now or late in the tenure of Robert Colebrand, to John Shelley. For 53s. 4d.

2136.)   26 *March* 1577.   The like for Lewis Grevyll and Thomasine his wife to alienate lands in Welneford *alias* Welford, co. Gloucester, to Thomas Welles. For 4s. 4¾d.

2137.)   26 *March* 1577.   The like for Lewis Grevill and Thomasine his wife to alienate lands in Welneford *alias* Welford, co. Gloucester, to John Welles the elder. For 5s. 4d.

2138.)   12 *Feb.* 1577.   Pardon of alienation: by fine in the Common Pleas in the quinzaine of Easter, 17 Eliz., Richard Guldeford and Benedicta his wife for them and the heirs of Benedicta conveyed the manor of Kenarton *alias* Kenardington, lands in Kenarton, Woodchurch, Appledore   [*m.* 38] and Warehorne and the advowson of Kenarton church, co. Kent, to Stephen Cowper and Thomas Davys and the heirs of Cowper, and Cowper and Davys by the same fine conveyed them back to Richard and Benedicta for life in survivorship, with successive remainders to the heirs male of Richard by Benedicta and to his right heirs. For £6 13s. 4d. paid to the Queen's farmer.

2139.)   12 *Feb.* 1577.   The like: by fine in the Common Pleas in the quinzaine of Easter, 14 Eliz., Richard Walwyn, knight, conveyed to Thomas Walwyn, his son, in tail, with successive remainders to Jane Walwyn, Richard's daughter, in tail, to the heirs of the body of Dorothy Hyett, deceased, another daughter of Richard, to Elizabeth ap Harry, another daughter of Richard, in tail, to the heirs male of the body of Thomas Walwyn the elder of Luggartine, deceased, and to the Crown, the manors of Great Marcle *alias* Moche Markell Awdeleys, Helens and Calohill, lands in Moche Marcle Awdeleys, Helens, Calohill, Hasill, Ledbury Deren, Ledbury Foren, Asportan, Bilmile and Weston under Penyarde and a moiety of the manor of Hasill, co. Hereford, (which manor of Moche Markell Awdeleys and the rest of the lands belonging thereto, parcel of the premises, are held of the Crown in chief). For £5.

2140.)   19 *April* 1577.   Licence for Henry Knolles and Edward   [*m.* 39] Williams to alienate the manor of Breedon, co. Worcester, once of the bishopric of Worcester, and the advowson of Breedon church, which were granted to them by patent, 5 April, 19 Eliz., to Thomas Coppley and George Hornyolde. For £20 1s. 8¼d., paid to the Queen's farmer.

2141.)   11 *June* 1577.   Pardon of alienation: John Dancastell *alias* Dancaster, Griffith Barton, James Braybrooke and William Palmer by indenture, 23 Aug., 17 Eliz., acquired from Henry Blanchard and Matthew Haylocke, 'yeoman', the capital messuage, farm and site of the manor called 'le Graynge' in Shawe, Cheveley and Curradge or elsewhere, co. Berks, and lands (*named with tenants' names*) belonging thereto, except certain lands (*specified*) in Curradge. For £5 10s. paid to the Queen's farmer.

2142.)   18 *June* 1577.   Licence for Nicholas Bacon, knight, keeper of the great seal, and William Cecill, knight, lord Burghley, treasurer, councillors, Henry, earl of Huntingdon, Walter Myldmay, knight, chancellor of the Exchequer, councillor, Ralph Sadler, knight, chancellor of the duchy of Lancaster, councillor, Alexander Nowell, dean of St. Paul's cathedral, London, Thomas Bromley, solicitor general, William Fletewood, recorder of London, Adrian Stokes, Henry Knolles the elder, John Harryngton, Edward Elrington, John Hastinges, George Carleton, Robert Creswell, Richard Hurleston and Thomas Norton to alienate the manor of Old   [*m*. 40]
Byland, co. York, to Edward Wotton and Hester his wife and his heirs by Hester, with successive remainders to the heirs of the body of Hester and to the right heirs of Edward Wotton. For £4 paid to the Queen's farmer.

2143.)   18 *June* 1577.   The like for the same to alienate the manor of Byland, co. York, and all lands late of William Pykeringe, knight, deceased, in Southborne, co. York, and in the city of London to Hester now wife of Edward Wotton in tail. For £10.

2144.)   1 *May* 1577.   The like for Christopher Nelson and Mary his wife to alienate the manor or capital messuage, site or cell of Skewkirke *alias* Skokirke in the county of the city of York, late of the monastery of St. Oswald of Nostell, co. York, the church, belfrey and churchyard of the late cell or priory of Skewkirke in the county of the said city and in the county of York, lands (*named*) at Tockwith and in the parish of Bilton in the county of the said city and in Kirkhamerton, co. York, late of the said priory or cell, and the tithes of a mill (*named*) in Tockwith in the county of the said city and in the county of York, late of the said priory or cell, to Thomas Harryson. For £3 6s. 8d.   [*m*. 41]

2145.)   1 *May* 1577.   The like for Denise Mannocke, widow, to alienate the manor of Wormyngford and all appurtenances thereof in Wormyngford and Fordham or elsewhere, co. Essex, the rectory of Wormyngford, the advowson of the vicarage of Wormyngford and woods (*named*) there to Francis Mannock and Thomas Walgrave to the use of Denise for life, with successive remainders to Edmund Mannocke, Anthony Mannocke, Thomas Mannock and Edward Mannock, her sons, in tail and to the right heirs of her said sons. For £7.

2146.)   1 *May* 1577.   The like for Ralph Sadler, knight, chancellor of the duchy of Lancaster, Walter Myldmay, knight, chancellor of the Exchequer, William Cordell, knight, master of the rolls, James Dyer, knight, chief justice of the Common Pleas, and Roger Manwood, a justice of the Common Pleas, to alienate the manor and rectory of Sellinge, all appurtenances thereof in Sellinge, Boughton under le Bleane and Faversham or elsewhere, co. Kent, and the tithes of corn in the borough of Rode in Boughton aforesaid to Michael Sondes and Richard Sondes. For £12.

2147.)   11 *June* 1577.   Pardon of alienation: John Temple by indenture, 15 Nov., 13 Eliz., acquired from Thomas Gyfford *inter alia* lands in Lamporte, co. Buckingham, which he purchased of Thomas Abbett, and in Buckingham, co. Buckingham. For 45s. paid to the Queen's farmer.

2148.)   28 *Nov.* 1576.   Manumission of William Wanklen of Saint   [*m*. 42]
Katheryns next London, co. Middlesex, 'hatmaker', a villein regardant to the manor of Leompster, co. Hereford, and Richard Wanklen, his son, and Susan Wanklen and Judith Wanklen, his daughters, and all his other issue. At the suit of Henry Lee *alias* Leae, knight, the Queen's servant, according to a warrant made to him by patent, 17 Jan., 17 Eliz.

The like of the following, viz,—

2149.)   7 *June* 1577. Joan Warren of Wreasbury, co. Buckingham, villein regardant to the manor of Langley Marreys, co. Buckingham.

2150.)   19 *June* 1577.   Robert Bolytowt of Molton, co. Norfolk, villein regardant to the manor of Forncett, co. Norfolk, and Thomas Bolytowte and William Bolytowte, his sons, and Margaret Bolytowte and Elizabeth Bolytowte, his daughters.

2151.)   12 *Feb.* 1577. Nicholas Weringe of Trevy in the parish of Lanteglos, co. Cornwall, villein regardant to the manor of Helston in Trigg, co. Cornwall, and Michael Weringe and Hugh Weringe, his sons.

2152.)   7 *Feb.* 1577.   Thomas Powlle of Leompster, co. Hereford, villein regardant to the manor of Leompster, and Richard Powlle, John Powlle and Thomas Powlle, his sons, and Anne Powlle, Christian Powlle, Dorothy Powlle, wife of Thomas Robyns, and Maud Powlle, wife of Richard Childe, his daughters.

2153.)   7 *Feb.* 1577.   Walter Wanklen of Warton in the parish of Leompster, co. Hereford, villein regardant to the manor of Leompster, and Joan Wanklen and Alice Wanklen, his daughters.

2154.)   7 *Feb.* 1577.   Henry Powll of Stagbach, co. Hereford, villein regardant to the manor of Leompster, co. Hereford, and William Powll and John Powll, his sons, and Maud Powll, wife of William Browne of Ivington, his daughter.

2155.)   19 *Nov.* 1576.   John Charke of Rillaton in the parish of Lenkynhorne, co. Cornwall, villein regardant to the manor of Rillaton.

2156.)   19 *Nov.* 1576.   John Blache of Hendra in the parish of Lanteglos, co. Cornwall, villein regardant to the manor of Helston in Trigg, co. Cornwall.

2157.)   19 *Nov.* 1576.   William Bache of Stockton in the parish of Kymbalton, co. Hereford, villein regardant to the manor of Leompster, co. Hereford, and William Bache and Thomas Bache, his sons, and Agnes Bache, his daughter.

2158.)   19 *Nov.* 1576.   John Powle of Le Hide, co. Hereford, villein regardant to the manor of Leompster, co. Hereford, and John Powlle, his son.

2159.)   20 *Nov.* 1576.   Thomas Powle of Le Hyde in the parish of Leompster, co. Hereford, villein regardant to the manor of Leompster and William Powle, his son.

2160.)   20 *Nov.* 1576.   John Prowte of Calistocke, co. Cornwall, 'batchelor', villein regardant to the manor of Calistocke.

2161.)   20 *Nov.* 1576.   John Prowte of Calistocke, co. Cornwall, 'batcheler', son of Walter Prowte, deceased, villein regardant to the manor of Calistocke.

2162.)   28 *Nov.* 1576.   Richard Wanklen of London, 'brewer', villein regardant to the manor of Leompster, co. Hereford.

2163.)   19 *Nov.* 1576.   Roger Prowte of Codda in the parish of Alternone,   [*m.* 43] co. Cornwall, villein regardant to the manor of Calistocke, co. Cornwall, and William Prowte, John Prowte and Thomas Prowte, his sons.

2164.)   19 *Nov.* 1576.   Robert Werynge of Trevy in the parish of Lanteglos, co. Cornwall, villein regardant to the manor of Helston in Trigg, co. Cornwall, and John Weryng and Michael Wering, his sons.

2165.)   19 *Nov.* 1576.   Henry Hicke of Fenterwanson in the parish of Lanteglos, co. Cornwall, villein regardant to the manor of Helston in Trigg, co. Cornwall, and William Hicke, John Hycke, Stephen Hycke, Nicholas Hycke and Henry Hycke, his sons.

2166.)   9 *May* 1577.   John Wanklen of Kymbalton, co. Hereford, villein regardant to the manor of Leompster, co. Hereford, and John Wanklen, Thomas Wanklen the elder, William Wanklen, Edmund Wanklen and Thomas Wanklen the younger, his sons, and Anne Wanklen, wife of John Carpenter, Joan Wanklen and Jane Wanklen, his daughters.

2167.)   17 *May* 1577.   Pardon for William Grene late of Thorneton in Pickeringlithe in the North Riding, co. York, detained in York castle for the death of William Boyes. It is reported by the record of John Mounson, a justice of the Common Pleas, and Thomas Meade, serjeant at law, justices of gaol delivery of the said castle, remaining in the Chancery files, that he killed Boyes in self defence.

2168.) 8 *May* 1577.   Pardon of outlawry for Roger Bonnet *alias* Bonnett late of Wenhaston *alias* Wenneston, co. Suffolk, 'tanner', who was put in exigent in the city of Norwich for non-appearance in the Common Pleas to satisfy Thomas Annott of Leystoft, co. Suffolk, merchant, touching a debt of £40, and 20s. damages, recovered in the said court and has now surrendered himself to the Flete prison.

2169.) 14 *May* 1577.   The like for Lewis Evans, clerk, late of Westmeane, co. Southampton, *alias* rector of Westemeane, who was put in exigent in the husting of London for non-appearance in the Common Pleas to satisfy Edward Compton, citizen and 'clothworker' of London, touching a debt of £20, and 28s. damages, recovered in the said court and has now surrendered himself to the Flete prison.

2170.) 13 *June* 1577.   The like for Thomas Spragges late of Brockton, co. Salop, 'yoman' *alias* 'husbondman' *alias* 'sonne to the said John', who was put in exigent in the county of Worcester for non-appearance in the Common Pleas to answer Thomas Taylor, son and sole executor of Edward Taylor the elder late of Harley 'in the countye aforesaid', 'yoman', in pleas of debt of (1) £25 6s. 8d. and (2) £40 and has now surrendered himself to the Flete prison.

2171.) 18 *July* 1577.   The like for Richard Noble late of York, 'chapman', who was put in exigent in the husting of London for non-appearance in the Common Pleas to answer Anthony Gamage and Wolstan Dyxe *alias* Dixey, aldermen of London, administrators and surveyors   [*m.* 44] named in the will of Robert Cage, citizen and 'saulter' of London, during the minority of Robert Cage, John Cage and Samuel Cage, executors of the said Robert, in a plea for payment of £16 4s. 2d. and has now surrendered himself to the Flete prison.

2172.) 21 *June* 1577.   The like for (1) Edmund Dighton late of London *alias* late of Stunston, co. Lincoln, who was put in exigent in the husting of London for non-appearance in the Common Pleas to satisfy Thomas Blackewey and John Woodward, citizens and 'clotheworkers' of London, touching a debt of £30, and 60s. damages, recovered in the said court; (2) Thomas Dighton late of London *alias* late of Stonston, co. Lincoln, who was put in exigent in the husting of London for non-appearance in the Common Pleas to satisfy Blackewey and Woodward touching a debt of £30, and 60s. damages, recovered in the said court; (3) the said Edmund, late of Sturton, co. Lincoln, who was put in exigent in the husting of London for non-appearance in the Common Pleas to satisfy John Harryson of London, 'goldsmyth', touching a debt of £9 8s. 4d., and 23s. 4d. damages, recovered in the said court; and (4) the said Edmund, late of Sturton, who was put in exigent in the county of the city of Lincoln for non-appearance in the Common Pleas to satisfy Robert Rochefourthe and Helen his wife, executrix of Edward Halleley of Lincoln, touching a debt of £14, and 44s. damages, recovered in the said court; they have now surrendered themselves to the Flete prison, and the said Blackway, Woodward, Harryson, Robert and Helen have severally acknowledged satisfaction.

2173.) 22 *June* 1577.   Pardon for Frederick Smyth late of Cardif, co. Glamorgan, 'maryner'. It was found by an inquisition taken at Bristoll before John Faye and John Feilde, coroners of the same city, on 1 Jan., 19 Eliz., on the body of Albert van Lynnenbergh late of Cardif, 'maryner', at Hungerode within the jurisdiction of the said city that Smyth killed him by misadventure on 24 Dec., 19 Eliz., in a ship called '*Le Mary* of Danske' lying in Hungerode (*details given*); which inquisition was certified into the Queen's Bench, and Smyth was committed to the Marshalsea prison to await the Queen's grace.

2174.)   *Undated.*   Pardon for William Thomas Agllewelin of Llanmellyn, co. Monmouth, 'yeoman'. It was found by an inquisition taken at Cayrwent, co. Monmouth, before William Coxe, a coroner of the county, on   [*m.* 45] 23 May last on the body of Henry David late of Cayrwent that the said William Thomas Agllewelin, while practising archery in the company of Rowland Kemys, clerk, and George James, at Crycke in Cayrwent by misadventure shot David on 12 May last so that he died on 21 May at Llanmellyn, co. Monmouth (*details given*).

2175.)   28 *June* 1577.   Pardon for Thomas Bullock late of Hawkeherst, co. Kent, 'taylor'. It was found by an inquisition taken before Thomas Mascall, coroner of Henry Carye, K.G., lord of Hunsdon, in the liberty of his royal manor of Wye, at Hawkeherst on 19 Feb., 19 Eliz., on the body of Andrew Mercer of Hawkeherst, 'taylor', that, after a quarrel in the house of John Freland there, Bullock killed Mercer in self defence at Hawkeherst near the house of Thomas Petter on 17 Nov. (*details given*).

2176.)   20 *April* 1577.   Pardon for Thomas Parker, citizen and 'haberdassher' of London, and William Parker, citizen and draper of London, for all offences committed before the present date in respect of the export of gold, silver and treasure.

   By the keeper of the great seal by virtue of a patent granted to Ralph Lane.

      (*The dorse of this roll is blank.*)

PART V

C. 66/1155

2177.)   21 *Nov.* 1576.   Grant in fee simple to Stephen Hadnoll of the   [*m.* 1]
undermentioned rents reserved under grants of lands etc., co. Salop, all late of the
monastery of Wenlocke, by patents dated as follows—

(1) 8 July, 32 Hen. VIII, to Thomas Lockier and William Bromeley of (*a*) lands in
Caldebroke in the lordship and parish of Madeley, (*b*) the site and capital messuage of the
manor of Marshe in Much Wenlocke and the tithes thereof, (*c*) the site and capital messuage
of the manor of Caughley in Much Wenlocke and the tithes thereof, (*d*) lands in Much
Wenlocke and (*e*) lands in Burwardesley, to hold by service of the twentieth part of a
knight's fee and by a yearly rent of 25*s.* 7*d.* [*Letters and Papers, Henry VIII*, vol. XV, no. 942
(35)].

(2) 29 July, 36 Hen. VIII, to William Whorwood *inter alia* of lands and tithes of corn in
Walton and Atterley in the parish of Wenlocke Magna and lands etc. in Barrowe in the
parishes of Wenlocke Magna and Marshe, to hold by   [*m.* 2]
service of the thirtieth part of a knight's fee and by a yearly rent of 26*s.* 6*d.* [*ibid.*, vol. XIX,
part I, no. 1035(157)].

(3) 14 July, 35 Hen. VIII, to James Leveson *inter alia* of the manor, farm and tenement of
Sutton in the parish of Sutton and lands in Sutton and Colnham, to hold by service of the
twentieth part of a knight's fee and by a yearly rent of 19*s.* 4*d.* [*ibid.*, vol. XVIII, part I, no.
981 (53)].

(4) 5 May, 37 Hen. VIII, to George Tressham and Edmund Twynyho *inter alia* of lands
in Wigwyke and Harley, to hold in socage and by a yearly rent of 6*s.* [*ibid.*, vol. XX, part I,
no. 846(11)].   [*m.* 3]

To hold of the manor of Estgrenewiche, co. Kent, in socage. Release of arrears from 12
July, 4 & 6 Ph. & Mary.   By p.s.

2178.)   14 *Dec.* 1576.   Lease for 31 years to John Cely, a yeoman of the scullery, of the
reversions and rents of the lands etc. comprised in a lease and grants as follows—

(1) Lease by patent, 4 Dec., 4 & 5 Ph. & Mary, to John Stewarde of marshes (*named*) and
a windmill [in the lordship of Fobbing, co. Essex,] for 25 years from Michaelmas then next
at a yearly rent of £14.

(2) Grant by patent, 4 Nov., 5 & 6 Ph. & Mary, to George Tirrell and Joan his wife of
the reversion and rent of the premises leased to Stewarde, and the manor of Fobbinge, co.
Essex, late of Edward,   [*m.* 4]
duke of Buckingham, attainted of treason, for life in survivorship, to hold in socage as of the
manor of Estgrenewiche, co. Kent, and by a yearly rent, after the death of George, of £28.

(3) Grant by patent, 16 July, 7 Eliz., to Robert Tirell, son and   [*m.* 5]
heir of the said George, of the reversion and rent of the premises leased to Stewarde, and the
said manor, lands (*named*) in Stanford in le Hoope, co. Essex, and the premises leased to
Stewarde, for life at a yearly rent, after the death of George and Joan, of £28.

Also the lands and manor aforesaid and all appurtenances thereof, including 'lez havens
and crekes' called Hole Haven and Shell Haven, in Fobbinge or elsewhere, co. Essex. Yearly
value £52 12*s.* 2¼*d.* Timber reserved. From the deaths of George, Joan and Robert. Yearly
rent £28.   [*m.* 6]

For his service.   By p.s.

2179.)   14 *Dec.* 1576.   Lease for 21 years to Thomas Hanbury of (1) the rectory of
Lanteglos *alias* Lanteglas, co. Cornwall, late of the priory   [*m.* 7]
or hospital of St. John in Bridgwater, co. Somerset, (2) the rectory of Wydcombe, co.
Somerset, once of the monastery of Bath, and (3) lands in Paridice and Northlode in the
lordship of Glaston, co. Somerset, once of the office of warden of the anniversary of Walter
Monyton in the monastery of Glaston and late of Edward, late duke of Somerset; with
reservations; from Lady Day next; yearly rents (1) £20, (2) £8 and (3) £4 12*s.* 8*d.* In
consideration of the surrender (*a*) by Hanburye of a patent, 5 April, 10 Eliz., leasing (1) to
John Mylner for 21 years from Michaelmas then last at the same rent and a patent, 30 March,
12 Eliz., leasing (2) to John Mylner for 21 years from Michaelmas then last at the same rent
and (*b*) by William Doddington of a patent, 18 April, 12 Eliz., leasing (3) to the said Mylner
inter alia for 21 years from Michaelmas then last at the same rent; and for a fine of £46 13*s.* 4*d.*
paid at the Exchequer by Hanbury.   By p.s.

2180.)   28 *Nov.* 1576.   Grant in fee simple to Edward Grymeston the elder and Edward
Grymeston the younger, his son and heir, of concealed lands etc. (*tenants named*) as
follows—lands in Lambeth Marshe, co. Surrey, late of the guild of the Assumption of St.
Mary the Virgin in the church of St. Margaret, Westminster, co. Middlesex; a free chapel
called 'chappell de Bulleye' and lands thereof in Bulley in the parish of Churcham, co.
Gloucester; lands   [*m.* 8]
in Burye St. Edmunds (*described*), late of the abbey there, in Washebroke (*named*), given for
'the Trynytye guylde of Hadley', co. Suffolk, in the parish of St. Helen in Ipswich (*described*),
given by Gilbert de Tudenham, knight, to the rector or curate of St. Helen's church for an
obit and mass on St. Helen's Day and a light in the said church, in the parish of St. Clement
in Ipswich (including 'Seynt James chappell'), given to the rector or curate of St. Helen's
church aforesaid by Oliver Spycer of Tudenham, co. Suffolk, for mass on St. James's Day in
the said chapel and certain other services for souls, in Westerfeild (*described*), given (1) by
Lawrence Code for a lamp and lights in Westerfeild church, (2) by [—] Ussherwood for an
obit in the said church on St. Blaise's Day and (3) by Robert Paishmore for a light in the said
church on St. Dunstan's Day, in the parish of St. Margaret, Ipswich, and Westerfeild
(*described*), in Akenham ('Lampe Lande', *described*), in Cockefield (*described*, including 'the
Towne Howse'), given by Thomas Kempe, clerk, rector there, for masses, dirges and
obsequies on 'Maundaye Thursdaye' in Cockfelde church, in Henley (*described*), given by
William Woddewarde of Henley for a lamp and other lights in Henley church, in
Thorneham Magna (*described*, including 'the Guyldehall'), near Eye Bridge (*described*), given
by John Dunche for masses and the like in the church of Thorneham aforesaid, in Laiston
                                                                        [*m.* 9]
(*described*), once of the monastery of Laiston, and in Bakwell next Burye St. Edmunds (a toll
at Tollocote), once belonging to the office of sacrist of the monastery of Burye St. Edmunds,
all in the county of Suffolk; lands (*named*) in Kirkbye Cayme or elsewhere, cos. Norfolk and
Suffolk, given by Thomas Jackson and Richard Swanne of Kirbye aforesaid for masses and
the like in Kirbye church; lands in Culpho, co. Suffolk, late a fee of the house of St. John of
Jerusalem in England; lands in Culpho aforesaid and Playford, given for a light in Culpho
church; the church of Stratton All Saints, co. Suffolk, and all tithes belonging thereto; a view
of frankpledge or leet in Wilbye, co. Suffolk, once of Butley priory, co. Suffolk; lands in
Barkinge, given for the discharge of a payment for candles at the purification of women, in
Metfielde (*named*), given by Thomas Maplehed for obits and the like in Metefielde church,
and in Acton *alias* Alpheton (*described*), given for a lamp before the sacrament in Alpheton
church, all in the county of Suffolk; a graveyard or small parcel of land wherein is the church
or chapel of Culpho, co. Suffolk, and the tithes of hay and other small tithes and the
oblations and other profits in Culpho, once of the monastery of Layston, co. Suffolk, from

which was paid to the curate there a yearly stipend of £5 10s.; the rectory of Farneham with all its appurtenances in Ferneham and Benhall, co. Suffolk, once of Butley priory, co. Suffolk; lands (named) in Swestlinge and Cransford, given for a lamp in Swestlinge church, in Southwolde, given by [—] Godbold for incense, lamps and other lights in Southwolde church, in Swestlinge and Crainsforde, [m. 10]
given for lamps or other lights in Swestlinge church, and in Cransford, given for a lamp in Cransford church, all in the county of Suffolk; the tithes of corn of lands (named) in Wingefield and Statebroke, co. Suffolk, once of Eye priory, co. Suffolk; lands (named) in Alderton, co. Suffolk; lands and tithes in Ormesbye, co. Norfolk, and in the parish of St. Paul, Norwich, the advowson of the rectory of Ormesbie and all possessions in Ormesbie and elsewhere, co. Norfolk, of the late hospital of the Normans or of St. Paul in Norwich; lands (described) in Cirencester, co. Gloucester; lands in Horscombe within the precinct of the city of Gloucester or elsewhere, co. Gloucester, given for lamps and the like in the church there; 'le Churchehowse' in Wichester, co. Gloucester, given for mass and the like; lands (including 'Our Ladyes Lande') in Little Barryngton, co. Gloucester; lands (described) in Burvorde, co. Oxford; lands in Shipton under Wichewood, co. Oxford, (including a former chapel and 'le Church Howse'), given for masses and the like; lands in Kethermoster (named) and Trymply, co. Worcester, given for the services of the Blessed Trinity, Jesus [m. 11]
Christ, All Saints and the like in Kethermoster or elsewhere, co. Worcester; lands in Pendocke, given for lights and the like in Pendocke church, in Churchehill, given for a lamp in Stowton church, co. Worcester, in Austley (named), belonging to Badston hermitage, co. Worcester, and in Elmesbridge (named), given for lights in Elmesbridge church, all in the county of Worcester; lands (described) in Wymondam alias Womondham, co. Worcester or Leicester, late of the monastery of Kerkby Bellowes; lands (named) in Padstowe, co. Cornwall, given for lights or the like in 'Saynte Bennettes chappell' in Padstowe; the tithes of fish on the river of Padstowe, once of Bodman priory; lands in Horlinge in the parish of Constantyne, co. Cornwall; the rectory of Pinforde, co. Dorset, once of the monastery of Shirborne, co. Dorset; burgages (described) in Craucombe, co. Somerset, given for (1) a lamp with oil therein in the nave of Craucombe church before the high cross and (2) two wax tapers before the images of Holy Trinity and St. Mary in the chancel of the said church; lands (named) in Chippinge Barnett, Easte Barnett and St. Albans, co. Hertford, once of the monastery of St. Albans; 'a hermitage' and lands called [m. 12]
'Lampelande' within the manor of Maden Crofte in a hamlet called Goose More in the parish of Hippolittes, co. Hertford; lands in Burnham Norton, late of the Carmelite friars there; in Midleton (described) and Sechey and Westwynche (described), late of Blackboroughe priory, co. Norfolk, in Hindringham, given for lights and the like in Bynham church, co. Norfolk, in Holkeham, late of the monastery of Westdereham, co. Norfolk, (beyond lands, named, leased to Roger Hopkyns by the said monastery by indenture, 21 March, 28 Hen. VIII, for 60 years still enduring), in Holcham aforesaid and Burnham Overey, once of Walsingham priory, co. Norfolk, in Warrham, late of Edward, late duke of Buckingham, attainted of treason, and in Warford, given by William Reve for a vestment in Easte Walton church, co. Norfolk, called 'a whyte albe', all in the county of Norfolk; the tithes of demesne lands of manors in Little Walsingham and Great Walsingham, co. Norfolk, by virtue of stat. 35 Hen. VIII leased by copy of court roll according to the custom of the manors; lands in Pertenstoke, co. Wilts, given for masses and the like; lands (described) in the parish of St. Mary in Readinge, co. Berks, late of the monastery of Readinge; lands (named) in Uffington alias Uffingdon or Ovington alias Offington, co. Berks; a free pasture in Wickeleis, Longnore and Bulholmes alias Belholmes or elsewhere, late of the nunnery of Goringe, co. Oxford; lands in Yattenden, given for lamps and the like in the church there, in Readinge ('the Sentuarye Lande'), [m. 13]

in Radley (*named*), late of the monastery of Abbendon, co. Berks, and in Sonnynge, given for obits and the like, all in the county of Berks; 'the Personage Howse' in Ornesbie, co. Norfolk; lands in Acle, co. Norfolk; 'the Guildhall' in Ryall, co. Lincoln, and lands in Ryall aforesaid, cos. Lincoln and Rutland; lands in Bellesthorpe and Greteford, cos. Lincoln and Rutland; lands (*named*) in Denton, co. Lincoln, parcel of escheat lands; lands in Dymbylbye *alias* Dymylbye, co. Lincoln; lands (*named*) in Skillington, co. Lincoln; lands (*named*, including 'the Guildhall') in Aslacton, co. Norfolk; a decayed chapel in Pullham, co. Norfolk; the site of 'Seynte Peters Gilde Hall' in Sutton, co. Lincoln; lands in Sutton aforesaid, bequeathed by Lawrence Male for an obit there; lands called 'the Decons Lande' in Sidebroke *alias* Sedgebroke, co. Lincoln; tithes in Sidebroke aforesaid, belonging to the Crown by the dissolution of monasteries; lands in Leake Magna *alias* Eastleake, co. Nottingham, escheated after the death of Julian Crosbye, clerk, without an heir; lands (*described*) in Great Broughton in Clevelande, co. York, given for lights before the rood and the images of St. Mary and St. Austin in Great Broughton church, prayer for the soul of John Longley *alias* Langley and others and other superstitious uses; lands in Cottestocke *alias* Cotlingestocke, co. Nottingham, escheated after the death of Julian Crosbye, clerk, without an heir; a cottage (*described*) in the town of Newcastle on Tyne, co. York [*sic*]; lands in Newton, co. York; lands (*named*) in Harlaxston, co. Lincoln, escheated; a decayed chapel or church with 'the churche yarde' and all possessions thereof in Wakton, co. Norfolk; lands in Aslackton (*named*), late of a guild there, in Heywood in the parish of Dysse (*named*), given for the 'Jesus masse prieste' in Dysse church, and in Albroughe (*described*), all in the county of   [*m.* 14]
Norfolk; lands in Shelforde Parva, co. Cambridge, late of [—] Orne, attainted of treason; lands in Fulbourne, co. Cambridge, given for an obit in Fulbourne church; lands in Brambre, West Grenested, Cowfielde, Fyndon, Stayninge, Shipley and Bidlington, co. Sussex, concealed before 20 April, 18 Eliz.; lands (*named*) in Horne *alias* Hourne, co. Sussex or Surrey, given by Andrew Twedham for an obit and two 'lez tapers' in Hourne church; a chapel and lands in Badshart *alias* Badshott or elsewhere, co. Sussex; a rent out of the manor of Okewodde *alias* Okenwood and out of lands in Shoreham, co. Sussex, late of the monastery of Nuneton, co. Warwick; lands in Lymefeld *alias* Lingefeild, co. Sussex [*sic*], given for two 'le tapers' in Lymeffield *alias* Lingefeld church; and a chapel called 'Seynte Gyles chappell', with the tithes belonging thereto, and a chapel called 'Marye Magdalens chappell' in Sotherham by Lewes, co. Sussex. Yearly value according to the several particulars thereof £14 7s. 2d. To hold as of the manor of East Grenewich, co. Kent, in socage. Issues from the times when the premises or any parcel thereof should have come to the Crown. The patent or the enrolment thereof to be sufficient   [*m.* 15]
warrant to officers of the Exchequer and the duchy of Lancaster to direct process in the Crown's name against occupiers of the premises for levying of the same issues, and to the grantees to have the same to their use and to dispense, compound and discharge for the making of such process. If the inheritance of the premises or any parcel thereof shall hereafter be lawfully taken from the grantees' possession, they may have in satisfaction of the grant other concealed lands of the same value as those taken. The grant to be void in respect of any of the premises which were not concealed before 1 May, 17 Eliz., on or after which day Grymeston the elder and Grymeston the younger and others or their assigns procured at their own costs the discovery thereof.

For £172 6s. paid at the Exchequer by Grymeston the elder and Grymeston the younger; and at the suit of William Drurye, knight, the Queen's servant.   By Q.

2181.)   19 *Nov.* 1576.   Grant in fee farm to Thomas Boynton of Barmeston, co. York, Nicholas Broke of Waltham Holycrosse, co. Essex, and Percival Gounson of Aske, co. York, their heirs and assigns of the following in the county of York—(1) the manor of

Romanbye and lands (*named with tenants' names*) in Romanby, late of Thomas Markenfeilde, attainted of treason;   [*m.* 16]
(2) lands (*tenant named*) in Thorpe, late of the said Markenfeilde; (3) lands (*tenants named*) in Resplith and Melmerbye, late of Richard Norton, attainted of treason; (4) lands (*named with tenants' names*) in Carleton Mynyott, Sandhooton and Aismonderby, late of Markenfeilde   [*m.* 17]
aforesaid; (5) lands (*tenants named*) in Owlcotes, Hawkeswicke in Litton Dale, Arnecliff in Litton Dale, Thorpe and Carperbye and rents in Arnecliffe and Thorpe, late of Leonard Metcalf, attainted of treason; and (6) the manor of Forcett and lands (*named with tenants' names*) in   [*m.* 18]
Forcett, late of Robert Lambert, attainted of treason. Advowsons, bells and lead, except lead in gutters and windows, reserved. To hold (1) by service of the hundredth part of a knight's fee and the rest as of the   [*m.* 19]
manor of Eastgrenewiche, co. Kent, in socage. Rendering yearly (1) £42 17s. 4d. (*detailed*), (2) £3 6s. 8d., (3) for the premises in Resplith 32s. 8d. during William Norton's life and £3 5s. 4d. after his death and for those in Melmerby 22s. 6d. during the said William Norton's life and 45s. after his death, (4) for the premises in Carleton £4 4d. (*detailed*), Sandhooton £3 4s. 4d. (*detailed*) and Aismonderby £2 10s. (*detailed*), (5) for the premises in Owlcotes £3 4s. 8d. (*detailed*), Hawkeswicke £3 14s. 3d. (*detailed*), Arnecliffe £3 (*detailed*), Thorpe £1 13s. 4d. (*detailed*) and Carperbye £2 12s. 8d. (*detailed*) and for the rents 13s. 1d. and (6) £25 8s. 11½d. (*detailed*). Issues from Pentecost last. The grantees charged with the yearly payment to William Brough and his heirs of a yearly   [*m.* 20]
rent of 6s. 8d. out of the premises in Forcett and to the said William Norton for life 32s. 8d. yearly out of the premises in Resplithe and 32s. 6d. yearly out of the premises in Melmerbye.
    In consideration and full satisfaction of £800 claimed by Walter Jobson of Kingston on Hull, merchant, from the Crown; and at the suit of Jobson.   By p.s.

2182.)   20 *March* 1577.   *Gorhambury.*   Grant in fee simple to John Fortescue, master of the great wardrobe, and John Walker of the following lands (*named with tenants names*) in Wellington, co. Somerset, late parcel of lands put in feoffment to the use of three priests in Ilmynster church; lands (*named*) in Warham, co. Dorset, once of the late church of St. Mary there; lands in Babcarye, co. Somerset, once of the late priory or hospital of St. John the Baptist in Wellis, co. Somerset; lands in Morelinche, co. Somerset, once of St. Mary Magdalen's chantry in Taunton; lands (*named*) in   [*m.* 21]
Buckminster and Sewsterne, co. Leicester, once of Kirkebiebellers priory; lands in Thurnebye, co. Leicester, once of the monastery of Pré, Leicester, co. Leicester; lands in Humberston, co. Leicester, late of the earl of Rutland and in the Crown's hands by exchange; lands in Houghton, co. Leicester, once of the Charterhouse next Coventry; lands in Markefeilde, co. Leicester, given for a light in Markefeild church; lands in Thurmaston, co. Leicester, once of the monastery of Pré, Leicester; lands (*named*) in Tottenhall, co. Buckingham, once of Snelshall priory; lands (*named*) in Morpeth, co. Northumberland, once of the monastery of Newminster, co. Northumberland; lands in Little Benton, co. Northumberland, leased by the present Queen by patent to William, marquess of Northampton, late attainted; lands (*named*) in Derington, co. Lincoln, once of the monastery of Haverholme; lands (*named*) in Derington, once of Catley priory; lands in Derington, once of Temple Brewer preceptory; lands (*named*) in Redcrewe, co. Merioneth, once of the monastery of Kynner; lands in Llanthewy or elsewhere, co. Monmouth, given for a light before the high altar in Llanthewy church; lands in Kemeis Comaunder, co. Monmouth, given for a light in Kemies Comaunder church by Walter ap Hoell ap Phipp; lands in Wolpitt, co. Suffolk, once of the monastery of Burye St. Edmunds; lands in Metfeilde, co. Suffolk, once of the monastery of Bury St. Edmunds; lands   [*m.* 22]

(*described*) in the parishes of St. Mary and All Saints in Huntingdon, co. Huntingdon, once of Huntingdon priory; and lands (*named*) in Edwardston, co. Suffolk, once of St. John's priory, Colchester. To hold as of the manor of Eastgrenewiche, co. Kent, in socage. Issues from Michaelmas, 17 Eliz. The grantees charged with the yearly payment of—out of the premises in Wellington 17*s*. 5*d*. to the bishop of Bath and Wells; and out of the premises in Buckminster and Sewsterne 54*s*. 10*d*. granted to Edward, lord Clinton and Saye, high admiral, and Leonard Irbye and 19*s*. 4*d*. to the lord of the manor of Framlonde.

In consideration of the bargain and sale to the Crown by Richard Lee, knight, deceased, of the manor of Abbottes Langley *alias* Lees Langley,   [*m*. 23]
co. Hertford.   By p.s.

2183.) 15 *Dec*. 1576. Grant in fee simple to Edward, earl of Lincoln, K.G., and Christopher Gough of Westhorseley, co. Surrey, of the following—the tithes of hay (*tenants named*) of a meadow in Severneham, co. Gloucester, once of the monastery of Tewkesburye, co. Gloucester; lands (*tenants named*) in Erthcote, co. Gloucester, once of St. Thomas's chantry in Cirencester church; a grange, farm or hereditament called Whittington Grange, co. Leicester, late of Henry, late duke of Suffolk, attainted of treason, and heretofore leased at a yearly rent of £9 13*s*. 4*d*.; lands (*tenant named*) in Claxton, co. Leicester, once of Belver priory, co. Lincoln, and leased at a yearly rent of 53*s*. 8*d*.; lands (*named with tenant's name*) in Bottesford *alias* Bottilleford, co. Leicester, once of Belver priory and leased at a yearly rent of 15*s*.; lands (*tenant named*) in Hose, co. Leicester, once of Belver priory; a moiety of the town of Overton, co. York, once of the monastery of St. Mary next the walls of York and afterwards of Thomas Henneage, knight, exchanged, and lands (*named with tenants' names*) in Overton, leased to Elizabeth Harbert, widow, now deceased, by patent, 11 Feb., 15 Eliz., *inter alia* for 21 years; a moiety of the said town of Overton, once of the said monastery and afterwards of Thomas Henneage, knight, exchanged, and lands (*named with tenants' names*) in Overton, leased to Isabel Ewstage, widow, by patent, 26 April, 12 Eliz., for 21 years; lands (*tenant named*)   [*m*. 24]
in Skaling, co. York, and all other lands there once of Helaugh priory, co. York; lands (*named*) in Warrhem, co. York, once of Haltemprice priory, co. York, and late leased to John Bathe; lands (*tenant named*) in Okebroke, co. Derby, once of the monastery of Dale, co. Derby; lands (*tenant named*) in Elvasten, co. Derby, once of the monastery of Darleigh, co. Derby; lands (*tenants named*) in Lamecote in the parish of Holme, co. Nottingham, and Ratcliff, once of the monastery of Newsted, co. Nottingham; lands in Ratcliff and Lamecote aforesaid of the yearly value of 20*s*., once of the monastery of Dale, co. Derby; lands (*tenants named*) in Burton, co. Warwick, once of Wroxall priory, co. Warwick; lands (*named with tenants' names*) in the borough of Wigmore, co. Hereford, once of the monastery of Wigmore; St Mary's chantry at the West end of Llantwight church, co. Glamorgan, a messuage adjoining, now or late in the tenure of John Taylor, clerk, late of the said chantry, and lands (*named with tenants' names*) in Llantwight, all late in the tenure of Thomas Bagland and parcels of lands exchanged by William, late earl of Pembroke, with Edward VI; a tenement (*described with tenants' names*) in the parish late of St. Olave (*Olati*) now of St. George of Colgate in Norwich, once of the priory of St. Faith of Horseham, co. Norfolk; lands in Esthanney, co. Berks, which the prior of Norton unjustly recovered from Hugh Sulgrave and Joan his wife, parcel of escheated lands in the said county; lands in Crowmershe Battall, co. Oxford, escheated by reason of the appropriation made thereof by the abbot of Battle to Peter de White without licence; lands in divers places, co. Southampton, called 'le Frary Rentes', once of the hospital of St. John of Jerusalem; lands (*named with tenants' names*) in Westhorseley, co. Surrey, once of the monastery of Newarke and late leased to Christopher Goughe; lands (*tenant named*) in Hanslopp, co. Buckingham, once of   [*m*. 25]

'Kiswike chaunterye', co. Buckingham; lands (*tenant named*) in Byfeild, co. Northampton, once of Catesbye priory; lands (*tenants named*) in Wynsley and Hope within the halmote of Ivington, co. Hereford, once of Leominster priory, co. Hereford, leased at yearly rents of 13*s*. 4*d*. and 9*s*.; lands (*tenant named*) in Appulby, co. Lincoln, once of the monastery of Thorneholme, co. Lincoln; the manor of Sewarby, co. Lincoln, late of Robert Constable, knight, attainted, lands etc. (*named with tenants' names*) in Sewarby, in the lordship of Owneby and in Limber Magna, co. Lincoln, some parcels of the said manor, a portion of tithes and a pension due from the rectory of Somerby for the same portion, and the perquisites and profits of courts in the said manor; lands (*tenant named*) in Sudbroke, co. Lincoln, once of the monastery of Barlinges, co. Lincoln; all lands in Winsby, Hagworthingham and Lusbye, co. Lincoln, late of Robert Leache, attainted of treason; a messuage in Harleston, co. Lincoln, parcel of the land of Andrew Chamber, who feloniously killed John Mylner; lands (*tenants named*) in Gouxhill and Thorneton, co. Lincoln, late leased to Thomas Reade at a yearly rent of 33*s*.; lands (*named with tenants' names*) in Welby, co. Lincoln, once of the monastery of Farleigh, co. Wilts, and late leased to the said earl of Lincoln by the name of Edward, lord Clinton; a messuage (*tenant named*) in Killingham, co. Lincoln, once of the monastery of Nunapleton, co. York; a half quarter of salt arising in Ludney, co. Lincoln, once of the monastery of Kirkested, co. Lincoln; lands (*described with tenant's name*) in Spaldinge, co. Lincoln, late leased to John Colchester; a garden (*described with tenant's name*) in Nottingham, once of St. Mary's chantry in the parish of St. Peter in Nottingham; lands (*tenant named*) in Saltefleteby, co. Lincoln, once of the monastery of Louth Parke, co. Lincoln; the rectory and rectories of Cadbury and Nethereux, co. Devon, once of the hospital or priory of St. Nicholas, Exeter, and a portion of tithes in Cadbury and Nethereux (*tenants named*), all leased to George Carew for a term of years still to run at a yearly rent of 53*s*. 4*d*.; lands (*tenants named*) in Westerkele   [*m*. 26] and Belchford, co. Lincoln, once of the hospital of St. John of Jerusalem; lands (*tenant named*) in Leverton, co. Lincoln, given by Thomas Kecher for an obit in Leverton church; lands (*tenant named*) in Leverton aforesaid; lands (*tenant named*) in Haddenham, co. Buckingham, once of the late brotherhood of Aylesburie, co. Buckingham, and leased to Charles Fitche for a term of years still to run; all lands in Northmerston and Aylesburie, co. Buckingham, leased to Edward Loughbourough by patent, 13 Feb., 3 Eliz., for 21 years, once of the brotherhood of Aylesburye; and lands (*tenant named*) in Mylton, co. Oxford, late of Thomas Pope, knight, exchanged, late leased to Richard Gyll *inter alia*. Advowsons, bells and lead, except lead   [*m*. 27] in gutters and windows, reserved. To hold as of the manor of Eastgrenewiche, co. Kent, in socage. Issues from Michaelmas last. The grantees charged with the yearly payment of—10*s*. for the fee of the bailiff of the manor of Sewarby; 26*s*. 8*d*. out of the said manor to Robert Benton, vicar of Somerby, and his successors; and 15*s*. out of the premises in Milton to William Davers and his heirs in right of his manor in Milton for quitrent.

In consideration of the surrender of lands in Milton, co. Oxford, in the tenure of Richard Gill, of the yearly value of 48*s*. 2*d*., late of Thomas Pope, knight, exchanged; also in consideration of lands in Sempringham and Gosberkirk *alias* Gosberton and elsewhere, co. Lincoln, parcel of the manor or grange of Neslam, co. Lincoln, bargained and conveyed to the Queen by the said earl of Lincoln; also for the said earl's service; and at his suit.

By p.s.

2184.)   22 *March* 1577.   *Gorhambury*.   Licence for 20 years for the mayor   [*m*. 28] and burgesses of the town of Kingston upon Hull to buy in the counties of York, Lincoln, Norfolk and Kyngston upon Hull 20,000 quarters of grain, that is to say, 5,000 quarters of barley, 5,000 quarters of malt, 5,000 quarters of wheat and 5,000 quarters of beans and pease, and export the same in ships of the realm or friendly countries from places in the said counties to Scotland or elsewhere beyond seas; from the present date; so that the wheat be bought at the price of 16s. the quarter or under and the residue of the grain at 12s. the quarter or under; no duties to be paid, notwithstanding stat. 13 Eliz. for the increase of tillage and maintenance of the navy, whereby it is provided that there shall be paid for custom and poundage of every quarter of wheat transported by force of that statute 12d. and of other grain 8d., and of every quarter of wheat transported by special licence and not by force of the statute 2s. and of other grain 16d.; quantities shipped to be set down on the back of this licence that it may be left on expiry with the officers of the port where the last portion shall be shipped. In consideration of their great costs about the maintenance of defences against the sea in the river of Humber, without which daily charges neither the said town or port nor the Queen's bulwarks or fortifications adjoining, with the repair of which the mayor and burgesses have been charged, can long continue in good state—which costs they are not now able to bear without relief by reason of great losses sustained by the inhabitants of late years through piracy, tempests, shipwrecks and other misfortunes upon the sea; also for their service to the Queen and her progenitors, especially in the time of the late rebellion in the North. *English.*   By p.s.

2185.)   10 *April* 1577.   *Gorhambury.*   Presentation of Richard Turswell, M.A., to the rectory of Waddingham St. Mary, Lincoln dioc., void by death.   By p.s.

2186.)   20 *March 1577.*   *Gorhambury.*   Grant for life in survivorship to Richard Harman and Margery his wife of an annuity of £10, payable at the Exchequer. In consideration of the surrender of a patent under the great seal of England   [*m.* 29] exemplifying a decree of the court of Augmentations, 20 June, 1 Edw. VI, whereby it was ordered that Harman should have £5 yearly so long as he should continue schoolmaster at the King's college in Cambridge called Trinity college and an annuity of £10 whenever he should depart or be removed from the place of schoolmaster; and that the grammar school in Trinity college was dissolved by the late visitors and commissioners of the same, so that Harman was removed from his place and by decree of the said court, 30 Oct., 3 Edw. VI, was awarded the said annuity of £10 for life; as appears by an endorsement on the said patent signed by the chancellor and general surveyors of the court.   *English.*   By Q.

2187.)   25 *March* 1577.   Pardon for Stephen Foxe late of London, goldsmith. Thomas Bellingham late of London, 'yoman', was indicted for that he burgled the house of Thomas Barrowe, goldsmith, on 10 Feb., 19 Eliz., in the parish of St. John Zakary in Aldrichgate ward, London, and stole plate (*described*) belonging to him, and Henry Foxe late of London, goldsmith, Ellis Lewys late of London, 'blacksmyth', and the said Stephen were indicted for procuring the said felony on 5 Feb., 19 Eliz., in the said parish. At the suit of Joan Foxe, Stephen's wife.   By Q.

2188.)   18 *March* 1577.   *Gorhambury.*   Lease for 31 years to Robert   [*m.* 30] Payne, a yeoman of the chamber, of—(1) lands (*named with tenants' names*) in Little Wilbram, co. Cambridge, parcel of the manor of Anglesey, co. Cambridge, once of Anglesey priory and leased by patent of the Exchequer, 6 Nov., 8 Eliz., to Payne for 21 years from Michaelmas then last; (2) lands (*named*) in Wintringham in the parish of St. Neots, co. Huntingdon, and in a field called Bargrave in the said parish, leased by patent of the Exchequer, 1 July, 8 Eliz., to Payne for 21 years from Lady Day then last; (3) lands (*named with tenants' names*) in St. Neots, leased by patent of the Exchequer, 6 Nov., 8 Eliz., to Payne for 21 years from Michaelmas then last; (4) three water mills (*named*) in Paxston and St. Neots, co. Huntingdon, leased by patent, 7 Feb., 6 Eliz., to Edward Skegges for 21 years from Michaelmas 1567; (5) lands (*named with tenant's name*) in St. Neots, leased by patent of

the Exchequer, 13 April, 10 Eliz., to Payne for 21 years from Lady Day then last; (6) lands (*named with tenant's name*) in Hardwick in the parish of St. Neots, parcel of the manor of St. Neots and leased by patent, 2 July, 11 Eliz., to Payne for 21 years from Michaelmas then next; (7) lands (*tenants named*) in Bargrave in the parish of St. Neots, in the town of St. Neots (*described*) and in Eton, co. [*m.* 31]
Bedford, (*named*), which premises in Bargrave and St. Neots are parcels of the manor of St. Neots and were leased by patent of the Exchequer, 13 Dec., 14 Eliz., to Payne for 21 years from Michaelmas then last; (8) lands (*named with tenants' names*) in Wintringham aforesaid, leased by patent, 6 April, 10 Eliz., to Payne *inter alia* for 21 years from the termination of a lease thereof to Thomas Peck; (9) lands (*named*) in St. Neots, leased by patent, 2 July, 11 Eliz., to the said Robert Payne for 21 years from the termination of a lease thereof to John Payne; (10) a bakehouse called 'le common backhowse' in St. Neots (*tenants named*), leased by patent of the Exchequer, 1 July, 16 Eliz., to Robert Thorpe *inter alia* for 21 years from Lady Day then last; (which premises in Wintringham and St. Neots are parcels of the manor of St. Neots and once of the monastery of St. Neots); (11) the usual shops, stallage and picage of 'le bowthes' in the town of St. Neots, the profits of the weekly market held there on Thursday, the fairs there and the tolls of the said market and fairs, and lands (*named*) in Bargrave in St. Neots, all parcels of the manor of St. Neots and leased by patent, 6 April, 10 Eliz., to the said Robert Payne for 21 years enduring until Michaelmas 1579; and (12) lands (*tenants named*) in the town of St. Neots (*described*) and in Bargrave, all once of the monastery of St. Neots and afterwards assigned to the present Queen before her accession. With reservations. (1), (2) and (3) from [*m.* 32]
Michaelmas 1587; (4), (5) and (6) from Michaelmas 1588; (7) from Michaelmas 1592; (8), (9) and (10) from Lady Day 1597; (11) from Michaelmas 1600; and (12) from Michaelmas 1581. Yearly rents (1), (2) and (3) £9 2s., to wit, for (1) £2 13s. 4d., (2) £3 10s. (*detailed*) and (3) 58s. 8d. (*detailed*), (4), (5) and (6) £23 4s., to wit, for (4) £20 6s., (5) £2 10s. and (6) 8s. (*detailed*), (7) £4 8s. 2d., to wit, for the premises in St. Neots £4 5s. 2d. (*detailed*) and Eton 3s., (8), (9) and (10) £3 18s. 4d., to wit, for (8) 51s. 8d., (9) 25s. and (10) 20d., (11) £12 6s. 8d., to wit, for the shops etc. £9 6s. 8d. and the lands in Bargrave 60s., and (12) 72s. 6d. (*detailed*). The lessee to pay to the vicar, curate or minister in St. Neots church, both during all the terms of years in the premises still to run by force of former leases and during the term hereby granted, £8 yearly, in augmentation of his living, from Lady Day next. [*m.* 33]
    In consideration that Thomas, bishop of Lincoln, has certified that the said town of St. Neots is large and full of inhabitants and the living of the minister is very small, but the said Robert Payne, an inhabitant there, has undertaken to augment the stipend as aforesaid; and for the said Robert's long service. By p.s.

2189.)   30 *Aug.* 1577.   *Gorhambury.*   Grant for life to Henry Cary, the Queen's servant, of the office of keeper of Fremantill park, co. Southampton; from the death of Henry Kyngesmyll, late holder of the office; wages etc. as had by Kyngesmyll or before him by Thomas Brandon, knight, William, lord Sandes, Humphrey Foster, knight, Christopher Litcott or George Brediman; payable by the sheriff of the county; with 5 marks yearly, payable by the said sheriff, for the carriage of water for the Queen's wild beasts and game in the park in summer; also with herbage and pannage of the park, reserving sufficient pasture for the deer and wild beasts. For Cary's service. By p.s.

2190.)   6 *Sept.* 1577.   *Gorhambury.*   Presentation of William [Toft, clerk][1] to the perpetual vicarage of Amport *alias* Annaport with the chapels of [Choulderton and Appleshaw],[1] Winchester dioc. By p.s.

(*The dorse of this roll is blank.*)

---

[1] The roll is damaged at this point; reading from the warrant in Chancery Warrants, Series II (C. 82), no. 1318.

PART VI

C. 66/1156

2191.)   1 *July* 1577.   *Inspeximus* and exemplification, at the request of   [*m.* 1]
John Crooke, of the following (remaining in the files of Chancery):—
   (1) Petition to the Privy Council by Nicholas Cubbedge of Horton, co. Oxford, John
White of Staunton Sainte John, co. Oxford, and John Gome of Wormenhall, co.
Buckingham, on behalf of themselves and the other inhabitants of Horton, Studley,
Staunton, Wormenhall, Brill and Ocley, for redress: common of pasture in a great parcel of
woody and waste ground, cos. Oxford and Buckingham, called 'the Quarters' (2,000 ac.)
belonging to divers manors in the said counties and another parcel of woody and waste
ground called 'Stonehurste' (400 ac.) adjoining the same has been had from time
immemorial by the lords and tenants of other manors and townships adjoining, such as lord
Norris of Ricott for him, his tenants and farmers of his manor of Horton, co. Oxford, John
Crook for him, his tenants and farmers of his manors of Studley and Esses and for his
tenants of Horton, cos. Oxford and Buckingham, the warden and fellows of 'Sainte Marye
colledge of Wynchester' in Oxford for them, their tenants and farmers of their manor of
Staunton Sainte John, all the tenants, freeholders and farmers of the townships of Borestall,
Brill and Okeley, co. Buckingham, Thomas Typping for him, his tenants and farmers of his
manors of Wormenhall and Thomley, and all other the freeholders and inhabitants in the
said manors and townships; Vincent Curson of Waterpurye, co. Oxford, being seised in fee
of 200 ac. of the said woody and waste ground, John Dynham of Borstall being seised in fee
of 'Stonehurste'   [*m.* 2]
and parcel of 'the Quarters' (100 ac.) and Richard Leigh of Ocley being seised as of freehold
of another 200 ac. of the said woody and waste ground in right of his wife, the late wife of
George Tirrell, deceased, have under colour of preservation of wood enclosed the same not
leaving any part to the commoners, who have borne it for nine or ten years in hope that
Curson, Dynham and Leigh and those whose estate Dynham and Leigh now have would
not have kept the wood grounds in severalty for longer than a reasonable time for the saving
of the 'springes'; but they not only use the same as pasture for their own cattle, but also they
defraud both their own tenants and the petitioners and all other 'borderes' and commoners
of their lawful common in the same wood grounds, for they now fell them and sell them
again before they ever come to lie open to the commoners; and Curson has dug 40 ac. of the
waste having no wood at all growing on it and causes his servants to chase away the poor
commoners' cattle with dogs.   *English.*
   (2) Petition to the Privy Council by Edward Harte of Brill, a regarder of the Queen's
forest of Barnewood, Thomas Shurley of Lurgishall and Thomas Neele of Wootton
Underwood on behalf of themselves and   [*m.* 3]
all other inhabitants of Brill, Lurgishall, Wootton, Dorton and Hame, co. Buckingham, to
the number of 100 householders and over, for redress: the petitioners and their ancestors,
their tenants and farmers have had from time immemorial common of pasture in a parcel of
wood (1,000 ac.) called 'Mollens Wood' of the inheritance of John Denham within the view
of Barnewood forest, co. Buckingham, and also in the rest of the said forest until at several
times within the past six years Denham has unlawfully encoppiced and made several to
himself over 500 ac. being the greatest part of the said woods and commons, converting
from wood to pasture 50 or 60 ac., to wit, four closes (*described with tenants' names*); Denham

has also without warrant felled of the Queen's vert within the said woods at least 200 old oaks and ashes without coppicing and also the old 'standells' left at fellings heretofore within the coppices, whereby the Queen's game is greatly 'straigtned' and daily destroyed and the petitioners forebarred of their common; Denham has also encoppiced within the time aforesaid woods called 'Kinges Wood' in Lurgisham aforesaid, so that the petitioners are barred from their common there; also Shurley and Neele complain that Edward Grenefelde about 17 years past enclosed 10 ac. out of a parcel of common called 'Wotton Land' for which he was then indicted and made his fine, but notwithstanding has kept the same enclosed excluding them from their common there; Grenefelde has also enclosed two common ways leading from the said common to the towns aforesaid, so that the petitioners cannot at divers times of the year drive their cattle to and from it without miring and great peril, and has within these three years set two houses on the common and taken in a close to each of them; Grenefelde has also erected a tenement on a parcel of the said common, being the Queen's ground, called 'Tethersell' and has enclosed a parcel of the same ground to the disherison of the Queen and the hindrance of the inhabitants in their common; also there was kept for the   [m. 4]
Queen a swainmoot court for the said forest until within 20 years, and in default of keeping the same all good orders accustomed to be used for the forest and common have been utterly subverted. *English*.

(3) Commission by patent, 29 April, 19 Eliz., to Francis, earl of Bedford, councillor, Arthur, lord Grey of Wylton, Francis Knolles, knight, treasurer of the household, Robert Drurye, knight, Henry Lee, knight, Edmund Ashefeild, knight, Edward Umpton, knight, William Babington, knight, John Cheyney of Chessham Boyes, Michael Blunte, Griffith
                                                                  [m. 5]
Hampden and George Davers (or five of them, the earl, lord Grey, Knolles, Drurye, Lee or Ashefeild being two) to hear and determine the matters contained in the foregoing petitions (annexed to the commission), which were exhibited to the Council on 18 April last and on the same day, after examination by Nicholas Bacon, knight, keeper of the great seal, Edward, earl of Lincoln, high admiral, Thomas, earl of Sussex, chamberlain of the household, Francis, earl of Bedford, Robert, earl of Leicester, Francis Knolles, knight, aforesaid and James Crofte, knight, controller of the household, all councillors,—Curson, Dynham and Leigh and certain of the tenants aforesaid being present and specially summoned—it was ordered by the said councillors with the assent of the said lord keeper, that this commission should issue out of Chancery; meeting at Tame, co. Oxford, on 3 June next; if they cannot end the said controversies, they shall certify the Privy Council before Midsummer next, returning the petitions with this writ.

(4) Articles or interrogatories (*recited*) for the examination of witnesses on the part of the said Cubbidg and others, querents,   [m. 6]
against Vincent Curson, defendant. *English*.   [m. 7]

(5) Depositions (*recited*) of witnesses, as follows, on the interrogatories taken at Thame, co. Oxford, on 3, 4 and 5 June, 19 Eliz.,   [ms. 8-18]
before the aforesaid earl, lord Grey, Lee, Cheyney, Blunte, Hampden and Davers, commissioners:— Thomas Bonnar of Morcote in the parish of Charleton, co. Oxford, 'husbondman', (aged about 70); Thomas Bigges of Casington, co. Oxford, 'husbondman', (aged about 72); Roger Pyme of Morecott, co. Oxford, 'husbondman', (aged about 53); Thomas Beckleye of Horton, co. Oxford, 'laborer', (aged about 64); Gilbert Bawle of Heddenden, co. Oxford, (aged about 60); John Mondaye of Pedenton, co. Oxford, 'husbondman', (aged about 60); and William Clerke of Staunton, co. Oxford, 'laborer', (aged about 57). *English*.[1]

---

[1] For the circumstances of the enrolment of this entry *see* no. 2250 below.

2192.) 22 *Dec.* 1576. Lease for 21 years to John Myddlecott of   [*m.* 19]
(1) the rectory of Norton Bavent, co. Wilts, and lands there and (2) lands (*named*) there, once
of the monastery of Dartforde, co. Kent; with reservations; from Michaelmas last; yearly
rent £11 16s. 11d.; the lessee to pay yearly 6s. 8d. to the dean and chapter of Salisbury and
12s. 5d. to the archdeacon of Salisbury out of the rectory for proxies and synodals. In
consideration of the surrender by Myddlecott of an indenture, 6 Nov., 30 Hen. VIII,
whereby Joan Fane, prioress, and the convent of the monastery leased the premises, then
late in the tenure of John Dewe, to Thomas Lovell of Stratton, co. Hertford, 'husbondman',
for 40 years from Michaelmas then last at yearly rents of (1) £12 10s. and (2) 6s.; and for a fine
of £23 13s. 10d. paid at the Exchequer.   By warrant of the commissioners.

2193.) 5 *Jan.* 1577. *Gorhambury.* Lease for 21 years to John Baylye of the following in
the isle of Wight, co. Southampton,—(1) the site, farm or hereditament of Arreton, the
demesne lands thereof, the conies and the tithes of corn, lambs and hay arising therefrom
and common of pasture   [*m.* 20]
for 16 cattle and two mares with their foals in a pasture there called 'Lyn', once of the
monastery of Quarr in the said isle, (2) the site of the manor of Staplehurst, the farm or
hereditament of Staplehurste and the demesne lands thereof, the tithes and conies of the said
manor, a pasture called 'Powles' near Newporte and land North of 'Powles Lane' by lands
late of Thomas Oglonder, once of the said monastery, and (3) the rectory of Shalflete, parcel
of the lands assigned to Anne of Cleves; with reservations, including lands (*named*) in
Arreton; (1) from Michaelmas 1595, having been leased by Thomas, abbot, and the convent
of the said monastery by indenture dated on the eve of Candlemas, 16 Hen. VIII, to John
Lighe *alias* Lie, with reservations including the lands above excepted, for 70 years from
Michaelmas then next at a yearly rent of 16 quarters of wheat and 20 quarters of barley; (2)
from Michaelmas 1589, having been leased by the Queen, with the advice of Edward
Horsey, captain of the isle, by indenture, 21 Oct., 10 Eliz., signed by the said captain, to
John Baylye for 21 years from Michaelmas then last at a yearly rent of 60s.; (3) from Lady
Day 1581, having been leased by patent, 15 March, 2 Eliz., to Elizabeth Gyrlynge, late the
wife of William Gyrlynge, deceased, for 21 years from Lady Day then next at a yearly rent of
£14 14s. 4d.; same rents; the lessee to   [*m.* 21]
provide entertainment for the Queen's steward and surveyor coming to the said manor to
hold courts or make a survey. For the survice of John Baylye aforesaid and Henry Baylye.
          By p.s.

2194.) 14 *Jan.* 1577. *Gorhambury.* Grant in fee farm to Nicholas Bagnall, knight, his heirs
and assigns of the reversions and rents of—(1) lands in the town of Heredevaige in the
commote of Meney, co. Anglesey, leased by patent, 1 July, 7 Eliz., to Nicholas Bagnall,
knight, at a yearly rent of 102s. 6d. for 21 years from Michaelmas 1571 or the termination of a
lease thereof by patent of the court of Augmentations, 10 Feb., 5 Edw. VI, to William
Sackvyle for 21 years from Michaelmas then last at the same rent, and (2) the town of
Eskyvyock   [*m.* 22]
in the said commote with the coal mines in the said town, leased (*a*) by the said patent, 1 July,
7 Eliz., to Bagnall at a yearly rent of £7 8s. 8d. for 21 years from Michaelmas 1571 or the
termination of a lease thereof by patent dated at Caernarvon, 13 Sept., 23 Hen. VIII, to the
same Sackvyle for 40 years from Michaelmas then next at the same rent and (*b*) by patent, 16
Dec., 18 Eliz., to Henry Harvye *inter alia* for 30 years from Michaelmas 1596 at the same
rent; and all the premises in Heredrevaige and Eskyvyocke, parcels of the principality of
North Wales. To hold by   [*m.* 23]
service of the twentieth part of a knight's fee and rendering yearly (1) £5 2s. 6d. and (2)
£7 8s. 8d. For Bagnall's service.   By p.s.

2195.) 4 *Feb.* 1577. Lease for 50 years to Humphrey Poole, Thomas Poole and John Cowarde of (1) lands in Estbackweare, Westbackweare and Waterlease and (2) lands (*described with tenants' names*) in Glaston,   [*m.* 24]
Estbackweare and Brendham, once belonging to the office of almoner in the monastery of Glaston, and in Egersleigh and Kynyerd Meade, once belonging to the office of chanter of the said monastery, all which premises are in Glaston, Westpennarde, Mere and Edgarsleigh or elsewhere, co. Somerset, once of the said monastery and afterwards of Edward, late duke of Somerset, also common of pasture for all their cattle in the moors and commons of Glaston; with reservations, including lands in Backweare leased to Richard Poynes and Richard Soute at a yearly rent of 31*s.*; from Michaelmas last; yearly rent £20 2*s.* 2*d.*; the lessees to permit the present tenants of the premises to enjoy possession in their several tenements, so long as upon reasonable request they compound ratably for the lessees' costs about obtaining this patent or about buying the interest in the premises of Henry Ughtred. In consideration of the surrender by Ughtred by deed, 10 Dec., 19 Eliz.,   [*m.* 25]
enrolled in Chancery, of the interests of Thomas Smyth, Chidiock Wardure and Roger Northe, knight, lord Northe of Kyrtlynge: by patent, 30 March, 13 Eliz. the premises (1) and (2) were leased *inter alia* to Northe at yearly rents of (1) £15 5*s.* 6*d.* and (2) 57*s.* 5*d.* for 31 years from Michaelmas 1590, having been leased (1) by patent, 23 Nov., 12 Eliz., to Smyth and (2) by patent of the Exchequer, 18 Dec., 12 Eliz., to Wardure in both cases for 21 years from Michaelmas then last at the same rent.   By p.s.

2196.) 1 *Feb.* 1577. Lease for 21 years to William Lutton of lands (*tenants named*) in (1) Burton Flemmynge, parcel of the manor there,   [*m.* 26]
(2) Nafferton and Navye (*named*), (3) Wanesforth, (4) Beverley (*described*), (5) Buckton, (6) Gryndall, (7) Bysforth, (8) Speton, some parcel of   [*m.* 27]
the manor there, (9) Hylderthorpe, (10) Ryghton (*named*), (11) Gransmore, (12) Awborne and (13) Flyxston, co. York, once of the monastery of Bridlyngton, co. York; with reservations; from Michaelmas last; yearly rents (1) 124*s.* (*detailed*), (2) and (3) 65*s.*, (4) 6*s.*, (5) 24*s.*, (6) 20*s.*, (7) 8*s.*, (8) 114*s.* 8*d.* (*detailed*), (9) 37*s.* 4*d.* (*detailed*), (10) 24*s.*, (11) 30*s.* 8*d.*, (12) 18*s.* and (13) 24*s.* 4*d.*; the lease to be void in respect of any parcel of the premises, if the lessee shall expel the present tenant therefrom, so long as the tenants pay the lessee among themselves before   [*m.* 28]
Michaelmas next his costs about obtaining this patent. On surrender by Lutton of two patents, 15 Jan., 5 Eliz., (*a*) leasing (1)–(7) to William Mylton for 21 years from Michaelmas then last at a yearly rent of £12 15*s.* and (*b*) leasing (8)–(13) to Thomas Brygges for 21 years from Michaelmas then last at a yearly rent of £12 19*s.*; and for a fine of £50 12*s.* paid at the Exchequer.   By p.s.

2197.) 26 *Jan.* 1577. Grant to the burgesses and inhabitants of the town of Rychmond, co. York, of liberties as follows—The town to be a free borough by the name of the alderman and burgesses of the borough of Rychmond. Incorporation of the alderman and burgesses. There shall be an alderman and 12 chief burgesses, to be elected from among the inhabitants; James Cottrell, inhabitant, to be the first and present alderman from the present date until the feast of St. Hilary next and thereafter, if he shall so long live, until another burgess be appointed to the office and sworn; John Teasdall, Thomas Wraye, Lawrence Moyser, Ralph Ackrige, Ralph Ewbancke, Thomas Wyllance, John Barker, William Cowarde, William Heighyngton, James Clarkeson, Richard Key and Christopher Morland, inhabitants, to be the first and present chief burgesses from the present date during good behaviour. The alderman and burgesses to hold of the Crown all the liberties and lands heretofore enjoyed by the men and burgesses of the town by the several rents and ancient farm heretofore due to the Crown or others. There shall be two serjeants at mace [*m.* 29] attendant on the alderman for the execution of process and other business in the borough appertaining to his office; which serjeants shall be elected by the alderman and burgesses yearly on Monday after the feast of St. Hilary for one year and sworn before them; the serjeants to bear gilt or silver maces adorned with the arms of England everywhere within the bounds of the borough before the alderman. The alderman and burgesses may elect from time to time a man learned in the common law to be recorder or steward of the borough, to hold office at their pleasure, whenever the office shall be void; appointment of Robert Smelte to be recorder and steward for life. The alderman and governors of the town may elect yearly on Monday after the feast of St. Hilary for one year such constables and other officers as the men and burgesses of the town have heretofore had there, to be sworn before the mayor and chief burgesses; as often as one of these lower officers of the town shall die or be removed, the alderman and burgesses may within eight days elect another in his place for the rest of the year, to be sworn as aforesaid. The alderman and burgesses shall have a court of record in the borough on Monday every two weeks before the alderman, the recorder or steward and three chief burgesses (or two of them, the alderman or the recorder or steward being one) in a chamber called 'le Talboorth', or in any other house within the precinct of the borough which shall seem fitting to the alderman and chief burgesses, for all personal suits arising within the borough not exceeding the sum of £100, by such process as is accustomed in the court of Common Pleas or in any other court of record in any city, borough or town incorporate in England; the serjeants at mace to execute within the borough all process necessary to the said causes or other causes touching the borough, as shall be required by law or as is accustomed in the Common Pleas or any other court of record in England; the alderman to have all profits of the said court. The alderman and burgesses shall have a view of frankpledge of all inhabitants and residents within the borough twice yearly in a place accustomed there called 'Trinitye churche'. They shall also have a gaol in the town; and the alderman shall be keeper thereof. The borough shall extend to the same bounds as from time immemorial; and the alderman and burgesses may make perambulations as accustomed heretofore within the borough or elsewhere in the county of York to survey their boundaries. The alderman and   [m. 30] burgesses shall have the assize and assay of bread, wine, ale and other victuals, fuel and wood in the borough, both in the presence as well as in the absence of the Queen and her heirs, and victuallers, both inhabitants and those coming to the borough with victuals, shall be under the rule of the alderman and chief burgesses. The alderman and chief burgesses shall have power, assembled in court, to make ordinances for the government of the borough and enforce the same, so that they be not repugnant to the laws of the realm. Power for the chief burgesses yearly on the feast of St. Hilary to elect two of their number and for the inhabitants assembled to elect one of the two to be alderman, who shall be sworn on the Monday following before the last alderman, or in his absence before the recorder or steward, and shall hold office for a year; if the alderman shall die or be removed from office, another shall be elected and sworn in the manner aforesaid for the rest of the year. Whenever any of the chief burgesses shall die, be removed from his place or dwell outside the borough, the remaining burgesses may elect others of the inhabitants in their place, to be sworn before the alderman. Whenever the recorder or steward shall die or be removed, the alderman and burgesses may elect another man learned in the law in his place within 14 days, to hold office at their pleasure, being first sworn before them. The alderman and the recorder or steward during their time of office to be justices of the peace in the borough,   [m. 31] with power to inquire touching all felonies and other offences committed there, so that they do not proceed to the determination of any capital offence without special command of the Crown, and nonetheless to determine all other offences; the justices of the peace in the county not to intermeddle therein, save in default of the alderman and recorder. If anyone elected to the office of alderman or to other lower offices, except that of recorder or steward,

shall having notice of election refuse to exercise the office he shall forfeit to the burgesses 40s., and the alderman and burgesses may commit him to gaol until the fine is paid to the use of the borough. The alderman and burgesses may have yearly a fair for one day on 'Palmesonday Even', a market every Saturday, a fair or market on Saturday once a fortnight for all cattle and other wares between 'Palmeson' Evon' and Christmas, and all other fairs and markets which they ought formerly to have, with all rights and profits such as appertain to 'Bartholomewe Fayre' in Smythfeyld in the suburbs of London; the alderman to be clerk of the market and coroner in the borough, so that the clerk of the market of the household or any of the Queen's coroners shall not in the absence of the Sovereign intermeddle therein, but nonetheless in the presence of the Sovereign the clerk of the market of the household shall together with the alderman intermeddle with anything appertaining to the office of clerk of the market, saving the amercements and fines to the alderman and burgesses. Burgesses and inhabitants shall not be put on juries and the like with foreign men in foreign causes arising before the justices or other ministers of the Crown nor shall foreign men be put with burgesses and inhabitants on juries and the like in causes arising within the town, but juries and the like touching matters plainly arising within the town shall be done only by burgesses and inhabitants, unless the matter touches the Crown or the commonalty of the realm. The alderman and burgesses shall have the goods of felons and outlaws, deodands and other forfeitures concerning all burgesses and inhabitants residing and not residing within the borough, and, whenever anyone shall commit an offence for which he ought to forfeit his goods, wherever justice ought to be done therefore, his goods within the borough shall belong to the alderman and burgesses; and they may by the officers of the town take such goods to their use although already seized by the Crown or its ministers. There shall be two burgesses of   [m. 32]
Parliament elected by the burgesses of the borough. Licence for the alderman and burgesses to acquire lands not held of the Crown in chief or of the Crown or any other by knight service to the yearly value of £40.

At their suit: in consideration that Rychmond is an ancient and populous town—which has from time to time enjoyed divers liberties by prescription and by grants of the Crown—that there may be a sure way for keeping the peace and for the government of the people there.   By p.s.

2198.)   23 *Jan.* 1577.   Licence for Roger Northe, knight, lord Northe, baron of Kyrtelynge, his heirs and assigns to enclose and impark a several ground in Stechworth and Dullyngham, co. Cambridge, containing 400 ac. of pasture and wood, so that they be not within the bounds of the Queen's forest; no one without their leave to enter the said park and warren to hunt under the statutory penalties and under penalty of forfeiture to the Crown of £100. By advice of the Council and without fine, fee or other payment.
                                                                                     By p.s.

2199.)   31 *Dec.* 1576.   Assignment to Henry Cheeke, clerk of the Council, of a lease to the Queen by Robert, bishop of Winchester, by indenture, 5 Sept., 18 Eliz., of the site of the manor of Bentley, co. Southampton, at a yearly rent of £29 15s. 8d.. for 31 years from Michaelmas 1583 or the termination of a lease thereof by the same bishop to William
                                                                                     [m. 33]
Jephson of Froyle, co. Southampton, by indenture, 16 June, 4 Eliz., for 21 years from that date at the same rent. For his service.   By p.s.

2200.)   23 *Jan.* 1577.   Lease for 21 years to John Pryce of all lands in Llandilo Tale y Bont, Lougher, Llanruddion, Penmayne, Barry, Porteynon, Llangenyth, Oystermouth, Swansey

and Llansambett in or about the lordship of Gower, co. Glamorgan, once of the monastery
of Neath, co. Glamorgan;   [*m.* 34]
with reservations; from Michaelmas last; yearly rent £28 1*d.*. In consideration of the
surrender by Pryce of a lease by patent, 8 Oct., 14 Eliz., leasing the lordship or manor of
Gower *alias* Goore to William Pulvertofte for 21 years from Lady Day 1574 at a yearly rent
of £27 17*s.* 10*d.*, which patent was of no effect since the lordship always was and still is parcel
of the possessions of William, earl of Worcester, and the Queen had no title therein; and
because Pulvertofte paid £40 by way of fine for the said patent.   By p.s.

2201.)   1 *Feb.* 1577.   Lease for 21 years to James Verselyne, denizen, of a wood called
Kyngeswood lying in severalty or enclosed or in common in the parish of Hedlynge or
elsewhere, co. Southampton, and within or next the outer bounds of the forest of Wulmere,
co. Southampton, parcel of the ancient possessions of the Crown; with reservation of all
timber trees, all oak 'saplynges' fit to be timber and sufficient 'lez staddelles and storers'
according to statute; from Michaelmas last; yearly rent £15 4*s.*; the lessee to make two
cuttings only of the woods and at fitting times, to enclose them after cutting without putting
in any animals which could damage 'lez sprynges', and to leave sufficient 'lez staddelles' in
every acre according to statute; the lessee before any cutting be made shall cause this patent
to be enrolled before the auditor of the county for charging of the rent and before the
surveyor of woods this side Trent. In consideration that the woods must be enclosed for
seven years after cutting, the charges of which Verselyne offers to undertake and pay the said
rent; and also of great damage sustained by him when his glasshouse was burnt.   By p.s.

2202.)   1 *Feb.* 1577.   Grant to Robert Freake of the wardship and marriage of John
Ryves, son and heir of Robert Ryves; with an annuity of £6 13*s.* 4*d.* from 27 July, 18 Eliz.,
when Robert died. Yearly value of the   [*m.* 35]
inheritance £22 5*s.* 1*d.*   By Q.

2203.)   24 *Jan.* 1577.   Appointment during good behaviour of Robert Bell, knight,
serjeant at law, to be chief baron of the Exchequer, in place of Edward Saunders, knight.
                                                                                             By Q.

2204.)   22 *Dec.* 1576.   Lease for 21 years to Reginald Awderson the elder, Gabriel
Awderson, Edward Awderson, Robert Awderson and John Awderson of the demesne
lands of the manor of Barwyck on Teas, co. York, with a fishery in the water of Teas; with
reservations; from Michaelmas last; yearly rent £58. In consideration of their surrender of
an indenture, 11 July, 36 Hen. VIII, whereby William, earl of Essex, leased the premises, by
the name of the said manor and lands (*described*) belonging thereto, to Henry Avetson, his
servant, at the same rent for 10 years from the termination of a term of 40 years theretofore
granted to Avetson, to wit, from the Invention of Holy Cross 1576; and for a fine of £116
paid at the Exchequer.   By p.s.

2205.)   26 *Jan.* 1577.   Protection for one year for Nicholas Sayntleger   [*m.* 36]
alias Sellenger of Eastwell, co. Kent.   By p.s.

2206.)   1 *Feb.* 1577.   Licence for seven years for George Scott, the Queen's servant, to
export lists of woollen cloth, shreds of woollen cloth and all manner of 'hornes'; from the
present date; paying such custom as should be paid by any merchant alien; no other except
by assignment of the licensee to export such lists, shreds and 'hornes' on pain of forfeiture of
the same or the value thereof, one half of the forfeiture to be to the use of the Crown and the
other to the use of the licensee; the licensee may search all ships and also all books and

remembrances of the Queen's customers and other ministers to 'trye out their dilygence and dutye' touching the premises. For his service. *English*.   By p.s.

2207.)   26 *Jan*. 1577.   Grant for life to John Lytcott, a gentleman pensioner, of the office of keeper of Bagshott park in the forest of Wyndesor, co. Surrey; with an annuity of £5 6s. 8d., payable by the receiver general of   [*m.* 37] the county; from the death of Richard Stafferton, late holder of the office; with herbage and pannage of the park. For his service.   By p.s.

2208.)   1 *Feb*. 1577.   Grant to John Brooke, son and heir of James Brooke late of Adwalton, co. York, deceased, his heirs and assigns of a market at Adwalton, co. York, to be held every second Thursday between Easter and Michaelmas and two fairs to be held there yearly on the Thursday after Easter and the Thursday after Pentecost; so that they be not to the harm of neighbouring fairs and markets; the grantee may take at the market and fairs for every lamb sold 1d., for every five sheep sold 1d. and other customs and tolls on all wares sold; to hold at fee farm by a yearly rent of 26s. 8d. At his suit: he is seised in his demesne as of fee of the said town or hamlet of Adwalton in the manor of Dryghtlington, whither time out of mind many of the Queen's subjects have resorted from the counties of Lancaster and York and elsewhere in England every second Thursday between Easter and Michaelmas for the public market and on the Thursdays after Easter and Pentecost for the common fair held there; but the said market and fairs have been held without any right, and the names of sellers and buyers have been unknown, so that stolen goods have often been brought there and the thieves have escaped free.   By p.s.

2209.)   27 *Dec*. 1576.   Grant for life to Randall (*Randius*) Blacklock of the office of one of the gunners in the castle of Carlisle, with wages of 8d. a day, payable at the Exchequer, from the death of Reginald Warcoppe, late holder of the office.   By p.s.
        Vacated because surrendered, 1 *Aug*. [27] *Eliz., to commissioners by virtue of a writ of* dedimus potestatem, *as appears by the said writ and the return thereof enrolled on the dorse of this enrolment* [*no*. 3151 *below*]: *signed* G. Gerrard.

2210.)   22 *Dec*. 1576.   Lease for 21 years to Richard Warwyk of the   [*m.* 38] capital messuage and site of the manor of Scraptofte, the town of Scraptofte, co. Leicester, and the tithes of corn and hay of Scraptofte, once of Coventry priory; with reservations, including a pension of 26s. 8d., parcel of the manor; from Michaelmas last; yearly rent £30 10s. 6½d. from the time when he shall obtain possession. In consideration that Warwyck offers at his own costs to prove void a pretended lease of the premises by the priory to Henry Wyghley for 38 years still to run; and for a fine of £10 paid at the Exchequer.   By p.s.

2211.)   8 *Jan*. 1577.   *Gorhambury*.   Pardon for John Carlyll late of Great Cumersdell, co. Cumberland, indicted together with George Falder late of Carlisle, 'yeoman', for the theft of horses belonging to a man unknown at Sourebye, co. Cumberland, on 19 May, 18 Eliz., procured and abetted by Thomas Ryche and Richard Graun *alias* Hutchyns Ryche, 'yeomen', both late of Eske, co. Cumberland, on the same date at Carhill (*details given*). At the suit of Grace Carlyll, wife of John.   By p.s.

2212.)   24 *Jan*. 1577.   Grant for life to Thomas Burges, the Queen's servant, of the office of keeping the Queen's great clocks of Westminster and   [*m.* 39] her great clocks in her houses of Grenewich, Hampton Courte, Otelandes, Rychemond and other her ordinary houses of access, whereof Nicholas Urcean, deceased, late had the keeping; with wages of 12d. a day, payable at the Exchequer, from Urcean's death. In consideration of his pains in keeping the said great clocks in the latter days of Urcean and since his death. *English.*   By p.s.

2213.)   30 *Jan.* 1577.   Grant to Walter Hyckman of the wardship and marriage of John Leighe, son and heir of John Leigh; with an annuity of £10 from 20 Jan., 18 Eliz., when John the father died.   By Q.

2214.)   18 *Jan.* 1577.   Grant for life to Lewis Stewar, a yeoman of the guard, of the offices of bailiff and collector of (1) the manors of Southstock   [*m.* 40] and Corston, co. Somerset, once of the monastery of Bathe, and (2) all pensions and portions of tithes in the said county once of the same monastery; so that he answer for the issues thereof at the Exchequer yearly; with yearly fees of (1) 73s. 4d. and (2) 73s. 4d., payable by himself or by the receiver general of the county. On the determination, hereby declared, of the appointment during pleasure to the said offices of Richard Puller by patent of the Exchequer, 1 June, 5 Eliz. For his service and by mainprise of Edward Wyngate of Dunstable, co. Bedford, and Robert Seale of the parish of St. Clement Danes, co. Middlesex, found in the Exchequer.   By Q.

2215.)   1 *Feb.* 1577.   Grant to Susan Talmache, widow, of the wardship and marriage of Lionel Talmache, son and heir of Lionel Talmache; with an annuity of £13 6s. 8d. from 11 Dec., 18 Eliz., when Lionel the father died, until the death of the said Susan, wife of Lionel the father, who holds   [*m.* 41] certain lands for life; and thereafter a further annuity of £6 13s. 4d.   By Q.

2216.)   14 *Jan.* 1577.   *Gorhambury.*   Grant during pleasure to Valentine Dale, LL.D., the Queen's servant, of an annuity of £100, payable at the Exchequer, from Michaelmas last. For his counsel and attendance about the Queen's person.   By p.s.

2217.)   18 *Jan.* 1577.   Grant for life to William Bowll, a yeoman of the chamber, of the office of bailiff of the bailiwicks and hundreds of Sutton at Hone and Twyford, co. Kent; so that he account to the sheriff of Kent yearly for the profits of the bailiwicks and hundreds; from the present date. For his service.   By p.s.

2218.)   21 *Dec.* 1576.   Pardon for Richard Crompton late of London,   [*m.* 42] 'grocer', for the undermentioned felony and all other offences. He was indicted for that he burgled the house of lady Joan Laxton, widow, she with her family being at rest within, in the parish of St. Mary of Aldermarye in Cordwaynerstreete ward, London, on 17 April, 18 Eliz., and stole £480 belonging to her, and at the session held at the Guyldhall of London on 28 April, 18 Eliz., before Ambrose Nicholas, knight, mayor of the city, John Southcote, a justice of the Queen's Bench, William Cordell, knight, master of the rolls, William Fletewood, recorder of the city and others, justices of oyer and terminer, pleaded not guilty and was condemned. At the suit of Thomas Scriven of Frodsley, co. Salop.   By p.s.

2219.)   22 *Dec.* 1576.   Lease for 21 years to John Ellys of the rectory of Holme on the Wold, once of Nunapleton priory, co. York; with reservations; from Michaelmas last; yearly rent £10 12s. 8d.; the lessee to pay 'lez thraves' called 'Saynte John thraves' of Beverley and all proxies and synodals. In consideration of his surrender of a patent, 10 Feb., [*m.* 43] 6 Eliz., leasing the rectory to him for 21 years from Michaelmas then last at the same rent; and for a fine of £10 12s. 6d. paid at the Exchequer.   By warrant of the commissioners.

2220.)　22 *Dec.* 1576.　Lease for 21 years to Roger Thorpe of the rectory and grange of Bierdsall, co. York, and glebe land belonging thereto, once of the monastery of Watton, co. York; with reservations; from Michaelmas last; yearly rent £17; the Crown to discharge the lessee from the yearly payment of 40s. to the dean and chapter of York; the lessee to pay all other charges and to find a sufficient minister in Birdsall church. In consideration of his surrender of a patent, 6 April, 10 Eliz., leasing the premises to his father, Francis Thorpe, for 21 years from Lady Day then last at the same rent; and for a fine of £25 10s. paid at the Exchequer.　　　　　　　　　　　　　　　　　　　　　　　　　　　　By p.s.

2221.)　14 *Jan.* 1577.　*Gorhambury.*　Grant in fee simple to Thomas　　　[*m.* 44] Sekeforde, a master of the Requests, of (1) the rectory called Barnes in Thurleston, co. Suffolk, late of St. Peter's priory, Ipswich, and afterwards of cardinal Wolcey, now or late in the tenure of Sekeforde at a yearly rent of £9 18s. 2d., (2) the site of Felixtowe priory, in the tenure once of Anthony Girlinge and now of Philip Browne, and lands (*named*) adjoining the same and (3) the rectories of Felixstowe and Walton, co. Suffolk, once of Felixstowe priory, with the advowson of the vicarage of Walton; as formerly held by cardinal Wolcey, any duke of Norfolk or any other; to hold in socage as of the manor of Estgrenewiche,　[*m.* 45] co. Kent; issues from Michaelmas last. In consideration of a yearly rent of £30 out of the manor of Parham, co. Suffolk, now or late of William Willoughbye, knight, lord Willoughbye of Parham, bargained and sold to the Crown by Sekeforde; and for his service.　　　　　　　　　　　　　　　　　　　　　　　　　　　　　　　　　By p.s.

2222.)　24 *Dec.* 1576.　Lease for 21 years to Edward Butler of (1) lands (*named*) in Great Sonkye, co. Lancaster, parcel of the manor of Great Sonkye and leased by patent, 1 June, 3 & 4 Ph. & Mary, to Ranulph Worseley for 21 years from Michaelmas then next at a yearly rent of £18 19s., and (2) the manor of Great Sonkye, once of Walter Buckler, knight; with reservations, including wards, marriages, advowsons and all other regalities belonging to the manor; from Michaelmas 1578; yearly rent £30. For a fine of £120 paid at the Exchequer.　　　　　　　　　　　　　　　　　　　　　　　　　　　　　　　　　　By Q.

2223.)　2 *Jan.* 1577.　Grant for life to Henry Dynne of the office of one of the seven auditors of the Exchequer which shall next be void; with a yearly fee of £20, payable at the Exchequer. The present auditors are Francis Southewell, John Osborne, John Thompson, Thomas Neale,　　　　　　　　　　　　　　　　　　　　　　　　　　　　　　[*m.* 46] William Fuller, William Neale and Robert Hodgeson, each appointed by a several patent for life; the reversion of Southwell's appointment has been granted to Anthony Roue by patent, 5 Nov., 5 & 6 Ph. & Mary, for life and that of Osborne's to Robert Multon by patent, 8 Nov., 5 & 6 Ph.　　　　　　　　　　　　　　　　　　　　　　　　　　　　　　　　[*m.* 47] & Mary, during good behaviour.　　　　　　　　　　　　　　　　　　　　　By Q.

2224.)　20 *Dec.* 1576.　*Hampton Court.*　Grant to John Scudamore and his wife, Mary Scudamore, a lady of the privy chamber, their heirs and assigns of—the reversion and rent of a coney warren within Cranborne park, co. Dorset, and without in the demesne lands there leased (1) by patent, 7 [*recte* 27] June, 9 Eliz., *inter alia* to Henry, lord Herbert, for 21 years from Lady Day then last at a yearly rent of £13 6s. 8d. and (2) by patent, 16 July, 16 Eliz., (being therein described as parcel of the manor of Cranborne) to William Herle for 31 years from Lady Day 1588 at the same rent; the park of Blagedon *alias* Cranborne Parke, co. Dorset,　　　　　　　　　　　　　　　　　　　　　　　　　　　　　　　　　[*m.* 48] late parcel of the jointure of Catherine, Queen of England; and the coney warren within the said park and without in the demesne lands of the manor of Cranborne, late parcel of the same jointure. To hold in fee farm by service of the twentieth part of a knight's fee and by a yearly rent of £18 7s. 6d. Issues from Michaelmas last. The Crown to discharge the grantees from the payment of a yearly fee of £3 10d. granted to Henry, now earl of Pembroke, for the keeping of the park, 40s. yearly allowed to the keeper of the park for the sustenance of the wild beasts therein in winter and all other charges, except the rent and service above reserved.

For the said Mary's service. By patent, 24 Nov., 16 Eliz., the manors of Cranborne and Cranborne Aldersholte, co. Dorset, were leased to Edward Fitzgarrett with divers reservations including the demesne lands of the manor (being of the yearly rent of £13 6s. 8d.) and the coney warren of the manor (being of the yearly rent of £13 6s. 8d.) for 30 years from Michaelmas then last at a yearly   [*m.* 49]
rent of £30 7s. 11¼d.   By p.s.

2225.)   28 *Jan.* 1577.   Grant for life to Charles Arundell, the Queen's servant, of the offices of warden or keeper of the forest of Gillingham, co. Dorset, steward of 'le wodewardes courte' in the county of Dorset, keeper of the park of Gillingham, with herbage and pannage of the same park, and bailiff of the town of Gillingham and manor of Gillingham; with the wages etc. accustomed, payable out of the issues of the said manor; as now held by John Zouche, knight, or formerly by John Rogers; from the death, forfeiture or surrender of the said Zouche, to whom, by the name of John Zouche, the King's servant, the offices were granted by patent, 29 May, 31 Hen. VIII, for life.

Also grant (1) for life of the office of keeper of the park of Mere, co. Dorset, parcel of the duchy of Cornwall, and (2) for 60   [*m.* 50]
years, if he shall so long live, of the herbage and pannage of the same park; with the wages etc. accustomed for (1) payable out of the issues of the duchy; (1) as now held by the said John Zouche, knight, or formerly by Henry, late marquess of Exeter; (1) from the death, forfeiture or surrender of the said Zouche, to whom were granted (*a*) by patent, 10 Jan, 30 Hen. VIII, by the name of John Zouche, the King's servant, the offices of steward of the manor of Mere, bailiff of the same manor and keeper of the said park with the herbage and pannage thereof, for life, and (*b*) by patent, 21 Dec., 4 & 5 Ph. & Mary, the office of keeper of the said park, with the herbage and pannage, for life, the office of keeper of the said park, with the herbage and pannage, having also been granted *inter alia* by patent, 24 March, 1 Eliz., to John Zouche, his son, now deceased, for life in reversion rendering yearly for the herbage and pannage £5; (2) from the death, forfeiture or surrender of the said John Zouche, knight, and the end of the interest of Roger North, knight, lord Northe of Kyrtlinge, to whom by patent, 11 Jan., 16 Eliz., the herbage and pannage were leased *inter alia* at a yearly rent of 100s. for 31 years from the termination of the interest therein of John Zouche, knight, and his son aforesaid; rendering yearly for (2) £5 to the receiver general of the duchy or the bailiffs and receivers of the premises.

Also grant for life of the offices of steward of the manor of   [*m.* 51]
Mere, parcel of the said duchy, and bailiff of the said manor; as now held by the said John Zouche, knight, or formerly by the said Henry, late marquess of Exeter, or Edward Walgrave, knight; from the death, forfeiture or surrender of Zouche, to whom the offices were granted by patent, 26 April, 1 Eliz., for life.

Also grant for life of the office of steward of the manor of Gillingham and keeper of the courts held therein; with the wages etc. accustomed, payable out of the issues of the manor; from the death of the said John Zouche, knight, now holder of the office.   [*m.* 52]
For his service.   By p.s.

2226.)   1 *Feb.* 1577.   Grant to Edward Osborne, John Gresham and William Leveson, citizen and [—] of London, of the wardship and marriage of John Leveson, son and heir of Thomas Leveson; with an annuity of £10 from 21 April, 18 Eliz., when Thomas died.

By Q.

2227.) 9 *Jan.* 1577. *Gorhambury.* Licence for one year for William Drynker of Nordiam, co. Sussex, yeoman, to gather alms in the counties of Kent and Sussex; from the present date. For his service to Henry VIII by sea and land in the wars: he is very poor, aged, impotent and almost blind by 'mayhems' sustained in the wars, so that he is unable to help himself, his poor wife and children. *English.*   [*m.* 53]

By p.s.

2228.) 27 *Feb.* 1577. Lease for 21 years to William Hodgeson *alias* Hodshon of the deanery and vicarage of Lanchester church in the bishopric of Durham; with reservations; from Michaelmas last; yearly rent £28 10s.; the lessee to pay to the curate of Lanchester a stipend of £7 6s. 8d. yearly. In consideration of his surrender in Chancery of a patent, 29 April, 5 Eliz., leasing the premises to him for 21 years from Michaelmas then last at a yearly rent of £35 16s. 8d.; and for a fine of £28 10s. paid at the Exchequer.   By p.s.

2229.) 27 *Feb.* 1577. Lease for 21 years to Richard Easte of the rectory of Westwycombe, co. Buckingham, parcel of the possessions   [*m.* 54] late granted to Anne of Cleves; with reservations; from Lady Day next; yearly rent £21; the lessee to discharge the Crown from all proxies, synodals and other payments ordinary and extraordinary. In consideration of his surrender in Chancery of a patent, 3 July, 9 Eliz., leasing the rectory to him for 21 years from Lady Day then last at the same rent; and for a fine of £21 paid at the Exchequer.   By p.s.

2230.) 25 *Feb.* 1577. Lease for 21 years to Thomas Lancaster of a park called Dacre Parke in Dacre, co. Cumberland; with reservations, including the deer and wild beasts in the park, if any there be, and pasture for the same; from Michaelmas last; yearly rent £17. In consideration of the surrender by Lancaster of the interest therein of William Fitzwilliams and Robert Wiseman, to whom the park was leased *inter alia* by patent, 20 Dec., 15 Eliz., for 21 years from Michaelmas then last at the same rent; and for a sum paid at the Exchequer.

By p.s.

2231.) 25 *Feb.* 1577. Lease for 21 years to Philip Paskin and William   [*m.* 55] Rawlyns and the parishioners of the church of St. Stephen in Colmanstreate, London, of the rectory of St. Stephen aforesaid, once of the monastery of Butley, co. Suffolk; from Lady Day next; yearly rent £10; the lessees to pay all charges ordinary and extraordinary. In consideration of the surrender by Paskyn and Rawlins in Chancery of a patent, 10 July, 7 Eliz., leasing the rectory to Thomas Hargrave and Cuthbert Beiston and the said parishioners for 21 years from Lady Day then last at the same rent; and for a fine of £20 paid at the Exchequer.   By warrant of the commissioners.

2232.) 8 *Feb.* 1577. Pardon for Anne Abbes, wife of Thomas Abbes of Cawson, co. Norfolk, 'spynster', indicted at the sessions held at Norwich in 'le Shirehouse', co. Norfolk, on 9 Jan., 19 Eliz., before Thomas Gawdye, a justice of the Queen's Bench, Christopher Heydon, knight, William Paston, Ralph Shelton, Francis Wyndham and Edward Flowerdewe and their fellows, justices of the peace and of oyer and terminer in the county, for that she broke and entered the close and house of George Peters at Cawson on 30 Dec., 19 Eliz., and stole malt etc. (*described*) belonging to him.   By p.s.

2233.)   12 *Aug.* 1577.   *Gorhambury.*   Grant to Elizabeth Notte, widow,   [*m.* 56]
of the wardship and marriage of Anthony Notte, son and heir of William Notte; with an
annuity of 40*s.*, from 25 Nov., 19 Eliz., when William died. Yearly value of the inheritance
£18 10*s.* 1¼*d.*   By Q.

2234.)   16 *Aug.* 1577.   *Gorhambury.*   Commitment to Henry Mackwilliam of the custody
of John Mordaunte, a younger son of Philip Mordaunte, deceased, and his family and lands
during his lunacy. He was found by an inquisition taken at Brayntre, co. Essex, on 28 May,
17 Eliz., to be a lunatic enjoying lucid intervals.   By Q.

2235.)   16 *Aug.* 1577.   *Gorhambury.*   Lease for 21 years to John Moore,   [*m.* 57]
Thomas Cooke and Margaret Curteys, late relict of Henry Curteys, of—(1) lands (*named*) in
the lordship of Barkhampsted, co. Hertford, parcel of the duchy of Cornwall, and leased by
patent of the Exchequer, 10 May, 11 Eliz., for 21 years from Lady Day then last to William
Axtell at a yearly rent of 43*s.* 4*d.*; (2) lands (*named*) in Barkyng, co. Essex, parcel of the manor
of Barkynge and late of the monastery of Barkyng, leased by patent of the court of
Augmentations, 24 Feb., 5 Edw. VI, *inter alia* to Nicholas Celye, the King's servant, for 40
years from Lady Day then next at a yearly rent of £4 7*s.* 4*d.*; (3) the site of the manor of
Estymanner and a mill called Melyn Estymanner in Estymanner, co. Merioneth, parcel of
the principality of North Wales and leased by patent, 25 June, 7 Eliz., *inter alia* to Humphrey
Gylbert for 31 years from 25 April, 1573, at a yearly rent of 70*s.*; and (4) the site of the manor
of Burford, co. Oxford, parcel of the manor there and late of John, earl of Warwick,
exchanged, now in the hands of Edward Unton, knight, in right of Anne, countess of
Warwick, his wife, for life and conveyed by Unton and the countess to Edmund Harman,
now deceased, at a yearly rent of £11 3*s.* 4*d.* With reservations, (1) from Lady Day 1589; (2)
from Lady Day 1591; (3) from 25 April 1603; and (4) from the death of the said Anne,
countess of Warwick. Same rents.   [*m.* 58]
    For the service of the said Moore, Cooke and Henry Curteys, the Queen's servants; and
for a fine of £42 8*s.* paid at the Exchequer.   By p.s.

2236.)   26 *July* 1577.   *Gorhambury.* Lease for 21 years to Clement Gyles of lands (*named with
tenants' names*) in Melton Mowberye, co. Leicester, parcel of the lordship of Lewes, co.
Leicester, and once of the monastery of Lewes, co. Sussex, and late of Thomas, lord
Cromwell, late earl of Essex; with reservations; from Michaelmas next; yearly rent £6 12*d.*
(*detailed*). In consideration of the surrender by Gyles of the interest in the premises of
Anthony Gonson, to whom was granted by patent,   [*m.* 59]
10 Jan., 36 Hen. VIII, the Crown's interest in a lease of the said lordship in Melton
Mowberye to his father, William Gonson, esquire for the King's body, by Robert, prior,
and the convent of the said monastery by indenture, 17 April, 23 Hen. VIII, for 55 years
from the Invention of Holy Cross then next at a yearly rent of £14 12*s.* 1*d.* (payable at the
monastery or at the prior and convent's house in Southwarke in London called 'Wallnutt
Tree')—which William feloniously killed himself, by reason whereof his interest under the
indenture came to the Crown; and for a fine of £6 12*d.* paid at the Exchequer.
                                                        By warrant of the commissioners.

2237.)   16 *Aug.* 1577.   *Gorhambury.*   Commitment to Henry Mackwilliam, a gentleman
pensioner, of the custody of James Mordaunte, brother and heir of John Mordaunte, son
and heir of Philip Mordaunte, son and heir of Robert Mordaunte, and his family and lands
during his lunacy. He was found by an inquisition taken at Brayntree, co. Essex, on 28 May,
17 Eliz., to be a lunatic enjoying lucid intervals.   By Q.

2238.)   26 *July* 1577.   *Gorhambury*.   Presentation of Anthony Whyterowe, clerk, to the vicarage of Maddern with the chapel of Morva, Exeter dioc.   By Q.

2239.)   24 *July* 1577.   *Gorhambury*.   Pardon for Abraham Fowler and   [*m.* 60] John Fowler, late of London, 'yeomen', indicted for that they burgled the house and shop of Lawrence Atkynson, 'draper', on 22 May, 19 Eliz., in the parish of St. Gregory in Baynerdescastell ward, London, and stole goods (*described*) belonging to him.   By p.s.

2240.)   12 *Aug.* 1577.   *Gorhambury*.   Grant for life to Simon Bowyer, a gentleman usher, of the office of keeper and captain of St. Andrew's castle on the sea coast at Hamull, co. Southampton; with power to appoint 'a porter', 'a mayster gonner' and six 'soldyors' or 'gonners' there and for reasonable cause to remove them; with a yearly fee of £19 3s. 4d., and wages of 8d. a day each for 'le porter' and 'le master gunner' and 6d. a day each for the 'soldyors' or 'gonners', payable by the receiver in the county; from Midsummer last; as formerly held by William Hawkes, deceased, or John, marquess of Winchester. For his service.   By p.s.

2241.)   12 *Aug.* 1577.   *Gorhambury*.   Protection for one year for John Rowsse of Lenne Regis, co. Norfolk, merchant. In consideration of grievous losses suffered by him by robbers and in his wares and ships upon the sea, according to the testimony of George Baker, major of the borough of Lenne Regis, Christopher Grant, Robert Gerves, John Pell, Thomas Grave, John Grebbye, Francis Shaxton and Thomas Laborne, justices of the peace, and others, burgesses of the said town.   [*m.* 61] By p.s.

2242.)   2 *Aug.* 1577.   *Gorhambury*.   Pardon and discharge for William Morgan of Llanternam, co. Monmouth, late keeper of the seal of the Common Pleas, for all wrongful detentions and concealments of money and other offences committed in his office up to Michaelmas, 1 Eliz.   By p.s.

2243.)   6 *Sept.* 1577.   *Gorhambury*.   Pardon for Christopher Barwyke of London, 'maryner', indicted for piracy in that he with many others attacked a ship '*The Willyam*' belonging to Thomas Smyth of Great Yarmouth, co. Norfolk, 'merchaunt', on 2 June, 18 Eliz., on the high sea within the jurisdiction of the Admiralty and stole 'a crosse sayle' belonging to Smythe. By report of Thomas Gawdye, a justice of the Queen's Bench, William Paston, Francis Wyndham and William Heydon, justices of the peace in the county of Norfolk.   By p.s.

2244.)   7 *Sept.* 1577.   *Gorhambury*.   Grant to Margaret Denton, widow, and George Phetyplace of the wardship and marriage of Thomas Denton,   [*m.* 62] son and heir of Alexander Denton; with an annuity of £13 6s. 8d. from 7 Jan., 19 Eliz., when Alexander died.   By Q.

2245.)   6 *Sept.* 1577.   *Gorhambury*.   Pardon for Richard Horton late of Rochester, co. Kent, 'myller', indicted and convicted for treason in that on 1 Jan., 18 Eliz., at Rochester he struck four counterfeit 'twelve peny peeces' and uttered the same there, for all forfeitures by reason thereof.
By patent, 27 Oct., 18 Eliz., he had a pardon for the said offence.   By p.s.

2246.)   13 *Sept.* 1577.   *Gorhambury*.   Presentation of Charles Mathue, LL.B., clerk, to the rectory of Portlemouth, Exeter dioc., in the Queen's gift *jure devoluto*.   By p.s.

2247.) 30 *Aug.* 1577. *Gorhambury.* Grant for life to George Austen of   [*m.* 63]
the office of clerk of the peace in the county of Surrey.   By p.s.

2248.) 20 *Sept.* 1577. *Gorhambury.* Lease for 21 years to John Kynge of (1) demesne
lands (*named*) in Wyngham, co. Kent, late parcel of possessions of the archbishop of
Canterbury in the Crown's hands by act of Parliament, (2) demesne lands (*named*) in
Wyngham, parcel of the manor of Wyngham and late of the said archbishop and in the
Crown's hands by exchange, (3) woods etc. (*named with tenant's name*) by 'le Downe' in the
parish of Boxley or elsewhere, co. Kent, late of Thomas Wyatt, knight, attainted of treason,
parcel of the manor of Boxley, (4) woods (*named with tenants' names*) in Boxley, late of the said
Wyatt, parcel of the manor of Boxley, and   [*m.* 64]
(5) lands (*named)* in Boxley; with reservations; (1) and (2) from Lady Day 1591, having been
leased by patents, (1) 1 July, 12 Eliz., to William Oxenden and Henry Oxenden at a yearly
rent of £10 13*s.* 4*d.* and (2) 10 May, 12 Eliz., to Henry Jones the elder at a yearly rent of £8, in
both cases for 21 years from Lady Day then last; (3) from Lady Day 1594, having been leased
by patent of the Exchequer, 2 May, 15 Eliz., to Thomas Fludde for 21 years from Lady Day
then last at a yearly rent of 73*s.* 4*d.*; (4) from Lady Day 1590, having been leased by patent of
the Exchequer, 13 May, 11 Eliz., to Richard Eyre for 21 years from Lady Day then last at a
yearly rent, for them and other lands, of 51*s.* 10*d.*; (5) from the termination of a lease thereof
by the monastery of Boxley by indenture, 29 Feb., 27 Hen. VIII, to William Webbe for 60
years from Candlemas then last at a yearly rent of 20*s.*; yearly rents (1) £10 13*s.* 4*d.*, (2) £8,
(3) 73*s.* 4*d.*, (4) 18*s.* and (5) 20*s.*; the lessee to repair and maintain a bridge   [*m.* 65]
called 'Damebridge'; also to make two cuttings only of the woods and at fitting times, to
enclose and preserve 'lez sprynges' after cutting, and to leave sufficient 'lez staddelles' in
every acre according to statute. For the service of Matthew Kynge now deceased, and John
Kynge aforesaid, his son, farmer of the premises (1)—(4), the Queen's servants. By p.s.

2249.) 22 *Aug.* 1577. Confirmation of—a lease for 99 years by William Cordell, knight,
master of the rolls, by indenture, 26 March, 19 Eliz., to John Duddeley of Newyngton, co.
Middlesex, of (1) a portion of the great garden belonging to 'le Rolles' and adjoining Fewter
Lane, to wit, a garden in the tenure of John Thomwood and a garden in the tenure of [—]
Hoppes, widow, and (2) gardens in several pieces adjoining Fewter Lane, now or late in the
several tenures of Christopher Whichcote, William Strowde, Anthony Hyckmote,
deceased, William Pratte, Edmund Bradshawe, Thomas Marshe, Henry Elsynge and
Richard Tottell, containing about 1 ac., and (3) a tenement, 'a yarde' and a garden in
Chauncerie Lane, London, now or late in the tenure of Elizabeth Newman, widow; (1) from
Lady Day following the termination of a lease thereof by Robert Southwell, knight,
deceased, late master of the rolls, by indenture, 4 July, [2] Edw. VI, to William Honnynge
for 99 years from Lady Day then next at a yearly rent of a red rose at Midsummer if
demanded, which indenture was confirmed by patent, 10 Oct., 2 Edw. VI; (2) and (3) from
Lady Day last; yearly rents (1) a red rose at Midsummer if demanded, (2) 3*s.* 4*d.*
(Whichecote), 7*s.* 6*d.* (Strowde), 5*s.* (Hyckmote), 2*s.* (Pratte), 2*s.* (Bradshawe), 18*d.*
(Marshe), 18*d.* (Elsynge) and 2*s.* 6*d.* (Tottle) and (3) 6*s.* 8*d.*   By Q.
    Vacated, because surrendered by Duddeley, [. . .] *Feb., 21 Eliz. signed*: 'Wyll'm Cordell'.[1]

2250.) 7 *March* 1745. Petition to the master of the rolls by the   [*m.* 18*d.*]
warden and scholars of St Mary college of Winchester, commonly called New college,
Oxford, lords of the manor of Stanton St. John, co. Oxford, and of their tenants and farmers
and all owners of lands in the said manor and parish of Stanton St. John for the enrolment by

---

[1] The marginal note is partly illegible.

the clerk of the Chapel of the Rolls of a patent of the year 19 Eliz. exemplifying a commission, 29 April, 19 Eliz., and depositions taken thereon [*see* no. 2191 above]. The warden and scholars have been seised from time immemorial of a considerable estate in Stanton St. John which it has been customary to grant for three lives by copy of court roll, and they and their tenants there have common of pasture in the wood or coppice called 'Stonyhurst' and the woody and waste grounds called 'the Quarters', 'Menmarshe' and 'Waterperry Common', which have always laid together open and been enjoyed as one entire common; by virtue of the said commission witnesses were examined to prove the present petitioners' right to the common; search has been made in both the Tower and the Chapel of the Rolls for the original records exemplified, but they cannot now be found and are supposed to have been destroyed by a fire which burnt down the Six Clerks' Office in the reign of James I; the petitioners' property would be greatly affected by any loss or accident which might happen to the exemplification, as it is now very ancient and in a decaying condition. *English.*

    Noted in margin:—'Be it so. W. Fortescue'.

(*Ms.* 1d.—17d. and 19d.—36d. *are blank.*)

2251.)   9 *July* 1585.   Writ of *dedimus potestatem* to John Braddill,   [*m.* 37d.] John Chowe and John Haworth (or two of them) to receive the surrender of Rand Blacklock's patent [no. 2209 above].

    Return (*English*) by Braddill and Haworthe certifying that they received the surrender at Grymstongarth, co. York, on 1 Aug.   [*m.* 38d.]

(*The rest of the dorse is blank.*)

PART VII

C. 66/1157

2252.) 22 *July* 1577. *Gorhambury*. Grant in fee simple to Robert, [*m.* 1]
earl of Leicester, councillor, his heirs and assigns of lands (*named with tenants' names*) (1) in
Festynyock, in Llanvrothen, in Mantoroge, [*m.* 2]
in Llandekwyn, in Llanvihangell, in Trawsevenyth, in Llanvrothen, [*m.* 3]
in Nanmor, in Trawsevenyth, in Keysswyn, in Keven Rhos, in Rhiwogo, [*m.* 4]
in Brone y Price, in Pennall, in Kynvell, in Llanvaier, in Llanbeder, [*m.* 5]
in Llanenddwyn, in Llanaber, in Llanvachred in the commote of Talpont, in Nanney, in
Penerose, in a place called y Copple, called y Rhunvelyn and Dole y Kynhavon, in Blayne
Glynne, adjoining Maes y Carreg, in Nanney, in Dolgelly, in Brichdir, in Garthgynvawre, in
Diffredan, in Garthginvaure, in Dolgleder, in Diffredan, in Keven yr Owen, in [*m.* 6]
Kregennan, in Pennyarth, in Tremorna, in Rederewe, in Penaran, in [*m.* 7]
Llanthervell, in Y Garne, in Rhewedocke, in Nanfrire, in Keven Cum Iskadewe, in
Nanllidiocke, in Maystrane, in Strevelyn, in Gwernevell, in Kiltalgarth, in Gwernevell, in
Pennaran, in Maystrane, in Llanickill, [*m.* 8]
in Kyffdy, in Penmayne, in Llanbeder, in Llanvayer, in Trawsevenith, in the forest of
Snoden, in Llanbeder, in Llanvihangell, in Llandeckwyn, in [*m.* 9]
Llandanocke, in Llanvihangell, in Llandeckwyn, in Festynyock, in Trawsevenyth, in
Mantoroge, in Llanvayre, in Llanendwyn, in Llanvayre, in Trawsevenyth, in Corys, in
Kysewin, in Maysetrenaunt, in [*m.* 10]
Llanvihangell, in Kevenrhos, in Towen, in Llanglenyn, in Llanvawr, in Llanthervell, in
Llanuthlin, in Llanvawre, in Llanthervell, in [*m.* 11]
Llanvawre, in Llanuthlin, in Llanvawre, late of the monastery of Strata Marcella, in
Llanickell, late of the said monastry and in Llangowre, late of the said monastery, all in the
county of Merioneth, and (2) in Penvro, in Castle, in Llanbeder, in Llanglennyn, in Eryauns,
in Lleghan, [*m.* 12]
in Dwi Gevilly, in Llanvayre, in Bodselyn, in Treffelane, in Dolle [*m.* 13]
Paderne and Treffelane, in Reege, in Denorwecke within the parish of Llanberis or
elsewhere, in Dynlley, in Llangean, in Rhw, in Bodrith, in Llanvayre, called Twenymaine-
bras, in Llanvayer, in Penrhin, in [*m.* 14]
Roesveygh, in Llangwstenyn, in Llanwayer and (*or* in) Rhike, in Dihlley, in Elerneon, in
Cornegeough, in Penaghan, in Penaunt, in Penenett, adjoining 'le Frith' of Lloyne Llenor
Ucha, in Nantwhynan, in Lleghan and in Trevellon, all in the county of Carnarvon, all
which premises [*m.* 15]
were unlawfully enclosed or encroached upon by divers persons; to hold as of the manor of
Estgrenewich, co. Kent, in socage and by yearly rents of (1) £7 4s. 8½d. and (2) £5 12s. 1⅞d.;
the grant to be void in respect of any parcel of the premises of which the issues have before
this date been answered to the Crown; if the grantee cannot enjoy the issues of any parcel of
the premises, he shall be discharged of the rent thereof according to an apportionment made
in the Exchequer. For his service. By Q.

2253.) 20 *Feb.* 1577. Presentation of John Costerdine, M.A., to the rectory of
Litterworth, co. Leicester, Lincoln dioc., void by resignation. By p.s.

2254.) 7 *March* 1577. *Gorhambury*. Grant to John Farneham, a   [*m.* 16]
gentleman pensioner, his heirs and assigns of—(1) Plaxstoll *alias* Plaston chapel and 'le
chappell yarde' adjoining in Wrotham, (2) a decayed chapel called 'Saynte Margarettes
chappell' with 'le chappel yarde' and all lands belonging thereto in Daraunt *alias* Darnth
[*alias*] Darrant *alias* Drent, (3) lands (*tenant named*) in Grenestrete in Daraunte aforesaid,
Stone or elsewhere, given for obits and the like in the churches of Darrante or Stone or
elsewhere, and (4) lands (*named with tenant's name*) in Daraunt, given for lamps and the like, all
in the county of Kent; (5) a small ruinous cottage, chapel or hermitage in Heighgate in the
parish of Harensey *alias* Harningey or St. Pancras in the Fields, (6) lands (*named with tenant's
name*) in Ikenham, late of Hillyngdon or Woxbridge chantry, (7) lands (*named with tenants'
names*) in Uxbridge and Hillingdon, once of St. Mary's brotherhood or guild in the church or
chapel of Uxbridge, and (8) lands (*tenants named*) in Uxbridge, late of 'Sheryngtons chauntry'
in the church or chapel of Uxbridge, all in the county of Middlesex; (9) the chapel of
Cressage, co. Salop, and all its possessions in Hernage Graunge, Cressage or elsewhere, with
a small tenement there, now or late in the tenure of [—] Eldershawe, rector, or others; (10)
lands (*named with tenant's name*) in Northleverton, given for lamps and the like, (11) a small
ruinous cottage, where 'Saynt Laurence chappell' once stood, with land adjoining in Fenton
in the parish of Great Stourton (*named with tenant's name*), (12) lands (*named with tenant's name*)
in Fenton and (13) lands (*named with tenants' names*) in Northleverton and the lordships of
Northleverton and Hablestrope, given for obits and the like, all in the county of
Nottingham; (14) lands (*named with tenants' names*) in the parishes of Lancaster, Maverne and
Muggleswicke in the county of the bishopric of Durham, late of the monastery of Durham
or given for superstitious uses; (15) lands (*named with tenant's name*) in Flategate in the parish
of Howden, late of St. John the Baptist's chantry in Howden, (16) lands (*tenants named*) in
Rocliffe in the parish of Snaythe, late of St. Mary's guild in Rocliff, (17) lands (*tenant named*)
in Northgrymston, late of Grimston chantry or given for superstitious uses, (18) lands
(*tenant named*) in Grimston aforesaid, late of the monastery of Malton, and (19) 'Saynte
Ellyns chappell' and lands (*tenants named*)   [*m.* 17]
in Barnebye and Knedlyngton or elsewhere in the parish of Howden, given for priests and
the like, all in the county of York; (20) lands (*named*) in Bigleswade, (21) lands in Bigleswade,
Holme, Stratton and Langforde, called 'le Brotherhoode Landes and Tenementes' in
Bigleswade, (22) lands (*named with tenant's name*) in the parish of Sowthyell, called 'le
Brotherhoode Meadowe', (23) 'le Chapell Landes and Tenementes' of Holme in Holme in
the parishes of Bigleswade and Langford, (24) lands (*named*) in Bigleswade, (25) lands (*named
with tenant's name*) in Stratton in the parish of Bigleswade, (26) 'le Churche House *alias* le
Townehouse' (*tenant named*) in Old Wardon, (27) 'le Chappell Land of Stratton' in the parish
of Bigleswade, (28) lands (*named with tenant's name*) in Old Warden, (29) 'le Chauntrye
Landes' (*tenant named*) in Sondey, (30) 'le Churche Landes' (*tenant named*) in Sondey, (31)
'Lampe Landes *alias* le Lampelighte Landes' (*tenant named*) in Sondey, (32) 'Churche Close
alias le Close' (*described with tenants' names*) in Beeston *alias* Beson in the parishes of Norrell
and Sondey, (33) all lands in Bigleswade, Holme and Stratton late of the brotherhood of
Bigleswade, (34) lands (*named with tenant's name*) in Bigleswade, (35) lands (*named with tenant's
name*) in Holme in Bigleswade, (36) lands (*named with tenants' names*) in Bigleswade, (37) 'le
Churche Landes *alias* le Towne Landes' in Old Wardon, (38) lands (*named with tenant's name*)
in Wardon aforesaid, (39) lands (*named with tenant's name, including* 'le Churche Close *alias*
Towne Close', 'Lampe Pightell', 'Lampe Lande' and 'Churche Medowe and Churche
Lande' *alias* 'le Towne Meadowe and le Towne Lande') in Ravensden, (40) 'le Chappell
Close *alias* le Personage Close *alias* le Close' and 'le Chappell Land *alias* le Parsonage Land
alias le Land' (*tenants named*) in Beeston in the parishes of Norrell and Sondey, (41) a
messuage (*tenant named*) in Bigleswade, given for an obit in Bigleswade church, (42) 'Saynte
Leonardes' hospital and all its possessions in Bedford and (43) 'Saynte Leonardes Landes'

(*tenant named*) in Sondey, all in the county of Bedford; (44) lands (*tenant named*) in [m. 18] the parish of Trowell, co. Nottingham, some late of Cossall chantry, the others called 'Lampe Lande' and 'the Church Lande'; (45) a tenement in Lockington, co. Leicester, and (46) the advowson of the vicarage of Lockington, once of the monastery of Pré, Leicester; (47) lands (*tenants named*) in Forde and Fresford (*named*), once of the monastery of Bathe, co. Somerset, (48) two chapels, one called 'Capners chappell', and lands belonging thereto (*tenant named*) in Porteshed and Wynford *alias* Wynesforde, (49) a moiety of lands (*tenants named*) in Blackedowne, Yatton, Kyngeston Seymor and Bedmyster, given for priests in the churches of St. Werburgh (*Beat' Warborough*) and Ratclyff in the city of Bristoll or the like, (50) lands (*named with tenant's name*) in Glastonburye or elsewhere, once of the monastery of Glaston, (51) lands (*tenant named*) belonging to the late hospital of St. Mary Magdalen next Bathe, (52) a cottage in Kelneston *alias* Kelveston and (53) the advowson of the rectory of Kelneston, once of the monastery of Shafton, co. Dorset, (54) wastes (*named*) within the manors of Langport, Estover, Huishe and Pitney and (55) a chapel in Edgestocke *alias* Ichestocke and lands (*tenant named*) belonging thereto, all in the county of Somerset; (56) woods (*named with tenant's name*) in the parish of Bytton, co. Gloucester, once of the monastery of Kaynesham; (57) a moiety of lands (*named with tenants' names*) in Magotesfield *alias* Magnersfeld, co. Gloucester, in the parish of St. Philip without Laffordes Gate, Bristoll, and in Highe Streate in the city of Bristoll, given for chantries called 'Kemys chauntrye' and 'Fortheys chauntrye' in the parish of St. Philip aforesaid and to a brotherhood or guild called calenders in All Saints church, Bristoll, for obits in the same church or the like; (58) the rectory of Preston on Stower, co. Gloucester, and (59) the advowson of the vicarage of Preston on Stower, both once of the monastery of Tewkesbury, co. Gloucester; (60) the free chapel of Lynley, co. Salop, and all its possessions; (61) lands (*described with tenants' names*) in Evesham, co. Worcester; (62) lands

[m. 19]

(*named*) in Sutton Bonnyngton, co. Nottingham, given for lights and the like; (63) lands (*described with tenants' names*) in the parishes of St. Edmund, St. Sidwell and St. Mary in the county of the city of Exeter and the parish of St. Thomas, co. Devon, given for superstitious uses; (64) lands (*tenants named*) in a place called Kirkeland Hollyn (*alias* lands in Lepton in the parish of Kirkehead aforesaid), co. York; (65) lands (*named with tenant's name*) in the parish of Ekyngton, co. Derby, once of the guild or brotherhood of Ekyngton; (66) a wood (*named*) in Nashe in the lordship or parish of Whaddon, co. Buckingham; (67) lands (*tenants named*) in Spittlegate, co. Lincoln, late of St. George's guild, co. Lincoln, and lands (*described with tenants' names*) in Grantham aforesaid [*sic*], late of (*a*) St. George's guild aforesaid and (*b*) Holy Trinity chantry in Grantham or other superstitious uses; (68) a fowling or fishery in the manor of Barrowe and (69) lands etc. (*named with tenants' names*) in Barrowe, late of Thornton Curtesse college, co. Lincoln; (70) lands (*named with tenants' names*) in Barrowe, Barton and Burneham, late of Barrowe church, (71) lands (*named with tenant's name*) in Barrowe Ynges, late of Thomas Beckett's chantry in Barton, (72) lands (*tenant named*) in Barrowe, late of St. Mary's chantry or guild in Barrowe, and (73) lands etc. (*named with tenants' names*) in Barton and Witton, late of the monastery of Barney, co. Lincoln, all

[m. 20]

in the county of Lincoln; (74) all lands in Shirborne in the county of the bishopric of Durham or elsewhere, co. York, assigned to the late master or warden of Shirborne hospital for priests or chaplains or the like in the hospital chapel or in any chapel, place, church or oratory celebrating for the souls of Hugh, once bishop of Durham, all founders and benefactors of the hospital or others departed; (75) the free chapel of St. James of Duffield in the parish of Skipwith, co. York, and lands (*tenant named*) belonging thereto; (76) lands (*named with tenant's name*) in Cleabroke, co. Leicester, given for lamps in Cleabroke church; and (77) lands (*named with tenants' names*) in Gillmoreton, co. Leicester, given for lamps in

Gillmoreton church. Yearly value, according to several particulars thereof, £9 4s. 1d. To hold as of the manor of Estgrenewich, co. Kent, in socage and by year rent of (1) 4d., (2) 6d., (3) 4d., (4) 4d., (5) 4d., (6) 6d., (7) 3s. 4d., (8) 12d., (9) 2s ., (10) 6d., (11) 8d., (12) 4d., (13) 16d., (14) 2s. 4d.,   [m. 21]

(15) 4d., (16) 12d., (17) 12d., (18) 8d., (19) 16d., (20) 6d., (21) 6d., (22) 3d., (23) 6d., (24) 6d., (25) 4d., (26) 4d., (27) 4d., (28) 4d. and 4d., (29) 4d., (31) 4d., (32) 4d., (33) 6d., (34) 1d., (35) 4d. and 2d., (36) 4d., 2d. and ½d., (37) 2d., (38) 2d., (39) 6d., (40) 16d., (41) 4d., (42) 2s. 2½d., (43) 4d., (44) 4d., 12d. and 2s. 6d., (45) 12d., (47) 12d., (48) 8d., (49) 2s., (50) 2s. 6d., (51) 3s. 4d., (52) 12d., (54) 6d., (55) 12d., (56) 12d., (57) 12d., 12d. and 6d., (58) 20s., (60) 2s., (61) 4d., 2s., 4d. and 4d., (62) 2d., (63) 2d., 6d., 12d., 8d. and 6d., (64) 8d., (65) 12d., (66) 12d., (67) 12d., 6d. and 6d., (68) 3s., (69) 4s. and 12d., (70) 3s. 4d., 12d., 16d. and 4d., (71) 12d., (72) 3s., (73) 3s. 4d.,
                                                                                          [m. 22]

3s. 4d., 8d., 16d. and 6d., (74) 60s., (75) 10s., (76) 2s. and (77) 12d. Issues from the times when the premises or any parcel thereof should have come to the Crown. Power to sue in the Exchequer in the Crown's name for the premises and the rents thereof as the Crown could have done if the present grant had not been made. If any of the premises shall hereafter be lawfully recovered from the grantee's possession, he may in satisfaction of this grant have other concealed lands of the same value as those recovered, at a like rent. The patent to be void in respect of any   [m. 23]
of the premises which were not concealed at and down to the time of the first inquisition or of the first certification or information of the same premises.

   For his service.   By Q.

2255.) 8 *March* 1577.   *Gorhambury*.   Grant to Peter Greye, the Queen's servant, and Edward Greye, his son, and the heirs and assigns of Peter of—(1) lands in Fordham, co. Cambridge, held by tenants (*named*) by colour of a demise of certain inhabitants of Fordham; (2) lands in Billington, in Lynton (*tenants named*), late of Gresselye priory, co. Derby, and in Latton (*named*), late of the late chapel of Hatton, all in the county of Derby; (3) lands (*named, including 'le Churche Howse'*) in Brodweye, co. Worcester; (4) a third part of the tithes of corn (*named*) in Comotoyher, co. Radnor, late of the monastery of Stratflor; (5) the rectory of Hussington with all its appurtenances (*tenant named*) in Hussington or elsewhere, cos. Montgomery and Salop; (6) lands in Corvedon, co. Montgomery, and (7) a mine called 'a quarrell of slates' in Corvedon forest; (8) lands (*named with tenants' names*) in Crigiogg, co. Denbigh, late of the monastery of Vale Crucis, co. Denbigh; (9) lands (*tenant named*) in Mustwire in the parish of Corwen, late of the monastery of Vale Crucis, (10) lands (*named with tenant's name*) in the parish of Llandrillo, late of the said monastery, and (11) pools (*named with tenant's name*) in the parishes of Trawsevenyth and Llandrillo, all in the county of Merioneth; (12) lands in Kellynyock, (13) lands (*named*) in Cowrnowllys and (14) lands (*named*), late found by William Stinpe (*alias* Stympe), in Cowrne, all in the county of Anglesey and late of the monastery of Cowrnowe, co. Anglesey; (15) lands (*tenants named*) in Mels, co. Somerset; (16) view of frankpledge in Clifton, co. Bedford; (17) lands, including a cottage once used for a chapel and 'the chaple yarde', in Berick Solon, co. Oxford; (18) 'Lampe Meadowe' and a free fishery in Whitechurche, co. Oxford; (19) the chantry of Charnelhowse of the foundation of Andrew Jones   [m. 24]
and all other chantries in Hereford cathedral of the foundation of Roger Collebridge, Thomas Posforde, John Stambye, the dean and chapter, John Bacon, Joan Bohun, Andrew Seculer, Philip Haye, Thomas Absolon, John Middleton, William Radnor and Simon Radnor or others, St. Mary Magdalen's chantry there whereof John Batman was late chantry priest, the wax and oil used in the same cathedral for lights and lamps and all hereditaments given for the said chantries, wax, oil, lights and lamps, now or late in the

tenure of the dean and chapter and the vicars choral there; (20) lands in Madley, co. Hereford, given by Roger Beale for his obit in the church there; (21) lands (*tenant named*) in the parish of St. Nicholas in Hereford, given by the said Beale for obits and lights there and elsewhere; (22) lands (*tenant named*) in Kentchurche, co. Hereford, given for lights in Kentchurche church; (23) lands (*named*) in Brampton in the parish of Rosse, co. Hereford, given for a lamp in Brampton chapel; (24) lands (*named with tenant's name*) in Rosse aforesaid, given for a light before St. Mary the Virgin's image in Rosse church; (25) lands (*tenant named*) in the parish of Bristowe, co. Hereford, given for a lamp before 'le rode' in the said cathedral; (26) a rent (*tenant named*) in the parish of All Saints in Hereford, given for a lamp before 'le rode' in Hereford cathedral; (27) 'a chauntrie howse' in the graveyard of Hereford cathedral, built by Edmund Awdeley, late bishop of Salisbury; (28) lands (*named with tenants' names*) in the parish of Goodriche, co. Hereford, belonging to the late free chapel of Glewston; (29) lands (*tenant named*) in Lyngen, co. Hereford, late of the hospital of St. John of Jerusalem; (30) lands (*named with tenants' names*) in Byfelde, co. Northampton, given for obits and the like in Byfelde church; (31) lands (*tenants named*) in Wapnham, co. Northampton, given for lamps in Wapnham church; (32) lands, once of Horkesley Parva priory, co. Essex, (33) lands, late of the guild of Stoke next Nayland, co. Suffolk, and (34) lands, given by John Markes for an obit in the church of Stoke aforesaid, all (*named with tenants' names*) in Stoke aforesaid; (35) 'the gildehall' in Erlstonham, co. Suffolk; (36) 'the gildhall' in Erle Soham aforesaid and land there called 'Lampland' (*tenant named*); (37) lands in Cotton, co. Suffolk, given for guilds and the like; (38) woods (*named*) in Studham and Flamsted, co. Hertford, late of the monastery of Dunstable, co. Bedford; (39) lands (*named*) in Sandrishe, co. Hertford, late of the monastery of St. Albans, co. Hertford; (40) lands (*tenant named*) within the site of the manor *alias* 'le Deirey Howse' in Hemylhamsted, co. Hertford, late of the late college of Assheridge; (41) a tenement in the parish of St. Michael in Saynte Michelles Lane by Crooked Lane in Candelwike Strete ward, London, now or late in the tenure of James Jackson, escheated to the Crown; (42) a tenement in Iremonger Lane in London, in the tenure once of Ambrose Barker and now or late of Stephen Duckett, given for priests to sing for souls; (43) a parcel of pasture called 'Lame Pittes' with a conduit

[*m.* 25]

belonging thereto in the parish of St. Leonard in Shordishe, co. Middlesex, abutting to the South of 'le Spittle Fielde' and to the [—] on land called 'Mayhue', now or late in the tenure of Richard Acworth; (44) a yearly rent of 8*d.* out of tenements in Markelane in London once of [—] Coston, given by him for obits and the like; (45) a guild or brotherhood called 'Saynte Marie gilde' in the parish of St. Peter in Maldon, co. Essex, and all its possessions in Maldon or elsewhere; (46) a guild or brotherhood called 'Saynte Georges gilde' in the parish of St. Mary in Maldon aforesaid and all its possessions; (47) lands (*tenant named*) in Welton, co. Northampton, given by Richard Englond for an obit in Welton; (48) lands (*tenant named*) in Houton Magna, co. Northampton, late of the monastery of St. James; (49) land in Preston Stonowey, co. Northampton, escheated to the Crown; (50) lands (*named*) in Wotton, co. Bedford, late of the monastery of Harrolde, co. Bedford; (51) lands in Sutton, co. Bedford, given for an obit in Sutton church; (52) the rectory of Castelthorpe, co. Buckingham; (53) all lands in Petishoo, Eckney, Emerton, Craulye, Chicheley, Astley and other places, co. Buckingham, given by Richard Lyster, John Cottysford, clerk, and others in mortmain without licence; (54) lands (*named*) in Milton, co. Northampton; (55) lands (*tenants named*) in Poukesley, co. Northampton, once of the earl of Warwick, attainted; (56) lands (*named with tenants' names*) in Okeley, co. Buckingham; (57) 'the Churche House' and 'the Churche Lande' in Brill, co. Buckingham; (58) the tithes of conies, wood and underwood in the parish of Luton, co. Bedford, late of the monastery of St. Albans; (59) lands (*named with tenants' names*) in Okeley, co. Buckingham, some given for lamps and lights in Okeley church; (60) lands in Lamcote Ende in Tempesford, co. Bedford, given by William Gimber for an obit in Tempesford church; (61) lands (*described*) in the parish of Buckingham, co. Buckingham, parcel of the hermitage there; (62) lands in Ufford and Baynton, co. Northampton, escheated by the death of Joan Bayllie without an heir; (63) lands (*tenants named*) in Richemond, co. Bedford, given for anniversaries or the like in the church there; (64) woods (*named*) in the parish of Edsborough, co. Buckingham, late of the monastery of Dunstable, co. Bedford; (65) lands in Castor, co. Northampton, given for priests and

[*m.* 26]

other superstitious uses in Caster church; (66) 'le Holy Lofe Medowe' in Biddenham, co. Bedford; (67) lands (*named with tenants' names*) in the parish of Ouldwarden, co. Bedford; (68) 'the Churche House' in Henlowe, co. Bedford; (69) 'the Churche Howse' in Southill, co. Bedford; (70) 'the Churche Hedlondes' in Wodell, co. Bedford; (71) 'le Churche Grene' in Milton Harnes, co. Bedford; (72) 'le Churche Barne' in Milton Harnes; (73) 'Ravensden Churche Landes' in Wylden, co. Bedford; (74) a late chapel called 'Cressage chappell' with 'le chappell yarde', all hereditaments in a grange called Harrage Graunge in Cressage, co. Salop, belonging to the said chapel, and a cottage (*tenant named*) in Cressage; (75) a late chapel called 'Edstaston chappell' in Eddestaston, co. Salop, and lands (*tenant named*) belonging thereto; (76) the late chapel of Lynley with 'le chappell yearde', co. Salop, and the tithes (*tenants named*) belonging thereto; (77) the chapel of St. Mary of Broughton in Clauverley, co. Salop, and lands (*tenants named*) in the said county, given by [—] Chuckewell for priests in the said chapel; (78) 'Saynte Lawrence chappell' and the land whereon it now stands in the parish of Weston, co. Somerset; (79) all lands in Shrewsbury or elsewhere, co. Salop, now or late in the tenure or disposition of the wardens of the late guild of Holy Trinity or the brotherhood or mistery of drapers there, given for priests celebrating for souls in the chapel of Leybourne in St. Mary's church in Shrewsbury or other superstitious uses; (80) 'Saynte Giles chappell' and lands (*tenant named*) in Aston, co. Salop; (81) lands (*described*) in Westenslowe or in Stokesey, co. Salop, late of Ludlowe priory; (82) 'Lampe Acre' in Brodeweye, co. Salop, now or late in the tenure of the vicar there; (83) tenements (*tenant named*) by 'Owre Ladies priestes chamber' in Shrewsbury; (84) a cottage or 'le smythes forge' adjoining St. Nicholas's chapel in Shrewsbury (*tenant named*); (85) lands (*named with tenants' names*) in Willyngton, co. Hereford, late of Dimmore preceptory, co. Hereford; (86) 'le Churche Howse' (*described with tenant's name*) in the parish of St. Mary in Marleboroughe, co. Wilts; (87) the manor of Acton Pigott, co. Salop; (88) 'le Chauntrye House' in the parish of Comrawlye, (89) 'le Churche Howse *alias* le Gilde Howse' in Sidmoute, (90) a fair held yearly in the borough or town of Totnes, late of the monastery of St. Nicholas in Exeter, (91) lands in Herbarton *alias* Hamberton, given for obits and the like, and (92) lands called 'le Tynworke' or 'Wolworke Tinworke' in Raytre, given for lamps in the church there, all in the county of Devon; (93) lands (*named*) in the parish of Bray, co. Berks; (94) 'le Churche Acre *alias* Lampe Acre' (*tenant named*) in Oldwynsor, co. Berks; (95) 'an osyer platte *alias* the Churche Eight' in Oldewynsor; (96) lands in Newe Wyndsor, co. Berks; (97) lands (*tenants named*) within the lordship of Eglaston in 'le farrea' of Brimigam, late of the guild or brotherhood in Birmigham aforesaid, (98) lands in 'le   [*m.* 27] farrea' of Birmigham within the lordship of Dueston or Asson, given by William Lynche and Agnes his wife for priests and the like, (99) lands in Lapworth, Hampton Arden and Meriden and adjoining places, given for chantries and the like in the church of Asson aforesaid, (100) all lands in Edgebaston given by lady Middelmore, widow, for a priest celebrating for her soul's health in Edgebaston church, (101) a cottage (*tenant named*) in Brimigham, (102) lands in Harborne, given for obits and the like, (103) lands (*named with tenant's name*) in Edgebaston, escheated to the Crown, (104) lands (*tenant named*) in Lynyngton, late of the monastery of Kenelworth, (105) all lands in Barkeswell given for masses or the like in Weedon church, co. Northampton, and (106) lands (*tenants named*) in Willoughby, Dunchurche and Thurlaston, all in the country of Warwick; (107) lands (*named with tenants' names*) in Newton, given by Henry England of Newton for obits and the like in Newton church, (108) 'Churcheland' in Newton, given for obits in St. Catherine's church in Newton, (109) a fishery and waters (*named*) at Benwicke, late of the monastery of Huntingdon, (110) a water (*named*) in Benwick, late of the monastery of Crowland, (111) marshes (*named*) at Litleporte, given for obits and the like in Lytleport church, (112) land at Benwicke on which stood a chapel now decayed, 'le priestes chambre' belonging to the chapel and lands etc. (*named*), given for priests and the like, (113) six 'le swanne markes' with the swans, cygnets and other appurtenances thereof, of which two belonged to the monastery of Eley and one each to the monasteries of Barnewell, Anglesey, Denny and Chateris, and (114) lands (*named*) by Apshall in Litleporte, given for obits in Lytleporte church, all in the isle of Eley, co. Cambridge; (115) lands (*named*) in Eley in the parish of St. Marion, co. Cambridge, given for obits in Litleporte church; (116) a chapel and lands in Sibton, co. Oxford, given for priests and the like; (117) lands in Cleydon, co. Oxford, given for priests to pray for souls; (118) 'le Churchehouse' in East Hatley, co. Cambridge, (*tenant named*); (119) a late chapel and lands called 'Parsonnes Flattes' in Atterton in the parish of Witherle, co. Leicester; (120) lands (*named with tenants' names*) in Northlewerton, co. Nottingham, given for a light in Northlewerton church; (121) lands late parcel of the brotherhood of Gamlyngay, co. Cambridge; (122) lands (*tenants named*) in Asselby, (123) lands (*tenants named*) in Saffrone Gate in the parish of Howden, (124) 'Saynte Ellens chappell' and lands belonging thereto in Barneby and Knedlyngton or elsewhere in the parish of Howden (*tenants named*), given for a priest in the chapel, (125) lands (*tenant named*) in Howden, (126) lands (*tenant named*) in Wighton, given for 'the ladie Joyce Constables obite', (127) lands (*tenant named*) in Asselby, given for the same obit, (128)   [*m. 28*] lands (*named with tenant's name*) in Falgate in the parish of Howden, given to St. John's chantry in Howden, (129) lands (*tenant named*) in Bromefelde in the parish of Howden, late parcel of St. John the Baptist's chantry there, (130) a cottage (*tenant named*) in Hayelgate in the parish of Howden, parcel of the said chantry of St. John there, (131) lands (*named with tenants' names*) in Asselby in the parish of Howden, late parcel of St. Mary's guild in Howden, (132) lands (*named with tenants' name*) in Skilton in the parish of Howden, late parcel of St. John the Baptist's chantry in Howden, (133) lands (*tenants named*) in Rockyff in the parish of Snayth, late of St. Mary's guild in Roclyff aforesaid, (134) a cottage called 'Skelton chappell' (*tenant named*), (135) a cottage (*tenant named*) in Howden, late parcel of the said chantry of St. John in Howden, (136) lands (*tenants named*) in Wighton, given for obits and the like in Wighton church, (137) 'the Churche Close' (*tenant named*) in Wighton, given by lady Constable for her obit in Wighton church, (138) lands (*tenants named*) in Wighton, given for 'the ladie Constables obytt' aforesaid, (139) cottages (*tenants named*) in Wighton, (140) lands (*tenant named*) in Knedlyngton in the parish of Holden, belonging to the late chapel of St. Ellen, (141) lands (*tenant named*) in Barneby in the parish of Howden, late of Lymton chantry, (142) lands (*tenant named*) in North Grymston, late of Grymeston chantry, (143) lands (*tenant named*) in Northgrymston, late of the monastery of Malton, co. York, (144) lands (*tenant named*) in Kelweeke, given for obits and the like in Kelweeke church, (145) lands (*tenant named*) in Skerynge, given for priests, and (146) the guild or brotherhood in Rippon and its possessions, all in the county of York; (147) the rectory of Pynford and possessions thereof in Pinford, Sharneborne, Marborne, Castleborne or elsewhere, co. Dorset; (148) a chapel at Saynte Margarettes Hill in the parish of Darnte *alias* Darrant *alias* Drante, the site thereof with 'le chappell yarde' and two bells hanging in the chapel (*tenant named*), and lands (*tenant named*) there, given for priests and the like there, (149) a chantry in St. Mary's church in Feversham and all its possessions, (150) the manor of Estwickham, late of viscount Lovell, attainted, (151) a marsh (*described with tenants' names*) in Iwade, late of the monastery of Boxley, and (152) lands (*named with tenants' names*) in Newyngton, given for 'le rode lighte' there, all in the county of Kent; (153) a chapel in Melcom Turges *alias* Melcom

Hesey (*alias* Melcome Horsey), co. Dorset, and lands (*named*) in Melcom aforesaid, Armeswelles and Blackallers; [(154) lands (*named*) in Luttington in the said county][1]; (155) lands (*named with tenant's name*) in Lewes, (156) lands in Borne, (157) lands (*tenant named*) in Willington, (158) 'Brambylby *alias* Brambleby chappell' and lands (*tenant named*) in the parish of Grenestreate, (159) a chapel and lands (*tenant named*) in Ryngmere, (160) lands in Borne, (161) (*named with tenants' name*) in Hamsey, (162) lands in Marsefelde, in the

[*m. 29*]

tenure of the rector there, (163) 'Baldesden chappell' and lands (*tenants named*) in the parish of Rothingden, (164) 'Saynte Giles chappell' and the lands and tithes belonging thereto in Lynfelde (*alias* Lamfeilde), (165) 'a brewehouse' (*tenant named*) in the parish of Wynchelsey, (166) lands (*tenant named*) in Westhadly, (167) all lands in Mychyndy in the tenure of the vicar there, (168) lands (*tenants named*) at Blackhill in Lynfeld and in Lynfeld, (169) a chapel and lands called 'Wallyngworth chappell' in the parish of Chawley (*tenant named*), (170) all lands in the parish of Pecocke in the tenure of the inhabitants of Chawley aforesaid, (171) 'Owre Ladies chappell' in the parish of St. Michael in Lewes, (172) lands in the parish of Kyngstone by Lewes (*tenant named*), (173) lands in Mychenhame *alias* Newhame, in the tenure of the rector of Mychendhame, (174) 'Chaunterye Lande' (*tenant named*) in the parishes of Horsted or Hedley and (175) a sheep pasture in Plumton, all in the county of Sussex; (176) two cottages in Holstone in the parish of Rockland and all lands belonging thereto in Holstone *alias* Hollestone, Rocklound, Hellyngstone or elsewhere, co. Norfolk, (*tenants named*); (177) a messuage with a garden, co. Middlesex, called 'le signe of the Squerrell' in the parish of St. Botolph without Algate in Portsoken ward, London, once in the tenure of Robert Bradshawe and now or late in that of John Shaerd, once of the priory of 'le Minoris' in London; (178) a messuage in Newgate Markett in the parish of Christes Churche, London, between the tenements of Robert Crockett and Bartholomew Yardeley, in the tenure of [—] Spencer, widow; (179) lands (*tenant named*) in Banburye, co. Oxford; (180) 'the Churchefelde' (*tenant named*) in Southe Mymmes, co. Middlesex; (181) lands (*tenant named*) in Kentishe Towne, co. Middlesex; (182) woods (*named*) in Bissiter, co. Oxford, late of the monastery of Bissiter; (183) a cottage called 'the Bores Heade' in Candelwike Strete in London, now or late in the tenure of James Elye; (184) a cottage called 'the White Horse' in the same street and city, now or late in the tenure of William Drakes; (185) a messuage called 'the Horseshewe' in Candelwike Strete aforesaid, now or late in the tenure of Henry Lewes; (186) a small cottage in the parish of St. Bartholomew next West Smythfelde, London, late in the tenure of [—] Moreton; (187) two closes in the parish of St. Andrew in Holborne, now or late in the tenure of Richard [—], once parcel of the possessions of John Banister; (188) a tenement called 'the White Beare' in Candelwike Strete aforesaid, now or late in the tenure of William Castelton; (189) all lands in Creplegate ward, London, in the several tenures of Christopher Fulke, Elizabeth Hillyard and John Gilpyn; (190) all lands once belonging to a service called 'Foster service' in the church of St. Werburgh (*Sancti Warborowe*) in Bristoll in the said city or elsewhere; (191) 'Balleys chauntrie' in the church of Trinity *alias* Christeschurch in Bristoll with all its possessions; (192) all lands given for divers obits in the said church of Trinity *alias* Christchurche; (193) Trinity chapel or hospital in the parish of St. Philip in Bristoll and all its possessions in Bristoll or elsewhere; (194) 'the chappell of the Three Kynges of Culloyne' in the parish of St. Michael in Bristoll and all its possessions in the said city or elsewhere; (195) St. Catherine's chapel in the parish of the Cross of the Temple in Bristol with all its possessions in Bristoll or elsewhere; (196) the chapel of the Assumption of St. Mary the Virgin on the bridge of Bristoll in the parish of St. Michael aforesaid with all its appurtenances and the advowson belonging thereto; (197) the chapel of St. John the Evangelist *alias* 'Knappe chappell' in or next the church of St. Michael

---

[1] Omitted on the roll, and on the Originalia Roll (*E.* 371/474, no. 128) but a rent is specified below for lands so described. The relative part of the warrant (in *C.* 82/1322) is indecipherable.

aforesaid with its appurtenances and the advowson belonging thereto; (198) the chapel of Radcliff in the said city with its appurtenances and the advowson belonging thereto; (199) all lands in Gloucester or elsewhere in England given to the late master or warden of St.

[*m.* 30]

Bartholomew's hospital in Gloucester for a chaplain or chaplains in the church or chapel of the said hospital or elsewhere in any other chapel, place, church or oratory belonging to the Crown by stat. 1 Edw. VI but concealed; (200) the hospital or brotherhood of Holy Trinity in Wickrisington, co. Gloucester, with all its possessions in Wickrisington or elsewhere; (201) lands (*tenants named*) in Broughton, co. Chester; (202) a capital messuage called Balles Farme in Upton and Wirwyn, co. Chester, (*tenant named*); (203) lands in Mosten, Upton, Salghton *alias* Saughton, Farnall *alias* Teston Farnall and Tarven or elsewhere, co. Chester; (204) lands (*named with tenants' names*) in Muggleswick in Lancaster in the dioceses of York and Durham, once of the monastery of Durham; (205) lands (*tenants named*) in Dimolbye *alias* Dimbelby or elsewhere, co. Lincoln, given in mortmain; (206) lands (*named with tenant's name*) in Northstocke, late of the monastery of Owescrofte *alias* Owson, (207) lands (*tenants named*) in Grantham, late of 'the Trinitie chauntrie' in Grantham, (beyond lands of the said chantry granted by patent in the year 3 Edw. VI *inter alia* to Edward, lord Clynton), (208) lands (*named with tenant's name*) in Grantham, belonging to the Queen in right of her manor of Panton, co. Lincoln, (209) lands (*tenant named*) in Panton Parva, given for lights before St. John's image in the church there, (210) lands (*named with tenant's name*) in Harlaxton, belonging to the Queen by escheat in the manor of Paunton, and (211) lands (*named*) in Corby, given for a chaplain celebrating 'a masse of requiem', all in the county of Lincoln; (212) the rectory of the church or chapel of Garbouldsham All Saints, co. Norfolk; (213) the church or chapel of New Buckingham, co. Norfolk; (214) lands (*named with tenant's name*) in Flichinge *alias* Fletchinge, co. Sussex; (215) 'Seynte Flesshers chappell' in Stokeblisse, co. Hereford, and lands (*tenant named*) there, given for oblations and prayers in the said chapel; (216) waste land between Barnesley and Audesley Loore *alias* Audesley Lane or elsewhere in the parish of Barnesley and liberty of mining coal thereon; (217) lands (*named*) in the manor of Ecclesall in the parish of Sheffelde, co. York; (218) lands (*named*, including 'the Chappel Garth') in Ayskarth, co. York, in the lordship of Middleham; (219) lands (*tenants named*) in Woodford next Thrapstone and Denford, co. Northampton, given for obits and the like in Woodford church by John Goodson and Thomas Porchett; (220) lands (*named with tenants' names*) in the parish of Writtle, co. Essex; (221) lands (*named*) with the   [*m.* 31] tithes thereof in Wotton in the county of the city of Gloucester (*tenant named*), late of St. Oswald's priory; (222) lands (*named with tenants' names*) in Readinge, co. Berks, and all lands there late of the monastery of Readinge, reserving to the Crown certain lands (*specified*, including 'Saynte Edmondes chappell' and 'le Scole House'); (223) tenements (*named*) in the parish of Sonnyng, co. Berks, and all lands there late of the monastery of Readinge; (224) lands in Bridgenorth, co. Salop, late of a chantry in St. Leonard's church in Bridgenorth; (225) lands in Bridgenorth, given for a priest in Quatt church; (226) lands (*described with tenant's name*) in Bridgenorth, late of chantries in Bridgenorth and Worvild, co. Salop; (227) the tithes of corn and hay of lands (*named*) in Hencote (*alias* Hencottesty) and Shrewsbury, co. Salop, (*tenant named*), late of the monastery of Lilleshull, co. Salop; (228) 12 oak trees yearly to be taken by the prior of the late hospital of St. John the Baptist of Bridgenorth out of Morff forest, co. Salop, in allowance of as much dead wood and dry wood as a horse could draw in a day to the prior's hearth, granted by the Queen's progenitors; (229) lands (*tenants named*) in Spittlegate, co. Lincoln, late of St. George's guild in Grantham, co. Lincoln; (230) a cottage (*described with tenant's name*) in Grantham, late of St. George's guild aforesaid; (231) a cottage (*tenant named*) in Grantham, late of Holy Trinity chantry in Grantham; and (232) lands (*tenants named*) in London Thorpe and Manthorpe in the parish of Grantham, late of Holy Trinity chantry aforesaid. Which premises were concealed   [*m.* 32] from the Queen or from Henry VIII, Edward VI or Queen Mary up to 12 Feb., 18 Eliz., and are of the yearly value according to the several particulars thereof of £53 10s. 11d. To hold in fee farm as of the manor of Estgrenewich in socage by yearly rents of (1) 2s.. (2) (the premises in Billington, Lynton and Hatton) 2s. 6d., (3) 20d., (4) 2s. 6d., (5) 3s. 4d., (6) 12d., (7) 10d., (8) 3s. 4d., (9) (the premises in Mustwrid) 3s. 4d., (10) 2s. 6d., (11) 20d., (12) 2s., (13) 12d., (14) 3s. 4d., (15) none specified, (16) 20 d., (17) 12d., (18) 6d., (19) £4, (20) 8d., (21) 12d., (22) 16d., (23) 8d., (24) 2d., (25) 2d., (26) 6d., (27) 12d., (28) 2d., (29) 3d., (30) 12d., (31) 4d., (32) 8d., (33) 1d., (34) 2s., (35) 4d., (36) 6d., (37) 4d., [m. 33]

(38) 10s., (39) 26s. 8d., (40) 12d., (41) 3s. 4d., (42) 10s., (43) 6d., (44) 8d., (45) 20s., (46) 20s., (47) 10s., (48) 2s., (49) 4d., (50) 2d., (51) 12d., (52) 26s. 8d., (53) 26s. 8d., (54) 3s. 4d., (55) 16d., (56) 12d. (detailed), (57) 5s., (58) 2s. 6d., (59) 22d. (detailed), (60) 12d., (61) 6d., (62) 13s. 4d., (63) 3s. 4d., (64) 3s. 4d., (65) 6s. 8d., (66) 4d., (67) 12d., (68) 12d., (69) 12d., (70) 12d., (71) 16d., (72) 12d., (73) 4d., (74) 2s. 6d., (75) 12d., (76) 12d., (77) 2s., (78) 4d., (79) £4 6s. 8d., (80) 3s. 4d., (81) 3s. 4d., (82) 8d., (83) 2s., (84) 8d., (85) 6s. 8d., (86) 12d., (87) £3 6s. 8d., (88) 6d., (89) 4d., (90) 2s., (91) 20d., (92) 12d., (93) 10s., (94) 12d., (95) 8d., (96) 6s. 8d., (97) 12d., (98) 12d., (99) 2s., (100) 12d., (101) 4d., (102) 6d., (103) 4d., (104) 6s. 8d., (105) 23s. 4d., (106) 3s. 4d., (107) 2s., (108) 18d., (109) 20d., [m. 34]

(110) 3s., (111) 2s., (112) 8d., (113) 3s., (114) 6d., (115) 4d., (116) 6s. 8d., (117) 5s. 8d., (118) 2s. 6d., (119) 6d., (120) 8d., (121) 20d., (122) 3d. and 4d., (123) 6d., (124) 12d., (125) 6d., (126) 6d., (127) 12d., (128) 2d., (129) 2d., (130) 2d., (131) 2d., (132) 2d., (133) 6d., (134) 2d., (135) 2d., (136) 4d., (137) 2d., (138) 3d. and 2d., (139) 4d., (140) 4d., (141) 12d., (142) 6d., (143) 12d., (144) 6d., (145) 2s., (146) 20s., (147) 13s. 4d., (148) 8d., (149) 20s., (150) £3 6s. 8d., (151) 2s., (152) 2d., (153) 5s., (154) 3s., (155) 12d., (156) 4d., (157) 20d., (158) 12d., (159) 12d., (160) 6d., (161) 6d., (162) 8d., (163) 6d., (164) 6d., (165) 6d., (166) 4d., (167) 4d., (168) 6d., (169) 6d., (170) 4d., (171) 3d., (172) 6d., (173) 6d., (174) 6d., (175) 6d., (176) 10s., (177) 2s., (178) 3s. 4d., (179) 6s. 8d., (180) 2s., [m. 35]

(181) 3s. 4d., (182) 3s. 4d., (183) 2s., (184) 2s., (185) 3s. 4d., (186) 20d., (187) 3s. 4d., (188) 3s. 4d., (189) 2s. 6d., (190) 6s. 8d., (191) 2s., (192) 4s., (193) 20s., (194) 13s. 4d., (195) 6s. 8d., (196) 2s., (197) 2s., (198) 2s. 6d., (199) 20s., (200) 20s., (201) 20d., (202) 3s. 4d., (203) 10s., (204) 5s., (205) 2s., (206) 12d., (207) 2s. 6d., (208) 4d., (209) 3s. 4d., (210) 3s. 4d., (211) 6d., (212) 12d., (213) 3s. 4d., (214) 5s., (215) 3s. 4d., (216) 2s., (217) 12d., (218) 3s. 4d., (219) 4s. and 12d., (220) 31s. 6d. (detailed), (221) 2s. 6d., (222) 20s. (beyond £4 heretofore reserved to the Queen), (223) 10s., (224) 2s. 6d., (225) 3s. 4d., (226) 12d., (227) 2s., (228) 3s. 4d., (229) 12d., (230) 4d., (231) 6d. and (232) 12d. Issues from the times when the premises or any parcel [m. 36] thereof should have come to the Crown. This patent or the enrolment thereof to be sufficient warrant to the officers of the Exchequer to issue process in the Crown's name for the recovery of the premises to the grantees' use. If any of the premises shall hereafter be lawfully recovered from the grantees' possession, they may in satisfaction of this grant have other concealed lands of the same value as those recovered, at a like rent. The patent to be void in respect of any of the premises which were not concealed at and down to 12 Feb., 18 Eliz. For the said Peter's service. By Q.

(The dorse of this roll is blank.)

PART VIII

C. 66/1158

2256.)   8 *June* 1577.   Grant that Robert, earl of Leicester, baron   [*m.* 1]
of Denbigh, K.G., K.M., master of the horse, James Crofte, knight, controller of the
household, and Francis Walsingham, one of the principal secretaries, all councillors, Henry
Cobhame, Thomas Gresshame, William Wynter, William Allen, Lionel Duckett, John
Ryvers and James Hawes, all knights, Thomas Blanck, Anthony Gamage, Edward
Osborne, William Kympton, Thomas Pullyson, George Barne, Francis Bowyer and
Thomas Starkye, all aldermen of London, Henry Sackeford, Thomas Dudley, John Mershe,
Thomas Smyth, Gerrard Goore, Richard Merten, John Barne, George Bond, Richard
Saltonstall, John Spencer, George Heaton, Blaise Saunders, Arthur Dawbeny, Richard
Reynold, Robert Dowe, Christopher Hoddesdon, William Wydnell, Edmund Huggan,
Anthony Garrard, Thomas Braneley, Richard Stapers, Thomas Altham, Anthony
Jenkinsonne, Thomas Aldersey, John Heydon, William Hewett, Robert Brooke, William
Massam, William Whytemore, Richard Hale, Matthew Coulcloughe, William Merrick,
William Towresonne, Thomas Wilford, Hugh Offeley, Richard Maye, William Cockayne,
Olave Bur, Lawrence Mellowe, Edmund Ancelline, Henry Wallys, Henry Richardes, John
Hawes, John Hall, Richard Venables, John Byrd, John Wattes, George Holmes, John
Cage, Reginald Barker, Robert Howe, Michael Barker, William Wyntroppe, Henry Hewett,
Thomas Cordell, William Salter, Giles Fludd, Richard Rowed, Reginald Hollingworthe,
Thomas Cambell, Thomas Searl, Richard Goodard, Philip Smythe, Thomas Gore, Henry
Isame, John Hillyard, William Shacrofte, Jane Symcottes, John Watson, John Castlyn,
Thomas Castlyn, Roger Bodname, Richard Hewsonne, Richard Reynold the younger,
Thomas Myllyngton, Francis Wyght, George Clough, Jarvey Thurland, Cuthbert Brand,
William Mylford, Hugh Ingram, Robert Bringborne, George Howlmer, James Moreley,
William Barker, John Barker, Thomas Robynsonne, Nicholas Atkins, William Atkyns,
John Thomas, William Thomas, John Studderd, William Skydmore, Robert Chamberlayn,
Percival Hassell, Thomas Russell, Gregory Yonge, Anthony Peniston, Paul Bannynge,
William Harebrowen, Richard Foster, Martin Gosnall, George Kyrwyn, Thomas Audeley,
Edward Staper, William Weekes, James Staper, John Hawkes, John Rowles, Robert Jakes,
Oliver Growne, William Hylls, Edmund   [*m.* 2]
Anceline the younger, William Skevyngton, Emanuel Wyllys, Thomas Forman, William
Kevell, John Harvye, William Coole, William Welden, John Melowes, Robert Thomas,
William Jenynges, Ralph Crompe, Austin Fowlkes, John Sparke, Thomas Sparke, Geoffrey
Daines, John Newman, William Hamford, William Boroughe, William Gebbons, Robert
Sparke, Arthur Jervys, William Blag, John Bowrne, Anselm Beckett, Michael Locke,
Robert Pecock, John Johnsonne, Robert Cobbe, George Cullymer, Richard Barrett,
Ranulph Mannyng, Thomas Rosse, John Gardener, Alexander Avenon, Nicholas Hewett,
Ranulph Symmes, Baldwin Durrham, George Sutherton, Robert Walkedyne, Anthony
Key, William Typper, Bernard Hylls, William Harryes, John Hunt, John Newton, John
Chappell, Simon Brooke, Michael Barton, Henry Barwicke, John Wyght, Godfrey
Wylsonn, Richard Colwell, John Allen, John Audeley, John Whyttall, William Reynoldes,
Guy Howke, Robert Shorte, Robert Handley, Robert Philipson, Henry Brooke, John
Suragold, Hugh Layton, Thomas Clerke, William Asteley, Francis Shawe, John Rycarbye,
William Kelynge, William Vyllers, William Radford, Andrew Fones, Richard Glascocke,

Hugh Merske, Pierce (*Pirseus*) Salysburye, Peter Collyn, Henry Cowltres, George Turnor, Clement Draper, Hugh Johnson, John Thomas, John Audeley and Michael Boyle of the city of London, merchants, Robert Shappey, Thomas Chester, Thomas Kelke, John Browne, George Snigge, Thomas Aldworthe, William Yonge, Richard Yonge, Walter Pykes, Thomas Rowland, William Hygges, William Gyttyns, Robert Ketchyn, William Saltren, Robert Hubbtyn, John Ashe, Walter Stanfast, William Coxe, Robert Presey, William Kyrke, Edmund Smythe, John Carr, John Draper, Robert Tyndall, Thomas Symons, Richard Fawance, William Warford, Ranulph Wylborn, Thomas Meyllyn, Robert Hambyn, Edward Culemore, Robert Taylor, Robert Samford, Edward Chester, Andrew Cotterell, Richard Bennett, Richard Saltren, Bartholomew Poyner, Richard Langford, Thomas Deconson, John Saunders, George Wylson, Miles Deconson, John Bysse, Walter Dull, Robert Sheward, Henry Robertes, Thomas Cutt, Robert Cable, Thomas Lacye, William Sparte, Rice Johnes, Robert Powey, William Smythe, Richard Berrett, John Powell, Nicholas Gamsheford, Richard Dane, Nicholas Hylckes, Miles Yevans, Francis Rowley, John Clerke, Thomas Davys, Henry Goughe, Nicholas Cutt, Richard Kelke, Henry Collymer, John Hopkyn, George Badram, Robert Allyn, Nicholas Thorne, Nicholas Ware, John Geruys, John Bradshawe and John Sachefield, merchants of Bristoll, John Peter, William Chappell, Simon Knyght, Nicholas Martyn, Eustace Oliver, Thomas Martyn, George Perryman, William Martyn, Thomas Chappell, John Peryam, John Hackwell, Thomas Spycer, Nicholas Spycer, Richard Hardyng, John Chappell, John Fallett, John Levermore, John Huchyns, Henry Paramore, John Crosse, Richard Newman, Richard Swete, Francis Tucker, Henry Ellys, Philip Yard, William Perrye, Richard Perrye, John Sandye, Valentine Tucker, Richard Dorchester and John Applyn, merchants of Exeter, John Thorneton, James Clerkesonne, John Smythe, William Wylsonne, John Fawether, Luke Thurscrosse, John Loggyn, Christopher Loggyn, Geoffrey Gefferdsonne, John Gee, Edward Thorneton, George Smyth, Richard Loggyn and Christopher Thorneton, merchants of Kyngestonne on Hull, Oliver Lison, Humphrey Ryckthorne, Philip Best, Richard Wanden, Walter Leson, Richard Solder, Hugh Typpton, Thomas Sparke, William Golding, Edward Lewys, John Fletcher, Robert Clerke, John Deane, Leonard Chylton, Alexander Hamon, Robert Byrd, Ralph Cotton, Edward Burnell, John Altroppe, Edmund Bowne, John Coldwell, John Curton, William Wyld, Simon Burman, Henry Hawkes, Botolph Holder, Hugh Johnson and William Otborowe, merchants residing in divers places in Spain and Portugal, John Crooke, William Staveley, Nicholas Chapelyn, Richard Goddard, John Bullycard, Robert Moore, John Favor, Peter Stoner, Richard Bysonne, Emery Lakes, Alexander Peynton, John Addyson, Robert Norman, John Erington, Paul Staveley, Thomas Demerecke, Peter Jaunrynne, Bernard Courtmell, Richard Elner, Andrew Harryes, John Harper, Walter Earle, William Chydley, John Carewe, Stephen Bartye, John Sedgeswyck and John Marche the younger, merchants resident in Southampton, and all others the Queen's subjects engaged in trade in Spain and Portugal before 1 Jan. 1568 [/9], together with their children and apprentices, may be a fellowship by the name of the president, assistants and fellowship of merchants   [*m.* 3] of Spain and Portugal; and incorporation of the same. The society to have a president and 40 assistants. John Mershe to be and continue in the office of president from the present date until Monday before Lady Day 1578 and thereafter until another be appointed and sworn, if he shall so long live. There shall be 40 of the better persons of the fellowship, whereof ten at least shall be inhabitants in places outside London, who shall be called the assistants and chief councillors, assisting the president or his deputy or deputies in all matters touching the fellowship; appointment of James Hawes, knight, Edward Osborne, Thomas Poolyson, George Barne, Francis Bowyer and Thomas Starkye, aldermen of London, Richard Saltonstall, John Spencer, Thomas Aldersey, Richard Reynoldes, Blaise Saunders, Arthur Dawbney, William Wydnall, Anthony Garratt, William Towerson, Christopher Hodsdon,

Thomas Wylford, William Hewett, John Heydon, William Massam, William Cockayne, Thomas Branbey [*sic*], Richard Staper, Richard Venables, John Hawes, George Homes, Richard Goddard, John Wattes, William Salter and Richard Rouyhedd, citizens of London, Thomas Chester, Thomas Aldeworthe and William Gyttyns, citizens of Bristoll, Eustace Oliver, citizen of Exeter, John Crooke and William Staveley, merchants of Southampton, John Barker of Gipswiche, merchant, and John Hornton and John Fowether of Kingeston upon Hull, merchants of the fellowship, to be the first and present assistants and chief councillors during good behaviour. Power for the president or his deputy or deputies, with the assent of the assistants or a majority of them, to appoint at will anyone in the fellowship to be their president or presidents in the parts of Spain and Portugal; which president and presidents, with six other merchants of the fellowship there whom he or they shall associate with himself or themselves as assistants in the place where the said president or presidents in those parts shall reside, shall have power in the said realms, within limits prescribed for them by the president and assistants resident in England, to govern all merchants, subjects of the Crown, whether of the fellowship or not, and their factors, agents and servants trading in Spain or Portugal, to administer to them full and speedy justice in all causes arising between themselves in the said realms and to do all things which shall by the president or his deputy and the assistants be ordered according to the ordinances of the fellowship. Power for the assistants yearly on Monday before Ascension to elect one of themselves as president for one year, to be sworn before his predecessor, if present, in the presence of a majority of the assistants and fellowship; if the president shall die or be removed from office, the assistants may elect another from among themselves for the rest of the year, being sworn as aforesaid. Whenever any of the 40 assistants shall die, be absent from their place of assistant or be removed, the other assistants and the fellows of the fellowship may elect others of the commonalty of the fellowship in their places, to be sworn before the president and a majority of the other assistants. The president or his deputy or deputies and the assistants and fellowship may convene courts and assemblies of the whole fellowship at a convenient place in London or elsewhere both in England and in   [*m.* 4]
Spain and Portugal whenever it shall seem necessary to the president or his deputy or deputies for the good of the fellowship. Power for the president of his deputy or deputies and the assistants to make ordinances for the government of the fellowship, so that they be not repugnant to any treaties between the Crown and any prince or power, for the government both of the president, assistants and fellowship and of all others the Crown's subjects trading in the regions aforesaid, to revoke the same and to cause them to be executed both in England and in the regions aforesaid. Power for the president or his deputy or deputies and the assistants to impose levies on wares carried to or from Spain or Portugal or the isles belonging to the said realms to the South or West or ships laden therewith. If any of the fellowship summoned by officers of the fellowship to appear at any court or assembly appointed by the president or his deputy or deputies shall not come, or if any of the fellowship or any of those trading in the said realms shall not pay the levies imposed on their wares or ships, or if any commit any trespass against the liberties of the fellowship hereby granted or any ordinance made aforesaid, or if any attempt by any manner or craft or understanding with any alien prince or magistrate or alien born to infringe the privileges contained in these presents, the president or his deputy or deputies and the assistants may commit him to prison and detain him there until he be released by them or punished by such fine or penalty as they shall award. Also—whereas divers the Queen's subjects, inexpert in the order and practice of trade, in the laws of Spain and Portugal and in customs, weights and measures and other things appertaining to the merchant, commit by their ignorance many great inconveniences to the offence of the Queen and of the Kings of Spain and Portugal—order that none of the Queen's subjects not of the fellowship shall intermeddle in trade in the parts of Spain and Portugal from Fuenterrabia (*Oppido Fontrabi*) in the realm of

Biscay (*Biskaye*) throughout the coasts of Spain and Portugal as far as Barcelona (*Barsilonam*) or in the isles thereto belonging to the South or West, who shall not keep all such ordinances and be subject to the president or his deputy in all such things as those of the fellowship should be, under pain of the Queen's indignation and payment of the penalties due for[*m.* 5] transgression of the ordinances aforesaid; the president or his deputy or deputies and the assistants may by fines, imprisonment and other penalties and means according to their will compel all subjects of the Crown not of the fellowship to desist from trading there contrary to these presents; penalties levied to be to the use of the fellowship. The president, assistants and fellowship shall not admit into the fellowship a professor of any mechanical craft or craftsman, nor the sellers of wares piecemeal called retailers (*retalliatores*); but they shall not refuse to admit merchants not being of another fellowship of merchants because on 1 Jan. 1568 [/9] they had transported wares of England into Spain or Portugal by way of trade, provided that within one year after the present date they seek to be admitted and at the time of admission they are willing to pay to the fellowship £5 by way of fine and that they take such oath either in England or in Spain or Portugal, where it shall seem more convenient to him that seeks admission, as any others being admitted there shall be bound to take; they shall also admit all other merchants subjects of the Crown (except those aforesaid) who shall seek it and shall at the time of admission pay by way of fine £10 to the use of the fellowship and take oath as aforesaid; but, notwithstanding any supposed exception, other merchants subjects of the Crown being of some other fellowship shall be admitted into this fellowship also, so long as they seek it and at the time of admission pay by way of fine or recognisance such sums to the use of the fellowship as are wont to be paid by those being admitted by redemption into that fellowship from which they are passing into this one, and take oath in the manner aforesaid. The president or his deputy and the assistants may expel anyone of the fellowship therefrom for offences against its ordinances, and persons so excluded shall thenceforth not intermeddle with the fellowship, with the exercise of trade or with any traffic of merchandise there. Power for the president or his deputy or deputies and the assistants to appoint such officers and ministers as shall seem necessary both in London and elsewhere in the Queen's dominions and in the regions overseas aforesaid to levy impositions and penalties from persons found guilty of offences contrary to this patent and any ordinance made by the president or his deputy or deputies and the assistants; such officers and ministers to have power for default of payment or for disobedience to apprehend the bodies and goods of offenders and detain the same until they make satisfaction or compound for their default with the president or his deputy or deputies and the assistants. All officers and ministers of the Crown to assist the president or his deputy or deputies and the assistants in the execution of the said ordinances, and, if   [*m.* 6] the president or his deputy or deputies shall send any of the fellowship or other subject of the Crown to any gaol, the wardens and keepers thereof shall receive them and keep them at the transgressor's costs until the president or his deputy or deputies give consent to their release; and the Crown will not release them without such consent and until they have obeyed in all things and paid, to the use of the fellowship, such penalties as by the president or his deputy or deputies have been awarded. Licence to acquire in mortmain lands to the yearly value of 100 marks not held of the Crown in chief or of the Crown or others by knight service. The patent to be interpreted in the courts of the Crown and all other places within the Crown's dominions to the benefit of the president, assistants and fellowship against the Crown.

By patent, 1 Sept., 22 Hen. VIII, divers liberties were granted to the merchants trading in Spain in the parts of Andelasia; but that patent procured not so good an effect as was hoped, because of the imperfection thereof and because the merchants for lack of full incorporation had no power to make ordinances for their better government.   By Q.

2257.)   8 *June* 1577.   Licence for 30 years for William Waade of Hampsted, co. Middlesex, and Henry Mekyns *alias* Pope of London, jeweller, to make sulphur, brimstone and oils in any places in England and Ireland   [*m.* 7]
with any manner of minerals, seeds, herbs, fruits, roots, nuts, berries and other things there growing or being; from the present date. With power in the Crown's name to take up young persons of 20 years or under and keep them apprentice for eight years to work and learn the art of making sulphur, brimstone, oil or soap; also to take up other persons to work in the said occupations, for such reasonable wages as by law labourers ought to have; also to take up, by consent of the parties being owners and having interest, any wood, timber, empty casks, land, houses, mills, buildings, carriage and other necessaries belonging to the Crown or its subjects; also power to do all things necessary for the growing or getting of seeds, minerals and other things and the making and keeping of sulphur, brimstone, oils or soap; so as they at their own costs first compound with persons having interest in the woods, timber, lands and other things taken up. If the licensees cannot agree with such persons having interest, then   [*m.* 8]
upon complaint made by the licensees a justice of the peace in the place where the things are shall make agreement between them; and, if controversy in any such case cannot by that means be speedily agreed, four, three or two of the Privy Council (the chancellor of England, the keeper of the great seal, the treasurer or the principal secretary being one) shall with the consent of the parties make agreement between them. Order—hereby openly published—that all persons in England and Ireland shall yearly from St. Bartholomew's Day next during the term of this licence till and sow with hempseed and flaxseed *alias* linseed so much of their best ground, in such manner and under such penalties as is appointed in stats. 24 Hen. VIII and 5 Eliz. for the sowing of hempseed and flaxseed; printers to the Crown to print during the said term such a number and so many of the Queen's proclamations for tilling and sowing with hempseed or flaxseed as to the treasurer and principal secretary shall be thought good; justices, mayors and other head officers to receive the same and in the Queen's name to command that all her subjects during the term shall observe the said statutes in every place within their several jurisdictions where the treasurer and principal secretary shall appoint that proclamation be made. No persons other than the licensees shall directly or indirectly exercise the arts of working or making sulphur, brimstone or oil with things growing or being within the Queen's dominions whereof sulphur, brimstone or oil may be made; no persons other than the licensees shall buy any such things, but only such persons as shall sow the same so bought on their own ground or therewith feed their own birds, fowls or cattle or use the same in their medicines, man's meat or sauce; no persons to ship any things growing or being within   [*m.* 9]
the Queen's dominions whereof sulphur, brimstone, oil or soap may be made or any fresh or corrupt butter or waste foul soap, ashes or empty cask to the intent to transport the same overseas, on pain of imprisonment for one year and forfeiture of £40 for every offence. No person that shall be owner, master or taking any charge of a ship or shall be customer, controller or searcher for the Crown, or any person using the authority of any their several offices, permit any soap but such as they know to be good and sweet Syvyll soap during the said term to be landed at any place within the Queen's dominions, or permit anyone to ship overseas or from port to port within her dominions any things whereof sulphur, brimstone or oil may be made or any waste foul soap, ashes, corrupt, curd or fresh butter or any empty cask, or make any entry thereof, receive any subsidy or custom or give any cocket or other warrant for the same, on pain of imprisonment for one year, forfeiture of £40 for every offence and forfeiture of every office or deputation held at the time of the offence. No one during the said term shall bring into any place in the Queen's dominions or to cause to be made, boiled or sodden or to offer for sale in any place in the Queen's dominions any manner of soap wherein shall be used train oil, whale oil or other fish oil or tallow, suet, fat or

kitchen stuff, fresh, corrupt or other butter, or shall use in the making of cloths, kerseys or bays any train oil, whale oil or other fish oil, or shall offer for sale in any place in the Queen's dominions any train oil, whale oil or other fish oil to persons other than shoemakers, curriers and such as use the same about the making, currying or perfecting of leather or such as use it about the making of friezes or cottons, on pain of imprisonment for one year and forfeiture of £40 for every offence. Also—that good butter shall hereafter be made as in time past—order that all persons in the Queen's dominions shall during the said term make perfect, good, sweet and wholesome butter for man's body, make it only of perfect, good and sweet cream and perfectly make and salt it with good, perfect white salt upon salt so that it shall continue good, and shall not put any unsweet, corrupt or fresh butter, curd or whey butter or any butter made of curds or whey into any butter that may be for man's sustenance nor make or offer for sale any butter wherein shall be put any fresh, whey or curd butter or any butter made of whey or curds or unwholesome, unsweet, unsalted or ill salted butter, on pain of imprisonment for one year and forfeiture of £20 for every offence. Also—in consideration of the licensees' great charges about the provision of mills and houses, workmen and the like, and that there may be sufficient minerals and seeds   [*m.* 10] for the more abundant making of sulphur and brimstone, oil and soap, and that mills and workmen that be idle may be set on work about the same—grant to the licensees of a moiety of forfeitures due to the Crown from any persons in respect of offences against the orders contained in this patent. If any person shall resist the licensees concerning the execution of the premises or commit any offence hereunder and shall not compound with the licensees, they may in their own name or the Crown's prosecute him in any of the Queen's courts of record at Westminster. Also—forasmuch as the licensees will not be able at any one place to provide so many mills, workmen and other things as will serve to make all the minerals, seeds and other things growing or being in the Queen's dominions into sulphur, brimstone, oil and soap—they may buy any empty cask and any fresh, corrupt, curd and whey butter, fat, grease and kitchen stuff and mix them with the said oils to delay the heat of the same and use the casks about the said oils and mixtures, and may sell the oils whether by themselves or so mixed in any place in the Queen's dominions; and any person may buy the same and use them about the making of cloth, kerseys or other woollen commodities. The licensees may ship from   ·   [*m.* 11] port to port within the Queen's dominions any fresh or corrupt butter, waste foul soap, ashes and empty cask and such minerals, seeds and other things whereof sulphur, brimstone, oil or soap may be made; and every person that is officer or subject to the Crown shall suffer them to ship the same and speedily make entry thereof and give them such cocket or other warrant, taking sufficient bonds for discharging the same stuff on land, as in such cases of transporting from port to port is commonly used, notwithstanding any law or restraint or any order in these presents expressed. The licensees may with any searcher or other ordinary officer in any place within the Queen's dominions in the Queen's name search any ship, house and place and provide and see that no things whereof sulphur, brimstone or oil may be made are carried out of the Queen's dominions, also that no fresh, corrupt, curd or whey butter, waste foul soap, ashes or empty cask are shipped out of the Queen's dominions, and that no soap wherein shall be used any train, whale or other fish oil or fish liver oil, tallow, suet, kitchen stuff, fresh, corrupt, curd, whey or other butter shall be brought in and offered for sale in the Queen's domions; and may search out offences against anything licensed or granted in this patent. The Crown will not grant any licence or pardon other than to the present licensees touching anything done contrary to these presents. All judges and other officers and subjects of the Crown shall upon sight of these presents or the duplicate, exemplification or enrolment thereof aid the licensees in the execution of the premises for the best advantage of the licensees. The licensees to deliver to the Crown at the Tower of London in Hilary term yearly a tenth part of all sulphur and brimstone made by them or by

any other to their use; and also likewise from time to time to deliver all the rest   [*m.* 12]
of such sulphur and brimstone to the Queen at the places where the same shall be made,
upon ready payment for the same after the rate of a twelfth cheaper than the ordinary price
thereof. The patent to be construed to the benefit of the licensees. Provided that, if it shall
appear to the Queen that anything in this patent will be prejudicial to her or to her realm, the
licensees, being called before the Council to answer thereunto, shall stand to obey such
order as they shall take therein; or otherwise after one half-year's warning given to the
licensees under the signet or sign manual the present grant shall be void. Provided also that,
if the licensees shall not before the end of three years from the present date make within the
Queen's dominions so many tons of oil of rape seed and others things as in any one year
these three years past tons of train, whale or other fish oil have been brought in from
overseas and have been entered in the custom books of the port and city of London, it shall
be lawful for any person within the Queen's dominions to use train, whale and other fish oil
about the making of Northern cloths and Northern kerseys until the licensees shall make
that quantity of oil yearly of rape seed and other things.

In consideration of the surrender in Chancery by the said William Waade, son and heir
and sole executor of Armigell Waade, of a patent, 18 June, 7 Eliz., granting to the said
Armigell and William Hearle (who before Armigell's death released by deed his right to
him) a licence to make sulphur and oil in England for 30 years from that date.   *English.*

By p.s.

2258.)   3 *June* 1577.   *Gorhambury.*   Lease for 21 years to Nicholas Arrington, provost or
undermarshal of the town of Berwick, of (1) the tithes of corn (*tenants named*) of the towns of
Shaftowe and Belforthe, co. Northumberland, parcels of the cell of Banboroughe, co.
Northumberland, parcel of the monastery of St. Oswald, co. York, (2) lands (*tenants named*)
in Stannyngton and Meresen, co. Northumberland, once of the monastery of Newmyster,
(3) the rectory of Mydleton, co. Warwick, once of Tamworth college, co. Warwick, (4)
lands (*named*) in Walton, co. Stafford, once of Stone   [*m.* 13]
priory, co. Stafford, and (5) lands (*named with tenants' names*) in Wetherby, co. York, once of
the hospital of St. John of Jerusalem; with reservations; (1) from Lady Day 1584, having
been leased by patent, 10 July, 5 Eliz., to Robert Constable for 21 years from Lady Day then
last at several yearly rents of 100s. and 106s. 8d.; (2) from Lady Day 1583, having been leased
by patent, 20 June, 4 Eliz., to Hugh Storye for 21 years from Lady Day then last at a yearly
rent of £4; (3) from Lady Day 1588, having been leased by patent, 13 May, 11 Eliz., to
George Willoughby for 21 years at a yearly rent of £8; (4) and (5) from Michaelmas 1590,
having been leased (4) by conventual indenture, 10 Feb., 20 Hen. VIII, to Thomas Leycrofte
and Margery his wife for 61 years at a yearly rent of 60s. and (5) by patent, 12 April, 12 Eliz.,
to William Sysson for 21 years from Michaelmas then last at a yearly rent of 106s. 8d.; same
rents. For his service.   By p.s.

2259.)   1 *June* 1577.   *Gorhambury.*   Lease for 40 years to John Zouche,   [*m.* 14]
knight, of—(1) the rectory of Ratclyf on Trente, co. Nottingham, late of the monastery of
Thurgarton, co. Nottingham; (2) the rectory of   [*m.* 15]
Heynor, now or late in the tenure of George Zouche, and all lands in the parish or lordship
of Codnor belonging thereto, (3) lands (*tenants named*) in Mapley *alias* Mapperley, (4) the
tithes of corn (*tenants named*) in Penteriche and Rypley and (5) the tithes of corn (*tenants
named*) in Codnor, parcel of the rectory of Heynor, all in the county of Derby and once of the
monastery of Dale, co. Derby; and (6) lands (*tenants named*) in Ratclyf on Trent, once of St.
Mary's guild or brotherhood in Bingham, co. Nottingham. With reservations, including
certain tithes in the parish of Shepeley and in Heinor. From Lady Day last. Yearly rents (1)
£20, (2) £4, (3) 13s. 4d. (*detailed*), (4) £4, (5) 33s. 4d. and (6) 13s. 4d.. The lessee to pay a yearly
pension of £9 to the vicar of Heynor.

On surrender by the said John of (*a*) a patent, 8 Nov., 8 Eliz., leasing (1) to Edmund Dryver for 21 years from Michaelmas then last at the same rent, (*b*) a patent of the Exchequer, 5 Dec., 10 Eliz., leasing (2) and (3) to John Zouche, knight, with reservations including the tithes in Shepeley and Heynor above-reserved, for 21 years from Michaelmas then last at the same rents, (*c*) a patent, 23 Nov., 17 Eliz., leasing (4) and (5) to John Zouche, knight, for 21 years from Michaelmas then last at the same rents and (*d*) a patent of the Exchequer, 31 Jan., 12 Eliz., leasing (6) to Francis Howlyn *inter alia* for 21 years from Lady Day then last at the same rent. For his service; and for a fine of £62 paid at the Exchequer.

By p.s.

2260.)   29 *May* 1577.   *Gorhambury.*   Lease for 31 years to William Gourley, one of the Queen's captains, of—(1) lands (*tenants named*) in Netherdonsford, parcels of the manor of Myton, co. York, once of the monastery of St. Mary next the walls of York, leased by two several patents of the Exchequer, 8 July, 7 Eliz., to Christopher Malthouse for 21 years from Lady Day then last at yearly   [*m.* 16] rents of 53*s.* 4*d.* and 56*s.* 10*d.*; (2) the rectory of Skelton, co. York, and all tithes there late of the monastery of St. Mary next the walls of York, leased by patent, 30 June, 5 Eliz., for 21 years from Lady Day then last to Christopher Herbarte at a yearly rent of £8; (3) the tithes of corn and hay in Shipton in the parish of Overton, co. York, late of the monastery of St. Mary next the walls of York, leased by patent, 1 May, 9 Eliz., to Thomas Newton for 21 years from Lady Day then last at a yearly rent of £5 6*s.* 8*d.*; (4) the tithes of corn in Bolton, co. York, late of the said monastery of St. Mary, leased by patent of the Exchequer, 28 March, 3 Eliz., to Michael Kettlewell for 21 years from Lady Day then last at a yearly rent of 66*s.* 8*d.*; (5) the site or capital messuage of a manor called Dringehousehall in Dringhouses and lands (*named with tenants' names*), parcel of the manor of Dringhouses, in Dringhouses in the parish of Holy Trinity and elsewhere in the county of the city of York, parcel of the possessions of Francis Englefeld, knight, exchanged, and leased by patent, 9 April, 10 Eliz., to Richard Vavesor for 21 years from Lady Day then last at a yearly rent of £8 16*s.* 8*d.*; (6) the rectory of Norton near Malton, co. York, once of the monastery of Malton, leased by patent, 30 April, 9 Eliz., to Ralph Johnsonne for 21 years at a yearly rent of £8; (7) a tenement (*named*) in Westewyke or elsewhere in the bishopric of Durham, parcel of the lordship of Barnarde Castell, leased by patent, 17 Oct., 9 Eliz., to Thomas Bowbancke for 21 years at a yearly rent of £5; (8) a tenement (*named*), parcel of the manor or honour of Ewelme, co. Oxford, leased by   [*m.* 17] patent of the Exchequer, 16 Dec., 13 Eliz. to Ralph Spyer for 21 years from Michaelmas then last at a yearly rent of £4 2*s.*; (9) the rectory of Churchhonyborn, co. Worcester, once of the monastery of Eveshame and leased by patent, 28 May, 11 Eliz., to Robert Throgmerton, knight, for 21 years from Lady Day then last; (10) the rectory of Bilaughe *alias* Belhaghe *alias* Beloughe, co. Norfolk, once in the tenure of John Byrde, clerk, and afterwards in that of Henry Mynne, once of the monastery of Butley, co. Suffolk, and leased by patent of the Exchequer, 15 April, 7 Eliz., to William Mynne for 21 years from Lady Day then last at a yearly rent of 26*s.* 8*d.*; and (11) Berforde grange, co. Wilts, once of the priory of St. Denis, co. Southampton. With reservations, including the tithes of hay of Wellome belonging to the said rectory of Norton. To hold (1) and (10) from Lady Day 1586, (2) from Lady Day 1584, (3), (6) and (7) from Lady Day 1588, (4) from Lady Day 1582, (5) from Lady Day 1589, (8) from Michaelmas 1592, (9) from Lady Day 1590 and (11) from Michaelmas next or the   [*m.* 18] termination of any lease or grant thereof for life or years enduring after that date. Yearly rents (1) £5 10*s.* 2*d.*, (2) £8, (3) £5 6*s.* 8*d.*, (4) 66*s.* 8*d.*, (5) £8 16*s.* 8*d.*, (6) £8, (7) £5, (8) £4 2*s.*, (9) £7 6*s.* 4*d.*, (10) 26*s.* 8*d.* and (11) £5. The lessee discharged from all other yearly payments, except out of the rectory of Churchehonyborn £5 for the salary of the curate there and 56*s.*

8*d.* for the salary of another curate in Churchehonyeborne chapel and except the salary of a chaplain in Bilaughe church.

In consideration of Gourley's surrender of an annuity of £60   [*m.* 19]
granted to him by patent, 6 Feb., 10 Eliz., for life; and for his service in the wars. By Q.

2261.)   24 *May* 1577.   *Gorhambury.*   Pardon and release to John Thomas, clerk, of all entries and intrusions into the vicarage of Stebunheath,   [*m.* 20]
co. Middlesex, and the parsonage of Roche, co. Cornwall, of all penalties arising by reason of stat. 21 Hen. VIII concerning the holding of benefices in plurality and of all other defaults heretofore arising since 4 March, 2 Eliz., concerning the said vicarage and parsonage; also of all revenues thereof received since the said 4 March. This patent to be sufficient warrant to the keeper of the great seal to issue a patent of presentation of Thomas to the vicarage of Stebunheathe, in the Queen's gift *hac vice* by lapse; which vicarage appears in the Queen's books to exceed the yearly value of £30. Licence also for Thomas to hold the said vicarage, although he be not a bachelor of divinity or allowed a preacher, notwithstanding stat. 13 Eliz. or any other law to the contrary. Grant also that he may during his life hold both the said vicarage and the said parsonage.

Thomas, being vicar of Stebunheath, about 1 Oct., 3 & 4 Ph. & Mary, became a chaplain of the late earl of Pembroke, as appears by letters of passport of the said earl testifying that he was then his chaplain; later he was presented by the Queen to the parish church of Roche and was thereto lawfully admitted and instituted; Matthew, late archbishop of Canterbury, granted him letters, 22 Feb., 2 Eliz., of dispensation to hold two benefices; the Queen by patent, 4 March, 2 Eliz., confirmed the said dispensation, and on 28 April, 2 Eliz., he was inducted in the said church of Roche; after the death of the said earl of Pembroke, Robert, earl of Leicester, councillor, took him to be his household chaplain, as appears by letters testimonial, 4 April, 12 Eliz., of the said earl of Leicester; the said archbishop granted him other letters, 10 Nov., 15 Eliz., of dispensation, containing a clause of *perinde valere*, and the Queen confirmed the said dispensation by patent of the same date. Doubts have now arisen whether the vicarage has not now become void; by stat. 21 Hen. VIII it was enacted that, if any person having a benefice with cure of souls of the yearly value of £8 or above, should take another and be instituted and inducted in the same, the first benefice should thereupon be void, notwithstanding any licence, union or other dispensation to the contrary; by the same statute it was also enacted that every spiritual person promoted to any dignity in a monastery or cathedral church or other church conventual or collegial or beneficed with any parsonage or vicarage from Michaelmas then next should be personally resident in one of them at least, and that, if he should absent himself wilfully for one month together or two months accounted at several times in any one year, he should forfeit for every default £10, half to go to the King and half to the party that would sue for the same in the King's courts; by stat. 13 Eliz. it was enacted that no one thenceforth should be admitted to any benefice with cure of souls above the yearly value of £30 in the Queen's books unless he should be then a bachelor of divinity or a preacher lawfully allowed by some bishop within this realm or by one of the universities of Cambridge or Oxford, all admissions contrary to the act and all dispensations and the like contrary thereto to be void. *English.*   By p.s.

2262.)   10 *Dec.* 1576.   Lease for 21 years to Thomas Hennaeg *alias* Henneage of the site of the manor of Elmeswell *alias* Helmeswell on the Wold, co. York, now or late in the tenure of Ralph Buckton, Margaret his wife and Robert Henneag, once of the monastery of St. Mary next the walls of York; with reservations; from Michaelmas last; yearly rent £29 7*s.*; the
[*m.* 21]
lessee to provide entertainment for the Queen's steward and surveyor coming to hold courts there or survey the manor. For £58 14*s.* paid at the Exchequer.   By p.s.

2263.)   31 *May* 1577.   *Gorhambury*.   Licence for life for Paul French, S.T.B., prebendary of Canterbury cathedral, to absent himself from his canonry or prebend in the said church and any other benefices which he now or hereafter holds and from the general chapter of Canterbury cathedral held yearly on 25 Nov., without loss of emoluments; provided that he personally and continually resides in his canonry or prebend in St. George's collegiate church in Windesor castle. In consideration of his advanced age and feeble health.

By p.s.

2264.)   29 *May* 1577.   *Gorhambury*.   Lease for 21 years to Nicholas Bacon, son and heir apparent of Nicholas Bacon, knight, keeper of the great seal, of the tithes of sheaves of lands (*named with tenants' names*), parcel of the tithes belonging to the rectory of Myldenhall, co. Suffolk, assigned to Queen Mary before her accession and formerly of the monastery of Burie, co. Suffolk; from Lady Day last; yearly rent £12 4s. In consideration of the surrender by the said Nicholas the son of a patent, 25 June, 9 Eliz., leasing the premises to Thomas Androwes for 21 years from Lady Day then last at the same rent; and for a fine of £20 paid at the Exchequer.   [*m.* 22]

By p.s.

2265.)   27 *May* 1577.   *Gorhambury*.   Presentation of Thomas Mawdesley, clerk, to the rectory of Stangrave, York dioc., void by the translation of Richard Barnes, bishop of Carlisle, to the bishopric of Durham.   By p.s.

2266.)   29 *May* 1577.   *Gorhambury*.   Grant for life to Herbert Westfalinge, S.T.P., of a canonry or prebend in the royal collegiate church or free chapel of St. George in Wyndesor castle, void by the death of Anthony Rushe.   By p.s.

2267.)   24 *May* 1577.   *Gorhambury*.   Lease for 21 years to Nicholas Sullyard of Clyffords Inne, London, of a wood called Whytley Woode, parcel of the manor of Otford, co. Kent; with reservations; from Michaelmas next; yearly rent £9 15s.; the lessee to make two cuttings only of the woods and at fitting times, to enclose and preserve them after cutting for the term appointed by statute, and, before any cutting is made, to cause this patent to be enrolled before the auditor of the county for charging of the rent and before the surveyor of woods this side Trent for performance of the covenants. In consideration that he offers to undertake the enclosures of the woods, which must be enclosed for seven years after cutting, and pay the said rent; and for a fine of £19 10s. paid at the Exchequer.

By warrant of the commissioners.

2268.)   24 *May* 1577.   *Gorhambury*.   Lease for 21 years to Edmund Ratclyff of the rectory of Crossethwayte *alias* Crostwayte, co. Cumberland, once of the monastery of Fountance in the archdeaconry of Richemond; reserving to the Crown a yearly pension of 20 marks payable by the vicar there; from Lady Day last; yearly rent £14 6s. 8d. In consideration of his
[*m.* 23]
surrender of a patent, 15 June, 4 Eliz., leasing the rectory to him for 21 years from Lady Day then last at the same rent; and for a fine of £28 13s. 4d. paid at the Exchequer.   By p.s.

2269.)   3 *June* 1577.   *Gorhambury*.   Lease for 21 years to Michael Coles of the rectory of Wolverston, co. Buckingham, once of the monastery of Shene, co. Surrey; with reservations; from Lady Day last; yearly rent £20. In consideration of the surrender by Coles of a patent, 27 March, 10 Eliz., leasing the rectory to Anthony Rotsey for 21 years from Lady Day then last at the same rent; and for a fine of £20 paid at the Exchequer.   By p.s.

2270.) 7 *June* 1577. Order until the Queen shall signify her pleasure to the contrary to the bishop, dean and chapter of Durham, to pay out of the tenths payable by the clergy of the diocese at Christmas last £300 to John Clopton, receiver of the county of Northumberland, bishopric of Durham and archdeaconry of Richmond, for payment to the treasurer of Barwycke as his first half-year's assignment for the wages of the garrison there, and to make a similar payment yearly in May. The receiver is unable by £300 to meet the requirements of the said treasurer at every first half-year on account of the later days of payment usual in those places than in the South. *English*   By p.s.

2271.) 3 *June* 1577. *Gorhambury.* Lease for 21 years to William   [*m.* 24] Adam of the rectory of Awsten *alias* Austen, co. York, late of the monastery of Welbeck, co. Nottingham; with reservations, including a parcel of land (*tenant named*) and the tithes and other profits belonging of old to the vicar of Awsten; from Lady Day last; yearly rent £17 6*s*. 8*d*.; the lessee to pay 13*s*. 4*d*. yearly to the archdeacon of York and 6*s*. 8*d*. for a pension yearly to the archbishop of York. In consideration of the surrender by Adam of a patent, 20 July, 11 Eliz., leasing the rectory to Leonard Wraye and him for 21 years from Lady Day then last at the same rent; and for a fine of £20 paid at the Exchequer.   By p.s.

2272.) 7 *June* 1577. Pardon for Richard Lewys of Wakerley, co. Northampton, 'yoman', for the felonious killing of John Walton late of Wakerley, 'yoman'.   [*m.* 25] By p.s.

2273.) 7 *June* 1577. Order until the Queen shall signify her pleasure to the contrary to the archbishop, dean and chapter of York to pay out of the tenths payable by the clergy of the diocese at Christmas last £700 to John Jenkyns, receiver of the county of York, for payment to the treasurer of Barwicke as his first half-year's assignment for the wages of the garrison there, and to make a similar payment yearly in May. The receiver is unable by £700 to meet the requirements of the said treasurer at every first half-year on account of the later days of payment usual in the said shire than in the South. *English.*   By p.s.

2274.) 10 *Feb.* 1577. *Hampton Court.* Pardon for Thomas Hylles late of Chichester, co. Sussex, 'yoman', for all libels specified in a bill late exhibited in the court of Star Chamber by Richard, bishop of Chichester, and others and all penalties due by reason of the premises, except a fine of £50 imposed in the said court; the pardon to be interpreted in his favour.   By p.s.

2275.) 3 *June* 1577. Presentation of Robert Patynson, M.A., to the rectory of Stevenage, Lincoln dioc., void by lapse.   By p.s.

2276.) 14 *March* 1577. *Gorhambury.* Presentation of Richard Elkes, B.A., to the rectory of Westyldesley, Salisbury dioc., void by lapse.   By p.s.

2277.) 7 *Dec.* 1576. *Gorhambury.* Lease for 21 years to John Briskoe   [*m.* 26] of a farm or lands called Plompton Heade, parcel of a park or lawn called Plompton in the forest of Inglewoode, co. Cumberland; with reservations; from Michaelmas last; yearly rent £10 13*s*. 4*d*.; the lessee to serve by himself or a sufficient man with horse and arms when summoned by the warden or lieutenant of the West marches towards Scotland, to occupy the premises by himself or a sufficient man, to cultivate the same and to fence them as ordered by the steward of the Queen's court or other her commissioners there. In consideration of his surrender of a patent, 17 April, 10 Eliz., leasing the premises to him for

21 years from Lady Day then last at the same rent; and for a fine of £10 13s. 4d. paid at the Exchequer.   By warrant of the commissioners

2278.) 7 *Dec.* 1576. *Gorhambury.* Lease for 21 years to Peter Temple and John his son of lands (*named*) in the parish of Lutterworth, co. Leicester, late   [*m.* 27] of Henry, late duke of Suffolk, attainted of treason; with reservations; from Lady Day 1600, having been leased by patent, 10 Aug., 4 & 5 Ph. & Mary, to the said Peter for 40 years from Michaelmas or Lady Day first occurring after the death of Frances, duchess of Suffolk, now deceased, once wife of the said duke, at a yearly rent of £37; same rent. For the service and at the suit of John Dyer, a yeoman of the bakehouse, John Walker and William Conn, grooms of the bakehouse.

2279.) 10 *Dec.* 1576. *Gorhambury.* Grant for life to John Osborne of Lincolnes Inne, son of Peter Osborne, of the reversion of the office of treasurer's remembrancer of the Exchequer, now held by his said father, to whom it was granted by patent, 7 Sept., 6 Edw. VI, for life; as held by   [*m.* 28] his father or formerly by Clement Smythe, knight. In consideration of his knowledge and experience in the office both by instruction of his father and by continuance in the work of the office.   By p.s.

2280.) 26 *Jan.* 1577. Lease for 21 years to Nicholas Bacon of Redgrave, co. Suffolk, of (1) the hundred of Baber, the rents of free tenants and the fines of leets arising therein, a rent of 9 quarters, 2 bushels and 3 'le peckes' of oats payable by the free tenants therein and a yearly rent of 18s. 8¾d. payable for the same rent, (2) the hundred of Thingoo and the rents of assize of free tenants therein, (3) the hundred of Ricebridge, the rents of assize of free tenants therein and the fines of leets belonging thereto and (4) the hundred of Cosford, the rents of assize of free tenants belonging thereto, the oats and the moveable rent payable by tenants of the hundred, the leets in the hundred and the perquisites and profits of the leets and a yearly rent of 12d. payable to the hundred, all in the county of Suffolk and once of the monastery of Bury St. Edmunds, co Suffolk; from Michaelmas last; yearly rent £15 12s. 7¾d.   By p.s.

2281.) 3 *Dec.* 1576. Lease for 21 years to Thomas Burroughe of the manor of Upton Snoddesbury *alias* Upton Snoddisby, co. Worcester,   [*m.* 29] and woods (*named*) in Upton Snoddesbye, which premises Anthony Kyngeston, knight, held for life; great trees, mines and quarries of the premises and advowsons reserved; from the present date; yearly rent £23 19s. 8½d.   By p.s.

2282.) 4 *Dec.* 1576. *Gorhambury.* Grant in fee simple to Francis, earl of Bedford, councillor, of the reversion of the borough of Denbury and the manors of Denburie and Borington, co. Devon, the manor of Hawkeswell, co. Somerset, and other lands in Borington and Denburye, co. Devon, and Hawkeswell and Cutcombe, co. Somerset, granted *inter alia* in tail male by patent, 4 July, 31 Hen. VIII, to John Russell, knight, lord Russell, afterwards earl of Bedford, to hold by knight service and by a yearly rent for them and other lands specified in the said patent; reserving to the Crown the said tenure by knight service and the said rent; without fine or fee. For the service of Francis, to whom the premises have descended as son and heir male of the body of John.   By p.s.

2283.) 14 *Dec.* 1576. Grant in fee simple to Christopher Hatton, the Queen's servant, of the keeping of Moulton park and the warren of Moulton Parke and the keeping of all the warren of Moulton and Molton Parke in the fields of Moulton, Kingesthorpe, Pisforde, Boughton and Northampton, co. Northampton, and the office of the game of wild beasts of

the park; as held by William Parre, knight, lord Parre of Horton, deceased; also herbage and
pannage of the park. For   [*m.* 30]
his service.   By p.s.

2284.)   23 *Jan.* 1577.   Lease for 21 years to Kenelm Digby and Everard Digby, his son, of
(1) the demesne lands of the manor of Preston, (2) lands (*named*) in Pissebroke Fielde, parcel
of the manor of Preston, and (3) lands in Uppingham, all in the county of Rutland and
parcels of Warwycke and Spencers Landes, and (4) a cottage (*tenant named*) in Uppingham
and (5) lands (*tenant named*) in Pissebroke, all once of Dingley preceptory; with reservations,
including all courts and profits of the said manor of Preston and Uppingham; from
Michaelmas last; yearly rent £6 3*s.* 6*d.* In consideration of the surrender by Kenelm of a
patent, 30 May, 9 Eliz., leasing the premises to him for 21 years from Lady Day then last at
yearly rents of (1) 102*s.* 9*d.*, (2) 20*s.*, (3) 3*d.*, (4) 2*d.* and (5) 4*d.*; and for a sum paid at the
Exchequer by way of fine.   By p.s.

2285.)   21 *Nov.* 1576.   Pardon for John Tregidiowe, 'taylor', and Matthew Tregidiowe,
'grome', both late of Bodmyn, co. Cornwall. At the general gaol delivery of Launceston
castle, co. Cornwall, made there before Roger Manwoode, a justice of the Common Pleas,
and John Jefferey, a justice of the Queen's Bench, justices of gaol delivery, on 12 Aug., 17
Eliz., they were indicted (1) together for that they with others on 8 March, 17 Eliz., burgled
the house of George Stutridge at Temple, co. Cornwall, assaulted him, Joan his wife and
Blanche their daughter and stole 20 marks and plate etc. (*described*) belonging to him, (2)
John for that he with others on 24 March, 17 Eliz., at Treglithe West, co. Cornwall, burgled
the house of John Packett and stole 13*s.* and clothing etc. (*described*) belonging to
                                                                                    [*m.* 31]
him and (3) John for that he with others on the said 24 March at Treglith West burgled the
house of William Fosterd and stole clothing (*described*) belonging to him; they pleaded not
guilty, were convicted and were condemned and afterwards were for divers causes
committed back to gaol. At the suit of Florence Tregidiowe, widow, their mother.   By Q.

2286.)   15 *Dec.* 1576.   Grant in tail to James Merwyn, knight, an esquire for the body, of
the office of bailiff, forester and keeper of Selwoode forest, co. Wilts, late of Walter
Hungreforde, knight, late lord Hungreforde, deceased, attainted of treason; to hold in
socage as of the manor of Eastgrenewich, co. Kent. For his service.   By p.s.

2287.)   14 *Dec.* 1576.   Pardon for Edward Robson late of Chepsted, co. Kent, 'laborer',
indicated for that on 23 Dec., 18 Eliz., in the highway at Chepsted he robbed Richard Baker
of £11 belonging to him. At the suit of Elizabeth Robson, widow, his mother.   [*m.* 32]
                                                                                    By p.s.

2288.)   19 *Dec.* 1576.   Lease for 21 years to Robert Thwaytes of mills in Barnesley, co.
York, parcel of the manor of Barnesley and once of the monastery of Pontefract, co. York;
from Michaelmas last; yearly rent £8. In consideration of his surrender by deed, 17 Dec. last,
enrolled in Chancery, of his interest in the premises by virtue of a patent, 18 June, 17 Eliz.,
whereby they were leased to him *inter alia* for 21 years from Lady Day then last at the same
rent.   By warrant of the commissioners.

2289.)   14 *Dec.* 1576.   Confirmation for Cecily now the wife of Ranulph Pickemere of a
pardon granted her, by the name of Cecily wife of Robert Bostocke, by patent, 15 Jan., 16
Eliz. [*Calendar*, 1572–75, no. 1299] for the murder of Joyce Browne, widow. At the suit of
Ranulph and Cecily.   [*m.* 33]

Grant also to Cecily and Ranulph and the heirs of Ranulph—for the relief of great losses sustained by them—of a salt pan called a 'wychehouse' in Midlewych, co. Chester, and two cottages and gardens there, with arrears of issues from the attainder of Robert Bostocke; and restitution of all goods of Robert and Cecily forfeited by reason of the said murder; to hold in free burgage of the borough or town of Mydlewyche.   By p.s.

2290.)   14 *Dec.* 1576.   Lease for 21 years to George Bredyman, the Queen's servant, of all lands in Shrewsbury or elsewhere, co. Salop, late of the brotherhood or guild of Holy Trinity of the mistery of drapers of Edward IV's town of Shrewsbury, in the Crown's possession by stat. 1 Edw. VI for the dissolution of chantries; with reservations; from Michaelmas last; yearly rent £15 15*s.* 2*d.* from the time when he shall obtain possession.

[*m.* 34]
By p.s.

2291.)   19 *Nov.* 1576.   Lease for 21 years to Thomas Shipman of the rectory of Cropwell Butler, co. Nottingham, late of Thurgarton priory, co. Nottingham; with reservations; from Michaelmas last; yearly rent £9 6*s.* 8*d.* In consideration of his surrender of a patent, 11 Nov., 11 Eliz., leasing the rectory to him for 21 years from Michaelmas then last at the same rent; and for a fine of £18 13*s.* 4*d.* paid at the Exchequer.   By p.s.

2292.)   23 *Jan.* 1577.   Lease for 21 years to Robert Hopton of the hundred of Blythinge, co. Suffolk, late assigned to Anne of Cleves for life and formerly of the late duke of Suffolk, and all fines and the like of inhabitants thereof before the Queen's justices and clerk of the market and others justices and commissioners, goods of felons and outlaws, execution

[*m.* 35]
of writs and all other profits in the hundred; as formerly held by Hugh ap Howell, Charles, late duke of Suffolk, or Anne of Cleves; from Michaelmas last; yearly rent £12. In consideration of his surrender of a patent, 13 May, 9 Eliz., leasing the premises to him for 21 years from Lady Day then last at the same rent; and for a fine of £24 paid at the Exchequer.

By p.s.

2293.)   20 *Nov.* 1576.   Pardon for Thomas Legg late of Chard, co. Somerset, 'weaver', indicted for that (1) he with Francis Mannyng late of Chard, 'weaver', on 20 Oct., 17 Eliz., broke and entered the house of William Colles at Chard and stole cloth (*decribed*) belonging to Thomas Cogan and (2) he received and comforted Francis Mannyng late of Yercombe, co. Devon, on 21 Oct., 17 Eliz., at Chard, knowing that he had burgled the house of William Colles at Charde on 17 Oct., 17 Eliz., and stolen 40*s.* 4*d.* belonging to Austin Warrey.
By Q.

2294.)   17 *Dec.* 1576.   Appointment of Henry Lea, knight, as the Queen's commissioner and grant to him of power from time to time to inquire, or otherwise by commissions under the great seal of the Exchequer to such persons as he shall nominate and the treasurer and chancellor of the Exchequer   [*m.* 36]
(or one of them) shall allow, cause inquiry to be made, of lands and chattels alienated during seven years from the present date by bondmen or bondwomen in blood of the Crown, as well in gross as appertaining or regardant to lordships and lands of the Crown, in England and Wales. Lea, his heirs and assigns to have all lands and chattels which by force of any such commission shall be certified or otherwise by Lea's diligence shall be discovered to have been so alienated; to hold such lands as of the manor of Eastgrenewiche in socage. The chancellor and keeper of the great seal shall upon certificate made by Lea under his hand and seal of compositions with any persons for any of the said lands or chattels pass grants thereof

by patent according to the tenor of such certificates. The Crown will at the suit of Lea, his heirs or executors grant under the great seal to him, his heirs, executors and assigns or any other persons named by him or appointed by the chancellor or keeper of the great seal all lands or chattels so found to be alienated; the lands to be held as of the manor of Estgrenewich in socage. Upon every certificate made by force of these presents or by force of such commissions as are above mentioned the treasurer and chancellor   [*m.* 37] of the Exchequer (or one of them) shall issue sufficient particulars and warrants for the conveying by patent of all such lands and chattels to Lea, his heirs, executors and assigns or to such other persons as he shall nominate to the treasurer and chancellor of the Exchequer (or one of them). This patent to be sufficient warrant and discharge in all the premises at all times hereafter; upon which patent and all other patents made by virtue of these presents like provision and reservation shall be made as is mentioned in the Queen's former patent dated 17 Jan., 17 Eliz. For his service.   *English.*   By Q.

2295.)   28 *Jan.* 1577.   Lease for 21 years to Anthony Rose of the rectory of Alfryston, co. Sussex, late of Anne of Cleves and afterwards granted to cardinal Pole and the clergy of England by act of Parliament; with reservations; from Michaelmas last; yearly rent £16 13*s.* 4*d.* In consideration of his surrender of a patent, 10 May, 3 Eliz., leasing the rectory to his father, Robert Rose, citizen and merchant taylor of   [*m.* 38] London, for 21 years from Michaelmas then last at the same rent; and for a fitting sum paid at the Exchequer.   By p.s.

2296.)   29 *July* 1577.   *Gorhambury.*   Pardon for Thomas Lee late of   [*m.* 39] Wynchelowe, co. Buckingham, *alias* of Granborowe, co. Buckingham, for all robberies, felonies and burglaries committed between 1 May, 18 Eliz., and 8 July, 19 Eliz.; also for all felonies, robberies and burglaries committed before the present date. At the suit of Henry Lee, knight.   By Q.

2297.)   2 *Aug.* 1577.   *Gorhambury.*   Grant to Christopher Hatton, captain of the guard, his heirs and assigns of—(1) the house and site of Breamore priory, co. Southampton, lands (*named with tenants' names*) in Bremore, once of the said priory, and other lands (*named with tenant's name*) there; (2) lands (*named with tenants' names*) in Tewkesburye, co., Gloucester,
          [*m.* 40]
late of Thomas, late lord Seymor; (3) land (*described with tenants' names*) in Tewkesbury, once parcel of Warwykes and Spencers Landes; (4) lands (*named with tenants' names*) in the parish of Whitechurch, co. Somerset, and the site and capital messuage of the grange of Filton *alias* Whitchurche, in the tenure of Hugh Smyth, all late of Catherine, late Queen of England, and formerly of the monastery of Keinsham; (5) lands (*tenants named*) in Corston, co. Somerset, once of the monastery of Bath; (6) lands (*named with tenants' names*) in Tyntenhull, co. Somerset, once of Mountague priory; (7) lands (*named with tenants' names*) in Burton, co. Dorset, once of the late college of St. Stephen, Westminster, co. Middlesex; (8) lands (*named with tenant's name*) in Easby in the archdeaconry of Richmond, co.   [*m.* 41] York, once of the monastery of St. Agatha in the said archdeaconry; (9) a grange in Bengeworthe, co. Worcester, parcel of the manor of Bengeworth, and lands (*described with tenants' names*) there, all once of the monastery of Evesham; (10) lands etc. (*tenants named*) in Totterton *alias* Tuderton and Wydbache *alias* Vydbache, co. Salop, and woods called Astwood in Bishop's Castle or elsewhere, co. Salop, all late of the bishopric of Hereford and in the Crown's hands by act of Parliament; (11) 'the chapell of Shawbery', co. Salop, and lands (*tenant named*) belonging to the said chapel; (12) lands (*tenant named*)in Eltington *alias* Ellington, co. Hereford, leased to Edward Crowther by patent of the Exchequer for a term of years still enduring, late parcel of Wigmore and Wigmores Landes, once of the earl of

March; (13) the manor of Roidon, co. Suffolk, once of the late college of Wyngfeld, co. Suffolk; (14) the advowson of the rectory of Blislande, co. Cornwall; and (15) a wood called 'la Hay Wood' within the precinct of the old forest called 'the forest de la Hay', co. Hereford, and the reversion and rent of the same wood, leased by patent, 11 March, 14 Eliz., to Hatton for 21 years from Lady Day then next at a yearly rent of £9 from the time when he should   [m. 42]
obtain possession. To hold (15) in fee farm by a yearly rent of £9 and the rest as of the manor of Eastgrenewich, co. Kent, in socage. Issues from Lady Day last. The grantee may with reasonable hedges and ditches assart, enclose and encoppice all woods within Haye Wood or the forest called 'de la Hay forrest', and likewise may cut them, keep them enclosed and reduce them to tillage after cutting, without leave of the Crown or its ministers.

In consideration of lands in Tyllington, Lurgishall and Snapeland, co. Sussex, late parcel of the Queen's manor of River, lands, late parcel of the manor of Frampton, co. Dorset, in the liberty of Frampton   [m. 43]
and the advowson of the rectory of Upton Episcopi, co. Hereford, heretofore granted by the Queen to Hatton and late bargained and sold by him to the Crown.   By Q.

2298.)   16 *Aug.* 1577.   *Gorhambury.*   Pardon and release for Robert Sherington, clerk, rector of St. Margaret Moyses in Fridaye Strete, London, and his successors of a yearly pension of 5 marks payable out of the rectory of St. Margaret Moyses aforesaid to the Crown in right of the late monastery of Horsham, co. Norfolk, and of all arrears of the same, also of all   [m. 44]
other charges due to the Crown out of the rectory, first fruits only excepted; the rectory to remain and continue of the yearly value of £12 13s. 4d. and no more, and after that rate to pay first fruits and yearly tenths and otherwise stand chargeable to the Crown. The rectory being but small, no incumbent would accept it by reason of the said pension and the arrears thereof, which for the 30 years ending Michaelmas, 18 Eliz., amount to £100, and it has become void for sundry years past, whereby the Crown has lost the first fruits thereon upon the change of every incumbent, and the parishioners have not been well served. *English.*
                                                                                                    By p.s.

2299.)   28 *Oct.* 1577.   *Windsor Castle.*   Grant to John Farnham, a gentleman pensioner, his heirs and assigns of—(1) a chapel with the close in which it stands in Glenne Parva, co. Leicester, and land there belonging to the chapel; (2) a chapel in a small toft in Walcote, co. Leicester; (3) lands (*tenant named*) in Swynford, co. Leicester, given for lights in the church there; (4) land in Sharnforde, co. Leicester, given for lamps there; (5) the site of the priory of St. Kynmark *alias* Kynmarkez next Chepstowe, co. Monmouth, now in decay, the manor of St. Kynmark and parcels of demesne land (*tenant named*) of the same priory in St. Kynmark; (6) lands (*tenants named*) in St. Arvans, (7) lands (*tenants named*) in Herdwick (*alias* Hardwick) in the parish of Chepstowe, (8) lands (*tenant named*) near Pont Vayne, (9) lands (*named*) in the parish of St. Lawrence, (10) lands (*tenant named*) in Mathern, (11) land called Cockshott (*tenant named*), (12) lands (*tenant named*) in Llanyssen,   [m. 45]
(13) lands (*tenant named*) in St. Arvans, (14) lands (*tenant named*) in Chepstowe, (15) lands (*tenant named*) in Llandevenyo (*alias* Llandavenye), (16) lands (*tenant named*) in Llanyssen, (17) a weir etc. in the parish of Llanicoute (*alias* Llancawte), (18) the rectory of the church or chapel of St. Arvans and (19) the rectory of the church or chapel of Llanyssen, all in the county of Monmouth and late of the priory of St. Kynmark; (20) lands (*tenant named*), including a croft in which there is an old chapel, in Burton on the Wolds and Wymesold, (21) lands (*named*), including St. James's chapel, in Drayton and (22) lands (*named*) in Heather, by Sivepston and towards Raunson, all in the county of Leicester; (23) the tithes of the demesne lands of the manor of Hertf', co. Huntingdon, and of other lands (*named*) in

Hertf', once of St. Mary's priory in Huntingdon; (24) lands (*named with tenants' names*), including the old site of the castle, in Upsall, co. York, once of Leonard Dacres, attainted of treason; (25) the manor of Seamer with lands in Seamer, Kilvington, Thornbargh and Northkilvington, co. York, once of Leonard Dacres, attainted of treason; (26) the tithes of corn, hay, wool and lambs in the late parish of Salisburye, co. Monmouth, once of Chepstowe priory, co. Monmouth; (27) lands (*named with tenants' names*) in Llanguarde (*alias* Llangwade), co. Carmarthen, late of John Reade, attainted of treason; (28) lands (*named with tenant's name*) between Kithinock and Elvett, co. Carmarthen, given for masses and other superstitions to Llanllownye priory; (29) lands in Llangathen, co. Carmarthen, now or late in the tenure of John Talley, clerk, vicar there, given by Edmund Blunte, deceased, for dirges and other superstitious uses in Llangathen church; (30) marshes etc. (*named*) in Westham, co. Essex, late of the monastery of Stratford Langthorne, co. Essex; (31) four cottages with a stone wall and a small garden in the parishes of St. Martin and St. Anne within or by Luddgate, London, now or late in the tenure of Richard Arnolde; (32) 'Saynct Michaelles hospitall' or 'chappell' with lands belonging thereto (*tenant named*) in the parish of Dixtonn, late of Monmouth priory and given for superstitious uses, (33) lands (*tenant named*) in Sherenewton, given for a light in Sherenewton church, (34) lands (*tenant named*) in Whittstonn, given for mass and matins in Whittston church, (35) lands (*named with tenant's name*), in Penhowe, given for a light in Penhowe church, (36) lands (*named with tenant's name*) in Caldecott,   [*m.* 46]
given for a light in Caldecott church, and (37) lands (*tenant named*) in Llanhennock, given for a light in Llanhennock church, all in the county of Monmouth; (38) the rectory of St. Anne within the precinct of the late house of friars preaches, London, with the advowson of the vicarage of St. Anne aforesaid; (39) lands (*named with tenant's name*) in Bramber, given for masses for the donors' parents, (40) lands (*named*) in Wadhurste, given for obits in Wadhurst church, (41) lands (*tenants named*) in New Shorham, given for the maintenance of ornaments and vestments in the church of St. Mary of Shorham, and (42) lands (*named*) in Rodding Deane near Brightelmeston, given for a superstitious use in Preston church, all in the county of Sussex; and (43) lands (*named with tenants' names*) in the parish of St. Mary Magdalen in Southwarke, co. Surrey, late of the monastery of Barmondsey, co. Surrey. Which premises were concealed from the Queen or from Henry VIII, Edward VI or Queen Mary hitherto or down to 8 Oct., 17 Eliz., and are of the yearly value, according to the several particulars thereof, of £12 7s. 8d. To hold as of the manor of Eastgrenewich, co. Kent, in socage and by yearly rents of (1) 2s., (2) 20d., (3) 3s. 4d., (4) 2s. 6d., (5) 6s. 8d., (6) 3s. 6d. (*detailed*), (7) 2s. 2d. (*detailed*), (8) 2d., (9) and (10) 2s., (11) 16d.,   [*m.* 47]
(12) 4d., (13) 2s., (14) 8d., (15) 6d., (16) 2s., (17) 6d., (18) 2s. 6d., (19) 2s. 6d., (20) 4s. (*detailed*), (21) 4d. (22) 4d., (23) 6s. 8d. (*detailed*), (24) 40s., (25) £5, (26) 5s., (27) 5s., (28) 3s. 4d., (29) 2s. 6d., (30) 14s., (31) 13s. 4d., (32) 12d., (33) 12d., (34) 8d., (35) 4d., (36) 12d., (37) 6d., (38) 20d., (39) and (40) 12d., (41) and (42) 12d. and (43) 3s. 4d. Issues from the time when the premises should have come to the Crown's hands. The lessee to have power in the Crown's name to sue in the Exchequer for any of the premises and for the levying of the rents thereof. If any of the premises shall hereafter be lawfully recovered   [*m.* 48]
from the grantee's possession, he may in satisfaction of this grant have other concealed lands of the same value as those recovered, at a like rent. The patent to be void in respect of any of the premises which were not concealed at and down to the time of the first inquisition or the first certificate or information thereof. For his service.   By Q.

2300.)   27 *Sept.* 1577.   *Windsor Castle.*   Grant for life to Christopher Barker of London, printer, of the office of printer of all statute books, libels of acts of Parliament, proclamations, injunctions and Bibles and New Testaments in the English tongue of any translation with or without notes, printed or to be printed by royal command, and of such service books for churches as shall be ordered and other volumes and things whatsoever, by whatever name they be called, or issued by command of Parliament, in English, or English and another tongue mixed (except the rudiments of Latin grammar); no others to print such books or reprint them abroad and import them, under pain of forfeiture of 40s. for each book and confiscation   [*m.* 49]

of the books; the grantee may seize such books; the grantee may take up workmen when needed; with an annuity of £6 12s. 4d., payable at the Exchequer.   By p.s.

(The dorse of this roll is blank.)

PART IX

C. 66/1159

2301.)   29 *April* 1577.   Grant in fee farm to Thomas Warcoppe, a   [*m.* 1]
gentleman pensioner, and Robert Warcoppe, their heirs and assigns of—(1) lands (*tenants named*) in Wombewell, co. York, once of Synnyngthwaite priory, co. York; (2) lands (*tenants named*) in Wombewell, once of Helaughe priory, co. York; (3) a messuage (*tenant named*) in Alwoodley, co. York, once of the monastery of Kirkestall, co. York, and all lands there belonging to the said monastery; (4) lands in Grynsthorpe and Brearley, co. York, and lands (*named*) in the parish of Normanton, co. York (*tenant named*), once of St. Mary's chantry called 'Lakes chauntrie' in Normanton; (5) lands (*tenant named*) in Leverton, co. York, once of the monastery of Whitbye, co. York; (6) lands (*tenant named*) in Leverton, once of Handale priory, co. York; (7) tithes of corn and hay in the lordship and territory of Kiplinge, co. York, late leased to Henry Scroope, knight, lord Scroope of Bolton, at a yearly rent of 12*s.*, once of the monastery of St. Agatha in the archdeaconry of Richemonde, co. York; (8) lands (*named with tenants' names*) in Steresbye, co. York, late leased to Roger Chomley, once of Marton priory, co. York; (9) lands (*tenant named*) in Whenbye, co. York, late leased by the Queen to Nicholas Fairfax, knight, once of Marton priory aforesaid; (10) lands (*tenants named*) in Flaxton, co. York, late leased to Christopher Kenne by patent, once of the priory of St. Andrew   [*m.* 2]
next York; (11) a cottage (*tenant named*) in Tollerton, co. York, late leased to Richard Hebborne, once of the priory of Austin friars in York; (12) a cottage (*tenant named*) in Whorleton, co. York, late leased to Thomas Ellys by patent, once of the hospital of St. John of Jerusalem; (13) lands (*named with tenant's name*) in Hoton on Darwent, co. York, once of Malton priory, co. York; (14) lands (*tenant named*) in Pottowe, co. York, once of the monastery of St. Mary next the walls of York; (15) lands (*tenant named*) in Rillington, co. York, once of the monastery of Bylande, co. York; (16) lands (*named with tenant's name*) in the parish of Addle, co. York, once of the monastery of Kirkestall aforesaid; (17) a mill (*named with tenant's name*) in Radforde, co. Nottingham, once of the monastery of Lenton, co. Nottingham; (18) lands (*tenants named*), including Tickenhall grange, in Tickenhall, co. Derby, once of the monastery of Repingdon, co. Derby; (19) lands (*named*) in Wotton Wawyn and Tonworthe, co. Warwick, parcel of the possessions of Baldwin Ilshawe, attainted of felony, once of a chantry in Tonworthe and Lapworthe, co. Warwick; and (20) the grange of Comothorder *alias* Comotherer, co. Radnor, once of the monastery of Strata Florida, co. Cardigan. Bells, lead (except in   [*m.* 3]
gutters and windows) and advowsons reserved. To hold as of the manor of Estgrenewiche, co. Kent, in socage and by yearly rents of (1) 94*s.* 2*d.* (*detailed*), (2) £4, (3) 13*s.* 4*d.*, (4) 66*s.* 8*d.*, (5) 16*s.* 8*d.*, (6) 10*s.*, (7) 12*s.*, (8) 31*s.* 2*d.* (*detailed*), (9) 20*s.*, (10) 80*s.* 4*d.* (*detailed*), (11) 2*s.*, (12) 18*d.*, (13) 60 *s.*, (14) 13*s.* 4*d.*, (15) 5*s.* 4*d.*, (16) 10*s.*, (17) £4 9*s.*, (18) 66*s.* 4*d.* (*detailed*), (19) 10*s.* and (20) £6. Issues from Lady Day last. The grantees discharged from all other charges.

For the service of Thomas Warcoppe aforesaid and at his suit.   [*m.* 4]
By Q.

2302.)   3 *May* 1577.   Lease for 21 years to Richard Barton of the site of the manor of Deane, once of the monastery of St. Augustine by the walls of Canterbury, the land of Hengrove, lands etc. (*named*) and all other appurtenances of the said manor in the parishes of

St. John, St. Lawrence, St. Peter and Minster in the Isle of Thanet and in the parish of Chistlett and elsewhere, co. Kent; with reservations; from Lady Day last; yearly rent £42 2s. 11½d. On the surrender in Chancery by Barton of a patent, 13 July, 4 & 6 Ph. & Mary, leasing to John Shepparde and Richard Edwardes the manor of Deane and land of Hengrove at a yearly rent of £42 17½d. and two hens for 21 years from Michaelmas 1563 or the termination of a lease by the Crown by indenture, 16 Feb., 34 Hen. VIII, for a term of years. For a fine of £66 13s. 4d. paid at the Exchequer.   [m. 5]

By p.s.

2303.)   1 *May* 1577.   Exoneration and discharge of Thomas Thurland, clerk, one of the Queen's chaplains and master of the royal hospital of the Savoy, and Daniel Houghstetter, a German born, and their partners, assistants and assigns named in a certificate remaining in Chancery from all sums due by reason of any subsidy, fifteenth or tenth granted to the Crown in the Parliament held from 8 Feb. to 15 March, 18 Eliz.; this patent with a true copy of the enrolment of the said certificate to be sufficient warrant in this behalf. By indenture, 10 Oct., 6 Eliz., the Queen covenanted with Thurland and Houghstetter that they and their partners and assigns, being the first enterprisers of certain mineral works, not exceeding 24 in number, 16 to be English and born in England, should be discharged for life from all taxes, save from such as were thereby reserved, so that the names of the said 24 should be certified in Chancery within six months; by patent, 7 Oct., 7 Eliz.,—because they could not within the time limited in the indenture agree on their partners and assistants and make certificate thereof—it was granted that they and their partners and assigns to the number aforesaid should be discharged for life from taxes as aforesaid, so that the names of the said 24 persons should be certified into Chancery within six months from that date; which certificate has been certified into Chancery under the hands and seals of Thurland and Houghstetter within the time limited in the patent.   *English.*   [m. 6]

By Q.

2304.)   29 *April* 1577.   Lease for 21 years to Andrew Smythe, clerk of the bakehouse, of (1) the rectory of Winterton, co. Lincoln, once exchanged with John Lyon, alderman of London, and (2) the site of the rectory and the rectory of Ockley, co. Northampton, once of the monastery of Pipwell, co. Northampton; with reservations; (1) from Lady Day 1588, having been leased by patent, 12 July, 9 Eliz., to Peter Geringe for 21 years from Lady Day then last at a yearly rent of £30 and (2) from Michaelmas next or the termination of any lease or grant thereof for life or years enduring after that date; yearly rent (1) £30 and (2) 100s. For his service.   [m. 7]

By p.s.

2305.)   1 *May* 1577.   Grant to Oliver Scaunderett of the wardship and marriage of James Hodges, son and heir of Philip Hodges; with an annuity of 20s. from 18 Aug., 17 Eliz., when Philip died. Yearly value of the inheritance £3.   By Q.

2306.)   2 *May* 1577.   Grant for life to Richard Bearde, M.A., of the rectory of All Saints, Northampton, void by the resignation of William Smythe.   By p.s.

2307.)   29 *April* 1577.   Lease for 21 years to Francis Harvey, a gentleman pensioner, and Mary his wife of the manor of Wytham, co. Essex, once of the hospital of St. John of Jerusalem; with reservations, including wards, marriages, a moiety of escheats and goods of felons and fugitives, and a yearly rent of 20s. issuing from the manor of Wickeham; from Lady Day last; yearly rent £72; the lessees discharged from all other charges; they are to provide entertainment at the manor for the Queen's steward and surveyor coming to hold

courts or survey the manor. For a fine of £100 paid at the Exchequer by Harvye. [*m.* 8]
By p.s.

2308.) 29 *April* 1577. Pardon for William Ludford, M.A., late of the city and university of Oxford, co. Oxford, for manslaughter. It was found by an inquisition taken at Oxford on 5 Aug., 18 Eliz., before William Tilcocke, then mayor of the city, and Richard Williams, coroner in the city, on the body of Randolph Francklyn late of Oxford, Ludford's servant, that on 25 July, 18 Eliz., Ludford wounded him so that he died there on 29 July (*details given*). By Q.

2309.) 27 *April* 1577. Grant to Thomas Knyvett, one of 'le gromes' of the privy chamber, of the wardship and marriage of Robert Trappes, son and heir of Robert Trappes, mercer of London; with an annuity of   [*m.* 9]
£20 from 2 Nov., 18 Eliz., when Robert the father died. By Q.

2310.) 27 *April* 1577. Grant to Thomas Bradgate of the wardship and marriage of Richard Bradgate, son and heir of William Bradgate, 'yoman'; with an annuity of 40*s.*, from 1 Jan., 18 Eliz., when William died. Yearly value of the inheritance £20. By Q.

2311.) 27 *April* 1577. Presentation of James Taylor, S.T.B., to the rectory of Bownes, co. Cumberland, Carlisle dioc., void by the cession of Arthur Key. By p.s.

2312.) 1 *May* 1577. Presentation of William Absolon, M.A., one of the Queen's chaplains in ordinary, to the rectory of St. Olave, co. Surrey, next London, [London] dioc., void by death. By Q.

2313.) 23 *Jan.* 1577. Lease for 21 years to George Woddroffe of the tithes in Notton and Chevete *alias* Chete and a tithe barn in Notton in the parish of Ruston, co. York, once of the monastery of St. John the Evangelist,   [*m.* 10]
Pontefract; from Michaelmas last; yearly rent £8 13*s.* 8*d.* [*sic*]. In consideration of the surrender by Woodroffe of an indenture, 8 Aug, 12 Hen. VIII, whereby the prior and convent of the said monastery leased the premises to the prior and convent of the monastery of Monkbretton for 60 years from Midsummer then last at a yearly rent of £8 13*s.* 4*d.*; and for a fine of £17 6*s.* 8*d.* paid at the Exchequer. By warrant of the commissioners.

2314.) 21 *Jan.* 1577. Lease for 19 years to Richard Williams of the site of the manor of Wukeburnell, late of Anthony Kingston, knight, and all lands, courts and other appurtenances of the said manor in Wykeburnell, Wyke, Parshore, Crickelaunton, Pensham, Camerton Parva, Ekington, Brockton Hackett, Collesden, Pepilton and elsewhere, co. Worcester; timber, mines and quarries reserved; from Lady Day next; yearly rent £15 6*d.* For a fine of £5. By p.s.

2315.) 23 *Jan.* 1577. Lease for 21 years to William Harbert of the mansion house of Belthrope and lands (*named*), parcels of the manor of Belthrope, co. York, late of Thomas Hennage, knight, exchanged; with reserva-   [*m.* 11]
tions; from Michaelmas last; yearly rent £21 4*s.* (*detailed*); the lessee to provide entertainment for the Queen's surveyor and steward coming to the manor to hold courts or make a survey. In consideration of the surrender by the said William of a patent, 19 March, 5 Eliz., leasing the premises *inter alia* to John Harbert for 21 years from Michaelmas then last at a yearly rent for them and other lands of £26 2*s.* 2*d.*; and for a fine of £42 8*s.* paid at the Exchequer. By p.s.

2316.)   18 *Jan.* 1577.   Pardon for John Wever late of the parish of St. Leonard in the precincts of St. Martin le Graunde, London, mercer, for manslaughter. It appears by the information of trustworthy persons living in the county of Warwick and in London that Wever by misadventure shot and killed Hugh Barlowe, clerk, with a 'dagge' in the house of Edmund Carter, 'inholder', one Hugh Warner being present, at Dunchurche, co. Warwick,

[*m.* 12]

on 15 Dec. last (*details given*).   By p.s.

2317.)   30 *Jan.* 1577.   Pardon for Anthony Gonne late of Newton St. Cyres, co. Devon, 'yoman', indicted for the theft of a mare belonging to Christopher Bodley, clerk, at the parish of St. David on the Hill in the county of the city of Exeter on 15 March, 18 Eliz. At the suit of Robert Denys, knight, recorder of Exeter, John Peter, Thomas Bruarton and others, justices of the peace in the city.   By Q.

2318.)   23 *Jan.* 1577.   Lease for 21 years to Robert Lawe of (1) the rectory of Luddington *alias* Lullington, co. Somerset, and (2) lands (*tenant named*) in Sevage *alias* Seveageton, co. Southampton, all conveyed by Thomas Henage, knight, and lord Willoughbye or one of them to Edward VI in exchange; with reservations; from Michaelmas last; yearly rents from the time when he shall enjoy possession (1) 40*s.* and (2) £4 5*s.*

By warrant of the commissioners.

2319.)   28 *Jan.* 1577.   Appointment for life in survivorship of Ralph   [*m.* 13] Nateby and Thomas Nateby, his son, to be bailiffs and collectors of the Queen's lands in Litington and Cutherston, co. York, late of William, late marquess of Northampton, deceased; as heretofore held by the said Ralph or Bartholomew Nateby.   By Q.

2320.)   22 *Jan.* 1577.   Order to Robert Bell, knight, to take the rank of serjeant at law, to which the Queen by advice of the Council has appointed him, on the octave of Hilary next; under pain of £1,000 for omission.   By Q.

2321.)   23 *Jan.* 1577.   Presentation of Richard Dernlove, clerk, to the perpetual vicarage of Boovetracei, Exeter dioc.   By p.s.

2322.)   18 *Jan.* 1577.   Grant for life to William Coxe, a yeoman for the mouth in the pantry, of an annuity of 12*d.* a day, payable at the Exchequer. For his service.   By p.s.

2323.)   26 *Jan.* 1577.   Grant for life to William Damano of wages of 20*d.* a day, as had by Baptist Bassano, deceased, with £16 2*s.* 6*d.* yearly for his livery, payable at the Exchequer; from the death of Bassano. For his service in the science or art of music.   By p.s.

2324.)   19 *Jan.* 1577.   *Honour of Hampton Court.*   Pardon for John Bell late of Leicester, co. Leicester, 'yoman'. Christopher Croftes late of Leicester, 'yoman', and he were indicted before the justices of gaol delivery in the county or other competent justices for that on 3 Feb., 18 Eliz., in the highway at Lubsethorpe, co. Leicester, they robbed William Jempson of 37*s.* 9*d.* belonging to Catherine, countess of Huntingdon, late deceased, and 4*s.* 7*d.* belonging to Jempson.   By Q.

2325.)   29 *Jan.* 1577.   Grant for life to William Darrett, the Queen's servant, of the office of master of the barge and 'le botes'; as late held by William Scarlett, deceased, or by Richard Drewe, Thomas Coxe, John Bundie, Thomas Ragge, John Carter, John Johnson or John

Thurston; with the wages accustomed, payable at the Exchequer; from Midsummer last. For his service.   By p.s.

2326.) 1 *Feb.* 1577.   Presentation of William Palmer, M.A., to the rectory of Wheldrake, York dioc., void by resignation and in the Queen's gift *sede vacante*.   By p.s.

2327.) 12 *July* 1577.   *Gorhambury*.   Lease for 21 years to William   [*m.* 14] Wyclyff of the tithes of corn in Tallentyre, parcel of the rectory of Birdkirke, co. Cumberland, once of the monastery of Gysborne, co. York; from Lady Day last; yearly rent £6 13*s.* 4*d.* In consideration of his surrender of a patent, 18 May, 3 Eliz., leasing the rectory to him for 21 years from Lady Day then last at the same rent; and for a fine of £6 13*s.* 4*d.* paid at the Exchequer.   By p.s.

2328.) 5 *July* 1577.   *Gorhambury*.   Lease for 50 years to Roger James of eleven tenements on the West side of Tower Hill in the parish of Hallows Barkinge in London (between tenements belonging to the fellowship of mercers of London on the South, tenements and gardens belonging to Christopher Allen, knight, on the North, a garden belonging to Thomas Spyke on the West and 'le Tower Hill' on the East), now or late in the several tenures of Edmund Mundaye (or Modye), Joan Streat, widow, Joan Barkar (or Baker), widow, Thomas Fakes, William Adamson, Edmund More, Nicholas Abraham, Thomas Bulleyn, John Andwey and Margaret Chester, late belonging to the parish of St. Dunstan in the East, London, by gift of Joan Wykes, widow, and in the Queen's hands by stat. 1 Edw. VI for the dissolution of chantries and the like; from Lady Day last; yearly rent of £6 10*s.* In consideration of the surrender by James of an indenture, 20 May, 37 Hen. VIII, whereby John Pallesgrave, late rector, and John Daye and Thomas Custable, churchwardens, of St. Dunstan in the East, with the assent of the greater part of the parishioners, leased the premises to Rowland Dee, citizen and mercer of London, for 60 years from Midsummer then next at the same rent.   By p.s.

2329.) 5 *July* 1577.   *Gorhambury*.   Lease for 21 years to Thomas Yonge   [*m.* 15] of lands (*tenants named*) in Axhey, Epworthe and Estlande in Axhey, co. Lincoln, late of the chantry of Axhey in the isle of Axholme; with reservations; from Lady Day last; yearly rent £7 5*s.* In consideration of the surrender by Yonge of the interest in the premises of Thomas Newlande, to whom they were leased by patent, 22 Jan., 8 Eliz., *inter alia* for 21 years from Michaelmas then last at a yearly rent for the premises and other lands of £7 18*s.* 4*d.*; and for a fine of £14 10*s.*, to wit, £7 16*s.* 8*d.* paid at the Exchequer and £6 13*s.* 4*d.* to Thomas Warren allowed for a like sum heretofore paid by Warren for the fine of a lease of Mermonde priory, co. Cambridge, which lease he could not enjoy because the priory had been granted in fee simple, as appears by a bill signed by Christopher Smythe, clerk of the pipe, annexed to the particular whereon this patent issued.   By warrant of the commissioners.

2330.) 15 *July* 1577.   Pardon for—Ellis Smythe late of Hungerford, co.   [*m.* 16] Berks, 'yeoman', indicted with others for that at Hungerford Downe in the highway leading towards Kyntburye, co. Berks, on 8 Dec., 19 Eliz., he robbed Roger Fyggyns of 33*s.* 4*d.* belonging to him; George Price late of Hardwick, co. Worcester, 'husbandman', indicted with others for that he broke and entered the close of Robert Goodman at Aston on Carrant, co. Gloucester, on 28 June, 18 Eliz., and stole a gelding belonging to him; John Clarke late of Uffenam, co. Worcester, 'milner', indicted with others for making two counterfeit 'Elizabeth shillinges' at Uffenam on 9 April, 18 Eliz.; Thomas Barbor late of Malverne Magna, co. Worcester, 'laborer', for the theft of a gelding belonging to George Barnes at Hanley Castell, co. Worcester, on 3 Oct., 18 Eliz.; Henry Langston late of Evesham, co.

Worcester, 'taylor' *alias* 'hosyer', for that in the highway at Emley, co. Worcester, on 22 Jan., 18 Eliz., he robbed (1) William Baynton of 4*s*. and a sword belonging to him and (2) Thomas Bande of 26*s*. 8*d*. belonging to him; Eleanor Thomas late of Hereford, 'spynster', for the theft of two oxen belonging to a man unknown at Mockas, co. Hereford, on 1 July, 18 Eliz.; Ralph Eyton late of Uttoxetur Woodland, co. Stafford, 'laborer', for the murders of (1) Thrustancia Laughtenhouse and (2) Agnes Eyton, his wife, at Uttoxeter Woodland on 7 Sept., 17 Eliz. (*details given*); and Jane Ketle *alias* Ensor of Narrowdale, co. Stafford, indicted with others for that she burgled the house of [*m*. 17] John Stone at Wynyates, co. Stafford, on 30 March, 18 Eliz., and assaulted the said John, Isabel his wife and Richard Stone, their son. By consideration of Edward Saunders, knight, late chief baron of the Exchequer, and William Lovelace, late justices of assize in the said counties, and of Robert Bell, knight, now chief baron of the Exchequer, justice of assize in the said counties. By p.s.

2331.)   17 *July* 1577.   *Gorhambury*.   Pardon for John Tegan *alias* Irishe late of St. Albans, co. Hertford, 'laborer', indicted for the theft at St. Albans of (1) a sword belonging to Giles Livezan on 20 Nov., 19 Eliz., (2) 'an ewe shepe' belonging to Simon Baldwyne on 30 Jan., 19 Eliz., and (3) a sack of corn belonging to Richard Woodwarde on 2 Feb., 19 Eliz.
By Q.

2332.)   22 *July* 1577.   *Gorhambury*.   Pardon for Alice Ashe of Taunton, co. Somerset, 'spinster'. At the general gaol delivery of Yvelchester, co. Somerset, made before Roger Manwood, a justice of the Common Pleas, and John Jefferay, a justice of the Queen's Bench, and their fellows, justices of gaol delivery, at Taunton on Wednesday in the third week of Lent, 19 Eliz., she was indicted for the theft of cloth etc. (*described*) and 2*s*. belonging to John Peter from the said Peter's shop at Taunton on 10 Dec., 18 Eliz.; she pleaded not guilty, was convicted and for divers causes was committed back to gaol. At the suit of James Williams.
By Q.

2333.)   12 *July* 1577.   *Gorhambury*.   Grant for life to Thomas Payne of the   [*m*. 18] office of bailiff and collector of the possessions late of the monastery of St. Neots, co. Huntingdon; with a yearly fee of £10, payable out of the issues of the office; as held by Thomas Neale, deceased, or Robert Payne. In consideration of the surrender in the Exchequer by the said Robert, a yeoman of the chamber and father of the said Thomas Payne, of a patent of the court of Augmentations, 24 March, 36 Hen. VIII, granting him the office for life. By p.s.

2334.)   15 *July* 1577.   Pardon for George Sherington late of Taunton, co. Somerset, 'shearman'. At the general gaol delivery of Winchester castle, co. Southampton, made before Roger Manwood, a justice of the Common Pleas, and John Jefferay, a justice of the Queen's Bench, and their fellows, justices of gaol delivery, at Winchester castle on Monday in the second week of Lent, 19 Eliz., he was indicted for the theft of a mare belonging to a man unknown at Warmford, co. Southampton, on 20 Nov., 19 Eliz.; he pleaded not guilty, was convicted and condemned and for divers causes was committed back to gaol. At the suit of Alice Sherington, his wife. By Q.

2335.)   12 *July* 1577.   *Gorhambury*.   Grant for life in reversion to John Allen of the office of yeoman tailor in the great wardrobe, now held by Thomas Ludwell for life by patent, 3 Sept., 15 Eliz.; with wages of 6*d*. a day, payable at the great wardrobe, and the usual livery; as held [*m*. 19] by Ludwell, Richard Tisdall and John Bonyard, deceased. By p.s.

2336.)   22 *July* 1577.   *Gorhambury*.   Pardon for William Snape late of Bromley Hurste, co. Stafford, weaver, indicted with others for making counterfeit coins (*described*) on and about 13 Dec., 19 Eliz., at Bromley Hurste. By consideration of Robert Bell, knight, chief baron of the Exchequer, justice of assize in the said county.   By p.s.

2337.)   20 *July* 1577.   *Gorhambury*.   Pardon for John Bunsoll late of Botesfliminge, co. Cornwall, 'glover'. At the general gaol delivery of Launceston castle, co. Cornwall, made there on Monday in the fifth week of Lent, 19 Eliz., before John Jefferay, a justice of the Queen's Bench and his fellows, justices of gaol delivery, he was indicted for that (1) in the highway at Pillaton, co. Cornwall, on 26 Feb., 19 Eliz., he robbed John Baylye of 3*d.* belonging to him and (2) on 4 Feb., 19 Eliz., he broke and entered by night the fulling mill of Nicholas Howe at Mutton Myll, co. Cornwall, and stole cloth (*described*) belonging to him; he pleaded not guilty, was convicted and condemned and for divers causes was committed back to gaol.   [*m.* 20]
                                                                          By Q

2338.)   17 *July* 1577.   *Gorhambury*.   Grant in fee simple to William West, knight, lord de la Ware, Francis Walsingham, one of the Queen's principal secretaries, and Henry Wallopp, knight, of the South part of Winchester castle, co. Southampton, enclosed with walls (140 feet long and 110 feet wide), with all buildings and other appurtenances thereof, and a small 'ditche' in the North part of the said South part, for the building, within the next seven years, of a house of correction for vagabonds at the costs of the inhabitants of the county; to hold by fealty only, as of the manor of Estgrenewiche, co. Kent; licence for the grantees (or two or one of them) to demolish or rebuild any of the walls, towers, building or 'vaultes', as they think necessary; also to sell materials not needed for the construction of the house of correction and spend the proceeds on the building of a better house and to no other use; the governor, censor or warden of the wanderers and vagabonds in the said house, and the vagabonds themselves with the leave of the governor, censor or warden, may have free entry by a door in the East part of the said small ditch in the outer wall of the castle, also access both within the green (*viridam*) of the castle called 'le grene' in the North part of the said ditch to draw water in the well in the green and do other necessary business and within all other greens and ditches without the castle and belonging thereto for the conserving of their health and other necessary business; provided that, if such buildings hereafter to be erected are not used for the sole purpose of a house of correction, the Crown may re-enter the said South part of the castle. At the suit of many inhabitants of the county both within and without the city of Winchester for a house of correction, according to the form of a statute thereof lately made, for vagabonds, wanderers and others leading an idle and useless life, that they may be assisted in the building of a fitting house.   By Q.

2339.)   9 *July* 1577.   Order to Richard Martyn, warden of the mint, John Lawinson, master worker of the moneys, and the other officers of the mint to begin again to set the moneyers on work, and to proceed with the coinage and continue the same as it was the month before the last stay thereof, until the Queen or such other as she shall appoint shall take further order therein. Order also that the warden of the mint shall take up to the Queen's use the benefit arising by the 'sheare' of the said moneys, answering to the said master the value of the half remedy of the same, as before the last stay. Also—whereas of 11 journeys of coined moneys or thereabout received from the moneyers on 21 July 1576, which was the time of the last coinage (the subjects being then fully paid) there remain in the joint custody of the warden and the master worker £571 for current money or thereabouts, challenged by the master worker to appertain to him and detained by the warden as belonging to the Queen—the warden is to deliver the said £571 to the master worker, he

first putting in sufficient bonds of £100 more than the sum to be delivered to the Exchequer, to be answerable for the same, if it be found due upon his account when it shall be taken and finished. Order also to the worker of the moneys to deliver his account forthwith to the warden, which, after declaration thereof made, is to be delivered to the principal secretary for the Queen's consideration; and—if the Queen has any law or ordinance or has taken any bonds of Martyn or any other in his behalf which he or they have broken by suffering the master   [*m.* 21]
worker to alter the Queen's standard in making her moneys not so rich as the standard and yet within the remedies—he and they shall be discharged from such penalties as they have incurred, or in the obeying of the premises hereafter shall incur, against their bonds or the laws or ordinances aforesaid.

For the relief of the poor workmen, the moneyers, the coinage in the mint having stayed a long time, to their great hindrance. *English.*   By Q.

2340.)   22 *July* 1577.   *Gorhambury.*   Licence for 10 years for Christopher Saxton, servant to Thomas Sekeford, master of the requests, to be the sole printer and seller of all maps of England and Wales or of any county or other part thereof by him already, or hereafter to be, set forth; from the present date; no persons, other than the licensee or such other as by him shall be appointed, shall print or set forth any such maps or import any such made in a foreign country, on pain of the Queen's displeasure; offenders to forfeit to the Crown's use £10 for every offence, and to the licensee all maps printed, sold or uttered contrary to the meaning of these presents; the master and wardens of the mistery of stationers in London and all other the Queen's officers and subjects to assist the licensee in the exercising of this licence. Saxton has, at the great costs of his said master, already travelled through the greatest part of England and has 'to the greate pleasure and commoditie' of the Queen and her subjects set forth divers 'trewe and pleasainte mappes, chartes or plattes' of the counties, and intends further to travel therein throughout all the residue of the realm and cause the 'plattes' to be engraved in copper plates and printed. *English.*   By Q.

[*Printed in* Thoresby Society Publications, *vol.* xxviii, *p.* 378.]

2341.)   8 *July* 1577.   *Gorhambury.*   Lease for 21 years to Richard Todde of lands in Hampton Courte, co. Middlesex, parcel of the lordship and honour of Hampton Courte; with reservations; from Lady Day last; yearly rent £10 10s. (*detailed*); the lessee to re-stock, maintain and preserve   [*m.* 22]
the hare warren at Hampton Courte. In consideration of his surrender of a patent, 18 Dec., 9 Eliz., leasing the premises to him from Michaelmas 1567 for so long as he should remain keeper of the wardrobe at Hampton Courte at the same rent; and for a fine of £10 10s. paid at the Exchequer.   By warrant of the commissioners.

2342.)   26 *July* 1577.   *Gorhambury.*   Lease for 21 years to Henry Bristowe of (1) the site of the manor of Hertford, co. Huntingdon, now or late in the tenure of Thomas Hardinge, and (2) lands in Stewekley, co. Huntingdon, now or late in the tenure of Thomas Anthonie, all late of Huntingdon priory, co. Huntingdon, and (3) the rectory of Apulton, co. Norfolk, now or late in the tenure of Thomas Colt, once of the monastery of Westacre; with reservations; from Lady Day last; yearly rents (1) £4 6s. 8d., (2) 50s. and (3) 66s. 8d.; the lessee to pay to the vicar of Apulton a yearly pension of £7. In consideration that Bristowe will undertake the repair and maintenance of the house and buildings of the site of the manor of Hertford and the chancel of Apulton church, now ruinous; and for a fine of £16 13s. 4d. paid
                                                                                                  [*m.* 23]
at the Exchequer.   By warrant of the commissioners.

2343.) 8 *July* 1577. *Gorhambury*. Lease for 21 years to John Peache, John Scott the younger, Henry Newman, Thomas Killingworthe, Simon Love, William Lamberd, John Kinge the elder, Simon Kinge, John Englishe and Robert Kinge the elder, to the use of them and all other the Queen's tenants and inhabitants of Hallywell and Nedingworthe, co. Huntingdon, of (1) the first cutting of marsh and meadows (*named*) in Hallywell and Nedingworthe and (2) meadows (*named*) in the said manor of Hallywell and Nedingworthe, all (*tenants named*) late of the monastery of Ramsey; with reservations; from Lady Day last; yearly rents (1) £5 12*s*. 1*d*. and (2) 16*s*. 4*d*. On the surrender by Peache and the others above-named of a patent, 7 Nov., 6 Eliz., leasing the premises to William Mynne for 21 years from Michaelmas then next at the same rents; and for a fine of £10 10*d*. paid at the Exchequer.   By warrant of the commissioners.

2344.) 8 *July* 1577. *Gorhambury*. Lease for 31 years to John Collingwood of (1) a corn mill and (2) a fulling mill in the lordship of Etall, co. Northumberland, parcel of the manor of Etall and late of the late earl of Rutland exchanged; with reservations; from Lady Day last;
[*m*. 24]
yearly rents (1) £6 and (2) 26*s*. 8*d*.; the lessee to serve in the North by himself or sufficient men with horse and arms when commanded by the Queen's warden or lieutenant, to occupy the premises by himself or sufficient men and to cultivate and fence the same. In consideration of the surrender by Collingwood of a patent, 8 Nov., 8 Eliz., leasing the premises to Rowland Forster for 21 years from Michaelmas then last at the same rents; also because they are near the borders of Scotland and have been subject to invasions and devastations of thieves and wicked Scots; and because Collingwood offers to new build them within four years at his own costs.   By warrant of the commissioners.

2345.) 8 *July* 1577. *Gorhambury*. Lease for 21 years to Ralph Grey   [*m*. 25]
of the tithes of corn in (1) Sinderlande in Bamburgheshire and (2) Dichende, parcels of the rectory of Bamburghe, co. Northumberland, once of the monastery of St. Oswald, co. York; from Lady Day last; yearly rents (1) £10 and (2) 40*s*. In consideration of the surrender by the said Ralph of a patent, 17 May, 6 Eliz., leasing the premises to Thomas Grey, knight, for 21 years from Lady Day then last at the same rents; and for a fine of £24, to wit, £6 8*s*. paid at the Exchequer and £17 12*s*. to William Bedingfeild in satisfaction of a like sum paid by Bedingfeild for the fine of a lease of lands in Brampton, co. Huntingdon, which he could not enjoy, because the lands had been conveyed by the Crown to John Rade, as appears by a bill signed by Christopher Smythe, clerk of the pipe, annexed to the particular whereon this patent issued.   By warrant of the commissioners.

2346.) 27 *April* 1577. Lease for 40 years to Richard Master, M.D., the Queen's servant, of—(1) the site of the manor of Hallywell, parcel of the manor of Hallywell with Nedyngworthe, co. Huntingdon, late assigned to the Queen before her accession, formerly of the monastery of Ramsey, co. Huntingdon, and leased by conventual indenture, 24 Oct., 27 Hen. VIII, for 60 years from Michaelmas 1539 to Robert Emottes at a yearly rent of £6 6*s*. 8*d*., payable in wheat or malt at St. Ives, co. Huntingdon, at the rate of 8*s*. a quarter of wheat and 3*s*. 4*d*. a quarter of malt; (2) lands in Bokested in the beadlery of Framfeld and in Bokested and Framfeld, parcel of the manor of Framfeld, co. Sussex, parcel of the possessions of the archbishopric of Canterbury in the Queen's hands by act of Parliament, leased by John, late archbishop, by writing, 29 Oct., 12 Hen. VII, for 100 years from that date to Henry Calleys at a yearly rent of 43*s*. 2½*d*.; (3) a coney warren in Barnabye, co. Lincoln, parcel of the duchy of Cornwall and leased by patent, 25 Feb., 10 Eliz., *inter alia* to Thomas Bellingham at a yearly rent of 40*s*. 8½*d*. for 21 years from the termination of a lease to Richard Brokelsbye by patent of Edward VI; (4) lands (*tenants named*) in Inningham, co.

Lincoln, in the Crown's hands by the dissolution of chantries and the like and leased by patent of the Exchequer, 8 July, 11 Eliz., for 21 years from Lady Day then last *inter alia* to Thomas Yeoman at a yearly rent of 26*s.* 8*d.*; (5) lands (*tenants named*) in Northickham, co. Lincoln, once of the monastery of St. Catherine, co. Lincoln, and leased to William Dove by patent of the Exchequer, 25 May, 10 Eliz., for 21 years from Lady Day then last at a yearly rent of 11*s.*; (6) the rectory of Wykes, co. Essex, once in the tenure of William Bretton, late of cardinal Wolcey, attainted, once of Horkesey priory, co. Essex, and leased to George Gascoigne by patent of the Exchequer, 29 May, 10 Eliz., for 21 years from Lady Day then last at a yearly rent of 55*s.* 8*d.*; (7) lands (*named with tenants' names*) in Tofte and Newton, co. Lincoln, once of the monastery of Sixhyll and leased *inter alia* to Anthony Cowper by patent, 1 July, 10 Eliz., for 21 years from Lady Day then last at a yearly rent of 31*s.* 4*d.*; (8) lands (*tenants named*) in Tofte and Newton aforesaid, once of the monastery of Sixhyll and leased *inter alia* to Robert Sanderson by patent of the Exchequer, 6 Dec., 11 Eliz., for 21 years from Michaelmas then last at a yearly rent of 46*s.* 2*d.*; (9) lands (*tenant named*) in Shalston, co. Buckingham, given for an obit in the church there, and (10) lands in Dedington, co. Oxford, given for a light in Dedington church, all leased to Paul Darell by patent of the Exchequer, 12 March, 11 Eliz., for 21 years from Michaelmas then last at a yearly rent of 12*s.*; (11) lands (*described with tenants' names*) in Rapley *alias* Ropley, co Southampton, parcel   [*m.* 26] of possessions of chantries and the like dissolved, leased *inter alia* to John Izerne by patent of the Exchequer, 8 April, 11 Eliz., for 21 years from Michaelmas then last at a yearly rent of 8*s.*; (12) land (*named with tenants' names*) in Laleham, co. Middlesex, parcel of the manor of Laleham and Billettes and now parcel of the honour of Hampton Courte, leased *inter alia* to Thomas Woodwall by patent of the Exchequer, 25 June, 9 Eliz., for 21 years from Michaelmas then last at a yearly rent of 12*d.*; (13) a tenement in the parish of St. Mary at Strond, co. Middlesex, once in the tenure of William Buttrye, formerly of Edward, late duke of Somerset, leased to William Pereson by patent of the Exchequer, 16 March, 10 Eliz., for 21 years from Michaelmas then last at a yearly rent of 20*s.*; (14) a water mill (*named with tenant's name*) in Ricmersworthe, co. Hertford, parcel of the manor of Rickmersworthe and of the lands late taken out of the bishopric of London by act of Parliament, leased to John Wylson by patent of the Exchequer, 21 Feb., 6 Eliz., for 21 years from Michaelmas then last at a yearly rent of 66*s.* 8*d.*; (15) the tithes of the manor of Ardenhall in the parish of Hornedon, co. Essex, (*tenants named*), once of the monastery of Barmondesey, co. Surrey, and leased to Henry Pollyver by patent of the Exchequer, 7 July, 5 Eliz., for 21 years from Lady Day then last at a yearly rent of 53*s.* 4*d.*; (16) lands (*named*) in Cardigan, co. Cardigan, late of Rees Griffith, attainted, and leased *inter alia* to Griffith Rees by patent, 14 Oct., 5 Eliz., for 21 years from Lady Day then last at a yearly rent of 18*s.* 4*d.*; and (17) the rectory of Skidbroke, co. Lincoln, once of the monastery of Torre, co. Devon, and leased to John Gerbray by patent, 10 Feb., 3 Eliz., for 21 years from Michaelmas then last at a yearly rent of £5 19*s.* 2*d.* With reservations. From (1) Michaelmas 1599, (2) Michaelmas 1596, (3) Michaelmas 1583, (4) Lady Day 1590, (5), (6) and (7) Lady Day 1589, (8), (9), (10) and (11) Michaelmas 1589, (12) Lady Day 1588,   [*m.* 27] (13) Michaelmas 1588, (14) Michaelmas 1584, (15) and (16) Lady Day 1584 and (17) Michaelmas 1581. Yearly rents (1) £6 6*s.* 8*d.* payable in wheat or malt at the election of the Crown at St. Ives at the rate of aforesaid, (2) 43*s.* 2½*d.*, (3) 40*s.* 8½*d.*, (4) 26*s.* 8*d.*, (5) 11*s.*, (6) 55*s.* 8*d.*, (7) 31*s.* 4*d.*, (8) 46*s.* 2*d.*, (9) 9*s.*, (10) 3*s.*, (11) 8*s.*, (12) 12*d.*, (13) 20*s.*, (14) 66*s.* 8*d.*, (15) 53*s.* 4*d.*, (16) 18*s.* 4*d.*, (17) £5 19*s.* 2*d.* The lessee to pay yearly a stipend of £6 13*s.* 4*d.* to a priest or curate in Wykes church and 9*s.* 4*d.* for proxies and synodals to the archdeacon of Colchester out of the said rectory and to bear the costs of wine, wax and other necessaries for Wykes church; also to pay 7*s.* 6*d.* for proxies to the archdeacon of Lincoln out of the rectory of Skidbroke; also to do suit and service at the court of the manor of Southmallynge, co. Sussex; the lessee and all others hereafter holding the premises in Framfeld and Bokested shall at the death of every tenant in possession pay his best beast by way of relief or heriot; the lessee to provide entertainment for the Queen's steward and surveyor at the manor of Hallywell coming to hold courts or make a survey for three days yearly.   [*m.* 28]

    For Master's service.   By p.s.

2347.)   15 *April* 1577.   Licence for Francis Walsingham, one of the principal secretaries of state, his executors, administrators and assigns, and all other persons, as well aliens and strangers as English and denizens, by them appointed, to export 30,000 woollen cloths 'unrowed, unbarbed and unshorne and not fullie and readie dressed or wroughte' made in England or other the Queen's dominions, coloured cloths to be above £3 in value and uncoloured or white to be above £4; notwithstanding stats. 3 Hen. VII, 3 Hen. VIII, 5 Hen. VIII, 21–27 Hen. VIII and 33 Hen. VIII; aliens who   [*m.* 29] are assigns or other agents of the licensee to pay duties as aliens, and the licensee and persons born within the Queen's dominions who are his assigns or agents to pay duties as subjects born within the realm. For his service.   *English.*   By Q.

2348.)   15 *April* 1577.   Appointment of the master, wardens and commonalty of the mistery of tallow chandlers of London to be searchers, weighers, examiners, viewers and triers of all soap, vinegar and barrelled butter made, brought and kept within the city of London and the liberties thereof, the borough of Southwarke and St. Katherens near the Tower of London, Whyte Chappell, Shordiche, Sainte Jones, Clarkenwell, and Sainte Giles in the Feilde, Westminster, for sale and also of all oil and hops brought from foreign parts into the city of London or the liberties aforesaid or any way kept there for sale; every firkin of butter to contain 64 pounds with the cask. With power for them or their sufficient deputies to enter all places where such things are kept for sale and from time to time make view and trial of the same. Within two months from the present date this patent or the effect and contents thereof under the hands of the master and wardens shall be openly notified in print or writing within the city and the liberties aforesaid, and those using that trade there shall have two months after such publication to do away corrupt things and provide others of good and wholesome stuff; after which two months the master, wardens and commonalty may seize all soap found by them or their deputies and proved before the lord mayor of London and the head officers of Sainte Katheryns and liberties aforesaid to be mingled with tallow or other corrupt things and offered for sale, and all oils, hops, vinegar and salt butter found and proved by like means to be faulty, and may consume them by   [*m.* 30] fire in the sight of the people with the assistance of the chief officer of the place where the same shall be found. Power also to mark all vessels of good, sweet and perfect soap, oil, vinegar and butter and sacks and pockets of good and perfect hops with the rose and crown imperial upon it, and to mark all vessels of soap made and boiled with train oil or rape oil commonly called coarse soap, which is to be occupied about woollen cloth and other things of that nature, and all mingled oils with the letter C betokening 'coarse'; sellers of the same wares not to use fraud in weighing of butter and soap, but the allowance of the lack to be restored to the buyer, or in the uttering or changing thereof, or in abusing the same marks after marking, upon pain of imprisonment and further fine as the offences shall deserve. Every person to forbear to put to sale any soap, vinegar, barrelled butter, oil or hops until such time as the master, wardens and commonalty or their deputies have tried and marked the same in manner aforesaid; so as they be always ready to make such trial and marking and do the same upon warning given by those bringing those things into the city, Saincte Katherens or the liberties aforesaid or keeping them there for sale, upon pain of forfeiting such as shall be put to sale before trial and marking; one moiety of the forfeitures to be paid into the Exchequer by the master, wardens and commonalty, and the other moiety to be distributed by them to the poor of the place where the forfeitures shall happen by the discretion of them with the chief officers or persons of the place. The master, wardens and commonalty and their deputies for the several places above-named may take of owners for the trying and marking the fees following: for every barrel of good soap 2*d*., half barrel 1*d*., firkin ½*d*. and half firkin ¼*d*.; for every tun of good vinegar 8*d*., puncheon 4*d*. and hogshead 2*d*.; for every barrel of good barrelled butter 2*d*., half barrel 1*d*. and firkin ½*d*.; for every tun of good 'Civill' oil or train oil 8*d*., pipe 4*d*. and hogshead 2*d*.; for every barrel of good rape oil or whale oil 2*d*.; for every barrel of 'sallet' oil 2*d*.; for every sack of good hops 8*d*. and pocket 4*d*. If any of the said things allowed by marks set on as aforesaid for good shall by the buyer thereof be proved not good by default of the marker, the master, wardens and commonalty shall not only pay the said buyer the price he paid for it, but also one moiety of the price for damages and costs. Provided that, if it shall be thought good to the Queen for any lawful cause that this grant should be revoked, or if the master and wardens or any of their deputies shall misuse it, the Queen may by patent repeal and stay the execution thereof or of so such of it as shall be thought convenient.

For the reformation of abuses: 'unmeate devises' are practised by makers of soap and vinegar by mingling 'unkyndlie and hurtfull stuffe' instead of wholesome and good things, as in making soap to mix tallow and other 'impartynente and unswete thinges' not meet for the washing of linen for the body and yet is sold for good and sweet soap; also to weigh every vessel of soap that for every pound and other weight over and above the due weight in timber, the soap maker to allow for every such lack in every vessel so much soap as shall lack in the same; likewise by making vinegar of corrupt beer and ale mingled with 'unholsome dredges' for the colouring of it, where it ought to be made only of perfect 'eger wyne'; also oils and hops brought from foreign parts and uttered in the realm are often found mingled and impaired from their natural goodness; also the like abuse is used in packing barrelled butter by mingling corrupt and musty butter in the heart of vessels of butter and so not meet to be uttered to be eaten; also lack of weight in firkins of butter. *English*.   By p.s.

2349.)   19 *April* 1577.   Pardon for George Strutte late of Colchester, co. Essex, 'maryner', late owner of a fourth part of a ship called '*The Anne* of Colchester' *alias* '*The Anne* of Quynboroughe' and master of the same, William Johnson late of Snettisham, co. Norfolk, 'maryner', and Thomas Smythe late of Redrithe, co. Surrey, 'maryner', for that on 21 July, 17 Eliz., in the said ship on the river Thames by Tilberye Hope within the jurisdiction of the Admiralty sailing from the port of Dunkirke in Flanders towards the port of London they piratically seized and broke open (1) 'a case' and stole therefrom cloths etc. (*described*) belonging to John de la Barr, merchant of Antwerp, dwelling in London, (2) 'a drye fatte' and stole therefrom thread etc.   [*m.* 31]
(*described*) belonging to Abraham Elinge, merchant of Antwerp, residing in London, (3) 'a packe' and stole therefrom cloths etc. (*described*) belonging to Livinus van Stelte, merchant of Ghent, and (4) 'a case' and stole therefrom silks (*described*) belonging to Peter de Coster, merchant of Antwerp, dwelling in London, as appears by indictments and presentments remaining in the court of Admiralty; to be interpreted in their favour.   By p.s.

2350.)   25 *April* 1577.   Pardon for Charles Wrighte late of Campton,   [*m.* 32]
co. Bedford, 'taylor', indicted with Robert Cramfelde late of Shefford, co. Bedford, 'yoman', for that in the highway at Mauldon, co. Bedford, on 6 Nov., 17 Eliz., they robbed Robert Gaddesdon, 'yoman', and Joan Hunte, 'spynster', both of Mauldon, of articles (*described*) belonging to Gaddesdon. At the suit of Clara Wrighte, wife of Charles.

By p.s.

2351.)   22 *April* 1577.   Pardon for William Horne late of Barningham in the North

Riding, co. York, 'laborer', indicted for the theft of sheep (*described*) belonging severally to (1) George Cattericke and (2) William Wicliffe at Barmingham on 18 Dec., 19 Eliz.

By p.s.

2352.)   24 *April* 1577.   Grant to Thomas Horwell of the wardship and marriage of John Pynnoke, son and heir of William Pynnoke; with an annuity   [*m.* 33] of £5 from 20 Jan., 18 Eliz., when William died.   By Q.

2353.)   24 *April* 1577.   Lease for 21 years to William Hungate of the rectory of Tadcaster, co. York, late of Arthur Darcye, knight, exchanged; with reservations; from Michaelmas next; yearly rent £30. In consideration of William's surrender of an indenture, 1 May, 34 Hen. VIII, whereby Darcye leased the rectory to Thomas Hungate, father of William, for 41 years from St. Mark's Day then last at the same rent; and for a fine of £60 paid at the Exchequer.   By p.s.

2354.)   17 *April* 1577.   Grant to John Carye, the Queen's servant, of £200 owed to the Crown by Thomas Francke of Hatfeilde Regis, co. Essex,   [*m.* 34] for a fine imposed on him in the Star Chamber in Hilary term last and 40 marks in which the said Francke and William Smythe and William Davyes, both of the parish of St. Michael in Bassieshawe ward, London, were bound before Thomas Greke, a baron of the Exchequer, on 28 Feb. last for payment of the said fine in Trinity term next, as appears by their recognisance remaining in the Exchequer with the Queen's remembrancer; with power to sue in the Exchequer in the Crown's name or his own for the recovery of the said sums. For his service.   By p.s.

2355.)   19 *April* 1577.   Lease for 40 years to Thomas Blethen of (1) all tenements in Moore Lane in the parish of St. Giles without Creplegate, London, once in the tenure of Thomas Alsope and now or late in that of Robert Fryer, given by William Kente for superstitious uses in the parish of St. Peter the Little next Brokenwharfe, London, and (2) all lands in the said parish of St. Giles called Master Howes Rentes, or parcel of the same, now or late in the tenure of Geoffrey Ibgrave *alias* Hisberde and heretofore leased to William Grene and Thomas Gaye, once belonging to the late fellowship of clerks of London; from Lady Day last; yearly rents from the time when he shall obtain possession (1) £6 and (2) 26s. 8d. For a fine of £3 paid at the Exchequer.   By warrant of the commissioners.

2356.)   22 *April* 1577.   Presentation of William Irelande, M.A., to the perpetual vicarage of St. Michael in Coventry, Coventry and Lichfield dioc., void by death.   By p.s.

2357.)   19 *April* 1577.   Presentation of John Robynson, S.T.B., to the rectory of Fulbeck, Lincoln dioc., void by lapse.   By p.s.

2358.)   20 *June* 1577.   Lease for 21 years to Nicholas Sherwood of   [*m.* 35] lands (*tenants named*) in (1) Stixwold, co. Lincoln, once of the monastery of Stixwold, (2) Spaldinge, co. Lincoln, once of the monastery of Spaldinge, and (3) Southraye, co. Lincoln, late of John Belloo, exchanged;   [*m.* 36] with reservations; from Lady Day last; yearly rents (1) £6 2s. 6d., (2) 52s. 4d. and (3) 58s. In consideration of his surrender in the Exchequer of a patent of the Exchequer, 21 July, 13 Eliz., leasing certain of the premises in Stixwold to him for 21 years from Lady Day then last at a yearly rent of £5; also because he will undertake the repair and maintenance of the rest of the premises, which are in great decay; and for a fine of £5 paid at the Exchequer.   By warrant of the commissioners.

2359.)   10 *June* 1577.   Lease for 21 years to John Mildmaye of (1) the site of the manor of Harroldes in Cretingham, co. Suffolk, and lands (*tenant named*) in Cretingham and (2) lands (*named with tenants' names*) in Brandeston, co. Suffolk, all once of St. Philip's chantry called 'the olde chaunterie of Donnyngton' and afterwards of Richard Fulmerston, exchanged, (3) lands (*tenants named*) in Shelley, co. Suffolk, once of St. John's monastery, Colchester, and (4) lands (*named with tenant's name*) in Whitwicke, co. Leicester, parcel of the manor of Whitwicke, late of Henry, duke of Suffolk, attainted; with reservations; from Lady Day last;

[*m*. 37]

yearly rents (1) £8, (2) 69s. 8d. (*detailed*), (3) 12s. and (4) 30s. In consideration of his surrender of a patent, 10 May, 5 Eliz., leasing (1), (2) and (3) to him for 21 years from Lady Day then last at the same rents; and for a fine of £18 1s. 8d. paid at the Exchequer.   By p.s.

2360.)   17 *June* 1577.   Lease for 21 years to Thomas Smythe of (1) the site and capital mansion of the manor of Southstoke, co. Somerset,   [*m*. 38]
and stock (*described*) thereof and (2) a stock of 280 sheep and pasture for the same on 'le stalles', hills or 'downes' and other lands, all once of the monastery of Bathe, co. Somerset; with reservations; from Michaelmas next; yearly rent £12 2d.; the lessee to deliver the stock aforesaid at the end of the term to the receiver general or surveyor of the county or the steward of the Queen's manor of Southstoke; also to provide entertainment for the Queen's steward and surveyor coming to the manor to hold courts there or survey the same two days yearly. In consideration of his surrender of a patent, 25 Nov., 7 Eliz., leasing the premises to Ellis Wynne for 21 years from Michaelmas then last at yearly rents of (1) £6 19s. 4d. and (2) 100s. 10d.; and for a fine of £16 paid at the Exchequer.

By warrant of the commissioners.

2361.)   15 *June* 1577.   Licence for two years for Goumer van Osterwick, the Queen's servant, to buy and export in English or friendly bottoms from any English port to friendly countries 200 broad woollen cloths or kerseys, counting three kerseys to one broad cloth, as well 'Kentishe clothe' or 'Suffolk clothe' as any other sort, white as well as coloured, undressed or dressed; from the present date; duties to be paid as by English-born merchants and citizens of London; the licence to have the amounts shipped endorsed on it that it may be left, when expired, with the customers of the port where the last part shall be shipped.   *English.*

2362.)   18 *June* 1577.   Pardon for Arthur Drinkwater late of Dunham, co.   [*m*. 39]
Chester, 'yoman', for manslaughter. He was indicted by an inquisition taken at Dunham on 24 Sept., 18 Eliz., before John Maisterson, a coroner of the county, on the body of James Cooke late of Dunham, 'yoman', for that he wounded Cooke at Dunham on 13 Sept., 18 Eliz., so that he died there on 23 Sept. (*details given*). At the suit of Thomas Butler. By Q.

2363.)   10 *June* 1577.   Pardon for Thomas Stranguishe late of Asshe, co. Surrey, for all offences committed before the present date (murder, burglary and rape excepted). He was indicted for that at Purbrighte, co. Surrey, on 21 Dec., 19 Eliz., in the highway he robbed John Russell of a mare and £19 belonging to him.   By Q.

2364.)   18 *June* 1577.   Pardon for Robert Tuyll of Dunhevit Burgh *alias* Launceston, co. Cornwall, 'cordiner'. At the gaol delivery of Launceston castle, co. Cornwall, made there on [—] in the fifth week of Lent, 19 Eliz., before John Jeffraye, a justice of the Queen's Bench, and his fellows, justices of gaol delivery, he was indicted for the theft of a mare belonging to

John Luckys at St. Stephins next Launceston, co. Cornwall, on 7 Feb., 19 Eliz., pleaded not guilty, was convicted and for divers causes was committed back to gaol. At the suit of his son,   [*m.* 40]
William Tuyll.   By Q.

(The dorse of this roll is blank.)

PART X

C. 66/1160

2365.)   19 *Nov.* 1576.   Licence for Edward Blount, son and heir of   [*m.* 1]
Thomas Blount, to enter upon his lands; issues from the time when   [*m.* 2]
Edward attained the age of 21.   By bill of the court of Wards.

2366.)   26 *Nov.* 1576.   The like for Oliver Seynt John and Dorothy his wife, as in right of
the same Dorothy, daughter and heir of John Reade; issues from the time when Dorothy
attained the age of 14.   [*m.* 3]
          By bill of the court of Wards.

2367.)   27 *Nov.* 1576.   The like for James Hannam, son and heir of William Hannam;
issues from William's death.   [*m.* 4]
          By bill of the court of Wards.

2368.)   24 *Jan.* 1577.   The like for Simon Parrott and Mary his wife, as in right of the same
Mary, daughter and heir of Francis Barrantyne; issues from the time when Mary attained the
age of 16.   [*m.* 5]
          By bill of the court of Wards.

2369.)   5 *Feb.* 1577.   The like for Peter Courteney, son and heir of Margaret Buller,
widow; issues from Margaret's death.   [*m.* 6]
          By bill of the court of Wards.
          [*m.* 7]

2370.)   7 *Dec.* 1576.   *Gorhambury.*   The like for John Waryner and   [*m.* 8]
Catherine his wife, as in right of the same Catherine, sister and heir of Richard Robson;
issues from Robson's death.   [*m.* 9]
          By bill of the court of Wards.

2371.)   2 *July* 1577.   The like for John Jackman, son and heir of Edward Jackman,
alderman of London; issues from the time when John   [*m.* 10]
attained the age of 21.   By bill of the court of Wards.

2372.)   15 *Nov.* 1577.   Pardon of outlawry for Richard Aynsley late of Kylnewyck, co.
York, 'taylor', who was put in exigent in the said county for non-appearance in the Common
Pleas to answer William Fyssher in a plea of trespass and has now surrendered himself to the
Fleet Prison.

2373.)   7 *May* 1577.   Licence for Thomas Leveson, son and heir of John Leveson, to enter
upon his lands; issues from John's death.   [*m.* 11]
          By bill of the court of Wards.

2374.)   20 *May* 1577.   *Gorhambury.*   The like for Richard Barthelet, son and heir of John
Barthelett; issues from the time when Richard attained   [*m.* 12]
the age of 21.   By bill of the court of Wards.

2375.)   7 *May* 1577.   The like for Robert Acton, son and heir of Henry Acton; issues from
the time when Robert attained the age of 21.   [*m.* 13]
                                                    By bill of the court of Wards.

2376.)   3 *May* 1577.   *Gorhambury.*   The like for George Wylkyns, kinsman and heir of
John Wylkyns, to wit, the son of Mark Wilkyns, brother of   [*m.* 14]
John; issues from John's death.   By bill of the court of Wards.

2377.)   20 *June* 1577.   The like for John Tyndall, son and heir of William Tyndall; issues
from the time when John attained the age of   [*m.* 15]
21.   By bill of the court of Wards.

2378.)   17 *June* 1577.   The like for Edward Denton, son and heir of John Denton and
brother and heir of John Denton, son and heir apparent (while he lived) of the said John;
issues from the death of John the father and   [*m.* 16]
John the son.   By bill of the court of Wards.

2379.)   7 *June* 1577.   The like for John Michell, son and heir of Alfred Michell; issues from
the time when John attained the age of 21.   [*m.* 17]
                                                    By bill of the court of Wards.

2380.)   14 *June* 1577.   The like for John Hawarde, son and heir of   [*m.* 18]
William Howard; issues from the time when John attained the age of 21.
                                                    By bill of the court of Wards.

2381.)   16 *Feb.* 1577.   Pardon of outlawry for John Waight late of   [*m.* 19]
Oxford, co. Oxford, 'chapman', who was put in exigent in the husting of London for
non-appearance in the Common Pleas to satisfy (1) John Eyer, citizen and 'clothworker' of
London, in respect of a debt of £8 16*s*., and 26*s*. 8*d*. damages, recovered in the said court and
(2) John Wyddell alias Wadham, citizen and 'haberdassher' of London, in respect of £14,
and 26*s*. 8*d*. damages, recovered in the said court; he has now surrendered himself to the
Fleet prison, and Eyer by John Turnor, his attorney, and Widdell by Thomas Gardney, his
attorney, have acknowledged satisfaction.

2382.)   1 *Feb.* 1577.   The like for William Nelson late of Hollme, co. York, 'yoman', who
was put in exigent in the husting of London for non-appearance in the Common Pleas to
answer Christopher Walker of Picall, co. York, husbandman, in a plea of debt of £18 and has
now surrendered himself to the Fleet prison.

2383.)   21 *June* 1577.   Order to all etc. to permit the men and tenants of the manor of
Bremysgrove, co. Worcester, to be quit, according to custom, as tenants in ancient demesne,
of toll and other dues (*named*), contributions to expenses of knights of Parliament and juries
etc. outside the court of the manor. They are found to be tenants in ancient demesne by a
certificate (*recited*) sent into the Chancery by the treasurer and chamberlains of the
Exchequer.

2384.)   28 *May* 1577.   Licence for the dean and chapter of Carlisle cathedral to elect a
bishop to that church, void by the translation of Richard, the last bishop, to the see of
Durham.   By p.s.

2385.)   9 *Aug.* 1577.   Signification to Edwin, archbishop of York, of the royal assent to the election of John Maye, S.T.D., to the bishopric of Carlisle; and order to confirm the election and do all other things incumbent on the archbishop in this behalf according to statute.　　　　　　　　　　　　　　　　　　　　　　　　　　　　By p.s.

2386.)　8 *Oct.* 1577.　*Windsor.*　Writ to the escheator in the county of Northumberland to deliver to John Maye, S.T.P., bishop elect of　　　　　　　　　　　　　　　　[*m.* 20]
Carlisle, the temporalities of his see; the Queen having assented to his election, received his fealty and restored the temporalities to him hereby; issues from 17 May last.　　By p.s.

2387.)　8 *Oct.* 1577.　*Windsor.*　The like to the escheators in the following counties— Cumberland; Surrey; Westmorland; Lincoln; Derby; Middlesex.

2388.)　8 *Oct.* 1577.　*Windsor.* Order to the tenants of the see to be intendant accordingly.
　　　　　　　　　　　　　　　　　　　　　　　　　　　　　　　　By p.s.

2389.)　10 *March* 1577.　*Gorhambury.*　Licence for the dean and chapter of St. Paul's cathedral, London, to elect a bishop to that church, void by the translation of Edwin Sandes to the archbishopric of York.　　　　　　　　　　　　　　　　　　By p.s.

2390.)　18 *March* 1577.　*Gorhambury.*　Signification to Edmund, archbishop of Canterbury, of the royal assent to the election of John Aylmer, S.T.D., to the bishopric of London; and order to confirm the election and consecrate him and do all other things incumbent on the archbishop in this behalf according to statute.　　　　　　　　　　　By p.s.

2391.)　10 *May* 1577.　Writ to the escheator in the county of Middlesex to deliver to John Aylmer, S.T.P., bishop elect of London, the temporalities of his see (except any lands now taken into the Queen's hands by stat. 1 Eliz.); the Queen having received his fealty and restored the temporalities to him hereby; issues from Michaelmas last.　　　By p.s.

2392.)　10 *May* 1577.　The like to the following escheators—cos. Essex and Hertford; cos. Surrey and Sussex; co. Worcester; co. Huntingdon; John Langley, mayor and escheator of London.

2393.)　10 *May* 1577.　Order to the tenants of the see to be intendant accordingly.
　　　　　　　　　　　　　　　　　　　　　　　　　　　　　　　　By p.s.

2394.)　25 *June* 1577.　Pardon of outlawry for William Snellinge late of Wenham Magna, 'yoman', who was put in exigent in the husting of London for non-appearance in the Common Pleas to answer John Snellinge *alias* Snellynge of the same town in a plea of debt of £8 and has now surrendered himself to the Fleet prison.

2395.)　18 *June* 1577.　Licence for Andrew Foster, son and heir of　　　　[*m.* 21]
John Foster, to enter upon his lands; issues from John's death.　　　　　　[*m.* 22]

2396.)　18 *May* 1577.　The like for John Strangwayes, son and heir of Giles Strangwayes, knight; issues from Giles's death.　　　　　　　　　　　　　　　　[*m.* 23]

2397.)　12 *June* 1577.　The like for Henry Bradburie, brother and heir of Robert Bradburie; issues from Robert's death.　　　　　　　　　　　　　　　　[*m.* 24]

2398.)　14 *Feb.* 1577.　The like for Francis Wynchecombe, son and heir of John Winchecombe; issues from the time when Francis attained the age of 21.　　　[*m.* 25]

2399.) 8 *May* 1577. The like for Nicholas Girlington, son and heir of Nicholas Girlington; issues from Nicholas the father's death.   [*m.* 26]

2400.) 12 *June* 1577. The like for Alexander Shepperde, son and heir of Robert Shepperde; issues from the time when Alexander attained the age of 21.   [*m.* 27]

2401.) 26 *Nov.* 1576. The like for Henry Kendall, son and heir of   [*m.* 28]
George Kendall; issues from the time when Henry attained the age of 21.

2402.) 15 *Nov.* 1577. The like for Edmund Allen, son and heir of   [*m.* 29]
John Allen; issues from the time when Edmund attained the age of 21.   [*m.* 30]

2403.) 6 *Feb.* 1577. The like for John Lane, son and heir of John Lane; issues from the time when John the son attained the age of 21.

2404.) 27 *Nov.* 1576. The like for William Underhill, son and heir   [*m.* 31]
of William Underhill; issues from the time when William the son   [*m.* 32]
attained the age of 21.   By bill of the court of Wards.

2405.) 26 *Nov.* 1576. The like for Richard Cooke, son and heir of Anthony Cooke, knight; issues from Anthony's death.   [*m.* 33]
By bill of the court of Wards.

2406.) 7 *Feb.* 1577. The like for Richard Fenys, son and heir of Richard Fenys, knight; issues from the time when Richard the son   [*m.* 34]
attained the age of 21.   By bill of the court of Wards.

2407.) 20 *Jan.* 1577. The like for John Crispe, son and heir of William Crispe; issues from William's death.   [*m.* 35]
By bill of the court of Wards.

2408.) 7 *Dec.* 1576. The like for Robert Wingfelde, son and heir   [*m.* 36]
of Robert Wingefelde; issues from Robert the father's death.
By bill of the court of Wards.

2409.) 15 *May* 1577. The like for Philip, now lord Wharton, son   [*m.* 37]
and heir of Thomas Wharton, knight, late lord Wharton; issues from the time when Philip attained the age of 21.   [*m.* 38]
By bill of the court of Wards.

2410.) 27 *April* 1577. The like for John Stafford, brother and heir of Humphrey Stafforde, knight; issues from Humphrey's death.   [*m.* 39]
By bill of the court of Wards.

2411.) 24 *March* 1577. *Gorhambury.* Licence for the dean and chapter of Worcester cathedral to elect a bishop to that church, void by death.   By p.s.

2412.) 9 *April* 1577. *Gorhambury.* Signification to Edmund, archbishop of Canterbury, of the royal assent to the election of John Whitgifte, S.T.P., to the bishopric of Worcester, void by the death of Nicholas, the last bishop; and order to confirm the election

and consecrate him and do all other things incumbent on the archbishop in this behalf
according to statute.   By p.s.

2413.)   10 *May* 1577.   Writ to the escheators in the county of Anglesey to deliver to John
Whitgifte, S.T.P., bishop elect of Worcester, the temporalities of his see (except any lands
now taken into the Queen's hands by stat. 1 Eliz.); the Queen having received his fealty and
restored the temporalities to him hereby; issues from Michaelmas last.   By p.s.

2414.)   10 *May* 1577.   The like to the following escheator — co. Salop; co. Middlesex; co.
Middlesex [*sic*]; co. Worcester; co. Hereford; co. Buckingham; co. Sussex; co. Oxford; co.
Warwick; co. Gloucester; John Langley, knight, mayor and escheator of London.

2415.)   10 *May* 1577.   Order to the tenants of the see to be intendant accordingly.
                                                                                     By p.s.

2416.)   29 *April* 1577.   Licence for John *alias* Seynt John Boroughe, son   [*m.* 40]
and heir of Richard Boroughe, to enter upon his lands; issues from the time   [*m.* 41]
when John attained the age of 21.   By bill of the court of Wards.

2417.)   17 *June* 1577.   The like for Thomas Welbore, son and heir of   [*m.* 42]
Michael Welbore; issues from Michael's death.   By warrant of the court of Wards.

2418.)   20 *June* 1577.   The like for George Gilberte, son and heir   [*m.* 43]
of Ambrose Gilberte; issues from the time when George attained the age of 21.
                                                     By warrant of the court of Wards.

2419.)   5 *June* 1577.   The like for Robert Wilbrahame, kinsman   [*m.* 44]
and heir of Robert Chidley late of London, to wit, the first born son of Barbara Wilbrahame,
deceased, late the wife of Thomas Wilbrahame, deceased, daughter and heir of Chidley;
issues from Chidley's death.   By warrant of the court of Wards.

2420.)   2 *July* 1577.   The like for Elizabeth Randell, widow, late   [*m.* 45]
the wife of Vincent Randyll, daughter and sole heir of lady Elizabeth Dennys, widow; issues
from lady Elizabeth's death.   By bill of the court of Wards.

2421.)   11 *June* 1577.   The like for Thomas Lane, son and heir of   [*m.* 46]
John Lane; issues from John's death.   [*m.* 47]
                                                     By warrant of the court of Wards.

2422.)   12 *June* 1577.   The like for Edward Seymor, kinsman and heir of John Walshe, late
a justice of the Common Pleas, to wit, the   [*m.* 48]
son and heir of lady Mary Seymor, daughter and heir of Walshe; issues from the time when
Edward attained the age of 21.   By warrant of the court of Wards.

2423.)   *Undated.* Licence for the president and chapter of Salisbury cathedral to elect a
bishop to that church, void by death.   By p.s.

(*The dorse of this roll is blank.*)

PART XI

C. 66/1161

2424.) 1 *May* 1577. Licence for William Bolles, Benjamin Bolles, [*m.* 1]
son of William, and Anne his wife, William Hodges *alias* Bolles, and Roger Balles to alienate
the manor of Osberton called Osberton Grange and all lands in Osberton and Worksoppe,
co. Nottingham, once of the monastery of Worksoppe, the manor of Newthorpe and all
lands in Newthorpe and Gresby, co. Nottingham, once of Lenton priory, co. Nottingham,
and 10 messuages and lands in the parish of St. Leonard in Shordiche, co. Middlesex, to
William Buckley and George Smyth and the heirs and assigns of Buckley. For £4 18*s.* 5*d.*
paid to the Queen's farmer.

2425.) 1 *May* 1577. The like for William Dummer, Catherine his wife, Humphrey
Bridges and Dorothy his wife to alienate lands called the grange or farm of Dummer in
Dummer, Nutley and Basinge, co. Southampton, to William Bridges; and for him by the
same fine to convey them back to William Dummer and Catherine for life in survivorship,
with successive remainders to Humphrey and Dorothy and the heirs of her body and to the
right heirs of William Dummer. For 50*s.*

2426.) 1 *May* 1577. The like for Richard Broke and Mary his wife to alienate lands in
Ledom *alias* Leddom *alias* Lydom, co. Salop, to Thomas Leveson and Humphrey Nycolls
and the heirs and assigns of Leveson; and for them by the same fine to convey them back to
Richard and Mary and heirs of the body of Richard, with successive remainders to the heirs
male of the bodies of Robert Broke, knight, deceased, and Dorothy his wife, to the heirs
male of the body of Robert and to the right [*m.* 2]
heirs of Robert. For £7 6*s.* 8*d.*

2427.) 1 *May* 1577. The like for John Parker to alienate the manor of Nonney Glaston
and all appurtenances thereof in Nunney, Cleverd, Wytham, Marston *alias* Maston Bygott,
Mells, Trotoxhill, Sharpshawe and Leighe, co. Somerset, and the advowson of the rectory
of Nonneye to Richard Prater. For 56*s.* 8*d.*

2428.) 29 *May* 1577. The like for Edward Clyston and Alice his wife to alienate a shop, a
rood of land and a rood of pasture in the parish of St. Clement Danes without the bars of the
New Temple, London, co. Middlesex, to William Kindesley and Anthony Cave and the
heirs and assigns of Kindesley. For 3*s.* 4½*d.*

2429.) 26 *March* 1577. The like for Lewis Grevill and Thomasina his wife to alienate
lands in Welneford *alias* Welford, co. Gloucester, to John Haltam the younger. For 3*s.* 6¾*d.*

2430.) 26 *March* 1577. The like for the same to alienate lands in Welneford aforesaid to
Richard Harrys and Alice his wife and the heirs and assigns of Alice. For 3*s.* 10*d.* [*m.* 3]

2431.) 1 *Oct.* 1577. The like for Richard Crayford, William Digby and Henry Nowell to
alienate the manor, farm and hereditament of Surfflete, co. Lincoln, conveyed *inter alia* to

Crayford and Digby by Robert Markham, and all other lands in Surfflete likewise conveyed, to William Sparke of London, scrivener. For £3 7s. 9½d.

2432.) 26 *March* 1577. The like for Lewis Grevill and Thomasina his wife to alienate lands in Welneford *alias* Welford, co. Gloucester, to Richard Mylles the elder. For 11s. 2½d.

2433.) 1 *Oct.* 1577. The like for Thomas Farnell, citizen and 'sadler' of London, to alienate a moiety of the rectory of Graysthurrocke, co. Essex, now or late in the tenure of John Webbe, and of the advowson of the vicarage of Graysthurrocke, both late of the hospital of St. John of Jerusalem, to Simon Farnell, citizen and merchant taylor of London. For 46s. 8d. [*m.* 4]

2434.) 1 *Oct.* 1577. The like for Silvester Bellowe to alienate the site of the monastery of Newested, the manors of Cadney and Howsam, lands in Cadney, Howsam and Newsted and free fishery in the water of Ancolne, co. Lincoln, to William Pelham and Dorothy his wife and the heirs and assigns of William. For £6 13s. 4d.

2435.) 1 *Oct.* 1577. The like for Henry Brodridge to alienate lands in Clayton, Keymer *alias* Kydmer, Patcheham and Pycombe, co. Sussex, to Richard Culpeper. For 55s. 8d.

2436.) 26 *March* 1577. The like for Lewis Grevyll and Thomasina his wife to alienate lands in Welneford *alias* Welford, co. Gloucester, to John Hewes. For 10s. 2d.

2437.) 1 *Oct.* 1577. The like for Robert Carr the elder to alienate lands in Durington *alias* Durrington, co. Lincoln, to Gregory Wolmer. For 13s. 4d. [*m.* 5]

2438.) 1 *Oct.* 1577. The like for Urian Verney and Lettice his wife to alienate lands in Barkhamsted, Northchurche and Hammelhamsted, co. Hertford, to Richard Yonge, clerk and writer of leases to the great seal, to the use of the same Richard and Catherine his wife and his heirs and assigns. For £4 9s.

2439.) 1 *Aug.* 1577. *Gorhambury.* The like for Edward Braye, knight, and Reginald Braye, his son and heir apparent, to alienate the reversion of the manor of Westland in Wotton and elsewhere, co. Surrey, to Thomas Godman. For 13s. 4d.

2440.) 1 *Oct.* 1577. The like for Richard Waver *alias* Over and Anne his wife to alienate lands (*described*) in the city of Coventry, late of St. Mary's priory or cathedral there, to Henry Breres, 'draper'. For 13s. 4d.

2441.) 1 *Oct.* 1577. The like for Gilbert Hyde, Eleanor his wife and Thomas Wylde to alienate lands in Elmeley, co. Kent, to [*m.* 6] William Cromer. For 26s. 8d.

2442.) 1 *Oct.* 1577. The like for Anthony Whytharte, Jane his wife, John Bright, Alice his wife, John Sympson, Catherine his wife, William Jones, Clara his wife, Roger Baker, Jane his wife, William Sadler and Joan his wife to alienate the manor of Westdeane, lands in Westdeane and Grymstede and the advowson of Westdeane church, co. Wilts, and lands in Westdeane, Deane All Saints and Lokerley, co. Southampton, to Henry Gyfford. For £5 12d.

2443.) 20 *July* 1577. The like for Richard Bonny to alienate a messuage and grange called

Loscoo Grange, co. York, late of the monastery of Kirkstall, co. York, now or late in the tenure of John Readman, lands (*named*) in Ayketon, co. York, late of the same monastery, and all his lands in Loscoo to John Leigh, 'yeoman'. For 19*s.*

2444.)   1 *Oct.* 1577.   The like for Thomas Gressham, knight, and Anne his wife to alienate lands in Wodmore, co. Somerset, to Thomas Baylie, clerk, and Elizabeth daughter of Fulk Eton, deceased, now wife of Baylye, and the heirs and assigns of Baylye. For 3*s.* 2*d.*

2445.)   1 *Aug.* 1577.   *Gorhambury.*   The like for William Hardinge to alienate lands (*described*) in the parish of Aishe, co. Surrey, to John Baker. For 40*s.*   [*m.* 7]

2446.)   1 *May* 1577.   The like for Nicholas Philpott to alienate lands in Mangottesfelde, More End and Downe Ende, co. Gloucester, to Joan Goore, widow. For 10*s.*

2447.)   20 *June* 1577.   Pardon of alienation: Thomas Wyseman in Hilary term, 15 Eliz., by fine in the Common Pleas acquired from Walter, earl of Essex, lands in Totham Magna, Goldanger and the isle of Ovesey, co. Essex. For £10 paid to the Queen's farmer.

2448.)   12 *Aug.* 1577.   Licence for George Byrde to alienate lands (*described*) in Estgrenewiche, co. Kent, to Brian Annesley. For 46*s.* 8*d.* paid to the Queen's farmer.

2449.)   7 *Nov.* 1577.   Pardon of alienation: Edward Cary, a gentleman of the privy chamber, and William Dodington by indenture, 31 Dec., 16 Eliz., acquired from Thomas Gressham, knight, the manor of Burton Hyll, co. Wilts. For £22 6*s.* paid to the Queen's farmer.

2450.)   1 *Oct.* 1577.   *Gorhambury.*   Licence for Thomas Bartlam *alias* Sale to alienate lands in Odingley, co. Worcester, to Edward Mathowes and   [*m.* 8]
Thomas Parker to the use of Bartlam *alias* Sale for life and thereafter of Mathowes. For 17*s.* paid to the Queen's farmer.

2451.)   1 *July* 1577.   *Gorhambury.*   The like for Hugh Griffithe, one of the six clerks of Chancery, to alienate the manor or grange of Llanvithen and two mills belonging thereto, co. Glamorgan, to William Herde and William Mores. For £4.

2452.)   1 *Oct.* 1577.   The like for William Rudhale to alienate lands (*named with tenants' names*) in the lordship of Wilton, co. Hereford, to Richard Webbe and Thomas Underwood. For 20*s.*

2453.)   20 *June* 1577.   Pardon of alienation: Thomas Emeley *alias* Emley by indenture, 10 Jan., 19 Eliz., acquired from John Dennys the manor or manors of Sowthouse and Sawyers and all lands called Sowthouse and Sawyers in the parishes of Malden, Munden and Purley, co. Essex, and lands (*named*) in Purley. For 53*s.* 4*d.* paid to the Queen's farmer.

2454.)   1 *Oct.* 1577.   Licence for Henry Josselyn and Anne his wife to alienate a moiety of the manors of Manyngtre, Shyddinghoo *alias* Shedinghoo, Oldehall *alias* Oldhall, Newhall and Abbottes *alias* Edlinges, of lands in Manyngtre *alias* Manytre, Mistleigh *alias* Mistley, Brodfeld, Colchester, Stanwaye, Wrabney *alias* Wrabnes,   [*m.* 9]
Wikes, Badowe Parva, Lawford, Bromley Parva and Ardleighe, of view of frankpledge, free warren and liberties in Mistleigh and Manyngtre, of the rectory of Bradfeld, of the

advowson of Mistleigh church and of the advowson of the vicarage of Bradfeld, co. Essex, to John Barker. For £6 13s. 4d. paid to the Queen's farmer.

2455.) 1 *Oct.* 1577. The like for George Penruddock, knight, and Anne his wife to alienate lands in Compton Chamberlayne, co. Wilts, to George Elrington and Thomas Lathburye and the heirs and assigns of Elrington; and for Elrington and Lathburye by the same fine to convey them back to Pendruddock. For 33s. 4d.

2456.) 1 *Oct.* 1577. The like for Roger Frape and Margaret his wife to alienate the rectory of Thorney, lands and the tithes of corn, hay and woods in Thorney and Wiggesley and the advowson of the vicarage of Thorney, co. Nottingham, to Austin Earle the elder and Austin Earle the younger and the heirs and assigns of Austin the elder. For £3.

2457.) 10 *Sept.* 1577. *Gorhambury.* The like for Arthur, lord Gray of Wylton, to alienate lands (*named with tenants' names*), parcels of   [*m.* 10] the demesne lands of the manor of Wylton on Wye, co. Hereford, to Richard Cockes. For 17s.

2458.) 1 *Oct.* 1577. The like for Richard Brakyn, Alice his wife, Thomas Brakyn and Jane his wife to alienate lands in Chesterton, co. Cambridge, to John Stywarde. For £3 11s. 4d.

2459.) 1 *Oct.* 1577. The like for Thomas Staveley and Margaret his wife to alienate the manor of Lyndby *alias* Lymby, lands in Lyndby, Paplewicke *alias* Paxlewik and the forest of Sherwoodd and free fishery in the water of Lyne, co. Nottingham, to John Savile. For £4 8s. 11d.

2460.) 1 *Oct.* 1577. The like for John Thynne and Dorothy his wife to alienate lands in Longleate, Deverell Longebrigge, Hornyngesham, Mayden Bradlegh, Baycliff and Hill Deverell, co. Wilts, to Robert Creswell and John Lacy and the heirs and assigns of Creswell. For 37s. 7d.

2461.) 10 *Sept.* 1577. *Gorhambury.* The like for Arthur, lord Grey of Wylton, to alienate lands (*named with tenants' names*), parcels   [*m.* 11] of the demesne lands of the manor of Wylton on Wye, co. Hereford, to William Ruddall. For 39s. 8d.

2462.) 13 *Nov.* 1577. Pardon of alienation: Thomas Baskervyle by feoffment, 10 May, 14 Eliz., enfeoffed William Tompkyns, John Seborne and James Wynton of all his lands in While and Hamnashe, co. Hereford, and Stoke Blisse, co. Worcester, (except the manor of Little Kyre, co. Worcester, and all the lands which he late purchased from John Combes and Joyce his wife in Stoke Blisse, cos. Worcester and Hereford, and the manor of Hull, co. Worcester, and all the lands which he late purchased from Thomas Hackluytt and Fortune his wife in Stoke Blisse, co. Worcester) to hold to the use of the feoffor in tail male, with successive remainders to Thomas Baskervile of Nethwood, the feoffor's illegitimate son, in tail, to Eleanor Pichard, wife of George Pichard, the feoffor's illegitimate daughter, in tail male, to William Good of Nethwood in tail and the feoffor, his heirs and assigns. For £3 10s. paid to the Queen's farmer.

2463.) 1 *Oct.* 1577. *Gorhambury.* Licence for Henry Cheyne, knight, lord Cheyne of

Toddington, to alienate lands in the parish of Mynster in the isle of Scapei *alias* Shepei, co. Kent, to William Henman and Thomas Henman. For £3 6s. 8d. paid to the Queen's farmer.

2464.)   1 *Oct.* 1577.   *Gorhambury.*   The like for the same to alienate lands in Mynster aforesaid to William Allen and Robert Allen. For   [*m.* 12]
£6 13s. 4d.

2465.)   29 *April* 1577.   The like for Richard Yonge to alienate a tenement with a yard and stable, now in the tenure of John Parker, in Charterhouse Lane in the parish of St. Sepulchre (between a tenement of Matthew Peryne on the East and a tenement of the same Peryne on the West) to Roger, lord North, baron of Kirtelinge. For 13s. 4d.

2466.)   1 *Oct.* 1577.   The like for Thomas Blechenden, Anne his wife and John Blechenden to alienate lands in Aldington, co. Kent, to John Spycer. For 10s.

2467.)   13 *Nov.* 1577. Pardon of alienation: John Huggon by feoffment, 22 April, 19 Eliz., enfeoffed Lucy Huggon, his wife, and Robert Curteys of lands in Longludfurth and Tevelbye, co. Lincoln, for life in survivorship, with remainder to John Curteys, son of Robert and heir of the feoffor. For 18s. paid to the Queen's farmer.

2468.)   1 *May* 1577.   Licence for William Warde and Lucy his wife to alienate the manor of Pillardington *alias* Pillarton Priorye and lands in Pillardyngton *alias* Pyllarton Priorye, Oxhull and Halford, co. Warwick, to Thomas Webbe   [*m.* 13] and Edmund Hooper and the heirs and assigns of Webbe; and for Webbe and Hooper by the same fine to convey them back to Warde. For £5 12s. 4d. paid to the Queen's farmer.

2469.)   1 *Oct.* 1577.   The like for John Palmer to alienate lands in Hucknoll Torcard, co. Nottingham, to Richard Palmer. For 10s.

2470.)   26 *Aug.* 1577.   The like for Thomas Everarde the elder, Dorothy his wife and Thomas Everard the younger to alienate the manor of Aston Thurrolde and lands in Aston Thurrolde, co. Berks, to Thomas Stampe. For 37s. 4d.

2471.)   1 *Oct.* 1577.   The like for George Gorynge to alienate lands (*named*) in Barcombe, co. Sussex, parcel of the manor of Barcombe, which manor he late purchased from Francis Carewe, knight, to Thomas Shurley. For 6s. 8d.

2472.)   1 *Oct.* 1577.   The like for Thomas Culpon, Richard Smyth and William Thomas to alienate lands (*tenants named*) in Ayringden Parke in the parish of Hextonstall, co. York, to Edward Byns. For 6s. 8d.   [*m.* 14]

2473.)   26 *Aug.* 1577.   The like for John Yate to alienate the manor of Aston Thorrolde and lands in Aston Thorrolde, co. Berks, to Thomas Stampe. For 37s. 4d.

2474.)   1 *Oct.* 1577.   The like for Robert Cobbe and George Colymore to alienate the manor of Valence, all appurtenances thereof in Valence and Blaxhall, co. Suffolk, and all their other lands there called Valence, late of the monastery of Campesse *alias* Campesey, co. Suffolk, to Francis Saunders the elder. For £3 6s. 8d.

2475.)   1 *Oct.* 1577.   The like for William Roper to alienate lands in Skalstete in Burgh *alias* Burrowe, co. Lincoln, to William Dawtre. For £6 13s. 4d.

2476.)   1 *Oct.* 1577.   The like for William Ascough and lady Anne his wife to alienate lands in Bushopburton, Killome, Rustone and Lockington, co. York, to Ralph Hansbye. For £6 13s. 4d.   [*m.* 15]

2477.)   1 *Oct.* 1577.   The like for William Poulett, son and heir of Chidiock Poulett *alias* lord Chidiocke Poulett, to alienate the manor of Warneford, lands in Warneford and Lomer and the advowson of Warneford church, co. Southampton, to William Neale and Agnes his wife and the heirs and assigns of Neale. For £16 13s. 4d.

2478.)   1 *Oct.* 1577.   The like for John Clerke and Elizabeth his wife to alienate two messuages and six cottages in Whitcrosstrete *alias* Whitcrowchstrete in the parish of St. Giles without Crepulgate, London, to John Lacye, citizen and 'clothworker' of London, and Rowland Lacy, his son. For 51s. 1½d.

2479.)   1 *Oct.* 1577.   The like for Nicholas Heyman and Alice his wife to alienate a third part of the manor of Wolborough, of lands in Wolborough, Comyntynhed, Buckland, Wydecombe, Ilsington, Hughweke, Newton Abbott, Forde, Gamerocke, Maynbowe and Rowses Hill and of a free fishery in the water of Teynge, co. Devon, to Henry Gildon and Geoffrey Babbe and the heirs and assigns of Gildon. For £4 14s. 4d.

2480.)   1 *Oct.* 1577.   The like for William Overton, S.T.D., to alienate the site of the house of friars preachers called 'le Black Fryers'   [*m.* 16] of Chichester, co. Sussex, to Rooke Overton. For 44s. 6d.

2481.)   1 *July* 1577.   The like for Matthias Draper to alienate lands called Gannoxke *alias* Gannockes in the parish of Southmyms, co. Middlesex, now in the tenure of Henry Parkyns by a lease dated 18 Nov., 9 Eliz., by Thomas Blackwell for 21 years, and all his other lands there to Edmund Bowyer of Lincolns Inne, co. Middlesex, and Catherine his wife and the heirs and assigns of Edmund. For £8.

2482.)   1 *May* 1577.   The like for Richard Sowthbie and Jane his wife to alienate the manor of Newnton and lands in Newnton, Bokelande and Pusey, co. Berks, to John Fetyplace, knight. For 46s. 8d.

2483.)   1 *Oct.* 1577.   The like for William Andrewe, Audrey his wife, Thomas Gyllett, John his wife, Lewis Sympson, Mary his wife, Thomas Nowell *alias* Reve, Martha his wife and Sarah Cowley to alienate lands in Bury St. Edmunds, Nowlton, Lacford, Whepsted, Whelstlee, Rushbrooke and Mydden Hall and the advowson of a chapel called Saint Parnells without the South gate of Bury St. Edmunds, co. Suffolk, to John Hatton and Hugh Andrewe and the heirs and assigns of Hatton. For 33s. 4d.

2484.)   1 *Oct.* 1577.   The like for John Morley to alienate lands in Royston, co. Hertford, to William Burdall. For 13s. 4d.   [*m.* 17]

2485.)   1 *Oct.* 1577.   The like for Margaret Bowghey, widow, John Hide and Jane his wife to alienate lands in Hampsted, co. Middlesex, to Thomas Harbert. For 13s. 4d.

2486.)   1 *Oct.* 1577.   The like for Christopher Jackson to alienate the site of 'le Grey Fryers' *alias* 'le Freeres Minors' and lands in Castelgayt in the city of York to Joan Hewitson, widow. For 9s.

2487.)   1 *Oct.* 1577.   The like for George Fairfaxe to alienate the rectory of Thorpe by Waynflete, co. Lincoln, the advowson of the vicarage of Thorpe aforesaid and lands (*tenant named*) there belonging to the rectory to William Garner. For £4.

2488.)   1 *Oct.* 1577.   *Gorhambury.*   The like for William Skipwith, Edward Skipwith and Henry Skipwith to alienate the manor of Radwell, lands etc. in Radwell and Norton and the advowson of Radwell church, co. Hertford, to Edward Potton to the use of the said William. For £6 5s. 10d.   [*m.* 18]

2489.)   15 *May* 1577.   Pardon of alienation: George Peckham of Denham, co. Buckingham, knight, late had by feoffment, 19 Dec., 16 Eliz., of Christopher Rythe of Elinge, co. Middlesex, and Marlian Rythe, his son and heir apparent, lands (*named with tenant's name*) in or near Oxford, late of 'le Grey Fryers' in Oxford. For 20s. paid to the Queen's farmer.

2490.)   1 *Oct.* 1577.   Licence for Henry Woodhouse to alienate the rectory of Paston, the advowson of the vicarage of Paston and all appurtenances of the said rectory in Paston, Knapton, Bromholme and Edingthorp, co. Norfolk, to William Paston. For £4 paid to the Queen's farmer.

2491.)   1 *Oct.* 1577.   *Gorhambury.*   The like for Innocent Reade to alienate lands in Wilsden, Hampsted, Paddington, Kilborne and Fulham, co. Middlesex, to Thomas Harbert. For 29s.

2492.)   1 *Oct.* 1577.   The like for Robert Losemore to alienate lands in Deyhowese, Overham, Netherham, Batler, Netherpytland, Overpytland and Willande, co. Devon, to John Snowe, 'clothier'. For 14s. 10d.

2493.)   2 *Sept.* 1577.   The like for Christopher Allen to alienate the site of the manor of Brikendon Bury in the parish of All Saints in the town and county of Hertford, the mansion house of the manor and lands (*named*), parcels of the demesne lands of the manor, to Roger Coys,   [*m.* 19]
Christopher Cory and James Smyth to the use of Allen until a marriage between him and Elizabeth Coys, daughter of the said Roger, should be consummated and thereupon to the use of him and Elizabeth for life in survivorship, with successive remainders to their heirs male begotten between them and to the right heirs of Allen. For 49s. 8d.

2494.)   7 *June* 1577.   The like for Thomas Cony the elder and Alice his wife to alienate a third part of a great and capital mansion house lately inhabited by Thomas Leigh, knight, deceased, in Old Jewry, London, and of six tenements in and by Old Jewry, by the name of a third part of seven messuages in the parish of St. Olave in Old Jewry, to John Thembleby, Bartholomew Armyn, Thomas Ellis and James Hewishe and the heirs and assigns of Thembleby to the use of the said Thomas Cony and Alice for life in survivorship, with successive remainders to Thomas Cony, elder son of Thomas the elder, in tail male, to Richard Cony, second son of Thomas the elder, in tail male, to George Cony, third son of Thomas the elder, in tail male, to Peregrine Cony, fourth son of Thomas the elder, in tail male, to the heirs male of the bodies of Thomas the elder and Alice, to the heirs of the bodies of Thomas the elder and Alice, to Catherine Baber, wife of Edward Baber, and Winifred Bond, wife of George Bond, Alice's sisters, in tail male, to the heirs of the body of the said Thomas Leigh, knight, and to Edward Leigh, kinsman of the said Thomas Leigh, knight. For 14s. 10d.

2495.)   1 *Oct.* 1577.   The like for Elizabeth Amyas, widow, to alienate the manor of Charlington *alias* Charleston, the capital messuage thereof, other lands (*tenants named*) in Charlington, the tithes of the premises and of 'custumery landes' in Charlington and all appurtenances of   [*m.* 20] the said manor in Charlington and Cothey or elsewhere, co. Gloucester, late of the monastery of Winchelcombe, co. Gloucester, to John Tracy, knight. For £7 5*d.*

2496.)   1 *July* 1577.   The like for Mathias Draper to alienate the manor of Camerwell *alias* Frerne *alias* Camberwell, and a tenement called Frerne, co. Surrey, late of the monastery of Hallywell by London, lands (*named with tenants' names*) and all appurtenances of the said manor in Camerwell and Peckham or elsewhere, co. Surrey, and in Depford *alias* Westgrenwiche, co. Kent, lands (*named*) in Camerwell and Peckham, late of the said monastery, and lands in Hatcham, co. Surrey, to Edmund Bowyer of Lincolns Inne, co. Middlesex. For £10.

2497.)   30 *April* 1577.   Pardon of outlawry for Richard Holcombe late of St. Decumans, co. Somerset, 'husbondman', who was put in exigent in the husting of London for non-appearance in the Common Pleas to answer William Torryton in a plea for payment of £40 and has now surrendered himself to the Fleet prison.

2498.)   19 *June* 1577.   The like for Thomas Alon late of Yfton, co. Monmouth, 'husbondman', who was put in exigent in the said county for non-appearance in the Common Pleas to answer Richard Thomas in a plea of trespass and has now surrendered himself to the Fleet prison.

2499.)   4 *May* 1577.   The like for Walter Pollington late of Halton, co. Oxford, 'yoman', who was put in exigent in the county of Suffolk for non-appearance in the Common Pleas to answer Ralph Pollington in a plea for payment of £29 and has now surrendered himself to the Fleet prison.

2500.)   25 *Sept.* 1577.   *Windsor Castle.*   Lease for 40 years to George   [*m.* 21] Kirkeham, the Queen's servant, of—(1) the site and demesne lands of the manor of Borscombe, co. Wilts, once of the monastery of Ambresbury and leased to William Goble by patent, 16 Dec., 13 Eliz., for 21 years at a yearly rent of £7 18*s.* 6*d.*; (2) lands in Freisbye, co. Leicester, leased to William Gamble by patent of the Exchequer, 5 Feb., 10 Eliz., for 21 years at a yearly rent of 30*s.*, (3) lands in Freisbye, leased to John Hubbarde by patent of the Exchequer, 5 Feb., 10 Eliz., for 21 years at a yearly rent of 20*s.* 8*d.*, (4) lands (*tenant named*) in Freisbye, leased to Robert Mylner by patent of the Exchequer, 5 Feb., 10 Eliz., for 21 years at a yearly rent of 26*s.* 8*d.*, (5) lands in Freisbye, leased to John Kirton and William his son by patent of the Exchequer, 5 Feb., 10 Eliz., for 21 years at a yearly rent of 33*s.* 8*d.*, and (6) lands (*named*) in Freisbye, leased to William Oswyne by patent of the Exchequer, 23 Feb., 10 Eliz., for 21 years at several yearly rents of 51*s.* and 7*s.*, which premises in Freisbie are parcels of the manor of Freisbie, once of the monastery of Launde; (7) lands (*named*), now or late in the tenure of the inhabitants of Ibstocke, co. Leicester, parcel of the manor of Whitwick and late of Henry, late duke of Suffolk, attainted of treason, leased to Robert Hodgson by patent of the Exchequer, 11 April, 5 Eliz., for 21 years from Michaelmas then last at a yearly rent of 8*s.*; (8) the site of the manor of Stewcley Parva and lands (*named with tenant's name*), parcels of the manor of Stewcley Parva, co. Huntingdon, once of the monastery of Ramsey and leased to John Nycolles by patent, 1 June, 10 Eliz., *inter alia* for 21 years at a yearly rent of 13*s.* 4*d.*; (9) tenements (*named with tenants' names*) in the town of Penmeneth within the bailiwick of Kellynyock, co. Anglesey, leased to William ap John ap Hoell ap Robyn, (10) a tenement

(*named*) in Penmeneth, leased to Lewis ap Res ap Richard, (11) tenements (*named*) in Penmeneth, leased to Sir Morgan ap David ap Llewelin, David ap Sir Morgan ap David and Lewis ap Sir Morgan ap David, (12) a tenement (*named*) in Penmeneth, leased to Thomas ap John ap Griffith ap Grono and William ap John ap Griffith ap Grono by patent of the Exchequer, 2 July, 9 Eliz., for 21 years at a yearly rent of 16s. 8d., (13) a tenement (*tenant named*) in Bodyner in Penmeneth, leased to Griffith ap Jevan ap Hoell *alias* Griffith Ridd, and (14) the yearly perquisites of the Queen's courts in Penmeneth within the bailiwick of Kellyniock,   [*m.* 22]
all which premises in Penmeneth were once of the monastery of Conwey; (15) lands (*tenant named*) in Pynchebeck, co. Lincoln, parcel of the manor of Pynchebeck and once of the monastery of Spalding; (16) a manor called Southouse in Kedington, all appurtenances thereof in Kedington, Alvingham, Cockerington and Louthparke, co. Lincoln, and lands in Kedington (*named*), in Whillworthe, co. Lincoln, (*named*) and in the lordship of Louthparke, once of the monastery of Louthparke, leased to Thomas Seintpole by patent, 12 July, 10 Eliz., for 21 years at a yearly rent of 66s. 8d.; (17) lands in Welton, co. Lincoln, once of the monastery of Nunormesbye, co. Lincoln, and leased to Gilbert Blanchard by patent, 9 Nov., 8 Eliz., for 21 years at a yearly rent of 19s.; (18) lands etc. (*tenant named*) in Kislingbury and Harpolle, co. Northampton, once of the monastery of St. Andrew next Northampton, and (19) lands (*tenant named*) in Kislingbury, once of the monastery of St. James next Northampton, leased to William Tanfeld by patent of the Exchequer, 20 Feb., 10 Eliz., for 21 years at several yearly rents of 40s. and 6s. 8d.; and (20) lands (*tenants named*) in Watford, co. Northampton, once of the monastery of St. James next Northampton and leased to Richard Burneley by patent, 1 April, 12 Eliz., *inter alia* for 21 years at a yearly rent of 58s. With reservations. From (1) Michaelmas 1591, (2), (3), (4), (5), (6), (18) and (19) Michaelmas 1588, (8) and (16) Lady Day 1589, (7) Michaelmas 1583, (12) Lady Day 1588, (9), (10), (11), (13), (14) and (15) Michaelmas next or the termination   [*m.* 23]
of any lease or grant thereof heretofore made for life or years enduring after that date, (17) Michaelmas 1587 and (20) Lady Day 1591. Yearly rents (1) £7 18s. 6d., (2) 30s., (3) 20s. 8d., (4) 26s. 8d., (5) 33s. 8d., (6) 58s., (7) 8s., (8) 13s. 4d., (9) 20s. 11d., (10) 16s. 8d., (11) 19s. 9d., (12) 16s. 8d., (13) 8s. 8d., (14) 3s. 4d., (15) 30s., (16) 66s. 8d., (17) 19s., (18) 40s., (19) 6s. 8d. and (20) 58s. For his service.   [*m.* 24]

2501.)   29 *May* 1577.   Licence for William Deveroux, knight, to alienate a farm and grange called Owreston grange and all lands in Owreston, Shustocke, Crudworth and Dunton, co. Warwick, now or late in the tenure of George Butler, late of the monastery of Meryvall, co. Warwick, to Edward Deveroux. For 40s. paid to the Queen's farmer.

2502.)   14 *Nov.* 1577.   The like for Stephen Barnam, citizen and 'draper' of London, to alienate all the lands in Snawe, Ivechurche, Brockland and Romley Marshe *alias* Romney Mershe, co. Kent, which he late had of Richard Patricke, citizen and 'haberdasher' of London, to Alice Barnam, widow. For £6.

2503.)   2 *July* 1577.   *Gorhambury*.   Pardon for Annabel Wadeson, 'spynster', and John Wadeson, 'shomaker', both late of Staunforde, co. Lincoln.   [*m.* 25]
She and Helen Faux and Catherine Croftes, both late of Staunforde, 'spynsters', are indicted for that on 8 April, 19 Eliz., at Staunforde they stole linen etc. (*described*) belonging to John Allen of Staunforde, and John Wadeson for that he received and abetted them there on the same date.   By Q.

2504.)   29 *June* 1577.   Pardon for Richard Browne of Estharlsey in the North Riding, co.

York, 'laborer', indicted for that he stole horses belonging severally to Thomas Granger and John Mason at Estharlsey on 2 May, 19 Eliz. (*details given*).   By Q.

2505.)   28 *June* 1577.   Pardon for Adam Hyndley late of Haghe, co. Lancaster, 'laborer'. At the sessions held at Lancaster, co. Lancaster, before Richard Harpur, a justice of the Common Pleas, and Christopher Wraye, a justice of the Queen's Bench, the Queen's justices at Lancaster, on Monday after the Assumption, 16 Eliz., the said Adam, Ralph Atherton late of Pemberton, co. Lancaster, 'laborer', and John Rogerson late of Catterall, co. Lancaster, 'laborer', were indicted for that on 26 Jan., 16 Eliz., at Aspull, co. Lancaster, in the highway they robbed Ralph Jollye of 20*s*. belonging to him (*details given*), and Roger Bradshaghe late of Haghe,   [*m. 26*]
Gilbert Hyndley late of Aspull, 'yoman', William Hyndley late of the same, 'yoman', and William Hollinsheade late of Hyndley, co. Lancaster, 'husbondman', procured and abetted them towards committing the said felony on 25 Jan., 16 Eliz., at Haghe and on and after 27 Jan. at Haghe and Werington, co. Lancaster, received and maintained them; at the session held at Lancaster before Harpur and Robert Mounson, another justice of the Common Pleas, on Monday after the Assumption, 17 Eliz., Adam pleaded not guilty, was convicted and, because the justices wished to consider their judgment, was committed back to prison in Lancaster castle. At the suit of Gilbert Hyndley, Adam's father.   By p.s.

2506.)   28 *June* 1577.   Pardon for Griffith Wyn *alias* Griffith ap Rice ap David Wyn late of Birgedinge, co. Montgomery, 'laborer', indicted for the theft of a horse belonging to Edward ap Jevan Gwyn at the city of Coventry on 8 Nov., 18 Eliz. (*details given*). By consideration of James Dyer, knight, chief justice of the Common Pleas, and Nicholas Barham,   [*m. 27*]
the Queen's serjeant at law, justices of gaol delivery of the said city.   By p.s.

2507.)   1 *July* 1577.   Pardon for Richard Sampson late of Bascombe, co. Southampton, 'husbondman', indicted for that he burgled the house of William Buddon at Mannington, co. Dorset, on 21 March, 17 Eliz., assaulted Buddon and stole clothing etc. and 25*s*. belonging to him (*details given*). At the suit of Matthew Colchester.   By p.s.

2508.)   1 *July* 1577.   Pardon for John Baylye late of Blanforde Forum, co. Dorset, 'husbondman', At the general gaol delivery of Fisherton Anger, co. Wilts, made before Roger Manwoode, a justice of the Common Pleas, and John Jefferaye, a justice of the Queen's Bench, and their fellows, justices of gaol delivery, at New Salisbury, co. Wilts, on Thursday in the second week of Lent, 19 Eliz., he was indicted for that on 28 Jan., 19 Eliz., at Eastharnam, co. Wilts, he stole a horse and fowls belonging to William Forde (*details given*); he pleaded not guilty, was convicted, was condemned and for divers causes was committed back to gaol. At the suit of John Baylye the elder.   By p.s. [*m. 28*]

2509.)   1 *July* 1577.   Pardon for John Riley of London, haberdasher, of the receiving of a profit of £43 10*s*. above the statutory rate of 10% for a year, as specified in the undermentioned information, and all penalties due to the Crown in respect of the same. John Leeke of London, mercer, laid an information in the Exchequer on 27 Oct., 17 Eliz., that Riley (1) on 28 March, 15 Eliz., at Westminster sold to Richard Pickman cloth and other goods, worth not more than £336 16*s*., for £404, so receiving in profit £67 4*s*., whereby he should forfeit to the Crown and the informer the treble value of the goods to the value of £1,010 8*s*., (2) on 4 March, 16 Eliz, at Westminster sold to the same Pickman cloth and other goods, worth not more than £217 10*s*., for £260 10*s*. [*sic*], so receiving in profit £43 10*s*., whereby he should forfeit £652 10*s*., (3) on 31 July, 15 Eliz., sold to Edward Woode velvets and other goods, worth not more than £186, for £223 4s., so receiving in profit £37 4s., whereby he should forfeit £558, and (4) on 31 July, 15 Eliz., sold to John Case cloth and other goods, worth not more than £151, for £281 4s. [sic], so receiving in profit £30 4s., whereby he should forfeit £453; a jury found that he did receive the said sum of £43 10s., but not the other three. *English.*   [m. 29]

By Q.

2510.) 1 *July* 1577. Presentation of Edward Griffith, M.A., to the perpetual vicarage of Fordingbridge with Ebesley chapel annexed, Winchester dioc.   By p.s.

2511.) 29 *June* 1577. Lease for 21 years to Edward Flowerdewe of lands and woods (*named with tenants' names,* including the site of a late chapel called Westwade) in Wymondham, Crounthorpe and Bonwell, co. Norfolk, parcels of the demesne lands of the manor of Wymondham and once of the monastery of Wymondham; with reservations; from Lady Day last; yearly rent £7 11s. 3½d.; the   [m. 30] lessee to cut the woods only at fitting times, to enclose and preserve them after cutting and to leave sufficient 'lez staddelles' in every acre according to the custom of the country for this kind of wood. For a fine of £30 5s. 2d. paid to the Exchequer.

By warrant of the commissioners.

2512.) 1 *July* 1577. Lease to Thomas Gresham of (1), for 21 years, the toll of markets and fairs in the manor of Preston and Uppingham, co. Rutland, and (2), for 40 years, a mill in the said manor, parcels of Warwick and Spencers Landes; from Lady Day last; yearly rents (1) 106s. 8d. and (2) 26s. 8d. For a fine of £10 13s. 4d. paid at the Exchequer;   [m. 31] and in consideration, in respect of (2), that the mill is in great decay, so that no rent has been answered for the same for a long time, as appears by certificate of the auditor of the county.

By warrant of the commissioners.

2513.) 5 *July* 1577. *Gorhambury.* Lease for 21 years to Richard Stathom of the following in the county of York—(1) the rectory of Darton, once of the monastery of Monkebretton, co. York, and the tithes of corn in Regeworthe, Birthwaite, Beighe, Heghame and Hey, the profit of the Easter roll of Darton church, the tithes of hay in the parish of Darton and all lands and tithes belonging to the said rectory leased to George Savell by patent, 17 Dec., 11 Eliz., for 21 years; (2) the rectory of Kernetbye, once of the monastery of Bridlington, co. York, leased to John Carlell by patent, 15 May, 6 Eliz., for 21 years at a yearly rent of £12 3s. 4d.; and (3) the manor of Foston, once of the monastery of St. Mary next the walls of York, a yearly pension out of the rectory of Foston due to the Crown in right of the manor and all appurtenances of the manor in Foston, Thorneton, Flaxton and Claxton or elsewhere, leased to Ralph Bagnall, knight, still surviving, and lady Mary Cotton, now deceased, by patent of the court of Augmentations, 16 March, 37 Hen. VIII, *inter alia* for life in survivorship. With reservations, including the tithes of lands (*named*) in Kernetbye, the tithes of certain lands annexed to the vicarage of Kernetbye and all other profits heretofore paid to the vicar there. From (1) Michaelmas 1589, (2) Lady Day 1585 and (3) Bagnall's death. Yearly rents (1) £9 14d.,   [m. 32] (2) £12 3s. 4d. and (3) £28 17s. 7d. The lessee to pay yearly £12 10s. to the curate or vicar of Darton.

For a fine of £200 8s. 4d. paid at the Exchequer.   By p.s.

2514.) 5 *July* 1577. *Gorhambury.* Lease for 50 years to Thomas Hobson and Edmund Thorneton of tenements, cottages and gardens in the parish of St. Olave next the house of crutched friars by the Tower of London in London, once in the tenure of Clement

Killingworth and now or late in that of Hobson and Thorneton, given for the maintenance of certain uses in the parish of St. Martin Orgar in London and in the Crown's hands by the dissolution of chantries and the like; from Lady Day last; yearly rent £6. In   [m. 33] consideration of the surrender by Hobson and Thorneton of an indenture, 18 May, 36 Hen. VIII, whereby Thomas Withers, rector, and John Hopkines and Thomas Hewett, citizens of London, churchwardens, with the consent of the parishioners of the church of St. Martin le Orgar, leased to the said Killyngworth, citizen and 'pewterer' of London, the premises, by the name of a tenement and three cottages lying together in the parish of St. Olave by the Tower of London with the gardens belonging thereto (containing in length from the tenement with a cellar then in the tenure of George Hutson, 'pewterer', at the South end along the street there to Woodrofe Lane at the North end leading from the highway called Hertstreate to London Wall 89 feet), two gardens lying together there (containing in length from London Wall to a cottage belonging to the said church 113 feet and in width from the South side to the North side 73 feet), four tenements lying together (adjoining the gate called 'le Alyegate' on the South and so leading by the highway on the East to a tenement once of Ralph Worsley formerly called 'le Bull' on the North) and six tenements lying together (adjoining St. Catherine's college on the South and so leading by the highway on the East to a tenement in which the said Killyngworth once dwelt belonging to the church of St. Martin le Orgar on the North) for 50 years from Michaelmas 1548 at the same rent.

By warrant of the commissioners.

2515.) 5 July 1577. *Gorhambury*. Lease for 21 years to Roger Allen of the chantry of St. Mary the Virgin in Great Driffeld church, co. York, and lands (*tenants named*), including 'the chauntrye house', in Great Driffelde; with reservations; from Lady Day last; yearly rent £6 5d.; the lessee to pay yearly rents of 25s. 2d. to Christopher Danby, knight, 18d. for ¾lb. of pepper to the said Danby, 7d. to George Swillington and 4d. to the rector of Great Driffelde; the lease to be void in respect of any parcel of the premises whereof the lessee shall not before Lady Day next make a lease by deed to the present tenant for the whole term, so long as the tenants pay him among themselves his costs about obtaining this patent. For a certain sum paid at the Exchequer. By warrant of the commissioners.

2516.) 5 July 1577. *Gorhambury*. Lease for 31 years to Thomas Fountayne and Joan his wife of a tenement in the parish of St. Lawrence Powltney next 'le Olde Swanne', London, late in the tenure of Robert Wakerfeild, deceased, once belonging to the parish of St. Peter in Westcheape, London, and in the Crown's hands by the dissolution of chantries   [m. 34] and the like; from Lady Day last; yearly rent £7. In consideration of the surrender by the said Thomas of a patent, 4 Dec., 8 Eliz., leasing the tenement to Joan Wakerfield, widow, for 21 years from Michaelmas then last at the same rent. By warrant of the commissioners.

2517.) 29 June 1577. Lease for 40 years to William Sisson of (1) the two water corn mills of Wetherbye and (2) a fulling mill with two shops in Wetherbye, co. York, (*tenants named*), parcels of the manor of Wetherbye, parcel of Ribston preceptory, co. York, with suit, soc and multure of the tenants of Wetherby and others; from Lady Day last; yearly rents (1) £13 6s. 8d. and (2) 53s. 4d. In consideration of his surrender of a patent, 14 Nov., 13 Eliz., leasing (1) to Geoffrey Walkeden for 21 years at   [m. 35] the same rent; and for a fine of £16 paid at the Exchequer. By p.s.

2518.) 5 June 1577. *Gorhambury*. Lease for 21 years to Richard Broughton, Thomas Newporte and William Barroll, to the use of Robert,   [m. 36] earl of Essex, son and heir of Walter, late viscount Hereford, of the grange of Havodwen, the grange of Blanarian *alias* Blaniairon, the grange of Pennarth, the grange of Comustwith, the grange of Mevenneth, the granges of Morva Mawre and Henhynocke and the grange of Dovorthen, co. Cardigan, all heriots, strays, casualties and perquisites of court therein, the custom called 'le comortha' therein and all issues payable by the tenants every third year amounting to £38 14s. 8d. and all other appurtenances of the granges, all late of the monastery of Strataflorida; with reservations; from Lady Day last; yearly rent £112, with a triennial rent of £38 14s. 8d. for the 'comortha' when it falls due; the Crown to discharge the lessee from all other payments, except the fee of bailiffs and collectors of the premises. In consideration of the surrender by Broughton, Newporte and Barroll in respect of the premises of a patent, 11 Dec., 5 Eliz., leasing *inter alia* to the said viscount lands and rents, parcels of the granges of Havodwen, Blanarian, Pennarth, Comustwith, Mevenneth, Morva Mawre and Hannynock for 21 years from Michaelmas then last at yearly rents of £6 5s. 10d. (Havodwen), 9s. 10d. (Blanarian), 77s. 1d. (Pennarth), 50s. 4d. (Comustwith), £6 8s. 8d. (Mevenneth) and £6 (Morva Mawre and Hennynock) and rendering every third year for 'comortha' the sums accustomed; and for a fine of £53 2d. paid at the Exchequer.

By p.s.

2519.)   20 *Nov.* 1576.   Licence for Edward Glemham, brother and   [*m.* 37] heir of John Glemham, deceased under age, to enter upon his lands; issues from the time when Edward attained the age of 21.   By bill of the court of Wards.

2520.)   27 *Nov.* 1576.   The like for Nicholas Seynt John, son and heir of John Seynt John late of Lyddiarde Tregoze, co. Wilts; issues from   [*m.* 38] John's death   By bill of the court of Wards.

2521.)   28 *June* 1577.   The like for Michael Dormer, son and heir of Ambrose Dormer; issues from the time when Michael attained the age of   [*ms.* 39, 40] 21.   By bill of the court of Wards.

2522.)   27 *March* 1577.   Licence for the dean and chapter of Durham cathedral to elect a bishop to that church, void by death.   By p.s.

2523.)   29 *April* 1577.   Signification to Edwin, archbishop of York, of the royal assent to the election of Richard, bishop of Carlisle, to the bishopric of Durham, void by the death of James, the last bishop; and order to confirm the election and do all other things incumbent on the archbishop in this behalf by statute.   By p.s.

2524.)   29 *May* 1577.   *Gorhambury.*   Writ to the escheator in the county of York to deliver to Richard, bishop of Carlisle, bishop elect of Durham, the temporalities of his see with all waters and fisheries in the manor of Norham and Norhamshere in the county palatine of Durham, being part of the same manor of Norham (except the residue of the same manor of Norham and Norhamshere and except Norham castle), the Queen having assented to his election, received his fealty and restored the temporalities (except as above) to him hereby; issues from Martinmas last.   By p.s.

2525.)   29 *May* 1577.   *Gorhambury.*   The like to the escheators in the following counties—Northumberland; Middlesex.

2526.)   29 *May* 1577.   *Gorhambury.*   Order to the tenants of the see to be intendant accordingly.

2527.)   19 *Jan.* 1577.   Licence for the dean and chapter of York cathedral to elect an archbishop to that church, void by the translation of Edmund Gryndall to the archbishopric of Canterbury.   By p.s.

2528.)   8 *March* 1577.   *Gorhambury*.   Signification to Edmund, archbishop of Canterbury, Thomas, bishop of Lincoln, Edmund, bishop of Norwich, John, bishop of Rochester, and Richard, bishop suffragan of Dover, of the royal assent to the election of Edwin, bishop of London, to the archbishopric of York; and order to them (or three of them, the archbishop of Canterbury being one) to confirm the election and do all other things incumbent on them in this behalf by statute.   By p.s.

2529.)   16 *March* 1577.   *Gorhambury*.   Writ to the escheator in the county of York to deliver to Edwin Sandes, late bishop of London, archbishop elect of York, the temporalities of his see, the Queen having assented to his election, received his fealty and restored the temporalities to him hereby; issues from Michaelmas last.   By p.s.

2530.)   16 *March* 1577.   *Gorhambury*.   The like to the following escheators—city of York (the mayor and escheator); town of Kyngeston upon Hull (the mayor and escheator); co. Lincoln; co. Surrey; co. Middlesex; co. Northumberland; co. Gloucester and the adjacent marches of Wales; co. Nottingham; town of Notingham (the mayor and escheator); co. Westmorland; co. Cumberland; co. palatine of Lancaster (the chancellor of the county palatine that he may give order to the escheator).

2531.)   16 *March* 1577.   *Gorhambury*.   Order to the tenants of the see to be intendant accordingly.

2532.)   6 *May* 1577.   Licence for Richard Gratewycke, son and heir   [*m.* 41]
of Thomas Gratewycke, to enter upon his lands; issues from the time   [*m.* 42]
when Richard attained the age of 21.   By bill of the court of Wards.

2533.)   5 *Dec.* 1576.   *Gorhambury*.   The like for Anne Shakerley, heir of Rowland Shakerley the younger, to wit, the sister of the said Rowland, son of Ralph Shakerley, son of Rowland Shakerley the elder, deceased;   [*m.* 43]
issues from the time when she attained the age of 14.   By bill of the court of Wards.

2534.)   4 *Feb.* 1577.   The like for Edward Rookewood, son and heir of Nicholas Rookewood; issues from the time when Edward attained the age   [*ms.* 44, 45]
of 21.   By bill of the court of Wards.

2535.)   25 *June* 1577.   The like for Richard Raysinge, son and heir of Ralph Raysinge; issues from Ralph's death.   [*m.* 46]
                                                             By bill of the court of Wards.

(The dorse of this roll is blank.)

PART XII

C. 66/1162

2536.) 1 *March* 1577.   Lease for 21 years to William Webbe, citizen   [*m.* 1]
and salter of London, of (1) meadows etc. (*named with tenant's name*) parcel of the manor of
Battell, co. Berks, and (2) lands etc. (*named with tenants' names*) in Readinge, co. Berks, all late
of the monastery of Readinge; with reservations; from Michaelmas last; yearly rents (1) 52*s.*
and (2) £5 16*s.* (*detailed*); the lessee to cut yearly the grass of the first vesture of certain of the
meadows and deliver the hay therefrom to the Queen's barn at Reading for the maintenance
of her horses. For a fine of £3 paid at the Exchequer. By warrant of the commissioners.

2537.) 28 *June* 1577.   Lease for life in succession to Thomas Dutton   [*m.* 2]
the elder and Thomas Dutton and William Dutton, his sons, of (1) the site of the manor of
Aldesworth, co. Gloucester, now or late in the tenure of Richard Lisley, Elizabeth his wife
and Thomas their son, (2) a flock of 360 'wethers' at Aldesworthe, the tithes of wool thereof
and appurtenances (*described*) thereof at Aldesworthe and in the lordship of Keymesford, co.
Gloucester, and (3) a flock of 240 'ewes' at Aldesworth, the tithes of wool and lambs thereof
and appurtenances (*described*) thereof at Aldesworthe and at Maysmore in the county of the
city of Gloucester, all parcels of the manor of Aldesworthe and once of the monastery of St.
Peter, Gloucester; with reservations; yearly rents (1) £4 13*s.* 4*d.* and (2) and (3) £20 and
heriot the best beast; the lessees to leave a stock of sheep to the same number at the end of the
term or pay £66 for the price thereof at the election of the Crown; the lessees to have an
allowance of 40*s.* off the rent for mowing the hay in the   [*m.* 3]
meadow of Keynsham in the manor of Ampney St. Peter, co. Gloucester, and 10*s.* for the
livery of the shepherds there, but they shall mow and make the said hay at fitting times and
deliver it to the Crown's other farmers and the shepherds there, as accustomed; the lessees
shall not keep more than 240 sheep by reason of the site of the manor of Aldesworth; they
shall also provide entertainment for the Queen's steward and surveyor at the manor when
they come to hold courts there or make a survey thereof. In consideration of the surrender
by Thomas Dutton the elder of an indenture, Michaelmas, 24 Hen. VIII, whereby William,
abbot, and the convent of the said monastery leased the premises to John Taynton, Alice his
wife and Thomas, Edmund, William, Henry and John, their sons, in succession for 70 years,
if they or one of them should so long live, at yearly rents of (1) 7 marks and (2) and (3) £20;
and for a fine of £44 6*s.* 8*d.* paid at the Exchequer.   By p.s.

2538.) 2 *March* 1577. *Gorhambury.*   Lease for 21 years to Francis Manners of lands
(*named*) in Litlyngton, co. Bedford, once of the monastery of Barkynge, co. Essex, and
afterwards annexed to the honour of Ampthill,   [*m.* 4]
co. Bedford; with reservations; from Michaelmas last; yearly rent £11 11*s.* 4*d.* In
consideration of the surrender by Manners by deed, 1 March last, enrolled in Chancery, of a
lease of the premises *inter alia* by patent, 22 March, 6 Eliz., to Ralph Symons *alias* Wilkynson
at the same rent for 21 years from Michaelmas 1564 or the termination of a lease thereof by
indenture of the court of Augmentations, 2 June, 35 Hen. VIII, to John Lyons for 21 years
from Michaelmas then next at a yearly rent of £12 6*s.* 4*d.*; and for a fine of £23 2*s.* 8*d.* paid at
the Exchequer.   By warrant of the commissioners.

2539.)   14 *Feb.* 1577.   Lease for 21 years to—(1) John Francke of the free chapel of Fitleton, co. Wilts, lands there and the tithes of corn and two parts of the tithes of wool and lambs from the farm of Hackeceston *alias* Hackleston, co. Wilts, late of Edward Darrell, knight, in the Crown's hands by the dissolution of chantries and the like and leased to Francke by patent of the Exchequer, 14 June, 16 Eliz., for 21 years from Michaelmas then next at a yearly rent of 65*s.*; (2) Henry Wylman of   [*m.* 5] lands (*named*) in Stepleashton, co. Wilts, parcel of the manor of Stepleashton and late of Thomas, lord Seymor, attainted of treason; (3) Edmund Broadway of the site and demesne lands of the manor of Cleve Episcopi and lands (*named*) there and elsewhere, co. Gloucester, all late of the bishopric of Gloucester and leased by indenture, 1 Aug., 33 Hen. VIII, to Thomas Yardington for 60 years; and (4) Thomas Holte of lands in Waybridge, co. Surrey, parcel of the manor of Otelandes and late purchased from John Reade, now annexed to the honour of Hampton Court and leased by patent, 20 Feb., 3 Eliz., to William Denton for 21 years and by patent, 9 Feb., 12 Eliz., to John Emeley in reversion for 21 years ending Michaelmas 1602. With reservations, including, in respect of the manor   [*m.* 6] of Cleve Episcopi, certain lands etc. (*named with tenant's name*), and also certain lands enclosed within Otelandes park and Hampton Courte chase respectively. From (1) Michaelmas 1595, (2) the termination of any former lease remaining in force, (3) the termination of Yardyngton's interest and (4) Michaelmas 1601 [*sic*]. Yearly rents (1) 65*s.*, (2) 22*s.* 3*d.*, from the time when Wylman shall obtain posessions, (3) £12 and (4) 105*s.* 1½*d.*

For a fine of £40 paid at the Exchequer by Francke, Wylman, Broadway and Holte.

By p.s.

2540.)   11 *Feb.* 1577.   Lease for life in succession to Thomas Buckland, Anne his wife and Francis Buckland, their son, of the rectory, the house of the rectory and the dovecote of Westharpetree, co. Somerset, once of the monastery of Keynsham, co. Somerset; with reservations; yearly rent £6 6*s.* 8*d.*; rendering also 6*s.* 8*d.* yearly to Wells cathedral. In consideration of the surrender by the said Thomas of an indenture, 8 July, 23 Hen. VIII, whereby John, abbot, and the convent of the said monastery leased the rectory, the tithes of the rectory and the dovecote of Westharptree (then late held by John Goodman, clerk) to Thomas Horner, John Buckland, Joan his wife and John Buckland, elder son of John and Joan, (reserving to the lessors the rents of tenants and the fines, heriots and other perquisites of courts) for life in succession at a yearly rent of £6, rendering also 6*s.* 8*d.* yearly to Wells cathedral; and for a fine of £19 paid at the Exchequer. By warrant of the commissioners.

2541.)   14 *Feb.* 1577.   Lease for life in succession to Thomas Bradley,   [*m.* 7] William Bradley, his son, and Grace Bradley, daughter of Thomas, of lands in the wapentake of Amoundernes, co. Lancaster, of the yearly rent of 18*s.* 5*d.*, the tithes of corn and hay in Great Pulton, Little Pulton, Great Marton, Little Marton, Stallmyn *alias* Strawaigne, Presoo, Hakensall *alias* Hagensey, Haston *alias* Hastayne and Peele, a moiety of the tithes of corn in Byspam *alias* Bispayne, the tithes of hay of 'le Poole' and a moiety of the pension of Preston in the said wapentake, once of the monastery of Syon, co. Middlesex; with reservations; from Michaelmas last; yearly rent £25 and heriot the best beast; the lessees to pay yearly all pensions and other charges out of Pulton church. In consideration of the surrender in Chancery by the same Thomas of a patent, 1 March, 13 Eliz., leasing the premises to him for 21 years from Michaelmas then last at the same rent; and for a fine of £25 paid at the Exchequer.

By p.s.

2542.)   7 *Feb.* 1577.   Lease for 21 years to Robert Sheffelde of (1) a chantry called 'Kennalferye chauntrie' in the parish of Owston and all   [*m.* 8] its possessions in Owston and Butterwike or elsewhere, co. Lincoln, late in the tenure of lady Anne Sheffeld, and (2) Holy Trinity chantry in Epworth and all its possessions in Epworth or elsewhere, co. Lincoln, late in the tenure of the same lady Anne Sheffelde, widow, and now or late in that of Anthony Cowper; with reservations; from (1) Lady Day 1586 and (2) Michaelmas 1587; yearly rents (1) £8 15s. 11d. and (2) £4 6s.; the lessee to pay yearly 9s. 10d. out of (1) for rents resolute to divers persons. In considerations that the said Robert has undertaken to maintain during his term the waterworks of Kennalfery chantry, which lands are greatly charged with defence against the river Trent; and for a fine of £26 3s. 10d. paid at the Exchequer.   By p.s.

2543.)   14 *Feb.* 1577.   Lease for 21 years to William Farley of (1) a moiety of all tithes, oblations, profits and hereditaments in Mollescrofte, co. York, once in the tenure of Robert Towrye and once belonging to the late   [*m.* 9] prebend founded at St. Stephen's altar in the collegiate church of St. John of Beverley, co. York, and (2) lands (*described*) at Beverley, once of Kelkes chantry in the parish church of St. Mary in Beverley; with reservations; from Michaelmas last; yearly rents (1) £7 6s. 8d. and (2) 30s.; the lessee discharged from all other charges. In consideration of the surrender by Farley of (*a*) a patent, 12 Dec., 4 Eliz., leasing (1) to John Smythe for 21 years from Michaelmas then last at the same rent and (*b*) an indenture, 6 Nov., 37 Hen. VIII, whereby John Wright and Richard Taylor, merchants, masters and receivers of the lands belonging to the late guild or 'le Hansehouse' of Beverley, by assent of Robert Grey, Robert Thomson, William Pounderson, John Spens and their fellows, the twelve governors, masters and wardens of the town and commonalty of Beverley, leased (2) to James Awsten for 40 years from Candlemas then next at the same rent; and for a fine of £17 13s. 4d. paid at the Exchequer.
                                                            By warrant of the commissioners.

2544.)   16 *Feb.* 1577.   Presentation of Robert Garret, S.T.B., to the perpetual vicarage of Eglingham, Durham dioc., void by the resignation of Thomas Bennett, clerk, and in the Queen's gift *sede vacante.*   By p.s.

2545.)   5 *Feb.* 1577.   Grant to John Ramsden and Elizabeth Beamonde (*alias* Beamonte)
                                                                                    [*m.* 10]
widow, of the wardship and marriage of Richard Beamonde, son and heir of Edward Beamonde; with an annuity of £13 6s. 8d. from 3 Jan., 17 Eliz., when Edward died.
                                                                                    By Q.

2546.)   7 *Feb.* 1577.   Grant to Bartholomew Clerke, LL.D., of the wardship and marriage of George Smyth, son and heir of Thomas Smyth; with an   [*m.* 11] annuity of £6 13s. 4d. from 10 Jan., 18 Eliz., when Thomas died.   By Q.

2547.)   7 *Feb.* 1577.   Grant to Thomas Cecill, knight, of the wardship and marriage of Edward Dennye, brother and heir of Robert Denny, deceased under age; with an annuity of £53 6s. 8d. from 12 Aug., 18 Eliz., when Robert died.   By Q.

2548.)   12 *Feb.* 1577.   Grant to John Jewrie of the wardship and marriage of Ralph Wighte the younger, son and heir of John Wighte; with an annuity of 20s. from 13 June, 15 Eliz., when John died. Yearly value of the   [*m.* 12] inheritance 60s.   By Q.

2549.)   11 *Feb.* 1577.   Grant to Thomas Browne and William Glasyer of the wardship and marriage of Matthew Ellys, son and heir of Matthew Ellys; with an annuity of 33s. 4d. from 20 April, 17 Eliz., when Matthew the father died. Yearly value of the inheritance £3 8s. 4d.
                                                                                    By Q.

2550.)   11 *Feb.* 1577.   Grant to John Puckering of the wardship and marriage of Thomas Draper, son and heir of John Draper, citizen and 'bruer' of London; with an annuity of £3 6s. 8d. from 12 May, 18 Eliz., when   [*m.* 13]
John Draper died. Yearly value of the inheritance £14.   By Q.

2551.)   8 *Feb.* 1577.   Grant for life to William Packer of the office of one of the clerks of the privy seal which shall be void by the death, surrender or forfeiture of Edmund Clerke, Thomas Kery, Richard Oseley or Hugh Allington, the present clerks, and after a grant for life by patent, 5 Jan., 15 Eliz., to Thomas Clerke of the reversion of the office of the said clerks has taken effect. For his service for now nearly 20 years past in the office of the privy seal.   By p.s.

2552.)   8 *Feb.* 1577.   Pardon for William Danyell of Sittlesham, co. Sussex, 'maryner', indicted for that he with many others on 2 June, 18 Eliz., piratically boarded a ship named *The William* belonging to Thomas Smythe of Great Yarmouth, co. Norfolk, 'merchante', on the high seas within the jurisdiction of the Admiralty and stole 'a crosse saile' belonging to Smythe. By information of Thomas Gawdye, a justice of the Queen's Bench, Christopher Heydon, knight, Francis Wyndham and Charles Calthrope,   [*m.* 14]
justices of the peace in the county of Norfolk.   By p.s.

2553.)   9 *Feb.* 1577.   Licence for Edward Baeshe, surveyor general of victuals for the navy, his heirs and assigns to impark 300 acres of land in his manor of Stansteade Abbott, co. Hertford, and have free warren in all demesne lands of the manor; no one to enter to hunt or take anything appertaining to park or warren without his licence, under pain of £10 to be levied to the use of the licensee; so that the lands be not within the bounds of the Queen's forest.   By p.s.

2554.)   15 *Feb.* 1577.   Licence for William Tovy of Phillipes Norton, co. Somerset, to exercise in any place in England where he shall inhabit the mistery of making woollen cloth, long or short, and kersies, pinned whites or plain straights, and to weave, put to rowing and weaving and put to sale the same, although he has not been apprenticed to the   [*m.* 15]
occupation for seven years or exercised the same for seven years, as required by stat. 4 & 5 Ph. & Mary; from 1 May following the making of the said statute. On information by justices of the peace of great credit in the county of Somerset that he is an honest man, has traded in making woollen cloth of his wools and keeps many men at work in Norton.   *English.*   By p.s.

2555.)   8 *Feb.* 1577.   Licence for one year for Peter Bones and his deputies, bearers hereof, to gather alms in the cities of York and Lincoln, for the relief of William Fortherley, William Hinderwell, William Johnson, William Foxe, John Tomson, William Redhed, George Maugham, William Carre, Janet Rainer, widow, and the said Bones of Scawby in Pickeringe Lethe, co. York, who about 20 Aug., 16 Eliz., had their houses (to the number of 17) burnt.   *English.*   By Q.

2556.)   12 *Feb.* 1577.   Licence for 20 years for the governor or governors, consuls, assistants and fellowship of English merchants for the discovery of new trades to exercise the killing of whales in any seas whatsoever and to make train oil thereof; from the present date; no persons, denizens or strangers and others subject to the Crown of England being not of the said fellowship to kill whales to make oil thereof, or to hire or set on work any person so to do, upon pain of imprisonment until discharged by special warrant of the Crown and forfeiture of £5 for every ton of oil so made, one moiety to the use of the Crown

and the other to the use of the fellowship; customers and other ministers of the ports not to take   [*m.* 16]
any entry or make any composition for train oil made of any whale killed or caused to be killed by any person inhabiting within the realm and brought into the realm other than the said fellowship upon pain of the Queen's displeasure; provided that, if the fellowship for five years in time of peace shall discontinue the killing of whales and making of train oil, it shall be lawful for others to enterprise the killing of whales and making of train oil. Rowland Heyward and Lionel Duckett, knights, governors of the fellowship, have given the Queen to understand that the fellowship mind shortly to attempt the said enterprise and have already at great cost procured certain expert 'Biskeins men' to instruct her subjects therein; and she likes of it as a thing likely to be beneficial for the increase of her navy and mariners and the furnishing of her dominions with so necessary a commodity. *English.*   By p.s.

[Printed in *Select Charters of Trading Companies, 1530–1707.* (Selden Society Publications, Vol. XXVII) pp. 28–30.]

2557.) 5 *Feb.* 1577.   Pardon for William Lyndon late of Ileton, co. Somerset, 'glover'. At the general gaol delivery of Dorchestre, co. Dorset, made there on Monday in the third week of Lent, 18 Eliz., before Roger Manwood, a justice of the Common Pleas, John Jefferay, one of the Queen's serjeants at law, and their fellows, justices of gaol delivery, he with others was indicted for that on 4 Oct., 17 Eliz., he burgled the house of Thomas Myller at Pottwell in the parish of Brodwynsor, co. Dorset, put Myller, Agnes his wife and their servants in fear and stole plate etc. (*described*) belonging to Myller; he pleaded not guilty, was convicted and was condemned, but for divers causes was committed back to gaol. At the suit of Thomas Lyndon, his brother.   By Q.

2558.) 15 *Feb.* 1577.   Grant to Lettice Baker, widow, of the wardship and marriage of Robert Baker, son and heir of Robert Baker; with an annuity of £3 6s. 8d. from 27 Oct., 17 Eliz., when Robert the father died.   [*m.* 17]
Yearly value of the inheritance £15 16s. 9d.   By Q.

2559.) 2 *March* 1577.   Pardon for Richard Harrye *alias* Resoga late of Pawle, co. Cornwall, 'husbandman', indicted before the justices of gaol delivery in the county for that on 28 August, 18 Eliz., he burgled the close of John Rawe at Ruyn Wartha in the parish of Peran in Zabulo, co. Cornwall, and stole two geldings belonging to him.   By Q.

2560.) 8 *Feb.* 1577.   Pardon for John Collyns late of Garsdon, co. Wilts, 'laborer', indicted for stealing a mare belonging to George Wadroffe at Cleverton, co. Wilts, on 23 July, 18 Eliz.   [*m.* 18]
       By p.s.

2561.) 17 *Feb.* 1577. *Gorhambury.*   Pardon for William Gilberte of Dover, 'maryner', for manslaughter. It was found by an inquisition taken at Dover on 11 July, 18 Eliz., before Thomas Warren, deputy of John Robins, mayor of the town and port of Dover, and the jurats thereof, coroners there, (*jury named*) on the body of John Nicholas that Gilbert wounded Nicholas in a fight at Penelesse Benche in the liberty of Dover on 7 July so that he died at Dover on 11 July (*details given*). At the suit of Mary Gilbert, William's wife.
       By p.s.

2562.) 27 *Feb.* 1577.   Licence for life for Edward, earl of Rutland, to retain in his service 40 gentlemen or yeomen, over and besides household servants and persons under him in any office held by him, although they be tenants of the Queen or any other or resident within the

Queen's honours, manors, 'domynyons', leets or hundreds; provided that his licence shall not authorise him to retain any of the Queen's servants; and pardon of all offences committed before the present date against acts of retainer. *English.*   [*m.* 19]

By p.s.

2563.)   6 *Feb.* 1577.   Pardon for John Eyre late of Christechurch, co. Southampton, 'wever', indicted for treason in that he made four counterfeit 'sixe pennye peeces' at Christechurche on 12 Jan., 16 Eliz., and uttered the same there on 20 Jan. following. By p.s.

2564.)   11 *Feb.* 1577.   Lease for 21 years to Robert Lloyd, a yeoman of the chamber, and Helen his wife of all lands, tithes and other spiritual possessions in the county of Denbigh of the late college of St. Peter in Ruthyn, co. Denbigh; with reservations; from Michaelmas last; yearly rent £7; the lessees to pay yearly to two chaplains or curates in   [*m.* 20] the church of St. Peter in Ruthyn and the church of Llanruth, co. Denbigh, £13 for their stipend as accustomed. In consideration of the surrender by Robert of a patent, 24 Feb., 3 Eliz., leasing the same to John Rogers for 21 years from Michaelmas then last at the same rent; and for a fine of £14 paid at the Exchequer by Robert.

By warrant of the commissioners.

2565.)   20 *Feb.* 1577.   Lease for 31 years to Nicholas Jones of (1) seven tenements and a barn in Grubstreate in the parish of St. Giles without Creplegate, London, and (2) a tenement and a stable adjoining there, all now or late in the tenure of John Watson, parcels of possessions coming to Edward VI by the dissolution of chantries and the like; from Michaelmas last; yearly rents (1) £5 4s. and (2) 26s. 8d. Jones offers to repair and maintain the premises, at present in such decay that they cannot be repaired without great cost.

By warrant of the commissioners.

2566.)   4 *March* 1577.   *Gorhambury.*   Lease for 21 years to George Erington of a third part of the site of the manor of Ellington, co. Northumberland, now or late in the tenure of Thomas Graye, late of John Swynborne, attainted of treason; with reservations; from Michaelmas   [*m.* 21] last; yearly rent £6; the lessee to serve by himself or a sufficient man with horse and arms in the North when summoned by the Queen's warden or lieutenant, to occupy the premises by himself or a sufficient man and to fence the same as ordered by the steward of the Queen's court or others her commissioners there. For a sum paid at the Exchequer.

By warrant of the commissioners.

2567.)   20 *Feb.* 1577.   Lease for 21 years to Clement Ogle of the tithes of corn in Estylborne, Bassynden, Tyllington and Westylborne, parcel of the rectory of Ellinghame *alias* Eglingham, co. Northumberland, and a moiety of the tithes of corn of Olde Bewick, Weperden, Hedgley, Benleye, Eglinghame, Crawlye, Harrope and Newbewick belonging to the said rectory; from Michaelmas last; yearly rent £12 10s. In consideration of his surrender of a patent, 29 May, 16 Eliz., leasing to him a moiety of the said rectory for 21 years from Lady Day then last at the same rent.   By warrant of the commissioners.

2568.)   11 *Feb.* 1577.   Lease for 21 years to John Wilson of the   [*m.* 22] demesne lands (*tenants named*) of the manor of Uglebarbye, co. York, late of John Swynborne, attainted of treason; with reservations; from Michaelmas last; yearly rent £40 (*detailed*).   By p.s.

2569.)   20 *Feb.* 1577.   Lease for 15 years to Henry Bowyer, citizen and mercer of London,

of all lands in Kington Maundefelde *alias* Knighton Maundesfeld, Babcary, Estlydford and elsewhere, co. Somerset, late of the prior or hospital of St. John the Baptist, Wells, co. Somerset; with reservations; from Lady Day last; yearly rent 109*s.* 8*d.* In consideration of the surrender by Bowyer of a patent, 18 July, 12 Eliz.,   [*m.* 23] leasing to Richard Barnard all lands in Kyngton Maunfelde and elsewhere, co. Somerset, late of the said priory or hospital for 21 years from Lady Day then last at the same rent.
By warrant of the commissioners.

2570.)   11 *Feb.* 1577.   Lease for 21 years to Ellis Markham of the tithes of corn and hay of Milford, Steton and Lomby, parcel of the prebend of Newthrope, co. York, parcel of the possessions of Edward, late duke of Somerset, exchanged, once belonging to the office of treasurer of York cathedral; from Michaelmas last; yearly rent £13 6*s.* 8*d.* In consideration of the surrender by Markham in respect of the premises of an indenture, 20 May, 37 Hen. VIII, whereby William Cliffe, LL.D., treasurer of the said church and prebendary of the said prebend, leased the premises *inter alia* to him for 55 years from Lammas then next at the same rent; and for a fine of £13 6*s.* 8*d.* paid at the Exchequer.
By warrant of the commissioners.

2571.)   14 *Feb.* 1577.   Lease for 21 years to Richard Price of (1) the rectory of Brecknock, co. Brecknock, and (2) a mill called Heldmyll, co. Brecon, now or late in the tenure of John Price, knight, once of Brecknock priory; with reservations; from Michaelmas last; yearly rents (1) £11 16*s.* 8*d.* and (2) 12*s.*; the lessee to pay the stipend of a chaplain   [*m.* 24] in St. Arbeta's chapel in the parish of Brecknock and all other charges. For a fine of £24 17*s.* 4*d.* paid at the Exchequer.   By warrant of the commissioners.

2572.)   19 *Feb.* 1577.   *Gorhambury.*   Grant to John Biest of Acham, co. Salop, and Agnes his wife for life in survivorship and the heirs and assigns of John of—the reversion and service of the manor, the rectory, the advowson of the vicarage and the grange of Attingham *alias* Acham aforesaid, granted by patent, 28 June, 1 Mary, *inter alia* to John Gage, knight, for life, with successive   [*m.* 25] remainders to William Gage, his son, in tail and to the said John Gage, knight, in tail, to hold by service of fortieth part of a knight's fee; and the said manor, rectory and advowson of the vicarage, once of the monastery of Lilleshill, co. Salop, and afterwards of Thomas Palmer, knight, attainted of treason, and the said grange. The grant to be void of William Gage shall die without heirs of his body and if heirs of the body of John Gage shall fail.
By p.s.

2573.)   22 *Feb.* 1577.   Grant in fee simple to William Powlett, knight, marquess of Winchester and earl of Wiltshire, of the Crown's interest in the undermentioned lands; to hold as of the manor of Estgrenewich, co. Kent, in socage. John Cooke late of South Tudworth, co. Southampton, by indenture, 18 May, 7 Eliz., enrolled in Chancery, covenanted with Ralph Scroope that the said John and his heirs should be seised of lands (*tenants named*) in South Tudworth to the use of the said John for life, with successive remainders to George Cooke, a son of John, and Eleanor wife of George and the heirs male of George's body, to the said Ralph for life, to Adrian Scroope, then son and heir apparent of Ralph, in tail male, to Richard Scroope, second son of Ralph, in tail male, to Thomas Sandys   [*m.* 26] in tail male, to the said John in tail male, to the said John in tail female, to the said Ralph in tail, to the said Sandys in tail and to the Crown; and also by the said indenture the said John covenanted for himself and his heirs with the said Ralph and his heirs that the said John and his heirs and all other persons and their heirs who should be seised of the manor of South

Tudworth, cos. Southampton and Wilts, and certain lands in the said counties (which were all the lands whereof the said John was seised in his demesne as of fee) should stand seised thereof to the use of John for life, with remainder to George in tail male, with remainder to Ralph for life, with remainders over as aforesaid; afterwards John and Ralph died, and the lands (*tenants named*) came to George and Eleanor and the heirs male of the body of George, and the manor and the rest of the premises to George in tail male; George bargained and sold all the premises to the marquess and his heirs; but perfect assurance thereof cannot be made by George so long as the remainder to the Crown stands.   By p.s.

2574.)   11 *Feb.* 1577.   Lease for 31 years to James Mervyn, knight, one of the four esquires for the body, of the rectory and vicarage of the   [*m.* 27] collegiate and parish church of Chester in le Strate *alias* Chester in the Streate in the bishopric of Durham, the house of the deanery and vicarage of the said church, the tithes of hay and other tithes and hereditaments in the parish of Chester in the Streate assigned to the vicarage and parish or colleagiate church there and the tithes of corn and other tithes in the said parish heretofore assigned to the prebends of Lamley, Lammesley, Pelten, Chester, Tanfield, Birtley and Urpeth in the said late collegiate church; from Easter 1590, being the termination of a lease thereof by patent, 4 Feb., 6 Eliz., to Mervyn at a yearly rent of £77 2s. 8½d. for 21 years from Easter 1569 or the termination of the interest of Ralph Copynger; same rent; the Crown to discharge the lessee from payment of the stipends of chaplains serving in the said church and any chapels annexed thereto, and all charges other than the rent. For his service.   By p.s.

2575.)   7 *Feb.* 1577.   Lease for 21 years to John Warde of lands (*named*   [*m.* 28] *with tenants' names*) in Balderby, co. York, parcels of the manor of Balderby, once of the monastery of Fountaunce, co. York; with reservations; from Michaelmas last; yearly rent £7 8½d. (*detailed*). In consideration of the surrender by Warde of two several leases of certain of the premises by patents of the Exchequer, 17 Feb., 12 Eliz., to William Stockdale *inter alia* for 21 years from Michaelmas then last at yearly rents of 53s. 9½d. (*detailed*) and 84s. 11d. (*detailed*); and for a fine of £7 8½d. paid at the Exchequer.

By warrant of the commissioners.

2576.)   1 *March* 1577.   Lease for 21 years to Henry Brabant (*alias* Braban) of (1) a capital messuage called (or in) Pedgbanck in the lordship of Brancepeth in the bishopric of Durham, (2) lands in Hedley in the said bishopric and (3) lands in Eastbrandon and Thelme (*alias* 'le Helme' in Eastbrandon), all parcels of the lordship of Brancepeth and late of Charles, late earl of Westmorland, attainted of treason, and (4) a tenement (*named with tenant's name*) in the said lordship, once of St. Mary the Virgin's chantry in   [*m.* 29] the church of St. Margaret in Crossegate dependent on the church of St. Oswald in Durham; with reservations; from Michaelmas last; yearly rents (1) £10, (2) 10s. 4d., (3) 11s. 4d. and (4) 30s.; the lessee to serve by himself or sufficient men with horse and arms in the North when summoned by the Queen's warden or lieutenant, to occupy the premises by himself or sufficient men and to fence them as ordered by the steward of the Queen's court or others her commissioners; the lease to be void in respect of any parcel of the premises if the lessee shall expel the present tenant therefrom, or if he shall not before Midsummer next make the tenant a lease thereof for his whole term and for the rent above-reserved, so long as the tenants pay him among themselves his costs about obtaining this patent. In consideration of the surrender by the said Braban of (a) an indenture, 8 Oct., 2 Eliz., whereby Henry, earl of Westmorland, leased to Henry Braban of Brancepeth, 'yoman', his servant, (1), then in the tenure of William Norton, for 21 years from Lady Day then next at the same rent, (b) an indenture, 1 Jan., 9 Eliz., whereby Charles, earl of Westmorland, leased to Margaret Steylye (*alias* Steley), widow, (2), then in her tenure, for 10 years from the Invention of Holy Cross then next at the same rent and (*c*) an indenture, 3 July, 7 Eliz., whereby the same Charles leased to Martin Sowerby of Eastbrandon, 'husbandman', (3), then in Sowerby's tenure, for 13 years from the Invention of Holy Cross then last at the same rent; and for a fine of £17 5s. 8d. paid at the Exchequer.   By warrant of the commissioners.

2577.)   1 *March* 1577.   Lease for 21 years to Walter Vaughan of (1) all   [*m*. 30] lands in Uchoide Kidwellie in the parish of Llangoner, co. Carmarthen, late of Rice Griffith, attainted, and (2) lands in Cliggin, co. Carmarthen, parcel of the manor of Clyggyn, late of the same Griffith; with reservations, including a tenement (*tenant named*) late leased to Francis Lloyde by patent at a yearly rent of 53s. 4d., also a yearly fee farm rent of 38s. 7d. in Clyggyn and a yearly rent of 46s. 8d. of the farm of a mill in Clyggin; from Lady Day next; yearly rents (1) £9 9s. 6½d. and (2) £6 19s. 5d.; the lessee to pay yearly in respect of (1) to the bailiff of Kidwellie 29s. 9½d. for a rent to the duchy of Lancaster and 7s. 6½d. for a 'comortha' to the said duchy. In consideration of the surrender by Vaughan of a patent, 26 Jan., 8 Eliz., leasing the premises to Lloid aforesaid for 21 years from Michaelmas then last at the same rents; and for a fine of £32 17s. 11d. within a sum of £39 7s. 3d. paid at the Exchequer. By p.s.

2578.)   11 *Feb*. 1577.   Lease for 21 years to William Holstock, controller   [*m*. 31] of the Admiralty, of the site of the manor of Orsett and a messuage called Hongershall, co. Essex, late taken by the Queen by force of an act of Parliament out of the bishopric of London; with reservations; from the termination of a lease by indenture, 4 Sept., 37 Hen. VIII, by Edmund, late bishop of London, confirmed by the dean and chapter of St. Paul's cathedral, London, to John Broughton then of Orsett, the said bishop's servant, of the premises, by the name of the site of the manor of Orsett and lands (*described with tenants' names*), for 60 years from Michaelmas then next at a yearly rent of £20; same rent. For his service.   By p.s.

2579.)   18 *Feb*. 1577.   Lease for 21 years to Richard Chamond of the sheaf and the tithes of sheaves, grain, wool and lambs and the small tithes in the parish of Launcelles, co. Cornwall, once of the monastery of Hartland, co. Devon; from Lady Day next; yearly rent £17 8s. 2d. On surrender   [*m*. 32] by the said Richard of an indenture, 6 April, 27 Hen. VIII, whereby Thomas Pope, abbot, and the convent of the said monastery leased the premises, by the name of the sheaf and the tithes of grain of the parish of Launcelles, belonging to the monastery by the impropriation thereto of the rectory of Launcelles, and 'lez peason' and the tithes of all corn and grain and other things whatsoever belonging to them by reason of the said rectory, to John Chamonde, knight, Jane his wife and Richard Chamonde, their son, for 50 years from SS. Peter and Paul then next at the same rent. For a fine of £34 16s. 4d. paid at the Exchequer.
                    By p.s.

2580.)   20 *Feb*. 1577.   Lease for 50 years to Michael Blake of a messuage called 'the Castle' in Newfyshstrete in the parish of St. Magnus near London Bridge, late in the tenure of Roger Wendon, and now in that of Blake or his assigns, which came to Edward VI by the dissolution of chantries and the like; from Lady Day next; yearly rent £16; the lessee discharged from all other payments. In consideration that Blake offers to repair and maintain the messuage, at present in great decay.   By p.s.

2581.)   7 *Feb*. 1577.   Grant for life to Lancelot Thexton, S.T.B., of the first canonry or prebend in Norwich cathedral, void by the death of   [*m*. 33] Thomas Tedmonde.   By p.s.

2582.)   7 *Feb.* 1577.   Presentation of Gervase Carington, clerk, to the ninth canonry or prebend in Worcester cathedral, void by the resignation of Arthur Dudley, clerk, S.T.P.

By p.s.

2583.)   14 *Oct.* 1577.   *Windsor Castle.*   *Inspeximus* and confirmation of a patent dated at Dublin, 30 June, 29 Henry VI, granting, by assent of James le Bottiler, earl Dormond, deputy of Richard, duke of York, lieutenant of Ireland, and the Council there and by authority of a Parliament held at Drogheda on Friday after the feast of St. Benet, in fulfilment of the intention of James le Bottiler, earl of Ormond (*Ermon'*), Michael, archbishop of Dublin, Edmund, bishop of Meath, William, prior of Holy Trinity cathedral, Dublin, James Aleyn, knight, Robert Dovedall, John Cornewalsh, Edward Somerton, John Chever, John Goghe, William Sutton, Robert Burnell, knight, Nicholas Woder, knight, John Blacktonn, Nicholas Strangwayes, Ralph Pembroke, Thomas Newlye, John Fitz Robert, John Bennett, James Dovedall, Philip Bedelowe, master Thomas Walshe, Richard Eustace, John Tankard, John Warynge, William White, John White, Nicholas Clerke, John Bateman, David Rowe, Thomas Savage, William Crampe, Walter Doughner, Thomas Boyes, Thomas Barbye, Arnold Ussher, John Archedeakyn, John Paslewe, Stephen Harroulde, Simon Fitzrery, John West, John Foyle, William Bryne, Thomas Shortales, Nicholas Elliott, John Shynnagh, William Galwey, Roger Walter, Robert Syward, William Beyram and Robert Lange, that—the same persons or the survivors of them may to the honour of the Holy Trinity found anew a brotherhood or guild of the craft of merchants of the city of Dublin in perpetual succession of themselves and others both men and women in Holy Trinity chapel in Holy Trinity cathedral, Dublin, and may admit as brethren and sisters of the same brotherhood those persons and others whatsoever desiring to join them, and name that chapel in honour of the Holy Trinity, Dublin; the brethren may elect yearly two masters and two wardens from among themselves, to have the government of the brotherhood and the keeping of its possessions, and put others in their place at their pleasure, and make a perpetual brotherhood or guild of the craft aforesaid and have a common seal; the masters and wardens may plead by that name before all judges secular and ecclesiastical; the persons above-named and the brethren of the brotherhood and their successors, masters and wardens and brethren, may assemble at fitting places and times at their pleasure to take order among themselves, with others for counsel, for the government of the brotherhood and craft and make and amend ordinances for the same; no alien born shall buy wares in retail or in gross within the city or the franchises thereof save from merchants of the city dwelling there, and, if any such alien born shall be convicted thereof by lawful means before the masters and wardens, they may commit him by warrant under

[*m.* 34]

their seal to the prison of the city and the keeper of the prison shall keep him there until released by a like warrant; the persons above-named or the survivors of them may found to the honour of the Holy Trinity a chantry of four priests in the same chapel to celebrate daily for the healthy estate of the King, the deputy, the founders and the brethren and sisters of the brotherhood as long as they shall live and for the souls of the King's progenitors, all those above-named who has passed away and the brethren and sisters and their successors and benefactors and all the faithful departed, with power to replace the said chaplains at their pleasure and to assemble at opportune places and times to take order for the chantry according to the ordinance to be made in this behalf; when the brotherhood shall be established, the masters and wardens and brethren and sisters may acquire in mortmain lands to the yearly value of £40, although held of the Crown in chief or of others, for the maintenance of the chantry, so long as it be found by inquisitions to be returned into the Chancery of Ireland that it can be done without damage of the King or any other.

Also grant—at the suit of Christopher Fagan, John Ussher, John Levan and Simon

Grove, masters and wardens, —to the masters, wardens, brethren and sisters of liberties as follows—Incorporation by the name of the masters, wardens, brethren and sisters of the brotherhood or guild   [*m.* 35]
of Holy Trinity, Dublin. They and all persons admitted into the brotherhood shall alone have power of buying and selling in retail or in gross all wares (victuals excepted) brought into the city or the franchises thereof; no alien born, stranger merchant, or any other not admitted into the brotherhood shall buy or sell any such wares within the city or the franchises thereof, the precinct of the cathedral of St. Patrick in or near Dublin, the place called 'the Bisshopps Glebe', the precinct of the cathedral of Holy Trinity in Dublin called Christes Churche, the precinct of St. Sepulchre or the abbey of St. Mary the Virgin or the abbey called Thomas Courte or any other places within the city or its franchises except from or to merchants of the brotherhood, under pain of forfeiture of the wares. Aliens born, stranger merchants and others not admitted into the brotherhood shall bring their wares (except as aforesaid) to 'le Commen Hawle' of the city or whatsoever other place or places shall be assigned by the masters and wardens thereto, under pain of forfeiture of all wares put elsewhere, and there only sell them; and where the wares are so placed they shall remain for sale and not be removed for 40 days without special licence of the master and wardens in writing, under pain of forfeiture of the wares. The masters and wardens may search, or may appoint others their officers and ministers to search, whether any person has dealt with wares otherwise than is above prescribed, and may seize any found to have been bought or sold contrary thereto to the use of the brotherhood. The masters, wardens, brethren and sisters may keep all their liberties heretofore accustomed, and may make and amend ordinances for the government of the brotherhood and provide fitting   [*m.* 36]
penalties for offences against the same. They may also have all fines and forfeitures by reason of the privileges aforesaid, and the moneys arising therefrom shall be spent by the masters and wardens with the advice of the brethren and sisters on the needs of the brotherhood and not otherwise. No officers or subjects of the Crown to intermeddle herein to the prejudice of the grantees.   By Q.

2584.)   7 *Sept.* 1577.   *Gorhambury.*   Grant during pleasure to John Puckeringe of the office of justice of the counties of Carmarthen, Pembroke and Cardigan in the principality of Wales; with a yearly fee of £50, payable at the Exchequer of Carmarthen; in case he cannot exercise the office on account of ill health or any other urgent cause to be approved by the president or vice-president and council in the principality, he may exercise it by a deputy or deputies appointed in writing by the said president or vice-president and council; from Lady Day last; he shall endeavour to be present with and assist by his counsel the president and council in all their general sessions, unless given leave of absence by the said president or vice-president and council.   By Q.

2585.)   12 *Oct.* 1577.   *Windsor Castle.*   Licence for the mayor and   [*m.* 37]
commonalty and the citizens of London that every freeman of the said city now using the trade of tavern-keeper or retailer of wines within the said city, the city of Westminster, the borough of Southewarke or the liberties of the duchy of Lancaster without Temple Bar, and also all that now are or hereafter shall be freemen of the city of London by birth or by service of seven years as apprentice and brought up in the trade of retailing wine, and every widow of such a freeman, and every freeman as aforesaid hereafter marrying the widow of any other freeman lawfully occupying the said trade being not the widow of a vintner, and now or hereafter inhabiting in the said city, the city of Westminster, the said borough or the said liberties, may keep a tavern for the sale of any manner of wines by retail by the gallon or less or greater measure and may buy or sell by small measures in retail or in gross all manner of wines to be spent or drunk in or out of their houses, notwithstanding stat. 7 Edw. VI

entitled an act to avoid the great prices and excess of wines or any other act or ordinance; release for such freemen and widows of penalties incurred under the said acts and ordinances; provided that—for the avoiding of an excessive number of tavern-keepers and retailers of wine—no person to whom this licence may extend not being free of the company of vintners shall keep more than one tavern or retail wines contrary to the said statute within the cities of London or Westminster or the borough or liberties aforesaid without first obtaining allowance of the mayor and aldermen of London, to the intent that before such allowance the mayor and aldermen may take good assurance of such persons for obeying the good ordinances hereafter mentioned, and they are specially charged to see that the number of [*m.* 38] taverns do not inordinately exceed and that they are only allowed in convenient places and are orderly governed, and that retailers are bound to obey such ordinances of the vintners' company as the mayor and aldermen see fit for search and the good governance of tavern-keepers; provided that nothing in this patent shall extend to take from any citizen free of the said company or from any person licensed to sell wines by virtue of any patent granted to Edward Horsey any liberty which they have by any patent or by the ordinances or customs of the city of London or otherwise. At their suit: by the ancient liberties of the city of London every citizen and freeman thereof might exercise what lawful trade he thought best, which liberties have been confirmed by the Queen's progenitors by charter and by acts of Parliament and amongst others by the great charter of the liberties of England; but the said liberties were by stat. 7 Edw. VI aforesaid greatly impeached and the trade of many citizens straightened or taken away; wherefore upon suit made to Queen Mary and the present Queen the penalties of the said act have to the master, wardens and freemen of the mistery of vintners of London and to others, being citizens and freemen of other companies in the city and using the trade of wine selling, been dispensed; yet the dispensation made to the said citizens being freemen of other companies does not extent any further than to themselves during their lives and not to their children and apprentices. *English.*

By p.s.

2586.) 4 *Oct.* 1577. *Gorhambury.* Lease for 21 years to William Raynes of the rectory of Northflete, co. Kent, late of the archbishop of Canterbury, exchanged; with reservations; from Lady Day last; yearly rent £28. In consideration of his surrender of the interest of Richard Robson, to whom by patent, 29 May, 12 Eliz., the rectory was leased for 21 years from that date at the same rent; and for a fine of £20 paid at the Exchequer. By p.s.

2587.) 8 *Oct.* 1577. *Windsor Castle.* Grant for life, in full chapter of the order of the garter, to Francis Walsingham, councillor, of [*m.* 39] the office of chancellor of the said order within Wyndesore castle, co. Berks, or elsewhere, with the keeping of the seals of the order, void by the death of Thomas Smyth, knight; with a fee of £100 yearly, payable at the Exchequer, from Midsummer last. For his service.

By p.s.

Vacated because surrendered, 6 June, 31 Eliz., by Walsingham, now knight; signed: G. Gerrard; Fra. Walsingham.

2588.) 27 *Sept.* 1577. *Windsor Castle.* Grant to Edward Sudlowe of the wardship and marriage of Thomas Bullocke, son and heir of Lancelot Bullocke; with an annuity of £3 6s. 8d. from 30 Aug., 18 Eliz., when Lancelot died. Yearly value of the inheritance £15 15s. 8d.

By Q.

2589.) 27 *Sept.* 1577. *Windsor Castle.* Grant for life to Andrew Grey of the office of receiver general of lands in the counties of Northampton and Rutland late in the survey of the court of Augmentations and now in that of the Exchequer; from Easter last; with an annuity of £20, and 20*s.* for portage on every £100 paid into the Exchequer or by virtue of

[*m.* 40]

any warrant to the Queen's use, payable out of the issues of his office.   By Q.

2590.)   12 *Oct.* 1577.   *Windsor Castle.*   Appointment during good behaviour of John Jefferay, knight, a justice of the Queen's Bench, to be chief baron of the Exchequer; with fees etc. as received by Edward Saunders, knight, or Robert Bell, knight, late holders of the office.   By Q.

2591.)   25 *Sept.* 1577.   *Windsor Castle.*   Lease for 21 years to George Lee, a groom of the privy kitchen, of a tenement called 'le Savage' in Wannesworth, parcel of the manor of Batrichsey and Wannesworth, co. Surrey, and once of the monastery of Westminster and now annexed to the honour of Hampton Courte; from Michaelmas 1585, having been leased by patent, 13 [*recte* 23][1] Feb., 7 Eliz., to William Emerson for 21 years from Michaelmas then last at a yearly rent of £5 10*s.*; same rent. For his service.   [*m.* 41]

By p.s.

2592.)   11 *Oct.* 1577.   *Windsor Castle.*   Grant for life to John Wolley, secretary for the Latin tongue, of the office of dean in Carlisle cathedral, void by the death of Thomas Smyth, knight; with dispensation—because the Queen has admitted him into her household and has been wont to use his service in her weightier and more secret business—though he is not in holy orders and has married a widow still living and may chance to be absent from the deanery, that he may not be bound to personal residence and may notwithstanding receive all the profits of the office.   By p.s.

2593.)   8 *Oct.* 1577.   *Windsor Castle.*   Grant for life in survivorship to George Carey, knight, the Queen's kinsman, and Robert Hopton, both the Queen's servants, of the office of marshal of the marshalsea of the household; with fees etc. as formerly had by John Carewe, John Turbevyle, Henry Sherborn, John Digby, John Russell, Thomas Wentworth, William Pickeringe, or Ralph Hopton, knight, deceased.   By p.s.
      Vacated because surrendered, 22 May, 39 Eliz., by Carey, now lord Hunsdon; signed: Tho. Egerton, C.S.

2594.)   11 *Oct.* 1577.   *Windsor Castle.*   Grant for life to Griffith Lewes, S.T.P., of the [—] prebend in the collegiate church of Westminster, void by the death of [—] Jones.

By p.s.

2595.)   8 *Oct.* 1577.   *Windsor Castle.*   Grant for life to Ralph Pichaver, M.A., the Queen's subalmoner, of the canonry or prebend in Christ Church cathedral, Oxford, which shall next be void.   By p.s.

2596.)   28 *Sept.* 1577.   *Windsor Castle.*   Presentation of Hugh Boothe, S.T.B., to the canonry and third prebend in Ely cathedral, void by the promotion of John Whitegifte, S.T.P., to the bishopric of Worcester and in the Queen's gift *hac vice*.   By p.s.

2597.)   11 *Oct.* 1577.   *Windsor Castle.*   Presentation of John Kington, clerk, to the perpetual vicarage of Alton, Winchester dioc., void by lapse.   By p.s.

---

[1] Cf. *Calender,* 1563–66, no. 1937.

2598.)   11 *Oct.* 1577.   *Windsor Castle.*   Presentation of Lawrence Bridger, M.A., to the rectory of Slimbridge, Gloucester dioc., void by lapse.   [*m.* 42]

By p.s.

(*M.* 1*d. is blank.*)

2599.)   17 *June* 1577.   Commission during pleasure to Edwin, archbishop of   [*m.* 2*d.*] York, Henry, earl of Huntington, president of the council in the North, George, earl of Shrewsburye, Henry, earl of Derbye, Edward, earl of Ruttland, the bishops of Durisme, Chester and Carlile for the time being, Henry, lord Scroope, warden of the West marches towards Scotland, William, lord Ewrie, Henry, lord Hunsden, warden of the East marches towards Scotland, Thomas Smyth, knight, chancellor of the order of the garter, Matthew Hutton, D.D., dean of Yorke, Thomas Gargrave, John Foster, Henry Gates, George Bowes, William Fairefax, Simon Musgrave, William Mallerye, William Bellasis, Robert Stapleton, Robert Constable and Thomas Stanape, knights, William Whittingham, dean of Durisme, Robert Bowes, treasurer of Barwicke, John Longworth, dean of Chester, John Walker, D.D., John Gibson, LL.D., John Vaughan, Lawrence Meres, Ralph Rokebye, Francis Rodes, Thomas Eynns, George Blythe, Robert Longhorne, LL.D., Leonard Pilkinton, D.D., William Palmer, chancellor of the church of York, John Biron, Christopher Hilliarde, Thomas Feyrefax, John Dawny, Thomas Bointon, Martin Birck-hedd, Robert Ramsden, archdeacon of York, John Lowthe, archdeacon of Nottingham, Ralph Coulton, archdeacon of Cleveland, the archdeacon of East Riding, Henry Wright, subdean of Yorke cathedral, Christopher Wandsfurth of Kirlington, Ralph Boucher, John Hussie, Thomas Caverley, Thomas Layton, John Lamplugh, Richard Dudlie, Richard Gooderick, Richard Bunye, John Hotham, Roger Dalton, John Lambarte, Anthony Samond, Avery Uedall, William Burnand, recorder of York, William Paler, William Hilliarde, John Moore, Anthony Taylboyse, Richard Mallerie, Robert Brigges, Robert Twiste, prebendary of Durisme, Robert Tower, B.D., Christopher Lynlie, B.D., Anthony Foord, B.D., Edmund Bunye, B.D., Christopher Ashborne, M.A., Walter Jones, LL.B., Richard Persie, LL.B., Ralph Tunstall, M.A., Edward Hanbye, M.A., Thomas Burton, chancellor to the bishop of Carlile, Thomas Tewkie, LL.B., Ralph Haule, Gregory Pecock and Hugh Graves, aldermen of York, and John Thorneton, James Clarcksone and John Fawther, aldermen of Hull, (or three of them, the archbishop, any of the earls, any of the bishops, any of the lords, Hutton, Gargrave, Whitingham, Walker, Gibsone, Longhorne, Palmer, Ramsden, Coulton, Tower or Jones being one) to inquire in the province of York touching offences against stat. 1 Eliz. restoring to the Crown the ancient jurisdiction over the state ecclesiastical and spiritual, stat. 1 Eliz. for the uniformity of common prayer, stat. 5 Eliz. for the assurance of the Queen's Majesty's royal power over all within her dominions and stat. 13 Eliz. for the reformation of disorders touching ministers of the church, and of all heretical, erroneous or offensive opinions, seditious books, contempts, conspiracies, false rumours or tales, seditious misbehaviours, slanderous words and libels against the Queen, her magistrates, officers or ministers or others contrary to the laws of the realm or against the quiet governance of the people or against the received order for government in the church of England and of all coadjutors and abettors of such offenders. Power to hear and determine all the premises, also to inquire, hear and determine all enormities and disturbances committed in any church or chapel, church yard or chapel yard or against divine service or any minister of the same contrary to law; also to search out and correct persons obstinately absenting themselves from the church and the divine service and sacraments appointed by law by censures of the church or fines to the Queen's use or any other   [*m.* 3*d.*] means appointed by the said act for uniformity or any laws ecclesiastical of the realm; also to take order by their discretions that the penalties limited by the said act for uniformity may be duly levied by churchwardens to the use of the poor of the parish by ways of distress according to the said statute, to punish churchwardens neglecting or refusing to do their duty in that behalf, and, where churchwardens need assistance, to command in the Queen's name by letters such mayors, sheriffs and other offices as the commissioners shall think convenient to aid the churchwardens for the levying of such distresses. Also power to correct all errors and offences spiritual or ecclesiastical which may lawfully be corrected by censures ecclesiastical, deprivation or otherwise. Also power to search out and call before them every person having a living in the province who shall maintain any doctrine directly contrary to any of the articles of religion which only concern the confession of the true Christian faith and the doctrine of the sacraments, comprised in a printed book of the articles agreed in the convocation held at London in the year A.D. 1562, and, if he persists therein, to deprive him. Also power to inquire of, hear, determine and punish incests, adulteries, fornications, outrageous misbehaviours and disorders in marriages and all other offences reformable by the ecclesiastical laws of the realm. All politic ways to be used for the trial of the premises, and, upon due proof had, punishment to be awarded by fine, imprisonment, censures of the church or otherwise. Also power to summon offenders and suspects, examine them on oath and proceed against them as the cause shall require; also to summon witnesses and examine them on oath; and to punish contempts by excommunication and other censures ecclesiastical or by fine or imprisonment at their discretion. Also—because there is a great diversity in the persons to be summoned, some dwelling far off, some being fugitive and some to be charged with grievous faults the speedy redress whereof is most requisite, and therefore more effectual process than by the commissioners' letters missive is required in most part of those causes—power to command justices and others to apprehend them and to take sufficient bonds for their appearance; if any person so apprehended is unable or refuses to give sufficient bond, the commissioners may in the Queen's name

[*m.* 4*d.*]

give commandment to those in whose charge he is for bringing him before them or committting him to ward until they take further order for his enlargement. Also power to receive from offenders and suspects recognisances both for appearance and for performance of the commissioners' orders. The archbishop and the dean of York, by their discretions and in consideration of the time and place judged most meet, to appoint a registrar or registrars for the registering of all acts, decrees and proceedings by virtue of this commission, limiting them a fitting allowance for the pains of them and their clerks from the parties summoned or from fines levied by force of this commission as the case shall require; and to appoint advocates, procurators, solicitors, messengers and other officers to attend upon them, limiting them allowances as for the registrars. Also power for the commissioners to appoint a receiver or receivers of the fines assessed by them; paper books indented to be made, one to remain with every receiver and another with the registrar or registrars, in which shall be entered all fines assessed, every entry being signed by the commissioners (or three of them as aforesaid) and the receivers thereby charged; by bills signed as aforesaid the commissioners may assign to the receivers and to the registrars and other their officers fitting sums for their rewards and pains; the names of the receivers and a note of all fines assessed to be certified every Michaelmas into the Exchequer, that the receivers may be charged thereby and upon termination of their account the Queen may be answered of the residue over and besides the allowances limited to the registrars and other officers.

Commission also to the same (or six of them, the archbishop, Hutton, Longhorne, Palmer, Towers or Jones being one) to examine the statutes and evidences of cathedral and collegiate churches, grammar schools and other ecclesiastical corporations in the province founded by Henry VIII, Edward VI, Queen Mary and cardinal Poole, the ordinances and statutes whereof are either none at all or imperfect or being made when the realm was subject to the see of Rome are in some points contrary to the prerogative of the Crown, the laws of the realm and the present state of religion within the same, to certify without delay the defects in them and to advertise the Queen of such good orders as they think should be made by her for the said foundations according to stat. 1 Eliz.

Commission also to the same (or three of them, the archbishop or   [*m. 5d.*] Hutton being one) to administer the oath of supremacy to all persons appointed by the acts above mentioned to take it, refusals to do so to be certified into the court commonly called the King's Bench.

The letters missive, decrees and the like of the commissioners to have affixed to them a seal engraved with the Rose and the Crown over the Rose and the letter E before and the letter R after the same with a ring or cirumference about the same seal containing as follows—'*Sigill' commissar' ecclesiastic' Reg' infra provinc' Ebor'*.'

The commissioners faithfully to execute this commission according to the true meaning thereof, notwithstanding any pretended privilege or exemption or any laws or other grants or ordinances which may seem contrary to the premises.   *English*.   By Q.

2600.)   4 *Feb.* 1577.   Commission to David Lewes, LL.D., master of the court of Chancery, to the cognisance of and to proceed in the Queen's name and by her command in all causes concerning charter-parties, bills of lading, exchange and insurance of ships, freight or bottomry (*chartas partitas, chirographa onerationum, navium excambiorum et assecuracionum quarumcumque, naula pro navibus conductis et locatis debita, pecuniam trajecticiam seu nauticum faenus aliquo modo concernentibus*) and to hear and determine the same summarily and without appeal, also to arrest ships, persons, wares and other things pledged for the furnishing of ships, to enforce his orders by imprisonment or fine and to do all other things necessary for the settlement of such causes; and appoint as commissary and judge in the premises, with power to appoint a surrogate or surrogates; Roger Parker, notary public, to be writer and registrar of his acts; inhibition of the Queen's justices, the mayor and sheriffs of London   [*m. 6d.*] and all other the Queen's officers and ministers having jurisdiction in such causes from taking cognisance thereof or doing any hindrance to Lewes or his deputies or to litigants therein.   By p.s.

2601.)   20 *June* 1577.   Commission during pleasure to William Cordell, knight, master of the rolls, David Lewes, LL.D., judge and president of the high court of Admiralty and master in Chancery, Valentine Dale, LL.D., master of the Requests, William Awbrey, LL.D., John Hammond LL.D., Thomas Randolphe and Henry Killegrew to be commissaries and judges delegate with power for them (or three of them, Cordell, Lewes, Dale, Awbrey or Hammond being one) to hear and determine, summarily and without appeal, the causes of Scottish subjects for piracy and depredation; power to imprison for contempt, power to fine and every other power of coercion fitting for the expedition of the premises; inhibition of any other having jurisdiction in the said causes to intermeddle therein while this commission endures. Because of many complaints by Scottish subjects and by the Regent of Scotland that their ships and wares while they are sailing in the course of trade are seized and despoiled by the Queen's subjects.   By Q.

2602.)   23 *April* 1577.   Commission to John, bishop of London, John, bishop of Rochester, Christopher Wray, knight, chief justice of England, Robert Bell, knight, chief baron of the Exchequer, William Cordell, knight, master of the rolls, Thomas Wilson, LL.D., master of the Requests, John Gibbons, LL.D., master of Chancery, and John Gryffyth, LL.D., (or two of them) to hear and determine, summarily and without appeal, a cause between William Wilson, S.T.B., a scholar in the university of Oxford, and Thomas,

bishop of Lincoln, and others concerning a claim of the said William Wilson to be admitted rector of Lincoln college, Oxford; statutes, canons and customs to the contrary, and the suit pending, notwithstanding. At the suit of the chancellor, doctors, masters and scholars of Oxford university: they complain that, according to the liberties of the university, all pleas (except mayhem and felony and assises and pleas of free tenement) arising within the precinct of the university where one party is a master, scholar or scholar's servant or otherwise privileged person belongs to the chancellor of the university, that doctors, masters and scholars are free from the jurisdiction of judges of bishops and other ordinaries touching all contracts or the like entered into within the university, touching all crimes or the like and the punishment thereof (except as aforesaid) and touching all scholastic acts so long as they remain in the university, and that the chancellor has all jursidiction ecclesiastical and spiritual over the said scholars; all graduates on admission to their degree have sworn to observe the statutes and liberties of the university; but the said William Wilson, claiming to have been elected rector of Lincoln college and to have been refused admission to the office by the said bishop of Lincoln, sought before Bartholomew Clarke, LL.D., official of the court of Arches, a summons to the bishop to show cause why he should not admit him and an inhibition of the bishop and Herbert Westfallinge, S.T.P., Lawrence Humphrye, S.T.P., Thomas Bicklye, S.T.P., Walter Baylye, M.D., Oliver Whitington, M.D., and William Smyth, LL.D.,   [m. 7d.]
the bishop's commissaries as visitor of the college, from doing anything to the prejudice of the complainant; afterwards Edmund, archbishop of Canterbury, at Wilson's suit, called the cause before him and committed the determination thereof to David Lewes, LL.D., Henry Jones, LL.D., Lawrence Husse, LL.D., and Nicholas Steward, LL.D., advocates of the court of Canterbury, (or two of them); the bishop's party has made allegations by way of defence and sought for a time for proving the same, but the said commissaries of the archbishop have refused to assign it; Thomas Underhill, M.A., proctor of the university, has appeared, under protest of not consenting to the commissaries as judges, and has sought for the cause to be remitted to the chancellor of Oxford, but the commissaries have refused and have proceeded to further acts to the prejudice of the university's liberties.   By Q.

2603.)   11 June 1577.   Commission to Nicholas Bacon, knight, councillor, keeper of the great seal, William, lord Burghley, councillor, treasurer of England, Thomas, earl of Sussex, councillor, chamberlain of the household, Robert, earl of Leicester, councillor, master of the horse, Francis Walsingham, councillor, one of the principal secretaries, and Walter Myldmay, knight, councillor, chancellor of the Exchequer, (or four of them) to peruse the book of values and rates of wares imported and exported made by virtue of a commission under the great seal in the year 4 & 5 Ph. & Mary, signed by Queen Mary, sealed with the great seal and sent into the Exchequer for the charging of the custom and subsidy, to inquire by the oath of skilful men of London or other port towns or otherwise which are undervalued or not valued, to set reasonable values upon them, and to cause a book of them newly valued to be written in parchment, to be signed by the Queen and sent under the great seal into the Exchequer for the charging of the custom and subsidy (the subsidy of poundage, that is to say, 12d. of every 20s. value of certain wares imported and certain wares exported, having been granted to the Queen by stat. 1 Eliz.); also to sent the tenor of the same book to every custom house under the Exchequer seal, if it   [m. 8d.]
shall so seem expedient to the treasurer and chancellor of the Exchequer.   English.   By Q.

2604.)   22 March 1577.   Gorhambury.   Commission for Martin Furbysher of London, to whom the Queen has given command of her ship The Ayde and other ships for a voyage to the Northwestward for the discovery of Cathay, or his deputy, the bearer hereof, to press in the Queen's name for her service only mariners, soldiers, gunners, shipwrights and other needful artificers and workmen and all manner of carriage, for the Queen's reasonable wages and payment; also to take into his charge the said ships and the whole company appointed for his service, to govern them and punish them by imprisonment and violent means, and by death if the fault shall so deserve, upon obstinate withstanding of such orders and articles as are delivered to him by the Queen or her Council, and to lead them to such places as he shall think expedient for the Queen's said service; provided that he shall not take up any principal man that is very meet for the Queen's own service in the wars, or any more persons than shall be necessary for the voyage. *English.*   By Q.

2605.)   11 *Feb.* 1577.   Commission to Christopher Wraye, knight, chief justice of the Queen's Bench, William Cordell, knight, master of the rolls, James Dyer, knight, chief justice of the Common Pleas, and David Lewes, LL.D., judge of the court of Admiralty, (or two of them) as special commissaries, judges and delegates to hear and determine, summarily and without appeal, the undermentioned complaint of John Cage, George Holmes, William Salter, Reginald Hollingworth, Giles Flud, William Kelinge, Henry Osmonde, William Weldon, Thomas Allet, William Hollyday and Percy Salisbury, merchants of London trading to Spain and Portugal. In March last they loaded goods worth £4,302 on a ship, *The Harrye* of London bound for Spain, which was seized on the high seas and taken to Vlissingen in Zeeland, where the goods were sold to the use of the Prince of Orange and the States of Holland and Zeeland; not long afterwards other ships sailing both from England to Antwerp and to England from Antwerp, laden with goods belonging to English merchants of the society of merchants adventurers of London trading in Antwerp and other parts of Belgia, were detained at Vlissingen by order of the same Prince and States, as George Holmes and his fellows were informed by Cage, their proctor; but other merchants adventurers by Martin Calthrop and Richard Goddarde interceded with the Prince of Orange and other magistrates in those parts for the restitution to the said merchants of their ships and goods; the Queen also by special deputies demanded their restitution; but when Calthropp and Goddard heard that the said Prince had decreed that the goods of Cage and his fellows should first be restored, while those of the merchants adventurers should be detained until they should lend a great sum of money to the Prince and States, they pleaded with the Queen's deputies that separate restitution to Cage and his fellows should not be considered, and with the mediation of the Queen's spokesmen they came to an agreement with Cage in the name of him and his fellows that Cage should no longer press his petition for the restitution of the goods of him and his fellows, but should permit the retention of the money from the sale thereof by the Prince and States towards the sum asked as a loan by them of the merchant adventurers; Calthorpe and Goddarde promised to Cage that they would see that the value of the goods in *The Harrye* would be restored to Cage and his fellows in England; but having obtained the release of their own ships and goods, and having been required by Cage and his fellows to carry out the agreement, they plead reasons for refusing to do so;   [*m. 9d.*]
Cage and his fellows therefore ask for their cause to be committed to some discreet and learned men.   By p.s.

2606.)   19 *Aug.* 1577.   *Gorhambury.*   Commission to Nicholas Bacon, knight, councillor, keeper of the great seal, William, lord Burghley, treasurer of England, Thomas, earl of Sussex, councillor, lord chamberlain, Edmund, bishop of Norwich, Thomas, lord Wentworth, Roger, lord North, Robert Bell, knight, chief baron of the Exchequer, William Cordell, knight, master of the rolls, Christopher Heydon, knight, Thomas Seckford, a master of the Requests, the dean of Norwich for the time being, Robert Wingfeld, knight, William Buttes, knight, William Walgrave, knight, John Still, D.D., William Foulke, D.D., Nicholas Bacon, Edward Grymston, Drew Drewrie, Robert Aishefieild, Ralph Shelton,

John Higham, the chancellor of Norwich for the time being, Matthew Carew, LL.D., Michael Bresley, LL.D., Edward Flowredewe, James Ryvett, William Heydon, Richard Wingfeld, Francis Windham, Robert Jermyn, Thomas Andrewes, Thomas Poley, Nathaniel Bacon, Richard Davye, John Reynoldes, Charles Caltrop and Hugh Castleton, B.D., (or four of them, the bishop being one) to hear and determine causes ecclesiastical in the diocese of Norwich,   [*m.* 10*d.*]
(*With duties and powers recited as in the like commission for the province*   [*m.* 11*d.*]
of York, no. 2599 *above, first paragraph*). Appointment of Anthony Alcocke to be registrar of the commission or in his absence or default a notary or notaries public to be named by the bishop; who is also to appoint messengers and a receiver (*duties and fees as in the commission for the province of York*).

Commission also to the same (or four of them, the bishop being one) to administer the oath of supremacy (*as in the commission for the province of York*).   [*m.* 12*d.*]

The letters of the commissioners to have affixed a seal with the Rose and the Crown (*as in the commission for the province of York, but the legend reading 'Sigill' Commissar' Ecclesiastic' Reg' infra dioces' Norwic''*).

The commissioners faithfully to execute this commission (*as in the commission for the province of York*). *English.*   By Q.

2607.) 22 *July* 1577. *Gorhambury.* Commission to Richard, bishop of Durham, Henry, lord Hundesdon, warden of the East marches towards Scotland, Cuthbert, lord Ogle, William, lord Ewrie, John Foster, knight, Robert Munson, a justice of the Common Pleas, Thomas Meade, serjeant at law, William Whittingham, dean of Durham, George Bowes, knight, William Hilton, knight, Robert Constable, knight, Leonard Pilkington, D.D., William Fletewood, recorder of London, Thomas Calverley, chancellor of the county palatine of Durham, Robert Swifte, clerk, John Barnes, clerk, Thomas Burton, clerk, Thomas Leyton, John Savill, John Heath and Thomas Myddleton (or four of them, the bishop, Swifte, Burton, Calverleye or Barnes being one) to hear   [*m.* 13*d.*]
and determine causes ecclesiastical in the diocese of Durham. (*With duties and powers recited as in the like commission for the province of York, no.* 2599 *above, first paragraph.*) A notary public to be appointed as   [*m.* 14*d.*]
registrar by the bishop; who is also to appoint messengers and a receiver (*duties and fees as in the commission for the province of York*).   [*m.* 15*d.*]

Commission also to the same (or four of them, the bishop being one) to administer the oath of supremacy (*as in the commission for the province of York*).

The letters of the commissioners to have affixed a seal with the Rose and the Crown (*as in the commission for the province of York, but the legend reading 'Sigill' commissar' ecclesiastic' Reg' infra dioc' Dunolm''*).

The commissioners faithfully to execute this commission (*as in the commission for the province of York*). *English.*   By Q.

2608.) 13 *Sept.* 1577. *Gorhambury.* Commission for two years to Francis, earl of Bedford, councillor, Charles, lord Howard of Effingham, John, lord Russell, Roger, lord Northe, Valentine Dale, a master of the Requests, Gabriel Goodman, dean of Westminster, Alexander Nowell, dean of St. Paul's, Roger Manners, esquire to the Queen's person, Henry Harvie, D.C.L., John Cotton, knight, John Cuttes, knight, Francis Hinde, John Hutton, John Gill, Ralph Barton, Robert Shoote, Matthew Bradburye, Thomas Homes, Charles Morison and Christopher Yelverton (or three of them) to receive such complaints by bills in writing as Ciris Ruse of Grays Inn, co. Middlesex, and William Ruse, his father, shall exhibit against their creditors and the creditors' answers, and to make final orders by such composition that the creditors may in due time be answered and yet Ciris, his wife and children in the meantime be something relieved; the orders to be certified into Chancery, that they may there remain to be caused to be executed. At the suit of Ciris: by colour of two several recognisances of 200 marks and £40 his lands worth £30 a year are extended, but only to the yearly value of 20s.; notwithstanding that the said sums and a great deal more are already discharged, his copyhold lands, goods, corn, cattle and leases are taken and kept from him, divers evidences concerning the premises and casually come into his adversaries' hands are likewise kept from him, and also divers other great bonds and the like concerning and belonging to him and his father are detained from him by divers persons. [m. 16d.] *English.*   By Q.

2609.)   17 *Aug.* 1577.   *Gorhambury.*   Commission to John, bishop of London, William Cordyll, knight, master of the rolls, Thomas Sackford and Valentine Dale, masters of the Requests, David Lewes, president of the high court of Admiralty, Thomas Yale, auditor of causes of the court of audience of Canterbury, Bartholomew Clarke, official of the court of Arches, and   [m. 17d.]
Lawrence Hussey, LL.D., (or two of them, the bishop, Cordell, Sakeford or Dale being one) to hear and determine a complaint by Edmund, bishop of Norwich, that John Parkhurst, his immediate predecessor, while he lived, committed and suffered great dilapidations in the cathedral of Norwich and the episcopal palace there; calling before them Walter Baspole and Robert Phillippes, Parkhurst's executors, and others who of right should be summoned; with power to enforce their orders by ecclesiastical coercion or secular incarceration. By Q.

(The rest of the dorse is blank.)

PART XIII

C. 66/1163

2610.) 28 *Oct.* 1577. *Windsor.* *Inspeximus* and confirmation of a patent dated at Dublin, 26 Jan., 3 Eliz., under the great seal of Ireland, [*m.* 1] granting (by assent of Thomas, earl of Sussex, lieutenant general of Ireland, according to the tenor of instructions signed by the Queen, delivered to the said lieutenant and enrolled in the Chancery of Ireland) to Conat, earl of Tomon, for his service, in tail male the castles, forts, manors and lordships of Clare More, Croverkayn, Dayngne in Ybeicke, Cahir, Menan, Inistimayn, Bunratte, Dromebye, Corcomrowe, Rosmonagher, Moghan, Belahignan and Coewlrioughe in Tomon in Ireland, as formerly held by Donnell O'Brien, to hold by service of one knight's fee, when scutage runs in the realm of Ireland, the grant to be interpreted in his favour. [*m.* 2]

By p.s.

2611.) 21 *Nov.* 1576. Lease for 31 years to William Herle of (1) the rectory of All Hallows the Less in Thamestreate, London, once of St. Lawrence Poultney college, London; (2) lands (*named*) within the manor [*m.* 3] of Mouncton, co. Brecon; (3) lands late of John Mason of Ree, co. Hereford, and the herbage in Hereford castle; (4) lands in Anstie, co. Leicester, once of the monastery of Pré, Leicester; (5) the manor of Ives in Maydenheath in the parish of Braye, co. Berks, once of Bustleshame priory; (6) fisheries and three 'lez eightes' in the river of Thames (*described*), co. Berks, parcel of the manor of Ives in the lordship of Braye, late of Anne of Cleves; and (7) lands in Longeworth, co. Berks, parcel of lands annexed to the honour of Ewelme, co. Oxford; with reservations, including courts etc.; (1) from the termination of a lease thereof by patent of the Exchequer, 2 July, 3 Eliz., to Thomas Rigges, Robert Rose, Thomas Anderson and John Miles, inhabitants of the parish of All Hallows the Less, to the use of the parishioners, for 21 years from Lady Day then last at a yearly rent of £4 10s. 11½d.; (2) from the termination of a lease thereof by patent, 29 July, 4 Eliz., to Edward Powell for 21 years from Lady Day then last at a yearly rent of 13s. 4d.; (3) from the termination of a lease thereof by patent, 16 April, 11 Eliz., to George Tirrell *inter alia* at a yearly rent of 11s. 8d. for 30 years from the termination of a lease thereof by patent, 9 June, 7 Edw.VI, to George Berington and John Grene; (4) from the termination of a lease thereof by patent, 11 April, 3 Eliz., to Peter Duckett for 21 years from Lady Day then last at a yearly rent of 16s. 6d.; (5) from the termination of a lease thereof by patent, 10 Aug., 4 & 5 Ph. & Mary, to Robert Noke for 30 years from Lady Day then last at a yearly rent of £7 13s. 4d.; (6) from the termination of a lease thereof by patent of the Exchequer, 2 March, 12 Eliz., to Roger Amice (*alias* Amyre) *inter alia* for 21 years from Michaelmas then last at a yearly rent of [*m.* 4] 8s.; (7) from the termination of a lease thereof by patent of the Exchequer, 7 June, 9 Eliz., *inter alia* to Edward Fetiplace for 21 years from Lady Day then last at a yearly rent of 7s.; yearly rents (1)—(6) the same and (7) 7s. 11½d.

By p.s.

2612.) 18 *March* 1577. *Gorhambury.* Lease for 21 years to Richard [*m.* 5] Aunger of lands (*named*) in Waterbeche and Dennye, co. Cambridge, once of Edward Elrington; with reservations, including free warren of beasts, fish and fowl; from Michaelmas last; yearly rent £9. On the surrender by Aunger of a patent, 25 Feb., 1 & 2 Ph.

& Mary, leasing the same to Edward Norton at the same rent for 21 years from Lady Day 1560 or the termination of a lease thereof by Elrington by indenture, 12 March, 30 Hen. VIII, to William Hawkyns and John Stocklyng for 21 years. For a fine of £27 paid to the Exchequer.   By the commissioners by virtue of the Queen's warrant.

2613.)   18 *March* 1577.   *Gorhambury*.   Lease for 40 years to Robert Constable, knight, the Queen's servant, of a capital messuage called Overton Hall, all appurtenances thereof in Overton and elsewhere, co. York, and woods called Overton Wood and the herbage and pannage thereof, all once of the monastery of St. Mary by the walls of York and late exchanged with Thomas Henneage, knight; with reservations; from Michaelmas 1593, being the termination of a lease thereof by patent, 11 Feb., 15 Eliz., to Elizabeth Harbert, widow,   [*m. 6*]
for 21 years from Michaelmas then last at a yearly rent of £68 8s. 6d.; yearly rent £61 17s.; the lessee to cut the woods at fitting seasons, to enclose 'lez springes' thereof and to leave 12 'lez staddelles' in every acre according to statute. For his service.   By p.s.

2614.)   5 *April* 1577. Lease for 21 years to Henry Worrall of the rectories of (1) Ranworth, co. Norfolk, once of Langley priory, and (2) Midleton, co. Suffolk, once of the monastery of Laiston and late of Charles, late duke of Suffolk; with reservations; from Lady Day last; yearly rents (1) £4 10s. and (2) £5 10s. In consideration that he has undertaken the repair and maintenance of the chancels of the rectories and will find sufficient priests or curates to serve in the churches.   By the commissioners by virtue of the Queen's warrant.

2615.)   11 *April* 1577.   *Gorhambury*.   Lease for 40 years to John Redwoodd of the water mill of Watford, co. Hertford, and the suit belonging thereto, late in the tenure of Robert Brande, parcel of the manor of Watford and once of the monastery of St. Albans, co. Hertford; from Michaelmas last; yearly rent £13. In consideration of the surrender by Redwood of a   [*m. 7*]
patent, 5 March, 3 Eliz., leasing the mill to Ralph Hope for 21 years from Midsummer 1570 at the same rent; also because he will repair and maintain the mill; and for a fine of £13 paid at the Exchequer.   By the commissioners by virtue of the Queen's warrant.

2616.)   22 *March* 1577.   *Gorhambury*.   Lease for 21 years to Reginald Turner, serjeant of the bakehouse, and Walter Freman, yeoman of the   [*m. 8*]
kitchen, of (1) the mills of Pentrighe *alias* Pentirgh and Disserth, co. Flint, and (2) St. John's chantry in Ruthland of the Prince's foundation, co. Flint, which mills and the rest were late of the late earl of Chester, (3) a messuage and a mill (*tenants named*) in Hallywell and Whitford, once of the monastery of Basingwerke, co. Flint, (4) the tithes of corn in Glothaithe in the parish of Eglusse Rosse, co. Caernarvon, given for a chaplain celebrating in the house of Thomas Mosten, in the Crown's hands by the dissolution of chantries and the like, and (5) lands (*named with tenants' names*) in Penmenith in the commote of Dindd, co. Anglesey, late of the monastery of Conwey, co. Caernarvon; with reservations; (1) from Michaelmas 1597, having been leased by patent, 26 June, 7 Eliz., to Reginald Turner, John Emerson and Walter Freman *inter alia*, with (2) and (3), for 21 years from (3) Michaelmas 1572 or the termination of the interest of Peter Mosten, (2) Lady Day 1579 or the termination of the interest of Margaret Griffyth, widow, (to whom it was leased by patent of the Exchequer, 30 June, 4 & 5 Ph. & Mary, for 21 years from Lady Day then last at a yearly rent of 24s. 4d.) and (1) from Michaelmas 1576 or the termination of the interest of John Daunce, knight, at yearly rents of (3) 105s., (2) 24s. 4d. and (1)£13 6s. 8d.; (2) from Michaelmas 1600; (3) from Michaelmas 1593; (4) from Michaelmas 1586, having been leased by patent of the   [*m. 9*]

Exchequer, 15 March, 8 Eliz., to Margaret Mosten for 21 years from Michaelmas then last at a yearly rent of 53s. 4d.; (5) from Lady Day 1596, having been leased by patent, 29 March, 17 Eliz., to John Hill *inter alia* for 21 years from Lady Day then last at a yearly rent of 2s. 1d.; same rents. For their service.   By p.s.

2617.) 22 *March* 1577. *Gorhambury.* Grant for life to Robert Knolls, one of the sons of Francis Knolls, knight, vice-chamberlain, and Catherine late his wife, of the reversion of the offices of (1) keeper of the capital house of Syon or site and house of the late monastery of Syon, co. Middlesex, (2) keeper of the woods in Istelworthe, Braynforde, Twickenham, Heston, Whitton, Sutton and Aydestones, co. Middlesex, (3) steward of the manor of Istelworthe and of all the Queen's lands aforesaid there and (4) bailiff of the same manor and lands, which offices were granted by patent, 27 May, 2 Eliz., (1) and (2) to the said   [*m.* 10] Francis, still surviving, and Catherine, now deceased, for life in survivorship and (3) and (4) to Francis for life; with wages of (1) 8d. a day, (2) 8d. a day, (3) 100s. a year and (4) 2d. a day, payable out of the issues of the manor and lands, from the death of Francis.   By p.s.

2618.) 22 *Aug.* 1577. *Gorhambury.* Lease for 21 years to Edward Nettleton of the site of the manor of Elmeswell *alias* Helmeswell on the Wold, co. York, late of the monastery of St. Mary next the walls of York; with reservations; from Michaelmas next; yearly rent £29 7s.; the lessee to provide entertainment for the Queen's steward and surveyor coming to the said site to hold courts or survey the manor. In consideration of the surrender by Nettleton of a patent, 10 Dec., 19 Eliz., leasing the site to Thomas Henneage for 21 years from Michaelmas then last at the same rent.   By p.s

2619.) 22 *March* 1577. *Gorhambury.* Lease for 21 years to Robert   [*m.* 11] Knolles, one of the sons of Francis Knolles, knight, of (1) lands (*named with tenants' names*) in Istellworthe Syon, (2) lands (*named with tenants' names*) in Istleworthe, Twickenham, Heston and Howndeslowe, (3) lands, including two water mills under one roof in Istleworth, now or late in the tenure of Thomas Wrothe, knight, (4) lands (*named with tenants' names*) in Istleworthe and Heston, once of the late chapel of All Angels   [*m.* 12] of Westbrainford Ende, (5) a cottage (*tenant named*), (6) lands (*named with tenant's name*) and (7) a tenement (*named with tenant's name*) in Istleworth, all parcels of the manor of Syon, co. Middlesex, and   [*m.* 13] late of Edward, late duke of Somerset, attainted of felony; with reservations; from Michaelmas 1591, being the termination of a lease by patent, 27 May, 2 Eliz., to the said Francis, then vice-chamberlain of the household, and Catherine his wife of all the premises (including the reversion and rent of (1), leased by patent, 14 Sept., 2 & 3 Ph. & Mary, to James [*recte* Joyce][1] Wastell *alias* Page for 21 years from Michaelmas then next at a yearly rent of £10) *inter alia* for 31 years from Michaelmas then next at yearly rents of (1) £10, (2) 10s., (3) £20 for the mills and £12 3s. 4d. for the rest and certain other lands, (4) £7 8s. 6d., (5) 1d. and a rose, (6) 66s. 8d. and (7) 20s.; yearly rents (1) £10, (2) 10s., (3) £20 for the mills and £9 12s. 4d. for the rest, (4) £7 8s. 6d.,   [*m.* 14] (5) 1d. and a rose, (6) 66s. 8d. and (7) 20s.; the lessee to have in consideration of the repair of the mills an allowance of 100s. yearly on payment of the rent before the auditor and the receiver of the county, and the Crown will bear the charges of repairing and maintaining the watercourses and other things concerning the mills without and beyond the mill houses and without and beyond 'le hedde and tayle' of the mills.   By p.s.

---

[1] Both the enrolment and the warrant (in Chancery Warrants, Series II, (C.82) 1312) read 'Jacobus'; but this appears to be a misreading for 'Jocosus', *cf. Calendar of Patent Rolls*, 1555–1557, p. 121, and 1558–1560, p.350.

2620.)   29 *March* 1577.   Lease for 21 years to Richard Broughton, Thomas Newporte and William Barroll, to the use of Robert, earl of Essex, of (1) the agistment and herbage of the park of St. Florence, co. Pembroke,   [*m.* 15]
(2) lands called Kingeswoode and Gauden *alias* Golden and meadows in Kingeswoode *alias* Kingesbridge, co. Pembroke, late of Jasper, late duke of Bedford, (3) a tenement (*tenant named*) called Elliottes Parke, co. Pembroke, late of Rice Griffith, attainted, (4) the rectories of Mancloughocke *alias* Manclohog, Llandylo and Llancolman, co. Pembroke, once of the monastery of St. Dogmael, co. Pembroke, (5) Iscoide grange and lands (*tenant named*), parcel thereof, co. Carmarthen, (6) Castle Cossam grange and lands (*named with tenants' names*), parcel thereof, some in the parishes of Llanuyno *alias* Llanony, Henllan Amgoid and Llanbedy, co. Carmarthen, (7) Courtmanorvorion grange and lands etc. (*named with tenants' names*), parcel thereof, some in the parish of Llangeller, co. Carmarthen, (8) Kilbargonne grange, co. Carmarthen, and (9) Lloynereball grange,   [*m.* 16]
co. Pembroke, with lands (*named with tenants' names*), parcel thereof, some in the parish of Ludchurche, co. Pembroke, which granges aforesaid were once of the monastery of Whitlande, co. Carmarthen; with reservations; from Lady Day last; yearly rents (1) 27*s.* 6*d.*, (2) £8 6*s.*, (3) 20*s.*, (4) £8, (5) £11 16*d.*, (6) £18 17*s.* 9½*d.*, (7) £18 1*d.*,   [*m.* 17]
(8) 2*s.* and (9) £11 5½*d.*; the Crown to discharge the lessees from all other payments. In consideration of the surrender by Broughton, Newporte and Barroll in respect of the premises of a patent, 17 Feb., 4 Eliz., leasing them *inter alia* to Walter, viscount Hereford, and Lettice his wife for 21 years (1) and (2) from Michaelmas 1562 or the termination of the interest therein of Francis Sowthwell and the rest from Michaelmas then next at the same rents.   By p.s.

2621.)   5 *April* 1577.   Grant to Henry Knolls, an esquire for the body, and Edward Williams of the Inner Temple, London, their heirs and assigns of —(1) lands (*named with tenants' names*) in Bury, co. Suffolk, once of the monastery of Bury St. Edmunds; (2) the rectory of Shenstone, co. Stafford, once of the monastery or the dean and canons of Christ Church and St. Mary the Virgin, Oxford; (3) lands in Bitteswell, co. Leicester, (reserving to the Crown the glebe lands and tithes belonging to the rectory of Bitteswell), once of the monastery of Pré, Leicester; (4) lands in Shemesbye *alias* Shesbye, co. Leicester, once of the monastery of Chacombe, co. Northampton; (5) lands (*tenant named*) in Normanton Feild, co. Leicester, once of St Mary's chantry in Bottesford; (6) lands (*tenant named*) in Westrington, co. York, once of the hospital of St. John of Jerusalem; (7) a tenement ((*tenant named*) in Alne, co. York, once of the house of Austin friars in York; (8) lands (*named with tenant's name*) in Bradwell, co. Buckingham, once of Snelleshall priory; (9) lands (*tenant named*) in Ratclyff, co. Nottingham, once of Bingham chantry, co. Nottingham; (10) lands (*tenants named*) in Degerburton in Mapperley, co. Derby, once of the monastery of Dale, co. Derby; (11) the manor of Bredon, co. Worcester, once of the bishopric of Worcester; (12) the advowson of the rectory of Bredon aforesaid; and (13) the manor of   [*m.* 18]
Knighton, co. Leicester, once of the bishopric of Lincoln. Advowsons, other than (12), and lead, except in gutters and windows, reserved. To hold in fee farm the manors of Bredon and Knighton with their appurtenances by service of the fortieth part of a knight's fee and the rest as of the manor of Estgrenewich, co. Kent, in socage, and by yearly rents of (1) 22*s.* (*detailed*), (2) £5 19*s.* 2½*d.*, (3) £5 12*s.* 7½*d.*, (4) £4 9*s.* 9*d.*, (5) 14*d.*, (6) 2*s.*, (7) 4*s.*, (8) 14*d.*, (9) 13*s.* 4*d.*, (10) 13*s.* 4*d.*, (11) £59 12*s.* ½*d.* and (13) £21 9*s.* 1½*d.* Issues from   [*m.* 19]
Michaelmas last. The grantees to pay 9*s.* yearly out of (11) by John Cooke for a tenement in his tenure to the farmer of the demesne lands of the manor allowed for 'lez plowirons' and other necessaries by covenant of his indenture. For the service of Knolls.   By Q.

2622.)   5 *April* 1577.   Presentation of Toby Walkewooke (*alias* Walkewood), M.A., to the rectory of Lymmyngton, co. Somerset, Bath and Wells dioc., void by the death of John Wigwoode and in the Queen's gift by the minority of William Rooswell.   By Q.

2623.)   3 *April* 1577.   Presentation of Adam Squier, S.T.P., to the rectory of Bosworth, co. Leicester, Lincoln dioc., void by the promotion of John Ailmer, S.T.P., to the bishopric of London.   [*m.* 20]
        By p.s.

2624.)   10 *April* 1577.   *Gorhambury.*   Grant for life to Toby Mathew, S.T.P. the Queen's chaplain, of the deanery of Christ Church cathedral, Oxford; as held by John Piers, the late dean.   By p.s.

2625.)   12 *April* 1577.   *Gorhambury.*   Licence for life for John Anson, clerk, rector of Weston Turvile, co. Buckingham, to absent himself from his said rectory and any other ecclesiastical benefices which he shall hereafter lawfully possess, as he could have done before stat. 21 Hen. VIII against pluralities of benefices; and licence to demise at farm the rectory and any of his benefices, as he could have done before stat. 13 Eliz. touching leases of benefices.   By p.s.

2626.)   26 *March* 1577.   Protection for one year for Ciriack Ruse.   By Q.
        [*m.* 21]

2627.)   5 *April* 1577.   Protection for one year for George Themilthorpe. Because he is deputed to travel about the Queen's business, to wit, the levying of arrears of clerical tenths and subsidies in the diocese of Norwich.   By p.s.

2628.)   12 *April* 1577.   *Gorhambury.*   Grant for life to Bartholomew Musgrave of the office of a gunner in Carlisle Castle, held by James Brigham, deceased; with wages of 8*d.* a day from Brigham's death, payable by the receiver general of the county of Cumberland or at the Exchequer.   By Q.

2629.)   22 *March* 1577.   *Gorhambury.*   Grant to Ralph Shelton of the next presentation to the rectory of Pulham Marie with its chapel, Norwich dioc., co. Norfolk.   By p.s.

2630.)   22 *March* 1577.   *Gorhambury.*   Grant for life to Elizabeth Jones, widow, of an annuity of £30, payable at the Exchequer, from Midsummer last.   By p.s.

2631.)   12 *July* 1577.   Grant in fee simple to Henry Campyon of   [*m.* 22]
London, mercer, and William Campyon, his son, of—lands in Harveryn, Kethinock, Widigada, Cayo, Rosemayn, Mallayne, Althegare, Dursloyn and Glyncothy, co. Carmarthen, late of Rice Griffith, attainted of treason, and leased by several patents to Walter, viscount Hereford, for divers years still enduring; lands (*tenants named*) in Uchoyd Kydwelly in the parish of Llangonnor in the commote of Kydwelly, co. Carmarthen, and in Abergwilly, co. Carmarthen, late of the said Griffith, attainted, and leased at several yearly rents of 53*s.* 4*d.* and 8*s.*; lands (*tenants named*) in Trathnegan *alias* Trathnelgan (*named*) and Kevenlleth *alias* Kevenblayth, co. Carmarthen, once of the monastery of Talley, co. Carmarthen; lands (*named*) in the lordship of Kydwelly, co. Carmarthen, late of the said Griffith, attainted of treason, and leased at a yearly rent of 26*s.* 8*d.*; lands (*named with tenants' names*), parcels of the grange of Custoda *alias* Gwastoda, co. Carmarthen, once of the monastery of Talley; lands   [*m.* 23]

(*tenants named*) in Trathnegan aforesaid, once of the monastery of Talley; lands (*named with tenants' names*) in Abbergwilly aforesaid, late of the said Griffith, attainted; lands (*named*), parcel of the grange of Mairedreff, co. Cardigan, once of the monastery of Talley and leased by patent, 2 June, 18 Eliz., to Thomas Wigmore for 21 years; lands (*named with tenants' names*) in Shurley, Lymbroke and Wigmore, co. Hereford, once of Lymbroke priory; the site of the manor of Bemerton and Quidhampton and the sites of the manors of Bemerton and Quidhampton, co. Wilts, once of the priory of St. Denys, co. Southampton, and late leased to Thomas Pacie at a yearly rent of £11; lands (*named with tenants' names*) in Bridgewater, co. Somerset, once of St. George's chantry there; and lands (*named with tenant's name*) in Barking, co. Essex, once of the monastery of Barking and leased by patent, 7 April, 10 Eliz., to Francis Stacy *inter alia* for 21 years. With reservations of the chief rents called 'westva'

[*m.* 24]

payable yearly to the Crown out of the premises belonging to the said Griffith in right of the principality of Wales and the duchy of Lancaster, advowsons and lead, except lead in gutters and windows. To hold the site of the manor of Bemerton and Quidhampton by service of the fortieth part of a knight's fee and the rest as of the manor of Estgrenewiche, co. Kent, in socage, and rendering yearly to the Crown for the premises late of the said Griffith such several rents called 'westva' as were payable before his attainder to the principality of Wales and duchy of Lancaster, and for the premises late of the chantry in Bridgewater 4s. as in right of the monastery of Athelney. Issues from Lady Day last. The grantees to pay yearly out of the premises in Althegare and Dursloyn 10s. to the Crown as in right of the principality of South Wales, and out of the premises in Bridgewater 17s. to the bailiff and burgesses of the fee of the

[*m.* 25]

borough of Bridgwater, 4d. to John Michell and his heirs and 4s. to the Crown in right of the monastery of Athelney.

In consideration of the manor of Brymfield, co. Hereford, and the manor of Chelworth and hundred of Staple, co. Wilts, bargained and conveyed to the Queen by James Crofte, knight, councillor, controller of the household; also for Crofte's service and at his suit.

By p.s.

2632.) 21 *Aug.* 1577. *Gorhambury.* Assignment to Thomas Leighton, captain of the isle of Guernesey, of a lease of fisheries in the water of Twede called Halewellstile, Twedemouth Steile, Goode, Blackwell, Yeresforde, Newewater, Waltham, Wilforde, Grenehill and Pedwell in the liberties of Norham and Norhamshire or elsewhere, co. Northumberland, granted to the Queen by Richard, bishop of Durham, by deed, 31 May, 19 Eliz., for 100 years from that date for such rent and under such covenants as are contained in the said deed enrolled in Chancery. For his service. *English.*

By p.s.

2633.) 2 *Sept.* 1577. *Gorhambury.* Presentation of Clement Forthe, M.A., to a canonry or prebend in Bristol cathedral, void by the resignation of John Bridgewater. By p.s.

2634.) 19 *Aug.* 1577. *Gorhambury.* Presentation of Stephen Nevinson, D.C.L., to the rectory of Romaldkirke, Chester dioc., void by the death of John Rudde. By p.s.

2635.) 20 *Aug.* 1577. *Gorhambury.* Grant for life to Edward Plankney of the office of a gunner in the Tower of London; with wages of 6d. a day, payable at the Exchequer; from the present date if such office shall be void or from the date of the next vacancy; the grant not to be to the prejudice of any person having a previous grant of the like place of a gunner. By Q.

(*The dorse of this roll is blank.*)

20 ELIZABETH I

17 November 1577–16 November 1578

PART I

C. 66/1164

2636.)   28 *Nov.* 1577.   Licence for Arthur Goldinge, brother and heir   [*m.* 1]
of Henry Goldinge, to enter upon his lands; issues from Henry's death.   [*m.* 2]
                                                            By bill of the court of Wards.

2637.)   5 *Dec.* 1577.   *Windsor Castle.*   The like for Anthony Dryden and Anne his wife as
in right of the said Anne, one of the three sisters and co-heirs of Robert Wilkes; issues from
Wilkes's death.   [*m.* 3]
                                                            By bill of the court of Wards.

2638.)   12 *Feb.* 1578.   The like for Francis Bowier *alias* Turner, son and heir of John
Bowyer *alias* Turner; issues from the time when Francis attained   [*m.* 4]
the age of 21.   By bill of the court of Wards.

2639.)   28 *Jan.* 1578.   The like for John Harpur, son and heir of Richard Harpur, a justice
of the Common Pleas; issues from Richard's death.   [*m.* 5]
                                                            By bill of the court of Wards.

2640.)   1 *Feb.* 1578.   The like for William Clerke, son and heir of Henry Clerke; issues
from the time when William attained the age of 21.   [*m.* 6.]
                                                            By bill of the court of Wards.

2641.)   5 *Dec.* 1577.   The like for Walter Harecourte, son and heir of   [*m.* 7]
Simon Harecourte; issues from Simon's death.   By bill of the court of Wards.

2642.)   26 *April* 1578.   The like for Francis Vaughan, son and heir of John Vaughan;
issues from John's death.   [*ms.* 8 and 9]
                                                            By bill of the Court of Wards.

2643.)   5 *May* 1578.   The like for Thomas Loveys, son and heir of Leonard Loveis; issues
from Leonard's death.   [*m.* 10]
                                                            By bill of the court of Wards.

2644.)   6 *May* 1578.   The like for Edward, lord Morley, son and heir of Henry Parker, late
lord Morley; issues from Henry's death.   [*m.* 11]
                                                            By bill of the court of Wards.

2645.)   18 *June* 1578.   *Gorhambury.*   The like for Robert Gale, son and   [*m.* 12]
heir of Francis Gale; issues from the time when Robert attained the age   [*m.* 13]
of 21.   By bill of the court of Wards.

2646.)   6 *June* 1578.   The like for Nicholas Wadham, son and heir of John Wadhame; issues from John's death.   By bill of the court of Wards.

[*m.* 14]

2647.)   6 *June* 1578.   The like for William Thornehull, son and heir of Robert Thornehull; issues from the time when William attained the age   [*m.* 15] of 21.   By bill of the court of Wards.

2648.)   12 *June* 1578.   The like for Thomas Skelton, son and heir of Thomas Skelton; issues from the time when Thomas the son attained   [*ms.* 16 and 17] the age of 21.   By bill of the court of Wards.

2649.)   *Undated.*   The like for Richard Carewe, son and heir of Thomas Carewe; issues from the time when Richard attained the age of 21.   [*m.* 18] By bill of the court of Wards.

2650.)   28 *April* 1578.   The like for Edmund Braye and Agnes his wife and William Johnson and Mary his wife, as in right of the wives as daughters and co-heirs of Edmund Harman; issues from Harman's death.   [*m.* 19] By bill of the court of Wards.

2651.)   28 *April* 1578.   The like for Vincent Barrey, son and heir of Lawrence Barrye; issues from Lawrence's death.   [*m.* 20] By bill of the court of Wards.

2652.)   5 *Aug.* 1578.   The like for Anthony Brakenburye and Mary his   [*m.* 21] wife, in right of the said Mary, daughter and heir of Hugh Thornhill;   [*m.* 22] issues from the time when Mary attained the age of 14.   By bill of the court of Wards.

2653.)   26 *Feb.* 1578.   The like for John Jobson, son and heir of   [*m.* 23] Francis Jobson, knight; issues from Francis's death.   [*m.* 24] By bill of the court of Wards.

2654.)   29 *Jan.* 1578.   The like for Edmund Longe, son and heir male of Richard Longe; issues from the time when Edmund attained the age   [*m.* 25] of 21.   By bill of the court of Wards.

2655.)   24 *Jan.* 1578.   The like for Henry Clyfford, son and heir of Thomas Clyfford; issues from the time when Henry attained the age of 21.   [*m.* 26] By bill of the court of Wards.

2656.)   27 *Nov.* 1577.   Signification to Edmund, archbishop of Canterbury, of the royal assent to the election of John Piers, bishop of Rochester, to the bishopric of Salisbury, void by death; and order to confirm the election and do everything incumbent on the archbishop's pastoral office in this behalf according to statute.   By p.s.

2657.)   23 *Dec.* 1577.   Order to the tenants of the bishopric of Salisbury to be intendant to John, bishop of Rochester, bishop elect of Salisbury; the Queen having received his fealty and restored to him hereby the temporalities of his see, except lands chosen and taken into the Queen's hands by force of stat. 1 Eliz. if such there be.   By p.s.

2658.)   23 *Dec.* 1577.   The like writs [*sic*] to the following escheators—co. Sussex; cos. Somerset and Dorset; cos Southampton and Wilts; co. Gloucester and the adjacent marches of Wales; cos. Oxford and Berks; co. Lincoln; Thomas Ramsey, knight, mayor and escheator of the city of London.

2659.)   22 *Nov.* 1577.   Licence for Nathaniel Harford, brother   [*m.* 27]
and heir of Richard Harford, to enter upon his lands; issues from Richard's death.
                                                                                  [*m.* 28]
                                                      By bill of the court of Wards.

2660.)   7 *Aug.* 1578.   The like for George Sayer, son and heir of George Sayer; issues
from George the father's death.   [*m.* 29]
                                                      By bill of the court of Wards.

2661.)   26 *Nov.* 1577.   The like for Thomas Cotton, son and heir of   [*m.* 30]
Thomas Cotton; issues from Thomas the father's death.   [*m.* 31]
                                                      By bill of the court of Wards.

2662.)   11 *Feb.* 1578.   The like for William Averye, son and heir of William Averye; issues
from William the father's death.   [*m.* 32]
                                                      By bill of the court of Wards.

2663.)   21 *April* 1578.   The like for Thomas Henslowe, son and heir of Ralph Henslowe;
issues from Ralph's death.   [*m.* 33]
                                                      By bill of the court of Wards.

2664.)   30 *April* 1578.   The like for Philip Babyngton, son and heir of William
Babington, knight; issues from William's death.   [*m.* 34]
                                                      By bill of the court of Wards.

2665.)   12 *June* 1578.   The like for Richard Mylle, kinsman and heir of George Mylle,
being son of Thomas Mylle, George's brother; issues from the time when Richard attained
the age of 21.   [*m.* 35.]
                                                      By bill of the court of Wards.

2666.)   9 *June* 1578.   The like for Innocent Reade, son and heir of Richard Reade, knight;
issues from Richard's death.   [*m.* 36]
                                                      By bill of the court of Wards.

2667.)   15 *June* 1578.   The like for James Calthorpe, son and heir of Christopher
Calthorpe; issues from the time when James attained the age   [*m.* 37]
of 21.   By bill of the court of Wards.

2668.)   20 *June* 1578.   The like for Timothy Lowe, son and heir of Simon Lowe; issues
from Simon's death.   [*m.* 38]
                                                      By bill of the court of Wards.

2669.)   12 *May* 1578.   The like for Nicholas Sutton, son and heir of   [*m.* 39]
Hammond Sutton; issues from the time when Nicholas attained the age   [*m.* 40]
of 21.   By bill of the court of Wards.

2670.)   18 *April* 1578.   The like for Anthony Clifford, son and heir of Henry Clifforde; issues from Henry's death.   [*m.* 41]

By bill of the court of Wards.

2671.)   12 *June* 1578.   The like for Edward, lord Zouche, Saint Maure and Cantilupe, son and heir of George, late lord Zouche, Saint Maure and Cantilupe; issues from the time when Edward attained the age of 21.   [*m.* 42]

By bill of the court of Wards.

2672.)   12 *May* 1578.   The like for John Caryll, kinsman and heir of John Caryll, to wit, the son and heir of Thomas Carill, son and heir of the same John the elder; issues from the time when John the younger   [*ms.* 43 and 44]
attained the age of 21.   By bill of the court of Wards.

2673.)   16 *June* 1578.   The like for Francis Newporte, son and heir of Richard Newporte, knight; issues from the time when Francis attained   [*m.* 45]
the age of 21.   By bill of the court of Wards.

(*The dorse of this roll is blank.*)

PART II

C. 66/1165

2674.) 18 *July* 1578. *Gorhambury*. Grant in fee farm to George   [*m.* 1]
Turpyn, knight, and Matthew Farneham and their heirs and assigns of the manor of
Knighton and lands (*named with tenants' names*) in Knighton and the meads of Leicester and
elsewhere, co. Leicester,   [*m.* 2]
late of the bishopric of Lincoln; reserving to the Crown advowsons, lead (except in gutters
and windows), free rents, rents of assize, services of free tenants and perquisites and profits
of court of the manor, and the common fine there; to hold as of the manor of   [*m.* 3]
Estgrenewiche, co. Kent, in socage and by a yearly rent of £18 1*s.* 5*d.* (*detailed*); issues from
Michaelmas last. In consideration of the said manor of Knighton granted to the Queen by
Turpyn and Farneham.   By p.s.

2675.) 23 *June* 1578. *Gorhambury*. Lease for 21 years to John Bell of (1) lands (*tenants*
named) in Wicke in the parish of Eaton, co. Buckingham,   [*m.* 4]
(2) lands (*named with tenants' names*), parcels of the manor of Eaton and now annexed to the
honour of Wyndesore, and (3) a water and fishery in the Thames late belonging to 'le locke'
and 'weare' of Boveney (*described*) and lands etc. (*described*, including a house next to St. Mary
Magdalen's chapel called 'Boveney chappell') and (4) a water and 'le broke' called Westmyll
Broke in the parish of Eaton, and appurtenances thereof (*described*), parcels of the manor of
Burneham and once of the monastery of Burneham, co. Buckingham, and now annexed to
the honour of Wyndesore; with reservations; from Michaelmas next; yearly rents (1) 66*s.*
8*d.*, (2) 78*s.* 4*d.*, (3) 100*s.*   [*m.* 5]
and (4) 40*s.* In consideration of the surrender by Bell of (*a*) the interest in (1) and (2) of
George Steede, to whom they were leased by patent, 22 March, 10 Eliz., *inter alia* at the same
rents for 21 years from the termination of leases thereof (1) to Sampson Butler and (2) to
Thomas Nicolles and (*b*) the interest in (3) and (4) of Bell himself, to whom they were leased
by patent, 25 June, 10 Eliz., for 21 years from Lady Day then last at the same rents; and for a
fine of £14 5*s.* paid at the Exchequer.   By p.s.

2676.) 18 *July* 1578. *Gorhambury*. Foundation of a college in Manchester in the county
palatine of Lancaster, to be called Christ's college in Manchester founded by Queen
Elizabeth, with a warden, being a priest and at least a bachelor of sacred theology, and four
fellows, being priests and at least bachelors of arts, able to instruct the Queen's subjects
there and in neighbouring places. Appointments of John Wulton to be first warden and of
John Mullyns, Alexander Nowell, Oliver Carter and Thomas Williamson to be the first
fellows. Incorporation of the warden and fellows. Successors of the present warden to be
appointed by the Crown by letters under the great seal; whenever the place of one of the
fellows shall hereafter become void, his successor shall be elected by the warden and
remaining fellows, or a majority of them of whom the warden shall be   [*m.* 6]
one, and shall be declared to be fellow by letters under the common seal of the college. There
shall be two chaplains or vicars in the college, who shall visit the sick and celebrate the
sacraments and other divine service in the college and parish of Manchester, and four
laymen and four boys skilled in music, who shall perform daily service in the church of the
college; appointment of Robert Barber and Thomas Richardson to be the first chaplains or

vicars, Robert Leighe, Charles Leighe, Philip Gosnall and John Glover to be the first men skilled in music and Anthony Glover, Hugh Shalcrosse, Mark Lenard and William Ellam the first boys skilled in music; whenever any of their places shall be void, a successor shall be elected by the warden and fellows, or a majority of them the warden being one. The said warden and fellows, chaplains, laymen and boys shall have such yearly stipends, with such deduction, as are assigned to them by these presents, to wit, the warden for every day he shall be present 4s. or 48d. and each of the fellows for every day he shall be present 16d., out of the rents and profits of the college, each chaplain 6¾d. a day, each man skilled in music 4½d. a day and each boy 2¾d. a day. Provision to be made of a collegiate house, in which the warden if he be present or in his absence the subwarden shall reside rent free. Also—because it is reported that the college has received very heavy damage by the absence of wardens who, being absent and not performing the office of warden, have nevertheless drawn to themselves most of the revenues of the college—hereafter neither the warden nor any of the fellows shall receive from the moneys of the college anything save only for the days on which he shall have been present in the college and in the church or shall have preached or shall have visited the sick in the town or parish; and the money collected by their absence shall be to the use of the college until provision be made of a common collegiate house and until the college has been brought to a good state; but thereafter for every day that the warden shall have been absent 2s. or 24d. of his stipend and for every day that any of the fellows shall be absent 8d. of his stipend shall go towards the better furnishing of the daily table of the fellows who shall be present on those days when the warden and the rest shall be absent; but the rest of the warden's stipend, that is, 2s. or 24d., as long as he shall be absent and the other 8d. of the stipend of each fellow absent shall be faithfully distributed by the fellows or fellow present in bread, drink, food or money to the poor of the town or parish; and, if the warden himself be present, he shall receive 4d. daily of the stipend of every fellow absent and the fellows present another 4d. thereof, but the remaining 8d. they shall distribute to the poor of the town or parish. Neither the warden nor any fellow shall receive anything of the money or goods of the college or have any voice in chapter until by oath before the remaining fellows present and also two or three gentlemen as witnesses they shall bind themselves to observe this the Queen's statute of not receiving anything save for days when they shall have been present and not to obtain or seek dispensation from observance thereof from the Crown or any other persons ecclesiastic or lay or accept such dispensation offered, under pain of perjury; and, if they do or attempt to do to the contrary, they shall be held as perjurors *ipso facto* and as not warden or fellow, and the Crown may in such case substitute another warden, and the warden and fellows another fellow, in place of the perjuror as if he were dead. The warden may nevertheless be absent from the college, visiting friends or on other business necessary to him, 20 days every quarter or in the whole year 80 days and receive his daily stipend of 4s. for so many days, and likewise every fellow may be absent 15 days every quarter and in the whole year 60 days and receive his daily stipend of 16d.; and, when the warden or any fellow shall chance to be absent on necessary business of the college by consent of the warden and chapter, his whole stipend shall be paid him as if he were present. Power for the bishop of London, the bishop of Rochester, the dean of St. Paul's, London, and the dean of the collegiate church of Westminster (or two of them) to make other ordinances for the government of the college; so that they be not contrary to the ordinances set out in this patent. Grant to the warden and fellows of messuages (*tenants named*) in Manchester, Newton, [*m. 7*]
Denesgate and Kirmanshulme in the parish of Manchester, lands (*named with tenants' names*) in Manchester, Newton and Salforde, the tithes of corn in Manchester and in Broughton, Chetam, Chorelton, Tetlowe, Hulme next Manchester, Dydisburie, Withington, Salforde, Lensholme, Openshawe, Trafforde, Stretforde, Cholerton, Barlowe, Blackley, Hulme next Stopforde, Clayton, Faylesworthe, Stryledale *alias* Drylesdale, Moston, Ancotes, Gorton,

Bexwicke, Reddishe, Denton, Haughtonne, Haughe, Inde, Harpethy, Keyrshall, Kirdins-mansholme, Bradford, Ardwike, Risheholme, Cromeshall, Hayfeild, Newton, Bromage, Ordeshall, Hardy, Honparke, Collyhurst, Claydon, Hopwoode Claydon and Heaton Norrys, co. Lancaster, belonging to the former college of Manchester, the tithes of lambs, calves, hay, flax and hemp and all profits of the dead, mortuaries and Easter book, small tithes and oblations in Manchester or the parish of Manchester (*tenants named*), messuages (*tenant named*) in Dunham Massy, co. Chester, late of the late college of Manchester, and all manors, lands, rectories, vicarages, the church once called the church of St. Mary of Manchester with all the chapels thereof, advowsons and other possessions spiritual and temporal in Manchester, in the counties of Lancaster or Chester or elsewhere in England once belonging to the said late college; to hold in frankalmoign, paying to the Crown at every vacancy of the warden and fellows such sums for first fruits as by law ought to be paid, and rendering also to the Crown yearly such sums as have heretofore been paid. Licence for the warden and fellows to acquire in mortmain, besides the premises above-granted, lands to the yearly value of £30 not held of the Crown immediately   [*m.* 8]
in chief or otherwise by knight service; they may nevertheless purchase lands of the former college of Manchester granted to the Crown by stat. 1 Edw. VI although held of the Crown in chief or by knight service; they may likewise purchase lands now belonging to the school in Manchester although held of the Crown in chief or by knight service. Provided that the Crown and its assigns may enjoy all the tithes and portions of tithes and grain specified in an indenture, 18 Dec., 18 Eliz., between the Crown and the master or warden and the fellows chaplains of the college, by the name of Thomas Hearle, master or warden, and the fellows chaplains of the college of St. Mary of Manchester of the foundation of King Philip and Queen Mary, as leased to the Queen, according to the intention of the same indenture that persons to whom the Queen should assign them by patent should be able to enjoy them without impeachment of the master or warden and fellows or of any other person by their consent or command; so nevertheless that the Queen's assigns shall pay to the warden and fellows the rents reserved in a patent, 20 Sept., 18 Eliz.

At the suit of the parishioners of Manchester, for the continuance and better establishment of the college, founded by King Philip and Queen Mary, of a master or warden, eight fellows chaplains, four clerks and six choristers; in the church whereof daily prayers and other divine service are celebrated for the Queen and realm and the parishioners, to the number of 10,000, and other neighbouring people are instructed; which college has by stat. 1 Eliz. either come to the Queen's hands as altogether dissolved or has no sure foundation by judgment of men skilled in law.   By p.s.

2677.)   28 *June* 1578.   *Gorhambury.*   Lease for 21 years to William Horton of lands (*named with tenants' names*) in (1) Modbury, (2) Newton Ferris, (3) Deane *alias* Deane Prior, (4) Hartford, (5) Ilsington, (6) Newton   [*m.* 9]
Abbottes and (7) Otterton, co. Devon; with reservations; from Michaelmas next; yearly rents from the time when he shall obtain possession (1) £7 13s. 2½d., (2) 7s. 1d., (3) 26s. 8d., (4) 3s. 4d., (5) 2s. 6d., (6) 16s. 8d. (*detailed*) and (7) 3s. 4d.; the lessee to pay yearly 26s. 4½d. out of (1)   [*m.* 10]
for chief rent to the lord of the manor and borough of Modburye. In consideration that the premises have been concealed for many years and no rent or profit answered therefrom.
                          By warrant of the commissioners.

2678.)   28 *June* 1578.   *Gorhambury.*   Lease for 21 years to Owen Gwynne of the house and site of the priory or cell of Kydwelly, co. Carmarthen, lands (*named*) in Kydwelly, late of the priory, all other lands belonging to the priory, the rectory of Kydwelly, late of the priory, the tithes and oblations in Estvailye, Moone, the parish of Lleghwen, the field of Welchien,

Penwarne, 'le Holwaye', the field of Horsestone, 'le Croftes', Westhiell, Westvailye and Middle Baylye, co. Carmarthen, the tithes of two mills in Kydwelly and a yearly pension out of the rectory of Penbray, co. Carmarthen, once of the same priory, which formerly belonged to the monastery of Shirborne, co. Dorset; with reservations; from Lady Day last; yearly rent £30 6s. 8d.; the lessee to pay yearly to the vicar of Kydwellye a pension of £8 and

[m. 11]

9s. 9d. for proxies and synodals to the archdeacon of St. Davids. In consideration of the surrender in the Exchequer by Gwynne of a patent, 4 Feb., 8 Eliz., leasing the premises to him for 21 years from Michaelmas then last at the same rent; also of a payment of £20 to William Morton and Thomas Twiste, grooms of the stable, by order of the treasurer and chancellor of the Exchequer; and for a fine of £40 paid at the Exchequer.   By p.s.

2679.)   7 July 1578.   *Gorhambury*.   Lease for 21 years to William Stonynge of lands (*named with tenants' names*) in Sidmouthe, co. Devon, late of Henry, late duke of Suffolk; with reservations; from Lady Day last; yearly rent £5 10s. 8d. For a fine of £16 12s. paid at the Exchequer.   By warrant of the commissioners.

2680.)   17 July 1578.   *Gorhambury*.   Lease for 21 years to Elizabeth Powell, widow, of the tithes and oblations in Raglan, co. Monmouth, and a   [m. 12] fishery in the water of Uske, once of Uske priory, co. Monmouth; from Michaelmas next; yearly rent £7 13s. 5d. In consideration of the surrender by the said Elizabeth of a patent, 3 July, 3 Eliz., leasing the premises to Elizabeth Jones, widow, for 21 years from Lady Day then last at the same rent; and for a fine of £23 3d., to wit, £15 3d. paid at the Exchequer and £8 to Anthony Wall allowed in satisfaction of a like sum paid by Wall for the fine of a lease of lands in Ingleton in the bishopric of Durham which he could not enjoy by reason of a former lease, as appears by a bill signed by Christopher Smythe, clerk of the pipe, and annexed to the particular whereon this patent issued.   By warrant of the commissioners.

2681.)   18 *July* 1578.   *Gorhambury*.   Lease for 41 years to Richard Tottill and Bartholomew Brokesbye of a tenement in the parish of St. Dunstan in the West by Temple Barre, London, now or late in the tenure of Henry Eve, once of St. Mary's brotherhood in St. Dunstan's church, six tenements in the said parish, now or late in the several tenures of Catherine Johnson, Catherine Hadley, Roger Bande, Robert Thomson, William Edmondes and John Dawson, and a tenement called 'the Brotherheadhall of Sainte Dunstane' in Fewterlane in the said parish and a garden in the same parish, late in the tenure of the churchwardens of St. Dunstan; from Lady day last; yearly rent   [m. 13] £8 4s. In consideration of the surrender by Tottill and Brokesbye of an exemplification of a patent of the court of Augmentations, 18 Oct., 2 Edw. VI, leasing *inter alia* to William Honnynge, the King's servant, whose interest they hold in the premises, 'Saint Dunstones Hall' aforesaid and the rest of the premises, all in the King's hands by stat. 1 Edw. VI for the dissolution of chantries and the like, for 41 years from Michaelmas then last at a yearly rent of £7 19s.; and because some of the tenements are in great decay, as appears by certificate of the Queen's surveyor there.   By warrant of the commissioners.

2682.)   23 *June* 1578.   *Gorhambury*.   Lease for 21 years to John Cole, son of Richard Cole, deceased, of the rectory of Stokenham, co. Devon, late assigned to Anne of Cleves, formerly of Bustlesham priory, co. Berks, and leased to the said Richard by patent, 22 Feb., 6 Eliz., for 21 years from Michaelmas then last at a yearly rent of £58; with reservations; from Michaelmas 1584; same rent. For a fine of £116 paid at the Exchequer.   By p.s.

2683.)   14 *July* 1578.   *Gorhambury*.   Lease for life in succession to John Goodwyn the

younger, Thomas Throkmerton and John Throkmerton, Thomas's son, of the rectory of
Ravenston *alias* Raunston, co. Buckingham, late of   [*m.* 14]
cardinal Wolcey; with reservations; yearly rent £14; the Crown to discharge the lessees from
all other payments. In consideration of the surrender by Goodwyn of a patent, 30 May, 9
Eliz., leasing the rectory to Robert Throkmerton, knight, for 21 years from Lady Day then
last at the same rent; and for a fine of £42 paid at the Exchequer.   By p.s.

2684.)   4 *July* 1578.   *Gorhambury*.   Lease for 21 years to David Lewes, LL.D., judge of
the court of Admiralty, of (1) the rectories of Brentles and   [*m.* 15]
Llandevallie, co. Brecon, once of Clifford priory, co. Hereford, and (2) lands (*named with
tenants' names*) in Mendham, co. Suffolk, once of the monastery of Bury St. Edmunds, co.
Suffolk; with reservations; from Michaelmas next; yearly rents (1) £16 and (2) 12*s.* 2*d.*
(*detailed*). (1) In consideration of the surrender by Lewes of a patent, 24 July, 6 Eliz., leasing
the rectories *inter alia* to John Asterley for 21 years from Lady Day then last at the same rent;
and for a fine of £32, to wit, £27 4*s.* paid at the Exchequer and £4 16*s.* to John Bathe allowed
in satisfaction of a like sum paid by Bathe for the fine of a lease of lands in Secklinge, co.
York, which he could not enjoy, as appears by a bill signed by Christopher Smythe, clerk of
the pipe, and annexed to the particular whereon this patent issued. (2) For a fine of 48*s.* 8*d.*
paid at the Exchequer.   By p.s.

2685.)   30 *June* 1578.   *Gorhambury*.   Licence for Christopher Hatton, knight, councillor,
captain of the guard and vice-chamberlain, his heirs and assigns to enclose and impark 300
ac. of arable land, 200 ac. of meadow and 700 ac. of of pasture belonging to him in Holdenby
alias Haldenbye, Churchebrampton and Chappelbrampton, co. Northampton, and to have
free warren and free chase in the demesne lands of his manors of Haldenbye,
Churchebrampton and Chappelbrampton and all other his lands there and several fisheries
in the waters thereof; no one to hunt or fish therein without his licence under forfeiture to
the Crown of £10, although they be within the bounds of any forest of the Queen; he may
not only enclose the said lands, but may take land from husbandry and convert it to pasture
and may destroy buildings of husbandry belonging thereto; notwithstanding stat. 5 Eliz. for
the maintenance of tillage, stat. 13 Eliz. for the reviving of certain statutes, stat. 27 Hen. VIII
concerning the decay of houses   [*m.* 16]
and enclosures, stat. 7 Hen. VIII to avoid letting down of towns and stat. 4 Hen. VII for the
maintenance of houses of husbandry; pardon of all offences heretofore committed in this
regard and grant to him of   [*m.* 17]
all forfeitures due for such offences. For his service.   By Q.

2686.)   30 *June* 1578.   *Gorhambury*.   Grant in fee simple—for the performance of the
purposes specified below—to Christopher Hatton, knight, councillor, vice-chamberlain
and captain of the yeomen of the guard, of a piece of land partly built on (containing about
153 feet by 182½ feet by 142 feet), and all the buildings thereon (*described with tenants' names*),
parcel of the palace or house of the bishop of Ely in Holborne, co. Middlesex, called Elye
Place, and 'le Gate House' and other chambers and places (*described with tenants' names*)
adjoining the said piece, a great garden adjoining the hall (about 295 feet 4¾ inches long), an
orchard adjoining the garden (containing on the West side about 221 feet, the South side 226
feet, the East side 256 feet and the North side 216 feet 3 inches), a close adjoining the orchard
or garden enclosed with 'a mudde walle' (about 14 ac.) and all other hereditaments conveyed
by the bishop by the undermentioned charter to the Crown; to hold as of the manor of
Eastgrenewiche in socage; issues from Michaelmas last. It is recited in a charter, 10 Sept., 19
Eliz.,   [*m.* 18]
made by Richard, bishop of Ely, confirmed by the dean and chapter of Ely cathedral and

enrolled in Chancery, that the bishop at the Queen's request by indenture, 20 March, 18 Eliz., leased to Hatton, by the name of Christopher Hatton, captain of the yeomen of the guard and a gentleman of the privy chamber, for 21 years from Lady Day then next certain parts of Elye Place, to wit, 'le Gate House', 'the first courte yearde' and divers chambers and other places belonging thereto mentioned in the indenture; also that Hatton thereafter spent large sums in building and repairing the premises and in purchasing the interest of divers persons in gardens and the like mentioned in the indenture and in a house adjoining the premises, as appears by a certificate tripartite of John, bishop of London, Christopher Wray, knight, chief justice of the Queen's Bench, William Cordell, knight, master of the rolls, and John Southecote, a justice of the Queen's Bench, by virtue of a commission to them in this behalf under the privy seal enrolled in the court of Requests; also that there were doubts of the validity of the said lease, whereby Hatton could to his great damage lose possession under the said lease and his expenditure, contrary to the intention of the lease, the Queen's intention and will, the intention of the bishop and all equity; also that the Queen therefore requested the bishop by her letters in this behalf and other ways that a conveyance might be devised whereby Hatton might have a good estate in fee simple in the premises until the bishop should repay him his expenditure aforesaid incurred or to be incurred about the

[m. 19]

premises; also that, by advice of learned counsel of the Queen and the bishop, the bishop was very ready to perform the Queen's request with liberty for redemption on repayment of the said expenditure; and by the said charter the bishop conveyed to the Crown the piece of land and buildings thereon aforesaid, certain other buildings and places adjoining the said piece, the said great garden, orchard and close and all hereditaments then in Hatton's tenure both leased by the said indenture and expressed by the charter to be conveyed to the Crown in or about that part of Ely Place then remaining to the bishop (except the liberties granted by the Crown to the bishops of Ely in Holborne or in or upon the premises).   By Q.

2687.)   10 *July* 1578.   *Gorhambury.*   Grant in fee simple to Robert Newdigate of Hawnes, co. Bedford, and Arthur Fountayne of Salle, co. Norfolk, of—woods (*named*) in the parishes of Clophilles and Hawnes, co. Bedford, (now in the tenure of Robert Newdigate), once of the monastery of Chickesandes; lands in Hungarton and Wyvell, co. Lincoln, of the yearly rent of 20s.,   [m. 20]

a yearly rent or pension of 10s. out of the rectory of Ropesley, co. Lincoln, and a portion of tithes out of the rectory of Collwicke, co. Nottingham, of the yearly value of 18s., all once of the monastery of Belvea, co. Lincoln; lands (*named with tenants' names*) in Bedford, co. Bedford, once of the monastery of Newenham, annexed to the honour of Ampthill; the manor of Great Brickill *alias* Brickhill, co. Bedford, and lands (*named with tenants' names*) in Great Brickell, once of the monastery of Woborne and afterwards annexed to the honour of Ampthill; lands in Goldington, co. Bedford, of the yearly value of 19d., late of chantries and the like; the rectory of Stanton Barye, co. Buckingham, formerly leased to William Hyde, once of the monastery of Goringe, co. Oxford; the manor of Parys Garden, co. Surrey, rents of assize and all other rents of free and customary tenants there of the yearly value of £8 7s. 8d. and the mansion house thereof and lands (*named*) there, parcel of possessions purchased from the late abbot of Barmondsey; lands (*tenant named*) in Parys Garden, in the Crown's hands by escheat; the manor of Asshested, co. Surrey, and all lands in Asshested now or late in the tenure of John Holgate, once of the monastery of Marton; the chantry or rectory of Wapenham and lands (*named*) in Wapenham, co. Northampton, in the Crown's hands as escheated; lands (*tenant named*) in Muscam, co. Nottingham, once of the monastery of Newested, co. Nottingham; lands in Spandy (*alias* Spanby), co. Lincoln, leased to William Lee by patent, 12 March, 10 Eliz., for 21 years at a yearly rent of 9s., once of the monastery of Sempringham, co. Lincoln; the manor of Farriett Monacorum *alias* Foriat Monachorum

next Shrewsbury, co. Salop. once of the monastery of SS. Peter and Paul in or by Shrewsbury, the rents of assize of free tenants thereof, rents called 'hognell rentes' out of lands in or by Foriett Monachorum or elsewhere, co. Salop, and   [*m.* 21] all other appurtenances of the manor; the grange of Blayne Annerthe and Aberporthe, cos. Carmarthen and Cardigan, once of the monastery of Talley, co. Carmarthen; lands (*tenants named*) in Thurlaston and Elvaston and in Ambaston in the parish of Elvaston, co. Derby, once of the monastery of Derleighe, co. Derby; lands (*named with tenants' names*) in Bedford, co. Bedford, some once of the monastery of Elvestowe and afterwards annexed to the honour of Ampthill and the rest once of the monastery of Caldwell and afterwards annexed to the same honour; lands (*tenant named*) in Sharpenhoo in the parish of Stretley, co. Bedford, once of a late free chapel called 'St. Gyles chappell' in Sharpenhoo, concealed from the Crown; lands (*tenants named*) in Bedford, once of the monastery of Elvestowe and afterwards annexed to the honour of Ampthill; lands (*tenant named*) in Luton, co. Bedford, concealed from the Crown; lands (*described*) in Easton next Stamford, co. Northampton, once of the chantry of Eston and concealed; burgages (*described*) in Richemonde, co. York, late of John Gower, attainted of treason; and the manor of Wanstrowe Rogers, co. Somerset, the capital messuage thereof and lands adjoining the same messuage, late of Charles, late lord Sturton, attainted of murder. Reserving to the Crown the manor of Wanstrowe Bullers *alias* Churche   [*m.* 22] Wanstrowe in Wanstrowe, co. Somerset, of the yearly value of £6 23*d.* To hold the manor of Parys Garden and its appurtenances by service of the fortieth part of a knight's fee and the rest in socage as of the manor of Estgrenewiche, co. Kent. Issues from Lady Day [*sic*].
    [*m.* 23]

    At the request of Henry Carie, K.G., lord of Hunsdon: in consideration of the manor and castle of Westharlesey, the manor of Daletowne, lands in Petto, Gobton, Swayneby, Faceby and Scruton and the manor of Aiselaby, co. York, and the manor of Eckington, co. Derby, late of Leonard Dacre, outlawed for treason, bargained and sold by lord Hunsdon to the Queen, having been formerly granted to him by her; and for his service.   By Q.

2688.)   2 *Sept.* 1578.   *Ipswich.*   Grant to John Farnham, a gentleman pensioner, his heirs and assigns of—(1) lands (*described with tenants' names*) in the parish of Richemond, co. York; (2) lands (*named with tenants' names*) in the parish of Hipeswell, co. York; (3) lands (*named with tenants' names*) in Bellerby, co. York, late belonging to the rectory of Spenythorne *alias* Spennyngthorne, co. York, for the support of a chaplain there; (4) lands (*tenants named*) in Bellerby, late of 'St. Oswoldes chappell *alias* Saint Oswoldes ermitage' in Bellerbye; (5) all lands in Brecon, co. Brecon, given for two masses called the morrow mass and St. Mary's mass in the church or chapel of St. Mary in Brecon and for St. Michael's mass celebrated for the departed in 'the Charnell House' in Brecon; (6) the chapel of Totenhoe, co. Buckingham, with all tithes, lands and fruits in Totenhoe (late of Snelshall priory); (7) lands (*named*) in the parishes of East Cleydon, Hodshawe (*alias* Hogshawe) or Queynton, co Buckingham; (8) lands (*named*) in Queynton; (9) a sheep pasture in Temmysforde, co. Bedford,   [*m.* 24] once given by Hugh de Caron to the church of St. Neots and the monks there for the salvation of his soul; (10) lands (*tenant named*) in Kempston, co. Bedford, given for a priest in Wavenden church, co. Buckingham; (11) a portion of the tithes of corn in Lethelay, co. York, the advowson of Lethelay church and all glebe lands there belonging to the Crown by the attainder of Henry Johnson for treason; (12) lands (*tenant named*, called 'the Anker Churche Howse', 'the Anker Churche Close' and 'Anker Churche Poole') in Ingolbie within the manor of Repington, co. Derby; (13) lands (*described with tenant's name*) in Bayldon, co. York, and all other lands in Bayldon, late of the chantry there, still remaining besides those lands there heretofore granted to any person by the Crown since the dissolution of the chantry; (14) lands (*tenants named*) in Farneley in the parish of Otley, co. York, belonging to the Crown by the attainder of Henry Johnson aforesaid; (15) the free chapel or chantry of the Lord's Ascension and the Assumption of Our Lady in Noseley, co. Leicester, and all its possessions there; (16) lands (*tenant named*), late of Richard Golden, in Beaumaris (*Bello Marisco*) and Llanvaies, co. Anglesey; (17) lands (*named with tenants' names*) in the parish of Fennystaunton, co. Huntingdon; (18) lands (*named*) in the parish of Istradveltey, occupied by Jankyn Thomas and others unknown for the past 30 years, (19) lands (*named with tenant's name*) in the parish of Devynnock and (20) lands (*named with tenant's name*) in the franchises of Brecon, all in the county of Brecon and once of Edward, late duke of Buckingham, attainted of treason; (21) lands (*named with tenant's name*)   [*m. 25*] in the parish of Trallionge, co. Brecon, which Owen Thomas Goz, being seised thereof in his demesne as of fee within the past 30 years and holding them of the Crown as of the honour of Brecon by fealty only, bequeathed to David ap Owen, his bastard son, and his heirs, which David died seised thereof in the year 9 Eliz. without an heir of his body, whereby they now belong to the Crown as escheat; (22) lands (*named with tenant's name*) in the parish of Llywell, co. Brecon, late of the said duke of Buckingham, attainted of treason; (23) lands called Capell Rydd Bryw in Llywell aforesaid, given from time immemorial, and in the year 37 Hen. VIII converted, for a mass and matins in Ryd Bryw chapel, co. Brecon; (24) lands (*tenant named*) in Southleighe in the manor of Stoke St. Noctan, co. Devon, given for a mass priest in Stoke St. Noctan church and other supersitious uses there; (25) Bramblety *alias* Brambeltye *alias* Brambiltye chapel or chantry in the parish of Eastgrenested *alias* Grenested, co. Sussex, (*tenant named*) and all its possessions there; (26) lands in Byton, co. Southampton, given for lights or other superstitious uses in Byton church; (27) the tithes, except those of corn, in the manor of Burton Constable in the parish of Swyne, co. York, (*tenant named*); (28) lands (*tenants named*) in Elstrunwick in the parish of Humbleton, co. York, late of Elstrunwick chapel; (29) lands (*named with tenant's name*) in Hallowghton, co. Leicester; (30) all lands in Felthrope *alias* Felthorpe, Braundeston, Swenyngton and Cawston, co. Norfolk, once of Mountjoy (*Sancti Laurencii de Monte Gaudio*) priory in Heveringland, co. Norfolk; (31) lands (*named with tenants' names*) in Cawston aforesaid; (32) lands (*described*) in Lugwarden, the advowson of Lugwarden church and the chapel of Llangarren, Henthlan and St. Winard annexed to the same church, co. Hereford; (33) lands (*tenants named*) in the parish of St. Mary in Bedford, given for superstitious uses, (34) lands (*named*) in Welton, given for anniversaries in Welton church, (35) lands (*named with tenants' names*) in Potton, some given for 'lez banners' in Potton church, (36) lands (*named with tenant's name*) in Eyworth, (37) a tenement (*tenant named*) in   [*m. 26*] Beeston *alias* Beeson in the parishes of Norrell and Sonday, (38) 'le Churche Howse *alias* le Towne Howse' in Goldington and (39) lands (*named with tenant's name*) in Beeston, Thornecote and Hatche in the parish of Northyell, all in the county of Bedford; (40) lands (*named with tenant's name*) in Ecopp in the parish of Addle, co. York; (41) lands (*tenant named*) in Tynshill and Addle (*named*), co. York; (42) lands (*named with tenants' names*) in Addle aforesaid; (43) six messuages and six gardens in the parish of All Hallows *apud Fenum* in London, once of the monastery or commandery of Coggeshall *alias* Coxhall, co. Essex; (44) lands (*described with tenant's name*) in Tyntenhull, co. Somerset, once of the monastery of Mountegewe, co. Somerset; (45) lands (*named with tenant's name*) in Wells, co. Somerset, given for 'le morrowe masse prest' and 'le Ladye service' in Wells cathedral for 90 years; (46) a ruinous water mill in Wells, once of St. John's priory or hospital in Wells; (47) lands (*described with tenant's name*) in Bristoll, given for lights and anniversaries in St. Michael's church in Bristoll; (48) lands (*tenants named*) in Pryn Pabean, co. Brecon; (49) lands (*tenant named*) in Llanganten (*alias* Flanganten), co. Brecon; (50) lands (*tenant*   [*m. 27*] *named*) in Byellth, co. Brecon; (51) the rectory of Darenth, co. Kent, and appurtenances (*tenant named*) thereof; (52) lands (*described with tenants' names*) in Aylesburye, co. Buckingham, once of St. Mary's brotherhood in Aylesburie; (53) lands (*tenant named*) in

Willington *alias* Willingdon, co. Sussex, given for lamps or lights in Eastborne church, co. Sussex; (54) a messuage called 'the Signe of the Redcrosse' in the parish of St. George the Martyr in Southwarke, co. Surrey, once in the tenure of Thomas Warde, deceased, and now or late in that of Edward Streete; (55) lands (*tenant named*) in Richemonde *alias* West Shene, co. Surrey, given for an obit in Richemonde churche; (56) a tenement (*described with tenant's name*) in Rye, co. Sussex; (57) lands in Blechington *alias* Blechingdon, co. [—], given for superstitious uses in the church there; (58) lands (*described*, now or late in the tenure of Thomas Swayne, clerk, rector of Farleighe, and Thomas Swayne, his son) in Farleighe, co. [—], given for prayers for the departed in Farleighe church by Robert Lyndweys of Wynchelsey, co. Sussex; (59) lands (*tenant named*) in Pacham, co. Sussex, given for lamps in the church there; (60) lands in Crawlye *alias* Crawley, co. Sussex, given for superstitious uses in the church there; (61) lands (*named with tenant's name*) in Micham, co. Surrey; (62) lands (*tenants named*) in Little Boroughinges, in Sturton Uppering (*named*) and in Upperstickes and Netherstickes, co. Nottingham; (63) woods called Cookriggwood in Addell or elswhere, co. York, once of the monastery of Kirkstall, co. York; (64) 'St. James chappell' and lands in Kingeston Lacie in the parish of Wymborne Mynster, co. Dorset, (*tenant named*); and (65) lands (*named*) in Appleton *alias* Appilton and Hillington *alias* Hillingdon, co. Norfolk, once of Flytcham *ad Fontes* priory. Which premises were concealed from the Queen or from Henry VIII, Edward VI or Queen   [*m.* 28] Mary down to 8 Oct., 17 Eliz., or the profits thereof not answered now or before that date. Yearly value according to the several particulars thereof £19 4*s.* 10*d.* To hold as of the manor of Eastgrenewiche in socage and by yearly rents of (1) 5*s.* 6*d.* (*detailed*), (2) 3*s.*, (3) 2*s.* 6*d.*, (4) 3*s.*, (5) 20*s.*, (6) 10*s.*, (7) 2*s.* 6*d.*, (8) 2*s.* 6*d.*, (9) 2*s.*, (10) 26*s.* 8*d.*, (11) 5*s.*, (12) 3*s.* 4*d.*, (13) 4*s.* 4*d.* (*detailed*), (14) 3*s.* 4*d.*, (15) 10*s.*, (16) 10*s.*, (17) 6*s.* 8*d.* (*detailed*), (18) 18*s.* 4*d.*, (19) 6*s.* 8*d.*, (20) 20*d.*, (21) 10*s.*, (22) 2*s.*, (23) 2*s.* 6*d.*, (24) 2*s.* 4*d.*, (25) 2*s.*, (26) 2*s.* 6*d.*, (27) 19*s.* (28) 12*d.*, (29) 26*s.* 8*d.*, (30) 10*s.*, (31) 28*d.* (*detailed*),   [*m.* 29] (32) 6*s.* 8*d.*, (33) 2*s.* 10*d.* (*detailed*), (34) 12*d.*, (35) 4*s.* 7*d.* (*detailed*), (36) 2*s.*, (37) 12*d.*, (38) 4*d.*, (39) 4*d.*, (40) 10*s.*, (41) 12*d.*, (42) 18*s.* 10*d.* (*detailed*), (43) 30*s.*, (44) 20*d.*, (45) 2*s.* 6*d.*, (46) 12*d.*, (47) 18*d.*,   [*m.* 30] (48) 2*s.*, (49) 2*s.*, (50) 12*d.*, (51) 20*s.*, (52) 16*d.* (*detailed*), (53) 8*d.*, (54) 5*s.*, (55) 2*s.*, (56) 2*s.*, (57) 12*d.*, (58) 2*s.*, (59) 12*d.*, (60) 12*d.*, (61) 12*d.*, (62) 5*s.*, (63) 5*s.*, (64) 6*s.* 8*d.* and (65) 13*s.* 4*d.* Issues of the premises and any parcel thereof from the time when they should have   [*m.* 31] come to the Crown. Power to sue in the Crown's name in the Exchequer for the levying of revenues or arrears of the premises. This patent or the enrolment thereof to be sufficient warrant to the officers of the Exchequer to issue process against occupiers of the premises and to deliver to the grantee moneys recovered. If any parcel of the premises shall hereafter be recovered from the grantee's possession, he shall in fulfilment of this grant have other concealed lands to the same value as those recovered, at like rents. The patent to be void in respect of any parcel of the premises not concealed at   [*m.* 32] the time of the taking of the first inquisition or the time of the first certifying or information thereof. For his service.   By p.s.

2689.)   16 Oct. 1578.   *Gorhambury.*   Lease for 21 years to Robert Jones, a yeoman of the chamber, of (1) the rectory of Loddon and the tithes of corn in the parish of Holy Trinity in Loddon, (2) lands (*named*) in Carleton Feild and (3) land called 'Gannockes Yarde' and fishings etc. (*described*, including a swan 'marke'), all in the county of Norfolk, once of the monastery of Langley, co. Norfolk, and (4) the site of the manor of Cartemeale, co. Lancaster, and lands (*named*) belonging thereto, exchanged with Henry VIII by Thomas Holcrofte and formerly of the monastery of Cartemeale; with reservations; (1), (2) and (3) from Michaelmas 1592, having been leased by patent, 23 Nov., 14 Eliz., to Nicholas Harrison for 21 years from Michaelmas then last at a yearly rent of £5 4*s.* 2*d.*; (4) from Lady

Day 1596, having been leased by patent, 16 April, 18 Eliz., to Christopher Preston for 21 years from Lady Day then last at a yearly rent of £8 13s. 4d.; yearly rents (1) 100s., (2) 3s. 2d., (3) 12d. and (4) £8 13s. 4d.; the lessee to provide entertainment for the Queen's   [m. 33] steward, surveyor and other officers coming to the manor of Cartemeale to hold courts or make a survey; the lessee to leave five 'lez cooples' of white swans of 'lez marke' aforesaid at the end of the term. For his service.   By p.s.

2690.)   30 June 1578.   Gorhambury.   Grant in fee simple to Thomas Kerye, a clerk of the privy seal, of—the reversion and rent of a sheep house on Launcesdowne called 'Launcesdowne Shepehouse', a close thereto adjoining   [m. 34] and parcel of 'le downe' called Launcesdowne, co. Somerset, in the fields of Langridge and elsewhere for pasture of 'le eweflocke', with 630 ewes and wethers (price 16d. each), leased (a) by William Birde, prior, and the convent of the monastery of Bathe by indenture, 28 Oct., 14 Hen. VIII, to Thomas Richeman of Corston, co. Somerset, Isabel his wife and John their son for life in survivorship at a yearly rent of £6 15s. and (b) by William, prior, and the convent of Bath cathedral by deed, 11 Oct., 21 Hen. VIII, to Richard Horsington, 'husbandman', and Agnes his wife inter alia at a yearly rent of £6 13s. 4d. for life in survivorship from the termination of the said previous lease; and the said sheep house and lands and the flock of 342 ewes and 18 wethers. To hold as of the manor of Eastgrenewiche, co. Kent, in socage. The grantee may sue in his or the Crown's name for the recovery of the rent and arrears thereof and whatever shall be recovered shall be paid to him. For £100 paid at the Exchequer.   By Q.

2691.)   15 Jan.   1578.   Hampton Court.   Grant to Edward, earl of Oxford, great chamberlain, his heirs and assigns of the following in the county of Norfolk—the manor of Rysinge ad Castrum, the castle of Rysinge alias Rysinge Castell, the site of the said castle and a close (named) in Rysinge aforesaid, late of Thomas, late duke of Norfolk, attainted of treason, and all the Crown's lands in Rysinge aforesaid, late of the said duke; a chase and free warren called   [m. 35] Rysinge Chase, late of the said duke; the advowsons of the rectories of Rysinge and Rydon; the manor of Geywood and lands etc (named) in Geywood, late of the said duke; the advowson of the rectory of Geywood; the manor of Easte Rudham and manors of Easte Rudham and Houghton, late of the said duke, and all the Crown's lands in Eastrudham, Westrudham, Gestwicke, Folsham, Woodnorton, Sydersterne, Oxwiche, Houghton, Harpley, Thorpe Markett and Burneham late of the said duke; the site and 'lez demeane landes' of Coxforde priory; the rectory of Easterudham, late of the said duke, the advowson of the vicarage of Estrudham, a water mill in Estrudham and all the Crown's lands in Estrudham, Westrudham, Lynne, Houghton, Hillington and Bromisthrope late of the said duke; the rectory of Westrudham, late of the said duke; the advowson of the vicarage of Westrudham; all tithes in Bradfild late of the said duke; lands (named) in Westrudham and all the Crown's lands in Hawtboys Magna, Coteshall and Harstead late of the said duke; and 7½ quarters of barley yearly in Estrudham and Westrudham. To hold the manor and castle of Rysinge   [m. 36] and the rest of the premises in Rysinge, the manor of Geywood, the manor of Estrudham and Houghton and the site of Coxford priory by service of the fortieth part of a knight's fee and by yearly rents of £60 11s. 3¼d.. and 1lb. of pepper for the manor and castle of Rysinge and the rest of the premises appertaining to the said manor of Rysinge ad Castrum, £58 13s. 3⅞d. for the manor of Geywood and the rest of the premises appertaining thereto, £34 5s. 10d. for the site and demesne lands of Coxford priory, the rectory of Estrudham and the water mill belonging to the said priory, £10 for the rectory of Westrudham and £52 16s. 9¼d. for the manor of Estrudham and Houghton and the rest of the premises belonging thereto;

and to hold the rest as of the manor of Estgrenewiche in socage. Issues from Michaelmas last. The grantee to pay yearly £9 2s. 6d. to the keeper of the castle and chase and the bailiff of the manor of Rysinge ad Castrum, £3 10d. to the bailiff of the manor of Geywood, £4 to the bailiff of the manor of Estrudham and Houghton, 15s. 3d. for the proxies and synodals

[m. 37]

of Estrudham and Westrudham churches and 13s. 4d. for a pension to the vicar of Estrudham. For his service.   By Q.

2692.) 15 Jan. 1578. Hampton Court. Lease for 50 years to Thomas Cornewallys, a gentleman pensioner, of (1) demesne lands (named with tenants' names) called 'the demaines of Prynces Risborough' in the lordship of Prynces Risborough, co. Buckingham, (2) the rectory of Chitterne All Saints, co. Wilts, late of the late college of Vaux, co. Wilts, (3) the tithes in Hamwood   [m. 38]
and elsewhere, co. Somerset, parcel of the rectory of Trull, once of the monastery of Taunton, co. Somerset, and (4) all lands in the disparked park of Kirribullock, parcel of the manor of Stoke Clymeslande, co. Cornwall, parcel of the duchy of Cornwall; with reservations; from the several terminations of leases thereof by patent, (1) 1 July, 1 Eliz., to Elizabeth Pygott, widow, late the wife of Francis Pigott, at a yearly rent of £3 12s. 2¼d. for 20 years from the termination of a lease thereof to the said Francis by indenture, 10 May, 2 & 3 Ph. & Mary, for 21 years from Michaelmas then last, (2) 2 March, 15 Eliz., to William Moulton for 21 years from Michaelmas then last at a yearly rent of £13 6s. 8d., (3) 3 July, 7 Eliz., to Edmund Tymewell for 21 years from Lady Day then last at a yearly rent of £7 and (4) 6 Jan., 14 Eliz., to Arthur Champernowne, knight, for 21 years from Michaelmas then last at a yearly rent of £6; yearly rents (1) £16 11s. 7½d.,   [m. 39]
(2) £13 6s. 8d., (3) £7 and (4) £6; the lessee to discharge the Crown of all payments out of (2) and (3). For his service.   By p.s.

2693.) 21 Sept. 1578. Redgrave. Lease for 31 years to Christopher Chute of the rectory of Hilmorton, co. Warwick, once of the late college of Astley, co. Warwick, and afterwards of lady Mary Grey, deceased, as one of the daughters and heirs of Henry, late marquess of Dorset, afterwards duke of Suffolk, attainted, and Frances his wife; with reservations;

[m. 40]

yearly rent £16 15s.; the Crown to discharge the lessee from the yearly payment of pensions of 28s. 4d. to the dean and chapter of Lichefeilde cathedral and 15s. for the appropriation of Hilmorton church and all other payments except the rent. In consideration that Chute, farmer or occupier of the said rectory,—who has by assignment of the treasurer and the Queen's command or consent chattels of the said lady Mary valued at £179 11s. 10d.—offers, in consideration of the same chattels (or the value thereof if he cannot have them according to the Queen's intention) and that the present lease may be granted him, to pay in such manner and at such dates as shall be ordered by the treasurer and the chancellor of the Exchequer sums to the amount of the £179 11s. 10d. aforesaid and such other sums as amount with the £179 11s. 10d. to £612 13s. 6d. for lady Mary's debts to divers persons named in a schedule to the particular on which this patent issued, signed by the treasurer.

By p.s.

2694.) 15 Nov. 1578. Richmond. Grant for life to Richard Blacklock of the office of a forester and keeper of the forest of Galtrees, co. York, held by John Nelson, deceased; with wages of 4d. a day, payable by himself or by the Queen's farmers etc. there; as formerly held by Francis Aselibye or Nelson.   By p.s.

2695.) 28 April 1578. Commitment for 21 years (on security found before the barons of the Exchequer) to David Boste, Thomas Boste, William Burbancke, Thomas Burbanke and John Burbanke of the farm or custody of a close called Warsmorton *alias* Warmorton in the forest of Inglewood, co. Cumberland; from Michaelmas last; yearly rent £4 5*s*. and 15*s*. beyond of increase; provided etc.   By warrant of the commissioners.

2696.)   24 *March* 1578.   Commission to John Southcote and William   [*m.* 41] Aylyff, two justices of the Queen's Bench, to examine and determine in the guildhall of London an appeal of error in the record, process and judgment of a suit before the mayor and aldermen of London in the chamber of the guildhall between James Turnor, executor of Henry Androwes, and Thomas Cliffe concerning a trespass on the case committed against Turnor by Cliffe: at the suit of Clyff.

2697.)   *Undated.*   The like to John Jeffreys, knight, chief baron of the Exchequer, and Thomas Gawdye, a justice of the Queen's Bench, to determine an appeal of error in (1) the record and process of a precept of *scire facias* before John Langley, knight, then mayor, and the aldermen in the chamber of the guildhall by John Pawlett of Frefok, co. Southampton, against George Puttenham for the restitution of 100 marks recovered by Puttenham against Pawlet by virtue of an original bill concerning a plea of debt of 1,000 marks affirmed before Ambrose Nicholas, late mayor, and the aldermen in the said chamber at the suit of Puttenham against Pawlett and (2) the judgment on the said original bill and the said precept: at the suit of Puttenham.

2698.)   10 *Oct.* 1578.   The like to John Southcote and William Ayliff, two justices of the Queen's Bench, to determine an appeal of error as above (no. 2696).

2699.)   26 *Nov.* 1577.   The like to Robert Mounson, a justice of the Common Pleas, and Thomas Gawdye, a justice of the Queen's Bench, to determine an appeal of error in the record, process and judgment of a suit before John Langley, knight, late mayor, and the aldermen of London in the chamber of the guildhall by William Walter and Elizabeth his wife, daughter of John Clarke, late citizen and draper of London, against William Morgan and Julian his wife, executor of Clarke, touching the detention of a   [*m.* 42] moiety of a third part of Clarke's chattels amounting to £1,034 10*s*.: at the suit of Morgan and his wife.

2700.)   4 *June* 1578.   The like to Thomas Gawdye, a justice of the Queen's Bench, and Thomas Meade, a justice of the Common Pleas, to determine an appeal of error as above (no. 2697).

2701.)   13 *March* 1578.   The like to Christopher Wraye, knight, chief justice of the Queen's Bench, and John Southcote, a justice of the Queen's Bench, to determine an appeal of error in the record, process and judgment (1) of a suit before the mayor and aldermen of London in the chamber of the guildhall by William Homden of Strowde, co. Kent, and James Whyte, 'buttenmaker', administrators of the goods of Roger Storye of Staple Inne, co. Middlesex, not administered by Thomas Corwyn, late executor of Storye, against Richard Foster, scrivener, and Thomas Hawkes, 'pewterer', touching the detention of £25 13*s*. 4*d*. and (2) on the attachment of £25 13*s*. 4*d*. belonging to Storye at his death in the keeping of Foster and Hawkes: at the suit of Foster and Hawkes.

2702.)   20 *Oct.* 1578.   *Chenies.*   The like to James Dyer, knight, chief justice of the Common Pleas, and Robert Mounson, a justice of the Common Pleas, to determine an appeal of error in the record and process of a suit between Nicholas Moseley, clothworker, and Richard Southworth, 'clothworker', and Anne his wife before Nicholas Backhouse, alderman, late a sheriff of London, in the city court, afterwards at the instance of Moseley for speed of justice taken before Thomas Ramsey, knight, mayor, and the aldermen of London in the chamber of the guildhall, and judgment of the same suit before them: at the suit of Southworth and his wife.   [*m.* 43]

2703.)   13 *Feb.* 1578. Order to all sheriffs etc. that the men and tenants of the manor of Chesterford, co. Essex, may be quit, according to custom as tenants in ancient demesne, of toll, contributions to expenses of knights of Parliament and juries etc. except in the manor court, except for lands not so held. They are found to be tenants in ancient demesne by certificate of the treasurer and chamberlains of the Exchequer sent into Chancery.

2704.)   12 *Dec.* 1577.   The like for the men and tenants of the manor of Stanley *alias* Stonley, co. Warwick.

2705.)   2 *July* 1578.   *Gorhambury.*   Pardon for Richard Wilkinson late of London, 'yoman', for all treasons and misprisions of treason by the removal of the wax of two old seals from two old writs sealed with the great seal and the enclosing in the wax of the two old seals two new writs of 'sub penis' made by him in place of the two old writs, and for all counterfeitings of the great seal.   By Q.

(The dorse of this roll is blank.)

PART III

C. 66/1166

2706.) 1 *March* 1578. Licence for Robert Everard, Margaret his wife,   [*m.* 1] Richard Everard and Jane his wife to alienate all lands in Shenton, co. Leicester, now or late in the tenure of Robert, late of Wolvescrofte priory, co. Leicester, and all lands there late of the said priory to Richard Wheler and Sampson Wolverston and the heirs and assigns of Wheler. For 21s. 4d. paid to the Queen's farmer.

2707.) 24 *April* 1578. The like for Edward Skipwith to alienate the manor of Haburghe, co. Lincoln, to John Thymbleby. For £6 13s. 4d.

2708.) 24 *April* 1578. Pardon of alienation: by indenture, 1 Feb., 18 Eliz., Luke Adyn acquired from Robert Reade, knight, lands (*named with tenants' names*) in the parish of Catestoke, co. Dorset. For £4 8s. paid to the Queen's farmer.

2709.) 22 *April* 1578. The like: Robert Tayler in Easter term, 14 Eliz., by fine in the Common Pleas acquired from Thomas Jones *inter alia* a house and lands in or by Oswester *alias* Oswalter called Spitty St. John *alias* the monastery of Spitty Abbi, co. Salop, to the use of Thomas Swalman, as appears by an indenture, 15 March, 14 Eliz., between Jones of the one part and   [*m.* 2] Swalman and Tayler of the other leading the uses of the said fine. For 53s. 4d.

2710.) 22 *April* 1578. The like: Thomas Beckingham by indenture, 24 Nov., 17 Eliz., acquired from John Barker lands (*tenants named*) called Hyams and Joyces, co. Essex. For £4.

2711.) 24 *April* 1578. The like: Martin Bowes, citizen and goldsmith of London, by indenture, 16 Nov., 13 Eliz., acquired from Thomas Bowes, his brother, citizen and goldsmith of London, *inter alia* a capital messuage called 'le Balle', then in the tenure of William Chappell, citizen and merchant taylor of London, three messuages adjoining the same, then or late in the several tenures of John Kyndon, skinner, Anthony Tryvett, goldsmith, and William Stiper, merchant taylor, and all the small tenements in Porche Alley then or late in the several tenures of John Williams, Agnes Gresham, widow, Mary Nicolles, widow, William Wilkynson, John Brisco, Elizabeth Edwardes, widow, and Richard Smyth, all in 'le Old Change' in the parish of St. Augustine, London. For £5.

2712.) 16 *April* 1578. The like: Urian Brereton, knight, by indenture, 17 Sept., 17 Eliz., for performance of covenants in an indenture tripartite, 20 Aug., 17 Eliz., between him of the one part, John Savage, knight, Hugh Cholmondley, knight, and Thomas Hanmer, knight, of the second part and Richard Brereton, George Brereton and Henry Manwaringe of the third part, enfeoffed Savage and the others above-named of all his lands in the counties of Chester and the city of Chester late of 'le nunnerye' of Chester to the use of the feoffor for life, with remainders in tail male successively to William Brereton, his second son, Edward Brereton, his third son, Urian Brereton, his fourth son, Urian Leighe, elder son of Sibyl his daughter, Thomas Leighe, Sibyl's second son, Edward Leighe, Sibyl's third son, and Ralph Leighe, Sibyl's fourth son, with remainder over to the feoffor's right heirs. For £13 19s. 3½d.

                                                                       [*m.* 3]

2713.)   1 *Oct.* 1578.   Licence for James Dyer, knight, chief justice of the Common Pleas, to alienate lands (*named*) in Great Staughton, Kymbalton, Hayleweston, Southoo and 'le Charterhouse Yarde', cos. Huntingdon and Middlesex, to William Fitzwilliam, knight, Edward Dyer, William Fytzwilliam (esquire) and John Farwell to the use of himself for life, and thereafter to Lawrence Dyer for life, with successive remainders to Richard Dyer, son and heir apparent of Lawrence, in tail male, to the heirs female of Richard by Mary Fytzwilliam, first born daughter of the same William Fitzwilliam, knight, and to the right heirs of James. For £5 8s. 11d. paid to the Queen's farmer.

2714.)   21 *July* 1578.   The like for Robert Losse to alienate 'Crashemylle Meadowe' in the parish of St Botolph without Algate, London, (between a garden of Robert Wade on the South and a garden late in the tenure of William Roy on the North, and abutting on Nightingale Lane towards the East, containing in length from the North side 28 rods, from the East 35 rods, from the South 24 rods and from the West 15½ rods), late of the monastery of St. Mary of Graces by the Tower of London and purchased by Hugh Losse, deceased, father of Robert, and Thomas Bocher unto them and the heirs of Hugh *inter alia* from Henry VIII as appears by patent, 10 May, 35 Hen. VIII, to Richard Robynson. For 3s.

2715.)   1 *May* 1578.   Pardon of alienation: John Thomas, a clerk of Henry Waldron, one of the six clerks of Chancery, by indenture, 22 April, 15 Eliz., acquired from Thomas Rysdon and Henry Skynner lands   [*m.* 4]
(*named with tenants' names*) in Colompton, co. Devon. For 12s. paid to the Queen's farmer.

2716.)   10 *May* 1578.   The like: Henry Coringdon in Michaelmas term, 15 Eliz., by fine in the Common Pleas acquired from Thomas Raymond and Julian his wife lands in Wethycombe Rawleighe, co. Devon. For 40s.

2717.)   12 *May.* 1578.   The like: John Gilberte, knight, Bernard Drake and John Upton by indenture, 20 Nov., 17 Eliz., acquired from Humphrey Gilberte, knight, the manors of Postelinge *alias* Postlinge and Badelsmere *alias* Batelsmere, lands in Postelinge, Badelsmere, Shelwiche, Selling, Challocke, Throughley, Stallesfeilde, Charinge, Burfeild, Buckland, Stanfourth, Lyminge, Wytperlinge, Leveland and Chilham, the advowson of Badelsmere church and lands called Rigeshall and Rigeshall Barne, co. Kent, to the use of the said Humphrey for life and any persons to whom he should by deed lease any of the premises for 21 years or three lives, and after his death to the use of Anne then his wife for life, with successive remainders to the heirs of Humphrey's body, to Anne in tail, to John Gilberte, knight, in tail, to Adrian Gilberte, brother of John and Humphrey, in tail male and to the right heirs of the said John Gilberte, knight. For £3 6s. 8d.

2718.)   1 *May* 1578.   The like: John Thomas, a clerk of Henry Waldron, one of the six clerks of Chancery by indenture, 1 Dec., 19 Eliz., acquired from Thomas Rysdon and Henry Skynner, 'yeoman', lands (*named with tenants' names*) in Colompton, co. Devon. For 3s.

2719.)   1 *March* 1578.   The like: Norton Grene and John Clarke of   [*m.* 5]
London, goldsmith, by indenture, 6 May, 15 Eliz., acquired from Robert Grene lands in Upchurche and Halstowe, co. Kent, late of Boxley abbey, co. Kent, and granted by patent, 29 July, 31 Hen. VIII, to Thomas Grene, father of Robert and Norton, and Alice then wife of Thomas and the heirs of Thomas. For £5.

2720.)   1 *Oct.* 1578.   Licence for Arthur, lord Grey of Wilton, and Jane Sibyl his wife to alienate lands (*named*) in the lordship of Wilton and parish of Bridstowe, co. Hereford, to William Rudehale. For 7*s*. 8*d*. paid to the Queen's farmer.

2721.)　20 *Sept*. 1578.　The like for George Evelyn to alienate the manor of Staners and Fordes in the parish of Chobham, co. Surrey, to John Evelyn to the use of George for life and thereafter of John in tail male, with remainder to the right heirs of George. For 47*s*. 8*d*.

2722.)　1 *June* 1578.　Pardon of alienation: Roger Predeaux by indenture, 2 Oct., 13 Eliz., acquired from Thomas Rysedon the manor of Milton Damerell, co. Devon, late of John Seintleger, knight. For £5 paid to the Queen's farmer.

2723.)　15 *Nov*. 1578.　The like: Richard Powell of Shrowesbury,　　　　　　[*m*. 6] co. Salop, 'mercer', by indenture, 5 May, 14 Eliz., acquired from Edward, lord Stafford, the forest of Le Haye adjoining Caurys castle, lands called Mulsoppe and Rose Goughe and all appurtenances of the premises in the parish of Worthyn *alias* Wurthyn, Westprye and Alverberrye, cos. Salop and Montgomery. For 53*s*. 4*d*.

2724.)　9 *June* 1578.　Licence for Thomas Gawdye, knight, a justice of the Common Pleas, and Thomas Baxter and Elizabeth his wife to alienate a moiety of the manors of Netherhall and Stowes and of lands in Styffeley, Langham Magna, Langham Parva, Bynham, Warham, Hindringham, Marston, Wighton and Cockethorpe, co. Norfolk, to Nicholas Bacon, knight, keeper of the great seal, and Nathaniel Bacon and the heirs and assigns of Nicholas.

2725.)　1 *Oct*. 1578.　Licence for Roger Cave and Margaret his wife to alienate the manor of Stanford, cos. Northampton and Leicester, with the rectory there, the advowson of the vicarage of Stanford and all their other lands in Stanford and Downe, co. Northampton, and in Stormesworth and Boresworth, co. Leicester, to Anthony Cave and William Cave and the heirs and assigns of Anthony. For £20 paid to the Queen's farmer.

2726.)　1 *Oct*. 1578.　The like for William Bushe to alienate lands in the parish of Dundrey, co. Somerset, to John Bushe and Thomas Bushe, 'yomen'. For 17*s*. 10*d*.

2727.)　24 *April* 1578.　Pardon of alienation: William Clopton by indenture, 12 Jan., 15 Eliz., acquired from Martin Bowes, citizen　　　　　　　　[*m*. 7] and goldsmith of London, *inter alia* a capital messuage called 'le Balle' and other messuages as above (no. 2711) in 'le Oulde Chaunge' in the parish of St. Augustine, London, acquired by him from Thomas Bowes, his brother, by indenture, 16 Nov., 13 Eliz. For £5 paid to the Queen's farmer.

2728.)　1 *May* 1578.　The like: John Thomas, a clerk of Henry Waldron, one of the six clerks of Chancery, by indenture, 28 June, 14 Eliz., acquired from Thomas Rysdon and Henry Skynner, 'yeoman', lands (*named with tenants' names*), parcel of a farm called the rectory of Upton Wever, in Colompton, co. Devon. For 15*s*.

2729.)　4 *June* 1578.　The like: Edward Clere by indenture, 17 May, 15 Eliz., acquired from Henry Carye, knight, lord Hunsdon, the manors of Hawes and Morehall with lands in Salle, Rayfham, Whitwell, Causton, Cardeston, Wooddaling and Geyst or elsewhere, co. Norfolk, all which lord Hunsdon late acquired from Clere. For £8.

2730.)　29 *May* 1578.　The like: John Burgoyne in Hilary term, 18 Eliz., by fine in the

Common Pleas acquired from John Spencer and Mary his wife   [*m.* 8]
lands in Dunton, Mylnhoo, Bigleswade and Stratton, co. Bedford. For 30*s.*

2731.) 3 *May* 1578. The like: Brian Parker by indenture, 9 Dec., 15 Eliz., acquired from John Robynson a moiety of the manor of Malham *alias* West Malham and of lands (*named with tenants' names*) in Malham and on West Malham More, co. York. For 31*s.*

2732.) 10 *May* 1578. The like: William Savyle by indenture, 31 Aug., 15 Eliz., acquired from John Paslewe lands (*named with tenants' names*) in Harden *alias* Harding in the parish of Byngley, co. York. For 49*s.* 4*d.*

2733.) 7 *May* 1578. The like: William Savyle in Easter term, 15 Eliz., by fine in the Common Pleas acquired from George Barwell, Elizabeth his   [*m.* 9]
wife, William Wright and Joan his wife *inter alia* the manor of Sapperton, lands in Sapperton and the advowson of Sapperton church, co. Lincoln. For £3 6*s.* 8*d.*

2734.) 12 *May* 1578. The like: William Howppill and Richard Bodleighe by fine in the Common Pleas levied in Easter term and granted and recorded in Trinity term, 16 Eliz., acquired unto them and the heirs of Howppill from Thomas Raymond and Julian his wife lands in Hill *alias* Bill in the parish of Whithycombe Rayleighe, co. Devon. For £4.

2735.) 1 *May* 1578. Licence for John Berrowe to alienate lands (*tenants named*) in Walton Cardyff, Fyddyngton, Treddington and Northey, co. Gloucester, to Nicholas Smythsen. For 16*s.* 8*d.* paid to the Queen's farmer.

2736.) 1 *May* 1578. The like for the same to alienate lands (*tenant named*) in the same places to Thomas Edwardes. For 6*s.*

2737.) 1 *May* 1578. The like for the same to alienate lands (*named with tenant's name*) in the same places to John Hyatt and Margaret his   [*m.* 10]
wife and the heirs and assigns of Hyatt. For 53*s.* 4*d.*

2738.) 1 *May* 1578. The like for John Keck and John Toms to alienate lands (*named with tenants' names*) in Marston Sicca *alias* Dry Marston, co. Gloucester, parcel of the manor of Marston Sicca, to Thomas Couper the elder and Thomas Couper the younger and the heirs and assigns of Thomas the younger. For 46*s.* 8*d.*

2739.) 1 *May* 1578. The like for the same to alienate lands (*tenant named*) in Marston Sicca, parcel of the manor there, to John Knight. For 2*s.*

2740.) 1 *May* 1578. The like for the same to alienate lands (*named with tenant's name*) in Marston Sicca, parcel of the manor there, to Richard Holtam. For 13*s.* 4*d.*

2741.) 1 *May* 1578. The like for the same to alienate the site of the   [*m.* 11]
manor of Marston Sicca and lands (*named with tenant's name*) there, parcel of the manor, to Thomas Holtam. For 13*s.* 4*d.*

2742.) 1 *March* 1578. The like for Paul Wood to alienate lands (*named*) in Sywell and Holcot, co. Northampton, to Anthony Jenkynson. For 50*s.* 8*d.*

2743.) 12 *June* 1578. Pardon of alienation: Richard Nicholls, being seised in his demesne as of fee of the manor of Westderham in Tylney, all lands belonging thereto in Tylney, Tyrryngton and Islyngton, co. Norfolk, and lands with 'le ferrye' in Clenchewarton and Westlyn, co. Norfolk, by his will, 12 Jan., 16 Eliz., bequeathed two parts of his manor of Westderham in Tylney and Islyngton and of his lands with the ferry rights belonging thereto in Clenchwarton and Westlynne to Anne his wife to pay his debts and perform his will until the child with which she then was should come to the age of 21 and thereafter

[m. 12]

to such child and its heirs, with remainder in default of such issue to his cousin, George Nicholls, after Anne's decease in tail male; after Richard's death Anne entered the said two parts. For £5 15s. 7d.

2744.)   4 *June* 1578.   The like: John Morgan in Easter term, 15 Eliz., by fine in the Common Pleas acquired from Nicholas Turbervyle lands in Winterborne Masterton *alias* Maston *alias* Abbottes Courte and Winterborne Kingston, co. Dorset. For £10.

2745.)   10 *June* 1578.   The like: William Lyster and Henry Farrer by indenture, 6 April, 13 Eliz., acquired from Henry Darcye, knight, the manors of Gisborne and Grange Mere, a water mill in Gysborne, a fair and market there and lands (*named*) in Bolton and Paythorne, with lands (*tenants named*) belonging to the premises, co. York. For £12.

2746.)   9 *June* 1578.   The like: Richard James in Hilary term, 14 Eliz., by fine in the Common Pleas acquired from Edward Wyndesor, knight, lord Wyndesor, and Catherine his wife land in Okbrocke, co. Derby. For £5 2s.

2747.)   4 *May* 1578.   The like: Clement Fyssher by indenture, 31 May, 13 Eliz., acquired from John Mendham a great capital messuage in Great Pakington, co. Warwick, formerly occupied by John Fyssher, deceased, (except a great close called Pakington Close), all which Mendham late had by bargain and sale of the said John Fyssher, as appears by an indenture,

[m. 13]

15 Feb., 11 Eliz. For 20s.

2748.)   9 *June* 1578.   The like: Thomas Barkelett and Richard Birde in Trinity term, 18 Eliz., recovered against Giles Poole, knight, lands in Cricklade, Great Chelworth and Little Chelworth, co. Wilts, which recovery was to the use of the said Giles, as appears by an indenture, 28 Sept., 17 Eliz., between Edward Poole and Giles leading the use of the recovery. For £5.

2749.)   13 *June* 1578.   The like: Giles Tracye and Thomas Best by indenture, 10 May, 16 Eliz., acquired from Giles, lord Chandos, baron of Sudley, the manors of Brymesfeld and Craneham and the park of Brymesfeld, co. Gloucester. For £5.

2750.)   9 *June* 1578.   The like: John Laverens by fine in the Common Pleas levied on the morrow of Ascension and granted and recorded on the morrow of Trinity, 16 Eliz., acquired from Henry, earl of Huntingdon, and Catherine his wife lands in Holfoun *alias* Holfome, Norcombe *alias* Norcome, Dipford *alias* Dupford and Dipford Downes, co. Devon. For £4 19s. 8d.

2751.)   10 *June* 1578.   The like: Thomas Browne and Brutus Browne, his son and heir apparent, by indenture, 31 Aug., 17 Eliz., acquired from Arthur Bassett, knight, a third part of the rents and services of all lands in Langtree, co. Devon, of the inheritance and in the several tenures of the said Thomas, Nicholas Stabledonne, Richard Martyn and John

Prudham, which they severally hold freely in fee simple of the manor of Frythelstocke, co. Devon, and the portion and purparty of Bassett of the seignorial rents and services which he has of the said tenants by reason of any lands which they hold of him in fee simple as of their [*sic*] capital house in Langtre, also a third [*m.* 14]
part of all lands in Langtre, parcel of the said manor, now or late in the tenure of Henry Yoeland, Humphrey Huckmore, Richard Collacott, John Baronfeild, Abraham Baronfeild and John Bacheler, with a third part of all lands in Frythelstocke leased or occupied by the said persons or parcels of their said several lands in Langtree, which were heretofore known as part of the inheritance of Bassett. For 50*s.*

2752.) 9 *June* 1578. The like: Robert Denys, knight, John Seyntabyn, Richard Prediaux, Robert Carye and Henry Geare by feoffment indented, 26 Nov., 14 Eliz., had of William Harrys *inter alia* the manor of Liston, co. Devon, to hold to the use of Harrys until he should marry Honor Milliton, widow, then to her use for life, and after her death to the use of Harrys. For £13 6*s.* 8*d.*

2753.) 12 *June* 1578. The like: Jerome Dybbyn by indenture, 7 March, 14 Eliz., acquired from Charles Zouche and Robert Kemys a moiety of lands (*named with tenants' names*) in the parish of Wincaulton, co. Somerset. For 12*s.* 1¼*d.*

2754.) 13 *June* 1578. The like: Edmund Harding and Elizabeth his wife in Michaelmas term, 17 Eliz., acquired unto them and the heirs of Edmund from Edward Sudleyr and Anne his wife lands in Aspeley Guyse, co. Bedford. For 53*s.* 4*d.* [*m.* 15]

2755.) 1 *March* 1578. Licence for Anthony Skutte to alienate the manor of Offington *alias* Uffington, lands in Uffington, Wolston, Bawkyng *alias* Battelking, Kingeston, Falter and Hardwell, the rectory of Uffington and the advowson of the vicarage of Uffington, co. Berks, to Thomas Haynes and Lawrence Byssee and the heirs and assigns of Haynes. For £20 paid to the Queen's farmer.

2756.) 1 *March* 1578. The like for Leonard Pygott and Catherine his wife to alienate the manors of Kempeley and Oxnall and Okeley Gransham and lands in Kempeley, Oxnall and Okeley Gransham, co. Gloucester, to Samuel Danvers and Anne Pygot in tail, with remainder to the right heirs of Samuel. For £11 6*s.* 8*d.*

2757.) 6 *May* 1578. Pardon of alienation: William Kirke in Easter term, 12 Eliz., by fine in the Common Pleas acquired from Kelham Kirke *inter alia* lands in Stokehamond and Salburye, co. Buckingham. For £4 paid to the Queen's farmer.

2758.) 1 *March* 1578. Licence for Lionel Skypwith to alienate the manor of Gayton and lands in Gayton, Weltoun, Beskenthorpe and Grangehomes, co. Lincoln, to Richard Hansharte the younger. For £7 16*s.* 8*d.* paid to the Queen's [*m.* 16] farmer.

2759.) 10 *May* 1578. Pardon of alienation: Thomas Brende in Trinity term, 17 Eliz., acquired from Francis Polsted lands in Cowdham *alias* Cudham, co. Kent. For £6 paid to the Queen's farmer.

2760.) 10 *May* 1578. The like: Roger Monoxe and Richard Vincente of London, 'yeomen', by indenture, 31 March, 16 Eliz., acquired from William Wynter, knight, lands (*named*) in Lydney, co. Gloucester. For 18*s.*

2761.)   17 *Jan.* 1578.   Licence for Edward Clifton and Alice his wife to alienate a messuage, a garden and 3ac. of pasture in Fyckettesfield *alias* Fyckattes Feild in the parish of St. Dunstan in le West, co. Middlesex, to Henry Garnett the elder and Edward Rust and the heirs and asigns of Garnett. For 12*d.* paid to the Queen's farmer.

2762.)   1 *May* 1578.   The like for William Waller to alienate a third part of the manors of Skelton, Marske *alias* Maske, Brotton and Easton and of lands in Skelton, Marske, Brotton, Easton, Redkarr, Uxledum, Stanghowe, Skynnyngreve and Gerricke, co. York, to Robert Trotter and Isabel his wife and the heirs and assigns of Robert. For £13 6*s.* 8*d.*

2763.)   16 *May* 1578.   The like for John Tufton to alienate the manors of Sturrey and Luyston *alias* Luerston, co. Kent, and lands (*tenants named*) in Leneham *alias* Lenham, co. Kent, late of Warham Seyntleger, knight,   [*m.* 17]
to Thomas Wotton. For 30*s.*

2764.)   1 *March* 1578.   The like for John Tufton and Christian his wife to alienate a third part of the manor of Hokenhanger *alias* Kympton and lands in Kympton, Barkelowe and Redborne, co. Hertford, to Edward Peede the younger and Thomas Peede, his son, and the heirs and assigns of Edward. For 27*s.* 6½*d.*

2765.)   1 *March* 1578.   The like for William Sheldon of Wadborowe and Elizabeth his wife to alienate lands in Arkecall, Willisland and Suggedon, co. Salop, to William Savage, William Sheldon of Abberton and Reginald Williams and the heirs and assigns of Savage. For 13*s.* 4*d.*

2766.)   1 *March* 1578.   The like for Francis Buller to alienate a moiety of the manors of Treglasca, St. Tethe, Tregarrecke, Killiowe and Pensight *alias* Pensith and of lands in Treglasca, St. Tethe, Tregarrecke, Killiowe, Pensith, Polletha, Tredwene, Treworsse, Trevantres, Tremure, Soveragonan, Treythycke, Treslyn, Trelaye, Trewynnock, Foymer, Trevyvyan, Trewenowe, Treasawicke, Tregollan, Lamperke, Henera *alias* Hender, Bokelley, Lyckham, Saynt Marye Wyke Towne, Pound Parke, Osmondowne, Launcaston, Lowe, Saynt Austill, Saynt Kewe, Tregnyhan *alias* Tregnethan, Bodmyn, Borowgh, Cadwyn, Bedell, Wethell, Killowe, Killowe Milles, Penhall *alias* Penhewe, Penwithe and Wynsore and common of pasture in Foymore, co. Cornwall, to William Cornewe and Edward Symon and the heirs and assigns of Cornewe. For 53*s.* 4*d.*

2767.)   28 *April* 1578.   Pardon of alienation: Simon Harecourte by   [*m.* 18]
indenture, 31 May, 13 Eliz., acquired from Edward, lord Stafford, the manor of Tillington, co. Stafford, and all his other lands late of Francis Warde in the said county. For £13 6*s.* 8*d.* paid to the Queen's farmer.

2768.)   14 *May* 1578.   The like: Richard Veale by indenture, 12 Nov., 13 Eliz., acquired from John Alsopp *inter alia* his interest in portions of all messuages then in the several tenures of Elizabeth Fryer, widow, Thomas Page, John Tighte and Thomas Juxe in Walbrooke, of all messuages then in the several tenures of Edmund Muschampe, John Brayne, William Brokebancke, Edward Gwynne and James Mounsie in Bucklersbury and of all messuages then in the several tenures of Ralph Phesey and William Fulwood within 'le Barge' in Bucklersbury, all in the parish of St. Stephen in Walbrooke, London. For £3 6*s.* 8*d.*

2769.)   1 *May* 1578.   Licence for Nathaniel Tracye of London, 'haberdasher', to alienate his moiety of Clifford priory, of Benefeildes grange, of all other lands in the county of

Hereford which he had by the will of Richard Tracye, his father, and of all other his lands in Clifford and Bradwarden, co. Hereford, to Samuel Tracye. For 100*s.* paid to the Queen's farmer.

2770.)   1 *May* 1578. The like for Peter Roos to alienate the manor of Laxton and lands in Laxton, Laxton More House, Ossington and Ollerton, co. Nottingham, to James Harvie, alderman of London, Michael Flemynge and Francis Cradock and the heirs and assigns of Harvie. For £13 6*s.* 8*d.*

2771.)   1 *May* 1578.   The like for John Alderford to alienate lands (*named*)   [*m.* 19] in Knight Weke, co. Worcester, to John Washeborne. For 4*s.* 5½*d.*

2772.)   1 *May* 1578.   The like for George Leighe and Mary his wife to alienate the tithes in Duddleston and Elsmere, co. Salop, to Edward Jones. For 13*s.* 4*d.*

2773.)   1 *May* 1578.   The like for John Keck and John Tomes to alienate lands in Marston Sicca, co. Gloucester, to John Davyes. For 3*s.* 4*d.*

2774.)   1 *May* 1578.   The like for the same to alienate lands in Marston Sicca to Agnes Busshell, widow. For 26*s.* 8*d.*

2775.)   1 *May* 1578.   The like for the same to alienate lands in Marston Sicca to Henry Cowper. For 20*s.*

2776.)   1 *March* 1578.   The like for Richard Garnet and Frances his   [*m.* 20] wife to alienate lands in Overstratforth and Netherstratforth, co. York, to Bartholomew Garnet. For 20*s.*

2777.)   1 *March* 1578.   The like for Arthur, lord Grey of Wilton, and Jane Sibyl his wife to alienate lands in Wilton and Bridstowe, co. Hereford, to Nicholas Wright. For 13*s.* 4*d.*

2778.)   1 *May* 1578.   The like for Edward, earl of Rutland, to alienate lands in Claston *alias* Clauson and Hose, co. Leicester, to George Manchester and Thomas Hooe. For 10*s.*

2779.)   1 *May* 1578.   The like for Henry Nevell, knight, to alienate the manors of Wargrave, Warfeild *alias* Warveld and Colham *alias* Culham, co. Berks, and all other lands in Wargrave and Warfeild which were within the last 50 years parcel of the possessions of the bishopric of Winchester, (the manor of Laurence Waltham and the capital mansion house and farm of Pellingbeare, co. Berks, reserved) to Thomas Andrewes and Bartholomew Kempe to hold to the use of Nevell until his marriage with Elizabeth Doylie, widow, and thereafter to hold the premises in Wargrave and Warfeld to the use of Nevell and Elizabeth and the heirs of the body of Nevell, with remainder to his right heirs, and the premises in Culham to the use of Nevell and Elizabeth and the heirs male of Elizabeth by him, with

[*m.* 21]

remainder to his right heirs. For £13 6*s.* 8*d.*

2780.)   1 *May* 1578.   The like for William Arondell, Humphrey Clarke and Margery his wife to alienate the manor of Chawton, lands in Chowton and Kyngesclere and the advowson of Chawton church, co. Southampton, to Nicholas Knight. For £10 14*d.*

2781.)   6 *June* 1578.   Pardon of alienation: John Freke by indenture, 30 Nov., 17 Eliz., acquired from John Pawlett, knight, earl of Wiltshire and marquess of Winchester, lands (*tenants named*) in Woodcotes, Gussage St. Andrewes, Minchinton and Hanleighe *alias* Hanley, co. Dorset. For £3 16s. 9½d. paid to the Queen's farmer.

2782.)   1 *April* 1578.   Licence for Ralph Sadler, knight, chancellor of the duchy of Lancaster, Walter Mildmaye, knight, chancellor of the Exchequer, William Cordell, knight, master of the rolls, James Dyer, knight, chief justice of the Common Pleas, and Roger Manwood, a justice of the Common Pleas, to alienate the manors of Sturrey and Luyston *alias* Luerston, lands (*tenants named*) in Leneham *alias* Lenham and lands (*named with tenant's name*) in Hedcrone *alias* Hedcorne, Ulcombe and Est Sutton, co. Kent, all late of Warham Seyntlegers, knight, to   [*m. 22*]
Stephen Thymylby and Thomas Denne. For £5 6s. 8d. paid to the Queen's farmer.

2783.)   2 *Jan.* 1578.   The like for John Harte, grocer, and Michael Barker, merchant taylor of London, to alienate the manor of Chetham, co. Kent, and all other their lands in the said county to Reginald Barker, citizen and merchant taylor of London, and Anne his wife and the heirs and assigns of Reginald. For £12 6s. 8d.

2784.)   16 *April* 1578.   Pardon of alienation: Richard Cholmeley, knight, in Easter term, 19 Eliz., by fine in the Common Pleas acquired from Ralph Salven lands in Bamton and Neswick on the Wold and the advowson of Bampton church, co. York. For 35s. 8d. paid to the Queen's farmer.

2785.)   2 *May* 1578.   The like: William Steane and Edward Riplyngham in Michaelmas term, 14 Eliz., by fine in the Common Pleas acquired unto them and the heirs of Steane from Benet Shuckborowe and Alice his wife, daughter and sole heir of Richard Fawkener, deceased, George Boddington and Elizabeth his wife lands in Cubbington, co. Warwick. For £6 12s.

2786.)   16 *April* 1578.   The like: Philip Gunter and Francis Gunter, his son and heir apparent, by fine in the Common Pleas in Trinity and Michaelmas terms, 14 Eliz., acquired unto them and the heirs of Philip from William Stanley, lord Mountegle, and Gregory Moore the reversion of a third part of lands in Riskington, Stopwike, Tymberland *alias* Tomberland and Hanworth, co. Lincoln, which Richard Barne and Catherine, duchess of Suffolk, hold for the duchess's life. For £3 10s.   [*m. 23*]

2787.)   1 *May* 1578.   The like: William Churchill and John Draper by indenture, 15 Oct., 15 Eliz., acquired from Thomas Sydenham lands (*named*) in Wynford Egle, co. Dorset. For 13s. 4d.

2788.)   1 *March* 1578.   Licence for Elizabeth Stonyng, widow, and Edward Stonyng, her son, to alienate lands in the city of Lichefelde to Francis Farrowe. For 13s. 4d. paid to the Queen's farmer.

2789.)   20 *Dec.* 1577.   The like for Edward More and Mary his wife to alienate a third part of the manors of Holworthe, Knyghton, East Ryngsted, Little Byndon, East Forcell, Eastlullworth and West Burton and of lands in Haworthe, Knyghton, East Ryngsted, Little Byndon, East Forcell, East Lullworth, West Burton, Mylton and Chalden, co. Dorset, to Thomas Covert, and for him by the same fine to convey it back to Edward and Mary and the heirs and assigns of Mary. For £4.

2790.)   19 *Nov.* 1577.   The like for John Shelley, Edward Gage and Richard Guldeforde to alienate lands (*described with tenants' names*), late of Thomas Guldeforde of Hempstede, co. Kent, knight, deceased, in the marsh of Guldeford in the parish of Eastguldeforde, co. Kent, to Robert Hare   [*m.* 24]
and Ralph Hare. For £8 6*s.* 8*d.*

2791.)   20 *Dec.* 1577.   The like for James Duffeld to alienate lands in Medmenham, co. Buckingham, to William Rice. For 29*s.* 5½*d.*

2792.)   1 *March* 1578.   The like for Thomas Copley and Margaret his wife to alienate the manor of Lynton and lands in Lynton, Howdan, Estrington, Greneake, Barneby and Blacketofte, co. York, to John Gate, Isabel his wife and Henry Gate and the heirs and assigns of John. For £3 6*s.* 8*d.*

2793.)   1 *March* 1578.   The like for Valentine Browne, knight, and Thomasina his wife to alienate lands in Horton and Pontland *alias* Pont Iland, co. Northumberland, to George Tonge. For £6 13*s.* 4*d.*

2794.)   1 *March* 1578.   The like for Roger Mennell the elder to alienate the manor of Normanby, co. York, and all other lands in Normanby to Thomas Tankard, William Beckwith, Solomon Swaile, Matthew Conyers and   [*m.* 25]
James Tanckard to the use of himself and Edmund Mennell, his son, and the heirs of Edmund. For £5 6*s.* 8*d.*

2795.)   1 *March* 1578.   The like for John Adice to alienate lands in Lusshecotte and Longvyll *alias* Longfelde, co. Salop, to John More, clerk. For 40*s.*

2796.)   1 *March* 1578.   The like for Charles Hall and Anne his wife to alienate the manor of Knowke *alias* Knooke and lands in Knowke, Upton Lovell and Hacheburye *alias* Heytredsbury, co. Wilts, to John Lacye and Rowland Lacye. For 46*s.* 8*d.*

2797.)   1 *March* 1578.   The like for Edward, lord Souche, Saintmaure and Cantelope, and Eleanor his wife to alienate a fourth part of lands in Wincaulton and Marshe, co. Somerset, to Thomas Rolffe the elder and Thomas Rolffe the younger and the heirs and assigns of Thomas the elder. For 33*s.* 4*d.*

2798.)   1 *March* 1578.   The like for Ralph Warylowe to alienate lands in Stallington in the parish of Stone, co. Stafford, to James Porter. For 6*s.* 8*d.*

2799.)   1 *May* 1578.   The like for William Waller to alienate the   [*m.* 26]
manor and farm of Darnebrooke in Malhomedale in Craven and lands (*named with tenants' names*) in Darnebroke, in Fountancefelles, in Craven and in the parish of Kirkeby in Malhomedale, co. York, and all other his lands in the said parish or elsewhere within the limits of Craven (certain lands reserved) to James Tenante, John Bentham, John Tenante and John Wallocke. For £5 6*s.* 8*d.*

2800.)   10 *Feb.* 1578.   Pardon of alienation: Richard Goddarde by indenture, 28 May, 13 Eliz., acquired from Clement Tanfelde the reversion of a moiety of the manor of Midcham in Thacham, co. Berks, and of the lands belonging thereto (*tenants named*). For 51*s.* 6*d.* paid to the Queen's farmer.

2801.)   1 *Oct.* 1578.   Licence for Thomas Tiringham the elder and Thomas Tiryngham the younger to alienate the manor of Nether Wynchingdon, co. Buckingham, and the rectory of Nether Wynchyngdon to Anthony Tyringham, Edmund Pryce, Edward Saunders and William Saunders to the use of Thomas the younger and Elizabeth his wife for life in survivorship, with remainder to the right heirs of Thomas the younger. For

[*m.* 27]

£12 3*s.* 2*d.* paid to the Queen's farmer.

2802.)   1 *Oct.* 1578.   The like for William Ireton, Jerman Ireton and John Ireton to alienate Muldrige *alias* Muldrigge grange in the parish of Bradborne and Cardelhaye in the parish of Hartington, co. Derby, now or late in the tenure of Luke Longland, pastures called Muldrige and Cardelhaye in Hartington and all tithes and profits belonging to the premises, now or late in the tenure of Longland, all once of Dunstable priory, co. Bedford, to Humphrey Bradborne, knight, and Elizabeth his wife. For 17*s.* 9½*d.*

2803.)   1 *Oct.* 1578.   The like for Henry Hall and Eleanor his wife, one of the daughters and heirs of Francis Neale, to alienate a moiety of the manor of Tugbie *alias* Tokeby, of lands in Tugbie, Estnorton, Mysterton, Burton Overe and Mounstrell *alias* Mountsorell and of the rectory of Tugbie and the advowsons of the vicarage of Tugbie and free chapel of Estnorton, co. Leicester, to Robert Wingfeld and William Sutton and the heirs and assigns of Wingfeld. For £3 6*s.* 8*d.*

2804.)   13 *June* 1578.   The like for Edward, lord Zouche, Seintmaure and Canteloupe, and Eleanor his wife to alienate a fourth part of the manors of Hartilond *alias* Hartland, Hartilond Biddell *alias* Hartland Biddell, Hartiland Castle and Hartiland Beterisbery and of the borough of Hartiland *alias* Hurton Boroughe and the hundred of Hartiland, co. Devon, to William, Earl of Bath. For £8 6*s.* 8*d.*

2805.)   1 *Feb.* 1578.   The like for John Abrahall, Blanche his wife and John Abrahall, his son and heir apparent, to alienate the manor of   [*m.* 28] Brompton *alias* Brampton and lands in Brampton, co. Hereford, to David Woodroff and Robert Woodroff and the heirs and assigns of David. For 47*s.* 9*d.*

2806.)   1 *Oct.* 1578.   The like for Francis, earl of Bedford, and Bridget his wife to alienate lands in Doggesthroppe *alias* Dosthropp, the city of Peterboroughe, Passon *alias* Paston, Peykirke, Walton, Estfeild and Newarke, co. Northampton, to William Fitzwilliams and Winefrid his wife and the heirs and assigns of William. For 48*s.* 8*d.*

2807.)   21 *July* 1578.   The like for Robert Losse to alienate two messuages and a garden belonging thereto, late in the tenure of Robert Hudson, in the parish of St. Botolph without Algate, London, once of the monastery of Graces by the Tower of London, whereof one tenement was late occupied by Robert Hudson and the other with the garden by Thomas Derycke, (containing in width from the North abutting on a tenement called 'le Foxe' 14 feet and in length from the North side to the South 95 feet abutting on the highway in Eastmythfeild leading from Towerhill towards Ratcliffe)—which premises are now in the tenure of Geoffrey Spychman at a yearly rent of 40*s.* and were purchased by Hugh Losse, deceased, Robert's father, and Thomas Bocher unto them and the heirs of Hugh *inter alia* from the Crown, as appears by patent, 10 May, 35 Hen. VIII,—to Thomas Potter. For 13*s.* 4*d.*

2808.)   3 *Jan.* 1578.   The like for Alice Barnam, widow, Stephen Barnam and Anne his wife to alienate all their manors and lands in Snawe, Ivechurche, Brockland and Romley *alias* Romney Marshe, co. Kent, to John Garrard, citizen and 'haberdassher' of London. For £6.

2809.)   20 *Dec.* 1577.   The like for William Rice and Barbary his wife to alienate lands and a fishery in the Thames in Medmenham, co. Buckingham, to James Duffeild. For 29*s.* 5½*d.*
[*m.* 29]

2810.)   8 *Feb.* 1578.   Pardon of alienation: Alice Leighe, widow, late the wife of Thomas Leighe, knight, alderman of London, by indenture, 7 Sept., 15 Eliz., enrolled on 8 Sept. following in Chancery, bargained and sold to Thomas Cony, Edward Baber, serjeant at law, and George Bonde, alderman of London, (by the names of Thomas Conye of Basingthorpe, co. Lincoln, Edward Baber of Lincolnes Inne, co. Middlesex, and George Bond, citizen and 'haberdasher' of London) Mylborne grange in Stoneley or elsewhere, co. Warwick, the capital mansion house thereof, lands (*named*) in Stoneley, all lands reputed parcel of the premises in Milborne, Stoneley and Killingworthe or elsewhere, co. Warwick, and all other lands late of Anthony Throckmerton, citizen and mercer of London, in Stoneley. For £7 10*s.* paid to the Queen's farmer.

2811).   15 *Feb.* 1578.   The like: Robert Rotherforth by fine in the Common Pleas levied in Michaelmas term, 14 Eliz., and granted and recorded on the octave of St. Hilary, 15 Eliz., acquired from John Salwen and Helen his wife *inter alia* lands in Newhey, co. York. For 13*s.* 4*d.*

2812.)   13 *Feb.* 1578.   The like: George Ognell and Richard Loftis by indenture, 28 Oct., 15 Eliz., acquired from Robert Bowshare manors, granges and lands called Cruelfeild *alias* Crefeld in Cruelfeilde and Stoneley or elsewhere, co. Warwick, and all other his lands there. For £20.   [*m.* 30]

2813.)   13 *Feb.* 1578.   The like: Edward Halfehide and Anne his wife by indenture, 12 Feb., 17 Eliz., acquired unto them and the heirs of Edward from Thomas Smyth and Alice his wife the reversion or remainder of the manor of Barkesdon *alias* Bardon, co. Hertford, then held for life by lady Mary Judde, then wife of James Altham and late the wife of Andrew Judde, knight, deceased, and all lands of the said Thomas or Alice in Barresden, Aspeden, Westemyll, Laston, Throkinge, Wydiall and Benington, co. Hertford. For £26 13*s.* 4*d.*

2814.)   20 *Jan.* 1578.   The like: William Norrys and William Babington, knight, by indenture, 20 July, 19 Eliz., acquired from Thomas Wenman the manor of Water Eaton *alias* Eaton Hastinges, co. Berks, with the advowson of Water Eaton church, and all his other lands there. For £194.

2815.)   19 *Feb.* 1578.   The like: William Veale and Arthur Veizer in Hilary term, 15 Eliz., by fine in the Common Pleas acquired unto them and the heirs of Veale from William Butler lands in Stoke and Hawkesburye and the tithes of corn in Stoke, Upton and Hawkesburie, co. Gloucester. For £9.

2816.)   15 *Jan.* 1578.   Licence for William Skipwith and Frances his wife to alienate the manor of Radwell, lands in Radwell and Norton and the advowson of Radwell church, co. Hertford, to Rowland Hayward, knight.   [*m.* 31]
For £6 6*s.* 8*d.* paid to the Queen's farmer.

2817.)   20 *Dec*. 1577.   The like for Henry Norreys, knight, lord Norreys of Ricott, and Margery his wife to alienate the manors of Sullamsted, Sheffelde, Uphton, Greishull, Arbor, Amnor Courte, Abbas Burfeilde and Sugworthe and lands in Sullamsted, Sheffield, Uphton, Greishull, Arbor, Sugworthe, Amnor Courte, Sonnyngwell and Bayworthe, co. Berks, and the manor of Sydenham and lands in Sydenham, co. Oxford, to George Cawfylde and Henry Bridgwater and the heirs and assigns of Cawfylde. For £38 13s. 6d.

2818.)   1 *Feb*. 1578.   Pardon of alienation: Henry Norreys, knight, lord Norreys of Ricott, by indenture, 16 Oct., 19 Eliz., acquired from William Norryes the manor of Eaton *alias* Eaton Hastings, the advowson of Eaton church and lands in Eaton, co. Berks. For £194 paid to the Queen's farmer.

2819.)   10 *Feb*. 1578.   The like: Alice Leigh, widow, late the wife of Thomas Leigh, knight, alderman of London, being seised for life of the manor of Newenham *alias* Kinges Newenham, co. Warwick, the rectory of Kinges Newenham, the tithes of corn and hay in the parish of Kinges Newenham and the advowson of the vicarage of Newenham aforesaid, the manor of Churche Lawforde, co. Warwick, and the manor of Swynforde, co. Leicester, the rectory of Swynforde, all tithes in the parish of Swynforde and the advowson of the vicarage of Swynforde, with remainder to William Leigh, Thomas's and her son, for life, with remainder over to divers other persons, by indenture quadripartite, 5 May, 17 Eliz., enrolled in Chancery, surrendered her interest therein to William, which surrender he agreed. For £28 5s.   [*m*. 32]

2820.)   1 *Oct*. 1578.   Licence for Stephen Hadnoll to alienate lands (*tenants named*) in Cleobury Mortymer and Cleoburie Barnes, co. Salop, to Francis Kynaston. For 40s. 6d. paid to the Queen's farmer.

2821.)   1 *Feb*. 1578.   Pardon of alienation: William Bruncker, Michael Garneley and William Marten in Hilary term, 17 Eliz., by fine in the Common Pleas acquired unto them and the heirs of Bruncker from Thomas Stevens, Elizabeth his wife and Nicholas Stevens the manor of Inglesham and lands in Inglesham and Burwardescott, co. Wilts, and the manor of Inglesham and lands in Inglesham and Burwardescott, co. Berks. For £20 paid to the Queen's farmer.

2822.)   17 *Jan*. 1578.   Licence for Edward Clifton and Alice his wife to alienate 2ac. of land in Ficketsfild *alias* Fickatsfyld in the parishes of St. Dunstan and St. Clement Danes, co. Middlesex, to Ralph Bossevyll. For 2s. paid to the Queen's farmer.

2823.)   1 *Oct*. 1578.   The like for Denise Mannock, widow, Edmund Mannock, Anthony Mannock, Thomas Mannock and Edward Mannock to alienate lands in Wythermonford *alias* Wormyngford, co. Essex, to William Waldegrave, knight, and Elizabeth his wife and the heirs and assigns of William For 13s. 4d.   [*m*. 33]

2824.)   13 *Feb*. 1578.   Pardon of alienation: Henry Cassye by indenture, 26 Oct., 15 Eliz., acquired from Roger Martyn, knight, alderman of London, the manor of Asschurche, the farm of Asschurche and all his lands called Asschurche, co. Gloucester, once parcel of Warwickes Landes and Spencers Landes, and all other his lands in the said county. For £25 paid to the Queen's farmer.

2825.)   26 *Feb*. 1578.   The like: Richard Forster and William Snowe by fine in the Common Pleas levied in the octave of St. Martin and granted and recorded in the octave of

St. Hilary, 14 Eliz., acquired unto them and the heirs and assigns of Forster from Solomon Prowghte four messuages in the parish of all Hallows ad Fenum, London. For £4.

2826.)   1 *May* 1578.   Licence for Robert Tomsone to alienate a moiety of a messuage and a ferry over the Thames called Tilbery *alias* West Tilbery ferry in West Tillberye, co. Essex, to James Crypse, 'yeoman'. For 13*s*. 4*d*. paid to the Queen's farmer.

2827.)   1 *March* 1578.   The like for Anthony Maxey and Dorothy his wife to alienate lands in Rayne Parva *alias* Reighnes Parva, co. Essex, to John Maxey and Thomas Renoldes and the heirs and assigns of John, and for them by the same fine to convey them back to Anthony and Dorothy and the heirs male of Dorothy by Anthony, with remainder to the right heirs of Anthony. For 22*s*. 3*d*.   [*m*. 34]

2828.)   1 *March* 1578.   The like for Anthony Martyn, Edward Clifton and Alice his wife to alienate a garden and ½ ac. of pasture in the parish of St. Dunstan in le West, co. Middlesex, to Henry Martyn, and for him by the same fine to convey them back to Anthony for 100 years from Lady Day last at a yearly rent of 20*s*., with remainder to Edward and Alice and the heirs of Edward. For 6*s*. 8*d*.

2829.)   20 *March* 1578.   The like for Innocent Rede, John Rede and Nicholas Rede to alienate the manor of Tangley *alias* Sydenhams Tangley and view of frankpledge with the court baron in Tangley, co. Southampton, to Thomas Rede. For 15*s*. 7*d*.

2830.)   1 *May* 1578.   The like for John Pelham, knight, William Pelham and James Spencer to alienate two third parts of the manor or grange of Collowe and of lands in Leggesbye, Callowe, Lissington, Lynwood and Holton, co. Lincoln, to Thomas Seyntpoule. For 44*s*. 11*d*.

2831.)   1 *March* 1578.   The like for Robert Forest to alienate lands in Stilton, co. Huntingdon, to Robert Aprece. For 3*s*. 4*d*.   [*m*. 35]

2832.)   1 *March* 1578.   The like for John Temys to alienate the manor of Buisshoppestrowe and lands in Buisshoppestrowe, Warmester and Westbury under le Playne, co. Wilts, to John Middlecott. For £8 17*s*. 9½*d*.

2833.)   13 *June* 1578.   Pardon of alienation: by fine in the Common Pleas levied in Michaelmas term, 16 Eliz., and granted and recorded in the octave of St. Hilary, 17 Eliz., Thomas Wisse and Anne his wife conveyed lands in Somerton, co. Somerset, to James Hodges and Richard Cowpper and the heirs of Hodges, who by the same fine conveyed them back to Thomas and Anne and the heirs of Thomas. For £7 paid to the Queen's farmer.

2834.)   20 *Nov.* 1577.   Licence for James Altham to alienate the manor of Buckland, co. Hertford, all his lands in Buckland, Barkwaye, Throcking, Wyddiall and Chipping Nova, co. Hertford, the advowson of Buckland church and the manor or mansion place called 'le Horne' in Buckland to Edmund Robertes, Thomas Altham, citizen and 'clothworker' of London, Emmanuel Wolley of London, grocer, and Anthony Waddington to the use of James and Mary his wife, late the wife of Andrew Judde, knight, for life, with successive remainders to Edward Altham and Elizabeth, daughter of John Barne, and the heirs of Edward by her, to the heirs of the body of   [*m*. 36]
Edward, to Thomas Altham, son of James, in tail male, to James Altham, another son of

James, in tail male, to John Altham, another son of James, in tail male, to Matthew Altham, another son of James, in tail male and to the right heirs of James the father. For £13 6s. 8d. paid to the Queen's farmer.

2835.)   20 *Nov.* 1577.   The like for John Barne to alienate a farm called the manor of Borstall, now or late in the tenure of William Cooke *alias* Bartelette, in Plumsted, co. Kent, and lands (*tenants named*) in Estwickham and Becksley, co. Kent, to Edmund Robertes, Thomas Altham the elder of London, 'clothworker', Emmanuel Wolley of London, grocer, and Anthony Waddington to the use of John for life, with successive remainders to Edward Altham and Elizabeth daughter of John and the heirs of Elizabeth by Edward, to Elizabeth in tail, to Mary Robertes, wife of Francis Robertes, and the heirs of Mary by Francis, to the heirs of the body of Mary and to the right heirs of John. For £6 13s. 4d.

2836.)   13 *June* 1578.   Pardon of alienation: William Spencer, one of the sons of Thomas Spencer, by indenture, 17 July, 14 Eliz., acquired from the said Thomas a portion of the manor or capital messuage of Ouldemalton, then inhabited by Thomas, late the site of Ouldmalton priory, of lands (*named*) in Oulde Malton, Wicham and Howehouse, of lands called Bissett House or Bisset Landes in the parish of Hemsworth, of lands in Huggatt, of a grange or capital messuage called Sandhuton Grange, of all other lands in Olde Malton, Wicham, Howe, Bissett, Hemsworth and Huggatt and of lands (*named*) in Packering Lieth and Pickering Inges, all in the county of York. For 20s. paid to the Queen's farmer.

[*m.* 37]

2837.)   3 *Jan.* 1578.   Licence for Henry Blage and Hester his wife to alienate the manor of Goldes and lands in Maydstone and Shofford, co. Kent, to Thomas Hendle and Anne his wife and the heirs and assigns of Thomas. For £5 6s. 8d. paid to the Queen's farmer.

2838.)   1 *May* 1578.   The like for Thomas Graye and Melucine his wife to alienate a moiety of lands in Basedale and Westerdale, co. York, to Thomas Yowertt. For 46s. 8d.

2839.)   10 *Feb.* 1578.   Grant to Christopher Nelson of the wardship and   [*m.* 38] marriage of William Nelson, son and heir of William Nelson; with an annuity of 40s. from 17 June, 13 Eliz., when William the father died. Yearly value of the inheritance £3 9s. 4d.

By Q.

2840.)   21 *Sept.* 1578.   *Redgrave.*   Pardon for John Handye late of Mowlton, co. Norfolk, 'laborer', indicted at the sessions of the peace held at Norwich in 'le Shirehouse', co. Norfolk, on 3 June, 19 Eliz., before Christopher Heydon, knight, William Buttes, knight, William Paston, Henry Woodhouse, Francis Wyndham and William Blenerhasset and their fellows, justices of the peace and of oyer and terminer in the county, for that he burgled the close and house of William Hardingham at Mowlton on 23 Feb., 19 Eliz., assaulted Hardingham and stole 35s. 6d. and goods (*described*) belonging to him.   By Q.

2841.)   11 *Sept.* 1578.   *Redgrave.*   Pardon for Elizabeth Muse late of   [*m.* 39] Horsham St. Faith, co. Norfolk, 'spynster', indicted for the theft at Horsham St. Faith on 2 Sept., 18 Eliz., of £13 and a silver ring in a purse belonging to William Skott.   By Q.

2842.)   24 *April* 1578.   Grant in fee simple to Thomas Leighton—who by patent, 14 April, 12 Eliz., was granted *inter alia* the office of captain, keeper and governor of the isle of Garnesey and castle of Cornett and of all other isles and places in those parts—of the rents, customs, profits and hereditaments called 'le campart' or 'campars' in the fee called 'Saint

Michaelles Fee' in the isle of Garnsey, the custom and profit of the twelfth sheaves of all manner of corn growing in the said fee called 'campart' or 'campars de blayes' and the custom and profit of the twelfth bundle of flax called 'le campert' or 'campars de lyne' arising in the said fee, all late of Mount Saint Michaell abbey in the said isle; to hold in socage as of the castle of Cornet in the said isle. For his service in the said office.   By p.s.

2843.)   23 *Sept.* 1578.   *Redgrave.*   Grant for life in survivorship to Hugh Drewe and Robert Note of the office of a gunner in the Tower of London now held by Drewe; from the present date; with wages of 6d. a day, payable at the Exchequer. In consideration of the surrender by Drewe of a patent, 10 Aug., 11 Eliz., granting him for life the office of a gunner in the Tower of London which should next be void;   [*m.* 40]
and for his service.   By p.s.

2844.)   11 *Sept.* 1578.   *Redgrave.*   Pardon for John Harlewyn of Fransham Parva, co. Norfolk, 'hoopmaker', and Robert Harlewyn *alias* Rudd of the same, 'hoopmaker', indicated for that with many others they burgled the close and house of John Wyskard at Fransham Parva on 7 Feb., 20 Eliz., and stole £200 and plate (*described*) belonging to him. At the suit of Wiborrowe Harlwyn, wife of John.   By p.s.

2845.)   6 *Oct.* 1578.   *Chenies.*   Pardon for Peter Alexander late of the parish of St. Peter in the isle of Jersey, 'husbandman', for the under-mentioned felony and robbery. On 8 July, 20 Eliz., the constable, the centenier and six men called 'ho[m]i[n]es s[er]vientes' [?*recte* 'hommes sermentes'] of the said parish declared on oath that they found in his house two lambs marked with his mark belonging to Edmund le Brym and wool of about 10 fleeces exceeding the number of sheep which Alexander then had, on the finding and seizing of which goods by them Alexander fled, wherefore they believed him to be a thief; and so according to the custom of the isle he is indicted for the felonious taking of the lambs.
          By p.s.

2846.)   14 *April* 1578.   *Greenwich.*   Grant for life to William Croft of the office of serjeant or bailiff of the honour of Wigmore,   [*m.* 41]
parcel of the lands called 'Wigmore and Wigmores Landes', co. Hereford, and collector of the revenues of the honour; so that he answer yearly for the said revenues to the receiver general of the county; with a yearly fee of 20s., payable out of the said revenues. On surrender in Chancery by John Braye of a patent of the court of Augmentations, 22 June, 4 Edw. VI, granting him the said office, then held by William Frosell, for life.   By p.s.

2847.)   12 *April* 1578.   *Greenwich.*   Appointment for life of John Scudamore, a gentleman pensioner, to be (1) steward and keeper of the courts of the manor of Fanhope, co. Hereford, late of the bishopric of London, which office was held by John Kirle, deceased, and (2) steward and keeper of the courts of the manors of Cradley, Ledbury, Ross Burgus and Ross Foreign, co. Hereford, and the manor of Busshopscastle, co. Salop, late of the bishopric of Hereford; with yearly fees of (1) 66s. 8d. and (2) 60s., payable out of the issues of the manors; as formerly held by John Hornyolde or Kirle. For his service.
          By p.s.

2848.)   19 *April* 1578.   Grant for life to Edmund Chapman of the offices of (1) chief joiner of the works in England and (2) chief joiner   [*m.* 42]
in the Tower of London; with (1) wages of 12d. a day, payable at the Exchequer, and (2) wages of 12d. a day and £16 2s. 6d. yearly for a robe of the suit of the other esquires of the

household at Christmas, payable at the Exchequer, and the house in the Tower anciently belonging to the said office; with arrears in respect of (2) from the date of the undermentioned patent, 13 March, 10 Eliz. In consideration of the surrender by Chapman in Chancery of a patent, 13 March, 10 Eliz., granting the said offices to Richard Pye, now deceased, and him for life in survivorship, in the case of (2) from the death, forfeiture or surrender of John Ripley, now deceased, to whom it was granted for life by patent, 12 March, 1 & 2 Ph. & Mary; and for his service.   By p.s.

2849.)   10 *Nov.* 1578.   *Richmond*   Grant for life to Thomas Graves of the reversion of the office of surveyor of the works in the Tower of London and in all honours, castles, lordships and manors reserved for the Queen's abode; which office was granted to Lewis Stocket

[*m.* 43]

by patent, 11 March, 6 Eliz., for life from 11 Dec. then last; with wages of 2*s.* a day for himself and 6*d.* a day for his clerk, payable at the Exchequer, and for diet, boat hire and riding as accustomed 4*s.* a day, payable by the paymasters that pay the books of the works; provided that he shall not intermeddle with the receipt or payment of any other money for the said works or paymaster, nor have any other fees of the Queen's provision and buildings other than are or shall be ordained by the Queen or by such of the Council as shall have care thereof to appertain to the said office of surveyor, and that he shall obey such orders as are or shall be established by the Queen for reformation of divers disorders and surcharges in the office of the works and the order of all other her officers appertaining to the works.   *English.*   By p.s.

2850.)   19 *April* 1578.   Pardon for Thomas Wilson late of Glasson, co. Lancaster, 'yoman'. It was presented by an inquisition taken at Wigan, co. Lancaster, before John Wrightington, a coroner in the county, on 16 Dec., 20 Eliz., on the body of John Curtis that Wilson murdered Curtis on 15 Dec., 20 Eliz., at Ince in Makerfeilde, co. Lancaster, (*details given*); before Thomas Meade, a justice of the Common Pleas, at the sessions held at Lancaster on Monday in the fourth week at Lent, 20 Eliz., he pleaded not guilty, and was found guilty of the said killing but not of murder. At the suit of Richard Shirborne,

[*m.* 44]

knight, and Robert Dalton, justices of the peace in the county.   By Q.

2851.)   4 *April* 1578.   *Gorhambury.*   Grant for life to Thomas Hanburye of the office of one of the seven auditors of the Exchequer which shall next be void after the death of Francis Southwell, John Thompson, Thomas Neale, William Fuller, William Neale, Robert Moulton or Henry Dynne, the present holders of the office for life by several patents, of Anthony Roue, to whom the reversion of Southwell's office was granted for life by patent, 5 Nov., 5 & 6 Ph. & Mary, or of William Spencer, to whom the office of auditor which should next be void was granted for life by patent, 18 Sept., 19 Eliz.; with a yearly fee of

[*m.* 45]

£20, payable at the Exchequer.   By Q.

2852.)   4 *April* 1578.   *Gorhambury.*   Grant for life to Henry Knolles, the Queen's servant, of the offices of (1) keeper of the manor of Newelme *alias* Ewelme, co. Oxford, with the garden there, (2) keeper of the park there, with herbage and pannage of the park and 'le bruse' and 'windefalles' there, (3) bailiff of the same manor, (4) keeper and surveyor of the woods of the said manor, (5) constable of the castle and manor of Wallingford, co. Berks, parcel of the honour of Ewelme, (6) steward of the said honour, of the four hundreds of Celtri and of all manors, hundreds and lands in the counties of Oxford and Berks or elsewhere parcel of the said honour and (7) master of the game of wild beasts of Ewelme

park, with herbage and pannage of the same park and power to appoint the keeper there when there is a vacancy; (5), (6) and (7) from the death, forfeiture or surrender of Francis Knolles, knight, to whom [*m.* 46]
they were granted for life by patent, 7 March, 4 Edw. VI; with (1) wages of 2*d.* a day, (2) wages of 2*d.* a day, (3) wages of 3*d.* a day and (4) wages of 2*d.* a day, payable out of the issues of the manor of Ewelme, and (5), (6) and (7) an annuity of £50, payable out of the lands of the honour of Ewelme; as held by (1), (2), (3) and (4) Edmund Asshefeilde, knight, deceased, or (5), (6) and (7) Francis Bryan, knight, deceased. For his service. By p.s.

2853.) 29 *April* 1578. Pardon for John Lovelace late of the city of Oxford *alias* late of Sandwich, co. Kent, indicted with others unknown for piracy, as appears by indictments in the court of Admiralty, as follows—(1) on 12 March, 19 Eliz., in a ship called *The Peter* of Sandwich by Flamborowgh Hed they attacked 'a flye boate' once called *The Fatte Swyne* of Ostende, George Curtes master, and took the same with its tackle to the value of £100 belonging to Curtes and others unknown; (2) on 15 March, 19 Eliz., in *The Fatte Swyne* off Scarborowghe they attacked a ship of Havre [*m.* 47]
(*Portus de Graciis*) in Normandy sailing to Newcastle and took the same with its tackle to the value of £50, four 'hogsheddes' of prunes worth £8 and a cask of vinegar worth 20*s.* belonging to Frenchmen unknown; and (3) on 21 March, 19 Eliz., in a ship of Havre in a place at sea called 'The Well' they attacked a pink (*pinca*) of Hull, Robert Clerck master, and took the same with its tackle to the value of £100, five packs containing 'broade clothes' worth £500, 100 quarters of barley worth £50 and 6 quarters of hemp seed worth £5 belonging to Christopher Ellis, John Ellis and Robert Ramsey, merchants of Hull, and Clarck; the pardon to be interpreted in his favour. By p.s.

2854.) 24 *April* 1578. Pardon for Thomas Thickbrome late of Cannall, [*m.* 48]
co. Stafford, indicted for that he with others unknown on 4 March, 18 Eliz., burgled the house of John Adcock of Nether Stannell, co. Stafford, and assaulted him, Alice his wife and Thomas Adcock. Also pardon and release for Edward Basset of Hyntes, co. Stafford, John Harman and Thickbrome of all sums due by reason of the forfeiture of a recognisance into which Basset and Harman entered before John Bowes, a justice of the peace in the county, for Thickbrome's appearance at the next assize and goal delivery at Stafford, each of the said mainpernors under a penalty of £40 and Thickbrome under a penalty of £80. By p.s.

2855.) 3 *May* 1578. Pardon for John Clyfford late of Bodmyn, co. Cornwall, 'inholder'. He was indicted at the general gaol delivery of Launceston castle, co. Cornwall, before Roger Manwood, a justice of the Common Pleas, and his fellows, justices of gaol delivery, on 17 Sept., 18 Eliz., for that he burgled the house of Richard Davye at Bodmyn on 30 April, 18 Eliz., and stole from the shop thereof velvets etc. (*described*) belonging to William Turney; he pleaded not guilty, [*m.* 49]
was convicted and was condemned, and afterwards for divers causes was committed back to gaol. By Q.

2856.) 24 *Feb.* 1578. *Hampton Court.* Pardon for Thomas Temple late of London, 'cooke', indicted for stealing horses (*described*) (1) belonging to Thomas Ayliff at Skeres in the parish of Lawrens Wotton, co. Southampton, on 29 Nov., 19 Eliz., (2) belonging to John Collins at Basingstoke, co. Southampton, on 21 Dec., 19 Eliz., and (3) belonging to the same Collins at Basingstoke on 21 Dec. By Q.

2557.) 26 *Sept.* 1578. (*No place.*) Grant for life to Robert, earl of Leicester, councillor, of the office of chancellor and chamberlain of the counties of Anglesey, Carnarvon and

Merioneth in North Wales; with a yearly fee of £20, payable out of the revenues of the principality of North Wales; as held formerly by John Salsburye, knight, Edward, late duke of Somerset, Henry, late duke of Richemonde, Richard Talbott, knight, Richard Poole, knight, William Gruffithe, knight, and Henry Norres. For his service.   By Q.

2858.)   7 *Nov.* 1578.   *Richmond.*   Presentation of John Colshill, one of the Queen's chaplains, to the rectory of Burston, Bristol dioc., co. Dorset, void by death.   By p.s.

2859.)   14 *Nov.* 1578.   *Richmond.*   Presentation of Bartholomew   [*m.* 50] Chambrelain, S.T.B., to the perpetual vicarage of Burforde, Oxford dioc., void by the resignation of William Maisters.   By p.s.

2860.)   24 *April* 1578.   Licence for four months for George Hopper of Edinboroughe in Scotland, burgess, to export from England to Scotland 200 quarters of barley, 200 quarters of malt, 400 quarters of beans and pease and 200 quarters of rye; from the present date; duty free; customers and searchers to note the quantities shipped on the back of the licence and also in their books, that on expiry of the licence it may be delivered again into the Queen's hands and that no further quantity be carried than is therein contained. At the special request of the earl of Morton, Regent of Scotland, for relief of the present want of corn there and upon his 'reciprok' offer of the like at any time that the Queen might require it.   *English.*
          By p.s.

(The dorse of this roll is blank.)

PART IV

C. 66/1167

2861.)   19 *April* 1578.   Lease for 21 years to Edmund Froste   [*m.* 1]
of the rectory of Wrangle, co. Lincoln, once of the monastery of Waltham; with
reservations; from Lady Day last; yearly rent £10. For a fine of £40, to wit, £21 18*s.* 8*d.* paid
at the Exchequer and £18 16*d.* to John Lane in repayment of £18 16*d.* paid by him for the
fine of a lease of lands in Lintón, co. Derby, which he could not enjoy by reason of a prior
lease to Anthony Grene dated 27 Nov., 6 Eliz., as appears by a bill signed by Christopher
Smyth, clerk of the pipe, and annexed to the particular whereon this patent issued.

By Q.

2862.)   19 *April* 1578.   Lease for 21 years to William Hicklinge of lands (*named*) in the
parish of Towcestre, co. Northampton, parcel of the manor of Aldington, co. Northampton, now annexed to the honour of Grafton; with reservations; from Michaelmas last; yearly
rent £10. In consideration of his surrender of a patent, 4 June, 10 Eliz.[1], leasing the premises
to him for 21 years from Lady Day then last at the same rent; and for a fine of £20 paid at the
Exchequer.   By Q.

2863.)   25 *Feb.* 1578.   Pardon for Thomas Weare *alias* Browne, Clement Wearè *alias*
Browne, Robert Weare *alias* Browne, Roger   [*m.* 2]
Apparry, Thomas Pynock, 'yeoman', and Edmund Whiteyate, 'yoman', all late of
Marleborough, co. Wilts, for the felonious killing of William Brynde.   By p.s.

2864.)   21 *Feb.* 1578.   *Honour of Hampton Court.*   Lease for 21 years to Nicholas Bacon,
knight, councillor, keeper of the great seal, of the hundred of Thedwardstree, co. Suffolk,
once of the monastery of Bury St. Edmunds, co. Suffolk, from Michaelmas next; yearly rent
£9 11*s.* 11½*d.*; the lessee to pay 10*s.* yearly to the farmer of   [*m.* 3]
the premises for livery. For a fine of £9 11*s.* 11½*d.* paid at the Exchequer.   By Q.

2865.)   9 *May* 1578.   Lease for 21 years to Henry Bristowe of (1) the rectory of Sherborne,
co. Norfolk, once of Pentney priory, and (2) the tithes of corn and hay of lands in
Teryngton, co. Norfolk, now or late in the tenure of Robert Wentworth (esquire), late
incumbent of St. James's chapel, Teryngton, which came to the hands of Edward VI by the
dissolution of chantries and the like; with reservations; from Lady Day last; yearly rents (1)
66*s.* 8*d.* and (2) £7 10*s.*; the lessee to pay a pension of £4 13*s.* 4*d.* yearly to the vicar of
Shirborne in augmentation of his stipend. For a fine of £10 16*s.* 8*d.* paid at the Exchequer.

By Q.

2866.)   9 *May* 1578.   Lease for 21 years to James Androwes of lands (*named with tenants'
names*) in Baynton, co. York, parcel of the manor of Baynton, late of Francis Bigod,
attainted; with reservations;   [*m.* 4]
from Lady Day next; yearly rent £10 1*s.* 4*d.* (*detailed*); the lease to be void in respect of any
parcel of the premises whereof the lessee shall not before Christmas next make a lease by

---

[1] In the enrolment of this patent (*cf. Calendar*, 1566–1569, no. 1012) the lands are described as being in Foxcote.

deed to the present tenant for the whole term and at the rent hereby reserved, so long as the tenants pay him themselves his costs about obtaining this patent. For a sum paid at the Exchequer.   By Q.

2867.)   3 *May* 1578.   Pardon for John Killam (*alias* Kylham) late of Norwich, 'locke-smythe', indicted by two indictments at the sessions of the peace held at Norwich in the guildhall on 23 July, 19 Eliz., before Thomas Cully, mayor of the city, Edward Flowerdewe, steward of the city, Thomas Layer, John Aldriche, Thomas Sotherton and their fellows, justices of the peace and of oyer and terminer in the county of the said city, for receiving and abetting (1) John Allen, 'taillor', Thomas Allen, 'lockesmyth', and Robert Raynoldes, 'taillor', all late of Norwich, after they had at Norwich on 28 Jan., 19 Eliz., stolen cloth etc. (*described*) belonging to Thomas Fyshman and (2) the same John and Thomas Allen after they had at Norwich on 15 April, 19 Eliz., stolen cloth (*described*) belonging to John Thegrave.   [*m.* 5]

2868.)   10 *March* 1578.   *Gorhambury.*   Grant to Francis Coote, the Queen's servant, of the Crown's moiety in the counties of Norfolk and Suffolk of (1) the arrears and mean profits of lands in England and Wales found by Henry Middlemore within seven years from 5 May, 13 Eliz., to have been withheld and concealed from the Crown, (2) chattels of dissolved monasteries, chantries and the like found by Middlemore to have been concealed before that date and (3) moneys collected from the clergy for subsidies, tenths and first fruits [*m.* 6] between 3 Nov., 27 Hen. VIII, and 8 July, 1 Mary, found by Middlemore within the said seven years to have been concealed. By patent, 5[1] May, 13 Eliz., one moiety of the said moneys and chattels in England and Wales was granted *inter alia* to Middlemore.   *English.*
                                                                                                    By p.s.

2869.)   10 *March* 1578.   *Gorhambury.*   Grant to William Lane of Horton, co. Northampton, and Edward Lane of Waldegrave, co. Northampton, of—all chattels forfeited by the departure of any person out of the Queen's dominions since the first day of the first year of her reign without her special licence or by reason that a person having licence so to depart has remained outside her dominions above the time limited in the licence, which are concealed from the Crown; and of all chattels forfeited by the attainder of any person before 10 March last for treason or misprision of treason, which are likewise concealed.   [*m.* 7] This patent or the enrolment thereof to be sufficient warrant to the barons of the Exchequer or others for delivery of the premises to the grantees. Licence for the grantees to levy and recover all such chattels by course of law. Power for the grantees to compound with any person for the premises, to grant the same to any person and to discharge any person, his lands and possessions of the same; such composition, grant or discharge in writing signed by the grantees or one of them to be sufficient bar against actions by the Crown and sufficient warrant to the chancellor or keeper of the great seal to issue by patent to any person with whom such compositions or agreements shall be made discharges of such of the premises as they shall extend to and pardons of the forfeitures. Power for the grantees to sue in the Crown's name or otherwise; the Queen's ministers to permit   [*m.* 8] them or such as they shall appoint by consent of the treasurer and chancellor of the Exchequer to have access to records of the Crown and to have exemplifications or copies thereof at their own 'travaill', and at the grantees' request to permit any process or commission to be awarded concerning the premises, the commissions being directed to the grantees or either of them and such other persons as to the keeper of the great seal, treasurer or chancellor or barons of the Exchequer shall seem best. Provided that the grantees shall

---

[1] Reading from the warrant, in Chancery Warrants II (C.82), 1327; the roll reads 'first'.

pay to the Crown at the Exchequer the value of a third part of all the premises received and of all sums hereafter arising by any composition made by them; provided also that they shall not only from time to time make privy the treasurer or chancellor of the Exchequer of every composition or agreement had or made by them for the premises above-granted, but also that they shall within six months from the present date be bound before the barons of the Exchequer in such sums as by the said treasurer and chancellor shall be thought convenient for the answering of the said third part and that they shall not make any composition or discharge to any person without the privity of the said treasurer and chancellor.

For the service of Edward Stafford, a gentleman pensioner, and at his suit.   *English.*

2870.)   19 *April* 1578.   Assignment to William Sutton, master of the ordnance in the North, of a lease to the Queen by Richard, bishop of Durham, by deed, 1 Feb., 20 Eliz., enrolled in Chancery, for 79 years from Martinmas last of the manors of Gateside and Whickhame, co. Durham, and all lands, mines and hereditaments in Gateside and Wickham belonging to the bishopric of Durham.   *English.*   [*m.* 9]
                                                                                        By p.s.

2871.)   19 *Feb.* 1578.   Lease for 21 years to John Lytcote, a gentleman pensioner, of the chantry of Wappenham, co. Northampton, and woods and lands (*named*) in Wappenham, in the Crown's hands by escheat; with reservations; from Michaelmas last; yearly rent 107s. 2d. (*detailed*); the lessee to make two cuttings only of the woods and at fitting times, to enclose them after cutting and to leave sufficient 'lez staddelles' in every acre according to statute.
                                                              By warrant of the commissioners.

2872.)   17 *March* 1578.   *Gorhambury.*   Grant for life to Richard Bingham of an annuity of 50 marks out of the manors of Bodrigam and Trevelen, Penstrasowe, Tregriam *alias* Tregriham, Thelowthes, Trevorock, Casawis, Trevergh, Resogowe, Dorsett, Enois, Peringborough, Pencois, Huntingdone Castell, Trebullock, Cruckvalaunce, Trevesthok and Truruburgh, co. Cornwall, which was granted to the Crown by Thomas, cardinal, archbishop of York, chancellor, John Heron, knight, Baldwin Mallett and Adam
                                                                                        [*m.* 10]
Rayleigh by charter indented, 3 June, 11 Hen. VIII, enrolled in Chancery; with arrears from the death of George Stonehouse, the Queen's servant. For his service.   By p.s.

2873.)   26 *Feb.* 1578.   *Gorhambury.*   Pardon for Ninian Watson. He, Robert Watson and William Dixon, all late of Somerhouse, co. Durham, 'yomen', are indicted for that they broke and entered the closes of (1) Matthew Dennome at Layton, co. Durham, (2) William Prowdlock at Bushopton, co. Durham, and (3) Richard Marshall, clerk, at Stainton in le Streate, co. Durham, on 21 Nov., 20 Eliz., and stole cattle (*described*) severally belonging to them.   By p.s.

2874.)   17 *Feb.* 1578.   Pardon for Peter Greneway late of Mynsted, co. Southampton, clerk. He was indicted at the general gaol delivery of Winchester castle, co. Southampton, made there before Roger Manwood, a justice of the Common Pleas, and John Jefferay, a justice of the   [*m.* 11]
Queen's Bench, and their fellows, justices of gaol delivery, on 26 Aug., 19 Eliz., for that with another he stole a mare belonging to John Iles at Mylton, co. Southampton, on 20 March, 19 Eliz.; he pleaded not guilty, was convicted and condemned and for divers causes was committed back to gaol. At the suit of Mary Greneway, his wife.   By Q.

2875.)   7 *March* 1578.   Pardon for Reginald Yorke of Hasketon within the liberty of St.

Etheldreda, co. Suffolk, 'husbandman', for manslaughter. It was found by an inquisition taken at Hasketon on 26 July, 19 Eliz., before Simon Mawe, coroner in the said liberty, on the body of Anne Yorke, late the wife of Robert Yorke of Hasketon, 'yoman', that Reginald assaulted her on 4 June, 19 Eliz., in his house at Hasketon so that she died there on 25 June (*details given*).   [*m.* 12]
At the suit of divers justices of the peace in the county.   By p.s.

2876.) 22 *Feb.* 1578.   *Hampton Court.*   Pardon for Nicholas Bosgrove late of Chitterum, co. Wilts, who was indicted at the general gaol delivery of Fysherton Anger, co. Wilts, made by Roger Manwood, a justice of the Common Pleas, and John Jefferay, a justice of the Queen's Bench, and their fellows, justices of gaol delivery, at New Salisbury on Thursday in the second week of Lent, 19 Eliz., for that he with others on 13 Dec., 19 Eliz., at Tilshed, co. Wilts, in the highway leading from Market Lavington robbed (1) Tristram Skete, (2) David Myller, (3) Hugh Hopkins and (4) Roger Tutt of money (*detailed*) severally belonging to them, pleaded not guilty, was convicted and condemned and was for divers causes committed back to gaol.   By Q.

2877.) 24 *April* 1578.   Lease for 21 years to Nicholas Snowe, keeper of the wardrobe at Richemond, of (1) the rectory of Woodford, co.   [*m.* 13]
Northampton, late of the monastery of Rocester, co. Stafford, and leased to Snowe by patent, 13 Oct., 9 Eliz., for 31 years from Michaelmas 1573 or the termination of the interest of Leonard Parrett at a yearly rent of £13 6s. 8d. and (2) lands (*named*) in the parish of Eaton, co. Buckingham, parcel of the honour of Windsor, co. Berks, and leased to Snowe by patent, 10 May, 3 Eliz., for 21 years from Michaelmas then last at a yearly rent of 66s.; with reservations; from (1) Michaelmas 1604 and (2) Michaelmas 1581; same rents. For his service.   By p.s.

2878.) 17 *April* 1578.   Lease for 21 years to Owen ap Roberte Owen of (1) all the spiritualities late belonging to Berkellet *alias*   [*m.* 14]
Berkellert priory in the county of Carnarvon and the rectory of Berthkellert, the rectory of Llanviangell y Penaunt, the rectory of Llanvar Isgair and Bettus, the rectory of Aberch, the chapel of Kynvill and the chapel of Doloweddelan, co. Carnarvon, and (2) the rectory of Llanydan, the rectory of Lloinedwyn, the rectory of Llaneniell Vab and the rectory of Llanvayer y Comot, co. Anglesey, all late of the said priory of Berkellet, once belonging to the monastery of Bysham *alias* Bustlesham, co. Berks, and afterwards granted to Anne of Cleves for life; with reservations; from Michaelmas last; yearly rents (1) £9 7s. 8d. and (2) £21 17s. 3d. In consideration of the surrender by the said Owen in respect of the premises of a patent, 20 Feb., 3 Eliz., leasing to John Tamworth the house and site of Bethkilhart priory and all lands then or late in the tenure of John Gough in the counties of Carnarvon and Anglesey or elsewhere in North Wales once of the said priory for 21 years from Michaelmas then next at a yearly rent of £42; and for a fine of £62 9s. 10d. paid at the Exchequer.
                                                                                By p.s.

2879.) 2 *May* 1578.   Lease for 21 years to Richard Hodgeson of coal mines (*named with tenants' names*) in Benwell and the lordship of Benwell, co. Northumberland, once of the monastery of Tynmouth,   [*m.* 15]
co. Northumberland; from Lady Day last; yearly rent £20; the lessee may dig pits and watergates there, with sufficient 'wayleve' across the fields of Benwell and liberty of having timber in the woods of the manor of Benwell by assignment of the Queen's auditor, receiver, surveyor, steward and bailiff or two of them there for the support of the mines; he may dig coal there according to the custom of the country there by survey of the auditor,

receiver, surveyor and viewer of the county; he shall leave sufficient 'pillers' for the support
of the pits; if he shall by any 'le styth' or other cause be hindered from working the mines, or
if the mines come to ruin for lack of 'seme and myne' (so long as it be not by his negligence)
by reason whereof he shall wish to leave the mines, he shall give sufficient warning thereof to
the auditor and receiver of the county one year before his leaving.   By p.s.

2880.) 22 *April* 1578. Pardon for persons indicted for felonies as follows—Agnes
Aspurner late of London, 'spinster', for the theft of clothing etc. (*described*) belonging to
Richard Angor at Highe Holborne, co. Middlesex, on 7 Jan., 18 Eliz.; Henry Bracher *alias*
Corbett late of London, 'yeoman', for the theft from the person of Helen wife of Anthony
Chadesley of a purse and 4*s.* 2*d.* belonging to the said Anthony at St. Giles in the Fields, co.
Middlesex, on 16 July, 18 Eliz.; Agnes Woorte late of London, 'spinster', for the theft of
clothing etc. (*described*) belonging to Nicholas Haynes at Hacney, co. Middlesex, on 10 June,
18 Eliz.; John Hickes late of London, 'yoman', for the theft of a gelding belonging to
Thomas Baxster at Holborne, co. Middlesex, on 28 Sept., 18 Eliz.; Agnes Laurence late of
London, 'spinster', for the theft of clothing (*described*) belonging to David Jones at
[*m.* 16]
Kensington, co. Middlesex, on 6 Feb., 18 Eliz.; Joan Smyth late of London, 'spinster', for
the theft of clothing (*described*) belonging to Thurstan Basford at Goldinge Lane, co.
Middlesex, on 28 Jan., 18 Eliz.; Alice Gilbert late of London, 'spinster', for the theft of
sheets etc. (*described*) belonging to John Stepps at Westminster, co. Middlesex, on 7 June, 18
Eliz.; Jane Phillipps *alias* Clerk late of London, 'spinster', for the theft of clothing etc.
(*described*) belonging to John Northend at Clerkenwell, co. Middlesex, on 20 May, 18 Eliz.;
Roger Jenckes late of London, 'armorer', for the theft of canvas (*described*) belonging to a
man unknown at St Martin in the Fields, co. Middlesex, on 16 Oct., 18 Eliz.; Hugh
Gaddesby late of London, 'yoman', for that he broke and entered 'the warehouse' of
Ferdinand Steynton, mercer, in the parish of St. Mary Aldermanbery in Creplegate ward,
London, on 8 Oct., 18 Eliz., and stole cloth etc. (*described*) belonging to him; Mary Lyngay
alias Carter late of London, 'spinster', for the theft of plate etc. (*described*) belonging to
Henry Rolf, 'letherseller', in the parish of St. Lawrence in Old Jewry in Chepe ward,
London, on 18 May, 18 Eliz.; Thomas Dashe late of London, 'yoman', for the theft of a
purse and 4*s.* from the person of a woman unknown in the parish of Christeschurch in
Farringdon Within ward, London, on 19 Nov., 19 Eliz.; John Evans late of London, baker,
for the theft of a mare belonging to a man unknown in the parish of St. Giles without
Creplegate in Creplegate ward, London, on 3 Nov., 18 Eliz.; Margaret Pynnyale late of
London, 'spinster', for the theft of linen etc. (*described*) belonging to Henry Kinge,
'yeoman', in the parish of St. Magnus the Martyr in Bridge ward, London, on 27 Nov., 19
Eliz.;   [*m.* 17]
Richard Smytheck late of London, 'yoman', for the theft of a purse and 2*s.* 6*d.* belonging to
John Johnson, draper, from the person of Elizabeth wife of the same John in the parish of
Christeschurche in Farringdon Within ward, London, on 18 Sept., 18 Eliz.; Edward
Mottershed late of London, 'bricklayer', for that he robbed James Cuttes of a sword
belonging to him at Islington, co. Middlesex, in the highway near Raige Crosse on 15 Jan.,
19 Eliz.; John Longe late of London, 'yeoman', for the theft of cloth (*described*) belonging to
a man unknown in the keeping of Thomas Stanford, 'taylor', in High Holborne, co.
Middlesex, on 18 Dec., 19 Eliz.; Henry Fysher *alias* Banker late of London, 'yoman',
indicted for the theft of two horses belonging to William Kent at Mylende, co. Middlesex,
on 28 Feb., 19 Eliz.; Richard Westerman late of London, 'laborer', indicted for the theft of a
gelding belonging to Richard Hodgis at Islington, co. Middlesex, on 19 Feb., 19 Eliz.;
Hugh Elwood late of London, 'yoman', indicted for the theft of (1) £5 13*s.* 4*d.* belonging to
William Smythe and £3 5*s.* belonging to Richard Thorpe, (2) 30*s.* belonging to Robert

Peayes and (3) 30s. belonging to William Hill at Wilsdon, co. Middlesex, on 4 April, 19 Eliz.; Joan Snellinge late of London, 'spinster', indicted for the theft of clothing (*described*) belonging to Christopher Preston, lord of Gormanston, in the parish of St. Sepulchre in Farringdon Without ward, London, on 12 April, 19 Eliz.; James Massy late of London, 'carpenter', indicted for the theft of (1) a timber vessel bound with iron called 'a water tankerde' belonging to Simon Hearing, goldsmith, in the parish of All Hallows in Honylane in Chepe ward, London, on 19 Dec., 19 Eliz., and (2) a like vessel belonging to James [—], 'waterbearer', in the parish of St. Michael on Cornehill in Cornehill ward, London, on 20 Dec., 19 Eliz.; Catherine Bonnyard late of London, 'spinster', for that she broke and entered the house of Anne Boddy, widow, in the parish of St. Mary Aldermary in Cordweynerstrete ward, London, on 7 March, 19 Eliz., and stole linen etc.(*described*) belonging to her; Philip Morgan   [*m.* 18]
late of London, 'yoman', for the theft of two steers belonging to Nicholas Melton at Woxbridge, co. Middlesex, on 8 May, 19 Eliz.; Margaret Lewes late of London, 'spinster', for the theft of rings etc. (*described*) belonging to William Nyseham at Halliwell Streate, co. Middlesex, on 1 May, 19 Eliz.; and Catherine Francklyn late of Westminster, co. Middlesex, 'spinster', for that she broke and entered the close of Edward Deverne at Westminster on 19 May, 19 Eliz., and stole two piglets belonging to him. By information of John Langley, knight, mayor of London, and others, justices of gaol delivery of Newgate.   [*m.* 19]
By warrant of the commissioners.

2881.) 2 *April* 1578.   *Gorhambury*.   Presentation of Simon Canham, M.A., to the rectory of Norton Fitzwarren, Bath and Wells dioc., void by death and in the Queen's gift by the minority of William, earl of Bath, her ward.   By Q.

2882.)   1 *Oct*. 1578.   Presentation of Geoffrey Crosse, M.A., to the rectory of Symondes Borne, Durham dioc.   By p.s.

2883.)   24 *March* 1578.   *Gorhambury*.   Grant for life to John Elliott of wages of 8d. a day, payable at the Exchequer, late held by George Awdelam, deceased; from Michaelmas last. For his service in war.   By p.s.

2884.)   26 *Feb*. 1578.   Dispensation for John Snowe, clerk, rector of Kyngston Seymer *alias* Semerke, co. Somerset, to retain his said rectory with absolution from all excommunications and other ecclesiastical penalties incurred by his *de facto* institution as perpetual vicar of Est Claydon, Lincoln dioc., into which vicarage he refused real induction until he could obtain sufficient dispensation to hold both livings together and which vicarage he later resigned, since when he has held the said rectory for many years. At his suit, for the removal of all scruple of doubt.   By Q.

2885.)   27 *Sept*. 1578.   *Gorhambury*.   Commission to Richard Martyn,   [*m.* 20] warden of the mint, and John Lovyson, master worker of the moneys,—whereas by indenture, 19 April, 14 Eliz., Lovison was authorised to make three kinds of gold moneys of the standard of 23 carats 3½ grains of fine gold and ½ grain of alloy and four kinds of silver moneys of the standard of 11 oz. 2 dwt. troy of fine silver and 18 dwt. of alloy, with remedies specified in the indenture, and Martyn was commanded to take to the Queen's use 4s. on every pound troy of gold moneys made and 18d. on every pound troy of silver, paying Lovison 18d. out of the said 4s. and 8d. out of the said 18d. received towards his working and other expenses, and now the Queen is minded for urgent reasons to tolerate for a short time some variation from the express words of the said indenture, and yet not much varying from the said ancient standard but rather better both in alloy and in the shear than much of the money commonly current — to make and convert bullion, of such gold and silver as shall be brought into the mint by the Queen or others of the goodness of the said standards to be received upon the Queen's bills, into the said three moneys of gold and four moneys of silver and for Lovison to make besides the aforesaid four moneys of silver one other money of silver called the penny (a want of which is commonly complained of), 720 to the pound weight troy and of the same fineness as the rest of the said silver moneys. Which moneys of gold and silver shall be made, commixed, alloyed, melted and shorn in fineness, weight and tale as follows: the gold to be commixed and melted at a standard now limited of 23 carats 3¼ grains of fine gold and ¾ grain of alloy and the silver at the standard of 11oz. 1 dwt. of fine silver and 19 dwt. of alloy in the pound weight troy; the said warden and master to be present at the casting of the bullion out of the pot and with the assay master the assays made of the ingots, and to cause moneys thereof to be made and shorn at the standard for gold of £36 10s. 10½d. the pound weight troy and for silver 60s. 3d. the pound weight troy. Remedy is to be allowed of ⅛ carat in the pound weight troy of gold and 2 dwt. in the pound weight troy of silver, after the old computation of 20 dwt. to the ounce. For every 100 pound weight troy of the silver bullion   [*m.* 21] to be coined there are to be made 1 pound weight of three-halfpence, 2 pound weight of pence and 1 pound weight of three-farthings. After the said moneys shall be by the said warden and the assaymaster tried and pyxed as ordered by the said indenture, the said master worker shall make true deliverance and payment of the same to every person by weight by the same balance and weight whereof he shall receive the same bullion, taking again his said bills; which payment shall be within 14 days according to the form of the indenture, if the said master be not letted by the said warden or assaymaster, for any bullion of the Queen's subjects and for her own bullion within as convenient time as may be; which money of the Queen's own bullion shall be delivered to the warden and the rest to the owners according to the form of the indenture. When the said moneys shall be assayed before the council as prescribed for the moneys mentioned in the said indenture and found good according to the tenor of these presents, the said master shall, without fee and without any other warrant than the showing of these presents, have letters patent under the great seal for his acquittance, specifying the said assays to be made and found as is above-said; but, if any fault be found at the assays in fineness and weight or either of them over and above the remedies ordained by these presents, he shall make fine and ransom at the Queen's will. The warden shall take of both the Queen's bullion and the bullion of other persons so converted into coin upon every pound weight troy of gold 5s. 10½d. and of every pound weight troy of silver 21d. by tale; out of which he shall cause to be paid to the master worker upon every pound weight troy of gold so coined 3s. 4½d. and of every pound weight troy of silver 12¾d. by tale, over and besides 1/16 carat of gold of every pound weight troy of the gold aforesaid and 1 dwt. fine silver of every pound weight troy of silver to be by the said master retained from the commixion of every pound weight troy; which the said master worker shall enjoy to his own use upon pound weight, together with the 3s. 4½d. for gold and 12¾d. for silver as aforesaid for the diets, wastes and other charges by him to be borne by reason of the said indenture and schedule thereunto annexed, without any account to be yielded by him for the same; the residue of all the profits rising both by the coinage of others and by the shear and coinage of the Queen's own bullion to be retained to the Queen's use and account thereof to be yielded. In which account defalcation and allowance shall be had of such diets, fees and payments as the Queen has agreed to bear by the schedule annexed to the said former indenture, and the same may be paid accordingly, provided that there be no expenses made for any diet but at such time as shall be needful for attendance about making of moneys or otherwise when the Council shall have just cause to be there for the affairs of the mint. The warden or his deputies to keep the ledger, meltings book and shear book of the said moneys as is requisite, so that the Queen may know how much of the said moneys and in what sort have been made, and of what alloy, and what is due to her for the same. The warden and master worker and all other officers and ministers of the mint, and any persons standing bound with them, are discharged from all penalties for infringements of articles in the said indenture incurred by the execution of this present commission. Provided that this patent extend   [*m.* 22] not to authorise the warden and master worker to receive any bullion into the mint after 16 Nov. next nor by virtue hereof to coin into the said moneys any other bullion but such as shall be received into the mint before that date. The warden may have a duplicate of this grant under the great seal, which shall be sufficient warrant for anything to be done by him or his deputies by force hereof.   *English.*   By Q.

2886.)   21 *March* 1578.   *Gorhambury.*   Licence for Martin Forbiser of London, the Queen's servant,—who has been appointed to have the order, rule and government of the Queen's and other ships in his company for the voyage to be made Northwestward for the discovering of Cathay and all other lands and islands already discovered and hereafter to be discovered by him—and his deputies, bearers hereof, to press and take up in the Queen's name for her only service ships, vessels, mariners, soldiers, pioneers, miners, gunners, shipwrights, smiths, carpenters and all other needful artificers and workmen for the voyage and also carriage by sea and land and post horses for the Queen's reasonable wages and payment to be made in that behalf; power for the licensee to take into his charge and government the said ships and also his whole company to be appointed for his service and them to govern and correct by imprisonment and violent means and by death if the greatness of the fault and necessity shall so deserve upon obstinate withstanding such orders and articles as are delivered to him by the Queen or her Council; also to lead them to such places as he shall think meet for this service, and to leave so many of the company to inhabit land discovered according to such orders and articles as shall be delivered to him by the Queen or her Council; also power to take by violence or other means all persons and ships with their goods which he shall find trafficking into harbours or creeks parcel of any land or islands by him lately discovered to the Queen's use to the Northwestward and to detain and dispose of them according to such orders and articles as shall be delivered to him by the Queen or her Council; provided that he shall not take up any principal man very meet for the Queen's own service in the wars or more persons than shall be necessary for the voyage. *English.*   By Q.

2887.)   28 *March* 1578.   *Gorhambury.*   Licence for life for John Smythe of Semyngton in the parish of Stepleashton, co. Wilts, 'yoman', who has married Sibyl Long, widow, sometime wife of William Longe of Seymyngton, 'clothier', who in her widowhood continued the trade of cloth making, whereby her servants work and the poor of the country about are much relieved, to exercise the occupation of making, working, weaving and rowing woollen cloth in any place in the Queen's dominions where such work has been commonly done for 10 years before 8 Feb., 18 Eliz.,   [*m.* 23] without incurring any penalty laid down in stat. 5 Eliz. forbidding any one not then engaged in the craft to engage in any craft after 1 March [*recte* May] then next who had not served seven years as apprentice therein. *English.*   By p.s.

2888.)   31 *Oct.* 1578.   *Chenies.*   Grant to the bailiff, jurats and commonalty of the town of Hastinge, co. Sussex, of power to make new and finish a haven in such place or places near the said town and port as to them shall seem most convenient, and licence for Richard Calveley and John Jeffrey, jurats of the said town, and William Relfe of Ore and all persons thereunto deputed by them (or two of them) by writing under the common seal of the town to collect a contribution and benevolence towards the same throughout the realm; some of the Privy Council shall upon sight of these presents or the exemplification thereof at the

request of Calveley, Jeffrey and Relfe direct letters to the lord mayor of London, the justices
of the peace of the same city, all sheriffs in the counties and all mayors and head officers of
franchised places commanding them at the next quarter sessions or general assembly within
their several limits to require the justices of the peace therein to appoint one constable in
every hundred, rape, lathe or wapentake at least and one churchwarden in every parish and
command them to be liberal themselves in their contribution and also to write the name of
every parish and every man of ability therein and exhort them to contribute, writing the sum
which every man shall give, the money which they shall receive with the names of the givers
and the names of those that refuse to contribute, and within one month deliver the same to
the justice of the peace of whom they received their charge if he be living or otherwise to
such justices as shall be next dwelling thereabouts; the said justices shall by their warrant call
before them persons refusing to contribute liberally and exhort them to conformity, which
if they shall notwithstanding obstinately refuse then to certify their names and dwelling
places to the Queen or Privy Council; the said justices at the next sessions or general
assembly shall deliver to the said head officers by bill indented to which their hands or marks
shall be set (one part to remain with the justices, the other with the head officer) the money
[*m.* 24]
received and the writing made of the names and money-givers; the head officers shall within
one month after receipt cause the money received and the bills indented to be delivered in
London to Thomas Smythe, a customer of the city, John Heynes, serjeant of the Queen's
catery, and William Heynes, purveyor of her provision of sea fish, (or one of them) at the
house of Smythe, who shall give acquittances thereof and keep the money and bills in a chest
to remain with Smyth under three locks, one key to remain with Smyth, another with the
said John Haynes and another with the said William Heynes; and they shall upon demand
made at Smyth's house deliver the money and bills to Anthony, viscount Mountague, K.G.,
William, lord Cobham, warden of the Cinque Ports and constable of Dover castle, Thomas,
lord Buckhurst, and the said Calveley, Jeffrey and Relfe (or three of them, one of the lords or
his deputy being one), who are appointed surveyors of the work, with power to direct the
work and pay the workmen and of their proceedings therein to certify the Queen or Privy
Council every half-year. At the suit of the bailiff, jurats and commonalty: the said town and
port, being the ancient town of the Cinque Ports and situated on the main sea between the
two points of land called 'the Beachy' and 'the Nasse', 30 miles apart, is well placed and
furnished for defence against the French, for a safe haven for mariners, for the manning of
the navy and for the provision of fish for the Queen's household, the city of London and the
adjoining country; but its pier or harbour always maintained by the inhabitants, has lately
been carried away by the violence of the sea, since when the town is much decayed; divers of
the Privy Council and nobility and divers skilful artificers report that a very good haven may
be made near the port, but the inhabitants by themselves cannot finish so great a work,
which is likely to cost about £4,000. *English.*   By p.s.

    [Printed (in part), from an exemplification, in *Sussex Archaeological Collections,* vol. XIV,
p.84.]

2889.)   27 *Sept.* 1578.   *Baldock.*   Remission for John Smyth, knight, the Queen's
servant, of £508 4*s.*, parcel of £2,508 4*s.* payable by him in redemption of a mortgage on the
manors of Mugdenhaule *alias* Muckedenhaule and Graces in Owting, Hatfeild Peverell and
Little Badewe, co. Essex, and other lands at the lord treasurer's house near the Savoye on 29
Sept. 1578 according to the terms of an indenture, 28 Sept., 19 Eliz.,   [*m.* 25]
between Smyth on the one part and lord Burghley, councillor, treasurer, and William
Cordell, knight, master of the rolls, on the other. Grant also to Smyth of respite of payment
of the remaining £2,000 until 29 Sept. 1579, Smythe entering into a bond of £3,000 for the

payment of the said £2,000 at the Exchequer on the day named; Burghley and Cordell thereupon to regrant the manors and lands to him and cancel the indenture.

For his service. *English.* By p.s.

2890.) 28 *March* 1578. *Gorhambury.* Licence for Dennis Robynson, the Queen's farmer of the ferry of Barton, co. Lincoln, to export from any port in the county of Lincoln 3,000 quarters of barley, beans and pease, at the rate of 1,000 quarters this year and 1,000 in each of the next two years, in English or friendly ships; the usual duties to be paid; amounts shipped to be entered on the back of the licence, that it may be left, when expired, with the customers of the port where the last part shall be shipped; provided that, if the price of barley rises in the next market town to Barton above 12s. a quarter and beans and pease above 11s. a quarter, the licensee shall forbear to use the licence until the same grains shall be sold there at or under the said prices. In consideration that the creek called Barton Haven, whereunto at every tide the Queen's ferry boats of Kyngston upon Hull, Hasell and Barton and other vessels have access, is growing dangerously blocked, and Robynson offers as a condition of a lease of the ferry to undertake the repair and scouring of the haven, which is certified by Robert Tirwhitt, knight, and other commissioners, to be done at the Queen's charge and to be likely to cost £192 6s. 8d. *English.* By p.s.

2891.) 28 *March* 1578. *Gorhambury.* Licence for 10 years for Richard [*m.* 26] Watkyns and James Robertes and the survivor of them to print all such almanacks and prognostications as being allowed by any of the commissioners for causes ecclesiastical shall be printed in England; from 12 May 1581; no others to print the same or any other almanacks or prognostications, or to buy, utter or sell any except such as the licensees shall print, on pain of forfeiture of those printed, bought, uttered or sold contrary to this patent and forfeiture of 12d. for every one, one moiety of which forfeitures shall be to the use of the Crown and the other to the use of the licensees; the master and wardens of the mistery of stationers in London and all others to aid in the execution of this licence. In consideration that by the diligent foresight of Watkins and Robertes many fantastical and fond prophesyings which have been accustomed to be sent forth in former times in almanacks and prognostications are now left unprinted, notwithstanding that divers such yearly come to their hands to be printed. *English.* By p.s.

2892.) 13 *Oct.* 1578. *Chenies.* Licence for Amy Wynter, widow, mother of John Wynter, and Marion his wife to collect alms in the city of Bristowe and the liberties of the same and in all places where they shall travel between this and the said city, for the ransom of John Wynter late of Bristowe, shipwright, a very good workman in his art, who about three years and more ago, sailing in a hulk of Ratclyff into Barbara about true trade of merchandise, was taken captive by the Turks, still remains in Allorochia in Turkey and has been sold three times since, whereby his ransom is amounted to £40 and more. *English.* By p.s.

2893.) 27 *Feb.* 1578. *Gorhambury.* Licence for two years for Richard Kirforde, Richard Selwood, Nicholas Clapp and John Bampton, inhabitants of Charde, co. Somerset, and persons deputed by any of them in writing to [*m.* 27] collect charitable gifts and contributions in all places in the Queen's dominions towards the re-building of the said town, which was wasted by fire about 22 June last, most of the buildings necessary for the cloth trade being destroyed and goods lost to the value of more than £9,000; all archbishops and bishops in England to whom these presents or the exemplification thereof under the great seal shall be shown shall in their several jurisdictions at the request of the licensees appoint such persons as the licensees or one of them shall name and within such limits as to them and the licensees shall be thought best to gather the contributions in every church and parish; the said persons shall yearly within 14 days after Easter and Michaelmas cause to be delivered in London to Robert House and Alexander Everie, clothworkers, dwelling in Breadstreate in the parish of All Hallows, or one of them (or, if it happen that either of them die, then to such persons dwelling in London as the licensees or one of them shall appoint) the moneys collected, with a certificate of the names of contributors and their contributions and dwelling places, deducting to the collectors for portage according to the usual allowance upon payments made to the Queen's use; the moneys to be paid over to George Speake, knight, Humphrey Walrond, Nicholas Wadham and John Brytt, esquires, dwelling in the county of Somerset, and William Symms and William Everie, merchants, inhabitants of Charde, (or two of them), which persons (some of the esquires being always two) the Queen will by her letters appoint to oversee the works and make payment for the same and once every half-year advertise the Queen or Privy Council what shall   [m. 28] have been done; ministers and churchwardens shall use their best endeavours to exhort their parishioners to be liberal and to advise wealthy persons in time of sickness to further the said works by way of legacies. The town has long had a great and most profitable trade in making of woollen cloth, is the 'convenientest' town in the West for people trading between London and Devon and Cornwall and is used for the holding of the assizes in the county. *English*.   By p.s.

2894.)   19 *April* 1578.   Grant to John Lytcott, a gentleman pensioner, of the advowson of the rectory of Wappenham, co. Northampton, for the next vacancy only.   By p.s.

2895.)   23 *April* 1578.   Grant to Nicholas Bacon, esquire, of the wardship and marriage of Anne Dowbbes, daughter and heir of John Dowbbes, with an annuity of £10 from 20 Sept., 19 Eliz., when John died.   By Q.

2896.)   5 *May* 1578.   Pardon for Thomas Duporte for his intrusion into the free chapel of Whithall, Bath and Wells dioc., and its possessions being of the yearly value of £16 10s. and belonging to the Crown by stat. 1 Edw.VI concerning chantries and the like; this patent and the enrolment thereof in the Exchequer to be sufficient warrant to discharge him, his heirs, executors, administrators and farmers from all charges and penalties. The premises were concealed until Duporte, late farmer and tenant of the chapel, gave intelligence of the true estate thereof.   By p.s.

2897.)   23 *April* 1578.   Grant to John Reade, M.A., of a canonry or prebend in the collegiate church of St. Peter, Westminster, void by the death of Humphrey Parkyns.
                                                                    [m. 29]
                                                                    By p.s.

2898.)   26 *April* 1578.   Licence for William Periam, his heirs and assigns to enclose and hold in severalty, for the enlargement or necessary use of his dwelling or otherwise for his convenience, a common way or lane leading from the town of Credie *alias* Credie Perror in the parish of Newton St. Cyres towards the bridge of Credie and the town of Crediton *alias* Kerton, co. Devon, (by and under Periam's dwelling called Fulford there new-built, from the South end or corner of a close of his in the parish of Shobroke on the East of his said dwelling to another way on the West and North of his said dwelling leading from Shobroke towards the said bridge and Crediton by and under the dwelling), and that a new way made by Periam on his ground (from the said South corner of the close on the East of the dwelling between the said close on one side and land of the manor of Shobroke now in the tenure of

James Browne of Shobroke, 'husbandman', on the other as far as Periam's orchard, and thence between the orchard and other demesne lands of Periam's dwelling on either side as far as the said way leading from Shobroke to the bridge and Crediton) may be the common way in place of it; pardon of all offences committed in respect thereof. By an inquisition taken at Crediton before the sheriff of the county on a writ of *ad quod dampnum*, returned in Chancery, it was found that it was not to the damage of the Crown or any other if Periam enclosed the said old way, so that he made a way in its place not far distant; which new way he has now made at great cost.   By p.s.

2899.)   22 *Feb.* 1578.   *Hampton Court.*   Discharge and pardon for Thomas Smythe of all accounts and all demands by the Crown in respect of (1) divers subsidies in the port of London, whereof he was appointed collector during pleasure by patent, 12 June, 1 Eliz., and (2) the new impost on French wine for divers years to Michaelmas 10 Eliz., whereof he was collector; provided that this do not extend to discharge him from any arrears of rents owed to the Queen.

2900.)   24 *Oct.* 1578.   *Chenies.*   Presentation of William Jeninges, M.A., to the rectory of All Saints and St. Gregory in Northampton,   [*m.* 30]
Peterborough dioc.   By p.s.

2901.)   1 *May* 1578.   Presentation of Hugh Lloid, clerk, LL.B., to the perpetual vicarage of Charlbury, Oxford dioc., in the Queen's gift *sede vacante*.   By p.s.

2902.)   30 *Oct.* 1578.   *Chenies.*   Presentation of Hugh Williams, B.A., to the vicarage of Yalding, Rochester dioc.   By p.s.

2903.)   24 *March* 1578.   *Gorhambury.*   Presentation of Edward Bragdon, clerk, to the canonry and prebend of Northmustone in the collegiate church of Sowthwell, York dioc., void by the promotion of John Yonge, S.T.P., to the bishopric of Rochester.   By Q.

2904.)   2 *April* 1578.   *Gorhambury*   Presentation of Thomas Howell, clerk, B.A., to the rectory of Pagglesham, London dioc.   By p.s.

2905.)   10 *March* 1578.   *Gorhambury.*   Presentation of Robert Jackson, clerk, preacher of God's Word, to the rectory of Singlesthorne *alias* Sigleston, York dioc.   By p.s.

2906.)   25 *Feb.* 1578.   Pardon for Richard Gybbins late of the city of Gloucester in the county of the said city, 'tucker', indicted for the theft in the parish of Brookeruppe in the said county of a mare belonging to John Nyblett on 9 Aug., 18 Eliz. (*details given*). By consideration of Robert Bell, knight, chief baron of the Exchequer, and Nicholas Barham, late the Queen's serjeant at law, late justices of assize in the county.

2907.)   7 *Feb.* 1578.   Lease for 21 years to Robert Constable the   [*m.* 31]
younger of the following (*tenants named*)—(1) St. John's chapel, house or hospital in Bondgate next Aysmonderby and a capital messuage called St. John House and land in Bondgate, (2) lands (*named*) in Bondgate, (3) lands in Northe Stayneley, (4) lands in Netherstudley, (5) lands (*named*) by Busshopton, (6) lands in Eveston and (7) lands (*described*) in Bondgate, all in the county of York and once belonging to the said chapel; (8) St. Mary Magdalen's chapel, house or hospital next Rippon and 'le Mansion House *alias* le Hospitall House' and lands next Rippon, (9) lands in Sharrowe and Rippon and (10) lands in Malwath, all in the county of York and once belonging to the said chapel; (11) lands (*named*)

in Melton on the Hill, co. York; (12) a house and grange called Balderby Grange, co. York, and the advowson of Leathley church, co. York, late of Francis Norton and [—] Nevell, attainted of treason; (13) lands (*named*) in the parish of Sheffelde, co. York; (14) lands (*named*) in Whittlewood, co. York; (15) lands (*named*) in Sheffelde; (16) lands (*described*) in Rippon, (17) lands in Newby, (18) lands in Rippon, (19) lands in Netherstudley and (20) lands

[*m.* 32]

in Ilton, all in the county of York and once belonging to St. Mary Magdalen's chapel aforesaid; (21) woods in Wetherby, co. York, once of the hospital of St. John of Jerusalem; (22) a free chapel in Skelton, co. York, and lands given thereto; (23) lands ('Chauntrie Acre') in Bondgate; (24) a free chapel in Netherstudley; (25) lands in Rippon and Bondgate, once of the chantry of Holy Trinity at the high altar in the collegiate church of Rippon; (26) lands (*named*) in Rippon, once of 'Oure Ladye chauntrie' in Scambergate in Rippon; (27) a chantry of two priests founded by John Warrener of Netherstudley in St. Mary Magdalen's chapel aforesaid and lands in Netherstudley and (28) lands (*named*) by Rippon, all once of the said chantry; (29) lands (*named*) in the parish of Adeley, co. York, once of the monastery of Kirkestall *alias* Cristall; (30) lands in Northedalton, co. York; (31) lands in Home Churche in

[*m.* 33]

the parish of Beverley, co. York; (32) lands in Cheriburton, co. York; (33) lands in the parish of Etton, co. York; (34) lands (*named*) in Wetherby, co. York, once of the hospital of St. John of Jerusalem; (35) lands (*named*) in Adeley aforesaid, once of the monastery of Kirkstall; (36) lands in Wetherby in the parish of Spofforth, co. York, once of the hospital of St. John of Jerusalem; (37) lands (*named*) in West Witton next Middleham, co. York; (38) lands (*described*) in the parish of Wighill and Essedick, co. York, once of the monastery of Helaugh; (39) lands (*named*) in the parish of Whixle, co. York, once of the hospital of St. John of Jerusalem; (40) lands (*named*) in Ledes Wodehouse, co. York, given for obits and the like; (41) lands (*named*) in Ledes Wodehouse, (42) lands (*named*) in Hedingley and (43) lands (*named*) in the parishes of Ledes and Adeley, all parcels of the barony of Cookeridge, co. York and once of the monastery of Kirkstall and the priory of Arthington, co. York; (44) a burgage (*described*) in Ledes, once of St. Mary's chantry in Ledes church; (45) lands in Rawclyff, co. York, once of a chantry or chapel in Skelton in the parish of Rippon; (46) woods (*named*) in Darrington, co. York, once of the late college of Holy Trinity in Pontefract, co. York; (47) land in Cloughton, co. York, once of the   [*m.* 34]

late chapel or church of Cloughton; (48) lands in Stanbury, co. York; (49) lands (*named*) in Secrofte, co. York; (50) lands (*described*) in Middleton in Teysdale in the bishopric of Durham, given for lights and the like; and (51) lands in Middleton aforesaid, once of the monastery of Ryvers. With reservations. From Lady Day next. Yearly rents, from the time when he shall enjoy possession, (1) 3*s.* 4*d.*, (2) 5*s.* 8*d.* (*detailed*), (3) 4*s.* 6*d.*, (4) 7*s.* 8*d.* (*detailed*), (5) 8*s.* 4*d.*, (6) 4*d.*, (7) 3*s.* 9*d.* (*detailed*), (8) 12*s.* 6*d.*, (9) 4*s.*, (10) 14*s.*, (11) 21*d.* (*detailed*), (12) 5*s.* 1*d.*, (13) 3*s.* 8*d.*, (14) 3*s.* 10*d.*, (15) 8*s.* 10*d.* (*detailed*), (16) 7*s.* 3*d.* (*detailed*), (17) 7*s.*, (18)3*s.* 6*d.* (*detailed*), (19) 4*s.*, (20) 17*s.* 7*d.* (*detailed*), (21) 18*s.* 8*d.*, (22) 6*d.*, (23) 4*d.*, (24)2*d.*, (25) 2*d.*, (26) (*none specified*), (27) 18*s.* 4*d.* (*detailed*), (28) 2*s.* 5*d.*, (29) 33*s.* 3*d.* (*detailed*), (30) 23*s.* 6*d.*, (31) 2*s.* 6*d.*, (32) 21*d.*   [*m.* 35]

(33) 2*s.* 4*d.*, (34) 7*s.* 10*d.* (*detailed*), (35) 103*s.* 10*d.* (*detailed*), (36) 41*s.* 4*d.*, (37) 64*s.* 4*d.*, (38) 4*s.*, (39) 41*s.* 8*d.*, (40) 3*s.* 6*d.* (*detailed*), (41) 12*d.*, (42) 42*s.* (*detailed*), (43) 83*s.* 9*d.* (*detailed*), (44) 16*d.*, (45) 4*s.* 4*d.*, (46) 2*s.* (47) 15*d.*, (48) 15*s.* 10*d.*, (49) 14*d.* (*detailed*), (50) 3*s.* (*detailed*) and (51) 6*s.* 4*d.* The lessee to make two cuttings only of the woods and at fitting seasons, to enclose them after cutting and to leave sufficient 'lez staddelles' in every acre according to statute.

In consideration that the premises have been concealed and no rents or profits answered therefrom.   By p.s.

2908.)   11 *Feb.* 1578.   Pardon for George Barefoote late of Buckerell,   [*m.* 36] co. Devon, 'yoman'. It was found by an inquisition (*jury named*) taken at Buckerell on 26 June, 19 Eliz., before Gregory Mawrye, a coroner of the county, on the body of Philip Yeames that Barefoote killed Yeames on 24 June, 19 Eliz., at Buckerell in self defence (*details given*).

2909.)   10 *Feb.* 1578.   Pardon of outlawry for William John Thomas late of Huntingdon, co. Hereford, son and heir of John Thomas of Huntyngton, who was put in exigent in the husting of London for non-appearance in the Common Pleas to answer Stephen Vaughan, son and sole executor of Helen Vaughan, late the wife and sole executrix of Richard Vaughan of Harpton, in a plea for payment of £40 and has now surrendered himself to the Fleet prison.

2910.)   10 *Feb.* 1578.   The like for Griffith Payne late of Nantwell, co. Radnor, and David Lloyd ap Hoell late of Llanvyhangell Helegen, co. Radnor, who were put in exigent in the husting of London for non-appearance in the Common Pleas to answer William ap Jevan in a plea of debt of £40 and have now surrendered themselves to the Fleet prison.

2911.)   5 *Feb.* 1578.   The like for Zachary Catchpoll of Erle Stonham, co. Suffolk, 'yeoman', who was put in exigent in the county of Suffolk for non-appearance in the Common Pleas to answer Robert Bowrman in a plea of debt of £20 and has now surrendered himself to the Fleet prison.

2912.)   [—] *Feb.* 1578.   The like for Catherine Lynekre of London, widow, administratix of John Lynekre, who died intestate, which Catherine was put in exigent in the husting of London for non-appearance in the Common Pleas to answer George Hunt, citizen and 'haberdasher' of London, in a   [*m.* 37]
plea for payment of £41 1s. 10d. which on 3 Dec., 18 Eliz., at London she promised to pay him in consideration that he sold to the said John in his lifetime goods to that value, and has now surrendered herself to the Flete prison.

2913.)   10 *Feb.* 1578.   Pardon for Henry Morgan of Saynt Ellyn, co. Cornwall, 'yeoman'. It was found by an indictment taken before John Garrett, coroner of the liberty of Gyllyngham, co. Dorset, at Mocomb, co. Dorset, on 9 Dec., 20 Eliz., on the view of the body of John Morrice, that Morgan killed Morrice in self defence at Motcomb aforesaid on 8 Dec., 20 Eliz. (*details given*).

2914.)   25 *Nov.* 1577.   Pardon of outlawry for Gabriel Cornewall of Hemmyngham *alias* Hevenyngham, co. Suffolk, clerk, who was put in exigent in the county of Buckingham for non-appearance in the Common Pleas to satisfy (1) Thomas Weller in respect of a debt of 100s., and 25s. damages, and (2) Thomas Allen in respect of a debt of 40s., and 25s. damages, recovered in the said court: Weller and Allen have now acknowledged satisfaction and Cornewall has surrendered himself to the Flete prison.

2915.)   25 *Nov.* 1577.   The like for William Hylton late of London *alias* of Hylton, co. Durham, who was put in exigent in the husting of London for non-appearance in the Common Pleas to answer Walter Whalley of Twygmore, co. Lincoln, in a plea of debt of 200 marks and has now surrendered himself to the Flete prison.

2916.)   25 *Nov.* 1577.   The like for Silvester Hayne of Lynne, co. Dorset, merchant, who was put in exigent in the husting of London for non-appearance in the Common Pleas to satisfy William Townerowe, citizen and grocer of London, in respect of a debt of £18, and

40s. damages, recovered in the said court: Townerowe has now acknowledged satisfaction and Hayne has surrendered himself to the Flete prison.

2917.)   27 *Nov.* 1577.   The like for Christopher Golton late of Enderby, co. York, clerk, vicar of Enderby, who was put in exigent in the county of York for non-appearance in the Common Pleas to answer John   [*m.* 38] Thompson (suing both for the Crown and for himself) in a plea for payment of £80 and has now surrendered himself to the Flete prison.

2918.)   28 *Nov.* 1577.   The like for Richard Thymbleby of London and Alice his wife, who were put in exigent in the husting of London for non-appearance in the Common Pleas to answer John Rychardson the elder, administrator of Margaret Rawlynson, widow, intestate, in a plea of trespass by seizure of chattels of the said Margaret in his keeping to the value of £24 16s. 10d., to the retarding of the execution of the said administration and against the peace, and have now surrendered themselves to the Flete prison.

2919.)   18 *Nov.* 1577.   Pardon for John Aron late of Bylston, co. Stafford. It was found by an inquisition taken at Bylston on 26 June, 19 Eliz., before John Gervyse, a coroner in the county, on the body of Richard Pyrrye late of Bylston, 'laborer', that Aron shot Pirrye with 'a handgonne' by misadventure in 'the chappell yarde' at Bylston on 24 June, 19 Eliz., so that he died at Bylston on 25 June (*details given*).

2920.)   25 *Nov.* 1577.   Pardon for Richard Aburne of Tytchmarshe, co. Salop. It was found by an inquisition taken at Tychmershe on 20 March, 19 Eliz., before John Fosbrooke, a coroner in the county, on the body of Marion Tue late of Tytchmershe, 'spynster', servant of Aburne, that   [*m.* 39] Aburne by misadventure killed her at Tytchmershe on 19 March, 19 Eliz. (*details given*).

2921.)   25 *Nov.* 1577.   Pardon of outlawry for William Musgrave late of Haddyngley, co. York, 'yeoman', who was put in exigent in the county of York for non-appearance in the Common Pleas to answer Edward Walker in a plea of trespass and has now surrendered himself to the Flete prison.

2922.)   23 *Nov.* 1577.   Pardon for John Ingram of Redyngton, co. Nottingham, 'laborer'. It was found by an inquisition taken at Redyngton on 1 July, 19 Eliz., before John Samon, a coroner in the county, on the body of John Lowe late of Redyngton, 'laborer', as appears by the tenor of a record of James Dyer, knight, chief justice of the Common Pleas, and Francis Wyndham, serjeant at law, justices of gaol delivery at Nottingham, that Ingram killed Lowe in self defence at Redyngton on 29 June, 19 Eliz., Brian Redferne of Rodyngdon aforesaid, 'husbandman', being the first finder of the body (*details given*).

2923.)   11 *Feb.* 1578.   Pardon of outlawry for John Kever late of Okehampton, co. Devon, and Roger Bowdon late of Belston, co. Devon, 'husbandmen', who were put in exigent in the county of Devon for non-appearance in the Common Pleas to satisfy the Queen for their ransom for a trespass done to Geoffrey Kever whereof they were convicted: they have surrendered themselves to the Flete prison and have satisfied the said Geoffrey in respect of the damages awarded them.

2924.)   12 *Feb.* 1578.   The like for William Undern of Nottyngham, clerk, who was put in exigent in the husting of London for non-appearance in the Common Pleas to answer

Nicholas Plumptree, an attorney of the said court, in a plea of debt of 40s. and has now surrendered himself to the Flete prison.

2925.)   11 *Feb.* 1578.   The like for Thomas Arrundell late of London *alias* of Wotton, co. Kent, who was put in exigent in the husting of London for non-appearance in the Common Pleas to answer John Baker of Sauntor Cosme and Damian of Bleame, co. [—], in a plea of debt of 20 marks and has now surrendered himself to the Flete Prison.   [*m.* 40]

2926.)   22 *April* 1578.   The like for Charles Jackson, who was put in exigent in the husting of London for non-appearance in the Common Pleas (1), by the name of Charles Jackson of Snydall *alias* Snythall, co. York, to answer Robert Cryplyng *alias* Criplyn of York in a plea of debt of £20 and (2), by the name of Charles Jackeson late of Mansefeild Woodhouse, co. Nottingham, to answer William Hammond of Skethyngwell, co. York, in a plea of debt of £6 and has now surrendered himself to the Flete prison.

2927.)   10 *June* 1578.   Pardon for Thomas Aggeborough of Bewdley, co. Worcester, 'boocher'. It is reported by the record of Roger Manwood, a justice of the Common Pleas, and Francis Wyndham, one of the Queen's serjeants at law, and their fellows, justices of gaol delivery of Worcester castle, that he killed Richard Redferne late of Rydnoll in the parish of Kythermyster, co. Worcester, in self defence.

2928.)   1 *June* 1578.   Pardon for Hoell Morgan of Newport, co. Monmouth, 'yeoman'. It is reported by the record of Roger Manwood, a justice of gaol delivery of Monmouth castle, that Morgan killed John Thomas Watkyn in self defence.

2929.)   10 *June* 1578. Pardon for Thomas Pawfreyman (*alias* Palfreyman) of Stanforth, co. Norfolk, 'husbandman'. He was indicted at the sessions of the peace held at Norwich in 'le Sherehowse', before Christopher Heydon, knight, William Buttes, knight, William Paston, Drew Drewry, Ralph Shelton, Thomas Townesend, Henry Doyley, William Heydon, Thomas Gawdye, William Blenerhassett and others, justices of the peace and of oyer and terminer in the county, on 20 May last for the manslaughter of John Ketteryngham by assaulting him at Stanforth on 5 Sept., 19 Eliz., so that he died there on 13 Sept. (*details given*); he pleaded not guilty, and on the following day a jury found that he was not guilty of manslaughter, but killed Ketteryngham in self defence.   [*m.* 41]

2930.)   11 *June* 1578.   Pardon for Richard Fulstowe late of London. He was indicted before Robert Hodgeson, late a coroner of the city, on 21 Feb., 18 Eliz., in the parish of St. Giles without Creplegate in Creplegate ward, London, on the view of the body of James Eaton for the murder of Eaton by assaulting him in Barbycan Strete in the said parish on 17 Feb., 18 Eliz., so that he died in the said parish on 21 Feb., 18 Eliz., (*details given*); which indictment was caused to be brought into the Queen's Bench and Fulstowe surrendered himself to the Marshalsea prison; before Christopher Wraye, knight, chief justice of the Queen's Bench, Martin Bryghowse being associated with him according to statute, Fulstowe pleaded not guilty, and it was found that he killed Eaton in self defence, as has been certified in Chancery by Wraye.

2931.)   14 *June* 1578.   Pardon of outlawry for Simon Wylley late of Newsomme, co. York, also was put in exigent in the husting of London for non-appearance in the Common Pleas to answer Alice Lawsynby, widow, executrix of William Lawsynby, and Thomas Wraye and Alice his wife, co-executrix with the said Alice Lawsynby, in a plea of detinue of a writing indented and has now surrendered himself to the Flete prison.

2932.)   5 *May* 1578.   Pardon for Andrew Levandula late of Newport in the isle of Wight, co. Southampton, 'baker'. It was found at the general gaol delivery of Winchester castle, co. Southampton, held before John Jefferey, knight, chief baron of the Exchequer, and Edmund Anderson, one of the Queen's serjeants at law, and their fellows, justices of gaol delivery, at the said castle on Monday in the second week of Lent last by an inquisition taken at Cosham in the parish of Caresbrooke in the said isle on 22 Aug., 19 Eliz., before Edward Horsey, captain of the isle and coroner there, on the body of Martin Banchett and certified to the said justices that Levandula murdered Banchett at Cosham on 21 Aug., 19 Eliz. (*details given*); he pleaded not guilty and it was found that he killed Banchett in self defence, whereupon he was committed back to the said gaol to await the Queen's grace hereon.

[*m.* 42]

2933.)   29 *April* 1578.   Pardon of outlawry for Philip Aldersaye late of London *alias* of Horton, co. Chester, 'yeoman', who was put in exigent in the husting of London for non-appearance in the Common Pleas to answer Hugh Calveley of Bulkeley, co. Chester, in a plea of debt of £100 and has now surrendered himself to the Flete prison.

2934.)   29 *April* 1578.   The like for Alice Anderson late of London, spinster, who was put in exigent in the husting of London for non-appearance in the Common Pleas to answer William Chappell *alias* Whypple, citizen and skinner of London, in a plea of debt of £12 and has now surrendered herself to the Flete prison.

2935.)   23 *May* 1578.   *Gorhambury.*   The like for Robert Rosse of Ingmanthorpe, co. York, who was put in exigent in the city of York for non-appearance in the Common Pleas to answer Thomas Tanckerd, son and executor of William Tanckerd of Burghbryge, in a plea for payment of £340 and has now surrendered himself to the Fleete prison.

2936.)   19 *June* 1578.   The like for Hugh Ratclyffe late of Nuland next Ayre, co. York, who was put in exigent in the county of York for non-appearance in the Common Pleas to answer William Nelson and John Taylor, both of Nuland, 'yeomen', in a plea for payment of £100 and has now surrendered himself to the Fleete prison.

2937.)   16 *June* 1578.   The like for Richard Lyllyngton late of Yealmeton, co. Devon, clerk, *alias* vicar of Yealmeton, who was put in exigent in the county of Devon and in the city of Exeter for non-appearance in the Common Pleas to answer (1) John Furland, 'yeoman', John Collett, 'maryner', and Baldwin Wolcombe, 'yeoman', all of Newton Ferres, Exeter dioc., and Martin Sterle of Woodley, 'yeoman', administrators of Alfred Holbeton of Newton Ferres, 'husbandman', in a plea for payment of £6 13s. 4d. and (2) Richard Hals *alias* 'Rycharde of Kenneton' [*sic*] in a plea for payment of £8 and has now surrendered himself to the Fleete prison.

2938.)   16 *May* 1578.   *Gorhambury.*   The like for John Pelson late of Stebynheth, co. Middlesex, 'yeoman', who was put in exigent in the   [*m.* 43] husting of London for non-appearance in the Common Pleas to satisfy Simon Edmondes, citizen and goldsmith of London, in respect of £80, and £5 18s. damages, recovered in the said court; Edmondes has now acknowledged satisfaction and Pelson has surrendered himself to the Fleete prison.

2939.)   14 *Feb.* 1578.   The like for William Whyttyngton *alias* Whyttenton late of Natgrave, co. Gloucester, who was put in exigent in the county of Buckingham for non-appearance in the Common Pleas to answer Thomas Pyggott in a plea for payment of 80 sheep and 80 lambs worth 100 marks and has now surrendered himself to the Fleete prison.

2940.)   10 *March* 1578.   *Gorhambury*.   The like for Hugh ap John ap Jevan late of Thysserth, co. Montgomery, 'yeoman', and Robert Gennowe, Robert ap John Cadwalyder and Anthony ap John Cadwalyder, all of London, 'yeoman', who were put in exigent in the husting of London for non-appearance in the Common Pleas to answer John ap Lewys in a plea of debt of 40s. and have now surrendered themselves to the Fleete prison.

2941.)   1 *Oct.* 1578.   The like for John Eden, citizen and merchant taylor of London, who was put in exigent in the husting of London for non-appearance in the Common Pleas to answer Simon Edmondes, citizen and goldsmith of London, in a plea of debt of 200 marks and has now surrendered himself to the Fleete prison.

(Mm. 1d. to 35d. are blank)

2942.)   30 *May* 1578.   Commission to Francis Wylford, Nicholas Sayntleger,   [*m. 36d.*] Thomas Barham, William Aucher and Michael Berysforde, feodary of the county, (or two of them, the feodary being one) to inquire *post mortem* William Lovelace, serjeant at law, in the county of Kent.

   The like to the following, viz.-
2943.)   30 *May* 1578.   George Hastynges, knight, William Cave, Thomas Pagytt and Robert Braham, feodary of the county of Leicester, (or two of them); *p.m.* Thomas Goldeston.
2944.)   3 *June* 1578.   Henry Gates, knight, William Bellases, knight, Thomas Boynton, knight, Richard Aldburghe, Thomas Dowman and Thomas Willyamson (or two of them); *p.m.* Roger Cholmeley.
2945.)   3 *June* 1578.   The same; *p.m.* Jane Cholmeley, widow, late the wife of Roger Cholmeley.
2946.)   4 *June* 1578.   Henry Myldemaye, John Latham, John Glascocke and William Ramme (or two of them); *p.m.* Edward Madyson.
2947.)   10 *May* 1578.   George Turpyn, knight, Adrian Stokes, Edward Lee, Henry Turvyle and Robert Braham, feodary of the county of Leicester, (or two of them); *p.m.* John Wylson.
2948.)   24 *May* 1578.   *Gorhambury*.   George Salkeld, John Myddleton, Richard Dudley, George Gylpyn and William Atkynson (or two of them); *p.m.* Alan Bellyngham.
2949.)   24 *May* 1578.   *Gorhambury*.   Nicholas Bacon, John Hygham and Thomas Andrewes (or two of them); *p.m.* Francis Boldero.
2950.)   2 *Sept.* 1578.   *Ipswich*.   John Foster, kmight, John Foster (esquire), John Selbye, Christopher Lewyn, Thomas Bates and John Lawson (or two of them); *p.m.* Thomas Ilderton.
2951.)   14 *Oct.* 1578.   Henry Wallop, knight, William Bowyer, Thomas Uvedale and Richard Hore (or two of them); *p.m.* John Larymere.
2952.)   11 *Oct.* 1578.   Thomas Penny, M.D., Richard Taylor, M.D., Nicholas Wheler and William Necton, feodary of the city of London, (or two of them); *p.m.* Gerson Hylles.
2953.)   8 *Sept.* 1578.   Charles Walcott, Arthur Salwey, Thomas Staunton and Charles Bowthe (or two of them); *p.m.* George Hopton.
2954.)   12 *Sept.* 1578.   William Clopton, Clement Fysher, Arthur Gregorye and Richard Hall (or two of them); *p.m.* William Starkey.
2955.)   12 *Sept.* 1578.   The same; *p.m.* Julius Nethermyll.

2956.)   26 *Aug.* 1578.   Thomas Morgan, Edward Holte, John Lyle, Arthur Gregorye, John Sergeaunt and Robert Brytten (or two of them); *p.m.* Richard Turnor.

2957.)   3 *Oct.* 1578.   Thomas Dockwraye, Henry Butler, Ralph Ratclyff and Walter Tooke (or two of them); *p.m.* John Alwaye.

2958.)   3 *Oct.* 1578.   Thomas Stevens, Robert Freake, William Grove, Thomas Nooke, Anthony Hynton and Richard Cocke (or two of them); *p.m.* Henry Edes.

2959.)   22 *May* 1578.   Robert Dennys, knight, Thomas Southcott, William Poole, John Harrys and John Eveleygh (or two of them); *p.m.* John Wadham.

2960.)   26 *April* 1578.   Griffith Hampden, Thomas Pyggott, Alexander Hampden and Peter Palmer (or two of them); *p.m.* Edmund Ashefeyld, knight.

2961.)   26 *April* 1578.   Henry Scroope, Ralph Lawson, Thomas Grymston and Thomas Williamson (or two of them); *p.m.* Christopher Wyvell.

2962.)   26 *April* 1578.   William Buttes, knight, Francis Southwell, Robert Bozome and Christopher Dawbeney (or two of them); *p.m.* Thomas Townsend.

2963.)   5 *May* 1578.   Robert Crane, William Pooley, Thomas Edon and Thomas Andrews (or two of them); *p.m.* Francis Clopton.

2964.)   5 *May* 1578.   William Bellasses, knight, John Vavasor, William Myddleton, Christopher Vavasor and Brian Hamond (or two of them); *p.m.* William Atterton.

2965.)   20 *April* 1578.   Thomas Lucye, knight, Fulk Grevyll, knight,   [*m.* 37*d.*] Edward Eglyonbye and Arthur Gregorye (or two of them); *p.m.* John Somervyle.

2966.)   22 *April* 1578.   Benjamin Tycheborne, Richard Beconsawe of Henton and Richard Hore (or two of them); *p.m.* Thomas Shelley of Maplederham.

2967.)   29 *April* 1578.   William Buttes, knight, Francis Southwell, Robert Bozome and Christopher Dawbeney (or two of them); *p.m.* Richard Edwardes.

2968.)   29 *April* 1578.   John Hyckeford, Christopher George, Simon Codryngton and Humphrey Dyke (or two of them); *p.m.* John Somervyle.

2969.)   29 *April* 1578.   Edmund Coles, William Chylde and Gilbert Blunt (or two of them); *p.m.* John Somervyle.

2970.)   29 *April* 1578.   George Peckham, knight, John Cheney, Alexander Hampden, Thomas Lee and Peter Palmer (or two of them); *p.m.* Ralph Lee.

2971.)   16 *April* 1578.   Clement Cysley, John Glascock, Thomas Lodge and William Ram (or two of them); *p.m.* Benjamin Gunston.

2972.)   18 *April* 1578.   William Inglebye, Ralph Hansbye, William Gee and Walter Jobson (or two of them); *p.m.* Robert Dalton.

2973.)   18 *April* 1578.   The same; *p.m.* Ralph Watman.

2974.)   18 *April* 1578.   Robert Aske, Marmaduke Constable, William Inglebye and Walter Jobson (or two of them); *p.m.* Christopher Stevenson.

2975.)   18 *April* 1578.   Edmund Hall, Edward Herne, Edward Combes and Anthony Kyme (or two of them); *p.m.* Simon Lowe.

2976.)   20 *April* 1578.   Francis Molyneux, Francis Manbye, Alexander Hamcotes and Anthony Kyme (or two of them); *p.m.* Richard Dysney.

2977.)   23 *April* 1578.   James Washyngeton, William Barnebye, Gervase Cressye, Roger Portyngton and Humphrey Hanmer (or two of them); *p.m.* Philip Copley.

2978.)   20 *April* 1578.   Thomas Pyggott, John Burgoyne, William Thomas and George Wyngate (or two of them); *p.m.* Robert Jacobbe.

2979.)   28 *March* 1578.   Henry Barkeley, Richard Lygon, Thomas Handford, William Chylde and William Bell (or two of them); *p.m.* John Follyott.

2980.)   7 *April* 1578.   *Gorhambury.*   Arthur Bassett, knight, John Eveleygh, Hugh Wyott and Stephen Braddon (or two of them); *p.m.* William Bellewe.

2981.)   7 *April* 1578.   *Gorhambury.*   William Fytzwilliams, knight, Henry Graye, Richard Cuttes, James Morrice and John Glascocke (or three of them, Glascocke being one); *p.m.* Edward Eldryngton.

2982.)   7 *April* 1578.   *Gorhambury*.   John Trefrye, John Rasheley, John Whythell and Thomas Browne (or two of them); *p.m.* Robert Rasheley.

2983.)   14 *March* 1578.   Thomas Escourte and Christopher George; *p.m.* Maurice Mallett.

2984.)   24 *Feb.* 1578.   William Parteryche, Francis Coolepeper, Francis Kempe and Michael Berysford (or two of them); *p.m.* Walter Hendley.

2985.)   24 *Feb.* 1578.   Gervase Clyfton, knight, Ralph Barton, Thomas Bullock and Humphrey Hanmer; *p.m.* Hugh Armestronge.

2986.)   24 *Feb.* 1578.   William Wynter, knight, Christopher George, Joseph Bayneham and John Maddocke (or two of them); *p.m.* Edward Bell.

2987.)   17 *March* 1578.   *Gorhambury*.   John Follyott, William Childe, Henry Willough-bye, Henry Feylde and Henry Hyckeford (or two of them); *p.m.* William Sparrye.

2988.)   17 *March* 1578.   *Gorhambury*.   The same; *p.m.* Thomas Greve.

2989.)   17 *March* 1578.   *Gorhambury*.   Edward Eglyonbye, Clement Fysher, John Fysher the younger, Henry Jeffereys and Arthur Gregorye (or two of them); *p.m.* John Hunckes.

2990.)   17 *March* 1578.   *Gorhambury*.   James Altham, Edward Turnor and John Glas-cocke (or two of them); *p.m.* Elizabeth Barker.

2991.)   17 *Feb.* 1578.   Thomas Sadler, Thomas Leventhorpe, Thomas Bowles and Walter Tooke (or two of them); *p.m* Edward Chester.

2992.)   17 *Feb.* 1578.   William Watson, Alexander Skynner, Robert Towneley and Anthony Kyme (or two of them); *p.m.* Robert Pynder.

2993.)   17 *Feb.* 1578.   Thomas Skympsher, Thomas Broughton, Matthew Craddock and Richard Repyngton (or two of them); *p.m.* Francis Roos.

2994.)   12 *May* 1578.   John Tracye, knight, Thomas Throgmerton, John Hygford and Christopher George (or two of them); *p.m.* William Lorwynge.

2995.)   1 *May* 1578.   Robert Pyggott, Thomas Staunton and George   [*m.* 38*d.*] Smythe (or two of them); *p.m.* Thomas Poyner.

2996.)   1 *May* 1578.   John Carmynowe, Thomas Mallett, John Harrys, John Trevanyon, William Samuell and Thomas Browne (or two of them); *p.m.* John Vyvyan.

2997.)   1 *May* 1578.   Henry Wallopp, knight, William Kyngesmyll, knight, and Richard Hore (or two of them); *p.m.* Henry Seymor, knight.

2998.)   17 *June* 1578.   John Hygham, Robert Ashefeyld and Thomas Andrews (or two of them); *p.m.* Thomas Sharpe.

2999.)   17 *June* 1578.   Arthur Gregorye, Edward Underhyll, Richard Hall and Edmund Peirs (or two of them); *p.m.* Richard Dalbye.

3000.)   17 *June* 1578.   Thomas Handford, Vincent Coventrey and Thomas Ryccardes (or two of them); *p.m.* Thomas Turnor.

3001.)   12 *June* 1578.   Henry Anderson, Robert Myddleton, Henry Woodryngton, Thomas Baytes and John Lawson (or two of them); *p.m.* Thomas Elderton.

3002.)   12 *June* 1578.   Francis Curson, Thomas Knyveton, Henry Foljambe, Godfrey Foljambe and Anthony Gell (or two of them); *p.m.* John Barker.

3003.)   12 *June* 1578.   George Purefrey, Francis Browne and Robert Braham (or two of them); *p.m.* Richard Wyghtman.

3004.)   12 *June* 1578.   George Stratford, George Rawley, Edward Fysher and Arthur Gregorye (or two of them); *p.m.* Peter Temple.

3005.)   12 *June* 1578.   Simon Musgrove, knight, William Musgrove, Thomas Denton, John Brysco and Henry Tolson (or two of them); *p.m.* Anne Berwyse, widow.

3006.)   16 *June* 1578.   Humphrey Mychell, Edmund Waller and Peter Palmer (or two of them); *p.m.* John Saunders.

3007.)   15 *June* 1578.   James Altham, Richard Barlee, John Glascock and Thomas Bedell (or two of them); *p.m.* Henry Fortescue.

3008.)   14 *June* 1578.   John Lambert, Richard Tompson, Thomas Williamson, Brian Hamond and Cuthbert Pepper (or two of them); *p.m.* John Marshall.

3009.)   3 *June* 1578.   Thomas Gargrave, knight, John Manners, Francis Manbye, Martin Byrkhed and Brian Hamond (or two of them); *p.m.* William Atherton.

3010.)   12 *May* 1578.   William Tooke, William Gerrard, William Necton and William Lee (or two of them); *p.m.* Thomas Castell.

3011.)   9 *June* 1578.   John Cupper and William Ryccardes; *p.m.* Simon Harecourt.

3012.)   9 *June* 1578.   Robert Crane, Thomas Andrews, Thomas Eden and William Pooley (or two of them); *p.m.* Robert Gurdon.

3013.)   18 *June* 1578.   Francis Slyngesbye, Christopher Wansforthe, John Doddesworthe and Thomas Williamson (or two of them); *p.m.* George Clarke.

3014.)   18 *June* 1578.   Richard Bolles, Alexander Skynner, Anthony Kyme and Richard Shutte (or two of them); *p.m.* John Sugar.

3015.)   8 *May* 1578.   Nicholas Arnold, knight, Thomas Porter, knight, Richard Pates, Thomas Atkyns and Christopher George (or two of them); *p.m.* Thomas Robyns.

3016.)   8 *May* 1578.   Clement Cyslee, Israel Ameys, Thomas Barscott and John Glascock (or two of them); *p.m.* Thomas Yale.

3017.)   6 *Feb.* 1578.   Edward Eglyonbye, Thomas Dabrydgecourt and Arthur Gregorye (or two of them); *p.m.* William Wygston, knight.

3018.)   6 *Feb.* 1578.   Nicholas St. John, William Grove, Thomas Stephens and Edward Waldron (or two of them); *p.m.* Thomas Brynde.

3019.)   6 *Feb.* 1578.   Kenelm Dygbye, Henry Skypwythe, Anthony Dygbye and Robert Braham (or two of them); *p.m.* Thomas Payne.

3020.)   6 *Feb.* 1578.   William Watson, Anthony Kyme, Robert Towneley and Alexander Skynner (or two of them); *p.m.* John Bawdrye.

3021.)   6 *Feb.* 1578.   Richard Moore, Robert Chomley, Alexander Skynner and Anthony Kyme (or two of them); *p.m.* Simon Serson.

3022.)   6 *Feb.* 1578.   John Manners, Matthew Hutton, Thomas Metham, Alfred Copley and Brian Hamond (or four of them); *p.m.* Ingram Clyfford, knight.

3023.)   6 *Feb.* 1578.   Thomas Pyggott, John Burgoyne, William Thomas and George Wyngate (or two of them); *p.m.* Richard Jacobbe.

3024.)   6 *Feb.* 1578.   Fulk Grevyll, knight, Edward Eglyonbye and Arthur Gregorye (or two of them); *p.m.* Robert Whodd.

3025.)   6 *Feb.* 1578.   Humphrey Ferrers, Edward Hole, Clement   [*m.* 39*d.*]
Fysher and Arthur Gregorye (or two of them); *p.m.* Thomas Fysher.

3026.)   14 *Jan.* 1578.   Brian Annesley, Francis Kempe, John Fynes and Richard Berysford (or two of them); *p.m.* Christopher Danbye, knight.

3027.)   28 *Jan.* 1578.   John Gardyner, Richard Gadbury, Robert Wrote and William Necton (or two of them); *p.m.* John Reade.

3028.)   25 *Jan.* 1578.   John Eveleygh, Edward Mereddyth, Thomas Heale and Henry Luscombe (or two of them); *p.m.* Richard Saverey.

3029.)   25 *Jan.* 1578.   Henry Scroope, Marmaduke Wyvell, John Doddesworth and Thomas Williamson (or two of them); *p.m.* Adam Tenant.

3030.)   25 *Jan.* 1578.   William Brounker, John Eyre and William Grove (or two of them); *p.m.* Robert Flower.

3031.)   25 *Jan.* 1578.   John Manners, Alfred Copley, William Byrnand, Richard Thompson and Brian Hamond (or two of them); *p.m.* Ingram Clyfford, knight.

3032.)   6 *Dec.* 1577.   *Windsor.*   Thomas Harwood, Edward Eglyonbye, Thomas Dabrydgecourt and Arthur Gregorye (or two of them); *p.m.* Francis Warren.

3033.)   6 *Dec.* 1577.   *Windsor.*   William Buttes, knight, Thomas Croftes and Christopher Dawbeney (or two of them); *p.m.* Thomas Clyfton.

3034.)   6 *Dec.* 1577.   *Windsor.*   John Watkyns, clerk, Edward Cowper, clerk, William Garnons, Thomas Jones, William Bagard and John Parry (or two of them); *p.m.* Walter Lyngen.

3035.)   21 *Nov.* 1577.   William Garnons, George Parry and John Parry (or two of them); *p.m.* Richard Perle.

3036.)   21 *Nov.* 1577.   James Whytney, knight, John Breynton and John Parrye (or two of them); *p.m.* John Baskervyle.

3037.)   21 *Nov.* 1577.   Nicholas Poynes, knight, Henry Poole, Thomas Escourte, Richard Gore and Christopher George (or two of them); *p.m.* William Butler.

3038.)   21 *Nov.* 1577.   John Tracye, knight, Thomas Throgmerton, Christopher George and Thomas Atkyns (or two of them); *p.m.* William Lorwyng.

3039.)   26 *Nov.* 1577.   John Strowde, George Trenchard, Thomas Mullens, Robert Napper and James Sharrocke (or two of them); *p.m.* John, late marquess of Winchester.

3040.)   22 *Nov.* 1577.   Richard Barkeley, knight, William Reade, Thomas Dennys and Christopher George (or two of them); *p.m.* Maurice Sheppard.

3041.)   22 *Nov.* 1577.   Walter Aston, knight, Richard Baggott, Edward Lytleton, Thomas Gresley, Ralph Adderley and Richard Repyngdon (or two of them); *p.m.* Francis Agard.

3042.)   22 *Nov.* 1577.   Richard Barkley, knight, William Reade, Thomas Dennys and Christopher George (or two of them); *p.m.* Henry Lygon.

3043.)   22 *Nov.* 1577.   James Washyngton, Robert Barnebye, Gervase Cressye, Roger Portyngeton and Ralph Barton (or two of them); *p.m.* Philip Copley.

3044.)   22 *Nov.* 1577.   Edward Unton, knight, Hercules Raynsford, Thomas Penyston, John Cupper and Thomas Ryccardes (or two of them); *p.m.* Edmund Harman.

3045.)   22 *Nov.* 1577.   Thomas Meade, serjeant at law, Matthew Bradbury, John Glascocke and Thomas Newman (or two of them); *p.m.* Edward Meade.

3046.)   22 *Nov.* 1577.   Edward Unton, knight, Hercules Raynsford, Thomas Penyston, John Cupper and Thomas Ryccardes (or two of them); *p.m.* Edmund Sylvester.

3047.)   25 *Nov.* 1577.   Thomas Kyme, Anthony Kyme, Robert Towneley and William Roche (or two of them); *p.m.* Brian Curteys.

3048.)   25 *Nov.* 1577.   The same; *p.m.* William Larkes.

3049.)   22 *Nov.* 1577.   Richard Barkeley, knight, Thomas Dennys, William Bassett and Christopher George (or two of them); *p.m.* Thomas Dorney.

3050.)   20 *Nov.* 1577.   George Mallynrey, Robert Harryson, Roger Portyngton, Christopher Copley and Brian Hamond (or two of them); *p.m.* William Frobysher.

3051.)   20 *Nov.* 1577.   Robert Shutt, Francis Hynde, John Hutton and Henry Lawrens (or two of them); *p.m.* Thomas Pyggert.

3052.)   18 *Nov.* 1577.   Henry Capell, Thomas Leventhorpe, Edward Hubbard and John Glascocke (or two of them); *p.m.* lord Morley.

3053.)   22 *Nov.* 1577.   Thomas Andrews, John Bacon and Roger Barbor (or two of them); *p.m.* Leonard Tyllett.

3054.)   23 *Nov.* 1577.   Thomas Uvedale, William Bythell, William Lawrence and Richard Hore (or two of them); *p.m.* Ralph Henslowe.

3055.)   23 *Nov.* 1577.   Benjamin Tycheborne, John Fysher and Richard Hore (or two of them); *p.m.* Richard Knyght.

3056.)   23 *Nov.* 1577.   Richard Rogers, knight, Thomas Moreton, John Skerne and John Shorrocke (or two of them); *p.m.* Thomas Turvyle.   [*m.* 40*d.*]

3057.)   29 *Nov.* 1577.   Hercules Raynsford, Cromwell Lee, Richard Lee, John Cupper and Thomas Ryccardes (or two of them); *p.m.* Lawrence Barrye.

3058.)   29 *Nov.* 1577.   Edward Stradlynge, knight, Henry Lewes, Miles Button and Rice Meyricke (or two of them); *p.m.* Hugh Griffyth.

3059.)   28 *Nov.* 1577.   Francis Kynaston, Richard Prynce and Thomas Staunton (or two of them); *p.m.* Fulk Crompton.

3060.)   28 *Nov.* 1577.   Roger Brereton, Robert Puleston, John Roydon and John Byllett (or two of them); *p.m.* Anthony Gravenor.

3061.) 28 *Nov.* 1577. Henry Wallopp, knight, John Hastynges, Giles Escourte and Richard Hore (or two of them); *p.m.* Catherine, late countess of Huntingdon.

3062.) 28 *Nov.* 1577. William Merynge, knight, Thomas Markeham, Cuthbert Bevercottes and Edmund Thurland (or two of them); *p.m.* John Williamson.

3063.) 28 *Nov.* 1577. Henry Cocke, knight, William Tooke, Henry Conysbye and Walter Tooke (or two of them); *p.m.* James Paver.

3064.) 28 *Nov.* 1577. Hercules Raynsford, Thomas Penyston, John Chylde and Thomas Ryccardes (or two of them); *p.m.* Thomas Wayneman.

3065.) 3 *Feb.* 1578. Ralph Rookesbye, Francis Slyngesbye, Brian Hamond and Thomas Williamson (or two of them); *p.m.* Peter Thomlynson.

3066.) 30 *Jan.* 1578. Francis Harryngton, Anthony Browne, William Rudd and Richard Shutt (or two of them); *p.m.* William Stubbes.

3067.) 30 *Jan.* 1578. James Boyle, John Parry, John Gerry and John Baker (or two of them); *p.m.* John Deyos.

3068.) 30 *Jan.* 1578. William Dounche, Michael Mollens, John Doyley and Thomas Ryccardes (or two of them); *p.m.* Anthony Pollard.

3069.) 3 *Feb.* 1578. William Inglebye, Marmaduke Constable, William Danyell and Walter Jobson (or two of them); *p.m.* Anthony Langdale.

3070.) 30 *Jan.* 1578. Richard Franckeland, Thomas Williamson, Thomas Jackson and John Farley (or two of them); *p.m.* George Conyers of Pynchyngthorpe.

3071.) 30 *Jan.* 1578. Thomas Savell, Thomas Williamson, Robert Nendyke and William Nendyke (or two of them); *p.m.* Francis Dobson.

3072.) 30 *Jan.* 1578. John Tracye, knight, John Hyckford, Charles Brydges and Christopher George (or two of them); *p.m.* Richard Wyggett.

3073.) 30 *Jan.* 1578. Robert Shutt, John Hutton, Richard Auger and John Peppes (or two of them); *p.m.* Edward Slegge.

3074.) 30 *Jan.* 1578. Robert Shutt, Francis Hynde and John Hutton (or two of them); *p.m.* Luke Godfrey.

3075.) 30 *Jan.* 1578. Brian Annesley, Francis Kempe, John Fynes and Michael Berysford (or two of them); *p.m.* David Polhill.

3076.) 30 *Jan.* 1578. Christopher Wyvell, Henry Scroope, Nicholas Gyrdlyngton and Thomas Williamson (or two of them); *p.m.* Peter Maunsell.

3077.) 30 *Jan.* 1578. John Barloe, Alban Stepneth, Erasmus Saunders, John Phillyppes and Hugh Lewes (or two of them); *p.m.* Rice Morgan Bowen.

3078.) 30 *Jan.* 1578. Griffith Whyte, Morgan Phillyppes, John Woogan, John Phillyppes and John Vaughan (or two of them); *p.m.* the said Rice.

3079.) 10 *Feb.* 1578. William Grove, Lawrence Hyde, Edward Lanford and Thomas Sayntbarbe (or two of them); *p.m.* Robert Thytherleygh.

3080.) 10 *Feb.* 1578. William Chylde, Henry Feylde and Henry Hyckford (or two of them); *p.m.* John Chambers.

3081.) 25 *Jan.* 1578. John Glascocke, William Necton and Israel Amyas (or two of them); *p.m.* Edward Randall.

3082.) 12 *Feb.* 1578. William Barnybye, Brian Hamond, Hugh Bethell and William Daynley (or two of them); *p.m.* Thomas Hardwyck.

3083.) 12 *Feb.* 1578. Marmaduke Constable, Marmaduke Therkyll, Marmaduke Lacye and Walter Jobson (or two of them); *p.m.* Walter Cawood.

3084.) 12 *Feb.* 1578. Godfrey Bossevyle, Godfrey Foljambe, Henry Foljambe, Anthony Gell, Edward Berysford and John Longe (or two of them); *p.m.* George Lynacre.

3085.) 15 *Feb.* 1578. John Manners, John Souche, knight, Godfrey Foljambe, Anthony Gell and Robert Fletcher (or two of them); *p.m.* Ingram Clyfford, knight.

3086.) 15 *Feb.* 1578. John Manners, Gervase Clyfton, knight, Anthony Strelley and Humphrey Hanmer (or two of them); *p.m.* the said Ingram Clyfford, knight.

3087.) 15 *Feb.* 1578. Ralph Barton, Humphrey Hanmer, Charles Fytzwilliam, Anthony Brakenburye and William Barwyck (or two of them); *p.m.* William Frobysher.

3088.) 11 *Feb.* 1578. John Glascock, John Rochester and Thomas Bedell (or two of them); *p.m.* George Sache.

3089.) 13 *Feb.* 1578. William Parteryche, Francis Culpepper, [*m.* 41*d.*] Francis Kempe, William Tonge and Michael Berysford (or two of them); *p.m.* John Podadge.

3090.) 11 *Feb.* 1578. Francis Leeke, knight, Godfrey Bossevyle, Francis Curson, Henry Foljambe and Anthony Gell (or two of them); *p.m.* George Selyocke.

3091.) 12 *Feb.* 1578. Richard Warre, Gabriel Warre, John Coles and Richard Farwell (or two of them); *p.m.* William Hoodye.

3092.) 12 *Feb.* 1578. Thomas Morgan, Thomas Lee, Arthur Gregorye and William Baldwyne (or two of them); *p.m.* William Astyll.

3093.) 15 *Feb.* 1578. Thomas Throgmerton, William Bassett and Christopher George (or two of them); *p.m.* Thomas Daunte.

3094.) 13 *Feb.* 1578. Henry Nevyll, knight, Thomas Stafford, Roger Yonge, John Dowlman and Thomas Noke (or two of them); *p.m.* Richard Warde.

3095.) 12 *Feb.* 1578. John Burlacye, William Ryce, Thomas Noke and Peter Palmer (or two of them); *p.m.* Robert Doyley, knight.

3096.) 12 *Feb.* 1578. Godfrey Bossevyle, Henry Foljambe, Anthony Gell and Richard Nedeham (or two of them); *p.m.* John Barker.

3097.) 12 *Feb.* 1578. Thomas Badby, Thomas Andrews, John Bacon and Roger Barbor (or two of them); *p.m.* Leonard Tyllett.

3098.) 12 *Feb.* 1578. Rowland Lacon, Richard Cressett, Edward Corbett, Robert Acton and Thomas Statunton (or two of them); *p.m.* John Baker.

3099.) 12 *Feb.* 1578. Richard Cressett, Edward Corbett and Thomas Staunton (or two of them); *p.m.* William Gatacred.

3100.) 12 *Feb.* 1578. William Hollys, knight, George Nevyll, Ellis Markeham, Thomas Babyngton and Humphrey Hanmer (or two of them); *p.m.* Origenalis Babyngton.

3101.) 3 *June* 1578. Thomas Gargrave, knight, John Manners, Francis Wortley, Martin Byrkhed and Brian Hamond (or two of them); *p.m.* William Atherton.

3102.) 10 *May* 1578. John St. John, William Warneford, Robert Straunge and William Grove (or two of them); *p.m.* Edward Poole.

3103.) 10 *May* 1578. Henry Cocke, knight, William Tooke, William Brockett and Walter Tooke (or two of them); *p.m.* Richard Lee, knight.

3104.) 7 *May* 1578. John Crocker, Christopher George, Simon Coodryngton and William Whytney (or two of them); *p.m.* Anthony Alborowghe.

3105.) 7 *May* 1578. Nicholas Poynes, knight, William Reade, Christopher George and Simon Coodryngton (or two of them); *p.m.* William Ryppe.

(The rest of the dorse is blank.)

PART V

C. 66/1168

3106.) 1 *March* 1578.   Licence for John Marshall, citizen and draper   [*m.* 1] of London, to alienate two messuages, now or late in the several tenures of himself and [—] Culins, one called the Sign of 'le Two Legges' and the other the Sign of the Eagle and Boy, in Watlingstrete in the parish of St. Antholin (*Sancti Antonii*), London, late of Higham Ferris college, co. Northampton, to Alice Barnam, widow. For 28*s.* 11*d.* paid to the Queen's farmer.

3107.) 15 *Feb.* 1578.   The like for Henry Norreis, knight, lord Norreis of Ricott, and William Norreis to alienate the manor and farm of Water Eaton *alias* Eaton Hastinges *alias* Water Hastinges, co. Berks, once of Richard Wenman, knight, with the advowson of Water Eaton church, to John Danvers, knight. For £64 13*s.* 4*d.*

3108.) 1 *March* 1578.   The like for Thomas Gyfforde and Margaret his wife to alienate the manor of Fulbrooke Kynsham and lands in Fulbrooke and Hogshawe, co. Buckingham, to Francis Powre. For 44*s.* 5½*d.*

3109.) 1 *Feb.* 1578.   The like for Joan Lloyd *alias* Yale, widow, late the wife of Thomas Lloyd *alias* Yale, LL.D., Henry Jones, LL.D., Hugh Lloyd *alias* Yale, Roger Lloyd *alias* Yale, David Lloyd *alias* Yale and William Mason, executors of the said Thomas Yale, and Thomas Yale, kinsman and heir of the said Thomas, to alienate a capital messuage called Newberye in Barkinge, co. Essex, lands (*described*) in Barkinge and three messuages by Temple Barr in the parish of St. Clement,   [*m.* 2] co. Middlesex, to Joseph Haynes. For 33*s.* 4*d.*

3110.) 2 *April* 1578.   Pardon of alienation: Richard Becke by indenture, 24 April, 18 Eliz., acquired from William Cockes lands (*described with tenants' names*) in Freisley, co. Warwick. For 7*s.* paid to the Queen's farmer.

3111.) 7 *May* 1578.   The like: Thomas Gyffarde and Margaret his wife by indenture, 12 June, 15 Eliz., acquired from Nicholas West, Francis Powre and Thomas Colwell the reversion of the manor of Fulbrooke Kynsham and of all lands in Hogshawe and Fulbrooke, co. Buckingham, late of the monastery of Kynsham, co. Oxford, (which premises ought after the death of lady Philippa Gyffarde to revert to West, Powre and Colwell by virtue of a bargain and sale made to them by the said Thomas Gyffard) to hold for life in survivorship, with successive remainders to the heirs male of the body of the said Thomas Gyffard, the heirs female of his body and his right heirs. For £6 13*s.* 4*d.*

3112.) 2 *April* 1578.   The like: John Barker by indenture, 18 June, 16 Eliz., acquired from William Whetcrofte the manor of Valens and all lands parcel thereof in Blaxhall and Ashe next Campsey, co. Suffolk, now in the tenure of Henry Cocke and John Cocke as farmers of the manor. For £5.

3113.) 1 *Feb.* 1578.   Licence for Robert Ryche, knight, lord Ryche, to alienate the manor

of Wansted *alias* Waunsted, the park of Wanstede and other lands (*named*) there, the advowson of the rectory of   [*m.* 3]
Wansted and all lands in Woodford, Walthamstoe, Leyton and Ilford, co. Essex, to Robert, earl of Leicester, councillor. For £6 13*s.* 4*d.* paid to the Queen's farmer.

3114.)   4 *March* 1578.   *Gorhambury.*   Pardon of alienation: John Nicholson and Humphrey Broke by indenture, 5 May, 15 Eliz., acquired from Warham Seintleger, knight, a great capital messuage called Sellenger Place in the parish of St. Olave in Sowthwark, co. Surrey. For 60*s.* paid to the Queen's farmer.

3115.)   11 *June* 1578.   The like: Arthur Manwaringe, knight, Robert Corbett, Richard Cotton, Hugh Cholmeley and George Manwaringe in Michaelmas term, 14 Eliz., by fine in the Common Pleas acquired unto them and the heirs of Arthur from John Aston lands in Assheley, Water Eaton and Longnor, common of pasture for 200 sheep in Assheley Heath and free fishery in the water of Asheley Poole, co. Stafford, and lands in Walselowe, co. Salop, (of which premises those in Assheley and Walselowe only are held of the Crown in chief). For £6 13*s.* 4*d.*

3116.)   13 *June* 1578.   The like: Clement Paman the younger in Trinity term, 17 Eliz., by fine in the Common Pleas acquired from Thomas Kytson   [*m.* 4]
and Elizabeth his wife lands in Chevington and Hardgrave *alias* Hargrave, co. Suffolk. For 16*s.*

3117.)   7 *June* 1578.   The like: Edward Heron by fine in the Common Pleas levied in Michaelmas term and granted and recorded in Easter term, 16 Eliz., acquired from Thomas Vyncent and Henry Vyncent lands in Staunford, co. Lincoln, and in the parish of St. Martin *alias* Staunford Bacon, co. Northampton. For £4.

3118.)   1 *May* 1578.   Licence for Thomas Copley, Margaret his wife, George Horniolde and Alice his wife to alienate lands (*named with tenants' names*) in Bredon, co. Worcester, parcel of the demesne lands of the manor of Bredon, and for the same George and Alice to alienate a moiety of certain other demesne lands in Bredon, to Thomas Cockes and Seth Cockes, his son. For 20*s.* paid to the Queen's farmer.

3119.)   16 *April* 1578.   Pardon of alienation: Alexander Rygbye by indenture, 26 Oct., 17 Eliz., acquired from Thomas Moore, citizen and mercer of London, lands (*named with tenant's name*) in Totenham, co.   [*m.* 5]
Middlesex. For £7 paid to the Queen's farmer.

3120.)   1 *May* 1578.   The like: Thomas Randall, citizen and mercer of London, by indenture, 31 Aug., 19 Eliz., acquired from Alexander Rygbye lands (*named*) in Tottenham, co. Middlesex. For £7.

3121.)   1 *March* 1578.   Licence for Edmund Longe to alienate the rectory of Lineham and lands (*named*) in Lyneham, Bradstocke, Clacke, Preston and Westakenham, co. Wilts, to William Baylyff and William Partridge. For £6 9*s.* 4*d.* paid to the Queen's farmer.

3122.)   1 *May* 1578.   The like for Michael Blunte to alienate two third parts of the manor of Heale Poore and of lands in Heale Poore and Mythe, co. Devon, to Edmund Parker. For 20*s.*

3123.)   26 *April* 1578.   The like for Robert Gybbes, Catherine his wife and Anthony Gybbes to alienate the manor of Honyngton, lands in Honyngton, the rectory of Honyngton and the advowson of the vicarage of Honyngton,   [*m.* 6] co. Warwick, to John Bartram and Edmund Porter and the heirs and assigns of Bartram. For £16 13*s.* 4*d.*

3124.)   1 *May* 1578.   The like for William Fytzwilliams, knight, to alienate lands (*named*) in Pinchbeck, co. Lincoln, to Richard Ogle. For 20*s.*

3125.)   1 *May* 1578.   The like for John Constable, knight, to alienate the manor of Hacknes, lands in Hacknes, Silso, Suffeild, Erley and Harwood Dall and the rectory of Hacknes, co. York, to John, lord Darcie, Cuthbert, lord Ogle, Christopher Wraye, knight, chief justice of the Queen's Bench, William Pelham, Thomas Tresham, knight, Robert Dormer, Thomas Farmer and John Chamberlayne and the heirs and assigns of lord Darcie. For £24.

3126.)   1 *May* 1578.   Pardon of alienation: Ambrose Jermyn, knight, bequeathed by his will, 28 March 1577, a moiety of the manor of Caxton, co. Cambridge, to Anthony his fourth son in tail male, with successive remainders in tail male to Robert his eldest son, Ambrose his second   [*m.* 7] son, Edmund his third son, William his younger son and John Jermyn, his brother, with remainder over to the testator; afterwards he died and Anthony entered the premises. For £4 paid to the Queen's farmer.

3127.)   9 *June* 1578.   The like: William Dalison by indenture, 17 April, 15 Eliz., acquired from Archibald Barnard lands (*named with tenants' names*) in Hagnabie, co. Lincoln. For £4 5*s.*

3128.)   9 *June* 1578.   The like: Edward Nevill and Francis Nevyll, his second son, by indenture, 1 Nov., 15 Eliz., acquired from Archibald Barnard lands (*tenants named*) in Sybsey, Stickford, Steepinge and Hagnabie, co Lincoln, and all his other lands in Sybsey, Stickford and Steepinge. For £4 5*s.*

3129.)   9 *June* 1578.   The like: Archibald Barnard by indenture, 7 Nov., 15 Eliz., acquired from Edward Nevill and Francis Nevill, his second   [*m.* 8] son, lands (*tenants named*) in Sybsey, Stickeford, Steepinge and Hagnabie, co. Lincoln, and all other lands in Sybsey, Stickford and Steeping which they late had by bargain and sale of Barnard. For £4 5*s.*

3130.)   6 *June* 1578.   The like: Henry Shawe by a feoffment, 16 June, 15 Eliz., acquired from Edmund Anderson of the Inner Temple, London, part of a pond called Fogwell Ponde in the parish of St. Sepulchre without Newgate, London, (extending on the North from the corner of 'a brickewall' of George Hyde to the West end of the pond and extending on the South from a post newly fixed in the South side of the pond straight across the said corner of the wall to the said West end), which part Anderson purchased from Edmund Clere by a charter of feoffment, 22 May, 13 Eliz. For 13*s.* 4*d.*

3131.)   9 *June* 1578.   The like: Archibald Barmarde by indenture, 6 Nov., 18 Eliz., acquired from William Dalison lands (*named with tenants' names*) in Hagnabie, co. Lincoln. For £4 5*s.*

3132.)   1 *May* 1578.   Licence for John Kecke and John Tomes to alienate lands in Marston Sicca, co. Gloucester, to John Johnson. For   [*m.* 9] 6s. 8d. paid to the Queen's farmer.

3133.)   29 *April* 1578.   The like for Thomas Wrenne and Anne his wife to alienate the manor of Henghton and lands in Henghton, Haddenham, Wilberton, Sutton, Wicham and Wentworth, co. Cambridge, to Robert Peyton and Thomas Ithell, LL.D., and the heirs and assigns of Peyton. For £4 13s. 4d.

3134.)   1 *May* 1578.   The like for Ellis Crymes and Thomas Crymes to alienate two third parts of the manor of Buckland *alias* Buckland Monachorum, of lands in Buckland Monachorum, of the rectory of Buckland Monachorum and of the advowson of the vicarage of Buckland Monachorum, co. Devon, to John Hewes and William Yardley and the heirs and assigns of Hewes to the use of Ellis in tail, with remainder to Thomas in tail, with remainder to the right heirs of Richard Crymes, father of Ellis and Thomas. For £13 6s. 8d.

3135.)   1 *May* 1578.   The like for John Kecke and John Tomes to alienate lands in Maston Sicca, co. Gloucester, to Nicholas Riland and John Ryland, his son. For 26s. 8d.   [*m.* 10]

3136.)   1 *May* 1578.   The like for John Trobridge to alienate lands (*tenant named*) in Knyghtcote in the parish of Brusheford, co. Somerset, to Humphrey Trobridge. For 3s. 4d.

3137.)   30 *May* 1578.   Pardon of alienation: James Hanam by indenture, 18 Aug., 17 Eliz., acquired from Robert Ludlowe lands (*tenant named*) in Horewood in the parish of Horsington, co. Somerset. For 20s. paid to the Queen's farmer.

3138.)   1 *May* 1578.   Licence for Thomas Whetenhall to alienate the manor of Fange and lands in Fange, co. Essex, to Thomas Newman. For 53s. 4d. paid to the Queen's farmer.

3139.)   1 *March* 1578.   The like for Ralph Sheldon and William Childe   [*m.* 11] to alienate lands in Bradway *alias* Bradwayes, co. Worcester, to Robert Logon and William Logon to hold unto the said Robert for life, with remainder to the said William Logon in tail, with remainder to the right heirs of Robert. For 10s.

3140.)   1 *March* 1578.   The like for the same to alienate lands in Bradwaye to Robert Hodges. For 10s.

3141.)   1 *March* 1578.   The like for the same to alienate lands in Bradwaye to Thomas Streche. For 13s. 4d.

3142.)   1 *March* 1578.   The like for the same to alienate lands in Bradwaye to Robert Logon and Thomas Logon to hold unto the said Robert for life, with remainder to the said Thomas Logon in tail, with remainder to the right heirs of Robert. For 10s.

3143.)   1 *March* 1578.   The like for the same to alienate lands in Bradwaye to John Sambege. For 10s.   [*m.* 12]

3144.)   1 *March* 1578.   The like for the same to alienate lands in Bradwaye to Nicholas Hobdaye. For 13s. 8d.

3145.)   1 *March* 1578.   The like for the same to alienate lands in Bradwaye to John Hodges. For 20*s.* 2*d.*

3146.)   1 *March* 1578.   The like for the same to alienate lands in Bradwaye to Nicholas Blabie. For 16*s.* 8*d.*

3147.)   1 *March* 1578.   The like for the same to alienate lands in Bradwaye to Thomas Severne. For 20*s.*

3148.)   1 *March* 1578.   The like for the same to alienate lands in Bradwaye to John Harrys. For 17*s.* 9½*d.*   [*m.* 13]

3149.)   1 *March* 1578.   The like for the same to alienate lands in Bradwaye to Richard Streche, Eleanor his wife, Philip Gardener and Jane his wife to hold unto Richard and Eleanor for their lives, with remainder to Philip and Jane in tail, with remainder to the right heirs of Richard. For 10*s.*

3150.)   1 *March* 1578.   The like for William Sheldon of Wadborowe, Elizabeth his wife, John Richardson the younger and Frances his wife to alienate the manor of Cherington and lands in Cherington, Tyberton and Aston, co. Salop, to William Savage, William Sheldon of Alberton and Reginald Williams and the heirs and assigns of Savage. For £4 8*s.* 11*d.*

3151.)   1 *March* 1578.   The like for Francis Cromwell to alienate lands in Eaton, co. Bedford, to John Webster. For 20*s.*

3152.)   1 *March* 1578.   The like for John Pakington to alienate the manor of Dunriche, with lands in Aston Cynton, Chesham and Wendover, co. Buckingham, to Henry Baldwyn and Richard Baldwyn. For £3 6*s.* 8*d.*   [*m.* 14]

3153.)   1 *March* 1578.   The like for Thomas Scovell and Alice his wife to alienate lands in Hemswourthe, West Hemsworth, Wickhampton, Shapwicke, Tarrant Abbye, Abbye Leynes and Keynston, co. Dorset, to George Turbervyle. For £6 13*s.* 4*d.*

3154.)   20 *Feb.* 1578.   The like for William Button and Ambrose Button to alienate lands in Christenmalford *alias* Christmalford, co. Wilts, to John Danvers, knight. For 23*s.*

3155.)   1 *March* 1578.   The like for Thomas Lee to alienate the tithes of corn and hay of the demesne lands in Donnyngton belonging to the farm of Dynton, co. Buckingham, to John Duncombe and Edward Duncombe. For 20*s.*

3156.)   1 *March* 1578.   The like for John Seyntleger, knight, to alienate lands (*named*) in the parishes of Iddesley and Brodewoodekellye, co. Devon, to Anthony Copleston and William Chapell, merchant. For 46*s.* 8*d.*

3157.)   1 *March* 1578.   The like for Edmund Spratt and Elizabeth his wife to alienate lands in Caldebroke and Madeley, co. Salop, to   [*m.* 15]
Thomas Lokyer. For 13*s.* 4*d.*

3158.)   1 *March* 1578.   The like for George Smethe to alienate the manor of Spynney *alias* Spynnyferme and lands in Snaylewell *alias* Snayleswell, co. Cambridge, to Martin Warren. For 42*s.* 3*d.*

3159.)   16 *April* 1578.   The like for Edward Smythe, Dorothy his wife, Humphrey Meade, Anne his wife, William Preston and Frances his wife to alienate three fourth parts of the manor of Chilwicke and of lands in Chilwick, Seynt Michells, Harpeden, Sandrige and Redborne, co. Hertford, to George Rotheram and William Toock and the heirs and assigns of Rotheram to the use of the said William Preston. For £10.

3160.)   1 *March* 1578.   The like for Humphrey Foster to alienate the manor of Iddesley, co. Devon, to Anthony Copleston the younger and Thomas Chapell the younger to hold one moiety unto each. For 6s. 8d.

3161.)   6 *May* 1578.   Pardon of alienation: Thomas Prediaux in Trinity term, 17 Eliz., by fine in the Common Pleas acquired from Henry   [*m.* 16] Compton, knight, lord Compton, a fourth part of the manor of Nutwell and of lands in Nutwell, Woodberie and Lympston, co. Devon. For £6 paid to the Queen's farmer.

3162.)   7 *May* 1578.   The like: by fine in the Common Pleas in Michaelmas term, 15 Eliz., Adrian Stokes and Anne his wife for them and the heirs of Adrian conveyed to William Hughes and Howell Aprice lands in Langarre and Brodecliste, co. Devon, and they conveyed the same back to Adrian and Anne in tail, with remainder to the right heirs of Anne. For £6.

3163.)   30 *April* 1578.   The like: Matthew Dale and William Webbe by fine in the Common Pleas levied in Trinity term and granted and recorded on the morrow of Martinmas, 19 Eliz., acquired unto them and the heirs of Dale from Thomas Sowth *inter alia* a moiety of the manor of Lamporte Westover and of lands in Lamporte Westover, co. Somerset, to hold to the use of Thomas Sowth, son and heir apparent of the said Thomas, and Martha his wife for life in survivorship, with remainder to the heirs of the body of Thomas the son by her, with remainder to the right heirs of Thomas the father, as appears by an indenture, 20 May, 19 Eliz., between Thomas the father and Thomas the son of the one part and Dale and Webbe of the other leading the uses of the said fine. For £7.

3164.)   1 *March* 1578.   Licence for William Butler to alienate lands in the parishes of St. Paul, All Saints, St. Peter and St. Cuthbert   [*m.* 17] in Bedford, co. Bedford, to William Langhorne, Elizabeth his wife and Robert Langhorne. For 10s. 8d. paid to the Queen's farmer.

3165.)   19 *Feb.* 1578.   The like for Benet Shukburgh and Alice his wife to alienate the manor of Cubbington and lands in Cubbington, co. Warwick, to Nicholas Tewe and John Blackburne to the use of Benet and Alice for life in survivorship and the heirs of their bodies begotten between them, with remainder to the heirs and assigns of Benet. For 33s. 7d.

3166.)   1 *March* 1578.   The like for John Mabbe the elder and Isabel his wife to alienate the manor of Waldeslade *alias* Netherwaldeslade and lands in Waldeslade *alias* Netherwaldeslade, Chetham, Luton and St. Margaret, co. Kent, to William Emes and Catherine his wife and the heirs and assigns of William. For 40s.

3167.)   9 *Feb.* 1578.   Pardon of alienation: Robert Smythe and William Cocke by fine in the Common Pleas levied in Trinity term and granted and recorded one month from Michaelmas, 17 Eliz., acquired unto them and the heirs of Smythe from Richard Rede, knight, and Innocent Rede and Elizabeth his wife the manor of Esthampsted, lands in Esthampsted, Warfyld, Bynfyld and Wynckfyld and the advowson of Esthampsted church, co. Berks, and the manor of Hollwaye and lands in Hollwaie, co. Dorset. For £10 10s. paid to the Queen's farmer.

3168.)   14 *June* 1578.   Lease for life in survivorship to John Coles   [*m.* 18]
and Edmund Coles, his son, with remainder for life to Richard Coles, son of Edmund Coles, John's brother, of the tithes of corn in Fyddington, Aston on Carrante, Walton Cardiff, Southweke and Tredington, parcel of the rectory of Tewkesburie, co. Gloucester, the small tithes, to wit, the tithes of hemp, pigs and piglets in the parish of Tewkesbury, the small tithes both spiritual and personal and oblations of the rectory and parish of Tewkesbury both in Lent and at Easter and on feast days and at marriages and burials in the parish and the tithe barn for the said tithes; yearly rent £44 11s. 5½d.; the lessees to pay yearly to the chaplain called 'le parish preist' in Tewkesbury church £10 for stipend, to the chaplain called 'the secondarie' £8, for bread, wine, wax and incense in the said church and chapel 33s. 4d., for oil and chrism in the same church and chapel 2s. and for the collection and stacking of the said tithes of sheaves and carriage thereof £8. In consideration of the surrender by John of a patent, 14 Jan., 11 Eliz., leasing the premises to him for 21 years from Michaelmas then next at the same rent; and for a fine of £44 11s. 5½d. paid at the Exchequer.   By p.s.

3169.)   2 *Dec.* 1577.   Pardon of alienation: Margaret Browne, widow, by indenture, 17 June, 15 Eliz., acquired from George Whetstone a great house called 'le Three Ankers' in Cheapside in the parish of St. Vedast, London, with all its appurtenances when it was in the occupation of Robert Whetston, deceased, George's father, or his farmers or assigns. For 40s. paid to the Queen's farmer.

3170.)   20 *Dec.* 1577.   Licence for Thomas Gressham, knight, and Anne his wife to alienate lands in Stoughton, Wedmore and Marke and   [*m.* 19]
common of pasture and common of turbary and fuel in moors (*named*) in Wedmore, Marke, Mere and Edington, co. Somerset, to John Councell and William Councell and the heirs and assigns of John. For 5s. 3d. paid to the Queen's farmer.

3171.)   13 *Feb.* 1578.   Pardon of alienation: George Whitestone by indenture, 20 May, 15 Eliz., acquired from Lawrence Barton *inter alia* a great capital messuage called 'le Three Ankers' in Chepeside in the parish of St. Vedast, London. For 20s. paid to the Queen's farmer.

3172.)   1 *March* 1578.   Licence for Henry Cheyne, knight, lord Cheyne, Jane his wife and Thomas Cheyne to alienate the site of the manor of Newhall and lands in Laysdowne in the isle of Shepey, co. Kent, to Richard Lucke the elder and Richard Lucke the younger and the heirs and assigns of Richard the elder to the use of the same Richard and Richard and their heirs and assigns. For £3 13s. 4d. paid to the Queen's farmer.

3173.)   1 *March* 1578.   The like for Edward Stanffeld and Hugh Halsted to alienate lands (*tenants named*) in Ayringden and Ayringden Parke in the parish of Heptonstall, co. York, to Nicholas Halsted and James Stanffeld to the use of the said Edward and Hugh for life in survivorship, with successive remainders to George Halstede, son of Richard Halstede, in tail male, to the heirs male of the body of Isabel Halstede, wife of the said Richard and daughter of the said Edward, and to the right heirs of Edward. For 20s. 11d.

3174.)   17 *April* 1578.   Pardon of alienation: Robert Grene and   [*m.* 20]
Thomas Gaske in Michaelmas term, 15 Eliz., by fine in the Common Pleas acquired unto them and the heirs of Grene from Arthur Robsarte the manors of Oldburye and Wallaxall

alias Langley Wallaxall *alias* Langley and Wallaxall and lands and all tithes and the fairs and markets and other liberties in the said places and Halsowen, co. Salop. For £22 paid to the Queen's farmer.

3175.)	29 *Jan.* 1578.	The like: Walter Hungerforde, knight, and Edward Hungerforde by indenture, 12 Feb., 17 Eliz., acquired unto them and the heirs of Walter from John Duddeley and John Ayscough the manor of Sutton, late of the monastery of Malmesbury, lands in Christmalford, lands (*named*) in the tithing of Foxley, given for a light before the altar in Christmalford church, and lands (*tenant named*) in Sutton, all the county of Wilts, granted *inter alia* to Duddeley and Ayscough by patent, 29 Jan., 17 Eliz. For £25.

3176.)	16 *April* 1578.	The like: Ambrose Jermyn, knight, by his will, 28 March 1577, bequeathed the manor of Westwrattham, co. Norfolk,					[*m.* 21]
inter alia to William Jermyn, his younger son, in tail male, with successive remainders in tail male to Robert the testator's son, Ambrose his second son, Edmund his third son, Anthony his fourth son, John Jermyn, the testator's brother, and Thomas Jermyn, his brother, with remainder over to the testator; afterwards he died and William entered the manor. For £3 6s. 8d.

3177.)	16 *April* 1578.	The like: Ambrose Jermyn, knight, by his will, 28 March 1577, bequeathed the manor of Bacons, co. Essex, *inter alia* to Ambrose his second son in tail male, with successive remainders in tail male to Robert the testator's eldest son, Edmund Jermyn, his third son, Anthony Jermyn, his fourth son, William Jermyn, his younger son, John Jermyn, the testator's brother, and Thomas Jermyn, his brother, with remainder over to the testator; afterwards he died and Ambrose the son entered the manor. For £6.

3178.)	16 *April* 1578.	The like: John Hungerford by a feoffment indented, 10 Dec., 16 Eliz., granted to Edmund Hungerford the manor of Great Rowlerighte and the advowson of the church there, co. Oxford, to hold one moiety in tail male and the other moiety for life, with remainder after his death to Ursula Hungerford, now his wife, for life, with remainder to the heirs male of his body, with remainder over of all the premises to the right heirs of John. For £16.

3179.)	1 *May* 1578.	Licence for John Banckes to alienate lands					[*m.* 22]
(*named with tenants' names*) in Shelford Parva, co. Cambridge, to Robert Frevill. For 46s. 8d. paid to the Queen's farmer.

3180.)	4 *June* 1578.	Pardon of alienation: by fine in the Common Pleas levied on the octave of Candlemas and granted and recorded in the quinzaine of Easter, 15 Eliz., Thomas Lucas, knight, and Mary his wife for them and the heirs of Thomas conveyed to William Markant and John Smythe and the heirs of Markant lands in Crudwell and Chelworthe, co. Wilts, and they by the same fine conveyed them back to Thomas and Mary and the heirs of Thomas. For 38s. 8½d. paid to the Queen's farmer.

3181.)	4 *June* 1578.	The like: Edward Hungerford and Jane his wife by indenture, 20 April, 17 Eliz., acquired unto them and the heirs and assigns of the said Edward from Edward Baynton, knight, the site of the manor of Rowdon and lands (*named with tenants' names*) in Rowdon					[*m.* 23]
and Chippenham, co. Wilts. For 50s.

3182.)	5 *June* 1578.	The like: Matthew Ewyns and Thomas Kelaway in Michaelmas term, 16 Eliz., by fine in the Common Pleas acquired unto them and the heirs of Ewyns from Richard Rogers and Andrew Rogers, his son and heir apparent, lands in Pimperne *alias* Pymperne, co. Dorset. For £6 20d.

3183.)   7 *June* 1578.   The like: John Danvers, knight, and Henry Knyvett, knight, in Easter term, 17 Eliz., by fine in the Common Pleas acquired unto them and the heirs of Danvers from Thomas Wroughton, knight, lands in Littletowne, Byncknoll *alias* Bynoll and Brodehenton, co. Wilts. For 26s. 8d.

3184.)   30 *May* 1578.   The like: William Hanam by indenture, 6 Dec., 14 Eliz., acquired from Charles Zouche and Robert Kemys a moiety of lands (*named*) in the manor of Mershe in the parish of Wyncaulton, co. Somerset. For 20s.   [*m.* 24]

3185.)   1 *March* 1578.   Licence for Thomas Saunders, son and heir of John Saunders, to alienate lands in Stewklye, co. Buckingham, to Thomas Duncombe. For 46s. 8d. paid to the Queen's farmer.

3186.)   1 *March* 1578.   The like for Charles Pagett to alienate lands in Morley called Morley Parke, co. Derby, to Thomas Whinyates and Mary his wife and the heirs and assigns of Thomas. For 4s. 5½d.

3187.)   21 *April* 1578.   Pardon of alienation: by fine in the Common Pleas in the quinzaine of Easter, 15 Eliz., Alexander Balam and Anne his wife for them and the heirs of Anne conveyed to John Balam and Thomas Brampton and the heirs of John *inter alia* lands, parcel of the manor of Northroughton, in Northroughton, Estwinche and Setche, co. Norfolk, late allowed by partition to Alexander, and they by the same fine conveyed them back to Alexander and Anne in tail male, with remainder to the right heirs of Alexander. For £3 paid to the Queen's farmer.

3188.)   21 *April* 1578.   The like: John Dalton by indenture, 30 June, 13 Eliz., acquired from Edward Eldrington, son and heir apparent of Thomas Eldrington, deceased, lands (*named*) in the parish of Abingworth *alias* Abingere, co. Surrey. For 40s.   [*m.* 25]

3189.)   16 *April* 1578.   The like: Henry Becher, Edward Becher and Fane (*Phanus*) Becher by indenture, 30 Oct., 15 Eliz., acquired from William Baxter the reversion of lands (*named with tenants' names*) in Mangerfeild *alias* Magottesfeild, co. Gloucester, which Richard Dennys of Siston, co. Gloucester, late had by bargain and sale of Edward Sherote of the city of Bristowe, 'tayler', by indenture, 15 Feb., 10 Eliz. For 25s.

3190.)   17 *April* 1578.   The like: Thomas Trentham, Richard Hussye, Richard Bagotte, Robert Colliare and Anthony Grene in Easter term, 15 Eliz., by fine in the Common Pleas acquired unto them and the heirs of Trentham from William Deveroux, knight, the manor of Adderston *alias* Atherston and lands in Atherston, Mancetur, Grendon, Meryvale and Whittington, co. Warwick. For £5 6s. 8d.

3191.)   20 *Feb.* 1578.   Licence for Thomas Webbe and Robert Webbe and Eizabeth his wife to alienate the manor of Rode and all the lands in the parish of Rode, cos. Somerset and Wilts, which the said Thomas and Margaret his wife once purchased from John Stowell and Richard Bampfeild to   [*m.* 26]
Nicholas Webbe and John Iles and the heirs and assigns of Nicholas to the use of the said Thomas and Margaret for life in survivorship, with successive remainders to Robert and

Elizabeth and the heirs of Elizabeth by Robert, to the heirs of the body of Elizabeth and to the right heirs of Thomas. For £4 paid to the Queen's farmer.

3192.) 10 *April* 1578. The like for Edward Herdson, citizen and skinner of London, to alienate his portion of the manors of Folkeston, Newton *alias* Newington Fe, Newington Bellowes *alias* Newton Belhous, Walton, Swetton and Tirlingham and of lands in Folkeston, Erpinge, Bartram, Newington Fe, Newington Bellowes, Ackhanger, Wolverton, Damycott, Halton, Walton, Swetton, Cherington, Brensell, Little Bexley, Terlingham and Romney Mershe, co. Kent, to William Ryche and Richard Wisedome. For £11 13*s.* 4*d.*

3193.) 23 *April* 1578. The like for Richard Wisdome and William Riche to alienate a third part of the same manors and lands (*last entry*) to Richard Ravencrofte to the use of Edward Herdson. For £11 13*s.* 4*d.*

3194.) 1 *March* 1578. The like for Thomas Smythe and Isabel his wife to alienate lands in Wheston *alias* Weston, co. Leicester, to Walter Hastinges. For 20*s.*

3195.) 1 *March* 1578. The like for Edmund Smythe and Elizabeth his   [*m.* 27] wife to alienate lands in Stukeley, co. Buckingham, to Richard Brytenell. For 20*s.*

3196.) 1 *March* 1578. The like for Arthur, lord Grey of Wilton, to alienate lands (*named with tenants' names*) in Kedyzam in the parish of Bredstowe and lordship of Wilton, co. Hereford, to Thomas Benet, 'yoman'. For 4*s.* 5*d.*

3197.) 19 *March* 1578. *Gorhambury.* Pardon of alienation: William Norton by indenture, 27 Sept., 18 Eliz., acquired from Stephen Hadnoll lands (*named with tenants' names*) in the parish and lordship of   [*m.* 28] Cleoberye Barnes *alias* Clebury Barnes, co. Salop. For 14*s.* 5*d.* paid to the Queen's farmer.

3198.) 19 *March* 1578. *Gorhambury.* The like: Richard Bisshopp, 'yoman', by indenture, 27 Sept., 18 Eliz., acquired from Stephen Hadnoll lands (*named with tenants' names*) in the parish and lordship of Cleobery Barnes *alias* Clebury Barnes, co. Salop. For 9*s.* 1*d.*

3199.) 20 *Dec.* 1577. Licence for Thomas Gressham, knight, and Anne his wife to alienate lands in Wedmore and Marke and common of pasture and common of turbary and fuel in moors (*named*) in Wedmore, Marke, Mere and Edington, co. Somerset, to William Sachell *alias* Martyn. For 30*s.* 6*d.* paid to the Queen's farmer.

3200.) 27 *Jan.* 1578. The like for John Snell, Jane his wife and Thomas Snell, his son, to alienate lands in Langley and Kington St. Michael, co. Wilts, to Richard Tanner. For 22*s.* 3*d.*

3201.) 13 *Feb.* 1578. Pardon of alienation: George Whiteston by indenture, 20 May, 15 Eliz., acquired from Thomas Harris, citizen and mercer of London, *inter alia* a great capital messuage called 'le Thre   [*m.* 29] Ankers' in Chepeside in the parish of St. Vedast, London. For 20*s.* paid to the Queen's farmer.

3202.) 1 *March* 1578. Licence for Thomas Thornton to alienate lands in Cleoberye Barnes and Cleoberye Mortimer, co. Salop, to Richard Bysshopp. For 36*s.* 6*d.* paid to the Queen's farmer.

3203.)   11 *Feb.* 1578.   Pardon of alienation: George Stratforde and Thomas Spencer in Hilary term, 19 Eliz., by fine in the Common Pleas acquired unto them and the heirs of Stratforde from Edward Andrewe the manor of Westhadden and lands in Westhadden, co. Northampton. For £20 paid to the Queen's farmer.

3204.)   2 *April* 1578.   The like: John Hichcockes by indenture, 28 Jan., 15 Eliz., acquired from Thomas Betterton lands (*tenants named*) in the parish of Astley *alias* Abbottes Astley and in Bridgnorthe (*described*), co. Salop, of the inheritance of Betterton. For 8s.

3205.)   3 *May* 1578.   The like: Henry Luscombe by fine in the Common Pleas levied on the morrow of Ascension and granted and recorded on the morrow of Trinity, 16 Eliz., acquired from Henry, earl of Huntingdon, and Catherine his wife lands in Dipford *alias* Dupford and Dipford Downes, co. Devon, and the advowson of Dipford church.

[*m.* 30]

For £4 9s. 4d.

3206.)   23 *April* 1578.   The like: William Baronsdall of London, M.D., and Thomas Traunsham the elder by indenture tripartite, 28 Oct., 18 Eliz., acquired from John Ayscough *inter alia* lands (*named*) in the parish of Minster in the isle of Sheppey (*Chapei alias Shepei*), co. Kent, and the tithes and profits appertaining thereto to hold to the use of Ayscough and Elizabeth his wife in tail, with remainder to Ayscough and his heirs. For 20s.

3207.)   16 *April* 1578.   The like: Edmund Hungerford etc. as above (no. 3178). *Vacated, because enrolled already on this roll.*

3208.)   31 *May* 1578.   Licence for Arthur Breame to alienate the   [*m.* 31] manor and rectory of Estham with the advowson of the vicarage of Estham, co. Essex, to Edward Stonley for the life of Breame, with successive remainders to Stonley for life, to Daniel Doonne, LL.B., in tail, to William Doonne, M.A., in tail, to William Uvedall the younger in tail, to Henry Uvedall in tail and to the Crown. For £4 paid to the Queen's farmer.

3209.)   1 *Oct.* 1578.   The like for Arthur, lord Grey of Wylton, and Jane Sibyl his wife to alienate lands in Wylton and Bridstowe, co. Hereford, to Richard Cockes. For 4s. 5½d.

3210.)   15 *Nov.* 1578.   Pardon of alienation: Thomas Hele and Stephen Hele, 'yoman', by indenture, 10 May, 16 Eliz., acquired from Henry, earl of Huntingdon, lands (*named with tenants' names*) in the parish of Dipford, co. Devon. For £3 paid to the Queen's farmer.

3211.)   16 *July* 1578.   The like: Thomas Smyth, knight, late one of the Queen's principal secretaries, by indenture, 4 Feb., 19 Eliz., between himself of the one part and Francis Walsingham, knight, James Altham, Henry Archer, Humphrey Michell and John Wood of the other part covenanted that he and every other person seised of (1) the manor of Oveston *alias* Overston, co. Northampton, and (2) the site and demesne lands of Ankerwicke priory, cos. Middlesex, Surrey and Buckingham, the manor of Parmyshe, cos. Middlesex, Surrey and Buckingham, and the site and demesne lands of the priory of St. Andrew, Northampton,   [*m.* 32] should stand seised of (1) to the use of the said Thomas for life, with successive remainders to George Smyth, Thomas's brother, and his heirs for the life of Philippa then Thomas's wife, to Wood in tail male, to the said George in tail male and to the right heirs of George and (2) to the use of the said Thomas for life, with successive remainders to Philippa for life in satisfaction of her dower, to the said George for life, to William Smyth, George's son for life, to the first born son of William for life, to the heirs male of the body of the said first born son, to the second son of William for life, to the heirs male of the body of the said second son, to the third son of William for life, to the heirs male of the body of the said third son, to John Smyth, George's son, for life, to the first born son of John for life, to the heirs male of the body of the said first born son, to the second son of the said John Smyth for life, to the heirs male of the body of the same second son, to the third son of the said John for life, to the heirs male of the body of the same third son, to Clement Smyth, another of George's sons for life, to the first-born son of Clement for life, to the heirs male of the body of the said first born son, to the second son of Clement for life, to the heirs male of the body of the same second son, to the third son of Clement for life and to the heirs male of the body of the same third son, by virtue of which covenant and the statute of uses the said Thomas is seised of all the premises *inter alia* for life with remainders as aforesaid. For £74.

3212.)   1 *Oct.* 1578.   Licence for Thomas Bysshopp and Anne his wife to alienate a third part of a moiety of the manors of Whytfeld, Lytle Pysynge and Wittresham, co. Kent, and of lands in Whytfeld, Lyttle Pysynge and Wyttresham to John Scott and Richard Scott and the heirs and assigns of John. For 100*s.* paid to the Queen's farmer.

3213.)   1 *Oct.* 1578.   The like for Edward Sadler and Anne his wife to alienate lands in Aspley Guyes, co. Bedford, to John Chardge and Thomas Norman and the heirs and assigns of Chardge. For 44*s.* 6*d.*   [*m.* 33]

3214.)   1 *Oct.* 1578.   The like for Robert Thwaytes to alienate lands in the lordship of Dodworthe in the parish of Sylkeston, co. York, to John Ramesden. For 5*s.*

3215.)   17 *Feb.* 1578.   Pardon for Christopher de Monte of London, an alien born, for all offences committed before the present date touching the transportation of gold, silver and treasure into foreign parts contrary to statute.
                    By the keeper of the great seal, by virtue of a patent granted to Ralph Lane.

3216.)   1 *Feb.* 1578.   Manumission of John Wall of Longwart in the parish of Kyngsland, co. Hereford, 'yoman', villein regardant to the Queen's   [*m.* 34]
manor of Leompster, co. Hereford, and John Wall, his son, and Maud Wall, his daughter, and all other his issue. At the suit of Henry Lee *alias* Leae, knight, the Queen's servant, according to a patent, 17 Jan., 17 Eliz.
                    By the keeper of the great seal by virtue of the Queen's warrant.

        The like of the following, viz.—
3217.)   1 *Feb.* 1578.   Robert Cowper of Colnesse in the parish of Felixstowe, co. Suffolk, villein regardant to the manor of Frostenden, co. Suffolk, and John Cowper, Peter Cowper and Robert Cowper, his sons, and Agnes Cooke, wife of Anthony Cooke, Alice Flynt, wife of John Flynt, and Mary Smyth, wife of Geoffrey Smyth, his daughters.
3218.)   1 *Feb.* 1578.   Marian Puntyng, daughter of Alexander Puntyng, deceased, now the wife of William Gosslyng of Bucklesam, co. Suffolk, she being a villein regardant to the manor of Walton, co. Suffolk.
3219.)   26 *Nov.* 1577.   William Elvye *alias* Elwy *alias* Elwyn of Mateshall, co. Norfolk, villein regardant to the manor of Wymondham, co. Norfolk, and Simon Elvye and Thomas Elvye, his sons, and Francis Elvye, Simon's son.
3220.)   26 *Nov.* 1577.   Thomas Elvye of Mateshall, co. Norfolk, villein regardant to the manor of Wymondham, and Edward Elvye, Richard Elvye, George Elvye, Thomas Elvye

and Christopher Elvye, his sons, and Grace Elvye, Catherine Elvye and Rachel Elvye, his daughters.

3221.)   29 *Jan.* 1578.   Richard Wynd the elder of Luston in the parish of Eye, co. Hereford, 'husbandman', villein regardant to the manor of Leompster, co. Hereford, and William Wynde, Richard Wynde, John Winde and Philip Wynde, his sons.

3222.)   29 *Jan.* 1578.   John Powll of Luston aforesaid, 'yoman', villein regardant to the manor of Leompster, and John Powll, Thomas Powll and Richard Powll, his sons.

3223.)   19 *June* 1578.   Thomas Powll of Eyton, co. Hereford, villein regardant to the manor of Leompster, and Thomas Powle and Hugh Powle, his sons, and Elizabeth Powle, his daughter.

3224.)   1 *May* 1578.   Thomas Wall of Byrcher, co. Hereford, son of Thomas Wall, deceased, villein regardant to the manor of Leompster.

3225.)   1 *May* 1578.   Hugh Wynde of Byrryngton in the parish of Eye, co. Hereford, villein regardant to the manor of Leompster.

3226.)   1 *May* 1578.   William Goodyer *alias* Goodethe and John Goodyer *alias* Goodethe of Ivyngton, co. Hereford, sons of John Goodyer *alias* Goodethe the elder, villeins regardant to the manor of Leompster.

3227.)   1 *May* 1578.   Richard Wynd the younger of Luston, co. Hereford, villein regardant to the manor of Leompster, and Richard Wynd, his son.

3228.)   3 *May* 1578.   John Higgyns of Hope, co. Hereford, son of Walter Hyggyns, deceased, villein regardant to the manor of Leompster.

3229.)   14 *Nov.* 1578.   Pardon for Ralph Smyth *alias* Dowsynge late of Fornecott, co. Norfolk, 'tallowchaundler'. At the session of the peace held at Ipswich, co. Suffolk, on 16 Sept., 20 Eliz., before Geoffrey Gylbert and John Moore, bailiffs of the town, and Robert Cutler, John Knappe, John Barker and Ralph Scryvener, justices of the peace in the same, and at the session of gaol delivery held then at the same place before the same bailiffs and justices and before James Ryvett, John Clenche, Robert Cutler, John Barker, William Smart, Richard Kynge, Ralph Scryvener and Austin Parker, justice of gaol delivery, it was presented that he stole a gelding belonging to John Curtes at Ipswich on 27 May, 20 Eliz.; he also broke and entered the dwelling house of John Marchant *alias* Tyler at   [*m.* 35] Framesden, co. Suffolk, and stole 'a sadle' belonging to him.   By p.s.

3230.)   1 *April* 1578.   Licence for Gregory Sprynte and Christian his wife to alienate the manors of Dotton *alias* Docton *alias* Dodington [and] Collaton *alias* Collaton Abbott *alias* Collaton Duke, the free chapel of Dotton, view of frankpledge and the like in Dotton *alias* Dodington [and] Collaton *alias* Collaton Abbott *alias* Collaton Duke and the tithes of corn, hay and wood in Dotton, co. Devon, to William Gorge and William Clarke and the heirs and assigns of Gorge to the use of Gregory and Christian and the heirs of Christian. For £5 18s. 4d. paid to the Queen's farmer.

3231.)   1 *Oct.* 1578.   The like for John Olmestede, citizen and grocer of London, to alienate lands (*named with tenants' names*) in Ging att Stone *alias* Yng att Stone *alias* Ingerstone, co. Essex, parcel of the manor of Yng att Stone and late of the hospital of St. John of Jerusalem, to Robert Johnson, clerk, William Charke of London, clerk, Robert Tayllor, 'haberdasher', and Richard Walter, girdler, citizens of London, to the use of Olmestede until his marriage with Elizabeth Cutlerde, widow, and thereafter of him and Elizabeth and the heirs of their bodies, with remainder to his right heirs. For 20s.

3232.)   29 *July* 1578.   The like for Thomas Thorrisbye to alienate a moiety of the manor of

Caxton, co. Cambridge, and of lands in the said county to Anthony Cage the elder and Anthony Cage the younger. For £5.   [m. 36]

3233.)   23 June 1578.   Gorhambury.   Pardon of alienation: John West, Thomas Lande the elder, Henry Wyatt, Richard Appowell, John Prowse the younger, Leonard Bowbyer, Nicholas Skynner and John Carselake (alias Karselake) by a feoffment indented, 20 Oct., 19 Eliz., acquired from John Waldron the elder inter alia the manor of Daccombe, co. Devon. For £8 paid to the Queen's farmer.

3234.)   1 Oct. 1578.   Licence for Francis Willughbye, knight, and Elizabeth his wife to alienate the manors of Wollaton, Sutton Passeys and Cossalle, co. Nottingham, and lands in Wollaton, Sutton Passeys and Cossall and the manor of Sellinge, co. Kent, and lands in Selling to Fulk Grevyll, knight, and Thomas Bromeley and the heirs and assigns of Grevyll. For £33 2s. 3d. paid to the Queen's farmer.

3235.)   1 May 1578.   The like for John Traves, merchant taylor of London, and Anne his wife to alienate the manor of Aldersbroke and lands in Great Ilford, Little Ilford and Wansted, co. Essex, to Henry, earl of Pembroke. For £3 6s. 8d.

3236.)   1 Oct. 1578.   The like for Thomas Seintpole to alienate the remainder or reversion of a third part of the manor and grange of Hackthorne, of a mill in Hackthorne, co. Lincoln, and of all other lands in Hackthorne and Redborne late of the monastery of Bullington, co. Lincoln, all late purchased by Seintpole from Miles Sandes and others, to Gerard Southill and Henry Southill and the heirs and assigns of Gerard.   [m. 37]
For 20s.

3237.)   1 Oct. 1578.   The like for John Eedes and Margaret his wife to alienate lands in Clyfforde, co. Gloucester, to John Payne and Robert Lever and the heirs and assigns of Payne to the use of John Grevyll, son of Lewis Grevill, in tail, with successive remainders to Charles Grevill, another son of Lewis, in tail, to Peter Grevill, another son of Lewis, in tail and to the right heirs of Peter. For 17s. 10d.

3238.)   15 Nov. 1578.   Pardon of alienation: Thomas Mores, a son of James Mores, late of Farryngdon Parva, co. Berks, by feoffment indented, 9 Sept., 20 Eliz., acquired from his said father the manor of Farryngdon Parva and all his other lands there, except certain lands (tenant named), to hold unto the said Thomas in tail male, with successive remainders to Edmund Mores of Coxwell Magna, co. Berks, in tail, to the first born son of John Mores, son and heir apparent of the said James, in tail male, to the first born son of James Mores the younger, another son of the said James, in tail male, to William Mores, another son of the said James the elder, in tail male and to Thomas in fee simple. For £10 paid to the Queen's farmer.

3239.)   1 May 1578.   Licence for Thomas Powle, clerk of the Crown of the court of Chancery, to alienate lands etc. (named with tenants' names), parcel of the manor of Rayhouse, in the ward of Great Ilford in the parish of Barkinge, co. Essex, purchased by him from Walter   [m. 38]
Morgan by indenture, 28 May, 17 Eliz., to Henry, earl of Pembroke. For 40s. paid to the Queen's farmer.

3240.)   1 Oct. 1578.   The like for Alice Barnham, widow, Stephen Barnham and Anne his wife to alienate a messuage and curtilage in Old Jewry in the parish of St. Mary Colchurche in Chepe ward, London, in the tenure of John Cage, to William Bennett and Richard Bennett to the use of Stephen and Anne and the heirs of the body of Stephen, with remainder to Benet Barnham, Stephen's brother, in tail, with remainder to the right heirs of Francis Barnham, alderman of London. For 26*s.* 8*d.*

3241.)   1 *March* 1578.   The like for Edward Madyson to alienate lands in Nettleton *alias* Nettylton, co. Lincoln, to Robert Turwhitt, knight. For £3 6*s.* 8*d.*

3242.)   3 *Nov.* 1578.   The like for John Talbott and Catherine his wife to alienate lands in Edgemonde *alias* Edgemondon, co. Salop, to William Yonge. For 33*s.* 4*d.*   [*m.* 39]

3243.)   1 *Oct.* 1578.   The like for William Porter the younger to alienate lands (*named*) in Castrope, co. Lincoln, to Thomas Forster and Austin Forster. For £3 6*s.* 8*d.*

3244.)   1 *Oct.* 1578.   The like for Henry Jernegam to alienate the manor of Veales in Fresingfeld, co. Suffolk, to Thomas Barrowe. For £8 13*s.* 4*d.*

3245.)   1 *Oct.* 1578.   The like for Stephen Hadnoll and Margaret his wife to alienate lands (*tenants named*) in Prestopp and Harley, co. Salop, to John Ball the younger. For 13*s.* 4*d.*

3246.)   1 *Oct.* 1578.   The like for Richard Cockes to alienate lands (*named with tenant's name*) in Wylton in the parish of Brydestowe,   [*m.* 40]
co. Hereford, to Robert Swayne, Henry Swayne, James Swaynee and William Tayllor. For 10*s.*

3247.)   18 *June* 1578.   The like for Richard Carewe of Anthonye, co. Cornwall, to alienate the manor of Hackney, a capital messuage in Hackney and all his other lands in Hackney and Totenham or elsewhere, co. Middlesex, to Henry Carey, knight, lord Hunsdon. For £6 19*s.*

3248.)   1 *Oct.* 1578.   The like for George Fermor and Mary his wife to alienate lands in Coscombe and Halstocke, co. Dorset, to Walter Sampson and John Elsdon and the heirs and assigns of Sampson. For £3 13*s.* 9*d.*

3249.)   1 *Oct.* 1578.   The like for Robert Evett and Henry Evett to alienate lands (*named*) in Bisleighe, co. Gloucester, to George Fletcher.

3250.)   1 *Oct.* 1578.   The like for Thomas Coppley and George Horniold to alienate lands in the parish of Bredon, co. Worcester, to Thomas Hyggens.

(The dorse of this roll is blank.)

PART VI

C. 66/1169

3251.)   24 *Feb.* 1578.   Grant to Edward, earl of Lincoln,   [*m.* 1]
K.G., councillor, and Christopher Gowffe, their heirs and assigns of—(1) the tithes of corn,
hay, hemp and flax in Bagworthe, co. Leicester, late leased to John Buxom *alias* Buckeshame
at a yearly rent of £4, once of the monastery of Pré, Leicester, co. Leicester; (2) all lands,
tithes and hereditaments in Shulton and Desforde, co. Leicester, once of the monastery of
Shene, co. Surrey, and leased to George Vincent at a yearly rent of £5; (3) the tithes of corn
of lands (*named with tenant's name*) in the parish of Lawruke, co. Cornwall, late leased to
Anthony Wille at a yearly rent of 53*s.* 4*d.* and once of St. Germans priory, co. Cornwall; (4)
the predial tithes in Bothamsall, all glebe lands and profits belonging to the rectory of
Bothamsall, the tithes and profits belonging to the church of Litleborough Ferrie, all
hereditaments in Litleborough belonging to the rectory of Litleborough aforesaid, a ferry in
Litleborough and a meadow (*named with tenant's name*), all in Bothamsall and Litleborough
Ferry, co. Nottingham, once of Welbecke abbey, co. Nottingham; (5) the rectory of Dore,
co. Hereford, once of Dore priory; (6) all tithes in Callowe, co. Hereford, once of Dynmore
preceptory, co. Hereford; (7) all tithes of hay, altarages and other tithes both privy and other
in Wombridge and Wokenyate or elsewhere in the parish of Wombridge, co. Salop, and all
tithes of demesne lands and other tithes and hereditaments there late in the tenure of William
Abottes at a yearly rent of 46*s.* 8*d.*, once of Wombridge priory; (8) the rectory of Newlande,
co, Worcester, once of the monastery of Malvern Major and now or late in the tenure of
John Robyns at a yearly rent of £3; (9) the rectory of Powicke, co. Worcester, once of the
monastery of Malvern aforesaid and afterwards exchanged with the said earl of Lincoln by
the name of Edward, lord Clynton and Saye; (10) the rectory of Burton in Kendall, co.
Westmorland, late in the tenure of William, late marquess of Northampton, at a yearly rent
of £24 or less, once of the monastery of St. Mary next the walls of York; (11) the chapel or
church of Ranwicke called 'Ranwicke chappell', co. Cumberland, once of the said
monastery of St. Mary and late leased to Thomas Owen at a yearly rent of 13*s.* 4*d.*; (12) the
rectory of Gilkirke, once of the monastery of Kirkestall, co. York, the tithes of corn in
Barlewicke *alias* Barnellwicke, Salterforde *alias* Salterforthe [and] the manor of Barnolf
called 'le Hall demaynes' and the tithes of corn of Brogden *alias* Brockden, the tithes of
wool, lambs, hay and pigs, small and privy tithes and oblations and tithes of mills there, the
tithes of corn of a tenement (*tenant named*) and all other tithes and profits, parcel of the rectory
of Gilkirk, now or late in the tenure of Richard Bannyster, the tithes of corn in Cootes and
all tithes and profits in Gilkirke, Barnollwicke, Salterforde, Brockden, Cotes and elsewhere,
co. York, belonging to the rectory of Gilkirke;   [*m.* 2]
(13) the rectory of Padburie, co. Buckingham, once of the monastery of Shene, co. Surrey,
and once leased to Roger Gifforde; (14) the rectory of Brackley Halfe, co. Northampton,
once of the monastery of Pré, Leicester, late leased to John Ruddinges; (15) the rectory of
Rodeston (*alias* Rodston), co. Northampton, once of the monastery of Shene aforesaid and
now or late in the tenure of [—] Cockes; (16) the rectories of Worle and Kewstocke, co.
Somerset, once of Worspringe priory, co. Somerset, and late leased to John Drewe at a
yearly rent of £12 13*s.* 4*d.*; (17) the rectory of Studley, co. Warwick, once of Studley priory,
co. Warwick, and now or late in the tenure of Thomas Knottesforde; (18) the rectory of
Harlingdon, co. Bedford, once of Dunstable priory and late leased to Anthony Stibbinge;

(19) the rectory of Utterby, co. Lincoln, once of the monastery of Nunormesbye, co. Lincoln, and now or late in the tenure of Thomas Cooke at a yearly rent of £5 6s. 8d.; (20) the rectory of Shernebroke, co. Bedford, once of the monastery of Leicester, now or late in the tenure of John Butler; and (21) the rectory of Canwicke, co. Lincoln, once of the priory of St. Catherine without the walls of Lincoln. Advowsons, bells and lead, except lead in gutters and windows, reserved. To hold   [m. 3]
as of the manor of Estgrenwiche, co. Kent, in socage and rendering yearly—(1) £4; (2) £5; (3) 53s. 4d.; (4) 10s., for the stipend of the curate of Bothamsall church £4 and for the stipend of the curate of Littleborough Ferry church £4 3s. 4d.; (5), (6) (7), (8) and (9) £6 5s. 3d., for the stipend of the curate of Dore church £4 18s., for the stipend of the curate of Callowe church 40s., for the stipend of the curate of Wombridge church 46s. 8d., for the stipend of the curate of Newlande church £5 6s. 8d., for a pension to the bishop of Worcester out of the rectory of Powicke 17s. 9d., for a pension to the dean and chapter of Worcester 13s. 4d. and for a pension out of the possessions of Dore priory to the dean and chapter of Hereford cathedral 6s. 8d.; (10) £9 7s. 8d., for the stipend of the curate of the parish church of Kendall aforesaid £4 12s. 10d., for the stipend of the curate of St. William's chapel in Kirby Kendall aforesaid £4 12s. 10d., for the stipend of the chaplain or curate of the church or chapel of Hewgill *alias* Benthowe £3 6s. 8d. and for proxies to the bishop of Chester 40s.; (11) 13s. 4d. and for the stipend of the curate of the church or chapel of Ranwicke such sums as the said Thomas Owen has paid; (12) £11 3s. 4d. and for the stipend of the curate there £4 13s. 4d.; (13) £6 3s. 6¾d., for proxies to the archdeacon of Buckingham 6s. 8d., for a pension to the bishop of Lincoln 2s. and for proxies to the said bishop 13¼d.; (14) £5 3d., for the stipend of the vicar of Brackley Half £7 13s. 4d. and for a pension to the bishop of Peterborough 9s. 9d.; (15) 33s. 4d. and for the stipend of the curate there £3; (16) 46s. 8d. and for a perpetual pension to the dean and chapter of Wells £10 6s. 8d.; (17) £9 14s. 5½d., for the stipend of the vicar of the parish church there £8, for the salary of a deacon in the same church 40s. and to the archdeacon of Worcester 9s. 8½d.; (18) £8 and for the stipend of the vicar of Harlingdon £4; (19) £5 6s. 8d.; (20) £5 9s. 6d., for a pension to the vicars and choristers of Lincoln cathedral £5 and to the archdeacon of Bedford for proxies 10s. 6d.; and (21) 39s., for a pension to the dean and chapter of Lincoln cathedral £7 16s. 10d., for a pension to the prebendary of Hungate All Saints 26s. 8d., for a pension to the vicars choral in Lincoln cathedral 24s., for a pension to the master and fellows of King's college, Cambridge, 10s. and for proxies and synodals to the archdeacon of Lincoln 10s. 2d. Provided that, if the farmer of any parcel of the premises is bound by any condition in his patent or lease to pay any of the said stipends and the like payable by these presents to curates or others, the grantees shall not be charged therewith during the term of such lease. Issues from Michaelmas last.

In consideration of lands (*named*) in the parishes of Sempringham and   [m. 4]
Poynton, co. Lincoln, conveyed to the Queen by the said earl of Lincoln; and at his suit.
           By Q.

3252.)   15 *March* 1578.   *Gorhambury.*   Lease for 31 years to John Somer, a clerk of the signet, of—(1) a close called Thorpeland, now or late in the tenure of John Freman, in the lordship of Molton, co. Northampton, parcel of the manor of Moulton and of Warwicke and Spencers Landes and leased by patent, 5 July, 8 Eliz., *inter alia* to Henry Fissher and Andrew Fyssher, his son, at a yearly rent of £11 for 31 years from Lady Day 1581 or the termination of a lease thereof by patent, 18 May, 3 Eliz., to Clemence Hasilwood, widow, for 21 years   [m. 5]
from Lady Day then last at the same rent; (2) lands (*named with tenants' names*) in the lordship or manor of Cligin, co. Carmarthen. late of Rice Griffith, attainted, leased by patent of the Exchequer, 26 Jan., 8 Eliz., to Francis Lloyd for 21 years from Michaelmas then last at a yearly rent of 21s. 8d.; (3) demesne lands of Denevor (*named*), co. Carmarthen, parcel of the

principality of South Wales and leased *inter alia* by patent, 12 April, 18 Eliz., to Walter Vaughan for 21 years at a yearly rent of 18*s*. 8*d*.; (4) lands (*tenant named*) in Bonialva, co. Cornwall, parcel of the manor of Bonialvei, once of the monastery of Lanceston, co. Cornwall, and now annexed to the duchy of Cornwall and leased by patent of the Exchequer, 19 Jan., 9 Eliz., to Robert Walles for 21 years at a yearly rent of 26*s*. 8*d*.; (5) a tenement in Horton, parcel of the manor of Stanwell, co. Middlesex, parcel of lands exchanged with the late lord Windesor, leased by patent of the Exchequer, 21 July, 7 Eliz., to Julian Mylles for 21 years at a yearly rent of 68*s*. 10*d*.; (6) lands (*named with tenants' names*) in Hucklescote, Marckfield and Staunton under Bardon, co. Leicester, parcel of the manor of Whitwicke and late of Henry, late duke of Suffolk, attainted; (7) lands (*named with tenants' names*) in Lutterworthe, co. Leicester, parcel of the manor of Lutterworthe and late of the same duke, leased by patent, 5 Nov., 7 Eliz., to John James for 21 years from Michaelmas then last at yearly rents amounting to £6 12*s*. 6½*d*.; (8) lands (*named with tenants' names*) in the lordship of Brecon, parcel of the demesne lands of the manor of Brecon, co. Brecon, late of Edward, duke of Buckingham,   [*m*. 6]

attainted, and leased by patent of the Exchequer, 4 July, 9 Eliz., to Richard Price for 21 years from Michaelmas then next at yearly rents amounting to 59*s*.; (9) lands (*named with tenants' names*) in the parish of Dyvynocke, co. Brecon, late of the same duke and leased to Richard Price by patent of the Exchequer, 4 May, 9 Eliz., for 21 years from Lady Day then last at yearly rents amounting to 26*s*. 10*d*.; (10) lands (*named with tenants' names*) in Beclyffe and Scales, parcel of the lordship of Mocheland, co. Lancaster, late of Henry, late duke of Suffolk, attainted; (11) the house and site of the house of Dominican friars in Newcastle under Lyme, co. Stafford, and lands (*tenants named*), leased by patent of the court of Augmentations, 4 May, 32 Hen. VIII, to John Smythe and Richard Smythe, his son, from Michaelmas then last for life in survivorship rent free; (12) lands (*named*) in Batrichesey and Bridgecourte, once of the monastery of St. Peter, Westminster, and now annexed to the honour of Hampton Courte, and all other lands in Batrichesey and Bridgecourte or elsewhere, co. Surrey, once of the said monastery and leased by patent, 23 Dec., 1 Mary, to William Roper for 30 years at a yearly rent of £5 6*s*. 8*d*.; (13) lands (*tenant named*) in Hartwell, co. Northampton, parcel of the manor of Hartwell, late purchased from William Mariott and now annexed to the honour of Grafton, co. Northampton, and leased by patent, 12 July, 3 & 5 Ph. & Mary, to Robert Parkins for 31 years from Lady Day then last at a yearly rent of £5 4*s*. 4*d*. and by patent, 16 March, 13 Eliz., to Andrew Stevens for 21 years from the termination of Parkins's lease at the same rent; (14) lands (*named with tenant's name*) in Lexden and Yeldham, co. Essex, late of the monastery of St. John, Colchester, and leased by patent, 4 June, 12 Eliz., to Roger Chadwicke at a yearly rent of 30*s*.; (15) lands (*tenants named*) in Gatefulforde, co. York, late of the monastery of St.   [*m*. 7]

Mary next the walls of York and leased by patent of the Exchequer, 11 June, 9 Eliz., to Edmund Metcalf for 21 years at a yearly rent of 74*s*. 1*d*.; and (16) lands in Cheriburton *alias* Northburton, co. York, late of Holy Trinity chantry in the church there and leased to Thomas Bayce *alias* Basse by patent, 20 April, 15 Eliz., for 21 years at a yearly rent of 13*s*. 4*d*. With reservations. From (1) Lady Day 1612 or the termination of the lease to Henry Fissher and Andrew his son, (2), (5) and (7) Michaelmas 1585, (3) Lady Day 1597, (4), (8) and (9) Michaelmas 1588, (12) Michaelmas 1583, (6) and (10) Michaelmas next or the termination of any lease or grant thereof for life or years enduring after that date, (11) the death of the said John Smythe and Richard his son, (13) the termination of the lease to Stevens,   [*m*. 8]

(14) Lady Day 1591, (15) Lady Day 1588 and (16) Lady Day 1594. Yearly rents (1) £11, (2) 21*s*. 8*d*., (3) 18*s*. 8*d*., (4) 26*s*. 8*d*., (5) 68*s*. 10*d*., (6) 55*s*. (*detailed*), (7) £6 12*s*. 6½*d*. (*detailed*), (8) 59*s*., (9) 26*s*. 10*d*., (10) 118*s*. 4*d*. (*detailed*), (11) 45*s*. 5*d*., (12) 106*s*. 8*d*., (13) £5 4*s*. 4*d*., (14) 30*s*., (15) 74*s*. 1*d*. and (16) 13*s*. 4*d*.   By p.s.
For his service.

3253.)   29 *March* 1578.   *Gorhambury.*   Lease for 21 years to John Wilson of the manor of Mauncefeild, co. Nottingham, late of Jasper, once duke of Bedford, and all lands and liberties belonging thereto; as formerly held by John Markham, knight; with reservations of woods, mines and quarries (except mines of stone), chattels of felons and outlaws, and advowsons;   [*m.* 9]
from Lady Day last; yearly rent £17 3s. 5d.   By p.s.

3254.)   28 *March* 1578.   *Gorhambury.*   Lease for 21 years to—(1) Thomas Grene of the site of the manor of Sydlesham, co. Sussex, late of the bishop of Chichester and now in the Queen's hands by act of Parliament, leased by Richard, late bishop of Chichester, to Anne Sawkins, widow, by indenture, 1 June, 30 Hen. VIII, for 61 years from Michaelmas then last at a yearly rent of £12 and now in Grene's tenure; (2) Thomas Master of lands called Great Pocton in the parishes of Newchurche and Hope or either of them in Romney Marshe, co. Kent, late of the late house or hospital of St. Mary in Dover called 'le Massendewe', leased to Master by patent, 11 March, 17 Eliz., for 21 years from Lady Day then next at a yearly rent of £21 6s. 8d.; and (3) Thomas Taylor of the site of the manor of Westwell, co. Kent, late of the archbishopric of Canterbury and in the Queen's hands by act of Parliament, leased by Thomas, late archbishop, to William Brent by indenture, 1 May, 37 Hen. VIII, for 32 years from Michaelmas then next at a yearly rent of £22 and by patent, 26 March, 10 Eliz., to John Fletcher and William Atkinson for 21 years from the expiry of Brent's lease at the same rent. With reservations, including lands etc. (*named*) in Westwell. From (1) the termination of the lease to Anne Sawkins, (2) the termination of the former lease by patent to Master and (3) Michaelmas 1598.   Same rents. The   [*m.* 10]
lessee in the case of (1) and (3) to provide entertainment for the Queen's steward and surveyor coming to the manors to hold courts or make surveys.
     For a fine of £221 6s. 8d. paid at the Exchequer by Grene, Master and Taylor, the tenants or farmers.   By Q.

3255.)   6 *May* 1578.   Lease for 21 years to John Celye, a yeoman of the scullery, of (1) a marsh (*named*) in Little Showburye *alias* Northshowburie, co. Essex, late of Pritwell priory, co. Essex, and (2) lands and marshes   [*m.* 11]
(*named*) in the isle of Fulnesse, co. Essex, late of a chantry in a chapel next the manor of Fulnesse in the said isle; (1) from the termination of a lease thereof by patent, 11 March, 10 Eliz., to Robert Hall *inter alia* for 21 years from Michaelmas then last or the termination of any lease or grant then in force at a yearly rent of 100s.; (2) from Lady Day 1595, having been leased by patent, 28 May, 16 Eliz., to Thomas Eyre for 21 years from Lady Day then last at a yearly rent of £8 (with a covenant that, if the Crown should cause the rectory or vicarage of Fulness to be annexed thereto, the lessee should pay to the rector, vicar or curate £10, to wit, 40s. of increase beyond the rent of £8); yearly rents (1) £5 and (2) 40s.; the lessee to pay yearly to the rector, vicar, minister or curate of Fulnesse for his better support £10. For his service; and for a fine of £25 paid at the Exchequer.   By Q.

3256.)   24 *April* 1578.   Lease for 50 years to James Bettes of lands (*tenants named*) in (1) Weke, co. Southampton, and (2) Chippenham, co. Wilts, all late in the tenure of William Bettes, deceased, late of the chantry of SS. Mary and Catherine in Chippingham; with reservations; from Lady Day last;   [*m.* 12]
yearly rent £10 8d., to wit, for (1) 8s. and (2) £9 12s. 8d. (*detailed*). In consideration of the surrender by James of three patents of the Exchequer, 1 July, 9 Eliz., severally leasing to the said William the premises comprised in (2) for 21 years from Lady Day then last at the same rent; and for a certain   [*m.* 13]
sum paid at the Exchequer.   By p.s.

3257.)   6 *May* 1578.   Lease for 21 years to—(1) William Atkyn of lands (*tenants named*) in Stoddon, parcel of the manor of Stoke *alias* Hartlande, co. Devon, once of the monastery of Hartland, co. Devon; (2) Richard Thekeston of the site of the manor of Helwell, co. Dorset, parcel of the jointure of Catherine, late Queen of England, and lands (*named*) in Helwell, all leased by patent of the Exchequer, 17 Feb., 13 Eliz., to John Payne for 21 years from Michaelmas then last at a yearly rent of 43s. 8d.; (3) Hugh Towers of the rectory of Southferibye, co. Lincoln, once of the monastery of Thorneholme, co. Lincoln, and leased by patent, 26 Nov., 10 Eliz., to Hugh Atkinson for 21 years from Michaelmas then next at a yearly rent of £4 15s. 1d.; (4) Richard More of lands (*tenants named*) in Cokerington, co. Lincoln, once of the monastery of Alvingham, co. Lincoln, and leased by patent, 12 March, 10 Eliz., to William Lee [for 21 years][1] from Michaelmas then·last at a yearly rent of 66s. 8d.; (5) Thekeston aforesaid of lands (*tenants named*) in Giddinges Abbott and elsewhere, co., Huntingdon, parcel of the demesne lands of the manor of Giddinges Abbott and leased by patent, 16 March, 12 Eliz., to William Button for 21 years from Michaelmas then last at a yearly rent of £12 3s. 10d.; and (6) lands (*named with tenant's name*) in Bowes in the lordship of Richemond, co. York, leased by patent of the Exchequer, 24 May, 10 Eliz., to Anthony Alderson for 21 years from Lady Day then last at a yearly rent of 68s. 8d. With reservations. From (1) Michaelmas next or the   [*m*. 14] termination of any lease or grant thereof for life or years heretofore made enduring after that date, (2) Michaelmas 1592, (3) Michaelmas 1588, (4) Michaelmas 1589, (5) Michaelmas 1591 and (6) Lady Day 1590. Yearly rents (1) 12s., (2) 43s. 8d., (3) £4 15s. 1d., (4) 66s. 8d., (5) £12 3s. 10d. and (6) £3 8s. 8d. The lessee to pay yearly £5 for the stipend of a vicar or chaplain in the parish of Southferibye and 4s. 11d. out of the same rectory to the archdeacon of Lincoln for proxies.

     For the service of Thomas Twyste, riding granger and purveyor of the stable, and Anne his wife, laundress for the body, and at their suit; and for fines severally paid by the lessees above-named at the Exchequer of (1) 24s., (2) £4 7s. 4d., (3) £9 10s. 2d., (4) £6 13s. 4d., (5) £24 7s. 8d. and (6) £6 17s. 4d.   By p.s.

3258.)   9 *April* 1578.   *Gorhambury.*   Lease for 31 years to Thomas Gower of—(1) lands (*named*), parcel of the manor of Bulteford, co.   [*m*. 15] Wilts, once of the monastery of Ambresburie, co. Wilts, and leased to William Marsheman and Isabel his wife at a yearly rent of 18s. 4d.; (2) a farm called Slaughter *alias* Slaughter Farme, parcel of the manor of Slaughter, co. Gloucester, once of the monastery of Syon, co. Middlesex, and leased to John Prowse and Silvester Prowse by patent, 24 May, 16 Eliz., for 21 years from Michaelmas then next at a yearly rent of £6 13s. 4d.; (3) lands (*named with tenants' names*) in Insworthe, parcel of the manor of Barton Regis, co. Gloucester, and once of the monastery of St. Peter, Gloucester, leased *inter alia* to Thomas Twynboroughe by patent of the Exchequer, 8 July, 16 Eliz., for 21 years at a yearly rent of 6s. 8d.; (4) lands (*tenants named*) in Lutterworthe, co. Leicester, leased to Richard Robson by patent of the Exchequer, 2 Nov., 7 Eliz., for 21 years from Michaelmas then last at a yearly rent of 40s. 3¾d. (*detailed*), (5) lands (*tenants named*) in Lutterworthe, leased *inter alia* to Henry Shilston by patent of the Exchequer, 2 Nov., 7 Eliz., for 21 years from Michaelmas then last at a yearly rent of 64s. 3d. (*detailed*), and (6) lands (*tenant named*) in Lutterworth aforesaid, leased *inter alia* to Richard Hodgeson by patent of the Exchequer, 1 July, 8 Eliz., for 21 years from Lady Day then last at a yearly rent of 13s. 6d., which premises in Lutterworthe are parcels of the manor of Lutterworthe and late of Henry, late duke of Suffolk, attainted; (7) a moiety of Exilby grange, co. York, parcel of the manor of Exelby, late of the monastery of St. Leonard in York, which moiety was leased to Leonard Snawden by patent of the Exchequer, 13 July,

---

[1] Omitted on the roll, but *cf.* the enrolment of the lease to Lee (*Calendar*, 1566–1569, no. 1527).

6 Eliz., for 21 years at a yearly rent of 43s. 4d.; (8) the other moiety of the same grange, which was leased to Christopher Thripland by patent, 10 July, 3 & 5 Ph. & Mary, for 30 years at a yearly rent of 43s. 4d.; (9) lands (*named with tenants' names*) in Lockington in 'le Estrithinge', co. York, late of Francis Bigod, knight, attainted, and leased to Robert Hodgeson by patent of the Exchequer, 12 Feb., 15 Eliz., for 21 years at a yearly rent of £4; (10) lands (*tenants named*) in Sutton in Galtres, co. York, once of Merton priory, co. York, and leased to Ralph Emson by patent of the Exchequer, 27 Nov., 5 Eliz., for 21 years for several yearly rents of 28s. and 8s.[1]; (11) lands (*tenants named*) in Thornamby, co. York, late of the monastery of Bylande, co. York; (12) lands (*tenants named*) in Austerfeild, parcel of the manor of Bawtrey, co. York, and late of George, late duke of Clarence, attainted, leased to Thomas Wentworth by patent of the Exchequer, 7 March, 11 Eliz., for 21 years from Michaelmas then last at a yearly rent of 26s. 8d.; (13) woods etc.(*named*) in Ledbury Forinseca, co. Hereford, parcel of the manor of Ledbury and late of the bishop of Hereford, leased to John Stretford by Edward, late bishop of Hereford, by indenture, 22 Dec., 29 Hen. VIII, for 60 years at a

[*m.* 16]

yearly rent of 60s.; (14) lands (*named*) in Ewelme, co. Oxford, parcel of the manor of Ewelme and leased to Thomas Carter by indenture of Charles, late duke of Suffolk, for a term of years at a yearly rent of £12 6s. 8d.; (15) a portion of the tithes of corn and hay (*tenant named*) in Derington, co. Lincoln, late of Westminster cathedral, leased to Francis Baldwyn and others by patent, 5 Aug., 12 Eliz., at a yearly rent of 53s. 4d. for 21 years from the end of a former lease to William Horseley; (16) lands (*named with tenants' names*), parcel of the manor of Stapleford, co. Wilts, parcel of the possessions of Henry, late earl of Arundel, exchanged, leased to John Stockman by patent of the Exchequer, 21 April, 12 Eliz., for 21 years from Michaelmas then last at a yearly rent of 40s.; (17) lands (*named*) in Hasilwood, co. Warwick, late of the cathedral or priory of St. Mary, Coventry, and leased to Henry Over by indenture, 8 May, 30 Hen. VIII, for 61 years at a yearly rent of 53s. 4d.; (18) lands (*tenants named*) in Stepingley, co. Bedford, parcel of the manor of Stepingley, late purchased from New College, Oxford, and annexed to the honour of Ampthill, leased to Thomas Style by patent of the Exchequer, 5 Dec., 13 Eliz., for 21 years from Michaelmas then last at a yearly rent of 12s. 2d.; (19) lands (*named*) in Kingesland, co. Hereford, parcel of the demesne lands of the manor of Kingesland and late parcel of lands assigned for the jointure of Catherine, late Queen of England, leased *inter alia* to Anthony Rotsey at a yearly rent of 26s. 4d.; (20) the rectory of Llanvelhadan *alias* Llanlloghayron, co. Montgomery, once of the monastery of Llanlligan, co. Montgomery, and leased to Nicholas Pursell; (21) tithes of corn and hay in Weston, co. Salop, (*tenant named*), once of the monastery of SS. Peter and Paul, Shrewsbury; (22) lands (*named with tenants' names*) in Grantham, co. Lincoln, parcel of the manor of Grantham and once of Jane, late Queen of England; (23) the site of the house of 'le grey fryers' in Carliell, co. Cumberland, leased to Mungo Smythe by patent of the Exchequer, 14 May, 16 Eliz., for 31 years at a yearly rent of 10s. 4d.; and (24) all the tenements in Distaffe Lane, London, late of the monastery of Bitlesden, co. Buckingham, and once leased to Richard Dobbes. With reservations, including all lands in Stepingley and Beckeringes parks, co. Bedford, enclosed, and 200 'younge saplinge okes', to wit, five score for every hundred, in the premises in Ledbury. From (2) and (3) Michaelmas 1595, (4), (5), (6) and (8) Michaelmas 1586, (7) and (10) Lady Day   [*m.* 17]
1584, (9) and (15) Michaelmas 1593, (12), (16) and (18) Michaelmas 1590, (13) the termination of Stretford's lease, after the lessee shall obtain possession, (1), (11), (17), (19), (20), (21), (22) and (24) Michaelmas next or the termination of any lease or grant thereof for life or years heretofore made enduring after that date and (14) and (23) Michaelmas 1604.

[*m.* 18]

---

[1] Reading from the warrant in Chancery Warrants, Series II, (C. 82), 1328; the roll reads '8d.'

Yearly rents (1) 18s. 4d., (2) £6 13s. 4d., (3) 6s. 8d., (4) 40s. 3¾d. (*detailed*), (5) 64s. 3d. (*detailed*), (6) 13s. 6d., (7) 43s. 4d., (8) 43s. 4d., (9) £4, (10) 36s., (11) 36s. (*detailed*), (12) 26s. 7d., (13) 60s., (14) £12 6s. 8d., (15) 53s. 4d., (16) 40s., (17) 53s. 4d., (18) 12s. 2d., (19) 26s. 4d., (20) £4 13s. 4d., (21) 40s., (22) 33s. 4d., (23) 10s. 4d. and (24) 1d.

In consideration of the surrender by Gower of his interest in the office of marshal of the town of Berwick, the fees due therefrom and an annuity of £40, granted to him by patent of Edward VI for life; and for his service.   By Q.

3259.)   1 *April* 1578.   *Gorhambury*.   Lease for 21 years to William Kyttes of the rectory of Swaton, co. Lincoln, late of the monastery of Barlinges, co. Lincoln; with reservations; from the present date; yearly rent £14 13s. 4d.; the lessee to pay 40s. yearly to the dean and chapter of Lincoln cathedral. For a fine of £10 paid at the Exchequer.   By p.s.

3260.)   21 *June* 1578.   Grant for life to George Frith of the office of a gunner in the Tower of London; with wages of 6d. a day from Midsummer last, payable at the Exchequer. On surrender in Chancery by Alexander Harison of a patent, 8 Nov., 1 Eliz., granting him the office for   [*m.* 19]
life.   By Q.

3261.)   24 *Feb.* 1578.   Lease for 21 years to William Ellys of the rectory of Harmeston, co. Lincoln, parcel of the possessions of the late lord Clynton, exchanged; with reservations; from Michaelmas last; yearly rent £29 3s. 4d.; the lessee to pay yearly £7 6s. 8d. to the vicar of Harmeston and 10s. to the archdeacon of Lincoln for proxies and synodals.   By p.s.

3262.)   24 *Feb.* 1578.   Lease for 21 years to Thomas Hanford of woods (*named*) in the parishes of Lurgurshall and Grindon, co. Buckingham,   [*m.* 20]
parcel of a wood called Kingeswood, reputed a member of the forest of Barnewood; with reservations; from Michaelmas last; yearly rent £7 6s. 4d.; the lessee to make three cuttings only of the woods and at fitting seasons, to wit, between Hallowmas and Lady Day, to enclose them after cutting, and to make such cuttings that a moiety of 'le springe' and of all trees 'used to be lopped and topped' are of the age of seven years at least at the end of the term; the patent to be enrolled within six months before the auditor of the county and before the surveyor of woods this side of Trent. In consideration of the surrender in Chancery by Hanford of a patent, 5 July, 11 Eliz., leasing the woods to John Jackson for 21 years from Michaelmas then next at the same rent; and for a fine of £14 12s. 8d. paid at the Exchequer.
By warrant of the commissioners.

3263.)   24 *Feb.* 1578.   Lease for life in succession to William Keblewhite and Francis Keblewhite and Peter Keblewhite, his sons, of the manor of Upton in the parish of Blewberie, co. Berks, late of the monastery of Barmondsey, co. Surrey; with reservations, including the common fine of 2s. 4d. payable by the tenants of the manor at the view of frankpledge, and all courts and perquisites of court and goods of felons and outlaws; from Michaelmas last; yearly rent £14 and heriot the best beast; the lessees to pay all charges, suits and services, except 'lez dismes' due to the Crown; also to provide entertainment for two days and two nights yearly for the steward, surveyor and other officers of the Crown coming to the manor to hold courts or make a survey. In consideration of the surrender by the said William of the interest of John Latton, to whom Robert, abbot, and the convent of the monastery by indenture, 20 Nov.,   [*m.* 21]
21 Hen. VIII, leased the manor (the said common fine reserved) for 60 years from Michaelmas then next at the same rent; and for a fine of £28 paid at the Exchequer.
By p.s.

3264.)   24 *Feb.* 1578.   Lease for life in succession to Henry Skipwithe and William Skipwithe and Francis Skipwithe, his sons, of the rectory of Prestwold, co. Leicester, late of Bullington priory, co. Lincoln; with reservations; from the present date; yearly rent £23; the lessees to pay all charges ordinary and extraordinary. In consideration of the surrender by Henry of a patent, 23 May, 4 Eliz., leasing the rectory to him at the same rent for 30 years from 10 Oct. 1563 or the termination of a lease thereof by conventual indenture to Edward Watson and Edward Watson, his son, for 30 years from 10 Oct. 1533 at the same rent; and for a fine of 40 marks   [*m.* 22] paid at the Exchequer.   By p.s.

3265.)   6 *May* 1578.   Lease for 21 years to Maurice Osberne of Piddington, co. Northampton, of the rectory of Brayfeild, co. Northampton, late of the monastery of St. Andrew in Northampton; with reservations; from Lady Day last; yearly rent £12; the lessee discharged from all other payments. In consideration of the surrender by Osberne of a patent, 8 March, 14 Eliz., leasing the rectory to William Marshe for 21 years from Michaelmas then last at the same rent; and for a fine of £12 paid at the Exchequer.
                                                     By warrant of the commissioners.

3266.)   6 *May* 1578.   Lease for 21 years to Lawrence Goulding and William Dove of lands (*tenants named*) in Hotton Crancewicke, co. York, late of   [*m.* 23] the monastery of Meux, co. York; with reservations; from Lady Day last; yearly rent £5 8s. (*detailed*). In consideration of the surrender by Goulding and Dove of the interest in the premises of William Dodington, to whom they were leased *inter alia* by patent, 16 Oct., 3 Eliz., for 21 years from Michaelmas then last at the same rent; and for a fine of £10 16s. paid at the Exchequer.   By warrant of the commissioners.

3267.)   6 *May* 1578.   Lease for 21 years to Maurice Browne of the demesne lands of the manor of Fordington, co. Dorset, parcel of the duchy of   [*m.* 24] Cornwall; with reservations, including lands (*named*) leased to William Herber by patent, 3 Nov., 13 Eliz., for 21 years at a yearly rent of 43s. 4d.; from Lady Day last; yearly rent £33 14d. In consideration of the surrender by Browne by deed, 4 May, 20 Eliz., enrolled in Chancery, of the interest of Thomas Warren, to whom by patent, 27 March, 16 Eliz., the premises were leased for 21 years at the same rent; for a fine of £66 2s. 4d. paid at the Exchequer by Warren for his lease; and for a fine of £13 6s. 8d. paid at the Exchequer by Browne.   By p.s.

3268.)   6 *May* 1578.   Lease for 21 years to John Catterall and Ralph Thompson of (1) the tithes of corn and hay in Withornesey, co. York, (2) the tithes of corn in Owthorne, co. York, and (3) lands (*named with tenants' names*) in Owthorne, all late of the monastery of Kirkstall, co. York; with reservations; from Lady Day last; yearly rents (1) £5 10s., (2) 100s. and (3) 49s. 4d. (*detailed*). In consideration of the surrender by Catterall and the said Ralph of the interest of John Thompson, to   [*m.* 25] whom the premises were leased by patent, 16 July, 7 Eliz., for 21 years from Lady Day then last at yearly rents of (1) £5 10s., (2) 100s. and (3) 41s. 4d. (*detailed*); and for a fine of £12 19s. 4d. paid at the Exchequer.   By warrant of the commissioners.

3269.)   2 *May* 1578.   Lease for 21 years to William Vaughan, the Queen's servant, and William Deathe of the site and capital messuage of the manor of Bignoures, co. Kent, all lands belonging to the same capital messuage in Derteforde and Wilmington, co. Kent, lands (*named with tenants' names*) in the parish of Stone, co. Kent, a stock of six cows there and two water mills (*named*), all once of Dertford priory; with reservations; from Michaelmas

1591, being the termination of a lease of the premises to Vaughan by patent, 15 Nov., 12 Eliz., for 21 years from Michaelmas then last at a yearly rent of £12; same rent; the lessees to provide entertainment for the Queen's steward and surveyor for two days and two nights

[m. 26]

yearly if they shall so often come to make a survey or hold courts; also to leave the said stock at the end of the term. For Vaughan's service.   By p.s.

3270.)   11 *Feb.* 1578.   Lease for life to Griffith Hampden, with remainder to Ruth Hampden and Mary Hampden, his daughters, for life in survivorship, of (1) all lands in Hyde, Chesham, Stockehamond, Horton, Potterowe and Ballinger, co. Buckingham, parcel of the manor of Missenden, co. Buckingham, once of the monastery of Missenden and afterwards assigned to the present Queen before her accession, and (2) the rectory of Missenden, once of the said monastery; with reservations, including the rents of assize of free tenants in Missenden, Hyde, Stokehamond, Potterowe, Ballinger, Chesham and elsewhere, parcel of the manor, and all customary or copyhold lands; from the present date; yearly rents (1) the premises in Hyde 43s. 5d., Chesham 57s., Stokehamonde 26s. 8d., Horton 40s. and Potterowe and   [m. 27]
Ballinger 47s. 1d. and (2) £12 19s. ¼d., and heriot the best beast or 5 marks; the lessees, in consideration of the diminution of the rent of the rectory, to pay yearly 7s. 7¾d. to the archdeacon of Buckingham for proxy and synodals. In consideration of the surrender by Griffith by deed, 27 Jan., 20 Eliz., enrolled in Chancery, of the interest of Richard Hampden, to whom by patent, 25 June, 2 Eliz., the premises were leased *inter alia* at the same rents for (1) and a yearly rent of £13 6s. 8d. for (2) for 21 years from (1) Michaelmas then last and (2) Michaelmas 1561 or the termination of a lease thereof by indenture of the court of Augmentations, 2 Feb., 32 Hen. VIII, to Richard Grenewaye for 21 years from Michaelmas then last; and for a fine of £40 paid at the Exchequer by Griffith.   By p.s.

3271.)   2 *May* 1578.   Lease for 21 years to Anthony Radclyff, citizen and merchant taylor of London, of a capital messuage called Stapleford Hall, with all lands belonging thereto in Stapleford Abbottes *alias* Stapleford   [m. 28]
Tuke, and lands (*named with tenants' names*) in Stapleford aforesaid, all parcels of the manor of Stapleford Tuke *alias* Stapleford Regis, co. Essex, and late purchased from Brian Tuke, knight; with reservations; from Michaelmas next; yearly rent £21 13s. 4d. In consideration of the surrender by Radcliff of a patent, 2 Aug., 5 & 6 Ph. & Mary, leasing the premises to Thomas Smythe for 30 years from Michaelmas then next at the same rent; and for a fine of £33 6s. 8d. paid at the Exchequer.   By p.s.

3272.)   28 *April* 1578.   Lease for 21 years to Simon Laborne and Robert Laborne of lands (*tenants named*) in Nafferton, co. York, (1) late of   [m. 29]
St. Nicholas's chantry in Wannesfourthe chapel, co. York, and (2) parcel of the manor of Nafferton and of possessions late of Marmaduke Constable, knight, exchanged; with reservations; from Lady Day last; yearly rents (1) 100s. 9d. [*sic*] and (2) 13s. 4d. In consideration of the surrender by Simon and Robert of the interest of Anne Laborne, widow, to whom the premises were leased by patent, 17 June, 6 Eliz., for 21 years from Michaelmas then last at yearly rents of (1) 100s. 5d. and (2) 13s. 4d.; and for a fine of £5 13s. 9d. paid at the Exchequer.   By warrant of the commissioners.

3273.)   16 *April* 1578.   Lease for 21 years to Thomas Tymperley of the manor of Doningworthe, co. Suffolk, late of Thomas, late duke of Norfolk, attainted; with reservations, including wards, marriages, reliefs, escheats, bondmen and their issue and goods of felons and outlaws; from Michaelmas   [m. 30]
last; yearly rent £23. For a fine of £69 paid at the Exchequer.   By p.s.

3274.)   18 *Feb.* 1578.   Lease for 21 years to William Myles Orrey of the rectory of Llannygon, co. Brecon, once of Brecknock priory, co. Brecon; with reservations; from Lady Day next; yearly rent £6 13s. 4d. On surrender by him of a patent, 1 March, 3 Eliz., leasing the rectory to his father, Miles Orrey, for 21 years from Michaelmas then last at the same rent. For a fine of £20 paid at the Exchequer.   By warrant of the commissioners.

3275.)   2 *April* 1578.   *Gorhambury.*   Lease for 50 years to John Francke of all lands now or late in the several tenures of [—] Stockinges, widow, relict of Peter Stockinges, Henry Nosken, 'cowper', Mother Myller, widow, Hubert Anthoney, 'bearebrewer', Tyse Hellybrand, Peter Cowper, Joan Dreywoman, widow, James Williamson, Bernard Harrison, 'cowper', Dericke Johnson, 'cowper', Thomas Hurton, 'taylor', and Rowley Johnson, 'cowper', in Eastsmythefeild next the Tower of London, co. Middlesex, two gardens in Eastsmythefeild now or late in the tenure of Lawrence Foxley (on the East and South sides by a brewhouse called 'le Swanne'), a tenement and 'le backeside' in Hounesdiche in the parish of St. Botolph without Algate, London, late in the tenure of the abbot [*sic*] of Minores, two gardens adjoining and a lodge in Hounesdiche now or late in the several tenures of Walter Assheley and Nicholas Cooke, two tenements lying together in the parish of All Hallows Steyninge, London, now or late in the tenure of Patrick Gallamor, 'frewterer', and Robert Prentyse, 'pewterer', and 5ac. of marsh in Popler Marshe, late occupied by the abbot and convent of the monastery of Graces, parcel of the manor of Popler, co. Middlesex, all once of the monastery of Graces next the Tower of London; with reservations of a tenement called 'the Gonnefownders House' in Hounesdiche in the said parish of St. Botolph late granted to John Owen and Robert Owen for life in survivorship and now or late in the occupation of George Elkyn, a garden called 'Kendalles Yarde' and a little house or lodge enclosed and adjoining the same garden in Eastsmythefeilde (to the East of the graveyard of the monastery of Graces), and a parcel of land called 'the Pyne Aple Garden' in Eastsmythefeild (on 'le Southest' by a garden called 'the Covent Garden' of the monastery of Graces); from Lady Day last; yearly rent £15 16s. 8d. In consideration of the surrender by Francke of a patent, 14 Jan., 14 Eliz., leasing to him and Peter Atkinson the premises, including 'Kendalles Yarde' and the lodge adjoining and 'the Pyne Aple Garden' (but reserving to the Crown 'the Gonnfownders House'), for 21 years from Lady Day then next at the same rent; also   [*m.* 31] because the premises hereby leased are in decay; and in consideration of £100 paid by Francke by the Queen's appointment to William Powell, serving in the wars in Ireland, to whom the said sum was by her special grace granted for his service.   By p.s.

3276.)   24 *April* 1578.   Lease for 21 years to William Hill the   [*m.* 32] younger of (1) the rectory of Pannall, co. York, late of the house of friars of St. Robert next Knaresboroughe in the archdeaconry of Richemond, co. York, and (2) the tithes of corn and hay in Willesdale, co. York, parcel of the rectory of Kirkbie Fletham, co. York, late parcel of the preceptory of Mount St. John the Baptist, co. York, and late of the hospital of St. John of Jerusalem; with reservations; from Lady Day last; yearly rents (1) £10 6s. and (2) 20s.; the lessee to pay yearly 100s. to the vicar of Pannall for his stipend. In consideration of the surrender by Hill of a patent, 8 July, 8 Eliz., leasing the premises to William Clopton for 21 years from Lady Day then last at the same rents; and for a fine of £22 12s. paid at the Exchequer.   By warrant of the commissioners.

3277.)   1 *May* 1578.   Grant to Robert Pister of the wardship and marriage of Richard Enderby, son and heir of James Enderby; with an annuity of 40s. from 18 June, 7 Eliz., when James died. Yearly value of the   [*m.* 33] inheritance £3.   By Q.

3278.)   30 *April* 1578.   Grant to Anthony Kerle and Richard Kearle, clerk of the wardship and marriage of John Kerle, son and heir of Thomas Kerle; with an annuity of £6 13s. 4d. from 30 July, 19 Eliz., when Thomas died.   By Q.

3279.)   30 *April* 1578.   Grant to Christopher Hatton, knight, councillor, vice-chamberlain of the household, of the wardship and marriage of John Cullyford, son and heir of Anthony Cullyford; with an annuity of   [*m.* 34]
£3 6s. 8d. from 10 April, 19 Eliz., when Anthony died. Yearly value of the inheritance £13 16s. 8d.   By Q.

3280.)   29 *April* 1578.   Grant to Edward Sudlowe of the wardship and marriage of William Vesye, kinsman and heir of William Vesye; with an annuity of £6 13s. 4d. from 4 July, 19 Eliz., when William the elder died.   By Q.

3281.)   28 *April* 1578.   Grant to Robert, earl of Leicester, K.G., baron of Denbigh, councillor, of the wardship and marriage of Frances Wilkes and Margaret Wilkes, two of the three sisters and co-heirs of Robert Wilkes, late the Queen's ward, son and heir of William Wilkes; with an annuity of 40 marks from 26 July,   [*m.* 35]
19 Eliz., when Robert died.   By Q.

3282.)   5 *May* 1578.   Grant to Mary Felton, widow, and Robert Sampson of the wardship and marriage of Anthony Felton, son and heir of Thomas Felton; with an annuity of £6 13s. 4d. from 4 Sept., 19 Eliz., when Thomas died.   By Q.

3283.)   5 *May* 1578.   Grant to Thomas Crompton of the wardship and marriage of Henry Hodgeson, son and heir of Robert Hodgeson; with an annuity of £5 from 26 May, 19 Eliz., when Robert died. Yearly value of the   [*m.* 36]
inheritance £13 10s.   By Q.

3284.)   5 *May* 1578.   Grant to William Peryam of the wardship and marriage of John Mallett, son and heir of Robert Mallett; with an annuity of £10 from 24 April, 19 Eliz., when Robert died, until John shall attain the age of 12 and thereafter an annuity of £13 6s. 8d.
By Q.

3285.)   26 *April* 1578.   Grant to Robert, earl of Leicester, councillor, and James Cressy and Jane Cressy, his wife, of the wardship and marriage of   [*m.* 37]
Richard Wenman, son and heir of Thomas Wenman; with an annuity of £12 from 23 July, 19 Eliz., when Thomas died, until the death of Isabel Wenman, now the wife of Richard Huddleston, and thereafter an annuity of £20.   By Q.

3286.)   24 *March* 1578.   *Gorhambury.*   Lease for 21 years to John Forster of (1) the site or capital messuage of the manor of Crambone, co. York,   [*m.* 38]
called 'the Hall Garth', late of Kirkeham priory, co. York, and the tithes of corn belonging thereto and 'lez demeanes' of the said manor and (2) a tenement (*tenants named*) in Sandehutton, co. York, once of the priory of St. Andrew next York; with reservations; from Michaelmas last; yearly rents (1) £5 19s. and (2) 8s. In consideration of the surrender by Forster of a patent, 10 Feb., 7 Eliz., leasing the premises to Richard Heyborne for 21 years from Michaelmas then last at the same rents; and for a fine of £12 14s. paid at the Exchequer.
By warrant of the commissioners.

3287.)   21 *March* 1578.   *Gorhambury.*   Lease for 40 years to Henry Cressye of cottages

and messuages (*tenants named*) in Blythe, co. Nottingham, some once of Roche priory, co. York, and others given for a stipendiary priest in Blythe, rents of assize in Blythe amounting with the rents of the same cottages and messuages to £15 9s. 2½d. and service, customs and works   [*m.* 39]
of tenants there amounting to a yearly rent of 9s. 6d. and service, and a cottage (*tenant named*) in Oldcottes, co. Nottingham, once of the monastery of Blythe; from Michaelmas last; yearly rent £16 14s. 11½d. In consideration that the cottages and messuages are in such decay that they cannot be repaired without great cost, the charges of which Cressye will undertake; and because the Queen will be better answered of the said rent.   By p.s.

3288.) 21 *March* 1578. Gorhambury. Lease for 21 years to William Warde of (1) the herbage of the park of Trowtebecke and (2) a pasture there called Dalehedd, co. Westmorland, leased *inter alia* to Henry, late earl of Cumberland, and now or late in the tenure of James Harrington, parcel of the barony of Kendall, co. Westmorland, late of William, late marquess of Northampton, and formerly parcel of Richemondes Landes; with reservations; from Michaelmas last; yearly rents (1) £20 and (2) £6 13s. 4d.; the lessee to serve according to the custom of the country with horse and arms when summoned by the Queen's warden or lieutenant. In consideration that Warde offers to answer the rents aforesaid.   By p.s.

3289.) 21 *March* 1578. *Gorhambury.* Lease for 21 years to Thomas Wyles, a gentleman of the chapel, of lands (*named with tenant's name*) in Rederith, co. Surrey, late exchanged with Henry Polsted; with reservations; from   [*m.* 40]
Michaelmas last; yearly rent £17 10s. In consideration that the premises are in great decay and Wyles will undertake the charge of repairing them; and for a fine of £17 10s. paid at the Exchequer.   By p.s.

3290.) 24 *March* 1578. *Gorhambury.* Lease for life to Thomas Parker of Northlache, co. Gloucester, with remainder to Maud his wife and Joan Parker, their daughter, for life in survivorship, of the site of the manor of Northlache, once of the monastery of St. Peter, Gloucester, all lands belonging to the manor once in the tenure of William Dyngley, James his son and Jane daughter of John More of Duncklyn, co. Worcester, the tithes thereof and 30 cartloads of hay yearly in a meadow called Kingesham at Ampney, co. Gloucester; with reservations; yearly rent £20 and heriot the best beast; the lessees to provide entertainment for the steward of the manor and steward of the court of view of frankpledge coming to hold courts there twice a year. For a fine of £13 6s. 8d. paid at the Exchequer.   By p.s.

3291.) 1 *March* 1578. *Gorhambury.* Lease for 21 years to Thomas Tallys and William Birde, gentlemen of the chapel, of—(1) the tithes of lands (*named with tenants' names*) in Oversley *alias* Osley, co. Warwick, late of Robert Throgmerton, knight, which tithes belonged to   [*m.* 41]
the cell of Alcester, co. Warwick, once annexed to the monastery of Evesham, co. Worcester, and were leased by patent of the Exchequer, 18 May, 6 Eliz., for 21 years from Lady Day then last to Throgmerton aforesaid at a yearly rent of 59s. 1d.; (2) the tithes of corn and hay in Willersley *alias* Willersey, co. Gloucester, once of the monastery of Evesham and leased by patent, 28 June, 11 Eliz., for 21 years from Lady Day then last to Humphrey Dyke at a yearly rent of £9 2s. 2d.; (3) the site of the manor of Billinge Magna, co. Northampton, and lands (*tenants named*) in Billinge Magna, parcel of Richemonde Landes and leased by patent, 10 July, 8 Eliz., for 21 years from Michaelmas 1571 at a yearly rent of £7 13s. 4d. to Charles Howarde, lord of Effingham, by the name of Charles Howard, the Queen's servant; (4) the site of the manor of Copford called Copford Hall in Copford, co. Essex, with lands

etc. (*named*) there, as formerly held by John Cokerell or Philip Mountjoye and Margaret his wife, late of the bishopric of London and in the Queen's hands by act of Parliament, leased by indenture of Edmund, late bishop of London, 20 Dec., 33 Hen. VIII, for 50 years from Lady Day then next at a yearly rent of £6 4s. 2d. to the said Philip and Margaret; (5) lands (*tenants named*) in Drayton and Est Camell, co. Somerset, given for an obit in Kingesberye, co. Somerset, and leased by patent of the Exchequer, 12 July, 8 Eliz., for 21 years from Lady Day then last at a yearly rent of 10s. to Roger Forte; and (6) the chantry of Newton Placie in the parish of Northe Petherton, co. Somerset, the tithes of lands (*named*) and all other tithes late in the tenure of William Ashe once belonging to the chantry, leased by patent of the Exchequer, 6 May, 19 Eliz., for 21 years from Lady Day then last *inter alia* to Margaret Annesley. With reservations. From (1) Lady Day 1585,   [*m.* 42] (2) Lady Day 1590, (3) Michaelmas 1592, (4) Lady Day 1592, (5) Lady Day 1587 and (6) Lady Day 1598. Yearly rents (1) 59s. 1d., (2) £9 2s. 2d., (3) £7 13s. 4d., (4) £6 4s. 2d., (5) 10s. and (6) 77s.. The lessees to provide entertainment at the manors of Billinge and Copford for the Queen's steward and surveyor coming to hold courts or make a survey.

     For their service.   By p.s.

(The dorse of this roll is blank.)

PART VII

C. 66/1170

3292.)   25 *Jan.* 1578.   Presentation of Christopher Ryley, B.A.,   [*m.* 1]
to the rectory of Holy Trinity, London dioc.

The like of the following, viz.—

3293.)   27 *Jan.* 1578.   Thomas Sowter, M.A., to the vicarage of St. Mary in Wygenhale,
Norwich dioc., void by death.

3294.)   27 *Jan.* 1578.   Thomas Lawrence, M.A., to the rectory of Shafton Peter, Bristol
Canterbury [*sic*] dioc., void by lapse.

3295.)   23 *Dec.* 1577.   Henry Parkyns, clerk, to the vicarage of Dormyngton with the
chapel of Bretwastre, Hereford dioc.

3296.)   13 *Jan.* 1578.   Harold Pachett, clerk, to the rectory of Thorpe next Newarke, York
dioc., void by resignation.

3297.)   13 *Jan.* 1578.   Robert Blunt, clerk, to the rectory of Walton, Lincoln dioc., void by
resignation.

3298.)   13 *Jan.* 1578.   William Hayward, clerk, to the vicarage of Northe Shobery,
London dioc., void by resignation.

3299.)   17 *Jan.* 1578.   Edward Moseley, clerk, to the vicarage of Raundys, Peterborough
dioc.

3300.)   24 *Jan.* 1578.   Francis Goldyngham, clerk, to the vicarage of Norbrogh, Norwich
dioc., void by death.

3301.)   18 *Nov.* 1577.   William Griffyth, M.A., to the vicarage of Mevern, St. Davids
dioc.

3302.)   4 *Feb.* 1578.   Philip Jones, clerk, to the vicarage of Aldermynster, Worcester
dioc., void by death.

3303.)   26 *Nov.* 1577.   John Thorneborough, clerk, to the rectory of Chilmarke,
Salisbury dioc., void by lapse.

3304.)   25 *Nov.* 1577.   Robert ap Rychard, clerk, to the rectory of Ludchurche, St. Davids
dioc.

3305.)   25 *Nov.* 1577.   Thomas Morrys, clerk, to the rectory of Leyrmerne, London dioc.,
void by death.

3306.)   22 *Nov.* 1577.   Griffith Toye, M.A., to the rectory of St. Florence, St. Davids
dioc., void by death.

3307.)   1 *Feb.* 1578.   Edward Turnor, clerk, to the vicarage of Melton Mowbery, Lincoln
dioc., void by resignation.

3308.)   1 *Feb.* 1578.   William Fayrchilde, clerk, to the rectory of Lucombe, Canterbury
dioc.

3309.)   1 *Feb.* 1578.   Humphrey Fen, clerk, to the vicarage of Holy Trinity in Coventry,
Coventry and Lichfield dioc.

3310.)   1 *Feb.* 1578.   Humphrey Cole, clerk, to the rectory of Staunwyke, Peterborough
dioc.

3311.)   1 *Feb.* 1578.   Richard Cosyn, clerk, to the vicarage of Sharnebrooke, Lincoln
dioc., void by resignation.

3312.)   3 *Jan.* 1578.   Zachary Hunte, clerk, to the rectory of Colleweston, Peterborough dioc.

3313.)   3 *Jan.* 1578.   Thomas Losebye, clerk, to the vicarage of Welham, Lincoln dioc., void by resignation.

3314.)   3 *Jan.* 1578.   John Savage, clerk, to the vicarage of Pollesworth, Coventry and Lichfield dioc., void by death.

3315.)   29 *Aug.* 1578.   *Ingatestone.*   John Thompson, clerk, to the vicarage of Ryseley, Lincoln dioc., void by resignation.[1]

3316.)   29 *Sept.* 1578.   *Gorhambury.*   Henry Yeenys, M.A., to the rectory of Ashehill, Norwich dioc.

3317.)   30 *Oct.* 1578.   *Chenies.*   Thomas Utye, clerk, to the vicarage of St. Mary in Beverley, York dioc., void by resignation.

3318.)   13 *Oct.* 1578.   *Chenies.*   William Nowell, clerk, to the vicarage of Welton, Peterborough dioc., void by death.

3319.)   7 *Nov.* 1578.   *Richmond.*   Simon Parratt, clerk, to the rectory of Burthorpe, Gloucester dioc., void by resignation.

3320.)   5 *Nov.* 1578.   *Richmond.*   Ralph Turnor, clerk, to the vicarage of Westhaddon, Peterborough dioc.

3321.)   5 *Nov.* 1578.   *Richmond.*   Robert Pirry, clerk, to the vicarage of Ratley, Coventry and Lichfield dioc., void by death.

3322.)   18 *July* 1578.   *Gorhambury.*   Ciriack [—], clerk, to the rectory of Muston, Peterborough dioc., void by death.

3323.)   18 *July* 1578.   *Gorhambury.*   John Wylles, clerk, to the vicarage of [—], Canterbury dioc.

3324.)   18 *July* 1578.   *Gorhambury.*   William Harvye, clerk, to the rectory of Weston, Norwich dioc., void by lapse.

3325.)   30 *April* 1578.   Thomas Sparke to the rectory of St. Cuthbert in Bedford, Lincoln dioc., void by death.

3326.)   26 *April* 1578.   John Ethryngton, clerk, to the rectory of Westoke, Chichester dioc., void by resignation.

3327.)   19 *June* 1578.   Ralph Mynton, clerk, to the vicarage of Overston, Peterborough dioc, void by lapse.

3328.)   19 *June* 1578.   Arthur Hassard, clerk, to the rectory of   [*m.* 2] Lassyngdon, Gloucester dioc., void by lapse.

3329.)   21 *April* 1578.   John Smythe, M.A., to the vicarage of Thorlowe Magna, Norwich dioc., void by death.

3330.)   4 *April* 1578.   *Gorhambury.*   Thomas Haberley, clerk, to the vicarage of Bradwell, Lincoln dioc., void by deprivation.

3331.)   4 *April* 1578.   *Gorhambury.*   Francis Langharne, M.A., to the rectory of Hoggeston, St. Davids dioc., void by death.

3332.)   4 *April* 1578.   *Gorhambury.*   James Hamerton, clerk, to the vicarage of Edlyngton, Lincoln dioc., void by death.

3333.)   21 *March* 1578.   *Gorhambury.*   Richard Clerke to the rectory of Marston, Gloucester dioc.

3334.)   7 *March* 1578.   *Gorhambury.*   James Sayer, clerk, to the rectory of Barmyngham, Canterbury dioc.

3335.)   19 *Feb.* 1578.   Edward Wylson, clerk, to the vicarage of Camerwell, Winchester dioc.

---

[1] This entry is repeated on the roll.

3336.)   22 *Feb.* 1578.   *Hampton Court.*   John Standen, clerk, to the vicarage of Egham, Winchester dioc., void by resignation.

3337.)   7 *March* 1578.   *Gorhambury.*   James Sayer, clerk, to the rectory of Barnyngham, York dioc.

3338.)   14 *March* 1578.   *Gorhambury.*   Michael Wharton to the vicarage of Wykewan, Gloucester dioc., void by resignation.

3339.)   12 *May* 1578.   Richard Maddock, clerk, to the rectory of Islyppe, Canterbury dioc., void by lapse.

3340.)   12 *May* 1578.   Henry Duxfeyld, clerk, to the vicarage of Bolum *alias* Bolun, Durham dioc., void by death.

3341.)   12 *May* 1578.   James Becher, clerk, to the vicarage of Chalke, Canterbury dioc., void by resignation.

3342.)   14 *June* 1578.   Thomas Puckerynge, clerk, to the free chapel of Frome Whytfeyld, Canterbury dioc.

3343.)   17 *June* 1578.   Henry Harryson, clerk, to the vicarage of Selsey, Chichester dioc.

3344.)   19 *Feb.* 1578.   Edward Wylson, clerk, to the vicarage of Camerwell, Winchester dioc.

3345.)   10 *Feb.* 1578.   John Barnes, clerk, to the vicarage of Mynterne, Canterbury dioc.

3346.)   13 *Feb.* 1578.   Ninian Fayrebarne, clerk, to the rectory of Thorner, York dioc.

3347.)   11 *Feb.* 1578.   Anthony Greneacres, clerk, to the rectory of Grafton, Peterborough dioc.

3348.)   11 *Feb.* 1578.   Robert Wytton, clerk, to the rectory of Fyttes, Coventry and Lichfield dioc., void by death.

3349.)   5 *May* 1578.   James Cottyngton, clerk, to the rectory of Acle, Norwich dioc.

3350.)   5 *May* 1578.   John Tyllye, clerk, to the vicarage of Brapole, Canterbury dioc., void by resignation.

3351.)   9 *June* 1578.   Christopher Fewell, clerk, to the vicarage of St. Mary in Beverley, York dioc., void by resignation.

3352.)   9 *June* 1578.   Bartimeus Andrews, clerk, to the rectory of Wenham, Norwich dioc., void by resignation.

3353.)   7 *June* 1578.   Philip Hatherley, clerk, to the vicarage of Stranton, with the chapel of Seton annexed, Durham dioc., void by death.

3354.)   7 *June* 1578.   Thomas Paynell, clerk, to the rectory of Stamborne, London dioc., void by death.

3355.)   13 *May* 1578.   Robert Norgate to the rectory of Fornecett St. Mary and St. Peter, Norwich dioc.

3356.)   13 *May* 1578.   William Gulson, clerk, to the rectory of Wymondham, Lincoln dioc.

3357.)   2 *June* 1578.   Richard Stanclyff, clerk, to the rectory of Esyngton, York dioc., void by resignation.

3358.)   2 *June* 1578.   Eustace Dowghtye, clerk, to the vicarage of Burgh on Baine, Lincoln dioc., void by death.

3359.)   17 *June* 1578.   Miles Humme, clerk, to the rectory of Fornecett St. Mary and St. Peter, Norwich dioc.

3360.)   10 *June* 1578.   Silvester Barber, clerk, to the rectory of Glandestrie, St. Davids dioc., void by resignation.

3361.)   11 *June* 1578.   Robert Bryan to the rectory of St. Clement in the suburbs of the city of Oxford, Canterbury dioc., void by resignation.

3362.)   11 *June* 1578.   John Wytter, clerk, to the rectory of St. Peter in Nottingham, York dioc., void by death.

3363.)   16 *June* 1578.   James Asheton, clerk, to the rectory of Thoreswaye, Lincoln dioc., void by resignation.

3364.) 16 *June* 1578. William Hobson, clerk, to the vicarage of Aldburgh, York dioc., void by resignation.

3365.) 16 *June* 1578. John Spencer, clerk, to the rectory of Waddyngworth, Lincoln dioc., void by death.

3366.) 16 *June* 1578. John Fawcett, clerk, to the rectory of Hormeade, London dioc.

3367.) 16 *June* 1578. Thomas Wood, clerk, to the rectory of Pynnock, Gloucester dioc., void by lapse.

3368.) 16 *June* 1578. Humphrey Browne, clerk, to the rectory of Rysom, Lincoln dioc.

3369.) 22 *April* 1578. Hugh Powell, clerk, to the vicarage of Tyddyngton, Gloucester dioc.

3370.) 22 *April* 1578. Christopher Baylden, clerk, to the vicarage of Baston, Lincoln dioc.

3371.) 19 *April* 1578. Robert Aldriche, clerk, to the vicarage of St. Mary in Nottingham, York dioc., void by resignation.

3372.) 19 *April* 1578. William Colson, clerk, to the vicarage of Waldnewton, York dioc., void by resignation.

3373.) 19 *April* 1578. Robert Cheveney, clerk, to the vicarage of Hornesey, void by resignation.

3374.) 19 *April* 1578. Richard Aldridge, clerk, to the rectory of Byford, Hereford dioc.

3375.) 19 *April* 1578. John Wattes, clerk, to the rectory of Chylcombe, Canterbury dioc.

3376.) 19 *April* 1578. Thomas Tarporley, clerk, to the rectory of Dunchyddock, Exeter dioc.

3377.) 17 *March* 1578. John Duncombe to the prebend of Cadyngton, York dioc.

3378.) 12 *May* 1578. James Becher, clerk, to the vicarage of Chalke, Rochester dioc.

3379.) 2 *June* 1578. Grant to John Mershe of London and John Turpyn   [*m. 3*] of London and the heirs and assigns of Mersche of—lands (*tenants named*) in Markington and Northstainley, in Essington ('le Guyld House' and 'Our Ladye House'), in Essington (*named*), given for a light, in Whitbye (*named*), late of the monastery of Whitby, in the parish of Kirkdale, late of the monastery of St. John on the Mount, in Kirbye (*named*), late of the said monastery of St. John, in the parish of Wadworth, in the lordship of Rilston (*named*), late of Richard Norton, attainted of treason, and in Killington, given for 'le Ladye service' and other superstitious uses in Killington church, all in the county of York; all lands in the manor of Compton Mordork, co. Warwick, late of the dissolved college of St. Mary in Warwick; the tithes of hay in the parish of Middleton Tyers, co. York, once of the monastery of St. Mary next the walls in York; a tenement (*described with tenant's name*) in York, given for 'le Ladye servyce' in Wakefeild church, co. York; lands (*tenants named*) in Wadworthe (*named*), in Sharlston, in Swyne ('the Ladye Gylde House' and a cottage given for a light in Swyne church), in Chappelthorpe in the parish of Sandall (including a former chapel), in Cawood (*named*), in Scagglethorpe in the parish of Cetrington (a former chapel), next Darfeld Brydge (a former chapel), in Wombewell, late of the monastery of Helye, co. York, in Rowton and Northskerlaughe (*named*), in Dowthorpe (*named*) in the parishes of Swyne and Ruston, late of the monasteries of Swyne and Thornton, in Stambrough (*named*), late of the monastery of St. John the Evangelist in Pomfrett, in Catton, Norbie, Stapleton on Teise, Whirshall, Estrounton and Romondbye, given for prayer for the souls of James Strangwaies, knight, his ancestors and successors in Northallerton church, co. York, in York, given by Helen Sesenax and others for superstitious uses in the church of St. Martin in Conystrete there, to wit, for their souls or otherwise, in Rowthe, given by Edward Roos for a priest to pray for him and the souls of his parents and all the faithful departed, in Wetheringsey, in Bolsterton and the manor of Bolsterton, late of the chantry of Bolsterton, in Netherstudley and elsewhere, given by John Warrener and others for a priest in the

chapel of Netherstudley and the chapel of St. Mary Magdalen, co. York, in Skelton, given
for a priest in Skelton chapel, and in Bondgate next Aismonderbie (a chapel or house called
Seynt John Baptystes and all its possessions) all in the county of York; lands (*named with
tenant's name*) in Eiton in the parish of Salley,   [*m.* 4]
co. Derby, late of Eiton chapel; lands (*named with tenant's name*) in the parish of Lydney, co.
Gloucester, once of the monastery of Lanthonye, co. Gloucester; lands in Farndon, co.
Nottingham, given for prayer for the soul of Alice Beckingham, widow, late of Farndon;
lands (*tenant named*) in Andesley Woodhouse, co. Nottingham, late of the monastery of
Felle, co. Nottingham; lands in the parish of Westburton, co. Nottingham; cottages (*tenants
named*) in the city of Oxford; lands (*tenants named*) in Denforde, co. Northampton, (*named*),
given for a light or obit in Denford church, in Little Bowden, co. Northampton, given by
[—] Chandler for an obit for his soul, in Emerton, co. Buckingham, in Compton, co.
Dorset, given for an obit in Compton church, in Billerica in the parishes of Bursted Magna
and Buttersburye, co. Essex, (*named*), given (1) by William Clerke *alias* Fuller for an obit and
prayer for his soul and (2) for a light in the church of Bursted aforesaid, and in Withecum,
co. Somerset, given for lights in Withecum church; a portion of tithes in Barrowe and
Atterley, co. Salop, late of Barrowe chapel or of the monastery of Wenlock; lands (*named with
tenants' names*) in Potters Hanley *alias* Castle Hanley, once of the late college or chantry of the
parish church of Potters Hanley, in Eston, given for a light, in Hanburie *alias* Hamburie,
given (1) for 'Our Ladye service' and (2) for a lamp, in the parish of Maumbell, in the parish
of Sapie, given for lights, in the parish of St. John by Worcester, given for a light, and in
Moseley in the parish of Kynges Norton (including 'the Ladye priestes chamber'), all in the
county of Worcester; lands (*tenants named*) in   [*m.* 5]
Southampton, co. Southampton, given for a priest celebrating for the souls of the departed
in the parish church of St. Michael in Southampton; lands (*tenants named*) in Harleston, late
of the monastery of St. James there, in Rockingham (*named*), in Oundell (*named*), parcel of
the guild there, in Whittleburie (*named*), given for a light, in Dallington, given for a salve
and other superstitious uses in the church of All Saints in Northampton, in Wedenbecke
(the site of a chapel), in Coldeashbye, late of the late manor [? *recte* monastery][1] of Sulby, in
Creeke, given for a lamp, and in Potterspurie (*named*), all in the county of Northampton;
lands (*tenants named*) in Item ('le Churche Howse'), in Bargemothe, given for 'le holybread'
in the church there, in Hawstowe, given for superstitious uses in the church there, in the
parishes of Warden and Estchurche in the isle of Sheppey, in Estchurche aforesaid (*named*),
in the parish of Mylton *alias* Middleton (*named*), given for a light in the church there, in
Northflet (*named*), given by William Blackman for an obit in the church there, and in
Sittyngborne, given by Catherine Daunce for superstitious uses in the church there; lands
(*tenants named*) in Marfeild Southe, co. Leicester, late of the late chapel there; lands (*named*) in
Oldbie, co. Leicester, given for prayer for the souls of the departed; lands (*tenants named*) in
Northam, co. Devon, given for the brotherhood of SS. John the Baptist and George in the
parish church of St. Mary of Northam and obits and the like in the same church; lands (*named
with tenant's name*) in Stichall *alias* Stivechall in the county of the city of Coventry, given for
lamps and the like; lands (*tenants named*) in Speeton, in Scampton in the parish of Ryllyngton
(*named*, and a ruined chapel), in Filinge Botham, given for lights in the church of Filinge
aforesaid, in Sharoe (*named*), in Kyrkby Malholmedale, given for 'le Ladie chauntrie' *alias*
'Stamforde chauntrye' in the parish of Gigleswick, co. York, and in Ryse and Ruston, given
for lights in Ryse church, all in the county of   [*m.* 6]
York; lands (*tenants named*) in Nonne, co. Somerset, (*named*) and in Wynsham *alias*
Wyncham, co. Somerset; lands (*named with tenants' names*) in Wyke in the parish of Barkeley,
co. Gloucester, and in Bucklesburie in the parish of Hawkesburie, co. Gloucester, given by

---

[1] Both the roll and the warrant, in Chancery Warrants II (C.82), 1330 read 'manerio'.

[—] Wymbole for masses and the like; lands etc. (*tenants named*) in Cullerne *alias* Collerne (*named*, including 'Seynt Saviers chappell'), given for priests and the like in Cullerne church or elsewhere, in Hangingestooke *alias* Stoke upon Aven (*named*, including 'Our Ladye of Lympleys chappell' and 'le Churche Howse'), given for 'le offrynge' and lights before 'the image of Our Ladye of Lympleystocke', in Cossham and Buddesdon St. Peter *alias* Bidesden (*named*, including the ruined free chapel of St. Peter and tithes belonging thereto and 'the Parsonage Howse'), in the parish of Polsholte (*named*), given for lights and the like, in the parish of Bushopston (*named*), given for lights and the like, and in Upton Skidmore (*named*), given for 'the lampe light' and other superstitious uses in Upton Skidmore church, all in the county of Wilts; lands (*named with tenant's name*) in Southe Hanningefeild, co. Essex; three messuages in London, whereof two are in Bucklersburye in the parish of St. Benet Sherehogge, now or late in the tenure of [—] Woodcock, and the other in the parish of St. John Walbrooke, once in the tenure of Robert Scott, 'laborer', given by Henry Woodcock for an obit in Strethall church, co. Essex; a messuage called 'the Dolphyn' in Candlewickstreete in the parish of Abchurche, London, now or late in the tenure of William Spycer; a cottage in the parish of St. George in Botulphe Lane, London, now or late in the tenure of John Boson; a decayed tenement late converted into a garden in the parish of St. Gabriel Fanchurche, London, given by Helmeng Leggett for singing the antiphon called 'Salve Regina' in the church of St. Gabriel aforesaid; a messuage or toft and a void parcel of ground with buildings thereon in the parish of St. Benet   [*m.* 7] Sherehogge, London, late of the late hospital of St. Mary without Bushoppesgate, London; two tenements and a piece of land in High Holborne in the parish of St. Giles in the Fields, co. Middlesex, now or late in the tenure of Henry Barnes and [—] James, widow, (240 feet long and 30 feet wide, abutting on a tenement of Henry Herne and Thomas Doughtye on the North and on the common sewer on the West), a tenement and piece of land in Highe Holborne in the said parish, now or late in the tenure of Robert Tucker, (480 feet long and 35 feet wide, abutting on the highway and a tenement in the tenure of Henry Amptill and late in the tenure of Roger Maskall on the North and the common sewer on the West), a piece of waste ground in the said parish (90 feet long and 24 feet wide, abutting on a tenement late of John Barnes on the North and on the West on a tenement in the tenure of John Birche), a close (about 6ac.) in the parishes of St. Giles aforesaid and St. Pancras, co. Middlesex, or one of them, now or late in the tenure of William Roper, and a close (about 2ac. 3rd.) in the parishes of Maribon and St. Pancras, co. Middlesex, or one of them, now or late in the tenure of Nicholas Holden, all once of the hospital of Burton St. Lazar and St. Giles in the Fields; a messuage (*tenant named*) in the town and county of Poole; all tenements in the parish of St. Mary at Hyll, London, once in the tenure of Prudence Crok, given by Robert Pickman for a priest there; all tenements and 'le brewhouse' once in the tenure of Robert Hamond in the parish of St. Andrew next Baynerescastle, London, given for five chaplains by William Walworth to celebrate for the souls of him and Margaret his wife and others; two tenements called 'the Kynges Head' in the parish of St. Magnus Bridgestreate, London, given by Andrew Hunt for a priest; all tenements once of Robert de Turney in Seynt Laurence Lane in Old Jewry, London, late in the tenure of Robert Whetstone, given by William Arderne for a chaplain in the church of St. Mildred Bredstreate, London; a shop with buildings thereover in Olde Fyshestreate in the parish of St. Nicholas Coldabbye, London; a tenement, a void piece of land and a garden in the same parish of St. Nicholas, once in the tenure of John Whyte, given by William Bromewell for superstitious uses; a tenement once called 'le Tannersseld' and now 'the Cowe Face' in Chepesyde, London, given for superstitious uses; a messuage called 'the Sonne' in the parish of St. Margaret in Bridgstreate, London, given for superstitious uses; all tenements in the parish of St. Mary Wolnoth, London, once in the tenure of Thomas Wetherell, James Crosse and others, given for a chantry by Thomas Nockett; a tenement, late in the tenure of Thomas Peerson, in the

parish of St. Benet Wodwharfe, London; a tenement, once in the tenure of Margery
Phillipps, in Bowe Lane in the parish of St. Michael Paternoster, London, given by John
Barnes, Simon Worsted and others for superstitious uses; lands in Blesbie (*named with tenant's
name*), given for a light before St. Mary's image in Blesbie church, in Whatton (*named*), given
for 'ploughe lightes' and like uses in Whatton church, in Skarrington (*named*), given for
lamps and the like in Skarrington church, in Hicklinge (*tenants named*), given for lamps and
the like in Hicklinge church, in Elton and Orston (*named*), given, being called 'Churche
House' and 'Churche Lande' of Elton, for lights and the like in Elton church, in Normanton
on Trent (*tenant named*), given for 'tapers' or 'seirgys' before the sepulchre and other places,
obits and the like in Normanton church, in Clarborow (*named with tenant's name*), given by
the ancestors of [—] Witton for an obit about Michaelmas in Clarborow church, in Hayton
(*tenant named*), given for lights and the like in Hayton church, in Upton in the parish of
Headon (a former free chapel), and in Everton (*named with tenants' names*), (1) given *inter*
[*m.* 8]

alia for 'a chauntrye preist, morrowe masse preist or stipendarye preist' in Everton church,
(2) given for a 'le dole' called 'Bolstons dole' in Everton church and (3) late of the monastery
of Mattersey, all in the county of Nottingham; lands (*described with tenants' names*) in Bawtry,
cos. Nottingham and York, (1) late of the chantry or stipendiary of Blighe, co. Nottingham,
(2) late of the monastery of Roche and (3) escheated; lands in Burton Joyes (*tenant named*),
late of Thomas Kinston, attainted of treason, in Thorpe next Newarke, late of the chantry or
hospital of St. Leonard of Stoke next Newarke, in Trowell (*named with tenant's name*), (1)
given for lights called 'sergeis' and the like in Trowell church, (2) late of the chantry of
Cossall, co. Nottingham, and (3) given for lamps and the like in Trowell church, in
Bassingfeild (a former free chapel called 'Seynt James chappell' and possessions thereof), in
Barnebye in Blythe (once 'Seynt Nicholas chappell'), in the parish of Carlton in Lindrick
(the site of a free chapel), in Wisall (*named with tenants' names*), given for lamps and the like in
Wysall church; in Willoughby (*named with tenant's name*), (1) given by Thomas Goodwyn to
Willoughbie church for lamps and the like, (2) given for lamps and the like in Willoughbie
church and (3) late of the donative of Lowdeham, in Beason (*named with tenant's name*), (1)
given for lamps and the like before images in the church of Beaston aforesaid, and (2) once
of St. John's brotherhood, in Basford (*named with tenants' names*), given (1) for lamps and the
like in Basford church and (2) *temp.* Hen. VIII by [—] Bigges to Lenton church for his obit,
in Owthorpe (*named with tenants' names*), given by the ancestors of William Birde and others
for obits and the like in Owthorpe church, in Darleton (*named with tenants' names*), given of
old in mortmain without licence for lights called 'sergeis' and the like in Darleton church, in
Laxton (*named*), given for a light in Laxton church, in Little Markham [*county not specified*]
(*named with tenant's name*), given for lamps and the like in the church there, in Bulwell
(*named*), escheated and of old given to rectors of Bulwell for lights and the like, in Bilborowe
(*named with tenant's name*), given for a lamp and the like in Bilborowe church, in Ragnell
(*named with tenants'* [*m.* 9]

names), given to the free chapel of Ragnell for masses and the like, in East Retford and
Grinley in the parish of Clarborow (*named with tenants' names*), given with other lands there
by Henry Crowder, clerk, to the use of the aldermen and masters of the guild of shoemakers
for an obit for him and his, in Serleby in the parish of Harworth (*tenant named*), given for 'a
morrowe masse preist', in Collingham, late of a guild or the like, in Worsapp (*tenants named*),
given for 'a morrowe masse preist' and lamps and the like in Worsapp church, and in
Egmounton (*named with tenants' names*), once of St. John's brotherhood, all in the county of
Nottingham; lands (*named with tenants' names*) in Nottingham in the county of the said town,
(1) given *inter alia* for 'Seynt Katheryns guilde preiste or stypendary' celebrating at 'Seynt
Katheryns altar' yearly in St. Mary's church in Nottingham, (2) given for lights and the like
in St. Nicholas's church, Nottingham, (3) once of the brotherhood called 'Seynt Johns

frarey' and (4) late of Holy Trinity guild in Nottingham; the chapel or messuage of St. Bartholomew, *alias* 'le pryorye' and brotherhood of St. Bartholomew and lands belonging thereto in the parishes of Chatham, Cliff, Higham and Seynt Margarete by Rochester, co. Kent, (*tenants named*), given for superstitious uses; 'Wilderton chappell' and its appurtenances in Throwley, co. Kent, (*tenant named*), given for superstitious uses; and lands (*tenants named*) in Warden in Sheppey ('Holybread Land'), at Thatchers Hyll in Rodmersham, given by the will, 3 Feb. 1491[/2], of John Aparke for an obit in the church there, in Chattham, and in Duddington and Newenham, given by John Huggen, once vicar of Duddington, for masses and the like. Which premises, all concealed from the Queen or from Henry VIII, Edward VI or Queen Mary,   [*m.* 10]
are of the yearly value, according to the several particulars thereof, of £16 17s. 2d. To hold in socage as of the manor of East Grenewyche, co. Kent, and by yearly rents of—for the lands in Harleston, co. Northampton, 5s. in right of the monastery of St. James; for the lands in Coldashbye, co. Northampton, 19½d. reserved by way of tenth by a patent, 3 July, 36 Hen. VIII, granted to Dorothy Dorrell, wife of Paul Dorrell, and George Tressam; for the lands in Normanton on Trent, co. Nottingham, 8s. 4½d. as in right of the monastery of Worsopp; and for the lands in Basford, co. Nottingham, 6s. as in right of Lenton priory. Issues from the time when the premises should have come to the Crown. This patent or the enrolment thereof to be sufficient warrant for the officers of the Exchequer and the duchy of Lancaster to issue process in the Queen's name for the levying of the issues of the premises and arrears thereof and the delivery of the same after recovery to the grantees; also for the grantees to dispense and compound for the issue of the same process. If any of the premises are hereafter lawfully withheld from the grantees' possession, they shall have other concealed lands to the value of those withheld. The patent to be void in respect of any of   [*m.* 11]
the premises which were not concealed on 1 Nov., 13 Eliz., and, being concealed, did not remain so until 12 Sept., 18 Eliz., about which time Mershe and Francis Greneham of London or their assigns procured the discovery thereof. If any of the premises concealed from 1 Nov., 13 Eliz., to 12 Sept., 18 Eliz., were afterwards conveyed or leased by the Queen to any person, the grantees shall have the reversion and rent thereof.

In consideration of—the Queen's promises in letters under her signature dated at Grenewyche on 1 Nov., 13 Eliz., touching lands to be granted to Mershe and Greneham and the heirs and assigns of Mershe; lands to the yearly value of £6 17s. 5d. surrendered by Mershe and Greneham by indenture, 27 April, 19 Eliz., to the Crown; and lands to the yearly value of £10 11½d. surrendered by the said John Mershe and William Mershe and Christopher Payton by indenture, 7 March, 20 Eliz., to the Crown.   By Q.

3380.)   19 *June* 1578.   *Inspeximus* and confirmation of a patent of confirmation, 18 June, 4 & 5 Ph. & Mary, inspecting and confirming for William Garrarde, knight, master of the mistery of 'haberdasshers' of London, and John Essex, John Rauffe, Edward Hall and Edward Withie, wardens thereof, a patent of confirmation, 12 Nov., 2 Hen. VIII, (1) inspecting and confirming a patent, 6 July, 17 Hen. VII [*Calendar,* 1494–1509, p. 261], confirming certain patents for the citizens and freemen of London of the mistery of 'marchaunte haberdasshers' and (2) (for the removal of disputes arising by reason of the unaccustomed name of 'marchaunte haberdasshers') changing the said guild or brotherhood of St. Catherine of 'marchaunte haberdasshers' in London into the guild or brotherhood of St. Catherine of 'haberdasshers' in London, incorporating the master and four wardens thereof, granting to the master and wardens the survey of all men of the brother-   [*m.* 12]
hood and of all persons in the said city and the liberties and suburbs thereof and within the space of three miles occupied in the making of hats and caps and all goods of the mistery of 'haberdasshers', granting also that the said persons shall pay 16d. quarterly to the master and

wardens, and that the said persons shall not put anyone to work in anything touching the mistery unless he be first admitted by the master and wardens as a competent workman (under pain of forfeture of the thing made, one moiety to go   [*m.* 13] to the mayor and commonalty of the city and the other to the mistery of 'haberdasshers').

[*m.* 14]

Also grant to George Barne, alderman of London, present master of the guild or brotherhood of St. Catherine of the craft of 'haberdasshers' in London, and Edmund Bragge, Henry Dale, Christopher Hoddesdon and John Whyte, present wardens of the same, of liberties as follows:—Change of the name of the said guild or brotherhood to the brotherhood, craft or mistery of 'haberdasshers' in London. Incorporation of the master and four wardens. Barne to be the first and present master, and Bragge, Dale, Hoddesdon and Whyte the first and present wardens. The master and wardens may have a hall or council house within the city, and may receive into the brotherhood such persons as they (or two of them) will as the master and wardens of the said guild of St. Catherine did; and they (or two of them) may hold assemblies of themselves and men of the brotherhood and all others making or selling caps, hats or any other thing concerning the mistery within the city or its suburbs or three miles about the city. The master and wardens may make ordinances for the government of men of the brotherhood and others using the mistery within the limits aforesaid; so that they be not repugnant to the laws and customs of the realm and of the city. The master and wardens (or two of them) with the assent of a majority of the assistants of the brotherhood may elect yearly from the men of the brotherhood a master and four wardens as often as pleases them or need is. The master and wardens may enjoy all their possessions

[*m.* 15]

heretofore obtained by them by any corporate name. Licence—for the maintenance of two preachers, two scholars studying theology in the universities of Oxford and Cambridge and divers poor of the brotherhood and for the better support of the brotherhood—for the master and wardens to hold lands in mortmain to the yearly value of £200 not held of the Crown or of others in chief or by knight service. The master and wardens (or two of them) with such knowledgeable persons of the brotherhood as they please, and no other, may have the entire survey within the limits aforesaid of all, both freemen of the craft, their servants and apprentices, foreigners, their servants and apprentices and others, using the craft of 'haberdasshers', and may for this purpose enter their houses and make such searches as the masters, governors and wardens of any incorporation of the fellowship aforesaid could do by law or by force of the patents aforesaid, notwithstanding the statute for the true making of cap and hats or any other statute; and the master and wardens (or two of them) may seize all wares found in their searches insufficient, and may apprehend and punish at their discretion all persons resisting or offending herein.

By advice of the Council and at the suit of the master and   [*m.* 16] wardens of the guild of St. Catherine aforesaid.   By Q.

3381.)   14 *June* 1578.   Lease for 21 years to William Pendlebury of all lands called Hutton Park, co. Westmorland, once or late in the several or joint tenures of Alan Bellingham, William Tarne and Edward Tarne, once parcel of Richmondes Landes and afterwards of William, late marquess of Northampton; with reservations; from Lady Day last; yearly rent £8. In consideration of the surrender by Pendlebury of a patent, 2 July, 16 Eliz., leasing to John Wylson the herbage and pannage of the said park, parcel of the manor of Hooton, for 21 years from Martinmas then next at the same rent.

By the commissioners by virtue of the Queen's warrant.

3382.)   14 *June* 1578.   Lease for 21 years to Matthew Ogle and John Howland of London, 'salter', of the rectory of Horseley, co. Northumberland, once of the monastery of Brenkebourne, co. Northumberland; with   [*m.* 17] reservations; from Lady Day last; yearly rent £15. In consideration of the surrender by Ogle in respect of the rectory of a patent, 26 March, 3 Eliz., leasing it *inter alia* to him for 21 years from Lady Day then last at the same rent; and for a fine of £40 paid at the Exchequer by Ogle and Howland.   By p.s.

3383.)   14 *June* 1578.   Lease for 21 years to William Gamble, Robert Wiche and George Addison of a fishery in the water of Pursant in a field called Stannynges, co. Lincoln, once of the monastery of Crowland, co. Lincoln; from Lady Day last; to hold one moiety unto Gamble to his use, and the other moiety unto Wiche and Addison, administrators of Nicholas Fygge, to the use of Richard and Robert Fygge, his sons; yearly rent for each moiety £7 3*s.* 4*d.* In consideration of the surrender by Gamble, Wiche and Addison of a patent, 1 July, 4 Eliz., leasing the fishery to Humphrey Burton for 21 years from Lady Day then last at a yearly rent of £14 6*s.* 8*d.*; and for a fine of £28 13*s.* 4*d.* paid at the Exchequer.
                                                                                   [*m.* 18]
                                                                                   By p.s.

3384.)   9 *June* 1578.   Lease for 21 years to John Cliffe, a clerk of the signet, of the rectory of Hockley, co. Essex, once of the monastery of Barkinge, co. Essex; with reservations; from Lady Day last; yearly rent £16. For a fine of £32.   By p.s.

3385.)   14 *June* 1578.   Lease for 21 years to George Rogers, knight, of the hundred of Kyngesberye, co. Somerset, late of the bishopric of Bath and Wells; from Lady Day last; yearly rent £7. In consideration of the surrender by the said George, son and heir of Edward Rogers, knight, of an indenture, 12 Oct., 1 Eliz., whereby Gilbert, bishop of Bath and Wells, with the approval of the dean and chapter of Wells cathedral, leased the hundred to the said Edward, then controller of the household and one of the Privy Council, for 21 years from Michaelmas then last at the same rent; and for a fine of £28 paid at the Exchequer.
                    By the commissioners by virtue of the queen's warrant.

3386.)   31 *May* 1578.   Lease for 31 years to Edward Turnor of—(1) lands   [*m.* 19] in Pensethorpe, Ploweland, Easthawfyeld and Hompton in Holdernes, co. York, once of the monastery of Bolton and leased by patent, 11 July, 3 Eliz., to Richard Hebborne and Christopher Jennyson for 21 years from Lady Day then last at a yearly rent of £6 13*s.* 4*d.*; (2) lands (*named with tenant's name*), parcel of the manor of Parrock, co. Kent, late of the monastery of Graces by the Tower of London, leased by conventual indenture, 1 Aug., 19 Hen. VIII, to Robert Stokemeade, Agnes his wife and others for 60 years from Michaelmas then next at a yearly rent of £4 5*s.* and afterwards by patent, 3 Oct., 5 Edw. VI, to John Fowler, now deceased, and Anne his wife *inter alia* for life in survivorship; (3) the tithes of corn in Weston, Hopton and Muckhall, co. Salop, (*tenants named*), once of the monastery of Wenlock, co. Salop, leased by patent, 29 Oct., 8 Eliz., to Richard Newporte, knight, for 21 years at a yearly rent of £4 13*s.* 4*d.*; (4) woods (*named with tenant's name*) in the parishes of Lurgashall and Gryndon, co. Buckingham, reputed parcel of a wood called Kingeswood in the forest of Barnewood and leased by patent, 24 Feb. last, to Thomas Hanford for 21 years from Michaelmas last at a yearly rent of £7 6*s.* 4*d.*; (5) the site and demesne lands of the manor of Parrock, co. Kent, once of the monastery of Graces, leased to William Wypeland and Edmund Page at a yearly rent of £11 6*s.* 8*d.* and granted by patent, 3 Oct., 5 Edw. VI, *inter alia* to John Fowler, now deceased, and Anne his wife for life in survivorship; (6) the site of the manor of Quinborough, co. Leicester, once of the monastery of Selbye, co. York, lands in Quinborough and all appurtenances of the said site, leased by patent, 27 Feb., 12

Eliz., to John Segrave at a yearly rent of 106s. 8d. for 21 years from the termination of a lease thereof to Anthony Dygby by patent, 29 Dec., 6 Edw. VI, for 21 years from the termination of a term of years therein of William Thorpe and Hugh Sharpe at the same rent; and (7) lands in Estnorton, co. Leicester, once of the monastery of Launde, co. Leicester, leased by patent, 10 June, 10 Eliz., to Henry, lord Cromwell, for 21 years from Lady Day then next at a yearly rent of £10 18s. 10d. With reservations. From (1) Lady Day 1582, (2) the termination of Stockmeade and the others' lease or the death of the said Anne Fowler, if she shall then be living, (3) Michaelmas 1587, (4) Michaelmas 1598, (5) the death of the said Anne Fowler, (6) the termination of Segrave's lease and (7) the termination of lord Cromwell's lease. Yearly rents (2) £4 6s. and the rest the same. The lessee to make three cuttings only of the woods, to enclose them after cutting, to leave sufficient 'lez staddelles' in every acre thereof according to statute, and to make such cuttings that a moiety of 'le springe'   [*m.* 20] and of all trees 'used to be lopped and topped' are seven years old at least at the end of the term.

For his long service; and in consideration of his surrender of a pension or annuity of £40 granted him for life.   By p.s.

3387.) 7 *June* 1578.   Lease for 21 years to John Collyer of Canford   [*m.* 21] of the manor of Canford Prioris and the rectory of Canford, co. Dorset, once of the monastery of Bradnestocke, co. Wilts; woods, mines and quarries and the advowson of the vicarage of Canford reserved; from Lady Day 1596 or the termination of a lease thereof by William Snowe, prior, and the convent of the monastery by indenture, 1 Sept., 28 Hen. VIII, to Richard Phillipp at a yearly rent of £14 13s. 4d. for 50 years from Lady Day 1546 or the termination of a lease thereof by Thomas Wallashe, prior, and the said convent by indenture to Thomas Horton, clerk, Richard Gay and Thomas Gaye, his son, from Lady Day, 6 Hen. VIII, for 32 years; yearly rent £27 6s. 8d. For £30 paid at the Exchequer by Collyer; and at the suit of George Caverley, now a knight of the chapel of Wyndesor castle.   By p.s.

3388.) 17 *June* 1578.   Lease for 21 years to John Moore of (1) the rectory of Hornesey, the tithes of corn and hay in Hornesey and Hornesey Beck and in Sowthorpp and Burton, co. York, the tithes of fish, with   [*m.* 22] 'le dole' customary there from all those occupied with things of the sea, and all other appurtenances of the rectory in the said places and elsewhere and (2) the site of the manor of Hornesey and lands (*named*) there, all once of the monastery of St. Mary next the walls of York; with reservations; from Lady Day last; yearly rents (1) £41 and (2) 26s. 8d.; the lessee to pay towards the repair of a 'le clowe' in Hornesey two parts of such sums as shall be assessed by the commissioners of 'le sewers' there. In consideration of the surrender by Moore by deed, 30 May last, enrolled in Chancery, of the interest of Richard Blunt, knight, to whom, then usher of the privy chamber, the premises were leased by patent of the court of Augmentations, 20 April, 7 Edward VI, at the same rents for 21 years from the termination of a lease thereof to him by the King dated 5 March, 31 Hen. VIII, for 21 years from Lady Day then next.   By p.s.

3389.) 5 *June* 1578.   Lease for 21 years to Edmund Frost of lands (*named with tenants' names*) in (1) Echingham, (2) Brightlinge and (3) Heathfeild, co. Sussex, once of the monastery of Beigham, co. Sussex, and concealed from the Crown; with reservations; from Lady Day last;   [*m.* 23] yearly rents, from the time when he shall enjoy possession, (1) £5 6s. 8d. (*detailed*), (2) 35s. (*detailed*) and (3) 10s. For a fine of £7 11s. 8d. paid at the Exchequer.

By the commissioners by virtue of the Queen's warrant.

3390.)   5 *June* 1578.   Lease for 21 years to Thomas Inkersell of woods (*named*), parcels severally of the manors of Dychingham, Southwalsham and Baryngham, co. Norfolk, and Donnyngworthe, co. Suffolk; with reservations; from Lady Day last; yearly rent £8 2*s.*; the lessee to make two cuttings only of the woods and at fitting seasons, to enclose them after cutting for nine years, to leave sufficient 'lez staddelles' in every acre according to statute, and to cause the patent to be enrolled within one year for charging of the rent before the auditor of the counties and before the surveyor general of woods this side Trent before any cutting is made. For a fine of £8 paid at the Exchequer.

By the commissioners by virtue of the Queen's warrant.

3391.)   5 *June* 1578.   Lease for 21 years to Walter Baylly, M.D., of Stanlake chantry, co. Oxford, and all its possessions, leased by patent,   [*m.* 24]
8 [*recte* 28][1] March, 11 Eliz., to William Castleman for 21 years from Michaelmas then next at a yearly rent of £6 21¼*d.*; with reservations; from Michaelmas 1590; same rent.   By Q.

3392.)   9 *June* 1578.   Lease for life to William Freke, with remainder to Robert Freke, the younger and John Freke, son of Robert Freke of Ewerne Courtney, co. Dorset, for life in survivorship, of the rectory of Frampton, co. Dorset, once of St. Stephen's college, Westminster, co. Middlesex; with reservations; yearly rent £20 10*s.* 3*d.*; the lessees to pay a yearly pension of 69*s.* 9*d.* to the vicar there.   [*m.* 25]
For a fine of £41 6*d.* paid at the Exchequer.   By p.s.

3393.)   30 *May* 1578.   Lease for 21 years to Richard Shute of all rents of assize in Newington, all rents now or once reputed parcel of the manor of Newington Bartram in Newington, a manor now or late called Newington Bartram in Newington, the moiety of a salt marsh in Newington (*tenant named*), a salt marsh now or once parcel of Newington Bartram or of the said manor and all demesne lands in Newington or elsewhere, co. Kent, called 'lez demeasnes' of Newington Bartram, late of the late earl of Essex; with reservations; from Lady Day last; yearly rent £14 4*s.* 9*d.* from the time when the premises shall come into his possession.   By p.s.

3394.)   26 *May* 1578.   Lease for 21 years to Edward, earl of Lincoln, councillor, and lady Elizabeth his wife of lands (*named with tenants' names*) in (1) Spaldinge, (2) Moulton and (3) Flete, co. Lincoln, parcel of the demesne lands there and late of Henry, late duke of Suffolk; with reservations; from Lady Day last; yearly rents (*detailed*) (1) 4*s.*,   [*m.* 26]
(2) 54*s.* and (3) 20*s.* 10*d.* For a fine of £11 16*s.* 6*d.* paid at the Exchequer by the said earl.
By the commissioners by virtue of the Queen's warrant.

3395.)   5 *June* 1578.   Lease for 21 years to John Senhouse and Peter Senhouse of the tithes of corn in (1) Dovenbie *alias* Dovingbie and Ribton in the parish of Bridekirke, co. Cumberland, and (2) Dereham and Rawe Hunrigge and Alneboroughe *alias* Elenboroughe in the parish of Dereham, co. Cumberland; to hold (1) unto Peter and (2) unto John; from Lady Day last; yearly rents (1) £5 and (2) £8 6*s.* 8*d.* In consideration of the surrender by Richard Senhouse, their brother, of a patent, 5 May, 15 Eliz., leasing to him the premises, by the name of the tithes of corn in Dovenbie and Ribton, the tithes of corn of Dereham and the tithes in Rawe Hunrigge and Ailboroughe, parcels of the rectories of Bridekirke and Dereham, for 21 years from Lady Day then last at a yearly rent of £13 6*s.* 8*d.*; and for a fine of £6 13*s.* 4*d.* paid at the Exchequer by John and Peter.
By the commissioners by virtue of the Queen's warrant.

---

[1] *Cf. Calendar,* 1566–1569, no. 2296.

3396.)   30 *May* 1578.   Presentation of William Rotherfoorthe, clerk, to the perpetual vicarage of Brixham, Exeter dioc., void by the resignation of Francis Cox, clerk. By p.s.

3397.)   30 *May* 1578.   Pardon for Henry Iselye *alias* Isley late of   [*m.* 27] Curringham, co. Essex, for the undermentioned felonies and all other offences committed between 18 Oct., 17 Eliz., and the present date. Reginald Peckham late of Curringham and he are indicted for that in the highway at Curringham they robbed (1) John Kinge of a gelding, two gold rings and £60 belonging to him on 18 Oct., 17 Eliz., (2) James Drakes of £38 and a gold ring belonging to him on the same date, (3) Thomas Lynsey of £115 belonging to him on the same date, (4) John Wakeman of £180 belonging to him on 16 Oct., 17 Eliz., and (5) William Jefferie of Rawreth, co. Essex, of £24 belonging to Edward Bartlett of Hocklye, co. Essex, on the said 16 Oct.   By p.s.

3398.)   30 *May* 1578.   Pardon for Jenkin Griffith late of Istradevodwg, co. Glamorgan, 'yoman', indicted with Richard David late of Langmor, co. Glamorgan, 'laborer', for that they broke and entered the close of Hopkin Myryke at Langmor on 6 Sept., 19 Eliz., and stole an ox   [*m.* 28] belonging to him.   By Q.

3399.)   14 *June* 1578.   Pardon for Thomas Emmynges *alias* Emmyngson late of Dysse, co. Norfolk, 'laborer', indicted at the general sessions of the peace held in 'le Sherehouse', co. Norfolk, at Norwich on 9 Jan., 20 Eliz., before Thomas Gawdye, a justice of the Queen's Bench, Christopher Heydon, knight, William Butte, knight, Francis Wyndam, serjeant at law, William Paston, Roger Woodhouse, Ralph Shelton and Edward Flowerdewe and their fellows, justices of the peace and of oyer and terminer in the county, for that he robbed James Sutton at Dysse on 13 Dec., 20 Eliz., of 40s. belonging to him. At the suit of Catherine his wife.   By p.s.

3400.)   12 *June* 1578.   Pardon for Thomas Herbert late of Penrise in the parish of Istradtevodocke, co. Glamorgan, clerk *alias* gentleman. It was found by an inquisition (*jury named*) held at Istradtevodock on 10 May, 20 Eliz., before Howell Mathewe, a coroner of the county, on the body of Meredith Llewelin late of Istradtevodock, 'laborer', that Herbert   [*m.* 29] feloniously killed him at Istradtevodocke on 7 May, 20 Eliz. (*details given*).   By p.s.

3401.)   3 *June* 1578.   Pardon for Lewis Phillipp of Seynte Brydes, co. Monmouth, and William Morgan of Marshefyeld, co. Monmouth, 'yomen', indicted for that they robbed Alexander Gaynor of £10 belonging to him in the highway at Marshefyeld on 29 May, 19 Eliz.   By p.s.

3402.)   26 *May* 1578.   *Gorhambury.*   Pardon for John Julius late of the city of Gloucester, physician, for treason in that on 1 Jan., 20 Eliz., at Gloucester he made two pieces of counterfeit money (*details given*).   By p.s.

3403.)   28 *May* 1578.   *Gorhambury.*   Protection for one year for Ciriack Ruse. By p.s.   [*m.* 30]

3404.)   6 *June* 1578.   Grant for life to Leonard Fryer of the room of a gunner in the bulwark or blockhouse of Estmersey, co. Essex; with wages of 8d. a day, payable at the Exchequer, from Christmas last; as held by Edmund Martyn, deceased. For service in the wars. *English.*   By p.s.

3405.)   28 *May* 1578.   *Gorhambury.*   Commission to lord Burghley, treasurer, the earl of Leicester and Christopher Hatton, knight, vice-chamberlain and captain of the guard, all councillors, Christopher Wraye, knight, chief justice of England, Walter Myldmay, knight, chancellor and undertreasurer of the Exchequer, and William Cordell, knight, master of the rolls, (or three of them, the treasurer or the earl being one) to hear and determine a controversy concerning the validity of the incorporation by Henry VIII of the dean and chapter of Chester cathedral; signifying their order to the Queen in writing that she may further ratify it if need be. Henry VIII endowed the dean and chapter at their erection with lands worth £800 yearly, which for the most part they granted by licence of Edward VI to Richard Cotton, knight, in fee farm, which by the said Richard in his lifetime and since his death by his son George have been mostly conveyed to Hugh Chomeley, knight, and George Calveley, knight, and others of the county of Chester in fee farm, and the dean and chapter have nothing but a certain yearly rent to maintain them; therefore the dean and chapter heretofore prayed the Queen to have the said lands reduced to them again according to the intent of Henry VIII, alleging that there are such imperfections in the incorporation that she might resume them and bestow them on the dean and chapter as she should think convenient; thereupon she caused the attorney general to exhibit an information of intrusion in the Exchequer against Chomeley, Calveley, Richard Hurleston and others to have validity of the incorporation bought in question; but now, upon complaint of Chomley and others that a great number of inhabitants of the county would be put to great charges before the suit could be ended, she has ordered the attorney general (and declares her pleasure hereby) that the suit shall be stayed and the matter determined by the commissioners.   *English.*   By p.s.

3406.)   13 *Jan.* 1578.   Order to Richard Martyn, warden of the exchange and money in the Tower of London and of the coinage of gold and silver there and elsewhere in England, and John Lovison, master worker of the money in the said Tower and elsewhere in England,—whereas certain goldsmiths trading the mint in the said Tower have delivered into the same certain bullion of gold and silver for which Lovison remains indebted to them to the value of about £1500, as appears by his deputy's bills, towards the answering whereof there remains a great part of the said bullion in the joint custody of Martin and Lovison yet unmolten and certain 'brokcage and sizell' remaining of other bullion molten in the sole custody of Lovison,—that Lovison shall forthwith satisfy the goldsmiths for their said bullion, for which they have the deputy's   [*m.* 31] bills, by redelivery to them of so much of the bullion as yet remains unmolten and of the 'brokcage and sizell' aforesaid, and for the residue to pay them ready money; and that thereupon he shall have his deputy's bills delivered to him. Also—whereas certain money growing of the profits by mintage in the said Tower and some other money coined by Eloie Mestrell for a trial are now remaining in the joint custody of Martyn and Lovison, which Martyn claims to belong to the Queen and Lovison challenges to be his—order that, after Lovison shall have given sufficient bonds to Martyn to the Queen's use for repayment of the same to the Queen if it shall be found due at the making of his account, Martyn shall deliver to Lovison or his assigns the said money.   *English.*   By p.s.

3407.)   19 *June* 1578.   Order to William, lord Burghley, treasurer, councillor, to order in the Queen's name to be taken into her hands the lands of Matthew, earl of Lyneux, deceased, and lady Margaret his wife, the Queen's cousin, in the county of York granted to them some in tail male by Henry VIII and King Philip and Queen Mary (as appears by the enrolment of the several patents thereof remaining in Chancery), the lady Margaret being also now dead; he shall cause the revenues thereof from lady Margaret's death during the Queen's pleasure to be paid into the Exchequer, shall appoint such stewards and other officers of the manors and other the premises as there were in lady Margaret's time and as he shall now think meet, shall take order that the capital and mansion houses used by lady Margaret are kept in sufficient repair, and shall see that none of the present farmers and occupiers are removed from their tenements without their consents or the Queen's special warrant. *English.*

By p.s.

3408.)   *6 June* 1578.   Grant for life to William Mompesson of (1) the offices of keeper of the house and gardens of the manor of Temple Hurste, co. York, and parker and keeper of the park there, with herbage and pannage of the park and with wages of 6*d.* a day for the keepership of the house and an annuity of £3 10*d.* for the office of parker out of the issues of the manor, and (2) the offices of keeper of the house and gardens of the manor of Temple Newson *alias* Newsham, co. York, and parker and keeper of the park there, with herbage and pannage of the park and with wages of 2*d.* a day out of the issues of the manor; the said fees payable from Michaelmas last at the Exchequer or by the bailiffs or receivers of the premises. For the removal of doubts whether grants of the premises   [*m.* 32] by Matthew, late earl of Lennox, lord Darnley in Scotland, and lady Margaret his wife (by the name of Matthew, earl of Levenox, lord of Rule in Scotland, and lady Margaret his wife) to Mompesson, their servant, for life, for his service, (1) by deed, 20 July, 36 Hen. VIII, from Lady Day then last and (2) by deed, 15 Oct., 36 Hen. VIII, from Michaelmas then last, are still of force since their deaths. *English.*   [*m.* 33]

By p.s.

3409.)   *4 June* 1578.   Licence for 12 years for Ralph Bowes and Thomas Bedingfeilde, the Queen's servants, to import playing cards into any of the Queen's dominions from friendly countries and sell the same in gross or by retail; from the present date; no others to import, sell or make playing cards during the term on pain of the Queen's high displeasure, punishment for contempt and forfeiture of the playing cards imported, sold or made, half of the forfeiture to be to the Crown and half to the licensees; power for the licensees to search ships, shops and other places and seize playing cards imported, put to sale or made contrary to this patent; customs officers not to receive from any others duty on playing cards imported or compound with them therefor, and the licensees   [*m.* 34] may have process out of the Exchequer to enforce this order; duties to be paid by the licensees. In consideration of 100 marks to be paid yearly at the Exchequer by the licensees, for which payment they have entered into bonds there. *English.*   By p.s.

3410.)   19 *June* 1578.   Assignment to William Appleton of Busshops Auckland, co. Durham, of a lease by Richard, bishop of Durham, by writing, 7 April, 20 Eliz., to the Queen of water mills at Darlyngton *alias* Darnton and Blackwell, co. Durham, and a tenement called Raker by the water of Wyske and lands (*described*), co. York, and all appurtenances of the said messuage held by James Metcalfe, knight, deceased, or Nicholas Thornell as parcel of the demesne lands of the lordship of Northallerton, co. York, for 40 years from Pentecost next for certain rents. *English.*   By p.s.

3411.)   12 *June* 1578.   Grant for life to Edward Carye, a groom of   [*m.* 35] the privy chamber, of the office of one of the four tellers of the Exchequer, which shall next be void by the death, surrender or forfeiture of Richard Stoneley, Henry Killigrewe, Robert Tayler and Robert Freke, who were appointed to the office of one of the said tellers by patents, 10 Feb., 1 Mary, 23 June, 3 Eliz., 7 [*recte* 27][1] May, 13 Eliz., and 8 May, 13 Eliz.,

---

[1] *Cf. Calendar,* 1569–1572, no. 2421.

respectively, Stoneley and Killigrew for life and Tayler and Freke during good behaviour. For his service.   [*m.* 36]

By p.s.

3412.)   26 *May* 1578.   *Gorhambury.*   *Inspeximus* of the following articles of agreement, [—] Jan., 19 Eliz., between Henry Sydney, K.G., president of Wales and the marches thereof, deputy general of Ireland and councillor in England, and Turlough (*Terentius*) Oneil:—

(1) Oneil submits to the Queen, acknowledges the duty and service of both himself and the rest of the barons, lords and captains in Ireland to her, and promises to obey her commands signified to him by the deputy or other governor of the realm and to help the deputy or governor against rebels, traitors or other persons undutiful towards her in Ulster and the neighbouring regions thereof; he also renounces all those called 'Uriaghs'.

(2) He will claim no followers from the Clandeboyes (*Clandeboycis*) inhabiting the Bann (*Banniam*) to the East or the Route (*Rowtam*) towards the Eastern region, but will send them back into their own country this side of the Bann to the East.

(3) He will not use traffice with the sons of the Baron and he will not exercise any jurisdiction over them or others between the great river and Bundalk [*sic*].

(4) He will foster no traitor or rebel in his country should any such come to dwell there, and when warned thereof by the governor or his commissioners he will speedily give care that they be apprehended and sent to the governor or commissioners.

(5) He will not permit theft to be done by inhabitants of his territory with impunity or thieves and robbers from elsewhere to flee across into his country, but will deliver them to the governor or his commissioners or make restitution fourfold for the thing stolen or prey committed.

(6) He will faithfully serve the Queen against all on whom she shall declare war, with soldiers hired by any captain appointed by him.

(7) He will give care that the Scots be cast out of his country, and he will not give them either wages or bonaght (*bonagium*) or receive goods imported by them, unless special licence be made to him by the governor to hire any of them.

(8) He will answer for all 'hostinges' with 50 horsemen and 100 footmen.

(9) He will behave peaceably towards Odonell (*Odonellum*) and all other faithful subjects of the Queen.

(10) Touching the performance of all these agreements he will give to the governor such hostages as the deputy shall demand of him; in consideration of the performance whereof it is granted him that he shall have for life by the Queen's grant all lands from Loughfoile to the great river and from the Bann to the boundaries [—] distant.

(11) He shall enjoy the regions of Clancan and Clanbresloughe as followers (*ut sequacibus*) and shall exact therefrom the same services which his predecessors were heretofore wont to exact.

(12) In consideration of his and his father's obedience and service to the Queen, for which they are worthy of her grace and good will, during his good behaviour and during the Queen's pleasure he shall by that law and condition have [——] that he shall pay 200 of the best oxen to the governor yearly.

(13) At his death his sons shall succeed to the portion of those lands called Nial Connilagh Oneil which in his father's lifetime belonged to him.

(14) He shall have part of the tribute of Loughfoile which is called in Irish 'coked' in as ample a manner as it can be proved that his predecessors were in lawful possession of the same tribute, likewise also to part of the Bann, so long as he settles with the fishermen coming thither according to the custom of the Bann, for which tribute he promises that he will aid and protect the fishermen who shall come there by virtue of a royal grant of fishing.

(15) The rent which he claims from Odochartay is granted to him, if it can be proved that such a rent was lawful and customarily due in the past.

(16) He shall have jurisdiction over Bernard Scahitus if the said Bernard shall dwell in his region across the Bann towards Tyrone, but, if Bernard shall come this side of the Bann into the parts of Clandboye to dwell, then he shall remain and shall give rent to the Queen for his country; but, if Bernard shall adhere to the Scots, then Oneil may possess his lands across the Bann and wage war on him.

(17) It is agreed between the parties that, if anyone's goods shall have been stolen and those whose goods they are pursue the same into the region or country of one of the parties, then the inhabitants of that region shall either restore the same to the true lords and possessors or compensate the damage fourfold.

Confirmation of the foregoing, on condition that Oneil will observe all those other articles and agreements to be performed on his behalf from time to time according to the articles above-recited.   By Q.

3413.)   12 *June* 1578.   Protection for one year for Raphael Veseye, citizen and grocer of London.   By Q.

                                                                                         [*m.* 37]

3414.)   18 *June* 1578.   Grant in fee simple to John Norton of the remainder and reversion of the manor of Wiarton and lands in Boughton Mounchelsey *alias* Monthensey and Langley, co. Kent; to hold as of the manor of East Grenewiche in socage. Norton was seised of the said manor and lands on 4 July, 4 Eliz., in tail male, with remainder to Robert Lambe of Ledes, co. Kent, Arthur Lambe, citizen and merchant taylor of London, Richard Lambe of London and Christopher Lambe of Ledes and their heirs, which Robert, Arthur, Richard and Christopher by indenture, 4 July, 4 Eliz., enrolled in Chancery, bargained and sold them, by the name of their messuage called Wiarton and all their lands in Bocton Montchensey and Langley, to William Lambe of London in fee simple, who by indenture, 6 July, 4 Eliz., enrolled in Chancery, bargained and sold them to Robert, Arthur, Richard and Christopher in tail, with remainder to the Crown.   By p.s.

3415.)   16 *June* 1578.   Grant for life to Humphrey Michell, the Queen's servant, of the office of waterbailiff of the river Severne and of all creeks, streams and ditches running into the Severne from Gloucester bridge to the river head; with all emoluments belonging to such office or had by any other waterbailiff in the river Thames or other place in England.
                                                                                         By p.s.
Vacated because surrendered, 22 *March,* 34 *Eliz.; signed:* G. Gerrard; Humfrey Michell.

3416.)   12 *June* 1578.   Presentation of John Knyghtley, B.A., to the vicarage of Tynmouth, Durham dioc.   By p.s.

3417.)   17 *June* 1578.   Lease for 21 years to Anthony Jackeson of   [*m.* 38] Killingwolde Graves, co. York, of a stock of 23 cows and a bull and lands etc. (*named*) in Fraisthorpe *alias* Fraistroppe, co. York, parcel of the manor of Fraisthorpe and once of the monastery of Bridlington, co. York; with reservations; from Lady Day last; yearly rent £6 13s. 4d.; the lessee to deliver back at the end of the term a stock of 23 cows and a bull or £12 for the same cows. In consideration of the surrender by Jackeson by deed, 21 Feb., 20 Eliz., in Chancery of his interest in the premises and of a deed, 2 June, 10 Eliz., whereby Richard Atkinson assigned to him his interest therein under a lease by patent, 29 May, 10 Eliz., to the said Atkynson *inter alia* of a stock of 46 cows and a bull and lands etc. (*named*) in Fraisthorpe, late of the said monastery, for 21 years from Lady Day then last at a yearly rent of £13 6s. 8d.; and for a fine of £13 6s. 8d. paid at the Exchequer.

By the commissioners by virtue of the Queen's warrant.

3418.)   26 *May* 1578.   *Gorhambury.*   Lease for 21 years to Martin Anne and William Moore of the tithes of corn in Hooton Pannell, Cleyton, Frickeley   [*m.* 39] and Shyppyns, co. York, once of Holy Trinity priory in the county of the city of York; from Lady Day last; yearly rent £9 6s. 8d. In consideration of the surrender by Anne of a patent, 22 Oct., 6 Eliz., whereby the premises were leased to Henry Jones for 21 years from Michaelmas then last at the same rent; and for a fine of £18 13s. 8d. paid at the Exchequer.

By the commissioners by virtue of the Queen's warrant.

(The dorse of this roll is blank.)

PART VIII

C. 66/1171

3419.)   6 *Dec.* 1577.   Licence for John Prior and Robert Prior to   [*m.* 1]
alienate lands (*tenant named*) in the manor of Upton Lovell, co. Wilts, to John Modye. For 5*s.*
4*d.* paid to the Queen's farmer.

3420.)   2 *Jan.* 1578.   The like for Edward Unton, knight, to alienate lands in Teynton, co.
Oxford, to John Tayller and Simon Tayller and the heirs and assigns of Simon. For 6*s.*

3421.)   6 *Feb.* 1578.   Pardon of alienation: Vincent Coventrye by indenture, 30 Jan., 14
Eliz., acquired from Thomas Norwood lands (*named with tenants' names*) in the manor and
parish of Carsington, co. Oxford. For 40*s.* paid to the Queen's farmer.

3422.)   20 *Dec.* 1577.   Licence for William Jenowaie to alienate lands (*described with
tenants' names*) in Ravensthorpe *alias* Rawnsthorpe, co. Northampton, and all other lands
there which descended to Richard Jenowaie, brother of William, on the death of William
Jenowaie, his father, to William Marten. For 8*s.* 11*d.* paid to the Queen's farmer.   [*m.* 2]

3423.)   12 *Jan.* 1578.   Pardon of alienation: Roger Dalton the elder, Anne his wife and
Roger Dalton the younger, his son and heir apparent, in Michaelmas term, 18 Eliz., acquired
unto them and the heirs of Roger the elder from James Rydley and Mabel his wife lands in
Kirkby Overkar *alias* Kirkby Mysperton, co. York. For £4 10*s.* paid to the Queen's farmer.

3424.)   6 *Feb.* 1578.   The like: Thomas Burdett by indenture, 20 Nov., 18 Eliz., acquired
from Francis Throckmerton, deceased, lands (*tenants named*) in Alcetter *alias* Awstrye, co.
Warwick, late of St. Sepulchre's priory, Warwick, co. Warwick. For 42*s.* 4*d.*

3425.)   5 *Feb.* 1578.   The like: Henry Pyle, 'yeoman', by indenture, 13 Nov., 16 Eliz.,
acquired from Richard Rede, knight, a fourth part of the site or farm of Pottrey Corte in
Wallopp Moyles *alias* Over Walloppe, co. Southampton, then or late in the tenure of John
Pyle, father of Henry, with the demesne lands belonging thereto (regalities and the like
reserved). For 36*s.* 8*d.*

3426.)   7 *Feb.* 1578.   The like: John Alwaye and Henry Alwaye by deed, 4 Nov., 14 Eliz.,
acquired from Richard Spicer *alias* Helder, 'yeoman', lands (*described with tenants' names*), late
parcel of the manor of Welles *alias* Welbury, in Great Offeley, Little Offeley, Lylley and
Little Hitchyn, co. Hertford. For 46*s.* 8d.   [*m.* 3]

3427.)   4 *Feb.* 1578.   The like: Richard Master by indenture, 28 April, 15 Eliz., acquired
from Thomas Parrye the manor of Preston and Northcote, co. Gloucester, once of St.
Mary's monastery, Cirencester. For £6 13*s.* 4*d.*

3428.)   20 *Dec.* 1577.   Licence for Richard Culpeper to alienate a moiety of a fourth part of
lands in Keymer *alias* Kydmer, co. Sussex, to John Moncke and John Michell. For 11*s.* 1½*d.*
paid to the Queen's farmer.

3429.) 3 *Dec.* 1577.   Pardon of alienation: Bridget late the wife of Stephen Woodroff, citizen and 'haberdasher' of London, entered under the will, 20 April, 18 Eliz., of her said husband a messuage (*named*) in St. Albans, co. Hertford, which he bequeathed to her for life, with remainder to Christopher Woodroff, his son. For 40*s.* paid to the Queen's farmer.

3430.) 2 *Jan.* 1578.   Licence for Francis Rydulphe to alienate a third part of lands in Canke *alias* Cannock, co. Stafford, late of Humphrey Salwey, to Matthew Salwey. For 1*s.* 2*d.* paid to the Queen's farmer.

3431.) 8 *Feb.* 1578.   Pardon of alienation: Thomas Kightley and Richard Yonge by indenture, 20 Dec., 14 Eliz., acquired from John Darcye, knight, lord Darcye of Chiche, the manors of Elmeswell and Wolpytt, lands (*named*), a warren and fairs and markets in Elmeswell and Wolpitt, the advowsons of the rectories of Elmeswell and Wolpitt and woods (*named*) in Elmeswell, Wolpitt, Tostocke, Whitherden, Ratelsden, Norton and

[*m.* 4]

Ashefeild, co. Suffolk. For £4 paid to the Queen's farmer.

3432.) 1 *Feb.* 1578.   The like: William Collingridge, 'yeoman', and Alice his wife by indenture, 5 Sept., 13 Eliz., acquired from Thomas Cheynye lands in Clopton, parcel of the customary lands of the manor of Kyntbury Ambresbury, and all appurtenances thereof in the parish of Kyntbury, co. Berks, to hold unto themselves for life in survivorship, with successive remainders for life to Joan Collingridge the elder, Joan Collingridge the younger, Mary Collingridge, Elizabeth Collingridge and Margaret Collingridge, daughters of William, with remainder over to the heirs of the bodies of the said Joan the younger, Mary, Elizabeth, Margaret and Joan the elder successively. For 20*s.*

3433.) 6 *Feb.* 1578.   The like: William Tomkyns in Easter term, 19 Eliz., by fine in the Common Pleas acquired from John Talbott and Catherine his wife a third part of the manor of Monyngton on Wye, of lands in Monyngton on Wye and Shutton and of the advowson of Monyngton on Wye church, co. Hereford. For £3 11*s.* 8*d.*

3434.) 29 *Nov.* 1577.   The like: John Stumpe by indenture, 30 June, 13 Eliz., acquired *inter alia* from Thomas Escorte—by the name of all lands late of Matthew Kinge or John Kinge in Malmesbury, Westporte, Brokenborough, Milborne and Burton—lands (*tenants named*) in Malmesbury in the parish of Westporte, once of 'Our Ladyes service' in Westporte,   [*m.* 5]
in Malmesbury, Westporte, Brokenborough, Mylborne, Charleton, Burton and Thornehill, co. Wilts, in Malmesbury (*described*) and in Brokenborough (*described*). For 18*s.*

3435.) 30 *Jan.* 1578.   The like: by fine in the Common Pleas in Michaelmas term, 14 Eliz., Benet Shuckburgh and Alice his wife conveyed to Thomas Skirroll and Henry Harryson and the heirs of Skirroll the manor or grange of Cubbington and lands in Cubbington, co. Warwick, and they by the same fine conveyed them back to Benet and Alice in tail, with successive remainders to the heirs of the body of Alice, to the heirs of the body of Benet and to the right heirs of Alice. For £5.

3436.) 18 *Dec.* 1577.   Licence for Adam Archerd, 'clothier', and Thomas Hall, 'yeoman', to alienate lands (*named with tenants' names*) in Burton Hill, co. Wilts, parcel of the manor of Burton Hill, to   [*m.* 6]
John Yonge, 'yeoman'. For 2*s.* 9*d.* paid to the Queen's farmer.

3437.)   18 *Dec.* 1577.   The like for the same to alienate lands (*named with tenants' names*) in Burton Hill, parcel of the said manor, to Richard Cowche. For 21*s.* 2*d.*

3438.)   18 *Dec.* 1577.   The like for the same to alienate lands (*named with tenants' names*) in Burton Hill, parcel of the said manor, to John Combe, 'yoman'. For 7*s.* 11*d.*

3439.)   18 *Dec.* 1577.   The like for the same to alienate lands   [*m.* 7] (*named with tenants' names*) in Burton Hill, parcel of the said manor, to Ralph Slyfelde. For 16*s.* 4*d.*

3440.)   26 *Dec.* 1577.   The like for Francis Rodes, serjeant at law elect, and Mary his wife to alienate the manor of Handley and lands in Staveley, Handley *alias* Hanley and Dranfeld, co. Derby, to Peter Fretchevile. For £3 6*s.* 8*d.*

3441.)   2 *Jan.* 1578.   The like for Henry Shepperd and Mary his wife to alienate lands in Swanbourne, co. Buckingham, to Andrew Wattes   [*m.* 8] and Elizabeth his wife and the heirs and assigns of Andrew. For 11*s.* 1⅜*d.*

3442.)   9 *Dec.* 1577.   Pardon of alienation: William Aucher by indenture, 15 July, 15 Eliz., acquired from William Rickthorne the manor of Kingeston, co. Kent, and the advowson of Kingeston church. For 26*s.* 8*d.* paid to the Queen's farmer.

3443.)   2 *Dec.* 1577.   The like: Margaret Browne, widow, by indenture, 15 June, 15 Eliz., acquired from Bernard Whetstone *inter alia* the rectory of Ratby and all his lands in Isley Walton and Ratbye or elsewhere, co. Leicester. For £4 9*s.*

3444.)   18 *Nov.* 1577.   Licence for Henry Cooke to alienate the manor of Knappwell, co. Cambridge, the advowson of Knappewell church and a wood called Knappwell Wood there to Thomas Marshe. For £4 9*s.* paid to the Queen's farmer.

3445.)   26 *Dec.* 1577.   The like for John Mychell to alienate a messuage called 'le Stewe', 'a stewe leade' (*fornac' plumbeam*), a lead cistern and a lead gutter from the Thames to the said house with 'a buckett' and chain belonging thereto in the parish of St. Michael at Quenehith, London, (extending from East to West 50 feet and from a tenement called 'le Signe of the Cuppe' on the North to the Thames on the South 76 feet) to John Richardson, citizen and
                                                                                          [*m.* 9]
'iremonger' of London. For 26*s.* 8*d.*

3446.)   20 *Jan.* 1578.   The like for Henry Cheney, knight, lord Chenye of Tuddington, to alienate the site of the manor of Calehill *alias* Calehill Felde and lands in Mynster in the isle of Shepe, co. Kent, to John Allen. For 53*s.* 4*d.*

3447.)   20 *Dec.* 1577.   The like for John Sparrye to alienate the manor of Monyhulls and all his other lands in the parish of Kinges Norton, co. Worcester, to William Sparrye. For 22*s.* 3*d.*

3448.)   20 *Dec.* 1577.   The like for Maurice Rodney to alienate a moiety of the rectory of Backewell, co. Somerset, with lands (*named*) belonging thereto and the advowson of the vicarage of Backewell, all late impropriated to the late hospital of St. John the Baptist without Ratcliffe Gate in the suburbs of Bristol, and all his other lands there late of the said hospital to John Bushe and Mary his wife for life in survivorship, with remainder to John

Norman the younger and his heirs male by Elizabeth late his wife, deceased, with remainder to the right heirs of Norman. For 33s. 4d.

3449.)   11 Jan. 1578.   Pardon of alienation: John Petre, knight, by indenture, 25 June, 13 Eliz., by the name of John Petre, esquire, acquired from Robert Petre and William Petre a third part of the manors of Odicknoll, Norton and East Alington and of all lands in Odicknoll, Kingeskarswell, Chymney Norton and East Allington, co. Devon, late

[m. 10]

of John Petre of Hayes in the parish of St. Thomas by Exeter, brother of Robert and uncle of William, late deceased. For 40s. paid to the Queen's farmer.

3450.)   13 Jan. 1578.   The like: Robert Petre by indenture, 8 Feb., 15 Eliz., acquired from John Petre a third part of the manors of Norton and East Allington, co. Devon. For 26s. 8d.

3451.)   20 Jan. 1578.   The like for Jane Kidwellie, late the wife of William Kidwellie, who had entered a moiety of the manor of Faccombe, co. Southampton, and lands (tenant named) in Abington, co. Berks, under his will, 20 Dec. 1574, whereby he bequeathed to her the said manor, all his other lands in Faccombe and the said lands in Abington. For 27s. 8d.

3452.)   2 Jan. 1578.   The like: George Fetiplace and Cecily his wife by indenture, 10 May, 19 Eliz., acquired unto them and the heirs of George from Edmund Cooke the manor of Little Resington, all hereditaments reputed parcel thereof on 28 Aug., 37 Hen. VIII, or since and all his other lands in Little Resington or elsewhere, co. Gloucester. For £20.

3453.)   20 Dec. 1577.   Licence for John Mershe, Alice his wife   [m. 11]
and William Mershe, his son and heir apparent, to alienate the manor of Sywell and lands and the advowson of Sywell church in Sywell, Barton, Willingboroughe, Halcott, Hanyngton, Asheby Maryes alias Meres Ashebye, Hardwyck, Overston and Ecletor, co. Northampton, to Anthony Jenkenson. For £9 6s. 8d. paid to the Queen's farmer.

3454.)   20 Dec. 1577.   The like for Adam Archerd, 'clothier', and Thomas Hall, 'yeoman', to alienate lands (named) within the manor of Burton Hill, late parcel of the manor of Burton Hill in the parish of Malmesbury, co. Wilts, to Henry Grayle, 'yoman'.

3455.)   18 Dec. 1577.   Pardon of alienation: Alice Leigh, widow, late the wife of Thomas Leigh, knight, deceased, by indenture, 28 Jan., 18 Eliz., enrolled within six months thereafter in Chancery, covenanted with Thomas Leigh of Stoneley Hall, co. Warwick, one of the sons of the said Thomas Leigh, knight, and her, that (for £600 paid by him to her) she and her heirs should stand seised of the manor, grange and capital messuage of Fletchampsted in the parish of Stonley or elsewhere, co. Warwick, late of the priory of St. John of Jerusalem in England, the capital messuage and chapel of Fletchampsted, all her other lands in Fletchampsted and Stoneley or elsewhere, co. Warwick, belonging to the said manor, grange or capital messuage and once of the said priory, lands (named) in Overfletchampsted and Stonley and all her other lands in Flethampsted late purchased by her said husband and her from William Humberston of Pakenham, co. Sussex [?recte Suffolk], deceased, to the use of Thomas the son for life, with successive remainders to Alice for life and to the heirs and assigns of Thomas the son, whereby under stat.   [m. 12]
27 Hen. VIII of uses Thomas the son is seised thereof. For £7 paid to the Queen's farmer.

3456.)   11 Jan. 1578.   The like: Richard Hardinge in Michaelmas term, 15 Eliz., by fine in the Common Pleas acquired from Richard Norton and Catherine his wife lands in Thursley and Witeley, co. Surrey. For £3 10s.

3457.)   21 *Jan.* 1578.   The like: Nicholas Swanton by indenture, 24 June, 13 Eliz., acquired from Robert Kemys lands (*named with tenants' names*) in the borough, town and parish of Wincalton, co. Somerset, and a moiety of the manor of Wincalton there. For £5 7s. 9½d.

3458.)   2 *Dec.* 1577.   The like: William Rickthorne by indenture, 16 April, 13 Eliz., acquired from William Aucher the manor of Kingeston, co. Kent, and the advowson of Kingeston, co. Kent, and the advowson of Kingeston church. For 40s.

3459.)   20 *Dec.* 1577.   Licence for Edward Ellys and William Ellys to alienate lands in Braunston in the county of the city of Lincoln to Richard Smythe and Leonard Carr. For 29s. paid to the Queen's farmer.   [*m.* 13]

3460.)   26 *Nov.* 1577.   Pardon of alienation: Thomas Neale and Richard Neale in Trinity term, 18 Eliz., by fine in the Common Pleas acquired unto them and the heirs of Thomas from Bernard Brocas and Anne his wife the borough of Buckingham, co. Buckingham, and lands and the fairs and markets, view of frankpledge, free warren and tolls etc. in the borough. For 44s. paid to the Queen's farmer.

3461.)   27 *Nov.* 1577.   Licence for William Barwell to alienate a house called 'le Graye Freers' and lands (*named*) in Great Grymsby, co. Lincoln, to Richard Thymbleby. For 6s. 8d. paid to the Queen's farmer.

3462.)   24 *Nov.* 1577.   Pardon of alienation: William Pelham in Michaelmas term, 13 Eliz., acquired from James Mussenden, Helen his wife and Richard Mussenden, his son and heir, lands in Lumber Magna and Stallingburgh, co. Lincoln. For £4 paid to the Queen's farmer.

3463.)   23 *Nov.* 1577.   The like: William Dennys and Richard Pickering in Easter term, 13 Eliz., by fine in the Common Pleas acquired unto them and the heirs of Dennys from Robert Longe and Barbara his wife lands in Malmesburyes, Charleton and North Kinges Hey, co. Wilts. For £3 6s. 8d.   [*m.* 14]

3464.)   19 *Nov.* 1577.   The like: by fine in the Common Pleas on the morrow of Trinity, 14 Eliz., John Wattes, Elizabeth his wife and John Tomlyn conveyed to John Adams lands in Swanborne, co. Buckingham, and he by the same fine conveyed them to Tomlyn for 1,000 years from Michaelmas then last at a yearly rent of 6d., if it should be sought, and the reversion and rent thereof to Wattes and Elizabeth and the heirs of Wattes. For 10s.

3465.)   20 *Nov.* 1577.   The like: William Merson in Easter term, 16 Eliz., by fine in the Common Pleas acquired from William Skipwith, knight, and Richard Skipwith and Mary his wife the manor of Woodhall in Hempsted *alias* Hemelhempsted, co. Hertford, and lands in Hemelhempsted. For £3 6s. 8d.

3466.)   20 *Jan.* 1578.   The like: William Fulwood, citizen and merchant taylor of London, by indenture, 17 April, 15 Eliz., acquired from Thomas Castle of London, 'feror', a messuage called 'Le Smythes Forge' *alias* 'le Ferrors House' at the North end of Longe Lane in the parish of St. Sepulchre in the suburbs of London, late in the tenure of William Bodley,

afterwards in that of Thomas Castle, deceased, the said Thomas's father, and now or late in that of William Maunsell, 'ferror', 13 other messuages in the said lane, now or late in the several tenures of Catherine Tomlynson, Robert Whaley, Elizabeth Idson, Christopher Mowsey, William Breadstrete, John Gascoigne, John Sedon, Robert Oswyn, William Pyckering, Leonard Smyth, William Baxter, David Nevell and Ralph Holford, a capital messuage called 'le Swane' and two gardens belonging thereto in the said lane, now or late in the tenure of Henry, lord Morley,   [m. 15]
a messuage in the said lane, now or late in the tenure of John Steepleford, and all other lands of the said Thomas in London, the county of Middlesex or elsewhere. For £4.

3467.)   19 Nov. 1577.   The like: by fine in the Common Pleas on the morrow of Trinity, 14 Eliz., John Wattes, Elizabeth his wife and John Adams conveyed to John Tomlyn lands in Swanborne, co. Buckingham, and he by the same fine conveyed them to Adams for 1,000 years from Michaelmas then last at a yearly rent of 6d., if it should be sought, and the reversion and rent thereof to Wattes and Elizabeth and the heirs of Wattes. For 10s.

3468.)   9 Feb. 1578.   The like: Philip Sture in Hilary term, 18 Eliz., by fine in the Common Pleas acquired from Henry, earl of Huntingdon, and Catherine his wife the manor of Dipford alias Dupford and lands in Dipford alias Dupford, co. Devon. For 4s. 6d.

3469.)   12 Jan. 1578.   The like: the same in Easter term, 16 Eliz., acquired from the same lands in Yoohayes, Morecoke alias Morecocke and Dipford, co. Devon. For 40s. [m. 16]

3470.)   8 Feb. 1578.   The like: Hugh Norrys in Easter term, 15 Eliz., by fine in the Common Pleas acquired from John, marquess of Winchester, and Winifred his wife lands in Westmounckton, co. Somerset. For £7.

3471.)   26 Dec. 1577.   Licence for Thomas Wiberde and Anne his wife to alienate lands in Westham, co. Essex, to John Glascock and John Meade and the heirs and assigns of Glascock. For 33s. 4d. paid to the Queen's farmer.

3472.)   29 Jan. 1578.   Pardon of alienation: Ralph Ewyre, son and heir apparent of William Ewrye, and John Horne in Hilary term, 19 Eliz., by fine in the Common Pleas acquired unto them and the heirs of Ralph from William, lord Ewrye, lands in Litle Broughton, Great Broughton, Inglebye and Kirkeby, co. York, which John Ewarden of Little Broughton, 'yeoman', held for 21 years from 30 Sept., 4 & 5 Ph. & Mary, at a yearly rent of £12 18s. 4½d. For £10 paid to the Queen's farmer.

3473.)   3 Feb. 1578.   Licence for Thomas Salwey, Arthur Salwey and Matthew Salwey to alienate a third part of lands in Canke alias Cannock, co. Stafford, to Thomas, lord Pagett of Beaudesert. For 1s. 2d. paid to the Queen's farmer.

3474.)   2 Jan. 1578.   The like for William Herde and William Mores to alienate the manor of grange of Llanvythen, and two mills belonging   [m. 17]
thereto, co. Glamorgan, to William Griffith. For £4.

3475.)   20 Nov. 1577.   The like for Arthur Golding to alienate the manor of Easthorpe, the advowson of Easthorpe church and lands (named with tenants' names) in Easthorpe, Messinge, Lyttle Birche, Great Birche, Capforde, Stanway, Layre de la Hay and Fordham or elsewhere, co. Essex, with reservations (specified), to Richard Atkyns and Eleanor his wife and the heirs and assigns of Richard. For £8.

3476.)   7 *Feb.* 1578.   Pardon of alienation: Richard Barkeley, knight, and John Tracye, knight, by indenture, 20 June, 17 Eliz., acquired from Thomas Throckmerton the manor of Wolston, the advowson of Wolston church and all his lands in Wolston and Gotherton, co. Gloucester. For £11 paid to the Queen's farmer.   [*m.* 18]

3477.)   20 *Dec.* 1577.   Licence for Robert Wykes and Elizabeth his wife to alienate the manor of Oldland *alias* Button *alias* Bytton and lands in Hannam, Downe Hannam, Westhannam, Oldland, Bitton and Upton, co. Gloucester, to Edmund Colthurst and Henry, his son and heir apparent, and the heirs and assigns of Edmund. For £3 6s. 8d. paid to the Queen's farmer.

3478.)   9 *Feb.* 1578.   Pardon of alienation: by indenture tripartite, 1 July, 15 Eliz., between Rowland Barker, Thomas Fortescue and Thomas Bromeley, solicitor general, Fortescue acquired from Barker *inter alia* the advowson of Hodnett church, co. Salop. For 20s. paid to the Queen's farmer.

3479.)   10 *Feb.* 1578.   The like: by indenture tripartite, 3 July, 16 Eliz., Rowland Barker acquired from Thomas Bromeley, solicitor general, and Thomas Fortescue the manor of Betton in Betton, Little Drayton, Tunstall, Rigerdyne and Norton or elsewhere, co. Salop, the manor of Ollerton *alias* Wollerton, co. Salop, all lands in Hopton and in the hamlet, grange or farm of Hopley or elsewhere, co. Salop, late of the inheritance of Rowland Hill, knight, deceased, and afterwards of Barker, and all lands which Bromley and Fortescue had of Barker and Vincent Randall, citizen and mercer of London. For £25.

3480.)   20 *Dec.* 1577.   Licence for Richard Purefey to alienate the manor of Netherworton *alias* Netherorton, co. Oxford, and lands (*named*) in Netherworton to Philip Babington. For £3 paid to the Queen's farmer.   [*m.* 19]

3481.)   20 *Jan.* 1578.   Pardon of alienation: George Downyng and Richard Elmy in Michaelmas term, 16 Eliz., by fine in the Common Pleas acquired unto them and the heirs of Dowyng from Reginald Rabet and Alice his wife *inter alia* lands in Bromefild *alias* Brampfyld and Wenhaston, co. Suffolk. For £10 paid to the Queen's farmer.

3482.)   30 *Jan.* 1578.   The like: John Samwayes and Bernard Samwayes, one of the sons of John, by indenture, 6 Feb., 18 Eliz., acquired from Richard Rede, knight, lands (*named with tenants' names*) in Holwaye in the parish of Cattestocke, co. Dorset, to hold unto them and the heirs of the body of Bernard, with successive remainders to John in tail, to Robert Samwayes, another son of John, in tail, to the heirs of the body of Elizabeth Gillett, deceased, one of the sisters of John, and to Alice Bonde, widow, another sister of John, in tail. For 55s.

3483.)   7 *Feb.* 1578.   Licence for William Gilberte to alienate lands in Great Over *alias* Mickleover and Finderne, co. Derby, to Edward Clere to the use of William and his heirs until the marriage of William and Anne Clere, and then to the use of William and Anne and the heirs of William's body by her, with successive remainders to the heirs male of the body of William and to his right heirs. For 40s. 11d. paid to the Queen's farmer.

3484.)   20 *Dec.* 1577.   The like for William Welden and Elizabeth   [*m.* 20]
his wife to alienate the manor of Wolston *alias* Wolverysheton *alias* Wolfrichton and lands in Wolston, co. Berks, to James Braybroke and Ralph Radcliff and the heirs and assigns of Braybroke. For £5 6s. 8d.

3485.)   20 *Dec.* 1577.   The like for the same to alienate lands in Whitewaltham, co. Berks, to Ralph Ratcliff and Thomas George and the heirs and assigns of Ratcliff. For 12*s.* 7*d.*

3486.)   9 *Feb.* 1578.   Pardon of alienation: Edmund Bray in Trinity term, 13 Eliz., by fine in the Common Pleas acquired from William Sandys, lord Sandis, and Catherine his wife the manor of Brode Rysingdon *alias* Rysingdon Magna, lands in Brode Rysingdon, Rysingdon Parva and Notgrave and the advowson of Brode Risingdon church, co. Gloucester. For £10 paid to the Queen's farmer.

3487.)   9 *Feb.* 1578.   The like: Giles Poole, knight, by indenture, 6 Sept., 18 Eliz., acquired from Edmund Bray the manor of Rysingdon Magna *alias* Brode Risingdon, co. Gloucester, the advowson of Rysingdon Magna church and lands (*named*) in Rysingdon Magna. For £3 6*s.* 8*d.*   [*m.* 21]

3488.)   5 *Jan.* 1578.   The like: Blaise Radberd by his will, 29 Sept. 1576, bequeathed to his brother, William Radberde, clerk, a moiety of the manor of Sowthpetherton, co. Somerset, late of the monastery of Brewton, co. Somerset, and of all his lands, and after Blaise's death William entered upon the same. For 34*s.* 9½*d.*

3489.)   1 *Feb.* 1578.   The like: John Winche in Michaelmas term, 17 Eliz., by fine in the Common Pleas acquired from Thomas Colbye and Elizabeth his wife lands in Estcottes *alias* Cotton Ende *alias* Heringes Ende, Cardington, Harrowden and Fenlacke, co. Bedford. For £7.

3490.)   1 *Feb.* 1578.   The like: John Felde, 'yoman', and Agnes his wife by indenture, 5 Sept., 13 Eliz., acquired from Thomas Cheynye lands (*named*) in Elcott, parcel of the customary lands of the manor of Kyntburye Ambresbury, and all appurtenances thereof in the parish of Kyntbury, co. Berks, to hold for life in survivorship, with remainders to John's sons, Robert Felde the elder, Robert Felde the younger, Richard Felde and John Felde the younger, for life successively, with remainders over to the heirs of the bodies of the said sons successively. For 26*s.* 8*d.*

3491.)   26 *Dec.* 1577.   Licence for George Burgoine the elder and Dorothy his wife to alienate the manor of Lannock, lands in Lannock, Weston and   [*m.* 22]
Graveley, the rectory of Weston and the advowson of the vicarage of Weston, co. Hertford, to George Burgoine the younger. For £8 17*s.* 9*d.* paid to the Queen's farmer.

3492.)   20 *Dec.* 1577.   The like for Henry Knyvett, knight, and Elizabeth his wife to alienate the manor of Houghton Magna, lands in Houghton Magna, Haughton Parva, Billingbye and Darfeild and free warren and view of frankpledge in Haughton Magna and Billingbye, co. York, to Francis Roodes. For £7.

3493.)   20 *Dec.* 1577.   The like for Richard Culpeper to alienate a moiety of a fourth part of lands in Keymer *alias* Kydmer, co. Sussex, to John Cheyle and Richard Cheyle. For 11*s.* 1½*d.*

3494.)   20 *Dec.* 1577.   The like for Thomas Lucas to alienate lands (*named with tenants' names*) in Mells *alias* Mellis in the parish of Bramptfeld, co. Suffolk, to Agnes Burrage, widow.   [*m.* 23]
For £8 6*s.* 8*d.*

3495.)   1 *Jan.* 1578.   The like for John Prowse of Brixham the elder and John Prowse the younger, son and heir of Nicholas Prowse, deceased, to alienate lands (*named*) in the parish of Totnes, co. Devon, to Richard Cliffe and John Srewner (*alias* Screwner) to the use of the said John Prowse the elder for life and thereafter of John Prowse the younger and Catherine his wife and the heirs and assigns of John the younger. For 46*s.* 8*d.*

3496.)   20 *Dec.* 1577.   The like for Thomas Kempe to alienate lands (*named*) in Charlewood, co. Surrey, to John Skynner. For 4*s.*

3497.)   20 *Dec.* 1577.   The like for John Conyers of London and Catherine his wife to alienate the manors of Carleton Magna, Carleton Parva and Castell Carleton, lands in Carleton Magna, Carleton Parva and Castell Carleton and the advowsons of Castell Carleton and Carleton Magna churches, co. Lincoln, to John Conyers of Sockbourne. For 53*s.* 4*d.*

3498.)   2 *Jan.* 1578.   The like for John Alwey and Henry Alwey to alienate lands (*named with tenants' names*), parcel of the manor of Welles *alias* Welburne, in Great Offeley, Little Offeley, Lytley and Little Hytchyn, co. Hertford, to Richard Spicer *alias* Helder   [*m.* 24] the younger. For 15*s.* 7*d.*

3499.)   20 *Dec.* 1577.   The like for Richard Cooke and Anne his wife to alienate lands in Dorset *alias* Dassett *alias* Birton Dorsett *alias* Byrton Dassett *alias* Dassett Magna, co. Warwick, to Francis Rame and John Skynner and the heirs and assigns of Rame. For £20.

3500.)   20 *Dec.* 1577.   The like for Philip, lord Wharton, to alienate the manor of Marston and lands in Marston, Huton and Tockwith in the county of the city of York to James Thwaite. For £4 2*s.* 2*d.*

3501.)   1 *March* 1578.   The like for John Tirrell and Mary his wife to alienate lands in Bacton, Cotton and Newton, co. Suffolk, to Thomas Pretyman. For 49*s.*

3502.)   1 *March* 1578.   The like for Roger Goodday to alienate lands (*named with tenants' names*) in Sandon, Easthaninfeild,   [*m.* 25]
Great Badowe and Springfeld, co. Essex, to Robert Goodday. For £9 13*s.* 4*d.*

3503.)   1 *March* 1578.   The like for Richard Cockes of Little Fawley, co. Hereford, to alienate lands (*named*) in Wilton in the parish of Bridstowe and in Bridstowe, co. Hereford, to William Edwardes, son of Thomas Edwardes, and George Penne. For 3*s.* 8*d.*

3504.)   1 *March* 1578.   The like for William Parker to alienate the manor of Overhall and all lands belonging thereto in Gelston and Overhall, co. Hertford, to Humphrey Corbett and Anne his wife and the heirs and assigns of Humphrey. For £5.

3505.)   1 *March* 1578.   The like for Thomas Gresham, knight, and Anne his wife to alienate lands in Mileham, co. Norfolk, to Christopher Crowe. For 26*s.* 8*d.*

3506.)   1 *March* 1578.   The like for John Nevell and Alice his wife to alienate the advowson of the perpetual vicarage of St. Peter the Apostle, Collshull, co. Warwick, to George Digby. For 10*s.*

3507.)   1 *March* 1578.   The like for Arthur Hall and Joan his   [*m.* 26]
wife to alienate a moiety of lands in Colchester, co. Essex, to John Watson. For 6*s.* 8*d.*

3508.)   23 *April* 1578.   Pardon of alienation: John Brograve and William Grove in Trinity term, 14 Eliz., by fine in the Common Pleas acquired unto them and the heirs of Brograve from Richard Marden lands in Wellowe, co. Southampton. For £5 6s. 8d. paid to the Queen's farmer.

3509.)   1 *March* 1578.   Licence for William Jaye, Elizabeth his wife, Robert Welles and Elizabeth his wife to alienate lands in Byllynghaye, co. Lincoln, to Richard Dycconson. For 19s. 10d. paid to the Queen's farmer.

3510.)   25 *Feb.* 1578.   The like for Roger Gryndon and Kenrick Davis and Alice his wife to alienate lands in Kaysho, parcel of the manor, capital messuage or farm called Grimsburye, co. Bedford, to Oliver, lord Seynt John of Blettisho. For 13s. 4d.

3511.)   24 *April* 1578.   Pardon of alienation: William Lambarde by indenture, 6 Feb., 15 Eliz., acquired from William Sydnor the   [*m.* 27]
manor of Brenchesley *alias* Cryells in Brenchesley *alias* Brencheley and Lamberherst and lands (*tenants named*) in Brenchesley, Yalding, Tonbridge and Lamberherst, co. Kent. For £3 6s. 8d. paid to the Queen's farmer.

3512.)   24 *April* 1578.   The like: the same by indenture, 10 April, 15 Eliz., acquired from the same lands (*named*) in Brenchley and Lamberherst, co. Kent. For 33s. 4d.

3513.)   21 *April* 1578.   The like: John Sames by indenture, 1 Nov., 16 Eliz., acquired from Thomas Beckingham the manor of Folyfans in Goldanger or elsewhere, co Essex, and lands (*named with tenants' names*) in Tollson Magna and Goldanger, co. Essex. For £4.

3514.)   23 *Nov.* 1577.   The like: William Fitzwilliams by fine in the Common Pleas levied in Trinity term and granted and recorded on the octave of Michaelmas, 13 Eliz., acquired from Robert Dymmock lands in Wythorne *alias* Withern, Mablethorpe, Maltbye, Strubbye, Woodthorpe, Carleton and Manby, four ninth parts of the manor of Wythorne, four ninth parts of lands in the places aforesaid and four parts of the advowson of Wythorne church, co. Lincoln. For £12.

3515.)   24 *April* 1578.   The like: Frances Bowes, widow, late the wife of Martin Bowes, by indenture, 18 Nov., 16 Eliz., acquired from William Clopton a capital messuage called 'le Ball' in 'le Ould Change' in the parish of St. Augustine in London, then or late in the tenure of William Chappell, citizen and merchant taylor of London,   [*m.* 28]
three messuages in 'le Ould Chaunge' adjoining the said messuage, then in the several tenures of John Kyndon, skinner, Anthony Trivett, goldsmith, and William Stiper, merchant taylor, and the small tenements in Porche Alley in 'le Ould Chaunge' then in the several tenures of John Williams, Agnes Gresham, widow, Mary Nicolles, widow, William Wilkynson, John Brisco, Elizabeth Edwardes, widow, and Richard Smyth. For £5.

3516.)   1 *May* 1578.   The like: Thomas Cheyne by indenture, 16 May, 16 Eliz., acquired from John Markeham all lands parcel of the manor of Woodcrofte in the parish of Luton, with all courts and franchises and all other lands, co. Bedford. For 40s.

3517.)   28 *April* 1578.   The like: George Catelyn in Michaelmas term, 14 Eliz., acquired from Everard Digbye and Margaret his wife the manors of Fortune, Lomewood *alias* Lamewood *alias* Bromes Hall Place, Ringes and Gore, the rectory of Hadlowe and lands in Aylesford, Est Peckham, Wateringham, Nettlested, Mereworth, Hadlowe, Est Barmyng,

Birling, Burham, Boxley, Woldham, Saynt Margarettes next Rochester, Sythingborne, Midleton and Tunstall, co. Kent. For 40*s*.

3518.)   1 *May* 1578.   The like: Thomas Cheyne in Michaelmas term, 17 Eliz., by fine in the Common Pleas acquired from George Rotheram the manor of Woodcrofte and lands in Luton, co. Bedford. For 40*s*.

3519.)   2 *April* 1578.   The like: Robert Freake and Thomas Freake, his son, in Michaelmas term, 17 Eliz., by fine in the Common Pleas acquired unto them and the heirs of Thomas from William Mighell   [*m.* 29]
and Adriana his wife lands in Iwerne Mynster, co. Dorset. For 20*s*.

3520.)   29 *April* 1578.   The like: William Tanckard and Ralph Tanckard by indenture, 20 July, 15 Eliz., acquired from Robert Ughtred, knight, and Dorothy Constable, widow, late the wife of John Cunstable, lands (*named with tenants' names*, including the inhabitants of Dunnyngton) in Kexbye. For 40*s*.

3521.)   1 *May* 1578.   The like: Henry Sympson, one of the clerks of William Cordell, knight, master of the rolls, by indenture, 15 Nov., 18 Eliz., acquired from William Crayford *inter alia* a third part of lands parcel of the manor of Madford, co. Devon. For 16*d*.

3522.)   1 *May* 1578.   Licence for Henry Alington and Anne his wife to alienate lands in Stratford le Bowe, co. Middlesex, to Peter Osborne and Hugh Alington and the heirs and assigns of Osborne. For 66*s*. 8*d*. paid to the Queen's farmer.

3523.)   10 *June* 1578.   Pardon of alienation: Charles Cornwallies by indenture, 13 May, 17 Eliz., acquired from William Fyncham the manors of Fyncham Hall *alias* Surpelles Hall and Baynerdes Hall, co. Norfolk. For £5 paid to the Queen's farmer.

3524.)   16 *June* 1578.   The like: Richard Musterd in Michaelmas term, 15 Eliz., by fine in the Common Pleas acquired from William   [*m.* 30]
Poulett, knight, lord Seynt John, and Agnes his wife a moiety of lands in Hemyngford Grey, co. Huntingdon. For 20*s*.

3525.)   1 *May* 1578.   Licence for Richard Hiltofte to alienate the manor of Cawkewell, lands in Cawkewell and the advowson of Cawkwell church, co. Lincoln, to Brian Eland. For £8 paid to the Queen's farmer.

3526.)   16 *June* 1578.   Pardon of alienation: Christopher Brome, knight, by indenture, 25 May, 18 Eliz., acquired from William Wyndesor lands (*tenants named*) in Princes Resboroughe, co. Buckingham, which Wyndesor purchased from Peter Palmer by indenture, 2 Feb., 6 Eliz. For 20*s*. paid to the Queen's farmer.

3527.)   17 *June* 1578.   The like: Matthew Smythe in Hilary term, 18 Eliz., by fine in the Common Pleas acquired from Richard Breton and Nicholas Breton, son[s?] of William Breton, deceased, ten messuages and a garden in the parish of St. Giles without Creplegate, London, whereof one messuage and a garden, once in the tenure of Thomas Smythe, are held of the Queen in chief. For 13*s*. 4*d*.

3528.)   1 *May* 1578.   Licence for Thomas Porter, knight, to alienate lands (*described*) in the city of Gloucester to Luke Garnons.   [*m.* 31]
For 20*s*. 9½*d*.

3529.)   1 *May* 1578.   The like for John Willoughbie to alienate a third part of the manor of Westdereham in Tilney and of lands in Tilney, Terrington and Ilsinginton, co. Norfolk, and a third part of lands with 'le ferry' in Clenchewarton and Westlyn, late of Robert Howardes, 'yeoman', co. Norfolk, to Charles Cornewallys. For 33*s*. 4*d*.

3530.)   9 *June* 1578.   Pardon of alienation: John Bayles in Hilary term, 19 Eliz., by fine in the Common Pleas acquired from Arthur Breame, Thomasina his wife, James Platte and Bridget his wife the manor of Stonehall and lands in Barkinge and Westham, co. Essex. For £4 paid to the Queen's farmer.

3531.)   10 *June* 1578.   The like: Balthezar Sanches of London, 'comfetmaker', by indenture, 25 June, 17 Eliz., acquired from John Bales, citizen and 'tallowchandler' of London, a corner messuage, then in the tenure of Thomas Parker, and the rest of the tenements adjoining thereto, then in the tenures of John Williamson, George Dodson, Matthew Wood and William Deman, in the parish of St. Dunstan in le Est, London, which Sanches late purchased from Thomas Ive of Kentyshetowne, co. Middlesex. For £10.

3532.)   13 *June* 1578.   The like: John Bales and Robert Garnett on Monday after the feast of St. Matthew, 18 Eliz., in the husting in the guildhall of the city of London before Ambrose Nicholas, knight, mayor, and the sheriffs of the city recovered against Peter Bales and Elizabeth Bales, widow, (by writ of right patent directed to the mayor and sheriffs according to the course of common recoveries at common law by custom of the city) two third parts of four messuages in the parish of St. Michael in Cornewall in Cornehill ward, London. For 100*s*.

3533.)   12 *June* 1578.   The like: John Willoughbye by indenture, 7 May, 16 Eliz., acquired from Robert Howarde a third part of the manor of Westdereham in Tilney and of all his lands in Tilney, Terrington and Islington, co. Norfolk, and a third part of lands with 'le ferrye' in Clenchewarton and Westlyme, late of the   [*m.* 32] same Howarde, co. Norfolk. For 100*s*.

3534.)   9 *June* 1578.   The like: John Bayles by indenture tripartite, 31 Dec., 18 Eliz., acquired from James Platt *inter alia* marsh lands (*named*), then or late in the tenure of Bayles, in the parish of Westham, co. Essex. For £4.

3535.)   17 *June* 1578.   The like: Henry Sadler, clerk of the hanaper of Chancery, by indenture, 1 June, 18 Eliz., acquired from John Philpott lands (*named*) in the parish of Aspiden, co. Hertford. For £9.

3536.)   1 *May* 1578.   Licence for Henry, earl of Arundell, John Lumley, knight, lord Lumley, Jane his wife, John Jackman and Jane his wife to alienate the manors of Wollavington *alias* Wolle Lavington, Wonworthe and Graffam *alias* Grafham and lands in Petworth, Shellingleighe, Wollavington, Kydford Grene *alias* Wisborowe Grene, Stopham, Pulborowe, Westburton and Lurgarsale, co. Sussex, to Giles Garton and Francis Garton and the heirs and assigns of Giles. For £18 8*s*. 4*d*. paid to the Queen's farmer.

3537.)   17 *June* 1578.   Pardon of alienation: Richard Charnock by indenture, 11 Dec., 16 Eliz., acquired from George Rotheram the reversion and remainder of a fourth part of the manor of   [*m.* 33] Bedlowe *alias* Bedloe *alias* Beawlowe, co. Bedford. For 40*s*. paid to the Queen's farmer.

3538.)   12 *June* 1578.   The like: Thomas Cecill, knight, by indenture, 27 Nov., 19 Eliz., acquired from Henry Darcye, knight, and Thomas Darcye the site and demesne lands of the monastery of Sawley, co. York. For £20.

3539.)   1 *May* 1578.   Licence for John Kecke and John Tomes to alienate lands in Marston Sicca, co. Gloucester, to Alice Campden. For 6s. 8d. paid to the Queen's farmer.

3540.)   21 *April* 1578.   Pardon of alienation: John Barker by indenture, 7 Nov., 15 Eliz., acquired from Thomas Beckingham two farms (*tenants named*) called Hyams and Joyces, co. Essex. For £4 paid to the Queen's farmer.

3541.)   2 *June* 1578.   Licence for Thomas Hayes to alienate lands (*named with tenants' names*) in the parish of Sandon, co. Essex, to John Glascocke. For 4d. paid to the Queen's farmer.

[*m.* 34]

3542.)   20 *June* 1578.   Pardon of alienation: John Jones the younger in Michaelmas term, 15 Eliz., by fine in the Common Pleas acquired from Thomas Jones and Rachel his wife lands in Kevell, Buckington and Sceane and common of pasture for four beasts in Oxenlease and Northwood, co. Wilts. For 26s. 8d. paid to the Queen's farmer.

3543.)   19 *June* 1578.   The like: Thomas Lucas, knight, by fine in the Common Pleas levied in Trinity term and granted and recorded in Michaelmas term, 17 Eliz., acquired from John Abell and Mary his wife lands in Fordam Magna, co. Essex. For 3s. 4d.

3544.)   1 *May* 1578.   Licence for John Blagrave and Anthony Blagrave to alienate two water mills and a fulling mill in the parish of St. Giles in Reding, co. Berks, the tithes thereof, lands and 'le locke' called Tanlocke in Redinge and mills called Mynster Milles and 'le locke' called Greys Locke, to Thomas Umpton. For 53s. 4d. paid to the Queen's farmer.

3545.)   12 *May* 1578.   Pardon of alienation: John Wooddye, citizen and skinner of London, by indenture, 10 July, 18 Eliz., acquired from Thomas Cockes of the Inner Temple, London, a messuage, then or late in Wooddye's tenure, in Fletstrete in the parish of St. Dunstan in le West in the suburbs of London (between the common way leading to the Inner Temple on the East, a tenement late in the tenure of Giles Atkynson and Richard Wheler on the West, the highway on the North and the garden of the Inner Temple on the South), late of the hospital of St. John of Jerusalem. For 20s. paid to the Queen's farmer.

3546.)   30 *June* 1578.   *Gorhambury.*   The like: Robert Byndlose by   [*m.* 35] indenture, 14 Dec., 14 Eliz., acquired from Henry Ayscoughe, Walter Ayscoughe and Edmund Ayscoughe *inter alia* the capital messuage and site of the priory of Seyton, co. Cumberland.

3547.)   28 *April* 1578.   Licence for Rowland Heyward, knight, and Joan his wife to alienate lands in Bildowes *alias* Bildwas, co. Salop, to Edward Harbert, knight. For £4 8s. 11d. paid to the Queen's farmer.

3548.)   23 *June* 1578.   Pardon of alienation: Anthony Blagrave by indenture, 1 Nov., 18 Eliz., acquired from John Blagrave two water mills and a fulling mill annexed thereto in the parish of St. Giles in Redinge, co. Berks, called Saynte Giles Milles, the tithes thereof, lands and 'le locke' called Tanlocke in Redinge and mills called Mynster Milles and 'le locke' called Greys Locke. For £8 paid to the Queen's farmer.

3549.)   2 *June* 1578.   Licence for Thomas Crompton and William Sparke to alienate lands (*named*) in Scalford *alias* Scalforthe and Waltom *alias* Waltam on le Wolde, co. Leicester, to Ralph Segrave. For £3 6s. 8d. paid to the Queen's farmer.

3550).   23 *June* 1578.   Pardon of alienation: John Lamberte by fine in the Common Pleas levied in Easter term and granted and recorded in Trinity term, 15 Eliz., acquired from John Robynson and Martha his wife a moiety of the manor of Malhome *alias* Westmalhome and of lands in Malhome and Malhome More, co. York. For 26s. paid to the   [*m.* 36] Queen's farmer.

3551.)   12 *May* 1578.   The like: Thomas Cockes of the Inner Temple by indenture, 12 April, 18 Eliz., acquired from John Wooddye, citizen and skinner of London, a messuage, then or late in Woddye's tenure, in Fleetstreete in the parish of St. Dunstan in le West in the suburbs of London (*described* as in no. 3545), late of the hospital of St. John of Jerusalem. For 20s.

3552.)   23 *June* 1578.   *Gorhambury*.   The like: John Northcote, John Weste, Thomas Laude and Richard Appowell by charter of feoffment, 20 Oct., 19 Eliz., acquired from John Waldron the elder *inter alia* the manor of Woneford *alias* Southwonford, co. Devon. For £4.

3553.)   17 *June* 1578.   The like: Richard Reade, knight, by indenture, 6 July, 13 Eliz., acquired from Henry Compton, knight, a fourth part of the manor of Wallopp *alias* Wallop Moyles *alias* Overwallopp, co. Southampton. For £4.

3554.)   18 *June* 1578.   The like: Thomas Rede and William Drurye in Trinity term, 16 Eliz., by fine in the Common Pleas acquired unto them and the heirs of the same Thomas from Innocent Rede and Elizabeth his wife a third part of the manors of Higheclere and Burghe Clere *alias* Borough Clere, of lands in Highclere and Borougheclere and of the advowsons of Highe Clere and Burghe Clere churches, co. Southampton. For £18.

3555.)   15 *May* 1578.   Licence for Edward Carill and Philippa his wife to alienate the manor of Shortefelde *alias* Shortesfelde and free warren therein, co. Sussex, to John Carill. For £4 8s. 11d.   [*m.* 37] paid to the Queen's farmer.

3556.)   1 *May* 1578.   Pardon of alienation: John Wolriche in Easter term, 18 Eliz., by fine in the Common Pleas acquired from Thomas Colbye and Elizabeth his wife lands in Estcotes *alias* Cottonende, Cardington *alias* Carington, Horroden *alias* Harrowden and Fenlake, co. Bedford. For 18s. 4d. paid to the Queen's farmer.

3557.)   1 *May* 1578.   Licence for Ingram Moyses to alienate lands (*tenant named*) in Leatheley and the reversion of a moiety of all lands in Leatheley, Farmeley and Elscome Botham, co. York, now in the tenure of Robert Moyses, his father, or himself to Anthony West. For 16s. 3d. paid to the Queen's farmer.

3558.)   1 *March* 1578.   The like for Henry Woodhouse to alienate the manor of Boylandes in Northwalsham and lands in Northwalsham, Worsted, Westwicke, Felmyngham and Bradfeld, co. Norfolk, to Thomas Gryme. For 40s.

3559.)   1 *May* 1578.   The like for Richard Pyncke and Maud his wife to alienate a moiety of the manor of Worting, of lands in Worting and Wotton and of the advowson of Worting church, co. Southampton, to James Rumboll. For 40s.

3560.)   15 *May* 1578.   The like for John Carell and Mary his wife to alienate the manors of Wythyham and Shipley, lands in Shipley, Somptinge and Cokeham, the rectory of Shipley, free warren in the said manors and the advowson of the vicarage of Shipley, co. Sussex, to Edward Carill. For £4 8*s.* 11*d.*   [*m.* 38]

3561.)   13 *May* 1578.   Pardon of alienation: William Wynter by indenture, 15 Feb., 14 Eliz., acquired from Edward, lord Stafford, lands (*named*) in Thornebury, co. Gloucester. For £4 paid to the Queen's farmer.

3562.)   3 *Feb.* 1578.   Licence for Robert, earl of Leicester, to alienate the site of the manor of Marston Sicca *alias* Dry Marston, co. Gloucester, in the tenure of John Warne and late in that of Thomas Warne, his father, and lands (*named with tenants' names*) in Dry Marston, all granted to him *inter alia* by patent, 29 June, 8 Eliz., (reserving to him the liberties and regalities belonging to the manor) to John Kecke and John Toms. For £6 13*s.* 4*d.* paid to the Queen's farmer.

3563.)   1 *March* 1578.   The like for Peter Tonge to alienate a tenement and garden, in the tenure once of Robert Lee, late of John Flower, merchant taylor, and late of Richard Stonley, in Aldersgatestreate in the parish of St. Botolph without Aldersgate *alias* Aldrichegate, London, to the said Stonley. For 6*s.* 7*d.*

3564.)   1 *March* 1578.   The like for Thomas Parker to alienate the manor of Belhouse in Northtuddenham, co. Norfolk, to Edward,   [*m.* 39]
lord Morley. For £3 15*s.* 3*d.*

3565.)   1 *March* 1578.   The like for Edward, lord Zouche, Seyntmaure and Canteloupe, and Eleanor his wife to alienate a fourth part of lands in Wincaulton and Marshe, co. Somerset, to Robert Kemys. For 33*s.* 4*d.*

3566.)   14 *Feb.* 1578.   Pardon of alienation: Bartholomew Quyney by indenture, 18 July, 18 Eliz., acquired from John Woodye, citizen and skinner of London, a messuage, now or late in Woodye's tenure, in Fletestrete in the parish of St. Dunstan in le Weste in the suburbs of London (*described* as in no. 3545), late of the hospital of St. John of Jerusalem. For 40*s.* paid to the Queen's farmer.

3567.)   14 *Feb.* 1578.   The like: Richard Mylward and Ralph Rogers by indenture, 28 July, 18 Eliz., acquired from Bartholomew Quyney a messuage, now or late in the tenure of John Woddye, citizen and skinner of London, in Fletestrete in the parish of St. Dunstan in le West in the suburbs of London (*described* as in no. 3545), late of the hospital of St. John of Jerusalem. For 40*s.*

3568.)   12 *March* 1578.   *Gorhambury.*   The like: Richard Onslowe, deceased, Thomas Godman and John Floyde by indenture, 14 Feb., 13 Eliz., acquired to the use of Onslowe from Gerrard Croker a grange called Barton Grange in the parish of Cirencester, co. Gloucester, late of the monastery of Cirencester, lands etc. (*named*) in the said parish and the first vesture of meadows (*named*) in Latton and Eysie, co. Wilts, and the customary works of Croker's tenants of the manor or manors   [*m.* 40]
of Latton and Eysie for cutting etc. the hay in the said meadows. For £10.

3569.)   13 *March* 1578.   *Gorhambury.*   The like: Richard Onslowe, being seised of the manor of Caughley and lands and free fishery in the water of Severn in Caughley and

Wenlock Magna, co. Salop, a grange called Barton Grange in the parish of Cirencester, co. Gloucester, late of the monastery of Cirencester, lands etc. (*named*) in the said parish and the first vesture of meadows (*named*) in Latton and Eysie, co. Wilts, and the customary works of the tenants of the manor or manors of Latton and Eysie for cutting etc. the hay in the said meadows, by his will, 20 March, 13 Eliz., bequeathed to Catherine his wife two parts of all his lands in England for life to the preferment in marriage of his five daughters at her discretion, and after his death she entered upon two parts of the premises. For £3 6s. 8d.

3570.)   15 *Nov.* 1578.   The like: Walter Powell in Trinity term, 19 Eliz., by fine in the Common Pleas acquired from Thomas Reynoldes lands in Llantrissen, co. Monmouth. For 14s. 5½d.

3571.)   10 *March* 1578.   Licence for Edward, lord Zouche, and Eleanor his wife to alienate a fourth part of the manor of Cardinham, of lands and of the advowson of Cardinham and all lands of the said lord Zouche in Cardinham, Bodman, Helland, Blisseland, Warlegan, St. Nyott, Brodeoke and Temple, co. Cornwall, to William Billinge and William Foorthe, clerk, and the heirs and assigns of Billing. For 38s. 11d. paid to the Queen's farmer.

(The dorse of this roll is blank.)

PART IX

C. 66/1172

3572.)   12 *Dec.* 1577.   *Hampton Court.*   Grant that the freemen   [*m.* 1]
of the misteries of merchant drapers and hosiers (*sutorum calligarum*) of the city of Chester
and the suburbs thereof may be one body corporate with a master and two wardens and the
commonalty of the misteries. Incorporation of the master and wardens. The master and
wardens may hold assemblies and make ordinances for the government of the misteries; so
that they be not contrary to the laws and customs of the realm and the privileges of the city.
Appointment of John Smythe, inhabitant of Chester, to be the first and present warden, to
execute the office according to his oath until Michaelmas next and thereafter until another be
elected and sworn. Appointment of John Allen and Humphrey Reignoldes, inhabitants of
Chester, to be the first and present wardens, to be sworn before the present master. The
master and wardens with the commonalty may assemble yearly on Monday before
Michaelmas between the hours of 9 and 12 a.m. in a convenient place within the city and
nominate two of the principal men of the misteries in order that the wardens may elect one
of them as master for one year; who after being sworn shall hold office until Michaelmas
following and thereafter until another be elected and sworn; if any master elect shall on
notice given of his election refuse to accept office without reasonable cause, the master and
wardens may commit him to gaol until he will exercise the office or may put a fitting fine
upon him and detain him in prison until he will pay it. The master elect shall be sworn before
his predecessor, if alive and present, and otherwise before the wardens and other principal
men of the misteries present; if a master shall die or be removed during his time of office, the
wardens and other principal men may assemble as aforesaid on an appointed day within
eight days following and nominate two of the principal men for election as aforesaid as
master until Michaelmas then next and thereafter until a new master be elected and sworn;
the person so elected to be sworn before the wardens and other principal men. Whenever the
wardens or either   [*m.* 2]
of them shall die, dwell outside the city or be removed from office, the master and other
principal men may within eight days following assemble as aforesaid and elect another or
others to be warden until Michaelmas then next and thereafter until a new warden or
wardens be elected and sworn; those so elected to be sworn before the master and other
principal men. The master and wardens to have within the city and the liberties and suburbs
thereof the entire survey and correction of all freemen of the city, denizens and foreigners
and aliens born of whatsoever mistery using the mistery of merchant drapers called 'drapers'
or the mistery of sewers of hose called 'hosiers' or of anything touching the same, both of
woollen cloths, rough and shaggy cloths called 'rugges and frises', other cloths and
garments called 'cadoes and mantelles', shaped hose (*calligis aptatis*), white cloths, cloths of
dark colour called 'russett and flannen' or other kinds of woollen cloths and of all goods
appertaining to either of the misteries, although such hose have been made within the city or
the liberties or suburbs thereof and the cloths bought or sold there having been brought by
anyone freeman or foreign from any part of England or from overseas to the city or the
suburbs thereof or one mile round about the city, and also of all others foreigners aliens born
using the misteries or anything appertaining thereto within the city or the suburbs or
liberties thereof; also to have the punishment of the same for faults in the making, buying
and selling of hose and the buying and selling of cloth, so that such punishment be executed

according to the law of the realm and the ordinances made by the master and wardens. No one to presume to search any the Queen's privileged liege frequenting those arts or lawfully admitted thereto by the master and wardens, or their goods, save only the master and wardens. No foreigner or alien born within the city or the suburbs thereof or within one mile of the city shall sell any cloths, whether rough cloths called 'rugges and frises', garments called 'cadoes, blankettes, mantelles and checkers', white cloths called 'whites', cloths of dark colour called 'russettes', other cloths called 'flannen' or other woollen cloths whatsoever or any shaped hose to any alien born or foreigner or to the use of any such by retail or in gross, under pain of forfeiture of 20s. for every yard of cloth sold, and no free denizen, unless first admitted to the mistery by the master and wardens shall sell such wares there to any alien or foreigner or any other person by retail or in gross under pain of forfeiture of £5 for every offence; provided notwithstanding that all freemen of the city dwelling within the city or the suburbs thereof may sell woollen cloths of their own and sole making by 'whole sale' or in gross to any alien born or foreigner or any other person; one moiety of the forfeitures to go to the mayor and commonalty of the city and the other to the use of the misteries of merchant drapers and hosiers. The mayor of the city to aid the master and wardens in the execution of the premises, and to distrain all persons rebellious in this behalf and, if need be, to arrest them and cause them to be kept in prison until they satisfy the mayor and the master and wardens of the forfeitures due, as the master and wardens shall on their part certify the mayor.

At the suit of the merchant drapers and hosiers of the city: they have from time immemorial been wont to regulate those misteries, order the estate of their servants of the same and correct their faults, and now for some time all saying they are of those misteries both strangers and others have taken shops in the city at will and great damage has arisen for many of the city and others by such strangers being unregulated and not corrected of their faults.　　　　　　　　　　　　　　　　　　　　　　　　　　　　　　　　　　　By p.s.

3573.)　18 *Nov.* 1577.　Grant for life in survivorship to Benjamin Gonson and John Hawkyns, the Queen's servants, of the office of　　　　　　　　　　　　　　　　[*m.* 3] treasurer of the marine causes; with an annuity of 100 marks and for two clerks under them 8d. a day each, and allowances of 6s. 8d. for every day they shall travel about the business of the office and £8 a year for boat hire; they shall also have allowance of all moneys spent about the marine causes, having the hands of two or three of the officers of the marine causes subscribed to their books of account testifying the expenditure thereof, and the showing of this patent and the books of account so subscribed shall be sufficient warrant for their discharge; they shall also have the costs of their clerks as often as they shall send them for the payment or receipt of money for the marine causes; all the sums above-granted to be payable at the Exchequer. In consideration of the surrender by Gonson in Chancery of a patent, 8 July, 3 Edw. VI, granting him the office for life; and for their service. *English.* By p.s.

3574.)　21 *Nov.* 1577.　Grant to Bridget Woodroff, widow, and William Webbe, merchant, of the wardship and marriage of Christopher Woodroof, son and heir of Stephen Woodroff, merchant; with an annuity of 53s. 4d. from 30 Nov., 19 Eliz., when Stephen died. Yearly value of the　　　　　　　　　　　　　　　　　　　　　　　　　　　　　[*m.* 4] inheritance £11 10s.　　　　　　　　　　　　　　　　　　　　　　　　　　　　By Q.

3575.)　21 *Nov.* 1577.　Grant to Thomas Hughes and Elizabeth Highgate, widow, of the wardship and marriage of William Highgate, son and heir of Thomas Higate; with an annuity of £13 6s. 8d. from 15 Aug., 18 Eliz., when Thomas Highgate died. Yearly value of the inheritance £19 10s.　　　　　　　　　　　　　　　　　　　　　　　　　　　　　By Q.

3576.)   20 *Nov.* 1577.   Grant to William Bedell of the wardship and marriage of Martha Bidell, a daughter and co-heir of James Bidell; with an annuity of 40*s.* from 25 Sept., 18 Eliz., when James died.   [*m.* 5]
Yearly value of the inheritance £10 4*s.* 4*d.*   By Q.

3577.)   21 *Nov.* 1577.   Grant to Walter Tooke of the wardship and marriage of John Howe the younger, son and heir of John Howe; with an annuity of £5 from 27 May, 16 Eliz., when John the father died. Yearly value of the inheritance £18.   By Q.

3578.)   27 *Jan.* 1578.   Lease for 21 years to William Spencer of the hundreds of Stone and Cattesash, co. Somerset, parcel of Richemondes Landes, and the cert rents or common fines amounting to £6 2*s.* 4½*d.* yearly and all other appurtenances of the hundreds; as held by any duke of Richmond; reserving to the Crown fines and the like arising in any court of record except the hundred courts, or before the Queen's justices of assize, justices of the peace or clerk of   [*m.* 6]
the market; from Michaelmas last; yearly rent £4 15*s.* 8½*d.*; the lessee to discharge the Crown from the several fees payable to the steward and bailiff of the hundred. In consideration of the surrender by Spencer of a patent of the Exchequer, 2 April, 13 Eliz., leasing the premises to George Agarde for 21 years from Lady Day then last at the same rent.
                                                       By warrant of the commissioners.

3579.)   30 *Dec.* 1577.   Lease for 31 years to Edward Fairechild of a mill called 'the Malt Mylne' in the parish of St. Michael in St. Albans, co. Hertford, once of the monastery of St. Albans; with reservations; from Lady Day next; yearly rent £10. In consideration of the surrender by Fairechild of a patent, 22 June, 4 Eliz., leasing the mill to Hugh Storye for 21 years from Lady Day then last at the same rent.   By warrant of the commissioners.

3580.)   1 *Feb.* 1578.   Lease for 21 years to John Byron of the manor of Huckenhall Torkarde, co. Nottingham, once of Newstede priory, and all courts and other appurtenances of the manor, timber, mines and quarries and advowsons reserved; from Michaelmas last; yearly   [*m.* 7]
rent £13 9*s.* 10*d.* For a fine of £13 9*s.* 10*d.* paid at the Exchequer.   By p.s.

3581.)   27 *Jan.* 1578.   Lease for 21 years to William Constable of the tithes of grain and parcel of the tithe barn in Burton Flemynge, co. York, once of the monastery of Bardney, co. Lincoln; from Michaelmas last; yearly rent £12. In consideration of the surrender by William of a patent, 2 July, 5 Eliz., leasing the premises to Francis Constable, father of William, for 21 years from Lady Day then last at the same rent; and for a fine of £20 paid at the Exchequer.   By warrant of the commissioners.

3582.)   18 *Nov.* 1577.   Lease for 21 years to Dowsabel Milles, widow, of 16 quarters of wheat and 20 quarters of barley yearly payable by John Leigh *alias* Lee or John Baylye, farmers of the site of the manor of Arreton in the isle of Wight, co. Southampton, under their several leases, parcel of the said manor and late of the monastery of Quarr and once leased by the monastery to George Mille *inter alia* at a yearly rent of £7 16*s.*; from Michaelmas last; yearly rent £7 16*s.* For a fine of £20 paid to the Exchequer.
                                                       By warrant of the commissioners.

3583.)   20 *Dec.* 1577.   Lease for 21 years to Richard Bryan of   [*m.* 8]
Iccombe chantry, co. Worcester, and all its possessions in Great Rysingdon *alias* Rysington and Barington Parva, co. Gloucester, or elsewhere in the counties of Gloucester and

Worcester; with reservations; from Michaelmas last; yearly rent £6 15s. 9d.; the lessee to pay all pensions, chief rents and other charges. In consideration of the surrender by Bryan of a patent, 10 Nov., 10 Eliz., leasing the premises to Richard Bernarde for 21 years from Michaelmas last at the same rent; and for a fitting sum paid at the Exchequer.

By warrant of the commissioners.

3584.)   12 *Feb.* 1578. Lease for 21 years to Robert Ludgater and John Cowper of a salt marsh or marsh land once enclosed in the East field of the river of Arundell, co. Sussex, parcel of the manor of Fourde, co. Sussex, parcel of the late honour of Petworthe and formerly of John Palmer in the Crown's hands by exchange; with   [*m.* 9] reservations; from Michaelmas last; yearly rent £19. In consideration of their surrender in Chancery of a patent, 24 July, 12 Eliz., leasing the premises to them for 21 years from Lady Day then last at the same rent; and for a fine of £19 paid at the Exchequer.   By p.s.

3585.)   28 *Nov.* 1577.   Lease for 21 years to Ralph Erington of the capital messuage of Cleisbie, co. York, and the demesne lands belonging thereto, parcel of the manor of Cleisbie and late of William, late marquess of Northampton; with reservations; from Michaelmas last; yearly rent £10 13s. 4d. In consideration of the surrender by Ralph by deed, 27 Nov. last, enrolled in Chancery, of a patent, 10 May, 14 Eliz., leasing the premises *inter alia* to John Erington, brother of Ralph, for 21 years from Lady Day then last at the same rent; and for a fine of £20 paid at the Exchequer.   By warrant of the commissioners.

3586.)   1 *Feb.* 1578.   Lease for so long as Thomas White is vicar of St. Dunstan in the West in London to the same White of the rectory of St. Dunstan in the West, late in the tenure of Thomas Broke and now in that of the same White, vicar there, once of the monastery of   [*m.* 10] Alnewick; the advowson of the vicarage reserved; from Michaelmas last; yearly rent £10; the lessee to discharge the Crown of £8 payable by way of pension to the vicar and all other charges.   By warrant of the commissioners.

3587.)   2 *Dec.* 1577.   Lease for 21 years to Richard Grey of the rectory of Yaxley, co. Suffolk, now or late in the tenure of Thomas Sherman and once of Eye priory, co. Suffolk; with reservations; from Michaelmas next; yearly rent £6; the lessee to pay 40s. yearly to the vicar of Yaxley.   By warrant of the commissioners.

3588.)   4 *Feb.* 1578.   Assignment to Thomas Wyndebank, a clerk of the signet, of a lease of the rectory of Warton, co. Lancaster, by Thomas Willson, D.D., dean, and the chapter of Worcester cathedral by indenture, 23 Sept., 19 Eliz., to the Crown, at the Queen's request,
                                                                      [*m.* 11]
at a yearly rent of £62 11s. and £7 9s. ¼d. yearly in discharge of the tenth due to the Crown—reserving to the dean and chapter the nomination of the vicar, and to the vicar such houses and the like as the vicar now there holds—for 21 years from the termination of a lease thereof by the dean and chapter by indenture dated on the feast of the Blessed Virgin Mary, 15 Eliz., to John Bradley and Christopher Preston, both of Howlker, co. Lancaster, with like reservations, for 21 years from that date at the same rent. For his service. *English*.

By Q.

3589.)   20 *Feb.* 1578.   Lease for 21 years to Richard Fugall of lands (*named*) in Hesill, Tranby, Anlaby, Anlaby Lyntoftes, Swanlande and Anlaby Marshe in the county of Kingston upon Hull, once of Haltemprice   [*m.* 12] priory; with reservations; from Michaelmas last; yearly rent £6 13s. 4d. On surrender by

Fugall of a patent, 7 [*recte* 27][1] July, 4 & 5 Ph. & Mary, leasing the premises to Margaret Haton, widow, for 21 years from Michaelmas then next at the same rent. For a fine of £26 13s. 4d. paid at the Exchequer.   By warrant of the commissioners.

3590.)   7 *March* 1578.   *Gorhambury.*   Lease for 21 years to Robert Marryat of the manors of Aston *alias* Asshen and Purye and all lands in Asshen *alias* Aston, Pallarspery *alias* Pawlespery and Hartwell and in Woodhall in the parish of Towcester, co. Northampton, late of Thomas Culpeper and now annexed to the honour of Grafton, co. Northampton, and leased to Marryat with the said manors at the undermentioned   [*m.* 13] rent, and all courts and other appurtenances of the manors; with reservations of all woods over eight years old, all woods called 'hardwood' to be felled as heretofore accustomed, the advowsons of the rectory of Aston and the chapel of Rande, and all lands parcel of the premises which have now or late been enclosed within Hartwell park for the enlargement thereof; from Michaelmas 1597; yearly rent £35 5s. 7d.; the Crown to discharge the lessee from all other charges, and to provide sufficient 'le slat'[2] for the repair of the buildings within 'le mote' of the manor of Asshen *alias* Aston when required; the lessee to enclose and preserve the woods and 'lez springes' thereof. For the service of Richard Jeffrey, one of the Queen's principal smiths; for a fine of 100 marks paid at the Exchequer by Jeffrey; and at his suit.   By p.s.

3591.)   20 *Feb.* 1578.   Lease for 40 years to James Metcalfe of a tenement called Estradale and Westradale *alias* Radale and Cragdale, parcel of the manor of Baynebrigge in the archdeaconry of Richemond, co. York, and all lands, parcel of the lordship of Midlam in the said archdeaconry, called Estradale and Westradale *alias* Radale and Cragdale, late in the tenure of Christopher Metcalfe, knight, deceased, and now in that of James; with reservations; from Michaelmas last; yearly rent £10 13s. 4d.; double the yearly rent to be paid as a fine or entry (*ingressus*) after the death of the Sovereign, after the death of every tenant and at the renewal of every lease; the yearly rent or value of lands alienated to be paid to the Crown on each alienation for the whole term of parcel of the premises; the lessee to pay suit and service to the Queen's court of Middleham or Bainbrigge, as accustomed, and to occupy the premises by himself or sufficient men; he is not to alienate or tavern any part of the premises for any longer term than his own life or six years after his death, if his term of 40 years shall last so long; but he may, with the consent of the chief steward of the lordship of Richemond or Midlam and the Crown's auditor, receiver and surveyor (or three of them, the chief steward being one) assign his title in the premises; he shall bear and do all other services and charges touching the Queen's service according to the custom of the lordship of Richemond and Midlam or the country there; he shall also fence the premises as ordered by the steward of the Queen's court or other her commissioners there; and, that the lessee may better serve the Queen henceforth, the eldest surviving son of James at the termination of this present lease shall have a new lease by patent on like terms, so long as the
                    [*m.* 14]
lessee shall observe the convenants in this patent. For a fine of £21 6s. 8d. paid at the Exchequer.   By warrant of the commissioners.

3592.)   10 *March* 1578.   *Gorhambury.*   Lease for 21 years to John Meade of (1) the rectory of Newporte Pownde, co. Essex, late of Westminster cathedral, and (2) the rectory of Shelley, co. Suffolk, once in the tenure of Philip Tyndall, knight, and now or late in that of Francis Framlingham, late of the late duke of Suffolk, exchanged, and formerly of the

---

[1] *Cf. Calendar,* 1557–1558, p. 19.
[2] Reading from the warrant in Chancery Warrants II (C.82), no. 1326. The roll has 'le stat'.

monastery of Butley, co. Suffolk; with reservations; from Michaelmas last; yearly rents (1) £18 and (2) 28s. In consideration of the surrender by Meade of the interest in (1) of Ralph Stannowe, to whom the dean and chapter of Westminster cathedral leased the same by indenture, 7 May, 36 Hen. VIII, for 41 years from Lady Day then last at the same rent; and for a fine of £41 12s. paid at the Exchequer.   By p.s.

3593.) 24 *March* 1578. *Gorhambury.* Lease for 21 years to James Sympson of the rectory of Middleton in Pykeringlyghe, co. York,   [*m.* 15] once of the monastery of Kirstall, co. York; with reservations, including the tithes and the like which the priests of Lockton and Cropton are wont to have for their salaries; from Lady Day next; yearly rent £30; the lessee to pay £10 13s. 4d. yearly to the vicar of Middleton and all other charges. In consideration of his surrender of a patent, 19 June, 6 Eliz., leasing the rectory to him for 21 years from Lady Day then last at the same rent; and for a fine of £30 paid at the Exchequer.   By p.s.

3594.) 24 *March* 1578. *Gorhambury.* Lease for 21 years to John Harrington of the manors of Henton and Norton, co. Somerset, late of Henton priory, woods (*named with tenant's name*), parcel of the said manor of Norton St. Philip, and the manor of Lyncombe and Wydcombe, co. Somerset, once of the monastery of Bathe, co. Somerset, and all courts and other appurtenances of the manors; with reservations of Henton grange, leased to Richard Davies *alias* Trahorne at a yearly rent of £49 8s. 3d., the capital mansion or grange of Norton St. Philip of a yearly rent of £20 2s. and certain other lands (*tenants named and rents specified*), parcels of the said manors, all woods, wards, marriages, mines and quarries (except the woods above-leased) and advowsons; from Lady   [*m.* 16] Day next; yearly rent £70 5s. 9½d. In consideration of the surrender by Harrington of a lease made by patent, 7 Jan., 8 Eliz., to Peter Smythe of the manor of Topsham, co. Devon, for 21 years.   By p.s.

3595.) 14 *March* 1578. *Gorhambury.* Lease for life in succession to William Godolphin, Francis Godolphin and William Beauchampe of the tithes and glebe lands belonging to the rectory of All Saints of Weneron and Stedean and either of them, co. Cornwall, once of the monastery of Rewley; with reservations, including the tithes of sheaves of the mansion of the rectory of Weneron heretofore leased to the vicar there by indenture; yearly rent £22. On surrender by the said William Godolphin of a patent, 20 March, 8 Eliz., leasing the said tithes to Robert Holmes for 21 years from Michaelmas then last at the same rent. For a fine of £66 paid by the said William Godolphin to Thomas Bostocke in full satisfaction of 100 marks paid by Bostocke for the fine of a lease of the rectory of Chippingwicombe, co. Buckingham, which he was not able to enjoy by reason of a prior lease to Rowland Buckley by indenture of the prioress of Godstowe, as appears by two several bills annexed to the particular upon which this patent issued.   By p.s.

3596.) 10 *March* 1578. *Gorhambury.* Lease for 21 years to John Gilbert, knight, of (1) the rectory of Brixham, (2) the tithes of corn and hay in Galmeton, Churcheton and Lockton in the parish of Brixham, (3) the tithes of corn and hay in Woodhouse, Brampton,   [*m.* 17] Bowley and Netherby and (4) the tithes in Northfield, Brixham and Wynston, and all appurtenances of the said rectory, co. Devon, once of the monastery of Totton *alias* Tottnes, co. Devon; with reservations; from Michaelmas last; yearly rent £36 6s. 8d., to wit, for (2) £13 6s. 8d., (3) £12 13s. 4d. and (4) £10 6s. 8d. In consideration of the surrender by Gilbert of a patent, 13 May, 3 Eliz., leasing the premises to William Gorge for 21 years from Lady Day then last at the same rent; and for a fine of £72 13s. 4d. paid at the Exchequer.   By p.s.

3597.)   20 *Feb.* 1578.   Lease for 21 years to Edward, earl of Lincoln, high admiral, K.G., councillor, and lady Elizabeth his wife of lands   [*m.* 18] (*named with tenants' names*) in Moulton, Whaplode and Flete, co. Lincoln, parcels of the manor of Moulton and late of Henry, late duke of Suffolk; with reservations; from the present date; yearly rent £23 10s. 8½d. For a fine of £50 paid by the earl at the Exchequer.

By p.s.

3598.)   10 *March* 1578.   *Gorhambury.*   Lease for 21 years to Arthur Creswell of lands (*tenants named*) in Swinhoo, co. Northumberland,   [*m.* 19] parcels of the manor of Swinhoo and late of Thomas, late earl of Northumberland, attainted of treason; with reservations; from Lady Day next; yearly rent £22 1½d. (*detailed*); the lessee to provide a sufficient man or sufficient men from every tenement to serve with horse and arms in the North when required by the Queen's warden or lieutenant there as accustomed, and to fence the premises as ordered by the steward or understeward of the Queen's court there; the lease to be void in respect of any parcel of the premises from which   [*m.* 20] the lessee shall expel the tenant or whereof he shall not by deed before Candlemas next make a lease to the tenant for the whole term at the rent hereby reserved, so long as the tenants before Candlemas next pay him among themselves such sums as he has paid for the fine of the premises or otherwise about obtaining this patent. For a sum paid at the Exchequer.

By p.s.

3599.)   21 *March* 1578.   *Gorhambury.*   Lease for 21 years to Arthur Dakyns of (1) the rectory of Rillington, co. York, late of the monastery of Byland, co. York, (2) lands (*named with tenants' names*) in Rillington, late of the monastery of Malton, co. York, and (3) lands (*tenant named*) in Warter, co. York, late of the monastery of Kirkham, co. York; with reservations, including the lands in Rillington belonging of old to the vicar there; from Lady Day next; yearly   [*m.* 21] rents (1) £18 11s., (2) £4 5s. 8d. and (3) 11s.; the lessee to leave 6 bovates of land well sown with winter corn and 'le ware corne' at the end of the term. In consideration of the surrender by Dakyns of (*a*) a patent, 5 March, 13 Eliz., leasing (1) to him for 21 years from Michaelmas then last at the same rent and (*b*) a patent of the Exchequer, 7 July, 10 Eliz., leasing (2) to Henry Saule for 21 years from Lady Day then last at the same rent; and for a fine of £30 paid by Dakins to Christopher Babham in full satisfaction of £80 paid by Babham at the Exchequer by tally levied on 21 May last for the fine of a lease of the manor and rectory of Wellwicke, co. York, which lease did not issue to Babham because a lease of the said manor and rectory issued to Robert Wright on the surrender of a former lease for a fine of £50, and the same £50 was allowed to Wright to the use of Babham as parcel of the £80 paid by him, as appears by a patent, 26 June last, made to Wright and by two several acquittances, signed by Babham and entered in the entry book of payments of such fines, remaining in the office of the clerk of the pipe.   By p.s.

3600.)   12 *Feb.* 1578.   Lease for 21 years to Henry Brouncker of (1) all lands in the county of Devon or elsewhere given for obits or anniversaries of Thomas Brentingham, Andrew Kylkenny, Peter, once bishop, John Wigar, knight, Thomas Hartford, Edmund Stafford, John Speake, knight, Thomas Bitton, once bishop of [Exeter], Thomas Bodham, Richard Marten and John Ryse in Exeter cathedral, (2) the rectory of Ellerby, co. Devon [*sic*], once of 'Crossewaters chauntries' in Exeter cathedral, (3) the rectory of Morthoo, co. Devon, once of 'Brentinhams chauntries' in Exeter cathedral, (4) the manor of Winterborne Wast and all lands in Bokehampton and Swanwyche, co. Dorset, given for two chantries called 'Staffordes chauntries' in Exeter cathedral, (5) the rectory of Upotterye, co. Devon, given for two chantries   [*m.* 22]

called 'Brewers chauntries' in Exeter cathedral, (6) the manor of Thorverton, co. Devon, given for two chantries called 'Brattons chauntries' in Exeter cathedral, (7) the rectory of Unely, co. Cornwall, given for two chantries called 'Bitton and Bodhams chauntries' in Exeter cathedral, (8) the rectory of Whithycombe and chapel of Spichwicke, co. Devon, given for 'Toridge chauntrie' in Exeter cathedral, (9) the rectory of Westanty, co. Devon, given for 'Kilkennys chauntrie' in Exeter cathedral, (10) the rectory of Estcoker, co. Somerset, given for 'Courteneys chauntrie' in Exeter cathedral, and (11) the manor of Langford Fishedd and all other lands in Fishedd and Ayshwell, co. Somerset, given for 'Speakes chauntrie' in Exeter cathedral; woods, wards, marriages, mines and quarries and advowsons reserved; from Michaelmas last; yearly rent £88 15s. 10d., to wit, for (1) 23s. 4d. (Brentingham), 22s. 4d. (Kelkenny), 10s. 5½d. (Peter, bishop of [—]), 5s. 6d. (Wigar), 5s. 6d. (Hartford), 24s. 6d. (Stafford), 44s. 11d. (Speake), 27s. 7d. (Bitton), 14s. ½d. (Bodham) and 17s. 8d. (Marten and Ryse), (2) £10, (3) £10, (4) £10, (5) £10, (6) £10, (7) £8, (8) £4, (9) £4, (10) £6 and (11) £7. In consid-   [m. 23]
eration that Brouncker offers to prove that the premises are the Crown's by stat. 1 Edw. VI for the dissolution of chantries and the like, where now an estate of fee simple or inheritance is claimed therein; and for a fine of £5 paid at the Exchequer.   By p.s.

3601.)   4 July 1578.   Gorhambury.   Grant in tail male to William   [m. 24]
Boxe of Marcham, co. Berks, with successive remainders to Thomas Boxe, William's brother, in tail male and to the heirs of William, of the reversions and rents of the lands etc. comprised in leases by patent to John Cobley for 21 years from Lady Day last as follows—
    (i) 18 Jan., 17 Eliz., (1) the rents of assize and services of free tenants of the manor of Moppercombe and Nettilcombe, co. Dorset, the customary lands and services of customary tenants of the same manor and the perquisites and profits of courts in the manor, (2) the rents of assize and services of free tenants of the manor of Milborne, co. Dorset, and (3) the customary lands and works and services of customary tenants of the said manor of Milborne and the perquisites and profits of courts in the manor, at yearly rents of (1) £9 12½d., (2) 7s. 9½d. and (3) 60s. 8½d.
    (ii) 20 April, 17 Eliz., (1) the site of the manor of Moppercombe and Nettilcombe, four customary tenements in the manor and live and dead stock (detailed) and (2) the site of the manor of Milborne, all lands and pasture for 100 wethers to be pastured with the wethers of the abbot and convent there and the works of customary tenants in the manor, with two cartloads of hay received yearly from the farmer of Affee Puddle and live and dead stock etc. (detailed), and pasture for 400 wethers (once reserved in the lord's hands and afterwards leased to Philip Vamvilder at a yearly rent of 30s.) at yearly rents of (1) £10 9s. 1d. and (2) £6 10s.
    Also grant of the said manors, once of the monastery of Cerne, co. Dorset.
    To hold by service of the fortieth part of a knight's fee and by yearly rents of 41s. 6d. for the manor of Moppercombe and   [m. 25]
Nettilcombe and 20s. 10d. for the manor of Milborne. Issues from the time of the attainder of Alexander Brete for treason. The grantees discharged from all payments and charges, except the rents and services above-reserved, leases and grants of the premises for life or years upon which the ancient rent or more is reserved, 2s. yearly paid to the reeve of the manor of Moppercombe and Nettilcombe for his fee, and all other sums which the farmer of the premises is bound to pay. For £315 15s. 6d. paid at the Exchequer.   By p.s.

3602.)   11 July 1578.   Gorhambury.   Lease for 21 years to (1) Freman Yonge, a yeoman of the chamber, of (a) the site and demesne lands of the manor of Ocley Clifford, (b) lands (named) and (c) groves (named), parcels of the said manor, late of the monastery of Lanthony, co. Gloucester, (which premises were leased (a) and (b) to John ap Morgan at several yearly rents of £4 and 20*s.* and (*c*) to John Arnolde at a yearly rent of 10*s.*), (2) Thomas Jones of the site and capital messuage of the manor of Whitleigh *alias* Whitley, co. Surrey, and lands (*named*) in Whitley and lands in the parish of Thursley (*named*) and Scottenham, co. Surrey, parcel of the manor of Whitley, all once of Jasper,   [*m.* 26] once duke of Bedford, now in the Crown's hands by exchange and leased by patent, 10 May, 10 Eliz., to Jones for 21 years from Lady Day then last at several yearly rents of 25*s.* 10*d.* and 76*s.* 8*d.*, (3) Matthew Glover of the site of the manor or mansion of Moulton, co. Northampton, parcel of Warwickes and Spencers Landes, lands (*named*) and all demesne lands belonging to the said site, leased by patent, 26 April, 16 Eliz., to Glover for 21 years from Lady Day then last at a yearly rent of £8 10*s.*, and (4) John Craven of the rectory of Shoplande, co. Essex, once of the monastery of St. Osyth, co. Essex, and leased by patent, 15 Oct., 4 Eliz., to Thomas Tenderinge for 21 years from Michaelmas then last at a yearly rent of 66*s.* 8*d.*; with reservations; from (1) Michaelmas next or the termination of any lease or grant thereof for life or years heretofore made enduring after that date, (2) Lady Day 1589, (3) Lady Day 1595 and (4) Michaelmas 1583; yearly rents (1) (*a*) £4, (*b*) 20*s.* and (*c*) 10*s.*, (2) £5 2*s.* 6*d.*, (3) £8 10*s.*   [*m.* 27] and (4) 66*s.* 8*d.*; the lessee of (3) to provide entertainment for the Queen's surveyor, steward and other officers coming to the manor of Moulton to hold courts or survey the manor, and to permit the tenants of the manor to enjoy among themselves the coney warren there as the farmers of the demesne lands of the manor have been wont to do. For Yonge's service, and as regards (2)—(4) at his suit.   By p.s.

3603.)   4 *July* 1578.   *Gorhambury.*   Lease for 21 years to Thomas Burgoyne of the rectory of Longestaunton, co. Cambridge, once of the late college of Asteley, co. Warwick, afterwards granted by Henry VIII to Henry, late duke of Suffolk, in tail and now in the Queen's   [*m.* 28] hands by the death of lady Mary Grey, one of the daughters and heirs of the body of the said duke, and 'the parsonage mansyon' and all other appurtenances of the rectory; with reservations; from Lady Day last; yearly rent £8 4*s.* 4*d.*; the lessee to pay £10 yearly to the vicar of Longestaunton and all other charges. In consideration of the surrender by Burgoyne of an indenture, 18 July, 29 Hen. VIII, whereby John Breerton, clerk, dean, and the chapter of the college leased the premises to Robert Sterlinge of Brampton, co. Huntingdon, 'yeoman', for 46 years from Lady Day then next at a yearly rent of £18 4*s.* 4*d.*, to wit, £5 to the vicar of Longestaunton at Candlemas, £8 4*s.* 4*d.* to the dean and chapter at Lady Day and £5 to the vicar at Midsummer; and for a fine of £49 6*s.* paid at the Exchequer.   By warrant of the commissioners.
   Vacated because surrendered, 7 *Dec.*, 22 *Eliz.*; *signed:* Wyll'm Cordell; Thomas Burgoyne.

3604.)   4 *July* 1578.   *Gorhambury.*   Lease for 21 years to Simon Wheler, the Queen's servant, of (1) the rectory of Astley, co. Warwick, now or late in the tenure of William Astell, and (2) the site of Astley college, a cow pasture in the great park of Asteley and lands, now or late in the tenure of Astell, all once of the said late college, with reservations; from Lady Day last; yearly rents (1) £4 13*s.* 4*d.*   [*m.* 29] and (2) 22*s.* For his service.   By warrant of the commissioners.

3605.)   4 *July* 1578.   *Gorhambury.*   Lease for 21 years to Thomas Allen of Staple Inne, London, and Alexander Allen of London, 'vintener', of lands (*tenants named*) in Northallerton, co. York, once of the monastery of Mountegrace, co. York; with reservations; from Michaelmas next; yearly rent £6 6*s.* 8*d.* (*detailed*). In consideration of the revival of a rent of 46*s.* 8*d.* which they have undertaken to pay.
          By warrant of the commissioners.

3606.)   11 *July* 1578.   *Gorhambury*.   Lease for 21 years to Christopher Hilliarde, knight, of lands (*named with tenants' names*) in Ottringham, co. York, parcel of the manor of Ottringham and once of the monastery of Meux *alias* Melsa, co. York; with reservations; from Lady Day last;   [*m.* 30]
yearly rent 100s. 4d. In consideration of the surrender by Christopher of a patent, 16 July, 7 Eliz., leasing the premises to John Hillyard for 21 years from Lady Day then last at the same rent; and for a fine of £15 12d., to wit, £7 12d. paid at the Exchequer and £8 to Thomas Newton allowed in satisfaction of a like sum paid by Newton for the fine of a lease of tithes of corn and hay in Overton, co. York, which he was not able to enjoy, as appears by a bill signed by Christopher Smyth, clerk of the pipe, and annexed to the particular on which this patent issued.   By warrant of the commissioners.

3607.)   28 *July* 1578.   Lease for 21 years to Thomas Pynner, a clerk of the kitchen, of the rectory of Wenlingboroughe *alias* Wedlingboroughe, co. Northampton, once of the monastery of Crowlande, co. Lincoln, and afterwards annexed to the honour of Grafton, co. Northampton; with reservations; from Lady Day last; yearly rent £40 6s. 8d. In   [*m.* 31] consideration of his surrender of a patent, 2 Nov., 13 Eliz., leasing the rectory to him for 21 years from Michaelmas then last at the same rent; and for a fine of £10 paid at the Exchequer.
By p.s.

3608.)   18 *July* 1578.   *Gorhambury*.   Lease for 21 years to William Gannocke of Muston chantry in Leake or elsewhere, co. Lincoln; with reservations; from Lady Day last; yearly rent £22. In consideration of his   [*m.* 32]
surrender of a patent, 15 May, 7 Eliz., leasing the chantry to him for 21 years from Lady Day then last at the same rent; and for a fine of £44 paid at the Exchequer.   By p.s.

3609.)   4 *July* 1578.   *Gorhambury*.   Lease for life in succession to William Edlynn the elder, William Edlynn the younger and James Edlynn, son of William the elder, of a messuage called Harwardes in the parish of Watforde, co. Hertford, parcel of the manor of Watford and once of the monastery of St. Albans, co. Hertford; with reservations; from Lady Day last; yearly rent £8 13s. 4d. and heriot the best beast; the lessees may dig clay (*lutum*) and dig and cut stone in the quarries of the premises for repairs. In consideration of the surrender by William the elder of a patent, 2 July, 10 Eliz., leasing the messuage to him for 21 years from Michaelmas then next at the same rent; and for a fine of £17 6s. 8d.
                                                                                    [*m.* 33]
paid at the Exchequer.   By warrant of the commissioners.

3610.)   4 *July* 1578.   *Gorhambury*.   Lease for 21 years to Henry Gardiner of the site and demesne lands of the manor of Kirton and land in Magelmore, parcels of the manor of Kirton in Lyndesey, co. Lincoln, parcel of the duchy of Cornwall; with reservations; from Lady Day last, yearly rent £15; the lessee to provide entertainment for   [*m.* 34]
the Queen's steward and surveyor two days and two nights yearly if they shall so often come to survey the premises or hold courts. In consideration of the surrender by him of a patent, 18 June, 10 Eliz., leasing the premises to Emma Brokilsbye for 21 years from Lady Day then last at the same rent; and for a fine of £30, to wit, £6 paid at the Exchequer and £24 to Nicholas Adams allowed in satisfaction of a like sum paid by Adams for the fine of a lease of tithes in Wylome, co. Northumberland, which he was not able to enjoy, as appears by a bill signed by Christopher Smythe, clerk of the pipe, and annexed to the particular on which this patent issued.   By p.s.

3611.)   21 *Aug.* 1578.   *Gorhambury*.   Lease for 21 years to Thomas Preston of a park

called Harte Parke, lands (*named*), a park called Shepe Parke, mills called Harte Mylne and Sey Mylne, a farm called Wheate Farme, late in the tenure of the prior of Coneshed, mines called 'le Yonre Mynes *alias* Iron Mynes' and fishings called Urswicke Terne in Urswicke and 'le Mayre' in Aldingham, being in Muchland, co. Lancaster, parcels of the castle and manor of Gleston in Haldingham in the lordship of Muchlande, late of Henry, late duke of Suffolk, attainted of treason; with reservations, including the herbage and pannage of Seywoode park; from Lady Day last; yearly rent £54 7s. In consideration of the surrender by Preston, except in respect   [*m.* 35]
of the said herbage and pannage, of a patent, 11 July, 3 & 5 Ph. & Mary, leasing the premises and the said herbage and pannage to William Curwen, son of Richard Curwen, for 21 years from Michaelmas or Lady Day following the death of Helen Curwen and the said Richard or the survivor of them at a yearly rent of £58 7s.; and for a fine of £40 paid at the Exchequer.
                                                                                    By p.s.

3612.)   28 *July* 1578.   Lease for 21 years to William Fitzwilliams, a gentleman pensioner, of lands (*named with tenants' names*) in Fodringhay or   [*m.* 36]
elsewhere, co. Northampton, parcels of the manor of Fodringhay, late parcel of the jointure of Catherine, late Queen of England, and formerly of Edward, late duke of York; with reservations; from Lady Day last; yearly rent £24 4d. In consideration that the tenements are in great ruin, as is certified by the surveyor of the county.   By p.s.

3613.)   23 *June* 1578.   *Gorhambury.*   Lease for life in succession to John Jenkins and Thomas Jenkins and Matthew Jenkins, his sons,   [*m.* 37]
of lands (*named with tenants' names*) in Clifton, co. York, parcels of the manor of Clifton and once of the monastery of St. Mary next the walls of York; with reservations; yearly rent £9 15s. 1d. (*detailed*). In consideration of the surrender by John of two   [*m.* 38]
patents of the Exchequer (*a*) 5 March, 13 Eliz., leasing *inter alia* to William Drewe certain of the premises (described as in Clifton in the county of the city of York) for 21 years from Michaelmas last at a yearly rent of 99s. 2d. (*detailed*) and (*b*) 23 March, 19 Eliz., leasing the rest to William Drewe for 21 years from Lady Day then next at a yearly rent of £4 15s. 11d.; and for a fine of £14 14s. 3d. paid at the Exchequer.   By warrant of the commissioners.

3614.)   4 *July* 1578.   Lease for 21 years to Thomas Coxe, yeoman of the pantry, of (1) a tenement on the North side of Sainte Stephens Alley in Westminster, co. Middlesex, late in the tenure of Margaret Atkins and now or late in that of Stephen Garrett, and a tenement in Sainte Stephens Alley, now or late in the tenure of Thomas Taylor, both once of the college of SS. Mary and Stephen in the palace of Westminster and leased by patent of the Exchequer, 17 Feb., 10 Eliz., to Fulk Mustion for 21 years from Michaelmas then last at yearly rents of 16s. 8d. and 16s. 8d. respectively, (2) lands (*named with tenants' names*) in Quinboroughe, co. Leicester, parcels of the manor of   [*m.* 39]
Quinboroughe, once of the monastery of Selbye, co. York, and leased by patent, 27 May, 10 Eliz., to Anthony Digbie for 21 years from Lady Day then last at a yearly rent of £19 22d., and (3) lands (*named with tenant's name*) in Foxcote or elsewhere, co. Northampton, parcels of the manor of Alderton and of the honour of Grafton, co. Northampton, and leased by patent of the Exchequer, 9 July, 10 Eliz., to Anthony Leeson for 21 years from Lady Day then last at a yearly rent of 58s.; with reservations; from (1) Michaelmas 1588 and (2) and (3) Lady   [*m.* 40]
Day 1589; same rents (*detailed*). For his long service to the Queen and her progenitors.
                                                                                    By p.s.

3615.)   30 *July* 1578.   Lease for 21 years to Peter Pawlyn, William Stone and John

Llewelin, grooms of the chamber, of (1) lands (*named with tenant's name*), parcel of the manor of Stanwell, co. Middlesex, late of the late lord Windsore and leased to Pawlyn by patent, 9 June, 9 Eliz., at a yearly rent of 73s. 10d. for 21 years from the termination of a lease thereof by patent, 12 April, 7 Edw. VI, to Dennis Vanharvan for 21 years from Michaelmas then next; (2) lands (*tenants named*) in the parish of Barnett, co. Hertford, once of the monastery of St. Albans, belonging to the office of new ordination of John Whethamstede, abbot thereof, and leased by patent of the Exchequer, 2 July, 17 Eliz., to Stone for 21 years from Michaelmas then next at a yearly rent of £4, (3) lands (*tenant named*) in the parish of Bromley, co. Middlesex, exchanged with Ralph Sadler, knight, and leased to Jane Jolles, widow, by patent, 3 May, 9 Eliz., for 21 years from Lady Day then last for a yearly rent of £4 16s., (4) lands (*tenant named*) in Bromeley Marshe, co. Middlesex, exchanged with Ralph Sadler, knight, and leased to Anthony Cowper by patent of the Exchequer, 2 July, 12 Eliz., for 21 years from Lady Day then last at a yearly rent of 6s. 8d., (5) all the demesne lands of the manor of Otforde, co. Kent, late of the archbishop of Canterbury and afterwards granted to cardinal Reginald Poole for life and a year after his death, and lands (*named*), parcels of the demesne lands of the said manor and leased to George Moulton the younger by patent, 16 April, 11 Eliz., for 21 years from Lady Day then last at a yearly rent of £12 6s. 8d., and (6) the free chapel of Blackeforde in the parish of Wedmore or elsewhere, co. Somerset, leased to John Franke by patent, 25 Jan., 16 Eliz., for 21 years from Lady Day then next at a yearly rent of £6; with reservations, including lands (*named*) enclosed in Otforde park; from (1) Michaelmas 1595,   [*m*. 41]
(2) Michaelmas 1596, (3) Lady Day 1588, (4) Lady Day 1591, (5) Lady Day 1590 and (6) Lady Day 1595; same rents. For their service.   By p.s.

(*The dorse of this roll is blank.*)

PART X

C. 66/1173

3616.)   5 *Dec.* 1577.   Lease for 21 years to Thomas Bellingham of   [*m.* 1]
the rectory of Crosbye, co. Westmorland, once of the monastery of Whitbye, co. York; with
reservations; from Michaelmas next; yearly rent £23. In consideration of the surrender by
Thomas of a patent, 2 July, 13 Eliz., leasing the rectory to Alan Bellingham for 21 years
from Lady Day then last at the same rent; and for a fine of £23 paid at the Exchequer.
By p.s.

3617.)   2 *Dec.* 1577.   Lease for 21 years to William Middleton and John Middleton of (1)
lands in Middleton *alias* Middleton on Leven, co. York, and (2) other lands in Middleton,
late leased to Thomas Middleton by James Strangweys, knight, all late of Leonard Dacres,
attainted of treason; with reservations; from Michaelmas next; yearly rents   [*m.* 2]
(1) £6 14*s.* 9*d.* and (2) 13*s.* 4*d.* In consideration of the surrender by James Middleton, their
brother, of a patent, 22 June, 19 Eliz., leasing the premises to him for 21 years from Lady
Day then last at the same rents; and because £14 16*s.* was paid at the Exchequer by Edmund
Engledaye on the grant of the said patent to James.   By warrant of the commissioners.

3618.)   5 *Dec.* 1577.   Lease for 40 years to John Pople of a water mill called Hamper Mill
in Watford, co. Hertford, purchased by Henry VIII; with reservations, including lands (*a*)
adjoining a river called Cloverstreame and (*b*) now enclosed in More park, parcel of the
duchy of Lancaster; from Michaelmas last; yearly rent £11 19*s.* 8*d.* In consideration of the
surrender by Pople of a patent, 12 April, 3 & 4 Ph. & Mary, leasing the premises (without
reservation of the lands above-excepted) to Francis Pitcher for 40 years from Lady Day then
last at a yearly rent of £13 6*s.* 8*d.*   By warrant of the commissioners.

3619.)   11 *Dec.* 1577.   Lease for 21 years to Catherine Throkmerton, widow, late the wife
of Clement Throkmerton, of lands etc. (*tenants named*) in (1) Hatton (*named*), (2) Haseley and
(3) Bewsall, co Warwick,   [*m.* 3]
once of the monastery of Wroxall, co. Warwick; with reservations; from Lady Day last;
yearly rents (1) 79*s.* 6*d.*, (2) 8*s.* and (3) 20*s.* In consideration of the surrender by her in respect
of the premises only of a patent, 9 Jan., 5 Eliz., leasing to Clement all lands in (1) Hatton, (2)
Haseley and (3) Bewsall once of Wroxall priory for 21 years from Lady Day then last at
yearly rents of (1) 105*s.* 8*d.*, (2) 8*s.* and (3) 20*s.* 11*d.*; and for a fine of £12 3*s.* 6*d.* paid at the
Exchequer.   By warrant of the commissioners.

3620.)   20 *Dec.* 1577.   Lease for 21 years to John Engelberd of the tenth part of all alum,
copperas, liquors of metals, minerals and commodities arising from three several houses and
mines or from the bowels of the earth within the precincts of (1) a mine at Bascombe, cos.
Southampton and Dorset, (2) a mine at Bruntsey in the isle of Bruntsey, co. Dorset, and (3) a
mine called Allame and Chyme, co. Dorset; with reservations of (*a*) 'a workehouse' and a
parcel of waste land (30 ac.) by the sea shore between places called Parkestone on the West
and Ockmans Close on the East in Canford, co. Dorset, which land adjoins a waste and
heath called Canford Landes and is parcel of the manor of Canford, and (*b*) a house and land
now in the tenure of Cornelius Stephenson to the use of Thomas Randolfe, Thomas Cotton,

George Carleton and Cotton Gargrave; from Michaelmas last; yearly rent £13 6s. 8d. By patent, 3 July, 6 Eliz., Cornelius de Vos of London, merchant, was granted a licence to open and work mines of alum, copperas or the like throughout the Queen's dominions especially in the isle of Wight for 21 years from 1 Aug. then next; by indenture of the same date between the Queen and him he covenanted that the Crown should in full satisfaction of all customs, dues and demands arising before transportation of the same out of the realm have a tenth part of all the alum, copperas and other commodities obtained to be delivered quarterly to the use of the Crown or such persons as should be appointed for the receiving thereof at the places where they were obtained; the interest of de Vos is now held by James, lord Mountjoye; by an inquisition taken at Wymborne Mynster, co. Dorset, on 14 July,
[m. 4]

19 Eliz., before Henry Aysheley, knight, Lawrence Hide and others by virtue of a commission out of the Exchequer it was found that three mines only had been opened, upon which three mine houses (domus minerales) had been built, to wit, a house and mine at Bascombe called Bascombe House, a house and mine at Bruntsey and a house and mine called Allam and Chyme, as appears by the same inquisition returned in the Exchequer and remaining with the Queen's remembrancer.   By warrant of the commissioners.

3621.)   20 Dec. 1577.   Lease for 21 years to Edward Littilton of (1) the prebend of Congreve (tenants named), (2) lands (described), the tithes of Otherton, a fourth part of the tithes of Preston (tenants named), a   [m. 5]
yearly rent of 4s. out of lands of Thomas Preston in Preston and the tithes and oblations of Dunston (tenant named), (3) the prebend of Copnall, (4) the prebend of Stretton, (5) the prebend of Penkeriche and (6) the prebend of Longruge alias Longnor, all in the county of Stafford and once of the late college of Penkeriche; with reservations, including the tithes of corn of a tenement (tenant named) parcel of the possessions of the prebend of Congreve; from Michaelmas last; yearly rents (1) £4 3s., (2) (the premises belonging to the prebend of Dunston) £9 18s., (3) £16, (4) £12, (5) £9 6s. 8d. and (6) 44s. 3d. In consideration of his surrender in Chancery of a patent, 31 May, 10 Eliz., leasing the premises to Edward Littilton, knight, his father, for 21 years from Lady Day then last at the same rents; and for a fine of £53 11s. 11d. paid at the Exchequer.   By p.s.

3622.)   11 Dec. 1577.   Lease for 21 years to John Dasset of the site and capital messuage of the manor of Yelvertofte, co. Northampton, parcel   [m. 6]
of the possessions assigned to the Queen by name of the lady Elizabeth and formerly of Warwicke and Spencers Landes; with reservations; from Michaelmas last; yearly rent £10 4s. 2d. In consideration of the surrender by Dasset of a patent, 24 June, 11 Eliz., leasing the premises to Thomas Everarde for 21 years from Lady Day then last at the same rent; and for a fine of £20 8s. 4d. paid at the Exchequer.   By warrant of the commissioners.

3623.)   11 Dec. 1577.   Lease for 40 years to William Thomas of (1) a tenement in the parish of St. Mary Wolchurche in London, now or late in the tenure of Richard Pelter, once belonging to the same parish, and (2) two tenements in the parish of St. Giles without Criplegate, London, now or late in the tenure of John Humfrye, once belonging to the parish of St. Martin Orgar, in the Queen's hands by stat. 1 Edw. VI for the dissolution of chantries and the like; from Michaelmas last; yearly rents (1) £4 and (2) 23s. 4d.
By warrant of the commissioners.

3624.)   11 Dec. 1577.   Lease for 21 years to John Freake of a water mill (tenant named) in the parish of St. Mary of Bromeley, co. Middlesex, late of Halliwell priory, co. Middlesex; with reservations; from Lady Day   [m. 7]
next; yearly rent £8.   By warrant of the commissioners.

3625.)   18 *Nov.* 1577.   Grant for life to William Wynter, knight, the Queen's servant, of the offices of constable of St. Briavels castle in the forest of Deane, co. Gloucester, and keeper of the woods in the said forest, parcel of Warwickes Landes; from the death of Henry Herbert, earl of Pembroke, or the forfeiture or surrender by him or other avoidance of the offices; with the fees and profits accustomed, payable out of the issues of the said forest and of the manor of Newland therein; power after the said offices became void to appoint bailiffs and other officers accountable to him for the same. For his service. By patent, 13 Dec., 3 Edw. VI, the offices of constable of the said castle, bailiff of the manor of Lydney, co. Gloucester, and keeper of the said woods, which offices were then late held by George Baynehame, knight, deceased, were granted to William Herbert, late earl of Pembroke, deceased, and the said present earl, by the names of William Herbert, knight, and Henry Herbert, for life in survivorship.   By p.s.

3626.)   18 *Nov.* 1577.   Lease for 21 years to John Clifton, knight, of the hundred of Barton *alias* Bathe Forinseca, co. Somerset, late of Edward, late duke of Somerset, the cert rents and fines of free   [*m.* 8]
suitors amounting to 101*s.* 4*d.* and all courts and other appurtenances of the hundred; with reservation of all fines, amercements and issues arising in any court of record, except the hundred court, or before the justices of assize, justices of the peace or clerk of the market and liberty to levy and collect the same; from Michaelmas last; yearly rent £6 8*s.*; the lessee to discharge the Crown from a yearly fee of 40*s.* payable to the bailiff of the hundred for the levying and collection of the rents, fines and profits of court there. In consideration of the surrender by Clyfton of a patent, 10 July, 7 Eliz., leasing the hundred to Robert Petre for 21 years from Lady Day then last at the same rent; and for a fine of £12 16*s.* paid at the Exchequer.   By warrant of the commissioners.

3627.)   11 *Dec.* 1577.   Lease for 21 years to Robert Pereson of the prebend of Howden in the late collegiate church of Howden, co. York, whereof Anthony Bellasys was once prebendary; with reservations; from Michaelmas last; yearly rent £21 13*s.* 4*d.* In consideration of the   [*m.* 9]
surrender by Pereson of a patent, 15 Nov., 6 Eliz., leasing the prebend to Robert Wolflete for 21 years from Michaelmas then last at the same rent; and for a fine of £43 6*s.* 8*d.* paid at the Exchequer.   By p.s.

3628.)   11 *Dec.* 1577.   Lease for 21 years to George Consett of the prebend of Thorpe Beilbye, co. York, once of the late collegiate church of Howden, co. York; with reservations, including the whole common of the said church; from Michaelmas last; yearly rent £18 6*s.* 8*d.* In consideration of his surrender of a patent, 15 May, 6 Eliz., leasing the prebend to him for 21 years from Lady Day then last at the same rent; and for a fine of £30 paid at the Exchequer.   By p.s.

3629.)   26 *Nov.* 1577.   Lease for 21 years to William Peighan and Alexander Blacklock of the rectory of Osmotherley, all the possessions in Osmotherley, Thymylbye, Ellerbeck and Westherlesey belonging   [*m.* 10]
to the said rectory and to the late three prebends in Osmotherley church, once in the several tenures of Richard Beck, Lawrence Thornell and John Taylfer, and lands thereof (*tenants named*) in the said places or elsewhere, co. York; with reservations, including a house in Osmotherley for the vicar there, and the mortuaries and profits of marriages, purifications of women and burials in Osmotherley church; from Michaelmas last; yearly rent £8; the lessees to pay the stipend of the vicar of Osmotherley and all other charges. In consideration of the surrender by Peighan and Blacklock of a patent, 1 July, 7 Eliz., leasing the premises to

James Conyers for 21 years from Lady Day then last at the same rent; and for a fine of £16 paid at the Exchequer.   By warrant of the commissioners.

3630.)   28 *Nov.* 1577.   Lease for 21 years to Robert Chabnor of the rents of assize of free tenants and service parcel of the manor of Swaffham, co. Norfolk, late assigned to the late duchess of Richemonde for life, an increase of rent and a parcel of land within the said manor newly approved amounting together to a yearly rent of £4 12s. 10d., four stalls about 'le tollehouse' in Swaffham heretofore leased at a yearly rent of 10s. 2d., a sore hawk yearly and from time to time arising or nesting   [*m.* 11] within the said manor and the yearly rents of faggots there amounting together to a yearly rent of 9s. 8d., 1½ quarters and 1 bushel of barley yearly of the said manor appraised at a yearly rent of 5s. 5d., the lands, tenements, rents and hereditaments called 'launcellettes' parcel of the said manor and a yearly rent of 79s. 11¾d., the tourns called by the several names of 'Richemonde turne' *alias* 'Narfforde turne' held every three weeks at Narfford and elsewhere within the fee of the honour of Richemonde, co. Norfolk, the lands and leets called 'the forreyne courtes' held yearly and from time to time in certain places, co. Norfolk, belonging to the said honour, the perquisites and profits, fines, reliefs, amercements and other casualties of the said tourns, courts and leets and all hereditaments in Swaffham *alias* Sopham *alias* Swaffham Market reputed parcels of the premises; with reservations, including 2 quarters of oats and divers several yearly rents payable to the said manor out of the following manors amounting to £9 13s. 5d., to wit, out of the manor of Northpickenham 60s. and 2 quarters of oats, Rednall 26s., Lynge 25s., Kipton Grene in Wesenham 5s., Foxley 10s., Cockley 10s., Bradingham 9d., Thirninge 8s. 6d., Feldallinge 5s., Horningtofte 5s., Fourdham 8s. and Hicklinge 10s. and out of the town of Narfforde 5s. 3d., also the demesne lands of the manor of Swaffham and the lands and pastures called Spynny Parke late called 'the warren of Swaffham' of the yearly rent of £14; from Michaelmas next; yearly rent £38 23¼d.; the lessee to pay yearly 40s. for the fee of the bailiff of the said manor and 60s. 10d. for the fee of the warrener or keeper of the warren there, and to collect the several rents above-reserved and pay them at the Exchequer or to the bailiffs or receivers of the premises. In consideration that the greater part of the premises consists of rents wherefrom little or no profit arises and the residue of them consists of amercements and other casualties which are reduced or arrented at a fixed yearly rent; and for a fine of £10 paid at the Exchequer.   By p.s.

3631.)   14 *Feb.* 1578.   Lease for 21 years to Thomas Plesaunce of the warren of Brandon Ferry, the conies therein, a lodge within the warren and lands (*named*) in Brandon aforesaid, parcel of the manor of Brandon Ferry, co. Suffolk, late taken from the bishopric of Ely by act of   [*m.* 12] Parliament; with reservations; from Lady Day next; yearly rent £20 15s.; the lessee may plough up such part of the land and pasture of the warren as shall seem convenient. In consideration of the surrender by Plesaunce of a patent, 22 Sept., 6 Eliz., leasing the premises to William Humberston for 21 years from Michaelmas then next at the same rent; and for a fine of £13 6s. 8d. paid at the Exchequer.   By p.s.

3632.)   7 *Feb.* 1578.   Lease for 21 years to Thomas Havers of (1) the site and demesne lands of the manor of Staverton with Bromeswall and (2) the warren there, co. Suffolk, late of Thomas, late duke of Norfolk, attainted of treason; with reservations; from Michaelmas last; yearly rents (1) £9 2s. 5d. and (2) 26s. 8d. For a fine of £41 16s. 4d. paid at the Exchequer.   By warrant of the commissioners.

3633.)   26 *Nov.* 1577.   Lease for life in succession to Thomas Rowles, John Rowles and

Margaret Rowles, the sons and daughter of Bartholomew Rowles the elder, of the rectory of Haresfeilde, co. Gloucester, late of the monastery of Llanthony and leased to Thomas Rowles, Eleanor his   [*m.* 13]
wife and Bartholomew, George, Walter and William, their sons, for 60 years if they should so long live; with reservations, including the tithes of Haresfeilde park; yearly rent £9 18*s.* 8*d.* For a fine of £19 17*s.* 4*d.* paid at the Exchequer.   By warrant of the commissioners.

3634.) 30 *Jan.* 1578.   Lease of life to Robert Pendelton of the tithes in Rocester, co. Stafford, once of Rocester priory; the advowsons of Bradley and Rocester churches reserved; from Michaelmas last; yearly rent £8 13*s.* 4*d.*; the lessee to discharge the Crown from the cures of souls of the parishioners of Bradley and Rocester and the stipends of the curates there. In consideration of the surrender by the said Robert of a patent, 10 Dec., 5 Eliz., leasing the tithes to Robert Pendelton, deceased, his father, for 21 years from Michaelmas then last at the same rent; and for a fine of £10 paid at the Exchequer.
By warrant of the commissioners.

3635.) 7 *Feb.* 1578.   Lease for life in succession to John Savage, Elizabeth his wife and John Golde of an inn called 'le George' in the high street of Glaston, co. Somerset, lands (*named*) once belonging to the office of chamberlain of the monastery of Glaston and six 'fetherbeddes' and five 'le bolsters' usually leased with the inn, all late of the late duke of Somerset; with reservations; from Michaelmas last; yearly rent £6 6*s.* 10*d.*; the lessee to leave at the end of the term the said bedding in good condition (*bona et apta stuffur' utend' et occupand'*) or the price thereof at the rate of 16*s.* for each 'le fetherbed' and 3*s.* for each 'le bolster' as shall be assessed by good men dwelling there with the assent of the bailiffs or other officers of the Crown there for the Queen's greater profit. In consideration of the surrender by the said John Savage of the interest in the premises of George Cowdrey, to whom they were leased *inter alia* by patent, 3 July, 4 Eliz., for 21 years from Lady Day then
                                                                                    [*m.* 14]
last at a yearly rent of £6 12*s.* 10*d.*; and for a fine of £25 7*s.* 4*d.* paid by the said John Savage, to wit, £18 15*s.* 4*d.* at the Exchequer and £16 12*s.* to Richard Dunkyn and Marmaduke Langdale in satisfaction of a like sum paid by them for the fine of several leases of lands which they could not enjoy, as appears by a bill signed by Christopher Smythe, clerk of the pipe, and annexed to the particular on which this patent issued.
By warrant of the commissioners.

3636.) 7 *Feb.* 1578.   Lease for 21 years to Roger Manwoode, a justice of the Common Pleas, Robert Honywood, John Boyes and Richard Bourne of London, merchant, of the rectory of Kemsinge and Seale, co. Kent, late of the monastery of Barmondesey, co. Surrey; with reservations, including certain lands in Kemsinge and Seale now imparked in the Queen's parks of Otforde and Knowlle, co. Kent, for the enlargement thereof; from Michaelmas last; yearly rent £9 13*s.* 4*d.*; the lessees to discharge the Crown from all charges. In consideration of the surrender by James Tebold, son and heir of Richard Tebold, son of John Tebold, of a conventual indenture, 28 Nov., 29 Hen. VIII, leasing the rectory to the said John Tebold for 30 years from the termination of a lease thereof by John, abbot, and the convent of the monastery   [*m.* 15]
by indenture, 19 Jan., 6 Hen. VIII, to the same John Tebold and William Cheseman for 40 years from Lady Day then last; and for a fine of £29 paid at the Exchequer by Manwoode, Honywood, Boyes and Bourne.   By warrant of the commissioners.

3637.) 4 *Feb.* 1578.   Lease for 21 years to Ambrose Smythe, citizen and merchant of London, of (1) the rectory of Foxton, co. Leicester, and the tithes of certain lands in Foxton belonging to the rectory of the yearly rent of 25s. 4d., once of the late royal college called 'Kinge Henrie Theightes colledge', Oxford, and (2) lands (*named with tenants' names*) in the parish of Westwell, co. Kent, parcel of the manor of Westwell and of possessions of the archbishop of Canterbury in the Queen's hands by act of Parliament; with reservations, including the tithes belonging to the vicarage of Foxton; from Michaelmas last; yearly rents (1) £14 4s. 5¼d. and (2) 13s. 4d.; the lessee to pay yearly out of (1) 7s. 6¾d. for synodals and proxies to the archdeacon of Northampton. In consideration of the surrender by Smythe of a patent, 6 May, 6 Eliz., leasing (1) to Dorothy Pole, widow, for 21 years from Lady Day then last at the same rent; and for a fine of £22 13s. 4d. paid at the Exchequer.   By p.s.

3638.)   12 *Feb.* 1578.   Lease for 21 years to Robert Shepperd and   [*m.* 16] Henry Dixe of the site of the manor of Halvergate called 'the Hall Yarde' and lands (*named with tenants' names*), some in Worthinge, Wikehampton and Halvergate, parcels of the demesne lands of the manor of Halvergate and Walsham, co. Norfolk, and of the jointure of Frances,   [*m.* 17] late countess of Surrey; with reservations; from Michaelmas last; yearly rent £29 11s. 5¼d. (*detailed*); the lease to be void in respect of any parcel of the premises from which the lessees shall expel the present tenant or of which the lessees shall not before Christmas next make him a lease by deed for their whole term and at the rent hereby reserved, so long as the tenants before Christmas next pay them among themselves their costs about obtaining this patent. For a sum paid by way of fine.   By p.s.

3639.)   27 *Jan.* 1578.   Lease for life in succession to Robert Thorpe, Humphrey Thorpe, his son, and Elizabeth Thorpe, his daughter, of the tithes of corn and hay in Hallyweston, co. Huntingdon, once of Huntingdon priory, co. Huntingdon; from Michaelmas last; yearly rent £6 13s. 4d. In consideration of Robert's surrender of the interest in the premises of Edward Woode, to whom they were leased *inter alia* by patent, 14 May, 10 Eliz., for 21 years from the feast of St. Dunstan 1577 or the expiry of a conventual indenture made to Oliver Leder at the same rent.   By warrant of the commissioners.

3640.)   2 *Jan.* 1578.   Lease for 21 years to Richard Molton of woods (*named*), parcel of the manor of Chertesey, co. Surrey, once of the monastery of Chertesey; with reservations, including herbage and pannage for the Crown's deer and wild beasts; from Michaelmas last;   [*m.* 18] yearly rent £6 5s. 4d.; the lessee to cut the woods at fitting seasons, to enclose them after cutting without putting in any horses or animals which could injure 'lez springes' during the time limited by statute and to leave sufficient 'lez staddelles' in every acre according to statute; also to permit the keepers of the Crown's deer and wild beasts to use and pasture the woods as accustomed; the patent to be enrolled before the auditor of the county within one year for charging of the rent and before the surveyor of woods this side Trent before any cutting be made for survey of the performance of the covenants aforesaid. In consideration that the woods must be enclosed for seven years after cutting, the charges whereof Molton offers to undertake.   By warrant of the commissioners.

3641.)   8 *Jan.* 1578.   Lease for 21 years to Henry Fyssher of the tithes of corn in (1) Tughall and (2) Swynnowe *alias* Swynehowe, co. Northumberland, parcel of the cell of Bambrough, co. Northumberland, and once belonging to the monastery of St. Oswald, co. York; from Michaelmas last; yearly rents (1) 106s. 8d. and (2) £9. In consideration of the surrender by Fyssher of the interest of Rowland Foster under a patent, 8 Nov., 8 Eliz.,—an exemplification whereof Fyssher has also surrendered—whereby the tithes were leased to

Foster for 21 years from Michaelmas then last at the same rents; and for a fine of £14 6s. 8d. paid at the Exchequer.   By p.s.

3642.) 28 *Nov.* 1577. Lease for 21 years to Robert Raunce of woods called St. Jones Woode in Chippingwicombe, co. Buckingham; with reservations; from Michaelmas last; yearly rent £24 4s. 8d.; with covenants for the preservation of the woods (as in no. 3640). In consideration that the woods must be enclosed for seven years after cutting, the charges whereof Raunce offers to undertake.   By p.s.

3643.) 11 *Dec.* 1577. Lease for 21 years to Humphrey Gilbert, knight,   [*m.* 19] of the lordship and manor of Nevyn, the town of Nevyn and the stewardship of the town and lordship of Nevyn, co. Carnarvon, parcel of the principality of North Wales, and all lands, courts and the like parcel thereof; reserving to the Crown the rents of the town of Morva, Penwyn, Cube and Treflegh, the town of Llanner with the hamlets of Ipistell, Bodelas, Bodowesson, Penwyn and Beno, Portegros and Pentirgh *alias* Pentagh, the townships of Crukenny, Niffrin, Kidio, Rosse, Venassaph, Tresgarnett, Bodronell [and] Bottagh, also three parts of the hamlet of Blythyocke, and the rents of the town of Herdreff in the commote of Dynnllayne, and woods, wards, marriages, mines and quarries; from Michaelmas last; yearly rent £15 12d. In consideration that Gilbert undertakes the revival of the ancient rent of £15 for the premises, for which a rent of £10 12d has been paid since 13 Hen. VIII, and the payment of a yearly rent of £15 12d.   By p.s.

3644.) 23 *Dec.* 1577. Lease for 21 years to John Purvey and John Cheeke of the rectory of Spaldinge, co. Lincoln, once of the monastery of Spaldinge; with reservations; from Michaelmas last; yearly rent £9 15s. 5d.;   [*m.* 20] the lessee to pay yearly 7s. 6d. to the archdeacon of Lincoln, £13 6s. 8d. for the wages of two curates in Spaldinge church, 13s. 4d. for the wages of the subdeacon in the said church for assiduous attendance in choir, 8s. for the wages of two clerks to assist in choir there on Sundays and feast days, 7s. 6½d. for a dinner for the priests and clerks of Spaldinge on 'Mawnedaye Thursdaye' by ancient custom and 35s. 5½d. for the provision of bread, wine and other necessaries in the church [*sic*] of Cowbytte and Spaldinge; provided that Purvey shall not alienate his interest to anyone but Cheke. In consideration of the surrender by Purvey and Cheke of a patent, 18 March, 3 Eliz., leasing the rectory to the said Cheke and Lawrence Eresbie at the same rent for 21 years from Michaelmas 1562 or the termination of the interest of Dennis Toppes; and for a fine of £19 10s. 10d. paid at the Exchequer.   By warrant of the commissioners.

3645.) 23 *Dec.* 1577. Lease for 21 years to Thomas Cowland of the rectory of Olney, co. Buckingham, and the mansion house of the said rectory, late of the monastery of Sion, co. Middlesex; with reservations, including the mansion, garden and pond of the vicarage of Olney, the advowson of the vicarage there, the nomination of the priest at Weston and the yearly tithe of wild beasts in the park there; from Michaelmas last; yearly rent £30 13s. 8d.; the lessee to pay yearly £13 6s. 8d. to the vicar of Olney, 10s. 8d. for synodals and proxies, 26s. 8d. to the bishop of Lincoln for his pension, 4s. to the dean and chapter of Lincoln cathedral, 2s. to the archdeacon of Buckingham, 6s. 8d. to be distributed in the Crown's name among the poor of Olney and Weston and in Warington, co. Buckingham, and a sufficient stipend to the curate at Weston. In consideration of the surrender by Cowland of a patent of the court of Augmentations, 20 April, 36 Hen. VIII, leasing the   [*m.* 21] premises to Ralph Copinger at the same rent for 40 years from the end of a term of 21 years specified in an indenture, 16 March, 22 Hen. VIII, made thereof by Agnes, abbess, and the convent of Sion to Thomas Lawe; and for a fine of £26 13s. 4d. paid at the Exchequer.   By p.s.

3646.)   4 *Jan.* 1578.   Lease for life in succession to George Nedeham, citizen and mercer of London, and Arthur Nedeham, citizen and 'draper' of London, of 'le key' or 'le wharffe' called 'the Newe Wolle Key' in Thames Street in the parish of All Hallows Barkinge in Tower ward, London, now or late in the tenure of John Kember, citizen and draper of London, and a tenement adjoining in the said parish, late in the tenure of George Thorneton and now or late in that of Kember, both purchased by King Philip and Queen Mary from John Lyme of Bassingborne, co. Cambridge; with reservation of a great chamber with a hearth therein and a 'le gallerie' adjoining in the South part of 'le Owld Custome Howse' there and access thereto; from Christmas last; yearly rent £40; the lessees shall pay also all other quit rents and charges; they shall also within one year (if either so long lives) repair 'le wharffe' with new campshots, stakes and defences (*cameshidis, stipis et defensor'*) for the better preservation of the stone work from damage by ships approaching 'le key' or 'le wharffe', and repair the stone work where ruinous with 'le tarr' and all other necessaries; they shall also pull down 'le jybett' now at the South end of the custom house and erect a new one nearer the water-side by 2 or 3 feet; they shall also pull down the other 'le jybett' now on 'le wharffe' and erect in its place a sufficient crane for the unloading of merchandise, and shall do all other necessary repairs and maintenance; they shall also make and keep a book of all goods loaded and unloaded at 'le wharffe' to inform the Crown's officers how the customs and subsidies of the same have been answered, if so required by the lord treasurer; the lease to be void at the treasurer's will if the lessees shall knowingly permit the customs and subsidies due to be withheld or diminished; if the Crown shall have need of any part of the premises on account of the enlargement of the places and offices of the customs and subsidies, it may take such part for that purpose, compensation being made to the lessees such as the treasurer at his discretion shall appoint.   By p.s.

3647.)   27 *Jan.* 1578.   Grant to Frances Lottisham, widow, late the wife of William Lottisham, of the wardship and marriage of William Lottisham, son and heir of William Lottisham; with an annuity   [*m.* 22] of £13 6s. 8d. from 2 Oct., 18 Eliz., when William the father died.   By Q.

3648.)   28 *Nov.* 1577.   Grant to William Swane of the wardship and marriage of James Gens, son and heir of Robert Gens, 'yoman'; with an annuity of £5 from 24 Nov., 18 Eliz., when Robert died. Yearly value of the inheritance £17.   By Q.

3649.)   4 *Feb.* 1578.   Grant to Amphilicia Faldo, widow, and George Fittes of the wardship and marriage of Robert Faldo, son and heir of Richard Faldo; with an annuity of £3 6s. 8d. from 6 Dec., 19 Eliz.,   [*m.* 23] when Richard died. Yearly value of the inheritance £16 6s. 8d.   By Q.

3650.)   8 *Feb.* 1578.   Grant to Thomas Lewknor of the wardship and marriage of George Gunter, son and heir of Arthur Gunter; with an annuity of 26s. 8d. from 23 June, 18 Eliz., when Arthur died.   By Q.

3651.)   1 *Feb.* 1578.   Grant to William Hamonde of the wardship and marriage of Thomas Browne, son and heir of Thomas Browne; with an   [*m.* 24] annuity of 26s. 8d. from 27 Aug., 17 Eliz., when Thomas the father died. Yearly value of the inheritance £14 10s.   By Q.

3652.)   19 *Nov.* 1577.   Grant to Anne Denton, widow, of the wardship and marriage of Ralph Denton, son and heir of Richard Denton, 'yoman'; with an annuity of 20s. from 22 Dec., 18 Eliz., when Richard died. Yearly value of the inheritance £8 18s. 4d.   By Q.

3653.)   6 *Dec.* 1577.   *Windsor.*   Grant to William Partridge of the wardship and marriage to William Steed the younger, son and heir of William Steed the elder; with an annuity of £6 13s. 4d. from   [*m.* 25]
28 Sept., 16 Eliz., when William the father died.   By Q.

3654.)   6 *Dec.* 1577.   *Windsor.*   Grant to George Dacres of the wardship and marriage of Thomas Mewtas, son and heir of Henry Mewtas; with an annuity of £13 6s. 8d. from 8 Aug., 18 Eliz., when Henry died, until Thomas reaches the age of 15, and thereafter an annuity of £20.   [*m.* 26]
                                                                          By Q.

3655.)   25 *Jan.* 1578.   Pardon for Philip Watkyn *alias* Gwatkyn late of Talgarthe, co. Brecon, 'yoman', for the theft of four oxen between 10 May, 19 Eliz., and 15 July following wherever committed.   By Q.

3656.)   8 *Jan.* 1578.   Pardon for Henry Newton late of Howden in the East Riding, co. York, 'joyner', indicted for the murder of Cuthbert Scate late of Howden, 'cordiner', at Howden on 13 April, 19 Eliz. (*details given*).   By p.s.

3657.)   29 *Nov.* 1577.   Pardon for John Callice for all piracies and other offences committed by sea or land before the present date.   [*m.* 27]
At the request of earl James, Regent of Scotland.   By p.s.

3658.)   12 *Dec.* 1577.   Pardon for John ap Hoell late of Bieston, co. Chester, 'laborer'. At the session of Chester held at Chester in the common hall of the county on 29 July, 19 Eliz., it was presented that Robert Clewlowe late of Bieston, 'laborer', stole from the person of Richard Rowe at Nantwich (*Wicum Malbani*) on 1 July, 19 Eliz., a purse with £3 belonging to him, and ap Hoell and Robert (*or* Richard) Greene late of Bieston, 'laborer', on the same date procured him to the commission of the said felony and afterwards received and abetted him.   By p.s.

3659.)   11 *Dec.* 1577.   *Hampton Court.*   Pardon for John Perrye late of Hastinges, co. Sussex, 'mariner', indicted for piracy in that (1) he with 24 others on the high sea within the jurisdiction of the Admiralty on 8 July, 19 Eliz., in 'a pynnes *alias The Runnegate*', whereof John Perse was master, boarded a ship called '*The Mawrice alias* a busse' (50 tons burthen) belonging to Adrian Williamson, stranger, of Skedam and Hendryke Johnson, stranger, of Delphe in the lordship of Holland, attacked Williamson and Johnson and stole 28 lasts of 'barrelled herringes', worth £200, 60 'herringe nettes' with ten ropes fixed thereto, worth £30, and the said 'busse', worth £100, belonging to them and (2) with others on 28 June, 19 Eliz., on the high sea boarded an unknown French ship and stole a pack containing 400 'thowsand pynnes', worth £4 6s. 8d., and other goods (*described*) belonging to a Frenchman unknown. By information of Thomas Gawdye, a justice of the Queen's Bench, Thomas Cornewallys, knight, William Buttes, knight, Henry Woodhouse, vice-admiral in the counties of Norfolk and Suffolk, William Masters, LL.D., Francis Windeham, Ralph Shelton, William Heydon, Nathaniel Bacon and Charles Calthrope, justices of the peace in the county of Norfolk.   By p.s.

3660.)   *Undated.*[1]   Pardon for John Fulford late of Borrington   [*m.* 28]
co. Devon, 'yoman', indicted (1) with Anthony Lawdye late of Heleconten, co. Devon,

---

[1] A marginal note states that the *teste* of this pardon was left out of the warrant.

'laborer', for that at Maritavy, co. Devon, on 22 Nov., 19 Eliz., they broke and entered a close (*named*) belonging to Walter Coade and stole a cow belonging to him and (2) with Anthony Lawdey late of Heighbekington, co. Devon, 'yoman', and Edward Bawden late of Borrington, 'laborer', for that at Aishrayney, co. Devon, on 23 Nov., 19 Eliz., they stole two hens and a cockerel belonging to Philip Gay.   By Q.

3661.)   13 *Feb.* 1578.   Grant to James Astyn of the wardship and marriage of Christopher Rogers, kinsman and heir of Francis Rogers; with an annuity of £4 from 3 Aug., 17 Eliz., when Dorothy Rogers, late the wife of Francis, died. Yearly value of the inheritance £13 6s. 8d.   By Q.

3662.)   27 *Dec.* 1577.   Pardon for William Androwes late of London,   [*m.* 29] 'yoman', for the undermentioned felony and all other offences. He is indicted for the theft of a gelding belonging to Owen Robertes at Heston, co. Middlesex, on 1 Feb., 18 Eliz. At the suit of the wife of [—].   By Q.

3663.)   30 *Dec.* 1577.   Grant for life to William Sparke of the offices of one of the ushers at the receipt of the Exchequer and keeper of the chamber of the Council of 'le Starre Chamber' in the palace of Westminster, with the mansions belonging thereto; fees payable at the Exchequer; from the death, when it shall happen, of Percival Harte, to whom the offices were granted by patent, 11 Feb., 24 Hen. VIII, and of Henry Broke *alias* Cobham, knight, to whom, by the name of Henry Broke *alias* Cobham, a gentleman pensioner, they were granted for life *inter alia* in reversion by patent, 15 Jan., 13 Eliz.; order   [*m.* 30] to the officers of the Exchequer that, if Harte dies during the lifetime of Broke, they shall admit Sparke to the offices as deputy of Broke, according to the intention of a writing, 3 April, 18 Eliz., whereby Broke appointed him his deputy.   By p.s.

3664.)   5 *Jan.* 1578.   Appointment during pleasure of Thomas Wilson, councillor, as one of the Queen's principal secretaries; with all dignities and emoluments belonging to the office. Also grant to him for life, towards his charges by reason of the office, of an annuity of £100 from Michaelmas last, payable at the Exchequer.   By p.s.

3665.)   14 *Jan.* 1578.   *Hampton Court.*   Grant to Edmund Hampshire, John Ball, Francis Baswycke and Cuthbert Rowll, four yeomen of the chamber in ordinary, of two fines of £100 and £40 imposed respectively on Leonard Bapthorpe and John Launder, both of York, in the Star   [*m.* 31] Chamber in Hilary term, 19 Eliz., as appears by an estreat thereof sent into the Exchequer by a writ under the great seal for the levying of the said fines *inter alia* and remaining with the Queen's remembrancer; power to sue for the same in the Exchequer in the Queen's name or their own. For their service.   By p.s.

3666.)   27 *Jan.* 1578.   Licence for two years for John Kyddall, Robert Brombey, Thomas Tofte, William Gryme, Christopher Westbye and Hugh Horringham, inhabitants of Southferibye, co. Lincoln, (or one of them), for and in the name of the inhabitants, to rebuild the parish church of Southferibye and to repair whenever necessary the bridge there; licence also for the same (or one of them) or their deputy or deputies, bearers hereof, to gather alms in the dioceses of Lincoln and York towards this work. At the suit of the inhabitants: the church is much decayed 'by occasion of the foundacion which is scytuate in the side of an hill and upon certayne springes, by reason whereof the sydes do flee from under the said churche'; the bridge is also decayed to the damage not only of the inhabitants, but also of two market towns, Barton upon Humber and Barton upon Trente Bancke, and other villages and hamlets in that angle, being the only passage over the river of Ancolne issuing out of certain 'carre groundes' and marshes in the county of Lincoln into the river Humber; also the Humber has so worn away the meadows and common pasture grounds of Southferybye that within the past 30 or 40 years the inhabitants have consumed their goods

[m. 32]

in maintaining the banks and yet have lost more than two parts of their said meadows and pasture grounds. *English*.   By p.s.

3667.) 27 *Jan.* 1578. Licence for two years for John Gunbye of the parish of St. Mary in Mawden *alias* Malden, co. Essex, to gather alms in the counties of Essex, Suffolk and Norfolk. It is reported by a certificate of William Vernon and Thomas Eve, bailiffs of the borough of Malden, that he suffered shipwreck about the end of May last while carrying coals from Newcastle to Malden in his hoy *The Fraunces* of Malden within Tylmouthe Haven on Durtwyke Sandes; it is also reported by certificate of John Barker and Matthew Rychardson, bailiffs of the borough of Scarborough, co. York, that he suffered like shipwreck about 17 Sept. next following in his hoy *The Jesus* of Maulden travelling from Staningborough, co. Lincoln, towards Newcastle for coals; which two shipwrecks being to the value of about £200, he, his wife and children are utterly impoverished. *English*.   By Q.

3668.) 11 *Jan.* 1578. Grant for life to Jonas Shutz, born at Annebergh in Saxony, of the office of master worker and principal workman of the minerals lately discovered in the North parts by Martin Furbusher and brought or to be brought into England from the said North parts or adjacent countries; the office to be occupied by himself or a deputy or deputies for whom he will answer; with a fee of £100 yearly, from the profits of the said minerals, from Michaelmas last. Grant also, at the suit of Shutz,   [m. 33] to Orothea his wife of an annuity of £20 for life, out of the same profits, from Michaelmas or Lady Day next after his death. In consideration that he has greatly travailed by land and sea for the service and profit of the Queen and her realm about the said minerals, and it is reported by Furbusher and others worthy of credit that he is very expert at melting the minerals and extracting richer metals; but especially because before members of the Privy Council he has undertaken to extract half an ounce of gold, fine, pure and nett, out of every hundredweight of the minerals brought into the realm from the same or like mines, and to deliver the same and all other gold, metals and profit therefrom to the use of the Crown and of others whose interest shall be in the premises to such officers as the Crown shall appoint, and that the charges that the Crown and others interested shall sustain about the extracting of the gold shall not amount to more than 10s. for every hundredweight of the minerals. *English*.   By Q.

3669.) 28 *Nov.* 1577. Grant during good behaviour to Christopher Muschampe of the office of a baron of the Exchequer; from the death of Thomas Greke, late a baron of the Exchequer.   By Q.

3670.) 27 *Jan.* 1578. Protection for one year for Nicholas Sentleger *alias* Sellenger of Eastwell, co. Kent.   By p.s.

3671.) 6 *Feb.* 1578. Pardon for Nicholas Dynham late of Holcomb Rogus, co. Devon, 'husbandman'. He was indicted at the general gaol delivery of Exeter castle held before Roger Manwood, a justice of the Common Pleas, and John Jefferay, a justice of the Queen's Bench, and their fellows, justices of gaol delivery, on Monday in the fourth week of Lent, 19 Eliz., for that he with Robert Dynham late of Holcomb Rogus,   [m. 34] 'husbandman', on 3 Oct., 18 Eliz., (1) broke and entered the close of Henry Barnarde at Uploman, co. Devon, and stole a mare belonging to Edward Churley and (2) broke and entered the close of Robert Yea at Sampford Peverell, co. Devon, and stole a mare belonging to Yea; he pleaded not guilty, was convicted and was condemned, but for divers considerations was committed back to gaol.   By Q.

3672.)   24 *Jan.* 1578.   Licence for 21 years for Peter Moris to make and put into use such engines for the raising of waters higher than nature not now or heretofore used within the realm as he has invented or shall within this term invent; no others except the licensee or such as he shall appoint to make or use any such engines or works; persons infringing the licence after warning given by the licensee shall be committed to ward without bail or mainprise until they have   [*m.* 35]
made fine to the Queen for such contempt and also paid to the licensee £100 for every month wherein they shall after warning given use the said engines; provided that all persons may make as hitherto any such engines or works as have been used within the last 20 years for drawing waters out of fen grounds or other conveying of waters within the realm; the licence to be void if the licensee do not within three years from the present date put it in use. At his suit.   *English.*   By Q.

3673.)   4 *Feb.* 1578.   Grant in fee simple to John Shelley, Edward Gage and Richard Guldeforde of lands (*named with tenants' names*) in the marsh of Guldeforde in the parish of Este Guldeforde, co. Sussex; to hold as of the manor of Eastgrenewich in socage; neither the lands nor the grantees will be charged with any demands by the Crown except the fealty due. Robert Hare and Ralph Hare of London by indenture enrolled in Chancery have conveyed to the Crown the said lands, late of Thomas Guldeforde late of Hempsted, co. Kent, knight, deceased, which they late purchased unto them and their heirs from the said Shelley, Gage and Richard Guldeforde, executors of the said Thomas Guldeforde.   By Q.

3674.)   18 *Nov.* 1577.   Licence for 30 years for Nicasius Yetsweirte, secretary for the French tongue and a clerk of the signet, to print all manner of books touching the common laws of England, already   [*m.* 36]
printed or not printed, whereof no other person except Richard Tottell has at present any special privilege or licence under the great seal; no others to print such books upon pain of forfeiture of 12*d.* on every book to the use of the Crown and of the books printed to the use of the licensee, and upon pain of the Queen's displeasure; from the death of Tottell or whenever a like licence granted by patent, 12 Jan., 1 Eliz., to Tottell for life (so long as he should behave well in using it) shall become void; grant also, in recompense of Yetswerte's industry and charges in that behalf, that no one shall during the term of this licence print any other book which the licensee shall first take in hand to print, upon the pains before-mentioned. For his service to Henry VIII, Edward VI, Queen Mary and the present Queen.   *English.*   By p.s.

3675.)   13 *Feb.* 1578.   Grant for life to Nicholas Wylkes of the office of a gunner in the Tower of London; with a fee of 6*d.* a day from Midsummer last, payable at the Exchequer. On surrender by Wylkes in Chancery of the interest, now held by him, of Edmund Crofte under   [*m.* 37]
a patent, 26 March, 13 Eliz., granting the office to Crofte for life.   By Q.

3676.)   23 *Jan.* 1578.   Protection until the feast of St. Luke next for Thomas Snagge, who is about to go to Ireland as attorney general there; he, his mainpernors and securities to be in the meantime quit of all pleas and suits, except certain forms of plea (*specified*), the presents not to be of force if it should happen that he does not take the journey or after he returns within the term to England out of that service.   By p.s.

3677.) 24 *Jan.* 1578.   Presentation of Ralph Pickhaver, M.A., to the rectory of Chylrey, Salisbury dioc., void by lapse.   By p.s.

3678.) 5 *Feb.* 1578.   Grant for life to Robert Knolles of the office of usher or porter of the mint in the Tower of London, when it becomes void by the death of Richard Farr, now porter of the mint, or otherwise; with a yearly fee of £10, payable by the undertreasurer or warden of the change, coinage and mint in the Tower. In consideration of the surrender by Knolles in Chancery of the interest, now held by him, of John Hammonde under a patent, 9 April, 18 Eliz., granting the office to Hammonde for life when it should become void as aforesaid.   By p.s.

3679.) 10 *Jan.* 1578.   Presentation of Richard Sutton, clerk, to the perpetual vicarage of Wellingborough *alias* Wendlingborough, Peterborough   [*m.* 38] dioc., void by resignation.   By p.s.

3680.) 24 *Dec.* 1577.   Presentation of Richard Guilpyn, M.A., to the rectory of Aldingham, co. Lancaster, Chester dioc., void by death.   By Q.

3681.) 23 *Jan.* 1578.   Grant for life to James Manuccio, Italian, the Queen's servant, of an annuity of £40, payable at the Exchequer, from Lady Day next. For his service. By p.s.

3682.) 23 *Jan.* 1578.   Presentation of Meredith Hanmer, M.A., to the rectory of Hunspill, Bath and Wells dioc., in the Queen's gift by the minority of William, earl of Bath.
                                                                                                By p.s.

3683.) 9 *Dec.* 1577.   *Windsor Castle.*   Presentation of Edward Norrys, clerk, to the perpetual vicarage of Tedburye, Gloucester dioc., void by lapse.   By p.s.

3684.) 21 *Feb.* 1578.   *Hampton Court.*   Lease for 21 years to Francis Whytney, a serjeant at arms, of enclosures and buildings thereon (*tenants named*) in (1) Utkington (*named*), (2) Clotton, (3) Helsbye (*alias* Heisbye), (4) Manley (in Dallamire forest), (5) Assheton,
                                                                                                [*m.* 39]
(6) Avenley, (7) Moldesworth, (8) Norley, (9) Kinisley,   [*m.* 40]
(10) Doddon, (11) Kellsawe and Tarvin, (12) Shotwicke (*named*), (13) Caponhurst and Willison, (14) Thorne on le Hughe, (15) Over Bonenton, (16) Brumlowe (*named*), (17) Thorne, (18) Cuddington, (19) Litle Budworthe, (20) Risheton, (21) Eaton, (22) Edisburie,
                                                                                                [*m.* 41]
(23) Minshawe, (24) Warrelson (*alias* Warrelston), (25) Powle (*alias* Poole), (26) Chompson, (27) Stoke, (28) Aston, (29) Desley   [*m.* 42]
alias Dislaie (some in Lyme Park), (30) Litle Moseley (*alias* Litle   [*m.* 43]
Mosseley), (31) Calveley, (32) Wordell, (33) Wymbosley, (34) Occason, (35) Croton, (36) Cuddington, (37) Norley, (38) Helsbie (*named*),   [*m.* 44]
(39) Gosworthe and Macklesfeilde forest, (40) Walley, (41) Taxall, (42) Wetnall (some in the manor of Maxfeild and given for a priest in the church or chapel of Disley Deine, some now or late in the tenure of the minister of 'Wetnall chappell') and (43) Saile and Crosstreate, co. Chester; with reservations; from Michaelmas last; yearly   [*m.* 45]
rents, after the premises shall come into his possession, (1) 3*s.*, (2) 9*d.*, (3) 12*d.*, (4) 6*d.*, (5) 18*d.*, (6) 6*s.*, (7) 18*d.*, (8) 2*s.*, (9) 3*s.*, (10) 6*d.*, (11) 5*s.*, (12) 12*d.*, (13) 6*s.* 8*d.*, (14) 6*s.* 8*d.*, (15)

18*d*., (16) 12*d*., (17) 3*s*., (18) 7*s*. 6*d*., (19) 37*s*. 6*d*., (20) 3*s*. 6*d*., (21) 9*d*., (22) 6*s*., (23) 6*s*., (24) 2*s*., (25) 3*s*., (26) 3*s*. 6*d*., (27) 2*s*., (28) 2*s*., (29) 10*s*., (30) 50*s*., (31) 2*s*., (32) 12*d*., (33) 3*s*., (34) 3*s*. 6*d*., (35) 7*s*., (36) 2*s*., (37) 12*d*., (38) 15*s*., (39) 12*d*., (40) 13*s*. 4*d*., (41) 13*s*. 6*d*., (42) 3*s*. and (43) 2*s*.[1] In consideration that the premises have been concealed, as appears by inquisitions remaining in the Exchequer, but Whytney will undertake to obtain them for the Crown and pay rent after they come into his possession.   By warrant of the commissioners.

(The dorse of this roll is blank.)

---

[1] The roll is in places illegible at this point, and readings have been supplied from the warrant, in Chancery Warrants Series II (C.82), no. 1326.

PART XI

C. 66/1174

3685.)   23 *May* 1578.   *Gorhambury*.   Lease for 21 years to John   [*m.* 1]
Lane of (1) lands (*named with tenants' names*, including a place once 'le hermitage', and 'the
Church House'), parcels of the manor of Dovercourte, co. Essex, and late of John, late earl
of Oxford, (2) lands (*named with tenants' names*) in Purleighe, co. Essex, (3) lands (*tenants
named*) in Malden. co. Essex, late of Bileigh priory, co. Essex, (4) the site of the manor of
Shalford, co. Essex, and all lands, courts and hereditaments belonging to the said manor,
now or late in the tenure of Richard Snowe, parcel of lands late assigned to Anne of Cleves,
(5) lands (*named with tenants' names*) in Thaxsted, co. Essex, (6) a cottage (*tenant named*) in
Dunmowe, co. Essex, and (7) two shops (*tenant named*) in Walden, co. Essex, late of Tiltey
priory, (8) lands (*tenant named*) in Westhurrock, co. Essex, (*named*) and Priors Marshe,
parcels of the manor of Purfleete, late of the priory of St. John of Jerusalem in England, and
(9) lands (*tenant named*) in Motesfounte, co. Southampton, parcel of the manor of
Motesfounte Thes[aurarii], late of Edward, late duke of Somerset, and formerly of the
treasurer of the metropolitan church of York; with reservations, including goods of felons
and outlaws and advowsons belonging to the manor of Shalforde: from Lady Day last;
yearly rents (1) 21*s.* 8*d.* (*detailed*), (2) 5*s.* 8*d.* (*detailed*), (3) 2*s.* 4*d.* (*detailed*), (4) £6 6*d.*, (5) 3*s.* 11*d.*
(*detailed*), (6) 6*d.*, (7) 14*s.*, (8) 26*s.* (Westhurrock) and 10*s.* (Priors Mershe) and (9) 10*s.*   [*m.* 2]
For (1)–(8) a fine of £40 18*s.* 4*d.* paid at the Exchequer by tally levied, 21 Feb., 20 Eliz., and
(9) a fine of 40*s.* paid at the Exchequer.   By warrant of the commissioners.

3686.)   23 *May* 1578.   *Gorhambury*.   Lease for 21 years to John Alured of (1) the tithes in
the lordship of Elsternewike in Holdernes, co. York, (2) the tithes of hay in Elsternewike
and (3) 24 hens and a cock which the tenants in Humbleton, parcel of the manor of
Frothinghame, co. York, render yearly as parcel of their rent, all once of the monastery of
Thorneton, co. Lincoln; the tithes of hay in Elsternewike belonging to the vicar there
reserved; from Michaelmas next; yearly rents (1) £6, (2) 10*s.* 8*d.* and (3) 3*s.* 4*d.* In
consideration of the surrender by Alured of a patent, 19 Feb., 3 Eliz., leasing the premises to
Joan Goldewell, widow, for 21 years from Michaelmas then last at the same rents; and for a
fine of £20 2*s.* paid at the Exchequer.   By warrant of the commissioners.

3687.)   13 *May* 1578.   Lease for 21 years to Walter Fysshe   [*m.* 3]
of the site or capital messuage of the manor of Yaresthorpe, co. York, parcel of the lordship
of Sherifhutton, co. York, parcel of the duchy of York; with reservations; from Lady Day
last; yearly rent £21 6*s.* 8*d.*; the lessee to provide entertainment for the Queen's steward and
surveyor coming to hold courts at the manor or survey the same. In consideration of the
surrender by Fysshe of a patent, 6 Dec., 12 Eliz., leasing the premises to Richard Sowtherne
for 21 years from Michaelmas then last at the same rent; and for a fine of £21 6*s.* 8*d.* paid at
the Exchequer.   By p.s.

3688.)   9 *May* 1578.   Lease for 21 years to Francis, earl of Bedford, councillor, of the
manor of Toppesham, late of Edward, late earl of Devon, and all lands, courts, ferries, fairs,
markets,   [*m.* 4]
tolls and other hereditaments in Toppesham and Weire or elsewhere, co. Devon, belonging

to the manor; with reservations, including the machines and cranage and cellars of the port with the fishery of the water of Clifte, being together of the yearly rent of £20, reliefs, fines, amercements and heriots, goods of felons and outlaws, wards, marriages and all other regalities; from Lady Day last; yearly rent £48 13*s*. 8½*d*.; the lessee to hold the manor courts at his own costs, to discharge the Crown of all charges and of the fee of any steward or bailiff of the manor, and to collect the fines and amercements and the reliefs, heriots and other profits hereby reserved, render account thereof before the auditor of the county and cause them to be paid yearly at the audit or before Christmas to the receiver general of the county.

By p.s.

3689.)   13 *May* 1578.   Lease for 21 years to Jasper Swifte, serjeant and marshal of the Admiralty, of a messuage and garden on 'le Tower Hill' in the parish of All Hallows Barkinge in   [*m*. 5]
Tower ward, London, late purchased by John Cornellis *alias* Cornelis from Lewis Williams of Abercarne, co. Monmouth, and a house late built by Cornellis on a void piece of ground adjoining the same messuage and garden, parcel of lands which ought to have come to the Crown after the death of the said Cornellis, an alien born, deceased, by reason of an inquisition or otherwise; from 1 Dec. 1592, being the termination of a lease thereof by patent of the Exchequer, 1 Dec., 14 Eliz., to Charles Smyth, page of the robes, whose interest Swyfte now holds, for 21 years from that date at a yearly rent of £5; same rent. For his service.   By p.s.

3690.)   16 *May* 1578.   *Gorhambury*.   Lease for 21 years to Henry Farror of Ewwoode, co. York, of the rectory of Kyrkebyfletham, co. York, late of the preceptory of Mount St. John, co. York; with reservations;   [*m*. 6]
from Lady Day last; yearly rent £20. In consideration of the surrender by Farrar of a patent of the court of Augmentations, 11 June, 7 Edw. VI, leasing the rector to William Bilmore, the King's servant, at the same rent for 21 years from the termination of a lease thereof by the prior of the hospital of St. John of Jerusalem in England and his brethren by indenture, 22 Nov. 1537, to Hugh Sterkey of Darley, co. Chester, and Leonard Warcopp, then serjeant at arms, for 29 years from Midsummer then next; and for a fine of £20 paid at the Exchequer.

By p.s.

3691.)   9 *May* 1578.   Lease for 21 years to Charles Smyth, page of the robes, of the mansion and demesne lands of the manor of Corston, co. Somerset, and the tithes of corn and hay of the demesne lands, all once of the monastery of Bathe and leased to Richard Horsington at a yearly rent of £12; with reservations, including a sheep house now built there, works of customary tenants in meadows by Bathe, common of pasture of sheep in the fields there at all times of the year for the ewe flock, and a winter pasture (*described*) of the demesne meadows and pastures for sheep; from Lady Day last; yearly rent £12. For his service; and for a fine of £12 paid at the Exchequer.   By warrant of the commissioners.

3692.)   16 *May* 1578.   Lease for 21 years to Thomas Sherley, knight, of 2,000 cords of 'beache, birchewood and okes' to be taken yearly in St. Leonard's forest, co. Sussex, which
                                                                                                                                      [*m*. 7]
forest is in the Queen's hands by exchange with Thomas, late duke of Norfolk, with access to the forest to cut and remove the said wood and convert it into charcoal; with reservations of all large oaks reputed timber and all fair 'lez saplinges' of oaks left for 'lez staddels' in the forest; from Lady Day last; yearly rent £66 13*s*. 4*d*.; the lessee to cut only by assignment of the surveyor general of woods this side of Trent and not to convert any cords to charcoal in any one year until viewed by the said surveyor or his deputy; he may cut more than 2,000

cords in any one year if it is convenient so to do, provided the total number taken under this lease is not more than 42,000; the patent to be enrolled within one year before the auditor of the county for charging of the rent and before the said surveyor before any cutting be made for survey of performance of the covenants. For a fine of £60 paid at the Exchequer.

By p.s.

3693.)   12 *May* 1578.   Pardon for Rachel Morecop late of London, 'spynster', wife of John Morecop late of London, 'barborsurgeon', and Elizabeth Cole, late the wife of Francis Cole late of London, 'yoman', for all offences committed before the present date. They are indicted for that they assaulted John Pullyn, 'yoman', on 14 Jan., 20 Eliz., in the highway in the parish of St. Gregory in   [*m.* 8]
Castell Baynard ward, London, and stole a coat (*described*) belonging to him. Because they are now pregnant.   By p.s.

3694.)   12 *May* 1578.   Grant to Marion Whistler, widow, late the wife of Edward Whistler, of the wardship and marriage of John Whistler, son and heir of Edward; with an annuity of £3 from 23 July, 19 Eliz., when Edward died. Yearly value of the inheritance £10 7s. 3d.   By Q.

3695.)   14 *May* 1578.   *Hampton Court.*   Pardon for David ap Howell Uryghe late of Rayader Goy, co. Radnor, indicted with others for that he burgled the mansion house of James ap Rees at Llanvyhangell Keven Llis, co. Radnor, on 12 Feb., 19 Eliz., assaulted James   [*m.* 9]
and stole £5 belonging to him.   By p.s.

3696.)   9 *May* 1578.   Grant for life to Thomas Cole, hereby accepted into the Queen's service, of the office of keeper of the 'pondes' in Westminster park and at the honour of Hampton Courte; with wages of 6d. a day and 22s. 6d. yearly for his livery coat, payable at the Exchequer. On resignation of the office by Thomas Bussard, to whom it was granted for life by patent, 20 June, 1 Eliz. *English.*   By p.s.

3697.)   12 *May* 1578.   Grant to Aunsel Samsford of the wardship and marriage of John Hedges, son and heir of Thomas Hedges; with an annuity of £6 13s. 4d. from 13 Nov., 18 Eliz., when Thomas   [*m.* 10]
died.   By Q.

3698.)   9 *May* 1578.   Grant to Edward Herne of the wardship and marriage of William Spenser, son and heir of William Spenser; with an annuity of 20s. from 18 May, 1 Eliz., when William the father died. Yearly value of the inheritance £4.   By Q.

3699.)   23 *May* 1578.   *Gorhambury.*   Grant for life in survivorship to Nicasius Yetsweirt and Charles Yetsweirt, his son, of the office of secretary for the French tongue; with a yearly fee of £66 13s. 4d., payable at the Exchequer. In consideration of the   [*m.* 11]
surrender in Chancery by Nicasius of a patent, 12 Nov., 37 Hen. VIII, granting the office to John Mason, now deceased, and him for life in survivorship; and for Nicasius's service to Henry VIII, Edward VI, Queen Mary and the present Queen.

Grant also for life to the said Charles of the office of one of the four clerks of the signet which shall next be void, the offices of clerk of the signet being now held for life by John Cliff, John Somer, Thomas Wyndebank and the said Nicasius, and the reversion of the one which shall first be void having been granted by patent, 15 June, 17 Eliz., to John Woode for life. Licence and admission also for Charles to write in the said office and pass all warrants as one of the clerks ordinary, that the Queen's subjects having to do in the same may have the better expedition in their affairs. *English.*   By p.s.

3700.)   9 *May* 1578.   Grant for the life of Anne Ayscough to William Aiscough and the said Anne, his wife, of the office of keeper of Byflete park, co. Surrey, and of all houses and lodges therein; from the death of Edward, earl of Lincoln, to whom, by the name of Edward Fynes, K.G., lord Clynton and Saye, the office was granted by patent, 18 Dec., 3 & 4 Ph. & Mary, for life; with fees etc. as held formerly by Anthony Browne, knight, or William Graye,   [*m.* 12]
knight, lord Graye of Wilton, or now by the said earl, payable by the receivers, bailiffs, farmers or occupiers of the manor of Biflete.   By Q.

3701.)   16 *May* 1578.   *Gorhambury.*   Licence for seven years for Andreas de Loo, born in Flanders and free denizen of the realm, to make or cause to be made pelts of sheep skins and lamb skins and to pull, clip, shear and take away the wool of any sheep skins or lamb skins to the number of 200,000 in any one year, and for any persons by the licensee's appointment and to his use to do likewise; also for the licensee to buy anywhere in the Queen's dominions pelts of sheep skins and lamb skins with the wool taken off and to export the same in ships of the Queen's dominions or friendly countries from the ports or havens of London, Sandwiche, Colchester, Ipswiche, Kinges Lynne, Yarmouthe or Southampton to the number of 200,000 yearly accounting every hundred of the same pelts after the rate heretofore accustomed; from the present date; stat. 5 Eliz. against the carrying of sheep skins and pelts overseas not being staple ware notwithstanding; the licensee to pay on the shipping of any of the pelts to the   [*m.* 13]
customer of the port 20*s.* for every 1,000 pelts over and above the duties accustomably paid; if by any restraint or other cause the licensee cannot in any year export the full number of 200,000 pelts, he may in following years of the term export the full residue of every year of the said number; no persons other than the licensee shall export such pelts or make them for any person other than the licensee, upon the pains limited in the said statute; officers of the ports where such shipping shall be to cause the number shipped with the day and time of shipping to be endorsed on the licence and yearly upon their accounts certify the number to the Exchequer. In consideration of great losses sustained by de Loo. *English.*   By Q.

3702.)   10 *May* 1578.   Grant for life to William Rylaund of the room of a yeoman waiter in the Tower of London which shall next be void; with wages of 8*d.* a day and a livery coat and a watch livery, payable as accustomed; the grant not to prejudice any person having a former grant of the like room, but to take place in due order. *English.*   By p.s.

3703.)   9 *May* 1578.   Grant for life to John Jonson of the office of a gunner in the Tower of London which shall next be void; with wages of 6*d.* a day, payable at the Exchequer; the grant not to be to the prejudice of any person to whom the like place   [*m.* 14]
has been granted, but to take effect in due order.   By Q.
      Vacated because surrendered, 16 *Oct.*, 21 *Eliz.; signed*: Wyll'm Cordell; John Johnson.

3704.)   23 *May* 1578.   *Gorhambury.*   Presentation of Anthony Haywood, B.A., chaplain in ordinary of the household, to the rectory of Resingdon Magna, co. Gloucester, Gloucester dioc., void by lapse.   By p.s.

3705.)   18 *May* 1578.   *Gorhambury.*   Grant for life to Daniel Rogers, the Queen's servant, of an annuity of £50, payable at the Exchequer, from Christmas last. For his service.
                                                                                      By p.s.

3706.)   9 *May* 1578.   Order to the treasurer for the appointment for seven years of William Fitzwilliam and George Delves, two of the gentlemen pensioners, to be alnagers of the new woollen cloths and other commodities called 'double, single and middle bayes, rashe or stamelles of Florence sorte, serge of the French sorte, sayes of Flaunders sorte, narrow woolsteddes, narrow grograynes, mockadoes of every sorte, plunnettes, frysadoes, carrell, fustian   [*m.* 15] of Naples, blankettes called Spanish rugges, knytte hose of wolstedde yarne' and all sorts of other new draperies and commodities now made only or mostly of wool, and to be collectors and farmers of the subsidy on the same, paying such yearly rent as the treasurer shall think convenient; such seals to be delivered to them for the office as shall be necessary; the treasurer—to whom the appointing and disposition of like offices and farms by ancient statutes appertains—to devise patents for so many shires, cities and places as he shall think convenient to be made to Fitzwilliam and Delves, and the same to certify to the keeper of the great seal to be passed under the great seal. The said new sorts of woollen commodities, chiefly devised and made by strangers that have resorted into the realm by reason of trouble in their own country, ought by the laws of the realm and the true meaning and equity of the same to be searched, measured and sealed and charged with a subsidy as other woollen cloths made in England have been, but no officers have as yet been appointed thereunto.   *English.*   By p.s.

3707.)   9 *May* 1578.   Licence for four years for Gilbert Gerrard (gentleman) to export 3,000 packs of linen yarn, counting 400 pound weight of the same yarn after the rate of six score pound weight thereof to every hundred pound weight for a pack and 200 pound weight of the same after the same rate for half a   [*m.* 16] pack, in English, Irish or denizen bottoms from Ireland to England; paying the usual duties payable since the beginning of the Queen's reign, but not any sum payable to the Crown or others under two Irish statutes lately enacted against the export of linen; the officers of ports to endorse quantities laden at any one time on the licence or the duplicate thereof, which is to be left at   [*m.* 17] the last port of lading.   *English.*   By Q.

3708.)   18 *May* 1578.   Appointment of William Drurye, knight, president of the province of Monster in Ireland, to be lord justice of Ireland during the absence of Henry Sidney, K.G., president of the council of Wales and deputy of Ireland, from Ireland, whom the Queen has licensed to repair to England for a season for the expedition of his private affairs and other causes; with power to do all things that customarily appertain to the office of lord justice in the absence of the deputy, and as if he had been elected to the office by the Queen's subjects of Ireland.   *English.*   By Q.

3709.)   21 *May* 1578.   Commission to Henry Sidney, K.G., president of the council of Wales and deputy of Ireland, William Drurye, knight, lord justice of Ireland, and William Gerrard, chancellor of Ireland, (or any of them) to invest, in the presence of such noble personages and men of honour of Ireland as they shall think fit, Tyrlaugh Lenaugh of that realm, whom the Queen has created by patents under the great seal of England a baron and earl of Ireland; causing to be inserted in the patents the several dates and the names of the noblemen present; the investiture as a baron to take place a day before that as earl and the patents to bear their dates accordingly.   *English.*   By Q.

3710.)   *Undated.* Creation of Tyrlaugh (*Terencius*) Lenaugh, baron of Clougher, as earl of Clanconneill in Ireland; in tail male;   [*m.* 18] provided that he or the heirs male of his body shall not have or claim any lands, jurisdictions, 'coyne and livery' or other profits, except those contained in articles agreed between Henry Sidney, K.G., president of Wales and the marches thereof and deputy general of Ireland, and him dated [—] and enrolled in the Chancery of Ireland. Witnesses: [—]   By Q.

3711.)   *Undated.*   Creation of Tyrlaugh Lenaugh, born in Ireland and noble by blood, as baron of Clougher in Ireland; in tail male; with proviso as above (no. 3710). Witnesses: [—].
     By Q.

3712.)   12 *May* 1578.   Commitment for 21 years (by mainprise found in the Exchequer) to Thomas Andrewes of the farm or custody of land in Ipswich in a street called Fyshemerkett, once the common gaol there; from Michaelmas last; yearly rent 12*d.* and 8*d.* beyond of increase; provided that, if anyone will without fraud give more of increase, Andrewes is bound to pay so much, if he wishes to hold the farm.   By treasurer's bill.

3713.)   9 *May* 1578.   Grant to Edward Horsey, knight, captain of   [*m.* 19] the isle of Wight, his heirs and assigns of the reversion and rent of the manor of Cramborne *alias* Craneborne, co. Dorset, (land called Hyde and Moloxden, co. Wilts, reserved), the rectory of Cramborne, the advowson of the vicarage of Cramborne and all appurtenances of the said rectory in Cramborne, Upwimborne,   [*m.* 20] Farneham, Blaydon, Rushton, Edmondesham, Hampreston, Gundevile, Chettell, Bage-bere, Steple, Purbecke, Knoll, Milborne, Dyvelishe, Estwood, Fairewood, Aldreholte, Blackedone *alias* Blagdon, Parkemeade and Bowridge, cos. Dorset and Wilts, all once of the cell or priory of Craneborne, parcel of the monastery of Tewkesbury, co. Gloucester, and leased by patent, 18 Jan., 2 Eliz., to Thomas Frauncis and Humphrey Frauncis and Nicholas Frauncis, both sons of William Frauncis, knight, for life in succession at a yearly rent of £28 16*s.* 10*d.*

Also grant of—(1) the said manor, rectory and advowson; (2) the rectory of Bremore, with the chapels of Charford and Hale, co. Southampton, once of Bremore priory; (3) tithes and lands (*named*) in Hampreston and Westporte, cos. Dorset and Southampton, (*tenants named*), once of the monastery of Christchurche Twyneham, co. Southampton; (4) lands (*named with tenants' names*) in Alencester hundred, co. Dorset, once of the monastery of Shaston; (5) lands (*described with tenants' names*) in Southampton, co. Southampton, once of St. Denys priory; (6) lands (*named with tenants' names*) in Ringwood, co. Southampton, once of the late free chapel of Bisterne, co. Southampton; (7) lands in Farnehamsdeane, co. Southampton, in the Crown's hands by the dissolution of chantries and the like; and (8) lands (*tenant named*) in Farleighe, co. Wilts, once of Iveschurche priory.

As formerly held by the abbots or priors of the said monasteries, Edward, late earl of Devon, any chantry priest or   [*m.* 21] others. To hold the manor and rectory of Cramborne by service of the fortieth part of a knight's fee, and the rest as of the manor of Estgrenewiche, co. Kent, in socage, and by yearly rents of (1) £28 16*s.* 10*d.*, (2) £4 17*s.*, (3) 30*s.*, (4) 20*s.* 4*d.*, (5) 6*s.* (*detailed*), (6) 61*s.*, (7) 3*s.* 4*d.* and (8) 4*s.* 8*d.* Issues from Lady Day last. The grantee to pay yearly out of (2) £11 3*s.*, to wit, in the stipend of a chaplain at Hale in the parish of Bremore £4 and of a curate at Bremore and Charford £6 and in a pension to King's college, Cambridge, for a portion of tithes 23*s.* For his service   By Q.

3714.)   28 *March* 1578.   *Gorhambury.*   Grant to John Hercey of   [*m.* 22] Andevor, co. Southampton, and John Haward of London, their heirs and assigns of—(1) lands (*named*) in the parishes of Colleshule and Aston, co. Warwick; (2) lands (*named with tenant's name*) in the parish of Rochefeilde, co. Leicester, late of the monastery of Stewkwell;

(3) lands in Twyforde in the parish of Thorpe Segefill, co. Leicester, given to the church for 'le holly breade loafe' and other supersititious uses; (4) lands (*tenants named*) in Birrington, co. Gloucester, given for prayer for the departed and other supersititious uses in Campden church, co. Gloucester; (5) the tithes of wool and lambs and other small tithes in the parish of Charleton Abbottes, co. Gloucester, late of the monastery of Winchecombe, co. Gloucester; (6) a ruinous chapel called 'Mawdlen chappell' and lands (*named with tenants' names*) in Brode Campden, co. Gloucester; (7) lands (*named with tenants' names*, including 'le Churche House'), given for lights and other supersitious uses in Le Lee church, co. Gloucester; (8) a parcel of tithes, late belonging to St. Oswald's priory, and lands in Wootton and Emesworth in the county of the city of Gloucester and lands (including the site of a chapel) in Twigworth in the county of the said city; (9) the advowson of the rectory of Wydcombe Magna in the county of the said city, late of St. Oswald's priory in the county of the said city; (10) all tenements once called 'a parte of a horsemyll' in the parish of St Peter in Cornehill, all tenements in the parish of St. Margaret Patenttes given by William Barrett for a chaplain celebrating mass in the church of St. Dunstan in the East, London, and a tenement in the parish of All Hallows Barkinge, once in the tenure of Thomas Blower, given by Barrett for the said uses, all in London; (11) three tenements in Milke Streate in London, once in the tenures of Matthew Dale, Thomas Thorne and William Knighte, given for a priest there by Thomas Kelsey; (12) a tenement in the   [*m.* 23] parish of St. Andrew, Holborne, once in the tenure of Hugh Woodall, a tenement adjoining the same, late in the tenure of Thomas Hylton, two tenements, once leased to Oliver Tatan in the same parish, a place once called 'a gate romme' in Grayes Inne Lane, late leased to John Beast, in the parish of St. Andrew in Holborne in the suburbs of London, given for superstitious uses, and a tenement in the parish of St. Peter in Cornehill, late in the tenure of Richard Kyrke, given for a priest there by lady Alice Brucknoll, widow, a shop and chambers in Old Fish Street (*Veteri Piscaria*) in the parish of St. Nicholas Coldeaby, once in the tenure of Robert Kinge, given by John Bryan for superstitious uses in the church of Holy Trinity the Less by Olde Fysshestreate, London, all houses once called 'Arthures Hall' in Longe Lane in the parish of St. Botolph without Aldrichegate, once of the Holy Trinity brotherhood or guild there, a tenement in the parish of St. Dunstan in the East at the West end and towards the South side of the graveyard of the same, once in the tenure of Edward Waters, given by Bartholomew James for superstitious uses, a tenement, once in the tenure of Thomas Bradforde, in the parish of St. Mary at Hill, given for superstitious uses in the church of St. Dunstan in the East by Roger Hall, a shop in Soperlane, once in the tenure of [—] Stagges, widow, given by Dennis Joyes for superstitious uses in the church of St. Dunstan aforesaid, three messuages, once in the tenure of Henry Hollande, in Thamestreate in the parish of St. Dunstan in the East, given by Matthew Earnest for superstitious uses, and four tenements in Thamestreate in the said parish of St. Dunstan, once in the tenure of Thomas Blower, Edward Waters, Thomas Constable, William Awgod, Ambrose Wolley, Thomas Warner, James Harryson and Henry Holland, given for the soul of William Hariett, knight, for superstitious uses, all in London; (13) lands (*tenants named*) in Northrode *alias* Northroade (*alias* Northwood), given for a mass in Gaiosworth church, in Northpevor (*named*) and in Dyssely *alias* Disleigh in the parish of Stoppord *alias* Stokeforth, given for superstitious uses, all in the county of Chester; (14) a tenement (*named*) in Lostwythell and Lanlyverye, co. Cornwall, given for a chaplain in the curiate chapel of St. Bartholomew in the borough of Lostwithell in St. Bartholomew's church there; (15) a tenement (*named with tenant's name*) in the parish of Marstowe, co. Devon, given for lights at the time of divine service every Sunday and other superstitious uses; (16) lands (*named with tenant's name*) in a parish called Saint Davys Doune, co. Devon, given for the brotherhood of the guild of the Assumption in the city of Exeter; (17) a messuage (*described with tenants' names*) in the parish of St. Olave in Exeter, given for bells, books and other ornaments in the chapel of St. Mary

the Virgin in the parish of St. John *de Arcubus* in Exeter; (18) a messuage (*described with tenants' names*) in Exeter, given for a chaplain celebrating for departed souls; (19) lands (*described*) in Ampton, co. Suffolk, belonging to Ampton chantry and a rent out of the same chantry, given by John Cockett and others for a chantry priest and other superstitious uses in Ampton church; (20) the rectory of Rendilsham, co. Suffolk, late of the monastery of Butley; (21) lands (*named with tenants' names*) in Walsham in le Willowes, co. Suffolk, given for lights in the church there; (22) lands in Blechenton *alias* Blechendon, co. Suffolk, given for superstitious uses in the church; (23) a messuage called 'le Katherin Whele' in Theame Strete in the parish of St. Dunstan in le Easte, London, with 'lez wharffes' and other appurtenances thereof (between a tenement once of Richard Halsted on the East, the common 'le ditche' of the city of the West, the Thames on the South and Thamestrete

[*m.* 24]

on the North), given for an obit in the church of St. Dunstan in le East for the souls of John Sabbe and his wife, John Searle and Margaret his wife, William Halbeck, 'draper', and all others departed, now or late in the tenure of Mary Bowlle, widow, as appears by the will, 15 April 1419, of Walter Heynes, citizen and 'woodmonger' of London, in performance of the will of the said Sabbe; (24) a cottage in Saint Nicholas Lane in the parishes of St. Nicholas Acon or St. Mary Abchurche by Candlewikestreate, London, now or late in the tenure of Thomas Rigges; (25) the rectory of Weston, co. Leicester; (26) lands in Grobe, co. Leicester, given for a lamp in Ratbye church; (27) lands (*named*, including 'le chappel yarde') in Bocheston (*alias* Becheston), co. Leicester, given for superstitious uses; (28) a portion of the tithes of hay in Clyffe Slades and in the parish of Thorneton, co. Leicester, belonging to the Queen by the dissolution of chantries and the like; (29) lands (*tenants named*) in Bonington Sutton, cos. Leicester and Nottingham, (*named*) and in Bonington Ende, given for superstitious uses; (30) lands (*named with tenants' names*) in Dreycote (including a small ruinous house once 'Saint James chappell'), Downefeild, Eaton, Netherfeild, Robin Holme, East Meadowe, Carfeilde, Northfeilde, Staunton and Borofeilde [*no county specified*]; (31) a grange called Sownlaye Cote in the parish of Kyrkedale, co. York, late of the monastery of Ryvalles, co. York; (32) woodlands (*named with tenant's name*) in the parish of Addell, co. York, once of the monastery of Kyrstall, co. York; (33) the rectory of Bylloughe, co. Norfolk, late of the monastery of Butley, co. Suffolk; (34) lands (*named*) in Nedeham, co. Norfolk, given by Robert Baylye of Waylred, co. Suffolk, for an anniversary for the souls of him and others his friends and other superstitious uses there; (35) a tenement (*named*) in Swaffham, co. Norfolk, given for a priest and other superstitious uses in the church there; (36) lands in Tybbenham, co. Norfolk, given by Rowland Targe and John Awbery, men of religion, to Hugh, prior, and the convent of the church of St. Faith of Horsham, and other lands (*described*) there; (37) six messuages in the parish of St. Augustine, London, in the several tenures of Ralph Porter, Thomas Browne, Gilbert Rydeo, William Raynerde, William Laurence and Catherine Yokins, widow, late of the house of crutched friars, London; (38) four small tenements in Goodrowe Lane in the parish of St. John Zacharye in London, given by William Hope, rector, and the wardens of the church there for superstitious uses; (39) the shops and tenements late belonging to the late new hospital of St. Mary the Virgin without Bysshoppesgate, London, in Westcheape in the parish of St. Pancras, London, (to wit, between void land once of the dean and chapter of St. Martin le Graunte, London, on the East and a tenement once of Robert Knowles on the West, one end thereof abutting on the highway of Westcheape towards the North and the other end on a great seld once of Richard Collyer called 'the Keyseilde' towards the South) and a great messuage called 'the   [*m.* 25]

Kaye seld' *alias* 'the Signe of the Kaye' in Westcheape and the rents issuing from the same messuage once belonging to the said hospital; (40) a piece of land (1 ac.), late belonging to the dissolved church of Aye, in the parish of St. Martin in the Fields, co. Middlesex,

(abutting on the highway from Westminster to Chelsey on the East and South, on a field called Eyburye Field on the West and on a footway from Westminster to Knightes Bridge on the North); (41) a messuage in the borough of Southwarke, co. Surrey, in Mylne Lane by a bridge called Battlebridge, now or late in the tenure of Garrett Edwardes, escheated because Peter Richard being seised thereof died on 21 June, 6 Edw. VI, at Southwark without an heir; and (42) two messuages in or by Mylne Lane and Battlebridge aforesaid, now or late in the several tenures of George Swayne and John Bylkyn, 'cowpers', whereof Henry Moreskyn was seised and by his will, 11 Dec., 5 & 6 Ph. & Mary, bequeathed them to Sarah Moreskyn, now wife of Roger James, and her heirs and he died on 10 Aug., 5 & 6 Ph. & Mary, seised thereof without an heir, which Sarah at that time and long before and after was an alien born dwelling outside the Queen's obedience, to wit, in Antwerp in the parts of Brabant, her father and mother being aliens, by reason whereof the messuages belong to the Queen by the law of the land and her prerogative. Which premises, all concealed from the Crown, are of the yearly value, according to several particulars thereof, of £7 11s. 6d. To hold in socage as of the manor of Eastgrenewiche, co. Kent, and by yearly rents, from the time when they or any parcel thereof come into the grantees' possession, of (1) 16s. 8d., (2) 20d., (3) 2s., (4) 3s., (5) 3s. 4d.,   [*m.* 26]
(6) 2s., (7) 3s. 4d., (8) 2s., (9) (the rectory of Wydecomb Magna) 2s. 6d., (10) 2s., (11) 3s., (12) 10s., (13) 4s., (14) 20d., (15) 20d., (16) 12d., (17) 20d., (18) 20d., (19) 12d., (20) 6s. 8d., (21) 18d., (22) 2s., (23) 6s. 8d., (24) 3s. 4d., (25) 6s. 8d., (26) 6d., (27) 6d., (28) 2s., (29) 3s. 4d., (30) 6s. 8d., (31) 6s. 8d., (32) 4s., (33) 6s. 8d., (34) 2s., (35) 2s., (36) 2s. 6d., (37) 10s., (38) 4s., (39) 3s. 4d., (40) 12d., (41) 2s. and (42) 3s. 4d. Issues from the time when the premises or any parcel thereof should have come to the Crown's hands until the making of the undermentioned
                                                                 [*m.* 27]
patent to lord Wentworth. This patent or the enrolment thereof to be sufficient warrant to the officers of the Exchequer and the attorney and solicitor general to direct process against occupiers of the premises as reasonably advised by the grantees and to try the same in the Exchequer as in causes on behalf of the Crown. The grant to be void in respect of any of the premises which were not concealed on 20 July, 12 Eliz., when lord Wentworth or any others by his procurement and charges caused discovery to be made thereof.

In part fulfilment of a patent, 24 July, 12 Eliz., whereby the Queen promised to grant in fee farm to Thomas Wentworth, knight, lord Wentworth, or such others as he, his heirs or executors should appoint concealed lands discovered by them to the yearly value of £200.
                                                                 By Q.

3715.)   31 *July* 1578.   Grant to Robert, earl of Leicester, councillor, his heirs and assigns of lands (*named or described with tenants' names*), late detained or encroached by divers persons (*named*), (1) in the commotes of Ardudwy, Estimanner, Talepont   [*mm.* 28–34] and Penllyn, co. Merioneth, and (2) in Tregoed, in Tregoyd Scycylt and Bodwilion, in Nant and Pestell, called Keaven Ybrayche, Kayucha, Kayissa, Byarthy, Glesyon and Karreg Yllam (*described*), in Nant and Carngioche, in Pistyll and Bodeilas, in Herdreff, in Ceidio of [? *recte* and] Madryn, in Madryn and Lleche, in Madryn, in Dwybor and Dwyverche, in Bodvyon, in Nant, in Pennyberthe, Krigau, Strootgyeeyarche, Bodvell, Bachelleth and Bodvyan, in Kidyo and Morva, in Rhosses and Lwynithe and Tregoyd Scycylt, in Penmayn Beno, Penmayn Kyttayle and Nevyn, in Nant,   [*m.* 35] in Tregoed, in Llavor and Bronhiocke, in Gwins and Gwinase, in Bachelleth, in Carnguch, in Llaneymon, in Newgulfe, in Rrav and Aberdaron, in Penlleghe, in Penlleche, in Pennarthe, in Glasevrin, in Pennant, in Geste and Penyvet, in Elernio, in Bulche yr Eysteye, in Elernyon, in Ddynlley, in Nantwynen and Dinorveg, in Llangian, in Trevruo, called Klayne Llone and Mangarw, in Treviw, in Gwider,   [*m.* 36] in Llan Virveghan, in Eniskyn, in Dygovylchye, in Llanvayre, in Llanvayr Vechan, in

Llechydyor, in Dinorwicke, in Llanvayre, in Penvro, in Castell, in Llanvayre Vechan, in Llanbeder, in Castell, in Penvro, in Castell, in Elernyon, in Elernyon and Glasevryn, [*m*. 37] in Tregoyd, in Castell, in Dynlley, in Bottache, in Penichin, in Ruge, in Tregoyd Scycilt, in Morva, in Penvro, in Clynocke, in Dygoyfilchye, in Llangian, in Dolbadarne, in Pennarthe, in Pennyvell, in Aberdaron, in Bryn Bras, in Dynlley, in Nancall, in Elernio, in Mynythe and in Llanvaire Vechan, co. Carnarvon; to hold in socage as of the manor of Estgrenewich, co. Kent, and by yearly rents of (1) £4 17s. 11⅛d. and (2) £5 10s. 6¼d.; the patent to be void in respect of any of the premises whereof the rents or   [*m*. 38] profits have heretofore been answered to the Queen; if the grantee cannot by reason of any person's interest enjoy the issues of the premises or any parcel thereof, the rents of the same may by the barons of the Exchequer upon the grantee's complaint be apportioned according to the quantity of the lands. For his service.   By Q.

3716.)   28 *June* 1578.   *Gorhambury*.   Lease for 21 years to William Holland of lands in Cotherstone in the archdeaconry of Richmond, co. York, late of William, marquess of Northampton, deceased; with reservations, including rents of free tenants, courts, reliefs and the like; from Lady Day last; yearly rent £16 15s. 5d. In consideration of the surrender by Holland in respect of the premises of a patent, 20 May, 14 Eliz., leasing the same *inter alia* to Christopher Newton for 21 years from Lady Day then last at the same rent; and for a fine of £16 15s. 5d. paid at the Exchequer.   [*m*.39]

3717.)   11 *June* 1578.   Pardon for William Downing late of Maristowe, co. Devon, 'mason'. He was indicted at the general gaol delivery of Exeter castle, co. Devon, made there before John Jefferay, knight, chief baron of the Exchequer, Edmund Anderson, one of the Queen's serjeants at law, and their fellows, justices of gaol delivery, on Monday in the fourth week of Lent, 20 Eliz., for that he with others burgled the dwelling house of Joan Hayne at Marstowe on 7 Oct., 18 Eliz., and stole money and wool (*described*) belonging to her; he pleaded not guilty and was convicted, but was for divers causes committed back to gaol.
By p.s.

3718.)   4 *Aug*. 1578.   Licence for 20 years for the mayor and burgesses of Boston, co. Lincoln, and their servants, deputies and assigns appointed by writing sealed, to buy and export from the port of Boston and its members or any port or haven in the counties of Lincoln or Norfolk in ships of the realm or friendly countries 40,000 quarters of corn and grain, wheat only excepted, to friendly countries; from the present date; 8d. to be taken in full discharge of duties on every quarter; the quantities   [*m*. 40] shipped to be written on the back of the licence, that it may be left on expiry with the customers of the port where the last amount is shipped; provided that the licence shall be suspended for the duration of any order that may be given by the Queen or Privy Council prohibiting the export of corn for a time. At their suit: for the relief of the borough, which is greatly impoverished by scarcity of traffic of merchants and damage to its port, bridge, wharfs, staithes and sea banks through inundation of both salt and fresh waters; and for the service of the mayor, burgesses and inhabitants. *English*.   By p.s.

3719.)   *Undated*. Pardon for Thomas Holland late of Facknam, co. Norfolk, 'yoman', indicted for the theft of a horse belonging to Henry Allsoppe at Lettwell, co. York, on 17 May, 18 Eliz.
By p.s.

3720.)   14 *Aug*. 1578.   Licence for three years for Margaret Hankin of Harwiche, co. Essex, widow, to export from any port in England in ships of the realm or friendly countries

500 quarters of malt duty free to friendly countries; from the present date; the licence to be endorsed with the quantities shipped, that   [*m.* 41]
it may be left on expiry with the customers of the port where the last amount is shipped. *English.*   By p.s.

3721.) 30 *June* 1578. *Gorhambury.* Grant for life in survivorship to Nicasius Yetsweirt and Charles Yetsweirt, his son, of the office of secretary for the French tongue and to Charles for life of the reversion of the office of one of the four clerks of the signet   [*m.* 42]
(in the same terms as above, no. 3699). *English.*   By p.s.

3722.) 23 *July* 1578. Pardon for Garrett Frayne late of Shordyche, co. Middlesex, 'yoman', indicated for that he broke and entered the dwelling house of Richard Walton at Shordiche on 28 May, 20 Eliz., Margaret Walton, Richard's wife, being within, and stole linen etc. (*described*) belonging to Richard. At the suit of Jane Frayne, his mother.
                                                                                                          By p.s.

3723.) 14 *Aug.* 1578. Grant for life to James Metcalf of the offices of (1) keeper or parker of Woodhall park in the forest of Wensladale, co. York, (2) keeper or parker of Wanles *alias* Vanles park, co. York, and (3) surveyor of the castle and lordship of Midleham and of all manors, lands, mines and tenements within the liberty of Richmond, co. York; as late held by Christopher Metcalf, knight, deceased, his father; with wages of 2*d.* a day for (1) and for the others the wages accustomed, payable out of the issues of the lordship of Midleham, from Christopher's death.   By p.s.

3724.) 2 *Aug.* 1578. Grant to Thomas White, LL.D., Giles Estcourte and John FitzJames of the Queen's interest in the manors of   [*m.* 43]
Sherborne, Wotton, Whitefelde, Burton, Holneste, Yatemyster, Candell Episocopi, Casteltone *alias* Casteltowne and Newlande, with the hundreds of Sherborne and Yatemyster and the castle and park of Sherborne, co. Dorset, in the Queen's hand by the attainder for treason by stat. 5 Edw. VI of Edward, late duke of Somerset, to whom they were leased by indenture, 8 March, 2 Edw. VI, by John, once bishop of Salisbury, confirmed by the dean and chapter of Salisbury cathedral by writing, 10 March following, for 99 years from Michaelmas then last at a yearly rent of £213 8s. ½d.; issues from the time when the premises came to the Crown.   By Q.

3725.) 26 *June* 1578. *Gorhambury.* Pardon for Rice Reede late of Ocestrye, co. Salop, 'yoman', indicted (1) at the great session held at Flint, co. Flint, on 22 April, 19 Eliz., [*m.* 44]
before John Throckmarton, knight, justice of the county, for that on 16 Aug., 18 Eliz., he broke and entered the close of John Lloid at Hopemedached, co. Flint, and stole a gelding belonging to him, (2) by the name of Rice ap John ap David late of Perkyngton, co. Salop, *alias* Rice Reade, for that he stole four bullocks belonging to John ap John on 13 Nov., 18 Eliz., at Hanmer, co. Flint, and (3) by the name of Rice ap John ap David late of Perkyngton *alias* Rice Reade, for that he stole a bull, a bullock, six cows and two heifers belonging to Edward ap Atha on the said 13 Nov. at Hanmer.   By Q.

3726.) 26 *July* 1578. Pardon for Timothy Challenger *alias* Challiner late of London *alias* late of the parish of St Mary, co. Kent, 'yoman', indicted for that with others on 27 Jan., 20 Eliz., he (1) stole £80 and plate etc. (*described*) belonging to Catherine Chelsam at Whitechappell, co. Middlesex, and (2) burgled the dwelling house of Catherine Kelsham at the said parish of St. Mary, she being within, and stole £75 and plate etc. (*described*) belonging to her. At the suit of the said Catherine Kelsham and of Julian Challenger, his mother.   By Q.

3727.) 26 *June* 1578. *Gorhambury*. Pardon for Robert Bunckar of Estneston, co. Northampton, 'cooke', for manslaughter. It was found by   [*m*.45] an inquisition taken before John Newport, a coroner of the county, at Estneston on 14 Dec., 20 Eliz., on the body of Philip Phelppes late of Estneston, 'yoman', that Bunckar struck Phelppes, while he was fighting with Christopher Barnes and John Bridges, both of Estneston, 'yomen', (*details given*), on 12 Dec., 20 Eliz., at Estneston so that he died there on 13 Dec.   By Q.

3728.) 7 *July* 1578. *Gorhambury*. Pardon for Thomas Tyrringham of Tyrringham, co. Buckingham, for all devastations of lands belonging to him in Tyrryngham and Filgrave, co. Buckingham, and of   [*m*.46] enclosures of lands lately cultivated there and converted to pasture contrary to stats. 4 Hen. VII for keeping up of houses for husbandry, 7 Hen. VIII to avoid letting down of towns, 27 Hen. VIII concerning the decay of houses and enclosures, 5 Eliz. for the increase of tillage and 13 Eliz. for the continuance of certain statutes; and licence for him, his heirs and assigns to hold all the said lands enclosed or converted to pasture without rebuilding of any house and without exercise of tillage therein.   By p.s.

3729.) 18 *Aug.* 1578. Grant for life in survivorship to Brian Hogg and George Hogg, his son, of the office of clerk of the deliveries of the ordnance within and out of the Tower of London and 'the Minorites', and out of any other storehouse appointed for the ordnance; with wages of 12*d.* a day, payable at the Exchequer, from Christmas last. In consideration of the surrender in Chancery by Brian of a patent, 28 Nov., 13 Eliz., granting him   [*m*.47] the office for life. *English*.   By Q.
    Vacated because surrendered, 7 May, 27 Eliz., by George Hogge; signed: Tho. Egerton, ...[1] Evelyn (*with note 'cognoscit Georgium Hogg'*) . . . .[1] Hogge.

3730.) 14 *May* 1578. Appointment, until the Queen shall declare it   [*m*.1d.] superseded, of Edwin, archbishop of York, Henry earl of Huntingdon, president in the North, Richard, bishop of Durham, John, bishop of Carlisle, lord Thomas Evers, Matthew Hutton, dean of York cathedral, William Mallory, knight, Robert Stapleton, knight, Robert Lougher, LL.D., vicar general of the said archbishop, John Gibson, LL.D., Christopher Waynsworth, Robert Ransden, archdeacon of York, and Robert Toures, S.T.B., (or five of them, the archbishop, the earl, the bishops of Durham and Carlisle or Evers being one) to be delegates and commissioners (without appeal) to—visit the cathedral church of Durham, inquire concerning the religion, life and conversation of the dean and chapter and of the canons, prebendaries, ministers and officers there, correct and punish those found delinquent or negligent by deprivation of office, sequestration of emoluments or other fitting coercion, and repress any found contumacious by ecclesiastical censures, imprisonment and other lawful remedies; examine the letters and muniments of the dean, prebendaries, canons and beneficed persons, both as regards their orders and their benefices, dismiss from office any found not sufficiently secured in that behalf, and the same persons and others serving in the church found unworthy of their offices or not embracing the true religion expel from the church and remove from office; receive resignation from office; restore to their old place those removed from the church, if right requires it; examine the privileges, statutes, registers, accounts and other muniments touching the foundation and

---

[1] The roll is illegible at this point.

endowment of the church, deliver in the Queen's name to the dean and others injunctions and statutes that seem suitable for the better government of the church, appointing fitting penalties for infringers of the same, and annul those found repugnant; receive from the dean and others the oath of obedience and fealty to the Crown, and especially concerning acknowledgment of the royal supremacy in all causes both ecclesiastical and temporal and renunciation of all foreign jurisdiction pursuant to stat. 1 Eliz., and all other oaths required by law, and remove those found contumacious; and generally do all things necessary for such a visitation or reformation.   By p.s.

(The rest of the dorse is blank.)

GENERAL INDEX

Numbers refer to entries and not to pages

A

Alderley—*cont.*
 and Poyntz of, *q.v.*
Aldermaston, Berks, Foster of, *q.v.*
Alderminster (Aldermynster), [Worcs], vicar
  presented to. *See* Jones, Philip
Aldersaye. *See* Aldersey
Aldersbrook (Aldersbroke) [in Little Ilford], Essex,
  manor, 3235
Aldersey (Aldersaye, Alldersey), Philip, of London
  alias of Horton, 2933
 Thomas, of London, 955, 1410
 Thomas, of London, assistant and chief councillor
  of fellowship of merchants of Spain and
  Portugal, 2256
Aldershot (Aylyshott), Hants, forest or chase, 1539
 lieutenants or keepers (*named*) of, 1539
Aldersley. *See* Alderley
Alderson, Anthony, 3257
Alderton (Aldington, Aldrington), Northants, 600
 manor, 600, 2862, 3614
Alderton, Suff, 2180
Alderyche. *See* Aldrich
Aldesworth, Aldesworthe. *See* Aldsworth
Aldewarke. *See* Aldwark
Aldeworthe. *See* Aldworth
Aldham, Thomas, 1623
Aldingham (Haldingham), Lancs, 3611
 fishing (Le Mayre), 3611
 mines, 3611
 rector presented to. *See* Gilpyn, Richard
 Hart Mill (Harte Mylne) and Sea Mill (Sey Mylne)
  in, 3611
 Baycliff, Gleaston, Hart Park, Muchland, Scales,
  Seawood Park and Sheep Park in, *q.v.*
Aldington (Aldyngton), Kent, 628, 2466
Aldington. *See* Alderton
Aldreholte. *See* Alderholt
Aldrich (Alderyche, Aldriche, Aldridge), John,
  alderman of Norwich, 449
 John, justice of peace and of oyer and terminer in
  Norwich, 2867
 Richard, rector presented to Byford, 3374
 Robert, vicar presented to St. Mary, Nottingham,
  3371
 Thomas, canon or prebendery of St Peter's,
  Westminster, 495
Aldringham with Thorpe (Alsingham and Thorpe),
  Suff, chapel, church, curate and rectory, 382
Aldrington. *See* Alderton
Aldsworth (Aldesworth, Aldesworthe), Glos, 2536
 manor, 2536
Aldwark (Aldewarke, Aldwerke) [in Alne], Yorks,
  621, 921
Aldworthe (Aldeworthe), Thomas, of Bristol,
  assistant and chief councillor of fellowship
  of merchants of Spain and Portugal, 2256
Aldyngton. *See* Aldington
ale. *See under* beer
Aleford. *See* Alford
Aleigh (Alie), Humphrey, 1570
 John, 1244
 Cf. Lee
Alencester, Dors, hundred, 3713
Alesburye, William, 831
Alesheath (*unidentified*) [in *or* near Malmesbury], Wilts,
  206
Aleston. *See* Alveston
Alexander, Nicholas, almsknight in college of St
  George, Windsor castle, 193
 Peter, of St Peter's, Jersey, 2845

Alexander—*cont.*
 Richard, [Herts], 1974
 Richard, justice of peace in Hertfordshire, 413
 Robert, *alias* Robert Zinzano, equerry of stable,
  1374
Aleyn. *See* Allen
Alford (Aleford, Alforde, Awforth), Lincs, 966
 grammar school of Queen Elizabeth, 1397
  governors (*named*), master and usher of, 1397
Alforde, Lancelot, surveyor of queen's lands in
  Ireland, 81
 Roger, 263
Alfreton, Derb, Birchwood in, *q.v.*
Alfriston (Alfryston), Sussex, rectory, 2295
Algarsthorpe (Agasthorpe) [?in Bawburgh], Norf,
  1192
Algarthorpe (Ulkarthorpe) [in Brampton], Derby,
  1331
Alie. *See* Aleigh
aliens, disfranchisement of merchants adventurers by
  marriage to, 53, 1531
 manufacture of goods by, 449, 3705
 regulation of trade by, 3485, 3572
 settlement in Ireland of, 59
 See also under merchants strangers
Alington. *See* Allington
Alisborowe. *See* Allesborough
Alkborough, Lincs, Walcot in, *q.v.*
Alkham, Kent, Halton and Wolverton in, *q.v.*
Alkington, Glos, Wick, Lower and Upper, in, *q.v.*
Alkyngton, William, 364
All Hallows. *See* Allhallows
Allame, Simon, Spanish subject, 726
Allame. *See* Alum
Allanbie, William, 892
Allard, Francis, Spanish subject, 1704
Allaston. *See* Alveston
Alldersey. *See* Aldersey
Allen (Aleyn, Alleyn, Alleyne, Allyn, Alon),
  Alexander, of London, 3605
 Christopher, 2493
 Christopher, knight, 2328
 Henry, 1347
 James, knight, 2583
 John, Edmund son of, 2402
 John, the elder, and John, the younger, his son and
  Edmund the latter's son, 437
 John, of London, 2256
 John, of Norwich, 2867
 John, of Stamford, 2503
 John, [Kent], 3446
 John, [Midd], 822
 John, warden of mysteries of merchant drapers and
  hosiers of Chester, 3572
 John, yeoman tailor of great wardrobe, 2335
 Richard, of London, 2069
 Richard, principal burgess of Daventry, 679
 Robert, of Bristol, 2256
 Robert, [Kent], 2464
 Roger, 2515
 Thomas, of Ifton, 2498
 Thomas, of London, queen's servant, 58
 Thomas, of Norwich, 2867
 Thomas, of Staple Inn, 3605
 Thomas, [Bucks], 2914
 William, knight, of London, 123, 1380
  alderman of London, 2256
 William, [Kent], 2464
 William, [Midd], 831
Allendale (East Allendell), Northumb,

Athelney [in Lyng], Som, monastery, 1350, 2631

Atherstone (Adderston, Atherston) [in Mancetter], Warw, 3190

manor, 3190

Hodgekyns and Knight of, *q.v.*

Atherstone on Stour (Atherston on Stowre), Warw, manor, 1334

Atherton, John, 1872

Ralph, of Pemberton, 2505

William, 3009, 3101

Cf. Atterton

Atherton. *See* Atterton

Athewick. *See* Adwick

Atkins (Atkyns), . . . , [Glos], 252–3

Margaret, 3614

Nicholas, of London, 2256

Richard, and Eleanor his wife, 3475

Thomas, 3015, 3038

Thomas, [Glos], 241

William, of London, 2256

Cf. Atkyn

Atkinston (Atkynson), Giles, 3545

Hugh, 3257

John, 1359

Lawrence, 2239

Peter, [Kent], and Margery Penreth his wife, 829, 1343

Peter, [Midd], 3275

Richard, 3417

Robert, 2058

William, 2948

William, [Kent], 3254

William, [Midd], 1631

William, (Westm], 1844

William, vicar presented to Kirby Hill, 1075

Atkyn, William, 3257

Cf. Atkins

Atkyns. *See* Atkins

Atkynson. *See* Atkinson

Atlebarowe. *See* Attleborough

Atley, Richard, 571

Cf. Hatley; Lee

Atram (Stock Atram) [in Netherbury], Dors, 638

Atsan. *See* Attisham

Atterley in Much Wenlock, Salop, 206, 2177, 3379

Atterton (Atherton) in Witherley, Leics, 2255

chapel, 2255

Atterton, William, 2964

Cf. Atherton

Attilborowe. *See* Attleborough

Attingham (Acham), Salop, 1629

grange, 2572

manor, 1629, 2572

rectory and advowson of vicarage, 1629, 2572

Berwick, Chilton, Cronkhill, Ernstrey and Uckington in, *q.v.*

Beast of, *q.v.*

Attisham (Adysham, Atsan) [in Broadwindsor], Dors, 930

Attleborough (Atlebarowe, Attilborowe) [in Nuneaton], Warw, 1293, 1590

attorney general. *See under* officers, king's or queen's

Atworth (Atforde, Atworthe), Wilts, 1348

Aubourn, Lincs, Haddington in, *q.v.*

Auburn (Awborne) [in Fraisthorpe], Yorks, 2196

Aucher (Ager, Awcher), William, 104–7, 1931, 1958, 2094, 2942, 3442, 3458

Alice wife of, 2094

Cf. Anger; Auger

Auckland, Bishop, (Burshops Auckland) [in

Auckland—*cont.*

Auckland St Andrew], Durh, Appleton of, *q.v.*

Auckland St. Andrew, Durh, Auckland, Bishop, and Hamsterley in, *q.v.*

Audeley. *See* Audley

Audesley. *See* Ardsley

Audley (Awdeley, Awdley), Staffs, 963, 1255

Audley (Awdley, Awdeley, Awedley), lord. *See* Tuchett

Audley (Audeley, Awdeley, Awdley), Christopher, and Thomas his son, 514

Edmund, bishop of Salisbury, 2255

Edmund, [Norf], 1902, 1923

Henry, 1399, 1539

James, *alias* James Tuchett, 963, 1255

James, [Norf], 1232

John, of London, 2256

Philip, and Margaret his wife, 1232

Richard, 1482

Thomas, 514

Thomas, of Berechurch, Robert son of, 1150

Thomas, of London, 123, 2256

Auger, Richard, 3075

William, 243, 247

Cf. Anger; Aucher

Aughton (Aghton), [Lancs], rector presented to. *See* Nutter, John

Aughton, Yorks, Cottingwith, East, in, *q.v.*

Aske of, *q.v.*

Aughton (Oughton) [in Aston cum Aughton], Yorks, 206

Augmentations, court of, chancellor of. *See* Rich, Richard

Aunger. *See* Anger

Austen (Astyn, Austyn, Awsten), George, clerk of peace in Surrey, 2247

James, 3661

James, [Kent], 104–5, 107

James, [Yorks], 2543

Cf. Aston

Austen. *See* Aston

Austenfeilde. *See* Alstonefield

Austerfield (Austerfeild) [in Blyth, Notts], Yorks, 3258

Austley. *See* Astley

Austrey (Alstrye, Alstwye, Awestrie, Awstrie, Awstrye), Warw, 844, 965

rectory and advowson of vicarage, 844, 965

Kendall of, *q.v.*

Austrie, Ralph, 276

Austyn. *See* Austen

Avecote. *See* Alvecote

Aveley (Alveley), Essex, 1165

Bretts in, *q.v.*

Avelyn, Edward and Joyce, 1279

Cf. Evelyn

Aven. *See* Avon

Avenals (Avenelles) [in Angmering], Sussex, manor, 1160

Avening Court (Avenons Courte) [in Avening], Glos, 2017

manor, 2017

Avenley. *See* Alvanley

Avenon (Avenor), Alexander, of London, 2256

Alexander, the younger, of London, 1293

Avenons. *See* Avening

Avenor. *See* Avenon

Averye, William, and William his son, 2662

Cf. Everie

B

Bodenham (Boddenham, Bodname), Nicholas, 2006
  Roger, of London, 2256
  Roger, [Heref], 1928, 1937
Boderocke. *See* Bodwrog
Bodewryd (Bodewred, Bodwred), Ang, rectory, 648
Bodfaes (Bodvais) [in Llanllechid], Carn, 212
Bodfean (Bodvyan, Bodvyon), Carn, 3715
  Penmaen in, *q.v.*
Bodfel (Bodvell) [in Llannor], Carn, 3715
Bodferin (Bodverryn), Carn, 830
Bodham. *See* Boddam
Bodington. *See* Boddington
Bodley (Bodleighe), Christopher, clerk, 2317
  Richard, 2734
  William, 3466
Bodmin (Bodman, Bodmyn), Corn, 2766, 2855, 3571
  chapel of St Nicholas, 1600
  priory, 2180
  Clifford and Tregidiowe of, *q.v.*
Bodname. *See* Bodenham
Bodowesson (*unidentified*), Carn, 3643
Bodrigam. *See* Bodrugan
Bodrith. *See* Bodwrdda
Bodronell (*unidentified*), Carn, 3643
Bodrugan (Bodrigam) [in Gorran], Corn, manor,
  2872
Bodsilin (Bodselyn) [in Aber], Carn, 2252
Bodvaio. *See* Bodfaeo
Bodvell. *See* Bodfel
Bodverryn. *See* Bodferin
Bodwilion. *See* Bodeilan
?Bodwrdda (Bodrith) [in Aberdaron], Carn, 2252
Bodvyan, Bodvyon. *See* Bodfean
Bodwred. *See* Bodewryd
Bodwrog (Boderocke, Bodwrocke), Ang, chapel or
  church, 820
Bodynys (Bodyner) in Penmynydd, Ang, 2500
Bodyngton. *See* Boddington
Bohun, Joan, 2255
  Cf. Bowne
Boilland, Richard, 2083
Bointon. *See* Boynton
Bokehampton. *See* Bockhampton
Bokelande. *See* Buckland
Bokelly (Bokelley) [in St Kew], Corn, 2766
Bokested. *See* Buxted
Bolam (Bolum, Bolun), [Northumb], vicar presented
  to. *See* Duxfeyld, Henry
Bolberry (Boltbery, Boltebery) [in Malborough],
  Devon, 930
  manor, 930
Bolde, William, 1243
Bolder. *See* Boldre
Boldero, Francis, 2949
  Francis, [Suff], 116
Boldre (Bolder), Hants, 1440
  Baddesley, South, Pilley, Sharpricks and
    Walhampton in, *q.v.*
Bolebec (Bulbeck, Bulbecke), barony, 424, 572
Bolham (Bollome) [in Clarborough], Notts, 1438
Bolholmes. *See* Bulholmes
Bollershaw [in Ripon], Yorks, 847
Bolles. *See* Bowles; Bowling
Bollome. *See* Bolham
Bolly, William, 1460
Bolney, Sussex, 1626
Bolnhurst, Beds, Greensbury in, *q.v.*
Bolsterstone (Bolsterton) [in Ecclesfield], Yorks, 3379
  chantry and manor, 3379
Bolston. *See* Bonvilston

Boltbery, Boltebery. *See* Bolberry
Bolton (Boulton) [in Edlingham], Northumb,
  hospital of St Thomas the Martyr, 831
Bolton [in Bishop Wilton], Yorks, 2260
Bolton Abbey (Bolton) [in Skipton], Yorks,
  monastery, 206, 3386
Bolton by Bowland (Bolton), Yorks, 2745
Bolton Percy, Yorks, Appleton, Nun, in, *q.v.*
Bolton upon Dearne (Bolton on Dearne), Yorks, 2047
  Goldthorpe in, *q.v.*
Bolton, Francis, 357
  George, of Great Wolford, 1437
  William, M.A., rector presented in Treswell, 1011
  William, [Yorks], 825
  William, rector presented to Priston, 1765
Bolton. *See* Boulton
Boltonsboroughe. *See* Baltonsborough
Bolum, Bolun. *See* Bolam
Bolytowt (Bolytowte), Robert, of Moulton St
    Michael, and Thomas and William his sons
    and Elizabeth and Margaret his daughters,
    2150
Bond (Bonde), Alice, sister of John Samwayes, 3482
  George, of London, haberdasher, 123, 2256
    alderman of London, 2810
  George, [London], Winifred wife of, 2494
  Nicholas, M.A., rector presented to Fulbeck, 556
  Nicholas, of St Stephens, and Richard his son and
    Elizabeth his daughter, 703
  Thomas, rector presented to Acrise, 165
  William, alderman of London, 123, 923
    Margaret wife of and William son of and Martin
    and Nicholas, William's sons, 923
  William, [Oxon], 1208
  Winefrid, 840
Bondgate (Bondgate next Aismonderbie, Bongate
    next Rippon) in Ripon, Yorks, 210, 2907,
    3379
  chapel, hospital or house of St John (Seynt John
    Baptystes), 2907, 3379
Bondleigh (Bawdeley), Devon, 638
bondmen in blood of the Crown, 3273
  inquiry as to alienation of lands and chattels by,
    3294
  See also under manumissions
Bonenton, Over, (*unidentified*), Ches, 3684
Bones, Peter, of Scalby, 2555
  Cf. Bowne
Bongate. *See* Bondgate
Bonham, John, and Mabel his wife, 1592
Bonialva, Bonialvei. *See* Bonyalva
Bonington End (Bonington Ende) [in Sutton
    Bonington], Notts, 3714
Bonner (Bonnar), Anthony, 2012
  John, 2068
  Thomas, the elder, of London, and Agnes his wife,
    932
  Thomas, of Murcott, 2191
  Thomas, the younger, and William, both of
    London, 932
Bonnet (Bonnett), Roger, of Wenhaston, 2168
Bonney. *See* Bunny
Bonny, Richard, 2443
  Cf. Bunney
Bonnyard. *See* Bonyard
Bonsall, Derb, 654
Bonvilston (Bolston, Bonvillston, Boulston), Glam,
  903
  manor, 903
Bonwell. *See* Bunwell

Bretonbye. *See* Brettanby

Brett, Robert, of London, 959

  Cf. Brete; Brytt

Brettanby (Bretonbye) [in Barton], Yorks, Wytham
  of, *q.v.*

Brettenham, Suff, 2091

Brettes. *See* Bretts

Bretton, Monk, (Monkbretton, Monkebretton), [in
  Royston], Yorks, monastery, 2313, 2513
  prior and convent of, 2313

Bretton (Breton), William, [Essex], 2346
  William, [London], Nicholas and Richard sons of,
  3527
  Cf. Bryton

Bretts (Brettes) [?in Aveley], Essex, manor, 442,
  1355A
  steward etc. of. *See* Cholmeley, Jasper; Hodgeson,
  Robert

Bretwastre. *See* Bartestree

Brevell (Brevall), Thomas, the younger, 615, 1264

Brewer, Thomas, 2071

Brewer. *See* Bruer

Brewere. *See* Bruern

Brewton. *See* Bruton

Breynton, John, 3036

Brian. *See* Bryan

Brichdir. *See* Brithdir

Brichett. *See* Birchitt

Brickell. *See* Brickhill

Brickendonbury (Brikendon Bury) in All Saints,
  Hertford, Herts, manor, 2493

Brickhill, Great, (Brickhill, Great Brickell, Great
  Brickill), Bucks, 1553, 2687
  manor, 2687

Brickhill, Little, Bucks, 35

Bridekirk (Birdkirke, Bridekirke), Cumb, rectory,
  2327, 3395
  Dovenby, Ribton and Tallentire in, *q.v.*

Bridge (Bredge), Kent, 913
  Lawrence of, *q.v.*

Bridge Court (Bridgecourte) [in Battersea], Surrey,
  3252

Bridge Town (Bridgetowne Feilde, Burgetowne) in
  Stratford upon Avon, Warw, 1345

bridge, licence to repair, 3666

Bridgecourte. *See* Bridge Court

Bridgenorth, Bridgenorthe. *See* Bridgnorth

Bridger, Lawrence, M.A., rector presented to
  Slimbridge, 2598

Bridges (Brydges), Charles, 3072
  Giles, knight, lord Chandos, 2012, 2054
  baron of Sudeley, 2749
  Henry, and Anne his wife, 2006
  Humphrey, and Dorothy his wife, 2425
  John, of Easton Neston, 3727
  John, [Worcs], 280
  Thomas, 1932, 1934
  William, 2425

Bridgetowne. *See* Bridge Town

Bridgewater. *See* Bridgwater

Bridgford, West, (Bridgforde), Notts, 206
  Bassingfield in, *q.v.*

Bridgnorth (Bridgenorth, Bridgenorthe,
  Bridgnorthe), Salop, 51, 1347, 1995, 2255,
  3204
  chantries (one in church of St Leonard), 2255
  church of St Mary Magdalen and its vicars choral,
  1347
  hospital of St John the Baptist, prior of, 2255

Bridgwater (Bridgewater), Som, 552, 1166, 2631

Bridgwater—*cont.*
  bailiffs and burgesses of, 2631
  chantry of St George, 2631
  priory or hospital of St John, 830, 1392, 2179
  Bower in, *q.v.*
  Blake of, *q.v.*

Bridgwater (Bridgewater), countess of. *See* Daubney

Bridgwater (Bridgewater), Henry, 2817
  John, canon or prebendary of Bristol cathedral,
  2633

Bridlington (Birdlington, Bridlyngton), Yorks,
  monastery, 407, 574, 597, 671, 1422, 2196,
  2513, 3417
  bursar of, 1422
  Buckton, Easton, Grindall, Hilderthorpe and
  Speeton in, *q.v.*

Bridport (Birpott), Dors, 1347
  chantry (Mundeynes), 1347
  Charde of, *q.v.*

Bridstow (Bredstowe, Bridstowe, Bristowe,
  Brydestowe, Brydstowe), Heref, 1683, 2255,
  2720, 2777, 3209, 3503
  Kedson and Wilton in, *q.v.*

Brierley (Brearley) [in Felkirk], Yorks, 2301

Brierton (Breereton) [in Stranton, Durh], 547
  vicar of, 547

Brierton. *See* Brereton

Brigg (Glamford Brigges) [in Wrawby], Lincs, 831
  chapel (Easte Chappell), 831

Brigge, John, 2104

Brigges (Brygges), Robert, ecclesiastical
  commissioner, York province, 2599
  Robert, steward or recorder of Kendal, 592
  Thomas, 2196

Brigham, James, gunner in Carlisle castle, 2628

Brighouse (Bryghowse), Martin, 2046, 2930

Bright, John, and Alice his wife, 2442
  Thomas, 831
  Cf. Brytt

Brightelmyston. *See* Brighton

Brightling (Brightlinge), Sussex, 3389

Brightlingsea (Brightlingsey), Essex, 1355A
  manor, 1355A
  bailiff of. *See* Baker, John
  collector of, 1355A

Brighton (Brighthelmyston), Sussex, 1576
  manor, 1576

Brightwalton (Bright Walton), Berks, 2082

Brightwell Baldwin *or* Britwell Salome (Brytewell,
  Butwell), [Oxon], rector presented to. *See*
  Westfallinge, Herbert

Brigstock, Northants, rectory and vicar of, 1458

Brikendon. *See* Brickendonbury

Brill, Bucks, 2191, 2255
  Moleyns in, *q.v.*
  Hart of, *q.v.*

Brimfield (Brymfield), Heref, manor, 2631

Brimham (Brambem, Bramham, Brymbem,
  Brymham) [in Kirkby Malzeard], Yorks,
  208, 847, 1212, 1216
  manor, 208–9, 631–4, 639, 641–4

Brimigam, Brimigham. *See* Birmingham

Brimpsfield (Brymesfeld), Glos, manor and park,
  2749

Brimpton Court *alias* Shalford (Brimpton Coorte) [in
  Brimpton], Berks, free chapel or rectory
  alias St Leonard's chapel, 206

brimstone, manufacture of, 2257

Brinckley, Brincklowe. *See* Brinklow

Brincknold, Brincknoll. *See* Bincknoll

Brindham (Brendham) [in Glastonbury], Som, 2195
Bringborne, Robert, of London, 2256
Bringhurst, Leics, Drayton in, *q.v.*
Brington, Northants, Gardiner *alias* Redy of, *q.v.*
Brimingham (Burnyngham), Norf, 845
Brinkburn (Brenkebourne), Northumb, monastery, 3382
Brinklow (Brinckley, Brincklowe), Warw, 210
    church, 210
Brinkworth (Brynkworth), Wilts, 617, 970, 1680
    manor, 970, 1680
Brinscombe, Roger, of Cameley, 1612
Brinton (Brynton), Norf, 845
Briscall. *See* Birstall
Brisco (Briskoe, Brysco), John, 3005
    John, [Cumb], 216, 2277
    John, [London], 2711, 3515
Brisiert. *See* St Clement's
Briskoe. *See* Brisco
Brisley, [Norf], rector presented to. *See* Hall, John
Bristol (Bristall, Bristoll, Bristowe), 51, 2173, 2255–6, 2688, 2892
    bridge, 2255
    brotherhood of St John the Baptist *alias* of tailors in, 1379
    cathedral, 1379
        canons or prebendaries in. *See* Bridgwater, John; Saunders, John; Wethered, Thomas
        canon or prebendary presented to. *See* Forth, Clement
    chamberlain of, 1379
    chapel of Redcliff (Radcliff) and advowson thereof, 2255
    church of All Saints, 2254
        calenders brotherhood or guild in, 2254
    church of Christchurch *alias* Holy Trinity (Christchurche, Christeschurche *alias* Trinity), 1379, 2255
        Balleys chantry in, 2255
    church of St Mary Redcliff (St Mary Ratclyff), 2254
    church of St Michael, 2255, 2688
    church of St Philip, vicar presented to. *See* Colman, Thomas
    church of St Werburgh, 2254–5
    coroners of. *See* Faye, John; Fielde, John
    feodary of. *See* George, Christopher
    High Street (Highe Streate) in, 2254
    hospital of St John the Baptist without Ratcliffe Gate, 3448
    house of Magdalen in, 1379
    mayor of. *See* Wade, John
    monastery of St Augustine next, 210, 666
    parish of St Ewin (St Ewen), 1379
    parish of St Michael, chapel of Three Kynges of Culloyne in, 2255
        chapels of Assumption of St Mary the Virgin and St John the Evangelist *alias* Knappe chappell, and avowsons thereof, 2255
    parish of St Philip (St Philip without Lawfords (Laffordes) Gate), 2254
        chantries (Fortheys and Kemys) in, 2254
        Trinity chapel *or* hospital in, 2255
    parish of Temple *or* Holy Cross (Cross of the Temple), chapel of St Catherine in, 2255
    port, 58
    St Augustine's Back (Saynt Augustynes Back) and St Augustine's Green (Saynt Augustynes Grene, Seynt Augustynes Grene), in, 1347
    staple, constables of. *See* Prewett, John; Saxey, Robert

Bristol—*cont.*
    mayor of. *See* Wade, John
    Aldworthe, Allen, Ashe, Badram, Bennett, Berrett, Bradshawe, Brown, Bysse, Cable, Carr, Chester, Clark, Collymer, Cotterell, Cox, Cutt, Dane, Davies, Draper, Dull, Dyckynson, Fawance, Gamsheford, Gervyse, Gittins, Gough, Hambyn, Hopkyn, Hubbtyn, Hygges, Hylckes, Jones, Kelke, Kirke, Kytchen, Lacy, Langford, Meyllyn, Powell, Powey, Poyner, Presey, Pykes, Robertes, Rowland, Rowley, Sachefield, Saltren, Samford, Saunders, Shappey, Sherote, Sheward, Smyth, Snegge, Sperte, Stanfast, Symons, Taylor, Thorne, Tucker, Tyndall, Ware, Warford, Wilson, Winter, Wylborn, Yevans and Younge of, *q.v.*
Briston. *See* Beeston
Bristowe, Henry, 2342, 2865
    John, justice of peace in Hertfordshire, 413
    Nicholas, 313, 1924
Bristowe. *See* Bridstow; Bristol
Britford, Wilts, Harnham, East, in *q.v.*
Brithdir (Brichdir) [in Dolgellau], Merion, 2252
Britwell Salome *or* Brightwell Baldwin (Brytewell, Butwell), [Oxon], rector presented to. *See* Westfallinge, Herbert
Brixham, Devon, 3596
    rectory, 3596
    vicar of. *See* Cox, Francis
    vicar presented to. *See* Rotherforth, William
    Brampton, Lockton, Nethway and Woodhuish in, *q.v.*
    Prowse of, *q.v.*
Brixton, Devon, Spriddlestone in, *q.v.*
Broad Meadow. *See under* Stratford upon Avon
Broad Oak (Brodeocke) [in Garway], Heref, 1643
Broadoak (Brodeoke), Corn, 3571
Broadway (Bradway), Som, 930
Broadway (Bradway, Bradwaye, Bradwayes, Brodweye), Worcs, 2255, 3139–49
Broadway, Edmund, 2539
Broadwell (Bradwell), Glos, 1233
Broadwindsor (Brodewynsere, Brodwynsor), Dors, 930
    manor, 930
    Childhay, Drimpton and Pottwell in, *q.v.*
Broadwindsor (Brodwynsere), Dors, hundred, 930
Broadwood Kelly (Brodewoodekellye), Devon, 3156
Brocas, Bernard, and Anne his wife, 3460
    Williams, 897
Brockden. *See* Brogden
Brockett, John, 266, 1913, 2127
    Nicholas, 82
    William, 3103
Brockhampton (Brokehampton) [in Bishop's Cleeve], Glos, 1350
Brockhampton (Brokehampton) [in Sevenhampton], Glos, 1350
Brockland. *See* Brookland
Brocklesby, Lincs, Limber, Little, in, *q.v.*
Brockton [?in Easthope], Salop, Spragges of, *q.v.*
Brockton. *See* Broughton
Brockworth (Brokeworthe), Glos, rectory, 648
Broddhinton. *See* Hinton
Brode, William, rector presented to Rendcomb, 1026
Brodebent (Bradebent), Lawrence, 674, 1347
Brodeblonsden. *See* Blunsdon
Brodecliste, Brodeclyste. *See* Clyst

Brodehenton. *See* Hinton
Brodemeadowe. *See* Broad Meadow
Brodeocke. *See* Broad Oak
Brodeoke. *See* Broadoak
Brodewey (*unidentified*), Salop, 2255
    vicar of, 2255
Brodewoodekellye. *See* Broadwood Kelly
Brodewynsere. *See* Broadwindsor
Brodfeld. *See* Bradfield
Brodgate. *See* Bradgate
Brodley, George, 1638
    Lewis, of Lostwithiel, 1600
    Cf. Bradley
Brodridge, Henry, 2435
Brodweye. *See* Broadway
Brodwynsere, Brodwynsor. *See* Broadwindsor
Brogden (Brockden) [in Barnoldswick], Yorks, 3251
Brograve, Henry, and John his son, 433
    John, [Hants], 3508
Brogyntyn. *See* Porkington
Broke. *See* Brooke
Brokebancke, John, governor of Alford grammar
        school, 1397
    William, 2768
Brokehampton. *See* Brockhampton
Brokelsbye (Brokilsbye), Emma, 3610
    Richard, 2346
Brokenborough (Brokenborowe), Wilts, 952, 3434
brokers, appointment of, 7
Brokesbye, Bartholomewe, 2681
Brokett (Broket), Nicholas, 1235, 1582
Brokeworthe. *See* Brockworth
Brokilsbye. *See* Brokelsbye
Brolton. *See* Brotton
Bromage. *See* Burnage
Brombey, Robert, of South Ferriby, 3666
Brome, Christopher, knight, 230, 3526
    See also Brame; Brown
Bromefeilde. *See* Broomfield
Bromefelde (*unidentified*) in Howden, Yorks, 2255
Bromefelde, Bromefield. *See* Bromfield
Bromefild. *See* Bramfield
Bromeham, Bromehame. *See* Bromham
Bromeholme. *See* Bromholm
Bromeley, Bromelye. *See* Bromley
Bromes. *See* Lomewood
Bromeswell (Bromeswall), Suff, 3632
    manor, with Staverton, 3632
    Staverton in, *q.v.*
Bromewell, William, 3379
Bromewich, Bromewiche. *See* Bromwich
Bromfield (Bromefelde, Bromefield, Bromfeld,
        Bromfelde), Denb, lordship, 812, 830
Bromham (Bromeham), Beds, Dyve of, *q.v.*
Bromham (Bromeham *alias* Bromeham Baynton,
        Bromehame *alias* Bromehame Baynton),
        Wilts, 629
    manor, 629
    Clinghill in, *q.v.*
    Baynton of, *q.v.*
Bromhill. *See* Broomhill
Bromholm (Bromeholme, Bromholme) [in Bacton],
        Norf, 2490
    priory, 1378
Bromisthorpe. *See* Broomsthorpe
Bromley, Midd, 3615
    Bromley Marsh in, *q.v.*
Bromley Hurst (Bromley Hurste) [in Abbots
        Bromley], Staffs, 2336
    Snape of, *q.v.*

Bromley, Little, (Bromley Parva), Essex, 2454
Bromley Marsh (Bromley Marshe) [in Bromley],
        Midd, 3615
Bromley St Leonard, Midd, St Mary of Bromley (St
        Mary of Bromeley) in, 3624
Bromley (Bromeley, Bromelye), George, attorney of
        duchy of Lancaster, 1848
    Hugh, 1948
    Thomas, [Notts and Kent], 3234
    Thomas, solicitor general, 381, 1427, 1633, 1635,
        2142–3, 3478–9
        justice of oyer and terminer, 539, 1507
    William, 2177
    Cf. Brameley
Bromley. *See* Broomley
Brompton, Yorks, 210
    church, 210
Brompton (Brompton next Northalverton) [in
        Northallerton], Yorks, 210
Brompton, East, (Eastbrompton), [in Patrick
        Brompton], Yorks, 621, 921
Brompton, Patrick, Yorks, Arrathorne, Brompton,
        East and West, and Newton le Willows in,
        q.v.
Brompton, West, (Westbrompton), [in Patrick
        Brompton], Yorks, 621, 921
Brompton, Bromptone. *See* Brampton
Bromsgrove (Bremysgrove), Worcs, manor, 2383
Bromwich, West, (Bromewich, Bromewiche,
        Westbromewiche, Westbromwiche), Staffs,
        681, 868
    rectory, 681
Bron y prys (Brone y Price) [in Tywyn], Merion, 2252
Bronhiocke. *See* Brynhynnog
Bronkehesey. *See* Brownsea
Bronllys (Brentles), Brec, 1347
    rectory, 2684
Brook (Brooke) [in King's Somborne], Hants, 1642
Brook (Brooke) [in Westbury], Wilts, 926
Brooke (Broke), Francis, [Glos], 1660
    Francis, [Salop], 1662
    George, *alias* George Cobham, clerk of council in
        principality of Wales and Welsh border
        counties, 1508
    George, vicar presented to Humbleton, 1814
    Henry, *alias* Henry Cobham, knight, 674
        gentleman pensioner, usher at receipt of
        Exchequer, keeper of chamber of Council
        of Star Chamber in palace of Westminster,
        3663
    Henry, of London, 2256
    Humphrey, 3114
    James, of Adwalton, John son of, 2208
    John, of London, 1593
    John, [Salop], 84, 2085
        Anne wife of, 2085
    Nicholas, of Waltham Holy Cross, 2181
    Reginald, vicar presented to Haselor, 1779
    Richard, [Glos], 225
    Richard, [Salop], and Mary his wife, 2426
    Richard, [Staffs], 288
    Robert, knight, and Dorothy his wife, 2426
    Robert and Simon, both of London, 2256
    Thomas, [London], 3586
    Thomas, [Northants], 1874
    William, lord Cobham, warden of Cinque Ports,
        constable of Dover castle, 2888
    Cf. Brookes
Brooker, Hugh, attorney in court of Marshalsea, 479
Brookeruppe. *See* Brookthorpe

Brookes, John, and Robert his son, 432
  Richard, of Bentley, 818
  Cf. Brooke
Brookland (Brockland), Kent, 2061, 2502, 2808
  manor, 2061, 2808
Brookthorpe (Brookeruppe), Glos, 2906
Broomfield (Bromefeilde), Essex, 206
Broomfield (Broomefeilde), Som, 2130
Broomhill (Bromhill) [in Westbury], Salop, 2117
Broomley (Bromley) [in Bywell St Peter], Northumb,
    572
  manor, 572
Broomsthorpe (Bromisthrope) [in East Rudham],
    Norf, 2691
Brothton. *See* Broughton
Brotton (Brolton), Yorks, 621, 921, 2762
  manor, 621, 921, 2762
  Skinningrove in, *q.v.*
Brough, William, 2181
  Cf. Borough; Burgh
Broughton [in Hawarden, Flint], Ches, 2255
Broughton [in Manchester], Lancs, 602, 2676
Broughton (Braughton), Lincs, 889
  Castlethorpe in, *q.v.*
Broughton, Yorks, Elslack in, *q.v.*
Broughton Gifford (Little Brothton *alias* Broughton),
    Wilts, 206
Broughton, Great, (Great Broughton in Clevelande)
    [in Kirby in Cleveland], Yorks, 2180, 3472
  church, 2180
Broughton, Great *or* Little, (Broughton), [in Kirby in
    Cleveland], Yorks, 621
Broughton Hackett (Brockton Hackett), Worcs, 2314
Broughton in Claverley, Salop, 206
  chapel of St Mary, 206, 2255
Broughton, Little, (Little Broughton), [in Kirby in
    Cleveland], Yorks, 3472
  Ewarden of, *q.v.*
Broughton (Broughton), John, of Orsett, servant of
    bishop of London, 2578
  Richard, [Card], 2518
  Richard, [Pemb], 2620
  Thomas, 2993
  Thomas, [Dors], 2059
Brouncker. *See* Bruncker
Broughton. *See* Broughton
Brounker. *See* Bruncker
Brown (Brome, Browne), . . . , 263
  Anthony, 3066
  Anthony, knight, keeper of Byfleet park, 3700
  Anthony, viscount Montague, K.G., 2888
  Catherine, [Essex], 898
  Catherine, [Glos], 916
  Catherine, [Wilts], 640
  Christopher, knight, 1981
  Christopher, of Hertford, 501
  Clement, *alias* Clement Weare, Robert and Thomas,
    of Marlborough, 2863
  Francis, 3003
  Francis, *alias* Francis Glover, of Great Malvern, 1
  Francis, [Leics], 96
  Henry, of Rowley, 43
  Henry, [Essex], and Alice Trappes his wife, 896
  Humphrey, rector presented to Riseholme, 3368
  James, of Shobrooke, 2898
  John, 1870
  John, (?*another*), 1980
  John, M.A., vicar presented to Dartford, 1010
  John, of Bristol, 2256
  John, [Dors], 2025

Brown—*cont.*
  John, [Leics], 2043
  John, [Lincs], 1169
  John, [Norf], 571
  John, [Yorks], 832, 1666
  Joyce, 2289
  Lancelot, 400
  Margaret, [Leics], 3443
  Margaret, [London], 3169
  Maurice, 3267
  Nicholas, 1281
  Philip, 2221
  Richard, 1860
  Richard, clerk of the peace in Essex, 387
  Richard, of East Harlsey, 2504
  Richard, [Essex], 1932–4
  Richard, [Heref], 238
  Robert, of Great Kelk, 42
  Robert, of London, 1293
  Robert, of Neasham, 39
  Robert, [Sussex], 1384
  Robert, vicar presented to Burton Agnes *or* Burton
    Fleming, 1020
  Thomas, (?*different men*), 1978, 2549, 2982, 2996
  Thomas, and Thomas his son, 3651
  Thomas, feodary of Cornwall, 109, 327, 1890, 1897,
    1940
  Thomas, knight, 250, 1317, 1554
  Thomas, [Devon], and Brutus his son, 2751
  Thomas, [London], 123, 210, 3714
  Valentine, knight, 124, 2793
    Thomasina wife of, 2793
  William, king's servant, and Thomas his son, 65
  William, of Ivington, Maud Powll wife of, 2154
  William, rector presented to 'St Peter', 1794
  Wistan, 637
Brownage. *See* Burnage
Browne. *See* Brown
?Brownlow (Brumlowe) [in Astbury], Ches, 3684
Brownsea Island (Bronkehesey, Bruntsey in the isle of
    Bruntsey) [in Studland], Dors, 3620
  castle, warden and governor of. *See* Hatton,
    Christopher
Broxholme, John, 1422
Bruarton, Thomas, justice of peace in Exeter, 2317
Bruce, Edward, 9
Brucknoll, lady Alice, 3714
Brudenell, Edmund, knight, 1889
Bruer, Temple, (Temple Brewer, Templebruer),
    Lincs, preceptory, 1347, 2182
Bruern (Brewere), Oxon, 2006
  Tangley in, *q.v.*
Brumlowe. *See* Brownlow
Bruncker (Brouncker, Brounker), Henry, [Berks],
    2082
  Henry, [Devon], 3600
  William, 3030
  William, [Berks], 2082
  William, [Wilts], 971, 1917, 2821
Brune, Ellis, French subject, 1696
Bruntsey. *See* Brownsea
Brushford (Brassheford), Devon, 638
Brushford (Brusheford), Som, Nightcott in, *q.v.*
Brusierd. *See* Brusyardes
Brustwick. *See* Burstwick
Brusyardes (Brusierd) in Babraham, Cambs, manor,
    1177
Bruton (Brewton), Som, 962, 1350, 2078
  monastery, 3488
Bryan (Brian), Francis, knight, constable of castle and

C

Chester—*cont.*
　　Catherine wife of, 1314
　　William, merchant of staple, and his wife, 206
Chesterford, Great *or* Little, (Chesterford), Essex,
　　　　manor, 2703
Chesterton, Cambs, 2458
Chesterton, [Oxon], vicar presented to.　*See*
　　　　Chapman, James
Chesterton (Chesteston) [in Wolstanton], Staffs, 963
Cheston, William, M.A., portionary presented to
　　　　Llanddewi Velfrey, 1795
　　William, M.A., rector presented to Llangeler, 1783
Cheswick.　*See* Chiswick
Chetam.　*See* Cheetham
Chete.　*See* Chevet
Chetewood, Richard, lady Agnes Calveley wife of,
　　　　276
Chetham.　*See* Chatham; Cheetham
Chetington.　*See* Cheddington
Chettle (Chettell), Dors, 3713
Chevalier, John, Spanish subject, 1716
Cheveley (Cheveleighe), Cambs, 954
　　rector presented to.　*See* Sendell, Robert
Cheveley.　*See* Chieveley
Cheveney, Robert, vicar presented to Hornsea, 3373
Chevening, Kent, Chipstead and Whitley Forest in,
　　　　q.v.
Chever, John, 2583
Chevet (Chete, Chevete) in Royston, Yorks, 2313
Chevington, Suff, 3116
Chew Magna *or* Stoke, (Chewe, Chiwe), Som, 1350,
　　　　1353
Chewton Mendip (Chewton, Chewton under
　　　　Mendipe), Som, chapel, rectory and
　　　　advowson of vicarage, 1353
Cheyle, John and Richard, 3493
Cheyne (Chayny, Cheney, Cheyney, Cheynie,
　　　　Cheynye), Giles, 281, 379–80
　　Henry, knight, lord Cheyne of Toddington
　　　　(Tuddington), 276, 669, 1291, 1347, 1668,
　　　　2463–4, 3172, 3446
　　　Jane wife of, 3172
　　John, 2970
　　John, *alias* John Parsmyth, the younger, and Mary
　　　　his wife, 1565
　　John, of Chesham Bois, 2191
　　John, [Berks], 248
　　Richard, bishop of Gloucester, 34
　　Thomas, [Beds], 3516, 3518
　　Thomas, [Berks], 3432, 3490
　　Thomas, [Kent], 3172
Chibborne, Christopher, 233
Chicheley, Bucks, 2255
Chichester, bishops of, 3254.　*See also* Curtis,
　　　　Richard; Sampson, Richard
Chichester, Sussex, house of the Black Friars in, 2480
　　port, 58
　　Hylls of, *q.v.*
Chichester, John, of Raleigh, 369
Chickesandes.　*See* Chicksands
Chicknell (Chuckewell), . . ., 206, 2255
Chickney, [Essex], rector presented to.　*See* Wale,
　　　　Philemon
Chicksands (Chickesandes), [Beds], monastery, 2687
Chiddingstone (Chydingstone), Kent, 1282
Chideock (Chidiocke), Dors, 638
Chidley, Robert, of London, and Barbara Wilbrahame
　　　　his daughter, 2419
Chieveley (Cheveley), Berks, 2004, 2126, 2141
　　Curridge and Leckhampstead in, *q.v.*

Chilcombe (Chylcombe), Dors, 1558
　　manor, 1558
　　rector presented to.　*See* Wattes, John
Childe (Chylde), John, 3064
　　John, [Oxon], 1981
　　John, [Surrey], 1350, 2116
　　Richard, Maud Powlle wife of, 2152
　　William, 2969, 2979, 2987–8, 3080
　　William, feodary of Worcestershire, 99, 242, 280,
　　　　353, 1846, 1922, 1982
　　William, [Worcs], 3139
Childhay (Chilehay) [in Broadwindsor], Dors, 930
Childrey (Chylrey), [Berks], rector presented to.　*See*
　　　　Pickhaver, Ralph
Childwick (Chilwick, Chilwicke) [in St Michael],
　　　　Herts, 3159
　　manor, 3159
Chilehay.　*See* Childhay
Chilham, Kent, 2717
Chilmark (Chilmarke), [Wilts], rector presented
　　　　to.　*See* Thornborough, John
　　vicar presented to.　*See* Babington, Zachary
Chilswell (Chelswell) [in Cumnor], Berks, Grenefeild
　　　　of, *q.v.*
Chiltern (Celtri), Berks, hundreds, stewards (*named*)
　　　　of, 2852
Chiltington, East, (Chyltington), [in Westmeston],
　　　　Sussex, 1626
Chiltington, West, (Chiltington), Sussex, 927
Chilton [in Atcham], Salop, 1629
Chilton ?Polden (Chelton) [in Moorlinch], Som, 207,
　　　　977
Chilton Trinity, Som, Idstock in, *q.v.*
Chilwick, Chilwicke.　*See* Childwick
Chinnock, East, (Estchynnock), Som, rectory, 1353
Chinnor, Oxon, Henton in, *q.v.*
Chiphill.　*See* Clophill
Chippenham, (Chipnam, Chippingham, Chypenham),
　　　　Wilts, 530, 629, 937, 1228, 3181, 3256
　　chantry of St Mary and St Catherine, 3256
　　manor, 629
　　Rowden, Stanley and Tytherton Lucas in, *q.v.*
Chipping (Chipping Nova) [in Buckland], Herts, 2834
Chippingham.　*See* Chippenham
Chippingwicombe.　*See* Wycombe
Chipsey, Thomas, 206
Chipstead (Chepsted) [in Chevening], Kent, 2287
　　Robson of, *q.v.*
Chirk (Chirke), Denb, manor of Chirkland and, 61
Chirrell.　*See* Cherhill
Chisbury (Chesburie, Chesburye) [in Little Bedwyn],
　　　　Wilts, 2020, 2120
　　chapel, 2120
Chiseldon (Chysylden), Wilts, 919
　　Badbury and Hodson in, *q.v.*
Chishill, Great *or* Little, (Chesell), Essex (*now in*
　　　　Cambs), 1407
Chislehurst (Cheseherste), Kent, Cavell and Cheseman
　　　　of, *q.v.*
Chislet (Chistlett, Chystlett), Kent, 1291, 2302
Chiswick (Cheswick) Midd, 954
Chitham, John, 1623
Chitterne (Chitterum), Wilts, All Saints rectory, 2692
　　Bosgrove of, *q.v.*
Chittynge, George, 1840
Chiute.　*See* Chute
Chiwe.　*See* Chew
Chobham, Surrey, Stanners and Fords in, *q.v.*
Chock (Chocke), Francis brother of Richard, and
　　　　John, of Shalbourne, 929

cloth—*cont.*
    Wiltshire, 56
    Worcester, 56
    worsteads, narrow, 3706
    See also woollen cloths
clothworkers, company of, 180, 656
Clotton Hoofield [in Tarvin], Ches, 3684
Clough, George, of London, 2256
Clougher. *See* Clogher
Cloughton [in Scalby], Yorks, 671, 2907
    chapel or church, 671, 2907
Cloverstreame (*unidentified*), Herts, river, 3618
Clowghe, Richard, Spanish subject, 1699
Cluddesdeane. *See* Cliddesden
Cluer. *See* Clewer
Clungunford (Langunford), Salop, 206
    church, 206
Clyff. *See* Cliff
Clyffe. *See* Cliffe
Clyfford, Clyfforde. *See* Clifford
Clyfton. *See* Clifton
Clyggin, Clyggyn. *See* Cloigyn
Clynnog (Clynocke), Carn, 212, 3715
    Cwm, Nancall and Nantcyll in, *q.v.*
Clynton. *See* Clinton
Clyst (Clifte), river, 3688
Clyst, Broad, (Brodecliste, Brodeclyste), Devon, 882,
    3162
    manor, rectory and advowson of vicarage, 1536
    Farthings, Loxbrook, Prior Court, Ratcliffes,
        Stileshame and Younghayes in, *q.v.*
Clyve. *See* Cleeve
Coade. *See* Code
coal mines, 576, 826, 830, 1342, 2255, 2879
coal trade, 3667
Coalbrook (Caldebroke) in Madeley, Salop, 2177,
    3157
Coates (Cotes), Lincs, 956
Coates (Cootes, Cotes) [in Barnoldswick], Yorks,
    3251
Coatham, East, (Estcottam), [in Kirkleatham], Yorks,
    210
Coatham Mundeville (Cottam Conyers) [in Haughton
    le Skerne], Durh, manor, 1353
Cobbe, Michael, serjeant at arms, 475
    Robert, of London, 2256
    Robert, [Suff], 2474
    Thomas, John son of, 114
Cobden, William, the younger, and John his son, 526
Cobham, lord. *See* Brooke
Cobham (Cobhame), George, *alias* George Brooke,
    clerk of council in principality of Wales and
    Welsh border counties, 1508
    Henry, *alias* Henry Broke, knight, 674
        gentleman pensioner, usher at receipt of
        Exchequer, keeper of chamber of Council
        of Star Chamber in palace of Westminster,
        3663
    Henry, knight, alderman of London, 2256
    William, knight, lord Cobham, 627
Cobley, John, 3601
Cobryse, Bastrian, Spanish subject, 795
Cock a Bowells. *See* Boyles
Cockayne (Cockeyn, Cockyn), Francis, 100
    William, of London, assistant and chief councillor
        of fellowship of merchants of Spain and
        Portugal, 2256
    William, [Staffs], 1892
Cocke, Henry, knight, 3063, 3103
    Henry, [Suff], and John, 3112

Cocke—*cont.*
    Richard, 2958
    William, [Berks], 3167
    William, [Midd], and Elizabeth his wife, 1618
    Cf. Cooke; Cox
Cockefield. *See* Cockfield
Cockerham, Lancs, Glasson in, *q.v.*
Cockerington, North and South, (Cockerington,
        Cokerington), Lincs, 2500, 3257
Cockerton (Cokkerton) [in Darlington], Durh, 42
Cockes. *See* Cox
Cockestones (*unidentified*), Midd, 1582
Cockethorpe. *See* Cockthorpe
Cockett, John, 3714
Cockeyn. *See* Cockayne
Cockfield (Cockefield, Cockfelde), Suff, 2180
    church, 2180
    rector of. *See* Kemp, Thomas
Cockley Cley (Cockley), Norf, 3630
Cockshoot (Cockshott) [in Usk], Monm, 2299
Cockson, John, 2103
    Cf. Cookeson
Cockthorpe (Cockethorpe, Cokthorpe, Cokthrope),
        Norf, 115, 2724
Cockyn. *See* Cockayne
Codda in Altarnun, Corn, Prowte of, *q.v.*
Coddenham (Cuddenham), Suff, 2091
Code (Coade), Lawrence, 2180
    Walter, 3660
Codnor [in Heanor], Derb, 2259
    lordship, 2259
Codrington (Codryngton, Coodryngton), Simon,
        2968, 3104–5
    Simon, [Wilts], and Agnes his wife, 867
    See also Cotherington
Coffer, John, 646
Coffinswell, Devon, Daccombe in, *q.v.*
Coffyn, John, 346, 1927
Cogan, Thomas, 2293
Coggeshall (Coxhall), Essex, monastery, 1994, 2688
Coggeshall (Ixnyng Coggeshall) in Exning, Suff,
        manor, 941
coin, clipping etc. of. *See under* commissions;
        pardons
coinage, export of, 430, 1480
    minting of, 1515, 2885
Coke. *See* Cooke
Cokeham [in Sompting], Sussex, 3560
Cokeham. *See* Cookham
Coker, East, (Estcoker), Som, rectory, 3600
Coker, Richard, and Anne his wife, 2082
Cokerell, John, 3291
Cokerington. *See* Cockerington
Cokkerton. *See* Cockerton
Cokthorpe, Cokthrope. *See* Cockthorpe
Colaton Raleigh (Collaton, Collaton Abbot, Collaton
        Duke), Devon, 3230
    manor, 3230
    Dotton in, *q.v.*
Colby (Colbye), Francis, 444
    Thomas, [Beds], and Elizabeth his wife, 3489, 3556
    Thomas, [Suff], 116
Colchester, archdeacon of, 2346
Colchester, Essex, 626, 2454, 3507
    monastery of St John, 1355A, 2182, 2359, 3252
    port, 3701
    ship of, *The Anne*, 2349
    Skynner and Strutte of, *q.v.*
Colchester, John, 2183
    Matthew, 2507

Conyers—*cont.*
Reginald, bailiff and collector of the monastery of
  Lenton, 1530
Conyngesby, Conysbye. *See* Coningsbye
Conyston. *See* Coniston
Coodryngton. *See* Codrington
Cooke (Coke), Anthony, Agnes Cowper wife of, 3217
  Anthony, knight, 233, 911, 2405
    Richard son of, 2405
  Edmund, 3452
  Henry, governor of Alford grammar school, 1397
  Henry, [Cambs], 3444
  Henry, [Herts], 313
  James, of Dunham, 2362
  John, of South Tidworth, and George his son and
    Eleanor George's wife, 2573
  John, [Bucks], 1347
  John, [Lincs], 2013
  John, [Wilts], 2020, 2120
    Dorothy wife of, 2020
  John, [Worcs], 2621
  Matthew, 1415
  Nicholas, 3275
  Richard, 440
  Richard, escheator in Nottinghamshire, 258
  Richard, keeper of St James's house, Westminster,
    bailiff of St James's fair etc., 463
  Richard, [Derb], 1896
  Richard, [Leics], 1204
  Richard, [Norf], 268
  Richard, [Warw], 1556, 1590, 3499
    Anne wife of, 3499
  Robert, coroner of Middlesex, 1601, 1615
  Robert, [Surrey], 831
  Stanfild, 1204
  Thomas, [Lincs], 3251
  Thomas, queen's servant, 2235
  Thomas, rector of Swanage, 30, 75
  Tilman, subject of duke of Cleves, 1721
  William, *alias* William Bartlett, 2835
  William, [Devon], 227
  William, [Som], 962, 2078
  Cf. Cocke; Cookes
Cookefeild. *See* Cuckfield
Cookerige. *See* Cookridge
Cookes, William, 1236
  Cf. Cooke; Cox
Cookeson, James, king's servant, 597
  Cf. Cockson
Cookham (Cokeham), Berks, 1640
  lordship, woodwards or keepers of woods (*named*)
    in, 1516
Cookridge (Cookerige), barony, 2907
Cookridge Woods (Cookriggwood) in Adel, Yorks,
  2688
Coole. *See* Cole
Coolepeper. *See* Culpepper
Coolreagh (Cowelrioughe) [in Kilnoe], co. Clare,
  2610
Coombe Bisset (Combe Bissett), Wilts, 1277
  manor, 1277
Coon, Alexandrin du, Spanish subject, 793
Cooper (Couper, Cowper, Cowpper, Cupper),
    Anthony, [Lincs], 2346, 2542
  Anthony, [Midd], 3615
  Edward, clerk, 3034
  Francis, *alias* Francis Godfrey, 1549
  Henry, 2775
  John, 3011, 3044, 3046, 3057
  John, of East Keswick, 39

Cooper—*cont.*
  John, [Oxon], 113, 1981
  John, [Surrey], 363
  John, [Sussex], 3584
  Peter, 3275
  Richard, of Hutton Henry, 39
  Richard, [Som], 2833
  Robert, of Colneis, and John, Peter and Robert his
    sons and Agnes Cooke, Alice Flynt and
    Mary Smyth his daughters, 3217
  Silvester, 981
  Stephen, 2138
  Thomas, bishop of Lincoln, 2188, 2528, 2602
  Thomas, the elder, and Thomas, the younger, 2738
  Thomas, rector presented to East Farndon, 995
  William, *alias* William Godfrey, 1549
Coote, Francis, queen's servant, 2868
  Cf. Cotes; Cott; Cowte; Cutt
Cootes. *See* Coates
Coowne. *See* Coln
Cope, Walter, 1175
Copeians, Daniel, Spanish subject, 735
Copford (Capforde), Essex, 3291, 3475
  manor (Copford Hall), 3291
Copinger (Copynger), Ralph, [Bucks], 3645
  Ralph, [Durh], 2574
Copledicke, John, 116
Copleston, Anthony, 3156
  Anthony, the younger, 882, 3160
Copley (Coppley), Alfred, 3022, 3031
  Christopher, 3050
  Philip, 2977, 3043
  Philip, of Sprotbrough, 359–60
    William son of, 359, 361
  Thomas, the elder, and Thomas, the younger,
    [Wilts], 2110
  Thomas, [Worcs], 2140, 3118, 3250
    Margaret wife of, 3118
  Thomas, [Yorks], and Margaret his wife, 2792
Coppenhall (Copnall) [in Penkridge], Staffs, prebend,
  3622
copperas mines, 3620
Coppice Lowhills (Coppesley Hills) [in East
    Claydon], Bucks, 1307
Copple. *See* Cyplau
Coppley. *See* Copley
Copynger. *See* Copinger
Corbett, Alice, 2033
  Edward, 3098–9
  Henry, *alias* Henry Bracher, of London, 2880
  Humphrey, and Anne his wife, 3504
  Jerome, 84, 217–21, 229, 306–7, 325, 378
  Miles, 2080, 2108
  Richard, Mary wife of, 660
  Robert, 364, 3115
  Vincent, 660
Corbridge, Northumb, Dilston in, *q.v.*
Corby, Lincs, 1571, 2255
Corby (Corbye), Northants, 858
  woods, keeper of deer and wild beasts in, 830
Corby, Little, (Litlecrokeby), [in Hayton], Cumb,
  1424
Corcomroe (Corcomrowe), co. Clare, 2610
Cordell (Cordyll), Thomas, of London, 2256
  William, 1525
  William, knight, 876
    governor of Thetford grammar school, 1396
    justice of oyer and terminer, 2218
    master of the rolls, 24, 123, 213, 250, 381, 383,
      394, 508, 833–4, 1259, 1391, 1396, 2146,

Courtoll. *See* Court Toll

Coventry (Coventre, Coventrie, Coventrye), [Warw], 51, 2114, 2440, 2506
  Charterhouse, 1187, 2182
  church of Holy Trinity, vicars presented to. *See* Fen, Humphrey; Fletcher, Anthony
  church of St Michael, vicar presented to. *See* Irelande, William
  feodary of. *See* Gregory, Arthur
  justices of gaol delivery in. *See* Barham, Nicholas; Dyer, James
  mayor of, 51, 1451
  parish of St Michael, 1350
  priory or cathedral of St Mary, 1350, 2210, 2440, 3258
  Willoughby of, *q.v.*

Coventry and Lichfield, bishop of, 1347, 1406

Coventrye (Coventrey), Vincent, 3000
  Vincent, [Oxon], 3421

Coverdale, William, 1881

Coverham, Yorks, Bradley and Carlton in Coverdale in, *q.v.*

Covert, Thomas, 2789

Cow Gill Cote (Cowgilhouses, Cowgillhouses) [in Burnsall], Yorks, 1267, 1269

Coward (Cowarde), John, coroner of Somerset, 1612
  John, [Som], 2195
  William, chief burgess of Richmond, 2197

Cowbit (Cowbytte), Lincs, church with Spalding, 3644

Cowche, Richard, 3437

Cowdham. *See* Cudham

Cowdrey, George, 3635

Cowelriougghe. *See* Coolreagh

Cowfold (Cowffelde, Cowfielde, Cowfolde), Sussex, 210, 848, 1384, 2180

Cowgilhouses, Cowgillhouses. *See* Cow Gill

Cowland, Thomas, 3645

Cowley, Sarah, 2483

Cowltres, Henry, of London, 2256

Cowpen (Cawpon) [in Horton], Northumb, 576
  manor, 576

Cowper, Cowpper. *See* Cooper

Cowrne. *See* Cornwy Llys

Cowrnowe. *See* Conway

Cowrnowllys. *See* Cornwy Llys

Cowsden (Collesden) [in Upton Snodsbury], Worcs, 2314

Cowte, John, Scottish subject, 132
  Cf. Coote; Cott; Cutt

Cowton, North, (Northcowton), [in Gilling], Yorks, 837

Cox (Cockes, Coxe), . . ., 3251
  Francis, 516
  Francis, vicar of Brixham, 3396
  Gregory, 1240
  John, of London, 525
  John, [Leics], 1240
  John, rector presented to Philleigh, 153
  Richard, bishop of Ely, 125, 1154, 2686
  Richard, of ?Fawley, 3503
  Richard, [Heref], 1992, 2457, 3209, 3246
    Sibyl wife of, 1992
  Thomas, the elder, [Leics], 1240
  Thomas, master of barge and boats, 2325
  Thomas, of Inner Temple, 3545, 3551
  Thomas, [Worcs], and Seth his son, 3118
  Thomas, yeoman of pantry, 3614
  William, coroner of Monmouthshire, 2174
  William, of Bristol, 2256

Cox—*cont.*
  William, [Warw], 3110
  William, yeoman for mouth in pantry, 2322
  Cf. Cocke; Cookes

Coxford (Coxforde) [in East Rudham], Norf, priory, 2691

Coxhall. *See* Coggeshall

Coxhed, Henry, and Margaret his wife, and James and Oliver, 1241

Coxwell, Great, (Coxwell Magna), Berks, Morris of, *q.v.*

Coxwold, Yorks, Byland Abbey, Newburgh and Thornton on the Hill in, *q.v.*

Coys, Roger, and Elizabeth his daughter, 2493

Coyton. *See* Chilvers Coton

Cracoll. *See* Crakehall

Cracrofte, Robert, 315

Craddock (Cradock), Francis, 2770
  Matthew, 2993

Cradley, Heref, manor, court of, stewards and keepers (*named*) of, 2847

Cradock. *See* Craddock

Craft (Crafte), Peter, Spanish subject, 1707, 1726

Cragdale and Raydale (Estradale and Westradale *alias* Radale and Cragdale) [in Aysgarth], Yorks, 3591

Cragges, William, 599

Craicall, Joan, 1201

Crainche, Burquot, 831

Crainsforde. *See* Cransford

Crakehall (Cracoll Magna) [in Bedale], Yorks, 837

Crakehall, Little, (Crakall Parva, Little Crakell), [in Bedale], Yorks, 621, 921

Crakehill (Crakehall) [in Topcliffe], Yorks, 419

Crakell. *See* Crakehall

Crambe (Crambone), Yorks, manor, (Hall Garth), 3286

Cramborne. *See* Cranborne

Cramfelde, Robert, of Shefford, 2350

Cramlington, Lancelot, 973

Crampe, William, 2583
  Cf. Crumpe

Cranborne (Cramborne, Craneborne), Dors, 1560, 3713
  cell or priory and advowson of vicarage, 3713
  manor, 2224, 3713
  park, *alias* Blagdon park, 1560, 2224
  rectory, 3713
  Aldersholt, Blagdon, Boveridge, Estwood, Holwell, Parkemeade, Verwood and Wimborne, Monkton Up, in, *q.v.*

Cranborne Aldersholte. *See* Alderholt

Cranbourne (Craneborn in Windesor forest in bailiwick of Battusbayly) [in Winkfield], Berks, le Newe Lodge in, keepers (*named*) of, 1516

Crane, Henry, and Anne his wife, 2091
  Robert, 2963, 3012
  Robert, [Suff], 1852, 2091

Craneborn. *See* Cranbourne

Craneborne. *See* Cranborne

Craneham. *See* Cranham

Cranesford. *See* Crayford

Cranham (Craneham), Glos, manor, 2749

Cranmer (Cranmere), Edmund, clerk, provost of Wingham college, 598
  Thomas, 678
  Thomas, archbishop of Canterbury, 414, 525, 678, 819, 3254
  servant of. *See* Bingham, Henry

D

Dowghtye. *See* Doughtye
Dowlman. *See* Dolman
Dowman, Thomas, 2944–5
Down (Downe) [in Stanford on Avon], Northants, 2725
Down St Mary (Marydowe), Devon, 638
Down, West, (West Downe), Devon, 2075
Downe in Towne (*unidentified*), Devon, 2075
Downe Mayne (*unidentified*), Ireland, 1351
Downe, Robert, 1201
   William, 1312
   Cf. Donne; Doonne; Downes
Downe. *See* Down; Downend
Downefeild (*unidentified*), 3714
Downefeild. *See* Dronfield
Downehall. *See* Downhall
Downend (Downe Ende) [in Mangotsfield], Glos, 2446
Downer (Doughner), John, of Piddinghoe, 1484
   Walter, 2583
Downes, Geoffrey, M.A., rector presented to Bishopsbourne and Barham, 454
   Robert, M.A., canon or prebendary presented to Norwich cathedral. 1518
   Robert, [Norf], 1192, 1232, 1902
   Cf. Downe
Downhall (Downehall) in Barrow upon Humber, Lincs, manor, 571
Downing (Downyng, Downynge), Arthur, and Susan his wife, 1232
   Edmund, [Essex], 1287
   Edmund, [Midd], 834
   Edmund, [Som], 1353
   George, 3481
   William, of Marystow, 3717
Dowsby (Dowsbye), Lincs, 831
Dowshill Gate (Dowsilgate) [in King's Lynn], Norf, 343
Dowson, Henry, and Richard his son, 4
   Cf. Dawson
Dowsynge *alias* Smyth, Ralph, of Forncett St Mary *or* St Peter, 3229
Dowthorpe in Long Riston and Swine, Yorks, 3379
Doyle (Doiley, Doyley, Doylie), Elizabeth, 2779
   Henry, justice of peace and of oyer and terminer in Norfolk, 1614, 2929
   James, 261
   John, 3068
   Robert, the elder, [Oxon], 113, 230
   Robert, knight, 3095
drains. *See under* sewers
Drake, Bernard, [Devon], 425, 1620
   Bernard, [Kent], 2717
Drakes, James, 3397
   William, 2255
Dranfeld. *See* Dronfield
Drante. *See* Darenth
Draper, Clement, of London, and John, of Bristol, 2256
   John, of London, and Thomas his son, 2550
   John, of London, alebrewer and innkeeper, 123, 295
   John, [Dors], 2787
   Matthias, 2481, 2496
drapers, guild of, 2290. *See also under* trades
Dratford. *See* Dartford
Drax (Draxe), Yorks, 573
   priory, rectory and vicar of, 573
   Camblesforth, Drax, Long, Newland, Rusholme and Stanhill in, *q.v.*

?Drax, Long, (Langredd), [in Drax], Yorks, 573
Drayton (Dreyton), [Berks], 210
Drayton [in Bringhurst], Leics, 2299
   chapel of St James, 2299
Drayton, Som, 1347, 1371, 3291
   manor of Westover and, 52, 833
   woods (Drayton Wood), 833
   Westover in, *q.v.*
Drayton [in Old Stratford], Warw, 1345
Drayton, Little, [in Market Drayton], Salop, 3477
Drayton, Market, Salop, Betton, Drayton, Little, Ridgwardine and Tunstall in, *q.v.*
Drempton. *See* Drimpton
Drent. *See* Darenth
Drewe, Hugh, gunner in Tower of London, 2843
   John, 3251
   Richard, master of barge and boats, 2325
   William, 3613
Drewrey, Drewrie, Drewry, Drewrye. *See* Drury
Dreycote (*unidentified*), 3714
Dreyton. *See* Drayton
Dreywoman, Joan, 3275
Driffield (Dryfeild), Glos, 916
   manor, 916
Driffield, Yorks, Driffield, Great and Little, Elmswell and Kelleythorpe in, *q.v.*
Driffield, Great, (Dryfeild Magna, Great Driffeld, Great Driffelde), [in Driffield], Yorks, 1355A, 2515
   chantry house, 2515
   church, chantry of St Mary the Virgin in, 2515
   rector of, 2515
Driffield, Little, (Dryfeilde Parva), [in Driffield], Yorks, 1355A
Drightlington (Dryghtlington) [in Birstall], Yorks, manor, 2208
Drimpton (Drempton) [in Broadwindsor], Dors, 930
Dringhouses in Holy Trinity, York [and Acomb], Yorks, 2260
   manor (Dringehousehall), 2260
Drinkell, Edward, 893
Drinkwater, Arthur, of Dunham, 2362
Drogheda, [cos. Meath and Louth], parliament at, 2583
   port, 503
Droitwich (Wych), Worcs, 1158
   Witton in, *q.v.*
Dromebye (*unidentified*), Ireland, 2610
Dronfield (Downefeild, Dranfeld, Dronefeilde, Dronsfeilde), Derb, 1406, 1637, 3440
   rectory and vicar of, 1406
   vicar presented to. *See* Bankes, Lawrence
   Apperknowle, Aston, Coal, Birchitt, Dronfield, Woodhouse, Holmesfield, Hundall. Povey, Stubley, Summerly, Totley and Unstone in, *q.v.*
Dronfield Woodhouse (Woodhowse) [in Dronfield], Derb, 1406
Drossecoyde, Drossecoydes. *See* Drwys-y-coed
Droylsden (Drylesden, Stryledale *alias* Drylesdale) [in Manchester], Lancs, 602, 2676
Drury (Drewrey, Drewrie, Drewry, Drewrye, Drurye), Drew, ecclesiastical commissioner, Norwich diocese, 213, 2606
   justice of peace and of oyer and terminer, Norfolk, 1614, 2929
   Drew, [Norf], 264, 343
   Drew, [Suff], and Elizabeth his wife, 2050
   Robert, knight, 263, 1952, 2191
   William, doctor of civil law, 123

Drury—*cont.*
  William, knight, lord justice of Ireland, 3708–9
    president of Munster, 3708
    queen's servant, 2180
  William, [Hants], 3554
Drws-y-coed (Drossecoyde, Frithe of Drossecoydes)
    [?in Beddgelert], Carn, 600
Dryden, Anthony, and Anne Wilkes his wife, 2637
  John, [Beds], 1834
  John, [Northants], 278, 377
Dryfeild, Dryfeilde. *See* Driffield
Dryghtlington. *See* Drightlington
Dryland, Thomas, 1306
Drylesdale, Drylesden. *See* Droylsden
Drynker, William, of Northiam, 2227
Dryslwyn (Dursloyn, Dursloyne) [in Llangathen],
    Carn, 1393, 2631
Drystocke. *See* Stoke
Dryver, Edmund, 2259
Dublin (Dublyn), archbishops of. *See* Loftus, Adam;
    Tregury, Michael
Dublin, co. Dublin, 44, 2583
  abbey of St Mary the Virgin and abbey *called*
      Thomas Courte, 2583
  brotherhood or guild of craft of merchants of, *alias*
      guild of Holy Trinity, 2583
    masters and wardens of, 2583. *See also* Fagan,
      Christopher; Grove, Simon; Levan, John;
      Ussher, John
  castle, 1351
  cathedral of Holy Trinity called Christ Church
      (Christes churche), 2583
    chapel.of Holy Trinity in, 2583
      chantry in, 2583
    William prior of, 2583
  cathedral of St Patrick, 2583
  patents dated at, 2583, 2610
  port, 503
  precinct of St Sepulchre, 2583
  prison, and its keeper, 2583
  the Bisshopps Glebe and Common Hall (le
      Commen Hawle), 2583
Duckett, Lionel, and Anne his wife, 1618
  Lionel, knight, of London, 1380
    alderman of London, 381, 2256
      governor of fellowship of English merchants for
        discovery of new trades, 2556
  Peter, 2611
  Stephen, 2255
Ducketts (Duckettes) [in Tottenham], Midd, manor,
    834
Duddeley. *See* Dudley
Duddelston. *See* Dudleston
Duddeston (Dueston) [in Aston, Warw], lordship,
    2255
Duddington. *See* Doddington
Duddon (Doddon) [in Tarvin], Ches, 3684
Dudeley. *See* Dudley
Dudleston (Duddelston) [in Ellesmere], Salop,
    2772
Dudley (Duddeley, Dudeley, Dudlie), Ambrose, earl
    of Warwick, K.G., 577, 837
  councillor, 1398
  master of ordnance, 124
  Anne wife of, 837, 1398
  Arthur, S.T.P., canon or prebendary in Worcester
      cathedral, 2582
  John, almsknight in college of St George, Windsor
      castle, 447

Dudley—*cont.*
  John, clerk of signet for writs and process touching
      suits in Wales and Welsh border counties,
      1508
  John, duke of Northumberland, 831–2, 1350
  John, earl of Warwick, 603, 660, 1264, 1503, 2235
    Anne wife of, 2235
  John, knight, 861–4, 871
  John, of Stoke Newington, 2249
  John, [Beds etc.], 1347
  John, [Wilts], 3175
  John, [Yorks], 419
  John, steward of five Cumberland manors, 1449
  John, surveyor in Suffolk, 466
  Richard, 2948
  Richard, ecclesiastical commissioner, York
      province, 2599
  Richard, [Cumb], 93, 366
  Robert, K.G. and knight of St Michael, earl of
      Leicester, baron of Denbigh, 1334, 1431,
      3562
    councillor, 61, 212, 648, 1357, 2191, 2252, 2261,
      3113, 3281, 3285, 3405, 3715
    chancellor and chamberlain of Anglesey,
      Caernarvonshire and Merionethshire, 2857
    master of the horse, 55, 124, 399, 608, 2256, 2603
    chaplain to. *See* Thomas, John
  Robert, [Northumb], 1358
  Thomas, of London, 2256
  Thomas, [Staffs], 868
Dueston. *See* Duddeston
Duffield (Duffeld, Duffyld), Anthony, 1628
  James, 2791, 2809
  Thomas, 2068
Duffield (Duffeilde), Derb, 654
  Belper, Bradshaw, Holbrook, Turnditch and
      Windley in, *q.v.*
Duffield, North, (Duffield), in Skipwith, Yorks, 2254
  chapel of St James, 2254
Duffyld. *See* Duffeild
Duforth. *See* Dwyfawr
Dufton (Duston), [Westm], rector presented to. *See*
      Walker, Christopher
Dugdayll, Christopher, rector presented to Poulshot,
      1741
Duke, Gilbert, clerk of council in principality of
      Wales and Welsh border counties, 1508
Dull, Walter, of Bristol, 2256
Dullingham (Dullyngham), Cambs, 2198
  manor, 1375
Dulong, William, French subject, 722
Dulverton, Som, 638
  Pixton in, *q.v.*
Dulwich (Dulwiche) in Camberwell, Surrey, 206
Duman, John, Spanish subject, 1718
Dummer, Hants, 2425
  grange, 2425
Dummer, William, and Catherine his wife, 2425
Dun. *See* Donne
Dunche (Dounche), Edmund, 267
  John, 2180
  William, 3068
Dunchideock (Dunchyddock), [Devon], rector
      presented to. *See* Tarporley, Thomas
Dunchurch (Dunchurche), Warw, 2255, 2316
  Thurlaston in, *q.v.*
Dunchyddock. *See* Dunchideock
Dunclent (Duncklyn) [in Stone], Worcs, Moore of,
      q.v.
Duncombe (Duncumbe), Edward, 3155

Dygovylchye, Dygoyfilchye. *See* Dwygyfylchi
Dyke, Austin, 2064
 Humphrey, 2968
 Humphrey, [Warw], 3291
 Humphrey, the younger, [Glos], 2017
 William, rector presented to Waterstock, 992
Dykeringe. *See* Dickering
Dykeyaites (*unidentified*) [?in Ripon], Yorks, 870, 918
Dylham. *See* Dilham
Dyllon, Gerald, of Swords, clerk of crown and of
  common pleas and keeper of writs and rolls
  in Queen's Bench of Ireland, 1532
 Lucas, chief baron of Exchequer [of Ireland], 81
Dylston. *See* Dilston
Dylton. *See* Dilton
Dymbylbye. *See* Dembleby
Dymchurch, Kent, Newington Fee in, *q.v.*
Dymmock (Dymmocke), Charles, 961
 Robert, 3514
Dymylbye. *See* Dembleby
Dyneley, Arthur, 606
 Henry, 2017
 Cf. Dyngley
Dynevor (Denevor) [in Llandeilo], Carm, 3252
Dyngley, William, and James his son, 3290
 Cf. Dyneley
Dynham. *See* Denham

Dynlley. *See* Dinllaen; Dinlle
Dynmore, Adam, almsknight in college of St George,
  Windsor castle, 447
Dynmore. *See* Dinmore
Dynne, Henry, auditor of Exchequer, 1535, 2223,
  2851
 Cf. Denne
Dynton. *See* Dinton
Dynyngton. *See* Dennington
Dyon, John, 284
Dysney, Daniel, 2019
 Richard, 2976
Dysse. *See* Diss
Dyssely. *See* Disley
Dysserth (Thysserth) [in Welshpool], Mont, Jevan of,
  q.v.
Dytheriche. *See* Ditteridge
Dytton. *See* Woodditton
Dyve (Dyves), Lewis, of Bromham, and John his son,
  1499
 Lewis, [Beds], 276, 1834, 1856, 1888
Dyvelishe. *See* Dewlish
Dyvenock. *See* Devynock
Dyves. *See* Dyve
Dyvynocke. *See* Devynock
Dyxe. *See* Dixe
Dyxson. *See* Dixon

E

Ealing (Elinge), Midd, Rithe of, *q.v.*
Eardington (Yardington, Yarton) [in Quatford],
  Salop, 1995
 manor, 1995
Eardisland (Earsland, Erdisland), Heref, manor, 2067
earl marshal of England, 1352
Earle, Austin, the elder, and Austin, the younger,
  2456
 Walter, 2256
 Cf. Hearle
Earnest, Matthew, 3714
Earsdon, Northumb, Blyth, South, and Newsham in,
  q.v.
Earsham (Rusham) in Wingfield, Suff, chapel, 206
Earsland. *See* Eardisland
Earthcott, Gaunts, [in Almondsbury], *or* Row
  Earthcott [in Alveston], Glos, 2183
Earthcott, Row, (Ercott, Ircote), [in Alveston], Glos,
  835, 2034
Easby, Yorks, 2297
 Aske and St Agatha in, *q.v.*
Easedike (Essedick) [in Wighill], Yorks, 2907
Easington (Essington), Yorks, [North Riding], 3379
 le Guyld House and our Ladye House in, 3379
 Liverton in, *q.v.*
Easington (Esynton) [Yorks, East *or* North Riding],
  rector presented to. *See* Stancliff, Richard
Easingwold (Easingwolde), Yorks, 206
 Raskelf in, *q.v.*
East Meadowe (*unidentified*), 3714
Eastanfeild (*unidentified*), Yorks, Warcopp of, *q.v.*
Eastbourne (Eastborne, Easteborne), Sussex, 1650
 church, 2688
 manor, 1650
Eastbourne (Eastborne), Sussex, hundred, 1650
?Eastbourne (Borne), Sussex, 2255
Eastbrandon. *See* Brandon
Eastbrompton. *See* Brompton

Eastchurch (Estchurche, Estchurche in the isle of
  Sheppey), Kent, 1668, 3379
Eastcote (Estecote) [in Pattishall], Northants, 1353
Eastcotts (Estcotes, Estcottes *alias* Cotton Ende *alias*
  Heringes Ende) [in Cardington], Beds,
  3489, 3556
Eastcourt (Escott) [in Crudwell], Wilts, 971
Eastdeane. *See* Dean
Eastdereham. *See* Dereham
Easte, Richard, 2229
Easteborne. *See* Eastbourne
Easten. *See* Easton
Easter, High, (High Ester), Essex, 896
Easter book or roll, Lent roll, 1347, 1406, 1410,
  2513, 2676
Eastergate (Gates), [Sussex], rector presented to. *See*
  Dyggones, Thomas
Easterudham. *See* Rudham
Eastfield (Estfeild) [in Peterborough], Northants,
  2806
Eastgrenested. *See* Grinstead
Eastgrenewich, Eastgrenewiche. *See* Greenwich
Eastguldeforde. *See* Guldeford
Eastham, Worcs, Orleton in, *q.v.*
Easthampstead (Esthampsted), Berks, 3167
 manor and advowson of church, 3167
Easthaninfeild. *See* Hanningfield
Easthawfyeld (*unidentified*), Yorks, 3386
Easthope, Salop, Brockton in, *q.v.*
Easthorpe (Esthorppe), Essex, 3475
 advowson of church, 3475
 advowson of rectory, 1328
 manor, 1328, 3475
Easthorpe (Yaresthorpe) [in Appleton le Street],
  Yorks, manor, 3687
Eastington (Estington) [in Worth Matravers], Dors,
  1347
 manor, 1347

F

Fellowe, John, 353
  Cf. Fallowes
Felmersham (Femersham), Beds, 605
Felmingham (Felmyngham), Norf, 3558
Felthorpe (Felthrope), Norf, 2688
Felton alias Whitchurch (Filton alias Whitchurche,
    Whitechurch), Som, 2297
  grange, 2297
Felton, John, and Catherine his wife, 2042
  John, and Elizabeth his wife, 851
  Mary, and Thomas, and Anthony his son, 3282
felts, importation of wool for making, 1421
Fely. See Philleigh
Femersham. See Felmersham
Fen, Humphrey, vicar presented to Holy Trinity,
    Coventry, 3309
fen grounds, engines for draining, 3672
Fencote [in Hatfield], Heref, 665, 830
Fenell, Simon, 1626
Fenelon, Sieur de la Mothe, French ambassador, 492
Fenlake (Fenlacke) [in Cardington], Beds, 3489, 3556
Fennar, Edward, 282
Fennemere (Fynymer alias Lynches) [in Baschurch],
    Salop, 1347
Fennycompton. See Compton
Fennystaunton. See Stanton
Fens, the, commons within, 1415
Fenterwanson in Lanteglos by Camelford, Corn,
    Hicke of, q.v.
Fenton, Lincs, 552
Fenton in Sturton le Steeple, Notts, 2254
  Saint Laurence's chapel, 2254
Fenton, Christopher, 206
  Edward, 1379
  William, canon or prebendary in collegiate church
    or free chapel of Holy Trinity, Norwich,
    1533
Fenwick (Fenwicke, Fenwyck, Fenwycke, Fenwyke),
    Cuthbert, of South Shields, 39
  John, 119, 275, 973, 1918
  William, 1918
Fenys. See Fiennes
Feock, Corn, Tresithick in, q.v.
feodary, appointment of, 488
Ferby. See Firby
Ferford. See Fairford
Ferlington. See Farlington
Fermor (Fermer, Fermour), George, [Dors], and
    Mary his wife, 3248
  George, [Northants], 1641
  Richard, 674
  Thomas, and Bridget his wife, 1625, 1627
  William, alias William Warde, 1337
  Cf. Farmer
Ferne. See Farne
Ferneham. See Farnham
Ferney alias Hiffarne (Hiffearne) (unidentified), Ireland,
    1351
  captain or chieftain of, 1351
Fernley, Ranulf, 1925
Fernyside, James, rector presented to Whickham, 31
Ferrabosco, Alphonso de, gentleman of privy
    chamber, 830
Ferrers, lord. See Devereux
Ferrers (Ferrys, Ferys), George, 266
  Henry, 263
  Humphrey, 3025
  Humphrey, [London], 1278
  Humphrey, [Warw], 342
  John, and Humphrey his son, 1142

Ferrors—cont.
  John, [Staffs], 322
  Cf. Farror
Ferriby, North, Yorks, Swanland in, q.v.
Ferriby, South, (Southferibye, Southferybye), Lincs,
    3666
  bridge, 3666
  church, 3666
  rectory and vicar of, 3257
  Brombey, Gryme, Horringham, Kyddall, Toft and
    Westbye, q.v.
ferries, 852, 1350, 1432, 2743, 2826, 2890, 3251, 3529,
    3539
Ferrys. See Ferrers
Fersfield (Faresfelde), Norf, 1396
Ferys. See Ferrers
Festiniock, Festynyock. See Ffestiniog
Fetiplace (Fetyplace, Phetyplace), Edward, 2611
  George, 2244
  George, justice of great session, 817
  George, [Essex], 1848
  George, [Glos], 241, 252-3, 615, 1264, 1969, 3452
    Cecily wife of, 3452
  John, knight, [Berks], 1329, 1641, 2482
Feversham. See Faversham
Fewell, Christopher, vicar presented to St Mary,
    Beverley, 3351
  Cf. Fowell
Feylde. See Fielde
Feyrefax. See Fairfax
Ffestiniog (Festiniock, Festynyock), Merion, 212,
    2252
Fiddington (Fyddington, Fyddyngton) [in
    Ashchurch], Glos, 2735-7, 3168
Fiddington (Fydington, Fyffehed Verdon) [in West
    Lavington], Wilts, 2044
  manor, 2044
Fielde (Feilde, Felde, Feylde), Henry, 2987-8, 3080
  John, coroner of Bristol, 2173
  John, [Berks], and Agnes his wife, and John the
    younger, Richard and Robert, the elder, and
    Robert the younger his sons, 3490
  Matthew, of London, 123, 1380
Fiennes (Fenys, Fynes), Edward, alias Edward
    Clinton, K.G., earl of Lincoln, lord Clinton
    and Say, 1630, 2183, 2255
  councillor, 552, 830, 3251, 3394
  High Admiral of England, Ireland and Wales,
    58, 2182, 2191, 3597
  keeper of Byfleet park, 3700
  Elizabeth wife of, 1630, 3394, 3597
  Gregory, lord Dacre, and Anne his wife, 1640
  Henry, lord Clinton and Say, 336-7, 344
  John, 3026, 3075
  Richard, knight, Richard son of, 2406
  Thomas, alias Thomas Clinton, lord Clinton,
    3261
Fifhedd. See Fivehead
Fifield (Fyfeild), Oxon, 2006
Figheldean, Wilts, Alton in, q.v.
Fildallinge, Fildallynge. See Dalling
Filgrave [in Tyringham with Filgrave], Bucks, 3728
Filinge. See Fylingdales
Filton. See Felton
Fincham (Fyncham), Norf, manor (Fyncham Hall
    alias Surpelles Hall), 3523
  Bainard Hall in, q.v.
  Cornwallies and Haynsworth of, q.v.
Finchley (Fyncheley), Midd, 1555, 1631
  manor, 1631

Frodsham—*cont.*
  Alvanley, Helsby, Kingsley, Manley and Norley in,
    q.v.
Frodsley. *See* Frodesley
Frogmore [in New Windsor], Berks, 1341
Frome (Frome Selwood, Fromeselwood,
    Fromeselwoode), Som, 210, 831, 1995
  church, 210, 831
  Vallis in, *q.v.*
  Harris of, *q.v.*
Frome, Bishops, Heref, Rhea in, *q.v.*
Frome, Canon, (Cannon Frome), Heref, manor, 1257,
    1674
Frome Whitfield (Frome Whytfeyld) [in Dorchester,
    Dors], chapel, chaplain presented to. *See*
    Puckering, Thomas
Frosell, William, serjeant or bailiff of honour of
    Wigmore, 2846
Frost (Froste), Edmund, [Lincs], 2861
  Edmund, [Sussex], 3389
  James, and Joan his wife, 1296, 2026
Frostenden, Suff, manor, 3217
Frothingham, Frothinghame. *See* Frodingham
Froxfield (Froxfeld), Wilts, 2020
  Rudge in, *q.v.*
Froyle, Hants, Jephson of, *q.v.*
Fruthesden. *See* Frithsden
Frye, William, of Stockland, 457
Fryer, Elizabeth, 2768
  Leonard, gunner in bulwark or blockhouse of East
    Mersea, 3404
  Robert, 2355
  William, 2102
Fryerning (Fryerninge), Essex, 206
  church, 206
Fryers. *See* Friar's
Fryngford. *See* Fringford
Frystock. *See* Frithelstock
Frythe. *See* Frith
Frythelstock, Frythelstocke. *See* Frithelstock
Fuenterrabia, [Spain], 2256
Fugall, Richard, 3589
Fulbeck (Fulbecke), Lincs, 2002
  manor, 2002
  rectors presented to. *See* Bond, Nicholas;
    Robinson, John
  rectory, 2002
Fulbourn (Fulbourne), Cambs, 2180
  church, 2180
Fulbrook (Fulbrooke) [in Hogshaw], Bucks, 3108,
    3111
Fulbrook Eynsham (Fulbrooke Kynsham) [in
    Hogshaw], Bucks, manor, 3108, 3111
Fulford, Gate, (Gatefulforde) [in Fulford Ambo],
    Yorks, 3252
Fulford, John, of Burrington, 3660
Fulham (Fullham), Midd, 954, 2491
Fulke, Fulkes. *See* Fowkes
Full, Hugh, 831
Fuller (Fulwere), William, *alias* William Clerke, 3379
  William, auditor of Exchequer, 1535, 2223, 2851
  William, [London], and Nathaniel his son, 1261
  Cf. Fowler
Fullestowe. *See* Fulstow
Fullham. *See* Fulham

Fulmerston, Richard, 2359
  Richard, knight, and Frances Clere his daughter,
    1596
Fulnesse. *See* Foulness
Fulnetby (Fulnetbye) [in Rand], Lincs, 961
Fulstow (Fullestowe), Lincs, advowson of church,
    1571
  rectory, 1572
Fulstowe, Richard, of London, 2930
Fulthroppe, Francis, 577
  John, and Robert and Thomas his brothers and
    Lucy his daughter, 577
Fulwere. *See* Fuller
Fulwood, William, of London, 2768, 3466
Funtington, Sussex, Oakwood in, *q.v.*
Furbusher, Furbysher. *See* Frobysher
Furland, John, of Newton Ferrers, 2937
Furness (Furnes) [in Dalton in Furness], Lancs,
    monastery, 210
Furtho, Thomas, 1347
Fussher. *See* Fisher
Fyddington, Fyddyngton, Fydington. *See*
    Fiddington
Fyfeelde, George, of Lowestoft, Grace Donne wife
    of, 710
Fyfehead. *See* Fyfield
Fyfeild. *See* Fifield
Fyffehed. *See* Fiddington
Fyfield (Fyfehead), Hants, 1642
  Redenham in, *q.v.*
Fygge, Nicholas, Richard and Robert sons of, 3383
Fyggyns, Roger, 2330
Fyldallynge. *See* Dalling
Fylingdales (Filinge, Filinge Botham), Yorks, 3379
  church, 3379
Fylley. *See* Philleigh
Fyn, Ralph, of Northampton, 1604
Fyncham, William, 3523
Fyncham. *See* Fincham
Fynche, Clement, 627
  George, of Norton, servant of. *See* Handley,
    Thomas
  Moyle (*Moilus*), 1577
  Nicholas, and William of Redbourn, his son, and
    Isabel, William's wife, 413
Fyncheley. *See* Finchley
Fynderne. *See* Findern
Fyndon. *See* Findon
Fynes. *See* Fiennes; Woolley *alias* Fynes
Fynmere. *See* Finmere
Fynny, William, 288
Fynton, John, Joan wife of, 900
Fynymer. *See* Fennemere
Fyshe (Fysshe), Walter, [Warw], 965
  Walter, [Yorks], 3687
  William, 1354
Fyshed. *See* Fivehead
Fysher. *See* Fisher
Fysherton. *See* Fisherton
Fyshman, Thomas, 2867
Fysshe. *See* Fyshe
Fyssher. *See* Fisher
Fytche. *See* Fitche
Fyttes. *See* Fitz
Fytzwilliam, Fytzwilliams. *See* Fitzwilliams

G

Gadbury (Gadburye), Richard, 3027
  Richard, [London], 321, 1847
Gaddesby, Hugh, of London, 2880
Gaddesden, Great, (Gaddesden), Herts, manor of,
  with Frithsden, 669
Gaddesden, Great *or* Little, (Gaddesden), Herts, 624
Gaddesden, Little, Herts, Ashridge in, *q.v.*
Gaddesdon, Robert, of Maulden, 2350
Gafflogian (Gaffogion), Carn, commote, 651
Gage, Edward, [Kent], 2790
  Edward, [Sussex], 310, 1160, 1626, 1930, 3673
  George, 1626
  John, knight, and William his son, 2572
  John, [Sussex], Richard, Robert and Thomas, 1626
  William, and Joan his wife, 1629
Gainford (Gayneford), Durham, manor, 1419
  Barnard Castle, Denton, Piercebridge,
    Summerhouse and Westwick in, *q.v.*
Gaiosworth. *See* Gawsworth
Gaitburton. *See* Burton
Gaite, Gaites. *See* Gates
Galbye. *See* Gaulby
Gale, Francis, Robert son of, 2645
Gallamor, Patrick, 3275
gallows, grant of, 813
Galmpton (Galmeton) [in Churston Ferrers], Devon,
  3596
Galtres (Galters, Galtrees, Galtries), Yorks, forest,
  206
  foresters and keepers (*named*) of, 2694
  stewards (*named*) of, 1452
Galwey, William, 2583
Gamage, Anthony, alderman of London, 2171, 2256
  lady Joyce, 1393
Gamble, William, [Leics], 2500
  William, [Lincs], 3383
Gamblesby (Gamlesby) [in Addingham], Cumb,
  manor, stewards and clerks of court (*named*)
  of, 1449
Game (Gamme), Robert, [Wilts], 1461
  Robert, [Yorks], 675
  Cf. Games
Gamerocke (*unidentified*), Devon, 2479
Games, Walter, 1370
  Cf. Game; James
games, lawful, power to licence houses for, 59
  unlawful, 59
  See also bowling; tennis
Gamlesby. *See* Gamblesby
Gamlingay (Gamlyngay), Cambs, brotherhood of,
  2255
Gamme. *See* Game
Gamon, John, vicar presented to Kirkby Green, 1746
Gamsheford, Nicholas, of Bristol, 2256
Gannocke, William, 3608
Gannockes Yarde (*unidentified*), Norf, 2689
Gannockes, Gannoxke. *See* Ganwick
Ganstead (Gansted) [in Swine], Yorks, 565, 596
Ganwick Corner (Gannockes, Gannoxke) in South
  Mimms, Midd, 2481
gaols, grants of, 392, 2197
Garboldisham (Garbouldsham All Saints), Norf,
  rectory, 2255
Garbray, Christopher, 2115
Gardiner (Gardener, Gardyner), Henry, 3610
  James, *alias* James Redy, of Brington, 1604
  John, 3027
  John, John son of, 416

Gardiner—*cont.*
  John, of London, 2256
  John, [Midd], 834
  Philip, and Jane his wife, 3149
  Stephen, bishop of Winchester, 1494
  Thomas, *alias* Thomas A Courte, and Margaret his
    wife, 2076
  Thomas, [London], 123
  William, of Southwark, 123
  William, [Surrey], 1368
Gardney, Thomas, attorney, 2381
Gardyner. *See* Gardiner
Garendon (Garryngton), Leics, monastery, 1240
Garford [in Marcham], Berks, 1207
  manor, 552, 1207
Garford (Garforthe), Anthony, rector presented to
  Washington, 1004
  John, 831
Gargrave, Yorks, Coniston, Cold, and Winterburn in,
  q.v.
Gargrave, Cotton, [Dors], 3620
  Cotton, [Yorks], 1979
  Thomas, knight, 3009, 3101
    ecclesiastical commissioner, York province, 316,
      391, 2599
    justice of oyer and terminer, 43, 1507
Garlande, George, 68
Garlands (Garnons) in Steeple Bumpstead, Essex,
  manor, 2102
Garlinge, Kent, Hengrove in, *q.v.*
garments, manufacture of, 3572
Garn (Garronwere) [in Westbury on Severn], Glos,
  fishery, 830
Garn (Garne) [in Llanfor], Merion, 2252
Garnans (Garnance, Garnannes, Garnnans, Garnons),
  James, 88, 108, 1838
  John, 256, 260
  Luke, coroner of Gloucester, 34
  Luke, [Glos], 3528
  William, 3034–5
  William, [Heref], 326, 1843, 1877
Garne. *See* Garn
Garneley, Michael, 2821
Garner, William, 2487
Garnesey. *See* Guernsey
Garnet. *See* Garnett
Garnethorpe. *See* Grainthorpe
Garnett (Garnet), Bartholomew, 2776
  Henry, the elder, 2761
  Richard, and Frances his wife, 2776
  Robert, 3532
  Thomas, 831
Garnnans. *See* Garnans
Garnons. *See* Garlands; Garnans
Garnsey. *See* Guernsey
Garrard, Garrarde. *See* Gerrard
Garrett (Garratt, Garret), Anthony, of London,
    assistant and chief councillor of fellowship
    of merchants of Spain and Portugal, 2256
  John, coroner of Gillingham liberty, 2913
  Robert, S.T.B., vicar presented to Eglingham, 2544
  Stephen, 3614
Garrettes, John, Spanish subject, 718
Garronwere. *See* Garn
Garryngton. *See* Garendon
Garsdon, Wilts, Collins of, *q.v.*
Garson, William, queen's drum, 498
Garstang, Lancs, Catterall in, *q.v.*

Gurdon (Gordon, Gurden), Robert, 3012
　　Robert, [Norf], 1967
　　Robert, [Suff], 91, 1852
Gurney, William, and Frances his wife, 1618
Gussage All Saints, Dors, Mannington in, q.v.
Gussage St Andrew (Gussage St Andrewes) [in
　　Handley], Dors, 2781
Guybon. See Gibbons
Guylliker, Francis, subject of duke of Cleves, 1700
Guylpyn. See Gilpyn
Guynes, John, 648
Gwastader (Custa, Custoda, Gwastoda) [in Talley],
　　Carm, grange, 552, 1519, 2631
Gwatkyn. See Watkyn
Gwedyr. See Gwydir
Gwenfo (Wenvoe), Glam, 903
Gwernefail (Grvenevell, Gwernevell) [in Llanycil]
　　Merion, 212, 2252
Gwestfa Cilfargen alias Cilfargen (Kilbargonne) [in
　　Llangathen], Carm, grange, 2620
Gwestfa Cil-san alias Cil-san (Kylsaen) [in
　　Llangathen], Carm, 1393
Gwider. See Gwydir
Gwillym, Morgan David ap, of, Llanfihangel, 254
　　Cf. Williams
Gwiniasa (Gwinase) [in Pistyll], Carn, 3715
Gwins. See Gwynys
Gwyddgrug (Gothegrigg, Gothgrige) [in
　　Llanfihangel ar Arth], Carm, grange, 1519
Gwydir (Gwedyr, Gwider) [in Llanrwst, Denb]
　　formerly in Carn, 212, 3715
Gwyn. See Gwynne
Gwynfaen (Gonvayne) [in Llandeilo Tal-y-bont],
　　Glam, 674
?Gwynfryn (Llanginsfryn) [in Llanystumdwy], Carn,
　　210

Gwynne (Gwyn), Edward, 2768
　　Edward ap Jevan, 2506
　　Owen, 2678
　　Thomas, 651
Gwynys (Gwins) [in Pistyll], Carn, 3715
Gybbes, Anthony, 3123
　　Robert, [Warw], and Catherine his wife, 3123
　　Robert, [Wilts], 1298
Gybbins, Gybbons, Gybbyns, Gybon, Gybons. See
　　Gibbons
Gybson. See Gibson
Gye, Anthony, alias Anthony Caverley, of London,
　　　and Elizabeth Caverley his mother, 1540
　　Peter, queen's servant, and Isabel his wife, 823
Gyffard, Gyffarde. See Gifford
Gyffin, Carn, Llechan in, q.v.
Gyfford, Gyfforde. See Gifford
Gylbert. See Gilbert
Gyles, Clement, 2236
　　John, of London, merchant adventurer, and Anne
　　　Hawkes his wife, 53
　　John, [Devon], 938
　　Robert, 1405
　　Thomas, vicar presented to Elberton, 986
Gyll. See Gill
Gyllett. See Gillett
Gyllyngham, Thomas, M.A., vicar presented to
　　Dartford, 1005
Gyllyngham. See Gillingham
Gylpyn. See Gilpyn
Gyrdlyngton, Nicholas, 3076
Gyrlynge. See Girlinge
Gyrlyngton. See Girlington
Gysborne. See Gisburn; Guisborough
Gysborughe, Gysburgh. See Guisborough
Gyttyns. See Gittins

H

Haarlem (Harlinge), [Holland], 137
Habberley (Haberley), Salop, 1632
Habblesthorpe (Hablestrope), Notts, lordship, 2254
haberdashers, company of, 3380. See also under trades
haberdashery, manufacture of, 3380
Haberley, Thomas, vicar presented to Bradwell, 3330
Haberley. See Habberley
Hablestrope. See Habblesthorpe
Habrough (Haburghe), Lincs, manor, 2707
Habton, Great, (Japton Magna), [in Kirby
　　Misperton], Yorks, 349
Haburghe. See Habrough
Haccombe, Devon, Carew of, q.v.
Hacconby (Haconby), Lincs, 2086
　　Stainfield in, q.v.
Hacculton. See Hackleton
Hacheburye. See Heytesbury
Hacheston, Suff, Bloomville Hall in, q.v.
　　Bull of, q.v.
Hackeceston. See Hacklestone
Hackensall (Hagensey, Hakensall) [in Lancaster],
　　Lancs, 2541
Hackforth (Hackforthe, Hackfourth) [in Hornby],
　　Yorks, 621, 921
Hacklestone (Hackeceston, Hackleston) [in Fittleton],
　　Wilts, 2539
Hackleton (Hacculton) in Piddington, Northants,
　　206, 1350
Hackley. See Hawkley

Hackluytt, Thomas, 1978
　　Thomas, [Worcs], and Fortune his wife, 2462
Hackness (Hacknes), Yorks, 3125
　　manor and rectory, 3125
　　Everley, Harwood Dale, Silpho and Suffield in, q.v.
Hackney (Hacney), Midd, 2880, 3247
　　manor, 610, 3247
　　Hartlake and Ruckholt (Rokeholte, Rookholte) and
　　　Temple mills, 610
　　London Fields in, q.v.
Hackthorn (Hackthorne), Lincs, 3236
　　manor, 3236
Hackwell, John, of Exeter, 2256
Hackwell. See Hawkwell
Hacney. See Hackney
Haconby. See Hacconby
Haddenham, Bucks, 2183
Haddenham, Cambs, 3133
　　Hinton in, q.v.
Haddes, Arnold, 104–7
Haddington [in Aubourn], Lincs, 1571
Haddling (Hedlinge in Waldershire, Hedlynge in
　　Waldershyre) [in Northbourne], Kent,
　　wood, 829, 1343
Haddocke (Hadock), John, 615, 1264
Haddon, West, (Westhadden, Westhaddon),
　　Northants, 3203
　　manor, 3203
　　vicar presented to. See Turner, Ralph

Handley (Hanley) (*unidentified*) [in Staveley], Derb,
    1637, 3440
  manor, 1637, 3440
Handley (Hanleighe, Hanley), Dors, 2781
  Gussage St Andrew, Minchington and Woodcutts
    in, *q.v.*
Handley (Hendle, Hendley), Robert, of London, 2256
  Thomas, [Kent], and Anne his wife, 2837
  Thomas, servant of George Fynche, 1607
  Walter, 2984
  Cf. Henley; Hyndley
Handsworth Woodhouse (Hannesworthe
    Woodhouse) [in Handsworth], Yorks, 1353
Handye, John, of Moulton, 2840
Hanford. *See* Handford
Hangingestooke, Hangingstoke, Hanginstoke. *See*
  Stoke, Limpley
Hanham, Downe, (Downe Hannam), [in Bitton],
  Glos, 3477
Hanham, West, (Hannam, Westhannam) [in Bitton],
  Glos, 2006, 3477
Hankerton (Hanckerton), Wilts, 971
  Cloatley in, *q.v.*
Hankin, Margaret, of Harwich, 3720
Hankye, Thomas, yeoman of wardrobe within
    principality of Wales and officer and clerk
    for bills for debt before Council there, 192
Hanleighe. *See* Handley
Hanley Castle (Castle Hanley, Hanley Castell, Potters
    Hanley), Worcs, 2330, 3379
  church, chantry or college of, 3379
  Hudson of, *q.v.*
Hanley. *See* Handley
Hanmer, Flint, 3725
Hanmer, Humphrey, 2977, 2985, 3086–7, 3100
  Meredith, M.A., rector presented to Huntspill,
    3682
  Thomas, knight, 2712
Hannah, Lincs, Hagnaby in, *q.v.*
Hannam (Hanam), James, 3137
  Thomas, 1929
  William, and James his son, 2367
  William, [Som], 1284, 3184
Hannam. *See* Hanham
Hannesworthe. *See* Handsworth
Hanney, East, (Esthanney, Esthannye), [in West
    Hanney], Berks, 210, 2183
Hanney, East, [in West Hanney], *or* Hanney, West,
    (Hannye), Berks, 831
Hanningfield, East, (Easthaninfeild), Essex, 3502
Hanningfield, South, (Southe Hanningefeild), Essex,
  3379
Hannington (Hanyngton), Northants, 3453
Hannye. *See* Hanney
Hannyshe. *See* Hamnish
Hansbye, Ralph, 2972–3
  Ralph, [Yorks], 2476
Hansharte, Richard, the younger, 2758
Hanslope (Hanslopp), Bucks, 2183
  Keswick in, *q.v.*
Hanworth, Potter, (Hanworth), Lincs, 2786
Hanyngton. *See* Hannington
Harbarte, Harbert. *See* Herbert
Harberton (Hamberton, Herbarton), Devon, 2255
  Belsford and Harbertonford in, *q.v.*
Harbertonford (Hurburnford) [in Harberton],
  Devon, 938
Harborne, [Staffs], 2255
Harbottell, Ralph and Thomas, 576
Hardcastell (Harcastell), Miles, 1213

Hardcastell—*cont.*
  Robert, and Christopher his son, 639
  William, and Margaret his wife, 642
Harden (Harding) in Bingley, Yorks, 2732
Harding (Hardinge, Hardyng, Hardynge), Edmund,
    and Elizabeth his wife, 2754
  Richard, of Exeter, 2256
  Richard, [Surrey], 3456
  Thomas, [Hunts], 2342
  Thomas, [Wilts], 1303
  William, [London], 1593
  William, [Surrey], 2445
Harding. *See* Harden
Hardingestorne. *See* Hardingstone
Hardingham, William, 2840
Hardingstone (Hardingestorne), Northants, vicar
    presented to. *See* Whalley, William
  Delapré Abbey in, *q.v.*
Hardwell [in Compton Beauchamp], Berks, 2755
Hardwick in St Neots, Hunts, 2188
Hardwick (Herdwick) in Chepstow, Monm, 2299
Hardwick (Hardwyck), Northants, 3453
Hardwick (Hardwyck) [in Burton Dassett], Warw,
  911
Hardwick [in Bredon], Worcs, Price of, *q.v.*
Hardwicke. *See* Kempston Hardwick
Hardwyck, Thomas, 3082
Hardwyck. *See* Hardwick
Hardy [in Chorlton cum Hardy in Manchester],
    Lancs, 2676
Hardy (Hardye), John, [Yorks], 1390
  John, rector presented to Kirkburn, 1751
  Ralph, 1221
  Robert and William, 1390
Hardyng, Hardynge. *See* Harding
Hare, Hugh, [Hants], 1546
  Hugh, [Midd], 1618
  Ralph, of London, 3673
  Ralph, [Kent], 2790
  Ralph, [Sussex], 310
  Robert, of London, 3673
  Robert, [Kent], 2790
  Robert, [Midd], 1618
Harebrowen, William, of London, 2256
Hareby (Harebye, Herbye), Lincs, 1525
Harecourt (Harecourte), Simon, 3011
  Simon, and Walter his son, 2641
  Simon, [Staffs], 2767
Harehope (Harrope) [in Eglingham], Northumb,
  2567
Harensey. *See* Hornsey
Harescombe, Glos, 831
  church, 831
?Harescombe (Horscombe), Glos, 2180
Haresfield (Haresfeilde, Haresfeld), Glos, 831
  church and church house, 831
  park and rectory, 3633
Harewood (Harwood), Yorks, 678
  Alwoodley and Keswick, East, in, *q.v.*
Harewood. *See* Harwood
Harflette *alias* Sepvaunce, Christopher, 105
Harford (Hartford), Devon, 2677
Harford, John, 1350
  Nathaniel, vicar of Chipping Campden, 555
  Richard, and Nathaniel his brother, 2659
  Richard, [Heref], 88, 108, 1257, 1674, 1838
    Anthony, Henry and Nathaniel brothers of and
      Martha wife of, [Heref], 1674
Hargrave, [Northants], rector presented to. *See*
  Smyth, John

Hesill. *See* Hessle
Hesket in the Forest, Ellerton and Hayclose in, *q.v.*
Hesleden, Monk, Durh, Hutton Henry in, *q.v.*
Heslington (Heslington near York) [in York], Yorks, 210, 1350
    manor, 1350
Hessle (Hasell, Heasill, Hesill), Yorks, 2890, 3589
    rectory, 1367
    Tranby in, *q.v.*
Heston, Midd, 1601, 2619, 3662
    woods, keepers (*named*) of, 2617
    Hounslow and Sutton in, *q.v.*
    Stockdoune of, *q.v.*
Heth. *See* Hoath; Hythe
Hether. *See* Haydor
Hetherdeane. *See* Hatherden
Hethersett (Hethesett), Norf, 1192
Hethorne. *See* Haydor
Heton. *See* Heaton
Hetton (Hetten) [in Burnsall], Yorks, 645, 1194, 1267–76, 1672
Heugh (Hewghe) [in Lanchester], Durh, 429
Hevatt. *See* Huthwaite
Heveningham (Hemmyngham, Hevenyngham), Suff, Cornewall of, *q.v.*
Heveringland. *See* Haveringland
Heward, Hewarde. *See* Hayward
Hewes. *See* Hughes
Hewett (Huett), Henry, of London, 2256
    John, French subject, 1733
    Nicholas, of London, 2256
    Thomas, of London, churchwarden of St Martin Orgar, London, 2514
    Thomas, [Notts], 1839
    William, of London, assistant and chief councillor of fellowship of merchants of Spain and Portugal, 2256
    William, rector presented to Ashley, 1045
Hewghe. *See* Heugh
Hewgill. *See* Hugill
Hewishe, James, 2494
Hewitson (Hewytsone), Joan, 2486
    John, *alias* John Hewson, of Bradshaw, 42
    William, 2089
Hewson (Hewsonne), John, *alias* John Hewitson, of Bradshaw, 42
    Richard, of London, 2256
Hewys. *See* Huish
Hewytsone. *See* Hewitson
Hexham, Northumb, chief steward and bailiff of, execution of offices of, 464. *See also* Erington, John; Trymmell, Walter
    Stowte of, *q.v.*
Hexhamshire, Northumb, 580
    chief steward and bailiff of, 464. *See also* Erington, John; Trymmell, Walter
Hexted. *See* Haxted
Hextonstall. *See* Heptonstall
Hey. *See* Haigh
Heyborne. *See* Hebborne
Heydon (Haydon), Christopher, knight, 115, 213, 264, 343, 1887, 1898, 2606
    justice of peace and of oyer and terminer in Norfolk, 1614, 2232, 2552, 2840, 2929, 3399
    Francis, [Bucks], 625
    Francis, [Herts], 1974
    Henry, 1316, 2080
    John, of London, assistant and chief councillor of fellowship of merchants of Spain and Portugal, 2256

John, [Devon], 1404
    William, 213, 1893, 1964, 1972, 1988, 2606
    justice of peace and of oyer and terminer in Norfolk, 1538, 1614, 2243, 2929, 3659
    Cf. Headon
Heyfeilde (*unidentified*) [?in Manchester], Lancs, 602
Heyford, Lower, (Neither Heyford, Nether Heyforde), Oxon, 210
    Caulcott in, *q.v.*
Heyland (Heylande), Humphrey, [Lincs], 206
    Humphrey, [Lincs], (*another*), 206
    Cf. Eland
Heyman, Nicholas, and Alice his wife, 2479
Heymesby. *See* Hemsby
Heynes. *See* Haynes
Heynor. *See* Heanor
Heyns. *See* Haynes
Heyshaw (Hayshaye) [in Ripon], Yorks, 847, 870, 918, 1213
Heytesbury (Hacheburye, Hatcheburie, Haytesbury, Heytredesburye, Heytredsburye), Wilts, 1675, 1995, 2796
Heytoft. *See* Huttoft
Heytredesburye, Heytredsbury. *See* Heytesbury
Heywar, Heyward, Heywarde. *See* Hayward
Heywood in Diss, Norf, 2180
Heywood (Haywood) [in Westbury], Wilts, 926
Heywood. *See* Haywood
Hibaldstow (Hybaulstowe), Lincs, 1320
    rectory, 1320
Hichecock (Hichcockes), John, of Compton *alias* of Caversfield, 445
    John, [Salop], 3204
    Robert, of London *alias* of Caversfield, 445
Hicke (Hycke), Henry, of Fenterwanson, and Henry, John, Nicholas, Stephen and William his sons, 2165
    Cf. Hickes; Huyck
Hickelton. *See* Hickleton
Hickes, John, of London, 2880
    William, [Glos], 241
    William, [Midd], 210
    Cf. Hicke; Hygges; Hylckes
Hickleton (Hickelton), Yorks, 2047
Hickling (Hicklinge), Norf, 3630
Hickling (Hicklinge), Notts, 3379
    church, 3379
Hicklinge, William, 2862
Hidcote Bartram (Hidcote, Hitcote) [in Mickleton], Glos, 1353
Hide (Le Hide, Le Hyde) [in Leominster], Heref, Powell of, *q.v.*
Hide. *See* Hyde
hides, 58. *See also under* staple; tanning
Hiegham. *See* Higham
Hiffarne (Hiffearne) *alias* Ferney (*unidentified*), Ireland, 1351
    captain or chieftain of, 1351
Higate. *See* Highgate
Higbedd, Michael, 1195
Higgons (Higgyns, Hyggens, Hyggyns), Anthony, canon or prebendary presented to Gloucester cathedral, 1476
    Thomas, 3250
    Walter, John, of Hope under Dinmore, son of, 3228
    William, 1350
    Cf. Huggons
Higgynson, Robert, coroner of Warwickshire, 976

Hormead—*cont.*
  rectory, 1292, 1294
  vicarage, advowson of, 1292
Hormead, Great *or* Little, (Hormeade), [Herts], rector
    presented to. *See* Fawcett, John
Hormer (Henton Hormere, Hormere) in
    Catherington, Hants, 674
Hornby (Hornebie), Yorks, 621
  Hackforth in, *q.v.*
Horncastle (Hornecastell, Hornecastle), Lincs, 210,
    336, 2040
  church, St Catherine's chantry in, 210
Hornchurch (Hornechurche), Essex, 655
Horndon, East, Essex, Heron Hall in, *q.v.*
Horndon on the Hill (Hornedon), Essex, Arden Hall
    in, *q.v.*
Horne (Hourne), Surrey, 1282, 1673, 2180
  church, 2180
Horne, John, 3472
  Robert, bishop of Winchester, 1154, 1494, 2199
  William, of Barningham, 2351
  William, of Redbourn, 405
  Cf Orne
Hornebie. *See* Hornby; Hornebye
Hornebye (Awdenbye, Haldenbye, Hawdenbie,
    Hawdenbye, Hornebie), Richard and
    Robert, of Stamford, 465
Hornecastell, Hornecastle. *See* Horncastle
Hornechurche. *See* Hornchurch
Hornedon. *See* Horndon
Horner, Thomas, 2540
Hornesey. *See* Hornsea
Horningsham (Hornyngesham), Wilts, 2460
  Baycliff in, *q.v.*
Horningtoft (Horningtofte), Norf, 3630
Horniold (Horniolde, Hornyolde), George, 2140,
    3118, 3250
  Alice wife of, 3118
  John, steward and keeper of courts of Fownhope,
    Cradley, Ledbury, Ross on Wye and
    Bishop's Castle manors, 2847
Hornsea (Hornesey), Yorks, 3388
  manor and rectory, 3388
  vicar presented to. *See* Cheveney, Robert
  Burton, Hornsea Mere and Southorpe in, *q.v.*
?Hornsea Mere (Hornesey Beck), Yorks, 3388
Hornsey (Harensey *alias* Harningey, Haringey *alias*
    Hernsey), Midd, 1555
  Highgate and Muswell Hill in, *q.v.*
Hornton, John, of Kingston upon Hull, assistant and
    chief councillor of fellowship of merchants
    of Spain and Portugal, 2256
Hornyngesham. *See* Horningsham
Hornyolde. *See* Horniold
Horringdon. *See* Horrington
Horringham, Hugh, of South Ferriby, 3666
Horrington, East *or* West, (Horringdon), [in Wells],
    Som, 1995
Horroden. *See* Harrowden
Horscombe. *See* Harescombe
Horseham, Horsehame. *See* Horsham
Horseley, George, of Acklington Park, 39
  William, [Lincs], 3258
  William, [Yorks], 545
Horseley. *See* Horsley
Horseman, Robert, 1215
  Thomas, 1259
Horsepool Grange (Horsepoole Graunge) [in
    Thornton], Leics, Raven of, *q.v.*
horses, queen's, hay for, 2536

horses—*cont.*
  master of. *See* Dudley, Robert
  theft of. *See under* pardons
Horsey Hill (Horsey) in Stanground, Hunts, 1350
  ferry, 1350
Horsey, Edward, knight, captain of isle of Wight,
    2193, 2932, 3713
  coroner of isle of Wight, 2932
  Edward, [London], 2585
  Edward, queen's servant, 523
  George, [Devon], 900
  George, [Herts], 279, 1968
Horsey. *See* Horkesley
Horsforth (Horsforthe, Horsfourth, Horsfurth) [in
    Guiseley], Yorks, 1658–9, 1661, 1664–7,
    2005, 2016, 2052, 2063
  chapel, 1661
Horsham, Sussex, 848
  Shortsfield in, *q.v.*
Horsham St Faith (Horsehame St Faith, Horsham, St
    Faith of Horseham, St Faith of Horsham),
    Norf, 2841
  church, 3714
  priory, 552, 2183, 2298, 3714
    Hugh prior of, 3714
  Muse of, *q.v.*
Horsington, Som, 854, 1284
  manor and advowson of church, 854
  vicarage, advowson of, 854
  Cheriton, South, Horewood and Horsington Moor
    in, *q.v.*
Horsington Moor (Horsington More) [in
    Horsington], Som, 812
Horsington, Richard, 2690, 3691
  Agnes wife of, 2690
Horsley (Horseley), Derb, 654, 1440
  Horsley Woodhouse and Kilburn in, *q.v.*
  Toweneson of, *q.v.*
Horsley, Long, (Horseley), Northumb, rectory, 3382
Horsley, West, (West Horseley, Westhorseley),
    Surrey, 1175, 2183
  Gough of, *q.v.*
Horsley Woodhouse (Woodhowse) [in Horsley],
    Derb, 654
Horstead (Harstead), Norf, 2691
Horsted Keynes *or* Horsted, Little, (Horsted), Sussex,
    2255
Horton, [Bucks], 3252
Horton [in Edlesborough], Bucks, 3270
Horton [in Tarvin], Ches, Aldersey of, *q.v.*
Horton, Dors, 866
  rectory, 866
Horton, Northants, Lane of, *q.v.*
Horton, Northumb, 2793
  Cowpen in, *q.v.*
Horton [in Beckley], Oxon, 2191
  manor, 2191
  Beckleye and Cubbedge of, *q.v.*
Horton, Richard, of Rochester, 550, 2245
  Thomas, clerk, 3387
  William, 2677
  Cf. Hurton
Horwell [in Severn Stoke], Worcs, 636
Horwell, Thomas, 2352
Hose, Leics, 2183, 2778
hose, manufacture of, 3572, 3706
hospitals and almshouses, foundations of, 1396, 1451
hostager for merchants strangers, appointment of,
    522
hostings. *See under* military service

Hotham (Hothome), John, ecclesiastical
    commissioner, York province, 407, 865,
    2599
  Nicholas, 1353
Hothe. *See* Hoath
Hothome. *See* Hotham
Hoton [in Prestwold], Leics, 552
Hoton. *See* Hooton; Huttons
Hottofte, John, chaplain in the Chapel Royal, rector
    presented to Paulerspury, 204
Hotton. *See* Hutton
Hough End (Haughe Inde) [in Manchester], Lancs,
    2676
Hougham (Hugham), Kent, Braddon *alias* Brydon
    Downe in, *q.v.*
Houghpark (Hoghe) [in Ashbourne], Derb, manor,
    chapel of St Mary (Glorious Virgin Mary)
    in, 206
Houghstetter, Daniel, German, 2303
Houghton (Howghton), Hants, rector presented
    to. *See* Bradford, Cuthbert
Houghton, Norf, 2691
  manor, and its bailiff, 2691
Houghton Conquest, Beds, 1347
Houghton, Glass, (Houghton), [in Castleford],
    Yorks, manor, 606
Houghton, Great, (Houton Magna), Northants, 2255
Houghton, Great, (Haughton Magna, Houghton,
    Houghton Magna), [in Darfield], Yorks,
    1424, 3492
  manor, 1424, 3492
Houghton le Spring, Durh, Herrington, East, Middle
    and West, and Offerton in, *q.v.*
Houghton, Little, (Haughton Parva), [in Darfield],
    Yorks, 3492
Houghton on the Hill (Houghton), Leics, 2182
Houghton St Giles (Houghton by Walsingham),
    Norf, 969
Houghton, Toby (Thoby), receiver general in Suffolk
    and Cambridgeshire, 394
  Cf. Hutton
Hounslow (Howndeslowe, Howneslowe, Hundesloo)
    [in Isleworth and Heston], Midd, 2619
  priory or house of friars, 1450
Hourde. *See* Hord
Hourne. *See* Horne
Hourstperpownd. *See* Hurstpierpoint
House. *See* Howes
household, queen's, 2592
  chief officers of, 482
  provision of fish for, 2888
  See also under officers, king's or queen's
Houton. *See* Houghton
Hovenden. *See* Havenden
Hovingham, Yorks, Coulton in, *q.v.*
Howard (Haward, Hawarde, Howarde, Howardes),
    Charles, lord Howard of Effingham, K.G.,
    553, 2608
  queen's servant, 3291
  Frances, countess of Surrey, 3638
  George, knight, steward of lordships and manors
    of Greenwich etc., 823
  usher of privy chamber, master of arms, 504
  John, of London, 3714
  John, [Salop], 1347
  Robert, 3529, 3533
  Thomas, duke of Norfolk, 831, 1396, 2691, 3273,
    3632, 3692
  William, John son of, 2380
  Cf. Harwarde; Haworth; Hayward

Howden (Holden, Howdan), Yorks, 2254–5, 2792,
    3656
  chantry of St John in, 2255
  chantry of St John the Baptist, 2254–5
  chapel of St Ellen (Saynte Ellyn), 2254–5
  collegiate church, 3628
    prebend of Howden in, 3627
      prebendary of. *See* Bellasis, Anthony
    prebend of Saltmarshe in, 1502
    prebend of Thorpe Belby in, 3628
  guild of St Mary, 2255
  Asselby, Barmby on the Marsh, Bromefelde,
    Cotness, Falgate, Flategate, Hailgate,
    Knedlington, Linton, Metham, Saffron
    Gate, Saltmarshe, Skelton and Yokefleet in,
    q.v.
  Newton and Scate of, *q.v.*
Howe [in Old Malton], Yorks, 2836
Howe House (Howehouse) [in Old Malton], Yorks,
    2836
Howe, John, and John, the younger, his son, 3577
  John, [Som], 222
  Nicholas, 2337
  Richard, of London, 966, 1176
  Robert, of London, 1176, 2256
  Cf. Hoo; Howes
Howell (Appowell, Hoell), David ap Res ap, 832
  David Lloyd ap, of Llanfihangel Helygen, 2910
  Griffith ap Jevan ap, *alias* Griffith Ridd, 2500
  Hugh ap, 2292
  John, and George, of London, and Samuel, his
    sons, 888
  John ap, of Beeston, 3658
  Richard, 3233, 3552
  Roger ap, vicar presented to Norton Canon, 1042
  Thomas, B.A., rector presented to Paglesham, 2904
  Thomas ap John Thomas David ap, 421
  William, 297
  See also Powell
  Cf. Hole
Howes (House, Howse), Robert, 123, 2893
  William, 567
  Cf. Hawes; Hughes
Howghton. *See* Houghton
Howke, Guy, of London, 2256
Howland, John, of London, 3382
Howlker. *See* Holker
Howlmer, George, of London, 2256
Howlyn, Francis, 2259
Howndeslowe. *See* Hounslow
Hownesfeilde. *See* Holmesfield
Howneslowe. *See* Hounslow
Howppill, William, 2734
Howsam. *See* Howsham
Howse. *See* Howes
Howsham (Howsam) [in Cadney], Lincs, 2434
  manor, 2434
Hoxton [in Shoreditch, Midd], prebendary of in St
    Paul's cathedral, London, 210
Hoy, John, of Tunstall, 1607
hoys, licence to send overseas, 18
Huband (Hubband), John, knight, 238, 256–7, 260,
    345, 1860, 1978
Hubbard (Hubbarde, Hubberd), Edward, 3052
  John, 2500
  Peter, Spanish subject, 1690
  Cf. Hobert
Hubberston (Hubbertyston), [Pemb], rector
    presented to. *See* Rogers, William
Hubbtyn, Robert, of Bristol, 2256

Hunt—*cont.*
  Zachary, rector presented to Collyweston, 1822, 3312
Hunter, John, rector presented to All Saints Pavement, York, 1028
Huntingdon, Hunts, parishes of All Saints and St Mary, 2182
  priory, 2182, 2255, 2299, 2342, 3639
Huntingdon, county, escheator in, 2392
  receiver in, 19
Huntingdon (Huntington), earl of. *See* Hastings
Huntingdon. *See* Huntington
Huntingdone Castell (*unidentified*), Corn, manor, 2872
Huntington (Huntyngton), Heref, Thomas of, *q.v.*
Huntington, English, (Huntingdon Englyshe, Huntington), [in Huntington], Heref, 836
  manor, 836
Huntington, Welsh, (Huntingdon Walshe, Huntingdon Welshe, Huntington), [in Huntington], Heref, 836
  manor, 836
Huntington. *See* Huntingdon
Huntley, George, 298–305
  Thomas, of Hadnock, 240
Hunton [in Crawley], Hants, 1188
  manor, 1188
Hunton (Huntyngdon), [Kent], rector presented to. *See* Wright, Anthony
Huntspill (Hunspill), Som, 1166, 1574
  rector presented to. *See* Hanmer, Meredith
  Withy in, *q.v.*
Huntyngdon. *See* Hunton
Huntyngton. *See* Huntington
Hunwicke, William, and Parnel his sister, 1443
Hunworth, Norf, 845
Hunys. *See* Hunnys
Hurburnford. *See* Harbertonford
Hurleston (Harleston), Richard, feodary of Cheshire, 306
  Richard, [Ches], 3405
  Richard, [Yorks], 1427, 1635, 2142–3
Hurleston. *See* Harlaxton
Hurley, Berks, 1640
Hursell, John, 1593
Hurst (Hurste), Berks, 601
  Winnersh in, *q.v.*
Hurste. *See* Hirst; Hurst
Hurstpierpoint (Hourstperpownd), Sussex, 1626
Hurton, Thomas, 3275
  Cf. Horton
Hurworth, Durh, Neasham in, *q.v.*
?Hurworth [in Trimdon], Durh, 400
Huslock, Lawrence, vicar presented to Wickwar, 1019
Hussey (Husse, Hussie, Hussye), John, ecclesiastical commissioner, York province, 2599
  John, [Lincs], and Elizabeth his wife, 2019
  Lawrence, LL.D., 2609
  Lawrence, LL.D., advocate of court of Canterbury, 2602
  Richard, 3190
  Thomas, of Topcliffe, 39
Hussington. *See* Hyssington
Hussye. *See* Hussey
Huthwaite (Hevatt) [in Whorlton], Yorks, 210
Huton. *See* Hutton
Hutson. *See* Hudson
Hutterfeilde. *See* Huddersfield
Huttoft (Heytoft), Lincs, 966

Hutton (Hooton) [in Kendal], Westm, manor and park, 3381
Hutton Cranswick (Hooton Crancewick, Hooton Crancewicke, Hootton Cranswick, Hotton Crancewicke), Yorks, 821, 3266
  rectory and vicar of, 821
Hutton Henry (Huton) [in Monk Hesleden], Durh, Cooper of, *q.v.*
Hutton in the Forest, Cumb, Morton in, *q.v.*
Hutton in the Hay (Hutton Hey) [in Kendal], Westm, 537
Hutton Rudby (Hutton) [in Rudby], Yorks, 210
Hutton, Sand, (Sandehutton, Sandhuton) [in Bossall], Yorks, 3286
  grange, 2836
Hutton, Sand, (Sandhooton), [in Thirsk], Yorks, 2181
Hutton, Sheriff, (Sherif Hutton, Sherifhoton, Sherifhutton), Yorks, castle, 597, 1366
  lordship, 1420, 3687
  Farlington in, *q.v.*
Hutton Wandesley (Huton) [in Long Marston], Yorks, 3500
Hutton, John, 2608, 3051, 3073–4
  Joshua, vicar presented to Reculver, 150
  Matthew, 3022
  Matthew, D.D., dean of York, 2599, 3730
  Cf. Hatton; Houghton
Hutton. *See* Hatton
Huttons Ambo (Hoton on Darwent), Yorks, 2301
Huxham Green (Huckesham) [in East Pennard], Som, 1239
Huyck, Thomas, LL.D., master of Chancery, and Dr Huyck his brother, 948
  Cf. Hicke
Huyde. *See* Hyde
Huyschampflower. *See* Huish
Hyams. *See* Highams
Hyatt. *See* Hyett
Hybaulstowe. *See* Hibaldstow
Hycheborne, Thomas, and Helen his wife, 947
Hycke. *See* Hicke
Hyckford (Hyckeford), Henry, 2987–8, 3080
  John, 2968, 3072
  Cf. Highford
Hyckman, Walter, 2213
Hyckmote, Anthony, 2249
Hydan (Hydon) in Castle Caereinion, Mont, 210
  chapel called 'le Palmant', 210
Hyde [in Great Missenden], Bucks, 3270
Hyde [?in South Damerham], Wilts, 3713
Hyde (Hide, Huyde, Hyed), George, 3130
  Gilbert, and Eleanor his wife, 2441
  John, and Jane his wife, 2485
  Lawrence, 3079
  Lawrence, [Dors], 1929, 3620
  Lawrence, [Wilts], 235
  Richard, 83, 1279
    Elizabeth wife of, 1279
  Thomas, M.A., rector presented to Saddington, 146
    vicar presented to Marston St Lawrence, 147
  William, [Berks], 1329
  William, [Bucks], 2687
Hyde. *See* Hide
Hydes, Geoffrey, 210
Hydon. *See* Hinton; Hydan
Hyed. *See* Hyde
Hyett (Hyatt), Dorothy, daughter of Richard Walwyn, 2139
  John, and Margaret his wife, 2737

I

J

K

Knolton. *See* Knowlton
Knook (Knooke, Knowke), Wilts, 1675, 2796
  manor, 2796
Knottesforde, Thomas, 3251
Knowke. *See* Knook
Knowle (Knowlle) [in Sevenoaks], Kent, park, 3636
Knowle, Church, (Knoll), Dors, 3713
Knowles. *See* Knollys
Knowlle. *See* Knowle
Knowlls. *See* Knollys
Knowlton (Knolton) [in Woodlands], Dors, 866
Knoyle, West, (Knoyle), Wilts, 1995
Knyfton. *See* Knyveton
Knyght. *See* Knight
Knyghtcote. *See* Nightcott
Knyghte. *See* Knight
Knyghtley. *See* Knightley
Knyghton. *See* Knighton
Knylmyngton. *See* Kilmington
Knyvet. *See* Knyvett
Knyveton (Knyfton), John, 611
  Thomas, 3002
  Thomas, [Derb], 1896, 1899
  Thomas, [Notts], 206, 611
  William, 1297
Knyveton. *See* Kniveton
Knyvett (Knevett, Knevitt, Knyvet), Edmund, of
    Buckenham Castle, bailiff, collector and
    receiver of Barking manor, bailiff, collector
    and surveyor of repairs of marshes between
    Bow Bridge and Mucking, 182
  Henry, knight, [Wilts], 3183, 3492
    Elizabeth wife of, 3492
    queen's servant, 1424, 1452
    steward of Galtres forest, 1452
  Henry, [Wilts], and Elizabeth his wife, 617–8, 952,
    970, 1680
  J., 1452
  Richard, 210
  Thomas, groom of privy chamber, 568, 1449, 2309
    steward of five Cumberland manors and clerk of
    courts thereof, 1449
  Thomas, knight, 1684
  William, 617
Kregennan. *See* Crogenen
Krigau. *See* Crugau
Kukby. *See* Kirby
Kydd, John, 1194, 1267–76
Kyddall, John, of South Ferriby, 3666
Kydford. *See* Wisborough
Kydmer. *See* Keymer
Kydwelley, Kydwellye, Kydwelly. *See* Kidwelly
Kyffdy. *See* Cyffty
Kyghley. *See* Kightley
Kylham. *See* Killam
Kylkenny (Kelkenny), Andrew, 3600
Kyllerbye. *See* Killerby
Kylnewicke, Kylnewyck. *See* Kilnwick
Kylpecke. *See* Kilpeck
Kylsaen. *See* Cil-san *alias* Gwestfa Cil-san
Kymbalton. *See* Kimbolton
Kyme, Lincs, monastery, 831

Kyme. *See* Keyme
Kympsey. *See* Kempsey
Kympton, William, alderman of London, 123, 2256
Kympton. *See* Kimpton
Kynaston, Francis, 3059
  Francis, [Salop], 2820
  Roger, 951
Kyndon, John, 2711, 3515
Kynewicke. *See* Kilnwick
Kyng, Kynge. *See* Kinge
Kyngesberye. *See* Kingsbury
Kyngesbridge. *See* Kingsbridge
Kyngesclere. *See* Kingsclere
Kyngesmyll. *See* Kingesmyll
Kyngesnothe. *See* Kingsnorth
Kyngeston, Kyngestonne. *See* Kingston
Kyngeswood. *See* Kingswood
Kyngsland. *See* Kingsland
Kyngsmyll. *See* Kingesmyll
Kyngston. *See* Kingston
Kyngstone. *See* Kingston
Kyngton. *See* Keinton; Kineton; Kington
Kyngwardeston, Kyngweston. *See* Kingweston
Kynlett. *See* Kinlet
Kynley. *See* Kinley
Kynmarkez. *See* St Kynemark
Kynner. *See* Cymmer
Kynnersley. *See* Kinnersley
Kynsham. *See* Eynsham
Kynsill. *See* Kinsall
Kyntbury, Kyntburye. *See* Kintbury
Kynvell. *See* Cynfal
Kynvill (*unidentified*), Carn, chapel, 2878
Kynyerd Meade [in Glastonbury], Som, 2195
Kyplyn. *See* Kiplin
Kyrbye. *See* Kirby; Kirkby
Kyre, Little, [in Stoke Bliss], Worcs, manor,
    2462
Kyrkblyfletham. *See* Kirkby
Kyrkby, Kyrkbye. *See* Kirby; Kirkby
Kyrkbymoreside. *See* Kirkby Moorside
Kyrke. *See* Kirke
Kyrkeborne. *See* Kirkburn
Kyrkebryde, Richard, 613
Kyrkeby. *See* Kirkby
Kyrkebybellers, Kyrkebye. *See* Kirby
Kyrkebyfletham. *See* Kirkby
Kyrkedale. *See* Kirkdale
Kyrkham. *See* Kirkham
Kyrkybedon. *See* Kirby
Kyrll. *See* Kirle
Kyrnyngton. *See* Kirmington
Kyrstall. *See* Kirkstall
Kyrton. *See* Crediton
Kyrwyn. *See* Curwen
Kysewin. *See* Ceuswyn
Kytchen (Ketchyn), John, 295
  Robert, of Bristol, 2256
Kythermyster. *See* Kidderminster
Kytson. *See* Kitson
Kyttes, William, 3259
Kyvernoe, Kyvernowe. *See* Kivernoll

L

Laborne, Anne, Robert and Simon, 3272
  Thomas, justice of peace in Norfolk, 2241
Labron. *See* Leyburn

Laceby (Lasbe), [Lincs], rector presented to. *See*
  Bradley, William
Lacford. *See* Lackford

M

Mounstrell.   *See* Mountsorrel
Mount Grace (Mountegrace, Mountgrace) [in East
    Harlsey], Yorks, monastery, 206, 210, 3605
Mount St John (Mount St John the Baptist, St John,
    St John on the Mount) [in Felixkirk], Yorks,
    preceptory, 210, 1353, 3276, 3379, 3690
Mountague, lord, 2004
Mountague (Mountagu), Edward, knight *alias*
    esquire, 417, 1458, 1889
Mountague.   *See* Montacute; Montague
Mounteagle.   *See* Monteagle
Mountegewe.   *See* Montacute
Mountegle.   *See* Monteagle
Mountegrace, Mountgrace.   *See* Mount Grace
Mountjoy in Haveringland, Norf, priory, 2688
Mountjoy (Mountjoye), lord.   *See* Blount
Mountjoy (Mountjoye), Philip, and Margaret his
    wife, 3291
Mountpellers (*unidentified*), Cambs, manor, 1318
Mountsorrel (Mounstrell, Mountsorell) [in Barrow
    upon Soar and Rothley], Leics, 2803
Mowden Hall (Muckedenhaule, Mugdenhaule) [in
    Hatfield Peverel], Essex, manor, 2889
Mowle, Lawrence, of London, 1598
Mowlton.   *See* Moulton
Mowse, William, LL.D., canon or prebendary of
    Halloughton in Southwell collegiate
    church, 1105
    Cf. Muse
Mowsey, Christopher, 3466
Mowthorpe [in Terrington], Yorks, Welborne of, *q.v.*
Mowyer, John, rector presented to Bagendon, 1091
Moyle, John, 1940
    Leonard, sewer of chamber, 1527
    Thomas ap Llewelin, 832
    Walter, 1295
Moyser, Lawrence, chief burgess of Richmond, 2197
Moyses, Robert, and Ingram his son, 3557
Muchelney (Mochelmer, Mochelney), Som, manor
    and rectory, 52
    monastery, 1371
Muchland (Muchlande) [in Aldingham and Urswick],
    Lancs, 3611
    lordship, 3252, 3611
Muckedenhaule.   *See* Mowden Hall
Muckhall.   *See* Monk Hall
Mucking (Mockinge Milles), Essex, 182
Mugdenhaule.   *See* Mowden Hall
Mugginton (Muggenton), Derb, chantry, 206
Muggleswick (Muggleswick in Lancaster,
    Muggleswicke), Durh, 2254–5
Muldridge, Muldrigge.   *See* Mouldridge
Mullens (Mollens, Mullyns), John, fellow of Christ's
    college, Manchester, 2676
    Michael, 3068
    Thomas, 3039
    William, Spanish subject, 743
Mullet, John, 2072
Mullyneux.   *See* Molyneux
Mullyns.   *See* Mullens
Mulshoo, Mulso.   *See* Moulsoe
Mulsop (Mulsoppe) [in Worthen], Salop, 2723
Multon.   *See* Moulton
Mulwith (Malwath) [in Ripon], Yorks, 2907
Mundaye.   *See* Mondaye
Mundon (Munden), Essex, 2453
Munke.   *See* Monke
Munslow (Mounslowe), Salop, 1347
    Hungerford in, *q.v.*
Munson.   *See* Mounson

Munster (Monster), Ireland, province, president
    of.   *See* Drury, William
Murcott (Morcote, Morecott) in Charlton on
    Otmoor, Oxon, Bonner and Pyme of, *q.v.*
Mursley (Moresley, Muresley), Bucks, 1347
Murton [in Dalton le Dale], Durh, Palmes of, *q.v.*
Murton [in Appleby St Michael], Westm, Blenkerne
    of, *q.v.*
Musbury (Musburye), Devon, 1620
Muscam.   *See* Muskham
Muschampe (Muschamp), Christopher, baron of
    Exchequer, 3669
    Edmund, 2768
    William, 1224
Muse, Elizabeth, of Horsham St Faith, 2841
    Cf. Mowse
Musgrave (Musgrove), Bartholomew, gunner in
    Carlisle castle, 2628
    Edward, 1497
    Simon, knight *alias* esquire, 1431, 2599, 3005
    William, 3005
    William, of Headingley, 2921
music, men and boys skilled in, 2676
    service in art of, 471, 2323
Muskham, North *or* South, (Muscam), Notts, 2687
Mussenden, James, and Helen his wife and Richard
    his son, 3462
Musterd (Musted), Richard, 3524
    Thomas, 831
musters, grant of power to take, 1412
Mustion (Mustian, Mustyan), Fulk, 3614
    John, of West Ham, 610
Muston (*unidentified*) in Leake, Lincs, chantry, 3608
Muston.   *See* Marston
Mustwire.   *See* Mwstwr
Mustyan.   *See* Mustion
Muswell Hill (Muswell *alias* Muswell Chappell) [in
    Hornsey], Midd, 1555, 2115
    manor, 1555, 2115
Mutley, George, vicar presented to Shustoke, 1089
    Cf. Motley
Mutton Mill (Mutton Myll) [in Botusfleming], Corn,
    2337
Muyth.   *See* Mythe
Mwstwr (Mustwire) in Corwen, Merion, 2255
Mychelholme (*unidentified*), Leics, 920
Mychell.   *See* Michell
Mychendhame, Mychenhame, Mychyndy.   *See*
    Newhaven
Myckfeild.   *See* Mickfield
Mydden Hall.   *See* Mildenhall
Myddlecott.   *See* Middlecott
Myddleton.   *See* Middleton
Mydgeley, Robert, and John his son, 2005
Mydleton.   *See* Middleton
Mydlewyche.   *See* Middlewich
Myers, Christopher, 1994
    Walter, of London, and Marion his wife, 1994
Myes, John, 855
Mygeham.   *See* Midgham
Mylborne.   *See* Milborne; Milbourne
Myldemaye.   *See* Mildmay
Myldenhall.   *See* Mildenhall
Myldmay, Myldmaye, Myldmey.   *See* Mildmay
Myle.   *See* Mile
Myleham.   *See* Mileham
Mylende.   *See* Mile End
Mylford, William, of London, 2256
Myll, Mylle.   *See* Milles
Myller.   *See* Miller

Northill—*cont.*
    Northwell, Northyell), Beds, 933, 1317,
        1354, 1554
  advowson of vicarage, 933
  church, St Mary's college in, 1317
  manor, 933, 1317, 1554
  rectory, 933, 1554
  Beeston, Caldecote, Caldecote, Lower and Upper,
    Hatch, Ickwell and Thorncote in, *q.v.*
Northill (*unidentified*), Yorks, 1359
Northkelsey. *See* Kelsey
Northkilvington. *See* Kilvington
Northleach (Northelache, Northlache), Glos, 831
  manor, 3290
  Eastington in, *q.v.*
  Parker of, *q.v.*
Northleverton. *See* Leverton
Northlew (Norlewe, Northlewe), [Devon], rector
  of. *See* Curtis, John
  rector presented to. *See* Phillipps, Richard
Northlewerton. *See* Leverton
Northleys. *See* Lees
Northload (Northlode) [in Wedmore], Som, 2179
Northmerston. *See* Marston
Northmolton. *See* Molton
Northottrington. *See* Otterington
Northpevor. *See* Peover
Northpickenham. *See* Pickenham
Northroade, Northrode. *See* Rode
Northroughton. *See* Ructon
Northshowburie. *See* Shoebury
Northskerlaughe. *See* Skirlaugh
Northstainley. *See* Stainley
Northstocke. *See* Stoke
Norththickham (*unidentified*), Lincs, 1571
Northtuddenham. *See* Tuddenham
Northtudworth. *See* Tidworth
Northumberland, county, auditor of, 2879
  escheator in, 2386, 2525, 2530
  feodary of. *See* Lawson, John
  receiver in, 464, 2879. *See also* Clopton, John
  surveyor and viewer of, 2879
Northumberland, duke of. *See* Dudley
Northumberland, earls of. *See* Percy
Northvell. *See* Northill
Northwalsham. *See* Walsham
Northway (Northey) [in Ashchurch], Glos, 1350,
    2735–7
  Cole of, *q.v.*
Northwell. *See* Northill
Northwey. *See* Northway
Northwickam. *See* Witham
Northwood. *See* North Wood; Rode
Northyell. *See* Northill
Norton (Norton Dawney) [in Townstall], Devon, 900
  manor, 900
Norton, Herts, 2488, 2816
Norton, Kent, Fynche of, *q.v.*
Norton (Norton by Daventre), Northants, manor
  (Mantells Manner), 1326
Norton, Suff, 3431
Norton, Wilts, 2012
Norton (Norton near Malton), Yorks, rectory, 2260
  Welham in, *q.v.*
Norton (*unidentified*), prior of, 2183
Norton Bavant (Norton Bavent), Wilts, 2192
  rectory, 2192
Norton Canon (Norton), [Heref], vicar presented
  to. *See* Howell, Roger ap
Norton Conyers [in Wath], Yorks, Norton of, *q.v.*

Norton, East, (Estnorton), Leics, 2803, 3386
  advowson of free chapel, 2803
Norton Ferris (Norton Ferrers) [in Kilmington,
    Wilts], *formerly in* Som, manor, 812
Norton Fitzwarren, [Som], rector presented to. *See*
  Canham, Simon
Norton in Hales (Norton), Salop, 3479
Norton juxta Kempsey (Norton), Worcs, 1633
  Newlands in, *q.v.*
Norton, Kings, (Kinges Norton, Kynges Norton),
    [Warw], *formerly in* Worcs, 3447
  Monyhull and Moseley in, *q.v.*
Norton, ?Lower, (Chymney Norton, Norton), [in
    East Allington], Devon, 3449
  manor, 3449–50
Norton St Philip (Norton, Phillipes Norton, Phillips
    Norton), Som, 869, 2554, 3594
  manor, 3594
  Tovy of, *q.v.*
Norton, Wood, (Woodnorton), Norf, 2691
Norton, Edmund, 208, 419, 658
  Edward, 2612
  Elizabeth, 429
  Francis, of Baldersby, 39
  Francis, [Yorks], 2907
  George, knight, 245–6, 362
  Henry, 1938
  John, 3414
  Richard, knight, and Catherine his wife, 1174
  Richard, of Hartforth, and Francis his son, 400
  Richard, of Norton Conyers, 39
  Richard, [Hants], 1174
  Richard, [Surrey], and Catherine his wife, 3456
  Richard, [Yorks], 210, 419, 2181, 3379
  Roger, 2046
  Thomas, [Midd], 210
  Thomas, [Yorks], 1427, 1635, 2142–3
  William, of Hartforth, 39
  William, [Durh], 2576
  William, [Salop], 218
  William, [Salop], (*another*), 619, 3197
  William, [Yorks], 2181
Norwich (Norwiche), bishopric, bishops of, 213,
    1396. *See also* Freake, Edmund; Parkhurst,
    John
  chancellor of, 213, 2606
  commissioners for ecclesiastical causes in, 213, 2606
  levying of arrears of tenths and subsidies in, 2627
  receiver of, 213
  registrars of, 213, 2606. *See also* Alcocke,
    Anthony; Andrews, Thomas
  seal of, 213, 2606
Norwich (Norwiche), Norf, 449, 1464, 2867
  aldermen (*named*) of, 449
  cathedral, 2609
    canons or prebendaries in. *See* Tedmonde,
      Thomas; Thexton, Lancelot; Toy, Griffith;
      Whitakers, William
    canon or prebendary presented to. *See*
      Downes, Robert
    dean of, 213, 2606
  collegiate church or free chapel of Holy Trinity,
    canons or prebendaries in. *See* Castleton,
      Hugh; Fenton, William
  episcopal palace, 2609
  gaol called le Shirehouse (le Sherehouse, le
    Sherehowse), 1614, 2232
    sessions of peace in, 2840, 2929, 3399
  guildhall, sessions of peace at, 1464, 2867
  hospital of Normans or of St Paul, 2180

O

P

Q

R

Rotherveld. *See* Rotherfield
Rothewell. *See* Rothwell
Rothingden. *See* Rottingdean
Rothley, Leics, Chadwell, Mountsorrel and Wycombe
in, *q.v.*
Rothwell (Rothewell), Lincs, 901
manor, 901
Greene of, *q.v.*
Rothwell, Northants, chantry or chapel, 206
Rotsey, Anthony, [Bucks], 2269
Anthony, [Devon], 674
Anthony, [Heref], 3258
Anthony, [Worcs], 1347
Rottingdean (Rodding Deane near Brightelmeston,
Rothingden, Rottingdene), Sussex, 1576,
2255, 2299
Balsdean in, *q.v.*
Roue. *See* Rowe
Rounton, East, (Easte Rounton, Estrounton) in
Rudby in Cleveland, Yorks, 206, 3379
Rounton, West, (Westeroungton, Westrington,
Westwoughton), Yorks, 210, 2621
rector presented to. *See* Greene, Christopher
Route, Ireland, river, 3412
Routh (Rowthe), Yorks, 831, 3379
Rouyhedd, Richard, of London, assistant and chief
councillor of fellowship of merchants of
Spain and Portugal, 2256
Rowden (Rowdon) [in Chippenham], Wilts, 3181
manor, 3181
Rowdon, John, of Steeple Langford, 530
Rowdon. *See* Rowden
Rowe (Roo, Roue), Anthony, auditor of Exchequer,
1535, 2223, 2851
Anthony, [London], and Audrey his wife,
2026
Anthony, [Yorks], 1387, 1450
Audrey wife and Edward son of, 1450
David, 2583
Richard, 3658
William, of London, 123, 1555
Cf. Rawe
Rowed, Richard, of London, 2256
Rowell. *See* Roel
Rowington, Warw, 874
Rowland, Thomas, of Bristol, 2256
Rowlandevy. *See* Rhuddlan Deifi
Rowlerighte. *See* Rollright
Rowles. *See* Rolles
Rowlett, Ralph, knight, 2051
Rowley [in Lanchester], Durh, 429
Rowley, Yorks, 43
Hunsley in, *q.v.*
Brown of, *q.v.*
Rowley, Francis, of Bristol, 2256
Richard, 317
Cf. Rawley
Rowley. *See* Rewley
Rowll. *See* Rolle
Rowse (Rowsse), John, of Kings Lynn, 2241
John, [Devon], 1875
Reginald, 116
Cf. Prowse; Roos; Rose; Ruse
Rowses Hill (*unidentified*), Devon, 2479
Rowshforde. *See* Rushford
Rowsley, Little, (Little Rollysley), [in Darley], Derb,
352
Rowsse. *See* Rowse
Rowsworth. *See* Rushford
Rowthe. *See* Routh

Rowton (Rowton in North Skarley) [in Swine],
Yorks, 210, 3379
Roxby cum Risby, Lincs, Risby and Sawcliffe in,
q.v.
Roxton [in Immingham], Lincs, 889
Roy, William, 2714
Roydon, [Essex], vicar presented to. *See* Glasse,
John
Roydon (Roidon) [in Diss hundred, Norf], *formerly in*
Suff, manor, 2297
Roydon (Rydon) [in Freebridge hundred], Norf,
advowson of rectory, 2691
Roydon Hall. *See* Fortune
Roydon, John, 3060
Royston, Herts, 1407, 2484
free chapel or hospital of St James and St John
and manor, 1407
Hall of, *q.v.*
Royston (Ruston), Yorks, 206
church, 206
Bretton, Monk, Chevet, Cudworth, Lower, and
Notton in, *q.v.*
Royton [in Lenham], Kent, 1259
Rozeaw *alias* Deblock, Francis, Spanish subject, 721
Rrav. *See* Rhiw
Ruckinge (Ruckinges), Kent, 628
Rudby (Rydby), Yorks, 210,
church, 206
Hutton Rudby, Middleton upon Leven and
Rounton, East, in, *q.v.*
Rudd (Rudde), John, rector of Romaldkirk, 2634
Robert, *alias* Robert Harlewyn, of Little Fransham,
2844
William, 3066
William, deputy feodary of Northamptonshire, 270,
281, 331, 356, 379–80, 1874, 1889, 1949
feodary of Northamptonshire, 102
William, [Northants], 278, 377
Ruddall. *See* Rudhale
Rudde. *See* Rudd
Ruddinges, John, [Leics], 673
John, [Northants], 3251
Cf. Ruding
Ruddington (Redyngton, Rodyngdon), Notts, 2922
chantry, 1347
Ingram, Lowe and Redferne of, *q.v.*
Rudehale. *See* Rudhale
Rudge [in Crediton], Devon, 930
Rudge [in Froxfield], Wilts, 2020
Rudgeway, Thomas, 1927
Rudhale (Ruddall, Rudehale), William, 2452, 2461,
2720
Rudham, East, [Easte Rudham, Easterudham,
Eastrudham, Estrudham], Norf, 2691
church, 2691
manor and its bailiff, 2691
rectory, advowson of vicarage and vicar of, 2691
Broomsthorpe and Coxford in, *q.v.*
Rudham, West, (Westrudham), Norf, 2691
church, rectory and advowson of vicarage, 2691
Ruding, Walter, keeper of houses of upper bailiwick
etc. in Windsor castle, 473
Cf. Ruddinges
Rudloe (Ridlowe) [in Box], Wilts, 1592
Rudston, John, 283
Rug (Reege, Rhike, Ruge) [in Llanrug], Carn, 2252,
3715
Rugg, John, M.A., canon or prebendary of St Peter's,
Westminster, 495
Ruley. *See* Rewley

Rumbles Moor (Rumbalde) [in Bingley and Ilkley], Yorks, Smytheson of, *q.v.*

Rumboll, James, 3559

Rumney. *See* Romney

Runckhorne, Alexander, 1195

Runcorn, Ches, Aston by Sutton in, *q.v.*

Runcton, North, (Northroughton), Norf, 3187 manor, 3187

Rundell, John, 1624

Ruse, Ciriack, 2626, 3403
William, and Ciris, of Grays Inn, his son, 2608
Cf. Roos; Rose; Rowse

Rusham. *See* Earsham

Rushbrooke, Suff, 2483

Rushden (Rusheden), [Northants], rector presented to, *See* Peake, Richard

Rushe, Anthony, canon or prebendary in St George's chapel, Windsor, 2266
Anthony, [Suff], 1840

Rusheden. *See* Rushden

Rusheholme. *See* Rushulme

Rushen. *See* Amwell

Rushford (Rowshforde, Rowsworth), [Norf] *formerly in* Suff, 2087

Rushock (Rosshock) [in Kington], Heref, 836

Rusholme [in Drax], Yorks, 573

Rushton (Risheton) [in Tarporley], Ches, 3684

Rushton, Tarrant, (Rushton), Dors, 3713

Rushulme (Risheholme, Rusheholme) [in Manchester], Lancs, 602, 2676

Ruskington (Riskington), Lincs, 2786

Russell, Bartholomew, clerk of crown and of common pleas and keeper of writs and rolls in Queen's Bench of Ireland, 1532
Charles, 1372
Christopher, of Swords, clerk of crown and of common pleas and keeper of writs and rolls in Queen's Bench of Ireland, 1532
Francis, earl of Bedford, 406, 936, 1568, 2024, 2075, 2123–4, 2129, 2806
councillor, 124, 2191, 2282, 2608, 3688
Bridget wife of, 2806
Francis, knight, 119, 572
John, knight, lord Russell, earl of Bedford, 2282, 2608
John, marshal of household, 2593
John, [Glos], 1660
John, [Surrey], 2363
Thomas, of London, 2256

Russhen. *See* Amwell

Rust, Edward, 2761

Rustat, William, master or warden presented to hospital of St John, Lutterworth, 1534

Rustington, Sussex, Preston, West, in, *q.v.*

Ruston Parva (Ruston, Rustone), Yorks, 831, 2476

Ruston, Sco', (Scoruston), [Norf], 1173
rectory and advowson of vicarage, 1173

Ruston. *See* Riston; Royston

Rustone. *See* Ruston

Ruswarp (Riswarpe) in Whitby, Yorks, 1347, 1440

Rutherland. *See* Rhuddlan

Ruthin (Ruthyn), Denb, church and college of St Peter, 2564

Ruthland. *See* Rhuddlan

Ruthyn. *See* Ruthin

Rutland, county, auditor of, 2512
receiver general in. *See* Grey, Andrew

Rutland (Ruttland), earls of, 2182, 2344. *See also* Manners

Rutter, Robert, 36

Ruttey, Philip, Spanish subject, 799

Ruttland. *See* Rutland

Ruyn Wartha. *See* Penwartha

Ryall. *See* Ryhall

Rycarbye, John, of London, 2256

Ryccarde. *See* Richard

Ryccardes. *See* Richardes

Ryce. *See* Rees

Rychard. *See* Richard

Rychardson. *See* Richardson

Ryche. *See* Rich

Rychefeld, Thomas, 368

Rychemond, Rychmond. *See* Richmond

Ryckthorne. *See* Rickthorne

Ryd Bryw. *See* Rhydybriw

Rydby. *See* Rudby

Rydcar. *See* Redcar

Rydeo, Gilbert, 3714

Rydinge. *See* Riding

Rydley. *See* Ridley

Rydnoll. *See* Wribbenhall

Rydon. *See* Roydon

Rydulphe, Francis, 3430

Rydynge. *See* Riding

Rye, Sussex, 1231. 2688
fletchers or archers of. *See* Bonyard, Robert; Hunt, George

Rye, river, 1167

rye. *See under* corn

Ryfam. *See* Reepham

Rygbye, Alexander, 3119–20

Ryghton. *See* Reighton

Ryhall (Ryall), Rut, *formerly also in* Lincs, 2180
guildhall, 2180
Belmesthorpe in, *q.v.*

Ryhill [in Burstwick], Yorks, 348

Rylah (Ryley) [in Scarcliffe], Derb, 1331

Ryland (Riland, Rylaund), Nicholas, and John his son, 3135
William, yeoman waiter in Tower of London, 3702

Ryley (*unidentified*), Derb, 352

Ryley. *See* Riley; Rylah

Ryllyngton. *See* Rillington

Rylstone (Rilston) [in Burnsall], Yorks, lordship, 3379

Ryman, Humphrey, 1347

Rynglethorpe. *See* Goldsmith

Ryngmere. *See* Ringmer

Ryngsted. *See* Ringstead

Rypley. *See* Ripley; Ripple

Ryppe, William, 3105

Ryppon. *See* Ripon

Rypyngton. *See* Repington

Rysam. *See* Riseholme

Rysdon. *See* Rysedon

Ryse, Nicholas, subject of duke of Cleves, 738

Ryse. *See* Rees

Rysedon (Rysdon), Thomas, 2715, 2718, 2722, 2728

Rysegrene. *See* Rise Green

Ryseley. *See* Riseley

Rysingdon. *See* Rissington

Rysinge. *See* Rising

Rysington. *See* Rissington

Ryskyns, William, subject of duke of Cleves, 720

Rysley, William, 902

Rysom. *See* Riseholme

Rysome (Risome in Holdernes) [in Hollym], Yorks, 1364

Rysyn, Nicholas, 1347

Rythe. *See* Rithe

S

Shaftesbury—*cont.*
    church of St Peter, rector presented to. *See*
        Lawrence, Thomas
    monastery, 1348, 2254, 3713
    abbess, abbot, prior or prioress of, 1348
Shaftoe, East *or* West, (Shaftowe), [in Hartburn],
      Northumb, 2258
Shafton. *See* Shaftesbury
Shaftoo, John, 86
Shaftowe. *See* Shaftoe
Shaftysburye. *See* Shaftesbury
Shakelton (Shakylton), Francis, rector presented to St
      Mildred in the Poultry, London, 1008
    William, the elder, and William, the younger, 888
Shakerley [in Leigh], Lancs, Shakerley of, *q.v.*
Shakerley, Peter, of Shakerley, Geoffrey, of Beeston,
      son of, 181
    Rowland, the elder, and Ralph his son and
      Rowland, the younger, and Anne, Ralph's
      children, 2533
Shakylton. *See* Shakelton
Shalbourne (Shalborne), Wilts, 929
    manor, 929
    Bagshot in, *q.v.*
    Chock of, *q.v.*
Shalcrosse, Hugh, 2676
Shalfleet (Shalfleete, Shalflete), Isle of Wight, Hants,
      2093
    manor and advowson of church, 2093
    rectory, 2193
Shalford (Shalforde), Essex, manor, 3685
Shalford. *See* Brimpton Court
Shalstone (Shalston), Bucks, 2346
    church, 2346
Shamborne. *See* Shernborne
Shapearrowe, John, rector presented to Shernborne,
      1761
Shappey, Robert, of Bristol, 2256
Shapwick (Shapwicke), Dors, 3153
    rectory, 1500
    Hemsworth, West, in, *q.v.*
Shapwick (Shapwicke, Shoppwick), Som, 1570, 1574
    manor, 1570
    vicar presented to. *See* Barnes, John
Shardlowe, John, 1222
Sharington. *See* Sharrington
Sharlston [in Warmfield and Wragby], Yorks, 3379
Sharnbrook (Sharnebrooke, Shernebroke), Beds, 831
    rectory, 3251
    vicar presented to. *See* Cosyn, Richard
Sharneborne. *See* Sherborne
Sharnebrooke. *See* Sharnbrook
Sharnford (Sharnforde), Leics, 2299
Sharow (Sharoe, Sharrowe) [in Ripon], Yorks, 2907,
      3379
Sharpe, Hugh, 3386
    Thomas, 2998
Sharpenhoe (Sharpenhoo) in Streatley, Beds, 2687
    chapel of St Giles, 2687
Sharpricks (Sharprickes, Shurpryckes) [in Boldre],
      Hants, 1440
    manor of, and South Baddesley, 1313
Sharpshaw (Sharpshawe) [in Nunney], Som, 2427
Sharrington (Sharington, Sheryngton), Norf, 905–6,
      1285, 2108
Sharrock (Sharrocke, Sherrock), James, 3039
    James, feodary of Dorset, 1883, 1900, 1929
    James, [Dors], 1185
    Cf. Shorrocke
Sharrowe. *See* Sharow

Shaston. *See* Shaftesbury
Shavington [in Moreton Say], Salop, 2033
Shaw (Shawe), Berks, 1238, 1657, 2004, 2126
    advowson of church, 1238, 1657
    manor, 1238, 1657, 2126, 2141
Shaw (Shawe), [Wilts], rector presented to. *See*
      Watkins, Thomas
Shaw Grange (Grange) [in Shaw cum Donnington],
      Berks, manor, 2004
Shawbury (Shabry, Shabrye, Shawbery), Salop, 206
    chapel, 2297
    church, 206
Shawe (Shaa), Christopher, of Cleadon, 39
    Francis, of London, 2256
    George, vicar presented to Bayton, 1787B
    Henry, 3130
    Thomas, 846
    Thurston, vicar presented to Stonehouse, 26
Shaxton, Francis, justice of peace in Norfolk, 2241
Shearsby (Shemesbye, Shesbye) [in Knaptoft], Leics,
      2621
Shebbear (Shebbeare), Devon, 187
Sheddon Hall (Shedinghoo, Shyddinghoo) [in
      Mistley], Essex, manor, 2454
Sheen (Shene) *alias* Richmond, Surrey, 2688
    church, 2688
    keeper of wardrobe at. *See* Snowe, Nicholas
    priory, 206, 603, 823, 1353, 1542, 2269, 3251
    queen's great clocks at, keepers of. *See* Burges,
      Thomas; Urcean, Nicholas
Sheep Park (Shepe Parke) in Aldingham, Lancs, 3611
    sheep, theft of. *See under* pardons
sheepskins, export of, 3701
Sheepy Parva, Leics, Moor Barns in, *q.v.*
Sheet (Shete) in Petersfield, Hants, 552
Sheffeilde. *See* Sheffield
Sheffeld (Sheffelde), lady Anne and Robert, 2542
Sheffield (Sheffelde) [in Burghfield], Berks, 2817
    manor, 2817
Sheffield (Sheffeilde, Sheffelde, Sheffielde, Sheiffield,
      Sheiffielde), Yorks, 37, 1353, 2907
    Ecclesall and Sheffield Lodge and Park in, *q.v.*
    Wigeley of, *q.v.*
Sheffield Lodge (Sheiffield Lodge) in Sheffield, Yorks,
      37
Sheffield Park (Sheffeilde Parke) [in Sheffield], Yorks,
      Baldwyn of, *q.v.*
Shefford [in Campton], Beds, Cramfelde of, *q.v.*
Shefford, East, (Est Shefford), Berks, 2082
Shefford, West, Berks, 2082
Sheiffield, Sheiffielde. *See* Sheffield
Sheinton (Sheynton), Salop, Amners Grounde in, 674
Sheldon, Ralph, [Salop], 1178
    Ralph, [Worcs], 242, 353, 1922, 3139
    William, of Abberton, 2765, 3150
    William, of Wadborough, and Elizabeth his wife,
      2765, 3150
    William, [Glos], 2017
    Cf. Shelton
Sheldwich (Shelwiche), Kent, 2717
Shelford, Little, (Shelford Parva), Cambs, 2001, 2180,
      3179
    manor, 2001
Shell Haven [in Corringham], Essex, 2178
Shelley, Suff, 2359
    rectory, 3592
Shelley, Edward, and Henry son of Henry his son,
      1115
    John, [Kent], 1295, 2135, 2790
    John, [Sussex], 3673

Stonegrave (Stangrave), [Yorks], rector presented
    to. *See* Mawdesley, Thomas
Stonehall [in Barking], Essex, manor, 3530
Stoneham. *See* Stonham
Stonehouse (Stonehowse), Devon, 1340
  manor and town, lord of. *See* Edgcombe, Peter
  market and fair, 1340
Stonehouse, [Glos], vicar presented to. *See* Shawe,
    Thurston
Stonehouse, George, queen's servant, 2872
Stonehurst (Stonehurste) [in Boarstall], Bucks, 2191
Stonehurst (Stonyhurst) [in Waterperry], Oxon,
    2250
Stoneleigh (Stanley, Stoneley, Stonely, Stonley),
    Warw, 2810, 2812, 3455
  almshouse of Thomas Leigh, knight, and its
    wardens, 1451
  church and its churchwardens, 1451
  manor, 2704
  Cryfield, Fletchamstead, Milborne, Milburn and
    Stoneleigh Hall in, *q.v.*
Stoneleigh Hall (Stoneley Hall) [in Stoneleigh],
    Warw, Lee of, *q.v.*
Stoneley (Stonely, Stonley), Edward, 3208
  Richard, [Bucks], 1503
  Richard, [Essex], 1250
  Richard, [London], 1235, 3563
  Richard, teller of Exchequer, 3411
  Cf. Stanley
Stonely (Stonley) [in Kimbolton], Hunts, priory, 648
Stonely. *See* Stoneleigh; Stoneley
Stonerd (Stonard, Stoner), Francis, escheator in
    Essex, 244, 296
  Francis, [Essex], 233, 335
  John, 236
  Peter, 2256
Stonham Aspall (Stoneham Aspall), Suff, 2091
Stonham, Earl, (Erle Soham, Erle Stonham,
    Erlstonham), Suff, 2255
  guildhall, 2255
  Catchpoll of, *q.v.*
Stonley. *See* Stoneleigh; Stoneley; Stonely
Stonnall, Lower, (Nether Stannell), [in Shenstone],
    Staffs, Adcock of, *q.v.*
Stonston. *See* Sturton
Stonyhurst. *See* Stonehurst
Stonyng (Stonynge), Elizabeth, and Edward her son,
    2788
  Thomas, rector presented to Purley, 1061
  William, [Devon], 2679
  William, [Som], 1347
Stonystratford. *See* Stratford
Stonywell, John, bishop of Pulati, commendatory of
    Tynemouth priory, 532
Stooke. *See* Stoke
Stopham, Sussex, 3536
Stoppord, Stopporte. *See* Stockport
Stopwike. *See* Scopwick
Stormesworth. *See* Starmore
Storrye. *See* Storye
Storthes, Thomas, 1203
Storye (Storrye), Hugh, [Herts], 3579
  Hugh, [Northumb], 2258
  Roger, of Staple Inn, 2701
  William, of London, 386
Stoterton. *See* Stottesdon
Stotfielde. *See* Statfold
Stotfold, Yorks, Shippens in, *q.v.*
Stottesdon (Scottesdon, Stoterton, Stotysdon), Salop,
    1178

Stottesdon—*cont.*
  vicar presented to. *See* Powell, John
  Walkerslow and Walton in, *q.v.*
Stoughton [in Wedmore], Som, 3170
Stoughton, Anthony, 95
  Lawrence, 1939
Stoulton (Stowton), Worcs, church, 2180
Stour Provost (Stower Provys), [Dors], rector
    presented to. *See* Cottesforde, Robert
Stourpaine (Stowre Payne), Dors, 2077
Stourton (Stowrton), Wilts [and Som], 1995
Stourton (Sturton), Charles, lord Stourton, 812, 1347,
    1353, 2687
Stourton. *See* Sturton
Stow, Lincs, Sturton by Stow in *q.v.*
Stow ?Bardolph (Stowe), Norf, Michell of, *q.v.*
Stow on the Wold (Stowe), Glos, 1233, 1520
  church, 1520
  Donnington in, *q.v.*
Stowe, Bucks, 931
  Dadford and Lamport in, *q.v.*
Stowe (Stowe Graunge) [in St. Briavels], Glos,
    Warren of, *q.v.*
Stowe (Stowes) [in Stiffkey], Norf, manor, 2724
Stowe, Christopher, 2057
  William, queen's servant, 1501
Stowell, John, 3191
  John, knight, 926
Stower. *See* Stour
Stowes. *See* Stowe
Stowey, Nether, (Netherstowey, Netherstowye),
    Som, 2023, 2027, 2065
Stowey, Over, (Overstowey, Overstowye), Som,
    2023, 2027, 2065
  Plainsfield in, *q.v.*
Stowre Payne. *See* Stourpaine
Stowres *alias* Towres, George, of Langport, 1606
Stowrton. *See* Stourton
Stowsler. *See* Stokesley
Stowte, John, of Hexham, 42
Stowton. *See* Stoulton
Strachie, William, 569
Stradbroke (Statebroke, Stradbrooke), Suff, 2180
  manor, 685
  Ingolf *alias* Ingle of, *q.v.*
Stradishall (Stradgehull), [Suff], rector presented
    to. *See* Eccleston, Nicholas
Stradling (Stradlinge, Stradlynge), Edward, knight,
    3058
  John, of Llantwit Major, 421
  Matthew, 2023, 2065
strangers. *See under* aliens
Stranguishe, Thomas, of Ash, 2363
Strangwayes (Strangwaies, Strangweys), Giles,
    knight, and John his son, 2396
  James, knight, 3379, 3617
  Nicholas, 2583
Stranton, [Durh], rectory, 547
  vicar presented to. *See* Rawelyn, Richard
  vicar presented to, with Seaton Carew chapel. *See*
    Hatherley, Philip
  Brierton and Seaton Carew in, *q.v.*
Strata Florida, Strataflorida. *See* Ystrad-fflur
Strata Marcella. *See* Ystrad Marchell
Strateford, Strateforde. *See* Stratford
Stratfield Mortimer (Stratfeld Mortimer), [Berks],
    vicar presented to. *See* Georges, David
Stratflor. *See* Ystrad-fflur
Stratford (Stratford Langthorne) [in West Ham],
    Essex, monastery, 2299

T

V

W

Welbore, Michael, and Thomas his son, 2417
Richard, 1869
Welborne (Welburne), John, 1932
Matthew, of Mowthorpe, 1663
Welburne. *See* Welborne; Wellbury
Welbury. *See* Wellbury; Westbury
Welby, Lincs, 1571, 2183
manor, 1571
Welchien (*unidentified*), [?in Kidwelly], Carm, 2678
Welcombstede. *See* Godstone
Weldon. *See* Weldon; Welton
Weldon, Great, Northants, 858
Weldon, Little, [in Great Weldon], Northants, 858
Weldon (Welden), Edward, gentleman at arms, 1404
Thomas, keeper of houses of upper bailiwick etc. in
Windsor castle, 473
William, of London, 2256, 2605
William, of Welton, 39
William, [Berks], and Elizabeth his wife, 3484–5
Cf. Welton
Weldyshe, Edward, 354
Welford on Avon (Welford, Wellneford, Welneford),
Glos, 2122, 2133–4, 2136–7, 2429–30, 2432,
2436
Welham, Leics, vicar presented to. *See* Losebye,
Thomas
Welham (Wellome) [in Clarborough], Notts, 1438
Welham (Wellome) [in Norton], Yorks, 2260
Welland (Willand), river, 206
Wellbury (Welburne, Welbury, Welles) [in Offley],
Herts, manor, 3426, 3498
Wellenger. *See* Wellingore
Weller, Thomas, 2914
William, 946
Wellerbye. *See* Welbery
Welles, Edmund, vicar presented to East Winch, 155
John, the elder, 2137
John, queen's servant, courier or post, 468
Robert, and Elizabeth his wife, 3509
Thomas, 2136
Welles. *See* Wellbury
Wellesbourne Mountford (Mountforde Wellesborne),
Warw, manor, 345
Welley. *See* Wellow
Wellingborough (Wedlingboroughe,
Wendlingborough, Wenlingborough,
Wenlingboroughe, Willingboroughe),
Northants, 206, 661, 1350, 3453
guild of Corpus Christi, St George, St Mary and St
Catherine, 206
rectory, 3607
vicar presented to. *See* Sutton, Richard
Wellingore (Wellenger), Lincs, 1525
?Wellington (Willyngton), Heref, 2255
Wellington, [?Salop], 51
Wellington, Som, 1350, 2182
Wellis. *See* Wells
Wellneford. *See* Welford
Wellome. *See* Welham
Wellow (Wellowe) [in Great Grimsby], Lincs, 831
monastery, 831
Wellow (Welley), Notts, 206
church, 206
Wellow (Willowe), Som, Baggridge in, *q.v.*
Wellow, East, (Wellowe), Hants, 3508
Wells (Wellis), Som, 1353, 1995, 2688
cathedral, 2540, 2688
dean and chapter of, 3251, 3385
hospital or priory of St John the Baptist, 1353,
2182, 2569, 2688

Wells—*cont.*
parish of St Cuthbert, 1353
Horrington, East *or* West, Southover and Wells,
East, in, *q.v.*
Bevell of, *q.v.*
Wells, East, (Estwalles), [in Wells], Som, 1353
Wellwicke. *See* Welwick
Welneford. *See* Welford
Welshe, Edward, 98
*Cf.*Walshe
Welshpool, Mont, Dysserth in, *q.v.*
Welton, Northants, 2255
vicar presented to. *See* Nowell, William
Welton (Welden) [in Ovingham], Northumb, 572
Weldon of, *q.v.*
Welton le Wold (Welton, Weltoun), Lincs, 2500,
2758
Welton, Henry, 101
Cf. Weldon
Welton. *See* Willington
Welwick (Wellwicke, Welwick in Holdernes,
Welwicke), Yorks, manor and rectory,
1428, 3599
Ploughland in, *q.v.*
Wem, Salop, Edstaston in, *q.v.*
Wembdon, Som, 1166
Wendens Ambo (Great Wendon and Little Wendon),
Essex, 206
Wendeover. *See* Wendover
Wendlingborough. *See* Wellingborough
Wendon, Roger, 2580
Wendon. *See* Wendens
Wendover (Wendeover), Bucks, 1625, 3152
vicar presented to. *See* Lyre, William
Bradshaw's and Wendover Forrens in, *q.v.*
Wendover Forrens (Wendover Foreign) [in
Wendover], Bucks, 1625
Wendron (All Saints of Weneron, Weneron), Corn,
rectory and vicar of, 3595
Wenesley. *See* Winsley
Wenham, Great, (Wenham Combust, Wenham
Magna), [Suff], rector presented to. *See*
Boothe, Robert
Snellinge of, *q.v.*
Wenham, Great *or* Little, (Wenham), [Suff], rector
presented to. *See* Andrews, Bartimeus
Wenhaston (Wenneston), Suff, 116, 3481
Mell's in, *q.v.*
Bonnet of, *q.v.*
Wenington. *See* Wennington
Wenlingborough, Wenlingboroughe. *See*
Wellingborough
Wenlock, Much, (Much Wenlocke, Much Wenloke,
Wenlock, Wenlock Magna, Wenlocke,
Wenlocke Magna), Salop, 206, 674, 2177,
3569
Amners Grounde in, 674
church, chaplain in, 206
manor, 674
monastery, 206, 674, 2177, 3379, 3386
Atterley, Callaughton, Caughley, Marsh, The,
Presthope, Walton, Wigwig and Wyke in,
q.v.
Wenman, Isabel, wife of Richard Huddleston, 3285
Richard, knight, 3107
Thomas, and Richard his son, 3285
Thomas, [Berks], 2814
See also Wayneman
Wenne, George, 969
Wenneston. *See* Wenhaston

Westley (Whelstlee), Suff, 2483
Westlington. *See* Westington
Westlutton. *See* Lutton
Westlyme, Westlyn, Westlynne. *See* Lynn
Westmalhome. *See* Malham
Westmeane. *See* Meon
Westmersh (*unidentified*), Wilts, 1669
Westmeston, Sussex, 1260
   Chiltington, East, and Middleton in, *q.v.*
Westmill (Westemyll), Herts, 2813
Westminster, [Midd], 822, 1409, 1540, 2509, 2585,
   2880, 3714
   church of St Margaret, brotherhood of Our Lady
     in, 822
     guild of Assumption of St Mary the Virgin in,
      2180
   collection of alms in, 452
   college or free chapel of St Stephen, 822, 2297,
     3392
   collegiate church (*formerly successively* monastery *and*
     cathedral) of St Peter, 2591, 3252, 3258,
     3592
     canons or prebendaries of, 197, 822. *See also*
      Aldrich, Thomas; Chaderton, William;
      Grant, Edward; Jones, . . .; Lewes, Griffith;
      Parkins, Humphrey; Ramsden, Robert;
      Reade, John; Rugg, John
     chapter of, 3592
     dean of, 123, 822, 2676, 3592. *See also*
      Goodman, Gabriel
   gaming houses in, 59
   hospital of Savoy (Le Savoye), 529
     chaplains or fellows of, 529
     masters of. *See* Absolon, William; Thurland,
      Thomas
   palace, 822
     chamber of Council of Star Chamber in, keepers
      of. *See* Brooke *alias* Cobham, Henry; Hart,
      Percival; Sparke, William
     royal free chapel of St Mary and St Stephen in,
      206, 822, 1353, 3614
   parishes in:
     St Clement Danes (St Clement, St Clement
      Danes without the bars of the New
      Temple), 1347, 2428, 2822, 3109
      Seale of, *q.v.*
     St Giles in the Fields (St Giles, Sainte Giles in
      the Feilde), 463, 831, 1195, 2348, 2880, 3379
     St Margaret, 463
     St Martin in the Fields (St Martin by Charinge
      Crosse, St Martin in the Fields by
      Charingcrosse, St Martin in the Fields by
      Charinge Crosse), 463, 948, 1416, 2880
      church of Aye in, 3714
     St Mary le Strand (St Mary at Strond), 2346
   queen's courts of record at, 2257
   queen's grammar school, master of. *See* Grant,
     Edward
   queen's great clocks of, keepers of. *See* Burges,
     Thomas; Urcean, Nicholas
   St James's fair (Seynte James Fayer), bailiffs
     of. *See* Astley, John and Catherine;
     Cooke, Richard; Mackwilliam, Henry and
     Mary; Morraunt, William
   streets and places in:
     le Brewhouse, 1416
     Charing Cross (Charinge Crosse), 463
     Ebury (Eyburye) Field, 3714
     Ficketsfild (Fickatsfyld), 2822
     Holywell Street (Holewaye Lane), 1347

Westminster—*cont.*
   streets and places in—*cont.*
     le Longe Wolstaple, 822
     lord treasurer's house near Savoy, 2889
     park, keepers of ponds in. *See* Bussard,
      Thomas; Cole, Thomas
     St James's (Seynte James) house, keepers
      of. *See* Astley, John and Catherine;
      Cooke, Richard; Mackwilliam, Henry and
      Mary; Morraunt, William
     St Stephen's Alley (Sainte Stephens Alley, Seynt
      Stephens Alley), 1353
     le Swanne, 948
     Temple Bar (Temple Barr) 3109
     taverns in, 523
     Knightsbridge in, *q.v.*
     Francklyn, Milburne, Singlehurst and Spencer of,
      q.v.
Westmorland, county, auditor of, 1381
   deputy feodary of. *See* Brathwaite, Thomas
   escheator in, 2387, 2530
   justices of peace in, 592
   sheriff of. *See* Clifford, George
Westmorland, earls of. *See* Neville
Westmounckton. *See* Monkton
Westoke. *See* Stoke
Weston (Weston by Baldock), Herts, 1280, 3491
   manor, 1280
   rectory and advowson of vicarage, 3491
   Lannock in, *q.v.*
Weston, Lincs, 1353
Weston [?in Monkhopton], Salop, 3386
Weston (*unidentified*), Salop, 3258
Weston, Som, chapel of St Lawrence, 2255
   lordship, 1347
Weston [Suff], rector presented to. *See* Smyth, James
Weston, Coney, (Conneston, Cunston, Weston), Suff,
   2087
   rector presented to. *See* Harvey, William
Weston, Hail, (Hallyweston, Hayleweston) Hunts,
   2713, 3639
Weston in Arden [in Bulkington], Warw, 681
Weston on the Green (Weston, Weston in le Grene),
   Oxon, 936, 1353
   manor, 936
Weston Turville (Weston Turvile), Bucks, rector
   of. *See* Anson, John
   rectory, 2625
Weston under Penyard (Weston under Penyarde),
   Heref, 2139
   Bilmile in, *q.v.*
Weston Underwood (Weston), Bucks, 3645
   park, 3645
Weston, Elizabeth, 1973
   Henry, knight, 1873, 1935
   Jerome, [Bucks], 935
   Jerome, [Leics], 1204
   Robert, LL.D., chancellor of Ireland, 503, 1364
     Alice wife of, 1364
   William, 1195
   William, knight, prior of hospital of St John of
     Jerusalem in England, 610
Weston. *See* Westover; Whetstone
Westover (Weston) [in Drayton], Som, 1371
   manor of Drayton and, 52
Westpennard, Westpennarde. *See* Pennard
Westport (Westporte) [in Wareham], Dors, 3713
Westport St Mary (Westporte), Wilts, 968, 3434
Westprye. *See* Westbury
Westradale. *See* Cragdale

Wrington, Som, church, 1353
Riding in, *q.v.*
writs etc.:
ad quod dampnum, 2898
covenant, 399
dedimus potestatem, 44, 2209, 2251
restitution of temporalities to bishop, 1135–6,
1155–6, 2386–7, 2391–2, 2413–4, 2524–5,
2529–30, 2658
scire facias, 1941,2697
subpoena, 2705
Writtle, Essex, 2255
Taverner of, *q.v.*
Wrongaye. *See* Wormegaye
Wroot (Wrote), [Lincs], rectors presented to. *See*
Dobson, Robert; Gregory, Richard
Wrote, Robert, 3027
See also Wroth
Cf. Woorte
Wroth (Wrothe), Robert, [Essex], 236
Robert, [Midd], 1966
Thomas, 2131
Thomas, knight, 1126, 2619
Robert son of, 1126
See also Worthe; Wrote
Wrotham, Kent, 2254
Plaxtol in, *q.v.*
Wrothe. *See* Wroth
Wrotton. *See* Wretton
Wroughton, Thomas, knight, 3183
Wroxall, Warw, priory, 2183, 3619
Wroxeter, Salop, Uckington in, *q.v.*
Wryne, Ralph, and Helen his wife, 1368
Wukeburnell. *See* Wick
Wuller. *See* Wooler
Wulmere. *See* Woolmer
Wulphett, Geoffrey, 1337
Wulton. *See* Woolton
Wurthyn. *See* Worthen
Wutton. *See* Wootton
Wyatt (Wiatt, Wyat, Wyate, Wyett, Wyott, Wyotte),
George, 1444
George, [Devon], 120, 369
Henry, 3233
Hugh, 2980
Hugh, [Devon], 120, 319
John, 1264
John, clerk, 615
Richard, governor of Alford grammar school, 1397
Thomas, 462
Thomas, knight, 210, 600, 2248
Wyberd (Wiberde), Thomas, and Anne his wife, 1682,
3471
Wych. *See* Droitwich
Wyche. *See* Wiche
Wycheford. *See* Witchford
Wyckham. *See* Wickham
Wyclyff (Wickliff, Wiclif, Wicliffe), Henry, 110
William, [Cumb], 2327
William, [Yorks], 215, 2351
Wycombe (Wickham) [in Rothley], Leics, 210
Wycombe, High, (Chepingwickham,
Chepingwicombe, Chippingwicombe),
Bucks, 1401, 3642
rectory, 1401, 3595
Wycombe, West, (Westwycombe), Bucks, rectory,
2229
Wydbache. *See* Woodbatch
Wydcombe. *See* Widcombe; Witcombe
Wyddell *See* Widdell

Wyddial (Wyddiall, Wydial), Herts, 2813, 2834
Wydecomb. *See* Witcombe
Wydecombe. *See* Widecombe
Wydeforde, Wydford. *See* Widford
Wydnall, Wydnell. *See* Widnell
Wye, Kent, liberty, coroner of. *See* Mascall, Thomas
Wyett. *See* Wyatt
Wyfold Court (Wivold Courte) in Checkendon,
Oxon, manor, 1569
Wygenhale. *See* Wiggenhall
Wyggeston. *See* Wigston
Wyggett, Richard, 3072
Wyghley, Henry, 2210
Wyght. *See* Wighte
Wyghtman. *See* Wightman
Wygston, William, knight, 3017
Wyke [in Much Wenlock], Salop, 1258
Wyke. *See* Week; Wick
Wykeburnell. *See* Wick
Wykeham (Wicham) [in Old Malton], Yorks, 2836
Wykes, George, *alias* George Wilkes, 1860, 1870,
1980
Joan, 2328
John, marshal of Marshalsea of Queen's Bench, 9
Richard, 1618
Robert, and Elizabeth his wife, 3477
Wykes. *See* Wix
Wyketon. *See* Wickton
Wykewan, Wykeware. *See* Wickwar
Wykham. *See* Whickham
Wylam (Wylome) [in Ovingham], Northumb, 393,
3610
Wylborn, Ranulph, of Bristol, 2256
Wylbraham. *See* Wilbraham
Wyld, Monkton, (Wyle), [in Wootton Fitzpaine],
Dors, 638
Wyld, Wylde. *See* Wilde
Wylden. *See* Wilden
Wyle. *See* Wyld
Wyles, Thomas, gentleman of chapel, 3289
Cf. Wylles
Wylford, Wylforde. *See* Wilford
Wylkes. *See* Wilkes
Wylkesbye. *See* Wilksby
Wylkinson. *See* Wilkinson
Wylkyns. *See* Wilkins
Wylkynson. *See* Wilkinson
Wyllance, Thomas, chief burgess of Richmond, 2197
Wyllerton, *See* Willoughton
Wylles, John, clerk, vicar presented to . . ., 3323
Cf. Wille; Wyles; Wyllys
Wylley, Simon, of 'Newsomme', 2931
Wylloughby, Wylloughbye. *See* Willoughby
Wyllson. *See* Wilson
Wyllyams. *See* Williams
Wyllyamson. *See* Williamson
Wyllys, Emanuel, of London, 2256
Thomas, 2036
Cf. Wylles
Wyllyston, William, 364
Wylman, Henry, 2539
Wylome. *See* Wylam
Wylsdon, Hugh, 983
Wylsfelde. *See* Wivelsfield
Wylson, Wylsonn, Wylsonne. *See* Wilson
Wylton. *See* Wilton
Wymberley, Thomas, 1347
Wymbledon, Wymbleton. *See* Wimbledon
Wymbole, . . ., 3379
Wymborne. *See* Wimborne

Z

Zeal Monachorum (Monckenzeale, Monken Seale,
    Monkenseale, Seale Monachorum, Zeale
    Monachorum, Zeale Monacorum), Devon,
    638, 1993
  manor and advowson of church, 638, 1993
  Loosebeare in, *q.v.*
Zealand. *See* Zeeland
Zeale. *See* Zeal
Zeals (Seles) [in Mere], Wilts, 1995
Zeeland (Zealand), 53, 2605
Zinzano *alias* Alexander, Robert, equerry of stable,
    1374
Zouche (Souche), Charles, 1218, 2078, 2753, 3184
  George, [Derb], 2259
  George, [Glos], 1916
  George, lord Zouche, Saint Maur and Cantelupe,

Zouche—*cont.*
    and Margaret his wife, 460
  Edward, lord Zouche, Saint Maur and
    Cantelupe, son of, 460, 2671, 2797, 2804,
    3565, 3571
    Eleanor wife of, 2797, 2804, 3565, 3571
  John, 2225
  John, knight, 235, 352, 1912, 2259, 3085
    king's servant, warden or keeper of Gillingham
      forest and park, steward of woodward's
      court in Dorset, bailiff of town and manor
      of Gillingham etc., 2225
  John, lord Zouche, Saint Maur and Cantelupe,
    Susan wife and Edward greatgrandson of,
    460

Printed in England for Her Majesty's Stationery Office at the Alden Press, Oxford.
Dd. 696382 C5